ISBN 978-1-5277-0166-3
PIBN 10882348

# THE
# CONTEMPORARY REVIEW

VOLUME XXXI. DECEMBER, 1877—MARCH, 1878.

STRAHAN AND COMPANY LIMITED,
34, PATERNOSTER ROW, LONDON
1878

LONDON
M'CORQUODALE & CO., "THE ARMOURY," SOUTHWARK.

# CONTENTS OF VOLUME XXXI.

DECEMBER, 1877.

PAGE



JANUARY, 1878.

FEBRUARY, 1878.



MARCH, 1878.

# RUSSIAN AGGRESSION,

PECIALLY AFFECTING AUSTRIA-HUNGARY AND TURKEY.

iot be amiss to ventilate a little the Eastern question. Not I could say anything new, but because purified notions lidate instinctive aspirations into convictions, and longings ses.

tern question is a European question. There is no power that would not feel that the phases of that question are more or less, mediately or immediately, with its own

comes the importance of this question?

d when did the Eastern question become a European ques-

increase of the Russian power and since the time when the diminution of the Turkish Empire, and the dismember-'oland—*increased to formidable proportions, and thus became o the freedom of Europe.*

ankfully indebted to the Porte. And I do not, like many nsider gratitude to be a burden, but to be a dear obliga-earned to esteem highly the noble qualities of the Turkish haracter. And I learned it the more from the admirable on, that this people of tenacious morals could not be cor-their rich social virtues even by the pestiferous air which l over them from Constantinople through a period of several during which this capital has been converted into a witch-European intrigues, fighting for the maintenance of the 1. This corrupt influence has found among the higher circles at kettle individuals accessible to bribery; but the country ain attached to the moral feelings and to the holy relics of ies, in the same way as in Hungary the eternal holy flame of nationality has been kept burning around the hearths of our people, whilst it has been extinguished in the palaces. It is true that the Turkish people remain still far behind in what we call civilization. This is not the fault of their susceptibilities, nor of their willingness. But it is quite certain that only national morality can supply a good soil for the roots of liberal institutions, and that they decay or become false without it. Quite as certain is it that the world would admiringly contemplate how easily the most liberal institutions would take root, how naturally they would become acclimatised among the Turkish people if Europe would but prevent the hereditary foe of the Turkish Empire from interfering with the spread of endeavours inspired by the warnings of time.

But these are my personal views, my individual sympathies. Sympathies, however, are no centre of attraction for the politics of the world; but self-interest is. And though for a long time the conservation of the Turkish Empire was a dogma of the politics of the European equilibrium, and is still so *in foro conscientiæ*, it does not follow that Europe is in love with the Turks, but only that it *abhors the increase of Russian preponderance.* And rightly so.

*The Eastern question is a question of Russian power.* "Hinc omne principium, huc refer exitum." This is the summary of European interests, considered from the European point of view. Every policy is either a cheat or a fallacy which does not take this fact as a starting point.

The Eastern question is a question of Russian power. If this line be struck out, the Eastern question ceases, *ipso facto*, to be a European question. It descends at once to the level of internal questions, whose changing phases may be followed sympathetically or antipathetically, according to the inspiration of political principles or instinctive feelings; but they will never disturb the sleep of any European Power. The Turkish Porte may succeed (and I wish from my innermost soul that she may succeed) in conciliating all her nationalities, of diverse races and creeds, either on the ground of equality of rights, surrounded by constitutional institutions, or by personal union, or on the ground of a strict federative system; or if she does not succeed, and on the ruins of her fallen power the nationalities of her Empire should rise to autonomy, asserting their national individuality, all this will not threaten the peace or the liberty of Europe—all this will never be converted by anybody into a European question.

On the contrary, the Eastern question lies in the actual situation. Every aggression, either on the integrity of the Turkish Empire or on her sovereignty, will always threaten the peace of Europe, because every direct or indirect increase of Russian preponderance in Europe will be a step to the fulfilment of that prophecy of Napoleon, that "*Europe will become Cossack.*"

They speak of humanity. Good God! where is the *Christian*

[illegible] unscrupulously disowned human feelings, [illegible] were concerned, but very often from [illegible] What bitter feelings and remembrances crowd into [illegible] feverish heat when I think that I am a Hungarian! [illegible] other terrible examples could I quote, through the long [illegible] atrocities, down to the insane brutality of the French [illegible] to the subsequent reprisals of loosened fury! And I [illegible] when has the trampling down of humanity, the traces [illegible] are visible all over the world, been made a European [illegible]?

[illegible] impossible not to feel indignation in our human bosoms [illegible] that the very same Power which rose by trampling down [illegible] of its people, from the Vistula to the Behring Strait, from [illegible] to the glacial sea, covers its dangerous schemes with the [illegible] humanity, and increases continually the giant stature of its [illegible] by such systematic consistency and pitiless cruelty as stand [illegible] in history.

[illegible] is no question of humanity here, but simply of the increase [illegible] ian preponderance. The one is only dust thrown into the [illegible] mankind that they may not see the other.

[illegible] speak of freedom, of self-government! But the thing [illegible] that whilst Russian power presses upon the south-eastern [illegible] Europe, the Christian nationalities of the Turkish Empire will [illegible] reconciled to the suzerainty of the Porte, nor can they [illegible] free and independent. They can only be instruments of [illegible] policy—sometimes by force, sometimes willingly, but always [illegible] instruments.

[illegible] at Servia. As far as the Porte is concerned Servia was a free [illegible], quite as much so as any other European nation, and she wanted [illegible] but the mere title to be entirely independent. She was more [illegible] dent than Hungary is at present with respect to her political, [illegible], and economical administration, in every point of view, even [illegible] rds the tribute payable to the Porte. But she was not [illegible] was not independent, with respect to Russia; she could not [illegible] Whoever has a protector, has a master too. Not that the [illegible] would not prefer to be free Servians, rather than vassals [illegible] Russian rule; but because they are unable to resist Russian [illegible]. This is the fatal necessity of the situation. The dust of [illegible] assurances was thrown into the eyes of Europe from St. Peters- [illegible] It was said that the Czar kept back Prince Milan from waging [illegible] but Russian agents stirred up the fire of war; the easily inflam- [illegible] passions of the Servian people were fanned by the prospect of [illegible] Bosnia, and by the phantasmagoria of a "great Servia." Russian [illegible] followed Servia, a Russian general was placed at the head of [illegible] army; Russian officers, and even such as were in active [illegible] service, were sent expressly on furlough; and thousands of

Russian soldiers crowded to Servia. And thus under the Servian mask it was that Russia began war against the Turks, in order to get a pretext to continue the war unmasked. The Servians were intoxicated with the war-cry of Slavonian liberty (which liberty blooms of course in Russia very nicely!) without perceiving that they fought, bled, and died not for freedom, but in the interests of Russian preponderance. And what has become of "free" Servia? There she hangs on Russia's pleasure. She is at present a vassal of Russia. Russian military patrols keep the Servians "in order" at Belgrade. These are very edifying things, and very instructive too.

Or, let us look at Roumania. I have here no room to draw up an epitome of history, but it would be very advisable if the diplomatists would do so and study it a little. They would learn therefrom what is meant when Russia guarantees "self-governmental reforms" by "occupation of territory." I wish only to recall to mind that since the time of the capitulation between Mircea and the Sultan Bajazet on the part of Wallachia, and between Bogdan II. and Selim I. on the part of Moldavia, the Porte has always respected the liberty and self-government of Roumania. She has respected them in such an unheard-of liberal way, that the mighty Porte, the sovereign power, conceded to her vassals the most unbounded religious liberty, excluding even from these vassal provinces her own creed, and did not grant to her own Mohammedan subjects even the right of possessing there any landed property. The Turks have never violated that treaty. *Never!* Roumania was free; she is indebted for all her troubles and misfortunes (and, alas, how much has she suffered!) to the meddling of Russia. And every Roumanian patriot feels that if Russian power surrounds Roumania—this island in the midst of a Slavonian sea—his fatherland will be broken to pieces by the folds of the boa constrictor. Every Roumanian dog knows it! And it was Europe that guaranteed the freedom and neutrality of Roumania!

And still Roumania is the high road by which Russia marches to wage war against Turkey. Roumania is still the basis of the Russian war-operations against the Porte, as it was in the year 1849 of those against the Hungarians. The Roumanian Government prayed, with clasped hands to the guaranteeing Powers that they would protect her neutrality. But the Russians are very clever politicians; they chose the right moment in which to stir up anew the Eastern question.

England is powerful. She can defend Constantinople and sweep the Russian flag from the seas. But she is not a Continental power. She *alone* cannot send an army of some hundred thousand men to Roumania.

France is still maimed; she begins to recover, but she suffers from [illegible] losses. If she were not maimed, Russia would not dare what [illegible]ow.

The German Imperial Government has polite words for every one, but it is its policy not to allow an alliance of any European power with Turkey against Russia, in order to localize the war. If this succeeds, it will be of the greatest service to Russia, as she will thus have an opportunity of preparing for the occupation of additional territory by raising internal convulsions in the Turkish provinces. And she will do it at the given time as well in Hungary as in Austria. And what is the key to this policy of Prince Bismarck? Nothing else but that he is afraid to offend Russia, as she might think of giving to France an aiding hand to procure revenge.

Lucky Italy, who deserves her luck for her constancy centuries ago, and who wins provinces by losing battles, is on the look-out to see whether there is visible on the horizon a completing ray of light for the "Stella d'Italia."

In the councils of Austria the traditional demon of "rapine" goes about, and where he does not appear, the paralysis of irresolution "hums and haws" from one day to the other.

Hungary is a province, and not a state; she cannot follow an independent policy. She has given up herself. She is treatiedto death.

They counted on all this at St. Petersburg, ere the "pacific" Czar Alexander became such a resolute "champion."

For Roumania the end will be that the free Roumania whose neutrality has been guaranteed by the Powers will be held in dependence by Russia, as she has been so many times before. The Roumanian-Russian alliance is an accomplished fact, and by it Roumania has become the auxiliary of Russia. What could the Roumanians have done? Could they, left alone to themselves, have resisted the Russian pressure? Could they, wolf-like, have shown their teeth to her whom the European powers regard with lamb-like patience? The situation coerced them.

This is the philosophy of the Eastern question. As long as Russia is conscious of her overwhelming power, and knows that she may press with all her might upon the Turkish Empire, nobody can there become free or independent. They may change masters, get a new patron, but the new patron's vital power consists in an autocracy in whose outspread arms Freedom dies, and only the weeds of the *Nihilismus* pullulate secretly. Such a "patron" they may get, but nobody can become free under "Russian protectorship."

And it is right that I should mention here what misconceptions there are as to the meaning of the tide of feelings and apprehensions that shakes the nerves of the Hungarian nation. They say the Hungarians are afraid of the freedom of their neighbours, the Slavonians. This is not true. It is only intrigue that can say so, only blindness or silliness that can believe it.

Hungary and the Hungarians' love of liberty are "twins born the same day." They have lived together a thousand years. The Hungarians nowhere and never feared, and do not fear liberty. And they were never exclusive in their love of liberty; they never accommodated even their privileges to certain races. And we are the less afraid of the liberty of our Eastern neighbours, since I feel thoroughly convinced that if these nations were to become free,—really free, not Russian serfs,—then Hungary (if she may still keep the mastership of her own destiny) would be quite ready to inaugurate with them such defensive combinations as, though in the interest of the European equilibrium, would also uphold and secure *their individual national independence.*

And I am convinced also that such a combination, in which the Turkish nation may very naturally join, is one of the chief necessities of the logic of history. Only in this order of ideas can be found security for the independence of minor nations against the pressure of the greater aggrandising powers.

We are not afraid of liberty, but of the increase of Russian power. That is what we Hungarians are afraid of. We fear that if the Turkish Empire should be dismembered, if its sovereignty should be undermined previous to the removal of this danger, and if this dismemberment and undermining should be provoked by Russia, and turned to her profit, the result would not be that free nations would rise out of the ruins of the Turkish Empire; but rather the result would be Russian occupation, or else (which is the same thing, though more dangerous) Russian servitude, accompanied, as a compensation, by the "grand idea" of affinity of race as a honeyed cake; and the Slavonian nations would be fettered to the Russian yoke. This would, in some inevitable way, have a tendency to enslave Hungary as well, and we should finally, after many and great struggles, be brought to perdition, as Poland was a century ago.

And I must observe that the danger that threatens us, threatens still more the Austrian Empire. There is between us such a community of interests as gives the power to secure the removal of this danger; and the Government can thus count on the whole nation, which would rise as if her millions were only one man, not merely in blind obedience, but with all the power which a nation can exert when it defends its existence, its very life.

This is the danger that shakes the heart-strings of the Hungarian nation. This makes it ready for every exertion, for every sacrifice, in order that the integrity of the Turkish Empire and the sovereignty of the Porte may not become a prey to Russian tyranny and aggrandisement.

Remove this danger, and we shall always approve the regenerational endeavours of the Turkish nationalities, and shall feel great pleasure if this regeneration succeed without destruction of races, language, or creed,—the old internal hatreds being superseded by equal laws and [illegible] We Hungarians shall thus acquire in the Turkish [illegible] friends as could not be found elsewhere on the surface of [illegible] earth. But if Fate, whose skein is composed of the thread of [illegible] past, should decide that all these endeavours shall be [illegible] to so many impediments being thrown in the way [illegible] by foreign intrigues, egotism, meddling, and passion, [illegible] very much afraid of the liberty of our neighbours. If the [illegible] happen, however, we will welcome them at the round table [illegible] independent nations; we will offer them our hands, and [illegible] that their liberty and independence may be secured [illegible] external aggression.

[illegible] my fatherland I live in solitary seclusion, and shall die [illegible] if I am forced to forget much, there is something I can [illegible]; it is that I know the Hungarian heart, on whose throb- [illegible] has so often rested.

* * *

[illegible] now state why I think that Hungarian public opinion should [illegible] determinate position on this Eastern question.

[illegible] diplomatically acknowledged during the crisis of 1854, how [illegible] Russian power had become to the liberty of Europe, and [illegible] seen that the future could only be secured against the [illegible] of this question by that power being reduced to lesser propor- [illegible] as would not endanger Europe.

[illegible] was what England aimed at in the Crimean war of 1854. But [illegible] programme could not be carried out then in consequence of the [illegible] *Austria*, as may be seen from some of the articles in the *Moniteur*, containing those official revelations with which [illegible] III. tried to soothe English public opinion, the fluctua- [illegible] which I then strove to direct, and which strongly demanded [illegible] ration of Poland.

[illegible] the programme not being carried out is the reason why this [illegible] now shows itself in a still more dangerous form than it has [illegible] since that time.

[illegible] more dangerous form, I say, because the Russian preponderance [illegible] has assumed such a character as against the liberties of [illegible] generally, and against those of our country particularly, as [illegible] aim to be new territorial annexations.

[illegible] Emperor of Russia has written upon his banner "The Slavonic [illegible] This was the phrase used by him on the occasion of his war- [illegible] ch at Moscow. This phrase had hitherto been paraded only [illegible] Slavonian dictionaries for private use; it had not before [illegible] in the plan of the confessed policy of the Russian Govern- [illegible] It now appears from beneath the ground, where it had before [illegible] mole-like,—rising, on the arms of the absolute autocrat of eighty-two millions of serfs, to the daylight as an active power. The Czar now occupies the position of the declared champion of Panslavism.

And what is this Panslavism? This is no merely national matter, no affair of national freedom. It absorbs the different Slavonic nations into one single race. It substitutes race for nationality; power of race for liberty.

The signification of "The Slavonic Cause" as a Russian war-cry is this: that the Cabinet of St. Petersburg seeks, wherever there are Slavonians, instruments wherewith to paralyze the policy of some other power, to cripple its force, and to find in the Panslavists wedges with which it may split States asunder, if they stand in the way of Russia's extension of power; and to create new combinations, either as her tools or her objects, for the sake of her aggrandisement.

At present it is the Turkish Empire that is the anvil upon which Russia strikes with her Panslavistic hammer. Her first object is the country which forms an angle betwixt the vital artery of our fatherland and Austria—the Danube, and her estuary on the coast of the Euxine.

That after the Turks, we and Austria would next be struck upon, is quite clear. Not to see this, is blindness. To see and not to prevent it, is suicide.

This is no mere question of sympathy or antipathy. It is a matter of vital importance for Hungary, that the integrity and sovereignty of the Turkish Empire should be secured, and that Russia, who is the enemy of the liberties of Europe, should have her poison-fangs torn out, before she can consolidate and increase her annexations for her own advantage.

This is the philosophy of the situation.

It is a fact, that with respect to this danger the workings of diplomatists afford to us Hungarians no comfort. They dissimulate; they will not even show that they are aware of the real danger.

The traditions of the past are very disquieting. It is an historical fact that there is not a single example of Austria having taken the part of Turkey against Russia. She has always been biassed in favour of Russia. She has always, indeed, declared openly for her. There have been cases when she acted as mediator, as at Nimierow; and as soon as she heard of the capture of Cracow by the Russians, and their invasion of the Crimea, she attacked with armed force the oppressed Turks. She made a treaty with the Russians for the dismemberment of Turkey. She had a share in the prey. She accepted the half of Moldavia (Bukovina) as a compensation for Poland, of which she got only a small part. So it was planned by Kaunitz and Gallitzin.

These are the traditions of Viennese policy on the Eastern question. That a continuation of this traditionary policy would be dangerous in the highest degree, to our fatherland and to the monarchy, is clear. To permit Russia to become either the direct lord or the dictator of the southern Slavonians, to be the steel hoop which compresses them, is equivalent to multiplying the splitting wedges.

I cannot believe that these dangerous traditions can be continued within the circles of a constitutional Government. But there are very influential circles, apart from constitutional bodies, that stick to this traditional policy. They are fond of those siren songs, which are always heard when Austria has lost something, and whose burden is, "Go for compensation to the East."

These are very disquieting things. And it is a fact, that the Hungarian Government has till now done little to soothe or to appease the mind of the nation. Its reservedness has transgressed the farthest limits. Though reservedness may be safe in some cases, when it overreaches itself it is a fault, a blunder.

Now, as the situation is full of danger, as diplomacy gives no comfort, as the traditions of the past are disquieting, and as the Government does nothing to appease the people, it is not only a natural consequence, but it is also a postulate of self-preservation, that the Nation should now occupy such a position on the Eastern question as should make the whole world aware what is the political tendency most conformable or most contrary to our national interests.

The interruption of the manifestations of public opinion caused by the very sinister proregation of the Hungarian Diet, was explained, if not as a change of mind, at least as a loss of interest, and gave rise to the apprehension that in the councils of the Viennese Cabinet certain influences, whose existence is an open secret, might gain the preponderance.

This apprehension was very well founded. The "taking up" of a position preparatory to becoming a sharer in the booty was nearly accomplished when, fortunately, the Turkish victories stopped these dangerous preparations, and Hungarian patriotism watchfully called out, "Be on thy guard, Hungarian! who will keep watch for thee, if thou thyself doest it not for thy fatherland?" And it spread all over the country, loudly proclaiming to friends and foes that the Hungarian nation wakefully watched.

When I speak of the Hungarian nation, I do not mean the Magyar race, but every faithful son of the fatherland, without distinction of race, tongue, or creed, who sticks patriotically to that type of government which has belonged to Hungary for a thousand years, and who wishes to see also Hungary remain as Hungary in the future, with her unity and indivisibility for ever secured.

This it is that serves as a criterion of the public opinion of the Hungarian nation. This, and not an inflamed sentimentality, sympathetic or antipathetic, is the starting point of the conviction, that dikes should be raised against the Russian extension; for if we do it not, we expose our fatherland and the monarchy, whose interests in this respect are identical, to the necessary consequence that the Russian power, increased already by the dismemberment of Poland to formidable proportions, would attack, after this new augmentation of force, the Austro-Hungarian monarchy as a boa constrictor that compresses her giant folds around the body of her prey, or as a hundred-armed polypus that screws itself into the flesh.

That this would be the unavoidable consequence of Russian extension cannot be doubted, considering the geographical position and ethnographical situation of the Austro-Hungarian monarchy.

Then it will no more be a question of the Hungarian race,—reduced by the Russophiles only to four millions of inhabitants; it will be a question whether Hungary shall remain Hungary.

* * *

And now it is necessary to point out a dangerous network which already hangs around us. This network is knitted out of that erroneous conception that the power of Russia can only become dangerous to us by territorial occupation.

They say, "The Czar has given his word that he will not *occupy;* and the Czar is an honest man" (Brutus is an honourable man); "let him then manage" (I very nearly wrote mismanage) "in the East. The present vocation of the Austro-Hungarian monarchy is to remain in readiness" (and of course only in the south, where we can do mischief to the Turks, but in no imaginable case to the Russians), "and only to step into action if the Czar should break his word, and want to occupy whilst the peace negotiations last. Oh! then we shall draw out the sword from the scabbard, and then we shall do—this and that."

The nation should be on its guard against this network. It is a very dangerous network.

Firstly, I say, if the Czar should come out victoriously from this war, then the Vienna Cabinet will not draw the sword to impede the Czar in his occupation, but only that it may participate in the booty. God save our poor country from this suicidal tingling of swords, where infamy would cover the suicide! But let us keep also in mind that God protects only those who defend themselves.

Secondly, I say, even if the Viennese Cabinet would impede at *such a time* the Russian occupation, it would not find a single ally to assist it to overthrow an accomplished fact, such as it could secure at present if it wished it, for the far easier task of preventing Russian occupation from becoming an accomplished fact. Prussia would not help her out of this difficulty with Russia; France would not help her; Italy would not help her. The Vienna Cabinet would then have, not an ally more, but *a mighty ally less,* one who under given circumstances [illegible] better than any other, *and this is the Turk.* We should [illegible] policy; we should lose him without replacing [illegible]. We should lose him, whether the Czar occupied [illegible] not. In the case of his raising army after army against [illegible] Turks, and finally conquering them—then, of course, a [illegible] would be out of the question. Or if the Turk, losing at the foul play of Europe, and above all of the Vienna [s]hould say, "Well, if Europe, and especially the Vienna Cabi[net] not care for me, I do not care for them either," and should [sep]arate peace with Russia—then the Vienna Cabinet might [illegible] wooden idol, chiselled by its own political wisdom, and [t]ools, which would be "set aside" by the "world's judge," [as] has always happened.

[T]his policy of looking out for the keeping or not keeping [Cz]ar's word is either bad calculation or criminal calculation; [cri]me or folly. Take your choice!

[The]re is a still more decisive view for us. This is, that the danger for the Austro-Hungarian Empire would not be [l]ess even if the Czar kept his word and did not occupy; for even [if he did] not occupy, but terminated the war victoriously, the fact that [he co]nquered would secure for him the power of leadership—that [mora]l influence which is his designed aim, and is written on his [banner]s "The Slavonic Cause." And for the Austro-Hungarian [Empire] the danger is not greater from the Czar extending his occupation than it would be if he showed by victory that [he i]s a mighty stronghold of "The Slavonic Cause," and thus [hi]s influence over the Eastern Slavonians and over those that [put] them in the same camp, viz., our neighbours on tho left [as w]ell as those on the right hand, and also in our own country. [He] could dispose of as their leader, their lord, their protector. [Mus]covite papers do not conceal that as the banner of "The [Slavonic] Cause" is unfurled, so after the Turkish "Slavonic Cause," the ["Slavoni]c Cause" of the Austro-Hungarian monarchy will follow. [This] is no idle boast; it is logic. This latter kind of Russian [conques]t is really more dangerous for us and for Austria than any [extensio]n of territory,—a mode of extension which does not win over, [but ir]ritates, those whose country is occupied. It is not a desirable [thing to be] a Russian subject, and an occupation is, at the worst, but a [boa-cons]trictor, against which it is still possible to struggle; but the [other] is the polypus: if he pierces into our flesh, there is no pos[sibility of] extrication left for us.

[The da]nger which arises from the Russian movement cannot be [averted e]ffectually from the Austro-Hungarian Empire by watching [the Czar's] promise; for in either case he will occupy a conspicuous [place on t]he page of history as the victorious leader of Panslavism. [All Slav]onian aspirations towards a universal monarchy will gather around Czarism; this will be the star that will lead the way, the Messiah to whose call they will listen, the idol they will adore, the lord who will command them, and whose obedient serfs they will be; and *thus Panslavism will develop into Panslavo-Czarism.*

But if we send the Czar who unfurled the Panslavonic banner back as a loser, then the wings of his Ghengis-Khanic flight will be clipped, the charm broken, and the Panslavic aspirations will lose their force. The Slavonians will perceive that it is not safe to carve for themselves an idol, in order to adore him as the god of liberty. The prop will be found broken, and the support will fall asunder like loosened sheaves. The different Slavonic nations will not seek salvation in the worshipping of the Czarism that leads to Russification, and therewith to the fetters of slavery, to drunken misery, and dreams of brutality; but, in the conservation of their individual nationality, in the elevation and maintenance of the vestal-fire of their self-esteem, they will find the road that leads to freedom. And we Hungarians will welcome them heartily on this road, accompany them with warm sympathy, as we accompanied them in past times, and as far as we are able aid every pulsation of the vital power of yon miraculous Slavonic "*living statue,*" whose national consciousness has never been broken, either by seduction or by the storm of long sufferings.

Really, if there be any situation that is clear, the present one is.

The Turk has understood the signs of the time. He gave a constitution to the communities of his empire, without distinction of race, tongue, or creed, on the basis of equality before the law. His enlightened statesmen provided that all the excrescences of exclusiveness which had been successively added to the morally pure civilization of Mohammedanism, should be buried in the grave of the past. The Czar of all the Russias threw his army into the midst of this peaceable undertaking, to prevent the Turks from realizing this liberty. He was afraid that when even the half-moon should reflect the glare of the sun of liberty, this glare might penetrate into the darkness of his servile empire, as the beams of the Hungarian peasant-emancipation had penetrated the night of Russian slavery.

The Austro-Hungarian Government must reckon with itself as to what can be claimed legally and fairly from the Turkish Government in the interests of its Christian subjects, without undermining thereby the existence of the Ottoman Empire. Let them come to a mutual understanding with each other. It will not be so difficult, since the Porte has intelligence and good-will as well. They should conclude a treaty of alliance on the basis of this understanding, for the repulse of the Russian attack which threatens our fatherland and the Austrian monarchy very dangerously. With this alliance consummated, let Austria-Hungary say to Russia, "Well, the Turks have administered justice to their subjects, and thou wouldst still continue the war. This can have no other meaning than that thou strivest to extend 'er. This we cannot permit in the interests of our monarchy, are firmly resolved not to allow it. Then let the bloodshed

• •

it would cease. The Russian would not expose himself to nce, that whilst the Turkish lion stood in front of him, the Hungarian military force should take up a position behind his d cut off his retreat. The fatherland and the monarchy would l without striking a single blow, or at a proportionately small ; which sacrifice might be reduced to the concentration of icuous army-corps. This demonstration should of course be the Danube and in Transylvania, but not in Dalmatia, nor on tian military frontier, which would be very ridiculous if it were the same time very suspicious. And with the safety of the nd and of the monarchy the demands of humanity would idered also, for it is indeed very shocking that there should ar in the nineteenth century, which, in its horrors, exceeds ngol invasion in the thirteenth century. And the protec- the Eastern Christians would also be vouchsafed, without g the integrity and independence of the Turkish Empire or nity of the State. These results, which can be attained thus, thus, would secure the weight, the authority, the splendour, fame of our monarchy in the highest degree.

e only tried to show the political bearings, not to lay down schemes of action. I feel convinced that the looming danger y be averted from our country and from the monarchy by a aving the above-named tendency.

t is certain that, with such a tendency, the Government could count on the self-sacrificing readiness of the entire Hungarian without exception of party.

why does not the Government attempt it? Such a chance is e. Why not use it? These circumstances open up to Count Andrassy the opportunity of covering himself with great and glory. He can become the saviour of his fatherland, of the hy, of the reigning dynasty, if he will understand the work hour. He will be their gravedigger if he does not do it, or res not do it.

hinders him from daring it?

r Prussia mentioned. Yes, ten years ago the nation was ed into the Delegations by the Russian hobgoblin, and now like to be driven into the arms of Russia by the terror of

not deny the Russian inclinations of the Berlin Cabinet. The leanings of the Emperor William have a share in this, pos- undoubtedly great weight in the decision of the Berlin policy. false position of Germany has also a share therein, into which osition she has been thrown by the conquest of Alsace and

Lorraine, which seems even to push into the background a consideration which should never be lost sight of by Germany, at present the first Power of Europe. This consideration is that every increase of the Russian power must necessarily compromise the primatial position of the German Empire in Europe; and that in the last analysis—against which personal inclinations struggle in vain—it may lead to a collision between the German and Slavonian races, the like of which has not yet been witnessed by the world. Rome and Carthage cannot exist side by side for long.

But however strong the present inclinations of the Berlin Cabinet may be, they cannot go so far as to compel Prussia to take Russia for her patron, and become the client of the latter. And, in the last resort, the German Imperial policy has to reckon with the other German princes and with the German nation; and among the former, as well as in the ranks of the latter, there are those who recollect Russian patronage and the significance of clientship for Germany under Russian rule. And those who recollect this would soon warn the Berlin Cabinet that German blood belongs to Germany, and not to the Russians.

The knowledge of the logic of history, which I have acquired by long study and painstaking (and the cares that whitened my hair have their own tale to tell), and, at last, experience, have taught me that the German Emperor might give advice in the shape of Russian inspirations, but that, whatever be the policy of the Vienna Cabinet in the Eastern question, it is certain, that, to favour Russia, the German Empire will never declare war against the Austro-Hungarian monarchy.

I take all that they say about Prussian threats for mere claptrap, originating from yonder camarilla, that strives—and alas! strives with great effect—*that the Vienna Cabinet should do the same things in aid of the aggressive Russian policy against Turkey that it did against Poland, when Russia undertook to annihilate the independence of that unhappy country, and for the same end—viz., that she should become a sharer in the robbery,* instead of allying herself with Turkey, as she ought to have done with the Poles, to frustrate the robbery.

This is the danger which I see, like a death-prophesying bird, with outstretched wings, fluttering over my country; and my patriotism stimulates me to call to mind other things in connection with certain premonitory reflections on the rising manifestations of public opinion.

* * *

I repeat, that the important point for the Hungarian nation in this question is this: that by the war which rages in our neighbourhood the vital interests of our fatherland as well as those of Austria are jeopardized.

I place weight on the fact that at present the vital interests of Austria are in harmony with our vital interests.

My views on the subject of the connection between Austria and Hungary are known. These interests are in such opposition with reference to reciprocal State-life and mutual State-economy, that it is utterly impossible even to fancy any form of connection that would be satisfactory to both countries. It is for this that I remain in exile—a living protest against this connection.

I do not, therefore, consider it to be my duty to feel sad forebodings for the special interests of Austria when its danger does not at the same time threaten the interests of our fatherland. But when the danger of the one walks arm in arm with that of the other, I put great weight thereupon, in order that Austria should feel the danger in union with Hungary.

We stand in the face of a war that threatens our country and Austria with mortal dangers if we do not aid the Turks in impeding the extension of Russian power. This war has found Austria in a State-connection with Hungary. I do not think that Russia would listen to us if we should tell her she should delay the war till this connection be dissolved. She would surely not delay. Then things stand thus: that the same King of Hungary whom our nation asks to frustrate the Russian aggressive policy is also Emperor of Austria. This Austrian Emperor stands very often in opposition to the King of Hungary. This time he is not so. And I think that the wishes of our nation can only gain in weight when she asks her Sovereign to fulfil his duty as saviour of the country, by acting as he ought to do as King of Hungary; also, in the meantime, pointing out that this is his interest as Emperor of Austria as well. It is for this reason—namely, that I like to appeal also to Austrian vital interests—that I repeat emphatically that the vital interests of Hungary and of Austria are identical.

This view is perfectly justified by the political significance and far-reaching importance of the Eastern question as it stands with reference to us.

If the Turkish Empire were to be under no pressure from the power that threatens the liberty of Europe,—a Colossus increased to formidable proportions by the dismemberment of Poland—then the Eastern question would be nothing else than a home question between the Turks and the other peoples of different races in the Turkish Empire.

And if this question stood thus, neither the integrity nor the dismemberment of the Turkish Empire, nor the reforms conceded or denied to the nations of that empire, would affect in the least, not the more distant countries of Europe, but not even us or Austria, who are her neighbours, except from a humanitarian, sympathetical or antipathetical point of view.

We have learned to appreciate justly the fundamental features of the Turkish character. We are aware, as I have said, that we possess in the Ottoman nation such reliable friends as we could not find anywhere else in the world, because our interests are so identical that there is not only no opposition, but not even a difference between us. We recollect gratefully the generosity shown to us by the Turks in the days of our sorrow; and it is honourable on our part to remember this warmly just now in the days of their sorrow. And so it is certain that we Hungarians should follow all regenerational endeavours of the Turks with heartfelt sympathy and blessing. We should feel gratified if they succeed in removing the obstacles in their way to liberty. On the other hand, if in consequence of Russian pressure the dismemberment of the Ottoman Empire should be identical with the aggrandisement of Russia, there would not be a single Hungarian who would not consider the territorial integrity of Turkey, and the upholding of its sovereignty, as a *conditio sine quâ non* of the maintenance of our own integrity and independence. No one would think of shedding his blood nor offering aid to the Turks if it were not for the threatening attitude of Russia; but for that we should not look with anxiety on the aspirations of the Slavonic nations.

Though all the provinces of Turkey should gain such an "autonomy" (!) as that which is prepared for the Bulgarians by Prince Cherkaski after the Russian pattern and in the Russian language, still the Eastern question would not be solved, but would then be revived in the face of Europe, and especially in that of Hungary and Austria, in such tremendous proportions as it has not yet reached.

Yes, because the Eastern question, I repeat again, is a question of Russian power; clearly, distinctly, a question of Russian aggrandisement.

And it will remain so until Europe, after a tardy repentance, shall at last determine the restoration of Poland, and thus avert the curse from herself which she has incurred by the crime of that partition.

Only by the restoration of Poland can Russia be pushed back upon her ancient boundaries, where she could in her still vast empire let her subjects become free men, and thus occupy a still glorious and prominent place at the round table of civilized nations, but a place whence she could no more threaten us and Austria and Europe with her Panslavo-Czaristical and universal-monarchical ambitions. Only when it shall be made sure on the banks of the Vistula that she can never more suffocate Turkey—only then will the Eastern question step down to an internal, and, if you like it, to a humanitarian level, and be solved in such a way as not to be dangerous to Europe.

But so long as this does not happen, the Eastern question will always remain a Russian question of power. If the Turkish Empire should be dismembered in consequence of Russian pressure, or even if it should be crippled, I repeat that every inch lost by the Turks would only increase Russian power. The diminution of Turkish sovereign independence would increase Russian influence, which would act as a dissolving poison on us and on Austria; and the unavoidable consequence would be that the nations which had been severed from the Turkish rule would not become free, but Russian serfs—forming the tail of that boa constrictor which presses us closely, the arms of that polypus which clings to our flesh.

These are the considerations which induce the Hungarians to adopt the view that their very existence is endangered by the war in their neighbourhood.

And these considerations are so momentous that, if we Hungarians should continue to look on in cowardly inactivity at the dismemberment of the Turkish Empire, or, which is identical, at the aggrandisement of Russian power,—if we should look on in cowardly inactivity while the boa constrictor gathers material to form a new tail from the southern Slavonians, while the polypus makes out of them new trunks,—it would be such suicidal insanity that I cannot find a word to designate it. We should be worse than the worms creeping upon the ground if we did not protect ourselves against it.

These are sad times. After so much blood has been spilt that the nations might become independent, we are still in the position that the fancy and the will of two or three purple-clad mortals are decisive, and not the will of the people. But the Hungarian people will live—they will not go so far in their resignation as to commit suicide for the sake of any mortal man whatever. We must raise *a dike against the extension of Russian power*. And to do that, we must *conserve and uphold the unity and the independence of the Turkish Empire*; for at present that is the practical way to construct a dike. This view is firmly upheld by the Hungarian nation, whatever form of expression they may use to state their will; and in this respect all the Hungarians are of the same opinion without difference of party. They are of the same opinion, for they are convinced that this *is a vital interest of our fatherland. And justly therefore Hungary feels indignation, and disavows—the whole Hungarian nation does it—that immoral and impolitic idea, that the Austro-Hungarian monarchy should become an accomplice in the occupation of any part of Turkey for the sake of the enemy of our country's vital interests.*

Governments should never be in opposition to the popular wishes when Governments wear the constitutional toga. It is the worse policy if they are. On the present occasion the wishes of the nation show themselves so unmistakably plain, that it would be a dangerously daring feat if the Government should try to elude them by some Parliamentary trick. It is a question of existence. The nation knows this well. And ours is a loyal nation. Therefore, I say to those in authority, Comply with her wishes. Don't force her to take in her own hands the insurance of her life. She will do it if she is forced to it, because she will not die. The Hungarian nation will not be a worm to be trampled upon by the heel of the trampler. She will not suffer that the bowing diplomatists of Czars and Cæsars should convert Hungary into a powder barrel to be exploded by Russian intrigues with a Panslavonic match.

They told thee, Hungary! "Be reconciled with Austria that thou mayest be safe from the Russian." Thou hast been reconciled: let us see the conciliator, where is he?

Almighty Father! if the Hungarians were but independent!

De profundis ad te, Domine, clamavi.

I know that what I have been saying is nothing new. But still I thought it right to speak my mind, as the Prime Minister of Hungary has made a very startling declaration.

When it was resolved in a public meeting of citizens that the integrity of the Turkish Empire should be upheld even by armed force, the Prime Minister of Hungary gave the following answer:— "*That it is not allowable to shed Hungarian blood for the interests of any other Power, and that the Government will never give its consent that the heroic sacrifice of the Hungarian nation should be made for others.*"

So the Hungarian Prime Minister still considers the upholding of the Turkish Empire against the Panslavonic standard-bearer, the Russian Czar, as being for the interests of "others."

Every inhabitant of Hungary, who wishes the conservation of our country, and those, also, who speculate on her overthrow, know that *our country's existence is at stake.* The Prime Minister is, perhaps, the only man in Hungary who does not see this.

But since the crippling of the integrity of the Turkish Empire is identical with the aggrandisement of Russian power, nobody in the world has the right to say that Hungarians are sacrificing Hungarian blood for the sake of others, when they offer to shed it for the upholding of the integrity of the Turkish Empire. The Prime Minister ought to know that this willingness is a flower that has grown in the soil of self-preservation, and opened its cup under the shining of the purest patriotic sunbeams.

The Hungarian Prime Minister has spoken a startling word. If this is to be the standpoint of the Government, I declare most emphatically that the interests of Hungary are in dangerous hands.

Whoever, *in this war*, considers the upholding of the Turkish Empire to be a foreign cause, *will not raise a dike to the extension of the Russian power: for he is not far from the thought of sharing with the Russians in the Turkish booty.*

But I should like to believe that this most unlucky expression was only an unconsidered pistol-shot, which went farther than it was intended. I do not say that the Hungarian Government has deliberately thrown itself into the arms of those who are undoubtedly stirring dangerous questions in the regions of diplomatic circles. I can doubt, but I cannot assert, for I don't know it. But alas! I neither in the declarations of the Hungarian Government, tions of the leader of the foreign policy, can a Hungarian comfort.

be amiss to call to mind now, when the representatives of assembled again, that the nation, without difference of ects that they will rise above party spirit and secure the the nation's will.

weighty declaration of the Hungarian Prime Minister has which (I quote it word by word) he assured the House tatives that *there is not a single person among the leaders who t to be the aim of our foreign policy that the power and sove- ey should be changed.*

aration has been greatly applauded, because (as I know n both sides of the House many persons who were present, earing interpreted the speech, full of diplomatically-clever as assuring them that the directors of the foreign policy rchy would hold it to be their task to see that the power gnty of Turkey should remain unchanged.

Hungarian Prime Minister did not only not say this, not not want to say it, but, on the contrary, when some days the representatives ascribed this sense to the declaration e Minister, the latter contradicted that explanation of his

lucem, ingemui que reperta."

amed ministerial declaration comes to nothing else but house of our neighbour is so situated with reference to our if his catches fire ours will catch fire too. The house hbour has been attacked by robbers and incendiaries s. Our household takes fright for our dwelling, and the watcher of the Hungarian household says, 'Don't be give you the assurance that amongst us, your watchmen, e who would hold that it is his task to burn down our house!'"

r declaration of the Prime Minister has been, that "*the has not given to any one, in any sense whatever, a promise lo; nor have they assumed any obligation, but they possess their of self-decision.*"

declaration we learn two things, but neither of them is We learn that the Government does not know yet what It has no fixed aim. Its policy has no certain tendency. t without a compass. It expects good luck wherever the low. If this be policy, it is a very improvident one.

r brings its own counsel" (*Kommt Zeit, kommt Rath*). This ary. Such determination according to the occasion may ood thing in itself, it is well to know *how* we shall reach the aim we have in view; but I don't think, in the present international imbroglio of affairs, which endangers the vital interests of the country, that to relegate the tendency of policy (not the *how*, but the *what!*) to the chance of future decision, can be advisable or even permissible.

And I am very fearful that the Prime Minister has told the truth. I see that the Minister of Foreign Affairs, by the consent of the leaders of both parties, has constructed for himself a scheme wherein he can indeed place many things, but what are these things? This he leaves to the future. "*Kommt Zeit, kommt Rath.*" The signification of the plan is the following: "Let the Russians do whatever they like. Our position towards them is a friendly neutrality." *Neutrality, and friendly:* a steel hoop, made of wood! *Contradictio in adjecto.* But, alas! still true. *Friendly* towards Russia; *hostile* towards Turkey; but no *neutrality.* When a country is affected in her vital interests by a war, as our country is now, neutrality is an absolute impossibility. Inaction is no neutrality. That this hitherto observed inaction has been of great service to the Russians is a fact crying to heaven and earth. But I will now continue the scheme. "If the Turks shall be victorious, everything will remain as it has been; and we shall mediate during the final negotiations, in order that the Turk may not press too hardly on the Russians, with whom we shall keep on 'friendly terms.' If, on the contrary, the Russians advance victoriously, 'we shall take up a position' in behalf of the conquered Turks; we shall strive to moderate the Russian exactions at the final negotiations: but in any case, if the Russians rob, we will rob too, *if possible down to Salonica!* And then we will say to Hungary and to Austria, '*Well, we have secured the interests of the monarchy in the face of the Russian extension-policy.* The Russians have annexed, but we have annexed also: the equilibrium which was upset by robbery has been restored by robbery."

Such is the "scheme" of the policy of "*freedom of self-decision,*" of which the Prime Minister has been boasting. I shall be very glad if the patriotism of the national representatives should give such a guarantee for the fulfilment of the people's wishes as may refute my suspicion—I had nearly written my "*certainty.*"

The second thing we learn from the quoted declaration is this, that our Government *has no ally.* I think that, under such circumstances, there are two things which are the chief duties of a Government. The one is that it shall see its way clearly with reference to the tendency of its policy,—of this I have spoken already; the other is that, in order to secure this policy, it should think of getting allies. It is a bad case that the Government has no allies. I could even call this also neglect of duty, because they could have had allies if they had had a good policy.

But it is still worse that the *untrammelled attitude,* of which the Prime

Minister has boasted, *favours the Russians.* Since the beginning of the complications we have heard of nothing so emphatically as the confederacy of the three Emperors, which was formerly styled "a friendly understanding." One of those three confederates is the Czar. My dear fatherland! thou art indeed in great danger from that *untrammelled attitude* which operates in friendly relations with Russia. Hitherto it has acted in that way. I could cite many testimonies; I will quote only a single one.

The Government says it has no obligations. What! Has it not entered into an engagement to let Roumania be occupied by Russia who unfurled the banners of "The Slavonic Cause," and so to convert this province into a place for her military operations, notwithstanding that the neutrality of that country has been guaranteed by the European Powers, under whose protectorate it has been placed? Yes, they have engaged themselves, and by a formal bargain, because they have expressly stipulated, as a reward, that the Czar shall not force Servia into war.

This fatal obligation is the source of all the evils which have happened hitherto and which will happen hereafter, and of all the dangers that threaten our country.

But the thing does not end here. The world is filled with anxiety lest even this stipulation should be omitted, and lest the Viennese Cabinet should not try to prevent the Czar from taking Servia into action. Lo! because the Turkish lion has struck the Czar over the fingers, the great Czar is in want of the perjury of little Servia, to whom Turkey the other day granted forgiveness. Thus the *untrammelled attitude leans* again *towards Russia.*

The representatives of Hungary will, no doubt, without party difference, feel the danger that menaces them through this new aggravation of circumstances.

I must now advert to a third governmental declaration, and I find it very weighty.

When an interpellation was directed to the Government with reference to its policy, instead of confessing its leanings, it avoided the question by declaring *that the interests of the Austro-Hungarian monarchy have led and will lead their policy, and that the interests of the monarchy under every circumstance will be considered.*

The Government, in fact, always serves up the same dish, nobody knowing whether it is fish or flesh, not even the butler who serves it. This is the question, in what direction (*not by what means, but in what direction*) the Minister seeks his policy? and whether he seeks it in a direction conformable to the interests of the monarchy?

If they should again serve a dish, which is neither "fish nor flesh," in the House of Representatives, and if the House should be contented with this assurance (as we heard out of doors), that "*the Government keep before their eyes the wish of the nation that the interests of the monarchy—in opposition to the Russian policy of extension—should be secured,*" the ambiguity of the situation would not be at all changed, and the door would still be left open; so that if events took another turn, the water would be turned to grind the mill for those "influences that wish to get a share," and our nation would some morning awake to find that, under the *pretence of securing the interests of the monarchy*, things had happened which the nation abhors as it does damnation.

I do not speak so because I have forebodings; it is not my object to enter into questions of principles. I don't want to quote the sad pages of our own history, nor the examples of Polignac or MacMahon, to show that it has always been so; and that there has never been any impiety without the reigning power invoking interests of State when committing it. But as we stand in view of the danger of Russian extension, I pray my countrymen to look for that page of history where they will see it written, *how the Viennese Cabinet understands the securing of the interests of the monarchy when face to face with Russian aggressive policy!* This has such an actuality of interest that I nearly shudder when I think of it.

Whoever looks at those pages must feel convinced *that the Viennese Cabinet never did understand the securing of the interests of the monarchy so that the Russian extension should not be permitted; but it so understood them as that whenever the Russians commit robbery, Austria must rob as well,—that when Russia extends herself, Austria ought to do the same.*

So, I repeat for the third time, it understood them at the division of Poland, and so it has understood them ever since, without exception, when face to face with the Russian policy of extension.

This is an awful remembrance.

And this they call the policy of restoring the equilibrium!

And what has history said of that awful policy? I do not speak even of morals, of honesty—which is always the best policy in the end, though it was a long time ago struck out of the vocabulary of diplomacy. I point to facts.

By this policy the Russian power has been swollen to giant-like proportions, which now menace the whole world. The consequence of this policy is the war of to-day, and Russia now smooths her way, through the Turkish "Slavonic cause," to the Hungarian and Austrian "Slavonic cause."

On the other hand, this policy of sharing has not saved the Austrian dynasty from withering. Russia has grown up; Austria has dwindled.

And what will be the result if the Vienna Cabinet should again follow this damnable policy of expediency?

In the past it has put a razor in the hand of Russia; now it would put this razor to the throat of Hungary, and also of Austria.

"Duo cum faciunt idem, non est idem."

There can be no doubt that what the Russians would rob from the Turks, what their influence would win on both shores of the Lower

Danube and on the Balkan peninsula, would form a real increase of their power, an augmentation of their strength; and the influence thus acquired would act upon the Slavonians of the Austrian Empire, and upon those of the Hungarian Crown, like the loadstone on iron. Those Slavonians that would be caught by Russia, she would take with her.

On the contrary, what the Viennese Cabinet would pilfer, under the shadow of the Russian highwayman, from the Turkish Empire, would only weaken us, and become eventually our death; because it would eternally multiply and put into further fermentation all the already fermenting and dissolving elements. The Slavonians who would be caught by the Viennese Cabinet would take the latter with them.

And what would be the infallible final result? The punishment of *talio*. If St. Petersburg and Vienna should divide the rags of the torn Turkish Empire, twenty-five years would not elapse before the Russians, the Prussians, and the Italians would divide Austria and Hungary among themselves, perhaps leaving something of the booty to Wallachia, as the reward of subserviency to Russia. This is as true as that there is a God.

Well, I feel no call to be anxious about the dismemberment of Austria, if free nations might step into her place; but I do feel it my duty to be anxious about a dissolution by which Russian power and Russian influence would be increased. I feel it so much my duty, that if our fatherland were connected with Austria only by the ties of good-neighbourly friendship, and if Austria were threatened by the Russians, I would most determinedly say to my countrymen, "Defend thy Austrian neighbour to the last drop of thy blood against Russia," just as I say now, "Defend thy Turkish neighbour to the last drop of thy blood against Russia."

The reigning dynasty of Austria must reckon with the logic of history. A time may come—it must come—when her German provinces—will go home. Well, well, I say: the royal throne of the palace at Buda is a very glorious seat. It will be good to think about how, after its thousand years' history, it may not be menaced by the Russian monster—neither in the form of a boa constrictor, nor in that of an hundred-armed polypus. The time is come to think of it, now that the Turkish lion is fighting his life or death struggle so gloriously. Let us not lose the opportunity. "Sero medicina paratur." "Mene! Mene! Tekel! Upharsin!"

I do not say that the Hungarian Government has given itself up to the impulses of robbery; I say only, that this is not excluded from the "scheme." This vampire sits on its bed, on its chest, on its arms. Shake off the vampire, I say. *Free your arms, and step at the head of the nation.* It is a glorious place. In such a great crisis it is a very small ambition to aim, by the cleverly construed phrase of "taking notice," at getting a vote of confidence from your party. You should act so that the confidence of the whole nation should surround you. You can do it. You should adopt the policy that has been pointed at by the whole nation. You should not contradict yourselves, for you said that your *hands were free.*

To the representatives of the nation I would like to cry out from my remote solitary place, "The fatherland is in danger,—in such danger as it has never been in before, viewing the irrevocability of the consequences. Then let the fatherland not be made a party question among yourselves, my countrymen! Let the genius of reconciliation hover over you when you stand arm in arm around the altar of our fatherland. I do not ask you to upset the Government, but I beg of you to place it in such a situation that its stability would be guaranteed by the fulfilment of the nation's wishes. *The action of Servia has supplied you with an opportunity which answers even diplomatical considerations.* Don't let this occasion escape you."

The fulfilment of the nation's will is the purest loyalty. I say so—I, who never yield. It is true I do not like the Austrian eagle in our fatherland. But I wish not that this eagle should be consumed in flame by the Russian; and I shudder at the thought that Hungary may be the funeral stake.

I am a very old man. I long ago overstepped the line assigned by Scripture as the limit to human life. Who knows whether this be not my last word? May it not be the voice of one who cries in the desert!

LOUIS KOSSUTH.

# MR. HERBERT SPENCER AND MR. G. H. LEWES:

## THEIR APPLICATION OF THE DOCTRINE OF EVOLUTION TO THOUGHT.

### PART I.—MR. SPENCER ON THE RELATION OF SUBJECT AND OBJECT.

AT the conclusion of an inquiry, recently published, into the course and result of that philosophical movement which is represented by the names of Locke, Berkeley, and Hume, I ventured to speak of the systems of philosophy, which since their time have found favour in England, as anachronistic, and to point by way of contrast to Kant and Hegel, as representing a real advance in metaphysical inquiry. Among many of the few persons who attended to it, such language naturally excited surprise or offence. With those who look to "mental philosophy" for discoveries corresponding to those of the physical sciences, the German writers referred to have become almost a by-word for unprofitableness, while the "empirical psychology" of our own country has been ever showing more of the self-confidence, and winning more of the applause, which belong to advancing conquest. It had seemed to me, indeed, that a clear exposition, such as I sought to furnish, of the state of the question in metaphysics, as Hume left it, would suffice to show that it has not been met but ignored by his English followers. A fuller consideration, however, might have taught me that each generation requires the questions of philosophy to be put to it in its own language, and, unless they are so put, will not be at the pains to understand them. An historical treatment of them, indeed, is challenged alike by the loud pretension of contemporary metaphysic (whether so called or not), and by its complacent disregard of the metaphysic of the past; but, when offered, though it may be commended, it does not persuade. The current theories about soul and mind have got too far apart from, if not ahead of the question which Hume (in effect) raised and Kant took up, to be brought back to it by any inquiry into the antecedents which rendered it inevitable, or by any exposition of the logical obligations which it imposed on the next generation, but which English psychology has hitherto failed to recognize. Only by a direct examination of that psychology itself, as represented by our ablest writers, can we expect to produce the conviction that this primary question of metaphysics still lies at its threshold, and is finding nothing but a tautological or preposterous answer.

What is that question? It cannot really be better stated than in the formula of the schools, "How is knowledge possible?" Let the reader withhold for a few moments the derision which this statement may possibly provoke. It is not to be confused with a question upon which metaphysicians are sometimes supposed to waste their time—"Is knowledge possible?" We are not inviting any one to inquire whether he can do that which he constantly is doing, and must do in the very act of ascertaining whether he can do it. Metaphysic is no such superfluous labour. It is no more superfluous, indeed, than is any theory of a process which without the theory we already perform. It is simply the consideration of what is implied in the fact of our knowing or coming to know a world, or, conversely, in the fact of there being a world for us to know. *Why* such a consideration should occupy the mind of man at all, is a question which comes strangely from a generation which has been taught by Positive Philosophy that the only reason why for anything is a sufficiently general and uniform *that*. At any rate, it is a question which may for the present be postponed. That the mind of man is inevitably so occupied, even unto weariness and vexation, whenever it has won sufficient shelter from the pressure of animal want, is what popularized materialism, no less than histories of philosophy, may be taken to show. How, indeed, should it be otherwise? How should that busy and boundless intellect, which is evermore accounting for things in detail on supposition of their relation to each other, avoid giving an account to itself of the system which renders it possible for them thus to be accounted for; in other words, of the process in virtue of which it is intelligent and they are intelligible? But though it must needs render such an account, there is room for much variety in the degree of clearness with which it understands what it is about in doing so. It is not really the case that one age, or one set of thinkers and writers, is metaphysical, another not, though one may addict itself to methods of inquiry obscurely called "transcendental," another to such as are experimental and "comparative." It requires little subtlety to read metaphysics between the lines of the Positive Philosophy. The difference lies between the metaphysic which recognizes itself as such, and that which does not; between the metaphysic which because it understands the distinctive nature of its problem, does not seek the solution of it from the sciences which themselves form the problem to be solved, and that which, unaware of its own [illegible] though unable to discard [illegible] then extracts from them, under the guise of a scientific theory of mental phenomena, what are after all but the first thoughts of metaphysic clothing themselves in a new set of mechanical or physiological metaphors.

Our grievance, then, against contemporary philosophy is, that whereas the movement of speculation, which issued in Hume's Treatise, had for one who, like Kant, could read it aright the effect of putting the metaphysical problem in its true and distinctive form, to our countrymen it has never been so put at all; and that thus we have never taken what is the first step, though only the first, to its solution. This merely means, it may be said, that we have been wise enough to drop metaphysics betimes and occupy ourselves with psychology. If psychology could avoid being a theory of knowledge, or if a theory of knowledge were possible without a theory of the thing known, the reply might be effective; but since this cannot be, it merely means that it is unaware of the assumptions which it uncritically makes in order to its own justification. It is not really, nor can be, the case that our psychology has cleared itself of metaphysics, but that, being metaphysical still, it is so with the metaphysics of a pre-Kantian or even of a pre-Berkeleian age. In that region where it is truly independent of metaphysical questions, and which may roughly be described as the border-land between it and physiology, it has doubtless gained much ground which can never again be lost, but this region, as we hope to show, has definite limits. Beyond them the alliance with physiology, so useful within them, becomes simply illusive. It has merely served to give a semblance of scientific authority to what is in fact a crudely metaphysical answer to questions on which, rightly understood, physiology has nothing to say, but which it is apt to fancy that it is answering when it is merely repeating under an altered terminology the see-saw metaphysics of Locke—of Locke in his first mind, as represented by the second book of his Essay.

We have already adopted, as the best preliminary statement of the question which Hume bequeathed to such of his successors as could read him aright, the formula "How is knowledge possible?" This formula, however, like every other of the kind, derives its meaning from the intellectual process of which it represents the result—a process preserved for us in the history of philosophy, and which the reader must in some simple and summary manner repeat for himself if the phrase is to be significant for him. When first presented to him, it will probably excite such reflections as the following:—"This seems to be an uncouth way of asking how I and other men have come by the knowledge we possess. The answer is that we have been taught most of it, but that ultimately, as our best psychologists teach, it results from the production of feeling in us by the external world and the registration of feeling in experience." To those acquainted only with the conventional "transcendentalist" whose views, undisturbed by their own rules of verification, Mr. Mill and Mr. Spencer develop with such easy generality out of their own consciousness—the lay-figure which they set up to knock down—it may seem strange to be told that no disciple of Kant or Hegel, who knows what he is about, would dispute the truth of the above answer, but only its sufficiency. The fact that there is a real external world of which through feeling we have a determinate experience, and that in this experience all our knowledge of nature is implicit, is one which no philosophy disputes. The idealist merely asks for a further analysis of a fact which he finds so far from simple. It is not to the purpose to tell him that consciousness is a simple ultimate fact. Knowledge is quite other than mere consciousness, and, being so, admits of and requires explanation. The fact just stated is not an explanation of it, but a summary of what requires explanation. It either merely amounts to the fact that we know because something makes us know—which we may leave to be dealt with by the logicians who are so fond of the story of the opium and its *vis dormitiva*—or is only more than this because the "something" is determined as a "world," as "real" and as "external," and as in some way reflecting itself in our experience.

It is the analysis of these further determinations and of all which they imply that is the proper task of the metaphysician. He is the inheritor of Plato's Dialectic, and has to give an account of the hypotheses which the sciences assume. The question before him is thus one relating to the *object* of knowledge—What are the conditions implied in the existence of such an object? and an answer to this question forms the necessary prolegomenon to all valid psychology. Till it has been fairly dealt with, an inquiry into the subjective process through which the individual comes by his knowledge can have only an illusive result, for it will be assuming an answer to a question of which the bearings have not been considered, and will therefore be at the mercy of crude metaphor and analogy in its assumption. It is this question which it is Kant's great merit to have clearly raised, and which he fixed in the formula, "How is nature possible?" The process by which it was forced upon him was one which it took philosophy some generations to traverse, but which an English reader who will acquaint himself with a few classical writers of his own country may readily apprehend. The object matter of all philosophy, physical or metaphysical, had been fixed by Locke once for all as in some sort consciousness. Whatever could be known or spoken of, in the Newtonian physics no less than in his own field of inquiry, was for him an "idea," or some order or combination of "ideas." The equivalent phrase that all "knowledge is of phenomena" has become an accepted commonplace of the modern enlightenment. Like every commonplace, it is of value [illegible] it is used it is or is not [illegible] is the true baptism into philosophy, but a polemic against "ontologists" who are supposed to dispute it is no proof that the baptism has been effectually undergone. If from the proposition, which all admit, that knowledge is of appearances, we go on to inquire into the nature of appearances, we find the natural man surviving in an explanation of them which neutralizes the admission that they are appearances, or that they are relative to consciousness at all. They are explained as molecular changes of a nervous organism. Beginning with a doctrine which, if it means anything, means that only as an element in a world of consciousness can any material relation be known, we are asked to explain consciousness itself as one sort of such material relation; which is as if a physiologist should explain the vital process by some particular motion of a muscle which it renders possible.

In Locke himself, the determination of the object of knowledge as lying in ideas is virtually cancelled on almost every page where it occurs. Ideas are the object of the mind in knowing, but ideas, again, are of something, and on their relation to this the nature of the ideas depends. What is it? Two accounts of it perpetually cross each other in Locke, as in the philosophy of the present day, which reproduces him without knowing it. Sometimes it is presented as the mere negation of the ideas which yet are supposed to derive their reality, truth, and adequacy from relation to it; sometimes, although supposed to be something else than ideas, it turns out, when some verbal disguises have been removed, to consist itself in certain constant relations between ideas. It is under the influence of the former notion of the object—as that of which we can only say that it is not ideas, not consciousness—that a prerogative of reality is supposed to belong to simple ideas, or to feelings as opposed to thought. Of these, in Locke's language, "we cannot make one to ourselves;" they "thrust themselves upon us whether we will or no;" and thus, since a representative within consciousness must needs be sought of the object determined by opposition to it, they are naturally fastened upon to do duty as such. So far, however, no characterization has been gained for the real which enables us to say anything about it, or which can constitute a knowledge. To say that I feel it tells nothing unless I can say what my feeling is. But in order to say this I must have recourse to relations. These form the nature of every feeling, whether we regard them simply as relations between it and other feelings, or as relations between it and some kind of matter; whether, after the prevailing manner of Locke's second book, we interpret them as representing (in the way either of likeness or effect) qualities of body, or in the more modern mode, which begins to appear in his fourth book, as "facts" in the way of coincidence with, or sequence upon, other phenomena. But these relations, in virtue of which alone feeling has any definite reality at all, derive their being from that from which feeling is supposed not to derive itself; that from which it could not derive itself without losing its supposed title to represent the real. We do not care to show here, as can be shown from Locke's own words, that according to him they are creations of thought, or to press that distinction between feeling and thought which does not apply to feeling in its reality, but only to feeling as it would be if what the sensationalists say of it were true. It is clear that relations between feelings can only exist for a combining consciousness, whether we call this feeling or thought; and the same would be equally clear of relations between feeling and motions or configurations of matter, if the combining action were not overlooked under the phrase which has come to cover it. A motion can only be a motion, or a configuration a configuration, for a subject to which every stage of the one, every part of the other, is equally present with the rest; and what is such a subject but conscious? We are thus brought to the contradiction which underlies all Locke's doctrine, and which current philosophy must show that it has overcome if it is to be proof against the charge of being anachronistic—the contradiction between that conception of the real on the one hand, which alone allows of its being knowable, but at the same time, by finding it in relations, implies that it is a work of thought, and a conception which leaves it the unknown negative of consciousness on the other hand. Only if the latter conception is the true one, is there any reason for taking feeling, on the ground of the mind's supposed passivity in it, to be the organ which reports the real; only if the former conception be the true one, has feeling anything real to report.

It was the presence of this contradiction in Locke's system that led to its disintegration at the hands of Berkeley and Hume. The process of this disintegration it would be superfluous here to trace. We have only to do with the elements which it left for assimilation by a new philosophy. Berkeley, it is well known, fastened on the supposed externality of the real something which with Locke feeling was taken to represent; but, as commonly understood, and as it is at least not very easy to avoid understanding him, he raised the wrong question about it. The true question is not whether there is such a thing as external matter, but what it is external to; whether its outwardness is an outwardness TO thought, or an outwardness of body to body only possible FOR thought. The great lesson which Berkeley has left for posterity to learn is the mischief of confusing these questions. That it has scarcely yet been learnt is shown by the general acceptance of Hume's dictum—the dictum of his unphilosophical maturity—that Berkeley's doctrine "admits of no answer and produces no conviction." In truth, the doctrine which "produces no conviction" is the doctrine that "there is no such thing as external matter," and it is one which admits of [illegible] [illegible] in [illegible] the doctrine that all externality is a relation of matter to matter, with which the relation between thought and its object can only be identified by a misleading metaphor, since thought alone furnishes the synthesis in virtue of which any relation of externality can exist; and in this doctrine, though the influence of familiar language may make it difficult to comprehend, there is nothing to repel popular conviction.

In default of a clear recognition of this first principle of a valid idealism, Berkeley achieved nothing but the exposure of Locke's equivocation between felt thing and feeling. In other words, he eliminated from the real world, as outward, those relations which cannot be given in feeling if the supposed title of feeling to represent the real, as derived from the distinction between it and the work of thought, is to be maintained. The outer world thus ceases to be explicable as a system of things acting on us and on each other, and becomes merely a sequence of feelings. So far, however, the work of scepticism was only half done. The inner causative substance, which Locke had put alongside of the outer as a co-ordinate source of ideas, still survived. To it Berkeley did not apply his master's canon of reality, and in it could be found a plausible explanation of the possibility of knowledge. The thinking thing might be supposed to hold together successive feelings as a connected experience. It was virtually in this supposition that Berkeley found rest, without attempting either to articulate it into an explanation of the sciences or to justify the exemption of the thinking thing from the same treatment which he had applied to the felt thing. The work which he had begun in the supposed interest of religion, Hume completed in an interest which it is the fashion to call one of pure scepticism, but which it is difficult to distinguish from that of personal vanity. Having disposed of the thinking thing by the same method by which Berkeley had disposed of unthinking matter—as a superfluous intellectual interpretation of the data of feeling—he was left in front of the question, How there comes to be a knowable world? But he rather showed the necessity of meeting it than met it himself. What was logically required of him, was to account for the appearance of there being those relations which seem to form the content of our knowledge, but which disappear from reality when reality is reduced to a sequence of feelings. In regard to the relations of cause and effect, and of identity, he seriously attempted this. He reduces them in effect to tendencies of memory and expectation, to instinctive habits consisting in this, that the recurrence of a feeling, upon which another has been constantly and closely sequent, recalls that other with special liveliness. His account of them, however, not only has the fault that it makes the actual procedure of the sciences inexplicable—a fault which may perhaps be considered a virtue in a system professedly sceptical: it is also inconsistent with the principle which led to such an account being attempted—the principle that whatever is not given in feeling, and in feeling from which all determination by thought is excluded, is unreal. It assumes, if nothing else, yet at least the relations of succession and coincidence, as that of which the experience generates the secondary impressions or tendencies described, and these relations are not so given. This feeling, and this, and this, *ad indefinitum*, do not constitute a succession except as held together by a conscious something else, present equally to each of them; and this something else is by the hypothesis excluded from reality. Thus the very proposition, that reality is nothing but a succession of feelings, is self-contradictory, for, in the absence of everything but such succession, the succession itself could not be. A system like Hume's which started from such a proposition—a proposition, we must not forget, to which philosophy had been brought in the attempt to work out consistently a conception of reality still current among us—was foredoomed to failure.

The failure, however, has not been generally recognized. Hume's natural history of ideas is often referred to as a forecast of the great "discovery," which, by those who have never understood the real point of the controversy about *a priori* ideas, is commonly regarded as its final settlement. The hereditary transmission of tendencies is supposed to give the order of nature time enough to produce in the human consciousness those elementary ideas of relation which seem to determine, not to result from, the experience of the individual, and Hume's doctrine, it is thought, only required reinforcement from the discovery of this law to become proof against all attack. Such a notion shows that the very essence of his doctrine has been misapprehended. It is being regarded as no more than an account of a process by which, given certain relations as objectively existing, a knowledge of them on the part of the individual has been gradually formed. In truth, what its history required it to be, and what it actually attempted to be, was an explanation of the process by which, in the absence of all such relations as objectively real, the "fiction" of their existence has come to be formed. Hume knows no distinction between fact and impression. The "impression of reflection," to which he reduces every case of necessary connection—the propensity, namely, to pass from one particular feeling to another—*is* itself the only relation of cause and effect which he can allow really to exist. He can recognize no unity of the world, no uniformity of nature, but the regularity, varying in every individual and at every age, with which one idea suggests another in memory or imagination. Hence the peculiar difficulty of adjusting his system, so far as it is faithfully maintained, to the procedure of the physical sciences—a difficulty from which the modern "experientialist" saves himself by assuming both the reality of an objective order, and an elementary consciousness of it, as antecedents of the process by which knowledge is attained. He cannot, however, claim any superiority over Hume for so doing. He is merely ignoring the previous question which Hume was trying to meet. Given a world of intelligible relations, it is easy to account for knowledge. The modern "experientialist" is taking the reality of such a world for granted along with a theory of reality which excludes it. Hume was trying to explain it away in order that the same theory of reality—the theory which identifies it with feeling—might be consistently maintained.

Where Hume has been misapprehended, Kant is not likely to be understood. As Hume's doctrine is thought to be completed, so Kant's is thought to be superseded, by recent discoveries in the natural history of man. Kant, it is supposed, in spite of his own disclaimer, believed in innate ideas, though, instead of using that term, he called them *a priori* forms. It is allowed that something was to be said for that belief so long as the work of experience on the individual consciousness was held to begin with the individual's own life, but the discovery that accumulated effects of experience can be transmitted, through modifications of structure, from generation to generation, fully explains all that Kant sought to explain by the supposition of forms, which render experience possible but are not its result. For the present we postpone the inquiry whether the psychological inferences drawn from the alleged fact of transmission do not mostly imply a *μετάβασις εἰς ἄλλο γένος*—a confusion between the transmission of habits, which is one thing, and the transmission of conceptions, which is quite another. What has here to be pointed out is that the question treated by Kant, and raised for him by Hume, is not such a question of "psychogenesis" as the supposed discovery meets. It concerns the objective relations which render experience possible, not the individual's convictions in regard to them. According to Mr. Lewes, "by showing that constant experiences of the race become organized tendencies which are transmitted as a heritage, Mr. Spencer shows that such *a priori* forms as those of space, time, causality, &c., which must have arisen in experience because of the constancy and universality of the external relations, are necessarily connate."* In other words, Mr. Spencer has shown that, given space, time, and causality, as constant and universal external relations, together with an experience of them, they become necessarily connate forms of experience. To have shown this, however, does not seem a great achievement, for it is difficult to see how the derived result differs from that from which it is derived, and, if it does not differ, what merit there is in the discovery which explains the derivation. Between relations, constant and universal, of which, though external, there is experience (the source) and "necessarily connate forms of experience" (the result) the difference is only verbal. Is it meant that the "relations" are external, the "connate forms" internal, and that the transmission of tendencies explains the process by which the external becomes

* Problems of Life and Mind, vol. i. p. 245.

internal? We should be sorry to believe that Mr. Spencer and Mr. Lewes regard the relation between consciousness and the world as corresponding to that between two bodies, of which one is inside the other; but apart from some such crude imagination it does not appear that the externality of the relations in question, which are brought within consciousness by the statement that we have experience of them, can mean anything else than that experience depends on them, not they on it—that they are constituents of it in its simplest possible mode, not its gradually-formed result. But this is the same thing as saying that they are its "necessarily connate forms." Kant held no other view of them, but instead of applying himself to the superfluous labour of showing how the external relations become the "connate forms" which they already are under another name, he sought to analyze, and, in his own language, to "deduce" them. He set himself, in other words, to ascertain what the relations are which are necessary to constitute any intelligent experience or (which is the same) any knowable world; and to explain *how* (not *why*) there come to be such relations—what is presupposed in the fact that there they are.

Of his success or failure in the work he undertook we are not here concerned to speak. For the present it is only important to point out the mistake of our "experiential psychologists" in putting their theory into competition with his, as if it dealt with the same question. He is at least trying to explain what they take for granted. It will perhaps be replied that it was just in this that his fault or misfortune lay; that, like other metaphysicians, he spent himself in seeking to solve the insoluble—to get behind or beyond the ultimate data of inquiry—and hence contributed nothing to the stock of positive knowledge which empirical psychology has so largely increased. In order to estimate the value of the received view which such language implies, we must look more closely at these "ultimate data." Are they really facts behind which we cannot penetrate, or merely familiar theories which, in default of further analysis and explanation, are vitiating the inferences drawn from them? So long as the dominant philosophy is allowed to represent the question between it and its "idealist" opponents in the mode which generally passes current, the continuance of its domination is assured. If the alternative really lay between experience and ready-made, unaccountable intuition as sources of knowledge; if the point in dispute were whether theories about nature should be tested merely by logical consistency or experimentally verified—whether "subjective beliefs" should be put in the place of "objective facts," or brought into correspondence with them—the "experientialists" would be entitled to all the self-confidence which they show. That the question does not so stand, they can scarcely be expected to admit till their opponents constrain them to it; and in England hitherto, whether from want of penetration or under the influence of a theological *arrière pensée*, their opponents have virtually put the antithesis in the form which yields the "experientialists" such an easy triumph. Both sides are in fact beating the air till they meet upon the question, What constitutes the experience which it is agreed is to us the sole conveyance of knowledge? What do we mean by a fact? In what lies the objectivity of the objective world?

According to Mr. H. Spencer's own statement, a certain conception of the relation between subject and object is the presupposition of his system:—

"The relation between these, as antithetically opposed divisions of the entire assemblage of manifestations of the unknowable, was our datum. The fabric of conclusions built upon it must be unstable if this datum can be proved either untrue or doubtful. Should the idealist be right, the doctrine of evolution is a dream."*

To those who have humbly accepted the doctrine of evolution as a valuable formulation of our knowledge of animal life, but at the same time think of themselves as "idealists," this statement may at first cause some uneasiness. On examination, however, they will find in the first place that when Mr. Spencer in such a connection speaks of the doctrine of evolution, he is thinking chiefly of its application to the explanation of knowledge—an application at least not necessarily admitted in the acceptance of it as a theory of animal life; and secondly, that what Mr. Spencer understands by "idealism" is what a raw undergraduate understands by it. It means to him a doctrine that "there is no such thing as matter," or that "the external world is merely the creation of our own minds"—a doctrine expressly rejected by Kant, and which has had no place since his time in any idealism that knows what it is about. Either Mr. Spencer's profound study of the physical sciences has not left him leisure, or his splendid faculty of generalization has relieved him from the necessity, for a thorough investigation of the history of philosophy. In lieu of it there are signs of his having accepted Sir W. Hamilton's classification of 'isms. His study of "idealism" at first hand would seem to have been confined to a hasty reading of Berkeley and Hume, of whom it is easy enough to show that their speculation does not agree with common sense, but not so easy to show that it is other than a logical attempt to reduce Locke's formulation of the deliverances of common sense, which is also virtually Mr. Spencer's, to consistency with itself. Of Kant it is hard to suppose that he would write as he does if he had read the "Transcendental Analytik" at all, or the "Transcendental Æsthetik" otherwise than hastily. This is not said in order to raise a preliminary suspicion against his system, which may very well have a higher value than could be given by a critical appreciation of other people's opinions—which must at any rate stand or fall upon its own merits, and will certainly not fall for any lack of intellectual energy or wide-reaching knowledge upon the part of its author. It is merely

* Principles of Psychology. Edition of 1872, § 387

said as a justification for ignoring his polemic against idealists, and passing straight to a consideration of his own account of his "datum," and of the consequences he draws from it.

Little as a well-instructed idealist of this century would recognize himself in the portrait which Mr. Spencer draws of him, he would readily admit that in the "datum" above stated, as understood by Mr. Spencer, lies the root of bitterness between them. To such an idealist all knowing and all that is known, all intelligence and intelligible reality, indifferently consist in a relation between subject and object. The generic element in his definition of the knowable universe is that it is such a relation. The value of this elementary definition, he is well aware, depends on its further differentiation; but he holds it to be the first step in any account that is to be true of the world as a whole, or in its real concreteness, in distinction from the accounts of its parts rendered by the several, more or less abstract, sciences. Neither of the two correlata in his view has any reality apart from the other. Every determination of the one implies a corresponding determination of the other. The object, for instance, may be known, under one of the manifold relations which it involves, as matter, but it is only so known in virtue of what may indifferently be called a constructive act on the part of the subject, or a manifestation of itself on the part of the object. The subject in virtue of the act, the object in virtue of the manifestation, are alike and in strict correlativity so far determined. Of what would otherwise be unknown, it can now be said either that it appears as matter, or that it is that to which matter appears. The reality is just this appearance, as one mode of the relation between subject and object. Neither is the matter anything without the appearance, nor is that to which it appears anything without the appearance to it. The reality of matter, then, as of anything else that is known, is just as little merely objective as merely subjective; while the reality of "mind," if by that is meant the "connected phenomena of conscious life," is not a whit more subjective than objective. "Matter," in being known, becomes a relation between subject and object; "mind," in being known, becomes so equally. It follows that it is incorrect to speak of the relation between "matter and mind"—"mind" being understood as above—as if it were the same with that between subject and object. A mode of the latter relation constitutes each member alike of the former relation. The "phenomena of matter," the "phenomena of consciousness," the connection between the two sets of phenomena, equally belong to an objective world, of which the objectivity is only possible for a subject. Nor is it to the purpose to say that, though matter *as known* involves the relation of subject and object, matter *in itself* does not. We need not inquire for the present into the meaning of "matter in itself." The matter which is in question, when we speak of a relation between matter and mind as equivalent to that between object and subject, is not "matter in itself," but matter as a "phenomenon" or as known; and since in this sense it is a certain correlation between object and subject, it may not be identified with one member of that relation to the exclusion of the other.

[illegible] the idealist's view, his quarrel with the doctrine of which Mr. Spencer is the most eminent representative is briefly this, that, taking, and rightly taking, the relation between object and subject as its datum, it first misinterprets this into a "dictum" on the part of consciousness that something independent of itself—something which can exist without consciousness, though not consciousness without it—is acting upon it; and then proceeds to explain that knowledge of the world which is the developed relation between object and subject, as resulting from an action of one member of the relation upon the other. It ascribes to the object, which in truth is nothing without the subject, an independent reality, and then supposes it gradually to produce certain qualities in the subject, of which the existence is in truth necessary to the possibility of those qualities in the object which are supposed to produce them. Instead of regarding subject and object as logical or ideal (though not the less real) factors of a world which thought constitutes, it "segregates" them as opposite divisions of the world, as two parts of the complex of phenomena, separate though capable of mutual interaction, of which one is summarily described as thoughts, the other as things. If we ask for the warrant of this antithetical division, a deliverance of consciousness is appealed to—a deliverance which is derived from the true correlation of subject and object, but is misinterpreted as evidence of the separate existence of the latter. "Thoughts" having been thus made the evidence for "things," no more questions are asked about the "things." On the strength of the admitted determination of subject by object—the converse determination being ignored—they are afterwards assumed to be the efficient cause of "thoughts." As apparent objects they are supposed to produce the intelligence which is the condition of their appearance. Through qualities which in truth they only possess as relative to a distinguishing and combining consciousness, and through the "registration" of these in the sentient organism, they are supposed gradually to generate those forms of synthesis without which in fact they themselves would not be.

The above we believe to represent the logical order which Mr. Spencer's philosophy follows. A happy instinct, however, has led him in the statement of it to put his presuppositions in regard to object and subject last. In his "Psychology" he first triumphantly explains, through three-fourths of the book, the genesis of "thought" from "things" on the strength of the assumed priority and independence of the latter, and defers the considerations likely to raise the question whether this assumption is correct—he never directly raises it himself—till he can approach them with the prestige of a system already proved adequate and successful. If the doctrine of evolution is true, the idealists are crushed already. If they are right, "the doctrine of evolution is a dream." Such being the alternative stated, the reader, to whom the doctrine has already been exhibited as an explanation of himself sanctioned by the collective authority of the sciences, is naturally ready to take the demolition of the idealists for granted. If, however, at the end of the hundred and fifty pages, full of logical sound and fury, through which the refutation of an idealism, unrecognizable by idealists, is carried on, he retains any curiosity about the doctrine which is to take its place and to justify all the preceding system, he will find a good deal to surprise him. Having gathered from Mr. Spencer's refutation of them that the idealists are people who perversely identify subject and object, and refuse to recognize the latter as a real world beyond consciousness, he naturally expects that the object according to the true doctrine of it will turn out to be such a world. But here Mr. Spencer leaves him in the lurch. The subject and the object, according to the account given of them, are as much or as little beyond consciousness the one as the other. Under the guise of a novel doctrine which is to reconcile all that is true in idealism with the opposite theory, we are offered a "realism," "transfigured" indeed, but so transfigured as to be scarcely distinguishable from the crude idealism of Locke.

Let us consider in detail the pertinent passages of his "Psychology," which it takes some sifting to arrive at. "Mysterious as seems the consciousness of something which is yet out of consciousness, the inquirer finds that he alleges the reality of this something in virtue of the ultimate law—he is obliged to think it. There is an indissoluble cohesion between each of those vivid and definite states of consciousness known as a sensation and an indefinable consciousness which stands for a mode of being beyond sensation and separate from himself."* Here it appears that the very ground asserted for the "reality of something out of consciousness" implies that this "something" is not "out of consciousness," and that the very proposition which is intended to state its outsideness to consciousness in fact states the contrary. The "something out of consciousness" is "something we are obliged to think," and is pronounced "real" on account of this obligation. It does not appear, indeed, whether the "obligation" is taken to constitute its reality, or merely to be an evidence of it as something extraneous; but this can only make a difference between the greater or less directness of the contradiction involved in the statement. It is a direct contradiction to call that "out of consciousness" of which the reality lies in the obligation to think it, but the other interpretation of Mr. Spencer's meaning only puts the difficulty a step further back. It is clear that the "something we are obliged to think" is something we do think, and therefore is not

* Principles of Psychology, § 448.

"out of consciousness." Nay, according to Mr. Spencer, the sole account to be given of it is that it is a necessity of consciousness. If, then, its "reality" is "out of consciousness," we have something determined solely as being that which its reality is determined solely as not being. Of the "something" we can only say that it is found in consciousness; of its "reality" we can only say that it is "out of consciousness." We look anxiously to the next sentence for an explanation of the paradox, but only find it stated more at large. The obligation to think the "something" now appears as its "indissoluble cohesion with each sensation," and, as was to be expected, the "something" thus cohering is now admitted to be itself a "consciousness." Its distinction is that it is "indefinable," and that it "stands for a mode of being beyond sensation." This "mode of being beyond *sensation*" might, indeed, be understood in a way which leads to a true conception of the object, but with Mr. Spencer it is merely equivalent to the "something out of consciousness" of the previous sentence. The only difference, then, which this further statement makes is, that the something out of consciousness which we are obliged to think is now explicitly broken into an "indefinable consciousness" on the one hand, and "a mode of being beyond consciousness, for which it stands," on the other. Now, an indefinable consciousness means a consciousness of which no account can be given, but simply that it is a consciousness. The result, then, is that the "object," about which Mr. Spencer undertakes to set the idealists right, is, according to him, something of which we can only say that it is consciousness, "standing for" something of which we can only say that it is not consciousness. In corresponding passages elsewhere, instead of "stands for," Mr. Spencer writes "symbolizes," but what becomes of the symbolical relation when of the symbol nothing can be said but that it is not the thing symbolized, and of this nothing but that it is not the symbol? A consciousness which is thus symbolical is indeed "mysterious," but there are mysteries which are near akin to nonsense.

So far we have merely a repetition of a notion familiar to students of Locke. According to it, simple feeling, of which nothing can be said but that it is feeling, is taken necessarily to represent a real something of which nothing can be said but that it is not feeling. We proceed to some other passages:—

"While it is impossible by reasoning either to verify or to falsify this deliverance of consciousness, it is possible to account for it. . . . This imperative consciousness which we have of objective existence, must itself result from the way in which our states of consciousness hang together. . . . Let us examine the cohesions among the elements of consciousness, taken as a whole; and let us observe whether there are any absolute cohesions by which its elements are aggregated into two antithetical halves, standing respectively for subject and object."*

* Principles of Psychology, § 449.

The result of the examination is thus stated :—

> "The totality of my consciousness is divisible into a faint aggregate which I call my mind; a special part of the vivid aggregate cohering with this in various ways, which I call my body; and the rest of the vivid aggregate, which has no such coherence with the faint aggregate. This special part of the vivid aggregate, which I call my body, proves to be a part through which the rest of the vivid aggregate works changes in the faint, and through which the faint works certain changes in the vivid."*

Here it is more clear that we have a contradiction of the passage previously quoted than that we have a more tenable view. There the characteristic of the "object," as being "something out of consciousness," is still retained, though retained under difficulties; but here it appears as itself an aggregate of certain elements of consciousness—as one half of the totality of consciousness, antithetical to another half which is the subject. It is true that at first these several "halves of consciousness" are said, not to be, but to "stand for" object and subject respectively. So far a verbal correspondence is maintained with the passage previously quoted, where the "indefinable consciousness" was said to stand for a mode of being beyond sensation, but it is merely verbal, for that which here "stands for" the object, being a vivid aggregate of elements of consciousness, is quite different from the "indefinable consciousness," expressly distinguished from sensation, there said to stand for it. Nor would it seem that Mr. Spencer himself attaches much importance to the distinction between "is" and "stands for," since he expressly identifies the distinction between the "vivid and faint aggregates" with that between body and mind, which again he elsewhere takes as equivalent to that between object and subject; and in the sequel the "separation of themselves" on the part of states of consciousness "into two great aggregates, vivid and faint," is spoken of as a "differentiation between the antithetical existences we call object and subject."†

If words mean anything, then, Mr. Spencer plainly makes the "object" an aggregate of conscious states, of which the distinction from the other aggregate, called the subject, is to be sought in the "cohesions" between the several states that form each aggregate. This search, however, is to end in the discovery of certain "absolute cohesions," which constitute the antithetical difference required; and we do not feel sure between what, in the context before us, these "absolute cohesions" are understood to lie. With a more scrupulous writer we should presume that, as the cohesions proposed for examination are cohesions among the elements of consciousness, the "absolute

* Principles of Psychology, § 462.

† Ibid. § 468: "While we are physically [illegible] separate themselves from instant to [illegible] each coherent within itself, having its [illegible] ways distinguished from the other. And [illegible] tical existences we call subject and object [illegible] possible, is made clearer by deliberate [illegible]

[illegible] we have to find would be so likewise; but it may [illegible] is here contemplating the discovery of an absolute [illegible] elements of consciousness and something which is [illegible]ciousness" altogether. Such a coherence, according to in that "deliverance of consciousness" which he under[illegible]unt for;* and though the process of examination, as he [illegible]ibes it, is one which could not possibly yield the account [illegible]st of, we shall not be surprised to find that, when it [illegible]upposes it to have done so. The process consists in a series of contrasts† between the states called "vivid" [illegible]lled "faint," which are pretty much the same as those by [illegible]ley, following Locke, distinguished "ideas of sense" of imagination," and Hume "impressions" from "ideas," [illegible]e often taken to constitute the difference between outer [illegible]se. Criticism of them may be postponed till a later stage [illegible]ry. All that we have to notice for the present is, that makes no pretence of treating the elements of the "vivid as other than states of consciousness. In one of his for instance, he speaks of making "the set of visual [illegible] he knows as his umbrella, move across the sets of he knows as the shingle and the sea," with a freedom [illegible]ley could not surpass. Nor is this all. It is only by a [illegible]ms, according to his own showing, that this vivid aggre[illegible]d an aggregate at all. The "states of consciousness" [illegible]t "have none of them any permanence." Each "changes to instant." To speak of such states "aggregating" or [illegible] themselves" is a contradiction in terms.

[illegible]ow to see how the "object," having been reduced to this [illegible]ting states—having become half of the totality of a con[illegible]hich, as described, does not admit of totality—is made to [illegible]n "beyond consciousness," as an "unknowable reality" [illegible]s our knowledge. An acquaintance with Locke will [illegible]oth for the result arrived at, and the process by which it The process is the simple one of putting alongside of the [illegible]onsciousness that what I feel is a feeling the counter[illegible] what I feel resists, and is there before and after my [illegible] attempt is made at such interpretation of the con[illegible] as might reconcile while it accounted for them; and, [illegible]e strange, whereas with Locke the former dictum is not [illegible]ted, with Mr. Spencer it is emphasized as strongly as [illegible]y and Hume, while yet his mode of dealing with it is, in [illegible]ther than a resort to Locke's confusion between feeling [illegible] judgment of solidity.

[illegible]d, as one of the leading contrasts between states of [illegible]elonging to the vivid aggregate and those belonging

[illegible] Psychology, § 449. † Ibid. § 458.

to the faint, that the former are "unchangeable by the latter in their qualities or order," he afterwards finds that one sort of "faint state" does "tend to set up changes in a certain combination belonging to the vivid aggregate." Further, "the changes which states in the faint aggregate"—which is in the vulgar the mind—"set up in this particular part of the vivid aggregate"—which in the boorish is the body—"prove to be the means of setting up special classes of changes in the rest of the vivid aggregate"—which in the common is the world. Thus "ideas and emotions, exciting muscular tensions, give my limbs power to transpose certain clusters of vivid states." Here we arrive at experiences which, according to Mr. Spencer, "give concreteness and comparative solidity to the conceptions of self and not-self;" and he proceeds, with an abundance of illustration which abridgment would spoil, to explain how the

"mutual exploration of our limbs, excited by ideas and emotions, establishes an indissoluble cohesion in thought between active energy as it wells up from the depths of our consciousness, and the equivalent resistance opposed to it: as well as between the resistance opposed to it and equivalent pressure in the part of the body which resists. Hence the root-conception of existence beyond consciousness becomes that of resistance *plus* some force which the resistance measures."*

But Mr. Spencer is counting his chickens before they are hatched. We shall not dispute that the process which he describes may "give concreteness to the conceptions of self and not-self," or that through it "the root-conception of existence beyond consciousness" may become what he says it becomes. In passing, indeed, we would commend a doctrine, which implies that the more abstract conception is prior to the more concrete, to the attention of any of Mr. Spencer's disciples who may still identify thought with abstraction. What we have to notice, however, is that if the conceptions of self and not-self, of existence beyond consciousness, are to be thus affected, they must be present; and that Mr. Spencer has not only not accounted for their presence, but has put in their stead certain successions of states of consciousness. We were waiting to see how either these successions were to be transformed severally into self and not-self, or the conceptions of these objects were to be otherwise accounted for; but instead of this, we are offered an account of a process which presupposes both the objects and the conceptions of them. Mr. Spencer, like Locke, "looks into his breast" and finds the experience of resistance (Locke's "solidity"), which at once reports to him the existence of a resistent something, independent of consciousness. He never considers what is implied in the transition from a succession of states of consciousness, distinguished as faint and vivid, to such an experience. His account of it in its simplest form is as follows:—

"I find that as to feelings of touch, pressure, and pain, when self-produced [*sc.*, produced by myself], there cohere those states in my consciousness which

* Principles of Psychology, §§ 461, 462, 466.

were their antecedents; it happens that when they are not self-produced, there cohere in my consciousness the faint forms of such antecedents—nascent thoughts of some energy akin to that which I used myself."*

The truth of this account is not now in question. The point to observe is, that it is only so far as what is still ostensibly an account of a succession of conscious states really presupposes something quite different, that it is an account of an experience of resistance. There are certain relatively vivid states—feelings of touch, pressure, and pain—which have their antecedents in certain relatively faint states—ideas or emotions. This is one proposition: but Mr. Spencer tacitly converts it into another—I become conscious, through mutual exploration of my limbs, of a power to produce changes in the vivid states of consciousness, known as my body—without apparently being aware of the difference. Yet he has really substituted for a proposition asserting a succession of feelings one expressing an experience determined by the conceptions of cause and substance. Again, vivid feelings, similar to those which have their antecedents in the relatively faint ones, have their antecedents in relatively vivid ones, and with these, notwithstanding their sequence upon vivid antecedents, there "were faint forms" of the antecedents belonging to the faint aggregate which like feelings have followed in other cases. This, on Mr. Spencer's authority, we are ready to accept as a phenomenon of mental association; but before it can become even the "nascent thought" of external energy, a reduplication of the substitutory process already noticed must be gone through. The antecedence of more faint states to more lively ones having been previously converted into a "consciousness of power, &c.," as above, the "coherence with the faint forms" of these antecedents becomes a coherence with such a consciousness. This alone, however, would merely account for the interpretation of the feelings of touch, pressure, and pain as products of "the mind" in the one case as much as in the other. To obtain the required result, we must suppose a combination effected between the faint imagined antecedents of these feelings, interpreted as consciousness of power, on the one side, and their actual vivid antecedents, interpreted as body, on the other; a combination which somehow yields the conception of a body exercising a power corresponding to that of which I am conscious in myself.

What is here supposed is a complex intellectual act—over and above feeling, if we like to call it so, but not beyond consciousness. Mr. Spencer's account, in short, of the experience of resistance, taken as it stands, while it fails to prove the existence of a real world beyond consciousness, or to give significance to that essentially unmeaning phrase, does show the experience which yields the consciousness to be not such a one as, in language virtually the same with that of Locke's idealist followers, he himself describes. If Berkeley and Hume could

* *Principles of Psychology*, § 463.

reappear among us, they might claim a good deal of the seventh part of the "Psychology" as essentially their own. They would seemingly have found a successor with a phraseology indeed more copious than theirs, and whose minute introspection of mental "cohesions" they had but imperfectly anticipated, but who was yet speaking with their voice. On further study, however, they would find that this was only his "forward voice," and that his "backward voice was to utter foul speeches of them and detract." "You agree with me," Berkeley might say, "that when we speak of the external world, we are speaking of certain lively ideas connected in a certain manner. You, indeed, prefer to call them vivid states of consciousness, but we need not quarrel about terms. You agree also that outward events are changes wrought among or upon these states of consciousness; and that our notion of the power which produces them is derived from our experience of such power as exercised by our own minds. If I could but induce you to say that the external force, which you have admitted to consist in a power of producing changes in consciousness and to be known only as corresponding to the like power in our own mind, itself belongs to a mind which is God!" Hume, on the other side, might put in a word for himself with still more effect. "You agree with me that what we call the world is a series of impressions, and what we call the mind a series of ideas and emotions, which differ from impressions in degree of liveliness.* And since you are as clear as I am that these states of consciousness have no continued existence, you can scarcely be serious in holding that there really is such existence in the world which you admit to be made up of such states. You see, too, that the production of change by mind in body is in fact the antecedence of certain elements of the fainter series to certain elements of the more lively; just as the production of change by one body in another is the antecedence of some elements to others within the more lively series. Only be consistent, and you must admit that inward power and outward force, energy of mind and energy of body, are phrases to which the corresponding realities are just these antecedences, *plus* an indefinite expectation of their recurrence."

Against such insinuations of the enemy, Mr. Spencer practically fortifies himself, as orthodox churchmen advise us to do under similar circumstances, by simply repeating his creed. He reiterates the fact—there is an object and there is a subject, there is a self and there is a not-self, there is mind and there is matter—without

* It should be observed in passing, that the distinction in respect of liveliness and faintness, as drawn by Hume, does not lie between sensations on the one side, and ideas *and emotions* on the other; but between impressions, whether primary (*i.e.* of sense), or secondary (*i.e.* desires and emotions), on the one side, and the ideas of these on the other. If the distinction is to be made at all, there is more to be said for it in this form than as put by Mr. Spencer, whose doctrine requires us to reckon "active energy as it wells up from the depths of our consciousness" among "the faint states."

The disturbance which the "emotions" cause in the classification of states into "vivid" and "faint," appears from a comparison of § 460 of the "Principles of Psychology" with § 43 of the "First Principles"—in particular page 151, third edition.

apparently being aware that the question is not *whether* there are such things, but *what* they are, and that he has conceded the premisses from which Hume's account of them is derived. Hume's explanation of them, it is true, explains them away, and is doubtless condemned by so doing. It is incompatible with the existence of a known world, and Mr. Spencer's analysis of the experience of resistance involves its contradiction as much as, but no more than, a valid theory of intelligent experience in any of its forms must do. But having satisfied himself by consideration of this experience that there are such things as "mind and matter," he contents himself with hurling this asseveration at the head of the Humists without considering its bearing on his own doctrine, which is also theirs, of what mind and matter are. His relation to Hume is in brief this: Hume, attempting to show what mind and matter are, did so by a theory which logically implied that they were not; *i.e.*, that there was no real unity corresponding to either of these names. Mr. Spencer adopts this theory, or at least repeats the propositions which contain it, but puts alongside of it another which implies that there really are such unities. He thus shows at once that the adopted theory is wrong, and that he misunderstands his own refutation of it. He takes this refutation for a proof that there is a world "beyond consciousness," whereas really it is a proof that consciousness is not what he takes it to be. It cannot at once be what Mr. Spencer's system requires it to be, and tell what his system requires it to tell. If it is to yield the "dictum" of its relation to an object, which he interprets as its announcement of a world independent of itself, instead of being a succession of states produced by such a world, it must itself be the condition of there being that world of which it tells.

The truth is, that "consciousness" with Mr. Spencer has two different meanings, and that his system really turns on an equivocation between them. It means one thing when it is found to tell of an objective world; another thing when this world is shown to be independent of it. So long as consciousness is understood to be a mere succession of states, it is easy to show that the objective world is independent of it, but the consciousness which can alone tell of such a world is not such a succession. We have already seen how, when Mr. Spencer, after condemning at large all who question the independent existence of the objective world, comes to give his own account of it, he describes what is neither an independent existence nor even a world at all, but a succession—an "aggregate" which is never aggregated—of vivid feelings. When, like Peter's brothers in the "Tale of a Tub," with this brown loaf before us we ask for the promised mutton, we are told that it is there already—"as true, good, natural mutton as any in Leadenhall Street." "Independent existence," it seems, "is implied in the vivid aggregate."* A "root-conception of

* Principles of Psychology, § 444.

existence beyond consciousness" is somehow given in and with the succession of conscious states, and this through a certain experience becomes the conception "of resistance *plus* some force which the resistance measures." But when we look to the account given of the experience which is thus to determine the conception of the relation between subject and object, we find it wholly different from the experience in which this distinction was supposed to be given. That was an experience consisting in successive states of feeling, distinguished as more or less vivid; this is a consciousness of power as exercised by oneself, and measuring a like power exercised by something not oneself. Mr. Spencer does not attempt to show how one sort of experience can "become" the other—how an antecedence of a fainter feeling to one more vivid becomes a consciousness of antagonism between agents of which just that has to be denied which is asserted of feelings. He simply at pleasure puts the one for the other. Yet the difference between them is no less than that between an experience which does and one which does not reveal a world. It is not, as Mr. Spencer sometimes puts it, a difference between a consciousness in which the relation between subject and object is given less concretely and one in which it is given more concretely, but between a consciousness in which the relation is not given at all and one in which it is given. In the consciousness which alone can give it, the object is not given as "beyond" this consciousness, but as immanent in it; as a determining factor of it, not an unknown opposite; not as independent of the subject, but as a correlative, implying and implied in it. It is only through equivocation between this sort of consciousness and another—that fictitious consciousness which the object is indeed "beyond," in the sense that for it neither subject nor object could exist—that the experience of resistance can be made to testify to a matter independent of thought, and from which thought results. This will become clearer when we consider more in detail the account which Mr. Spencer gives of the independence of matter.

"The conception we have of matter," he tells us, "is a conception uniting independence, permanence, and force." Now, we should be far from admitting that this was a sufficient account of "matter," or that "matter" and the "object" could properly be taken, as he seems to take them, to be equivalent terms. We should be equally far from saying that "mind and matter were the same." But it can be shown that, according to Mr. Spencer's own statements, the qualities here assigned to the matter, which he identifies with the object, are equally predicable of the mind, which he identifies with the subject. And these statements, which it would not concern us to examine merely for the sake of convicting an eminent writer of inconsistency, acquire a value when considered as involuntary witnesses to the truth that only the consciousness which is an object to itself can tell of the object misconceived as "beyond" it, and that thought, in knowing such a matter, is so far knowing itself. That he thinks of "permanence and force" as attributes of mind no less than of matter, his whole theory of resistance testifies.

> "The principle of continuity," he tells us, "forming into a whole the faint states of consciousness, moulding and modifying them by some unknown energy, is distinguished as the *ego*. . . . To the principle of continuity manifested in the *non-ego* there clings a nascent consciousness of force akin to the force evolved by the principle of continuity in the *ego*."*

When permanence and force have thus been ascribed to mind equally with matter, the "independence" of the latter becomes the more questionable. On this point it will be found, we think, that Mr. Spencer's premisses and conclusion do not tally. The conclusion is that matter is "something beyond consciousness, which is absolutely independent of consciousness," but in the premisses the independence of matter merely means that the "vivid aggregate" of conscious states is independent of the "faint." So far from being, as we had been led to expect, an independence of consciousness on the part of something other than consciousness, it turns out to consist merely in this, that the occurrence of any one of a set of feelings, distinguished as more lively, is not contingent upon the occurrence of one of another set, distinguished as less lively.† But as the occurrence of one of this latter set is on its part not contingent upon the occurrence of one more lively, the independence asserted in this sense of "matter" is equally predicable of mind. For if the "vivid aggregate," according to Mr. Spencer, is independent of the "faint," so likewise is the faint of the vivid. It too, as he expressively tells us, is "coherent within itself, has its own antecedents and its own laws." It is true that, according to him, the one aggregate is "absolutely independent," the other only "relatively or partially" so. But this distinction in favour of the vivid aggregate is afterwards cancelled by the account of resistance, which turns on the fact that changes in the vivid aggregate are initiated by changes in the faint. To whatever qualification, then, the independence of the faint aggregate is subject, that of the vivid must be so likewise. We are thus left with two sequences, each in the same sense independent of the other, but we are not offered any mark of distinction between the sequence which is "matter" and the sequence which is "mind," except such as equally distinguishes any two feelings differing in liveliness and not contingent the one upon the other. If this were really what Mr. Spencer meant, as it is undoubtedly what in effect he says, all that he urges against Hume could be retorted more strongly against himself. He would out-idealize Hume in Hume's own line of idealism; for whereas with Hume impressions are at least necessarily precedent to "ideas," Mr. Spencer's matter, as equivalent to the vivid

* Principles of Psychology, § 470.

† Ibid. §§ 454, 458, and 468.

aggregate, has no such prerogative over mind, as equivalent to the faint.

But there is reason to think that by the independence of matter Mr. Spencer means something else than what he says. He does not really believe either the vivid or the faint aggregate to be in any case independent. When he speaks of the vivid as independent, he does not mean either that it is subject to no determination proceeding from the faint, or that it is dependent on nothing. The true explanation of his language is that he holds that on which the one aggregate depends to be antithetical to that on which the other depends. If we are asked by what title we assume that he does not mean what he says, we answer that, on looking to the account given of any experience which he ascribes to the "vivid aggregate," we find two characteristics essential to its being what he takes it to be, each of which is incompatible with the "independence" of the aggregate. Every vivid feeling of the experience is determined by connection with modes of consciousness which, if Mr. Spencer's division is accepted, must fall to the "faint aggregate." And the whole experience is dependent on something which is not one of the conscious states forming the aggregate, nor all these together, but is persistent throughout the succession.

Before proceeding, however, to examine one of Mr. Spencer's "vivid" experiences, it is well to say that his division of states of consciousness into vivid and faint is one which can only be accepted under protest. That the "totality of consciousness" does not admit of being divided into "antithetical halves" on the basis of a distinction which at best is only one of degree, must be sufficiently obvious. The apparent significance of the distinction is, in truth, only derived from a tacit presupposition of the antithesis which yet, according to Mr. Spencer's account of the matter, we derive from it. Having already, for whatever reason, come to divide our experiences into those which are the product of outward things and those which belong merely to the mind, we may then find relative vividness to be characteristic of the one and relative faintness of the other; though it would be truer to say that to a great part of our mental experiences—those which we call intellectual as opposed to the emotional—the distinction between the faint and the vivid has no application at all. But if we had not the antithetical division already before our minds, there could be nothing in the constant transition from more to less lively feeling, and again from the less lively to the more so, to suggest it. If it suggested anything—and the possibility of its suggesting anything really presupposes that self-consciousness on the part of a subject distinguishing itself from the transition which, according to the empirical theory, is part of what is suggested—it would suggest, not two antithetical existences, but one existence of constantly varying intensity. That Mr. Spencer himself, instead of determining,

...with which an experience is to be classed on the ground ... or faintness of the experience, decides that it is vivid ... according to a preconceived view of the aggregate to which ... appears from his account of those "states of the faint ... which set up changes in the vivid." In regard to them, he ... "the classification by intensity fails."* He assigns them ... faint aggregate" on grounds which, whatever they may be ... nothing to do with degree of vivacity.

... to this proviso, let us consider, by way of example, the ... of the vivid experience on the sea-shore with which Mr. ... introduces his "partial differentiation of subject and object."† ... himself as sitting on a beach with the sea-breeze blowing ... face. "Sounds from the breakers, motions of the waves that ... away to the horizon, are at the same time present;" and he is aware of the sun's warmth and the odour of sea-weed." Before ... ere is a prospect of a "distant headland with a white cliff and ... of green down above;" of a pier to his right, and a cluster of ... anchored on his left. All that he thus, in common language, ... ears, and smells, Mr. Spencer regards as a vivid aggregate of ... of consciousness. Part of it, however, soon becomes "faint." ...-fog is supposed to drift in, and those "specially-shaped vivid ...s of green and white, which he distinguished as a distant head-... now remain with him as faint patches, having shapes and relative ...ons approximately the same; and the like holds with those pro-... in him by the pier and boats." Now, if we are to take as a ... of faint states that consciousness of the headland which ...s after the sea-fog has interfered with the sight of it, it is clear ... apart from such faint states, the experience which Mr. Spencer ... in the gross as vivid would lose all its real content. Abstract ... "the vivid patches of green and white which I distinguish as a ...nd" all determination by "ideas" as faint as these patches of ... are supposed to become in memory upon supervention of the ...nd it is distinguished as a distant headland no longer. Mr. ...er himself, to judge from his statements elsewhere, would admit ...s recognition as a headland implies a reference of the object seen ...lass, or the ascription to it of attributes which, since the shutting ... eyes makes no difference to them, must, according to his classifi-..., be reckoned faint states of consciousness. But this is not all. ...e not to suppose that the object seen, merely as a "vivid state" ...ation and apart from intellectual action, already has a nature, ... all that the intellect has to do is, in the act which naming ..., to class it with like objects previously observed. Intellectual ... necessary to constitute the individual object. All its elements, ...encer supposes it at any particular time to be "seen," would ... with the elimination from consciousness at that time of all

* ...Principles of Psychology, § 470. † Ibid. § 451.

but "vivid states." So far from its being a "cluster of vivid states," as Mr. Spencer apparently supposes not his umbrella merely but all sensible objects about him to be, it is an impropriety to call it a cluster of states of consciousness at all; a further impropriety to allow that, if it be such a cluster, any part of the cluster is, in Mr. Spencer's sense, "vivid;" and an impropriety than which error can no further go to reckon the whole cluster so.

We will deal with this worst impropriety first. The account given of the perception of an individual object by the school to which Mr. Spencer belongs, and which there is reason to suppose that he accepts,* is that it consists in the suggestion by a sensation of certain known possibilities of sensation, of which through past experience the given sensation has become symbolical. When, to return to the instance mentioned, I perceive a distant headland, what I actually see would be admitted to be but a small part of the perception. Certain present sensations—"vivid patches" of colour, specially coloured and shaped—are supposed to recall past experiences which have become indissolubly associated with them. Only as qualified by these do the sensations become representative of objects which can be recognized as of a certain nature—of the cliff, down, and sea, for instance—from which again, as related in a certain manner, results the total impression of a headland. To adapt this view to Mr. Spencer's way of speaking, for sensations we must write "vivid states of consciousness," and instead of saying that they become representative of the headland we must say that they become the state, or "cluster of states," which is the headland. Thus translated, the "doctrine of perception in which all psychologists concur"† implies that only as qualified by association with remembered facts, or by inference to what might be, but is not now, experienced, do the "vivid patches of green and white, &c.," become the state of consciousness called the headland, or any vivid states become the objects which make up Mr. Spencer's "vivid aggregate." Now memory and inference according to his classification must fall to the "faint aggregate." It may be objected indeed that the qualification of vivid states, necessary to constitute the perceived thing, is given not by memory but by remembered facts which once were sensations, not by inference but by facts inferred which are possibilities of sensation. Such an objection, however, would be inappropriate when, under Mr. Spencer's direction, we are considering the perceived object as a cluster of states of consciousness, into which we clearly cannot regard facts inferred or remembered as entering in distinction from the memory and inference. Nor, if appropriate, would it affect our conclusion, since neither the fact that a sensation once happened, nor the possibility of its happening again, are themselves sensations. Our conclusion then must be that, according to Mr. Spencer's own theory

* Principles of Psychology, § 315. † Ibid. § 315.

"vivid states of consciousness" must be qualified by ... to form the objects which he ascribes to the ... that if these objects are to be reckoned clusters ... at all, they are clusters into which faint ... qualifying the vivid, and into which the vivid states ... qualified.

... to follow Mr. Spencer in holding that "vivid states ...usness"—in plain English, sensations—are elements in the ... which we call sensible things or objects of the real world, ... forbidden from holding with him that such states are ... of the "faint." If vivid states contribute to form objects ...y do so as determined by faint ones; and if the "vivid ..." is to be identified with the objective world, we must say ... qualification by the "faint aggregate" or subject renders it ...rld at all. Can we explain how Mr. Spencer, in the face of ...eory of perception, comes to think otherwise? We answer that ...h confusion between an event in the way of sensation, which happens quite irrespectively of memory, imagination, or con... the part of the person to whom it happens and in that sense ...dent of "faint states," and the consciousness or existence of ... object or quality.* "In broad procession," he tells us, "the ...s—sounds from the breakers, the wind, the vehicles behind ...ing patches of colour from the waves, pressures, odours, and ... move on abreast, unceasing and unbroken, wholly without ... anything else in my consciousness."† Unfortunately the ...tes," of which this assertion is true, are not of a kind with ...ses given; nor can any "clustering" of them constitute ...ct of perception or an object perceived. It is only through ...h of statements, like Mr. Spencer's, as "broad" as the pro... which he describes, that any one is brought to think they ... talk of certain sensations, for instance, as sounds from the ...s changing patches of colour from the waves, without ... that merely as sensations—passing states of feeling—apart ...ard to something else in my consciousness" which at any ... a sensation, they are not for consciousness sounds from the ...r changing patches of colour at all. Neither the past ... under the influence of which a certain sensation of sight ... into a breaker, nor that which leads us to connect a ...nd with the sight thus translated, can be more vivid than ... which succeeds the sight when the sea-fog has shut the ... view, and which Mr. Spencer counts faint. As for the ... connection themselves—the acts of intellectual syn... inference by which known possibilities of sensation are

* ... or existence, for we shall find in the sequel that Mr. Spencer does ... existences out of consciousness within an aggregate which he expressly ... conscious states. † Principles of Psychology, § 454.

combined in an object and by which the sound becomes the sound of this object—whether "states of consciousness" at all or no, it is clear that something else than a "vivid state" renders them possible. In like manner successive sensations of colour are one thing, "changing patches of colour from the waves" quite another. With the occurrence of the sensations nothing else in my consciousness need have to do, but something else in it—the persistent something which consciousness of change presupposes—has everything to do with their becoming that which the description quoted assumes them to be.

How far Mr. Spencer in fact is from meaning by vivid states of consciousness those occurrences of sensation which can alone be truly said to be independent of operations that he would ascribe to the subject, appears from his language about the antecedents of such states. "When for any consequent in the vivid series we can perceive the antecedent, that antecedent exists in the vivid series. . . . Thus, in the vivid series, after the changing forms and colours which, as united, I call a curling breaker, there comes a sound made by its fall on the beach."* Now to say that both antecedent and consequent "exist in the vivid series"—if this means that series of events in the way of feeling which can alone be truly said to be independent of the faint aggregate—is a contradiction in terms. Coincident feelings may so exist, but not those related as antecedent and consequent. If the consequent be a sensation now occurring, the perceived antecedent cannot be so too, unless of two events one can both follow the other and accompany it. It may be replied perhaps that we are here arguing from a mere hastiness of expression on Mr. Spencer's part, which led him to put a present for a past; that by both antecedent and consequent he means sensations as they occur, and that though the antecedent is no longer vivid when the consequent follows, it previously was so; that thus it did exist in the vivid series, though it does not. Mr. Spencer, however, could scarcely accept this rendering of his thought. His polemic against Hume turns on the impropriety of using "existence" in a sense implying "absence of persistence,"† as it certainly would be used if of a mere sensation it were said that it did exist. So far as the loose abundance of his phraseology allows us to judge, "existence in the vivid aggregate" means with him the same thing as being a "member of the vivid aggregate," and an aggregate or member of an aggregate no sequent occurrences of feeling, by themselves, can form. Only so far as they become elements of a conception, in which they are no longer sequent, can they become an aggregate or parts of one. As little can such successive occurrence form the *perception* of antecedence which in the passage before us Mr. Spencer has in view. An antecedent, perceived as an antecedent, must be included in one conception with the consequent, and, as so included, cannot be that state of conscious-

* Principles of Psychology, § 455. † Ibid. § 467.

ness—a sensation at the time of its occurrence—which terminates when the state to which it is antecedent begins, and which is alone unaffected by the mind. In short, to say that two states of consciousness are perceived to be related as antecedent and consequent, and to say that either of them is "independent of the faint aggregate," are incompatible propositions.

If any doubt as to Mr. Spencer's meaning remained, his illustration, quoted above, must make it quite clear that the states of consciousness which he has in view are not sensations as they occur, but sensations as thought of—sensible objects, formed by conceived relations between feelings, not feelings as undetermined by thought or "independent." The antecedent, which he instances, is an object formed by the union of "changing forms and colours." That such an object can be a single sensation no one will for a moment suppose. That it is not a mere group of sensations, experienced at the same time, will be clear to any one who reflects that a coincident occurrence of several sensations cannot be also a consciousness of change from one to the other. Does it then consist in several successive sensations? It is clearly as impossible that successive events of any kind should form such an object, as it is necessary that they should occur in order to its formation. It could only seem possible to one who confused a succession of states of consciousness with that consciousness of succession which is its very opposite. If for no other reason than because a consciousness of succession is implied in the conception of a changing object, a consciousness consisting of a succession of states could never compass such a conception. The "antecedent," then, in Mr. Spencer's illustration is neither a sensation, nor several sensations coincident or sequent. As an object for consciousness—and it is as such alone that his account of the series in question allows us to consider it—it is formed by the thought of events in the way of sensation which have occurred successively, but are for thought equally present. If as thus equally present, as mutually qualifying members of a conception, they are still to be counted members of the vivid series, then it must be admitted that this series depends, for being what it is, on some act of consciousness which is not included in it.

T. H. GREEN.

*(To be continued.)*

# ARE THE CLERGY PRIESTS OR MINISTERS?

THE Bishop of Salisbury's article on the Divine Government of the Church, in the October number of this REVIEW, deserves the most serious attention and respect even from those who differ most widely from his conclusions. It would do so under any circumstances; for the claims advanced on behalf of the government of such a body as the Christian Church can never be a matter of indifference to persons who reflect seriously on the influence of religion upon human society; and the high reputation of the author both for learning and candour lends a peculiar weight to his words. But besides this, recent movements both within and without the Church have given to the subject a fresh interest and importance. On the one hand, recent discussions about priestly authority, recent discoveries, it may almost be said (for to many persons they have come with the surprise of a discovery), as to the practical assertion of claims, the exercise of which reaches to the very roots of society, have driven men to ask themselves what are the grounds on which such claims rest. On the other hand, the vexed question of Church and State faces us, look which way we will; and one essential part of this question, one of the hinges on which it turns, is the right which the Church may assert in matters of doctrine and discipline to govern herself. These are questions to which no class of the community can affect to be indifferent. The relations between the Church and the State are so complex, so manifold, so intertwined with the national fabric, that any change here must touch the heart of the national life. It may be well, therefore, as Bishop Moberly suggests, to deal with these subjects, "during the present comparatively quiet time," instead of waiting "for the exciting times, [illegible] will take the place of theory." These "exciting times [illegible] already we hear the muttering of the distant thunder; the air is full of it; the storm may burst sooner than we are aware; the present lull may usher it in. There are many indications that may put us on our guard. "Disestablishment" is not only the watchword of the advanced guard of a party; it is hinted at by statesmen in a responsible position. It is not only ardently desired and advocated by the Liberation Society; there is a shout for it in the Ritualist camp. There is in all but name an alliance, and it cannot be called an unnatural alliance, between opposite parties. And when the numbers are large enough and the organization complete enough to inspire some hope of success, the leader, we may be sure, will not be wanting; many eyes are already fixed upon him; the champion of Ritualism will put on the armour of Liberationism, and will not have to complain with a champion in another cause, "I cannot go with these, for I have not proved them."

Bishop Moberly's article was called forth by an article of Mr. Lyttelton's on the same subject in the August number of this REVIEW. Mr. Lyttelton had maintained, first, that there is given to the Church from Christ Himself a promise of Divine guidance into all necessary truth concerning God and man's relation to God. He admitted, indeed, that such a promise had its natural limitations, limitations of necessity imposed upon all Divine promises by the concurrent fact of human freedom. God gives, but never forces man to accept. Exceptions to the fulfilment of His promise, he remarks, are due to that "*crossing* of laws" which stamps the whole course of the Divine government.

But secondly, he had denied that this promise was to be restricted to any "privileged class" within the community. According to his view, this Divine illumination, this supernatural guidance, were intended for all, might be bestowed upon all, were the heritage of the laity as emphatically as that of the clergy, of each individual as truly as of assemblies of the Church gathered under any special sanctions.

This view of the Divine guidance of the Church, which regards it as diffused throughout the whole body, appears to Bishop Moberly both defective and dangerous. It is defective, he thinks, as confining itself to the single point of "truth respecting God and things eternal," and taking no account of "other gifts, such as that of absolution of sin and government within the Church," as well as in omitting all reference to "the historical origin of the gift as given to men." It is dangerous because it practically leaves us without guidance, without any standard of reference, any authority, when discordant voices are heard around us, all alike claiming our submission.

As regards the first charge, I shall have more to say further on. I only observe at present that it is somewhat difficult to understand in what sense "the gift of absolution of sin" can be separated as something different in kind from truth respecting God and things eternal. It would seem to be a part of that truth.

As regards the second charge, that the theory is a dangerous one which bids us look for truth and guidance, not in one direction only, but in *all*, I ask, with all respect, Why? Is there not in every man taught of the Spirit of God, an inner eye which distinguishes between the light and the darkness, an inner faculty which welcomes the truth and rejects the falsehood? Was not the appeal originally made to that faculty both by our Lord and by His Apostles? "He that is of the truth heareth my voice." "If any man think himself to be a prophet, or spiritual, let him acknowledge that the things that I wrote unto you are the commandments of the Lord." Such is at once our privilege and our responsibility. This does not leave us "in a wide and boundless sea." This does not expose us to be blown hither and thither "by every blast of doctrine." At least, if there is any such danger, it is a danger to which the Church of England herself exposes us. When she declares in her Sixth Article that "whatsoever is not read therein [*i.e.*, in Holy Scripture], nor may be proved thereby, is not to be required of any man that it should be believed as an article of the faith, or be thought requisite or necessary to salvation," she obviously charges every member of her community with the responsibility of what he accepts as an article of faith. The Church tells us what she has gathered on some questions out of Scripture; she leaves us free to accept or to reject her conclusions. She implies that we have within us a faculty of discernment and a faculty of interpretation. We must take our risk, but we may do it without fear, for we "have an unction from the Holy One," and we "know" or we may know "all things." And whenever a man is under the guidance of the Spirit of truth he recognizes the truth, and honours it, even though it be uttered by one whom some portion of the Church might brand as a schismatic or a heretic. The nobility of the Truth belongs to all her sincere worshippers. It is broader than all our divisions, larger than anything in the world, larger than intellect or heart of man. No man has the whole truth; no Church has the whole truth. Just as in all ages it has been given to certain great champions to draw the sword of some forgotten truth from its scabbard, or to put upon it fresh edge, and to wield it with a force that nothing could withstand, so it seems to be given to different Churches to assert most distinctly particular truths, or to bring into more vivid sunlight certain aspects of truth which others neglect or deny. To give a practical illustration of my meaning: if in the Church of England one aspect of the Lord's Supper is strongly emphasized—that it is our personal participation in the benefit of Christ's death—another aspect, scarcely less prominent in St. Paul's mind, is very much obscured, thrown into the background certainly, that the act is an act expressive [illegible] bolism of the broken loaf has disappeared. The unfortunate substitution of the singular for the plural of the original institution in the administration of the elements has perhaps made the individual believer more deeply conscious of his personal benefit, but only at the risk of isolating him from his fellow-communicants. This latter truth, on the other hand, finds its full recognition in the Presbyterian Churches. They do not forget, that the Eucharist teaches us "we, the many, are one loaf;" we do not forget, that as often as we eat that bread and drink that cup, we are made one with Christ, and Christ one with us. Thus one Church supplements another. Is it not possible to recognize the truth in both? Is it not possible to confess, without prejudice and without fear, "No system on earth is perfect; there is no exclusive heritage of the truth." A man may do this without any disloyalty to his own Church. He is not tempted to leave her community for another, because he sees in another some excellences which are wanting in his own, any more than he is tempted to forsake his own country for another, because the latter has some advantages of soil, of climate, of laws, of institutions, which his own has not. He recognizes a great principle of compensation. He believes that wherever there is life and light in the body of the Church, they are the life and the light of the Spirit of God; and he rejoices to think that he is a partaker of the treasure.

Bishop Moberly, however, does not deny that there is in some sense a diffusion of Divine illumination and of the knowledge of the truth throughout the whole Christian body. But he contends that along with this general guidance into the truth, there are special gifts vouchsafed originally to the Apostles, and through them to their lawfully constituted successors, which belong to the clergy alone, and not to the Church at large. He makes, it is true, some concessions, which appear hardly consistent with his argument. Thus, speaking of "the Divine guidance" as regards not only "the possession," but the "*authoritative teaching* of revealed truth when the Canon was closed, and the Church left 'for all the days' to the unseen presence of the Lord in the Holy Spirit," he observes—

"It resided, I do not hesitate to say, in the Body, the whole Body; in a graduated, no doubt, and proportionate manner in the different members of the body, yet not in such sort as absolutely to exclude any from some participation in the gift."

One would have thought that in this "authoritative teaching" of Divine Truth must have been included that which is of the very essence of the Gospel, the declaration of the forgiveness of sins. But it is clear that Bishop Moberly holds something more than a *declaration of forgiveness* as the prerogative of the clergy; they are, according to him, the channels, the divinely constituted channels, through which the forgiveness is conveyed. Hence he wholly severs from this "authoritative teaching" of Divine Truth "the other gift—the sacerdotal power of the remitting or the withholding the remission of sins." This gift he supposes to have been consigned to the Apostles, and to their successors, by the Lord Himself on the Resurrection-day, and here we have "the *real principle of the different positions of the clergy and the laity in the Church*, the inheriting body of Christ."

This "special gift to the clergy and their successors," he says,

> "consists of the impertition of the Holy Spirit for the forgiveness, and the withholding of forgiveness, of man's sins. Whatever falls within the scope and range of this great gift is the peculiar inheritance of the Apostles, and the clergy their ordained successors. That gift designated them, fitted them, prepared them to be holders in all time of that special power."

The Bishop goes on to explain that the clergy have thus been constituted the organs through which "the authoritative declaration of Divine forgiveness was to be conveyed to man in all the various methods and by all the different channels through which that forgiveness was to be given"—such, for instance, as the two Sacraments, or other rites of a "sacramental" character, such as confirmation and ordination, or the public or private forms of absolution.

The gift differed from the Pentecostal gift in this respect, that this latter, in the case of the Apostles, "filled up the great sacerdotal capacity which had been given them fifty days before."

And yet the Bishop says:—

> "There *is* a widely diffused participation of the whole Church in all its members in the Divine gift; but compatibly with this there is a sacred succession of men from the Apostles, appointed by Apostolic ordination, to exercise upon the individual members of the Church the sacred powers of the Church collective. There is an undeniable personal priesthood which belongs to every Christian man duly admitted into the membership of the Church, and still holding that membership entire; but that personal priesthood is in no degree incompatible with the existence of a priesthood, *collective* as I have called it, determined by successive ordination to those who inherit the position and gifts which were first given to the Apostles, not so much for their own personal sanctification as for the benefit of the whole organized body of the Church."

Certainly, there is no necessary incompatibility between a gift universally given and the concentration of that gift in particular persons. A State or an army may be full of enthusiasm, courage, devotion, but the spirit that animates it may be found in larger measure in its magistrates and officers. But this is not what the Bishop contends for, and we must not lose sight of his real meaning. He does not mean, unless I am very much mistaken, that the priesthood of the whole body appears in a concentrated form in its officers. He claims for them other gifts, the gifts of government and absolution, which belong to them, and not to the body at large; otherwise how are we to understand such words as "special gifts," "the peculiar inheritance of the Apostles and their successors," and the like? He is contending for the impartation of these gifts, not according to the law by which all gifts are given, but according to a law of special application in the Christian Church, the law of a priestly succession. These gifts are confined to Apostolic descent and an Apostolic order. How, then, can they be at once the inheritance of all and the exclusive privilege of a few? There can be no priestly succession of the individuals composing the body; there may be, if the theory is true, of the clergy by continuous ordination. According to this theory, that certain "special gifts" are bestowed on the clergy, and the clergy alone, I find it as difficult as my friend Mr. Lyttelton to understand how they can be regarded as "representatives" of the Church. But the Bishop does not insist on the word "representative," and in logical consistency it is hard to see how he could. If, indeed, he only means that whilst these gifts, the absolving and governing powers, belong to the whole Church, the *authority to exercise them* is bestowed on the Apostles and their successors, this is perfectly intelligible. But I do not feel warranted in putting such a construction upon the words: "The gift conveyed by the breath of Christ on the Resurrection-day is the *special gift* to the Apostles and the clergy their successors, and it consists of the impertition of the Holy Spirit for the forgiveness, and the withholding of forgiveness, of man's sins. Whatever falls within the scope and range of this great gift is the *peculiar inheritance* of the Apostles, and

importance to observe, that what he does insist upon is that the Christian ministry is essentially a priesthood, and that it is essentially in and by its priestly character that even while it represents, it is differentiated from, the rest of the Christian body.

And it is here that I feel myself constrained entirely to differ from him. Whatever else may constitute the essential difference between the Christian laity and the Christian clergy, it certainly does not lie in the fact that the clergy are in any other sense "priests" than the laity are. I am not going to say one word which shall lower the true dignity of the Christian ministry. I believe there is no earthly honour comparable to the honour of one who is sent to be an ambassador for Christ. But to regard the Christian ministry as a priesthood is, I also believe, to degrade it, and is most assuredly to represent it in a light in which it is never placed in the New Testament, or even in the Apostolical Fathers.

But as Bishop Moberly rests the claims which he has put forth on behalf of the Christian clergy on certain passages of Scripture which are very commonly supposed to favour his view, it is of importance to examine these somewhat in detail; and the more because centuries of misinterpretation have clouded the text, and the use of the passage in the Ordination Service of the Church of England has been held to favour the extreme sacerdotal theory.

Referring first to the passage in St. Luke's Gospel (xii. 41, 42) where Peter asks the question, whether the parable just delivered was spoken to the Apostles in particular or "even unto all;" and quoting the reply, "Who then is that faithful and wise steward, whom his Lord shall make ruler over his household, to give them their portion of meat in due season?"—the Bishop very truly observes, "The Lord's answer seems to carry at least this reply to the question,—there are to be stewards who are to rule over the household of God, to give them their meat (of all and various kinds as they need) in due season."

This, however, is what no one would question. Whatever may be our theories of Church government or of Apostolical succession, no one, unless in some extreme sects, would efface all distinction between laity and clergy. Certainly all would acknowledge that it is the distinct office and duty of the clergy to feed the Church of God, to give them their meat in due season. It is when we come to ask what is meant by the "feeding," and whence the authority to feed is derived, that the real difficulty presents itself.

What is the nature of the authority exercised, and by whom may it be exercised? these are the questions of paramount importance. On these Bishop Moberly very naturally appeals to the three cognate passages (Matt. xvi. 19; xviii. 18; John xx. 23), "which" (as he thinks) "refer to the great gift of the power of absolution." Here happily the field is so far narrowed that the question may now be stated thus: Is absolution the prerogative of the Christian ministry as lawfully constituted, and, if so, does this gift of necessity imply that the Christian ministry is a priesthood in the proper sense of that term? A careful comparison of the three passages just mentioned will I believe lead us to a very different conclusion from that to which the Bishop has been led.

Bishop Moberly appears to think that the essential difference between these passages consists in this: that in the two former passages, those in St. Matthew's Gospel, we have the *promise* of a gift, whereas in the last, that of St. John, we have the *fulfilment* of the promise. And this fulfilment he supposes furnishes the real commentary or explanation of the twofold promise. "He breathed on them, and saith unto them, Receive ye the Holy Ghost: whosesoever sins ye remit, they are remitted unto them; and whosesoever sins ye retain, they are retained." He lays stress on the difference of tenses and genders in the two cases. He remarks, "The future tenses and the neuter genders of the former passages (οἰκοδομήσω, δώσω, ὃ ἐὰν δήσῃς, ὅσα ἂν δήσητε, ἔσται δεδεμένα, ἔσται λελυμένα) have become present and past tenses and masculine genders (ἄν τινων ἀφῆτε τὰς ἁμαρτίας, ἀφίενται αὐτοῖς· ἄν τινων κρατῆτε κεκράτηνται)" as if this were the sole difference between them. But there is a much more important difference which he has entirely overlooked. He speaks of "the vaguer phrase of loosing and binding," as "now explained and superseded by the undeniably distinct expressions of forgiving and withholding forgiveness from the sins of men." But the simple fact is that the one neither explains nor supersedes the other; the two things are entirely different, and we have no right to regard them as synonymous. The one is not "the vaguer," the other the more "distinct expression" of the same power. The one might be possessed and exercised apart from the other. There are three different phrases employed by our Lord in the three passages, each having its several sense, though they are very frequently confounded. In Matt. xvi. the power bestowed upon St. Peter is twofold, the power of "the keys" and the power of "binding and loosing." The power of the keys has sometimes been explained* with a reference to the Jewish custom of delivering a key to the scribe when he was admitted to his office, in token that, holding "the key of knowledge" (Luke xi. 52), he was to open or to shut the treasures of Divine wisdom. If this be the meaning, our Lord intended to designate Peter as a scribe instructed unto the kingdom of heaven. I am more disposed, however, to think that the figure is to be explained by its use in such a passage as Isa. xxii. 22 (cf. Rev. i. 18), where it is so clearly the symbol of rule and government, there being thus given to St. Peter, as elsewhere to all the Apostles, the place of authority in the Church of God. The power of "binding and loosing" was of another kind. The phrase is one of constant occurrence in Jewish literature, and was employed with a perfectly definite and well-understood meaning in the Jewish schools. The expression applied to things, not to persons. This of course accounts for the difference of gender to which Bishop Moberly draws attention. To a Jew what was "bound" was forbidden; what was "loosed" was allowed; and both the one and the other were determined for him by his Rabbis, who based their authority on Deut. xvii. 8—11, and who might give conflicting decisions. Thus it was said, "The school of Hillel binds, the school of Shammai looses." But this had nothing to do with the forgiveness of sins; it was simply a question of discipline. Our Lord, in the second passage quoted (Matt. xviii. 18), extends this power to the whole Church. According to the Rabbinical notion, "the Celestial Court of Justice" decides only after and in accordance with "the Terrestrial Court of Justice." In like manner and in similar terms our Lord gave authority, first to St. Peter and afterwards to the Church in her collective capacity, to decide what was lawful or unlawful for her members, adding that their decisions should be ratified in heaven.†

In the third instance, the language has nothing in common with the first two, though it has been so strangely and so persistently confounded with them. Here there is not a word about "the keys," not a word about "binding and loosing:" instead of these we have now "the remitting and retaining of sins;" and this power is very differently consigned. It is connected with a significant act, "He

* As by Professor Plumptre, in an Excursus to his Sermon on "Confession and Absolution."

† I have repeated here what I have already said in an Excursus on John xx. 23, appended to a Sermon, "Confession in the Church of England," recently published by Macmillan & Co.

breathed on them;" it is conveyed in solemn words defining their high commission, "As my Father hath sent me, even so send I you." Thus the use of the past tense is no evidence, as the Bishop supposes, that the promise thus made on the two previous occasions was now fulfilled. This of course is out of the question, the gift being different *in kind* from the promise. But besides this, the past tense is that prophetic past of which the whole Hebrew Scriptures are full. To the Speaker to whose eye all things in heaven and earth are disclosed, that which shall be is already accomplished. And as the Prophet of old, contemplating the future deliverance, and sure of its accomplishment, exclaims, "Sing, O ye heavens, for the Lord *hath done it*," so the Divine Speaker here, beholding the course of His Gospel in all ages, exclaims, "If ye have forgiven, they *are* forgiven."

It must, however, be further remarked that, if the gift bestowed on the Resurrection-day was, as Bishop Moberly so earnestly contends, confined to the Apostles, and to the clergy their successors, it could not be a fulfilment of the promise in Matt. xviii., where the power given is given not to the Apostles, but to the whole body of believers. I quite agree with the Bishop that the absence of Thomas does not militate against his view as to the extent of the gift. It may be freely admitted that the gift being intended for all, in their representative capacity, "it might be conveyed to all though one of them was absent at the time." But there is another difficulty in the case, which is constantly overlooked by writers on this question. If we turn to St. Luke's narrative of the events which transpired on the Resurrection-day, we shall find that others besides the Eleven were present on this occasion. When the two disciples with whom our Lord conversed on the way to Emmaus returned to Jerusalem, they found "the eleven gathered together, and *them that were with them*" (τοὺς ἕνδεκα καὶ τοὺς σὺν αὐτοῖς). The scene which follows, in which the Lord shows the disciples His hands and His feet, is the exact counterpart of that in St. John (xx. 20), and there can be no reasonable doubt that the occurrence is the same. Yet if so, the question must be faced, Was the gift of the Holy Spirit for the remission of sins bestowed on others besides the Apostles? If it was, the whole fabric built on these words collapses. The gift of the remission and the retaining of sins is no longer the special and inalienable prerogative of the Christian priesthood deriving its descent and its consequent authority from the Apostles. And indeed it is very difficult to understand how this power, though unquestionably exercised through the ministers of the Church, as the proper and lawfully constituted organs by which all the spiritual gifts of the body are exercised, should be confined to them. No one will of course presume to assert that the clergyman possesses, any more than the layman, the power of forgiving sins. "None can forgive sins, but God only."

... words of a great master in theology) "is not denied ... by those whose language and practice appear to trench most ... prerogative. And from this it follows that no absolution ... can be anything more than a declaration, either general or ... that has been forgiven by God. Now such a declaration is ... terms whenever the Gospel is faithfully preached. Such ... substance a statement of the conditions on which forgiveness ... But if the declaration relates to a particular case, it is evident ... a special Divine revelation, it can only be a conditional declara... made on the supposition that the required conditions have ... Every Christian has a warrant to say to his brother, 'Repent ... and thy sins shall be forgiven thee;' but before he can say with ... thy sins are forgiven thee,' he must either have received some ... assurance of the fact, or he must qualify the declaration with ... 'If thou repentest and believest;' and this condition must ... understood to be implied where it is not expressed."*

... Christian" has this warrant. It is a part of that know... truth into which he is led by the Spirit of God, and, like ... is lodged in the whole Christian body; it is not the ... of a class. The absolving power rightly understood is of ... sence of Christianity; it is the sun-atmosphere of every ... which he shines and gives heat; it is that in which he ... oves and has his being. St. Paul could not have supposed ... the exclusive privilege of the clergy, when he wrote to ... ians, in reference to the excommunication and restoration ... stuous person, "To whom ye forgive anything I forgive it ... r. ii. 10). He obviously regarded it as belonging to all ... e Spirit of Christ.

... ems, then, no tenable ground for Bishop Moberly's dis... tween the possession of revealed truth and the possession ... r of absolution.

... the latter as the special gift, the undoubted prerogative, ... gy, appears to me to be a complete inversion of the true ... the Christian ministry.

... g to the view which I am commenting on, "authoritative ... s not so specially the prerogative of the clergy as are the ... of absolution and the administration of the sacraments. ... is be maintained? In the first place, what is preaching ... 'the authoritative declaration" of the forgiveness of sins ... aining of sins? St. Paul, speaking of the ministration of the ... large, but with special reference to the preaching of the ... s, "We are a savour of life unto life, or a savour of death unto ... or. ii. 12, 16). Unless, then, the power of preaching is a part ... rdotal" element in the ministry, it is in vain to contend that it ... dotal element which is the constituting force in the ministry. ... t place, taking St. Paul and the rest of the New Testament ... our guides, we shall find ourselves placed in this dilemma:

* Bishop Thirlwall's Remains, iii. p. 362.

of that which according to the theory is supposed to be the characteristic feature, the special and surpassing privilege of the Christian ministry, they are wholly silent; whereas the other, which is not regarded as any special prerogative of the ministry, is in their eyes its glory and its strength. Thus St. Paul, writing to the Corinthians, thanks God that he had baptized but few, adding, "For Christ sent me not to baptize, but to preach the gospel"—on any fair interpretation of the words, implying that in his estimation the preaching of the Gospel was more distinctively, more necessarily, a part of his office than the administration of the sacraments. Again, in that most solemn charge which he addresses to Timothy, as chief pastor of the Church, what is it that holds the first place in his thoughts?—the power of absolution?—the administration of the sacraments as channels of grace? No, the preaching of the Gospel: "I charge thee before God, and the Lord Jesus Christ, who shall judge the quick and dead at his appearing and kingdom; preach the word."

The Apostles must have known, one would suppose, what was the nature of their commission, as given them on the Resurrection-day. If they believed that they were then constituted priests, somewhere we should find them insisting upon this character of their office. But it is the entire absence of any trace of such a view of the Christian ministry in the Acts or the Epistles which, one would have thought, must strike the least attentive reader of the New Testament.

Nowhere is the name of "priest" given to the Christian minister, nowhere is his office described as "a priesthood." This is not because the mention of priests or a priesthood are few. It has been reckoned that there are no less than one hundred and forty of such references in the Acts and Epistles. Yet *not once*, I repeat, is the Christian minister ever called "a priest" (ἱερεὺς), or his office "a priesthood." St. Paul abounds in names and designations of the ministry. He calls the Christian clergy ambassadors for Christ, stewards of the mysteries of God, overseers of the flock, shepherds, evangelists, ministers, prophets, but never priests. When he speaks of the end and purpose for which that office was instituted, how does he describe those who hold it? "And he gave some, apostles; and some, prophets; and some, evangelists; and some, pastors and teachers; for the perfecting of the saints, for the work of the ministry, for the edifying of the body of Christ: till we all come in the unity of the faith, and of the knowledge of the Son of God unto a perfect man, unto the measure of the stature of the fulness of Christ" (Eph. iv. 11—13). It is impossible to conceive of an ampler description of the sublime purpose for which the Christian ministry was instituted. And yet those who are sent to do this work—surely the greatest work to which man can be called—are not designated as "priests." They are apostles, prophets, evangelists, pastors, teachers, who build up the body of Christ, and bring it to its destined perfection, but they are not "priests." Whereas if the later theory, and mediæval theory, be true, the building-power, the power the power of remitting sins, and of comforting and individual penitent, resides in the Christian minister as "a priest," not as "prophet," or "evangelist," or "teacher." It is scarcely possible to conceive of any ring contradiction than that which is to be found between total theory on the one hand, and the language of St. Paul ther. With the one, the pretension to be the sole channel forgiveness, and even, according to the mediæval scholastic sh doctrine, the power to offer sacrifice for the quick and upies the first, if not the exclusive place in the office of the With the other, there is not the most distant allusion to these prerogatives.

n next to the Epistles of St. Peter. If the Apostles as a e invested with the "priestly" character, to him individually ly powers were of course assigned in a very marked and manner. We should expect him to claim and to exercise vers if he deemed that they had solemnly been bestowed by his Lord. Yet what is his language? Addressing the the dispersion, without any distinction of order or office, he are a chosen generation, a royal *priesthood*" (1 Pet. ii. 9). have the spiritual priesthood of the whole body recognized. g the clergy, he writes, "The presbyters that are among ho am your co-presbyter, exhort" (chap. v. 1). In the rtion of the Epistle, where he is enlarging on the privileges istians, he tells them that they, "as living stones," are built a spiritual house, an holy priesthood, to offer spiritual sacri- he is Peter (a stone), so are they; if he is a member of a thood, so are they (chap. ii. 5). But, as an ordained Apostle ter, he calls himself a presbyter and nothing more.

istle to the Hebrews is full of the typical significance of the iesthood. But not once is it said that that priesthood has rpart in the Christian ministry; it is fulfilled in Christ, and alone. He is the One High Priest of the Church, offering erfect sacrifice for sin, making the one all-prevailing inter- heaven. Christians are spoken of as those who offer spiritual the sacrifice of themselves, the sacrifice of praise and thanks- id good works, through the One Eternal Mediator. In this are priests, but the Christian clergy are in no sense priests the Christian laity are not the same. And in the Epistle to the the only allusion to the Christian clergy is to them as having and exercising rule in the body (chap. xiii. 7), "Remember have the rule over you."

we are to interpret the passage in St. John's Gospel (xx. 23), so much stress is laid, by the light of the Epistles, we ie to the conclusion that the Apostles never regarded the commission of the Resurrection-day as a sacerdotal commission. They did, indeed, magnify their office. They looked upon it as one of unspeakable grandeur and importance, but mainly because they considered themselves as "ambassadors" of the King of kings. "As my Father hath sent me, even so send I you." Those words could only be understood with their proper limitations.* For, obviously, the Apostles were not sent to discharge that work of Redemption which was the one prerogative of their Lord. But they were sent as He was sent to proclaim God's love to sinners. This was how they understood their commission, and this was how they exercised it. When their Lord "breathed on them," what did the act signify? The "breath" is the "Spirit." The breathing is inspiration in its highest sense. But inspiration is in an emphatic sense the gift of the prophet, not of the priest. It is the gift of the preacher of righteousness. It is the power to discern spirits, it is the power to read the heart, it is the power to work mightily on the conscience, to penetrate beneath the hard crust of ungodliness and sin, to lay the sinner bare to himself and to God, whether that be done in the public preaching of the word or in the private ministration to individual men. The prophetical spirit is the spirit of the Christian ministry. It is as a prophet, as a messenger from God, that the Christian minister discharges every part of his office. There is no more force or efficiency in private absolution than there is in public; there is no more necessary conveyance of grace in the sacraments than there is in the preaching of the Gospel. All are parts of one great and merciful provision for the recovery of man to God. The grace of the sacraments, it is admitted, is not confined to their administration by the clergy. Why then draw this distinction? Why invest the sacramental remitting or retaining of sins with a priestly character, and regard the preaching that sins are remitted or retained as if it were inferior, because not sacerdotal in its nature? Neither is sacerdotal. The Christian ministry as depicted in the Acts and Epistles is incompatible with, is directly opposed to, the nature of a priesthood and sacrifices.

The question I have been discussing is not a question about words, but about things. There is a complete difference of conception as to the position of the clergy in the Church and the nature of the powers which they claim, according as we do or do not regard them as having the "priestly character." And this, I take it, is the real question we have now to face in the Church of England. All the other questions which have of late been debated with so much heat and acrimony, the use of vestments, of lights and incense and crucifixes, the ritual of Divine service, the Eastward position, these after all only mask the real question. That is behind all these, and they would have no import- [illegible] from it. What are the clergy? Are they the possessors

* [illegible] very clearly pointed out by Bishop Thirlwall, in the Sermon on "The [illegible]," already quoted.

of certain mysterious powers, special gifts, awful prerogatives which separate them from the laity? Are they "priests" to exercise at will the tremendous power of absolution, to call down Christ from heaven at their bidding, to offer sacrifice for sins? or are they ministers sent by Christ to preach His gospel, and solemnly set apart to this work by those "who have public authority given unto them in the congregation to call and send ministers into the Lord's vineyard?"* Are they intermediaries between man and God, without whose intervention pardon and grace cannot be obtained? or is it their office to preach not themselves, but Christ Jesus the Lord, to invite, to persuade, to entreat men, in Christ's name, to be reconciled unto God? Taking the New Testament as our guide, there can be no doubt about the answer. The answer which is given, by the Church of Rome, and by too many in our own Church, is drawn from the treatises of mediæval scholasticism, seeking to find support for a gigantic system of fraud, imposture, and corruption. The sacerdotal system is the fruit and the growth of ages of ignorance, superstition, immorality, and crime. That arrogant lording it over God's heritage is directly opposed to the Apostolic conception of the ministry. If the Church of England is true to herself, if she will shine forth in her Reformation splendour, if she will maintain her place as God's best gift to England, she can only do so by holding fast to that conception of the Christian ministry, its authority, and its nature, which is to be found in the inspired writings of those who first received and handed down the Apostolical commission.

J. J. STEWART PEROWNE.

* Twenty-third Article of the Church of England. The studied vagueness of the Article as to the source of the authority, and the entire absence of any reference to Apostolical succession as necessary to a lawful ministry, are not without significance.

# ON THE HYGIENIC VALUE OF PLANTS IN ROOMS AND THE OPEN AIR.

THE animal kingdom is, as we know, dependent on the vegetable kingdom, which must have existed on the earth before men and animals could live upon it. We may therefore rightly call plants children of the earth. But in so doing we use the language of metaphor, as when we speak of "mother earth." The earth does not directly bring forth either plants or animals. Every plant is the child of a mother plant, descends from one of its own kind like ourselves; but plants derive their nourishment directly from earth, air, and water, and, although generated by plants, are nourished directly by the inorganic breasts of nature, and imply no other organic life but their own. Had plants a voice, they would more correctly speak of "mother earth" than ourselves.

Plants live directly on the lifeless products of earth, and we live directly on the products of plants or on animals which live on them; our existence implies other organic life, and our nourishment is not derived so directly from the earth as that of plants. Since the vegetable world comes between us, *we* should rather call earth our grandmother than our mother. At all events it is an affectionate relationship.

We have a natural feeling of close affinity with the vegetable world, which expresses itself not only in our love of foliage and flowers, but in our fondness for metaphors derived from the vegetable world and its processes. If we were to reckon up how many metaphors in every-day life and in poetry are derived from the vegetable world, and how many from other spheres of nature, we should find a great excess of the former.

Our material relations to plants are also very numerous. The question we are now concerned with is not what food or what medicinal remedies plants provide us with, but the value of plants and plantations in dwellings and in the open air in conducing to health or preventing disease. We have given the subject very little consideration until quite recently, just as we have thought very little of the way in which the pleasures of the table, fine raiment, comfortable dwellings, and many other things, conduce to our well-being. Meanwhile we have been guided by our instincts, which, like nature in general, have, on the whole, guided us rightly. Even now there is not much scientific knowledge on the subject; still there is a little, and something is gained when we begin seriously to reflect on anything, for knowledge is sure then to increase. All that man has ever aspired to and attained, has always existed much earlier in idea than in reality. Ideas are never fully realized, as we all know, and it is only very gradually that they are realized at all.

It is generally asserted that vegetation purifies the air, and chiefly by three functions: firstly, because plants absorb carbonic acid; secondly, because under the influence of sunlight they exhale an equivalent in oxygen; and lastly, because they produce ozone. These facts I need not demonstrate, as they have been placed beyond doubt by vegetable physiologists, chemists, and meteorologists. My task is to show what the direct sanitary effect of these three functions is.

I must at once state that none whatever can be proved to exist. And as this assertion will contradict the prepossessions of many readers, I feel bound to prove my proposition.

As to carbonic acid, the first question is, what is the proper and normal proportion of this gas in the air, next how much more carbonic acid is contained in air which is notoriously bad, and, lastly, whether the air on a surface without vegetation contains essentially more carbonic acid than one having vegetation upon it.

The amount of carbonic acid in the open air has been often determined, and is confined within very narrow limits. It may be said—leaving severe storms or very thick fogs out of the question—to vary between 3 and 4 parts in each 10,000 of the volume of the air.

Experiments have also been made on the quantity of carbonic acid in apartments occupied by man, and it is generally taken as the criterion of the quality of the air, ventilation being regulated by it. In very bad air which is undoubtedly deleterious, it has been found to amount to from three to five per mille. One per mille marks the boundary line between good and bad air in a room.

We next inquire whether the atmosphere over a vast tract of country destitute of vegetation contains more carbonic acid than one abounding in vegetation, whether in the former case the amount of carbonic acid approaches one per mille. In 1830, De Saussure began to make researches into the variations in the quantity of carbonic acid in Geneva, and they were continued about ten years later by Verver in Holland, and Boussingault in Paris; in more recent, and very recent times, a great number of experiments have been made on the subject by Roscoe in Manchester, Schulze at Rostock, and myself and my pupils, particularly Dr. Wolffhügel, at Munich. The result is, in the main, that the variations—very small from the first—have been found to be still smaller as the methods of determining carbonic acid have been perfected.

Saussure, who worked by a method liable to give an excess, found from 3·7 to 6·2 parts in 10,000. He considered that there were also slight variations between summer and winter, day and night, town and country, land and sea, mountains and valleys, which might be ascribed to vegetation. Boussingault, however, found the carbonic acid in the air to be rather less, and the same on an average in Paris and St. Cloud; in Paris 4·13 and at St. Cloud 4·14 in 10,000, which surprised him the more as he had reckoned that in Paris at least 2,944,000,000 litres of carbonic acid were exhaled by men, animals, and fuel.

Roscoe made experiments on the air at a station in the middle of Manchester, and at two stations in the country. He was originally of opinion that the vast manufactures of Manchester, chiefly dependent on the consumption of coal, must produce a perceptible effect on the carbonic acid in the air; but he also discovered that the air in the space in front of Owen's College contained no more than the air at the country stations. He also observed occasional variations; but when the carbonic acid increased or diminished in the city, it was generally just the same in the country. Roscoe found the greatest amount of carbonic acid in the air during one of the thick fogs prevalent in England.

Schulze found the amount of carbonic acid in the air at Rostock to be between 2½ and 4 parts in 10,000. On an average it was somewhat higher when the wind blew off shore than off the sea.

In Munich, Wolffhügel found the carbonic acid to between 3 and 4 parts in 10,000. Now and then, but very seldom, he observed variations, the maximum being 6·9 parts in 10,000 in a very thick fog, the minimum 1·5 parts in 10,000 in a heavy snow-storm, when the mercury was very low in the barometer.

It may be asked how the immense production of carbonic acid in cities like Paris or Manchester can thus vanish in the air. The answer is very simple: by rarefaction in the currents of the atmosphere. We are apt not to take this factor into account, but think rather of the air as stagnant. The average velocity of the air with us is 3 metres per second, and even in apparently absolute calm it is more than half a metre. If we therefore assume a column of air 100 feet high and of average velocity, it may be reckoned that the carbonic acid from all the lungs and chimneys of Paris or Manchester is not sufficient to increase its amount so as to be detected by our methods.

From this fact it [illegible] concluded [illegible]

[illegible] acid of the air is observable, no diminution will be [illegible].

[illegible] recognised and incontrovertible fact that the [illegible] contained in all the vegetable life on earth is derived [illegible] acid in the air, in water, and the soil. Many [illegible] suppose that the air in a green wood must contain less [illegible] than that in a city or that of an extensive tract of waste [illegible] assure them that the air in the Sahara, so called, of [illegible] called the Dultplatz, contains no more carbonic acid [illegible] neighbouring Eschen grounds. Of this I can give incon-[illegible] an argument *ad hominem*. Dr. Zittel brought me several [illegible] of air in hermetically sealed glass tubes, from his travels in [illegible] desert, from sandy wastes and from oases, on which I [illegible] conveniently make experiments at Munich. The amount of [illegible] does not differ in the least in the air from the barren [illegible] the greenest oasis. The case is just the same with the [illegible] oxygen in the air. It was formerly thought, when im-[illegible] methods were employed, that perceptible variations could be [illegible] Thus, for example, the outbreak of cholera in 1831 was [illegible] to a diminution of oxygen in the air, and here and there [illegible] were made which seemed to confirm the opinion. The [illegible] did not seem improbable, for it was concluded with cer-[illegible] in tropical swamps, which are the home of cholera, the [illegible] the air might have been in course of time diminished by [illegible] of decaying matter. But since the method of gas [illegible] been arranged by Von Bunsen, the amount of oxygen in [illegible] summit of Mont Blanc has not been found to differ from [illegible] or in the swamps of Bengal. Neither is it greater in [illegible] air than in the air of the desert.

[illegible] of demonstrable variation, in spite of the production [illegible] by living plants and the absorption of it by the processes of [illegible] and decay, becomes intelligible when we consider first the [illegible] then the mass of the air encompassing our earth. The [illegible] this mass is, as the barometer tells us, equal to that of [illegible] which would cover the surface of the earth to the [illegible] millimetres (more than three-quarters of a metre). From [illegible] this, several billion kilos., some idea can be formed of the [illegible] air, when we consider that air, even beneath a pressure [illegible] of mercury is yet 10,395 times lighter than mercury. [illegible] like these, variations such as those we speak of go for [illegible] amount of carbonic acid and oxygen might perhaps be [illegible] changed in Paris or Manchester if all organic matter on and [illegible] were burning at once.

[illegible] granted, however, in face of these incontrovertible facts, [illegible] exercises no perceptible influence upon the composition [illegible] in the open air, many persons will not be disposed to give up the idea that the air in rooms can be improved by plants, because, as is well known, every green leaf absorbs carbonic acid and gives out oxygen under the influence of light. This idea may seem the more justifiable, because, although the production of carbonic acid is not perceptible in the greatest assemblages of human beings in the open air, it is always observed in confined spaces, although the actual production is but small. In the air of a closed apartment, every person and every light burning makes a perceptible difference in the increase of carbonic acid in the air. Must not, therefore, every plant in a pot, every spray, any plant with leaves, make a perceptible difference in a room? Every lover of flowers may be pardoned for wishing to see this question answered in the affirmative. Have not even medical men proposed to adorn schoolrooms with plants in pots instead of ventilating them better, in order that their leaves and stems might absorb carbonic acid from the mouths of the children, and give out oxygen in its stead? But Hygiene cannot agree even to this. Hygiene is a science of economics, and every such science has to ask not only what exists and whether it exists, but how much there is and whether enough. The power of twenty pots of plants would not be nearly sufficient to neutralize the carbonic acid exhaled by a single child in a given time. If children were dependent on the oxygen given off by flowers, they would soon be suffocated. It must not be forgotten what a slow process the production of matter by plants is,—matter which the animal organism absorbs and again decomposes in a very short time, whereby as much oxygen is used up as has been set free in the production of it. It is for this reason that such great extents of vegetation are required for the sustenance of animals and man. The grass or hay consumed by a cow in a cowhouse grows upon a space of ground on which a thousand head of cattle could stand. How slow is the process of the growth of wheat before it can be eaten as bread, which a man will eat, digest, and decompose in twenty-four hours! The animal and human organism consumes and decomposes food as quickly as a stove burns the wood which took so many thousand times longer to grow in the forest.

It would scarcely be intelligible if I were to calculate how much carbonic acid and oxygen a rose, a geranium, or a bignonia would absorb and give out in a room in a day, and to what extent the air might be changed by it, taking into account the inevitable change of air always going on. I will draw attention to a concrete case which every one can understand.

When the Royal Winter Garden in Munich was completed and in use, it occurred to me to make experiments on the effect of the whole garden on the air within it. There could not be a more favourable opportunity for experimenting on the air in a space full of vegetation. This green and blooming space was not exposed to the free currents of air which at once immensely rarefy all gaseous exhalations, but was kept warm under a dome of glass, through which only the light of heaven penetrated. Although not hermetically sealed, the circulation of air in such a building, compared with that in the open air, is reduced over a hundred-thousand-fold.

I asked permission to make experiments for several days at various hours of the day and night, which was readily granted. Now, what was the result? The proportion of carbonic acid in the air in the winter garden was almost as high as in the open air. This greatly surprised me, but I hoped at any rate to have one of my traditional ideas confirmed. I hoped to find less carbonic acid in the day than in the night, supported by the fact that the green portions of plants under the influence of light decompose carbonic acid and develop oxygen. But even here I was disappointed. I generally found carbonic acid increasing from morning till evening, and decreasing from night till morning. As this seemed really paradoxical, I doubled my tests and care, but the result remained the same. At that time I knew nothing of the large amount of carbonic acid of the air, in the soil, the air of the ground, or I should probably have been less surprised.

One day it suddenly became clear to me why there was always more carbonic acid by day than by night. I had been thinking only of the turf, the shrubs, and trees which consume carbonic acid and produce oxygen, and not of the men and birds in the winter garden. One day, when there were considerably more men at work there than usual, the carbonic acid rose to the highest point, and sank again to the average during the night. The production of carbonic acid by the working and breathing human beings was so much greater than that consumed by the plants in the same time.

The oxygen in the winter garden was rather higher than in the open air; there it was about 21 per cent., and in the winter garden 22 to 23 per cent.

I did not make any experiments on ozone, for reasons which I will give by-and-by.

The amount of carbonic acid in the air in the winter garden cannot be reckoned as telling for or against the hygienic value of vegetation in an enclosed space. Let us inquire, then, into the value of the slight increase of oxygen.

There is a widespread opinion that the breathing of air rich in oxygen effects a more rapid transformation of matter, a more rapid combustion, as we say, in the body. Even great inquirers and thinkers have considered that we only eat and imbibe nourishment to satiate the oxygen streaming through us, which would otherwise consume us. We know now well enough that the quantity of oxygen which we imbibe does not depend on the quantity in the air we breathe, but far more on previous changes in and the amount of transformation of matter in the body, which are regulated by the requirements of breathing. The inhalation of oxygen is not a primary but a secondary thing. When we inhale air at every breath richer than usual in oxygen—for example, when breathing highly compressed air, as divers do, or labourers on the pneumatic foundations of bridge piers—the result is not a larger consumption of matter and an increased production of carbonic acid, but merely a decrease in the number of inhalations. If in air of ordinary density we make about sixteen respirations in a minute, in air of greater density we should involuntarily make only twelve, ten, or eight, according to the density and our need of oxygen; all else remains the same.

Lavoisier, and half a century later Regnault and Reiset, placed animals for twenty-four hours in air very rich in oxygen, but they did not consume more of it than in the ordinary air. An increase of oxygen in the air, therefore, or pure oxygen gas, only produces an effect in certain morbid conditions, in cases of difficulty of breathing, or where breathing has been for some time suspended, because an inspiration communicates more oxygen to the blood than breathing ordinary air. A healthy person can, however, without difficulty or injury, compensate for considerable differences, and an increase or decrease of 1 or 2 per cent. of oxygen does no harm, for under ordinary circumstances we only inhale one-fourth of the oxygen in the air we breathe; we inhale it with 21 per cent. and exhale it with 16 per cent.

So far, therefore, as we feel ill or well in a winter garden, it does not depend on the quantity of oxygen in the air, and there is no greater appreciable quantity of oxygen in a wood of thick foliage than in a desert or on the open sea.

Let us, also, for a moment consider the ozone in the air, which may be looked upon as polarized or agitated oxygen. After its discovery, which has immortalized the name of Schönbein, was made known, it was thought for a time that the key had been found for the appearance and disappearance of various diseases, in the quantity of ozone in the air. But one fact, which was observed from the first, shows that it cannot be so; for the presence of ozone can never be detected in our dwellings, not even in the cleanest and best ventilated. Now, as it is a fact that we spend the greater part of our lives in our houses, and are better than if we lived in the open air, the hygienic value of ozone does not seem so very great. Added to this, the medical men of Königsberg long had several ozone stations there, during which time various diseases came and went, without, as appears from the reports of Dr. Schiefferdecker, ozone having the slightest connection with the appearance or disappearance of any of them.

Dr. Wolffhügel, assistant at the Hygienic Institute at Munich, has lately been occupied with the question of the sanitary value of ozone, but has arrived at only negative results.

But in saying this I have no intention of denying that ozone is of great importance in the atmosphere, for I am of opinion that it is. It is the constant purifier of the atmosphere from all organic matter, which passes into it and might accumulate. The air would have been long ago filled with the vapours of decomposition if it were not for ozone, which oxidizes all that is oxidizable, if only time enough is allowed for it, and too much is not expected at once; for, generally, the amount of ozone in the air is so small, that it is consumed in making its way into our houses, without disinfecting them, and we can no more dispense with the greatest cleanliness and best ventilation in our homes than we can essentially change the air in our rooms by means of plants in pots and foliage.

Some of my readers will perhaps ask in some disappointment, in what, then, does the hygienic value of plants and plantations consist? Or do I mean to say that all the money spent by one and another on a parterre of flowers in his house or on a garden, or by a community for beautiful grounds, or by a State for the preservation of forests, with the idea of promoting health, is mere luxury, without any hygienic value? These questions alter our standpoint, and I believe I shall be able to show that even hygiene does recognize a sanitary value in plants and flowers, in the laying out of grounds and plantations, only it offers a different explanation from the ordinary one.

I consider the impression which plants and plantations make upon our minds and senses to be of hygienic value; further, their influence on the conformation of the soil, with which health is in many respects connected; and, finally, their influence upon other qualities of the air than carbonic acid, oxygen, and ozone: among these may be mentioned, in passing, shade in summer, and decrease of wind and dust.

It is an old observation, needing no demonstration, that the cheerful and happy man lives not only an easier, but, on the average, a more healthy life than the depressed and morose man. Medical men, and especially "mad doctors," could tell us much of the great value of a certain relative proportion of pleasurable and painful impressions upon health, and how frequently some unfortunate position, an absence of pleasure, or too much of painful impression, are the causes of serious illness. Man always tries, and has an irresistible need, to balance painful sensations by some kind of pleasure or other, so that often, in order to get himself into a tolerable frame of mind, or to deaden his feelings for a time, he will have recourse to wine, beer, or spirits, though he knows well enough that he will be worse afterwards than before. A certain amount of change and recreation is indispensable, and, failing others, we seek them by injurious means. There are, doubtless, some unhappy and morbid natures who are always discontented, to whom everything comes amiss, and whom it is impossible to help; but the majority of men are easily pleased, find pleasure in little things, though it is but a sorry life they lead. It is something the same with the pleasures of life as with the pleasures of the table; we must relish our food if it is to do us good. What good will the most nourishing diet do me if it creates disgust? Professor C. Voit has clearly pointed out, in his experimental researches into diet, the great value of palatable food, as well as nourishment, and how indispensable a certain variety in our meals is. We think we are only tickling the palate, and that it is nothing to the stomach and intestines whether food is agreeable to the palate or not, since they will digest it, if it is digestible at all. But it is not so indifferent, after all; for the nerves of the tongue are connected with other nerves and with the nerve centres, so that the pleasures of the palate, or some pleasure, at any rate, even if it is only imagination, which can only originate in the central organ, the brain, often has an active effect on other organs. This is a matter of daily experience. If you put your finger down your throat, you produce retching; many people have only to think of anything disgusting to produce the effect of an emetic, just as the thought of something nice makes the mouth water just as much as tasting the most dainty morsel. Voit showed me one of his dogs with a fistula in the stomach. So long as this dog is not thinking of food, his stomach secretes no gastric juice, but no sooner does he catch sight of a bit of meat, even at a distance, than the stomach prepares for digestion and secretes gastric juice in abundance. Without this secretion the assimilation of nourishment would be impossible. If therefore some provocatives induce and increase certain sensations and useful processes, they are of essential value to health, and it is no bad economy to spend something on them.

I consider flowers in a room, for all to whom they give pleasure, to be one of the enjoyments of life, like condiments in food. It is certainly one of the most harmless and refined. We cannot live on pleasure alone; but to those who have something to put up with in life, their beloved flowers perform good service.

The same may be said of private gardens and public grounds, and of the artistic perfecting of them. The more tastefully laid out, the better the effect. Though tastes differ, there is a general standard of taste which lasts for several generations, though it varies from time to time and is subject to fashion. As their object is to give pleasure, public grounds should accord with the taste of the age, or aim at cultivating it. This is a justification for going to some expense for æsthetic ends.

The influence of vegetation on the soil is much more easy to determine than on the mind of man. Space fails me to go into all the aspects of this subject, and I will confine myself to some of the most obvious. The difference is most apparent on comparing the soil of a tract of land covered with wood with the soil outside, in other respects alike. The Bavarian Forest Department deserves great credit for having established meteorological stations with special reference to forest culture, under the superintendence of Professor Ebermayer of Aschaffenburg. He has published his first year's observations in a work on "The Influence of Forests on the Air and Soil, and their Climatic and Hygienic Importance,"* which may be recommended to every one who wishes to study the subject.

Modern hygiene has observed that certain variations in the moisture of the soil have a great influence on the origin and spread of certain epidemic diseases, as for instance cholera and typhoid fever—that these diseases do not become epidemic when the moisture in the soil is not above or below a certain level, and has remained so for a time. These variations can be measured with greater accuracy by the ground-water of the soil than by the rainfall, because in the latter case we have to determine how much water penetrates the ground, how much runs off the surface, and how much evaporates at once. The amount of moisture in the soil of a forest is subject to considerably less variation than that outside. Ebermayer has deduced the following result from his meteorological observations on forestry:—"If from the soil of an open space 100 parts of water evaporate, then from the soil of a forest free from underwood 38 parts would evaporate, and from a soil covered with underwood only 15 parts would evaporate." This simple fact explains clearly why the cutting down of wood over tracts of country is always followed by the drying up of wells and springs.

In India, the home of cholera, much importance has been attached in recent times to plantations as preventives of it. It has been always observed that the villages in wooded districts suffer less than those in treeless plains. Many instances of this are given in the reports of Dr. Bryden, President of the Statistical Office in Calcutta, and Dr. Murray, Inspector of Hospitals. For instance, Bryden† compares the district of the Mahanadda, one of the northern tributaries of the Ganges, the almost treeless district of Rajpoor, with the forest district of Sambalpoor. It is stated that in the villages in the plain of Rajpoor, 60 or 70 per cent. of the inhabitants are sometimes swept away by cholera in three or four days, while the wooded district of Sambalpoor is often free from it, or it is much less severe. The District Commissioner who had to make a tour in the district on account of the occurrence of cholera reports, among other things, as follows:—

"The road to Sambalpoor runs for sixty or seventy miles through the forest, which round Petorah and Jenkfluss is very dense. Now, it is a remarkable fact, but it is a fact nevertheless, that on this route, traversed daily by hundreds of travellers, vehicles, and baggage trains, the cholera rarely appears in this extent of sixty miles, and when it does appear it is in a mild form; but when we come to the road from Arang, westward to Chicholee Bungalow, which runs for about ninety miles through a barren treeless plain, we find the

* Die physikalischen Wirkungen des Waldes auf Luft und Boden und seine klimatologische und hygienische Bedeutung.

† Epidemic Cholera in the Bengal Presidency, 1869, p. 225.

cholera every year in its more severe form, the dead and dying lying by the wayside, and trains of vehicles half of whose conductors are dead."

In the same report Dr. Bryden continues:—

"I will mention one other fact as a result of my observations, namely, that places surrounded by those vast and splendid groves which are occasionally seen, lying in low and probably marshy situations, surrounded by hills, and which, from the mass of decaying vegetation, are very subject to fever in September, October, and November, are seldom visited by cholera, and, if it occurs there are but few deaths, while places on high ground, or in what are called fine airy situations, free from trees and without hills near, so that they are thoroughly ventilated, suffer very much from cholera."

Murray gives a number of instances showing the influence of trees on the spread of cholera. One of these may find a place here:—

"The fact is generally believed, and not long ago the medical officer of Jatiagar, in Central India, offered a striking proof of it. During the widespread epidemic of cholera in Allahabad, in 1859, those parts of the garrison whose barracks had the advantage of having trees near them enjoyed an indisputable exemption, and precisely in proportion to the thickness and nearness of the shelter. Thus the European Cavalry in the Wellington Barracks, which stand between four rows of mango trees, but are yet to a certain extent open, suffered much less than the 4th European regiment whose quarters were on a hill exposed to the full force of the wind; while the Bengal Horse Artillery, who were in a thicket of mango trees, had not a single case of sickness; and the exemption cannot be regarded as accidental, as the next year the comparative immunity was precisely the same."*

We need not, however, go to India to observe similar instances of the influence of a certain degree of moisture in the soil favoured by woods or other conditions; we can find them much nearer home. In the cholera epidemic of 1854, in Bavaria, it was generally observed that the places in the moors were spared, in spite of the otherwise bad condition of the inhabitants. The great plain of the Danube from Neuburg to Ingolstadt was surrounded by places where it was epidemic, while in the plain itself there were but a few scattered cases. The same thing has been demonstrated by Reinhard, President of the Saxon Medical College. Cholera has visited Saxony eight times since 1836, and every time it spared the northerly district between Pleisse and Spree, where ague is endemic.

In the English Garden at Munich there are several buildings, not sparsely tenanted—the Diana Baths, the Chinese Tower, with a tavern and outbuildings, the Gendarmerie Station, and the Kleinkessellohe. In the three outbreaks of cholera at Munich none of these places have been affected by it. This fact is the more surprising, as three of them comprise public taverns into which the disease germs must have been occasionally introduced by the public; yet there was no epidemic in these houses, although it prevailed largely immediately beyond the English garden and [illegible] Diana Baths in 1854 and 1873. It must have been [illegible]

* Report on [illegible]

Tower, or the Kleinkesselloche, might have as others did who came from a distance, but had cases, probably no epidemic would have occurred

deductions must be accepted with caution from an point of view, still, on the whole, they indisputably tell in and woods.

vegetation has also other advantages, besides its use in the moisture in the soil; it purifies it from the drainage of whereby it is contaminated and impregnated. If matter remains in soil destitute of growing vegetation, decomposition sets in, and other processes are induced, not of a salubrious nature, but often deleterious, the products of by means of air or water, and may penetrate into our But from this indisputable fact, false conclusions are some-. Many people imagine that if a few old trees are left in an open space their roots will absorb all the impurities houses around, and render the refuse which accumulates them innocuous. This idea is not only false in a sanitary view, but very injurious, as it prevents people from taking sures which alone can keep the ground under our houses

ill now explain why the shade of gardens and woods is at seasons so beneficial. The human race during its pilgrimage and wanderings over it has many difficult tasks to perform. the most difficult is involved in the necessity that all our organs, and the blood, whether at the Equator or the North ould retain an equable temperature of 37½° Centigrade (98° Deviations of but one degree are signs of serious illness. The the Negro and that of the Esquimaux is of the same tempera- ile the one lives in a temperature of 40° above and the other zero (Centigrade). A difference of 80° has therefore to be d.

rganism, doubtless, possesses a special apparatus for the per- e of this colossal task, self-acting sluices so to speak, by f which more or less of the heat generated in the body passes se consist mainly in the increase or diminution of the peripheric ion, and the action of the pores of the skin. But we soon the end of our natural regulating apparatus, and have to resort icial means. Against cold we have excellent methods in , dwellings, and fires; but at present our precautions against limited. This is doubtless the reason why higher civili- extended so much farther towards the Polar regions than Equator. The Germanic races, particularly, inevitably living for a few generations in the tropics, and must be renewed by immigration if they desire to retain supremacy, as is proved by the case of the English in India. They will not be able to settle there and maintain the characteristics which have made them dominant, until means have been found of diminishing the heat of the body at pleasure, as we are able to maintain it in the north. At present our remedies against heat are baths, fans, and shade.

We lose the heat of our bodies in three different ways—by the medium in which we are,—generally the air,—and which can be warmed; by the evaporation of perspiration; and by radiation from bodies of a lower temperature, not taking into account a small portion of heat which goes off in mechanical labour. Under ordinary circumstances in temperate climates, we lose half the heat generated by radiation, one-fourth by evaporation, and one-fourth by the conducting medium in which we are. In proportion as any of these methods is diminished, one or both the others must be increased. As long as possible, our organisms are so obliging as to open and close the sluices themselves without our cognizance, provided that our regulating apparatus is in order, that we are not ill. It is only when our good servant the skin, under certain conditions, has come to an end of its powers, that we begin to feel that we must lend our aid. And thus we have found by experience that in hot weather shade helps the body to keep cool to the needful extent. The chief effect of shelter is to prevent the sun's rays from striking us directly; but if this were all, it would be as cool in the height of summer indoors, or even under the leaden roofs of Venice—which have driven many to frenzy and desperation—as under the shade of a tree or in a wood. It also makes a great difference whether the sun's rays fall on thick foliage or on a roof of slate or metal. A great deal of heat is neutralized by evaporation from the leaves; another portion by the decomposition of carbonic acid, just so much as is set free when we burn the wood and other organic combinations into the composition of which it enters. The heat produced by burning wood in a stove is derived from the sun; it is but the captured rays of the sun again set free by combustion. We learn from Ebermayer's work that the temperature of the trees in a forest, and even in the tops of them, is always lower than the air in the forest.

Besides this, shade in the open air always causes a certain draught which acts as a kind of fan. All must have noticed when walking in oppressive heat, when the air seems still as death, that a refreshing breeze arises as soon as a cloud casts a shade. The same thing may often be observed in summer in walking through a street with close rows of houses, when the air is still, and one side is sunny, the other in shade. On the sunny side there is not a breath of air, [illegible] other there may be a light [illegible] the shade extends the [illegible] unequal warmth are [illegible] perature is the [illegible]

The shade of a single tree, therefore, cools not only by intercepting the sun's rays, but also by the effect of gentle fanning. The shelter of a thick wood, however, is much more agreeable than that of a single tree. The air in a wood is cooler than that of an open space exposed to the sun. The air from outside is drawn into the wood, is cooled by it, and cools us again. And it is not only the air that cools us, but the trees themselves. Observation has shown that the trunks of trees in a wood breast-high, even at the hottest time of day, are 5° Cent. cooler than the air. We therefore lose considerable heat by radiation to these cooler objects, and can cool ourselves more easily at a temperature of 25° Cent. in a wood than at a much lower temperature in an open space. When the objects around us are as warm as ourselves we lose nothing by radiation; what is radiated from us is radiated back by them. This is why we are so uncomfortable in heated and overcrowded rooms. It is generally set down to bad air, and this does certainly contribute to it, but it is chiefly the result of disturbed distribution of heat, as has been plainly shown by experiments on the composition of such air, which makes many people feel ill.

MAX VON PETTENKOFER.

# WILLIAM LAW, THE ENGLISH MYSTIC OF THE EIGHTEENTH CENTURY.

AMID all the change of feeling with which the last century has been regarded within the memory of men not yet old, it has remained unquestionably the Age of Rationalism. Whether as the age of shallowness, of poverty, as in those years when Carlyle's was the strongest influence in literature; whether as the age of sound and temperate good sense, of a wise respect for the limits of the knowable, as in our own day,—for blame, or for praise, the century which closed with the French Revolution remains as the undoubted blossoming time of all that part of human nature which belongs to the region of the understanding. It is the period of definiteness, of clear and limited apprehension, of sound logic and good taste, of what we may call the best daylight view of the world. From no point of view can any one who aims at understanding what is best in the past afford to treat such a period as a mere blank: and it is a curious illustration of its wealth that the great writer to whose disparaging estimate so much of the vague popular discredit into which it had fallen before the late reaction in its favour is due has spent his life in exploring and illustrating its history, and will always, probably, be the best known authority for some of its most striking figures. But the best daylight view of the world is not that which will ever be dear to the eyes of all thinkers. There will always be those to whom Wordsworth's noble address to Twilight as a power

> "[illegible]
> [illegible]"

and brings the unchanging features of the outward world into prominence, represents a truth for the inward no less than for the outward eye. To the merely literary critic any tendency towards sm is, in the eighteenth century, hardly discernible. But it , and its representative on English soil is worthy of more than attention from a student of the thought of the past.

ng the many influences which shut in William Law to the path h we seek to follow him we must not disregard that which the nt of our time regards as mere political superstition. It was gnificant fact with reference to the speculations which occupied er years, that the accession of George I. forced him, then a man,* to resign the Cambridge fellowship, which he could only e to hold on taking an oath of allegiance incompatible with victions as to the right of the exiled family. We are often ed by our mistakes. The nonjuring scruples which excluded om all paths that led to the world's high places, fenced in the where the mystic finds his home, and sheltered him from the e force of interests which, however valuable in themselves, are ited human minds hardly compatible with those which it was sion to diffuse in his generation. It is said that those who interpret spoken language by observing the motion of the lips e deaf. The eye will not do the work unless the ear refuses it. hing like this is true of all our perceptions. The thoughts which ed William Law could not have lived in an atmosphere of political life. They may be true, and the political creed may e, and all truth is mutually compatible, but all truth is not at oment the possible object of lively belief, and the public man st on the alert for voices which break in with fatal distraction e visions of the mystic. The nonjuring scruples of William were an instrument of detachment from a world with which he have kept no connection which would not have unfitted him work he had to do.

the other hand, the public life from which he was thus detached England, at the beginning of the eighteenth century, at its ebb. Between the principles which a glorious Revolution had ated and those which an impious Rebellion had branded with the boundary was so subtle and shifting that the only safe anywhere in its neighbourhood was to stop short whenever you in sight of anything that might be called an extreme. There universal sense that you must not lean hard on any principle. uld hold to a certain extent—the statesman, the practical man, ven the sound divine, would show his wisdom by keeping well the circuit of its influence; nothing could be more dangerous o imperil what was undoubted by carrying it too far. Perhaps eat literary excellence of this period has some connection with midity. It begets that temperance, that reserve, which forms so a part of literary excellence, and which our own age greatly and therefore highly values. But in an age when men fear

* He was born in 1686.

what is thorough, political life must be hollow; and it is perhaps well that those to whom any great protest for truth is committed should be at such a time cut off from politics.

This at all events seems to us the moral of a glimpse at the Cambridge where Law became a nonjuror. Such a glimpse is afforded us by one whom we venture to consider the most interesting medium through which we can contemplate his life. The reader who is aware that Gibbon is a rival, will probably be inclined to consider that the opinion according to which the great historian is cast into the shade by a certain John Byrom, the inventor of a system of short-hand, is mainly remarkable for its originality. To effect his conversion, we should demand nothing but space, for Byrom's journal is a self-revelation of one of the most charming characters of his time; nor would the attempt be irrelevant in a sketch of eighteenth-century mysticism, of which he was one of the most characteristic specimens, and for the history of which he is a chief authority. A portrait of Byrom's master, however, is enough for our canvas; and we must be content to leave our opinion of the disciple to be verified by those who will have patience to read in his journal (published by the Chetham Society) how many dishes of Bohea he took, and what difficulty he had in getting the washerwoman to darn his stockings properly. Mixed up with such details as these, themselves not wholly uninteresting to those who find the personality of the writer an engaging one, is a great deal of the most valuable information for the social life of his day, and especially for that movement towards mystic theology of which we learn so little from material more properly belonging to literature. Meantime the opinion here expressed of their writer may be at least supported by one high authority, who will not be suspected of any leaning towards mysticism. Listen to the terrible Warburton, and remember that Byrom's master has been bludgeoned without mercy for initiating an attack in which Byrom took part:—

> "I think you are the only honest man of all the number that have abused me. . . . Modesty should not hinder you from reflecting that a dash from your pen is not an indifferent matter. Your translation of the fine passage from Tully, equal to the original, gives me the opportunity of saying how much I think the literary world loses by your not applying your talents more to poetry, in which you appear naturally formed to excel."

We may have our own opinion about the loss to literature in Byrom not applying himself more to poetry; but if he is remarkable in nothing else, he may be remembered as the one human being who has received a gentle remonstrance from the author of the "Divine Legation." Fortified by this tribute, we may ask the reader to follow us in gathering up the reminiscences of one whom literature has forgotten, but whose picture of Law, for one reader at all events, has something of the charm of the biography that has made Dr. Johnson so much better known to us than the majority of our contemporaries.

Byrom's first impression of Law, however, is of interest only as a warning against first impressions; he speaks of him at this Cambridge stage (when he was Fellow of Trinity and Law of Emmanuel) as a "vain, conceited fellow," whose society he made no effort to cultivate, but he is of use to the student of Law's life at this early stage, in giving a specimen of the kind of reasoning Law failed to find convincing. A letter written in 1715 presents a curious picture of the confusion produced in an ingenuous mind by the conflicting claims of two monarchs, the right of one resting on a theory not yet overtly discarded, that of the other on the necessity of practical life. The sophistry by which Burke, seventy-five years later, tried to convince his readers that the Revolution of 1688 had only *more* emphatically proclaimed the doctrine of Divine Right, is curiously foreshadowed in this extract:—

"The abjuration oath hath not been put to us yet, nor do I know when it will be; nobody of our year scruples it, and *indeed in the sense they say they shall take it, I could.* One says he can do it and like the Pretender never the worse."

And so forth. Byrom had some difficulty in convincing himself that one might swear allegiance to a king whom one intended to drive out of the country at the first favourable opportunity. "But this oath," he writes, "I am not so well satisfied to take it." Then sweeping together some loose scraps of arguments for a course so thoroughly convenient, he goes on:—

"It has been always the custom of nations to set aside those whom 'twas found for the good of the people not to reign. Why do they make Kings of Sicily, &c.? And may I not rely on the judgment of thousands of learned and pious men for its being a lawful oath? 'Tis very hard, everything settled so orderly for posterity, and must all be undone for the sake of a man who has a disputed title to his birth and right? I saw a book in our library t'other day where the Pretender's birth is made very suspicious. The Commons I see have taken the abjuration oath—how is it likely the young fellow should ever come among us?"

This disjointed elliptical letter is worth notice as illustrating the influence of a theory which had forced the supporters of "a glorious Revolution" to keep in the background weighty considerations concerning the freedom of a great nation, and to bring into prominence silly fictions concerning the incidents of an accouchement.

There were many good men no doubt at Cambridge in 1715 who thought with Law that their rightful monarch was James III., and were yet convinced with Byrom that they might rely on the judgment of thousands of learned and pious men in swearing allegiance to George I. But no such compromise was possible to one who, whatever else he was, at least was one of the most consistent and thorough of men. "What can be more heinously wicked," he asks, contemptuously brushing away all these cobwebs, "than heartily to wish the success of a person on account of his right, and at the same time in the most solemn manner to declare that he has no right at all?" He must be witness to the uncompromising claim of truth, "not only with his lips, but in his life," and he turned aside from the path to all the world's high places, when the entrance fee was a form of words which in themselves were false, even though they deceived no one. "The sacrifice of interest to conscience," says Gibbon, in speaking of this action of Law's, "is always respectable." The sentence provokes a smile, and yet, no doubt, it expresses a very real feeling in the worldly man who, in order to make the most of his fortune, cut himself off from the political life of his country as completely as the consistent High Churchman had done in order to avoid telling a lie. In general too little respect is awarded to the nonjurors of the eighteenth century. Our knowledge of the martyr ends with the act which attests his courage and his trust. We can remember nothing about him which influences feeling as much as the fact that he gave up life rather than what he knew of truth. To give up, for a similar reason, the path to the world's high places does not in like manner strike the imagination, and yet, perhaps, a life of obscurity and dependence, borne without envy and without repining, would to many men prove a trial no less hard than a violent death.

If these words do not describe the life actually led by William Law, they at least point out that which, in declining the abjuration oath, he declared himself ready to accept. With that refusal he, the son of a grocer and Fellow of a College, turned away from all hope of a public career, and became tutor in the family of a rich merchant, formerly one of the South Sea Directors and victim to the outbreak of popular fury which followed the bursting of the bubble, but afterwards enabled to forget the confiscation of his first fortune in the acquisition of a second, which was equally large. This merchant was Gibbon's grandfather, a stout old Tory, who had, his grandson tells us, reluctantly contracted to clothe King William's troops in Flanders, and who, we presume, gladly opened his doors to a nonjuring ex-Fellow. The inconstant Flatus in the "Serious Call"—the worldling who tries to find happiness successively in a devotion to dress, hunting, polite society, building, travelling, and study—is said to be Law's portrait of his pupil. It would be a curious chance if the portraiture of an insignificant man like the historian's father had been taken by two men of genius, but at the time when Law described Flatus, Edward Gibbon the elder was an indolent youth cowed under the discipline of a severe father, and we do not see that at any time he exhibited the versatility of pursuit which is, in the character of Flatus, intended to bring out the steadfastness and calm of the Christian's ideal. However, the tradition may truly commemorate the tutor's disappointment with his pupil. Byrom tried to teach him shorthand, which it was the fashion at this time to learn of

"It is a pity he should be so slow for Law's sake." We however, that Law appears in this position as a mediator father and son; and once obtained forgiveness for his his father had gone the length of turning him out of him who has made the name famous he can have been known, except at second-hand, but he is probably familiar of our day mainly through his appearance in the auto- which may be regarded as the most polished literary the eighteenth century. The allusion, however familiar, may account taken from the reminiscences of one who stands opposite pole from Edward Gibbon, it must be confessed, in the literary finish as much as in every other respect. Byrom's ntains a mention of the historian at a very early stage of his it is from this source we learn that there were great doings hristening (May, 1737). It is as well, perhaps, that the notice occur at a period of life more suggestive of criticism! But was as just as he was generous, and his estimate of Gibbon ave been truer than Gibbon's of him. However, there is but slight touch of sarcasm in Gibbon's mention of his master. It possible for the writer of the famous sixteenth chapter to narrate bare fact that while the pupil, a youth of "warm and social ment," went on his travels, the tutor kept his place as spiritual in the family, without some such comment as the remark that nd of a saint is above or below the present world," but there little in this strain, and there is a good deal of unquestionable "In our family he had left the reputation of a worthy and an, who believed all that he professed, and practised all that ned. His theological writings, which our domestic connection pted me to peruse, preserve an imperfect sort of life, and I can ce with more confidence and knowledge on the merits of the His last compositions are darkly tinctured by the incompre- visions of Jacob Behmen, and his discourse on the absolute lness of stage entertainments is sometimes quoted for a ridi- intemperance of sentiment and language," of which he gives a n fully justifying these words, and goes on:—

These sallies of religious phrensy must not extinguish the praise which Mr. William Law as a wit and a scholar. His arguments on topics of ity are specious and acute, his manner is lively, his style forcible and had not his vigorous mind been clouded by enthusiasm, he might d with the most agreeable and ingenious writers of the times. Mr. ster-work, the 'Serious Call,' is still read as a popular and powerful votion. His precepts are rigid, but they are founded on the Gospel; is sharp, but it is drawn from the knowledge of human life, and his portraits are not unworthy of La Bruyère. If he finds a spark in his reader's mind, he will soon kindle it to a flame, and a philosopher that he exposes with equal severity and truth the strange contradic- the faith and the practice of the Christian world."

* Horace Walpole, as a youth, was one of his pupils.

The philosopher made that concession, we should imagine, without the very smallest reluctance, but it is no small tribute to the saint that he is brought in only as an exponent of this strange contradiction, and not as its illustration in his own person. Law's position in that household at Putney was one that was likely to expose all the weak points in the saintly character. It may seem, perhaps, that a position demanding only the maintenance of that spiritual attitude which at first inspired reverence and esteem, and conceding all the material advantages which are as necessary to the holiest as to the least holy of men, is almost the ideal for the spiritual teacher. Those who have seen the experiment tried will be inclined mournfully to confess that experience has here, as so often elsewhere, confuted their most natural and reasonable anticipations. Whether it is that we are apt to expect too much from those who have given us much—whether the expenditure of moral energy needed for thinking out religious truth hardly leaves an average amount available for its application to the everyday business of life—certain it is that the relation of spiritual director hardly ever bears such a strain upon it without a sense of jar. And here was the first of the Evangelicals, while the youth he was paid to teach was wandering on the Continent, ensconced in a luxurious home, and allowed to bring in his friends to dinner and order up bottles of wine to season their discussions in the library, and not apparently rendering any other service to his patron in return for this position of comfortable leisure, than choosing editions of the classics and the Fathers;* and the traditional respect he inspired is so little mingled with any other feeling, that not even Gibbon can describe it with a sneer! No eulogy of rapturous disciples would seem to us half so solid a testimony to a character of dignified uprightness and consistency.

His faults, such as they were, seem to have been of the very opposite nature to those of the conventional eighteenth-century chaplain. Through every glimpse we get of him we receive the impression of a certain rough and rather formidable independence; we sympathize with the gentle Byrom when on one visit to Putney, he sends in his companion first to explore the way and summon him "if Mr. Law gave occasion," although we can readily imagine Mr. Law's good-humoured scorn at these precautions as possible only to "one that was vapoured with drinking of tea." "You ask an absurd question," Byrom is told (very truly we must confess) when he asks if Ruysbrock, a contemporary of Tauler, is not the earliest mystic writer, and for the moment his visitor must have felt himself in the presence of the dangerous controversialist. In his controversial writings, Law often sinks into the mere polemic, and we shall pass them over with the mention of their existence. The roughness of nature expressed in these productions was felt in social intercourse so sensibly that one

* For which the historian remembers him gratefully.

[illegible] such matters as John Wesley administered a severe [illegible] to his old master, and Law's evidently sincere [illegible] receive it meekly does not quite conceal the pain [illegible] exchange of reverence for criticism. No change so [illegible] came over his intercourse with his more loyal disciple, [illegible] was a change, and, when he and Byrom were both [illegible] diffidence, so far as it existed, was perhaps on his side. [illegible] a good deal dropped out of society, and Byrom had sur[illegible] enthusiasm which had emboldened him to risk midnight [illegible] with foot-pads in the Putney lanes sooner than shorten his [illegible] the fountain of mystic divinity; and though he remembered [illegible] master"* still faithfully, years passed without his seeking [illegible] the life of Law's old age, as a sort of domestic chaplain [illegible] aunt and a female friend, was rather narrowing to a [illegible] narrow; certainly the letters of this period are uninter[illegible] change comes over their intercourse, and Byrom's Remains [illegible] interest.

[illegible] enable us, in the earlier years, when he is living in London [illegible] his family, teaching shorthand, and Law is an inmate of the [illegible] house at Putney or a sharer in the same coffee-house life, to [illegible]nto their intercourse as it is hardly possible to enter into the [illegible] of any but that of our contemporaries. We follow the [illegible] from its first start at Putney in an enthusiastic discussion [illegible] Malebranche, from which we excuse young Gibbon for very soon [illegible] escape (1729), to the discipleship of later years, when in [illegible] garden behind old Somerset House, shaded by fine old [illegible] by the unfinished but ruinous façade of Inigo Jones, and [illegible] from the Strand by dark and winding steps, which seemed, [illegible]e, a fit emblem of the distance that separated the mystic from [illegible]stling commonplace mind of that age, he watches day after day [illegible] chance of a word from the teacher. We enter into the satis[illegible] with which Byrom hears the great man propose a walk after [illegible] when Mr. Gibbon falls asleep; and into his regret at dis[illegible]g that Madame Guyon is gone down in the estimation of the [illegible] since it appeared that she was not averse to a game at cards. [illegible]tch them gliding down the Thames, or take up the conversation [illegible] garden at Putney, where Law is pacing the *green* grass beside [illegible], as Byrom with the cockneyism of his age sets on record; we [illegible] their conversation in all that abruptness of transition, so familiar [illegible] and unfamiliar to the eye, by which we pass in turning the [illegible] the most trivial to the most profound subjects of human [illegible] while a lament that the gardeners rolling the gravel "will [illegible] piety," or that people come to the Communion in patches [illegible] reminds us that we are listening, not only to the student [illegible] but to the author of the "Serious Call." However, it

* He thus addresses Law at this time.

appears from some specimens of the conversation that "the good man can joke," the pleasantry—an entreaty that Byrom would not damage the sale of the "Serious Call" by putting it all into verse as he had done a part—being certainly of the mildest description. We sympathize with Byrom in his perplexed half-annoyance at Law's tiresome greeting, "Well, what do you say?" which was, it would seem, his habitual form of accost, and brings home to the reader's imagination very vividly the attitude of a spiritual physician waiting to hear his patient's case. It was an accost somewhat repelling to a nature of feminine modesty like Byrom's; who sometimes told him he had much to say if he dared, and sometimes that he had nothing to say but "How-d'ye-do?"

Law had much the same thing to say always. He was ready at all times and in all places to preach that which he had found to be a gospel, "that this world was a prison into which we had fallen; that we had nothing to do but get out of it; that to be freed from it was all that we wanted; . . . . . that the philosophers, Epictetus, Socrates, &c., had, by the grace of God and their own search, observed that this world could not be what God made it; that there was a necessity for every one to feel the torment of sin, to die in this manner and descend into hell with Christ, and so rise again with him; that every one must pass through this fiery trial in this world or in another." However little such a gospel as this may seem to contain of help or consolation, it will always be found that one who believes in that history, not only as a series of events long ago and far away, but as a pattern of all human growth and a key to the most various individual experience, will always attract an eager, if not a large band of hungry disciples. The Gibbons' house at Putney, while Law was its inmate, was a kind of spiritual Delphi; and men who had hardly another experience in common might have exchanged their recollections of a common pilgrimage, and no doubt often of a common disappointment.

The following curious letter from John Wesley is worth inserting as a specimen of these applications. He writes, from Oxford, to beg him for counsel concerning the condition of one of his pupils, for whose spiritual state, which he considered a remarkable one, he seems to have felt himself responsible, and describes it with all the distinctness of a physician watching the progress of a fatal disease.

"When I asked him why he had left off the holy Eucharist, he said fairly 'because to partake of it implied a fresh promise to renounce himself entirely, and to please God alone, and he did not intend to do so.' I asked whether he was well convinced he ought to do so; he said, 'Yes.' Whether he wished he could desire it. He answered, 'No; he did not desire it.' From time to time I asked him to tell me upon what he grounded his hopes of salvation. He replied, after some pause, that Christ died for all men, but if none were saved by him without performing the conditions, his death would not avail one in a thousand, which was inconsistent with the goodness of God. But this answer, part of it, he soon gave up; adding with the utmost seriousness that not whether it was true or not. He was very happy, and desired rther. This morning I again asked him what he thought of his own He said he thought nothing about it. Nor could all I said move him. ed to all, but was affected with nothing. He grants, with all com- at he is not in a salvable state, and shows no degree of concern, while e cannot find mercy. I am now entirely at a loss what step to take. seem so much as to understand his distemper, it appears to me quite ensible. Much less can I tell what remedies are proper for it. I beseech you, sir, that you would not be slack, according to the ability gift, to advise and pray for him.

"And am, reverend sir,

"Your most obliged servant,

"JOHN WESLEY."

uses almost the same words a year or two later with to a less dangerous crisis—a young lady in whom he was d being resolved to turn Quaker. What was the result of the hese applications we do not learn, but imagine it to have more successful than the correspondence into which Law in order to retain the young lady in the Church of England. k a good-humoured view of their common failure. He greeted ccessful disciple on their next meeting—"Well, have you y more Quakers yet?" and we are glad to find him less an Dr. Johnson on a similar case of schism. He must have accustomed to such failures. He could have had but little entering into difficulties he had not himself known, and the s he had known could not have been various. His mental a remarkable one for its combination of great change and notony.

is no doubt that his was, on the whole, a monotonous nature. few men have passed across a spiritual chasm as wide as that parates the author of the "Serious Call" from the disciple Behmen. His forcible and florid denunciations of vice, his sketches of character, and his glowing exhortations, have a historic interest for those who seek to know William Law nglish mystic. But there is no question of the interest of itings to his contemporaries. The "Serious Call," which we n mentioned with a certain apparently sincere praise by was eulogized by Johnson as "the finest piece of hortatory e in any language," and we might add to this tribute that of were as unlike Johnson and Gibbon as Johnson and Gibbon like each other. Many who gave it no admiration afforded ually powerful tribute of angry criticism. Orthodox divines red they had prophesied when it came out that it would do d sure enough the Methodists sprung up on its track; young d gentlemen were ready to abuse it as "a silly, ridiculous nd rail at its author as "a whimsical, strange, impracticable in a way that showed it was not ignored by those for whom we should imagine it to have very little interest; and there was hardly a passage in it which some unknown correspondent did not write to tell him was either its blot or its gem. The truth was that this, and his other works belonging to what may be called his Methodist stage, were adapted to his age both by the qualities which were characteristic of the men of that time and those which were most wanting to them. The externality of these early works suited their readers. Mr. Stephen, in his entertaining account of Law, cites a passage which Pope appears to have borrowed from him, and the ideal which made Pope our great poet was at all events that which gave Law's style all its literary merit. There is a certain resemblance between all utterances that are didactic and definite; and whatever might be the difficulty of living up to the precepts of the "Serious Call," there was not a moment's preliminary doubt about their meaning. It is clear, sharp-cut, bold in outline, bare of all modifications, free from contemplation of perplexities. But the strength of Law as a popular writer lay in his combination of the outwardness characteristic of the age with the thoroughness which it utterly lacked. He represented to a generation who worshipped the golden mean the uncompromising character of Christianity, and must have taught some among them how much more practical an ideal we set before ourselves when we strive after perfection than when we aim at decency. The man who teaches this lesson will always have much forgiven him, but there can never have been an age when it was more necessary than the beginning of the eighteenth century. Something has been said of the half-heartedness of the political life of the day, and the same might be applied to the religious life. The feeling that holiness is something to be discovered by-and-by when we get to heaven is common in every age among a certain class, but the class was larger then than it is now, and the feelings characteristic of it were intensified by political influences which have passed away. It is impossible not to recognize in the commonplace orthodox sense that God would overlook much in those who recognized His Son as their Head some connection with the still insecure position of the House of Hanover on the throne. And Law's power over his generation lay in his vehement protest against the latent doubt at the root of this creed, and in the faith that was strong enough to disengage the idea of the love of God from that of His leniency. It would be no relief, he declared to the triflers of his day, to discover that God had made any exception in His laws against sin. Human nature was in the position of a child plucking poisonous berries. Would it be a blessing to that ignorant child to be only *seldom* checked in his quest for the fruit of death? God demanded the devotion of the whole nature, because He only could satisfy it. This was a new idea to the men of that day. Evil, in their eyes, was something to be subdued, to be [illegible]ader; there must have come to many minds a mysterious

... they were taught to look upon it as something to ... the roots. We shall understand Law's power over ... if we remember that the "Serious Call" was the first ... Evangelicism. In all its strength and in all its weakness ... contained in embryo what we may not inaptly describe as ... of Death—the religion that, regarding our sojourn in this ... anomalous episode in the career of eternity, makes it an ... strip it as bare as possible of everything but the anticipation ... there.

...is stage in Law's career, though it is that by which he is best ... is not that which is truly characteristic of him. At heart he ... was a mystic. Mysticism was, in that day, not so rare as we ...o suppose. Men who were going in and out of Westminster ... lounging in the Court of Requests, and in general leading a ...re not apt to credit with such yearnings, did, there is no doubt, ...ong craving after mystic thought, but Law was distrustful of ...nary utterances which satisfied them. Those who felt as they ... in truth ready to accept any witness, so that it was but dis... ...d unfaltering, that union with God was as possible as union ...n; and the least taste of the brine which orthodoxy then ... to such thirst as theirs will remove all wonder that the pools ... they quenched it were sometimes muddy. But while Law ...t would have allowed that any dream which contained the ...e of God's nearness to His creatures was truer than the most ...nd coherent system which excluded it, he was always on his ...gainst these visions even where they seem to the uninitiated ...e fanciful than those which were afterwards so much to him. ...e, as follows, in 1731 to a lady* who had apparently been ...pressed by the visions of Jane Lead, a sort of spiritualist of ... earlier time :—

...e fall of our first parents seems to be owing to the desire of a ...e not suitable to their state, so we sin in the same temper when our ... searches for a higher knowledge than that which is revealed to ... If all who are desirous to stop the growth of infidelity would oppose ...eir lives, and produce the practice of true Christian virtues in defence ...n, Christianity would be more than mathematically demonstrated to ... sense. But the misfortune is that in every attack we think there ...ing wanted in point of argument, and so are racking our thoughts for ... new in the way of reasoning; whereas the enemy is in his state of ... and we in our state of weakness, because we are doing nothing ..., and are contending for a *dead Christianity*; did we begin its defence ...g upon new lives, the old arguments would be sufficient."

...ortant to notice, just about the time he fell in with Behmen, ... he was on his guard against any but a directly practical ... how desirous he was to turn away the minds of all he could ... anything that might become a substitute for the simple

* ... Dodwell, daughter of the nonjuror, and sister of a clever pamphleteer.

effort after a holy life. If, afterwards, those writings became precious to him, which will seem as little helpful in this struggle as any of the visions against which he was warning his correspondent, we may be sure that it was not because he had changed his aim, but because he had discovered that effort was not the way of attaining it.

There are not many, probably, who have striven to bring into the life of every day the ideal of something high and pure, who have failed to discover, with more or less poignancy of disappointment, that success in this attempt is by no means proportionate to endeavour. Any sudden start that has been made in this path has been due, it will be acknowledged, less to a more arduous and self-sacrificing attempt than to some new influence which often has no obvious connection with that which yet is felt as its unquestionable result. We have no data for connecting Law's Behmenism with any conscious dissatisfaction with the outwardness of his earlier ideal, but we know that in proportion as a plan of duty is definite and formularized the earnest spirit must discover whatever in it is unsatisfying to the demands of the conscience, and we may be sure that one who felt as Law felt the need of a new life within must often have experienced the powerlessness of a set of rules to produce it. And it is evident that through the strange mystic utterances of the German seer there did come to him some mysterious waft of new life, putting a new spirit into what he must have felt in comparison a dead Christianity, and passing over a hard external system with a wonderful power of transformation and inspiration. The dry bones, under this wondrous influence, arose and lived, and the Religion of Death became the Religion of a Resurrection.

It was about two years after his warning to his female correspondent against her attraction towards the mystic visions which attracted many in that day, that, in looking over a bookstall, he came upon a work of Behmen's "Concerning the Three Principles of the Divine Essence," the perusal of which, he tells us, filled his soul with emotions so new and profound as even to result in physical agitation. And we can indeed well imagine the thrill of emotion at discovering that which Law imagined himself to find in this work—a link between the laws of the outward world and the laws of that which is invisible and eternal. The instinct which leads the human spirit towards unity is so strong that in our own day it triumphs over the instinct which attests the reality of the antithesis between the outward and the inward world, and makes the men of our time satisfied by the simple suppression of one member of this antithesis. A century and a half ago people felt differently. The accepted religion of the day, while it was much less spiritual a thing than with us, was yet in a sense more real; it had the hold on men's minds that a religion kept up by penal enactments cannot help having, whatever that may be worth. Moreover, there was the unquestionable advantage on its side that the set in our day are entirely hostile to every theological favourably inclined towards this set of ideas. scientific ideas is a very important element in such and though we can touch upon it very inade- must not entirely pass it over. The intellectual first half of the eighteenth century still palpitating of Newton's great discovery. The visible universe become more wonderful, more orderly, more full of There were some minds to whom the sudden and simplicity was almost like a physical declara- presence of one invisible Being throughout the whole which obeyed this law. This universal attraction— impressed upon mere brute matter—seemed a aspiration, call it faith or love, which was to bring spiritual world, and bid the creature revolve in its true the centre of all spiritual beings.* It seemed a clue to ous labyrinth that unites the two worlds in which we live. not have expected, perhaps, from a study of William works, that ideas like this would have laid a great hold this is no more than we may say of every influence new life into thought and belief, and gives momentum was previously no conscious want of light. There is in that change by which truth becomes dynamic. We the contrast between the poverty and outwardness of ideal and that which is embodied in the "Spirit of the "Spirit of Love," but to connect this transition with of the wonderful German shoemaker Jacob Behmen is a beyond the powers of the present writer. We shall speak of the thoughts which animated him as his own, in truth there was nothing in them that was original the force and fervour with which he was able to realize them, and which is often found greatest in a disciple.

which became charged with new meaning for Law by his state of mind was the word which has most meaning the world of our day. His special interest for our day is of *Nature* is a link between the views of those who assert, and emphatically deny, the very existence of the But in order to appreciate this interest we must the different associations which clustered round the word hundred or two hundred years ago, and those which belong To our mind it suggests mainly the sequences and of the material world. To the mind of our fathers it the associations which were impressed on it by the writings

* set forth in a work written at this time by the amiable Dr. George whose instrumentality it was that Law first became acquainted with the

of the Stoics, it suggested the tendencies of men and women, it meant, in short, *human* nature. Now human nature, in the views of those who may be directly affiliated with Law's earlier influence, was something to be repressed, to be subdued, to be utterly overcome. This is the whole preaching of the "Serious Call." The bad people are the people who do what is natural. Nature is a sort of inverted guide-post. There is a broad chasm between this view and that expressed in his later works. Under the teaching of Jacob Behmen, Law came to perceive as distinctly as any thinker of our day that what we mean by Nature is a system of cause and effect extending throughout the whole universe of phenomenal existence. But he continued to believe as firmly as any thinker of a past day that this system is not ultimate. While no scientific man looks upon the universe of being more as a unity than he did, no disciple of Plato is more decided in his belief that the only permanent form of being is spiritual. The moment that this system is cut off from the higher world to which it tends it becomes evil. Hence in one part of his belief Law still retained that earlier view, according to which human nature is a mere black background for the exhibition of Divine Grace. He would have had as little sympathy with Butler as he had with Warburton. Human nature was only in its right state when it was consciously what at all events it was actually, a continual travailing after a higher life. In itself, and cut off from this higher life, it was incapable of improvement.

This double view of Nature is expressed in the two following extracts from the "Spirit of Love:"—

"Nature is a birth or manifestation of the triune invisible Deity. And as it could only come into existence as a birth from God, so every creature, or beginning thing can only come forth as a birth from and out of nature. And no creature can have, or be anything, but by and according to the working powers of nature, and therefore strictly speaking, no creature can be put into an unnatural state. It may indeed lose or fall from its natural perfection by the wrong use or working of its will, but then its fallen state is the natural effect of the wrong use of its will, and so it only has that which is natural to it.

* * * * * * * *

"All evil is nothing else but nature left to itself, and under the divided workings of its own hunger, wrath, and contrariety. . . . Hence it is that that which is called the wisdom, the honour, and the religion of the natural man often does as much hurt to himself and others as his pride, self-love, and envy, and are subject to the same union and caprice; it is because nature is no better in one motion than in another, nor can be, till something supernatural is come into it. Self can have no motion but what is selfish. And be assured that nature in every man, whether he be learned or unlearned, is this very self, and can be nothing else, till a birth from the Deity is brought forth in it. There is therefore no possibility of having the spirit of love from any power of nature, or working of reason. It can only be had in its own time and place, and its time and place is nowhere but where nature is overcome by a birth of the life of God in the properties of the soul. And thus you see the absolute necessity of Christian redemption. The Deity must become man, take a birth in the fallen nature, become the life of it, or the natural man must of necessity be for ever and ever in the hell of his ow[illegible]iety, and self-torment. . . .

"Nature, and the first pro[illegible] the highest want of something,

... Nature, whether eternal or temporal, is that which for its own self, but for the sake of something that it has ... And this is the reason why nature is only a desire; it is ... the sake of something else."

... never read a line of Hegel will be reminded by these ... sentence often quoted from Hegel, that Nature is the ... Spirit." The truth which Law and Hegel thus saw from ...—one of the largest which the human intellect can ... seen by Law indistinctly, but in that day of mediocrity ... a mechanic Nature and an artificer-God, what insight it ... see it at all!

...ficult for any one in our day to realize fully the great ..., in any religious thinker of that time, of this idea of Nature. ...lent view of Christ's appearance on earth was nothing so ...nnatural. It recalled the most technical legal transactions, ... the harshest contrast to all the natural relations of human ... sons and brothers. Perhaps we cannot fully realize, and ...ne extent every one must realize, the relief which came to ... were taught to discover in these transcendent events, an ... of what, in the very deepest sense of the word, might be ... laws of Nature. The Incarnation, which the theology of ... regarded as a great interruption of the Divine system of ...nt—an isolated miracle in the course of nature—thus ...he type of all that is good in history, a representation in ... the world of that which must take place in every soul ...e delivered from its own misery, an outward event, corre... to that which must be exhibited in the history of every ...ing;—of every human being without exception, Law held ...r part of his life. .

... without scruple, declared to all the world," he writes to a friend in ... letter, written, probably, late in life, "that from eternity to eternity ... come from God but mere infinite love, and that he must eternally ...creature that which he willed at its creation."

...s a beloved friend who wrote to him on the subject of final ...—

"... know that I ever wasted my spirits in writing or thinking in the ... his letter before, and I trust I never shall again. But love to you, ...y zeal for your true growth in the spiritual life, has compelled me. ...r the purification of all human nature, either in this world or some ... I fully believe it. And as to that of angels, if it is possible, I am ...nd also sure that it will then also come to pass."

...ubject he spoke at first reluctantly, and with a sense of ...t as he drew near his own departure he seems to have felt ... need for the utterance of this hope. His last Easter Sunday ... wakened in him a sense of all that the event then com... implied for the whole human race; a width and range of anticipation probably mournfully contrasted with that opened by the sermon to which he had just been listening; and his companion narrates a walk with him after church with all that fallacious minuteness through which we so often seek to transfer the recollections that stir our hearts most deeply. He describes the way Law opened a gate into a field, and ascended the little elevation to which it led, as if he could thereby convey to the reader the incommunicable memories wrought up in his own soul with them. Any utterance that should justify his impression is reported quite inadequately; but the reader who is able to enter into the account with any sympathy whatever, readily expands into a solemn and prophetic utterance Law's belief in that divine spark shut up in lost and degraded natures, "in a sevenfold deeper or stronger compaction than fire is in a flint; yet as it *is* shut up and preserved in them, it will come forth." What it was in his day to believe not only that the divine spark lay hid in every human creature, but that in every human creature it was to be kindled, we can as little bring before the mind of the reader as we can make distinct the contrast between the comfortable assurance of our own time that everybody will come right at last and his awe-struck sense of a holiness that would not be satisfied till it had communicated itself to every spirit, how lost, guilty, and degraded soever.

The Incarnation, the Atonement, the Crucifixion, were to Law no doubt events in history, facts attested like any other facts, by witnesses and by their effects on the history of the world. But in their essence they were not events in time, they were the laws of the eternal holiness. "The schools," he says in a passage which might be taken from one of the early Fathers, "have given us accurate definitions of every vice, and shown us how to conceive them as notionally distinguished from one another, but the Christian has a much shorter way of knowing their nature and power. For call them by what names you will, they are all just that same thing and do that same work, as the scribes, the Pharisees, hypocrites, and rabble of the Jews were all but one and the same thing, and did one and the same work. They are nothing else but the murderers and crucifiers of the true Christ of God, not as the high priests did many hundred years ago, nailing his outward humanity to an outward cross, but crucifying afresh the Son of God, who is the Christ that every man crucifies as often as he gives way to wrath, pride, envy, or covetousness. For every temper that is contrary to the new birth of Christ is in the strictest sense of the word a murderer of the Lord of life; and where pride and envy are suffered to live, there the same thing is done as where Christ was killed and Barabbas saved alive. The Christ of God was not then first crucified, when the Jews brought him to the [illegible] but Adam and Eve were his [illegible] happened to them in the [illegible] the death of the Christ [illegible]

Christ had never come into the world as a second Adam to redeem it, had he not been originally the life and perfection and glory of the first Adam. And He is our atonement with God because by and through him, brought to life *in us*, we are set again in that first state of holiness and have Christ again in us, as our first father had at his creation."

There were many minds in the eighteenth century who came upon such utterances as these as wanderers in some newly-built town, wearied by its smug compactness and monotonous pettiness, might suddenly come upon an old Gothic church that had been spared in the midst of these encroaching streets and squares, and, entering its dim aisles, might forget the upstart vulgarity around them, and breathe the atmosphere of a nobler past. Wearied of evidences of the reasonableness of Christianity, wearied of exhortations to emancipate themselves from evils which held them as the magnet the needle, men were everywhere ready for any hope of *organic* change in the conditions of their life. Many found this hope in the outward violent manifestations of Methodist preaching—not so many, but not a few, and those of some influence, in the dim intense glow of Law's mystical teaching of the "Spirit of Love," a teaching the intense reality of which is testified by the words which he is said to have spoken, raising himself up in his bed, shortly before he died: "I feel within myself an inextinguishable fire of love, that has burnt up all within me contrary to itself, and changed it to its own nature."

Those words were no mere deathbed rapture. They were an utterance at once of a spirit quivering on the threshold of a new life, and a mind contemplating the source of its largest intellectual satisfaction. If the feeling they expressed was mainly the first, the fuller expression of the last given in the following extract from the "Spirit of Love" will prove the two things to have been inseparable:—

"Fire has but one nature throughout the whole universe of things. How easy to see that the fire of animal life is the same fire that burns in the kitchen! How else could the kitchen fire become serviceable to animal life? What good could it do you to come to a fire of wood where you wanted to have the heat of your own life increased? In animal life this fire is kindled and preserved in such a degree and in such circumstances as to be life; and this is its difference from fires kindled in wood, and burning to ashes. It is the same fire, only in a different state, that keeps up life, and consumes wood. The fire of this world overcomes its fuel, breaks its nature, alters its state, and changes it into flame and light. But why does it do this? Whence has it this power? It is because it is a true outbirth of the eternal fire, which overcomes the darkness and contrariety of nature, and changes all its properties into a life of light and joy. Not a spark of fire could be kindled in this world but because material nature is nothing but the very properties of eternal nature, standing for a time in a material state, and therefore they must work in time as they do in eternity; . . . . and consequently fire must do the same work in a material way which the eternal fire doth in spiritual nature."

The modern doctrine of the Correlation of Force is of course not present here in a sense which would have any value in the eyes of a scientific man. But surely this idea of a single power transforming itself to these widely diverse forms, and recoverable in its original form—this belief in a passage of energy from one manifestation to another—differs from the modern doctrine in nothing but its starting point and its goal. In Law's world, these were wholly spiritual. He looked, indeed, upon all that we call matter, as the sign of a mere transitory episode in the great cosmic drama; it was, like ice and snow, the sign of a low temperature of being; the summer of the spirit was to banish it in this form, though not to annihilate it. This part of his belief, even if it appear to the reader of our day only fantastic, has no mere individual significance, and we may conclude our sketch by an indication of the double vista opened by that part of Law's theory which is most visionary and mystical.

We turn most confidently to its historic interest. It was in common with a set of thinkers, whose thoughts—or if you will, whose dreams—have had no insignificant influence on the development of Christianity, that Law looked upon the existence of what we mean by matter as the result of the Fall, a view which of course makes the Fall itself mean something totally different from what most people mean by it. While all the spiritual creation remained in its right and natural position of conscious dependence, the thing that we mean by matter did not exist. It was potentially there, as ice is potentially in the ponds in July; but it was as little discernible to the senses of any conceivable spectator. Not that body had then no existence. Body is a sort of correlate of spirit: "every creaturely spirit must have its own body, for its body is that which makes it manifest to itself. . . . Its body is its first knowledge of its somewhat and somewhere." It is not more difficult to follow this distinction between body—the correlate of all finite spirit—and the thing we know as matter, than to grasp St. Paul's belief in "a spiritual body;" and if we were to attempt any ideal expansion of those words of the Apostle's, we should hardly know how to paraphrase them better than by "the creature's knowledge of its somewhat and somewhere." Whatever else he meant, he must have meant that which connects the creature with space. With the Fall, according to Law, this spiritual body became a material body. In all probability he never heard of the obscure heretics who taught that the coverings spoken of in the third chapter of Genesis were no more than these material bodies into which human spirits sank when they fell from their pristine holiness. But there is a substantial identity between their system and his; and his theories, however wild they may seem to us, must be judged as part of a Christian mythology at least as worthy of study as any other mythology. And the mere fact that without any direct affiliation there should exist this solidarity of belief between a thinker of the eighteenth century and a group of thinkers of the first and second [illegible] interest quite independent of our judgment of [illegible] the common produce of these different soils.

[illegible] more hazardous ground when we attempt to [illegible] connection between these speculations of William [illegible] of his successors. But the doctrine we have cited is, [illegible] developments, unquestionably similar to some specula[illegible] have in the last few years excited no small amount of [illegible] our own time. The anticipation of Law as to the ultimate [illegible] of the Cosmos is hardly to be distinguished from that set [illegible] thinkers not despised by the scientific world under the [illegible] "The Unseen Universe." The argument of that volume was [illegible] two beliefs of the scientific world of our day—the belief [illegible], as it can be transmuted alone, and not destroyed, reap[illegible] one form whenever it disappears from another; and the belief [illegible] is slowly but certainly disappearing from the whole physical [illegible]. Law was not qualified to form an opinion on either of these [illegible] but his conclusion is much the same as that which gave "[illegible] Unseen Universe" its whole interest.

> [illegible] and natural it is," he says, "to suppose all that is earth, and [illegible] be dissolved into water, the water to be changed into air, the air [illegible] and the ether rarefied into light! And how near a step is the next, to [illegible] changed, or exalted into that glassy sea, before the first angels [illegible] now is become of hard, heavy, dead, divisible, corruptible matter? [illegible]? No; and yet nothing of it is left, all that you know of it is [illegible] nothing but its shadowy idea will be known in eternity."

It is [illegible] by a mere coincidence that these words will recall to the [illegible] mind one of the most original works of our day. No doubt the authors of "The Unseen Universe" would have nothing to say [illegible] the fall of the angels. No doubt William Law would have had [illegible] to say of the degradation of heat and the correlation of force. [illegible] common belief in a future transmutation of all that we see [illegible] into something which shall be invisible and intangible, but [illegible] passing over of energy from that which affects the outer, to [illegible] affects the inner sense—is a much larger and deeper con[illegible] than either of those through which they reached it. Those [illegible] in it have a wide common ground, however far removed [illegible] their starting point.

[illegible] of William Law to any intellectual kindred with thinkers [illegible] time reckons among scientific men ought, perhaps, to be [illegible] forward with some diffidence. But we do not rest our claim [illegible] on any disputable ground. As a thinker who stood forward [illegible] of worldly good sense to bear witness to the realities which [illegible] good sense hides as daylight hides the stars, he remains, what[illegible] be taken of doubtful matters, a prominent and striking [illegible] representative of that school of thought of which the pedi[illegible], and for which a vista opens into the future hardly less distinctly than into the past. We do not conceal our own view that the interest of his thoughts belongs to a region deeper even than that which all thoughts may claim which have had a large interest in the past; that we consider them worthy of attention from the seekers for truth, as well as from the students of history. But we are content to rest his claim on that which is indisputable, and to demand attention for this sketch of his thoughts as an attempt to set forth the central ideas of one who was emphatically a mystic in an age when mysticism was even more despised than it is in our own day.

JULIA WEDGWOOD.

# NINETY YEARS' AGONY OF FRANCE.

ıinety years, since the time when Calonne called together Assembly of Notables, and when the voice of the Revolu- first heard announcing a reign of hope, love, freedom, and peace,—for ninety years has France struggled to attain a orm of constitutional government; and apparently she is om it now than she was in 1787,—apparently, but not, we , in reality. In this last crisis the mass of her people have not only a steadiness of purpose for which we were little , but a self-control which is full of the highest promise. In verything that the conspirators who had seized the govern- ıld do to provoke the nation to violence which might have a pretext for using the public force against the public. the nation has conquered by calmness. Conspiracy and have passed from the side of the people to that of the ary Government. This shows that considerable way has le since the days of the Faubourg St. Antoine.

rogress is to be measured, not by change of institutions, but ge of character. The Revolution made a vast change in nstitutions: it could not change French character, which as servile under the despotism of Robespierre as it had been at of Louis XIV. Character seems now, after ninety years ate effort and terrible experience, to be coming up to the nstitutions. Perhaps France has reason to be grateful to lie and his Marshal for giving her assurance of that fact, ıeir names will be infamous for ever.

ısons of the political failure of 1789 are manifest enough; ıot seek them in any mysterious incapacity of the Celtic race l or of the French branch of it in particular for constitutional government. These mysterious capabilities and incapabilities of races in truth are questionable things, and generally tend, upon closer inspection, to resolve themselves into the influence of circumstance perpetuated and accumulated through many generations. England, guarded by the sea, has had comparatively little need of standing armies, and she has thus escaped military despotism, since fleets cannot interfere with politics; yet even she might have fallen under a military despotism, and foreign critics might now be moralizing on the inherent incapacity of her people for any government but that of force, if when the army of James II. was encamped on Hounslow Heath there had not been a William of Orange to come over to our rescue. France has had frontiers; therefore she has had standing armies, and her rulers have been masters of legions. She was exposed to foreign invasion for a whole century, from the time of Edward III. to that of Henry VI.; and again, at the crisis of her destiny in 1791, she was assailed by the arms of the coalesced powers of Reaction. On each occasion her people, to secure national independence, were compelled to renounce liberty, and the Government was inevitably invested with a military dictatorship of defence, which, once acquired, was perpetuated in political despotism. It would be difficult to prove that, under more auspicious circumstances, the States-General, which at one period in the fourteenth century entered on a course of reform as bold and comprehensive as anything done by the framers of the Great Charter or the Parliaments of Henry III., might not have developed into a British House of Commons.

The political crisis of 1789 was in itself one of the most tremendous kind; it was nothing less than the collapse, amidst bankruptcy and general ruin, of the hereditary principle of government, the only principle which France or the greater part of Europe up to that time had known. But it was desperately complicated by its connection with a social and a religious crisis equally tremendous. It came upon a people totally untrained to political action, without political instruction, without a political press, without even the common information which a newspaper gives about passing events; without the means of judiciously choosing its political leaders, or even political leaders among whom a judicious choice could be made; without any good political writers, except Montesquieu, whose authority as we shall presently see, was practically misleading. At the same time this people had, in common with all intellectual Europe, been excited by visions of boundless and universal happiness, of new heavens and a new earth, to be attained by a change of the social system and of the form of government. Amidst such disadvantages, and in face of a reaction at once political, social, and religious, the desperate reaction of privilege, both social and ecclesiastical, fighting for its existence, and not scrupling, in its transports of rage and terror at the appearance of liberty and equality, to combine with Robespierre in order to defeat [illegible] success would have been almost a miracle. But then, to extinguish the last hope, came the coalition of the kings, hounded on by the too eloquent ravings of Burke, whose total failure to understand the difficulties under which the French reformers laboured was discreditable to him as a political philosopher, while his frantic invocations of war, and, in his own hideous phrase, of "a long war," were disgraceful to him not only as a political philosopher but as a man.

The Republican Constitution formed after the overthrow of the Terrorists was not a good one. The institution of two Chambers was a mistake, arising from an illusion of which we shall presently have to speak; a sufficient control over the Executive Directory was not secured to the representatives of the nation; the judiciary was not placed on a proper footing. Still it is probable that the Constitution would in time have worked and given to France law and order under a Republic, had it been administered by tolerably honest hands, and had it not been exposed to military violence. But a revolution, especially an abortive revolution, leaves behind it a fearful legacy not only of disappointment, lassitude, mistrust among the people, but of depravity among the chiefs. It gives birth to a race of intriguers, utterly selfish, utterly unprincipled, trained to political infidelity in the school of fortunate apostasy, steeped in perfidy by the violation of unnumbered oaths, and at the same time familiar with the revolutionary use of violence. Such was the offspring of the revolutionary periods of ancient history both in Greece and Rome. Thucydides saw and painted them; they impressed their character on Roman politics after the civil wars of Marius and Sylla. Such again was the offspring of the English Revolution; the Lauderdales and Shaftesburys, the scoundrels who formed the governments and led the factions of the Restoration, who carried on religious persecutions while themselves were infidels, shut up the Exchequer, made the Treaty of Dover, got up the Popish Plot, seized the municipal charters, judicially murdered Russell and Sydney. But never was there such a generation of these men as that which emerged from the wreck of the dreams of Rousseau and from the deadly struggle of factions which ended with the fall of Robespierre—Tallien, Fréron, Barère, Barras, Rewbell, Talleyrand, Merlin, Fouché, and their crew. Political corruption was aggravated by the corruption of morals, caused by the outburst of sensualism which naturally ensued after the dreadful repression and the savage Spartanism of the Terror. To this general depravity was added the volcanic fury, still unabated, of party passions raging in the breasts of factions which but yesterday had been alternately revelling in the blood of each other. It was by military violence, however, that the Constitution was at last overthrown, and its fall was the beginning of that supremacy of the army which unhappily has been from that hour, and still is, the fundamental fact of French politics. The hand which, at the bidding of traitors in the Directory, dealt the first blow, was that of Augereau, but the hand which planned it and dealt the final blow was that of Bonaparte. In estimating the result of the first experiment in Republican government, this must always be borne in mind.

The appearance of Bonaparte upon the scene with his character and his abilities may be truly called the most calamitous accident in history. An accident it was, for Bonaparte was not a Frenchman; he was made a French soldier by the chance which had annexed his country to France, without which he would have been a Corsican brigand, instead of being the scourge of the world. Little did Choiseul think that the rapacity which added to France Corsica, would be the cause a century afterwards of her losing Alsace-Lorraine. As to the greatness of the calamity, few doubt it except the train of mercenary adventurers whose existence in France, as a standing and most dangerous conspiracy against her liberties, is itself the fatal proof of the fact which they would deny. What may have been the extent of Napoleon's genius, political or military, is a question still under debate, and one of a kind which it is difficult to settle, because to take the measure of a force, whether mechanical or intellectual, we must know the strength of the resistance overcome. The Revolution had swept the ground clear for his ambition, and had left him in his career of aggrandisement almost as free from the usual obstacles without, as he was from any restraints of conscience or humanity within. Death removed the only three men who were likely to make a stand, Hoche, Marceau, and Kleber, from his path. He disposed absolutely of an army full of burning enthusiasm, and which, before he took the command, though it had recently met with some reverses, had already hurled back the hosts of the Coalition. In Europe, when he set out on his career, there was nothing to oppose him but governments estranged from their nations, and armies without national spirit, mere military machines, rusty for the most part, and commanded by privileged incompetence. England was the only exception, and by England he was always beaten. The national resistance which his tyranny ultimately provoked, and by which, when he had provoked it, he was everywhere defeated, in Russia, in Germany, even in decrepit Spain, was called into existence by his own folly. He ended, not like Louis XIV., merely in reverses and humiliations, but in utter and redoubled ruin, which he and his country owed to his want of good sense and of self-control, and to this alone, for he was blindly served, and fortune can never be said to have betrayed him, unless he had a right to reckon upon finding no winter in Russia. Before he led his army to destruction he had destroyed its enthusiastic spirit by a process visible enough to common eyes, though invisible to his. Nor was he more successful as a founder of political institutions. He, in fact, founded nothing but a government of the sword, which lasted just so [illegible] notorious and present. The instability of his political [illegible] was shown in a lurid light by the conspiracy of Malet. Of its effect on political character it is needless to speak; a baser brood of [illegible] was never gathered round any Eastern throne. At the touch of military disaster the first Empire, like the second, sank down in ignominious ruin, leaving behind it not a single great public man, not one above the level of Talleyrand. The Code survived; but the Code was the work of the jurists of the Revolution. With no great legal principle was Bonaparte personally identified, except the truly Corsican principle of confiscation, to which he always clung. The genius of the moral reformer is to be measured by the moral effect which he produces, though his own end may be the cup of hemlock. The genius of the adventurer must be measured by his success; and his success is questionable when his career, however meteoric, ends in total disaster. This is not the less manifest to reflecting minds because the pernicious brightness of the meteor still dazzles and misleads the crowd. But the greater Napoleon's genius was, the worse was it for France and for mankind. All his powers were employed in the service of the most utterly selfish and evil ambition that ever dwelt in human breast. It has been justly remarked that his freedom from every sort of moral restraint and compunction lent a unity to his aims and actions which gave him a great advantage over less perfectly wicked men. As to religion, he was atheist enough to use it without scruple as a political engine, and to regret that the time was past when he might, like Alexander, have given himself out as the son of a god. His selfishness is to be measured not merely by the unparalleled sacrifices of human blood and suffering which he offered to it; not merely by the unutterable scenes of horror which he witnessed without emotion, and repeated without a pang; but by the strength of the appeal which was made to his better nature, had he possessed one, and the splendour of the reward which was held out to him, if he would have kept his allegiance to the interests of his country and of humanity. What happiness and what glory would have been his if, after Marengo, he had given the world a lasting peace, and with it the fulfilment, so far as fulfilment was possible, of the social and political aspirations for which such immense and heroic efforts, such vast sacrifices, had been made! Never, in all history, has such a part been offered to man. Instead of accepting this part, Napoleon gave the reins to an ambition most vulgar as well as most noxious in its objects, and to the savage lust of war, which seems after all to have been the predominating element in this Corsican's character, and which gleamed in his evil eye when the chord was touched by those who visited him at Elba. The results were the devastation of Europe, the portentous development of the military system under which the world now groans, the proportionate depression of industry and of all pacific interests, the resurrection in a worse form of the despotisms around which the nations

government. These mysterious capabilities and incapabilities of races in truth are questionable things, and generally tend, upon closer inspection, to resolve themselves into the influence of circumstance perpetuated and accumulated through many generations. England, guarded by the sea, has had comparatively little need of standing armies, and she has thus escaped military despotism, since fleets cannot interfere with politics; yet even she might have fallen under a military despotism, and foreign critics might now be moralizing on the inherent incapacity of her people for any government but that of force, if when the army of James II. was encamped on Hounslow Heath there had not been a William of Orange to come over to our rescue. France has had frontiers; therefore she has had standing armies, and her rulers have been masters of legions. She was exposed to foreign invasion for a whole century, from the time of Edward III. to that of Henry VI.; and again, at the crisis of her destiny in 1791, she was assailed by the arms of the coalesced powers of Reaction. On each occasion her people, to secure national independence, were compelled to renounce liberty, and the Government was inevitably invested with a military dictatorship of defence, which, once acquired, was perpetuated in political despotism. It would be difficult to prove that, under more auspicious circumstances, the States-General, which at one period in the fourteenth century entered on a course of reform as bold and comprehensive as anything done by the framers of the Great Charter or the Parliaments of Henry III., might not have developed into a British House of Commons.

The political crisis of 1789 was in itself one of the most tremendous kind; it was nothing less than the collapse, amidst bankruptcy and general ruin, of the hereditary principle of government, the only principle which France or the greater part of Europe up to that time had known. But it was desperately complicated by its connection with a social and a religious crisis equally tremendous. It came upon a people totally untrained to political action, without political instruction, without a political press, without even the common information which a newspaper gives about passing events; without the means of judiciously choosing its political leaders, or even political leaders among whom a judicious choice could be made; without any good political writers, except Montesquieu, whose authority as we shall presently see, was practically misleading. At the same time this people had, in common with all intellectual Europe, been excited by visions of boundless and universal happiness, of new heavens and a new earth, to be attained by a change of the social system and of the form of government. Amidst such disadvantages, and in face of a reaction at once political, social, and religious, the desperate reaction of privilege, both social and ecclesiastical, fighting for its existence, and not scrupling, in its transports of rage and terror at the appearance of liberty and equality, to combine with Robespierre in order to defeat

true, but it does not save France from being, as a matter of fact, to a lamentable extent a stratocracy. How the army can be placed in safe hands is a problem of which it is almost impossible to suggest a complete and permanent solution. The reduction of its numbers by the definite adoption of a pacific policy is the only real security for the continuance of political liberty. In France the peril is greatest and its manifestations have been most calamitous, but it extends more or less to all the European nations. Everywhere in Europe public liberty and human progress are to a fearful extent at the mercy of the vast standing armies which are maintained by the mutual jealousies of nations, assiduously stimulated by courts and aristocracies in the interest of moral and political reaction. He who said that science could not be better employed than in devising means of destroying prætorians, gave utterance, in a cynical form, to a melancholy truth. It would be a happier way of escape from the danger if soldiers could possibly be made to understand their real duty to their country.

By the Restoration of the Stuarts, and the temporary recovery of its ascendency by a defeated and vindictive party, England was thrown back into political discord, violence, and intermittent civil war for three-quarters of a century. The same calamity befell France, though in her case the restoration was the work of foreign hands; and the same or even greater allowance for the disturbing influence must be made. As no institutions can be proof against military treason, so none can be proof against passions which go beyond political antagonism, beyond even the utmost violence of party, and are, in fact, the passions of civil war. The factions which encountered each other in the legislative assemblies of the Restoration were the same which not long before had encountered each other on the battle-fields of La Vendée. Their hostility, scarcely diminished since they met in arms, was incompatible with that common allegiance to the Constitution and its objects, in spite of divergences on special questions, which is the first condition of constitutional government. Both extremes in the assemblies of Louis XVIII. and Charles X. were striving, not to give effect to their respective policies by constitutional means, but to overthrow the Constitution itself, one extreme in the interest of absolutism, the other in that of democracy. It was then as it is now, when the monarchical and aristocratic party is manifestly using the Marshalate and the Senate, not to modify legislation in a conservative sense, but to overthrow the Republic, as, if it had been successful in controlling the elections, it would unquestionably have done. In such a case institutions can do no more than prolong for themselves a precarious existence by being so ordered as to prevent rather than facilitate a pitched battle between parties which, when it occurs, causes an outbreak of violence, and leads back to civil

leon, besides restoring superstition for his political ends,

restored aristocracy, though the fear of limiting his despotism made him dislike creating an hereditary House of Peers. This also has been a hostile and disturbing force, against which the Republic, founded on equality, has always had and still has to contend. The set of upstarts whom Bonaparte bedizened with tinsel dukedoms of course gave themselves greater airs than the old nobility of France. Such a fellow as Cambacères was very particular about being called Monseigneur; but a certain union of interest, if not a social union, has by this time been brought about between old privilege and new; and the attack on the Republic under De Broglie has been at least as much an aristocratic conspiracy as anything else. So manifest is this as to found a hope that the army, which is tolerably loyal to equality, if not to liberty, might recoil from supporting what it must see to be an aristocratic reaction. An aristocracy, while it exists, will never cease to intrigue against institutions based upon equality; and the total prohibition of hereditary titles was justly felt by the framers of the American Constitution to be essential to the security of their Republic.

Another adverse force, against which free institutions have to contend in France, too often noted to need more than recognition in its place, is the tendency, derived from the old *régime*, but handed on in an intensified form by the Bonapartes, to administrative centralization, which, notwithstanding the improvement of local institutions, still decidedly preponderates over local self-government. The influence exercised by De Broglie and his accomplices over the elections, through prefects of their appointment, is a fatal proof of the fact. From the same inveterate spirit of encroachment on one side, and submission on the other, arises the want of independence in the judiciary which has been so disgracefully displayed in the late political trials. The resistance made by the constituencies to the prefects shows that improvement is going on; but a century of effort is not too much to throw off maladies so deeply-seated as these.

The special influence, however, to which we wish here to point as having interfered with the success of elective government, and as still imperilling its existence in European countries generally, but notably in France, is the ignorant and fallacious imitation of the British Constitution. We wish we could hope that the few words we have to say on this point would meet the eye of any French statesman, and direct his attention to the subject.

Burke denounced the political architects of 1789 for constructing their edifice according to theoretic principles instead of building it on old foundations, and he contrasted their folly with the wisdom of the old Whigs. Considering that the old Whigs were aristocrats who had inherited the territorial plunder of the courtiers of Henry VIII. and who desired to preserve that [illegible]
power of an aristocracy, their [illegible]

... it would have tasked the sagacity of Burke to ... foundations for constitutional government there ... of 1789. France had then been, for at least a ... a despotism with a strictly centralized adminis- ... semblance of provincial government survived; but it ... really tempering the action of the satraps of the ... feudalism, crushed since Richelieu, had left behind no ... of local liberty, but only the antiquated machinery ... which Richelieu had done almost nothing to ... the political architects of 1789 did build on old founda- ... old foundations which anywhere presented themselves ... of the English Constitution. And it may con- ... said that, compared with that renowned, time-honoured, ... model, the newest creation of the brain of Sieyès ... been a safe and practical guide. The clockwork con- ... of Sieyès displayed a fatal ignorance of the real forces; but ... they involved no incurable self-contradiction. It was ... impossible to make them work. But it was abso- ... and had been actually proved to be so by English ... to make the British Constitution work, as the British ... was understood by Frenchmen and by Englishmen ...

... version of the British Constitution was that given by ... in perfect accordance with the forms of British con- ... law. Montesquieu, a great genius in his day, while he ... the forms with philosophic eloquence, failed to pierce ... to the real political forces. In this respect he is like ... whose work, admirable in many respects, is still an ... of the forms, not of the real forces, and consequently is of ... as a practical guide to American politics, and is seldom ... American politicians. The legislative power is the sovereign ... But Montesquieu believed that the sovereign power, in the ... of the British Constitution, was really divided among King, ... and Commons. He also believed that the legislative, execu- ... judiciary powers were not only distinct, but independent ... and that the mutual independence of those powers was ... of constitutional government.

... British Constitution is a single elective assembly, in which the ... of the legislative, and therefore the whole of the sovereign ... vested. This assembly virtually appoints the members ... who are the leaders of its majority, and through the ... ministers of justice. Round it still cling, as it were, the ... old feudal monarchy and of an old feudal House of ... both of them the power has long passed away, to ... Commons, though, strange to say, not only foreign ob- ... statesmen, long remained unconscious of the fact.

Whether the sovereign power, which could not be divided, should be vested in the Crown or in the representatives of the people, was the question which, after vain attempts to settle it by debate, was fought out with arms between the Parliament and the Stuarts. It was decided, after a century of conflict and several vicissitudes of fortune, in favour of the representatives of the people, who finally triumphed in 1688. From that time the monarchy has been *fainéant*, interfering with the government only by means of back-stairs influence, or by forming for itself, underhand, a party in the House of Commons, as it did during part of the reign of George III. William III., being the head and the general of a European coalition, kept for his life the Foreign Office and the War Office in his own hands; but after a slight resistance, ending with his attempt to veto the Triennial Act, he was obliged to relinquish every other kind of power; and, in the reign of his successor, the transfer of the sovereignty to Parliament was complete. As to the House of Lords, it has no power left in itself but that of obstruction on minor questions; on great questions it merely registers the vote of the majority of the House of Commons. This was settled in 1832, in the case of the Reform Bill, and again in 1846, in the case of the Corn Laws. On both those occasions the measures would notoriously have been rejected by an overwhelming majority had the House of Lords been an independent assembly. The result showed that it was nothing of the kind. King, Lords, and Commons work together harmoniously in England, not because each of them exercises its share of the sovereign power temperately, and with due respect for the rights of the others, which is the common and the orthodox belief, but because two of them are politically non-existent. Restore real sovereignty to the Crown, and you will have the Stuarts and the Long Parliament over again.

Following, however, as they thought the successful example of England, the framers of the French Constitution of 1789 attempted to divide the sovereign power, leaving a portion of it in the King, and vesting the remainder in the representatives of the people. The result, the inevitable result, was collision, and soon a conflict which, though neither party knew it, was essentially internecine. The weaker, that is to say, the Monarchy, fell; but in the desperate efforts necessary to get rid of the opposing force and to vindicate the sovereignty to itself, foreign intervention adding to the fury of the conflict and to the general difficulties of the crisis, the nation fell into convulsions, into a reign of violence, into the Terror, and after the Terror into military dictatorship and despotism. The same fatal situation was reproduced under the restored Monarchy; again an attempt [illegible] made to divide the sovereign power between the King [illegible] Assembly which represented the nation. In which of the [illegible] power should rest, was the issue once more really debated [illegible] those fierce sessions of the Restoration Legislature [illegible] heaved with conspiracy, and ever and anon the mutterings of civil war were heard in the streets. At last Charles X. made a desperate effort to cut the knot and render himself sovereign; by his failure and fall the question of sovereignty was decided for the time in favour of the representatives of the people. What power Louis Philippe retained, was retained not of right (for he subscribed to the doctrine that he was to be guided by Constitutional advisers assigned him by the majority in the Chambers), but by personal influence and corruption. It was in corruption, in fact, that monarchical power made clandestinely its last stand. Louis Philippe's fall, as we have already said, was due not so much to political causes, in the proper sense of the term, as to Chauvinism conspiring against a *bourgeois* King whose policy was peace, though he yielded too much to the fancied necessity of sacrificing, by military display and menace, to the idol of war. At the same time the fresh impulse given to the revolutionary movement in Europe by the struggles of oppressed nationalities caused an insurrection in France against the surviving forms of monarchy and the influences by which they were upheld. Chauvinism and the fear of anarchy together gave birth to the second Empire, under which the sovereign power reverted from the representatives of the nation to the monarch, who was in all but form a despot, as before the Legislature had been, in all but form and saving illicit influence, the King. The second Empire went to the grave of the first by the same road, the military aggressiveness which was the condition of its existence leading it on at last to ruinous defeat. Now again comes a nominal Republic; but, unfortunately, there is still a King, and the hopeless problem of carrying on government with a divided sovereignty presents itself afresh. The Marshal, having the command of the army, and being supported by those who desire a return to monarchy, struggles for the sovereign power; and the question at the late election was whether that power should belong to him and the Ministers of his personal choice, or to the nation. From 1789 onwards, there has been a chronic though intermittent struggle for the sovereign power several times; that power has been transferred and retransferred; there have been periods in which it was doubtful where it resided; but it has never been divided, nor is a division possible in the nature of things. The attempt can only lead to a conflict which will probably end, as it did in England, in civil war.

Those who found an elective government must not fancy that they can at the same time preserve monarchy. They must be logical, because they will find that in this case not to be logical is to plunge into practical confusion. They must vest the sovereignty absolutely and beyond question in the nation. Their first care must be to establish on an immovable foundation the principles, that the nation alone makes and alone can alter the Constitution; that to the nation alone all allegiance is due, and against it alone can treason be committed; that all other authority, however high, is merely derivative, responsible, and bounded by the written law; that the sovereignty of the nation is exercised through its representatives duly elected; and that to these representatives the obedience of all executive officers must be paid. This done, they may afford to make any conservative regulations with regard to the election of the National Assembly and the mode of its proceeding that they please; and where freedom is young, they will find careful regulations of this kind needful. It is the game of the Bonapartists, first to assert the sovereignty of the nation, and then to make the nation permanently divest itself of its sovereignty by a *plébiscite* in favour of the Bonaparte family and the brood of adventurers whose instruments the Bonapartes are. Of course, no legislation can prevent a national suicide; but clear declarations of principle are not barren because they are not endowed with force to defend themselves against treachery or violence: and it would be important to declare that the national sovereignty is inherent as well as entire, and that no single generation can by its act divest future generations of their right.

So long as there is a single head to the State there will always be some danger of a revival of monarchical pretensions, and of a dispute as to the seat of the sovereign power, at least in any country where monarchy has long existed and monarchical ideas have taken root. America is Republican soil, on which hardly any but democratic ideas can grow; the sovereignty of the nation is firmly established, not only in documents, but in the minds of the people; the President is elected for a short term, his powers are clearly bounded by the written law, he has hardly any military force at his command; yet Jackson showed a tendency to encroachment, and the jobbers who plundered the community under Grant betrayed their desire not only of increasing, but of perpetuating his power. A single head of the State is a fancied necessity; the Swiss Constitution, which, instead of a single man, has a Council with a President whose function is only to preside, presents great advantages in this respect, and is the safest model for adoption. It moreover gets rid of that which is the scourge even of America, but far more of any country where the questions that divide parties are so fundamental and party hostility is so deadly as in France—a Presidential election, which periodically stirs up from their depths all the most violent passions, excites the most turbulent ambitions, and brings all questions to a dangerous head. The framers of the American Constitution were in some degree misled, like the framers of the French Constitution, by their British model which they reproduced in a Republican form; they imagined that it was necessary to have something in place of the King, and the elective Presidency with all its evils is the result.

Another signal and calamitous instance of mistaken imitation of the British Constitution is the power of dissolution, which the other [illegible] of a disloyal President and Senate, was so nearly the [illegible] the Republic. In the days in which the power [illegible] the other attributes of sovereignty, resided in the Cro[illegible] instru- [illegible] of [illegible] ned only [illegible] as the [illegible] Our mo[illegible] of thin[illegible] King, or [illegible] other attri[illegible] exer- [illegible] a Parliamentary Minister, by whose advice the Crown is [illegible] on all other questions to be guided, for the purpose of [illegible] the relative position of parties in the country; and its exercise [illegible] to that object by restrictions which, though tacit and to be [illegible] book on constitutional law, are perfectly understood and [illegible] by both parties as the rules of the game. It is in fact the [illegible] which the House of Commons adjusts itself to the public [illegible] which is the basis of its power. This has not been seen by [illegible] thinking to reproduce the British Constitution, have vested [illegible] really external to the Parliament, such as the French [illegible] a power of dissolution, which is in fact a power of [illegible] for the time, and may in disloyal hands be used as a [illegible] extinguishing for ever, the organ of the national sovereignty, [illegible] national sovereignty itself. We know well that in the case [illegible] the fault does not lie with the friends of the Republic; but it is [illegible] the power of disso- lution [illegible] ailed.

Di[illegible] of old feud[illegible] the poli[illegible] ted, like [illegible] the pre[illegible] The exi[illegible] ty, and [illegible] to be [illegible] which ele[illegible] by bo[illegible] General ele[illegible] of [illegible] and pitched battles between parties, which when the differ- enc[illegible] Ultra- mo[illegible] France, a[illegible] plainly in[illegible] to [illegible] conflicts, to avoid pitched battles of opinion, to make the stream of political progress glide within its banks, and with as few cataracts as possible, ought to be the aim of all framers of elective constitutions. An elective assembly renewed, not all at once, but by instalments, and at regular periods fixed by law, independent of the will of any functionary, will fulfil the condition of uninterrupted life, without which usurping Governments, like that of De Broglie, may always be tempted to suspend its existence or get rid of it altogether; and it will conform steadily, yet promptly enough, to the changes of public opinion, without those violent revolutions which general elections are apt to produce, and without giving the excessive predominance which they are apt to give to the question or the cry of the day. The necessity under which party leaders find themselves of providing a question and a cry for a general election has had a bad effect even on English legislation.

Another illusion which has led to strange consequences in France, and in all other countries where the building of constitutions has been going on, including the British Colonies, is the notion that the House of Lords is a Senate moderating by its mature wisdom the action of the more popular House. As we have had occasion to say elsewhere, the House of Lords is not a Senate; it is an old feudal estate of the realm: its action has been, not that of ripe wisdom moderating popular impulse, but simply that of privilege combating, so far as it dared, all change, in the interest of the privileged order. Whether its influence is really conservative may be doubted; in the first place, because its resistance to change, being unreasoning and anti-national, is very apt, as the history of the first Reform Bill shows, to provoke the revolutionary spirit rather than to allay it; and in the second place, because it operates as a practical ostracism of the great landowners, who, under the circumstances of English society, would otherwise certainly find seats in the House of Commons. The real stronghold of English Conservatism is the preponderance of the aristocratic, or rather plutocratic element in the House of Commons. But at all events the House of Lords furnishes no model to any country which has not an hereditary and territorial aristocracy, or a privileged order of some kind, having its base, and presenting a fulcrum of resistance, outside the body of the nation. If both assemblies emanate from the nation, whatever diversities there may be in the mode of their election, and even if the Senate be not directly elected, but nominated by a Government itself the offspring of election, the attempt to make the national sovereignty check and restrain itself by acting through two organs instead of one, and confronting its own impulses with its own cooler wisdom, must ultimately fail. So long as the same party has a majority in both assemblies, the double machinery will work smoothly, but at the same time it will be ineffective. But when the party which is in a majority in the popular assembly is in a minority in the Senate, as soon as an [illegible] arises there will be a collision between the two [illegible] result will be a dead-lock, which will last till the [illegible] of the two assemblies to give way, declaring thereby [illegible] national sovereignty is delegated to the other. Nor [illegible] real advantage in the delay which the dead-lock causes, [illegible] compensate for the violence of the struggle, and the [illegible] agitation of turbulent and revolutionary passions. Such [illegible] of the British Colonies in Australia, while in Canada [illegible] a cipher, and its debates are not even reported. In Italy [illegible] party was at first in the majority in both Chambers; but the [illegible] a change took place in the popular Chamber, and at once [illegible] were symptoms of collision. In France, the Senate at each great [illegible] the constitution has proved impotent or useless, as the historian [illegible] Parliamentary Government in France admits; but it is now showing [illegible] tendency, as might have been expected, to become the citadel of a [illegible] or rather a group of parties, bent on overturning the Republic in [illegible] of some form of government more favourable to aristocracy; [illegible] this way it threatens to prove not a nullity, but a danger of the [illegible] magnitude, and an instrument of attempts, such as the attempt of [illegible] Broglie, which may plunge the country again into civil war. If [illegible] example of the American Senate is cited in favour of a second [illegible] Chamber, it must be remembered that the American Senate represents [illegible] Federal principle as opposed to the principle of population, and that [illegible] authority and usefulness, whatever they may be, thus depend on its [illegible] with a Federation.

[illegible] of what special elements do you wish your Senate to con[illegible]? What is to be the special character of its members compared [illegible] those who sit in the Lower House? Till this is distinctly settled, [illegible] for particular modes of election or appointment are devices [illegible] an object; they are machines for producing something which [illegible] is not determined. Do you wish your Senate to consist of old [illegible] in accordance with the literal meaning of the name, and with [illegible] of primitive nations? It will represent the infirmities of old [illegible]. Do you wish it to consist of the rich? It will be the organ of [illegible] interest, odious and the object of suspicion to all the rest of [illegible] nation. Or do you wish it to consist of the best and most trust[illegible] of your public men? If you succeed in putting these men [illegible] the Senate, you will deprive the popular Chamber of its guides [illegible] of those most able to control its impulses and passions, and [illegible] manner ostracize your legislative wisdom. Something like this [illegible] to Cromwell when he thought to temper the fractiousness [illegible] House of Commons by restoring the Upper House: to supply [illegible] for his Upper House he had to take his best men from the [illegible] the lead in the Commons was broken up; the two Houses fell [illegible] each other; and the Parliament was dissolved in a storm.

[illegible] of attempting to divide the sovereignty, which is really indivisible, and to make the nation perform the chimerical operation of producing by election a check upon itself, attention should, we venture to think, be directed, more carefully and systematically than it has ever yet been, to the constitution of the representative assembly, to the mode and rate of its renewal, to the securities for its deliberate action and for the exclusion from it of mere passion and impulse, to such questions as that between direct election and election through local councils or other intermediate bodies, to the qualifications for the franchise in the way of property, age, education, or performance of national duties. It is singular, for instance, that amidst all the discussions about vetoes, absolute or suspensive, to be reposed in kings or presidents, no one has thought of requiring an absolute majority of the whole house for the passage of an opposed measure, or of giving to a minority, if it amounts to a certain proportion of the House, a limited power of delay.

But of all the things borrowed by France and other nations from the British Constitution the most palpably absurd and calamitous, in its general application, is the system of party, which sets up the great offices of state as the prizes of a perpetual conflict between two organized parties, and relies upon the perpetual existence of these two parties and the ceaseless continuance of their conflict as the only available means of carrying on constitutional government. It is strange that any one should have fallen into such a trap who had studied the Parliamentary history of England. In this country there have throughout been two Parliamentary parties, and two only: while the objects sought by both have been so definite and of such importance as at once to ensure cohesion, and to justify, in some degree at least, allegiance to the party standard. The conflict of parties has, in fact, been the means of carrying on and regulating a series of organic changes and reforms in a democratic, or at least in a popular, direction. The adherents of each party have been able to say, with truth, that they were contending for the ascendency of certain definite principles in government and legislation. At the same time there have been certain principles common to both parties, which, with the remarkable aptitude of the nation, and the retention of the leadership on both sides by a section of the aristocracy, have always, in modern times, kept the contest within bounds. Even so, party has often shown that it is but a fine name for faction; and in the pauses of progress, when there was no great question before the country, the generous emulation of party leaders has sunk into a personal struggle for place with all its rancour and all its meanness. Such, however, as it is, the ground for the existence of the party system is peculiar to England, and has its explanation in her political history: the attempt to reproduce the system in other countries without the ground for its existence, will be not only senseless but noxious in the highest degree. To divide a nation for ever into two factions and to set these factions to wage [illegible] a war as that of factions always is, and with [illegible] of intrigue, mutual calumny, and corruption, is [illegible] plan ever deliberately adopted by a political [illegible] if we could be convinced that this was the only possible [illegible] constitutional government, we should regard the [illegible] government as hopeless. How can our political [illegible] in a system of which it is the inherent tendency, [illegible] the avowed object, to stir up discord, to excite [illegible] passions, to stimulate selfish ambitions, to deprave political [illegible] destroy that reasonable loyalty to the national govern- [illegible] the very existence of a free community depends? If [illegible] of such a theory is not manifest enough in itself, let [illegible] be made into the working of the system of party in the [illegible] where it has been retained for the personal benefit of [illegible] of politicians, when, all organic questions having been settled, [illegible] grounds for such combinations and for allegiance to party [illegible] to exist; it will soon become manifest what are its effects [illegible] efficiency, purity, and stability of government, on the morality [illegible] life, on the political character of the people. In the United [illegible] was ground enough, and more than enough, for the [illegible] of party while the nation was divided on the question of [illegible] and it is not surprising the party spirit should have prevailed [illegible] to the nation, or that there should have been a party [illegible] the utmost bitterness, which, being brought to a head by [illegible] to the Presidency, ended in a civil war. But the old [illegible] for party having been thus exhausted, and new materials [illegible] themselves, the combinations are breaking up, the lines [illegible] confused, and the present Government, in undertaking [illegible] of administrative reform, hardly relies more on the support [illegible] party, the regular managers of which are all against it, [illegible] of the best section of the other party, and less on either [illegible] of the nation at large.

[illegible] historian of Parliamentary Government in France, M. Duver- [illegible] de Hauranne, who tacitly assumes throughout his work the [illegible] of the party system, states its theory thus: "In free coun- [illegible] liberty is not of yesterday, there always exist, in the [illegible] society, two principal tendencies, one towards liberty, the [illegible] authority, which manifest themselves in all legal ways, [illegible] in the way of elections, and which usually produce two [illegible] having each its principles, its opinions, its flag. Of these [illegible] the majority, and governs, not directly but indirectly, [illegible] influence which it exercises, the choices which it indicates, [illegible] which it defends or combats. The other becomes the [illegible] and watches the Government, controls it, keeps it up to [illegible] such time as faults or a movement of public opinion [illegible] relative position of the parties, and give it in its turn the right and the power of governing." Two tendencies, according to this eminent writer, there must always be in the nation, one towards authority, the other towards liberty; and these tendencies are the foundations of the two parties, by the perpetual conflict of which government is to be carried on. But suppose a man to have an equal and well-balanced regard, both for authority and for liberty, to which party is he to belong? Or is he to remain in a state of suspension, and to be eliminated from politics, because he thinks rightly and is free from undue bias? Suppose the nation itself to have arrived at a reasonable frame of mind, to be practically convinced that, while the preservation of ordered liberty is the object for which authority exists, rational allegiance to authority was essential to the preservation of liberty—what then? Because the nation was all of one opinion, and that opinion evidently the right one, would the possibility of good government be at an end? Then, again, do not those who hold the view of M. Duvergier de Hauranne perceive that, while it is essential to their theory that there should be only two parties, that of authority and that of liberty, that of the Government and that of the Opposition, the fact is that in France there are a dozen, that the same is the case in other countries, and that even in England, though the Conservative party, which is a party of interest, retains its unity, the Liberal party, which is a party of opinion, is splitting into sections, which are becoming every day less amenable to party discipline, and therefore weaker as a whole? It is evident that, as intellectual activity and independence of mind increase, sectional differences of opinion will multiply, and party organization will become more impracticable every day. Nothing will be left us but hollow, treacherous, and ephemeral combinations of cliques which have no real principle of union, and which will be torn asunder again by mutual jealousies almost as soon as they are combined. Intrigue and cabal will continually gain force; the hope of a stable government will grow more faint; until at last the people, in sheer weariness and despair, will fling themselves at the feet of any one who promises to give them stability and security with the strong hand.

An executive council, regularly elected by the legislature, in which the supreme power resides, and renewed by a proper rotation and at proper intervals, so as to preserve the harmony between the legislature and the executive, without a ministerial crisis or a vote of censure, is the natural and obvious crown of an elective polity; and to something of this sort, we venture to think, all free communities will be ultimately compelled to have recourse, by the manifest failure of the party system. If further security for the responsibility of the executive to the legislative, and for the maintenance of harmony between the two, were deemed needful, it might be provided that, besides the limitation of office to a certain term, each member of the council should be liable to removal at any time for special cause, by the vote [illegible] proportion of the assembly. Such a provision would have [illegible] French Legislature to get rid of Barras and his two [illegible] the Executive Directory as soon as it became manifest [illegible] conspiring against the Constitution.

[illegible] assembly, elected under such conditions as may appear [illegible] favourable to the ascendency of intelligence and public [illegible] the undivided sovereignty of the nation, always in [illegible] renewed by such instalments as may preserve its popular [illegible] without rendering it the sport of temporary passion, legis- [illegible] the best that can be devised for securing deliberate [illegible] and in its turn electing the members of a responsible execu- [illegible], once more, seems the natural organization of a community [illegible] in the course of human progress, has discarded the hereditary principle, and adopted the elective principle in its stead. No constitution can protect itself against the external violence of a great army if the army is willing, at the bidding of a military usurper, to cut the throat of public liberty. No constitution can change the political character of a nation, or cure, as by magic, the weakness and servility [illegible] by centuries of submission to a centralized and arbitrary administration. No constitution can neutralize the bad effects produced on public spirit and on mutual confidence by the decay of religious belief in the minds of a great part of the nation, and the [illegible] imperfect development of any new faith. No constitution can eliminate the general vices of human nature, or the special vices of the particular nation. But such a constitution as we have indicated would at least not contain in itself the certain seeds of its own destruction; it would not be liable to legal dissolution by any external power; it would continue to exist, to do its work better or worse, to renew itself by an operation as regular as the seasons, and which there could never be a special temptation to interrupt; without inducing torpor, it would avoid anything like a violent crisis, such as is brought on by a general election, especially after a penal dissolution; it would keep the way always open to the reform of what is bad, by means of improved elections, and without a revolution; it would give full play to any increase of virtue and intelligence which there might be among the people; its course would no doubt be at first somewhat halting and unsatisfactory among a people whose training has been unfortunate, but it could hardly fall to the ground, or fail to answer in a tolerable way the ordinary ends of government.

With the present Constitution, unfortunately, the contrary is true. It does contain in itself the almost certain seeds of its own destruction. The quasi-monarchical power, Presidency, Marshalate, or whatever it is to be called, and the Senate, which is sure to have an aristocratic character, will probably remain, as they are now, the double basis of a [illegible] reaction in favour of the hereditary principle, to which [illegible] with good reason, clings; and recent experience renders it highly probable that the two, if firmly united, would be able by successive dissolutions, combined with the exercise of Government influence in the elections, to place in the utmost peril, and practically to annihilate, the organ of the national sovereignty and the national sovereignty itself. The constitution of "three Powers" is a constitution of civil war.

In discussing constitutions, however, and the revision of constitutions, we are haunted by the unwelcome apprehension that something of a sterner kind may yet be in store for France. We do not greatly fear that a soldier, whose name is associated with nothing extraordinary or great except defeat, will conceive the design of founding a military empire in his own interest. We do not greatly fear the Clericals, since the catastrophe of Eugénie and her priests, and when Ultramontanism, in spite of its recent spasm of aggressive energy, is manifestly losing ground throughout educated Europe. We do not even greatly fear Bonapartism in itself, simply as a movement in favour of the restoration of a military despotism for the benefit of a discredited dynasty. What we fear is the implacable hostility of aristocracy to a Republic based upon equality. In France the three aristocracies, Legitimist, Orleanist, and Bonapartist, are now collectively strong; their wealth has greatly increased; they begin to feel a common interest, social and political, though they are at present ranged under the banners of different pretenders, and have hitherto, by their disunion, saved the Republic. One and all, they instinctively hate equality, and those hate it most bitterly whose nobility is of yesterday. You may demonstrate as clearly as you please that aristocracy has had its hour, that humanity is passing into another phase, that the best and most glorious part which a man who inherits the influence of aristocracy can play is to smooth the transition into a new era: some of the finer minds, and of those who can hope to maintain their position by their own character and intellect, will perhaps listen to you; the mass will obey the bias of class, cling to privilege, and constantly conspire against equality and any institutions by which equality is upheld. Their feelings towards the democratic masses are not those of mere political difference, but of hatred more bitter than that which is felt by a foreign enemy, and aggravated by contempt. The aristocratic conspiracy, for such at bottom it was, of De Broglie and Fourtou has for the moment failed; but the attempt will be perpetually renewed: and it will be fortunate indeed if the question between the Republic and the aristocracy is finally decided without adding another convulsion to the ninety years' agony of France.

GOLDWIN SMITH.

# ETHICAL ASPECTS OF THE THEORY OF DEVELOPMENT.

THE Development Theory in its biological form, as it stands contrasted with the theory of the Logical Evolution of the universe, is best recognized under the name of Development of Species, as employed by Mr. Darwin. In brief outline the theory may be presented thus:—By survival of the fittest in the struggle for life, and by increasing adaptation to environment as this struggle proceeds, there is a gradual progression in the order of life, and in due course the appearance of new species or orders of beings. It is thus essentially a biological theory. As such, it includes man only in so far as the maintenance of individual life, and the continuance of the race through successive generations, depend upon conditions analogous to those which apply to lower orders of being. In so far as no acknowledgment is made of any break in the order of progression,—or hiatus between subordinate orders and the highest order of life,—it claims to include human life within its sweep. It must, indeed, be kept in mind that there are some upholders of the theory who grant a failure in the application of the law of selection to the human race. But the theory finds currency as one which is applicable to humanity, and which carries the true scientific account of the genesis and development of the race.

To what extent the theory may claim scientific worth, as a theory concerning the lower forms of animal life, I do not propose to inquire. But, looking at it as a theory which claims to apply to all life, including human, I wish to consider how it meets the tests which are to be encountered when it comes into the region of morals.

In raising this question, I am not seeking to carry the conditions of mental science into the province of physical science, where it may be said they cannot be legitimately applied. Specially it must be noticed, I am not attempting to apply ethical data beyond their proper sphere. I am not proposing—what I should readily allow would be unreasonable—to argue downwards from a moral law to the determination of the facts of biological science. The situation of things is this: biological science has not merely set itself to classify the forms of organic existence, and to enumerate the laws of life which apply to different orders, but it has risen above this to inquire as to the relations of the different orders. Beyond this, it has advanced to suggest that the higher orders have sprung from the lower. Pushing forward on this line, it has ventured the hypothesis that man is himself an illustration of this, being the last and crowning result in the history of evolution. By the launching of such a hypothesis, the biologist claims to include all the facts of human life within the sweep of his own domain. Thus it is that the moralist, within his own territory, is met with the question concerning the reasonableness of the hypothesis of the development of species. It devolves on him to grant the biological claim, or show cause for discrediting the hypothesis as applied to the characteristics of moral life. And here clearly the Evolution Theory must submit itself to ethical tests. For, if it be plain that we cannot argue from moral law to the determination of the facts of animal existence, it is just as plain that we cannot argue from a theory based only on facts observed in the lower forms of animal life to the determination of the facts of moral life. The hypothesis must meet the test it has summoned. It must show how it proposes to account for the distinctive features of moral life. For example, as it is given to speak much of the struggle for life, and survival of the fittest, it is required of it to show how it has come to pass, in the regulation of human life, that each one strives to sustain his own life, yet accounts it morally wrong to destroy a weaker life, if it be only human life. And, as giving greater vividness to the contrast, the biologist needs to explain how this sacredness of human life is acknowledged, when men take away so freely the life of all lower orders, and, in doing so, commonly prefer to kill the fittest.

These considerations are sufficient to show that the ethical philosopher does not ultroneously and unwarrantably encroach on the territory of biology when he proposes to meet a theory of development of species with ethical tests. It is the biologist himself who occasions the inquiry and courts it.

I may therefore inquire, *first*, in a more rigidly scientific manner, what biology offers us in the form of ethical science or theory of the genesis of ethical conceptions and consequent ethical actions; and then in a more general way, and very briefly, I may inquire what is the influence of this hypothesis on the moral phases of human life.

I shall restrict attention to one or two selected tests. I shall also waive all reference to the supernatural, and content myself with argument restricted to the area of experience. A reluctance to appeal to the supernatural is avowed by many upholders of the Evolution Theory, and, as there is ample common ground within the area of observed facts, we may restrict the argument accordingly. At the same time, it needs to be remembered that the Evolution Theory virtually professes to be a theory of the universe, and as such it goes beyond all experience in the very exposition of its meaning.

Accepting the limitation indicated, a glance at the facts of animal life out of which the theory has taken its rise will suffice for our purpose. It is well known that observation has been turned largely upon different orders of pigeons and of dogs. Facts concerning these animals may seem remote from the investigations of the moral philosopher. I think them very remote indeed. But if Evolutionists volunteer to instruct us in this matter, telling us that they have found a deeper meaning in pigeon-life and dog-life than has previously been recognized, we are willing to listen. Specially if they tell us that, in their study of pigeons and dogs, they have found clearly present the germinal forms of moral life, we must attend to them as a new order of moral philosophers.

The facts with which a beginning is made are sufficiently obvious and familiar to be accepted. They are such as these. Each animal seeks its own gratification, and in doing so struggles for precedence with others which are impelled by the same tendency. In this struggle the strongest prevail; the weakest are crushed aside. This temporary and occasional conflict illustrates a law of life for these animals, and really determines the issues in the struggle for life itself. The strongest live and flourish; the weakest die. Here is a law of natural selection which may be illustrated in a variety of ways. But further, animals not merely fight for precedence, they adapt themselves to their surroundings. Those exposed to uniform risks become skilful in escaping the danger. The experienced escape; the unwary are caught. Those needing special dexterity to secure their prey, or to reach the means of subsistence, make advances in the requisite adaptation. This acquired power is transmitted to their offspring, and by hereditary descent acquirements become permanent possessions of the species. These facts illustrate a law of natural acquisition. The facts are verified in the history of different orders of dogs—the sheep-dog, the pointer, and the setter. Further, this law of acquisition is aided in its operation by the intervention of training under the hands of men. The shepherd and the gamekeeper only utilize a natural law of the animal's life, and take advantage of hereditary transmission in the animals which they select for training. How much is involved here in human intervention, and what bearing it has on the theory of evolution itself, I do not at present inquire. But the facts are beyond doubt, and they give clear warrant for a theory of animal life in which natural selection and natural progression hold the chief places. It may also be granted that the facts give a *primâ facie* warrant for provisional extension of the theory beyond the range of actual observation. I will go further, and admit that there is reasonable ground for the inquiry whether human life, regarded as animal life, does not come largely under the sway of the laws enunciated. It cannot be thought wonderful if, in the enthusiasm of scientific generalizing, it be suggested that human life as a whole, including all that we mean when we speak of intellectual, moral, and spiritual life, may have its history—and consequently its true interpretation—wrapt up in these facts when rightly understood. This, then, is the suggestion actually made and pressed on our notice, as containing the new theory of morals which I am now to consider.

Granting that a basis has been found for the hypothesis in the facts briefly described, the next pressing demand is for attention to facts which seem to be adverse, or at any rate difficult to arrange under the hypothesis. The intervention of man in the training of animals is itself a difficult fact for the theory. It is in connection with this intervention that the clearest and most striking body of evidence in its support is gathered, but the evidence is associated with facts which lie along a different plane from that on which the suitable facts are found. For a theory coming from below upwards, proclaiming that evolution contains the explanation of all life, it is at least awkward theoretically (however serviceable practically) to have a helping hand stretched down from a higher elevation to aid evolution in its efforts to reach the height. But apart from this, and confining attention to human life alone, there are facts which constitute a great difficulty for an evolution theory, and upon these the discussion must largely turn. Human life does not look so like animal life as to make it quite easy to regard it as a mere enlargement and elevation of the lower form. There is indeed among men quite a sufficient experience of the struggle for life,—and, it must be added, quite enough of the practice of the strong pushing aside the weak,—to favour the analogy between lower animal life and human. But, on the other hand, there are in human life facts so different,—so completely contrary,—that it requires a great flight of imagination to represent them as the fruits of evolution in accordance with the laws of natural selection and heredity. Laying aside all influences of sex, and love of offspring, where analogies exist, and restricting attention to individuals engaged in the struggle for life, exactly as you observe animals in the same struggle, the strong do not as an invariable law of their life push aside the weak. Self-gratification is not seen to dominate individual action, involving disregard of others. On the contrary, the strong use their strength to protect and help the weak; and they approve the doing of this, and find pleasure in it,—and, what is more, onlookers admire it, and agree in calling it *right*. This is *moral*, and not animal life. It is moral in contrast with animal life. And it has no analogy with tenderness to offspring such as is witnessed among the lower animals.

... are facts peculiar to human life— ... life.

... will attempt to differentiate. It will ... as possible the most prominent distinctions ... of being. The scientific problem— ... answer—must be formulated on these ... is to be desired on both sides, is an ... differences between men and the lower ...re may be a tendency on the one side to exaggerate ...es, as there may be on the other a tendency to lessen ...en know what human nature is, and how it works,— ... their own life than they know of animal life; ... agreement, as a common ground for ... certainly there is sufficient harmony—though it ... formulated—as to the broad marks of distinction ... the lower animals.

...s may be adopted for throwing out in a general way ...erance. Having a regard to the governing power in ...ay that in the one case it is Reason; in the other ...nsidering the end in view, we may say a regulated life with moral law, in contrast with self-gratification as the ...ught. And these distinctions are clear enough and though it be admitted—as of course it is—that there ...f intelligence in the animals, as there is appetite in ... will appear that the law of regulation for the life may ...st of distinction. As, therefore, Evolutionists propose ...m their own data, a science of the genesis of moral ... who regard the promise as difficult of fulfilment will ... of moral life as those which present the best examples ... to be encountered.

...purpose will be sufficiently served by selecting a single ...aw of moral life, suggested by the references to animal Evolutionists. The law of animal life is self-gratifi... This law has also its application in human life, as ...mal; but not singly, because man is more than an ... of human life—animal, rational, and moral—a unity ... three—is regulated self-gratification; and in this self-...re is a law of *self-denial*, recognized and applied as a ...her than the law of self-indulgence. This law of self-...ential law of human life, and an exact type of moral ...

... think, we have a law of human life in complete con-... direct antagonism—to the law of animal life. If the ... contrariety of these two can be shown, the theory of ... in extreme difficulty. Either the theory is made ... a theory of human life, or it is proved that the history of life is not one of evolution, but something quite different.

How complete the distinction is between this higher law of self-denial and the law of animal life, may be easily shown. When we speak of the law of self-gratification and the law of self-denial, it is to be observed that in the latter case we are using the word "law" in a new and entirely different sense from that in which it is employed while we refer to lower forms of being. These two forms of law belong to distinct orders of things. Appetite is mere force, acting in a given way, capable of acting in no other, and subject to no check from within the organism, except by exhaustion. This is the law of physical organism, and it is the same in man as in the animal, in so far as man is regarded simply as possessed of organism. But in human nature there is a law which performs its function in checking that law of the physical nature which in the lower being plays its part unchecked. It is a law contemplated by the intellectual nature, accepted by the intelligence as a reason for restraining appetite, and put into application so as to bring about restraint of passion and guide activity in a different direction. There is nothing analogous to this in mere animal life; and it will be hard for that theory to endure scientific tests which proclaims that self-denial is a development of self-indulgence.

There is, however, an apparent semblance of analogy, which proves very attractive to an Evolutionist. It is said that animals also exercise self-denial. It is not professed that this is similar to what is in us, but it is thought sufficiently like to be the germ. Thus we are referred to the care which the bird has over her brood, or the ewe over her lamb. But such cases give no example of a law of self-denial; we have still but a special and temporary phase of the law of self-gratification. There is no approximation here to law in the higher sense, as when we speak of a law of self-denial. And so this semblance of self-denial in the bird or the ewe is not a law of life, but only at most a law of a special state, which soon ceases, so that the so-called self-denial passes off like an exhausted appetite. This every one may see who observes the determined and even harsh way in which a ewe casts off a lamb when it is able to take care of itself. And we find clear and ample confirmation of the same thing in the extreme difficulty which the shepherd experiences in getting the ewes to take charge of their lambs in a year of drought and scanty pasture, when the mothers are themselves in a weakened condition. We are only deluded by appearances when we speak of a law of self-denial operating in animal life, as a germ of the same law acting in moral life.

It is tantamount to surrender for a theory of natural selection to proclaim that a law of self-denial applies to merely animal life. For what is natural selection? It is survival of the fittest, and destruction weakest, in the struggle for life. And what is this but un-d struggle for self-gratification, or the negation of self-denial? room for self-denial, and the survival of the fittest becomes of doubt, in which case the foundations of the whole theory ken.

et us keep to survival of the fittest, and that is survival of the —survival of those most able to push others aside; most able n for themselves all that they desire. This is the test of one and muscle. No doubt men may also be estimated by st. But it would be far away from the true standard of nce among men if we reckon the "fittest" according to al proportions and strength of appetite. There is a vast stretch n physical and ethical quality. They are not on the same they are not even along the same line, to be reached one after ner in simple progression. They belong to distinct orders of ; there is a chasm between them, and there has been no really fic attempt to bridge it over. There has been no searching is of appetite, tending to prove that it operates naturally s a law of self-denial. The knowledge we have of appetite clearly and exclusively the other way. It presses on to self-ation; when that is found it dies away, but only to revive and prove that it is more clamant, more impatient of restraint. in which passions are regulated and curbed—in which intelli-seeks for some general rule of conduct—in which an ethical s admired and fought for—that is a life which may better be ted in any way rather than this, an evolution from animal life.

sense of scientific weakness and insufficiency here seems to ving Evolutionists on to the second position in their theory tation to environment—as if this were the main point, and better prospects for meeting the ethical tests. Thus it is we ome to hear more of "the interaction of social forces," as if were a willingness to let "survival of the fittest" drop out of or a time; while it is suggested that something nearer the level ical requirements, and giving higher promise for the future, be found in the doctrine that "man is the creature of circum-s." Still in a theory of evolution you cannot separate the two —struggle for life on the part of each, and interaction of out-forces as bearing upon all. And the scientific prospects of the are not in any way improved, but are rather beclouded, by all thers around it under the name of environment. A theory of ion as such must have its essential value in the evolution of g within the living organism itself. At best, we must take we have in the fittest individuals of the species. Environment ly supply outward conditions favourable to the unfolding of has already a germinal existence in the nature of the living And the case is in no degree better when we are referred to the "interaction of *social* forces." Society is but the aggregate of individuals. Any gain there is, is only that of combination. And when Evolutionists supplement their theory by calling in combination, they are deviating by another line from their favourite position concerning the struggle for life and survival of the fittest. They are strengthening a rampart by weakening the foundations. They are betraying a consciousness that combination performs a larger part in determining the life and experience of men than it does amongst lower orders of being. They are so far granting that after having found some advantage at the outset in giving prominence to the individual struggle for life, with selection of the fittest and destruction of the weakest, it becomes needful in unfolding the theory to allow these things to drop out of sight, and give prominence to some agency of a different kind.

But what is this "interaction of social forces?" It must be that which is illustrated in the lower orders of beings by the *gregarious*. That which is most seen among the sheep, and least among the dogs, though the latter have always been favourites with Evolutionists. Our attention is turned on the forces connected with the social element in human life, as that is an advance on the gregarious in animal life. What then is the theoretic value of this element in the process of evolution? How far does it promise to meet ethical requirements left unsatisfied by prior considerations? Beyond doubt, the interaction of social forces plays an important part as affecting the destiny of nations, and of the race as a whole. Account must be made of these forces in all ethical, as in all political, philosophy. On this all persons who give any thought to the matter must be agreed. But the question for an evolution theory is, How far does the play of these forces account for progression from animal life to human, and also for progression in the human race? I have already pointed out how subordinate is the influence of the gregarious in the history of the lower animals, and how obvious it is that the selection of the fittest is the predominant characteristic. I need not insist upon this, inasmuch as the Development Theory owes its whole position to this acknowledged fact. Granting this, it follows that development from animal life to human can draw but slightly for its support on the interaction of social forces.

Suppose, however, that we assume development into human life, with all the advantages of the higher intelligence belonging to the race, what value may we then assign to the interaction of social forces as a factor in human progress? To meet the requirements of the Evolution Theory, this must be allowed to be the main force operating. And if so, it becomes plain—in whatever way it can be vindicated under the theory—that the human race, as presenting the highest order of life, has somehow come to occupy a position, as to the conditions of progression, entirely different from subordinate orders at an earlier stage of development. Passing this, the question now is, How far does the interaction of social forces account for ethical conditions? I reply that the social forces of human life cannot be described without including ethical conditions not accounted for under the theory. We have in human life something more than mere gregariousness, and force of numbers. We have more than sense of common dangers and crowding together so as to gain solidarity for protection. We have more than sense of common attractions, and crowding together for co-operation in order to attain them. If these were all, there could be but a narrow theory of human life, and but a poor prospect for human progression. Human life as a whole would be swayed by the action and reaction of fears and expectations, and these determined by the mass of society, ever prone to be ruled by what is near and pressing, rather than by what may be more remote, but more important and enduring. There is, indeed, enough of this action and reaction in human life, but to say that this constitutes the whole of man is to misread human life, and at the same time to lose sight of the best prospects of our race. Such a theory, without attempting to vindicate itself by competent analysis, disparages worth of inward character, and favours an estimate of men solely by reference to brain and muscle. Under it, benevolence must be translated as meaning co-operation of the multitude for the attainment of a general good not otherwise to be secured, on condition of a division of profits at the end. Whether the individuals in that multitude really wish well to their neighbours, and really will what is good, are matters of which we can make no account—we must take men as we find them, and look only to the main result. We must keep our eye on that, and thence cast the auguries of the future. Well-wishing and practical regard to the good of others are things quite below the surface of the stream, and of no account, provided only the vessel of the State float securely, and carry a valuable cargo. In harmony with this, self-denial in the individual must be translated into a safe road for self-gratification. And when these translations have been made, what has been done, but to prove that the best thoughts of men have been read backwards by the theorist, and the theory proved insufficient to endure the strain of ethical requirements?

I shall say only one thing more. The Development Theory in its *earlier* stage magnifies the individual, in finding the fittest, and looks upon it as matter of course that there must be death for the weakest. In its *later* stage, it magnifies the general or combined life, even in disparagement of individual considerations. And yet it is so far consistent, that the selection of the fittest is for the progression of the species, and regard to the interaction of social forces is also for the general gain. But viewing it in its ethical aspects, and giving to it an ethical meaning so far as this can be done, it contains within it nothing but the barest scraps of material for an individual morality.

It does not affect to be specially concerned with ethical questions, and does not profess to formulate an ethical theory. It is a biological theory, and that alone. But in so far as it points towards a place where it must meet the questionings of intelligence as to an ethical theory, it is preparing the way for a slighter estimate of the individual, a magnifying of the interests of multitudes, and a reduction of what we have hitherto proclaimed as the indefeasible rights of man as man.

And now I close with a few more general considerations. I have been dealing with the question under discussion purely as matter of scientific theory. But theories on this question necessarily exercise influence on the popular mind. And it is only proper that in taking note of the scientific worth, we take some account of the wider popular effects of a theory which professes to give the genesis, and to forecast the destiny, of the human race.

I think it is clearly the practical result of the theory, so far as it finds acceptance, to lower the estimate of individual influence and personal right. It is at the opposite extreme from the theory of hero-worship, and may in a certain light be regarded as a reaction against that theory. And, as commonly happens in the history of reaction, it inclines decidedly to an opposite extreme. Its tendency is not to float, as by a rising tide, the great and best elements of individuality, and carry them on the centre of the stream, but to swamp and absorb them in the tide of force when a present and common interest is to be served. And, as each theory is born to suit the times, it is not to be overlooked that there are powerful social influences at work in the midst of all the nations of modern civilization, which show too decided an admiration of force, and too slight a regard for personal rights. It is well to speak of "*social duty* being raised to a higher significance." But if it be social duty alone which is magnified, and if it be treated or made to appear as if social duty were the sum of duty, the very ends sincerely and earnestly aimed at by those who exalt social duty will be lost. In eliminating the grander features of individual life, we prevent the manifestation of a higher individualism; and we sacrifice that most desirable of results, the combination of individuals with the intelligent design of seeking a higher ideal of social life on the type of a lofty ideal of individual life.

H. CALDERWOOD.

# HEREDITARY PAUPERISM AND PAUPER EDUCATION.

THE saying of Emerson, that "consistency is the hobgoblin of little minds," is doubtless true, in the sense that persons of narrow and consequently stubborn make will often be found ready to sacrifice anything, even conscience and truth, for the sake of being consistent. There is nothing they are more anxious to avoid than any appearance of contradicting themselves. But miserable as is this exhibition of little-mindedness, it is hardly less distressing to observe at times the complacent inconsistencies of better natures; their easy unconsciousness of the contradictions existing between principle and practice, as exemplified in their enthusiasms and earnest enterprises.

How indifferent, if not insensible, we English people are for the most part to those fluctuations of feeling, and those oppositions of sentiment or impulse, that may perhaps be said to characterize us, impelling the nation, now to bursts of almost Quixotic benevolence, and again to courses of active injustice and selfishness! The same complacent inconsistency appears often in other forms, as, for instance, in the provisions of some of our Acts of Parliament, or in the way in which these are applied and carried out; and a striking example of it is presented in the national arrangements for the education of the poorer classes of the community.

The Elementary Education Act of 1870, the result of long discussion and earnest consideration, secured for the children of the poorest a system of excellent instruction, the advantages of which it, at the same time, compelled the parents to accept. The principal portion of the cost of this elaborate system is defrayed out of the rates and taxes; and the burden, falling lightly enough on those immediately benefited, is very heavily felt by not a few belonging to the classes who, as a matter of fact, receive no direct benefit from the Board and State-supported schools.

Such persons find themselves placed in this anomalous position, that they are providing out of their hard earnings, with money which they can often ill afford to spare, far greater educational advantages for the children of others than they are able to secure for their own; the sole justification of an arrangement so apparently unfair being that the education of the lower strata of the poor is now recognized as a matter of importance, not merely in their own interest, but in the interest of the public.

It is generally admitted to be a national danger that any portion of the community should be allowed to remain in ignorance, and especially the children of destitute and demoralized parents, whose rescue and suitable instruction we have now learnt to regard as of the utmost moment for society. In addition, moreover, to the conviction that ignorance is one of the greatest promoters of vice, pauperism, and crime, we are beginning to feel that if competing nations are permitted to excel us in the education of the masses, our commercial position may come in time to be seriously affected, and there may be a danger of our losing the wealth which has hitherto flowed from our superiority in those arts and manufactures in which the intelligence of the workman tells.

Without denying that considerations of this kind may at times have been unduly pressed and have led to exaggerated fears, there is undoubtedly a large amount of truth in them, and we may congratulate ourselves upon any effect they have had in securing educational provision for the poorer classes of our countrymen at the public expense. But the practical acknowledgment of their force renders it the more incomprehensible and unpardonable that our legislature should have allowed one large class of children already under its control, and the class which perhaps most needs raising, to be excluded, not indeed from ordinary instruction, but from that particular education and training which is undoubtedly requisite for its elevation.

It must surely be perceived that if any one class requires more assistance than another, in order that it may be enabled to overcome its unhappy circumstances and to rise above the melancholy condition in which it has been placed by birth, it is that of pauper children. Yet in the case of the great majority of these, including the destitute orphans of the respectable poor, little effort has been made to promote their future welfare. We find, for instance, that while on the 1st of January, 1876, there were 48,511 pauper children in England and Wales, 40,000 of these were still in workhouses and receiving education in pauper schools, whilst 8,000 only were otherwise provided for in District Schools, or by being boarded out in Cottage Homes. In other words, of 48,000 children over whom the State had full control, 40,000 were being trained for a life of pauperism, surrounded with pauper associations, and exposed to all the contaminating influence of daily intercourse with bad and vicious characters.

Those best qualified to judge have repeatedly insisted that the pauper taint, once imbibed, is never thoroughly eradicated; that children brought up in connection with the workhouse lose all horror of the place, and are always lamentably deficient in that spirit of independence which is the greatest stimulus to exertion; and that nothing more degrades the character, in every way, than the pauper sentiment and temperament which the workhouse invariably induces.

It may here be noted that the influence of the poorhouse has proved itself no less baneful in the New World than in the Old. Not long since, at a time when labour was scarce and valuable, and the excuse of want of employment could not be pleaded, an hereditary pauper class was revealed in the United States of America as growing up wherever a workhouse had been erected. The Secretary of the State of New York Charities, in one of his reports, thus writes: "I visited one poorhouse in the western part of the State, in which there were four generations of females, all of whom were immoral women and confirmed paupers." We also find Professor Dwight stating, in a report on the county poorhouses, "that he found one of the most terrible diseases which can affect a country (hereditary pauperism) had begun to break out in the rural districts through the influence of the poorhouse." England is already suffering bitterly from this terrible disease, so justly dreaded by those free from it; and yet, with unaccountable infatuation, its rulers are perpetuating it by their unwise treatment of the children of the destitute poor. The persistency of the authorities, in this perverse course, is the more remarkable, since several well-tried and efficient methods are already in operation by which these pauper children might, at little, if any, extra cost, be so trained and educated as to cut off from them the sad entail and curse of their birth.

The question as to the best way of training pauper children has been more than once brought prominently before the public notice, but it has turned so much upon the comparative advantages of the Boarding-out and District School systems, that many, probably, even of those who take an interest in the matter, will be surprised to find how little either of these systems is resorted to, and that the workhouse is still the place in which the great majority of pauper children are being reared.

In the Report of the Local Government Board for 1876, we learn, from page xxxiv, that out of 32,943 attending school, there were only 5,817 attending District, as against 27,126 attending Workhouse or separate pauper schools:* we gather also, that on the 1st of January, 1876, the total number of indoor children was 48,511, so that in addition to the 27,126 at school in connection with the workhouses,

* The latest Local Government Board Report, issued October, 1877, states that at Lady-day, 1876, there were 5,582 children attending District Schools, as against 26,492 attending Workhouse, or Separate Pauper Schools.

there were 15,568 *in* the workhouses, to be included in that large number of children whom the State is thus carefully training to perpetuate the hereditary pauper caste with all the degradation, immorality, and waste inseparably belonging to it.

It is universally agreed on the part of those who have given careful attention to the subject,—whatever their differing opinions on other systems,—that no mode of bringing up young children is so bad as placing them in any connection with a workhouse. We find, for instance, in the journal of the Workhouse Visiting Society, a statement, by one of the Matrons, to the effect "that of 300 orphan children whom she had known brought up in this way, she did not believe one was doing well." Again, in the same journal it is stated "that out of 180 young persons who left Cork Workhouse, 60 returned within a brief period." And in Miss Florence Hill's book, "Children of the State," it is said that "out of 165 girls who had been apprenticed, from one workhouse, only 18 were reported as doing well; and that within three years 75 returned to it."

Such testimonies might be multiplied almost to any extent, but it is unnecessary, since public attention has already, from time to time, been called to them, while but slight defence of the system has ever been made by any person of authority. There is, indeed, considerable difficulty in understanding the persistent adherence to a practice, in condemnation of which so much has been advanced, and on behalf of which apparently so little can be said.

One thing, however, is certain, that if the people of England at all realized what the word *pauperism* implies, and what life in a poorhouse really signifies, they would at once cease to endure so complacently the sad prevalence of the former, and immediately demand that not another child should, in future, be brought up under the influence of the latter.

If we may judge from the general apathy prevailing on the subject, the popular idea, with regard to paupers, would seem to be that they are unfortunates, who, having become too old or too ill to work, receive charitable support out of the rates and taxes, and that poorhouses are places of comparative comfort where any unhappy "Lazarus" may find the refuge he needs and deserves, and at the same time spare "Dives" the annoyance and pain of seeing him daily at his gate full of sores.

But if the truth were more fully known, it would be found that in few, if any, instances, has the actual workhouse any resemblance to this ideal; that it is, on the contrary, a moral pest-house, which true charity should either abolish altogether, or at least reserve for the few whom it is compelled to regard as moral incurables, if any such there are; and with respect to the practical effects of a thorough and wide revelation of the truth, of one thing, surely, we might be confident, that it would rouse the community to forbid, in unmistakable tones, any [illegible] in the unwholesome workhouse atmosphere, of [illegible] lives which bereavement, or other crushing [illegible] upon the public charge, and whose future [illegible] upon the nurture the State provides for them.

[illegible] and design of the existing poorhouse are such [illegible] inevitably be more or less degrading. It is [illegible] irrespective of character, every destitute person can [illegible] and sustenance, and must needs, therefore, [illegible] numbers of the dissolute, the idle, and the [illegible] last home of the drunkard whose intemperance has [illegible] premature decay; the retreat of the lazy tramp who [illegible]; the final lodging of the abandoned woman [illegible] have driven from the streets; in a word the [illegible] which the drains and dregs of our population trickle. [illegible] as these we find a sprinkling of decent poor, who, [illegible] and starved till they can work and starve no longer, [illegible] at length to submit to this fate, which to them is as [illegible] undeserved.

[illegible] extracts from the writings of a lady who had [illegible] during a long course of visitation, the sufferings which [illegible] poor undergo in poorhouses, may present the subject [illegible] a new light, and will, at any rate, justify the urgency of [illegible] continually protest against the present system. It must [illegible] that, although the book was written for the purpose [illegible] treatment especially for the *sick* and *aged*, the [illegible] are not the less relevant to the question immediately [illegible] all authorities agree that it is impossible completely to [illegible] and children when under the same roof, even during [illegible] a rule, the same infirmary is common to both, so that [illegible] description of workhouse life applies to the children [illegible] adults.

[illegible]," says this writer, "of the respectable poor to go to the [illegible] need be a matter of very little surprise, on account of the intense [illegible] at the pauper nurses, and the mixing up of the vilest cha- [illegible] more respectable poor. . . . There were, by day and night, [illegible], in some of those sick rooms, which made them a hell upon [illegible] of the pauper nurses were as wicked and violent as the worst [illegible]; these pauper nurses being always present when the matron or [illegible] passed through the wards, any complaint from the victims of [illegible] would have brought the most savage reprisals from them, and, as [illegible] were hard to find, they knew that they would, even then, only be [illegible] not removed."

[illegible] further speaks of "the outcries of fearful language [illegible] in one room after another;" and then, after describing [illegible] as "women for the most part of ruined character, [illegible], living in an atmosphere of disease day and night, [illegible] they hated for bare food and clothing, their only hope being an occasional day out, when the poor wretches nearly always came back tipsy," the writer concludes thus:—

"The assortment of strange bedfellows, in a workhouse ward, is such as poverty and the Poor-law could alone bring together; men in convict-looking clothing are sitting on the sides of the beds; faces are amongst them on which one dare not look again. Strong, bad men are dying here, after lives of sin and shame, wild animals tracked to their lair, dying, savage to the last. Children are here; the little pale-faced boy of ten years old has been two years in that bed; the dying tramp lies quiet beside him; a burglar is in one bed, in the next a boy of sixteen with an innocent face."

She thus sums up:—

"A workhouse is a place where we find *childhood without its joys*, youth without its hope, age without its honour; a place the sight of which, more than anything else, tries our faith in the ultimate triumph of good over evil."

These sentences show how little the poorhouse has changed since Crabbe wrote regarding it:—

"There children dwell who know no parent's care,
Parents who know no children's love dwell there,
Heart-broken matrons in their joyless bed,
Forsaken wives and mothers never wed;
Dejected widows with unheeded tears,
And crippled age with more than childhood's fears,
The lame, the blind, and, far the happiest they,
The moping idiot, and the madman gay."

The following incident, recently related to the secretary of the Society for Promoting the Boarding-out of Pauper Children, will furnish another illustration of the feeling with which the respectable poor regard "life in the house." A woman of excellent character had lost her husband by an accident, and was left with five young children. She was of course quite unable, without assistance, to maintain so large a family, and applied to the Guardians for out-door relief. The chairman, however, told her that as they gave no out-door relief to able-bodied women, they could only offer her and her children the house. She then requested to know what constituted an able-bodied woman, to which the chairman replied, "Having all your joints right, and health to use them." On receiving this answer the woman retired, but presently returned, and, handing to the chairman something wrapped in a piece of paper, claimed *out*-door relief, as now she was not able-bodied. The paper was found, on examination, to contain the end of her finger, which she had deliberately chopped off, to save herself from being degraded and her children ruined by life in the workhouse.

This woman, without doubt, displayed a martyr's spirit in thus mutilating herself for her children's sake. It would be unjust, however, to condemn the Guardians for the consequence of their refusal, since severe restrictions on out-door relief are absolutely necessary to avoid imposture; our condemnation should rather fall on the woman's rich neighbours and the Christian Churches who failed to help her in her hour of need, and still more on the supporters of a system that provides no means, except the workhouse, by which the mother might, by being relieved of the charge of some of her children, be enabled to maintain the rest of her fatherless offspring by her honest labour.

The inconsistent conduct of the State in regard to pauper children will again appear, if we contrast its treatment of these young persons, many of whom, it must be remembered, are the orphan children of respectable parents, with the elaborate system that has been established for *reclaiming* juvenile criminals in reformatories, and for saving semi-criminal children, by maintaining them in Industrial Schools.

According to the latest Government Report, there are in England and Scotland 65 Reformatory Schools, in which each child costs on an average about £19, against an average cost of £12 in pauper orphan wards; there are also 118 Industrial Schools, in which the average cost of the inmates is about £16. It is a great mystery why the State should be so much more generous in its expenditure where the object to be attained is the reclamation of those who have gone wrong, than it is on behalf of the innocent who need to be guarded and saved from going wrong: why the work of preventing evil that threatens, should be practically treated as of inferior moment to the work of curing the evil when it has come to pass. The law provides its criminal youth with all the advantages of a model school, but immures its innocent wards in a workhouse home; it takes pains to secure these from contaminating associations, but leaves these to herd with the children of thieves, tramps, and vagabonds, exposes them to the peril of association with adults of the most vicious and depraved character, and at last sends them out into the wide world—without experience, without a friend—marked with the indelible pauper stamp. Is it to be wondered at if they speedily become absorbed in that criminal and worthless class for which they have been thus so carefully qualified? But such treatment of the fatherless and orphan is as cruel as it is needless, and as opposed to the Christian spirit, as it is to all patriotism and common sense.

It is only just to state that both Mr. Sclater-Booth and Mr. J. G. Goschen, during their presidency at the Local Government Board, endeavoured to alter this system, but, unfortunately, the ignorance and prejudice of many of the Guardians of the Poor defeated every effort towards reform; and little improvement can be hoped for till these Boards are brought to reason by our legislature making it illegal for any children to remain, except for a limited period, under the same roof with adult paupers; then, and not till then, will the majority of the Guardians be induced to bestir themselves and to adopt a better system.

There are three alternative methods of bringing up pauper children which have been tried with success; each has some special advantages to recommend it, and all are in every way superior to the workhouse. The first plan has been already, to a considerable extent, adopted in London and some other large towns, viz., that of the District Schools, under which the children are reared together in great numbers, and in large buildings erected generally outside the towns. The chief promoter of this scheme was Mr. Tufnell, so long and honourably known as an Inspector under the Local Government Board; and the rather bitter controversy between this gentleman and the late excellent Mrs. Nassau Senior, in consequence of the latter having reported unfavourably as to the working of the plan of congregating pauper children, especially girls, in such large masses, was recently published by the Local Government Board, and at the time attracted considerable attention. The facts brought out in this discussion would appear to indicate that there are peculiar dangers, both physical and moral, in collecting together large numbers of children belonging to one, and that the lowest class; that in the case of boys, however, these dangers may be guarded against by thorough and close supervision, and a generally satisfactory result attained; but that in the case of girls, who, from the very constitution of their nature, require more individual consideration, not to say affection, than can possibly be shown them in these large institutions, the result is often disappointing. Moreover, the routine of their daily life, and the machinery by which, in most cases, every domestic arrangement and industrial work, such as cooking and washing, is carried out, is a bad preparation for a future life of domestic service. There is also a danger lest any slight neglect may produce widespread and serious harm; such as those outbreaks of disease, especially ophthalmia, which have been so frequent in these institutions. Another great drawback to large District Schools is, that after the pupils have left them, they are, unless in exceptional cases, where the chaplain happens to be peculiarly devoted to his work, speedily lost sight of, and have no home to return to, and no friend from whom to seek advice and guidance at the most critical time of their lives.

But in addition to these drawbacks, the question of expense is a very serious one; the extensive buildings cost much, not only in the first outlay on their erection, but afterwards in keeping them in due repair; while the expense of the children's maintenance in them is so great, that nothing can justify its infliction on the ratepayers, unless it is proved that no other satisfactory method of dealing with this class is available.*

There is also a fear lest these handsome buildings with playgrounds, workshops, swimming-baths, bands of music, and abundance of food and clothing, should tempt struggling parents to throw themselves on the rates, in order to secure such advantages for their offspring. A tendency to seek to get rid of their children at the public cost has

* According to a recent Government Report, the comparative cost per child ranges from £16 10s. in Mile End school to £36 16s. 2*d.* in St. Pancras.

[illegible] among a certain class of the poor, in connection [illegible] Schools, which are somewhat similar in constitution [illegible] Schools. Parents have often been found endeavouring [illegible] children uncontrollable, to gain them admittance into [illegible] strong measures will be necessary to check the development [illegible] vil.

[illegible] w come to the second plan, that of boarding out the children [illegible] e homes. It consists in selecting respectable persons among the [illegible] classes and placing one, or at the most two, children to board [illegible] n. This method, wherever it has been carried out under the [illegible] provisions of an order issued by the Local Government [illegible] uring Mr. Goschen's presidency, has worked well, and for the [illegible] a real attachment has sprung up between the children and [illegible] er-parents, which has continued after the former have gone [illegible] the world. Mr. Goschen's order provides that when children [illegible] ed out *beyond* their own parish, a committee of two or more [illegible] sides the Poor-law officer, shall become responsible, first that [illegible] s are suitable, and secondly that the children are well cared [illegible] properly educated at some public elementary school. It [illegible] ly be said that, in addition to other advantages, the advice [illegible] ance of those ladies who have learnt to take an interest in the [illegible] during their early years, has proved most valuable, especially [illegible] n their first start in life, and has, without doubt, been the [illegible] saving many from ruin. The reports from the Guardians [illegible] or, in those parts of England where this system has been [illegible] are most encouraging, and may be said to afford a fair test [illegible] ue, since they come from such representative parishes as [illegible] am, Malvern, Worcester, Clifton, and Dartford.

[illegible] prejudice has, from time to time, been excited against the [illegible] -out system, by the occurrence of some sad cases of cruelty [illegible] ect which attracted a good deal of public attention. It [illegible] ound, however, on examination, that wherever these have [illegible] as in the recent case in Cheshire, the children had been [illegible] out without proper safeguards and supervision, which the [illegible] ppily permits to be done, so long as the children remain [illegible] parish boundary, a neglect which cannot be too strongly [illegible] ed, and should be immediately provided against, since inde- [illegible] upervision is equally essential to the safety of the children [illegible] hey are boarded out within or without the parish.

[illegible] be admitted that this system has, as yet, been only tried in [illegible] to a limited extent, but in Scotland it has been long in force, [illegible] the happiest results, and is now universally adopted there. [illegible] ount of its working will be found in an interesting book by [illegible] on, called "The Boarding-out System in Scotland."* Mr. [illegible], the Scotch Poor-law Inspector, also bears strong testimony

* Published by Blackwood & Sons, London and Edinburgh.

to its value, and in his Report states, that out of 923 children boarded out by the Glasgow Union only 40 have been lost sight of, and only 5 per cent. have failed. Similar testimony is borne by Mr. Greig, the Clerk to the Edinburgh Parochial Board. "It is," he says, "a rare thing for a child brought up thus to become afterwards chargeable to the parish." If those in authority would compare the results of this system with those that follow workhouse training, they would find that the moral advantages of the former are immense, while even the saving in the cost is considerable.*

The principal objection urged against the plan is that there is no reasonable prospect, in England, either of finding suitable homes, or the required supervision; this objection, however, has not been sustained by experience, which shows that wherever the system has been fairly tried, and wherever real efforts have been made to obtain them, both homes and proper supervision have been forthcoming. Should it, however, prove true that, in some localities, this difficulty exists, or that, for other reasons, such as the age of the children, Boarding-out is undesirable, there is a third system in operation which, from the success that has attended it, is well worthy of attention. This may be described as the Village Home, or Mettray system; it is to some extent already known to the public by the establishment of the Princess Mary Village Homes, and by the still larger establishment near Tours, in France, the latter, however, being only for the reformation of juvenile criminals. This system consists in bringing up the children, in small numbers, in separate but grouped cottage homes, so that the heads of each house, called parents, can exercise direct personal influence over the minds of all the inmates, and thus the life of the children is made to resemble home life as closely as possible. At Mettray, a village of such homes, the children attend a common day-school, and the whole village is under the careful supervision of one head, whilst industrial training and general education are equally attended to. One striking proof of the success of the plan is that in many cases the children and the so-called parents become so attached that the former frequently return to visit their homes in after-years, and the result of the training there, though exercised only on criminal children, may, when compared with the result of our treatment of those who are only destitute, cause us both shame and regret. It is stated in the official reports that, previously to this plan being adopted, 49 per cent. of the children once convicted relapsed into crime, while under it the relapses have for some time past been only 4 per cent. 4,500 youths have passed through Mettray, 850 being the children of criminals, 1,400 illegitimate, 580 the children of second marriages, and 850 being orphans. Of these, half have become agricultural labourers, one-fourth mechanics, and the remainder have joined the army and navy

* The cost is about £11 to £13 for those boarded out, as against £13 to £17 per child in Union and Pauper Schools.

of France. If such results can be obtained with children mostly of the lowest class, and already convicted of crime, how much might be hoped for by the adoption, in England, of a similar system of training and education for our pauper children?

Hereditary pauperism is at once a disgrace and a curse to our country, and, though now so prevalent, might soon be almost, if not entirely, extinguished by wiser treatment; for the more the causes of its prevalence are investigated, the more clearly does it appear that nothing contributes to it more largely than that wretched workhouse system which has so long been suffered among us; and which not only fails to aid, but positively hinders our pauper children from ever rising above the degradation of their birth.

The Local Government Report, October, 1877, shows that on the 1st July, 1876, there were 707,375 paupers in England and Wales, costing the country £7,335,858. It is difficult to say, for certain, how much of this pauperism arises from our present method of rearing pauper children, but the proportion is, undoubtedly, very large. The loss and discredit of such a state of things is only a just retribution upon the nation for the want of common sense and common charity exhibited in its treatment of those poor orphans, whose additional misfortune it is that they have been left to the tender mercies of this most Christian people, and have thus become hopeless and hapless paupers, by becoming the children of the English State.

FRANCIS PEEK.

[NOTE.—Since this article was written, the *Globe* of the 14th November contains the report of a case decided by the Sedgley magistrates, which shows how little security the sick poor have against ill-treatment when in the workhouse, and sadly illustrates the truth of the facts quoted above, from the book published by Bell & Daldy, "Sick and in Prison:"—

"Among the inmates of the workhouse at Upper Gornah, is a miserable old pauper seventy-five years of age, blind, dumb, paralyzed, and bedridden. People might have well imagined that a poor creature like this would have been sure of kind treatment, but one of the wardsmen named Povey, without any apparent provocation, fell upon this bedridden paralytic one night, and beat him so severely with a leather strap that there was some doubt next morning whether death would not result from the injuries. For this conduct the wardsman was brought before the magistrates at Sedgley, and the facts being proved, he could offer no more valid defence than that 'the old man had made a noise.' Whether this was the case or not, there could not be the slightest question that Povey had acted with shocking cruelty, and the bench therefore imposed the maximum punishment they had it in their power to award—two months with hard labour."]

# THE GREEK MIND IN PRESENCE OF DEATH,

## INTERPRETED FROM RELIEFS AND INSCRIPTIONS ON ATHENIAN TOMBS.

AT Athens the grave-stones of the ancient inhabitants are not only among the most interesting, but among the most extensive remains. Near Piræus, through all the Ceramicus, and in many other parts of the city, excavations have constantly brought to light a vast quantity of inscribed and sculptured slabs and columns, which have mostly, unlike antiquities of many other classes, remained at Athens, and now fill one wing of the new museum and the whole space in front. But there is a group of grave-stones of even greater interest which are left standing, just where they were disinterred, by the old road which led through the gate Dipylon, from Athens to Eleusis, the road annually trodden by the procession at the Eleusinia. These tombs, in size and beauty superior to the rest, are preserved for us, as is supposed, by a fortunate chance.* Sulla, when he attacked Athens and remorselessly massacred the miserable inhabitants, made his approach close to the gate Dipylon. There he erected the long *aggeres* by which his engines were brought close to the wall, and there his soldiers threw down several hundred yards of the city ramparts, which were formed of sun-baked bricks. Hence a vast mass of ruin which completely overwhelmed and buried the lines of tombs immediately without the gate, and preserved them almost uninjured until one day when they were once more brought to the light by a French archæological expedition in the year 1863. The suddenness with which these monuments were overwhelmed is indicated by the fact that some of them were and remain unfinished; the completeness of their disappearance is proved by the silence of Pausanias the traveller, who, passing through all quarters of Athens in the time of the Antonines, would appear to have seen no trace of them. All of the monuments

* See F. Lenormant's Voie Eleusinienne, vol. i.

in this group are of course indubitably Athenian, and furnish the best materials for the present paper. Of the stones in the museum it is sometimes impossible to trace the find-spot; some are Bœotian, some from Peloponnesus, some from the Islands. But this uncertainty need not debar us from freely referring to almost any as instances, for there is no great or essential difference between Athenian and other gravestones. It will be quite fair to treat, for the present purpose, all monuments preserved at Athens as Athenian, unless they be known to have come from a distance. Of the longer inscriptions a large proportion are from the tombs of foreign residents at Athens.

To the readers who are likely to peruse these pages, there are but two points in grave-stones likely to prove very interesting—firstly, the reliefs which they bear;* secondly, the inscriptions engraven on them.

The earliest of Athenian sepulchral monuments, if we leave out of account buildings like the Cyclopean tombs of Mycenæ, or mounds like those recently opened with such splendid results at Spata, in Attica, is the often-cited stêlê of Aristion. It represents the deceased on a scale somewhat larger than life, as standing clad in full armour, spear in hand. The ground of the relief is red; traces of colour may be seen, or rather might at the time of discovery be seen, on many parts of the body, and holes may be observed made by the pegs which fastened armour of bronze on to the body. The design or idea of this slab differs not much from that of a portrait statue. Clearly in early Greek times, for this statue is given to the very beginning of the fifth century B.C., the survivors wished to see in the monument the dead, as it were, still living among them, still to be seen in his daily dress, and about his daily business.

But it is from the fourth and succeeding centuries before the Christian era, that we inherit the great mass of the sculptured tombstones which crowd the museums. No one can spend a few hours among these without perceiving that the representations fall naturally into four or five classes.

The first class and the most extensive consists of formal groups wanting in distinctive character, which display the dead either alone or in company with others. The companions, where there are such, are sometimes other members of the family, sometimes slaves or attendants, who, in accordance with the well-known canon of Greek art, which gives larger stature to the person of more importance, are always represented as of diminutive size. Sometimes the companion is not a person at all, but a favourite animal, a pet dog or bird. Such subjects are common in Macedonian times. The grouping is usually simple and graceful, the attitudes natural and unforced, the

* On the subject of these reliefs there is no complete work, but several monographs, the best of which are those of Friedländer and Pervanoglu. Where my own notes fail I have quoted the descriptions of the latter writer.

movements, if movement there be, measured. But the execution is not of the best, save in a few remarkable cases, and there is a want of invention, nay, there is even vulgarity, in the designs. Like our modern photographers, the inferior Greek artists who condescended to this kind of work had a few cardinal notions as to possibilities of arrangement, and could not easily be induced to depart from them. I will give the details of a few reliefs of this class. (1.) A seated lady, who with her left hand holds the end of the veil which covers her face; before her stands a man, facing her. (2.) A pair of sisters, Demetria and Pamphile. Pamphile is seated, and turns her head towards the spectator; with her right hand she grasps the end of her veil. Demetria stands over against her, her right hand folded across her breast, and grasps her veil with her left hand. (3.) A man clad in long *himation* stands, in his hand a scroll. In front of him stands a small male figure, naked, holding a vessel, perhaps an oil-flask. The scroll which the master holds and the flask of the slave seem here to have as little meaning as the books and the flower-baskets of photographic rooms. (4.) A mother clad in flowing Ionian drapery is seated to left. Her left hand rests on the seat; with her right she lifts something from a little toilette-box which a servant holds out. Round her knees clings a little girl. (5.) A lad stands clasping to his breast a bird which a snake at his feet threatens and springs upward to reach. In other reliefs we find a dog in the place of the snake; sometimes a dog is standing elsewhere in the picture. Tame birds would seem to have been the usual playmates of Athenian children, and tame dogs the constant companions of young men, while in many houses a favourite which would be rarely appreciated in England, a snake, was nurtured.

As this is the commonest class of reliefs, so evidently it is the least original and interesting. Here most is left to the sorry invention and feeble sympathy of the sculptor, who knew nought of the deceased, and allows us to know no more than could be ascertained from the sources of information which among the old Greeks corresponded to the first column of the *Times* or the pages of Burke with us. But it is by no means rare to find on sepulchral slabs a more exact reference to the past life or the habits of the dead. Sometimes we are told more than the bare fact that the departed was father, mother, wife, or sister—was young, old, or in the prime of life. I select the following:—(1.) A youth, naked, or wearing the light chlamys only, stands holding in his hand the strigil and oil-flask, those invariable accompaniments of gymnastic exercises among the Greeks. No doubt the survivors, who chose the design, wished to indicate that their friend was prominent in manly sports and labours. In this, the field of his best energies, [illegible] wished him still to seem to live. (2.) A young man, clad in a [illegible] charges with spear advanced a wild boar, which is coming [illegible] lair; at his side is a dog, which leaps forward at the [illegible]

... We see at a glance that this is the tomb of ... the chase. (3.) On a rock sits a man in an attitude ... the sea, and on it a boat with or without sailors. ...ly received opinion that monuments of this character ... over those who had been wrecked at sea. (4.) A young ... in the light chlamys of the Athenian cavalry, charges, at ... beneath his horse's hoofs and transfixing with his spear ...e, who tries in vain with his shield to ward off the attack of ... enemy. From the accompanying inscription we know ... monument was erected in honour of Dexilaus, one of the five ... at Corinth—that is to say, as is supposed, one of the five ... who fell in the battle under the walls of Corinth, in which ...nians were engaged in the year B.C. 394. The relief thus ...ost from the best time of Attic art, and it is worthy of its ... does not, of course, represent the moment of the death of ...g warrior; we see him strong and triumphant, such as his ...ould fain have seen him always; to show him fallen would ...ed an enemy rather than a friend. (5.) Another relief, although ... honour of a man of Ascalon, is clearly of Athenian handi... d design. A sleeping man rests on a couch. Close to his ...s on its hind-paws a lion, who is clearly ready to slay or carry ... On the other side of the couch is a warrior who attacks and ... beast. In the background appears the prow of a ship. From ... metrical inscription which accompanies this relief, it would ...hat the Phoenician stranger here buried had incurred great ...ome previous period of his life from the attack of a lion, who ... have surprised him resting on the shore, but who was driven ...e timely arrival of friends just landed from their ship. (6.) ...d his wife, both muffled in ample garments, advance towards ...ator. Between them advances a priestess of Isis, clad in the ...er calling, holding in her right hand the sistrum, in her left ... of sacred water. It is possible, the inscriptions which ...ny this representation being illegible, that the monument was ...o a father and mother, and to their daughter devoted to Isis. ...ssible that we have here expressed in a symbolical form the ... of a man and woman to that mysterious worship which ... Ptolemaic times from the bank of the Nile over all lands, ... firm trust that in the next world Isis would recognize and ...er worshippers.

...re a few specimens of the reliefs which give us more precise ... with regard to the lives and habits of the dead. In the ... those who had devoted themselves to a profession appear ... with the badges of that profession; physicians, for ... the cupping-glass and other instruments of their daily ... priestesses of Apollo and Aphrodite appear with the ... guardian deities. And in this matter it is clear that the Athenians merely followed one of the most natural of all [illegible] leading to a custom common among all nations. Thus in the Odyssey the ghost of the drowned oarsman, Elpenor, begs Ulysses, when he reaches the island of Æsea:—

> "Raise thou a tomb upon the shore beside the hoary sea,
> Memorial of my blighted life for future times to be;
> Make thou my tomb beside the sea, and on it fix the oar,
> Which once among my comrades dear, while yet I lived, I bore."

And thus, even in our own day, what device is commoner on a soldier's grave than sword and cannon, or on a painter's than palette and brush?

But although the sculptors of tombs usually designed references to the past life of those they commemorated, such was not always the case. After all, past was past, and it were idle to deny that the moment of death brought a vast change over everything. The next class of reliefs have reference to the fact and the moment of death. Among the Romans that fact was symbolized in art frequently by sleep; and among all Christian nations it has become usual to speak of death in metaphorical language borrowed from the rest of night. But it was not usually merely as a deeper sleep that death presented itself to the imagination of Athenian sculptors. They considered death rather as a departure, a going far away from and losing sight of one's family and friends. Scenes of leave-taking are among the most frequent of all sepulchral reliefs. I am not, however, sure that this leave-taking is quite consciously adopted as the image of death. Indeed, all images of death were somewhat distasteful to the joyous sensuousness of Athenian taste. But when an artist had to represent the dead and the surviving friends of the dead in a group, this posture of farewell, which must have been one of the most usual and natural to think of, seems to have frequently suggested itself, and, in virtue of its inherent appropriateness to the occasion, to have become more and more common. This leave-taking presents itself in the least intrusive and gentlest form in those representations where a lady appears dressing herself with the assistance of her maids for an out-door journey, throwing over her head the ample veil, and perhaps handing to an attendant nurse the babe whom she cannot take out into the open air with her. Sometimes the preparations are more advanced; the lady sits or stands veiled and prepared for a journey, and gives her hand to husband or father who stands opposite. Sometimes two men grasp hands as if about to travel in different directions. Occasionally a horse appears in the background, or the head of a horse is seen through a window, which is destined to carry away the master of the house. In this very introduction of the [illegible] how much the notion of travel preponderates in the [illegible] that of death. For the [illegible] in no [illegible] Greeks with death [illegible] introduced to the popular imagination by the writer of the Apocalypse, who must have borrowed from a non-Hellenic source. Dwelling closely hemmed in by the sea, they never thought of the dead as travelling to other worlds by land, but usually as going over the waves mysterious and vast to some distant island, or perhaps as penetrating into deep abysses of the land. But for journeys from town to town in Hellas, the horse was the appropriate conveyer, from which fact he becomes the symbol of all moving and journeying.

The old opinion of archæologists with regard to these scenes of farewell, an opinion grounded on insufficient induction, was that in them the dead were represented as seated, the survivors as standing and taking leave of them. It is now acknowledged that this is not the case. It is true that most commonly in the groups one is seated, while of the standing figures one grasps his or her hand. But a careful study of the accompanying inscriptions proves that it is sometimes the dead person who stands while the survivor sits; and again, in other cases both the dead and the living stand, while sometimes, again, of the several dead persons commemorated some stand and some are seated. The fact is that any pedantic rule of uniformity is put out of the question by the circumstances under which sepulchral reliefs were designed and executed. It was essential to the composition of a group, thought the artists, that some of the figures should stand and others sit; but the question which should do each was settled, not by a desire to convey a careful meaning to the eyes of beholders, but by the study of a little graceful variety, within somewhat narrow limits, and the influence of every-day custom which made it far more natural and usual that a woman should be seated when taking leave of a man, than a man when taking leave of a woman. Sometimes a little life breaks in on the cold formality of the group. Children cling about their mother's knee, or daughters stand by in an attitude betokening their grief; but those circumstances which might move emotion in the spectator are quite banished or kept sedulously in the background. Here, as ever, the Greek abode by that motto, "Nothing in extremes," which expresses the ultimate law of all his art.

Another set of representations introduce us to a scene of banqueting.* (1.) A man reclines on a couch in the posture adopted by the Greeks at their meals; before him a three-legged table. Near his head sits a woman on a chair, holding in her hand the end of her veil. (2.) Similar two figures appear to those in the last relief, but in addition there is in the foreground a slave pouring wine from a larger into a smaller vessel. (3.) A man reclining at table holds a cup in his right hand; near him sits his wife, behind whom is a slave pouring wine

* M. Albert Dumont has published a volume on this class of monuments; the work has been crowned by the French Institute, but I have been unable to find a copy in English libraries.

from an amphora. Behind the couch stands a draped bearded figure; beneath it is a dog gnawing at some fragment of food. In the place of this dog we elsewhere find a snake. (4.) Two men recline side by side on a couch; in front of one is a three-legged table laden with food. At the two extremities of the couch sit two women. In the foreground is a galley, of which the oars, but not the rowers, are visible, in which is seated a weird figure with matted locks, clad in a short rough cloak, who stretches his hand towards one of the reclining banqueters. This latter figure has usually been taken for the ferryman of the dead, Charon, come to claim the feasters as his passengers into the next world. In scenes of this character, also, it is not unusual to find in the background a horse, or at least the head of one; here, too, the coming journey throws its shadow over the group.

With the sculptures of this class are frequently associated a set of representations, which would seem to have something more than a casual connection with them, though the exact nature of such connection is very obscure. I refer to the *ex voto* tablets commonly set up in Greek temples by those who had escaped from disease, peril, or death, in honour of the deity to whom they attributed their deliverance, and for a lasting memorial of their gratitude. Such tablets have been found in special abundance in the *temeni*, sacred to Hades or Sarapis, as god of the nether world, and of Asklepius and Hygieia. When Sarapis is the deity thus honoured, he appears on the tablet as reclining on a couch, on his head the *modius*, which is the symbol of his dominion in realms below, and sometimes as accompanied by his bride Isis or Persephone. A train of worshippers approaches from the side of the tablet, bringing in animals for sacrifice. Of the *ex voto* tablets dedicated to the deities of healing, perhaps the clearest specimen appears copied on certain coins of the city of Perinthus, in Thrace. On these we see Asklepius reclining on a couch. Beside him sits his daughter Hygieia, and in front is a three-legged table laden with food, at the feet of which is a serpent. From the side enters a train of votaries dragging in a sacrificial pig. Above, a cluster of arms hangs on a peg, and through a window appears the head of a horse who stands without. It is not easy to understand the symbolism of all parts of these pictures; but the general meaning cannot be doubtful. We see in them representations of the gratitude of those whose health was restored in the temples of the deity Asklepius, the hospitals of antiquity; the train of worshippers represents their family, and the pig of the reliefs had doubtless his original in an animal actually sacrificed to the god. Why the horse and the arms appear in the background, we need not try to ascertain.

It will be easily understood how difficult it sometimes be[illegible] the absence of inscriptions, to tell whether a relief is to be [illegible] among the *ex voto* tablets of [illegible] many cases we seem to [illegible] classes of monuments, as in the following:—Two men recline on a couch, each of them holding a drinking horn. By them sits a woman, while a slave in the foregound is engaged in pouring wine into a vessel. In front appears a three-legged table, beneath which is a snake; in the corner is seen a horse's head. Here horse's head and snake remind us of the *ex voto* tablets; although there can be little doubt that the subject is from a tomb. Both horse's head and snake reappear in the following, which seems to belong to the *ex voto* class of monuments:—Two men recline on a couch, one holds a drinking-horn. On either side a woman is seated. Three figures approach in the attitude of worshippers.

Now the greatest perplexity has arisen from the confusion of two classes of reliefs, which may indeed have something in common, but are widely different in meaning. To separate finally the classes, and to trace out their ultimate connection with each other, is a work still to be done, and one which will require patience and judgment. Meantime we may perhaps be permitted to express doubt whether there is a single relief proved by inscription or other circumstance to be from a tomb in which worshippers appear in the act of sacrifice or adoration. Wherever these are seen it seems reasonable, in the absence of evidence to the contrary, to assume that the monument is erected in honour of a deity, not in memory of a man. But all the scenes where simple feasting is going on, where servants are decanting wine, and wives seated, according to the Greek custom, near the couch on which their feasting husbands recline, may be presumed to be sepulchral until proved to be otherwise.

There are three theories, all well supported by the voice of learned men, as to the meaning of these scenes of feasting on tombs. According to the first view, what is represented is the dead supping in Hades. This theory was mainly based upon the confusion above pointed out. The person reclining on the couch was thought to be frequently receiving worship and sacrifice. Sometimes on his head he was supposed to bear the modius, the emblem worn by Sarapis in his character of deity of the lower world. Therefore it was assumed that the dead man was deified and represented as receiving high honour from the living. If, however, we allow as sepulchral only the scenes whence worshippers are excluded, then there remains nothing godlike or manes-like in the banqueting figure; we lose all reason for supposing the scene of the banquet to be Hades. Moreover, where the husband reclines there sits the wife; if this be in Hades, how is it that the wife was usually surviving, in fact often erected the tomb to the husband's memory? And indeed nothing could be more dissonant with Greek ideas than to ascribe a glorified existence after death to mortals indiscriminately; at the best Hades was shadowy and cold, and a banquet there would be but a faint and feeble echo of earthly banquets, quite untouched by any high exaltation or any worship from the happier living.

The second theory is that we have in these scenes, in emblematic form, pictures of those feasts at the tomb which the Greeks in ancient, as in modern days, spread from time to time, lest the departed should suffer hunger in the next world. That the dead have the same needs as the living, is a notion widely spread among barbarians and semi-civilized peoples. For this reason the savage buries with the dead chief his horse, perhaps his wife: for this reason many of the nations of antiquity stored bread and wine in the tombs with the corpse. The early Greeks not only buried weapons with the dead, but even whetstones to keep the edges of those weapons bright; and commonly placed in the mouth of each corpse a piece of money to defray the expenses of his journey to the next world. Thus, too, on certain days the survivors held a feast at the tomb of a departed friend, leaving place for the dead and supposing him to partake in the spirit.

It is quite possible that this may be the true account of the matter. Nevertheless, I am more inclined to accept the third of the suggested explanations, namely, that what we see before us on these reliefs is neither more nor less than a daily scene from the ordinary life of the dead person. If the toilet be represented on the tomb, why should not the family meal, that most charming and most characteristic of all daily scenes? How could husband and wife be shown us in more close and amiable proximity than when feasting together, and feeling the same thrill of pleasure from the enjoyment of earthly good? *A priori* we should have expected eating to be a favourite subject with the composers of sepulchral groups, and should beware of seeking a far-off explanation of our scenes when a nearer one will suffice. It is true that there are, even in the scenes undoubtedly sepulchral, some adjuncts which seem scarcely in keeping with the ordinary dinner-table—the snake, for instance, in the foreground and the horse in the background; but of these an explanation is possible. The snake was commonly domesticated among the Greeks, and so may appear only as a domestic animal. But I prefer the explanation which is ready to see in it an allusion to the future death of the banqueting master of the house, the snake being in many countries, on account of its habit of living in the ground, looked upon as the companion and representative of the dead. In the same way the horse may only convey a delicate allusion to future departure on a long journey. Such slight allusions would seem to suit Greek taste better than more direct references. More direct references, however, do sometimes appear, as in the relief mentioned above as No. 4, where Charon in his bark appears to summon the feasters from their wine.

There are still other ways in which, on the sepulchral reliefs which, so to speak, introduce us into the midst of life, a faint allusion to death, a slight flavour of mortality, is introduced. We often [illegible] urn placed in a corner, such an urn as when a body [illegible] received its ashes, or such as was set up, as we [illegible] thenes, over those who died unmarried. Like the skeleton at an Egyptian feast, this urn would seem meant to show that in the gayest moment of life death hovers near, waiting to strike. The same moral is conveyed in other cases, by the appearance at the side or in the foreground of a snake entwined round a tree; the snake being, as I have already remarked, the companion of the dead, sometimes even the embodiment of the dead man's spirit or ghost. And in scenes where there is no allusion to death so concrete or conventional as the above, there is over all an aspect of grief and dissatisfaction. Children or slaves are weeping without apparent cause, or women stand with an arm folded across their breast, their head resting on a hand, in an attitude consecrated by the Greeks to sorrow, not as among us to mere reflection.

All the scenes of which I have spoken have this in common, that they represent to us the deceased, with or without the living. But sometimes, though rarely, the Greeks substituted for these groups a merely symbolical figure of an animal or some fabulous creature. On a tomb at Athens, erected in memory of one Leon, stands a marble lion, evidently in punning allusion to his name. Over the tomb of the celebrated courtezan Laïs, in the suburbs of Corinth, was a group representing a lioness standing over a prostrate ram, a symbol the reference of which to the extraordinary career and splendid success of the woman is evidently appropriate. Stone snakes often guarded a tomb, in imitation of the living snakes sure soon to glide about it, on the same principle on which, when the Athenians sought a floral decoration for a stêlê, they selected the acanthus, which is notorious for freely growing among stones. But it was especially the forms of female monsters, sirens, sphinxes, and harpies, which were selected for the adornment of tombs. All these were spoken of in legend as fatal evils, carrying off to death young men and maidens. The sirens especially slew the young after attracting them by the sweetness of their singing, and so well became the graves of those who were lost in the mid ardour of their pursuit of the delights of youth.

Battles of heroes and Amazons, Dionysiac revels, and mythological scenes, occurring on sarcophagi, belong invariably to Roman times, and represent phases of thought quite other than those suggested by the reliefs inspired by genuine Greek feeling. It is extremely seldom that any mythological subject is found on Greek tombs at all. Indeed I am aware but of two instances. Charon is allowed, by the general consent of archæologists, to be represented in a scene above described. And in another very interesting representation, which however is not Athenian, Hermes appears as the conductor of souls, leading gently by the hand a young girl to the future world. So small is the part played by the gods in sepulchral scenes. Not a trace appears of scenes of future happiness or misery, no allusion to that future judgment of souls which is so prominently brought before us in Egyptian pictures. Only, in times when the Egyptian worship of Sarapis and Isis had penetrated to Athens, and served there to impart purer and higher views as to future punishment and reward, we do sometimes find the priestess of Isis going before the departed with all pomp of worship to guide them through the perils of the last journey, and lead them to a safe resting-place. But these scenes only illustrate the triumph of the religious notions of the Egyptians over the susceptible Greeks, at a time when their national city life was extinct, and they were driven by the fewer attractions of the present life to think more about the possibilities of the next.

It seems to be desirable, in view of the unfounded assertions so frequently set forth on the subject of Greek art, to gather what light we can on that most interesting subject from the facts above summarized. In doing so, however, it is above all things necessary to bear in mind the conditions under which sepulchral monuments were designed and executed. And first, it is quite clear that where several persons who died at intervals are buried in one tomb, they cannot all have been adequately represented in the relief which would naturally be the production of a single time. A citizen dies, and a relief is erected over his body, perhaps representing him as taking a farewell of his wife, while his infant son stands by. This same son, may be, dies in middle life and is buried with his father, and an epigram is inserted on the monument stating the fact. It may thus happen that a man of thirty or forty may appear in the sepulchral relief as an infant. Such slight inconsistencies are inseparable from the nature of these monuments. But it must be confessed that sometimes between inscription and sculpture there are contradictions which cannot be thus easily explained, and which raise serious reflections. The fact is that the conviction is forced upon us by the comparison of a multitude of instances, that very often the relief placed on a tomb did not possess much reference to its contents. There can be no doubt that the more ordinary sorts of representations were made in numbers by the sculptors, and, as we should phrase it, kept in stock by them for customers to choose from. And if the would-be buyer found a group of which the general outline and arrangement suited him, he would scarcely decline to purchase it because it was not entirely appropriate, because it made his wife look twenty years too young, or even turned the boys of his family into girls. Like a true Athenian he would probably be more disposed to make use of such a discrepancy as an argument to induce the seller to lower his price than to incur the expense of having a new slab executed on purpose for him. Those who are let into this secret will not be surprised if they occasionally find a subject repeated exactly on two tombs without variation, nor if a sculptured group is little in harmony with the inscribed list of the dead.

Even in those cases in which a relief was executed by special order on the death of a person, a relief adapted in plan and intended in [illegible] the deceased happy amid his family or pursuing [illegible] occupation, we must not expect too much. Even here, [illegible] himself to a generalized or idealized representa-[illegible] knew nought of the dead, almost certainly he took [illegible] imitate the living. Hence the same conventional [illegible] man, the veiled woman, the girl, the infant, repeat [illegible] almost without variety, through all the Macedonian period [illegible] graves. The men who appear on sepulchral reliefs of the [illegible] are as much alike one to another, as the horsemen of [illegible] the Parthenon, or the fighting heroes of the Ægina pedi-[illegible] Roman times this is far less the case; but among the [illegible] the fourth and third centuries B.C., the artist was careful [illegible] the type, and careless of the individual peculiarities; so far at [illegible] existing remains enable us to judge.

[illegible] it is quite an error to suppose that the Athenians were [illegible] one mould. They differed one from another quite as much [illegible] number of Englishmen taken at random. And of this the [illegible] conclusive. For there still exists at Athens a remarkable [illegible] portraits of those citizens who in succeeding years under-[illegible] office of gymnasiarch. This series stretches over a long [illegible] and while it is true that that period belongs to the decline, [illegible] flourishing greatness of the city, yet there is no reason to [illegible] that at the time Athenian blood had been very much mixed [illegible] of other races, or the type deteriorated. Taking these [illegible], as portraits of some of the most prominent Athenian [illegible] and probably some of the purest-blooded, what do we find? [illegible] is almost African in type, with thick lips and woolly hair; [illegible] be taken for that of an English judge; one for that of an [illegible]-musician. Looking on these faces one can scarcely [illegible] the artists did not grossly exaggerate the salient charac-[illegible] the faces of those they had to portray. And even if it were [illegible] safely affirm that an Athenian crowd of the period must [illegible] contained as many widely divergent types as an English or [illegible]. So of the Greek princes who reigned during the third [illegible] centuries before the Christian era over the *disjecta membra*, [illegible] fragments of the Empire of the Great Alexander, we possess quite [illegible] gallery in their numerous and excellent coins. Here, too, [illegible] widest variety of type, many coins presenting to us heads [illegible] one whose knowledge of Greek art was superficial would [illegible] be Greek at all. But although individual Greeks differed [illegible] one from another, and although, in the Alexandrine times [illegible] art, artists quite understood the art of taking portraits, yet [illegible] the forms and features of those sculptured on tombs are [illegible] conventionally rendered. And in nothing does one see more [illegible] there the blending of Attic good taste with Attic super-[illegible] and dislike of too deep or too persistent emotion. For a tombstone calling up in a general way past life and past happiness would be a constant source of emotion, gentle and melancholy, but not too intense in degree; while the sight of the very features of dead father, mother, wife, or child would be too startling and cause far more pain than pleasure. We moderns are less afraid of pain, and, when we place on tombs any representation of the dead at all, make it as exact a likeness as we can. But most, even now, prefer a mere slab in the graveyard and a portrait in the family-room or the bedroom.

The sources of these generalized types of man, youth, woman, and child are of course to be found in the common feeling of the Hellenic nation working through the brains and hands of the ablest statuaries. As in the accepted type of Zeus, the Greek sculptures embodied all that seemed to them most venerable, wise, and majestic; as in the accepted type of Apollo they combined youthful beauty with supreme dignity; so in the accepted type of matron they strove to embody all the matronly virtues, in the young girl all childish grace and promise, in the bearded man the dignity and self-control of a worthy citizen, such as Aristides or Epaminondas. The type was fixed in the case of human beings, as in the case of the Hellenic deities, by the sculptors of the generation which succeeded those who had fought at Marathon and Platææ, and altered but little after that until the collapse of Hellenic independence and Hellenic art.

Goethe has expressed, in a passage which cannot be too often quoted, the ultimate truth about Greek sepulchral reliefs:—

"The wind which blows from the tombs of the ancients comes with gentle breath as over a mound of roses. The reliefs are touching and pathetic, and always represent life. There stand father and mother, their son between them, gazing at one another with unspeakable truth to nature. Here a pair clasp hands. Here a father seems to rest on his couch and wait to be entertained by his family. To me the presence of these scenes was very touching. Their art is of a late period, yet are they simple, natural, and of universal interest. Here there is no knight in harness on his knees awaiting a joyful resurrection. The artist has with more or less skill presented to us only the persons themselves, and so made their existence lasting and perpetual. They fold not their hands, gaze not into heaven; they are on earth, what they were and what they are. They stand side by side, take interest in one another, love one another; and that is what is in the stone, even though somewhat unskilfully, yet most pleasingly depicted."*

It is a proof at once of the genius of Goethe and of his keen sympathy with all that is truly Greek, that at a time before Greek art was half understood, he was able to judge from the few inferior specimens known to him of the general character of these sepulchral reliefs. That on which he lays his master-hand is certainly their most essential character. Their whole aspect is turned, so to speak, from the future to the past, and from heaven to earth. We whose ancestors have been, for some twelve hundred years, taught constantly that death is but the entrance to wider life, that the world is [illegible]

* Italienische Reise, à propos of the museum at Verona. [illegible]

for eternity, can scarcely place ourselves position of men who seem to have found the delightful, and to have been well satisfied with their minds dwell on the enjoyments of the past future which at best was a cold and gloomy echo of world. It is not that they disbelieved in the unseen thought that the soul died with the body; such scepti- perhaps rarer in antiquity than in modern times, and antiquity as in modern times to a few of the highly But that inevitable future occupied comparatively very their time and thought; it was a cold shadow to be kept out life as much as might be. And when it was thought of, it was without very much either of hope or fear. Terrible punish- were reserved for terrible criminals, supreme pleasures for good, but for ordinary mortals an ordinary fate was sort of ghost or echo of their mortal life, made up, like pleasure and pain, but with both pleasure and pain diluted ghostly. From discontent with life and repining at the lot by fate, the Greeks would seem to have been singularly no nation ever thought life better worth living. I shall have on this subject further on.

to speak of the inscriptions which accompany or even place of the reliefs, and which have sometimes a considerable st for us. It will be convenient to quote these inscriptions in these who wish to compare the original Greek can easily do complete work of Kumanudes.*

ere are in the British Museum two sepulchral inscriptions on public † of considerable interest. Of these one contains lists of all the ns who fell in a single year at the various places where Athens carrying on war. We learn from Thucydides and Pausanias that the Athenian custom thus annually to honour with a public ment all those who had in the previous year fallen in the battles eir country—a custom which must have nerved for death many lier's heart, as he reflected that he was sure, if he fell, of a sort mortality before the eyes and in the memory of his countrymen. other inscription, which was written under a relief representing warriors, commemorates those Athenians who fell before ea, in the year B.C. 432. It runs thus:—

"Thus to the dead is deathless honour paid,
Who, fired with valour hot, in arms arrayed,
Felt each our fathers' valour in him glow,
And won long fame and victory o'er the foe.

"Heaven claimed their spirits, earth their bodies took,
The foemen's gate their conquering onslaught shook;
Of those they routed some in earth abide,
Some in strong walls their lives in terror hide.

* Ἐπιτύμβιοι. Athens, 1871.

† British Museum Inscriptions, i. pp. 102—107. The reading of the first few I follow Messrs. Newton and Hicks.

"Erechtheus' city mourns her children's fall,
Who fought and died by Potidæa's wall,
True sons of Athens, for a virtuous name
They changed their lives, and swelled their country's fame."

The smallness of the number of public epitaphs at Athens is well compensated by the abundance of private ones, of which upwards of 4,000 have been already published, while every year brings a multitude of fresh ones to light. I will attempt to class these, as I did the reliefs. The commonest inscriptions by far are those which simply record, in the case of a man, his name, his father's name, and his *deme* or clan; in the case of a woman, her name, that of her father, husband, or husband and father, with their respective demes. Of the numerous epitaphs which remain, perhaps nine out of ten are of this simple character. Probably in most cases they are of the poor, but not in all; for sometimes they accompany reliefs of an elaborate character, or are placed on tombs of great size and pretensions. Than such an epitaph nothing could possibly offend less against good taste, and it was probably thought somewhat sentimental and *gushing* at Athens to indulge in a longer metrical sepulchral inscription. When longer inscriptions occur, they seldom bear much sign either of taste or education. Their grammar is often doubtful, and, when in metre, they halt terribly. They clearly belong to the same class of compositions as the lame verses which abound in English graveyards. It would seem that the swans who sang thus only found their voice at death, but the death of friends, not their own. The chance of such publicity for one's verses as may be gained by placing them on a tomb proved too attractive for them to forego.

In the case of early reliefs we find usually not only the name of the dead, but also of the artist who did the work. In later times this custom dropped, and we have scarcely in any case a clue to the name of the sculptor. This fact is the more curious, inasmuch as in other remains of antiquity, vases, gems, and coins, to insert the artist's name becomes more usual as we approach the best time of art. Not many epitaphs of an earlier period than the year B.C. 400 are preserved, nor are these, except in the case of public tombs, of special importance. One is interesting to students of epigraphy as it bears an exact date, the year B.C. 430, when the plague, following in the wake of the Peloponnesian army, invaded Attica: "I am the tomb of Myrinê, who died of the plague." Another, of an ordinary Attic type, has a grace and charm which is seldom absent from the productions of Attica while yet unsubdued:—

"Let the reader pass on, be he citizen or stranger from afar, having pitied for a moment a brave man who fell in battle and lost his young prime. Having shed a tear here, go by, and good go with you."

To the period between the falling of Athens into Lysander's hands and the times of the Roman Antonines belongs the vast body of the epitaphs. For a more exact chronological classification the materials

...ly exist, it being especially hard to determine the ... inscriptions which are not accompanied by reliefs. It ... to divide them into classes, not by a determination ... but by a consideration of drift and content, and to ... belonging to one long period, a period when the ... had indeed passed away, and external conquests ... hoped for; but when Athens still ruled in the realm of ... attracted to herself the flower of the culture of Hellas and ... I have already said that the commonest sort of inscrip... ...ned only the name of the dead, his father's name, and that ... But not unfrequently a few words of comment were ... the person who paid for the erection of the tomb liked to ... record of his liberality. Thus a stone marks the spot where ... buried Julius Zosimianus, the head of the School of Zeno," ... head of the Stoics of Athens. Another records that ... set up this portrait in memory of his brother." We ... find the trade or calling of the deceased mentioned in his ... One Herakleides is stated to have been the greatest master ... catapult, a warlike machine which seems to have required some ... handling. Many other trades are mentioned in connec... ... the dead. One was a bathing-man, another a midwife and ... another a priestess of the all-producing Mother, probably ... another second in rank in joyous comedy, another a bull-... On one tomb the record ends quaintly, after mentioning that ...ve contained one or two named persons, with the phrase, "also ...ers who are represented in the relief," where the stonemason ... instructor seems to have grown tired of a bare list of names, ...pped short in the midst.

...he longer inscriptions which are found on Attic gravestones, ...cept only the class of minatory or deprecatory epitaphs, which ...re to the last, are in metre. To this rule there are few, if any, ...ons, so that the ancient epitaph-writer could at least, unlike the ..., claim the *dura necessitas* as a reason for attempting a metrical ...ition. I shall, however, render into English prose rather than ...e specimens of these selected for purposes of illustration, as it ...onvey quite a false impression if I were to disguise their oddities ...dities under the smooth mantle of English heroic verse.

...etrical epitaphs are of four kinds. Those of the first kind ... the form of a dialogue between the dead and the surviving ...or in some cases of a mere direct address to the dead. The ...t form which such an address can take is the χρηστὲ χαῖρε— ...well, lost friend"—which is so usual on tombs of a certain period, ... does not, apparently, appear on any which belongs certainly ...thenian. Of this simple and touching phrase we find a number ... amplifications:—

...well, tomb of Melitê; the best of women lies here, who loved her loving husband, Onesimus; thou wert most excellent, wherefore he longs for thee after thy death, for thou wert the best of wives. Farewell, thou too, dearest husband, only love my children."

But an inscription of this kind is necessarily of a late period, and but little in accord with the canon of Greek taste. No doubt when it was set up, it was at once condemned as vulgar by people of culture.

Far more usual and less extravagant is the following, which details a conversation not with the dead, but with his tomb:—"Whose tomb are we to call thee? That of famous Nepos. And who of the children of Cecrops begat him? say. He was not of the land of Cecrops, but from Thrace." Another epitaph, after proceeding in verse, suddenly breaks into prose: "And if you seek my name, I am Theogeiton, son of Thymochus of Thebes." Of course it is quite natural that the tombstone should thus speak in the first person in the name and on behalf of the deceased. In some of our commonest English epitaphs such as "Affliction sore long time I bore," we find the same peculiarity; but that a grave-stone should give information in reply to cross-questioning is less usual.

The second kind of metrical inscriptions, which is by far the most numerous, speaks of the past life and history of the deceased. Thus over the grave of a soldier we find:

"Of thy valour stands many a trophy in Greece and in the souls of men; such wert thou, Nicobolus, when thou leftest the bright light of the sun and passedst, beloved of thy friends, to the dwelling of Persephone."

Other triumphs besides warlike ones are elsewhere recorded; on the tomb of one Praxinus, *the doer*, we read the punning epitaph:

"My name and my father's this stone proclaims, and my country; but by my worthy deeds I attained such a name as few may obtain."

We are not aware in this case to what special kind of deeds the inscription refers; often it is more explicit as in the following, erected over a young statuary:—

"I began to flourish as a statuary not inferior to Praxiteles, and came to twice eight years of age. My name was Eutychides,* but that name fate mocked, tearing me so early away to Hades."

On the tomb of one Plutarchus, who seems to have been a merchant, we find a brief history of his life:—

"This is the tomb of the discreet Plutarchus, who, desiring fame which comes of many toils, came to Ausonia. There he endured toils on toils far from his country, although an only child and dear to his parents. Yet gained he not his desire, though longing much, for first the fate of unlovely death reached him."

Sometimes out of a whole life one event or circumstance of peculiar interest was taken, and commemorated as well by inscription as relief, as in the case of that Phœnician stranger already mentioned who narrowly escaped the jaws of a lion. The inscription on his tomb

* Child of good luck.

and explains the meaning of the representation

of the dead must always in all countries form the most subject of sepulchral inscriptions. Athens is no the rule. We find on the grave of a young man :—

having reached the goal of every virtue, lies entombed dear to father and mother, and loved by his sisters and all in the prime of his life."

from Crete has the simple and pleasing epitaph :—

to Sosinus, of his justice, his prudence, and his virtue, his death."

wing is from the tomb of one Sotius :—

earth lies Sotius, superior to all in the art he practised, virtuous of to his fellow-citizens; for ever he studied to please all, and his just towards his friends."

a few of the panegyrics bestowed on men after their death; stowed on women are fewer in number, but not less interesting. is commended for her serious and staid disposition :—

lies here coveted not, while alive, garments or gold, but desired virtue. But now, Dionysia, in place of youth and bloom, the awarded thee this sepulchre."

n once we find epitaphs which speak of the virtue and of nurses, evidently set up by young men who had never care for and respect them. The ancients evidently felt for nurse who cherished their infancy, slave as she might be, some- lasting and filial affection :—

is laid in earth the best of nurses, whose foster-child still misses her. se, nurse, when alive, and still I honour thee though thou art laid in d, and shall honour as long as I live."

characteristic of the Greek disposition than mere praise of are those praises of the good fortune of the departed, which most mocking to modern ears, and yet on a little reflection isplease. Of one, Symmachus, of Chios, we read on his tomb ough life his joys were many and his sorrows few, that he the extreme limit of old age, and lies in Athens, the city dear and men. On the tombs of women it is often stated that they comfortable circumstances, and that they lived to see children's All the happiness of past life seemed to the Greeks a gain, when it was over was to be regarded, not with bitter regret, le sympathy. In one inscription, though a late one, we find description of the beauty of the young wife buried below. hair, her bright eyes, her snow-white forehead, the ruddy teeth of her lovely mouth. These things were past, it even so they were something better to look back upon

Sometimes, however, through the general level of [illegible] sadder note breaks:—

> "My name is Athenaïs, and with grief I go to my place among the dead, leaving my husband and my darling children. A grudging web the Fates spin for me."

When youthful promise is early cut off it is scarcely possible that it should be spoken of without a sound of sad regret. Even the statement of the fact produces this impression:—

> "If fortune had continued thy life, Macareus, and brought thee to manhood, strong wert thou in the hope that thou wouldst become the guiding spirit of tragic art among the Hellenes. But thou diest not without fame for discretion and virtue."

Even here consolation comes in to modify regret, so true to the happy disposition of the Greeks was the charming saying of Spenser,

> "A dram of sweete is worth a pound of sowre!"

As in sepulchral reliefs, so in epitaphs, the Greek mourner usually turns his thought to the past, and dwells on the life which is over rather than on any which may be beginning. Nevertheless we do find, here and there, some allusions to the state of the departed which are of great interest, and which furnish us with evidence on a subject still obscure and much discussed, the beliefs of the ordinary minds among the Greeks as to the future life, and as to reward and punishment in it. The small space which these allusions occupy, compared with the whole body of epitaphs, shows how small a corner of the Greek thought was taken up with meditation on matters outside the present life. But the materialism of the Greeks was rather natural and practical than speculative, and we nowhere find any positive denial of future existence. In one or two epitaphs there is an appearance of such denial, but its meaning must not be pressed. Thus, in one case, we find the phrase, "Rising out of earth I am become earth again," and in another epitaph, one Nicomedes, who calls himself the servant of the Muses, says that he is "clad in wakeless sleep." Here we probably only have popular phrases used in a vague and indefinite sense, and without the least intention of theorizing on the nature of the soul. Commoner still are even more vague phrases as to the destination of the soul, which is said to fly to heaven, to air, or to æther.* It is æther which is said in the [illegible] inscription first quoted to receive the souls of the slain Athenian warriors. So in the following:—

> "Here Dialogus, student of wisdom, his limbs purged with pure fire [illegible] to the immortals. Here lie naked the bones of Dialogus the [illegible] practised virtue and wisdom; them a little dust hides, sprinkled [illegible] but the spirit from his limbs the broad heaven has received."

...bly a philosopher and had learned the differ... soul and body. The words, heaven and the immortals, ...im a somewhat vague meaning, representing rather some...ed for than believed in and expected. There is a stronger ...philosophic materialism in the following:—"Damp æther ...and mighty intellect of Eurymachus, but his body is in ..." The word αἰθήρ, æther, is certainly used by Homer to ...e abode of the gods, and no doubt the poet of our metrical ...n had Homer in his mind, but here the word "damp" (ὑγρός) ...oint to some materialist notion as to the nature of spirit and ...r to the upper air. A more popular interpretation must be ...in other cases, such as: "Earth sent thee forth to light, ...and earth holds thy remains, but æther, the source of thy ...received it again."

...e vulgar notions with regard to the future state were cer...rrowed from Homer, sucked in by the many with their ...milk, or at latest imbibed at school, where Homer occupied ...taken by the Bible in our Church schools. The Greeks ...were inclined to regard Homer as infallible, and so, when ...ght of the future state at all, pictured it according to his ... Hence they made it a shadowy realm under the govern... Hades and Persephone, a poor washed-out copy of the ...ife on earth. The dead go to the chamber of Persephone, ...o sometimes phrased, the chamber of the blessed. "The ...the flesh of our sweet son lie in earth, but his soul is gone to ...ber of the holy." It is clear, from some other inscriptions, ...at chamber rewards were supposed to await the good, and ...nts the bad. Thus one man writes on the grave of his nurse, ...now that, if below the earth there be rewards for the good, ...nurse, more than for any, is honour waiting in the abode of ...ne and Pluto." The suggestive *if* is again repeated elsewhere. ...is with Persephone any reward for piety, a share of that was ...on thee in death by Fate." The expression in both instances ...e rather of a wish or longing than of a sure and certain hope. ..., this wavering tone never becomes full and confident until ...down to the times of Christian inscriptions, when a sudden ...rellous change takes place. To the Christian the place of ...t is no longer a tomb, but a sleeping-place. When he speaks ...and heaven as receiving the soul, the words have quite another ...hough Christian epitaphs at Athens be somewhat beyond my ... I cannot avoid introducing one or two, if merely for the ...ntrast. The following charmingly combines the genial back... ...of the Greek with the forward glance of the believer:—

> ... on the sacred beauty of Asklepiodote, of her immortal soul ...both nature gave one undefiled beauty, and if Fate seized her ..., in her death she was not forsaken, nor did she abandon

her husband though she left him, but now more than ever watches him out of heaven, and rejoices in him and guards him."

Or take another :—

"His body is hidden here in earth, but his soul is escaped to heaven (αἰθήρ) and returned to its source, for he has obtained the reward of the best of lives."

Sometimes one catches a note of a still higher strain, "There, whence pain and moans are banished, take thy rest." I think no one can deny that these epitaphs are quite equal to the pagan ones in literary taste and felicity of language, while in sentiment they mark a striking advance.

It would have been natural to expect that the religion of Isis, which among all ancient faiths clung most closely to the belief in a future life, and which owed to that circumstance its great influence among the later Greeks, would have left in the epitaphs some traces of a surer hope and trust in what was beyond the grave. But such is not the case, and a still more remarkable omission is to be noticed. The great Eleusinian mysteries were celebrated annually, within a few miles of Athens. The whole population must have known more or less of the meaning of the ceremonies; and there were probably few adult Athenians who had not been initiated. But it has always been supposed that the resurrection of the dead and the life to come were the chief matters on which light was thrown during the celebration. It has been thought that the analogy between the sowing of wheat and the burying of the dead, that analogy which the Apostle Paul works out in full detail, was then insisted on. Cicero speaks of the mysteries of Eleusis as some of the noblest productions of Attic soil, and declares that they impart not only directions for leading a better life, but also a better hope in death. Polygnotus painted on the walls of the *Lesche* at Delphi the punishments suffered in Hades by those who neglected to have themselves initiated in the mysteries. Yet in all the Attic epitaphs which have come down to us, we discern not a trace of any such doctrine as we should have been disposed, from such indications, to attribute to the College of Priests who conducted the mysteries. When the next world is at all spoken of, it either appears as the Homeric realm of Hades and his bride Persephone, or else is mentioned in the vague language of the philosophers as æther and heaven. The conclusion seems inevitable. We are strongly warned against attributing too much influence over the ordinary mind, or any very lofty and spiritual teaching, to the mysteries. The wise men, like Cicero and Plutarch, may have found in them deep meaning and profound consolation, reading into them the results of their own philosophy and faith; just as able men of recent times have read into them most of the doctrines of Christianity. But to the common people they were probably a string of outward observances with little inner meaning. Like the sacraments of Christianity, to which in many respects they were parallel, they had a strong tendency to lose all life and become mere form. That their secret was so well preserved can but one cause—that their secret, such as it was, was that could be communicated. It is certain that throughout antiquity, the future life was by the common people with distaste, if not with dread; and that they had no tending to soften its repulsion.

Reflections and words of advice form a not unfrequent ending an epitaphs. Sometimes in these nothing more is expressed adly wish for the reader. Thus one stranger after stating was shipwrecked, adds in genial spirit, "May every sailor ch his home!" Another wishes for all wayfarers who read the osperous journey. Sometimes there is a general observation: for a woman to be at once noble and discreet;" or a quotation et, as in the case of the well-known line of Menander, "Those gods love die early." Sometimes the occasion is improved, h minister would say, and a little sermon read to the passer- advised to live virtuously, "knowing that the abode of Pluto s full of wealth and has need of nothing,"—virtues, that is to not riches, are the only things which will avail after death.

with regard to metrical inscriptions. The long inscriptions not metrical are nearly always of the same kind as the well- itaph of Shakespeare,—curses pronounced against those who ature time attempt to move or destroy the grave, curses of modern explorer makes very light, apparently supposing virtue has in the course of centuries departed. But in me they might be more effectual. They are always of a very ; so long as the people of Athens had a common feeling and pride in their city there was small fear of the violation of of a citizen, but under the Roman Emperors the Athenian and Greek nationality fell to pieces, and no one felt sure ire. Herodes Atticus, the wealthiest citizen of Athens in of Hadrian, who built the Athenians a splendid marble t up a monument to his wife Appia Annia Regilla, "the light use," which he thought it necessary to fence by a very t string of threats.

gods and heroes I charge any who hold this place not to move ; and if any destroy or alter these statues and honours (τιμάς), for rth refuse to bear fruit, and sea become unsailable, and may he and rish miserably!"

ption goes on to heap blessings on those who keep the tomb e and pay it honour. A lady who bears the Roman name hands over, in her epitaph, her tomb to keep to Pluto and nd Persephone and all the nether gods, calling down a curse violate it. In another epitaph we find a formidable list of ch are likely to seize the violator—palsy, fever, ague, , and the rest. In another instance the dimensions of are curtailed, and it is put neatly into two hexameter verses,

"Move not the stone from the earth, villain, lest after *thy* death, wretch, dogs mangle thy unburied body."

In the last-quoted epitaph it is evidently the writer's intention to threaten a punishment according to the *lex talionis*. To move a tombstone was an offence of the same class, though in degree of course slighter, as to leave the body of a dead man unburied. It is well-known how keenly every Greek dreaded that his body should after his death be deprived of burial-rites, and how bitterly he condemned all who through fear or carelessness abandoned dead friends to dogs and vultures. No doubt this dread was connected with the very ancient and widespread notion that those who remained unburied could not rest in the grave, were repelled from the gates of the world of spirits, and hovered as unhappy ghosts in the vicinity of their corpses. As the first step towards exposing a dead body was the tearing down of the stone which covered it, and as the stone was moreover closely associated with the dead, some of the mysterious horror which guarded the corpse was transferred to the gravestone above it. We may consider ourselves happy that among us gravestones are protected not by curses but by blessings, by cherished memories and associations; and so perhaps it was in the better times at Athens, only when the old civilization was falling into corruption, all gentler ties were loosed, and every man fought for himself and his, with any weapons which came nearest.

One closes the Corpus of the Sepulchral Inscriptions with a feeling of surprise—surprise that a people so gifted as the Athenians should be so helpless and tongue-tied in the presence of death. The reliefs do not disappoint a reasonable expectation; in execution at least they put our modern cemeteries to shame, if the range of ideas expressed is somewhat narrow. But the inscriptions are at a far greater depth below Greek poetry and oratory than the reliefs are below the best Greek sculpture. The reason may partly be that the reliefs are the work of professionals, the inscriptions of amateurs. But there are two other reasons of a more satisfactory character. The first of these I have already mentioned, that except in the case of soldiers and of public characters, such as eminent poets, it was considered bad taste at Athens to have an epitaph at all; those, therefore, which we find are mostly written by persons of the less respectable classes, [illegible] the later and worse times of the city. But the deepest reason, at [illegible] from the modern point of view, is that the Greek mind found [illegible] no inspiring power; they might regard its inevitable power [illegible] equanimity and even cheerfulness, but in any way to rejoice [illegible] presence, to look upon it with hope and warmth of heart, [illegible] consist with the point of view of their religion. Such [illegible] a time are inspired only by one or two religions of the [illegible] which there is no [illegible]

# ΓUART MILL'S PHILOSOPHY TESTED.

"....

the last few weeks the correspondence columns of the' ... have contained letters on the subject of the late Mr. ns about the Immortality of the Soul. The discussion a letter, in which an anonymous writer, G. S. B., asserted' ike of immortality as *probably an illusion*, although morally an illusion that it is better to retain it. He went on to urely time that all this scientific shuffling and intellectual for it is nothing else—should be exposed and exploded." t admirer of Mill was not unnaturally stung by this' replied in a letter, ably and warmly vindicating Mill's and "scrupulous accurateness." After showing, as he Mill never tried to uphold any illusion, he thus con-

difficult to misunderstand Mr. Mill, so anxious was he always to just, to keep back nothing, to examine both sides, to overstate understate nothing, so sensitively honourable was his mind, so honest his style. But these are commonplaces with respect to ntent to contrast the scrupulous accurateness of Mr. Mill with of that quality in 'G. S. B.'"

*ectator* of the following week (October 27th), I took the to express my dissent from both the correspondents,

the expression 'scientific shuffling and intellectual dishonesty' was used, for fear it should imply that Mill knowingly misled It is impossible to doubt that Mill's mind was 'sensitively whatever may be his errors of judgment, we cannot call in good faith and loftiness of his intentions. On the other difficult to accept what Mr. Malleson says as to the ...' of Mill's 'Essays on Religion.' He was scrupulous, but the term 'accurateness,' if it means 'logical accurateness,' cannot be applied to his works by any one who has subjected them to minute logical criticism."

I then pointed out that, in pp. 109 and 103 of his "Essays on Religion," Mill gives two different definitions or descriptions of religion. In the first he says that

"the essence of religion is the strong and earnest direction of the emotions and desires towards an ideal object, recognized as of the highest excellence, and as rightfully paramount over all selfish objects of desire."

In the second statement he says:—

"Religion, as distinguished from poetry, is the product of the craving to know whether these imaginative conceptions have realities answering to them in some other world than ours."

A week afterwards Mr. Malleson made an ingenious attempt to explain away or to palliate the obvious discrepancy by reference to the context. I do not think that any context can remove the discrepancy; in the one case the object of desire is an *ideal* object; in the other case the *craving*, which I presume means a strong desire, is towards realities in some other world; and the difference between ideal and real is too wide for any context to bridge over. Besides, I will ultimately give reasons for holding that Mill's text cannot be safely interpreted by the context, because there is no certainty that in his writings the same line of thought is steadily maintained for two sentences in succession.

Mill's "Essays on Religion" have been the source of perplexity to numberless readers. His greatest admirers have been compelled to admit that in these essays even Mill seems now and then to play with a word, or unconsciously to mix up two views of the same subject. It has been urged, indeed, by many apologists, including Miss Helen Taylor, their editor, that Mill wrote these essays at wide intervals of time, and was deprived, by death, of the opportunity of giving them his usual careful revision. This absence of revision, however, applies mainly to the third essay, while the discrepant definitions of religion were quoted from the second essay. Moreover, lapse of time will not account for inconsistency occurring between pages 103 and 109 of the same essay. The fact simply is that these essays, owing to the exciting nature of their subjects, have received a far more searching and hostile criticism than any of his other writings. Thus inherent defects in his intellectual character, which it was a matter of [illegible] difficulty to expose in so large a work as the "System of Logic" were readily detected in these brief, candid, but most ill-judged essays.

But, for my part, I will no longer consent to live silently [illegible]

morals, political philosophy, political economy, metaphysics, logic—he has expressed unhesitating opinions, and his sayings are quoted by his admirers as if they were the oracles of a perfectly wise and logical mind. Nobody questions, or at least ought to question, the force of Mill's style, the persuasive power of his words, the candour of his discussions, and the perfect goodness of his motives. If to all his other great qualities had been happily added logical accurateness, his writings would indeed have been a source of light for generations to come. But in one way or another Mill's intellect was wrecked. The cause of injury may have been the ruthless training which his father imposed upon him in tender years; it may have been Mill's own life-long attempt to reconcile a false empirical philosophy with conflicting truth. But however it arose, Mill's mind was essentially illogical.

Such, indeed, is the intricate sophistry of Mill's principal writings, that it is a work of much mental effort to trace out the course of his fallacies. For about twenty years past I have been a more or less constant student of his books: during the last fourteen years I have been compelled, by the traditional requirements of the University of London, to make those works at least partially my text-books in lecturing. Some ten years of study passed before I began to detect their fundamental unsoundness. During the last ten years the conviction has gradually grown upon my mind that Mill's authority is doing immense injury to the cause of philosophy and good intellectual training in England. **Nothing surely can do so much intellectual** harm as a body of thorou**ghly illogical writings, which are forced upon** students and teachers by the weight of Mill's reputation, and the hold which his school has obtained upon the universities. If, as I am certain, Mill's philosophy is sophistical and false, **it must be an indispensable** service to truth to show that it is so. This weighty task I at length feel bound to undertake.

The mode of criticism to be adopted **is one which has not been** sufficiently used by any of his previous **critics. Many able writers** have defended what they thought the truth against Mill's errors; but they confined themselves for the most part to skirmishing round the outworks of the Associationist Philosophy, firing in every here and there a well-aimed shot. But their shots have sunk harmlessly into the sand of his foundations. In order **to have a fair chance of** success, different tactics must be adopted; **the assault must be made** directly against the citadel of his logical reputation. His magazines must be reached and exploded; he must be hoist, like the engineer, with his own petard. Thus only can the disconnected and worthless character of his philosophy be exposed.

I undertake to show that there is hardly one of his more important and peculiar doctrines which he has not himself amply refuted. It will be shown that in many cases it is impossible to state what his doctrine is, because he mixes up two or three, and, in one extreme case, as many as six different and inconsistent opinions. In several important cases, the view which he professes to uphold is the direct opposite of what he really upholds. Thus, he clearly reprobates the doctrine of Free Will, and expressly places himself in the camp of Liberty; but he objects to the name Necessity, and explains it away so ingeniously, that he unintentionally converts it into Free Will. Again, there is no doubt that Mill wished and believed himself to be a bulwark of the Utilitarian Morality; he prided himself on the invention, or at least the promulgation, of the name Utilitarianism; but he expounded the doctrines of the school with such admirable candour, that he converted them unconsciously into anything rather than the doctrines of Paley and Bentham.

As regards logic, the case is much worse. He affected to get rid of universal reasoning, which, if accomplished, would be to get rid of science and logic altogether; of course he employed or implied the use of universals in almost every sentence of his treatise. He overthrew the syllogism on the ground of *petitio principii*, and then immediately set it up again as an indispensable test of good reasoning. He defined logic as the Science of Proof, and then recommended a loose kind of inference from particulars to particulars, which he allowed was not conclusive, that is, could prove nothing. Though inconclusive, this loose kind of inference was really the basis of conclusive reasoning. Then, again, he founded induction upon the law of causation, and at the same time it was his express doctrine that the law of causation was learned by induction. What he meant exactly by this law of causation it is impossible to say. He affirms and denies the plurality of causes. Sometimes the sequence of causation is absolutely invariable, sometimes it is conditional. Generally, the law of causation is spoken of as Universal, or as universal throughout nature; yet in one passage (at the end of Book III., chapter xxi.) he makes a careful statement to the opposite effect, and this statement, subversive as it is of his whole system of induction, has appeared in all editions from the first to the last. On such fundamental questions as the meaning of propositions, the nature of a class, the theory of probability, &c., he is in error where he is not in direct conflict with himself. But the indictment is long enough already; there is not space in this article to complete it in detail. To sum up, there is nothing in logic which he has not touched, and he has touched nothing without confounding it.

To establish charges of this all-comprehensive character will of course require a large body of proof. It will not be sufficient to take a few of Mill's statements and show that they are mistaken or self-inconsistent. Any writer may now and then fall into oversights, and it would be manifestly unfair to pick a few unfortunate passages out of a work of considerable extent, and then hold them up as specimens of the whole. On the other hand, in order to overthrow a philosopher's [illegible] requisite to prove his every statement false. If this [illegible] would require ten large ones to refute it. [illegible] to select a certain number of his more promi[illegible] doctrines, and to show that, in their treatment, he is [illegible] article, I am, of course, limited in space and can [illegible]y one test, and the subject which I select for treatment is [illegible] concerning geometrical reasoning.

[illegible]ience of geometry is specially suited to form a test of the [illegible] philosophy. Mill certainly regarded it as a crucial instance, [illegible] considerable part of his "System of Logic" to proving [illegible]netry is a *strictly physical science*, and can be learnt by direct [illegible]on and induction. The particular nature of his doctrine, or [illegible]*strines*, on this subject will be gathered as we proceed. Of [illegible] this inquiry I must not abstain from a searching or even a [illegible]nalysis, when it is requisite for the due investigation of Mill's [illegible]ethod; but it will rarely be found necessary to go beyond [illegible]y mathematical knowledge which almost all readers of the [illegible]ORARY REVIEW will possess.

[illegible]rst test of Mill's philosophy I propose this simple question of [illegible] there in the material universe such things as perfectly [illegible] lines? We shall find that Mill returns to this question a [illegible]al negative answer. There exist no such things as perfectly [illegible] lines. How then can geometry exist, if the things about [illegible] is conversant do not exist? Mill's ingenuity seldom fails [illegible]ometry, in his opinion, treats not of things as they are in [illegible]ut as we suppose them to be. Though straight lines do not [illegible] can experiment in our minds upon straight lines, as if they [illegible]. It is a peculiarity of geometrical science, he thinks, thus [illegible] of *mental experimentation*. Moreover, these mental experi[illegible]e just as good as real experiments, because we know that the [illegible]y lines exactly resemble real ones, and that we can conclude [illegible]m to real ones with quite as much certainty as we conclude [illegible] real line to another. If such be Mill's doctrines, we are [illegible] into the following position:—

[illegible]fectly straight lines do not really exist.

[illegible] experiment in our minds upon imaginary straight lines.

[illegible]se imaginary straight lines exactly resemble the real ones.

[illegible]hese imaginary straight lines are not perfectly straight, they [illegible] enable us to prove the truths of geometry.

[illegible]hey are perfectly straight, then the real ones, which *exactly* [illegible] them, must be perfectly straight: *ergo*, perfectly straight [illegible]exist.

[illegible]ld not be right to attribute such reasoning to Mill without [illegible]ntiating the statements. I must therefore ask the reader [illegible] me while I give somewhat full extracts from the fifth [illegible] second book of the "System of Logic."

Previous to the publication of this "system," it had been [illegible] thought that the certainty of geometrical and other [illegible] truths was a property not exclusively confined to these truths, but nevertheless existent. Mill, however, at the commencement of [illegible] chapter, altogether calls in question this supposed certainty, and describes it as an *illusion*, in order to sustain which it is necessary to suppose that those truths relate to, and express the properties of, purely imaginary objects. He proceeds:*—

> "It is acknowledged that the conclusions of geometry are deduced, partly at least, from the so-called Definitions, and that those definitions are [illegible] to be correct descriptions, as far as they go, of the objects with which geometry is conversant. Now we have pointed out that, from a definition as such, no proposition, unless it be one concerning the meaning of a word, can ever follow, and that what apparently follows from a definition, follows in reality from an implied assumption that there exists a real thing conformable thereto. This assumption, in the case of the definitions of geometry, is false:† there exist no real things exactly conformable to the definitions. There exist no points without magnitude; no lines without breadth, nor perfectly straight; no circles with all their radii exactly equal, nor squares with all their angles perfectly right. It will perhaps be said that the assumption does not extend to the actual, but only to the possible, existence of such things. I answer that, according to any test we have of possibility, they are not even possible. Their existence, so far as we can form any judgment, would seem to be inconsistent with the physical constitution of our planet at least, if not of the universe."

About the meaning of this statement no doubt can arise. In the clearest possible language Mill denies the existence of perfectly straight lines, so far as any judgment can be formed, and this denial extends, not only to the actual, but the possible, existence of such lines. He thinks that they *seem to be inconsistent with the physical constitution of our planet, if not of the universe.* Under these circumstances, there naturally arises the question, What does geometry treat? A science, as Mill goes on to remark, cannot be conversant with nonentities; and as perfectly straight lines and perfect circles, squares, and other figures do not exist, geometry must treat such lines, angles, and figures as do exist, these apparently being imperfect ones. The definitions of such objects given by Euclid, and adopted by later geometers, must be regarded as some of our first and most obvious generalizations concerning those natural objects. But then, as the lines are never perfectly straight nor parallel, in reality, the circles not perfectly round, and so on, the truths deduced in geometry cannot accurately apply to such existing things. Thus we arrive at the necessary conclusion that the peculiar accuracy attributed to geometrical truths is *an illusion*. Mill himself clearly expresses [illegible] result:‡—

* Book II., chapter v., section 1, near the [illegible]

† The word *false* occurs in the editions [illegible] ninth edition I find the words, not strictly [illegible]

‡ Book II. chapter v., section 1, at the [illegible]

eculiar accuracy, supposed to be characteristic of the first principles y, thus appears to be fictitious. The assertions on which the of the science are founded, do not, any more than in other sciences, rrespond with the fact; but we *suppose* that they do so, for the sake the consequences which follow from the supposition."

Mill's statements are consistent enough. He gives no evi- support his confident assertion that perfectly straight lines xist; but with the actual truth of his opinion I am not con- All that would be requisite to the logician, as such, is that, nce adopted the opinion, he should adhere to it, and admit which leads to an opposite conclusion.

uestion now arises in what way we obtain our knowledge of s of geometry, especially those very general truths called Mill has no doubt whatever about the answer. He says:*—

mains to inquire, what is the ground of our belief in axioms—what ence on which they rest? I answer, they are experimental truths; tions from observation. The proposition, Two straight lines cannot space—or in other words, Two straight lines which have once met, t again, but continue to diverge—is an induction from the evidence ses."

pinion, as Mill goes on to remark, runs counter to a scientific of long standing and great force, and there is probably no n enunciated in the whole treatise for which a more un- e reception was to be expected. I think that the "scientific " still prevails, but I am perfectly willing to agree with nand that the opinion is entitled to be judged, not by its but by the strength of the arguments which are adduced in f it. These arguments are the subject of our inquiry. Mill to point out that the properties of parallel or intersecting lines are apparent to us in almost every instant of our lives. nnot look at any two straight lines which intersect one without seeing that from that point they continue to diverge more."† Even Whewell, the chief opponent of Mill's views, hat observation *suggests* the properties of geometrical figures; s not satisfied with this, and proceeds to controvert the argu- which Whewell and others have attempted to show that e cannot *prove* the axiom.

ief difficulty is this: before we can assure ourselves that two lines do not enclose space, we must follow them to infinity. the difficulty with boldness and candour:—

the axiom? That two straight lines *cannot* enclose a space; once intersected, if they are prolonged to infinity they do not to diverge from one another. How can this, in any single by actual observation? We may follow the lines to any

* Same chapter, at the beginning of section 4.
† Same section, near the beginning of fourth paragraph.

distance we please; but we cannot follow them to infinity: for [illegible] can testify, they may, immediately beyond the farthest point to which we have traced them, begin to approach, and at last meet. Unless, therefore, we had some other proof of the impossibility than observation affords us, we should have no ground for believing the axiom at all.

"To these arguments, which I trust I cannot be accused of understating, a satisfactory answer will, I conceive, be found, if we advert to one of the characteristic properties of geometrical forms—their capacity of being painted in the imagination with a distinctness equal to reality: in other words, the exact resemblance of our ideas of form to the sensations which suggest them. This, in the first place, enables us to make (at least with a little practice) mental pictures of all possible combinations of lines and angles, which resemble the realities quite as well as any which we could make on paper; and in the next place, make those pictures just as fit subjects of geometrical experimentation as the realities themselves; inasmuch as pictures, if sufficiently accurate, exhibit of course all the properties which would be manifested by the realities at one given instant, and on simple inspection: and in geometry we are concerned only with such properties, and not with that which pictures could not exhibit, the mutual action of bodies one upon another. The foundations of geometry would therefore be laid in direct experience, even if the experiments (which in this case consist merely in attentive contemplation) were practised solely upon what we call our ideas, that is, upon the diagrams in our minds, and not upon outward objects. For in all systems of experimentation we take some objects to serve as representatives of all which resemble them; and in the present case the conditions which qualify a real object to be the representative of its class, are completely fulfilled by an object existing only in our fancy. Without denying, therefore, the possibility of satisfying ourselves that two straight lines cannot enclose a space, by merely thinking of straight lines without actually looking at them; I contend, that we do not believe this truth on the ground of the imaginary intuition simply, but because we know that the imaginary lines exactly resemble real ones, and that we may conclude from them to real ones with quite as much certainty as we could conclude from one real line to another. The conclusion, therefore, is still an induction from observation."*

I have been obliged to give this long extract in full, because, unless the reader has it all freshly before him, he will scarcely accept my analysis. In the first place, what are we to make of Mill's previous statement that the axioms are *inductions from the evidence of our senses?* Mill admits that, for aught our senses can testify, two straight lines, although they have once met, may again approach and intersect beyond the range of our vision. "Unless, therefore, we had some other proof of the impossibility than observation affords us, we should have no ground for believing the axiom at all."† Probably it would not occur to most readers to inquire whether such a statement is consistent with that made two or three pages before, but on examination we find it entirely inconsistent. Before, the axioms were inductions from *the evidence of our senses;* now, we must have "some other proof of the impossibility than *observation* affords us."

This further proof, it appears, consists in the attentive contemplation of mental pictures of straight lines and other geome[illegible]

* Book II., chapter v., section 5. [illegible]

† End of the [illegible]

... sufficiently accurate, exhibit, of course, all the ... real objects, and in the present case the conditions ... real object to be the representative of its class are ... fulfilled. Such pictures, Mill admits, must be *sufficiently* ... what, in geometry, is sufficient accuracy? The expres- ... mind, a new and puzzling one. Imagine, since Mill ... do so, two parallel straight lines. What is the sufficient ... which we must frame our mental pictures of such lines, ... they shall not meet? If one of the lines, instead of being ... is a portion of a circle having a radius of a hundred ... the divergence from perfect straightness within the length ...ot would be of an order of magnitude altogether imperceptible ...nses. Can we, then, detect in the mental picture that which ...be detected in the sensible object? This can hardly be held ... because he says, further on, that we are only warranted in ...ing observation of the image in our mind for observation of ...ity by long-continued experience that the properties of the ...re faithfully represented in the image.

...since we may (at least with a little practice) form mental ... of all possible combinations of lines and angles, we may, I ..., form a picture of lines which are so nearly parallel that they ... meet at a distance of 100,000 miles. If we cannot do so, ... we detect the difference between such lines and those that ...ally parallel? Mill meets this difficulty. If two lines meet at ... distance,

> ... transport ourselves thither in imagination, and can frame a mental ... the appearance which one or both of the lines must present at that ... we may rely on as being precisely similar to the reality. Now, ... we fix our contemplation upon this imaginary picture, or call to ... generalizations we have had occasion to make from former ocular ..., we learn by the evidence of experience, that a line which, after ... from another straight line, begins to approach to it, produces the ... on our senses which we describe by the expression, 'a bent line,' not ... expression, 'a straight line.'"*

...s passage we have somewhat unexpectedly got back to *the* ... We may call to mind the generalizations from former ocular ...tion, and we have the evidence of experience to distinguish ... the impressions made on our senses by a bent line and a ... line. But what will happen if the bent line be a circle with ... of a million miles? Have we the evidence of experience that ...h lines, which seem to be parallel for the first hundred miles, ... begin to approach, and finally intersect. If so, our senses ... us to see clearly and to exactly measure quantities a ... miles away. Or again, if there be two lines which close in

* Book II., chapter v., section 5, end of fourth paragraph.

front of me are one foot apart, but which a hundred miles away are one foot *plus* the thousandth of an inch apart, they are not parallel. Will my senses enable me to perceive the magnitude of the thousandth part of an inch placed a hundred miles off?

But we have had enough of this trifling. Any one who has the least knowledge of geometry must know that a straight line means a *perfectly* straight line; the slightest curvature renders it not straight. Parallel straight lines mean *perfectly* parallel straight lines; if they be in the least degree not parallel, they will of course meet sooner or later, provided that they be in the same plane. Now, Mill said that we get an impression on our senses of a straight line; it is through this impression that we are enabled to form images of straight lines in the mind. We are told,* moreover, that *the imaginary lines exactly resemble real ones*, and that it is long-continued observation which teaches us this. It follows most plainly, then, that the impressions on our senses must have been derived from really straight lines. Mill's philosophy is essentially and directly empirical; he holds that we learn the principles of geometry by direct ocular perception, either of lines in nature, or their images in the mind. Now if our observations had been confined to lines which are not parallel, we could by no possibility have perceived, directly and ocularly, the character of lines which are parallel. It follows, that *we must have perceived perfectly parallel lines and perfectly straight lines, although Mill previously told us that he considered the existence of such things to be "inconsistent with the physical constitution of our planet, at least, if not of the universe."*

Perhaps it may be replied that Mill simply made a mistake in saying that no really straight lines exist, and, correcting this blunder of fact, the logical contradiction vanishes. Certainly he gives no proper reason for his confident denial of their existence. But merely to strike out a page of Mill's Logic will not vindicate his logical character. How came he to put a statement there which is in absolute conflict with the rest of his arguments? No interval of time, no want of revision, can excuse this inconsistency, for the passage occurs in the first edition of the "System of Logic" (vol. i. p. 297), and reappears unchanged (except as regards one word) in the last and ninth edition. The curious substitution of the words "not strictly true" for the word "false" shows that Mill's attention had been directed to the paragraph; and a good many remarks might be made upon this little change of words, were there not other matters claiming prior attention.

We have seen that Mill considers our knowledge of geometry to be founded to a great extent on *mental experimentation*. I am not [illegible] that any philosopher ever previously asserted, with the same [illegible]ness and consciousness of his meaning, that the [illegible] ideas might be substituted for the [illegible]

* Same section, about thi[illegible]

uently spoken of their ideas or notions, but it was usually a n of speech, and their ideas meant their direct knowledge of Certainly this was the case with Locke, who was always bout ideas. Descartes, no doubt, held that whatever we can erceive is true; but he probably meant that it would be possible. I do not think that Descartes in his geometry ever ntal *experimentation.* But however this may be, Mill, of all ht not to have recommended such a questionable scientific if we may judge from his statements in other parts of the of Logic." The fact is that Mill, before coming to the subject try, had denounced *the handling of ideas instead of things* as e most fatal errors—indeed, as *the cardinal error of logical* s. In the chapter upon the Nature and Import of Proposi- , says:—

otion that what is of primary importance to the logician in a proposi- relation between the two *ideas* corresponding to the subject and (instead of the relation between the two *phenomena* which they y express,) seems to me one of the most fatal errors ever introduced hilosophy of Logic; and the principal cause why the theory of the s made such inconsiderable progress during the last two centuries. ses on Logic, and on the branches of Mental Philosophy connected e, which have been produced since the intrusion of this cardinal error, metimes written by men of extraordinary abilities and attainments, ays tacitly imply a theory that the investigation of truth consists in ting and handling our ideas, or conceptions of things, instead of the mselves: a doctrine tantamount to the assertion, that the only mode g knowledge of nature is to study it at second hand, as represented minds."

re denounces the *cardinal error* of investigating nature at and, as represented in our own minds. Yet his words exactly that process of mental experimentation which he has unques- advocated in geometry, the most perfect and certain of the

be urged, indeed, with some show of reason, that the method ight be erroneous in one science might be correct in another. hematical sciences are called the exact sciences, and they may culiar character. But, in the first place, Mill's denunciation ndling of ideas is not limited by any exceptions; it is applied ost general way, and arises upon the general question of the f Propositions. It is, therefore, in distinct conflict with Mill's nt advocacy of mental experimentation.

second place, Mill is entirely precluded from claiming the tical sciences as peculiar in their method, because one of the points of his philosophy is to show that they are not peculiar. outcome of his philosophy to show that they are founded on empirical basis, like the rest of the sciences. He speaks† of

* Book I., chapter v., section 1, fifth paragraph.
† Book III., chapter xxiv., section 7, about the tenth line.

geometry as a "strictly physical science," and asserts that every theorem of geometry is a law of external nature, and might have been ascertained by generalizing from observation and experiment.* What will our physicists say to a *strictly physical science*, which can be experimented on in the private laboratory of the philosopher's mind? What a convenient science! What a saving of expense in regard of apparatus, and materials, and specimens.†

Incidentally, it occurs to me to ask whether Mill, in treating geometry, had not forgotten a little sentence which sums up the conclusion of the first section of his chapter on Names.‡ Here he luminously discusses the question whether names are more properly said to be the names of things, or of our ideas of things. After giving some reasons of apparent cogency, he concludes emphatically in these words:— "Names, therefore, shall always be spoken of in this work as the names of things themselves, and not merely of our ideas of things." Here is really a difficulty. *Straight line* is certainly a name, and yet it can hardly be the name of a thing which is not a straight line. It must then be the name either of a real straight line, or of our idea of a straight line. But Mill distinctly denied that there were such things as straight lines, "in our planet at least;" hence the name (unless indeed it be the name of lines in other planets) must be the name of our ideas of straight lines. He promised expressly that names "in this work," that is, in the "System of Logic," should *always* be spoken of as the names of things themselves. It must have been by oversight, then, that he forgot this emphatic promise in a later chapter of the same volume. We may excuse an accidental *lapsus memoriæ*, but a philosopher is unfortunate who makes many such lapses in regard to the fundamental principles of his system.

But let us overlook Mill's breach of promise, and assume that we may properly employ ideal experiments. We are told§ that, though it is impossible ocularly to follow lines "in their prolongation to infinity," yet this is not necessary. "Without doing so we may know that if they ever do meet, or if, after diverging from one another, they begin again to approach, this must take place not at an infinite, but at a finite distance. Supposing, therefore, such to be the

* Same section, beginning of second paragraph.

† Since writing the above, I have made the significant discovery that in the first and second editions, a clause follows the passage quoted from Book I., chapter v., section 1, paragraph 5 (vol. i., middle of page 119), in the following words:—"A process by which, I will venture to affirm, not a single truth ever was arrived at, except truths of psychology, a science of which Ideas or Conceptions are avowedly (along with other mental phenomena) the subject matter." These words do not appear in the fifth and ninth editions. Now, as Mill could not possibly pretend to include geometry, *a strictly physical science*, under psychology, we find him implying, or rather asserting, that *not a single truth ever was arrived at* in geometry by the very method of handling our ideas on which he depends for the knowledge of the axioms of geometry. The striking out of these words seems to indicate that he had perceived the absolute conflict of his two doctrines; yet he [illegible] about *the cardinal error* of handling ideas, and merely deletes a [illegible] from it.

‡ Book I., chapter ii., section I, [illegible]

§ Book II., chapter v., section 5, [illegible]

[illegible] transport ourselves thither in imagination, and can [illegible] image of the appearance which one or both of the [illegible] at that point, which we may rely on as being [illegible] to the reality." Now, we are also told* that "neither [illegible] the human mind do there exist any objects exactly [illegible] the definitions of geometry." Not only are there no [illegible] lines, but there are not even lines without breadth. "We cannot conceive a line without breadth; we can form [illegible] picture of such a line: all the lines which we have in our [illegible] possessing breadth." Now I want to know what Mill [illegible] prolongation of a line which has thickness and is not [illegible] examine this question with some degree of care.

[illegible] place, if the line, instead of being length without [illegible] according to Euclid's definition, has thickness, it must be a [illegible] it had had two dimensions without the third, it would [illegible] been described as a surface, not a line. But then I want [illegible] how we are to understand *the prolongation of a wire*. Is the [illegible] the wire to be defined by its surface or by its central line, [illegible] line running deviously within it? If we take the last, then, [illegible] devious and uncertain, its prolongation must be un- [illegible] If we take a certain central line, then either this line has [illegible] or it has no breadth; if the former, all our difficulties recur; if [illegible] —— Well, Mill denied that we could form the idea of such a [illegible] same difficulty applies to any line or lines upon the surface, [illegible] surface itself regarded as a curved surface without thickness. [illegible] then, we can get rid of thickness in some way or other, I feel [illegible] understand what the prolongation of a line means.

[illegible] us overlook this difficulty, and assume that we have got [illegible] line—length without breadth. In fact, Mill tells us‡ that [illegible] reason about a line as if it had no breadth" because we [illegible] power, when a perception is present to our senses, or a [illegible] to our intellects, of *attending* to a part only of that perception [illegible] tion, instead of the whole." I believe that this sentence sup- [illegible] good instance of a *non sequitur*, being in conflict with the [illegible] which immediately follows. Mill holds that we learn the [illegible] of lines by experimentation on ideas in the mind; these [illegible] surely be conceived, and they cannot be conceived without [illegible] Unless, then, the *reasoning* about a line is quite a different [illegible] *experimenting*, I fail to make the sentences hold together [illegible] the other hand, we can reason about lines without [illegible] can only experiment on thick lines, would it not be much [illegible] to the reasoning process, whatever it may be, and drop [illegible] experimentation altogether?

[illegible] II, Chapter v., section 1, beginning of third paragraph.
[illegible] section, second paragraph, eleven lines from end.
[illegible] paragraph, seventeen lines from end.

N 2

But let that pass. Suppose that, in one way or other, we manage to *attend* only to the direction of the line, not its thickness. Now, the line cannot be a straight line, because Mill tells us that neither in nature nor in the human mind is there anything answering to the definitions of geometry, and the second definition of Euclid defines a straight line. If not straight, what is it? Crooked, I presume. What, then, are we to understand by the prolongation of a crooked line? If the crooked line is made up of various portions of line tending in different directions, if, in short, it be a zigzag line, of course we cannot prolong it in all those directions at once, nor even in any two directions, however slightly divergent. Let us adopt, then, the last bit of line as our guide. If this bit be perfectly straight, there is no difficulty in saying what the prolongation will be. But then Mill denied that there could be such a bit of straight line; for the length of the bit could scarcely have any relevance in a question of this sort. If not a straight line, it may yet be a piece of an ellipse, parabola, cycloid, or some other mathematical curve. But if a piece of an ellipse, do we mean a piece of a perfect ellipse? In that case one of the definitions of geometry has something answering to it in the mind at least; and if we conceive the more complicated mathematical curves, surely we can conceive the straight line, the most simple of curves. But if these pieces of line are not perfect curves, that is, do not fulfil definite mathematical laws, what are they? If they also are crooked, and made up of fragments of other lines and curves, all the difficulty comes over again. Apparently, then, we are driven to the conception of a line, no portion of which, however small, follows any definite mathematical law whatever. For if any portion has a definite law, the last portion may as well be supposed to be that portion; then we can prolong it in accordance with that law, and the result is a perfect mathematical line or curve, of which Mill denied the existence *either in nature or in the human mind.* We are driven, then, to the final result that no portion of any line follows any mathematical law whatever. Each line must follow its own sweet will. What then are we to understand by the prolongation of such a line? Surely the whole thing is reduced to the absurd.

But in this inquiry we must be patient. Let us forget the non-existence of straight lines, the cardinal error of mental experimentation, and whatever little oversights we have yet fallen upon. Let us suppose there really are geometrical figures which we can treat in the manner of "a strictly physical science," such as geometry [illegible] be. What lessons can we draw from Mill's Logic as to the [illegible] treating the figures? A plain answer is contained in the [illegible] extract from the second volume:—

"Every theorem in [illegible]

* Book III., [illegible]

might have been ascertained by generalizing from observation and experiment, which in this case resolve themselves into comparison and measurement."

Here we are plainly told that the solution of *every* theorem in geometry may be accomplished by a process of which measurement is, to say the least, a necessary element. No doubt a good deal turns upon the word "generalizing," by which I believe Mill to mean that what is true of the figure measured will be true of all like figures in general. Give him, however, the benefit of the doubt, and suppose that, after measuring, we are to apply some process of reasoning before deciding on the properties of our figure. Still it is plain that if our measurements are not accurate we cannot attain to perfect or unlimited accuracy in our results, supposing that they depend upon the data given by measurement. Now, I wish to know how Mill would ascertain by generalizing from comparison and measurement that the ratio of the diameter and circumference of a circle is that of 1 to 3·14159265358979323846 . . . . .

Some years ago I made an actual trial with a pair of compasses and a sheet of paper to approximate to this ratio, and with the utmost care I could not come nearer than one part in 540. Yet Mr. W. Shanks has given the value of this ratio to the extent of 707 places of decimals,* and it is a question of mere labour of computation to carry it to any greater length. It is obvious that the result does not and cannot depend on measurement at all, or else it would be affected by the inaccuracy of that measurement. It is obviously impossible from inexact physical data to arrive at an exact result, and the computations of Mr. Shanks and other calculators are founded on *a priori* considerations, in fact upon considerations which have no necessary connection with geometry at all. The ratio in question occurs as a natural constant in various branches of mathematics, as for instance in the theory of error, which has no necessary connection with the geometry of the circle.

It is amusing to find, too, that Mill himself happens to speak of this same ratio, in his "Examination of Hamilton,"† and he there says, "This attribute was discovered, and is now known, as a result of reasoning." He says nothing about measurement and comparison. What has become, in this critical case, of the empirical character of geometry which it was his great object to establish? A few lines further on (p. 372) he says that mathematicians could not have found the ratio in question "until the long train of difficult reasoning which culminated in the discovery was complete." Now, we are certainly dealing with a theorem of geometry, and if this could have been solved by comparison and measurement, why did mathematicians resort to this long train of *difficult* reasoning?

I need hardly weary the reader by pointing out that the same is

* Proceedings of the Royal Society (1872-3), vol. xxi. p. 319.
† Second Edition, p. 371.

true, not merely of many other geometrical theorems, but of all. That the square on the hypothenuse of a right-angled triangle is exactly equal to the sum of the squares on the other sides; that the area of a cycloid is exactly equal to three times the area of the describing circle; that the surface of a sphere is exactly four times that of any of its great circles; even that the three angles of a plane triangle are exactly equal to two right-angles; these and thousands of other certain mathematical theorems cannot possibly be proved by measurement and comparison. The absolute certainty and accuracy of these truths can only be proved deductively. Reasoning can carry a result to infinity, that is to say, we can see that there is no possible limit theoretically to the endless repetition of a process. Thus it is found in the 117th proposition of Euclid's tenth book, that the side and diagonal of a square are incommensurable. No quantity, however small, can be a sub-multiple of both, or, in other words, their greatest common measure is an infinitely small quantity. It has also been shown that the circumference and diameter of a circle are incommensurable. Such results cannot possibly be due to measurement.

It may be well to remark that the expression "a false empirical philosophy," which has been used in this article, is not intended to imply that all empirical philosophy is false. My meaning is that the phase of empirical philosophy upheld by Mill and the well-known members of his school, is false. Experience, no doubt, supplies the materials of our knowledge, but in a far different manner from that expounded by Mill.

Here this inquiry must for the present be interrupted. It has been shown that Mill undertakes to explain the origin of our geometrical knowledge on the ground of his so-called "Empirical Philosophy," but that at every step he involves himself in inextricable difficulties and self-contradictions. It may be urged, indeed, that the groundwork of geometry is a very slippery subject, and forms a severe test for any kind of philosophy. This may be quite true, but it is no excuse for the way in which Mill has treated the subject; it is one thing to fail in explaining a difficult matter: it is another thing to rush into subjects and offer reckless opinions and arguments, which on minute analysis are found to have no coherence. This is what Mill has done, and he has done it, not in the case of geometry alone, but in almost every other point of logical and metaphysical philosophy treated in his works.

W. STANLEY JEVONS.

# CONTEMPORARY LIFE AND THOUGHT IN FRANCE.

NOTHING is more difficult than to write about political events in a time of crisis. What I say to-day will perhaps have ceased to be true by the time it comes before the reader's notice, and were I to attempt to foretell events, facts would perhaps have already given the lie to my predictions before their appearance in print. It is therefore better I should content myself with trying to discover the causes of the present crisis, to define its real nature, and point out the permanent difficulties with which, whatever turn affairs may take, France will have to contend.

Nothing would be more unjust than to make the Ministry of the 16th of May alone responsible for the serious position in which France finds herself at present. No doubt its violent advent to power, the prorogation and subsequent dissolution of the Chamber of Deputies, the series of arbitrary and illegal acts committed by MM. de Broglie and Fourtou, the imprudent and anti-constitutional words they put into the mouth of the Marshal, the bad faith displayed by their partisans, and the unheard-of pressure exerted during the elections, greatly aggravated the evil and enhanced the difficulty of the cure, but the evil existed before, and must have broken out sooner or later. The crisis might have taken place under less dangerous conditions, but it could not have been averted, for it was inherent in the very nature of things. Since the fall of the old *régime* France has been in a state of revolution, in the sense that no government has ever been accepted by the whole nation; all the governments, more or less regular, that have succeeded each other have had their principles and origin called in question; they owed the short moments of tranquillity they enjoyed only to the momentary lassitude of their enemies, and the more or less unflagging energy of their leaders; but they were all obliged to use their chief strength in maintaining and defending their position instead of in governing wisely and well, and carrying out useful reforms and undertakings. Nor could it be otherwise in a country with four parties standing side by side,—Legitimists, Bonapartists, Orleanists, and Republicans,—and where the one of the four that seized the power was sure to see the three others coalesce at once against it.

After the disasters of 1870 and the fall of the Empire we might have hoped that things would change a little. The republican party, until then an energetic stirring minority, capable of making the long duration of any monarchical government impossible, but incapable of founding a government itself, all at once increased prodigiously. On the one hand a swarm of old monarchists, with M. Thiers at their head, seeing the impossibility of establishing a monarchy which would not be either a clerical absolutism or a military tyranny, ranged themselves on the side of the Republic, as being the only possible government if once legitimacy and the Empire were put out of the question; on the other hand a swarm of peasants, who had loved and upheld the Empire, their eyes being opened by our misfortunes, began to look on the Republic as a guarantee of peace and a safeguard against clericalism, the object of their instinctive aversion. At the same time, the old republicans had grown perceptibly calmer; the exercise of power during the tragical months of the war and the Commune, the discipline of M. Thiers' strong will, and the obligation they were under of fighting side by side with their new allies against the anti-republican majority of the National Assembly, had converted them, if not into men fit to rule, at least into a real political party instead of a revolutionary one. It was to this sudden increase of strength, as well as to the personal influence of M. Thiers, to the division of the monarchical parties, and the aversion and dread occasioned by the idea of a Bonapartist restoration, that the republican party owed all its successes: the failure of the monarchical attempts after the 24th of May, 1873, the vote of the republican constitution of the 25th of February, 1875, the election of the seventy-five permanent senators, two-thirds of whom were republicans, the republican elections of 1876, and the substitution of two republican cabinets—those of M. Dufaure and M. J. Simon—in the place of M. Buffet's.

Notwithstanding these successes the Republic was far from being sure of peaceable possession and stability. A primary difficulty arose, from the choice, in 1873, of Marshal MacMahon, as president of the Republic, a choice ratified in 1875. An honest soldier, but a man of narrow intelligence, incapable of understanding the delicate handling required by a political constitution, the Duc de Magenta's legitimist instincts, Bonapartist recollections and ties, and lastly the reactionary and clerical influences which had raised him to power and kept him there, rendered him naturally hostile to the Republic and especially to the republicans. He had been placed there as a sentinel to keep the place open for the first monarch who was to be had. He has been faithful to this charge, entrusted to him on the day of his election, when M. de Fourtou exclaimed with more frankness than elegance, "*Nous avons la botte,*" and under the influence of the coterie who diligently reminded him of his first engagement, he has continually impeded the action of the republican ministers. Still this danger was only a secondary one. M. de MacMahon would have accepted the maintenance of the Republic with Ministers who would not have alarmed his conservative instincts too much, had there not been in the country and in the Chambers elements of conflict always on the point of clashing.

It would be childish to be satisfied with declaiming against the reactionary intrigues, the occult action of the *camarilla*, and the ambitious passions of a few men. The difficulties which the republican party has to overcome are far more serious. They are of two kinds: the first proceed from the enemies it has to contend against; the others from the very elements out of which it is constituted.

The last elections of the 14th of October show, pretty exactly I think, the proportion of the political parties into which France is divided; for if on the one hand Government pressure made some electors vote for monarchical candidates who would be very ready to accept a Republic, the fact of the existence of the Republic, and the vague idea that the triumph of the clericals would entail a war, have, on the other hand, made electors, who would unquestionably accept a monarchy or the Empire, vote for republicans. Two-thirds of France therefore wish for a republic, and one-third wishes for its overthrow, or rather (for to the general mind ideas do not formulate themselves so precisely) does not wish to be governed by the republicans. It is idle to speak here of intrigues, corruption, and violence. Every one who knows France knows well enough that a considerable number of people are convinced that the republicans are incapable of governing, that they will be both weak and violent, that they will allow disorder to creep into all the public offices, and that the consequence of their advent to power will be discredit abroad and anarchy at home, and very shortly civil war and the Commune. To guard against these evils, whose near approach so alarms them, some (and these are the more numerous) wish to revert to the Empire, which alone does not shrink from any measures for securing order, which satisfies some of the democratic tendencies of modern societies, and which, in short, recalls to the mind of the peasant the time of prosperity and abundance; the others, swayed either by historical traditions or the interests of the Catholic religion, wish to return to a legitimate monarchy. What is still more serious is, that amongst these radical enemies of the Republic or at least of the republicans, are a great many representatives of the so-called leading classes, members of the magistracy, the clergy, and the army, landed proprietors, manufacturers, and commercial men. And the Senate, elected by the electoral colleges of notables, so to speak, seeing that it is elected by the deputies, the councillors-general, and the delegates of the municipal councils, shows an anti-republican majority, small it is true, but which would be very large if it were not that most of the permanent senators' seats had been given to republicans. Moreover, this conservative majority pretends to represent more fairly the permanent interests of France than the majority in the Chamber of Deputies, which they say represents more particularly numbers and the popular masses.

These elements hostile to the Republic, divided into Bonapartists, legitimists, and more or less constitutional monarchists, would not be very formidable, or rather would never have succeeded in organizing themselves at all, or carrying on any combined action, had it not been that they were all inspired and knit together, on the one hand by that sincere conviction I alluded to just now, of the impossibility ot establishing a regular and moderate republic, and, on the other, by clericalism. A passion with some, a habit with others, to others again an instrument of rule, clericalism has become a considerable power in France, and a formidable element of disturbance. The excesses and overbearing pretensions of the clergy and the Ultramontane party, and, on the other side, the hostile attitude assumed by a large section of the republicans with regard to religion itself, have brought things to such a violent head as to make almost all those who attach great value to the maintenance and the prestige of Catholicism range themselves on the monarchical side, and convert the pious women and timid spirits into blind enemies of the republican government.

The republican party, therefore, has to fight, not so much against historical traditions or political theories, as against prejudices, passions, and fears, very sincere, very real, and partly legitimate, which it will succeed in dissipating and allaying only by action and the help of time. Unhappily it finds obstacles and impediments in the very elements that constitute it. The hostility of the parties of the Right has obliged all the groups of the republican party to draw more closely together, and make common cause against the common foe, so that we see such men as M. Léonce de Lavergne and M. Nadaud, M. Léon Say and M. Naquet, acting in concert, although their opinions and their temperaments differ at least as widely as those of M. de Kerdrel and M. Rouher. The conservative and moderate elements in the republican party are, no doubt, numerous, and no one will take M. Hérold, M. Léon Renault, M. Calmon, and M. Waddington for radicals or revolutionists; but associated with these moderate elements are other and more numerous ones, not moderate, or, at best, very inexperienced and imprudent.

In addition to this, is it possible to govern a large country, centralized as France is, in the face of the ill-will if not the constant hostility of the greater part of the conservatives, the heads of the administration, the possessors of wealth, and the public interests? Is it even possible for a government to maintain its position whose centre of gravity would be not in the centre but quite to the left, that is to say, in the midst of elements purely progressive and consequently shifting and unstable? Such a thing is almost inadmissible, and yet since the Right and the Left have dug a pit between them it seems unavoidable.

The republican party itself has helped to aggravate the state of affairs. During the electoral contest, it was allowable even for M. Thiers to say that the majority in the Chamber of Deputies had not committed any fault, that all was going on as well as could be wished, and that the Ministries of MM. Dufaure and J. Simon had met with the most cordial support in the Chamber. In reality the Chamber of Deputies had shown itself wanting in experience and foresight. It had not known how to face the reality of things, grasp the situation, and direct its actions accordingly. It should have seen that, in keeping M. Dufaure, it was secure of a republican ministry until 1879, the date of the re-election of a third of the Senate, that neither the Marshal nor the Senate would dare to touch M. Dufaure if the Chamber supported him, whereas any other more advanced Ministry would arouse the susceptibilities of the Marshal and the Senate, and risk the bringing on of the conflict. The Chamber ought, therefore, to have given absolute support to M. Dufaure, to have proposed no law which he was not inclined to accept, and to have exacted nothing from him in return for this support but the gradual substitution of republican for reactionary functionaries. By this means the Chamber would have been sure of good senatorial elections in 1879, and a republican majority in the Senate, the only aim they ought to have had in view, seeing that, whatever the Ministry might be, so long as the majority in the Senate was monarchical, the Republic was paralyzed. Instead of this, the majority in the Chamber of Deputies has never acted like a government party, but always as an opposition party; it has allowed its members to [illegible]

[illegible]tions haphazard, which it approved of in reality, but [illegible] was obliged to vote at the last moment, in order not to [illegible]istry; it was constantly threatening the existence of [illegible], and then at the last moment, seized with remorse and [illegible] its rescue with a vote of confidence. Consequently, the [illegible] no weight either with the President or with the Senate, [illegible] sure of a majority in the Chamber; and the Chamber got [illegible] for its progressive ideas from the people, because it was [illegible]crificing them, nor for its moderation from the Senate, [illegible]owed too plainly that that moderation was forced upon it. [illegible] manner, although M. Dufaure retired after a vote of the [illegible]was really the Chamber that unsettled and discredited him, [illegible] cause of his fall. Nor was it more successful in supporting [illegible]imon Ministry, whose existence, precarious from the first, [illegible]longed agony. M. Gambetta was the chief culprit in these [illegible]d tactics of the Chamber of Deputies. Since 1870 he has [illegible]y made great strides as a politician. He has become more [illegible]as educated himself, has learnt to take a clearer view of the [illegible]ts of government, and his splendid oratorical talent has gone [illegible]ng; but his presence in the Chamber has been one of the great [illegible] the steady and regular action of the republican Ministries. [illegible]lity was too powerful, his influence too great, for it to be [illegible]t people should not have the feeling that the Ministries were [illegible]on his favour and his moods; nor could he himself resist the [illegible]pleasure of making them quake, that he might afterwards [illegible]ir rescue. By this he brought the proper representatives [illegible] party into discredit. A certain carelessness which he has [illegible] aside from the time when, the head of a small minority, he [illegible]f up to radical opposition, without having any responsi[illegible]incur, and a sturdy optimism, which is the basis of his [illegible]nt, blinded him to the danger of this parliamentary game. [illegible]h of May rudely aroused the republicans from their false [illegible]nd revealed to them the extent of their faults. That par[illegible] coup d'état did not, as has been said, create a crisis that [illegible] had no reason to foresee; it revealed, on the contrary, the [illegible] the evil, and the gravity of both the moral and political [illegible]f France. But now, if we turn our eyes from the repub[illegible]e Right, and to the Marshal, whom it made its tool rather [illegible]hief, the faults of the former will seem very slight compared [illegible]onduct of the latter. The republicans have been imprudent, [illegible] the conservatives have deliberately obstructed and overturned [illegible]. No constitution can work if the various powers of which [illegible] do not show a certain degree of consideration towards each [illegible] evince a desire to avoid shocks and conflicts, if each does [illegible] from pushing his claims and rights to their utmost limits [illegible]raining the springs of legality. The Chamber of Deputies [illegible] this spirit of condescension and moderation; not so the [illegible]d the President. Whilst the latter surrounded himself ex[illegible] with the avowed enemies of the Republic, and by his con[illegible]sition to the action of the Ministers gave people cause to [illegible] sincerity of his intentions, the Senate lost no opportunity of [illegible] conflict, deliberately rejected the most moderate motions [illegible]rward by the Cabinet, if they wore a liberal hue, and chose as permanent senators none but open enemies of the constitution. That these tactics should have been adopted by the Bonapartists and legitimists, whose sole dream is the overthrow of the republican system, is the most natural thing in the world; but that the Right Centre, styled constitutional, which had accepted the republic, should not have been able to lay aside its fears and its repugnance, in order to facilitate the action of the constitution it had voted,—that almost all its members, from M. Buffet to M. d'Audiffret Pasquier, should have made common cause with the Bonapartists and entered into a contest with the republican Left Centre, is an unpardonable fault, and may prove an irreparable one. The 16th of May aggravated the situation still further, by bringing the crisis on prematurely, and giving it a violent and illegal character unforeseen even by those by whom it had been desired.

The 16th of May was a surprise to every one. Many political men, not only of the Right Centre, but even of the Left Centre and the Left, had thought that a crisis must come, that the Chamber would treat all the Ministries in succession as it had treated M. Dufaure's and M. J. Simon's, that it would be necessary to have a dissolution, and the formation of a large Constitutional Conservative party out of all the moderate elements. Unfortunately, amongst those who cherished these ideas were men who, like M. de Broglie and M. de Fourtou, mingled them, the one with personal grudges, wounded vanity, and secret enmity against the Republic, the other with absolute and Bonapartist instincts. Throughout the whole winter the Marshal's mind was worked upon to get him to agree to a scheme for a dissolution; for a long while he resisted, partly from indolence, partly from respect for law, until the vote of the 4th May against Ultramontanism came. Then the clerical influences began to act; their chief tool was Mme. de MacMahon, and one morning the Marshal roughly discharged M. J. Simon, as he would have discharged his valet. Those who had driven him to it were the most surprised. They wanted the dissolution, but not until the Chamber had discredited itself, not until the extreme Left had irritated and separated from itself the Left Centre and part of the Left, not until the country was so wearied out as to accept the Conservative candidates of the constitutional party with joy. The wine had, however, once drawn, to be drunk. To desert the Marshal was to give up the game to the Republicans. M. de Broglie had enough presumption, M. de Fourtou enough contempt for the electoral body, to undertake the campaign of dissolution. They found colleagues, one of whom, M. Paris, did not deserve to find himself associated in such measures; and another of whom, M. Berthaut, remained in the Ministry of War from a sense of duty, to protect law, if necessary, against his unscrupulous allies. The Senate voted for the dissolution, and so did the Constitutionalists, though with "death in the soul," knowing that they were giving up France to fate, perhaps to adventurers. All the world knows the incredible series of violent, arbitrary, and illegal acts perpetrated by the Ministry and its agents, which followed: the overthrow of the administration by M. de Fourtou, of the magistracy by M. de Broglie; the impunity guaranteed to the most criminal acts of the Bonapartists; the transformation of the tribunals into the willing servants of the conservatives' vengeance; the dismissal of recalcitrant railway officials by M. Paris; the conversion of financial *employés* into electoral agents by M. Caillaux; and finally the restoration of official candidates with more effrontery even than [illegible]

[illegible] M. de Broglie becoming the patron of M. de Maupas, who [illegible] father; decorating the magistrates who, after the 2nd [illegible] part in the most daring outrages against the law, allow- [illegible] to be insulted by the agents of justice; and lastly, to [illegible] refusing to bring V. Hugo's "Histoire d'un Crime" before [illegible] thus taking the 2nd December under his direct protection. [illegible] condemnation of Europe has been passed upon this *Com-* [illegible], but it is already a very serious and disquieting fact [illegible] that it should ever have been able to exist and have found [illegible] obey it, and electors to approve it. I know one revolutionist [illegible] himself delighted with it, pretending that no one had [illegible] so much to discredit the principle of absolutism, the adminis- [illegible] the magistracy, the clergy, and the army, as MM. de Broglie [illegible] Fourtou.

[illegible] the republican party, having learnt wisdom by the blow [illegible] received, showed itself equal to the occasion. It manifested [illegible] it had until then been deficient in, and, with a firmness, [illegible] unanimity worthy of admiration, it entered on a campaign of legal [illegible] such as France had never before witnessed, and which was [illegible] with brilliant success at the legislative elections of the 14th of [illegible] and above all at the elections of the Councils-General of the [illegible] November.

[illegible] were in a constitutional country, the crisis would be over, and a [illegible] of the Left would already be in office; but we are in a Republic [illegible] quite a new Republic. The very men who, like M. de Broglie [illegible], most strongly insisted on the constitution being modelled on a [illegible] government, and on the President being irresponsible, [illegible] that in a Republic he is necessarily responsible, as he is in [illegible] United States. They have made it their object to render his retire- [illegible] impossible by making him declare beforehand, with a contempt [illegible] national will no head of the State has ever displayed before, that [illegible] neither govern with the Left nor yet resign, so that now if he [illegible] to be logical, suicide would be the only honourable alternative [illegible] The Constitutionalists in the Senate are greatly irritated with the [illegible], which has given up France to Bonapartist intrigues; but with [illegible] habitual want of decision, they do not dare to look the hypothesis [illegible] Marshal's resignation in the face, and their hesitation prolongs [illegible], at the same time that the Senatorial elections, in which they [illegible] wish to separate themselves from their old allies of the Right, [illegible] personal with political questions. If M. Thiers were still alive [illegible] would no doubt have rallied round him, but his death leaves [illegible] republicans without a head whose name inspires confidence. [illegible] it is probable that the crisis will have a pacific solution, [illegible] the Left will come into office. Then its real trial will begin. [illegible] real governing party forms itself in the bosom of the Left, [illegible] of rallying round it the liberal elements of the Right Centre, [illegible] a Ministry of energetic and intelligent men, and of steadfastly [illegible] them and perseveringly following them, the Republic may [illegible] elements of the Extreme Left will separate themselves, but [illegible] rendered powerless. If, on the contrary, the Left preserves its [illegible] of an Opposition party, overwhelms its Ministers with idle [illegible], impracticable projects and laws, makes it impossible for [illegible] any serious work by over-burdening them with a thousand useless matters and anxieties, the Republic will become unendurable to the country, which has need, above all, of work and rest. It is also necessary that the republican party should know how to keep itself resolutely distinct from the revolutionary and socialist party, to whom we owed the Commune, that it should show itself incapable of leaning towards those who had a share in that insurrection; for it should remember that if the memory of Sedan still protects us against the restoration of the Empire, the remembrance of the Commune is the chief obstacle to the hearty acceptance of the Republic by timid minds who love peace above everything. The easy relations, the outward politeness, the familiarity even, that usually reigns between political adversaries, make republican statesmen too ready to think that the situation is free from dangers and difficulties. They must recollect, on the contrary, that the present form of government has only been accepted by about two-thirds of France, that a great part of the living forces of the nation are opposed to it, that the political situation is still one of revolution, I would even say of civil war, from which intelligence, firmness, moderation, and wisdom can alone deliver us.

If I have devoted such a large space to the description of the political condition of France, it is because I am bound to put that which at present engrosses the thoughts of all, and for the moment throws all other interests into the background, into the foremost rank. What is yet more serious is that the political crisis has for the moment abruptly cut short reforms already in progress, particularly the educational reforms undertaken by M. Waddington, the one of the republican ministers who was most successful in economizing his time and his strength for the business of his department. These reforms are, nevertheless, too imperatively required by public opinion not to be carried on by the government, whatever it may be, that is about to be formed, and not to be furthered at the same time by the association of individual efforts. After the disasters of 1871, when people tried to discover the cause and the remedy for the reverses France had suffered, the desire for a reform of public instruction manifested itself most strongly on all sides. We awoke to a sense of the parsimony with which primary instruction was distributed; of the defects of our secondary instruction, still influenced, as it was, by Jesuitical traditions, and by exclusive attention to literary form; and lastly of the radical inadequacy of the higher education, or, to express it better, the almost entire want of the same. M. Renan in his "Réforme intellectuelle et morale," M. Bréal in his "Quelques Mots sur l'Instruction publique," pointed out the direction the reform should take: the foundation of Universities similar to the German, richly endowed, powerfully organized, enjoying a great autonomy, to which all the cultivated youth of the country would flock to acquire a taste for higher culture and habits of work and criticism; as regards secondary instruction, putting the substance before the form, spending less time on exercises of rhetoric and more on positive knowledge, developing the study of living tongues, destroying or at least relaxing the barrack system prevalent in the Lycées. Political and, particularly, clerical influences made the introduction of these reforms very difficult. Whilst compulsory primary instruction, which was included in the programme of all the members of the Left, was rejected by the Right of the National Assembly as one of the most dangerous

...modern spirit, the reform of secondary instruction, ... M. J. Simon, was abandoned immediately after the 24th ... the reactionary Ministry. As for the higher instruc-... taken of the general wish for reforms to get a law ... pretence of freedom, which only served to create Catholic ... rival the faculties of the State, and thus to divide the young ... hostile camps, living in perpetual defiance. In spite of these ... difficulties the cause of educational reform made some pro-... individual effort tried to take the place of State effort. The ... founded by M. Godard, a man with a great talent for ... and teaching, adopted quite a new plan of instruction, put ... of ancient languages for three years, substituted the study ... and philological exercises for most of the studies in ... composition, gave an infinitely more important place than the ... the State to the study of the sciences and living tongues. ... time the material wants of the pupils were most admirably ... In six years the number of its pupils rose to eight hundred. ... school founded with less capital, the *Ecole Alsacienne*, has put ... principles in practice, and has furthermore abolished the system ... boarders, and provided for the physical education of the ... is completely neglected at the *Lycées*. A private association ...*loppement de l'enseignement populaire* has imported into Paris ... of the Froebel system for the education of little children, ... them into the municipal schools. As regards the higher ... the establishment of the *Ecole libre des Sciences politiques*, of ... Boutmy is the founder and director, is likewise due to indi-... effort. The course of study is unlike any hitherto existing in ... it consists of what in Germany are called *Cameralien Wissen-*..., namely, the administrative, economical, political, and diplo-...sciences. Its courses of lectures on the history of finance, on ...entary, diplomatic, and constitutional history, ethnography, ...strative law, the law of nations, are all entrusted to specialists ... ability and authority, and its yearly increasing success ... it to become the future nursery of our administrators and ... And lastly, the Catholic Universities themselves, in spite ... narrow-mindedness and intolerance that presided over their ...ment and the dangers they present to national unity and ... have succeeded in enlisting the services of some men of ... as M. Allix, M. Terrat, M. l'Abbé Duchesne in Paris, and ...bert in Angers; new studies have been inaugurated, such as ...bé Duchesne's chair of Christian antiquity and ecclesiastical ..., and the emulation they cannot fail to excite in the faculties of ...te is sure to be productive of good result.

...over, as soon as the republicans were in power again, the projects ...m were resumed, and M. Waddington had the honour of drawing ...neral plan for the creation of new universities and of further ... out some partial reforms; many new Chairs were founded, ... subjects hitherto excluded from the faculties of the State, ... Sanskrit, old French, classical and Christian archæology, and ... seventy-five professorships and three hundred scholarships ... of poor students. The very day of his fall M. Waddington ... Faculty of Protestant Theology in Paris, intended to replace ... Faculty of Strasburg; and when we reflect that this faculty will necessarily become part of the future University of Paris, we can estimate the consequences of this innovation. Protestant theology placed side by side and on the same footing with Catholic theology is an implicit recognition of the freedom of thought,—the State declaring its neutrality in matters of doctrine, and giving up, for the first time, an official theology and consequently an official philosophy. Added to this, the vigorous critical method of the Protestant theologians, the serious and painstaking spirit of the students, cannot but excercise a good influence on the teaching of the faculty of letters. Finally, M. Waddington has encouraged and developed the *Ecole des Hautes Etudes*, perhaps the most original creation of later years, and the one that bears the most striking testimony to the irresistible power that is pushing France to the reform of her higher education. When M. Duruy founded the *Ecole des Hautes Etudes* in 1868, he first merely thought of founding new laboratories for the natural sciences, and providing scholars with larger subsidies. When he added the historical and philological section, his object was not so much to found a new branch of instruction as to furnish young scholars with means of studying freely; but he had the discernment to choose for this section of the school young men acquainted with the system of teaching at the German universities, and desirous of introducing it, in part, into France, and, besides, he had the wisdom to leave them free to organise their work as they should think best. Thanks to the efforts of M. L. Renier, M. Bréal, and M. Gaston Paris, a series of conferences was soon organized in which history, the classics, Roman, Semitic, Sanskrit, and Persian philology, Greek and Latin archæology, and Egyptology were studied, exactly as in the historical and philological seminaries of the German universities. Whilst the natural science, physical, and mathematical sections continue to consist merely of laboratories having no connection with each other, the philological and historical section form a regular school, which is self-administrative, draws up its own programmes and regulations at periodical meetings, and, thanks to the support of the Ministry, is extending its influence and teaching year by year, so that its action on the younger learned world is more considerable now than that of the Sorbonne or even the Collége de France. In 1869, the masters were only eleven in number, the weekly conferences eighteen; there are now twenty-four masters who hold between them fifty conferences weekly. It has added to its original branches of study, Celtic, Rabbinical Hebrew, the Zend tongue, and Semitic antiquities. It has published more than thirty volumes, written by its professors or pupils, most of them scientific works of the first order, such as "St. Alexis," by M. G. Paris; "Tables Eugubines," by M. Bréal; "Ormazd and Ahriman," by M. James Darmesteter. By degrees the *Ecole Pratique d'Histoire et de Philologie* has also founded, in the very heart of the old Sorbonne, a higher instruction quite new in France, which, though founded by the State, and furthered in its progress by several Ministers, especially M. Waddington, may be said to have developed itself by its own strength and its own resources, especially when we remember that during eight years the salaries of its professors did not exceed 2,000 francs.

The foundation, spontaneous so to speak, of the *Ecole Pratique d'Histoire et de Philologie* is the most striking sign of the intellectual movement which for some years past has been directing the [illegible]

[illegible] erudition. From 1820 to 1840 France had had a [illegible] renaissance, which had shown itself, simultaneously, in [illegible] Hugo, Lamartine, and Musset; in the drama, with Hugo [illegible] in history, with Aug. Thierry and Guizot; in philosophy, [illegible] in criticism, with Villemain and Ste. Beuve. This [illegible] was chiefly marked by its more especially literary [illegible] the attention paid to form, style, and eloquence, and to [illegible] brilliant and charming qualities. The men of that genera- [illegible] not deficient in science, but what they were chiefly [illegible] not so much truth of detail and the discovery of new [illegible] general ideas, wide views, the art of composition, and good [illegible] were all the qualities generally regarded as, *par excellence*, [illegible] predominance of the literary element had its advantage [illegible] with superior men like those we have just named; but when [illegible] passed into the hands of Epigones inferior to their [illegible] neglected serious and patient work in favour of charm of [illegible] perfection of form, a barren wordiness was the result, vague [illegible], a literature at once empty and pretentious. By a natural [illegible] as well as by the scientific movement that carried away the [illegible] Europe, the desire for accurate research, exact criticism, and [illegible] method began to be more and more manifest in France. [illegible] two most eminent writers of the present generation, MM. [illegible] Taine, are likewise, both of them, scholars. The theatre [illegible] the drama in favour of the comedy of observation of customs [illegible]; the novel laid aside its poetical dress to become a work [illegible] and exact representation; philosophy, forsaking eloquent [illegible], devoted itself, with the help of the natural sciences, to [illegible] research; history renounced vast pictures and general [illegible] favour of erudition; pure literary criticism made way for [illegible]. Even poetry submitted to the new influence of learning, and [illegible] revive past ages and paint them in their real colours.

[illegible] the French retain their taste for good style and artistic [illegible], but they have acquired a taste for facts and research, and [illegible] even disregard the qualities of form, to which in a great [illegible] they owed their glory and their intellectual influence. This [illegible] erudition, this tendency which I might qualify as German, [illegible] itself most strongly since the war. No other proof is needed [illegible] number of new reviews that have been started, all of which [illegible] contributors and readers. These reviews are all of a learned [illegible] so learned as to surprise the Germans themselves. Thus, [illegible] *de Philologie ancienne*, edited by MM. Tournier and Havet, [illegible] almost exclusively devoted until now to the driest parts of [illegible], such as conjectures, emendations of texts, the collation of [illegible]. The *Romania*, started by MM. G. Paris and P. Meyer, [illegible] more generally interesting, is nevertheless also of a very [illegible] philological character, and has seldom allowed itself to make [illegible] into the domain of literary history. The *Revue Celtique*, [illegible] M. Gaidoz, likewise by its very nature addresses itself to a [illegible] of specialists. These three reviews have all of them [illegible] weight, owing to the solid and able character of the [illegible] in them. An older review, the *Revue Critique*, [illegible] by MM. Paris, Meyer, Morel, and Zotenberg, gave the [illegible] this learned press. It confines itself to reports of the new literary and historical works published, but these reports, written by learned specialists, are often as valuable as the works themselves, and the severe impartiality that characterizes them contrasts with the customary indulgent and superficial politeness of criticism in France. Almost all the editors of the new reviews served their first campaign in the *Revue Critique*, and, what is no less striking, are also, almost all of them, professors or old pupils of the *Ecole des Hautes Etudes*.

Other reviews, of a much more general character and interest, were the offspring of this same movement which is leading serious minds in France towards works of erudition. The *Melusine* edited by MM. Gaidoz and Rolland, contains all the documents that may be useful in the study of mythology and popular literature. M. Ribot's *Revue de Philosophie*, though it has no avowed doctrinal tendency, is evidently strongly influenced by the contemporary school of English psychologists; it has rallied round it, not only all the young French philosophers, but a great number of the most eminent foreign philosophers. It does not aspire to general favour, and does not shrink from the most severe works on logic and mathematics. The *Revue Historique*, edited by MM. Monod and Fagniez, is conducted in the same spirit. It rejects all polemical works and does not court public favour by adapting its contents to passing interests. At the same time it furnishes those who are historians by profession with full information concerning all that is being done and published in the line of historical research. Geography as well as history has benefited by the zeal manifested for science in France since the war. The Geographical Society has doubled the number of its members. Unfortunately, M. Drapeyron's *Revue de Géographie* has not fulfilled all that it promised, and if it has been less successful than the above-named reviews, it is due to its being of too popular a character, too little scientific, and to its seeking what is piquant and of present interest, rather than what is solid and serious. Its rival, the *Revue Géographique Internationale*, edited by M. G. Renaud, is more especially a journal of information, fairly well supplied.

No less striking is it, that the reviews intended for the general public have begun to neglect literature too in favour of erudition. The eldest and most illustrious of all, the *Revue des deux Mondes*, every number of which used to contain one or two articles of literary criticism, finds no one who will occupy himself with pure literature now, and gives its readers nothing but history, archæology, in a word, learning. No doubt it is learning stripped of its briars and thorns, but often very serious learning all the same. Its best writers, MM. Renan, Boissier, Sorel, Soury, are scholars. The *Correspondant*, which is the *Revue des deux Mondes* of the Catholic party, has become a historical review; another organ of the same party is the *Revue des Questions Historiques*, a special review which, notwithstanding its sectarian and polemical character, contains works of great scientific value. Literature has been deserted by writers as well as by readers, so much so that not one of the purely literary magazines started during the last few years has been able to live. The *Revue Politique et Littéraire*, whose success is yearly increasing, lives chiefly by history, philosophy, and philology; the *Vie Littéraire* now devotes itself almost entirely to politics; and the *Courrier Littéraire*, notwithstanding M. Colani's first-rate talent as a writer, does not command a large circle of readers.

...daily press, we notice the same phenomenon. In ...newspapers published periodical articles of literary ...week under the empire, M. Schérer in the *Temps*, ...the *Constitutionnel*, M. Cuvillier Fleury in the *Débats*, ...the *Opinion Nationale*, pronounced judgment on the ...of the day, or published retrospective studies on some ...known or not rightly appreciated. Now most of the ...those, such as the *Temps* and the *Débats*, read by the ...only publish from time to time, and that unwillingly, ...of "Variétés," and confine themselves more and ...on current politics and letters from correspondents ...any chance a paper wishes to open its columns to ...questions, literature is not the chosen subject, but science ... Thus M. Soury was commissioned by the *Dix-neuvième* ...a review of the philosophical movement,—a series of ...that none but readers already acquainted with the ...treated of could appreciate: whilst the *République* ...almost banished the feuilleton novel to make room ...of the sciences, edited by specialists, that has no other ...that of requiring more sustained attention in the reader ...arily bestowed on a daily paper. Two eminent men, ...ist and physiologist, M. Paul Bert, the other a linguist, ...fère, edit this part of the paper, and are aided by a ...contributors. These articles keep the reader acquainted ...the intellectual movement; philosophy, history, philology, mythology, physical sciences, natural and medical, the ...of the sciences to industry, are all brought before him ...thing but literature properly so called. Chairs of erudi... being founded in all our faculties of letters; but when ...French literature in the Collége de France becomes vacant, ...cult to know whom to appoint.

...or, more correctly speaking, this disappearance of litera... ...ubt in some degree connected with the serious tendencies ...ds, but it is likewise connected with a very great change ...and social condition of France. Serious men are more ...pursuit of solid and profound science; but in society, in ...ellectual tastes and the taste for reading have declined. ...to instruct themselves, but no longer seek in books the ...most refined form of distraction. The *salons*, as they were ...gatherings whose one object was the direct and pleasant ...thoughts and opinions, whose subject was the literature of ...no longer. The women are steeped in bigotry or world... ...those who fly the two extremes are on the point of plung... ...ing. That polished society, semi-serious, semi-frivolous, ...ic, witty, and curious, that inspired literary works, or for ...y works were written, exists, so to speak, no longer. ...readers has become smaller, and the conversation of the ...longer fed by reading; and those who do still read want ...to furnish food for thought or for their work. From ...nevertheless, some purely literary work does make its ...one may be sure that it is some posthumous work by ...of the last generation, some far-off echo of a bygone ...the "Cahiers" of Ste. Beuve, sheets in which he noted his inmost thoughts and opinions on books or men; "L'Abélard" of M. de Rémusat, a living picture of the society of the twelfth century, and a profound description of the moral struggles of a Faust of the middle ages; the "Dernières Pages" of G. Sand, in which we recognize that magic pen that could paint nature with words, that imagination still wearing, in spite of years, the freshness almost of youth; and lastly, the "Lettres" of Doudan, the secretary and friend of Duc Victor de Broglie, a brilliant, cold, and, now and then, profound wit,—a true type of the literary epoch that, as I have shown, has come to a close, who looks on all events, persons, and books as subjects for pretty [illegible], brilliant dissertations, or topics of conversation or correspondence.

In a society in which pure letters have ceased to be in favour, and where the women read little, poetry must of necessity languish. A great deal of verse continues to be published in France, but I am inclined to think that, for the most part, the poets are only read by their brother-poets. Of course, I do not speak of Victor Hugo, whose name and glory carry universal weight; but except him, who is there that is known or read? Is it M. Leconte de Lisle, a writer, nevertheless, of the first order, who with the accuracy of a scholar has brought Greece, the ancient East, the barbarous ages, back to life again? Or M. de Banville, in spite of his refined and fantastic spirit? Or André Lemoyne, who is an exquisite artist nevertheless, and has produced some little masterpieces? Their fame does not extend beyond a very narrow circle. Though a mediocre poet, M. Deroulède has made a name for himself by his "Chants d'un Soldat," because the very day after the war, in which he bore a brave part, he stirred the patriotic fibres of every Frenchman's heart. François Coppée is known by the brilliant success on the stage of his play "Le Passant," and by his having put his talent, by no means inconsiderable, at the service of a very *terre à terre* kind of *bourgeois* poetry, requiring neither a very strong imagination nor a very refined taste to understand. Less known than Coppée, Sully Prudhomme, the first of our contemporary poëts, has succeeded in securing a place amongst known men; but this is owing to a philosophical depth and a faculty for understanding all the scientific questions of the day that make him the friend and confidant of all students, the echo of their thoughts and anxieties, intellectual or moral. What is he at work on at present? A poem on natural law, on Darwinism. Was I not right in saying that pure letters are dead, and that science has invaded everything?

Nor is it otherwise with fiction. The novel of adventure, sword-cuts, and plumes, such as Dumas conceived it, no longer exists. In its stead we have the judicial novel, the novel of the assizes,—in a word, [illegible]. The novel of passion and of ideal poetry, in which G. Sand [illegible] supreme, that too, has been forsaken. The most illustrious [illegible] present novelists are followers of Balzac, the implacable [illegible] "comédie humaine;" but they take great care, from incapacity [illegible] as from intention, not to give their creations that grandeur [illegible] that convert them into types and remove them from the real [illegible] ideal. What they strive after is pure reality, common[illegible] as the case may be. Some, like Alphonse Daudet, [illegible] choose interesting subjects which permit of [illegible] sympathetic characters; but their passion for [illegible] lengths that they will insert in their novels [illegible]

M. Daudet has just done in his "Nabab." There we meet the Deputy Bravay, Dr. Olif, and M. Daudet himself. The about it is that M. Daudet was Morny's secretary and a ; these, therefore, are the recollections of the friend-day, that he retails to the public. In fact, our writers anatomists, whose love of truth deprives them of all modesty. M. Zola goes much further. He will have nothing and of the real all that is lowest and most trivial. A writer, with a vigorous talent of observation, gifted in the with the sense of life, M. Zola takes immense pains to it is impossible to read without disgust and loathing. He feel it himself, and at the opening of his last novel, " that powerful, but outrageous, and all but slanderous of the Parisian working class, wherein he has endeavoured not only its habits but also its *argot*, he says that he to make a study of life and a philological study. To means physiology and philology. M. Flaubert, the head realist school, in his last volume, "Trois Contes," begins us a picture of a very insignificant little corner of provincial gives us a legend of the middle ages in a new dress; and into the third story all that archæology can tell us about Roman life at the end of the first century B.C. Photo-medicine, statistics, on the one hand, erudition on the other, are whence our present novelists draw their inspirations.

not think that the result on all the writings of the day is impartiality and coldness that quench passion. The of the day, whether political or religious, never cease to exert especially in critical times like the present, when all that respond to those preoccupations and passions, risks being over-. And yet it is strange that, excepting the daily polemics of the pure politics have produced no work worthy of notice. all the works of contemporary history owe their savour : M. Thureau Dangin's Studies on the Liberals and the of the Restoration; M. E. Daudet's on M. de Martignac, and on des Ministres en 1830;" M. Taine's great work on the de la France contemporaine;" and, lastly, that book written ago, but so present in its interest, "L'Histoire d'un Crime," the crushing and heartrending evidence of an eye-witness of December. Some surprise may have been occasioned by the taken by all the press of two works on Molière, by and M. de la Pommeraye; but if the public was excited (as to be) by this literary quarrel, it was not on account of its with Molière, but on account of the attack made by a clerical who held up to undying ridicule that religious hypocrisy lives, and now more than ever threatens danger to France.

contemporary passions make themselves less strongly of philosophy. The zeal with which philosophy is present day springs alike from the progress scientific study, and from political and religious not always either very well founded or party has made itself, generally, the defender of Evolutionist ideas and of the modern school of English psychologists, from mere opposition to the conservative party, which, when it is not *dévot*, adheres to the traditional spiritualism, and regards the doctrines of Darwin and Haeckel as the great modern heresy. It must nevertheless be acknowledged that the official spiritualism which, through M. Cousin, was made the compulsory doctrine of the University, has few adherents left. Those who still hold to it, like MM. Frank, Lévèque, Caro, whatever their merits as writers may be, have no great philosophical authority. M. Janet, on the contrary, who is a very vigorous dialectician and an earnest [illegible], has renounced the official doctrines on many points, and, in every respect, has very much widened the school's horizon by devoting constant attention to the new scientific theories and the works of the English psychological logicians. As for M. Taine, in his beautiful book, "L'Intelligence," he places himself at the same point of view as the English school. Amongst the young philosophers, some, headed by M. Ribot, have attached themselves completely to the latter school, and lately, one of them, M. Espinas, in his thesis for his doctor's degree, on the "Sociétés Animales," ventured to profess, for the first time at the Sorbonne, evolutionist doctrines. M. Nolen, the author of a remarkable study on "Kant et Leibnitz," shows tendencies similar to those lately so brilliantly represented in the *Revue Scientifique* and the *Revue Philosophique*, by M. Léon Dumont, snatched away by a premature death. A certain number of other young philosophers, struck by the difficulty of conciliating the data of science with the spiritualist theories of M. Cousin, have sought refuge in the vague, mystical, and intangible doctrines of M. Ravaisson. This almost religious idealism has enabled them to show themselves very daring in their examination into the most delicate problems of free-will, the separation of the soul and body, Providence, without nevertheless alarming the heads of the University, jealous though they are of maintaining the official *Credo*. They include some remarkable writers in their ranks: M. Lachelier, a logician of the first order; M. Fouillée, who is a true orator; M. Boutroux, a poet. I do not include amongst our philosophers M. Renan, who has plainly shown in his "Dialogues philosophiques" that he neither has nor wishes to have any doctrine; that he is satisfied with being a thinker, a poet, and a scholar. His chief work, "L'Histoire des Origines du Christianisme," the fifth volume of which, "Les Evangiles," was lately published, is a combination, often strange, always admirable, of imagination and science.

Philosophy, moreover, is in the act of pulling down its boundaries and allying itself with the natural sciences, which tends to nothing less than their being confounded together. The Positivist school, still [illegible] ably represented by MM. Littré and Wyrouboff's review, *La Philosophie Positive*, has long denied psychology the right of constituting itself [illegible] an independent science. The learned do not all go so far, but physiologists are making more and more frequent inroads into the [illegible] psychology, and the psychologists on their side seek in physiology [illegible] a groundwork for their labours, or at least a field of [illegible] elements of control. M. Luys' late book on the "[illegible] is the most remarkable [illegible] has hitherto made to [illegible] exclusive point of view [illegible] and furnishes psychology with important materials. The be said of Dr. Fournié, whose book, "La Bête et l'Homme," kind of stir, chiefly through his wanting to establish a sychology on scientific data. Spiritualism deserved a better Generally this desire to draw philosophical consequences gical, medical, physical, chemical researches, as from works tory, is apparent in all our learned men, and the names of steur, Claude Bernard, Würtz, and Quatrefages recur more often ophical writings of the day than those of Cousin or Jouffroy. icult until now to lay down very precisely what the ruling our learned men are. Amongst the doctors of medicine ysiologists, Positive (I do not say Positivist) tendencies, to official spiritualism, are clearly predominant, and the doctrines have many adepts. But several of our first learned steur, Würtz, Quatrefages, and Dumas, are spiritualists from others, such as Claude Bernard and Berthelot, confine themtrictly to the domain of experiment, but draw no conclusions ritualism. A book by M. Berthelot is, however, shortly ex- is to explain his general conception of the universe, and rnard will give us a deeper insight into his philosophical ideas ed book on the "Phénomènes Métaphysiques de la Vie." may with respect to these various tendencies, the scientific very active, and excites attention and interest far beyond the learned, properly so called. The proof is seen in the s of the *Association Française pour l'avancement des* nded on the model of the British Association, which held its eeting in Havre last August; and also in the rapid popu- by the *Bibliothèque Scientifique Internationale*. Many of contemporary science, even some of the most important, ized by the general public because they require attainments a kind; but all that is accessible is the object of lively have already spoken of physiological works; to them must se on anthropology, a science still in its youth, but which given birth in France to a society, a review, and even a which, based on geology and natural history, is linked on to history, archæology, and philology, by its researches into d into the primitive societies of man, and on the other to by the insight it gives into the origin of the earth and of M. Broca has constituted himself the apostle of anthropology nd is going to bring out soon an important book on the M. Hovelacque devotes himself to anthropology specially uistic point of view; finally, MM. Bertrand and De Mortillet, of the fine pre-historic museum of St. Germain, represent l and archæological side.

es of intellectual activity least influenced by the scientific and encies of the age are naturally those that address themselves the feelings and the emotions of the general public, namely, nd the arts. Not but that here too a pretence has been made to *ideal*, synonymous as it has become with the conventional and favour of true observation and pure reality; but in addressing has to be touched and charmed, the heart and the imagination ealed to. The most faithful of our painters of modern life,

Augier and Dumas, know this well; and though the theatre, like the whole of literature, has felt the influence of realism, it has not entirely succumbed to it. The two attempts to introduce pure realism on the stage, in "Henriette Maréchal" by the brothers De Goncourt, and "Thérèse Raquin" by M. Zola, have failed miserably. The piece lately played at the Gymnase, evidently inspired by M. Zola's "Assommoir," "Pierre Gendron," by MM. Lafontaine and Richard, is in reality a broad popular piece, in which vice is punished and virtue rewarded. Moreover since the war, side by side with the desire for serious work which drove the educated classes to science and learning, there was a general and very ardent desire for moral improvement, for healthy, manly, and pure emotions. Hence the enthusiasm, in part deserved, that welcomed such tragedies as "La Fille de Roland," by M. de Bornir, and "Rome Vaincue," by M. Parodi; the success of dramas such as "L'Hetman," by M. Déroulède, and "Jean Dacier," by M. Lomon; the tears and the applause excited by MM. Erckmann and Chatrian's pretty idyl "L'Ami Fritz." I believe that this purist tendency has produced real works of art, that it will take the learned tastes of our age into account, and find the principal sources of its inspiration in a resuscitation by historical criticism of our middle ages; just as it is in Germany with Wagner. We must not, however, think that the French public has suddenly grown so serious that it has forgotten how to laugh and be gay: it always needs distraction, and more especially now when the sadness and depression caused by politics have to be shaken off. Amusements are not wanting: Sardou is taking the lead and preparing for new successes with a sequel to "Dora;" and Meillac and Halévy have just been making all Paris laugh heartily with their fresh and charming "Cigale." Too often unhappily the merriment is not of the best kind, when, as in "Bébé," which had such a long run at the Gymnase, it is excited by subjects that cannot be alluded to in decent terms.

The desire for noble and pure emotions which has been increasing in the French public of late years, has shown itself more particularly in the growing taste for music. Some of the works of our young composers evince earnest striving after a high ideal; such, for instance, as "Le Roi de Lahore," by M. Massenet; "Dmitri," by M. Joncière; "Le Bravo," by M. Salvayre. But what is most noteworthy is the success of our great instrumental concerts. Every Sunday crowds collect in the Cirque d'Hiver and the Salle du Châtelet, to hear M. Pasdeloup's and M. Colonne's orchestras play the finest works of the great masters, amongst which public admiration has henceforth classed the orchestral compositions of Berlioz, and beside which the works of our young composers, Saint-Saëns, Massenet, Guiraud, deservedly take their place. A new series of concerts, called *Concerts Modernes*, has been begun in the Cirque Fernando [illegible] though the Conservatoire has doubled the number of its rehearsals [illegible] number of the favoured who gain admission is still very small [illegible] pared to the crowds who are excluded. Even frivolous music [illegible] of becoming less frivolous, and the operetta is coming back [illegible] the Opéra Comique.

What has been said of the theatre and music may [illegible] We see, on the one hand, the realistic tendencies [illegible] portance to execution and simple truth, and [illegible] talents like M. Vollon or M. [illegible]

...impressionists; on the other hand, the more ideal tendencies ... satisfaction either in the study of nature, in which our ... cherish the beautiful traditions of Rousseau, Dupré, ... or in the painting of grand historical subjects, where, ... learned tastes of the age combine with the research ... Jean Paul Laurens is at the present moment the most bril... ...tative of this phase of contemporary art, endeavouring to ...rical truth with the grand human emotions, whilst carrying ...cution to its highest perfection. The Administration of the ... done its utmost to encourage these strivings after high art, ... with that view, the decoration of the Panthéon by covering ... frescoes representing the life of Ste. Geneviève—that is to ... series of pictures of barbarian and Christian Gaul. The com... M. Puvis de Chavannes that have just been uncovered, and ... executed with true religious and picturesque feeling, augur ... undertaking that might appear hazardous. But we must not ... painting is now more than anything an art of ornament, ... with decorating the walls of the luxurious and elegant apart... ...he favourites of fortune. So that *genre* painting is the kind of ...at chiefly attracts young artists. A wealth of skill, cleverness, ...ion is expended upon it every year, and now and then, under ... of a genius of observation, like Meissonier, Detaille, or Neuville, ... the level of high art. We shall be able in the coming exhi... ... the changes that have taken place since 1867 in our modern painting. There also I fancy we shall see that learning has ... realms of art, and that the pictures of M. le Comte du Nouy, ...e, like those of M. Alma Tadema, are as learned and instructive ... of the *Revue Archéologique.*

... the pet attractions in Paris just now is also of a scientific ... I refer to the Esquimaux at the Jardin d'Acclimatation, ... crowds every day. They were brought hither, so people say, ...ests of anthropology. The same grass-plot was tenanted in ... by a party of Nubians, who presented the public with a ... African life. Now that the cold has come, we are transported ...ed. These Esquimaux—three men, a woman, and two little ... them a baby in arms—give us a very complete idea of life ... regions. They are dressed in their costumes of seal-skin; ... who is one of the belles of Greenland, carries her younger ... back in a bag made of skin. They have built two winter ...ods of earth, and pitched two summer tents of skin. They ...ght over with them ten seals, five white bears, and a dozen ...times they are to be seen in their *Kajak*, a canoe made of ... hole in the middle, in which the man sits, having a sham ...owing the javelin and the harpoon, sometimes driving in ... drawn by dogs round their little territory. Just now this ...ject that has any power to divert the Parisian mind from ... Blondin, the renowned Blondin, runs along his rope ... back, cooks an omelette, and drives a young girl in a ... height of 35 mètres from the ground,—no one takes ... there not Blondins far more daring to be seen ... antics on the tight-rope of politics, at the risk ...

GABRIEL MONOD.

# ESSAYS AND NOTICES.

---

## THE INDIAN CIVIL SERVICE EXAMINATIONS.

PROFESSOR BAIN'S interesting article in the last number of this REVIEW may be looked at as suggesting improvements either in regard to general education or in regard to the particular examination of which it treats. It is by no means necessarily the case that what is true or expedient for the one is also true or expedient for the other. A subject, which is of great value for training, may not lend itself easily to the purpose of examining, and *vice versa*. More than this, the objects of the two are distinct; the end of education is to make the most of the individual educated, the end of competitive examination is, ordinarily, to discover the ablest among a number of competitors. Thus, as regards the Indian Civil Service examinations, the object is simply to find out the best administrators for India. And the best administrator, we shall probably all agree, is not necessarily the man who is most highly instructed at the age of twenty-two, but the man who has the most natural force of character and intellect, controlled by high moral principle, and softened by sympathy and tact. If to these qualities we add a good presence and manner, bodily strength and activity, we have a man who is likely to do honour to England and to win the respect and affection of our Indian fellow-subjects. It must be confessed that the present mode of selection is only very partially effective in discovering such qualities in the candidates. No doubt there was ample reason for doing away with the old system. Relationship to a director could be no guarantee of a man's fitness for office, while on the other hand many admirable candidates were excluded from the service owing to the want of such connection. But if one mode of nomination was faulty, that is no reason why we should have rushed into the opposite extreme and given away appointments on the ground of intellectual attainments only, without regard to other and more important considerations. If it is asked, what other course was open? the answer is plain. Those who have the best opportunity of forming a judgment on the younger generation of English gentlemen are the heads of our great schools and colleges; whilst those have passed well through these are the most likely to possess the qualifications mentioned above as desirable for work in India. It would have been a simple course to have placed a number of nominations in the hands of the vice-chancellors of the Universities and the head masters of the chief schools. Other less distinguished bodies might have had partial nominations, *e.g.*, the right to nominate candidates, of whom a certain proportion should be selected by the Secretary of State for India. Unhappily, whether from jealousy, or the exigencies of party, or the mere ignorance and thoughtlessness of our public men, this course was not followed. Recourse was had to the universal panacea of competitive examination. This would not have been so mischievous if the subjects and times of examinations had been so arranged as to induce candidates to pass through school or college, as usual; but the limit of age was so fixed that it was almost impossible to get a degree at the University, and the examination extended over so wide a field that it could not be covered by the regular school training. Hence arose the necessity for "cramming" as it is called. Boys were removed from school, thrown loose among all the temptations of London life, not to be educated, but to cram themselves with miscellaneous facts and theories to be poured out on paper in the examination room. In saying this, we have no wish to join in the common abuse of the crammers. They are simply persons who have had the energy and intelligence at once to meet a sudden demand. But they would not themselves deny that, while schools and colleges profess to educate the whole man for future usefulness, and to prepare him, in the old phrase, to serve God in Church and State, the one object candidates have in view is to pass a particular examination, and that those whom they employ to prepare them for this end are [illegible] exclusively to that which will "pay." No doubt the same [illegible] of less, of the preparation for any examination in which [illegible] the result. How many candidates for a high place among [illegible] allowed to ask themselves what would be really the best [illegible] their own self-improvement? In their case, too, a means [illegible] substituted for the end. But at Oxford or Cambridge there [illegible] influences. There is the excellent tradition of accuracy [illegible] work, ensured where the attention is concentrated upon one [illegible] years of study. There is the variety of interests among [illegible] each free to follow his own taste, not all looking forward to the [illegible]. There is the presence of, perhaps familiar intercourse with, [illegible] to be animated by the love of knowledge and of truth, whose [illegible] recognized as those of the leaders in thought, or science, or [illegible] nothing else, there is at least the *religio loci* insensibly inspiring [illegible] selfish considerations.

[illegible] that it was an ill-judged step to make the Indian appointments [illegible] the results of a general competitive examination, and that it has [illegible] ill-judged, because the effect has been to substitute the hothouse [illegible] establishment for the invigorating atmosphere of the school and [illegible]. But the step once taken, it is difficult to draw back; probably all [illegible] is to alter the conditions of the examination, so as to make it [illegible] candidates to continue at school or college without injuring their [illegible] success. The changes which have been lately introduced have had [illegible]. It remains to be seen how far they are calculated to attain it. [illegible] simpler alteration would have been more effective. Since the schools [illegible] not adapt their system to your examinations, why not suit the [illegible] to their system? Be satisfied to examine in English, classics (allow[illegible] German as alternatives for Greek), and mathematics, to the extent [illegible] in Professor Bain's article. All you want to ascertain is mental [illegible] may be ascertained from three subjects as well as from a dozen. [illegible] agree with Professor Bain's other recommendations? Instead [illegible] weight to the public school training, he proposes to exclude from [illegible] that which is at present the main subject of school-training— [illegible] translation. If there were the least hope that the great schools [illegible] accommodate their system to the examination, it might be worth while [illegible] question on its merits; and if, on consideration, we were satisfied [illegible] would be really improved by cutting out the study of the classical [illegible] might then adopt this indirect means of introducing such an [illegible] into the schools; but since it is a matter of perfect indifference [illegible] whether the candidates remain with them or go to the crammers, it seems [illegible] who desire the good of India will not be disposed to welcome a [illegible] which would still further diminish the connection between the public [illegible] Indian Civil Service.

[illegible] to the consideration of the article as suggesting improvements in [illegible] While Professor Bain's remarks on the study of science have met with [illegible] assent from those who are best qualified to speak on the subject, we [illegible] that classical teachers will be satisfied with his statement of the [illegible] derived from the study of language. No doubt, in times past the [illegible] claims have been advanced in defence of the exclusive study of [illegible]. The most insignificant details of language, the merest dust of [illegible], have been insisted upon, not only as capable of utilization at the [illegible] philosopher or historian, but as intrinsically valuable, and even [illegible] ordinary student. But this cannon-ball protectionism is now [illegible]. There are few scholars who would dispute that German is in [illegible] as good an educational instrument as Greek; few teachers of [illegible] would deny that many of those who now learn Greek would have [illegible] spent the same amount of time in reading translations of the [illegible], and in gaining more familiarity with the best Latin authors. [illegible] seems to ignore the great advantage of studying the modes [illegible] in a language other than our own. If we investigate the [illegible] in our own language, the method is analytic: beginning with a [illegible] general meaning of the sentence, we gradually break it up into [illegible] account to ourselves of the relation of each part to the whole. [illegible] hardly an exciting process. There is none of the pleasure of [illegible] distinct problem awaiting solution to stimulate and reward the labour of the chase. In a foreign language it is different. There we begin with fragments of knowledge gathered from the lexicon and the grammar, which we build up by gradual synthesis into a complete sentence, revealing to us the total thought of the author. Take for instance such a writer as Demosthenes; to make out the meaning at all, it is necessary to examine with the utmost minuteness the exact relation of clause to clause, to weigh the force of particles, to consider the bearing of sentences and paragraphs on each other. Is there any better way in which an ordinary student may be trained in clearness and subtlety of thought? And, if further he is not satisfied with the bare understanding of the original, but endeavours to infuse the spirit of the Greek into his English translation, is there any better way of becoming acquainted with the capabilities of his own language, and acquiring a practical mastery over it? Lastly, if he analyses the course of the argument, if he watches the manner in which the subject is handled, and endeavours to understand the reason for the order in which the different points are introduced, even for the order of the different words in the same sentence, can we doubt that this supplies an excellent lesson in rhetoric?* Professor Bain asks rather contemptuously, Is logic, is universal grammar, is taste taught in practice? Are not these mere polemical pleas? We answer boldly, they are undoubtedly taught, and cannot but be taught, by careful study of any good foreign author, especially if the language in which he writes is as distinct from our own, in its syntactical formation, as the Greek, the Latin, or the German. Professor Bain continues, "Supposing that these various ends may be attained by the study of language, they will at any rate be better attained by being studied separately." Study them separately, by all means; get up your logic and rhetoric and grammar from the ordinary text-books; theory lends eyes to practice. And yet we may hold that an acquaintance with the informal logic of expression, as illustrated in the pages of Demosthenes, is not less valuable than a knowledge of Whately or of Mill; and that the impression of grandeur and of beauty which comes through the slow deliberate perusal of the Agamemnon or the Antigone, is worth any amount of theory learnt out of books on æsthetics. And so for the rest. We are far from denying the value of the abstract; but we prefer to learn and to teach through the concrete. The opposite view may be compared to a German's exaltation of the *Turn-verein* over our school-games, as affording a far more scientific exercise of the muscles; yet most Englishmen would hold that this was more than counterbalanced by the quickened life and the absorbing interest of the games, as well as by the scope which they give for the exhibition of character, and for the discipline of temper and courage. In like manner it is the union of many points of interest, the scope they afford for the development of various tastes and capacities, which constitutes, in our view, the peculiar excellence of the classics as a training for life.

On educational grounds, therefore, as well as on competitive grounds, we are compelled to dissent from Professor Bain's proposal to substitute ancient history for the ancient languages. Not that we at all approve of the recent minute, which runs into the opposite extreme, and limits the examination to translation and composition alone. But if we must have one-sided systems, we prefer that which, to say the least of it, cannot fail, in some degree, to test the active working of the individual mind, rather than that which, in the majority of cases, is likely to prove no more than a greater or less degree of receptive capacity; that which gives as its result the power to translate at sight from any Greek or Latin author, rather than that which calls forth only a *rechauffé* of the views of Mommsen or of Grote.

---

* Cicero's habit of translating from Greek into Latin, and his opinion of the value of this practice as improving his own Latin style, are familiar to every one. Dr. Arnold's view expressed in the following passage may be less generally known:—"My delight in going over Homer and Virgil with the boys makes me think what a treat it must be to teach Shakespeare to a good class of young Greeks in regenerate Athens; to dwell upon him line by line and word by word, in a way that nothing but a translation lesson will ever enable one to do; and so to get all his pictures and thoughts leisurely into one's mind, till I verily think one would after a time almost give out light in the dark, after having been steeped, as it were, in such an atmosphere of brilliance. And how could this be done without the process of construing, as the grosser medium through which all the beauty can be transmitted, because else we travel too fast, and [illegible] it escapes us?"—*Arnold's Life*, Letter cxliii. It was the same feeling [illegible] tion of Schlegel's translation of Shakespeare as the subject [illegible] the Sixth Form.

## PICTURES FOR CHILDREN.

persons, outside of literary and artistic circles no less than have shown themselves sensitive to the stupidity of a trick by too many recent writers for the young,—the trick, namely, of clumsy way with the simple thread of the work allusions, mostly public topics, quite out of the reach of children's minds. Much of the for the young is suspectible of applications which only the adult can make; for example, many if not most of Andersen's stories for philosophers and students as well as fables in which children can similar remark applies to most of the other fables. Nearly all, if not modern attempts in that kind are utter failures. The second or esoteric not well appreciable by any one who has not been in society and Thackeray. They please adults, but they fail to interest young readers been forewarned that they *ought* to be pleased. And here it may be the adults who provide reading for the young are far too apt to hint beforehand the occasions on which they are to try to feel gratified. Of from young readers extracted under such conditions are not worth

This criticism would apply with still greater force to the subject of " as they are called, though the word is in five cases out of ten quite mark. Confining our attention for the moment to books and pictures for young children, we may safely lay it down that, however the pictures grown-up people, the majority of them have, to say the least, no special to the young. This is stating the case at the lowest. A young child of high art, nothing of nice perspective, nothing of delicate work-nothing of subtle shades of expression. A picture which delights an adult, is worse than thrown away upon its untaught little eyes—it con-impressions. Nor is the case mended if the subject of the picture be which children themselves enter ever so largely. For instance Mr. Du children, or Sir Joshua Reynolds's, have, in a young chit's eyes, but a very interest. The best of the picture is thrown away upon it, and is too far from its sphere of apprehension to exercise any educating influence.

years ago, Sir Henry Cole, under the signature of Felix Summerley, edited charming editions of old nursery rhymes, with excellent woodcuts. The pic-a delight to many adults, but those who made experiments, as we did, discovered that young children greatly preferred coarse, simple work, get in the old-fashioned editions of "Æsop" and "Goody Two Shoes." who makes the trial will discover that a little one who can just read will Quarles's "Emblems" or an old Bunyan with greedy pleasure, while it nothing for the sort of pictures now-a-days provided in such plenty as for the young.

are of course limits here as elsewhere. If a child has reached the age at does not care how many syllables a word contains, and begins to have of caricature, it will have begun to understand pictures such as please We can mention an actual case in which the first *pointed* indication given child of its advanced growth in matters of art, was an instantaneous laughter at a set of pictures from the Bayeux tapestry. A child that is and clever enough to see the grotesqueness of those figures is old enough the well-known Struwwelpetter pictures as caricatures or humorous But it is different with a child that can just read Wordsworth's "Lucy perhaps. What such a child wants in pictures is simplicity, directness, straightforward actuality of presentation. If the letterpress tells the child that of the sun smote a sleeping traveller sorely on the head, he is not a bit pleased by a picture, however artistic, in which the sun is seen at the landscape quivering with heat, and a man lying down with a weary aside. What the child sees is actual beams coming down from the sun the man on the forehead like sticks. And so of other matters. Gulliver's "dear old Christian looking like a turtle," would delight a little infinitely more than the most artistic figure that Holman Hunt could a word, and once more, pictures such as those in Quarles's "Emblems" type to which illustrations for the very young should conform. The is, of course, not to be crude and incorrect, as Quarles's artist was; but he is, like that ancient draughtsman, whoever he was (Quarles himself perhaps), to avoid crowding his pictures: to be utterly simple and straightforward; and in fact to spend his force, not upon subtleties of expression and workmanship such as students of Millais, or Leech, or Du Maurier rightly enjoy, but upon the task of "illustrating" the text, or of conveying impressions apart from any text, with the vividness, aloneness, and materialistic force of a dream. These conditions leave ample room for the genius of the artist to make sport in, and if the letter-press cannot be illustrated upon those terms, it is not fit for the reading, or at least not fit for the delectation of young children.

---

## BLACK AND WHITE.

WE have before us five works, all illustrated in black and white; some appreciable portion of the art-work of this year, and of different degrees of merit, or the contrary. Some years ago these woodcuts would have been called works in light and shade; but as the Rembrandtesque tastes of Continental draughtsmen are fast prevailing over our own workmen, and the greater number of intermediate greys between black and white are now left out of a picture, black and white let it be. We do our artists no injustice when we suppose them to be influenced in all they do by the purest pecuniary motives. They have to work in black and white because it pays. These things the public will buy, because it gets them in quantities. They pay by their multitude; by means of electro-typed blocks and other means, they can be indefinitely multiplied, and people can have them cheap. And after careful inspection the question really occurred to our mind, in so many words, How far do the people care for these works, of greater or less merit? and what good are they likely to get from them? Before going into this question, the two monographs should be placed by themselves. Mr. Ernest George's Flemish etchings* are thoroughly worthy of him; they are of a fair standard of beauty and accuracy: they are printed in brown and not in black; there are evidences of sincere pleasure and the workman's honour in them; and that they command a good sale is a cheering symptom in public taste—much wanted. Mr. W. B. Scott's etchings from Blake,† however, claim a certain precedence in interest as ideal work of high aim. To reproduce Blake is, as may well be supposed, a labour of love to Mr. Scott, and no man can be better qualified for the task, as his own efforts as author and engraver place him at least in the same category as his great model, and the aim of all his labours has always been honourable to him. He is not himself a very strict draughtsman, and is none the less able to sympathize with the divine mania of Blake's pencil, which did so many things gloriously, but never did anything right. He is well known as both poet and painter, and has appeared as a somewhat vehement critic; but his little book on Albert Durer did him the greatest credit, and was quite exhaustive, from the engraver's point of view: nor was it by any means bad as a biography. Blake would most likely have accepted his last reproducer with even more satisfaction as a kindred spirit had he seen the illustrations to the Pilgrim's Progress, published by Mr. Scott and as we believe, not having the book before us, by an elder brother of great genius). We cannot help suggesting that a reissue, at least of the first part of that considerable work, would be a great boon to the English art-world: in giving it assurance of a thing much desired by many—a good Northern-Gothic genius with a dash of Scriptural Puritanism.

The etching of the "Nativity," No. 4, is perhaps the central work of all the ten. The treatment and idea are mystical. Blake's determined sense of the supernatural in that event perhaps led him too far from the thought of Him who was born as a man among men. But the fainting Virgin, the adoring Elizabeth, and the appearance of the Holy Child in glory show that intensity of imagination which must pass excused or blameless, *quia multum amavit*, in theology and art alike. There are enough elaborate draperies and highly-finished oxen in the

* Etchings in Belgium. By Ernest George. London: Seeleys

† William Blake. Etchings from his works, by William Bell Scott. London: Chatto and Windus.

ly; and certainly little enough of that spiritual conviction which the ...isposes of by labelling as mysticism.

... look at the "St. Matthew and the Angel," and think of what an oil-... great thought would have made, had Blake been taught or teachable ... men or things; or of the "Queen of Evil," painted in full sensuous ...y one who most obviously was "not of her order, but belonged to the ...s," and clad her quite decently against her will,—we are reminded ...h of a sentence in the "Stones of Venice," where the author does not ... what men *suffer*, so much as at what they *lose*." Blake never saw ... would he have cared for him. He must have seen Hogarth's works, ...ve seen Hogarth in life, as there are ten years overlapping, between ...ut he must only have included Hogarth in his long list of strong ... is extraordinary that while, as Mr. Scott says, every object in "Marriage ... is precisely studied and truthfully realized, Blake never took the trouble ...en drapery. No doubt, as he said, he found nature abominably in his ... could hardly have been otherwise in a mind literally "troubled" by ...ming fancies. We must needs pass by the invented vegetation which ...ing on earth, and Mr. Scott is right in claiming a kind of indulgent ...r reverent indulgence, for one who worked so truly from the Idea. ...rong, Blake had command of true Beauty; and the Eves now first ...re pure and lovely to a degree; though we really have measured, with ...viders, nine heads to the newly created mother of mankind in No. 7; ... Adam has no back whatever to his head in No. 8. Indeed, Mr. ... drawing, though fine in idea, repeats this smallness of head rather too ...ut these etchings are genuine work of art and labour of love, and ...ble old maniac the sort of honour which a kindred spirit only could

...est George's Belgian etchings show delicate and correct drawing ...ful sparkling quality, as in Nos. 1, 5, 6, and 10. The composition and ...empts at mass and light, with detail in both, remind us greatly of ... Rivers of France," or rather of the city-subjects therein; for Mr. ...he says, makes no attempt at the landscape of Belgium. He seems to ...ing for the past, and it must be genuine and hearty. It is worthy of ...n quay or canal scenes as Nos. 5 and 6, that there is an undercurrent of ...f Venice, which lives and must live for ever in every English painter who ...ere—and perhaps in some who have not. There is a sameness in the ...neat handling; but it is able and faithful: and Mr. George always ... difference between shade and sunshine. This seems happily to be a ...rk which the public can enjoy; and is in the highest grade of printed ...cally multiplied art-productions.

... come to a volume of "L'Art."* It contains, besides endless wood-... a certain merit in their kind, an excellent portrait in etching and ...ing of M. Thiers: autograph etchings by Saintin, Toussaint, Desbrosses; ...nes after Jules Breton, Orchardson, Burne Jones, Diaz,—one in par-...Champollion, after Fortuny's "Moors and Vulture,"—and, above all, an ...nally happy in subject and treatment, from Watts's portrait of Lady ... Balcarres. About the value of all these things there can be no doubt. ...ems to us a work in which the ideal and the real are quite wonderfully ...e pose and look are like those of "Joy" in Collins's underrated Ode†—...s just stopping the higher strings, and the dark eyes catch the spec-... full of delight in the notes just ringing out upon his ear; though ... half-pensive after all. It is no small matter to have this great work ...ndered for circulation in the commonwealth of French painters. ...e no doubt of what our artists learn from them, for good as well as for ...hey should at least see our best, whatever they may think of it. As an

---

* London: 135, New Bond Street.

† ". . . Last came Joy's ecstatic triad;  
He, with viny crown advancing,  
First to the lively pipe his hand addressed:  
But soon he saw the brisk awakening viol,  
Whose sweet entrancing sound he loved the best.  
And as his flying fingers kiss'd the strings . . ."

excellent colourist in the subdued or Continental scales, Mr. Watts is more likely to be understood than Mr. Burne Jones. And here we find most judicious and well-instructed remarks on the latter (in the articles on the Grosvenor Gallery by Mr. J. Comyns Carr), with a magnificent etching of the "Beguiling of Merlin," and several heads illustrative of his unique power of representing naturally beautiful faces under stormy or evil passion. Those named Sævitia and Crudelitas are extremely subtle, and anybody who wishes to understand the difference between spiritual power of expression and mechanical method, may compare them with Flaxman, in "Sir Charles Bell on Expression;" or, if that is not enough, with Lebrun's "Passions." No less is required of the draughtsman of such subjects than to make expression overpower distortion in a distorted face, so as definitely to appeal to the imagination of the spectator. This is done admirably in "Sævitia:" the face, all raging and agonized, tells you of the reaction of cruelty on itself, and the failure of reason under the inner torment of unsated blood-thirst, like Ezzelino's or the Cenci's. It would hardly be complete, either, without the premonitory stages of "Crudelitas"—cruelty of folly and of honesty; the latter pre-eminently good.* There are excellent papers on the last Salon, capitally illustrated (see in particular M. C. F. Gaillard's Head at p. 181; and opposite p. 85, from A. A. Montfort, and Gilbert's "Market Scene" at p. 86). The lovely drawing called "Un Charmeur" (Butin fils), and a head, "A Villageoise, Calvados," p. 83, by Ulysse Butin, give us much pleasure. And the woodcuts and autotypes from Rubens, with artistic biography by M. Paul Leroi, would also give value to the work. There are good papers on Sèvres China, and on early Faïence at Quimper and Rouen. In short, there is a wonderful amount of good art for the money. Some which seems to us bad in purpose is honestly given, and shows at all events what it is: we may notice, as instances of offensive coquetterie, skilful, beautiful, and mischievous, the etching opposite p. 210, and a woodcut called "Après le Bain." It is quite proper that these should be given in "L'Art;" but they are in themselves unwelcome to us. The design called "Les Muses," at p. 17, seems to indicate an enthusiastically profound exploration of the Bathos, which will certainly gratify the critics of that region. Nevertheless, with all our appreciation, it is hard to disguise from ourselves that all this really good work in black and white is not only beyond the unskilled public, but, in a real sense, unattractive. The strong and excellent woodcuts at pp. 4 and 39, and even that of Mr. Poynter's "Proserpine," are only *symbolic* of beauty. Those who have seen the pictures are reminded of them more or less, according to memory and knowledge of style. But the cuts possess no beauty; they are not much prettier than letterpress to a sharp eye, untrained to understand their import. Colour is more cruelly missed in these examples, because it is very delicate in the originals. When one comes to black cows and white cows, and Continental works never conceived in colour at all, but as light and shade tinted to conventional scales of harmony, one feels less of the change from what, in them, is called colour, to plain chiaroscuro; and the alternate depth and sparkle of the etching is pleasant, no doubt, to many who cannot etch. Still all these are tedious unless you have skill to conceive of them in colour. And when the horrors of M. J. Buisson's sketch-book stared, scowled, and jibbered at us,—however capitally done, all the more horrible because they were all awfully like,—we shut the book in much-amused despair. This periodical seems likely to be of the greatest value, as a medium of mutual understanding between French and English painters; and Mr. Comyns Carr is fully able to interpret between men of high aim on either side.

A great gulf has here to be passed, between artistic, or quasi-artistic works, done in some measure for art's sake, and commercial illustration produced to sell. There are better or worse things in both classes, and some very good in the latter, but the distinction holds for all that. "The Rhine"† is a work written by three German authors, and illustrated by ever so many artists. Its style is the best form of handbook; and Mr. Bartley seems to have wrestled not unsuccess-

---

* I only remember one ideal of the pitilessness of folly equal to this: the "Faithful led to Execution," in the Scotts' Pilgrim's Progress, where the Lord of Vanity Fair is dancing at the head of the procession with cap, bells, and bauble; a tall and graceful figure, with no expression but that of pure indifference, even to the spirit of the hour,—to anything but cap and bells.

† The Rhine: From its Source to the Sea. Translated by G. C. T. Bartley from the German. With 425 Illustrations. London: Bickers & Son.

[illegible] three gentlemen in one. The illustrations are [illegible] the Birket-Foster style of land[illegible] graphic power (and this is seldom the case) [illegible] natural enjoyment of a pretty scene. [illegible] "Sketch in the Odenwald with roe-deer;" [illegible] Heidelberg. One or two others are striking; [illegible] "the Bridge at Constance," and the "Schaffhausen." [illegible] curious contrast of paper versus ink; as the [illegible] the latter of which has a dash of the [illegible] in the trees and the smoke. The foregrounds are [illegible] the freshness of study from nature: and we notice [illegible] of tone and gradation, caused by abuse or over-use of [illegible] illustrations, as that of "Sitting in the Trenches at [illegible] to those who, like ourselves, have only seen the Rhine [illegible] Bridge," p. 261, and the drawings at pp. 306-7, may re[illegible] the book: the first by Mr. Pültney, who we think must [illegible] studied Turner in his time, and found out that the English [illegible] solid drawing as well as of cloud-compelling. In [illegible] book, though it might be better with fewer illustrations— [illegible] them are not so good, but because the reader would then [illegible] enjoy the majority, which have more or less merit. The [illegible] illustration which every year produces, is much against [illegible] of art. It all tends to make the public think that cheap [illegible] banged out of printing-presses; that because it is cheap [illegible] to; and that it leads to nothing higher or better.

[illegible] to be said in praise of the letter-press of "Great Painters of [illegible] the author appears to have gone to all the best authorities, [illegible] his references to them; and we have to thank him for ingeni[illegible] them in the text, instead of sending one's eye to notes at the [illegible]. His own observations, though rare, are distinguished [illegible] tells us that the real home of the English language was, [illegible] to be found in the Lowlands of Scotland, on which text we [illegible] to hear Dr. Freeman comment; and that Barbour's English [illegible] to Chaucer's. We suppose that the curious grammatical con[illegible] p. 10 (last paragraph) is an imitation of Barbour. It certainly is [illegible], or English either.

[illegible] compilation of other books, this may be useful; though we do [illegible] whom. Perhaps it will be of value to other book-makers or [illegible] by reference, through magazine articles, to papers for [illegible] and pupil-teachers. The book must have been published [illegible] wood blocks, and seems to be intended for a gift-book, for which [illegible].

[illegible] issue of machinery art is an evil of which Mr. Poynter and all [illegible] may well complain: but we see no cure for it. These books are [illegible] of the progress of art, but of indifference to it. The graphic part [illegible] on carelessness of inspection, and is not intended to be really [illegible] they will prosper till the English public has learnt from nature to [illegible], whether naturalistic or imaginative.

---

## CHARLOTTE WILLIAMS WYNN.†

[illegible]DERABLE portion of this volume of 400 pages had already been [illegible] for private circulation, and the edition was long ago exhausted. [illegible] Williams Wynn was the daughter of the Right Hon. Charles [illegible] Wynn, and was born in the year 1807. She died in 1869, of cancer,

---

[illegible] Painters of Christendom, from Cimabue to Wilkie. By John Forbes [illegible] Cassell, Petter, & Galpin.

[illegible] Charlotte Williams Wynn. Edited by her Sister. With a Portrait. [illegible], Green, & Co.

having had, apparently, much illness, largely neuralgic, in the course of her life. Her portrait, taken at fifty, shows a fine patrician face, the lips firmly set in the way which is so frequently to be noticed in those who have had much to undergo, either in mind or body, or both. It also shows a quick, apprehensive sensitiveness, but without much capacity of abandonment or self-illusion. Accordingly, the letters exhibit traces of intelligence that assume the look of downright [illegible]. She appears to have been a highly-cultivated woman, taking a deep interest in religious, political, and social questions, but, so far as we can judge, without any enthusiasm of accomplishment or pursuit. In her father's circle, she knew Heber, Southey, Hallam, Mackintosh, &c., &c., and later on she was intimate with Varnhagen von Ense, Bunsen, Rio, Carlyle, and Maurice. With the last of these distinguished men she formed a strong friendship, and a letter from him (side by side with one from the Baroness de Bunsen) forms part of the introductory matter of the book. She must have suffered a great deal,—at least we may probably infer as much from her sister's statement that she received with glad thanksgiving, "like a hymn of praise," the information that her end was very near—though the news came quite suddenly upon her.

It is impossible to study this noble countenance and the Memorials which follow the Introduction, without deep sympathy with the noble lady whose life they go far to make real to us. A strongly affectionate nature, very well balanced, with a deep-seated conscientiousness, and a consequent love of what is solid in human relations, is what meets us on almost every page. It is probable that the impression left upon the mind of a stranger would gain much in tenderness if it were not for omissions which were inevitable,—or which, at least, were quite natural to the high-toned reticence of good society. Her clear-sightedness and openness to truth were most remarkable. Take the following, relating to George Sand:—

"*Nice*, 1839.—To Baron Varnhagen von Ense.—'What's in a name?' Shakespeare is wrong there; there is a great deal in it. I should have read 'Les Lettres d'un Voyageur' long ago, had it not been for the bad name of their author. The book has perhaps struck me the more from my previous prejudices, but it has given me more pleasure than I have had for some time. How magnificent are some passages! One thing strikes me: I had always been told that her writings were so like those of a man that it was impossible to discern from them that the author was a woman. Now in this work it appears impossible to make such a mistake: every line bears the impress of a woman's writing."

And this about some one whose name is left blank:—

"With —— I cannot agree; but I have a singular faculty for admiring another person's faith, although I cannot make it my own. It is like viewing a fine prospect out of a window; I can think it beautiful, and even wish to be transported there, without finding it possible. I am not at all sure whether I am not in danger of carrying this too far, and may be becoming indifferent. If one is thoroughly and decidedly convinced of the truth of an opinion, is one not generally anxious to persuade others to adopt the same view?—and I am not."

Very good is this about Peel, and the subsequent touch about Mr. Gladstone is highly amusing:—

"The following sentence would form a good motto for a future life of Peel:—'In a higher world it is otherwise; but here below to live is to change, and to be perfect is to have changed often.' They say Mr. Gladstone has been given two offices, in order, if possible, to keep him quiet, and by giving him too much to do, to prevent him from troubling his head about the Church; but I know it will be in vain, for to a speculative mind like his, theology is a far more inviting and extensive field than any that is offered by the Board of Trade."

This was in 1842. As an instance of the humour of the writer, which often breaks out in capital touches, take this, written in June, 1843:—

"Ireland is indeed in an alarming state, and Father Mathew (although I believe unintentionally) has much increased the danger. It is a very different thing to have to deal with well-organized bodies of men who are all sober, to what it was when they were all drunk."

In March, 1845, the same doubt seems to have occurred to Miss Wynn which was the subject of a fine essay in the *Spectator* at the time of the death of Artemus Ward:—

"Poor Sydney Smith's death is a great loss to London. His wit will not easily be replaced; in a certain set he will be missed daily, and nowhere will his [illegible] come across one so often as at the great dinners of which he used to make the [illegible]

[illegible], and though perhaps a dinner-table is not the monument one [illegible] whether it is not a more enduring one than a stone with two [illegible] is to be done with Wit hereafter? If Sydney Smith had to [illegible] the grave, his individuality is gone; and yet there are few [illegible] in accordance with the ordinary ideas of heaven."

[illegible] railway travelling and the distance between friends is worthy [illegible] perhaps it is more like Leigh Hunt:—

"[illegible] of all these railroads? One is not a bit nearer one's friends when [illegible] your trunks before you go! I reckon my journeys now always by [illegible] required; it is far more exact than troubling one's head with [illegible] you are to go over. Mary laughed when I talked of a place I was [illegible] a 'carpet-bag' off, but it is very expressive."

[illegible] in 1856, we have a stroke of humour about the inutility of the [illegible] as good as anything of the kind could possibly be:—

"[illegible].—The streets had an odd appearance this morning—all the [illegible], nosegay sellers, match vendors, each armed with 'Form of Prayer, [illegible] of their usual articles; and the street so empty; you saw nothing [illegible] sheets of paper, excepting policemen, who, having evidently no work [illegible] come out on speculation. But they were a few hundred yards apart from [illegible] they expected an outbreak against the Fast."

[illegible] quainter than that notion of an outbreak against a fast, when [illegible] what nobody was compelled to, besides being in itself a negative? [illegible], but by no means surprising, to have the testimony of the [illegible] to the value of religious ministrations as a sanitary agent:—

"[illegible] Bunsen.—November 6th, 1854.—They are very desirous of sending out [illegible] army as soon as possible, and a fact mentioned by the Archbishop of [illegible] a great impression on me. He said that the Duke of Wellington told [illegible] ago, 'that he could have saved the lives of 2,000 men a year had he [illegible] any religious ministers. The uneasiness of their minds reacted on [illegible] kept up continual fever.' Such an opinion coming from the most prac[illegible] enthusiastic man that ever lived, has great weight, and I trust the object [illegible] out."

[illegible] to mind no memoir of a woman of any distinction of character [illegible] so strong an impression of the entire sanity of its subject. The [illegible], and kindness of the writer of these letters is strongly illus[illegible] she wrote about the time of the *coup d'état*, when she was actually [illegible] was by no means inclined to relinquish any of her just privileges [illegible], as far as we can judge, she used them with great sagacity. Mar[illegible] complained, or at all events recorded, that in "conversation" with [illegible] the reciprocity was all on one side, as the Irishman put it: in other [illegible] he would not allow you to interrupt him; but Miss Wynn seems boldly [illegible] to have laid her hand on the lion's mane:—"Burning incense [illegible] hero all day is so bad for him. Sooner or later it drags them down; [illegible] was with Carlyle I always felt it a matter of conscience, just because [illegible] love and admire him, to make a stand against what in any one else [illegible] have passed over. No sooner do we catch a lion than we gorge him [illegible] unwholesome food; and when it disagrees, and he makes a beast of [illegible] jeer and laugh, when, had we given him a dry bone to gnaw once a-day, [illegible] would have happened."

[illegible] was made in 1863. It would, we suppose, have been in 1847, or [illegible], that Margaret Fuller met Mr. Lewes, Mazzini, and the rest, at Cheyne [illegible] in the meantime Mr. Carlyle had learnt to intermit his thunders a [illegible]

[illegible]eral feeling left upon our mind by these Memorials may be stated [illegible] two heads. First, happy is the country where such women are, so to [illegible] very uncommon product of the soil, and yet make no stir. Secondly, [illegible] would have made an excellent political and social critic.

## LUTCHMEE AND DILLOO.*

"I FIND," says Emerson, in his Essay on "Goethe, or the Writer,"—"I find a provision in the constitution of the world for the writer or secretary. His office is a reception of the facts into the mind, and then a selection of the eminent and characteristic experiences."

Mr. Jenkins is not Goethe, and he is not "the writer" in this precise sense; but the description has a certain applicability to him and his books. He is an interesting complex—part journalist and part novelist. With his quality as a philanthropist we have here no particular concern; though we earnestly wish every success to his philanthropic labours. Nor have we any objection to a story with a purpose:—the author of such a book must take his risk openly, as Mr. Jenkins does, but he does no harm so long as he avoids pretence. To tell the truth, Mr. Jenkins does fail as an artist, fine as much of his writing is, and vividly as he tells his story. He stood in need, for his plan, of Dilloo's jealousy, but it is in working out Craig's relations with the beautiful Lutchmee that the author breaks down. He has been well advised in omitting the chapter entitled "A Temptation," which we read with stupefied amazement in the first draft (in magazine form), but even now these particular episodes want those last graces of art or simple nature which could alone justify them. The following passage is quite unnecessary:—

"Craig put his arm affectionately on her shoulder. She was a coloured woman, and he meant nothing by the action. But to the other it had an unpleasant and natural significance. Something that Dilloo's quick glance detected, of the subtle understanding almost inevitably created by sick-room intercourse between any two human beings who are ordinarily agreeable and of opposite sexes, sent a pang of jealousy through his heart of which he was immediately ashamed."

At all events, the case is ill-put, and we have not yet met one single reader of the book who does not feel with us upon the general question of this jealousy business. Mr. Jenkins could not spare something of the kind, and he was rightly anxious to make it truthful and natural. But he spoils all by his comments, which are those of a lawyer rather than those of a poet. Something similar may be said about the *effect* of the whole story considered psychologically. Mr. Jenkins is wonderfully intelligent and impartial; he never gives you a monster for a man, and he never shuts up all doors of sympathy: he is, besides, full of humour; and yet—and yet—the general outcome of his books is apt to be too nearly cynical. Of course he is no cynic—he is an earnest reformer; but there is something hybrid about his writings; he is too poetic for a man of the world, and too knowing for a poet. He writes as Charles Kingsley might have written if he had been less of a poet and student, and had been a magistrate or a newspaper editor all his life.

Lutchmee is a Hindoo coolie, wife of Dilloo, and the story is the story of their wrongs. Dilloo is entrapped by a Government agent into emigrating to British Guiana; Lutchmee follows him; the end of their sad, sad story is that Dilloo, dying, turns his face to the wall and scornfully rejects the clergyman's message from the *Christian's* God. The tale is told with unflagging power; the descriptive passages are all of great force and beauty; and the "native" episodes are full of humour. It is not only a deeply interesting book, but a very instructive one. We happen to know enough of such matters to feel the general truth of the picture drawn by the author, and can warmly commend "Lutchmee and Dilloo" as a work of solid value, though not as an artistic story.

---

## THE ART OF BEAUTY.†

IF this book had shown a little more severity of plan it might fairly have been ranked very highly indeed. Its title will bear amplifying; what the volume really treats of is the art of beautifully attiring the human body and tastefully decorating our homes. As the work stands, three hundred pages of letter-

---

* Lutchmee and Dilloo: A Story of West Indian Life. By Edward Jenkins. 3 vols. London: William Mullan & Son.

† The Art of Beauty. By Mrs. H. R. Haweis. London: Chatto and Windus.

[illegible] accompanied by nearly a hundred illustrations, cannot be [illegible]. What we wished to hint was this, that a more [illegible] of the miscellaneous gathering of learning, and mass [illegible] criticism and suggestion, would have made the [illegible] dress and household furnishing. In saying dress, [illegible] Men now, with the exception of two or three minor [illegible] Mrs. Haweis's use of the word—they only put on clothing. [illegible] high note at the beginning. She says that "the culture [illegible] right of every woman." The reason with which she backs [illegible] one: "A woman's natural quality is to attract, and, having [illegible]." Such slavery is of a kind no man can object to. Mrs. [illegible] step further: she quotes, and partially approves, the old [illegible] woman's *duty* to be beautiful. Again a male chorus of [illegible] be looked for. Men have always been willing for women [illegible] they like, and can have no objection to being told on this [illegible] have a right to larger expectations being fulfilled in this [illegible] misgiving that can possibly arise is, as to whether all [illegible] heavier dressmakers' and milliners' bills. Well, Mrs. Haweis [illegible] possibility of masculine meanness suggesting this. She very [illegible] protests against the present expensive bondage of fashion in [illegible] are, and is for having the dressing done, not only better, but [illegible] This, too, will be satisfactory to male readers.

[illegible] is to be made sure, it is to be hoped she sees clearly, for, if the [illegible] to be said, Mrs. Haweis's notions of what is wanted are not narrow [illegible] will be at once seen that she does not err on the score of lack of [illegible] we mention that at p. 28, she affirms that some not unelaborate [illegible]" which she has laid down, "may be as apparent in a gown as in [illegible] seems rather to hint at doing the thing thoroughly, and it may [illegible] scale. Indeed, it will be as well to state at once that Mrs. [illegible] the side of simplicity in any niggardly, stinting sense. With her [illegible] means getting the worth of your money in true ornament, not [illegible] quantity of it so long as it is effective. The object of the book, [illegible] in any way primarily to lessen the amount of dressmakers' bills, [illegible] dressed so as to make them look beautiful. Very good. It is [illegible]—we mean, of course, the husbands—at present are so fully [illegible] the sum totals of those bills, that they do not sufficiently look when they are dressed greatly to admire them; but, if this is all [illegible] Haweis's principles of taste not being observed in the dress, and [illegible] this is done, the men will admire only the women, and forget the [illegible] will be right. At any rate, Mrs. Haweis is only on the [illegible] so far as that helps richness of effect. Her notions, in fact, are [illegible] completely artistic, including not merely the remedying of every [illegible] shortcoming and defect, but the altering of every personal peculi- [illegible] the making a good personal impression. It may surprise some, [illegible] mastered her striking reasoning, to find that she has a word of [illegible] for the use of face-powder in the sad cases of an ill complexion, [illegible] glances at the enhancing effect of hair-powder, and cheek and [illegible] moderation. The increasing the quantity of hair, the replacing of [illegible] a mysterious skilled employment of "padding," naturally go along [illegible] counsels. In a word, Mrs. Haweis will spare nothing, and not [illegible] which will prevent our giving one another the least personal [illegible] using every means to make quite sure that everybody will visibly [illegible] else. It is very pleasant to think of. Certainly, there would [illegible] good deal of dressing going on for this, especially in some cases, and [illegible] all we could be guarded against being upset by glimpses of one [illegible] before the toilettes were completed, it is not easy to see. How- [illegible] can only deal with this world as she finds it.

[illegible] quite shake off a doubt as to whether Mrs. Haweis is not show- [illegible] of artistic devotion in laying it down that a woman, in choosing [illegible], should study the "surroundings of the room" in which she [illegible] other thing we have no doubt whatever,—that the authoress [illegible] book quite a store of sound wisdom, as well as a few views that [illegible]. All the sex will be the better for reading it; crowds of women [illegible] of its perusal. We have not space to quote either the well [illegible] general rules she lays down, or the very valuable detailed suggestions which she gives in such plenty. Some of the advice goes much deeper, too, than mere ornamentation; it runs into matters of health and includes questions of ethics.

In what we have said, we have only spoken of the first part of the book,—that bearing on personal attire. The later section, dealing with the furnishing and decorating of our home interiors, is full of capital advice. Mrs. Haweis rates the beautifying of our houses highly, asking "why Eastlake, Burges, and Cottier"—who excel in this—"are not Royal Academicians?" Let us further add that there is a fourth section, entitled "A Garden of Girls," which, besides its smart sketches of typical young women, gives excellent counsel.

Finally, the book is thoroughly readable from first to last. You often come upon passages where the piquancy is either witty or droll, for Mrs. Haweis is a courageous lady, and does not like a bold remark any the less for its shocking a prejudice. It asks a little self-denial not to quote some passages in which vulgarity, sham delicacy, and slavery to fashion, are very smartly taken off. The work cannot but have a healthy influence in the broadening and the heightening of taste. A word ought to be said in praise of the illustrations, which are by Mrs. Haweis herself. Some of those giving examples of past fashions are highly funny. The volume itself is a dainty one in several respects. Its silver binding, delicately-tinted frontispiece, good printing, and thick paper, make it a not bad exemplification of its own title.

---

## AUGUSTIN COCHIN.*

THE name of Augustin Cochin, the devout and highminded Catholic philanthropist and Liberal, the valued and trusted friend of Montalembert, Lacordaire, Berryer, Bishop Dupanloup, and the Abbé Perreyve, is one that deserves to be better known than it is on this side the Channel. He presents a type of character of which there of necessity exists hardly any exact counterpart amongst ourselves—an English Catholic, as such, finding in the politics of his own country but little scope for his activity;—and Count de Falloux's memoir of his departed friend and fellow-worker will be read with interest, not only as the record of a life singularly pure, unselfish, and noble, but for its bearing upon many of those politico-religious questions which are so profoundly agitating nearly the whole of the Continent, and are confessedly at the bottom of the fierce conflict of parties now raging in France. Augustin Cochin, born December 11th, 1823, was a descendant of one of those ancient families of burgesses which served, as it were, says his biographer, "to form the inner framework of French society." A Cochin had been alderman of Paris as far back as the days of St. Louis. Augustin's great-uncle, the Abbé Cochin, curé of St. Jacques du Haut Pas, had been eminent both as preacher and zealous parish-priest in the middle of the last century, and his father, Jacques Denys Cochin, Mayor of the Twelfth Arrondissement of Paris, was a man of note for many municipal services, and in particular for devotion to the cause of popular education, and to all measures tending to the amelioration of the lot of the poor. Under the Restoration he was created a baron, but neither he nor his son ever made use of their title. Care for the poor, then, may be said to have come to Augustin Cochin, who lost his father when only in his eighteenth year, almost by way of inheritance; and, young as he was, he threw himself at once into the support and furtherance of the many works of charity set on foot by his father with an untiring zeal and devotion that never flagged as long as life was left him. No man assuredly better merited that title of "benefactor of the poor," bestowed on him by the Sister of Charity who tended his death-bed, which he said was the only one after which he ever aspired.

A very large portion of Count de Falloux's narrative is occupied with an account of these charitable labours of M. Cochin's, and this is only as it should be, for the man would be ill brought before us by a biographical sketch which left out of sight what he regarded as the true work of his life. At the same time, admirable as Cochin was, viewed as a religious philanthropist, it is not as a religious philanthropist that he has most interest for us. Chiefly he attracts our

---

* Augustin Cochin. By Count de Falloux, of the French Academy. Translated from the French by Augustus Craven. London: Chapman and Hall.

a Catholic Liberal, a man who aimed at teaching and showing ... compatibility of Catholicism with what are called modern institutions. To his devout mind there was something repellent in ... lines of demarcation between the Church and the world—the ... secular spheres. For Cochin, Christianity comprised, in fact, as his ... "every sphere of human activity, for it acts upon every con... mind." In a letter to the Abbé Perreyve he says, "It seems ... younger days we inhaled the love of Christianity because it was ... as an opening of the soul, not as a penitentiary cell likely to confine ... his eyes was not only the means for bringing souls to heaven; it ... to make men good citizens on earth. Good citizens loving their ... seek to secure for her those free institutions in which experience ... welfare of States consists; they must crave liberty the more ... they become the fitter for its exercise. "The nearer men ...," writes Cochin, "the more they are capable of liberty." In ... its development and progress," he discerned "the providential ... race. In the *Correspondant*, which became the organ of that little ... of whom Montalembert was, perhaps, the chief, M. Cochin ... Catholic upholders of absolutism of the danger they incurred ... the defence of Christianity with a permanent and systematic ... the era of 1789," as though, he says, the Church had never ... and contradictions until that date. One of the conditions of ... is that "the past soon becomes irreparable, and attempts to ... imperfect and impotent." "Whatever happens, the Church in ... must endeavour to retrieve a portion of the privileged power ... has lost and never will recover, by a more active participation in ... of her general liberties." But, though "Christian liberty in poli... Cochin's ideal, he was not, as we gather from this memoir, in the ... Liberal Catholic," in the sense in which that phrase is sometimes ... was convinced of the importance, both on political and religious ... maintaining the Temporal Power, and looked with much disfavour on ...; nor do we read of any difficulty or hesitation on his part in accept... definition of the Pope's infallibility. How then was it, one may ask, that ... in spite of his zeal for religion and devotion to the Holy See, was, ... latter years of his life, regarded with inveterate distrust and hostility by ... party in France, and once even stigmatized as "a quasi-sectarian" by ... master "of gibes, and flouts, and sneers," M. Louis Veuillot? Simply, it ... because he declined to put that interpretation—a quite unnecessary ... strained one, as Bishop Dupanloup showed—upon the Syllabus of 1864 ... render it an attack upon modern institutions *en masse*, without ... definition, and in fact, amount to "a denial of the rights and almost ... of civil society," but remained firm in his attachment to political ... parliamentary government, notwithstanding that something called ..." had been condemned by the Pope. This reason seems so inade... one is tempted to suppose that M. Cochin's enemies must have had some ..., real or imaginary, to go upon; but no such ground is, however, to ... in M. de Falloux's memoir. Of course the question of the soundness ... belief in the perfect compatibility between Catholicism and free ... is one too wide to enter on here. It may be that the Curia and those ... claimed best to interpret its mind, followed a true instinct in looking ... and men who felt like him, as "dangerous" for all their good gifts. ... something, one can see, in zeal for political liberty and progress as ... in themselves, out of keeping with that temper of mind which ... seeks to create and cherish in its children. But this subject would ... Count de Falloux's thoughtful and often eloquent memoir will ... for all who can take delight in the contemplation of a saintly life, ... standards of excellence may not be their own, and are interested in ... movements and struggles of the time; and it is ably translated by ... Craven, himself a person of distinction in right of his wife, the ... fascinating "Sister's Story," which M. Cochin was one of the first

## VIRGINIA: A NOVELETTE.*

THERE is a distinct class of readers who like a slight volume, written rather artificially, if only there is enough ability shown in it to entertain throughout with a sense of cleverness, so giving the impression that the author could do a good deal more. A pleasant feeling is set up that both reader and writer are only half-serious—are a little playing with one another. The perusal is so made very light. In this division of books the present volume may be put.

On the title-page it is entitled "A Roman Sketch." The scenes of the story—for a complete one is told, having quite a finished little plot of its own—namely all pass in the Eternal City. An artist, Jack Travers—who, alas! is also gobbo (a certain vein of cynicism being attributed to the fact of his hump)—is the professed narrator. He was born in England, but has lived nearly ever since in Rome, following his art as a sculptor, and there he develops into a "cosmopolitan," which all the world knows means any other nationality but English. Some of the quiet entertainment of the book lies in its depreciatory criticism of English people seen as visitors at Rome. There is a humiliating kind of fun in finding Britons—in the persons of the Chiltons and the Du Boulay Browns—typically put forward as foreigners on that spot, and critically ranked (in all respects save womanly beauty and masculine bulk) low down—far below all whom they consider foreigners. True, a strong-minded American lady, Mrs. Cato B. Tappen, has quite as much reason to complain. But this setting down of the British reader by one who ought to be a compatriot is part of the light mystification of the book.

However, we are forgetting the story; or rather, we find that we have not space to give it. There is plenty of love-complication in it, and just a touch of dark Italian romance. It ought to be added that a real glimpse is afforded into the crafty naïveness of a Roman family.

But what drew our attention to the book is a certain artistic feeling in it. We do not simply mean that there is some picturesque writing. As specimens of a power of that kind, we might quote the description of out-door life in Rome with which chapter xi. opens, and the church interior at p. 142. There are also some examples of true dramatic force shown in the first parting of Travers and the *contessina*, the scene where the latter flies from Sir Wilfrid Malpus, and Travers's smashing of the marble figure. Still, we were chiefly thinking of a soft poetic illumination of style which now and then briefly occurs, suddenly lighting up a line or even a passage; and which further connects with a kind of "Bohemian" philosophy that is fitfully taught from first to last. An attempt is made to associate Art and Conduct. The general moral put forward—amidst not a few remarks showing keen cynical shrewdness, and something still higher—is that Love, when there is enough of it, sets everything right. Indeed, the book finishes as seriously as if it had been throughout earnestly advocating a new sort of gospel in this.

The final affectation of solemnity need not disturb the reader, any more than the earlier hints of the sadness of fate. If this had been really felt, a few very small disfiguring jokes which occur on the pages would hardly have been there, nor indeed the frequently-recurring smartness of criticism. As we said, there is a light literary mystification running through the book, to be found out in a holiday kind of way by the reader. As one hint towards this, we suggest that rather early we ourselves discovered that Jack Travers is most certainly a lady.

Those who know the Eternal City will soon find out that the book is written by one who loves her, and they will like it for that. The writer's next volume ought to be one of more importance, for the present work, despite its purposed slightness, clearly shows the faculty.

* Virginia: a Roman Sketch. London: Bentley and Son. 1877.

# "DISESTABLISHMENT."

LORD HARTINGTON'S admission that the policy of maintaining State Churches must be an open question in the Liberal party ought not to have been a surprise to anybody. It has been an open question for a long time. Most of the Liberal Cabinets which have been formed in recent years have had men in them whose opinions were known to be adverse to Church Establishments. It was not, however, a question of practical politics until the Cabinet of Mr. Gladstone felt itself called upon to deal with the case of the Irish Church. I was a party, and a willing party, to the course taken in the disestablishment of that Communion. I looked upon it as occupying precisely the same position in respect to the Irish people as the establishment of Episcopacy would have occupied in Scotland in respect to the people of that country. It was the embodiment of the triumph of external force. The maintenance of it was not just, and therefore it was not expedient. It is needless to say, therefore, that I look upon the question of Church Establishments as one that cannot be determined by any abstract principle whatever. Like all other human institutions, excepting the very few which rest on the primary laws of justice, religion, and humanity, they are the creatures of circumstance—not of one circumstance or of two circumstances, but of many. It is difficult to understand how they can be regarded in any other light. Who would propose to set up an Established Church in the United States, or in Australia, or in any one of the colonies which have grown up under similar conditions of society? These conditions of society we may regard as less happy and lower than those in which Established Churches have arisen and have flourished. And this is my own opinion. But, being what they are, State Churches are there impossible. In our own country there are various possible or conceivable changes which would cause men who are now eager in defence of Establishments to be quite as eager in attacking them. Some would be moved to this revolution of opinion and of feeling by one kind of change, others by another kind. For example, any general defection of the clergy of the Church of England from the theology of the Reformation would lead many men to desire the overthrow of the Establishment. Others might be incited to the same desire by any straining or tightening of the bonds which limit the free action of the Church as a spiritual Society. These are not imaginary causes, but causes which, to a certain extent, are now in actual operation, and may come to operate much more powerfully and much more widely than at present. The truth is, that the time may be not far distant, if indeed it has not already come, when a policy of Disestablishment may be as much an open question among Tories as it is now among Liberals.

Under these circumstances the declaration which Lord Hartington lately made in Scotland, that Disestablishment must depend on movements of opinion which are not yet decided, was nothing but a declaration of facts with which we have been long familiar.

I have already in another form stated very shortly my dissent from the view indicated by Lord Hartington that Patronage in Scotland was a system which tended to strengthen the connection between Church and State. This, however, is a very natural view on the part of an Englishman, because in England it may be true, and because there are very few Englishmen indeed who have any intimate acquaintance with the very different history and genius of the Presbyterian Church of Scotland. The subject, nevertheless, is one of great interest in itself, and will be found to have a most intimate bearing on the whole subject connected with the relations between Church and State.

I propose, therefore, in this paper to set before my friends in England, as shortly and as clearly as I can, the main facts and arguments connected with Patronage in Scotland, and the bearing which the abolition of it has upon the question of Disestablishment.

That the Reformation in Scotland was conducted, not under the influence of authority, but in the teeth of it, is well known. Perhaps it is pretty much all that is known by a great many Englishmen. They think and speak of the Scotch Church as a Democratic Church mainly in connection with this feature of its origin. And it is quite true that the circumstances of its early history have impressed themselves on its character. In England the Reformation marched to order; and by a happy combination of circumstances, successive Governments were able ultimately to carry with them the great [illegible] of the nation. In Scotland everything was different. The doctrines carried by storm the convictions of the peop were forced through long and desperate struggles up and the sanction of the Crown. The Church which arose convictions owed its success to popular support. Kings ts nursing fathers, nor Queens its nursing mothers. true, and it is a truth which has had its influence. But ntal peculiarity of the Reformation in Scotland, and of the which arose out of it, is something quite separate, and it from this. Popular insurrections against authority do sult in the establishment of popular government. Revolu- always—they do not even generally—lead to freedom. te reaction from long abuses is by itself no safe foundation it institutions. Least of all can a Church be founded on ns—not even on that most important of all negations, the false authority. Protesting and pulling down may be the ur hour, but they cannot be the work of life. They who the waste places must have some other instrument than their hand. It is a very great mistake to suppose that which arose in Scotland was a Church which made no le principle of authority, or that it was democratic in the g government by a mob. Its Reformers had a definite idea not only as to what it was needful to destroy, but also as was quite as necessary to set up again. It was in the s idea that their power lay. It was in the practical form y embodied it that the strength of their work consisted, nd its endurance. This idea was the conception they had he nature, foundation, and elementary constitution of the urch. It was a conception which placed the governing the Church not in the clergy, but in the whole body of its Theoretically, indeed, it has never been pretended in any mmunion that the clergy constitute the Church. But has not only been contended, but it has been assumed ully asserted, that the clergy have the sole right of govern- rection. At the present moment it is almost ludicrous to difficulty which is made in the Methodist body as regards n of the lay element in the management of its spiritual ith the Scotch Reformers this never was a question. The in any vague or abstract sense, but in the sense which con- ne authority and power, was the whole body of the believing were there any devices, such as that of separate voting by break the sweep or limit the operation of this fruitful prin- mit in its system of government was simply the Congrega- tself by its own elected members. Its representative body the Eldership." And the minister was only one among mong the rest. Except by the influence of superior nowledge, he had no greater authority than his brethren, ministered to them in holy things, and although as resident or chairman of the Eldership he had a special pre-eminence in virtue of that office. The appointment of ministers was declared to consist essentially in these three things: examination as to learning by the ministry, approbation of the people, and admission by the joint authority of both. Ordination followed upon election, or at least upon consent of the Congregation. This body, through its appointed organs, was the foundation of the whole edifice. Above this unit in the Government of the Church, the higher Courts and Tribunals rose in regular order, founded on the same representative system, and without a trace of any feeling or idea that the laity were not entitled to the most complete association in every act of administration, and in every exercise of discipline. The result was that the General Assemblies of the Church were a fuller representation of the nation than the Parliaments then were or could be. Every Burgh in Scotland as such sent, and to this day sends, its members to the General Assembly. It is obvious that this system in itself constituted a connection between Church and State which approached very nearly to complete amalgamation. Lord Minto has lately* said that the connection of the Church with the State in Scotland has never been very close. I hold, on the contrary, that it was closer than in any other country in the world. When two men or two Societies are in partnership, surely the closest association is not that in which one is kept under jealous subjection to the other; but that in which each works in its own province with mutual confidence and support. And not only was the connection between Church and State in Scotland closer than elsewhere because of this principle of association, but it was closer also because they were prone to work even too much together in the same field of operation. But more than this—the very definition of Church and State brought them very near each other. The aggregate of Congregations constituted the Church, and, if they did not also constitute the State, they tended more and more to do so in proportion as the Reformation extended, and in proportion as popular liberties were successfully asserted. Accordingly, as soon as the hostility of the Crown had been overcome, Parliament incorporated among the Statutes of the Realm the whole of the Confession of Faith which embodied the Reformed doctrine. The truth is that there was a real risk of the union of Church and State becoming only too close—so close as to endanger that distinction between the two which lies in the nature of things, and which can never be forgotten or put out of sight without peril to the interests of freedom and of truth. In the earliest Confession of the Scotch Church, which was adopted by the Legislature in 1567, powers are ascribed to the civil magistrate with which no secular Government can be safely trusted. It was expressly declared that Kings, Princes, and Magistrates were not appointed only for civil policy, but most principally "for the conservation and purgation of religion." Subsequent experience of rulers

* In a letter addressed to the *Times*.

... the action and with the opinions of the Church soon ... and, indeed, to the announcement of doctrines ... of this. But from the first period of its ... present hour, the Presbyterian Church has had that ... with the State which consists in the full and ...ociation of the laity in her government and discipline, wide popular basis on which the great body of the people ...ented in their General Assembly.

...less to observe that in a system such as this Patronage was wholly alien. The relation of pastor and people was ... to the whole; and this relation was conceived to depend, ...ne essential condition, upon the approval and assent of ...gation. The right of one man, by virtue of property in the ... to have a right of appointing arbitrarily to the cure of ...n idea which was abhorrent to the Reformers, and to the ... of the people. Instead, therefore, of being a bond of union ... Church and State it was in Scotland the one thing, the which weakened and impaired the foundation on which ...ested.

...gly the whole history of the Church in Scotland is a history of ...rring struggles to get rid of this system,—an object which ...accomplished in that Revolution Settlement under William ...hich closed the long contests of the British people with kings. Under that Settlement a system of appointing ...as established, in which the Kirk Session, as the constitu... of the Congregation, had a principal share, and in which Courts of the Church were left free to give full effect to ...ion of popular assent on which such value had been

...erefore, a Scotch Presbyterian of whatever kind—whether ... Free, or United—hears Englishmen speak of Patronage ...rtant bond of union between Church and State, he can ...and wonder. Scotchmen are often accused of a narrow ...n, and assuredly they have their own "Idols of the Den." ...nds on the other side of the Tweed are quite up to the ...s respect. Especially on a whole class of subjects which ...the most important in the world, there is no creature with ...range of vision as a genuine John Bull. In respect to these, ...er seems to have heard a sound or caught a glimpse coming ...d the ancestral trees and the village spire which bound the ...is pleasant or his stately home. This is especially true in ...everything connected with his Church. Results arising ...most peculiar, the most local, the most accidental history ...d are habitually regarded by him as results of the most ...nd necessary truth. And it is perfectly true that in that ... in the system which arose from it, Patronage has its own special significance and value. It has indeed its bad as well as its good side; and perhaps the bad is as dear to many Englishmen as the good. The coarse and literal sense in which appointments to the pastoral office are considered and dealt with as "property"—the sale of benefices, and the sale of them too often under circumstances which separate the transaction from simony by nothing but the shadow of a shade—these are not circumstances which can be contemplated with any satisfaction.

But, apart from this lower aspect of Patronage, it is perfectly true that there is another aspect in which the value set upon it by Englishmen of wider views is intelligible enough. It is the great peculiarity of the Church of England, and its special value in the eyes of many, that it passed over into the ranks of the Reformed with the whole furniture and apparatus of the Mediæval Church, *minus* only the supremacy of the Pope. Its priesthood remained without a "break," and, without a break too, its government might easily have become exclusively sacerdotal. Two things have stood in the way of this result—first and foremost the Supremacy of the Crown, and secondly lay Patronage. These two have represented, and they have been the only things which did represent, the rights of the laity in the government of the Church. Presbyterian writers generally have been accustomed to press home against the English Church the somewhat coarse and offensive forms in which the Supremacy of the Crown has sometimes been asserted. It has never appeared to me that this is just. The origin and real historical meaning of the claims asserted on behalf of the Crown in England, in the conduct of the Reformation, is an origin and a meaning with which Presbyterians ought to sympathize. The great object was to deny the usurped supremacy of the Pope. But negative propositions never make good popular watchwords; and so the best way of denying anything is very often simply to affirm its contradictory. On this principle the best way of denying the supremacy of the Pope was to affirm the supremacy of the King. It is true that the merely national element in religion is not the most important in itself. But it had in England a temporary importance out of proportion to its intrinsic value. Not only in this light, but also in the relation which it bore to the claims of the laity, it deserves the sympathy of all Protestants. Presbyterians cannot think it the best or indeed in any respect a convenient form for the expression of those claims. But in the system of the English Established Church there was no other expression given—no other method of operation provided for. Lay Patronage in respect to parochial charges, and the right of the Crown to appoint Bishops, overruling the purely clerical body with which the right of election nominally rests, may be regarded in England as compensatory provisions against the evils and dangers of a purely sacerdotal constitution.

Regarded from this point of view, it is perfectly natural that Englishmen should set a value upon Patronage which does not

it in Scotland, where the rights of the laity have been other-
more completely as well as much more fittingly provided for,
..., Patronage assumes the exactly opposite character
trary individual privilege inconsistent with the natural and
storical rights which, in the view of the Presbyterian Church,
to any one member of the Congregation, but to the Congrega-
hole. The system of Patronage is inseparably connected with
fortunate memories in the constitutional history of Scotland.
memories are more unfortunate than those connected with
f Queen Anne which re-imposed Patronage on the Church.
very fond of applying the word "reactionary" as a term
h to any policy. It is a favourite word with demagogues
feel that their power is waning. It is a favourite word
when they scent the first returning symptoms of reason
nscience after some delirious outburst of passion and of
A reactionary policy may be wise and just. Everything
n the character of that previous condition of things against
reaction comes. But when it is agreed, or when it is
d what our opinion is on this point, then the word may be
definite and intelligible meaning. Jacobitism has long
as a policy: but as a sentiment it will live for evermore.
lo young ladies still sigh over the "bonnie Prince Charlie,"
Episcopalians generally retain their natural preference for
patrons of their Church. Fidelity, although it be in a bad
never cease to attract the admiration of mankind. Even
that great Whig of Whigs, could pour out the sympathies
bite in most melodious verse. But among Presbyterians at
should be, and there can be, no difference of opinion on
ing and import of every step in that contest which the
nd the friends of the Stuarts, maintained against their com-
They know that every attempt to disturb and upset the
n Settlement was an attempt on the liberties of the nation.
this sense and with this end in view, that the policy of a
party in the reign of Anne was a reactionary policy. It was
which was at that time connected, not with any mere vague
timent of any kind, but with a definite desire to bring about
revolution. We know from Burnet, and Lockhart, and Car-
Swift, and Oxford, and a host of witnesses, that the Act of
ring Patronage in Scotland, in direct violation of the Revolu-
ement, was one of the measures devised by this party to
hat close alliance between secular and ecclesiastical liberties
made the Presbyterian Church so powerful an instrument
il wars, and in establishing the constitution which it was
t to secure. This was the meaning and the aim of Toryism
lays, and this was the meaning and the aim with which it
Act depriving the great body of the laity in Scotland of

that liberty in the choice of ministers which lay at the very root of the union between Church and State in the Presbyterian system.

And the Tories of that time were wise in their generation. The Act of Patronage has been the one source of strain, tension, and discontent in the Established Church from the year in which it was passed to the year of its final repeal. That Act, and that Act alone, has endangered the connection between Church and State, and has been the single cause of every division. Those who do not belong to the Established Church in Scotland are not generally "Dissenters" in the English sense of that word. They were in their origin, and for the most part they still are, simply Seceders, and they seceded for reasons which had connection almost exclusively with the action and the results of Patronage.

The same connection between movements for the extension of popular liberties and movements for the restraint of Patronage, has been conspicuous in our own time. That progress of events and of opinion which brought about the passing of the Reform Act of 1832 affecting the Parliamentary representation of the people, brought about also in the Church those endeavours to reconcile the existence of Patronage with the ancient rights of Congregations which resulted in the passing of the Veto Law by the General Assembly in 1834. The Voluntary Controversy, in which such yeoman's service had been done for the principle of Establishment both in England and in Scotland by Dr. Chalmers, had awakened the sense of Presbyterians to the breach which the unrestricted exercise of Patronage had effected in the armour of the Establishment, and the first aim of every friend of that Establishment was to heal and repair that breach.

Accordingly the Veto Law passed by the General Assembly in 1834 was a law which provided that, if any Presentee to a vacant parish were objected to by a majority of the Congregation, being heads of families and in full communion with the Church, his settlement should not be proceeded with. It is obvious that this was the most limited and moderate form in which effect could be given to the constitutional principle that the assent of the Congregation was essential to the completion of the pastoral tie. That assent was not to be asked affirmatively, but was to be assumed unless challenged by a positive majority. Thus in every case in which a Patron by the natural and legitimate influence of his position could prevent such a prevalence of opposition—in every case even when the Patron had one-half of the Congregation with him—his power of appointment held good. It ceased to be a power wholly despotic and arbitrary; but it remained a power of great weight, and capable of being worked in harmony with the liberties of the people. This law was in operation between five and six years before it was pronounced by the House of Lords to be *ultra vires* on the part of the General Assembly, on the ground that it contravened the great Jacobite Act of Patronage of 1712. During

parishes had been filled under its provisions, and out of this great number of presentations only rejected on account of the veto of the people. to a time and to transactions of which I have often and will now express again, the opinion I entertain. had been passed during a Whig administration. Its encouraged the leaders of the popular party in the liberal policy, and some of the most eminent lawyers had no doubt of its compatibility with the proper inter- even of the Act of Queen Anne. When ultimately lawyers this in the negative, the most obvious considerations of policy a modification of a statute so invidious in its origin and so its effects.

of this course being taken, the Liberal Government did Four more years of violent contest between the Assemblies urch and the Courts of Law were allowed to run their course, ng both parties more and more to extreme opinions, during was only too clear that feelings and passions purely pro- were deeply affecting the conduct and the language of the Body. Lord Cockburn, in his most interesting Memoirs, has ed, as it deserved to be stigmatized, the intemperate lan- some of his brethren on the bench. A very slight modifica- he Act of Patronage would have been then sufficient. But nment stood silent, and remained inactive.

n earliest recollections of Parliament are associated with this the scenes which were being almost weekly repeated in the f Lords are indelibly imprinted on my memory: Lord m thundering across the table, under the passionate excite- a lawyer who thinks that his own profession should be in every department of human conduct, and demanding overnment whether they meant to enforce the law; Lord , who represented the defeated minority opposed to the late novement in the Church, repeating the same demand; Lord e deprecating discussion, and pointing out the difficulties of urse, with that noble countenance and listless manner which perfect type of the history and condition of the Whigs,—the vices they had rendered in the past, the decrepitude into which fallen in the present. If ever there was a time or circumstances manded that "something must be done," it was the condition in 1839-40-1. But Lord Melbourne had no other resource than essed in the characteristic question, "Can't ye let it alone?" indeed high time that such a Government should be dis- It was followed by the Government of Sir Robert Peel. I no temptation to speak otherwise than with respect of that ent. All my own sympathies were with it. In many respects e of the greatest Administrations which England has ever seen. But its responsibility for the evils which were allowed to result in Scotland is a responsibility which can never be forgotten. It professed to be Conservative in that only sense in which Conservatism is rational, namely, that in which respect for ancient institutions is combined with a ready response to the necessities of adaptation and reform. It had in its hands the interests, and possibly the fate, of one of these institutions; and it was offered, from an independent but friendly hand, a measure which would have closed a dangerous controversy by a moderate and timely compromise. Moreover, that measure involved none of the risks and objections which might have been anticipated as almost inseparable from other methods of proceeding. During the heat of the contest, claims as to the nature and extent of what was called "spiritual independence" had been expressed in language of loose and dangerous import, and it might have been feared that some new call would be made on Parliament to define what is certainly not very easy of definition. But a Bill was offered to the Government, which the General Assembly accepted by a large majority as a settlement of the question, which did not enter at all upon this dangerous ground, which left that ground to be occupied by the ancient constitutional statutes of the country, and which did nothing but modify the Act of Anne so as to be compatible with the reasonable liberty of Congregations. With an infatuation which is really unaccountable, this measure was refused, and the well-known "Disruption" of 1843 followed. If the Government had determined to uphold the law of Patronage in the arbitrary operation which had been assigned to it by recent decisions, their conduct would have been irrational enough. But they had not even this excuse. They were willing to alter the law of Patronage, and they did persist in altering it after it had become too late to prevent the great secession. But this is not all. The alteration which they did make was one ingeniously devised to come as close as possible in appearance to the change sought for by the Church, but yet to fall short of it in a way which introduced difficulties and objections in the exercise of Patronage which had never existed before. This was the effect of the Act commonly called "Lord Aberdeen's Act;" and as this was the law of Patronage recently repealed, and which it is now pretended was of such fundamental value, I must explain what was its import and effect.

The fundamental principle of the new Patronage Act was this: that no amount of disapprobation of the Presentee on the part of the Congregation was to be a bar to his settlement, unless they could substantiate some objections of a definite and tangible nature before the Presbytery. But, on the other hand, every facility and even encouragement was to be given for the statement of such objections, if they could find any, and this on the part of any minority of the Congregation, however small.

[illegible] a law of this kind; first from an abstract, and [illegible] point of view.

[illegible] plausible or reasonable at first sight than the prin[illegible] is to be rejected except on account of objections [illegible]ated. But in reality nothing is more unreason[illegible] this principle, when applied to the appointment of men to [illegible] of souls. There are a great number of men of the highest [c]haracter, and of many good attainments, who are nevertheless [illegible] that position. Especially is this true in respect to the [illegible] preaching. It is not too much to say that this power [illegible] gifts, and the want of it depends upon defects, which [illegible] of definition. Has it not happened to all of us to feel, [illegible] first sentences of a sermon have been uttered, that the [illegible] belongs to the *genus* goose? And are there not other cases [illegible]ults of another kind, but of infinite variety, render it impos[illegible]at the minister should ever exercise any of that influence on [g]ood preaching depends? I know that there are many men [illegible] depreciate the value of sermons altogether, and to whom [illegible] under all circumstances, nothing but a bore. But this is the [illegible]nen who have only a languid interest in the greatest of all [illegible] It is not the feeling of the poor. Neither will it ever be the [illegible] of the great masses of mankind. The Gospel was spread by [illegible]g at the first, and preaching will be the most powerful instru[illegible] its maintenance to the last. In our own time there are no [illegible] the Pulpit having lost its power. Whenever and wherever [illegible] by men with any special qualifications for their great duty, [illegible] no standing-ground for those who press to hear. And so [illegible]e in all time to come, so long as the everlasting interests of [illegible] shall endure, and so long as there are men capable of speaking [illegible]orld of these.

[L]et it be remembered that if this is true of all Churches and [illegible]rms of worship, most of all is it true of that which prevails [illegible]resbyterian Churches. I have long ago expressed my own [illegible]at in that system so much is left to depend entirely on the [illegible] gifts of the minister. This dependence extends not only to the [illegible] but also to the prayers, and nothing is exempted from it except [illegible]mody, which, fortunately, is in itself a liturgy, and the one [illegible]tible storehouse of the noblest forms of devotional expression. [illegible]rayer" ought never, I venture to think, to be expunged from the [illegible] Christian worship; but I cannot think it ought to be left alone, [illegible] the relief and support of words which have their ever-living [illegible] in the very associations of age and use. But whatever may [illegible]elings or prejudices on this matter, we have to consider facts [illegible] And it is the fact that, as things are now ordered in [illegible] all of the Presbyterian Churches, the personal qualifica[illegible] minister, even those which are most subtle and least susceptible of definition, may be and often are all in all to the edification of the people in public worship. It is a gross absurdity and a grievous injustice to impose upon Congregations the obligation of finding or inventing some objection susceptible of formal definition, if they are to save themselves from Presentees whose unfitness might be evident without in any way resulting from faults which can be proved.

Let us turn now from the abstract to the practical aspects of the question. Look at the demoralizing effects which such a law must have upon Congregations. They are compelled to colour or exaggerate objections so as to bring them within the scope of legal definitions. Look again at its effects upon the Church Courts, upon whom the invidious duty was imposed of adopting or rejecting the objections of the people. They might reasonably hold that the mere fact of a certain amount and prevalence of opposition to a Presentee was in itself an objection, and a bar to any prospect of usefulness in the particular parish. And one clause in the Act was so drawn as to suggest the notion that this degree of liberty was left to the Presbytery. But a subsequent clause was as carefully drawn expressly to exclude it. Let me not be supposed to attribute this kind of double dealing to Lord Aberdeen. In later years I learned to know him: and that knowledge was inseparable from feelings of admiration and of love. No man ever was more transparently true, or more absolutely sincere. But in the drafting of this measure on Patronage, he was in the hands of lawyers as cunning as they were obstinate, whose great aim was to detach as many as possible from the ranks of the non-intrusion party in the Church, without really conceding the one essential principle for which they had contended. The statute has never come under judicial interpretation upon this point; and therefore it is to this hour uncertain what view would have been taken of it by the Civil Courts. But my own conviction is, that the wording of the Act was so drawn as to exclude any power of Presbyteries to give effect to any amount of opposition or dislike on the part of the people, unless for reasons which the Church Courts could themselves adopt. The Presbyteries therefore were also under the like temptation to give forced and fictitious colour to objections which they might wish to support, or else they were under obligation to refuse to give effect to objections which, nevertheless, they might consider valid under the special circumstances of the case. The ambiguities and doubts attaching to this condition of the law were in themselves a very great evil. The Church Courts had not only no rule to go by, but were in constant danger of being dragged into litigation in the Civil Courts; and their own decisions on cases as they arose were inconsistent and confusing to the popular mind. Neither Patrons nor Congregations knew what their respective rights were. No condition of things could be more unsatisfactory or more mischievous. Look, again, to the effect of such a law on the interests of Presentees themselves, including the [illegible] men educated for the ministry. Nothing could [illegible] to the interests of a Presentee than a disputed [illegible] operation of Lord Aberdeen's Act of Patronage. [illegible] disqualification which could be conceived was e dragged into the light of a public discussion. Faults [illegible] real, but temporary, and capable of amendment, [illegible] with exaggeration, and exposed to the view and [illegible] memory of every other Congregation in the Church. [illegible] might well be fatal to the prospects of any candidate [illegible]. Thus in every form and aspect this "amended" [illegible] tended to the demoralisation and scandal of the [illegible] to inflict real injury on the interests of religion.

[illegible] true that the settlements which were disputed, had to be dealt with under the provisions of this most [illegible]le law, were not very numerous. But the scandal and [illegible]ch these occasioned to the Church were out of all proportion [illegible] number of them. This result lies in the very nature of [illegible] case exposed the unjust and invidious restrictions which [illegible]ed by Statute upon the liberties of the Church both in its [illegible]rts and in its individual Congregations. Every case there[illegible]d the risk of new secessions, and was quoted as only a [illegible]agrant demonstration of the necessity of every secession gone before.

[illegible] was it, after all, that these cases were not more numerous were? It was because Patrons felt the necessity of con[illegible] wishes of Congregations before they presented, and because shrank from the ordeal of a disputed settlement, even when [illegible] minority of the Congregation had power to submit them [illegible] danger. I need not point out that this was practically [illegible] an abolition of Patronage, except as regards Patrons less than others, and except as regards Presentees who were [illegible]ster. It says much for the Patrons of Scotland generally, [illegible] such a law more numerous scandals did not arise. But it be remembered, that among the Patrons of Scotland there individuals and some public bodies who were not disposed [illegible]derate to the interests of a Church of which they were not [illegible]nd to which they had no cordial feeling. I will not say [illegible]tations were ever issued with the deliberate intention of strife, and doing injury to the Church. But I will say that [illegible] there was grave suspicion of unfriendly motive; and [illegible] the suspicion were well founded or not, the fact remained was the opportunity, the temptation, and the effect. If simple-minded enough to consider it too shocking even to [illegible] any men could act in so solemn a matter with such ends has not yet learned to estimate the subtle and powerful which make even men who are good and conscientious in all other matters, capable of any injustice to a Church to which they are opposed.

But now let me pass to the aspect of the system from another point of view—namely, that aspect in which it presented itself to Patrons. Of this I can speak from personal experience. I believe I had the honour and the misfortune of being almost, if not quite, the largest holder of Patronage in Scotland next to the Crown. So far as the law of Patronage could give it, I had it in my power to dispose of a very important item in the spiritual interests of more than thirty parishes. But if any Englishman supposes that Patronage could be administered in Scotland as it is administered in England, he is very much mistaken. It is true that historically the system had the same origin in both countries. Originally, I suppose, Patronage represented a power associated with the sources of benefaction and endowment. But considering the very distant and obscure connection between existing Patrons and the origin of Tithes, I never found it very easy to consider the powers which the law assigned to me as really resting on this foundation. Special circumstances moreover, connected with the history of Patronage in Scotland, made it impossible to derive any comfort from such a plea. And here, in passing, I must say that the connection between Patronage and endowment, even if it had been much more real and much more recent, is a connection which does not seem to commend itself to an enlightened conscience. If men do give of their substance to endow the Christian Church, they should not do it for valuable consideration and demand in return an equivalent in power. Above all, they should not regard this power as partaking of the nature of property saleable in the market. There is one and one only aspect in which Patronage ever appeared to me defensible, or even tolerable. As a trustee for the Congregation whose dearest interests were involved in the appointment of its minister, and as personally acquainted, as well as connected by old hereditary ties, with the people of a parish, it was possible sometimes to use this power without offence, and even with some indirect advantage. But it could only be so used when the feelings and interests of the Congregation were thus personally known, or could be anticipated with perfect confidence. Accordingly I have on one or two occasions presented to parishes without any formal consultation with the Congregation, and I have done so with success. But in the vast majority of cases such a course would have been impossible, and would, in my opinion, have been unjustifiable. Even if Patrons were disposed to have the most overweening confidence in their own judgment of the fitness of men for the most important of all duties, [illegible] have not generally had in Scotland that personal knowledge [illegible] candidates for the ministry which is common in England. In [illegible] a very large proportion of those who are presented [illegible] more or less nearly connected with, or at least [illegible]

, his family, or his friends. In Scotland any such connection rratively rare. Patrons had to act on the testimony of others, perience has been that this testimony is rarely to be trusted. , therefore, no excuse for Patrons imposing their own selec- communities who had probably better means of knowing the who had a natural and moreover a legal right to press any they might entertain. This legal right of objection, how- ght result, was at least conclusive as to a power of resistance rocesses of law which could not fail to inflict the most serious e Congregation, and possibly also on the Presentee. Patrons, recollect that any arbitrary insistance on their part in the nt of a minister might very probably lead to a secession ongregation and from the Church. Doors were always open ceive seceders, and no differences of doctrine or of discipline the naked eye were obstacles to the transfer of their allegi- der these circumstances the only course left to Patrons to s to request the Congregation through their Kirk Session, some other committee of their body, to select some candi- g the general support of the people. In all parishes where any strong popular element this was the course I invariably nd my experience was that this method of proceeding ays led to a satisfactory result.

not say that Patronage exercised on this principle is not, in h sense, Patronage at all. It is nothing more, at the most, ght of first nomination, and even this right subject to such ng conditions as to involve the maximum of objection with um of benefit.

s indeed one other aspect in which the position of a Patron regarded, which would have been very comforting if I e entertained it. Patrons, we are now told, were the special tives of "the public." It is quite intelligible how this a most grateful doctrine to the class to which Patrons . To feel that one's own individual will, and one's own per- ts of property, represented something far superior to the ongregations—something of such indescribable value that d Churches would be nothing without it—this is a doctrine eals to feelings which are not peculiar to lairds, or to any but to each and every class in turn, in proportion as it exceptional power over others. What strikes me most is Toryism—a character which belongs to it in its root and d is not at all affected by the accident that, in regard to a mber of parishes, the right of Patronage, such as it was, public bodies. If those public bodies exercised that right usly, they must have exercised it on precisely the same which were incumbent on an individual peer or landed pro- t was their duty to nominate ministers with a view to the interests of the people who were to profit by their ministrations. This is the only principle of administration which could reconcile Patronage with the public interests; and to pretend that Patrons could represent those interests by acting on any other principle betrays the presence of some other idea, which is unavowed and hidden under plausible forms of speech.

And so it is. When we come to analyse the dictum that Patrons represented the public, we soon find that under this phraseology lies the doctrine that Patrons were not trustees for the Congregation whose interests were at stake, but agents for those who did not belong to the Congregation at all, but who, on the contrary, were antagonistic to it. Surely the absurdity of this doctrine is apparent on the face of it. No Patron ever did act on this principle avowedly, and that any Patron acted upon it unavowedly was only a matter of dark suspicion. It is quite true that a great majority of the Patrons in Scotland were not members of its Established Church, but were Episcopalians. But I sincerely believe they never acted or wished to act except in what they believed to be the interests of the Congregations, who alone by law had any right of resistance or of objection. Moreover, it is to be remembered that the law of Patronage always assumed that the Patrons were members of the Church. It was never in the contemplation of the system that it should be otherwise. The only kind of Dissent which was known or thought of at the time when these matters were dealt with by the Legislature, was the Roman Catholic; and the principle of the law is indicated by the well-known fact that Roman Catholics having the right of Patronage were always expressly excluded from the exercise of this proprietary right. This exclusion is wholly inconsistent with the idea of any absolute property in Patronage, and equally inconsistent with the notion that it can ever be rightfully exercised except as a trust for the interests of the Church and people with which it stands connected.

The facts and arguments which have been now shortly noticed in this paper seem to prove conclusively these three things: 1st, That in the Reformed Church as established in Scotland, Patronage never did, directly or indirectly, represent anything but an element alien to its Constitution and wholly unconnected with the rights of the laity in its government and discipline. 2nd, That its restoration in the time of Queen Anne was a Tory measure conceived in a spirit of hostility to the Revolution Settlement and to the popular liberties of which that Settlement was the guarantee. 3rd, That in the form in which it survived under the Act of 1843, commonly called Lord Aberdeen's Act, it had become unworkable, and, in so far as it did operate at all, was accompanied with provisions which rendered it powerless for good and fruitful of evils which were wholly new.

Now let us examine the objections which can be raised to the abolition of a system such as this.

objection, which so far it goes, was and is intelligible possession of Patronage however nominal it had become, and possibly even to a few corporations (though this ), a sort of feeling of personal and proprietary interest which they might not themselves belong. They could parish as "my parish." And, no doubt, it is wonderful sort of feeling goes with some specimens of humanity. very many years ago at a dinner party in the country the house coming to me and saying, "Let me introduce to ndooted Pautron." "The what?" I said. "The undooted and forthwith I had the honour of being introduced to -looking little man, and of magnificent deportment. He be the Patron of everybody, and everything around him, ous of being the observed of all observers. The mystery xplained. The legal instrument by which presentations to e effected in Scotland always set forth that the author of it ndoubted patron" of the parish in question. In a very large parish full of magnates of much larger estate and of k, my new acquaintance had nevertheless the right of . The ever-present consciousness of this distinction which l his countenance and animated his steps, had procured for ; the people the appropriate nickname. This is a carica- eeling which had its influence and its value. Patrons who in effecting the settlement of a minister whom they had ere disposed to carry the sympathies of Patronage a little nd these sympathies gave them a degree of interest in the ent as a whole which they might not otherwise have had. velopment of what the metaphysicians call "the *Ego*," which natural. I am by no means disposed to deny or to under- e value of a feeling of this kind. Statesmen cannot afford or to forget the operation of motives which are trivial in . I fully admit that the sacrifice of an influence even such ich was a sacrifice involved, more or less, in the abolition ge, was in itself, and as far as it went, an evil. But my of the Patrons of Scotland assures me that this sort was the very least and weakest of the ties which bound ought to bind them, to take a personal interest in the Congregations with which they are generally connected the ties of property or of neighbourhood. The result of quiry led me to believe that the leading Patrons in Scot- senting the feelings of the general body to which they were quite sensible of the evils attending such poor f the system as remained under the Act of 1843. In t they made no resistance, and not a few of the most im- ong them willingly assented to the abolition of a privilege ined nothing but the name. I cannot believe, therefore, that any mere personal feelings on the part of former Patrons can effect any permanent alienation or estrangement. They must know, at all events, that the strength of the Presbyterian Church has always lain in its close association with popular rights, and they know that of late more than ever it is a Church which must throw itself for support on the great body of the people.

There was one other objection to the abolition of Patronage founded on considerations of the same kind, which also had its own importance. Rival Churches have a natural tendency to rejoice in each other's faults. To see any one of them get rid of a burden or impediment, is a real grievance to all the rest. This is the form in which we are very apt to fulfil towards each other the great law of love. And if any one Church may happen from accidental circumstances to need the help of others in getting rid of any impediment, excellent and even religious reasons are quite sure to be found for resisting and refusing. Just as Tories and, I am sorry to say, a few Liberals, have been generally maintaining of late that the interests of England require that some twelve or fourteen millions of Europeans should be kept under the demoralized and demoralizing government of Turks, so a considerable number of persons, chiefly clerical, held that it was for the interest of their own communions that the people of an Established Church should be kept under whatever disadvantages might arise from the system of Patronage. That system might be condemned by the most cherished principles of those whose assent as public men was asked for its abolition. It might be a real hindrance, not merely to the Church as an Establishment, but to the vital interests of religion. Never mind; keep it up —its evils were only the proper reward of belonging to an Established Church at all. I was astonished with the frankness with which this sort of language was held to me by a deputation of very worthy men whom I saw in London. And this is perfectly natural; so natural, indeed, that it seems a lively illustration of what theologians are accustomed to call "the natural man." Its naturalness, and therefore its prevalence, had to be kept in view. Hence any application to Parliament of any sort or kind, however just or otherwise expedient, was in itself an evil. Again, I admit that this, so far as it went, constituted a real objection. But it was overweighted by the probability that Parliament would not allow such influences to prevail, and that the public interests were best consulted by promoting a measure of unquestionable value in itself to the interests of the Established Church.

Passing, then, from these two objections, neither of which was by any means to be despised, but both of which were of a nature to be faced and set aside, I come to the only other objections, that I know of, which were of a higher character and deserve the fullest consideration. One of these objections is that the measure ought to have been so framed as to meet the views of all the Presbyterian

Churches; and the other is that it ought to have been so framed as to embrace not only the members of those Churches, but all men of all kinds, whether they belonged to one Church or another, or to none at all.

As regards the first of these objections my answer is simply this, that there can be no approach to the other Presbyterian bodies in Scotland until the decks are cleared of Patronage. The abolition of what remained of it is a preliminary measure without which nothing farther can be done. Moreover, and this is even more important, the abolition of Patronage has in itself an effect which goes very far beyond what is commonly understood or perceived by Englishmen, or indeed by Scotchmen who are not thoroughly conversant with the history and bearings of the whole question. What other Presbyterians have desired, is not merely the abolition of Patronage, but also some formal and effective return to those constitutional principles of connection between Church and State which were authorized in the more ancient statutes of the realm, and which had been injured and invaded by the Jacobite Act of Queen Anne. We live in times when Parliaments are necessarily very shy of dealing with any abstract questions of any kind, but especially of such a kind as defining the boundaries of civil and ecclesiastical jurisdiction. But the old Parliament of Scotland had no such shyness, and had embodied their opinions in statutes which are unrepealed, and of living force in the present day. Every violation or every alleged violation of the system thus established arose directly or indirectly out of the interpretation of that one Jacobite innovation, the Act of Anne. Consequently the repeal of it threw back the whole system and government of the Established Church upon its old foundations—foundations which were found strong enough to bear the strain of rougher times than these: and even those who think, as some Presbyterians do, that fresh buttresses are now required. must admit that the abolition of the only law that had practically interfered with the old system which they admire and love, was in itself an important and indeed the most important of all steps in the restoration of it. I will not conceal my own opinion of the extreme difficulty of getting anything fuller or better than we had, and which we now have again, standing just as it stood before. Patching and mending those old laws is a dangerous operation. But if there is anything within the bounds of "practical politics" which could remove doubts, however unsubstantial, it would have my cordial support. My own conviction is that the simple abolition of the Act of Queen Anne, and of the Act of 1843, had in itself a necessary sweep of operation on the relations between Church and State which has as yet been very imperfectly appreciated.

I pass then to the only other objection of a substantial character. namely, that the measure ought to have included in the constituency for the election of ministers, not only all Presbyterians, not only all Protestants, but all men of all Churches, or of no Church, even all the Ratepayers of a parish. I am the more bound to deal with this objection as it is connected with opinions which are sometimes called Liberal, and because there are, perhaps, some ingredients in it which may really be so.

My first answer to this objection is one entirely practical. It rests upon certain facts, and not on theories or opinions of any kind. That answer is simply this—that if the measure abolishing individual Patronage had placed the election of ministers in a plebiscite of Ratepayers, it would have been a measure not of comprehension but of exclusion. It would have in itself constituted an absolute and final separation between the Established Church and all the other Presbyterian Churches in Scotland. There is not one of them which would tolerate such a system for a moment, or indeed would regard it in any other light than as a system which would reduce the Establishment to the lowest depths of degradation. I am not now expressing any opinion on the reasonableness of this feeling. For the moment I am speaking of it simply as a fact—a fact which must be known to every one who knows anything of the past history and the living conditions of opinion in Scotland on the relation between Church and State. If there be any men among those Churches, and I trust there are very few, who are animated exclusively by the spirit of sectarian enmity, these men would have received such a measure with a shout of triumph. But the great majority of Presbyterians of all Churches would have been shocked that a communion with which they have so much in common, and which is connected with so many memories dear to them, had bowed its head so low.

And now passing from the fact to the reasons of it, let me explain that these reasons are very little connected with any of those obvious absurdities in practice to which the working of such a system would have been exposed. There are a few parishes in Scotland which the Reformation never overflowed and which are still mainly Roman Catholic. There are a good many more where the Roman Catholics are a considerable element in the population. That Roman Catholic Ratepayers should be electors of the Presbyterian minister is incongruous enough. But perhaps practically it is not more so than that any other men should be electors, who are from other causes hostile to the teaching and to the position of the Established Church. The very extent of the incongruity, and the natural promptings of ordinary good feeling, might prevent Roman Catholics from exercising their right of vote. But it is very doubtful whether this restraint would operate on others of much nearer kin.

But conclusive as these practical objections may be to the [illegible] of such a scheme, they are not the objections which [illegible] invincible and insuperable hostility with which it would [illegible] by all Presbyterians.

That hostility arises out of principles which I [illegible] regarded by all who hold them, as of [illegible] to think that it is no essential part of liberality, either in religion or in politics, to let go our hold of definite opinions on the fundamental principles of government either in Church or State. And there are opinions of this kind which, so far as I know, all Presbyterians hold in common, which make it impossible for them to assent to a Rate-paying franchise in the election of ministers. We believe, in a definite sense, that there is such a thing as the Church of Christ. We can repeat, with as much emphasis as any other communion, that clause in the Nicene Creed, "I believe in One Universal and Apostolic Church." In order to the holding of this doctrine it is not necessary to believe in the Romish theory of the Divine right of any one universal Bishop, nor in the Anglican theory of the Divine right of an indefinite number of Bishops with parity among them, nor in the Presbyterian theory of the identity of the offices of Presbyter and of Bishop, and of the equal right of Elders to be associated with these in the Government of the Church; nor indeed in the Divine right of any forms of organization absolutely fixed. It fell in the way of the Reformers both in England and in Scotland to define "The Church:" but neither in England nor in Scotland did they venture to make this definition turn on any particular method of appointing the Christian ministry. This in itself is one of the greatest of all "Confessions." It is enough to believe that our Lord did not merely promulgate doctrines, but that He also founded a Society: a Society having its own definite aims and ends in view, its own definite principles of government, its own kind of polity, and its own laws of membership. Nor is it necessary to hold that it is either wise or right to demand as the terms of admission to this Society, or to any branch of it, the assent of men to those long Creeds and Confessions which are one of the misfortunes of the Reformation, and which enumerate among the things of faith long strings of propositions which in their very nature are not matters of faith at all, but of opinion, and of very doubtful opinion, too. There are many of these propositions which, at best, can only be accepted as expressing, as they often do express in noble language, certain special and very important aspects of the truth. I am not now arguing for narrow or contracted terms of membership. On the contrary, I should be in favour of making them as wide as possible. But if the Christian Church is to be an organized Society at all, it must have some terms of membership—some principle of association. And when we consider the objects which it has in view, and the sphere within which it works, namely, the consciences and the minds of men, we must hold it, as the Westminster Confession declares it to be, a sphere in its own nature "distinct from the civil magistrate." But, again, it is to be remembered that this great principle is of no "private interpretation." It does not involve the proposition that the two spheres never overlap, nor even that they can ever be kept absolutely apart. Still less does it affirm that those who work and rule in each can never do so in close alliance or under limitations self-imposed. But there is one thing which this principle does absolutely exclude—and that is that the Christian Church should have imposed upon it terms of membership which are purely secular, and therefore wholly alien to its nature and its functions. The tie which binds men together as members of that Society is a tie peculiar to itself, and it cannot be confounded with those other ties which gather men together in the tap-room, or even in the polling booth. It is true, indeed, that in a far-off way and to a microscopic extent in connection with the Established Church in Scotland, and to a very much greater and palpable extent in connection with the Established Church in England, men have come to exercise some power in connection with its government who are not members of the body and may not be members of any Church at all. But this is an indirect and purely accidental effect of changes in the condition of society, which have arisen gradually and imperceptibly since the times when all Established Churches began to be. It was never contemplated, and it constitutes no part of the acknowledged and recognized principles of the institution in either country. This, of course, is a very different thing from a new Act of Parliament deliberately placing in the hands of men who are not members of the Church one of the most important duties connected with its duties and its constitution. Such a measure would have been intolerable to any Church which respects itself, or which places value on fundamental principles which are of much greater value than any connection with civil governments. If such a measure had been passed for Scotland, I should have been the first to enlist as a volunteer in the army of Disestablishment.

And yet the just and necessary refusal of the Government and of Parliament to listen to any proposal of this kind is the only foundation on which it is pretended that the Act for Abolishing Patronage had the effect of narrowing the basis of the Church. The facts are precisely the reverse. The Act not only widened that basis because of its recognition of greater power on the part of Congregations, but in so far as it affected the terms of membership at all, it enlarged and liberalized them in an important matter. The law as it stood before never did recognize the right of any persons to vote for or to object to Presentees who were not themselves members of the Congregation. Moreover, Lord Aberdeen's Act of Patronage, which the new Act repealed, had defined membership as requiring "full communion with the Church," thus making sacramental communion an indispensable test of membership. As originally framed, the Bill brought in by the Government followed this precedent, and limited the election of ministers by the same qualification. No blame is to be attached to the Government for having proposed this limitation. Beyond all question, the unexpressed understanding of the Church had been that membership in her body consisted in being in full communion with it in the dispensation [illegible] But apart from the objection which lay against [illegible] expressly embodied in a Statute, which would [illegible] on the freedom of the Church, there was [illegible] of a practical kind. "It is well known that in some [illegible] a superstitious feeling has arisen in respect to [illegible] Lord's Supper, almost akin to that which arose in the [illegible] respect to the sacrament of baptism. This feeling has [illegible] among Free Church congregations than among those [illegible] the Established Church. Under the influence of this [illegible] often happen, and it does happen, that a large part [illegible], including its most attached and constant members, [illegible] under the legal definition of communicants. Again [illegible] to believe that one of the most distinguished laymen [illegible] has served as an Elder in the General Assembly, [illegible] from other causes never did communicate in the Pres- [illegible]hurch. But he was an habitual member of a Congrega- [illegible] and adherent. It would be in the highest degree [illegible] the freedom of the Church in recognizing such men ing to her Congregations. On this, as well as on other [illegible] ventured to suggest to the Government that the word- Act should be such as to include the Congregation in the [illegible]sible acceptation of the term which the Church itself it wise and necessary to attach to it. The Government at ted this suggestion, and, by including "adherents," opened loor to all who consider themselves, and can be considered rethren, as in any sense members of the body.

rough consistency of the measure when thus modified, not the opinions and traditions of the people of Scotland, but fundamental principles of the universal Church, was well by the form of parliamentary resistance to which the of it were driven. It was difficult for members connected ne of the Presbyterian bodies to give any vote directly in naintaining Patronage. It was equally difficult for members with the Church of England who had any knowledge of, or hurch principles, to vote for any amendment embodying the ilarism of the Ratepaying franchise. It was difficult for embers of any kind to oppose a Bill, which, not merely on it but in its very nature, was in the direction of popular The result was that it could only be opposed by a flank Delay for the purposes of inquiry is always plausible. case it had nothing to recommend it, and everything to [illegible]ievous. No inquiry was needed to ascertain the fact bolition of Patronage, such as it had been always, and such as it had come to be, was not only just and expedient it the one indispensable preliminary to any possible union Presbyterian Churches. To make such a question matter of formal inquiry could only have deluged the country under floods of that kind of speaking and writing to which men resort when they dislike a measure upon grounds which are not easily avowed, and when, therefore, they are compelled by the conflict between their position and their principles, to say one thing when they mean another. To warn Established Churches to adopt the strategy of those creatures which lie motionless in order to escape from danger—not to lift a finger or move a muscle lest they should attract attention—this may be honest advice, but it does not seem a very hopeful policy in the fierce light which beats on every institution in our time. Movement is at least a sign of life: and the real objection lay in the doctrine that to do anything in favour of an Established Church, however just or reasonable in itself, is unjust to that portion of the public which does not belong to the Establishment, and which, therefore, has a vested interest in keeping up every disability or vexation to which its members may be exposed.

And this brings me to the real significance of the movement to disestablish the Church of Scotland, upon any ground connected with the Act abolishing Patronage. It is perfectly true, that if Established Churches are in themselves an injustice to those who have separated from them, then every action of Parliament which tends to make those Churches more efficient or more popular, is action in a wrong direction. There may be a little difficulty sometimes, in the minds of very scrupulous or very conscientious men in following up this argument to all its consequences; because much at least of the work, even of an Established Church, is, after all, work in the interests of religion, and opposition to all measures for promoting this work must run disagreeably close to the policy of doing evil that good may come. But there are none of us wanting in that kind of ingenuity which is sufficient to overcome this kind of difficulty. It is quite easy to draw a distinction between the Church as a religious society, and the Church as a political institution; and it is quite as easy to found on this distinction conclusions of which perhaps a very calm and a very enlightened conscience would detect the fallacy. Accordingly the doctrine which has been eagerly accepted by the "Liberation Society" in reference to the Act abolishing Patronage in Scotland, namely, the doctrine that it was unjust because it was passed in the interest of an Established Church, is a doctrine which, if it be accepted, will lead to very important, and moreover, perhaps, to very speedy applications. We are accustomed to say now of political questions which it is not convenient to discuss, such as the destruction of the Turkish Empire in Europe, that it is [illegible] a question of practical politics." And this is habitually said of the Disestablishment of the Church of England. No doubt the [illegible] of that Church are deep, and in some aspects its position may [illegible] impregnable—"Four-square to all the winds that blow." "I [illegible] know," it was said not long ago, "by what methods of [illegible] with what weapons of attack, such an operation as the Disestablishment of the Church of England could be accomplished." Well, but here is at least one weapon very handy for a commencement, and lending itself to immediate use. It so happens that under the existing constitution of the Church of England hardly anything can be done, however great, or however small, without the help of an Act of Parliament. Weaker in many other ways, the Established Church of Scotland is at least in this respect in a more favourable position. Reforms of the most extensive kind in her worship and discipline could be carried into effect without any application to Parliament, by the inherent and recognized authority of her own Assemblies. In all these matters the Established Church of England is bound hand and foot by a constant necessity of referring for everything to Parliament. Many members of her communion are already fretted by the practical difficulty of regarding the House of Commons, constituted as it is, as a body fitted to express the opinion of the laity, as distinguished from the opinions of a purely secular constituency. Yet to this body the Church must apply for every adjustment however small, and every amendment however necessary, of machinery which works with friction, and is in many parts out of date. The immense advantage which this will give to the new doctrine about the injustice of helping Established Churches, must be apparent at a glance. Already we are notoriously under conditions of society which render it impossible to think of any new endowments from the State. And if the doctrine be accepted that exactly the same principle is involved in any attempt to strengthen the position of religious endowments already existing, then "practical politics"—very practical indeed—will find in this condition of things, the incentive and the opportunities for immediate action. It is but a very few years ago since Parliament in the interests of the Established Church relaxed the terms of subscription to the Articles. This was a great boon—a great relief to burdened consciences, and therefore a great help to an institution which Liberationists condemn, as in its own nature unjust to Dissenters. "Whereas it is expedient," says the Act of 1865, "that the subscriptions and oaths required to be made and taken by the clergy of the Church of England should be simplified." This, no doubt, is the doctrine, and the only doctrine, which is truly liberal. But the new doctrine which is recommended to us as such is the opposite doctrine, which may be expressed as follows:—"Whereas it is unjust to Dissenters that the subscriptions or oaths taken by the clergy of any Established Church should be simplified." For myself, I can only say that I look upon such a policy as not only illiberal, but as unjust, unchristian, and immoral. Macaulay has given us a vivid account of the success of a policy of this kind, when the jealousies of Dissent, combined with the prejudices of High Churchism, combined to defeat the Comprehension Bill of 1689.* Dean Stanley has given us an

* Macaulay's History of England, chap. xi.

account equally vivid of the delight and relief expressed in Convocation when some part at least of this evil work was undone by the Relaxation Act of 1865.* It is an indication, we may hope, of the progress of morality in spite of sectarian temptations, that Dissenters do not seem to have thought themselves entitled to prevent or oppose a measure which, perhaps more than any other passed in our time, has tended to strengthen the Established Church. Again, it is but the other day since a "brand new" Bishopric was established by Act of Parliament in an English county—Cornwall—which is notoriously peopled thickly with Dissenters. In one of the principal towns of that county, a few years ago, I attended church in the forenoon, and the Methodist chapel in the afternoon. If the proportions in which the population over the county generally is divided between the two communions is a proportion at all like that which seemed to prevail in that town, the Established Church must be in a very decided minority. The new Bishop, a very distinguished man, has spoken in a late address of the "latent Churchmanship of the people;" and beyond all question this is an element on which all Established Churches which have any life in them do most naturally rely. But the appeal to this element is an appeal hostile to the interests of the Dissenting bodies, and necessarily aggressive as regards their membership. On the principles now laid down as regards the Act abolishing Patronage in Scotland, all such Acts as those I have referred to, affecting England, are Acts to favour the interests of "a sect," are in nature of re-endowment—of fresh buttresses to the Establishment, and as such a political injustice. Before any more such Acts are passed, the course of "practical politics" may probably be systematically to resist them, or to obstruct them by moving for Committees of Inquiry.

It is quite time, therefore, that men should make up their minds whether it is really true that the maintenance of ancient endowments, in connection with a particular Church, is in itself necessarily unjust to those portions of the community which have from time to time separated from it. No mere pleas for delay, no mere shirking, can save us from meeting this question in the face. Of course it is not a question at all, but an obvious fact, that when a great majority of the population have come to be hostile to an Established Church, they will, if they are so minded, be able to effect its overthrow. In this sense we must all accept the ultimate results of popular government; and no Church which is worthy of the name can ever speak or think of such a consummation as by any means the greatest calamity that could befall it. But this is not the question now pending as regards the doctrines of the Liberation Society. The question is touching the formation of opinion as yet undecided, and not as to the acceptance of a final verdict when the public mind has arrived at its conclusion. It is on this question that I venture to express my own

* Essays on Church and State: Essay IV. note iv. p. 216.

clear and decided opinion, that the maintenance of ancient national endowments, in connection with a Church which has been really national in its origin, which is still doing its work among a large portion of the people, and which is capable of doing the same work among a portion larger still, is a policy involving no injustice to those who have become Dissenters. I venture to think that even when an Established Church has many faults, and may justly be accused of many shortcomings, the resources which have been placed at its disposal are under such circumstances better employed than in any other work whatever,—better than in secular education, and better even than in the care of lunatics.

There is another part of this question on which it is also quite time to take our side. I observe that in recent speeches of members of the Liberation Society it has been announced that when Disestablishment does take place, it must be effected on conditions much less lenient than those on which the late Government disestablished the Church of Ireland. Now as the principle of that measure was little more than the guarding of life interests, and the retention of the ancient Buildings as belonging to the disestablished body, it would appear that in England this principle is not to be respected. And, indeed, it must be admitted that the demands of perfect religious equality would hardly be satisfied without going farther. The ancient Cathedrals of England, as national property, would have to be opened for the use of all. Nor could that use be confined to those who are usually called Nonconformists. There might be much good in this. But religious equality would not be satisfied with this. "The beautiful and the holy houses where our fathers worshipped" must be at the service equally of all sects—of those who, in this nineteenth century of the Christian era, are still building altars to the "Unknown God;" of those who think that there is no God to know or to be known; and of those who bow their heads in that strangest of all worships, the worship of Humanity.

There is one thing, however, to be well considered by those who advocate such extreme measures—and that is that even if they succeed in the policy of Disestablishment they will probably fail in this policy of spoliation. The Church of England is too strong for this. Unless that Church breaks up from internal dissensions, she will, when disestablished, be the richest and most powerful Corporation in the world. She will march out of her entrenchments not only with the honours but laden with the spoils of war.

The difficulty, indeed, of disendowing the Church of England with any approach to completeness, even if it were disestablished, is a difficulty which does not seem to have been sufficiently thought of by the members of the Liberation Society. Large as the amount of revenue is connected with that Church which Parliament would have a fair right, if it saw adequate reason, to dispose of otherwise, that property is not sufficient for the full performance of the Church's work in the growing population of the country. This is equally true, though on a smaller scale, with the Established Church of Scotland. The consequence is that both these Churches are compelled to supplement their endowments by voluntary effort, thus combining the stability and the territorial ubiquity which belongs to an Established Church with the life and activity of a Church which is largely dependent on its own exertions. If the sums were counted which within living memory have been poured into the lap of the Church of England by the devotion of her sons, they would be found to amount to millions. No measures, short of revolutionary violence, could deprive her of these vast accumulations, nor of that territorial and parochial organization which is the richest of all endowments, and which is the inalienable heritage of a Church which has been really national in its history and its origin.

Among the deep tap-roots which the English Church has struck into the land it occupies, I am well aware that lay patronage is one. Personally, I have little sympathy with the notion of property in benefices with cure of souls. But it is to be recollected that in England the Patrons are almost always members of the Church, and it is undeniable that this system is one of the few indirect methods in which the laity exert their influence in the government of their Church. Apart altogether therefore from the effect which it has in identifying Church endowments with the personal influence and interests of a powerful class, it has a real value as representing, however indirectly, a principle of fundamental importance in the organization of the Church. In Scotland it never has had this significance, but, on the contrary, it has been the symbol and the stronghold of a principle directly opposite, namely, that of a power external altogether to the Church and hostile to the liberties of its people. No Scotchman whose sympathy is with the feelings and opinions of the great body of his countrymen on these high matters can for a moment entertain the opinion that it is of the essence of an Established Church—the one thing which the State must stipulate for as its special compensation—that somebody must have the power of thrusting ministers on reluctant Congregations. This is a notion which comes from nothing but prejudice; and although it is a notion to which some countenance has been given in the language of a few Scotchmen, its origin is plain enough. It comes from English associations, and the difficulty of getting men who are not themselves Presbyterians to understand the possibility of any relation between Church and State other than those which were established in England by the Tudors and the Stuarts. No one who knew intimately the history of the contest which ended in the secession of 1843 could fail to feel that the greatest difficulties in the way of remedial legislation were due to those unfortunate circumstances which have alienated a large part of the aristocracy in Scotland from the Church of the people. The ideas fundamental to its constitution have become unfamiliar to their minds: and, truth to say, these ideas were not always presented in the most reasonable form. There was thus a combination of influences to raise an invincible barrier of prejudice. That kind of Toryism which hates the very idea of popular liberties in the Church, that kind of secular Liberalism which hates every Church alike, and that degree of Anglicanism which is prevalent among Episcopalian Patrons in Scotland, were equally opposed to any effective alteration of the Jacobite Act of Patronage.

Precisely the same influences, with some tributaries of an accidental origin, are at work again. From pure secularism, abhorrent to all Presbyterian principle, come all those suggestions, under whatever forms they may be disguised, which require that the Christian Church alone, of all other Societies on earth, is not to be the judge of its own terms of membership; that one of its highest privileges is to be exercised by those who do not belong to it; and that ministers of the Gospel are to be elected as men elect a Chief Constable or an Inspector of Nuisances. This is the real meaning of the phrase which has become so common with "heckled" candidates at meetings of electors, when there is sore need of words with some echo of a popular sound in them to cover any defence of Patronage—the phrase, namely, that the Act of 1874 has reduced the Church to the condition of a "sect." There is one method of testing this phrase which I would recommend to my countrymen, as at once eminently Scotch and perfectly Socratic. Let the question be put, What is the distinction between a Church and a sect? It would then appear that a Church is a body whose ministers are to be chosen by a few Tory lairds, or a few Whig Peers, and that a sect means a Church which is so illiberal as to depend on the whole body of its Congregations, which means the whole Presbyterian people who, unshackled by any test or any subscription, may choose to come to them.

Then as regards English prejudice, it is as strong as ever. Some metaphysicians derive all our ideas from what they call "inseparable association:" and such is the nature of the link which binds Englishmen generally to the grotesque idea that Patronage is essential to the very definition of a Church in connection with the State. I am not at all sure that there is not another influence at work—even less legitimate as affecting any question of politics in Scotland—namely, the feeling of Episcopalian High Churchism that a Presbyterian Church is not fit to have the support and acknowledgment of the State. Perhaps this phase of opinion has somewhat passed away. It is not, I think, a very active force. But that there would be some pleasure in some minds in seeing Episcopacy the sole form of ecclesiastical organization in alliance with the State, cannot well be doubted by any who have observed certain indications which are plain enough. It is for the Presbyterians of Scotland generally to say whether this is a result which they desire to see accomplished. To seek for it is no doubt a consistent course for those of them who have adopted the opinion that all Church Establishments are in themselves necessarily wrong. They may safely count upon the natural result that, when the Scotch Church has been disestablished, all Presbyterians would unite with the opponents of the Church of England. No doubt this would be the inevitable result. But not holding that Established Churches are unjust to those who have seceded, and not desiring to see these results attained, I am in favour of the opposite policy, which historically has been the policy of all Liberal politics in Scotland, namely, that of adapting the Church Establishment as completely as possible to the hereditary traditions and opinions of the people.

And this brings me, in conclusion, to the main reason which determined me to support the abolition of Patronage. I have spoken of some tributary and accidental sources of feeling which have caused that measure to be regarded with hostility, or at least with jealousy, by a great many Scotchmen who have not the smallest sympathy either with Secularism or with English prejudices on the subject of Patronage. Free Churchmen especially are disposed to regard it as an Act passed exclusively for the benefit of those particular men who happen to be ministers or members of the Established Church at the present time. But surely this is not a just or reasonable view to take of it. It is true of course that the extreme inconveniences to which I have referred as attending the operation of Patronage under the Act of 1843 were an evil affecting most directly and most immediately the interests of those who belonged to the Establishment. But they were also a public evil, as affecting the interests of all for whom that Establishment is intended, which is the whole Presbyterian people. The removal of this evil, and the avoidance of the danger of new secessions, was in itself, and by itself, a full justification of the abolition of that Act. And this was its primary object. But I admit that all legislative action on behalf of Established Churches ought, if possible, to have regard to the opinions, and even the tendencies of opinion, among those who have been led to separate or to stand aloof. Any movement ought, if it be possible, to be a movement in their direction—a movement to make it easier for them to take advantage of the ancient endowments of their country if they choose to do so, without compromise or sacrifice of their freedom to hold their own special opinions, whatever these may be. My own sympathies with those who seceded in 1843, in so far as their contention was based on constitutional law, were insufficient to constitute membership with the separate Church they formed, because I have never been able to hold the doctrine of "spiritual independence," or the Divine authority of ecclesiastical jurisdictions, in that absolute and dogmatic sense in which Free Churchmen profess to hold it. But I think it in the highest degree inexpedient to hinder those who do hold it from belonging to the National Establishment. It is an opinion in which there ought at least to be freedom of thought, and every obstacle to that freedom ought to be removed. Now to the establishing of this freedom the Jacobite Act of Queen Anne was not only the chief, but in my view it was the only obstacle. I do not say that the repeal of it amounted in itself to any new declaration on the part of the Legislature in favour of the doctrine of spiritual independence. But I do confidently affirm that this repeal did effectually revive all the old declarations of the Scottish Parliaments on this subject, and did remove the only statute which had ever practically interfered with the freedom of the Church,—the only statute which had been founded upon in the aggressions of the Civil Court. Free Churchmen cannot fairly ask that all other Presbyterians shall be compelled to affirm propositions which we think too wide, too absolute, to be theoretically true. All that they can fairly demand is that they shall be at least free to affirm their own view without any practical contradiction from the law. And this is precisely the liberty which all may now enjoy in the Established Church. Its connection with the State now rests solely upon the old Constitutional Statutes of the Parliament of Scotland. These statutes are certainly broad enough in their language on the freedom which is the birthright of the Church, and the like of these old statutes will probably never be passed again.

Practically it is not denied that freedom of action on the part of the Church is now complete. I am happy to observe that in a lecture lately delivered by Lord Moncreiff on the relations of Church and State this practical freedom was fully admitted; "it was not," he said, "the extent, but the source of the Jurisdiction that was called in question."* The admission as regards the extent of jurisdiction now enjoyed is as certainly true as it is important; and the qualification as regards the source of this jurisdiction is a qualification which cannot be sustained. There is nothing in the law of the Established Church to throw any doubt whatever on the source of what is called spiritual jurisdiction. There is nothing to impede any man who is in that Church, or who may choose to join it, from holding the very highest and extremest doctrine as to that source. I hold with the Confession of Faith, that the Founder of the Christian Church "hath therein appointed a government distinct from the civil magistrate." I do not hold that this doctrine, which seems to me to express an indisputable fact, involves all the consequences which some Free Churchmen assert. But there is nothing remaining in the law to prevent them from perfect freedom of opinion in this matter. The Established Church is now as free as any Church in the world,—perhaps a great deal more free than many which are purely voluntary,—in every kind of action and of movement which is requisite for the discharge of those functions for which all Churches exist. I trust that this freedom will be exerted gradually and with caution in many things that

* I quote from a report in the *Scotsman* newspaper.

require a genuine spirit of liberality and reform. Along with a firm adherence to the fundamental principles of the Presbyterian Church, and even an eager return to them in some things in which they have been obscured and lost, it is perfectly possible to make both our theology and our worship a good deal wider and more comprehensive than it has ever been. A great many ideas and practices have come to be associated with Presbyterianism which have nothing to do with anything essential to its doctrines. I am not among the number of those who think that any Church can exist without a definite theology, or that even the ethics of Christianity would long survive its Creed. But all the Churches of the Reformation have inherited difficulties from the minute and elaborate definitions which were common at that time, but which are now more and more felt to be a needless restraint on freedom. In meeting these difficulties all the Presbyterian Churches will have enough to do. And considering how important this duty is not only as regards the peace of particular communions, but as regards the interests of Christian truth, it ought to be matter, not of a narrow jealousy, but of sincere congratulation, that by the abolition of Patronage, the Established Church has not only been made accessible to many who could never otherwise have availed themselves of her services, but has been placed in a position which must make her both more able and more disposed still farther to include rather than to exclude, to conciliate rather than to offend.

And this brings me to a matter of far higher importance than the jealousies which have been aroused by the abolition of all that remained of Patronage under the Act of 1843. I refer to the effects, or alleged effects, of the present terms of subscription to the Westminster Confession of Faith. It is probable that any application to Parliament for a relaxation of those terms, in so far as they are regulated by statute, would come across the same party interests and the same illiberal feelings which animated the opposition to an Act establishing the liberty of Congregations in the election of ministers. I have no doubt that a number of politicians would discover that it is a liberal thing to do to repress even the most reasonable liberty of religious thought in connection with an Established Church, in order to prove that no such liberty can or ought to be enjoyed by any Church connected with the State. It is true, as we have seen, that this liberty has been accorded to the Church of England by a very recent statute. But this was passed before the doctrine had been promulgated that all statutes in the interest of such a communion are necessarily unjust to Dissenters. In view of this doctrine, [illegible] it becomes of some importance to inquire whether the Established Church of Scotland is under any necessity of going to Parliament [illegible] all in order to assert for its members a very large [illegible] in this most important matter.

In the first place, then, it is to [illegible]

recast the Creeds and Confessions of the Reformation is an attempt from which the unestablished Churches themselves instinctively recoil, and which if made would probably bring about disruptions in them all. One of the least of the difficulties attending such an attempt is the legal difficulty, from which none of these Churches can be wholly free. All Churches have property of some kind belonging to the communion; and all Churches, whether Established or not, must be identified and defined by some terms of association. Those who adhere to these terms of association when others depart from them, can always call in the power of the civil courts to keep the property which belongs to the body, and does not belong to those who leave it. This is one of the cases in which it is practically impossible so to "redd the marches" of temporal and spiritual things, that civil jurisdiction shall be wholly kept out even from a question so purely "spiritual" as definitions and interpretations of doctrine. And this is a practical, legal, and, so to say, a mechanical difficulty in the way of altering the Westminster Confession itself, or still more of departing from it altogether.

But putting this difficulty aside, there is another difficulty cutting far deeper. The Westminster Confession has taken a firm hold upon the mind of all Presbyterian Churches not only in Scotland, but throughout the world. And this arises not from its embodiment in statutes of any kind, but from the sources of its own inspiration, and the place which these occupy in the history of religious thought. It is not peculiarly Scotch, nor is it distinctively Presbyterian. There is only a small and comparatively insignificant portion of it which is marked by the influence of local and temporary circumstances. A learned and able defender of it in recent times has said with truth, "It is lined and scored with the marks of conflict, but the deepest and the broadest lines are those which run through all the Christian ages, and which appear distinctly either in the Creeds of the early Councils, or in the writings of the greatest of the Latin Fathers, or which, if they are not found so prominently there, appear broad and deep in the teaching both of the Greek and of the Latin Church and of the ablest theologians of the middle ages."* It is to this fundamental coincidence with the main stream of Christian teaching that it owes its strength, and the hold it has acquired over so large an extent of Christian ground. A corresponding width of interpretation must be given to it. This may be gathered from its history as well as from its words. It was not drawn upon the model of the old native Scotch Confession, but on the model of the Articles of the Church of England. And the amplification which it makes of these Articles is one which did not come from any Scotch or Presbyterian hands, but mainly from the hands of one of the most eminent divines of the Episcopal Church, Archbishop

* Lecture on the Westminster Confession. By Professor Mitchell, D.D., of St. Andrew's. Edinburgh, 1876.

Usher.* It represents his view, not of any local or provincial controversy, but of the sum and substance of the Reformed doctrine. Its relation moreover to the old Scotch Confession, which is very remarkable, shows how wide and liberal must be the understandings under which it not only may, but must be signed. The old Scotch Confession of 1560 is different in tone, and in texture, and even in the direction in which it looks on some questions of primary importance. Yet that old Confession of the Scotch Reformation has never been repealed, or modified, or departed from. The Assembly which accepted the Westminster Confession expressly did so on the ground that they interpreted it as "in nothing contrary to the received doctrine, worship, discipline, and government of this Church." Every man now signing the Westminster Confession is thus formally authorized so to read it as in all things to be consistent with the older Confession of the Scotch Reformation. And the effect of this authority is great. "I now dismiss this document," says Edward Irving after analysing the old Confession, "with the highest encomium which I am capable of bestowing upon a work of fallible man. It hath been profitable to my soul and to my flock. For several years I was in the habit of reading it twice in the year to my people; and once upon a time, when two men whom I wished to make Elders had their difficulties in respect to the Westminster Confession, I found them most cordial in giving their assent to this. Its doctrine is sound, its expression is clear, its spirit is large and liberal, its dignity is personal and not dogmatic, and it is all redolent with the unction of holiness and truth." Such is the high and fine eulogium passed upon the Confession of 1560 by a very remarkable man who himself fretted under the supposed yoke of the Westminster Confession. But that yoke is removed in all that requires removal when we recollect that the Westminster Confession was accepted, and only accepted, because it was held to be compatible with the older and, to Scotchmen, the more venerable standard of their own Reformers. If the Westminster Confession was so construed, and if this reasonable liberty of interpretation was asserted, by the able men who represented the Church of Scotland in 1647, assuredly it may be asserted now. Considering the weight and variety of authority represented in the Assembly at Westminster, and the power which it has carried with it over subsequent opinion, the Presbyterian Churches may well shrink from the dangerous and the needless task of revising formulas of such a character, and with such a history. Considering, too, the complete vagueness, and uncertainty, and aimlessness of what is called modern thought, it is not very easy to wish any rash lifting of the anchors by which so many have held on so long.

And after all, is there any real need of altering Confessions? The great fault of the Westminster Confession is not only its minuteness

* See Schaff's History of the Creeds of Christendom, chap. vii. in voc. Westminster Confession.

tion of detail, but its inclusion of matters which do not the domain of faith at all. I would venture to suggest, to young men, if there are any such, who are troubled by us scruples about signing such a document, that in this instance they may see the reasonable liberty with which ture must necessarily be consistent. Take, for example, r on the Civil Magistrate. This is naturally the great block and rock of offence to some of the seceding Presburches. And no wonder. It is wholly impossible to ret chapter with the abstract doctrines of spiritual indepen- it is the duty of the civil magistrate "to take order that peace be preserved in the Church, that the truth of God be and entire," and that "all corruption and abuses in worship line be prevented or reformed," then, in order to perform e must interfere, and authoritatively too, in the most purely atters. The non-established Churches have not dealt with lty, if it be one, in a very satisfactory manner. The Free s emitted a declaration that this chapter in the Confession involve certain obnoxious interpretations when "rightly d." But no vague declarations of this kind can explain plain meaning of very plain words. The United Presbyrch thinks it has got over the difficulty in two ways—first, aration that it accepts the Confession only as containing orized exhibition of the sense in which we understand the ptures." But no Church accepts it in any other or higher No Church accepts the Confession as having any indepenority other than as an authorized exposition of the sense in ipture is understood. The second mode of meeting the is like that adopted by the Free Church; viz.—a special n that the chapter on the Civil Magistrate is not to be d in the sense which it obviously bears.

It is a far more satisfactory way of meeting such a diffiis, to admit frankly the undoubted fact that in this matter, ot one of faith at all, the Westminster Assembly was influthe position and circumstances in which it found itself hich was that of an Assembly called together by the Parhich then represented the civil power, and called together press purpose of imposing, by authority of law, upon the the United Kingdom an uniformity both of worship and of This is the simple truth, and it is a truth of immense e, as demonstrating that, wholly irrespective of authorized ns of any kind, every man is perfectly entitled to sign the with those reservations of opinion which are inseparable ssent to documents of such a character.

ven authorized declarations on the part of Church Assemitiving or repudiating certain meanings, or apparent meanings of the Confession, are of any use to over-scrupulous consciences, such declarations are as competent to the Assemblies of the Established Church as to those of any other. Indeed, it is a circumstance not a little remarkable that in the very Act of Assembly which first sanctioned the Westminster Confession, there is a special reservation made for the purpose of excluding a possible interpretation of one part of it: and it is a powerful illustration of the jealousy with which the Scotch Church guarded the rights of its laity and of its Congregations, as against any exclusive powers vested in the ministry, that this reservation was made for the purpose of repudiating the idea that ministers alone could constitute Synods and Assemblies without delegation from the Churches, and a due representation of the Eldership.

I pass therefore, in connection with the same subject, to some matters which are really among the things of faith on which the utterances of the Confession may seem to require some latitude of interpretation. In the chapter on God's Eternal Decrees the Confession has certainly selected from the writings of St. Paul some of the things which are "hard to be understood," and has founded on them interpretations which are harder still. If there is any part of the Confession which might justify scruples of conscience on the part of those who are called to sign, it is part of this chapter. And yet there is one principle of interpretation of indisputable authority, which is sufficient of itself to establish the widest liberty of opinion on the incomprehensible mysteries to which this chapter refers. That principle is simply this, that every document must be interpreted in harmony with itself. If, therefore, we are staggered by any of the propositions of this chapter, we have only to turn to the first and leading proposition of them all, and to the other chapter on "Free Will," to be satisfied that as they must be reconciled, so each man is free to reconcile them as he can. If one sentence is Calvinistic, another is Arminian. The great question how to reconcile our ideas of the necessities of causation with our consciousness of our own responsibility and freedom, is not a question peculiar to theology; it is the most difficult of all questions in the history of philosophy: and never in any age of the world were men more bepuzzled and befooled than now by their own poor and thin logomachies concerning it. The theologians of Westminster have ventured on some very rash sayings on one aspect of the doctrine of Necessity, but not more rash than we may see every day repeated by the scientific dogmatists of our own days on another aspect of it. Indeed, I should be disposed to say that the Westminster Confession contains within itself by far the best antidote to any errors on this subject which it may contain, since, unlike our modern dogmatists in dealing with the same subject, it indicates with great precision and force of language the fundamental limitations under which the doctrine of Necessity can alone be accepted or under-the Westminster Confession is very much more than the corresponding Articles of the The tenth Article of that Church, which professes Will, contains no distinct affirmation of that free- the contrary perplexes us with a sentence which deny that free will exists at all; whilst in the on "Predestination and Election," the same involved which animates the rawest Calvinism. It is not pushed to its obvious conclusions; but any affirmation of the counter-propositions by which conclusions can be escaped. The Westminster Con- as vigorous, even more vigorous, in insisting under which the doctrine of Necessity is to be it is in affirming that doctrine in certain senses. declares that the Decrees of God are always to be such that "thereby neither is God the author of offered to the Will of the creatures, nor is the contingency of second causes taken away, but rather esta- there anywhere else that I know of a better, shorter, given of man's freedom than in this passage on Free hath endued the Will of man with that natural liberty, forced, nor by any absolute necessity of nature deter- good or evil." These propositions are the governing pro- the whole, and in proportion as they are contradicted or contradicted by others, either these others must be ex- way, or (and this is the most reasonable conclusion) we are native liberty to reconcile them in Theology as we prac- reconcile them both in Philosophy and in Life.

onsiderations, and others of a similar kind which apply to s of the Confession, go to show that men with the most conscience not only may but can only reasonably accept ssions as that of Westminster, with many reservations as ority of particular propositions, and this quite independent oritative declarations by the Church, either affirming or ial or obnoxious interpretations.

hese considerations are not enough to satisfy men's con- nd to establish a reasonable liberty in the matter, the ld seem to have another remedy in her own hands. The 1693, which gave effect to the wishes of the Church in terms of subscription, simply requires that the sub- thereby signify the acceptance of the Confession as "the his faith." The law requires nothing more than this. sign such a document as the confession of their faith, it as a confession of their Cosmogony, or of their more minute, elaborate, and entangling questions the "whole doctrines," &c., which are now put to candidates for ordination, rest, or seem to rest, not upon any statute, but upon an Act of the General Assembly, passed at a subsequent date, and by the authority of the Church alone. I apprehend that it must be perfectly competent to the General Assembly to alter and amend these questions, if it should seem advisable to do so, and to be satisfied with declarations less stringent and specific.

But lastly, even if there should be any doubt as to this, there can be no doubt of the exclusive power of the Church Courts over all matters of discipline. Their jurisdiction in all questions and in all Causes affecting doctrine is supreme and indisputable. Through this jurisdiction they could practically establish even the largest and widest modification of the terms of subscription. They can systematically discourage the work of petty hunters after Heresy. They can encourage a liberal spirit, which will be at the same time a tender and a scrupulous spirit in dealing with the most difficult of all subjects. This appears to be the solution which is being resorted to by the unestablished Churches, which have precisely the same embarrassments to deal with, and whose tendencies to liberal methods of dealing with "deviating" brethren seem to be sensibly quickened by the near neighbourhood of an Established Church with similar tendencies perhaps more pronounced. If the views which I have here ventured to express be sound, no very wide modification is required. What is really wanted is, not license or anarchy in Doctrine, but only that reasonable liberty in theological Belief which is needed by the progress of knowledge, and the well-considered development of religious thought.

In like manner as regards forms of worship, the courts of the Established Church are perhaps more free than any other to admit such changes and modifications as may be demanded by the feelings of Congregations, and may be justified by the gradual disappearance of prejudices which were temporary and accidental.

It is difficult to conceive of any Church with greater powers and liberties than these: they are greater, more unencumbered, than have been enjoyed at any former period of its history. It is now distinctly more free than in the days of Knox, or in the days of Melville, or in the days of Henderson. If its powers are wisely used they give to that Church singular facilities for meeting the requirements of its own country and of our time. It now represents with a fulness of measure in which it never represented before that ideal connection between Church and State which was the passion of its Reformers, and has been always the distinguishing aspiration of the whole Presbyterian people. And in this result the seceding Churches have at least an equal right to triumph. It is their testimony, helped by other causes, which has finally prevailed—not over their brethren in the Establishment, but over Anglicanism and Secularism, and the combined influence of both over too many Scotchmen. It is the whole

Presbyterian people who have gained the day. It is for them, or for as many of them as choose to do so, to enter in and take possession. They can do so if they like, with their drums beating and their banners flying. Or if they do not formally join, at least they can work alongside in peace, for there is room for all. What divided them is gone. What has always united them alone remains. Or if there be any step which can be taken, or any other measure which can be adopted to make this plainer than it now is, I can only say that no one would be more ready than myself to lend it a helping hand.

It would indeed be a strange and perverse reason for disestablishing a Church, that it has just been brought to coincide almost, if not altogether, with those who once thought themselves compelled to withdraw or to stand aside. If the Presbyterian laity of Scotland are now worthy of those who have gone before them, they will in this matter refuse to follow either secular politicians or ecclesiastical leaders who make it the sport of party. They will compel both sectarianism and faction to stand aside. They will not allow the abandonment of that public and national recognition of the principles of their Church which our ancestors highly valued, and which they dearly bought.

ARGYLL.

# JOHN STUART MILL'S PHILOSOPHY TESTED.

## PART II.

IN the previous article on John Stuart Mill's Philosophy, I made the strange assertion that *Mill's mind was essentially illogical.* To those who have long looked upon him as their guide, philosopher, and friend, such a statement must of course have seemed incredible and absurd, and it will require a great body of evidence to convince them that there is any ground for the assertion. My first test of his logicalness was derived from his writings on geometrical science. I showed by carefully authenticated extracts, that Mill had put forth views which necessarily imply the existence of perfectly straight lines; yet he had at the same time distinctly denied the existence of such lines. It was pointed out that he emphatically promised to use names *always* as the names of things, not as the names of our ideas of things; yet, as straight lines in his opinion do not exist, the name straight line is either the name of "just nothing at all," as James Mill would have said, or else it is the name of our ideas of what they are. It is by experimenting on these ideal straight lines in the mind that we learn the axioms and theorems of geometry according to Mill; nevertheless Mill had denounced, as *the cardinal error of philosophy*, the handling ideas instead of things, and had, indeed, in the earlier editions of the "System of Logic," asserted that not a single truth ever had been arrived at by this method, except truths of psychology. Mill asserted that we might experiment on lines in the mind by prolonging them to any required distance; but these lines according to Mill's own statements must have thickness, and on minute inquiry it was found impossible to attach any definite meaning at all to the *prolongation of a thick line.* Finally, it was pointed out that, when Mill incidentally speaks of an important mathematical theorem concerning the ratio of the diameter and circumference of the circle, he abandons [illegible] *pro tempore*, and speaks of the ratio in ques- [illegible] by a long train of difficult reasoning.

[illegible] of the first small instalment of my evidence. [illegible] I shall return to the subject of geometrical [illegible] far from being exhausted. It will then be proved [illegible] whether geometry is an inductive or a deductive [illegible] opinions of every phase; in one part of his writings [illegible] inductive; in another part it is improperly called [illegible], it is set up as the type of a deductive science, [illegible] a matter of direct observation and experiment; [illegible] discovers unexpectedly, that there is no difference at all [illegible] inductive and a deductive science; the true distinction [illegible] deductive and an experimental science. But Mill charac- [illegible] overlooks the fact that if the difference lies between a [illegible]nd an experimental science, and not between a deductive [illegible]uctive science, then a similar line of difference must be [illegible] an inductive and an experimental science, although [illegible] methods are the Four Experimental Methods.

[illegible]origin of our geometrical knowledge is a very slippery [illegible] before allowed. It would not be fair to condemn Mill [illegible]bles in which he involved himself in regard to such a [illegible] were no other counts proved against him. Certainly, [illegible] geometry as a critical test of the truth of his empirical [illegible] but he may have erred in judgment in choosing so trying [illegible] us, therefore, leave geometry for the present, and select [illegible]nt in this second article a much broader and simpler ques- [illegible]hich lies at the basis of the philosophy of logic and know- [illegible] will endeavour to gain a firm comprehension of Mill's [illegible]ncerning *the nature and importance of the relation of Resem-* [illegible]is question touches the very nature of knowledge itself. [illegible] who are considered to be quite competent to judge, have [illegible]at Mill's logic is peculiarly distinguished by the thorough [illegible]ich it presents of the cognitive and reasoning processes. [illegible]t restricted himself to the empty forms and methods of [illegible]ut has pushed his inquiry, as they think, boldly into the [illegible] and philosophy of reasoning. In the "System of Logic," [illegible]all find it clearly decided whether resemblance is, or is not, [illegible]ental relation with which reasoning is concerned. It was [illegible]e of Locke, as fully expounded in the fourth book of his [illegible]y, that knowledge is the perception of the agreement or [illegible]nt of our ideas.

[illegible] then," says Locke, "seems to me to be nothing but the per- [illegible] connection and agreement, or disagreement and repugnancy, of [illegible]. In this alone it consists. Where this perception is, there is [illegible] where it is not, there, though we may fancy, guess or believe, [illegible] come short of knowledge."

Many other philosophers have likewise held that a certain agreement between things, variously described as resemblance, similarity, identity, sameness, equality, &c., really constituted the whole of *reasoned knowledge*, as distinguished from the mere knowledge of sense. Condillac adopted this view and stated it with admirable breadth and brevity, saying, "L'évidence de raison consiste uniquement dans l'identité."

Mill has not failed to discuss this matter, and his opinion on the subject is most expressly and clearly stated in the chapter upon the Import of Propositions.* He analyzes the state of mind called Belief, and shows that it involves one or more of five matters of fact, namely, Existence, Co-existence, Sequence, Causation, Resemblance. One or other of these is asserted (or denied) in every proposition which is not merely verbal. No doubt relations of the kinds mentioned form a large part of the matter of knowledge, and they must be expressed in propositions in some way or other. I believe that they are expressed in the terms of propositions, while the copula always signifies *agreement*, or, as Condillac would have said, *identity* of the terms. But we need not attempt to settle a question of this difficulty. We are only concerned now with the position in his system which Mill assigns to Resemblance. This comes last in the list, and it is with some expression of doubt that Mill assigns it a place at all. He says:†—

> "Besides propositions which assert a sequence or co-existence between two phenomena, there are therefore also propositions which assert resemblance between them; as, This colour is like that colour;—The heat of to-day is *equal* to the heat of yesterday. It is true that such an assertion might with some plausibility be brought within the description of an affirmation of sequence, by considering it as an assertion that the simultaneous contemplation of the two colours is *followed* by a specific feeling termed the feeling of resemblance. But there would be nothing gained by encumbering ourselves, especially in this place, with a generalization which may be looked upon as strained. Logic does not undertake to analyze mental facts into their ultimate elements. Resemblance between two phenomena is more intelligible in itself than any explanation could make it, and under any classification must remain specifically distinct from the ordinary cases of sequence and co-existence."

It would seem, then, that Mill had, to say the least, contemplated the possibility of resolving Resemblance into something simpler, namely, into a special case of sequence and co-existence; but he abstains, not apparently because it would be plainly impossible, but because logic does not undertake ultimate analysis. It would encumber us with a "strained generalization," whatever that may be. He therefore accords it provisionally a place among the matters of fact which logic treats.

Postponing further consideration of this passage, we turn to a later book of the "System of Logic," in which Mill [illegible]sses pretty clearly his opinion, that Resemblance is *a minor kind* [illegible] to be treated

* Book I., chapter v. † Boo[illegible] [illegible]ction 6.

last in the system of Logic, as being of comparatively small importance. In the chapter headed "Of the remaining Laws of Nature,"* we find Mill distinctly stating that† "the propositions which affirm Order in Time, in either of its two modes, Co-existence and Succession, have formed, thus far, the subject of the present Book. And we have now concluded the exposition, so far as it falls within the limits assigned to this work, of the nature of the evidence on which these propositions rest, and the processes of investigation by which they are ascertained and proved. There remain three classes of facts: Existence, Order in Place, and Resemblance, in regard to which the same questions are now to be resolved."

From the above passage we should gather that Resemblance has not been the subject treated in the preceding chapters of the third book, or certainly not the chief subject.

Of the remaining three classes of facts, Existence is dismissed very briefly. So far as relates to simple existence, Mill thinks‡ that the inductive logic has no knots to untie, and he proceeds to the remaining two of the great classes into which facts have been divided. His opinion about Resemblance is clearly stated in the second section of the same chapter, as follows:—

"Resemblance and its opposite, except in the case in which they assume the names of Equality and Inequality, are seldom regarded as subjects of science; they are supposed to be perceived by simple apprehension; by merely applying our senses or directing our attention to the two objects at once, or in immediate succession."

After pointing out that we cannot always bring two things into suitable proximity, he adds:—

"The comparison of two things through the intervention of a third thing, when their direct comparison is impossible, is the appropriate scientific process for ascertaining resemblances and dissimilarities, and is the sum total of what Logic has to teach on the subject.

"An undue extension of this remark induced Locke to consider reasoning itself as nothing but the comparison of two ideas through the medium of a third, and knowledge as the perception of the agreement or disagreement of two ideas: doctrines which the Condillac school blindly adopted, without the qualifications and distinctions with which they were studiously guarded by their illustrious author. Where, indeed, the agreement or disagreement (otherwise called resemblance or dissimilarity) of any two things is the very matter to be determined, as is the case particularly in the sciences of quantity and extension; there the process by which a solution, if not attainable by direct perception, must be indirectly sought, consists in comparing these two things through the medium of a third. But this is far from being true of all inquiries. The knowledge that bodies fall to the ground is not a perception of agreement or disagreement, but of a series of physical occurrences, a succession of sensations. Locke's definitions of knowledge and of reasoning required to be limited to our knowledge of, and reasoning about, Resemblances."

We learn from these passages, then, that science and knowledge

* Book III., chapter xxiv. † First section, near the beginning.
‡ Same section.

have little to do with resemblances. Except in the case of equality and inequality, *resemblance is seldom regarded as the subject of science*, and Mill apparently accepts what he holds to be the prevailing opinion. The sum total of what logic has to teach on this subject is that two things may be compared through the intervention of a third thing, when their direct comparison is impossible. Locke *unduly* extended this remark when he considered reasoning itself as nothing but the comparison of two ideas through the medium of a third. Locke's definitions of knowledge and of reasoning require to be limited to our knowledge of, and reasoning about, resemblances.

In the preceding part of the third book of the "System of Logic," then, we have not been concerned with Resemblance. The subjects discussed have been contained in propositions which affirm Order in Time, in either of its modes, Co-existence and Succession. Resemblance is another matter of fact, which has been postponed to the twenty-fourth chapter of the third book, and there dismissed in one short section, as being *seldom regarded as a subject of science.* Under these circumstances we should hardly expect to find that Mill's so-called Experimental Methods are wholly concerned with resemblance. Certainly these celebrated methods are the subject of science; they are, according to Mill, the great methods of scientific discovery and inductive proof; they form the main topic of the third book of the Logic, indeed, they form the central pillars of the whole "System of Logic." It is a little puzzling, then, to find that the names of these methods seem to refer to Resemblance, or to something which much resembles resemblance. The first is called the Method of Agreement; the second is the Method of Difference; the third is the Joint Method of Agreement and Difference; and the remaining two methods are confessedly developments of these principal methods. Now, does Agreement mean Resemblance or not? If it does, then the whole of the third book may be said to treat of a relation which Mill has professedly postponed to the second section of the twenty-fourth chapter.

Let us see what these methods involve. The canon of the first method is stated in the following words,* which many an anxious candidate for academic honours has committed to memory:—

"If two or more instances of the phenomenon under investigation have only one circumstance in common, the circumstance in which alone all the instances agree, is the cause (or effect) of the given phenomenon."

Now, when two or more instances of the phenomenon under investigation agree, do they, or do they not, resemble each other? Is agreement the same relation as resemblance, or is it something different? If, indeed, it be a separate kind of relation, it must be matter of regret that Mill did not describe this relation of agreement when treating of the "Import of Propositions." Surely the propositions in

* Book III., chapter viii., section 1, near the end.

which we record our observations of "the phenomenon under investigation" must affirm agreement or difference, and as the experimental methods are the all-important instruments of science, these propositions must have corresponding importance. Perhaps, however, we shall derive some light from the context; reading on a few lines in the description of the Method of Difference,* we find Mill saying that

"In the Method of Agreement we endeavoured to obtain instances which agreed in the given circumstance but differed in every other: in the present method (*i.e.* the Method of Difference) we require, on the contrary, two instances resembling one another in every other respect, but differing in the presence or absence of the phenomenon we wish to study."

It would really seem, then, as if the great Experimental Method depends upon our discovering two instances *resembling* one another. Here resemblance is specified by name. We seem to learn clearly that Agreement must be the same thing as Resemblance; if so, Difference must be its opposite. Proceeding accordingly to consider the Method of Difference we find its requirements described in these words:†—"The two instances which are to be compared with one another must be exactly similar, in all circumstances except the one which we are attempting to investigate."

This exact similarity is not actual identity, of course, because the instances are *two*, not *one*. Is it then resemblance? If so, we again find the principal subject of Mill's Logic to be that which he relegated to section 2 of chapter xxiv. If we proceed with our reading of Mill's chapter on the "Four Experimental Methods," we still find sentence after sentence dealing with this relation of resemblance, sometimes under the very same name, sometimes under the names of similarity, agreement, likeness, &c. As to its apparent opposite, *difference*, it seems to be the theme of the whole chapter. The Method of Difference is that wonderful method which can prove the most general law on the ground of two instances! But of this peculiarity of the Method of Difference I shall treat on another occasion.

Perhaps, however, after all I may be misrepresenting Mill's statements. It crosses my mind that by Resemblance he may mean something different from *exact similarity*. The Methods of Agreement and Difference may require that complete likeness which we should call *identity of quality*. It is only fair to inquire then, whether he uses the word Resemblance in a broad or a narrow sense. On this point Mill leaves us in no doubt; for he says distinctly,‡ "This resemblance may exist in all conceivable gradations, from perfect undistinguishableness to something extremely slight."

Again on the next page, while distinguishing carefully between such different things as numerical identity and indistinguishable resemblance,

* Same chapter, second section.
† Same chapter, third section, third paragraph, fourth line.
‡ Book I., chapter iii., section eleven, paragraph four.

he clearly countenances the wide use of the word resemblance, saying,* "Resemblance, when it exists in the highest degree of all, amounting to undistinguishableness, is often called identity." It seems then, that all grades of likeness or similarity, from indistinguishable identity down to *something extremely slight*, are properly comprehended under resemblance; and it is difficult to come to any other conclusion than that the agreement and similarity and difference treated throughout the Experimental Methods are all cases of that minor relation, seldom considered the subject of science, which was postponed by Mill to the second section of the twenty-fourth chapter.

But the fact is that I have only been playing with this matter. I ought to have quoted at once a passage which was in my mind all the time—one from the chapter on the Functions and Value of the Syllogism. Mill sums up the conclusion of a long discussion in the following words :†— .

"We have thus obtained what we were seeking, an universal type of the reasoning process. We find it resolvable in all cases into the following elements: Certain individuals have a given attribute; an individual or individuals resemble the former in certain other attributes; therefore they resemble them also in the given attribute."

All reasoning, then, is resolvable into a case of resemblance; the word *resemble* is itself used twice over, and, as I shall hereafter show, the word *attribute*, synonymous with *property*, is but another name according to Mill, for resemblance. It is true that this quotation is taken from the second book of the System, not from the preceding part of the third book to which Mill referred as not having treated of resemblance. But this can hardly matter, as he speaks of the *universal type of the reasoning process*, which must include of course the whole of the inductive methods expounded in the third book.

But in case the reader should not be quite satisfied, I will give yet one more quotation, taken from the twentieth chapter of the third book, a chapter therefore which closely precedes the chapter on "The Remaining Laws of Nature," where Mill despatches Resemblance. This chapter treats nominally of analogy, but what must be our surprise to find that in reality it treats from beginning to end of Resemblance! This is the way in which he describes reasoning by analogy :‡—

"It is on the whole more usual, however, to extend the name of analogical evidence to arguments from any sort of resemblance, provided they do not amount to a complete induction: without peculiarly distinguishing resemblance of relations. Analogical reasoning, in this sense, may be reduced to the following formula;—Two things resemble each other in one or more respects; a certain proposition is true of the one; therefore, it is true of the other. But we have nothing here by which to discriminate analogy from induction, since this type will serve for all reasoning from experience. In the strictest

* Same section, fifth paragraph, third line.
† Book II., chapter iii., section 7, at beginning.
‡ Book III., chapter xx., beginning of second section.

[illegible] we conclude because A resembles [illegible] it does so in a certain other property."

[illegible] universal type of the reasoning process [illegible] resemblance. The stone which was [illegible] treated in a brief section of the twenty-fourth [illegible] the cornerstone of Mill's logical edifice. It would [illegible] Mill were one of those persons who are said to [illegible] with the two halves of their brain. On the one [illegible] must be held the doctrine that [illegible] a subject of science; on the other side, Mill [illegible] the important place which resemblance holds [illegible] type of the reasoning and inductive processes. [illegible] the Law of Obliviscence, or some *Deus ex ma-* [illegible] called in; for it is absurd to contemplate the possi- [illegible] Mill's statement of the *universal type of all reason-* [illegible] upon Locke's doctrine. Locke, he says in the [illegible] quoted, *unduly extended the importance of resemblance,* [illegible] *reasoning a case of it,* and Locke's definition of know- [illegible] reasoning required *to be limited to our knowledge of and* [illegible] *resemblances.* Yet, according to Mill himself, the [illegible] ALL *reasoning* turns wholly on resemblance. Under [illegible] it is impossible to discuss seriously the value of [illegible] of knowledge. Which part of the analysis are we to [illegible] in which resemblance is treated as the basis of all [illegible] that in which it belongs to the "remaining" and [illegible] of fact," which had not been treated in the books of [illegible] which therefore remained to be disposed of?

[illegible] t yet done with this question of resemblance; it is the [illegible] question as regards the theory of knowledge and rea- [illegible] at the risk of being very tedious, I must show that [illegible] Mill's inconsistency there is still a lower deep. I have [illegible] that some of his opinions concerning the import of [illegible] be thus formulated:—

[illegible] of attributes are names for the resemblances of our [illegible]

[illegible] propositions affirm the possession of properties, or attri- [illegible] peculiarities.

[illegible] propositions do not, properly speaking, assert resemblance [illegible]

[illegible] in the first place to prove that Mill has made state- [illegible] meaning attributed to him, we find the matter of the [illegible]* written by Mill in answer to Mr. Herbert Spencer, [illegible] rged Mill with confounding exact likeness and literal

[illegible] section 2, near the beginning of the third paragraph of the [illegible] does not occur in some of the early editions.

identity. With the truth of this charge we will not concern ourselves now; we have only to notice the following distinct statement: "What, then, is the common something which gives a meaning to the general name? Mr. Spencer can only say, it is the similarity of the feelings; and I rejoin, the attribute is precisely that similarity. The names of attributes are in their ultimate analyses names for the resemblances of our sensations (or other feelings). Every general name, whether abstract or concrete, denotes or connotes one or more of those resemblances." Mill's meaning evidently is that when you apply a general name to a thing, as for instance in calling snow *white*, you mean that there is a resemblance between snow and other things in respect of their whiteness. The general name *white* connotes this resemblance; the abstract name *whiteness* denotes it.

Let us now consider a passage in the chapter on the Import of Propositions, which must be quoted at some length.*

"It is sometimes said, that all propositions whatever, of which the predicate is a general name, do, in point of fact, affirm or deny resemblance. All such propositions affirm that a thing belongs to a class; but things being classed together according to their resemblance, everything is of course classed with the things which it is supposed to resemble most; and thence, it may be said, when we affirm that gold is a metal, or that Socrates is a man, the affirmation intended is, that gold resembles other metals, and Socrates other men, more nearly than they resemble the objects contained in any other of the classes co-ordinate with these."

Of this doctrine Mill goes on to speak in the following curious remarks,† to which I particularly invite the reader's attention:—

"There is some slight degree of foundation for this remark, but no more than a slight degree. The arrangement of things into classes, such as the class *metal*, or the class *man*, is grounded indeed on a resemblance among the things which are placed in the same class, but not on a mere general resemblance: the resemblance it is grounded on consists in the possession by all those things, of certain common peculiarities; and those peculiarities it is which the terms connote, and which the propositions consequently assert; not the resemblance. For though when I say, Gold is a metal, I say by implication that if there be any other metals it must resemble them, yet if there were no other metals I might still assert the proposition with the same meaning as at present, namely, that gold has the various properties implied in the word metal; just as it might be said, Christians are men, even if there were no men who were not Christians. Propositions, therefore, in which objects are referred to a class because they possess the attributes constituting the class, are so far from asserting nothing but resemblance, that they do not, properly speaking, assert resemblance at all."

I have long wondered at the confusion of ideas which this passage exhibits. We are told that the arrangement of things in a class is founded on a resemblance between the things, but not a "mere general resemblance," whatever this may mean. It is grounded on the possession of certain "common peculiarities." I pass by the

* Book I., chapter v., section 6, second paragraph.
† Same section, third paragraph.

oness of this expression; I should have thought that *common rity* is a self-contradictory expression in its own terms; but here is to mean merely *attribute* or *quality*. The terms then connote tribute, not the resemblance. Here we are in direct and abso- nflict with Mill's previous statement that *attribute is precisely that ity*—that common something—which gives a meaning to the l name, and that the names of attributes are, in their ultimate is, *names for the resemblances* of our sensations. Previously he at "every general name" connotes one or more of these resem- s; now he says that it is "these peculiarities" which the terms e, and which the propositions consequently assert, not the lances. But these peculiarities are *common peculiarities*—that is, on qualities or attributes. The self-contradiction is absolute mplete, except, indeed, so far as Mill admits that there is "some degree of foundation" for the remark which he is controverting. will afterwards consider what is this *slight degree of foundation;* oceeding for the present with the interpretation of the remark- ssage quoted, we learn that when I say, "Gold is a metal," I nply that if there are other metals it must resemble them; yet, e were no other metals, I might still assert that gold has the properties implied in the word metal. The "Law of Oblivis- " seems to have been at work here; Mill must have quite for- that he was speaking of propositions, "of which the predicate neral name," or the name of a class. Now if, as Mill sometimes a class consists only of the things in it,* there must be more than gold, else metal would not be a general name. If, as sewhere says, to the contrary effect, the class may exist whether ngs exist or not,† we still have him on the other horn of the na; for then the meaning of the general name must consist in notation, which consists of attributes, which are but another for resemblances. Yet, forsooth, the proposition does not ly speaking assert resemblances at all.

important passage quoted above is, as we might readily expect. istent with various other statements in the "System of Logic," instance most of the seventh section of the chapter on Definition, we are told ‡ that the philosopher, "only gives the same name gs which resemble one another in the same definite particulars," at the inquiry into a definition § "is an inquiry into the resem- s and differences among those things." Elsewhere we are told,‖ the general names given to objects imply attributes, derive whole meaning from attributes; and are chiefly useful as the

em of Logic, Book II., chapter ii., section 2, fourth paragraph.
k I., chapter vii., section 1, first paragraph.
k I., chapter viii., section 7, paragraph 4, about the seventeenth line. This s numbered 8 in some of the early editions.
e section, paragraph 8, line 7.
k IV., chapter iii., eight lines from end of chapter.

language by means of which we predicate the attributes which they connote." Again, in the chapter on the Requisites of a Philosophical Language, he says:*—

"Now the meaning (as has so often been explained) of a general connotative name, resides in the connotation; in the attribute on account of which, and to express which, the name is given. Thus, the name animal being given to all things which possess the attributes of sensation and voluntary motion, the word connotes those attributes exclusively, and they constitute the whole of its meaning."

Now, *the attribute, as we learned at starting, is but another name for a Resemblance, and yet a proposition of which the predicate is a general name, does not properly speaking assert resemblance at all.*

The inconsistency is still more striking when we turn to another work, namely John Stuart Mill's edition of his father's "Analysis of the Human Mind." Here, in a note † on the subject of classification, Mill objects to his father's ultra-nominalist doctrine, that "men were led to class solely for the purpose of economizing in the use of names." Mill proceeds to remark ‡ that "we could not have dispensed with names to mark the points in which different individuals resemble one another: and these are class-names." Referring to his father's peculiar expression—"individual qualities," he remarks very properly:—

"It is not *individual* qualities that we ever have occasion to predicate. . . . We never have occasion to predicate of an object the individual and instantaneous impressions which it produces in us. The only meaning of predicating a quality at all, is to affirm a resemblance. When we ascribe a quality to an object, we intend to assert that the object affects us in a manner similar to that in which we are affected by a known class of objects."

A few lines further down he proceeds:—

"Qualities, therefore, cannot be predicated without general names; nor, consequently, without classification. Wherever there is a general name there is a class: classification, and general names, are things exactly coextensive."

This is, no doubt, quite the true doctrine; but what becomes of the paragraph already quoted, which appeared in eight editions of the "System of Logic," during Mill's lifetime? In that paragraph he asserted that propositions referring an object to a class because they possess the attributes constituting the class, do not, properly speaking, assert resemblance at all. Now, when commenting on his father's doctrine, Mill says that the *only meaning of predicating a quality at all, is to affirm a resemblance.*

In a later note in the same volume Mill is, if possible, still more explicit in his assertion that the predication of general names is a matter of attributes and resemblances. He begins thus:§—

* Book IV., chapter iv., section 2, second line.
† Vol. i. p. 260. ‡ Page 261.
§ James Mill's Analysis of the Human Mind. New edition, vol. i. p. 288.

... that classes and classification would not have existed ... of economising names, we may say that objects are ... on account of their resemblance."

... he says, in the most distinct manner :—

"... stands in a very different relation to the definite resem- ... intended to mark, from that in which it stands to the various ... which may form part of the image it calls up. There ... common to the entire class, which the class-name was ... selected as a mark of, or, at all events, which guide us in ... of it. These attributes are the real meaning of the class-name ... we intend to ascribe to an object when we call it by that name."

... can be no possible mistake about Mill's meaning now. The ... *intended to mark definite resemblances.* These resemblances ... attributes which the class-name was either deliberately ... as a mark of, or which guide us in the application of it. ...tributes are the *real meaning* of the class-name—are *what ... to ascribe to an object*, when we call it by that name. Yet we ... in the passage of the "System of Logic" to which I invited ...er's special attention, that propositions in which objects are ... to a class, because they possess the attributes constituting ... are so far from asserting nothing but resemblance, that they ...*roperly speaking*, assert resemblance at all. A class-name is ...ken of as *intended to mark definite resemblances.* Previously we ...ormed that, in saying, "Gold is a metal," I do not assert ...nce, forsooth, because there might be no other metal but ...et *metal* is spoken of as a class, so that the word metal is a ...e, and the whole discussion refers to propositions of which ...icates are general names.

...ct is, the passage contains more than one *non-sequitur;* it tacitly ... that *metal* might continue to be a class-name, while there was ... kind of metal, so that there would be nothing else to resemble. ...ere is another *non-sequitur* when Mill proceeds straightway ...er example, thus—"just as it might be said, Christians are ...n if there were no men who were not Christians." The ...ust as" here mean that this example bears out the last; but ...s and men being plural, the predicate *men* is now clearly ...ame, and the meaning is that Christians all resemble each ... the attributes connoted by the class-name *man.* Mill ...eed, the words "even if there were no men who were not ...s." Here is unquestionable confusion of thought. Man is ...ame and connotes the definite resemblances of the ob- ... class, even if the class happens to be coextensive with ...Christians. If I say, "Men are capable of laughter," the ...dicate "capable of laughter" connotes a character in ... resemble each other, even though there be no beings capable of laughter who are not men. Thus, when we closely examine the passage in question, it falls to pieces; it has no logical coherence.*

I may remark incidentally that it is strange to meet, in a discussion of the fundamental principles of logic and knowledge, with things which have *a slight degree of foundation*. The elementary principles of a science either are true or are not true. There is no middle term. Degree in such matters is out of place. But in Mill's philosophical works, as I shall have various opportunities to show, there is a tendency to what may be called *philosophical trimming*. Instead of saying outright that a thing is false, he says too frequently that it is "not strictly true," as in the case referring to the primary ideas of geometry quoted in my last article. Mill's opinions, in fact, so frequently came into conflict with each other, that he acquired the habit of leaving a little room to spare in each of his principal statements: they required a good deal of fitting together. Now "the slight degree of foundation" for the remark that propositions, of which the predicate is a general name, do assert resemblance, seems to be explained in the two paragraphs which follow that quoted, and these we will now consider.

Mill proceeds to remark† that there is sometimes a convenience in extending the boundaries of a class so as to include things which possess in a very inferior degree, if in any, some of the characteristic properties of the class, provided that they resemble that class more than any other. He refers to the systems of classification of living things, in which almost every great family of plants or animals has a few anomalous genera or species on its borders, which are admitted by a kind of courtesy. It is evident, however, that a matter of this sort has nothing to do with the fundamental logical question whether propositions assert resemblance or not. This paragraph is due to the ambiguity of the word resemblance, which here seems to mean vague or slight resemblance, as distinguished from that incontestable resemblance which enables us to say that things have the same attribute. In fact, a very careful reader of the sections in which Mill treats of resemblance will find that there is frequent confusion between definite resemblance, and something which Mill variously calls "mere general resemblance" or "vague resemblance," which will usually refer to similarities depending on the degree of qualities, or the forms of objects.

There is, however, a second case bearing out Mill's opinion that there is "some slight degree of foundation" for the remark that propositions whose predicates are general terms affirm resemblance.

* In my own opinion, an affirmative proposition asserts resemblance in its highest degree, *i.e.*, identity, even when the subject and predicate are singular terms; but to prevent confusion, I argue the question on Mill's assumption that the predicate is a general or class-name.

† Book I., chapter v., section 6, fourth paragraph.

which we must inquire with some care, so that I the paragraph relating to it: *—

"...another exceptional case, in which, though the predicate is the ... in predicating it we affirm nothing but resemblance, that ... not on resemblance in any given particular, but on general ... resemblance. The classes in question are those into which our ... or rather simple feelings, are divided. Sensations of white, ... are classed together, not because we can take them to pieces, and ... alike in this, and not alike in that, but because we feel them to be ... though in different degrees. When, therefore, I say, The colour ... was a white colour, or, The sensation I feel is one of tightness, ... the attribute I affirm of the colour or of the sensation is mere ...—simple likeness to sensations which I have had before, and which ... names bestowed upon them. The names of feelings, like other ... names, are connotative; but they connote a mere resemblance. ... of any individual feeling, the information they convey is that of ... to the other feelings which we have been accustomed to call by the ... Thus much may suffice in illustration of the kind of propositions ... the matter-of-fact asserted (or denied) is simple resemblance."

a paragraph as the above is likely to produce intellectual in the steadiest thinker. In an off-hand manner we are told *much may suffice* in illustration of an *exceptional case*, in which ance happens to be predicated. This resemblance is mentioned gly as *mere* resemblance, or *general unanalyzable resemblance*. ıen we come to inquire seriously what this resemblance is, we o be that primary relation of sensation to sensation, which lies ıasis of all thought and knowledge. Professor Alexander Bain ıosed to be, since Mill's death, a mainstay of the empirical and, in his works on Logic, he has unfortunately adopted far :h of Mill's views. But, in Professor Bain's own proper writings, a vigour and logical consistency of thought for which it is ble not to feel the greatest respect.

we find Mr. Bain laying down, at the commencement of his s on the Intellect,† that the Primary Attributes of Intellect are sciousness of Difference, (2) Consciousness of Agreement, and :entiveness. He goes on to say with admirable clearness that ination or feeling of difference is an essential of intelligence. ginning of knowledge, or ideas, is the discrimination of one om another. As we can neither feel, nor know, without a ɔn or change of state,—every feeling, and every cognition, e viewed as in relation to some other feeling, or cognition. :annot be a single or absolute cognition.

, again, Mr. Bain proceeds to say that the conscious state from Agreement in the midst of difference is equally marked ...lly fundamental:—

* ... I., chapter v., section 6, paragraph 5.

† ... and Moral Science: a Compendium of Psychology and Ethics, 1868, pp. 82, ... doctrine of the nature of knowledge is stated in the treatise on the Senses ... Intellect, second edition, pp. 325—331; in the Deductive Logic, pp. 4, 5, 9, and

"Supposing us to experience, for the first time, a certain sensation, as redness; and after being engaged with other sensations, to encounter redness again; we are struck with the feeling of identity or recognition; the old state is recalled at the instance of the new, by the fact of agreement, and we have the sensation of red, together with a new and peculiar consciousness, the consciousness of agreement in diversity. As the diversity is greater, the shock of agreement is more lively."

Then Professor Bain adds emphatically:—

"All knowledge finally resolves itself into differences and agreements. To define anything, as a circle, is to state its agreements with some things (genus) and its difference from other things (differentia)."

Professor Bain then treats as the fundamental act of intellect the recognition of redness as identical with redness previously experienced. This is, changing red for white, exactly the same illustration as Mill used, in the example "The colour I saw yesterday was a white colour." Now Mr. Bain says, and says truly, that all knowledge finally resolves itself into differences and agreements. Propositions accordingly, which affirm these elementary relations, must really be the most important of all classes of propositions. They must be the elementary propositions which are presupposed or summed up in more complicated ones. Yet such is the class of propositions which Mill dismisses in an off-hand manner in one paragraph, as "still another exceptional case."

If we look into the details of Mill's paragraph, perplexity only can be the result. He speaks of "the class being founded not on resemblance in any given particular, but on *general unanalyzable resemblance*." The classes in question are those into which "our simple sensations, or rather simple feelings, are divided." Now, what can he possibly mean by *any given particular?* If the colour I saw yesterday was a white colour, that was the given particular in which resemblance existed. No doubt the resemblance is unanalyzable, because analysis has done its best, and the matter refers, Mill states, to a *simple sensation*. When we are dealing with the elements of knowledge, of course analysis is no longer applicable. But I confess myself unable to understand why he calls it *general unanalyzable resemblance*. If I understand the matter aright, Mill should have said *specific analyzed resemblance*. When one red flower is noticed to resemble another red flower in colour, the general resemblance *has been analyzed*, and found to consist in a specific resemblance of colour to colour. If I see an orange, I know it to be an orange, because it resembles similar fruits, which I have often heard so called. In the first instance the resemblance may be to my mind mere general resemblance, that is to say, I may not devote separate attention to the several points of resemblance. But if one asks me why I call it an orange, I must analyze my feeling of resemblance, and I then discover that the colour of the fruit resembles the colour of fruit formerly called oranges, and that in regard to the form, the texture of the surface, the hardness, the smell, and so forth, there are [illegible] knowledge, as Professor Bain says, finally [illegible] *differences and agreements*. But the agreements in [illegible] those resemblances, the base-work of all know-[illegible] *as still another exceptional case*.

[illegible] mystery or perplexity in the matter except such [illegible] by the perversity of his intellect. Mill has made [illegible] which is really the *summum genus* of knowledge. [illegible] knowledge to consist in the perception of [illegible] of our ideas, and Professor Bain has stated [illegible] a force and distinctness which leave nothing to [illegible] Mill, strange to say, has treated this all-fundamental [illegible] "the Remaining Laws of Nature," "Minor Matters of [illegible] Exceptional Cases." It is usually impossible to trace the [illegible] to Mill's perversities, but, in this important case, it is [illegible]xplain the peculiarity of his views on Resemblance. He was [illegible] under *hereditary prejudice*. His father, James Mill, in his [illegible], but usually wrong-headed book, the "Analysis of the [illegible] of the Human Mind," had made still more strange mis-[illegible] several curious passages the son argues that we cannot [illegible]semblance into anything simpler. These needless arguments [illegible]ntly suggested by parts of the "Analysis" in which the [illegible]fessed to *resolve resemblances into cases of sequence!*

[illegible]when James Mill is discussing* the Association of Ideas, he [illegible] Hume specifying Resemblance as one of the grounds of [illegible]. He says:—

[illegible]ance only remains, as an alleged principle of association, and it is [illegible] inquire whether it is included in the laws which have been above [illegible] believe it will be found that we are accustomed to see like things [illegible] When we see a tree, we generally see more trees than one; when [illegible] ox, we generally see more oxen than one; a sheep, more sheep than [illegible], more men than one. From this observation, I think, we may [illegible] to the law of frequency, of which it seems to form a par-[illegible].

[illegible] help regarding the misapprehension contained in this [illegible] perhaps the most extraordinary one which could be [illegible] the whole range of philosophical literature. Resemblance [illegible] to a *particular case of the law of frequency*, that is, to the [illegible]currence of the same thing, as when, in place of one man, [illegible] men. But how do I know that they are men, unless [illegible] that they resemble each other? It is impossible even to [illegible] without implying that there are various things called [illegible] resemble each other sufficiently to be classed together [illegible] by the same name. Nevertheless, James Mill seems to [illegible] actually under the impression that he had got rid of

* [illegible] first edition, vol. i. p. 79. Second edition, vol. i. p. 111.

Later on in the same work,* indeed, we have the following statement:—

"It is easy to see, among the principles of association, what particular principle it is, which is mainly concerned in Classification, and by which we are rendered capable of that mighty operation; on which, as its basis, the whole of our intellectual structure is reared. That principle is Resemblance. It seems to be similarity or resemblance which, when we have applied a name to one individual, leads us to apply it to another, and another, till the whole forms an aggregate, connected together by the common relation of every part of the aggregate to one and the same name. Similarity, or Resemblance, we must regard as an Idea familiar and sufficiently understood for the illustration at present required. It will itself be strictly analyzed, at a subsequent part of this Inquiry."

In writing this passage, James Mill seems to have forgotten, quite in the manner of his son, that he had before treated Resemblance as an *alleged* principle of association, and had referred it to a particular case of the law of frequency. Here it reappears as the principle on which the whole of our intellectual structure is reared. It is strange that so important a principle should elsewhere be called an "alleged principle," and equally strange that it should afterwards be "strictly analyzed." Before we get down to the basis of our intellectual structure it might be supposed that analysis had exhausted itself.

James Mill gives no reference to the subsequent part of the inquiry where this analysis is carried out, nor do I find that John Stuart Mill, or the other editors of the second edition, have supplied the reference. Doubtless, however, the analysis is given in the second section of chapter xiv., where, in treating of Relative Terms,† he inquires into the meaning of Same, Different, Like, or Unlike, and comes to the conclusion that the resemblance between sensation and sensation is, after all, only sensation. He says:—

"Having *two* sensations, therefore, is not only having sensation, but the only thing which can, in strictness, be called having sensation; and the having two and knowing they are two, which are not two things, but one and the same thing, is not only sensation, and nothing else than sensation, but the only thing which can, in strictness, be called sensation. The having a new sensation, and knowing that it is new, are not two things, but one and the same thing."

This is, no doubt, a wonderfully acute piece of sophistical reasoning; but I have no need to occupy space in refuting it, because John Stuart Mill has already refuted it in several passages which evidently refer to his father's fallacy. Thus, I have already quoted, at the commencement of this article, a statement in which John Stuart Mill argues that resemblance between two phenomena is more intelligible than any explanation could make it. Again, in editing his father's "Analysis," Mill comments at some length upon this section,‡ showing that it does not explain

* Analysis: first edition, vol. i. pp. 212, 213. Second edition, vol. i. pp. 270, 271.
† First edition, vol. ii. p. 10. Second edition, vol. ii. pp. 11, 12.
‡ Vol. ii. pp. 17—20.

[illegible] the likenesses and unlikenesses of our simple feel[illegible] facts than they were before.

[illegible] thus refuses to dissolve resemblance away altogether [illegible] probably warped in youth by the perverse doctrines father so unsparingly forced upon his intellect. Too early fibres received a decided *set*, from which they could not [illegible] all the power and acuteness of Mill's intellect were trying to make things fit, which could not fit, because [h]ad been made in the very commencement of the structure. [M]isapprehension of the Mills, *père et fils*, concerning resem[blance is c]ertainly one of the most extraordinary instances of perversity [i]t in the history of philosophy. That which is the *summum* [...]soned knowledge, they have either attempted to dissolve [alto]gether, or, after grudgingly allowing its existence, have [...]e position of a minor species and exceptional case. Yet [it is impos]sible to use any language at all without implying the relation [of resembl]ance and difference in every term. There is not a sentence [in his o]wn works in which this fact might not be made manifest [...] discussion. We cannot employ a general name without [...]he resemblance between the significates of that name, and [...]t select any class of objects for attention without discrimi[nating th]em from other objects in general. To propose *resemblance* [as th]e subject of inquiry presupposes that we distinguish it from [...]ible subjects of inquiry. Thus, when James Mill is engaged [...]ge already quoted) in dissipating the relation of resemblance, [he presup]poses resemblance in every name. What is a *new* sensation, [unless it] resembles other *new* sensations in being discriminated from [...]ions? What is a *sensation* unless it resembles other sensa[tions in b]eing separated in thought from things which are *not-sensa*[tions? Bu]t it is truly amusing to find that, in the very first sentence [of the par]agraph immediately following that quoted, James Mill uses [...] resemblance. He says:*—"The case between sensation [and sensa]tion resembles that between sensation and idea." Never[theless Ja]mes Mill sums up the result of the section of his work in [...]y the following:†—

> [...]s, therefore, to be made clear, that, in applying to the simple sensa[tions and i]deas their absolute names, which are names of classes, as red, [...]t, bitter; and also applying to them names which denote them in [...]ch and such; there is nothing whatsoever but having the sensations, [...] ideas, and making marks for them."

[This sen]tence, if it means anything, means that our sensations and [ideas] have no ties between them except in the common marks or [...]plied to them. The connection of resemblance is denied

This ultra-nominalism of the father is one of the strangest

* [A]nalysis: first edition, vol. ii. p. 10. Second edition, vol. ii. p. 12.
† [I]bid. first edition, p. 15. Second edition, p. 17.

perversities of thought which could be adduced; and though John Stuart Mill disclaims such an absurd doctrine in an apologetic sort of way, yet he never, as I shall now and again have to show, really shook himself free from the perplexities of thought due to his father's errors.

It may seem to many readers that these are tedious matters to discuss at such length. After all, the Import of Propositions and the Relation of Resemblance are matters which concern metaphysicians only, or those who chop logic. But this is a mistake. A system of philosophy—a school of metaphysical doctrines—is the foundation on which is erected a structure of rules and inferences, touching our interests in the most vital points. John Stuart Mill, in his remarkable Autobiography, has expressly stated that a principal object of his "System of Logic" was to overthrow deep-seated prejudices, and to storm the stronghold in which they sheltered themselves. These are his words:*—

> "Whatever may be the practical value of a true philosophy of these matters, it is hardly possible to exaggerate the mischiefs of a false one. The notion that truths external to the mind may be known by intuition or consciousness, independently of observation and experience, is, I am persuaded, in these times, the great intellectual support of false doctrines and bad institutions. By the aid of this theory, every inveterate belief and every intense feeling, of which the origin is not remembered, is enabled to dispense with the obligation of justifying itself by reason, and is erected into its own all-sufficient voucher and justification. There never was such an instrument devised for consecrating all deep-seated prejudices. And the chief strength of this false philosophy in morals, politics, and religion, lies in the appeal which it is accustomed to make to the evidence of mathematics and of the cognate branches of physical science. To expel it from these, is to drive it from its stronghold: and because this had never been effectually done, the intuitive school, even after what my father had written in his 'Analysis of the Mind,' had in appearance, and as far as published writings were concerned, on the whole the best of the argument. In attempting to clear up the real nature of the evidence of mathematical and physical truths, the 'System of Logic' met the intuitive philosophers on ground on which they had previously been deemed unassailable; and gave its own explanation, from experience and association, of that peculiar character of what are called necessary truths, which is adduced as proof that their evidence must come from a deeper source than experience. Whether this has been done effectually, is still *sub judice;* and even then, to deprive a mode of thought so strongly rooted in human prejudices and partialities, of its mere speculative support, goes but a very little way towards overcoming it; but though only a step, it is a quite indispensable one; for since, after all, prejudice can only be successfully combated by philosophy, no way can really be made against it permanently until it has been shown not to have philosophy on its side."

This is at least a candid statement of motives, means, and expected results. Whether Mill's exposition of the philosophy of the mathematical sciences is satisfactory or not, we partially inquired in the previous article; and in one place or another the inquiry will be further prosecuted in a pretty exhaustive manner. Mill allowed that

* Autobiography, pp. 225—227.

the character of his solution was still *sub judice*, and it must remain in that position for some time longer. But of the importance of the matter it is impossible to entertain a doubt. If Mill's own philosophy be yet more false than was, in his opinion, the philosophy which he undertook to destroy, we may well adopt his own estimate of the results. "*Whatever*," he says, "*may be the practical value of a true philosophy of these matters, it is hardly possible to exaggerate the mischiefs of a false one.*" Intensely believing, as I do, that the philosophy of the Mills, both father and son, is a false one, I claim, almost as a right, the attention of those who have sufficiently studied the matters in dispute to judge the arduous work of criticism which I have felt it my duty to undertake.

W. STANLEY JEVONS.

ERRATUM.—In the first article on John Stuart Mill's Philosophy, CONTEMPORARY REVIEW for December, 1877, vol. xxxi. p. 170, fifth line, for *Liberty* read *Necessity*.

# THE LITTLE HEALTH OF LADIES.*

IN the following pages I propose to speak, not of any definite form of disease, but of that condition of *petite santé*, valetudinarianism, and general readiness to break down under pressure, wherein a sadly large proportion of women of the higher classes pass their years. It is unnecessary, I think, to adduce any evidence of the prevalence of this semi-invalidism among ladies in England, or its still greater frequency abroad, and (emphatically) in America. In a very moderate circle of acquaintance every one knows a score of cases of it, of that confirmed kind which has scarcely any analogue in the physical condition of men. If we take a state of perfect soundness to be represented by 100, the health of few ladies will be found to rise above 80 or 90—that of the majority will be I fear about 75—and a large contingent, with which we are now specially concerned, about 50 or 60. In short, the health of women of the upper class is, I think, unquestionably far *below par*. Whatever light their burners were calculated to shed on the world, *the gas is half turned down* and cannot afford anything beyond a feeble glimmer.

Of the wide-extending wretchedness entailed by this *petite santé* of ladies it would be easy to speak for hours. There are the husbands whose homes are made miserable by unsettled habits, irregular hours, a cheerless and depressed, or else, perhaps, an hysterically excitable or peevish companion; the maximum of expenditure in their households, with the minimum of enjoyment. I think men, in such cases, are most sincerely to be pitied, and I earnestly wish that the moans which they, and also their mothers and sisters, not unnaturally spend over their hard lot, could be turned into short, sharp words, resolutely

* To avoid misapprehension, it may be well to say that this word is here used in its older sense of the "*Loaf-givers*." The ill-health of women who are *Loaf-winners* is, alas! another and still more sorrowful subject.

bodily or mental suffering, spring (as we all recognize) that which is most precious in human experience,—the gold purified in the furnace, the wheat threshed with the flail.

> "Only upon some cross of pain and woe
> God's son may lie,
> Each soul redeemed from self and sin must know
> Its Calvary."

But the high moral results of positive pain and danger seem unattainable by such a mere negation of health as we are considering. The sunshine is good and the storm is good, but the grey, dull drizzle of November—how is any one to gain much from it? Some beautiful souls do so, no doubt; but far more often chronic *petite santé* leads to self-indulgence; and self-indulgence to selfishness; and selfishness (invariably) to deceit and affectation, till the whole character crumbles to pieces with dry rot.

Now I must say at once that I consider the frequency of this valetudinarianism among women to be a monstrous state of things, totally opposed to any conception I can form of the intentions of Providence or the laws of beneficent Nature; and the contented way in which it is accepted, as if it were a matter of course, by society and the poor sufferers themselves, and even by such well-meaning friends of women as M. Michelet, strikes me as both absurd and deplorable. That the Creator should have planned a whole sex of Patients—that the normal condition of the female of the human species should be to have legs which walk not, and brains which can only work on pain of disturbing the rest of the ill-adjusted machine—this is to me simply incredible. The theory would seem to have been suggested by a study, not of the woman's *body*, framed by the great Maker's wisdom, but from that of her silly *clothes* sent home from the milliner, with tags, and buttons, and flounces, meant for show, not use; and a feather and an artificial flower by way of a head-gear.

Nay, my scepticism goes further, even into the stronghold of the enemy. I do not believe that even the holy claims of Motherhood ought to involve—or, if women's lives were better regulated, *would* involve—so often as they do, a state of invalidism for the larger part of married life; or that a woman ought to be disabled from performing the supreme moral and intellectual duties of a parent towards her first-born children, when she fulfils the lower physical part of her sacred office towards those who come afterwards. Were this to be inevitably the case, I do not see how a woman who has undertaken the tremendous responsibilities of a mother towards the opening soul of a child could venture to burden herself with fresh duties which will incapacitate her from performing them with all her heart and soul, and strength.

One of the exasperating things about this evil of female valetudinarianism is that the women who are its victims are precisely the

[illegible] our whole mortal race seem naturally most [illegible] want or danger, and ought to have enjoyed [illegible] or pain of any kind. Such ladies have pro-ever from their birth been exposed to hardship, or toil, or lation, or bad or scanty food, fuel, or raiment. They have fed fatness of the earth, and been clothed in purple and fine linen. e the true Lotos-eaters whom the material cares of the world [illegible] they

"live and lie reclined,'

[illegible] where (in a very literal sense)

"It seemeth always afternoon,"

ere they find a certain soothing æsthetic emotion in reading e the doleful tale of wrong of the "ill-used race of men that he soil,"—without dreaming of going down amongst them to [illegible] tale less dismal.

these women, these Epicurean goddesses of the drawing-room, be so often the poor, fragile, suffering creatures we behold nable to perform half the duties of life, or taste a third part of [illegible],—this is a pure perversity of things which ought surely [illegible] revolt.

are the causes of the valetudinarianism of ladies?

of course, there is a considerable class of inherited mischief, onstitutions, congenital tendencies to chronic troubles, gout, ia, and so on, due to the errors of either parent, or to *their* itage of the same. All that need be said here on this topic is ch cases must necessarily go on multiplying *ad infinitum* till regain the vigour which alone permits them to transmit a constitution to their children.

to hereditary *petite santé*, we come to cases where the habits sufferers themselves are the cause of the mischief; and these wo kinds—one resulting from what is good and unselfish, and n what is bad and frivolous, in the disposition of women.

en are generally prudent enough about their money; that is, own money, not that of their husbands. I have heard an nt man remark that he never knew a well-conducted woman her own fault, became bankrupt. But as regards their health, best of women have a propensity to *live on their capital.* ervous energy, stimulated either by conscience or affection or ual interests, suffices to enable them to postpone perpetually of their bodies for food, sleep, or exercise. They draw large n their physical strength, and fail to lodge corresponding sums ring rest and nutriment. Their physical instincts are not s, like those of men; and they habitually disregard them when they make themselves felt, till poor Nature, continually snubbed when she makes her modest requests, ceases to press for daily settlement of her little bill, and reserves herself to put in an execution by-and-by. The vegetative and the spiritual part of these women flourish well enough; but (as Kingsley's Old Sandy says) "There is a lack of healthy animalism," between the two. They seem to consider themselves as fire-flies issuing out of a rose, flitting hither and thither to brighten the world, not creatures of flesh and blood, needing to go to bed and eat roast mutton.

If we study the condition of Mr. John Bull in his robust middle age, we shall notice that for forty years, with few interruptions, he has enjoyed those "reg'lar meals," on which Tennyson's Northern Farmer lays such stress as the foundation of general stability of character. He has also walked, ridden, rowed, skated, smoked his cigar, and gone to his bed (as nearly as circumstances permitted) when the inclination seized him. If now and again he has omitted to gratify his instincts, it has been for a business-like reason, and not merely because somebody did not happen to wish to do the same thing at the same time. He has not often waited for an hour, half-fainting for want of his breakfast, from motives of mere domestic courtesy; nor sat moped in a hot room through a long bright day to keep some old person company; nor resolved his dinner into tea and muffins because he was alone and it was not worth while to trouble the servants; nor sat up cold and weary till three in the morning to hear about a Parliamentary debate wherein he took only a vicarious interest. At the end of the forty years of wholesome indulgence, the man's instincts are more imperious and plain-spoken than ever, and, as a reward for his obedience to them, his organs perform their respective offices with alacrity, to the great benefit of himself and of all dependent upon him. Pretty nearly the reverse of this has happened in the case of Mrs. Bull. Almost her first lesson in childhood was to check, control, and conceal her wants and miseries; and by the time she has grown up she has acquired the habit of postponing them, as a matter of course, to the smallest convenience of A, B, C, and D, father, mother, brothers, even servants, whom she will not "put out of their way" for herself, though no one would so much as think whether they had a way to be put out of, for her brothers. The more strain there is upon her strength, by sickness in the house or any misfortune, the more completely she effaces and forgets herself and her physical wants, recklessly relinquishing sleep and neglecting food. When the pressure is relieved, and the nervous tension which supported her relaxed, the woman breaks down, as a matter of course, perhaps never to enjoy health again.

It must be borne in mind, also, in estimating a woman's chances of health, that if she neglect to think of herself, there is seldom anybody to do for her what she does for her husband. Nobody reminds her to [illegible] they are damp; nobody jogs her memory as [illegible] of this or that beverage or comestible, or [illegible] little casetings which so often ward off colds and [illegible]. Unless the woman live with a sister or friend, it [illegible] against her chances as compared to a man, that *o wife.*

[illegible] must, of course, be set against all this the two facts, that the [illegible] man's wishes and wants leads them often not *only* to [illegible] wholesome things as those of which we have been speaking, [illegible] unwholesome excesses beside, for which in due time by various diseases, from gout up to *delirium tremens.* And [illegible]ndingly, women's comparative indifference to the pleasures of keeps them clear of the ills to which gormandizing and bibu[illegible] is heir. We all know scores of estimable gentlemen who [illegible]ely be prevailed on, by the prayers and tears of their wives, from drinking a glass of beer or port wine which will in all [illegible]ty entail a fit of the gout next day; but in my whole life I [illegible] known a woman who consciously ate or drank things [illegible] make her ill, save one mild and sweet old lady, whose pre[illegible] for buttered toast overcame every motive of prudence, and [illegible]n of religion, which I have reason to believe she endeavoured to bear against the soft temptation. But for the purpose we [illegible] in hand, namely, that of tracing the origin, not of acute but of general *petite santé*, this aspect of the subject is [illegible]ant. It is precisely *petite santé* which comes of the perpetual [illegible]f nature's hints—that she wants air, bread, meat, fruit, tea, [illegible]ep, a scamper or a canter. It is definite *disease* which results [illegible]-exercise, over-feeding, and over-drinking.

[illegible] it not be possible, I venture to ask, to cut off *this* source of invalidism, at all events, by a somewhat more respectful to the calls of healthful instinct? I am very far from that women should grow more selfish, or less tenderly re[illegible] the convenience and pleasure of those around them. Even [illegible]alth of body—immeasurable blessing that it is—would be [illegible]d too dearly if this should happen. But there ought surely to [illegible]quate reason, not a mere excuse of whim and caprice of her [illegible]f anybody else, why a woman should do herself hurt or [illegible]ate herself for future usefulness?

[illegible] source of *petite santé*, I fear, may be found resulting from a survival amongst us of the idiotic notion that there is some[illegible] "lady-like" in invalidism, pallor, small appetite, and mode of speech and manners. The very word "delicacy," a term of praise, being applied vulgarly to a valetudinary [illegible], is evidence that the impression of the "dandies" of sixty that refinement and sickliness were convertible terms, is not yet wholly exploded. "Tremaine" thought *morbidezza*—a "*charming morbidezza*"—the choicest epithet he could apply to the cheek of beauty; and the heroines in all the other fashionable novels of the period drank hartshorn almost daily, and died of broken hearts, while the pious young Protestants who converted Roman Catholics in the religious tales, uniformly perished of consumption. Byron's admiring biographer records how, at a large dinner-party, he refused all viands except potatoes and vinegar (horrid combination!), and then retired to an eating-house to assuage with a beefsteak those cravings which even Childe Harold could not silence with "chameleon's food" of "light and air."

We have advanced indeed somewhat beyond this wretched affectation in our day, and young ladies are not required by *les bienséances* to exhibit at table the public habits of a ghoul. In a few cases perhaps we may opine that women have gone to the opposite extreme, and both eat and drink more than is desirable. But yet we are obviously not wholly free from the "delicacy" delusion. We are not so clear as we ought to be on the point that, though Beauty includes *other* elements, yet Health is its *sine quâ non*, and that no statuesque nobility of form (much less a pinched waist and a painted face) can constitute a beautiful living human creature, who lacks the tokens of health—clear eyes, clear skin, rich hair, good teeth, a cool soft hand, a breath like a bunch of cowslips, and a free and joyous carriage of the head and limbs.

Have we not, in the senseless admiration of feebleness and pallor (to obtain which a fashionable lady not long ago literally bled herself by degrees to death), an illustration of the curious fact pointed out by Miss de Rothschild in her admirable essay on the "Hebrew Woman,"* namely, that the homage which Christianity won for weakness has tempted women to cultivate weakness to secure the homage? Just as Christian Charity to the Poor has fostered Mendicancy, so has chivalrous Tenderness to the Feeble inspired a whole sex with the fatal ambition of becoming Feeble (or of simulating feebleness) to obtain the tenderness. The misconstruction and abuse of the Beatitudes of the gospel, as manifested in the rise of the Mendicant Orders of Friars, is notoriously a sad chapter of history. I do not think it a less sorrowful one that an analogous abuse has led to a sort of canonization of bodily and mental feebleness, cowardice, and helplessness among women. Can we question which is the nobler ideal,—the modern, nervous, pallid, tight-laced, fine lady of Little Health,—or the "Valiant Woman" (as the Vulgate calls her) of whom King Lemuel saith, "She girdeth her loins with strength, and strengtheneth her arms. Strength and honour are her clothing; and she shall rejoice in time to come?"†

* New Quarterly Magazine, No. X.

† Proverbs xxxi.

We have now touched on the subject of Dress, which plays so important a part in the health of women that it must here be treated somewhat at length. A little girl in a London Sunday-school, being asked by a visitor "why God made the flowers of the field?" replied (not unconscious of the gorgeous paper poppy in her own bonnet), "Please, ma'am, I suppose for patterns for artificial flowers." One might anticipate some answer scarcely less wide of the mark than that of this sophisticated little damsel, were the question to be put to not a few grown women, "Why do you wear clothes?" Their most natural response would obviously be, "To be in the fashion." When we have visibly wandered a long way from the path of reason, the best thing we can do is to look back to the starting-point and find out, if possible, where we have diverged. In the matter of raiment that starting-point is not hard to find—indeed, to mark it is only to state a series of truisms.

Human clothing has three *raisons d'être*, which, in order of precedence, are these:—

I.—HEALTH.
II.—DECENCY.
III.—BEAUTY.

HEALTH demands—

1. Maintenance of proper temperature of the body by exclusion of excessive heat and cold.

2. Protection from injury by rain, snow, dust, dirt, stones to the feet, insects, &c.

3. Preservation of liberty of action to all the organs of the body and freedom from pressure.

DECENCY demands—

4. Concealment of some portions of the human frame.

5. Distinction between the habiliments of men and women sufficient to avert mistake.

6. Fitness to the age and character of the wearer.

7. Concealment, when possible, of any disgusting personal defect.

BEAUTY demands—

8. Truthfulness. The dress must be genuine throughout, without any false pads, false hair, or false anything.

9. Graceful forms of drapery.

10. Harmonious colours.

11. Such moderate consistency with prevailing modes of dress as shall produce the impression of sociability and suavity, and avoid that of self-assertion.

12. Individuality,—the dress suiting the wearer as if it were an outer body belonging to the same soul.

(Be it noted that the fulfilment of this highest condition of tasteful dress necessarily limits the number of costumes which each person should wear on similar occasions. No one body can be adorned in several *equally suitable* suits of clothes, any more than one soul could be fittingly housed in twenty different bodies.)

Glancing back over the above table, we find this curious fact. The dress of *men* in all Western nations meets fairly all the conditions of Health and Decency, and fails only on the side of Beauty. The dress of *women*, on the contrary, ever variable as it is, persistently misses the conditions of Health; frequently violates the rules of Decency; and instead of securing Beauty, at which it aims first instead of last, achieves usually—ugliness.

It is to be remembered for our consolation and encouragement that men have arrived at their present good sense in dress only within two or three generations. A hundred years ago the lords of creation set Beauty above Health or convenience, just as the ladies do now, and peacocked about in their peach-blossom coats and embroidered waistcoats, surmounted by wigs, for whose stupendous discomfort even a seat on the judicial bench can scarcely reconcile the modern Englishman. Now, when the men of every European nation have abjured such fantastic apparel, we naturally ask, Why have not the women followed their example? Why is the husband, father, and brother habited like a being who has serious interests in life, and knows that his personal dignity would be forfeited were he to dress himself in parti-coloured, be-ribboned garments, and why is the wife, mother, or sister bedizened like a macaw, challenging every observer to note how much of her time, thoughts, and money must have been spent on this futile object? The answer is one which it is not pleasant to make, discreditable as it is to both sexes. The women who set the fashions dress for admiration; and men like women who dress to be admired; and the admiration given and received is a very poor and unworthy admiration, not much better than a salmon gives to a glittering artificial fly, and having very little more to do with any real æsthetic gratification,—as is proved too clearly by the thoroughly un-beautiful devices to which fashion has recourse. It is the *well-got-up* woman (to borrow a very expressive phrase), not the really well-dressed woman, who receives by far the largest share of homage.

And now let us see how all this concerns the Health of Women—how much of their *petite santé* is due to their general neglect to make Health the first object of dress, or even an object at all compared to fashion.

Tight-lacing among habits resembles Envy among the passions. We take pride in all the rest, even the idlest and worst, but tight-lacing and an envious heart are things to which no one ever confesses. A small waist, I suppose, is understood to belong to that order of virtues which Aristotle decides ought to be natural and not acquired, and the most miserable girl who spends her days in a machine more cruel (because more slowly murderous) than the old "Maiden" of Seville, smiling through her martyrdom, that her clothes about her!" It would be waste of time to dwell folly. Mrs. Haweis, in her very noteworthy new of Beauty," has given some exceedingly useful diagrams, of the practice on the internal organs and skeleton* I earnestly recommend to the study of ladies who to perform this sort of English Suttee for a *living* Haweis says that sensible men do not love wasps, and to her their "overallishness" when they behold them. how effectively they have hitherto managed to display approval whenever women have attempted to introduce , it is a pity, I think, that they do not "pronounce" distinctly against this, literally mortal, folly.

already alluded to the brain-heating chignons, just gone out after a long reign of mischief; and along with them should the bonnets which expose the forehead to the cold, while of the head is stewed under its cushion of false hair, and the still more serious disadvantage of affording no to the eyes. To women to whom the glare of the sun is hurtful to the sight, the necessity for wearing these on pain of appearing singular, or affectedly youthful, con- almost a valid reason against living in London. And the forsooth, is to hold up perpetually a parasol!—a yet further to add to the care of the draggling train, so that both y be occupied during a whole walk, and of course all natural motion rendered impossible. In this as in a dozen other silly , the women who have serious concerns in life are hampered practice of those who think of nothing but exhibiting their and ladies of limited fortune, who live in small rooms and the streets on foot or in cabs, are compelled (if they wish to ing pointed at) to adopt modes of dress whose sole *raison* that they suit wealthy *grandes dames* who lounge in their

and 50. The preceding pages on what I conceive to be the *raisons d'être* of dress before I had seen this exceedingly clever, brilliant, and learned little book. the authoress thanks for her most sensible reprobation of many senseless not presuming for a moment to question her judgment in the matters of she speaks with authority, I must here enter my humble but earnest the over-importance which, I think, she is inclined to attach to the art of the pursuits of women; and (most emphatically) against her readiness to be only committed in moderation—the offence against both truth and wearing false hair (see p. 178). It seems to me quite clear, that here the of honesty in attire is sacrificed. If no woman would wish it to be known her head never grew there, but on the scalp of some poor French girl, bribed to part with it, or of some unkempt Russian peasant who rarely her life,—then the wearing of that false hair is an act of *deception*, and both morally, and even æsthetically wrong. I cannot conceive why which we are now perpetually told must shine on our architecture and nothing must appear stone that is iron, and so on *ad infinitum*, should hardly over the dress of women. Where no deception is meant, and supply a want, not to forge a claim to beauty—*e.g.*, in the case of is no harm involved.

barouches or display their trains over the carpets of forty-feet-long drawing-rooms. What *snobbery* all this implies in our whole social structure! Some ten millions of women dress, as nearly as they can afford, in the style fit at the most for five thousand!

The practice of wearing *décolletée* dresses, sinning equally as it does against Health and Decency, seems to be gradually receding—from ordinary dinners, where it was universal twenty years ago, to special occasions, balls, and court drawing-rooms. But it dies hard, and it may kill a good many poor creatures yet, and entail on others the life-long bad health so naturally resulting from the exposure of a large surface of the skin to sudden chills.

The thin, paper-soled boots which leave the wearer to feel the chill of the pavement or the damp of the grass wherever she may walk, must have shortened thousands of lives in Europe, and even more in America. Combined with these, we have now the high heels, which, in a short period, convert the foot into a shapeless deformity, no longer available for purposes of healthful exercise. An experienced shoemaker informed the writer that between the results of tight boots and high heels, he scarcely knew a lady of fifty who had *what he could call a foot at all*—they had mere clubs. And this is done, all this anguish endured, for the sake of—Beauty!

Bad as stays, and chignons, and high heels, and paint, and low dresses, and all the other follies of dress are, I am, however, of opinion that the culminating folly of fashion, the one which has most wide-spread and durable consequences, is the mode in which for ages back women have contrived that their skirts should act as drags and swaddling clothes, weighing down their hips and obstructing the natural motion of the legs. Two hundred years ago the immortal Perrette, when she wanted to carry her milk-pail swiftly to market, was obliged to dress specially for the purpose.

> "Légère et court vêtue, elle allait à grands pas,
> Ayant mis ce jour-là, pour être plus agile,
> Cotillon simple et souliers plats."

From that time to this the "cotillon simple,"—modest, graceful, and rational,—has been the rare exception, and every kind of flounce and furbelow, hoops and crinolines, panniers and trains, "tied back" costume, and *robe collante* has been successively the bane of women's lives, and the slow destroyer of their activity.

It has been often remarked that the sagacity of Romish seminarists is exhibited by their practice of compelling boys destined for the priesthood to flounder along the streets in their long gowns, and never permitting them to cast them aside or play in the close-fitting clothes wherein [illegible] lads enjoy their cricket and football. The obstruction to free [illegible] such perhaps slight in itself, yet constantly maintained, [illegible] l of ecclesiastical decorum. But the lengthiest of *soutanes* compared to the multitudinous petticoats which, up to the r or two, every lady was compelled to wear, swathing and about her ancles as if she were walking through the sea. Nor shion of these later days much better, when the scantier dress back"—as I am informed—with an elastic band, much on the that a horse is "hobbled" in a field; and to this a tail a yard dded, which must either be left to draggle in the mud or cupy an arm exclusively to hold it up. In youth these skirts enough, as exercising a constant check on free and healthful nt; but the moment that the elastic steps begin to give place assitude of middle life, the case is desperate. There is no nergy to overcome the impediments created by the ridiculous and the poor donkey of a woman hobbles daily round a and shorter course till at forty or fifty she tells her friends sigh that she finds (she cannot imagine why) that she cannot all!

Decency require such a sacrifice as this? Does the utmost f feminine modesty ask for it? If it were so, I, for one, should e matter with a sigh, as not to be remedied. But who in their dreams that such is the case? Who, in the age of *robes* and *décolletée* dresses, can pretend that a reasonably full, ut silk or cloth skirt, reaching to the ancles and *no longer*, ot fulfil immeasurably *better* than any fashion we have seen for day the requirements of true womanly delicacy? It is for not Decency, that the activity of women is thus crushed, alth ruined, and (through them) the health of their children. t to be an indubitable fact that if twenty years ago a rational dest style of dress had been adopted by English women and ged by English men, instead of being sneered down by fops s, the health not only of women, but of the sons of women, e entire nation, would now be on altogether a different plane at we find it.*

wing all these deplorable follies, we may learn to make for legislators who classify women with "Criminals, Lunatics, nd Minors." It needs all a woman's knowledge of the perni- cesses to which the opening minds of girls are commonly d,—the false and base aims in life set before them, the perverse

nquiry, How fashions originate and *with whom?* would lead us too far from t in hand, but some light is thrown on the way in which complicated arrange- ress are maintained under every variation and in defiance of the true principles s well as of health and economy, by the reflection that it would never pay drapers makers that their customers should readily calculate how much stuff they r each garment. For further criticism of the follies of female dress—the *frigid* zones of body and limbs—the "panniers" or "bustles" creating kidney he skewering down of the arms by tight armholes; the veils which cause &c., &c.—and also for some excellent suggestions of reform, see *Dress and* little book printed by Dougall & Son, Montreal, to be obtained in London for f only by sending 1s. 6d. in stamps to B., 15, Belsize Square, N.W.

distribution towards them of approval and blame, admiration and neglect, and even of love and dislike, from parents, teachers, servants, brothers, and finally from the ball-room world into which they are now launched in childhood,—to enable us to make allowances for them, and retain faith that there sometimes beats a real woman's heart under the ribs of a tightly laced corset, and that a head surmounted by a pile of dead women's hair is not invariably devoid of brains.

How is the remedy for this dreary round of silly fashions ever to be attained? No woman who knows the world and how severe is the penalty of eccentricity in attire, will ever counsel her sisters to incur it for any motive short of a distinct duty. But if the hundreds of ladies who recognize the tyranny of senseless and unhealthful fashions were to combine forces to obey those fashions *just as little as may be*, to go as near the wind in the direction of simplicity, wholesomeness, and ease in their dress, as they dare, there would by degrees be formed a public opinion, rising year by year with the numbers and social standing of the representatives of common sense. It must have been in some such way that our great-grandfathers dropped their swords and bag wigs and ruffles and embroidery, and took to dressing—as even the silliest and vainest men do in these days—like rational beings.

Next to unhealthful dress, women may lay their *petite santé* at the door of their excessive addiction to pursuits giving exercise neither to the brain nor yet to the limbs. If the problem had been set to devise something, the doing of which would engage the very fewest and smallest powers of the mind or body, I know not whether we should give the prize for solving it to the inventor of knitting, netting, crochet, or worsted work. Pursued for a reasonable period in the day, these employments are no doubt quite harmless, and even perhaps, as some have urged, may be useful as sedatives. But that a woman who is driven by no dire necessity to "stitch, stitch, stitch," who has plenty of books to read, and two legs and feet to walk withal, should voluntarily limit the exercise of her body to the little niggling motion of the fingers required by these works, and the labour of her mind to counting stitches, is all but incomprehensible. That the consequences should be sickliness and feebleness seems to follow of course. In old times the ever-revolving spinning-wheel had its full justification in its abundant usefulness, and also in the dearth of intellectual pursuits for women. But it is marvellous that a well-educated Englishwoman, not yet sinking into the natural indolence of age, should choose to spend about a fifth or fourth of the hours God has given her on this beautiful earth in embroidery or worsted work. A drawing-room crammed with these useless fads—chairs, cushions, screens, and antimacassars—is simply a mausoleum of the wasted hours of the female part of the family. Happily there

...ation in this perpetual needling, and no future ... will be kept for the best hours of her girlhood ... daily seam. More intelligent and more active ... multiplying, and the great philanthropist who invented ... done more to remedy the Little Health of Ladies ... doctors together.

... now glanced over a number of causes of *petite santé*, for ... sufferers themselves are more or less responsible. Let us ... the others regarding which they are merely passive.

... many years since in my early youth, I was struck by a singular ... lence. Several of my married acquaintances were liable to a ... of headache. They were obliged, owing to these distressing ... remain very frequently in bed at breakfast-time, and later ... to lie on the sofa with darkened blinds and a considerable ... of Eau-de-Cologne. A singular immunity from the seizures ... be enjoyed when any pleasant society was expected, or when ... usbands happened to be in a different part of the country. By ... putting my little observations together, I came in my own ... o call these the "Bad-Husband Headaches," and I have since ... reason to alter my diagnosis. On the contrary, I am of opinion ... incalculable amount of feminine invalidism arises from nothing ... e depressing influences of an unhappy home. Sometimes, of ... it is positive unkindness and cruelty which the poor creatures ... Much more often it is the mere lack of the affection and care ... nderness for which they pine as sickly plants for sunshine. ... imes it is the simple oppression of an iron will over them which ... their pleasant fancies, and lops off their innocent whims, till there ... ap left in them to bud or blossom any more. Not seldom the ... comes of frequent storms in the household atmosphere,—for ... the woman is probably as often to blame as her companion, but ... which she suffers doubly, since, when they have passed, he goes ... his field or his merchandise with what spirit he can muster, poor ... while she sits still where the blighting words fell on her, to ... their bitterness. Of course it is not only unkind *husbands* who ... women down-hearted. There are unkind people in every relation, ... e only speciality of a woman's suffering from unkindness is, that ... commonly almost like a bed-ridden creature, for whom a single ... or even a hard lump in her bed, is enough to create a soreness. ... se who can get up and walk away, the importance which she ... es to the thorn or the lump seems inexplicable.

... balking of the heart is, I suppose, the worst evil in life to nine ... out of ten, whether it take place after marriage in finding an ... nial husband, or before marriage when a lover leaves them in ... and causes them a "Disappointment." This word, I observe, is ... significantly used with reference to such events among a cer... ... of women, as *the* Disappointment *par éminence*. When a lady fails to get her book published or her picture hung at the Academy, nobody speaks of her as having undergone a "disappointment." I have no doubt the grief of losing the lover is generally worse than these; but I wish that pride would teach every woman under such circumstances not to assume the attitude of an Ariadne, or settle down after a course of sal volatile into languor and Little Health till she is found at sixty, as M. About deliciously describes an English Old Maid, "tant soit peu dessêchée par les langueurs du célibat." Of this kind of thing I would fain hope we might soon see the end, as well as of the Actions for Breach of Promise, which are a disgrace to the whole womanhood of the country.

But beside heart sorrows, real and imaginary, there are other departments of women's natures wherein the balking of their activities has a deplorable effect on their physical as well as mental condition. Dr. Bridges once gave an admirable lecture at the Royal Institution, concerning the labouring and pauper class of Englishmen. He made the remark (which was received with emotion by the audience) that it was not enough to supply a human being with food and shelter. "Man," he said, "does not live by bread alone, he must have *Hope.*" May we not say likewise, "Woman does not live by bread alone—nay, nor by the richest *cake?*" She, too, must have Hope—something to live for, something which she may look to accomplish for herself or others in God's world of work, ere her night shall fall. A Hindoo lady, lately speaking at a meeting in India, compared Mary Carpenter's beneficent existence to a river bearing fertility to many lands, while the life of a woman in the Zenana, she said, resembled rather a pond. Surely every woman worthy of the name would desire to be something more than the pool, were it only a little trickling rill! But in endless cases she is *dammed up* on all sides, and none the less effectually that the soft mud of affectionate prejudice forms the dam. If her friends be rich, she is sickened with excess of luxury, but prohibited from stooping down out of the empyrean of her drawing-room to lend a finger to lift the burdens of a groaning world. If the family income be small, and the family pride proportionately great, she is required to spend her life—not in inspiriting, honourable money-*earning*, but in depressing, heart-narrowing money-*saving*. When the poor soul has borne this sort of pecuniary stay-lacing for a dozen years, and her forehead has grown narrow, and her lips pinched, and her eyes have acquired a certain anxious look (which I often fancy I recognize) as if of concern about sixpences, then, forsooth, the world laughs at her and says, "Women are so stingy!" How gladly, in a hundred cases, would that poor lady have toiled to *earn*—and not to *save*—and have been nobly generous with the proceeds of her industry!

We have heard a great [illegible] te of the danger to women's health of over mental strain or [illegible] labour. I do not say there is never dange[illegible] dire[illegible] never [illegible] [illegible] too

...daughters of women who have never used their ...ot have inherited rather soft and tender organs of cogita... I am no enthusiast for excessive book-learning for ...er such, though in books read and books written I have ...f the chief pleasures of a happy life. Perhaps if it were ...upervise the education of girls I should be rather inclined ...e hero of Locksley Hall,

> "They shall ride and they shall run,
> Leap the rainbows of the brooks,
> Not with blinded eyesight poring over miserable books."

...thing I am sure, and that is, that for one woman whose ...ured by excessive study (that is, by *study itself*, not the ...ety of examinations superadded to study), there are ...ose health is deteriorated by *want* of wholesome mental ...ometimes the vacuity in the brains of girls simply leaves ...d spiritless. More often into those swept and empty ... their skulls enter many small imps of evil omen. ...se of the intellectual powers," says an able lady M.D., ... means of preventing and counteracting an undue ... of the emotional nature. The extravagances of imagi... ...eeling engendered in an idle brain have much to do with ... of girls." Another observer, an eminent teacher, says, ...aded, and my experience has been confirmed by ex... ...ysicians, that the want of wholesome occupation lies at ...e languid debility, of which we hear so much, after girls ...ool."* And another, the Principal of one of the largest ...women in England, adds, "There is no doubt whatever ...udy is an eminent advantage to young women's health; ...course, that the general laws of health be attended to at ...e."*

...n have larger interests and nobler pursuits, and their ...l become, not less strong and deep, but less sickly, less ...demonstrative tenderness in return, less variable in their ...s. Let women have sounder mental culture, and their ... long exclusively fostered—will return to the calmness of ...e shall hear no more of the intermittent feverish spirits, ... depressions, and all the long train of symptoms which ...otean-formed Hysteria, and open the way to madness on ...to sin on the other.

...in conclusion, I must touch on a difficult part of my ...o is to blame for all the misery resulting from the Little ...dies?

... large portion of the evil must be impartially distributed ...ciety, with its false ideals of womanhood. Another portion

* The Education of American Girls, p. 229.

rests on parents and teachers; and of course no inconsiderable part on the actual sufferers, who, in many cases, might find healthful aims in life, if they had the spirit to look for them, and certainly need not carry the destructive fashions of dress to the climax they reach in the red-hot race of vanity. There remains yet a share of guilt with the childish and silly men who systematically sneer down every attempt to make women something better than the dolls they play with (just as if they would be at a loss for toys, were the dolls to be transformed into rational creatures), and those others, even more cruelly selfish, who deliberately bar every door at which women knock in search of honourable employment. After all these, I find one class more.

There is no denying the power of the great Medical Order in these days. It occupies, with strangely close analogy, the position of the priesthood of former times, assumes the same airs of authority, claims its victims for torture (this time among the lower animals), and enters every family with a latch-key of private information, only comparable to that obtained by the Confessional. If Michelet had written for England instead of for France, he should have made a book, not on "Priests, Women, and Families," but on "Doctors, Women, and Families." The influence of the family medical man on wives and mothers, and, through them, on husbands and children, is almost unbounded, and if it were ever to be exerted uniformly in any matter of physical education, there is little doubt that it would be effective.

What, then, we may reasonably ask, have these omnipotent doctors done to prevent the repetition of deadly follies in the training of girls generation after generation? Now and then we have heard feeble cautions, given in an Eli-like manner, against tight-lacing, late hours, and excitement; and a grand display of virtuous indignation was, if I remember rightly, exhibited about a year ago in a medical round-robin, against feminine dram-drinking—a vice for which the doctor's own prescriptions are in too many cases responsible. But the steadily determined pressure on mothers and young women, the insistence on free, light petticoats, soundly shod feet, loose stays, and well-sheltered heads—when has it been exercised? An American medical lady says that at a *post-mortem* examination of several women killed by accident in Vienna, she found the internal organs of nearly all affected by tight-lacing. "Some ribs overlapped each other; one had been found to pierce the liver; and almost without exception that organ was displaced below the ribs. . . The spleen in some cases was much enlarged, in others it was atrophied,"[*] and so on. Do the male doctors, who behold these and other hideous sights continually, go out to warn the mothers who encourage girls to this ghastly self-destruction, as they do denounce the poor, misguided Peculiar People and Anti-Vaccinators who cheat Science of her dues?

At last, after the follies of lu[illegible] and fashion have gone on in a sort of *crescendo* like the descent of Vathek into the Hall of Eblis, till we seem nearly to have reached the bottom, a voice of warning is heard! It has pealed across the Atlantic, and been re-echoed on the shores of England with a cordiality of response which our men of science do not often give to American "notions." "Women, beware!" it cries. "Beware! you are on the brink of destruction! You have hitherto been engaged only in crushing your waists; now you are attempting to cultivate your minds! You have been merely dancing all night in the foul air of ball-rooms; now you are beginning to spend your mornings in study! You have been incessantly stimulating your emotions with concerts and operas, with French plays and French novels; now you are exerting your understanding to learn Greek and solve propositions in Euclid! Beware, oh beware! Science pronounces that the woman who—*studies*—is lost!"

Perhaps there are some women, now alive, who did study a little in youth, who even spent their nights occasionally over their books while their contemporaries were running from one evening party to another—who now in middle and advanced life enjoy a vigour which it would be very well for their old companions if they could share. These women know precisely *à quoi s'en tenir* concerning these terrific denunciations.

There is another point on which it seems to me that a suspicion of blame must attach to the medical profession. We all believe that our doctors do the utmost in their power to cure *acute* diseases. When any patient has scarlet fever or small pox or bronchitis, he may be sure that his medical attendant will exert all his skill and care to pull him through. But is it equally certain that out of the 20,000 men, or thereabouts, who are qualified to practise medicine and surgery in this kingdom, there are not a few who feel only a modified interest in the perfect recovery of chronic sufferers who represent to them an annual income of £50 or perhaps £200? A few months ago there appeared an article in one of the magazines expounding the way in which *legal* business was made to grow in hydra fashion. We have all heard similar accusations against slaters and plumbers, who mend one hole in a roof and leave another. In short, we unhesitatingly suspect almost every other trade and profession of *making work for itself*. Is it clearly proved that doctors are in this respect quite different from lawyers and other men, or that the temptation to keep a wealthy patient coddling comfortably with an occasional *placebo* for twenty years is invariably resisted? The question is not easy to answer unhesitatingly in the affirmative—"Suppose a really radical cure were discovered whereby all the neuralgic and dyspeptic and gouty patients could be made in an hour as sound as so many trivets, do we believe implicitly and *au fond du cœur* that that heaven-sent remedy would be rapturously welcomed by the whole medical profession?" Is there no truth at all in the familiar legend of the elderly lady whose physician, after many years of not unprofitable attendance, advised her to go to Bath, promising to give her a letter to the most eminent local doctor, his intimate friend, to whom he would thoroughly explain her case? The lady, armed with the introductory letter, it is said, proceeded on her way; but the curiosity of a daughter of Eve unhappily overcame her discretion. "It is only about myself after all," she said to pacify her scruples; "and once for all I will learn what dear Dr. D—— *does* think is my complaint. If I am doomed to die, it is better than this prolonged uncertainty." The seal was broken, and the lady read: "Keep the old fool for six weeks, and be sure to send her back to me at the end. Yours truly."

There are at this day in Mayfair and Belgravia, in Bayswater and South Kensington, a dozen houses in every street and square at the doors of which the doctor's carriage stops as regularly as the milkman's cart; and apparently there is just as little likelihood that either should cease to stop. If the old Chinese custom were introduced amongst us, and patients were to pay their physicians a salary *so long as they were in health*, and ceased to pay whenever they required medical attendance, I very much question whether we should see quite so many of those broughams about those doors. I cannot help fancying that if the clockmakers who undertake to wind up our domestic timepieces were to keep them in the same unsatisfactory and perpetually running-down condition as the inner machineries of these doctors' patients, we should in most cases bring our contract with the clockmaker to a close, and wind up our timepieces in future for ourselves.

But more, and in a yet more serious way, the doctors have, I conceive, failed, not only as guardians of the health of women, but as having (as a body) opposed with determined and acrimonious resistance an innovation which—*if medical science be good for anything*—they could scarcely doubt would have been of immense benefit to them.

No one is ignorant how often the most agonizing diseases to which female nature is liable follow from the neglect of early premonitory symptoms, and how often, likewise, lifelong invalidism results from disregard of the ailments of youth. It is almost equally notorious how often these deplorable catastrophes are traceable directly to the poor victim's modest shrinking from disclosing her troubles to a male adviser. When such events are spoken of with bated breath among friends, it is sometimes said that it was the sufferer's own fault—that she *ought not* to have felt any shyness about consulting a doctor—and that it is proper for everybody to "look on a doctor as an old woman." I confess I do not understand precisely such playing fast and loose with any genuine sentiment of modesty. The members of the Royal Colleges of Physicians and Surgeons and of the Society of Apothecaries are *not* "old women." They are not even all old, nor all

. A few months before they begin to practise—while they "Bob Sawyer" stage—they are commonly supposed to be e least steady or well-conducted of youths; and where a them congregate together—as in Edinburgh, for example— pt to obtain an unenviable notoriety for "rowdyism." I have once myself witnessed conduct on the part of these lads at etings which every man on the platform denounced as dis- I could not but reflect as I watched them: "And *these* ear hence will be called to the bedsides of ladies to minister f uttermost trial when the extremest refinement of tact and ust scarce make the presence of a man endurable! Nay, attend in crowds the clinical instructions in the female the hospitals, and are invited to inspect miseries of disease le operations on women, who, if of humbler class, are often e and modest as the noblest lady in the land!"

lings of Englishwomen on all matters of delicacy are pro- ner than those of the women of any other Western country, ne particulars may possibly be now and then overstrained. could wish them to be changed? Who questions their finite value? In every instance, except the one we are dis- ey receive from Englishmen the respect which they deserve. se deliberately to teach girls to set those sacred feelings ne point, and that point the one where they are necessarily immeasurably more closely than anywhere else, is simply They could not do it if they would, and they ought not to ey could. A girl who would willingly go to a man-doctor lt him freely about one of the many ills to which female flesh ould be an odious young woman. Violence must be done tural instincts, either by the pressure of the mother's per- who has undergone the same *peine forte et dure* before her), unendurable anguish, before she will have recourse to aid thinks worse than disease, or even death. And so the time lth and life might be saved is lost by delay, and when the s made at last, the doctor observes compassionately, "If you to me long ago I might have restored you to health,—or an could have been performed which might have saved your r, I grieve to say, it is too late."

e admission of qualified women to practise medicine is the d only effectual remedy for this evil is of course obvious to pposing such admission relentlessly, as they have generally ical men have incurred a responsibility which to me seems hort of tremendous. Whatever motive we may be willing to them above mere pitiful rivalry for practice and profit ely possible to suggest one which is not grossly injurious and to women, or which ought for a moment to weigh in the gainst the cruel woes to which I have referred, or the just claim of all women to receive, if they prefer them, the ministrations of their own sex in their hours of suffering and weakness.

Doctors are wont to speak—apparently with profound feeling—of the sympathy they entertain for their patients, and to express their readiness (in a phrase which has passed into cant) " to sacrifice a hecatomb of brutes to relieve the smallest pain of a human being." May not women justly challenge them to sacrifice something a little nearer to themselves,—their professional pride, their trades-unionism, and a certain fraction of their practice,—to relieve their entire sex of enormous pain, mental and physical ?

I rejoice to believe that the long contest draws to a close, and that, thanks to men like Mr. Stansfeld and Mr. Cowper Temple, there will soon be women-doctors, and women's hospitals attended by women-doctors, in every town in the kingdom. I rejoice to know that we possess already a few qualified ladies who every day, without wound to the feelings of the most sensitive, receive the full and free confidence of girls and women, and give in return counsels to which many attribute the preservation of life and health; and which—if medical science have any practical value—must afford the rising generation a better chance than ever their mothers have had of escaping the endless miseries to themselves and all belonging to them attendant on the Little Health of Ladies.

FRANCES POWER COBBE.

# ON THE TEACHING OF NATURAL PHILOSOPHY.*

: the very outset of our work two questions of great importance come prominently forward. One of these, I have reason to con- from long experience, is probably a puzzling one to a great of you: the other is of paramount consequence to us all. And are of consequence not to us alone but to the whole country, in esent feverish state of longing for what it but vaguely under- s and calls *science-teaching*. These questions are, *What is Natural ophy?* and, *How is it to be taught?*

ew words only, on the first question, must suffice for the present. term *Natural Philosophy* was employed by Newton to describe tudy of the powers of nature: the investigation of forces from otions they produce, and the application of the results to the nation of other phenomena. It is thus a subject to whose proper sion mathematical methods are indispensable. The "Principia" ences with a clear and simple statement of the fundamental laws tion, proceeds to develop their more immediate consequences by verful mathematical method of the author's own creation, and ds them to the whole of what is now called *Physical Astronomy*. in the Preface, Newton obviously hints his belief that in time ilar mode of explanation would be extended to the other pheno- of external nature.

many departments this has been done to a remarkable extent g the two centuries which have elapsed since the publication of Principia." In others, scarcely a single step of any considerable itude has been taken; and in consequence, the boundary be- that which is properly the subject of the natural philosopher's

* [illegible] from Notes of the Introductory Lecture to the ordinary course of Natural [illegible] in Edinburgh University, October 31st, 1877.

inquiries and that which is altogether beyond his province is at present entirely indefinite. There can be no doubt that, in many important respects, even life itself is dependent upon purely physical conditions. The physiologists have quite recently seized, for their own inquiries, a great part of the natural philosopher's apparatus, and with it his methods of experimenting. But to say that even the very lowest form of life, not to speak of its higher forms, still less of volition and consciousness, can be fully *explained* on physical principles alone—*i.e.* by the mere relative motions and interactions of portions of inanimate matter, however refined and sublimated—is simply unscientific. There is absolutely nothing known in physical science which can lend the slightest support to such an idea. In fact, it follows at once from the *Laws of Motion* that a material system, left to itself, has a perfectly determined future, *i.e.*, that upon its configuration and motion at any instant depend all its subsequent changes; so that its whole history, past and to come, is to be gathered from one almost instantaneous, if sufficiently comprehensive glance. In a purely material system there is thus *necessarily* nothing of the nature of a free agent. To suppose that life, even in its lowest form, is wholly material, involves therefore either a denial of the truth of Newton's laws of motion, or an erroneous use of the term "matter." Both are alike unscientific.

Though the sphere of our inquiries extends wherever matter is to be found, and is therefore co-extensive with the physical universe itself, there are other things, not only without but within that universe, with which our science has absolutely no power to deal. In this room we simply recognize them, and pass on.

Modern extensions of a very general statement made by Newton enable us now to specify much more definitely than was possible in his time the range of physical science. We may now call it the *Science of Matter and Energy*. These are, as the whole work of the session will be designed to prove to you, *the two real things* in the physical universe; both unchangeable in amount, but the one consisting of parts which preserve their identity; while the other is manifested only in the act of transformation, and though measurable cannot be identified. I do not at present enter on an exposition of the nature or laws of either; that exposition will come at the proper time; but the fact that so short and simple a definition is possible is extremely instructive, showing, as it unquestionably does, what very great advances physical science has made in recent times. The definition, in fact, is but little inferior in simplicity to two of those with which most of you are no doubt already to a certain extent familiar—that of Geometry as the *Science of Pure Space*, and of Algebra as the *Science of Pure Time*.

But, for to-day at least, our second question, viz., *How is Natural Philosophy to be taught?* is of more immediate importance. The answer, [illegible] like this, must of course be—"popularly." [illegible] has many senses, even in the present connection—one [illegible] the others of variously graduated amounts of badness. [illegible] begin with one or two of the bad ones. The subject is [illegible] one for you, and therefore must be considered care- [illegible] the celebrated dictum of Terence, *Obsequium amicos,* [illegible] (In other words, Flatter your audience and tickle [illegible] you seek to ingratiate yourself with them; tell them the [illegible] wish to raise enemies.) But science is one form of truth. [illegible] surgeon is convinced that the knife is required, it becomes [illegible] to operate. And Shakspeare gives us the proper answer to [illegible] serving caution of Terence and Cicero in the well-known [illegible] "Let the galled jade wince."

[illegible] these wholly bad methods was recently very well put by a [illegible] critic, as follows:—

"The name of 'Popular Science' is, in itself, a doubtful and somewhat [illegible] one, being commonly taken to mean the superficial exposition of [illegible] by a speaker or writer who himself understands them imperfectly, to [illegible] that his hearers or readers may be able to talk about them without [illegible] them at all."

[illegible] I need hardly say, is not in any sense science-teaching. It [illegible] however, that there is a great demand for it, more especially [illegible] audiences which seek amusement rather than instruction; and [illegible] demand of course is satisfied. Such an audience gets what it [illegible] and, I may add, exactly what it deserves.

[illegible] so monstrous as that just alluded to, yet far too common, [illegible] essentially vague and highly ornamented style of so-called [illegible] teaching. The objections to this method are of three kinds at [illegible] independently fatal.

[illegible] It gives the hearer, if he have no previous acquaintance with [illegible] an altogether erroneous impression of the intrinsic difficulty [illegible] subject. He is exhorted, in grandiloquent flights of laboured [illegible] to exert his utmost stretch of intellect, that he may com- [illegible] the great step in explanation which is next to be given; and [illegible] after this effort, the impression on his mind is seemingly quite [illegible] he begins to fancy that he has not understood at all— [illegible] must be some profound mystery in the words he has heard [illegible] has entirely escaped his utmost penetration. After a very few [illegible] he gives up in despair. How many a man has been driven [illegible] whose intellect might have largely contributed to [illegible] of Physics, merely by finding that he can make nothing [illegible] dicta of his teacher or text-book, except something so [illegible] it cannot possibly be what was meant!

[illegible] altogether spoils the student's taste for the simple facts [illegible] And it does so just as certainly as an undiluted course [illegible] or music-hall comic songs is destructive of all relish for the true art of Mozart or Haydn, or as sensation novels render Scott's highest fancies tame by contrast. And,

> ". . . . . as if increase of appetite
> Had grown by what it fed on, . . . ."

the action on the listener is made to react on the teacher, and he is called upon for further and further outrages on the simplicity of science. Sauces and spices not only impair the digestion, they create a craving for other stimulants of ever-increasing pungency and deleteriousness.

But, *thirdly*. No one having a true appreciation of the admirable simplicity of science could be guilty of these outrages. To attempt to introduce into *science* the meretricious adjuncts of "word-painting," &c., can only be the work of dabblers—not of scientific men, just as

> "To gild refinèd gold, to paint the lily,
> To throw a perfume on the violet,
> To smooth the ice, or add another hue
> Unto the rainbow; or with taper light
> To seek the beauteous eye of heaven to garnish,
> Is *wasteful and ridiculous excess*."

None could attempt such a work who had the smallest knowledge of the true beauty of nature. Did he know it, he would feel how utterly inadequate, as well as uncalled-for, were all his greatest efforts. For, again in Shakspeare's words, such a course

> "Makes sound opinion sick, and truth suspected,
> For putting on so new a fashioned robe."

"In the great majority of 'popular' scientific works the author, as a rule, has not an exact knowledge of his subject, and does his best to avoid committing himself, among difficulties which he must at least try to *appear* to explain. On such occasions he usually has recourse to a flood of vague generalities, than which nothing can be conceived more pernicious to the really intelligent student. In science 'fine language' is entirely out of place; the stern truth, which is its only basis, requires not merely that we should never disguise a difficulty, but, on the contrary, that we should call special attention to it, as a probable source of valuable information. If you meet with an author who, like the cuttle-fish, endeavours to escape from a difficult position by darkening all around him with an inky cloud of verbiage, close the book at once and seek information elsewhere."

But I must come back to the really important point, which is this:—*True science is in itself simple, and should be explained in as simple and definite language as possible.*

Word-painting finds some of its most appropriate subjects when employed to deal with human snobbery or human vice—where the depraved tastes and wills of mortals are concerned—not the simple and immutable truths of science. Battles, murders, executions;

political, legal, and sectarian squabbles; gossip, ostentation, toadyism, and such like, are of its proper subjects. Not that the word-painter need be himself necessarily snobbish or vicious—far from it. But it is here, as our best poets and satirists have shown, that his truest field is to be found. Science sits enthroned, like the gods of Epicurus, far above the influence of mere human passions, be they virtuous or evil, and must be treated by an entirely different code of rules. And a great deal of the very shallowest of the pseudo-science of the present day probably owes its origin to the habitual use, with reference to physical phenomena, of terms or synonyms whose derivation shows them to have reasonable application to human beings and their actions alone,—not at all to matter and energy. In dealing with such pseudo-science it is, of course, permissible to me, even after what I have said, to use word-painting as far as may be thought necessary.

The Pygmalions of modern days do not require to beseech Aphrodité to animate the ivory for them. Like the savage with his *Totem*, they have themselves already attributed life to it. "It comes," as Helmholtz says, "to the same thing as Schopenhauer's metaphysics. The stars are to love and hate one another, feel pleasure and displeasure, and to try to move in a way corresponding to these feelings." The latest phase of this peculiar non-science tells us that all matter is ALIVE; or at least that it contains the "promise and potency" (whatever these may be) "of all terrestrial life." All this probably originated in the very simple manner already hinted at; viz., in the confusion of terms constructed for application to thinking beings only, with others applicable only to brute matter, and a blind following of this confusion to its necessarily preposterous consequences. So much for the attempts to introduce into science an element altogether incompatible with the fundamental conditions of its existence.

When simple and definite language cannot be employed, it is solely on account of our ignorance. Ignorance may of course be either *unavoidable* or *inexcusable*.

It is unavoidable only when knowledge is not to be had. But that of which there is no knowledge is not yet part of science. All we can do with it is simply to confess our ignorance and seek for information.

As an excellent illustration of this we may take two very common phenomena—a *rainbow* and an *aurora*—the one, to a certain extent at least, thoroughly understood; the other scarcely understood in almost any particular. Yet it is possible that, in our latitudes at least, we see the one nearly as often as the other. For, though there are probably fewer auroras to be seen than rainbows, the one phenomenon is in general much more widely seen than the other. A rainbow is usually a mere local phenomenon, depending on a rain-cloud of moderate extent; while an aurora, when it occurs, may extend over a whole terrestrial hemisphere. Just like total eclipses, lunar and solar. Wherever the moon can be seen, the lunar eclipse is visible, and to all alike. But a total solar eclipse is usually visible from a mere strip of the earth—some fifty miles or so in breadth.

The branch of natural philosophy which is called *Geometrical Optics* is based upon three experimental facts or laws, which are assumed as exactly true, and as representing the whole truth—the rectilinear propagation of light in any one uniform medium, and the laws of its reflexion and refraction at the common surface of two such media; and as a science it is nothing more than the developed mathematical consequences of these three postulates.

Hence, if these laws were rigorously true, and represented *all* the truth, nothing but mathematical investigation based on them would be required for the complete development of the phenomena of the rainbow—except the additional postulate, also derived from experiment, that falling drops of water assume an exact spherical form—and, as data for numerical calculation, the experimentally-determined refractive index for each ray of light at the common surface of air and water.

Thus for instance we can tell why the rainbow has the form of a portion of a circle surrounding the point opposite to the sun; why it is red on the outer edge; what is the order of the other colours, and why they are much less pure than the red; why the whole of the background enclosed within it is brighter than that just outside; and so on. Also why there is a second (also circular) rainbow; why it is concentric with the first; and why its colours are arranged in the reverse order, &c.

But, so long at least as we keep to *Geometrical* optics, we cannot explain the spurious bows which are usually seen, like ripples, within the primary and outside the second rainbow; nor why the light of both bows is polarized, and so forth. We must apply to a higher branch of our science; and we find that *Physical Optics*, which gives the results to which those of geometrical optics are only approximations, enables us to supply the explanation of these phenomena also.

When we turn to the aurora we find nothing so definite to explain. This may, to some extent at least, account for our present ignorance. We remark, no doubt, a general relation between the direction of the earth's magnetic force and that of the streamers: but their appearance is capricious and variable in the extreme. Usually they have a pale green colour, which the spectroscope shows to be due to homogeneous light; but in very fine displays they are sometimes blood-red, sometimes blue. Auroral arches give sometimes a sensibly continuous spectrum; sometimes a single bright line. We can *imitate* many of the phenomena by passing electric discharges through rarefied gases; and we find that the streamers so produced are influenced by magnetic force. But we do not yet know for certain the source of the discharges which produce the aurora, nor d[illegible] even know what substance it [illegible] its light is due. We find by a statistical [illegible] like cyclones, are most numerous when there [illegible] the sun; but the connection between these is not yet known. Here, in fact, we are only *beginning* to [illegible] but confess our ignorance.

[illegible] that there is nothing about the rainbow which [illegible], even of that which is seen at once by untrained [illegible] the phenomena connected with it which we can ex[illegible] mathematical deductions from observed facts which are the investigation. But these facts are, in the main, them[illegible] yet explained. Just as there are many exceedingly expert who habitually and usefully employ logarithmic tables [illegible]ving the least idea of what a logarithm really is, or of the which the tables themselves were originally calculated; [illegible]ral philosopher uses the observed facts of refraction and without having as yet anything better than guesses as to [illegible]le proximate cause. And it is so throughout our whole [illegible]suming one result, we can prove that the others *must* follow. [illegible]ection great advances have been made, and every exten[illegible]thematics renders more of such deductions possible. But [illegible]ry to reverse the process, and thus to explain our hitherto [illegible]sults, we are met by difficulties of a very different order. [illegible]ject of *Physical Astronomy*, to which I have already alluded, [illegible]ce one of the most striking and one of the most easily illustrations of this point. Given the law of gravitation, [illegible] of the sun and planets, and their relative positions and *any one instant*,—the investigation of their future motions, disturbing causes come in, is entirely within the power of [illegible]natician. But how shall we account for gravitation? This [illegible]on of an entirely different nature from the other, and but [illegible]lausible attempt to answer it has yet been made. . .

[illegible]sume. The digression I have just made had for its object [illegible]u how closely full knowledge and absolute ignorance may [illegible] associated in many parts of our subject—absolute com[illegible]e necessary consequences of a phenomenon, entire igno[illegible] actual nature or cause.

[illegible] every branch of physics the student ought to be most [illegible]structed about matters of this kind. A comparatively small mathematical training will often be found sufficient to to trace the consequences of a known truth to a consider[illegible], and no such training is necessary to enable him to see [illegible] properly presented to him) the boundary between our [illegible] our ignorance—at least when that ignorance is not [illegible]ndent upon the inadequacy of our deductive powers.

[illegible] Lucretius is perhaps the only really successful attempt [illegible]. And it is so because it was written before there was any true physical science. The methods throughout employed are entirely those of *à priori* reasoning, and therefore worse than worthless, altogether misleading. Scientific poetry, using both words in their highest sense, is now impossible. The two things are in their very nature antagonistic. A scientific man *may* occasionally be a poet also; but he has then two distinct and almost mutually incompatible natures; and, when he writes poetry, he puts science aside. But, on the other hand, when he writes science, he puts poetry and all its devices aside. Mark this well! A poet may, possibly with great effect on the unthinking multitude, write of

> ". . . . the huger orbs which wheel
> In circuits vast throughout the wide abyss
> Of unimagined Chaos—till they reach
> Æthereal splendour . . . . . ."

(The word "unimagined" may puzzle the reader, but it probably alludes to Ovid's expression "*sine imagine.*" For this sort of thing is nothing if not *classical!* The contempt in which "scholars" even now hold mere "physicists" is proverbial. And they claim the right of using at will new words of this kind, in whose company even the "tremendous empyrean" would, perhaps, not be quite out of place.)

But, whether this sort of thing be poetry or not, it is in no sense science. "Huge," and "vast," and such-like (for which, if the rhythm permit, you may substitute their similars, "Titanic," "gigantic," &c.), good honest English though they be, are utterly unscientific words. In science we restrict ourselves to *small* and *great*, and these amply suffice for all our wants. But even these terms are limited with us to a mere relative sense; and it can only be through ignorance or forgetfulness of this that more sonorous terms are employed. The size of every finite object depends entirely upon the unit in terms of which you measure it. There is nothing absolutely great but the Infinite.

A few moments' reflection will convince you of the truth of what I have just said. Let us only go by easily comprehensible stages from one (so-called) extreme to the other. Begin with the smallest thing you can see, and compare it with the greatest. I suppose you have all seen a good barometer. The vernier attached to such an instrument is usually read to thousandths of an inch, but it sometimes leaves you in doubt which of two such divisions to choose. This gives the limit of vision with the unaided eye. Let us therefore begin with an object whose size is about 1-2000th of an inch. Let us choose as our scale of relative magnitude 1 to 250,000 or thereabouts. It is nearly the proportion in which each of you individually stands to the whole population of Edinburgh. (I am not attempting anything beyond the rudest illustration, because that will amply suffice for my present purpose.) Well: 250,000 times the diameter of our *minimum visibile* gives us a length of ten feet or so—three or four paces. Increased again in about the same ratio, it becomes more than 400 miles, somewhere about the distance from Edinburgh to London. Perform the operation again, and you get (approximately enough for our purpose) the sun's distance from the earth. Operate once more, and you have got beyond the nearest fixed star. Another such operation would give a distance far beyond that of anything we can ever hope to see. Yet you have reached it by repeating, at most *five* times, upon the smallest thing you can see, an operation in itself not very difficult to imagine. Now as there is absolutely nothing known to science which can preclude us from carrying this process farther, so there is absolutely no reason why we may not in thought *reverse* it, and thus go back from the smallest visible thing to various successive orders of smallness. And the *first* of these that we thus reach has already been pointed to by science as at least a rough approximation to that coarse-grainedness which we *know* to exist (though we shall never be able to see it) even in the most homogeneous substances, such as glass and water. For several trains of reasoning, entirely independent of one another, but based upon experimental facts, enable us to say with certainty that all matter becomes heterogeneous (in some as yet quite unknown way) when we consider portions of it whose dimensions are somewhere about 1-500,000,000th of an inch. We have, as yet, absolutely no information beyond this, save that, if there be ultimate atoms, they are at least considerably more minute still.

Next comes the very important question—*How far is experimental illustration necessary and useful?* Here we find excessively wide divergence, alike in theory and in practice.

In some lecture-theatres, experiment is everything; in others, the exhibition of gorgeous displays illustrative of nothing in particular is said occasionally to alternate with real or imagined (but equally sensational) danger to the audience, from which they are preserved (or supposed to be preserved) only by the extraordinary presence of mind of the presiding performers—a modern resuscitation of the ancient after-dinner amusement of tight-rope dancing, high above the heads of the banqueters, where each had thus a very genuine, if selfish, interest in the nerve and steadiness of the artists.

Contrasted in the most direct manner with these, is the dictum not long ago laid down:—

"It may be said that the fact makes a stronger impression on the boy through the medium of his sight—that he believes it the more confidently. I say that this ought not to be the case. If he does not believe the statements of his tutor—probably a clergyman of mature knowledge, recognized ability, and blameless character—his suspicion is irrational, and manifests a want of the power of appreciating evidence—a want fatal to his success in that branch of science which he is supposed to be cultivating."

Between such extremes many courses may be traced. But it is better to dismiss the consideration of both, simply on the ground that they are extremes, and therefore alike absurd.

Many facts cannot be made thoroughly intelligible without experiment; many others require no illustration whatever, except what can be best given by a few chalk-lines on a blackboard. To teach an essentially experimental science without illustrative experiments may conceivably be possible in the abstract, but certainly not with professors and students such as are to be found on this little planet.

And, on the other hand, you must all remember that we meet here to discuss science, and science alone. A University class-room is not a place of public amusement, with its pantomime displays of red and blue fire, its tricks whether of prestigiation or of prestidigitation, or its stump-oratory. The best and greatest experimenter who ever lived used none of these poor devices to win cheap applause. His language (except perhaps when non-experimenting pundits pressed upon him their fearful Greek names for his splendid discoveries) was ever the very simplest that could be used: his experiments, whether brilliant or commonplace in the eyes of the mere sight-seer, were chosen solely with the object of thoroughly explaining his subject; and his whole bearing was impressed with the one paramount and solemn feeling of duty, alike to his audience and to science. Long ages may pass before his equal, or even his rival, can appear; but the great example he has left should be imitated by us all as closely as possible.

Nothing is easier in extempore speaking, as I dare say many of you know by trial, than what is happily called "piling up the agony." For, as has been well said,

> ". . . . men there be that make
> Parade of fluency, and deftly play
> With points of speech as jugglers toss their balls;
> A tinkling crew, from whose light-squandered wit
> No seed of virtue grows."

Every one who has a little self-confidence and a little readiness can manage it without trouble. But it is so because in such speaking there is no necessity for precision in the use of words, and no objection to any epithet whatever, unless it be altogether misplaced. But the essence of all such discourse is necessarily *fancy*, and not *fact*. Here, during the serious work of the session, we are tied down almost exclusively to facts. Fancies *must* appear occasionally; but we admit them only in the carefully-guarded form of a reference to old opinions, or to a "good working hypothesis." Still, facts are not necessarily dry: not even if they be mere statistics. All depends on the way in which they are put. One of the most amusing of the many clever songs, written and sung by the late Professor Rankine in his moments of relaxation, was an almost literal transcript of a prosaic statistical description of a little Irish town, taken from a gazetteer! He was a truly original man of science, and therefore exact in his statements; but he could be at once both exact and interesting. And I believe that the intrinsic beauty [illegible] is such that it cannot suffer in the minds of a really intelligent audience, however poor be the oratorical powers of its expounder, provided only he can state its facts with clearness. Oratory is essentially *art*, and therefore essentially *not science*.

There is nothing false in the *theory*, at least, of what are called Chinese copies. If it could be *fully* carried out, the results would be as good as the original—in fact, undistinguishable from it. But it is solely because we cannot have the theory carried out in perfection that true artists are forced to slur over details, and to give "broad effects," as they call them. The members of the Pre-Raphaelite school are thoroughly right in one part at least of their system: unfortunately it is completely unrealizable in practice. But the "broad effects" of which I have spoken are true *art*, though perhaps in a somewhat modified sense of the word (which, not being a scientific one, has many shades of meaning). To introduce these "broad effects" into science may be artful, but it is certainly unscientific. In so-called "popular science," if anywhere, *Ars est celare inscientiam.* The "artful dodge" is to conceal want of knowledge. Vague explanations, however artful, no more resemble true science than do even the highest flights of the imagination, whether in "Ivanhoe" or "Quentin Durward," Knickerbocker's "New York" or Macaulay's "England," resemble history. And when the explanation is bombastic as well as vague, its type is the same as that of the well-known speech of Sergeant Buzfuz.

One ludicrous feature of the "high-falutin" style is that if you adopt it you throw away all your most formidable ammunition on the smaller game, and have nothing proportionate left for the larger. It is as if you used a solid shot from an 81-ton gun upon a single skirmisher! As I have already said, you *waste* your grandest terms, such as huge, vast, enormous, tremendous, &c., on your mere millions or billions; and then what is left for the poor trillions? The true lesson to be learned from this is, that such terms are altogether inadmissible in science.

But even if we could suppose a speaker to use these magnificent words as a genuine description of the impression made on himself by certain phenomena, you must remember that he is describing *not* what is known of the objective fact (which, except occasionally from a biographic point of view, is what the listener really wants), but the more or less inadequate subjective impression which it has produced, or which he desires you to think it has produced, on "what he is pleased to call his mind." Whether it be his own mind, or that of some imaginary individual, matters not. To do this, except perhaps when lecturing on psychology, is to be unscientific. True scientific teaching, I cannot too often repeat, requires that the facts and their *necessary* consequences alone should be stated (and illustrated if required) as simply as possible. The impression they are to produce on the mind of the reader, or hearer, is then to be left entirely to himself. No one has any *right* to suppose, much less to take for granted, that his own notions, whether they be "so-called poetic instincts" (to use the lowest term of contempt) or half-comprehended and imperfectly expressed feelings of wonder, admiration, or awe, are either more true to fact or more sound in foundation than those of the least scientific among his readers or his audience. When he does so he resembles a mere leader of a *claque*. "Hiss here, my friends; applaud these! Three cheers more! Three groans! Nine times nine!" And so forth *ad nauseam*. If your minds cannot relish simple food, they are not in that healthy state which is required for the study of science. Healthy mental appetite needs only hunger-sauce. *That* it always has in plenty, and repletion is impossible.

But you must remember that language cannot be simple unless it be definite; though sometimes, from the very nature of the case, it may be very difficult to understand, even when none but the simplest terms are used. Multiple meanings for technical words are totally foreign to the spirit of true science. When an altogether new idea has to be expressed, a new word must be coined for it. None but a blockhead could object to a new word for a new idea. And the habitual use of non-scientific words in the teaching of science betrays ignorance, or (at the very least) wilful indefiniteness.

Do not fancy, however, that you will have very many new words to learn. A month of *Botany* or of *Entomology*, as these are too often taught, will introduce you to a hundredfold as many new and strange terms as you will require in the whole course of natural philosophy; and, among them, to many words of a far more "difficult complexion" than any with which, solely for the sake of definiteness, we find ourselves constrained to deal.

But you will easily reconcile yourselves to the necessity for new terms if you bear in mind that these not only secure to us that definiteness without which science is impossible, but at the same time enable us to get rid of an enormous number of wholly absurd stock-phrases which you find in almost every journal you take up, wherever at least common physical phenomena are referred to. When we are told that a building was "struck by the *electric fluid*" we may have some difficulty in understanding the process; but we cannot be at all surprised to learn that it was immediately thereafter "seized upon by the *devouring element*, which raged unchecked till the whole was reduced to ashes." I have no fault to find with the penny-a-liner who writes such things as these: it is all directly in the way of his business, and he has been trained to it. Perhaps his graphic descriptions may occasionally rise even to poetry. But when I meet with any-thing like this,—and there are but too many works, professedly on natural philosophy, which are full of such things,—I know that I am not dealing with science.

...plaintive wail for definiteness often comes from those ...lecturers who are habitually the most vague. A few ...are shed, appearances are preserved, and they plunge ... greater mistiness of verbosity than before.

...the actual state of the great majority at least of our ...our elementary text-books, I should prefer that you came ...entirely untaught in physical science. You will then have ...unlearn. This is an absolutely incalculable gain. Unlearn... the hardest task that was ever imposed on a student, or ... else. And it is also one of those altogether *avoidable* tasks ... we have allowed them to become necessary, irritate us as ... does a perfectly unprofitable one—such as the prison crank ...mill. And in this lies by far the greatest responsibility of all ... and teachers. Merely to fail in giving instruction is bad ..., but to give false information can be the work only of utter ...nce or of carelessness, amounting, so far as its effects go, almost ...tical wickedness.

...y one of you who has habitually made use of his opportunities ...rvation must have already seen a great deal which it will be ...y to help him to understand. But I should prefer, if possible, ... the entire guidance of him in helping him to understand it. ...should commence by warning him in the most formal manner ... the study of books of an essentially unscientific character. ... means let him read fiction and romance as a relaxation from ... studies; but let the fiction be devoted to its legitimate ... human will and human action; don't let it tamper with the ... of science. From the "Arabian Nights," through "Don ...e," to Scott, the student has an ample field of really profit...ading of this kind; but when he wishes to *study*, let him care...schew the unprofitable, or rather pernicious, species of literary ... which is commonly called "popular science."

... have already said, in this elementary class, you will require ...ttle mathematical knowledge, but such knowledge is in itself ... those wholly good things of which no one can ever have too ... And, moreover, it is one of the few things which it is not very ...y teach badly. A really good student will learn mathematics ... *of* the badness of his teaching. No pompous generalities can ...ver an incorrect demonstration; at least in the eyes of any one ...tent to understand a correct one. Can it be on this account ...ere are so many more aspirants to the teaching of physics than ... of the higher mathematics? If so, it is a very serious matter ... progress of science in this country; as bad, at least, as was ...se in those old days when it was supposed that a man who ...iously failed in everything else must have been designed by ... the vocation of schoolmaster; a truly wonderful application

But even this queer kind of Dominie was not so strange a monstrosity as the modern manikins of *paper science*, who are always thrusting their crude notions on the world; the anatomists who have never dissected, the astronomers who have never used a telescope, or the geologists who have never carried a hammer! The old metaphysical pretenders to science had at least some small excuse for their conduct in the fact that true science was all but unknown in the days when *they* chiefly flourished, and when their *à priori* dogmatism was too generally looked upon as science. But that singular race is now well-nigh extinct, and in their place have come the paper-scientists (the barbarous word suits them exactly)—those who, with a strange mixture of half-apprehended fact and thoroughly appreciated nonsense, pour out continuous floods of information of the most self-contradictory character. Such writers loudly claim the honours of *discovery* for any little chance remark of theirs which research may happen ultimately to substantiate, but keep quietly in the background the mass of unreason in which it was originally enveloped. This species may be compared to midges, perhaps occasionally to musquitos, continually pestering men of science to an extent altogether disproportionate to its own importance in the scale of being. Now and then it buzzes shrilly enough to attract the attention of the great sound-hearted, but unreasoning because non-scientific public, which, when it *does* interfere with scientific matters, can hardly fail to make a mess of them.

Think, for a moment, of the late *vivisection crusade* or of the *anti-vaccinators*. What absolute fiends in human form were not the whole race of really scientific medical men made out to be, at least in the less cautious of these heated denunciations? How many camels are unconsciously swallowed while these gnats are being so carefully strained out, is obvious to all who can take a calm, and therefore a not necessarily unreasonable view of the matter.

But the victims of such people are not in scientific ranks alone. Every man who occupies a prominent position of any kind is considered as a fit subject for their attacks. By private letters and public appeals, gratuitous advice and remonstrance are perpetually intruded upon him. If he succeed in anything, it is of course because these unsought hints were taken: if he fail, it is because they were contemptuously left unheeded!

Enough of this necessary but unpleasant digression. I *know* that it is at least quite as easy to understand the most recondite mathematics as to follow the highest of genuine physical reasoning; and therefore, when I find apparently profound physical speculation associated with incapacity for the higher mathematics, I feel convinced that the profundity cannot be real. One very necessary remark, however, must be made here: not in qualification, but in explanation, of this statement. One of the greatest of physical reasoners, Faraday, professed, as most of you are aware, to know very little of mathematics. But in fact he was merely unacquainted with the technical use of symbols. His modes of regarding physical problems were of the highest order of mathematics. Many of the very best things in the recent great works on *Electricity* by Clerk-Maxwell and Sir William Thomson are (as the authors cheerfully acknowledge) little more than well-executed *translations* of Faraday's conceptions into the conventional language of the higher analysis.

I hope that the time is not far off when no one who is not (at least in the same sense as Faraday) a genuine mathematician, however he may be otherwise qualified, will be looked upon as even a *possible* candidate for a chair of Natural Philosophy in any of our Universities. Of course such a danger would be out of the question if we were to constantly bear in mind the sense in which Newton understood the term Natural Philosophy. There is nothing so well fitted as mathematics "to take the nonsense out of a man," as it is popularly phrased. No doubt a man may be an excellent mathematician, and yet have absolutely no knowledge of physics; but he cannot possibly *know* physics as it is unless he be a mathematician. Much of the most vaunted laboratory work is not nearly of so high an order of skilled labour as the every-day duty of a good telegraph clerk, especially if he be in charge of a syphon-recorder. And many an elaborate memoir which fills half a volume of the transactions of some learned society is essentially as unsightly and inconvenient an object as the mounds of valueless dross which encumber the access to a mine, and destroy what otherwise might have been an expanse of fruitful soil.

There are many ways in which these mounds may grow. The miner may be totally ignorant of geology, and may thus have bored and excavated in a locality which he ought to have known would furnish nothing. Or he may have, by chance or by the advice of knowing friends, hit upon a really good locality. Even *then* there are many modes of failure, two of which are very common. He may fail to recognize the ore when he has got it; and so it goes at once to the refuse-heap, possibly to be worked up again long after by somebody who has a little more mineralogical knowledge—as in the recent case of the mines of Laurium. Here he *may* be useful—at second-hand. Or, if it be fossils or crystals, for instance, for which he is seeking, his procedure may be so rough as to smash them irreparably in the act of mining. This is dog in the manger with a vengeance. But, anyhow, he generally manages to disgust every other digger with the particular locality which he has turned upside down; and thus exercises a *real*, though essentially *negative*, influence on the progress of mining.

The parallel here hinted at is a very apt one, and can be traced much farther. For there are other peculiarities in the modes of working adopted by some miners, which have their exact counterparts in many so-called scientific inquiries; but, for the present, we must leave them unnoticed.

There is but one way of being scientific: but the number of ways of being unscientific is infinite, and the temptations alluring us to them are numerous and strong. Indolence is the most innocent in appearance, but in fact probably the most insidious and dangerous of all. By this I mean of course not mere idleness, but that easily acquired and fatal habit of just stopping short of the final necessary step in each explanation. Faraday long ago pointed this out in his discourse on "Mental Inertia." Many things which are excessively simple when thoroughly understood are by no means easy to acquire; and the student too often contents himself with that *half* learning which, though it costs considerable pains, leaves no permanent impression on the mind, while "one struggle more" would have made the subject his own for ever after.

Science, like all other learning, can be reached only by continued exertion. And, even when we have done our utmost, we always find that the best we have managed to achieve has been merely to avoid straying very far from the one true path.

For, though science is in itself essentially simple, and is ever best expressed in the simplest terms, it is my duty to warn you in the most formal manner that the study of it is beset with difficulties, many of which cannot but constitute real obstacles in the way even of the mere beginner. And this forms another of the fatal objections to the school-teaching of physical science. For there is as yet absolutely no known road to science except through or over these obstacles, and a certain amount of maturity of mind is required to overcome them.

If any one should deny this, you may at once conclude either that his mental powers are of a considerably higher order than those of Newton (who attributed all his success to close and patient study) or, what is intrinsically at least somewhat more probable, that he has not yet traversed the true path himself. But it would be a mere exercise of unprofitable casuistry to inquire which is the less untrustworthy guide, he who affirms that the whole road is easy, or he who is continually pointing out fancied difficulties.

Here, as in everything to which the human mind or hand can be applied, nothing of value is to be gained without effort; and all that your teacher can possibly do for you is to endeavour, so far as in him lies, to make sure that your individual efforts shall be properly directed, and that as little energy as possible shall be wasted by any of you in a necessarily unprofitable direction.

P. G. TAIT.

# CHINA, ENGLAND, AND OPIUM.

THE CHEFOO CONVENTION.

convention agreed upon by Sir Thomas F. Wade on behalf Her Majesty, and the Minister of the Empire of China, 13th September, 1876, is understood to be at the present subject of consideration with Her Majesty's Government and Government of India. It has been the subject of represen- to the Foreign Office, made on behalf of the Shanghai r of Commerce, and of a memorial which has been described ating from "the Archbishop of Canterbury, the Duke of West- Cardinal Manning, Mr. Spurgeon, the two Messrs. Morley, of 'Professors,' Ritualists, and Quakers, Missionaries and , with some waifs and strays of the mercantile community," nation of usually divergent atoms, which must suggest some nd perhaps valid force of attraction to the one common point. gst other subjects, this Convention deals with the question of nd it is chiefly in that regard that I propose to discuss its ns.

Convention itself is not easy reading; and it is impossible to nd its meaning, or what it will do, without going a little way o the history of our diplomatic relations with China.

so-called opium war of 1840-2 was ended by the Treaty of by which Great Britain received six millions sterling for ue of opium seized by the Chinese Government in British nd unmistakeably threw the whole weight of her victorious support of the contraband trade, which was carried on by merchants and Chinese smugglers for the gain of India and of China. The smugglers were not isolated and sneaking als; they constituted organized bands capable of contending unequal terms with the Government authorities. "Every one," says Mr. Consul Robertson, writing under date of 16th May, 1877:—

"Every one who knows (*sic*) Canton previous to the signing of the Treaty of Tientsin, can recall the constant fights on the river between boats manned with from eighty to a hundred men, and pulling as many oars, armed and ready to engage whoever interfered with them, and Chinese Imperial cruisers. Scarcely a day passed without loss of life, and, the penalty for smugglers of opium when caught being death, the execution ground was in constant requisition."*

In 1857 occurred what is generally known as the affair of the Lorcha *Arrow*. I do not care to go into the historical details connected with that affair. It is only necessary for me to say that, as a consequence of it, we entered upon a war, which, in the opinion of many persons, was entirely unjustifiable on our part, and in the course and consequence of which we brought a great deal of pressure to bear upon China.

That war produced the mission to China of Lord Elgin, a man of the very highest character, and the Treaty of Tientsin, which bore date the 26th of June, 1858.

The Treaty of Nankin had provided that British imports having paid the tariff duties should be conveyed into the interior free of all further charges except a transit duty, the amount of which was not to exceed a certain per-centage on tariff value. Under this clause difficulties had arisen; no accurate information was furnished of the amount of such duty, and the British merchants constantly complained that charges were suddenly and arbitrarily imposed by provincial authorities as transit duties upon produce on its way to foreign market, and on imports on their way into the interior, to the detriment of trade. With these difficulties the twenty-eighth Article of the Treaty of Tientsin dealt by providing that within a specified and short time, the authorities appointed to superintend the collection of duties at the respective ports should be obliged, upon application of the Consul, to declare the amount of duties leviable upon produce between the place of production and the port of shipment, and upon imports between the consular port in question and the inland markets named by the Consul; and that a notification of this should be published in English and Chinese for general information.

This provision had no special reference to opium; and, indeed, the word does not, I believe, occur in the Treaty of Tientsin. That treaty was followed by a supplementary agreement concluded at Shanghai on the 8th of November, 1858, to which I must call my reader's attention, as it introduced a considerable modification into this matter.

The seventh rule is in part in these terms:—

"It is agreed that Article 28 of the Treaty of Tientsin shall be interpreted

* Blue Book, China, No. 5, 1877, p. 5.

... of transit dues legally leviable upon merchandise ... by British subjects to be one-half of the tariff duties, ... or duty-free goods liable to a transit duty of 2½ per cent. ... provided in Article 2 of these rules."

... that the rule which I have just quoted was couched ... language, but it was preceded by another clause in the ... Treaty, headed "Regarding certain Commodities here- ...," which was in the following terms:—

"... affecting trade in opium, cash, grain, pulse, sulphur, brim- ..., and spelter, are relaxed under the following conditions:— ... henceforth pay 30 taels per picul import duty. The importer will ... at port. It will be carried into the interior by Chinese only, and ... property; the foreign trader will not be allowed to accompany ... provision of Article 9 of the Treaty of Tientsin, by which British ... authorized to proceed into the interior with passports to trade will ... to it, nor will those of Article 28 of the same treaty by which the ... are regulated; the transit dues on it will be arranged as the Government see fit; nor in future revisions of the tariff is the same ... to be applied to opium as to other goods."

... history of our relations with regard to China and opium, ... is of the highest importance. It was the first occasion on ... Chinese Government legalized the importation of opium: ... shortly on the conclusion of the war raised about the ... *Arrow*. It is true that Lord Elgin postponed the considera- ... subject till the Supplementary Treaty because he could ... it to his sense of right to urge the Chinese Government ... its traditional policy under the kind of pressure which he ... to bear upon it at Tientsin.* But no one can doubt that the ... which operated on the Imperial Government at Tientsin in 1858, was also operating on them at Shanghai on the 8th of ...ber in the same year.

... next place it is to be observed that the clause with regard to ... places it, by the most emphatic language, in a position, both ... and prospective, entirely different from that of any other ...dity. The Treaty of Tientsin provided for a decennial revision ... duties; but this was not to apply to the sale of opium. All the ... with regard to the regulation of transit duties were not to ... opium. The amount of taxation upon opium was to be ...ed as the Chinese Government saw fit—in other words, they ... be the sole judges as to the amount of taxation which ... should bear after it reached their shores. All the provi- ... which the Treaty of Tientsin contained to facilitate British ... into the interior were inoperative as regards opium. Why was ...ne? It was done by Lord Elgin, because he would have said, ... no desire to give the slightest encouragement to the opium

* ... Elgin to Mr. Reed: Blue Book, Correspondence relative to Lord Elgin's Mission ... 397.

trade; I have no desire that British merchants should be enabled to sow opium broadcast over China. The state of things," he would have continued, "is shocking; the British merchants are carrying on, and have for a long series of years been carrying on, a trade which the Chinese Government do not recognize. But that Government have put upon the commodity what is called a 'squeeze;' and by so doing they get out of it a certain amount of revenue in the shape of taxation. Therefore the Chinese Government must be said to be accomplices to a certain extent in the evils which have resulted from the trade. Let us transfer the question from the region of fiction to that of fact; let us put upon paper the real truth; as a Government, let us rather legalize the trade than shut our eyes to it, and let us enable the Chinese Government also to legalize it if they be so minded." That this was in the mind of Lord Elgin when he introduced the provisions into the Supplementary Treaty is sufficiently apparent from his correspondence and utterances, and not least so from a speech which he made in answer to an address presented to him by a body of Shanghai merchants. In the course of his reply to that address, Lord Elgin said:—

"It must be distinctly understood that the modifications introduced into the new Chinese tariff in reference to opium do not in any degree fetter or restrict the discretion of Great Britain as regards the traffic in that article. If the British people and the British Government see fit to do so, they may still make it penal for a British subject to engage in it; and by so doing, although they will not probably in any material degree diminish the consumption of opium in China, they will no doubt do something more or less effectual towards preventing British subjects from being the importers. Short, however, of this extreme measure, of the likelihood of the adoption of which each man may form his own opinion, I am satisfied that the barren announcement by a foreign Government of its assent to the principle that the trade in opium is illegal is productive of nothing but mischief; that it is a delusion and a snare, both to the Chinese and those who have commercial dealings with them. It is notorious that, notwithstanding the clause in the Treaty of Wanghia which pronounces opium to be contraband, and the strong declarations of American statesmen on this head, the American flag has been in some instances used habitually, even by British subjects, to cover the traffic. In my recent discussions with the Chinese Imperial Commissioners, I have merely sought to induce them to bring the trade in opium from the region of fiction into that of fact, and to place within the pale of law, and therefore under its control, an article which is now openly bought, sold, and taxed by them beyond the pale. The effect of the change on the interests of the trade itself will be, I believe, either trifling or null."*

The transit dues which have caused so much trouble in our trade with China are levies in the nature of octrois, leviable at certain fixed points or barriers. The provincial Governments have no right to add to the levies or increase the places of collection without the authority of the Imperial Government. But the central authority in China is weak, the provincial Governments often strong in comparison; [illegible]

* Correspondence relative to Lord Elgin's Mission 1857-9, p. [illegible].

[illegible] in war, a slight necessity has furnished a reason [illegible] increasing these dues. They have been levied with [illegible] of amount in different places and times. Moreover [illegible] Government have kept scant faith with regard to these [illegible] information promised to the British authorities, so that [illegible] without doubt been harassing to the souls of our mer[illegible] in the sides of those who think that the great [illegible] nation is to push its grey shirtings and its opium.

[illegible] distressing still has been the *li-kin*, which was either [illegible] or was not an impost of a serious character at the time [illegible] Treaty of Tientsin. About 1860 it first attracted notice. It [illegible] properly an import duty, a transit duty, or an excise duty, but [illegible] something in the nature of a benevolence in the old English sense [illegible]. It was first imposed heavily with a view to the pay[illegible] the indemnity to England after the *Arrow* war, and then to [illegible] other extraordinary expenses.

[illegible] a long series of years the Chinese Government had to grapple [illegible] various troubles. There was the great Taeping rebellion, and [illegible] also rebellions simultaneously in various provinces of the Chinese Empire, which caused a considerable drain upon the Imperial finances, as well as lessened the returns from the provinces in which the rebellions occurred. The *li-kin* tax therefore became necessary for the maintenance of Chinese officials. The imposition or the increase of this tax naturally attracted notice and invited remonstrance, and the serious question arose as to whether its imposition came within the stipulations referring to the transit dues. That is a question on which much might be said on both sides. Sir Thomas Wade thought that it did not come within these stipulations. The British merchants in China contended that it did. I have already mentioned that in the Treaty of Tientsin provision was made for a decennial revision of the tariff. In 1869 the time arrived for this revision of the tariff. Sir Rutherford Alcock arranged for such revision, and in so doing dealt with this question of *li-kin*. To put it very shortly, it was agreed that certain commodities, which included cottons, linens, woollens, and other textile fabrics, should pay transit dues simultaneously with the import dues, and China agreed that when these commodities were imported by British merchants they should be exempted from all further taxes and charges whatsoever. The Convention further provided that opium should pay an import duty at an increased rate. This Convention excited the most lively apprehensions on the part of the merchants in China and of the Indian Government, and in the end, on the representations of the mercantile bodies in China and of England, Lord Granville, the then Foreign Secretary, determined, though with great regret, to refuse the ratification of that Convention, and it thus, in consequence, fell through.

It was during the course of these negotiations that the representations were made by the Chinese Government to Sir Rutherford Alcock with regard to the whole subject of this opium traffic, to which I have referred in my previous papers, and which I deeply feel ought to have had, and ought still to have, great influence with Her Majesty's Government.*

This abrupt failure of Sir Rutherford Alcock's convention left the *li-kin* question unsolved then. Over and above the question of the right of the Chinese Government to levy this *li-kin*, arose a further question as to the places where it could be levied. Could it be levied in the concessions occupied by the foreign merchants? Could it be levied at the ports which by treaty were opened to our commerce? What were the limits of these ports?

Meanwhile, other questions arose or remained still pressing for settlement. There was the old question of the etiquette which, in some form or other, has been a difficulty from the very first time when we barbarians forced ourselves upon the Chinese Empire down to the present hour. There was the new question which arose from that most lamentable event, the murder of a fine young Englishman, Mr. Margary, in Yunnan.

With all these questions the Convention of Chefoo deals.

The terms on which the Yunnan affair was concluded, included a pecuniary indemnity to the men killed at Yunnan, and the presentation of a letter of apology to Her Majesty's Government by a mission to be despatched on purpose. Every one knows that this condition has been fulfilled, and that the Chinese Embassy is located in Portland Place.

The provisions with regard to official intercourse are not of general interest, so I will not detain the reader with any observations upon them.

The third section of the Convention deals with trade. It opens in these terms:—

"With reference to the area within which, according to the treaties in force, *li-kin* ought not to be collected on foreign goods at the open ports, Sir Thomas Wade agrees to move his Government to allow the ground rented by foreigners (the so-called Concessions) at the different ports to be regarded as the area of exemption from *li-kin;* and the Government of China will thereupon allow I-ch'ang in the province of Hu Pei, Wu-hu in An-Hui, Wên-Chôw in Che-Kiang, and Pei-hai (Pak-hoi) in Kwang-Tung to be added to the number of ports open to trade, and to become Consular stations."

These words are somewhat singular no doubt. They express, not a stipulation of the treaty, but an agreement by the Ambassador to move his Government to a particular effect; and if this section be accepted, the principal questions which have hitherto been agitated

* See CONTEMPORARY REVIEW for February, 1876, p. 453.

... will be dealt with, not by any explicit declaration, but ... the suggestion of Sir Thomas Wade implies, first, that ... be levied, and secondly, that there are areas ... exemption from it.

... article provides for the ascertainment by arrangement ... foreign settlement area in all ports opened to trade at which no ... area has been previously defined.

... article deals with opium, and is in these words:—

> "... Sir Thomas Wade will move his Government to sanction an ... different from that affecting other imports. British merchants, ... is brought into port, will be obliged to have it taken cognizance of ... and deposited in bond, either in a warehouse or a receiving ... such time as there is a sale for it. The importer will then pay the ... upon it, and the purchasers the *li-kin*; in order to the prevention of ... of the duty, the amount of *li-kin* to be collected will be decided by ... provincial Governments according to the circumstances of each."

...t Her Majesty's Government to adopt and act upon the sug-..., which Sir Thomas Wade has, of course, made to them in ... of this pledge?

... to answer this, an earlier question must be asked—What is ... meaning of this stipulation? that is, what will it do? what ... will it effect?

...dy the Chinese Government have the right under the Supple-...y Convention of November, 1858, to place any duty they choose ...pium. But their power to lay very heavy charges upon it is in ... reality limited by the danger of smuggling between the ... import and the place of taxation. The higher the tax the ... is of course the temptation to smuggling; and the limit which ...poses on the Government is, I believe, considerable: for China ...ntry where the central authority is far from strong, and where ...ling is known as a science and a profession. But if the ... import and the place of taxation be one and the same, the ...lity of smuggling is extinguished, and the practical power of ...n proportionately increased: and this is what the clause in ... does.

...his clause be agreed to," write the Shanghai General Chamber to their ... Committee, under date of the 15th June, 1877, "the Chinese Govern-...ill have it in their power by the imposition of heavy duties to extin-...e India trade, and it is for Her Majesty's Government to decide whether ...ll permit the Tientsin Treaty to be modified in order to promote such a ...

...hose who, like myself, earnestly long to see such a result, the ... of Sir Thomas Wade's recommendation will seem highly .... The Chinese Government may, no doubt, use the power ... will be conferred on them in very different ways. They may ... use it for little more than to raise a slightly increased income;

or they may use it as a means for depressing the import of opium, in order to encourage its growth in China; and, lastly, they may use it for the sake of gradually discouraging alike the import and the growth of opium. The portions of Sir Thomas Wade's despatch bearing on this section of the treaty have not been published, and I have failed to trace anything like trustworthy information as to the present views on this question of the Chinese Government. I know no sufficient reason, however, for supposing that they are different from what they were in 1869 and 1870, or that the strong opinion expressed by Sir Rutherford Alcock as to the sincerity and reality of their desire and power to check its consumption is not as true now as it was a few years ago.* But be this as it may, and be the use of the power by the Chinese Government what it may, the adoption of Sir Thomas Wade's motion would lessen our complicity in the trade, and for that reason I answer that Her Majesty's Government ought to second and act upon it.

There are yet other and more detailed considerations which lead me to the same conclusion.

The proposed arrangement follows the lines of Lord Elgin's policy in the Convention of November, 1858. By that he left the amount of taxation to the absolute discretion of the Chinese Government: by this we should only corroborate that power and give effect to that discretion. And to me it does seem undignified and little to our credit that we should seek to avail ourselves of the aid of the smugglers as a check on China's power to do that which Lord Elgin emphatically maintained that China ought to have the liberty and the power to do.

I concede that the British Government are under no legal obligation to accede to the suggestions which their Minister undertook to make to them. The very fact that all the Convention contains as regards the *li-kin* is made to rest in a promise of a suggestion, and not in an operative stipulation, shows of itself that the British Government were to be at liberty to accede or not to the motions of their Minister; and the sixth paragraph of the section on trade makes this yet more clear; for it provides that whilst the stipulations as to the new ports, and certain others as to new places of landing and shipment, should have effect given to them within six months after receipt of an imperial decree approving of a memorial with regard to the Yunnan affair,

"the date for giving effect to the stipulations affecting exemption of imports from *li-kin* taxation within the foreign settlements, and the collection of *li-kin* upon opium by the Customs Inspectorate at the same time as the tariff duty upon it, would be fixed as soon as the British Government had arrived at an understanding on the subject with other foreign Governments."

It is within the power, then, of Her Majesty's Government to repel Sir Thomas Wade's motions to them. But would it be honourable or

* See CONTEMPORARY REVIEW for February, 1876, p. 455.

politic to do so? This is the second effort to settle this question of *li-kin*—the second convention upon the point that has been concluded. To the first the Government, with undisguised regret, refused their ratification, at the instance of the mercantile bodies. Is this second convention to meet with a like fate? Is the work of Sir Thomas Wade to fare no better than that of Sir Rutherford Alcock? The Chinese Government will soon think it a waste of time to bargain with our envoys.

The irritation left by the rejection of that convention has not yet died out in the minds of Chinese statesmen, and Sir Thomas Wade found it one of the antagonistic influences against which he had to contend.* Sir Charles Dilke has called attention to the extent to which our line of conduct has been lessening our influence in China, and throwing her Government into the arms of Russia. Will not a refusal to act on the Chefoo Convention accelerate this tendency?

Furthermore, the indemnity has been paid: the apology has been presented at St. James's by the special envoy, and the new treaty ports have been opened. Is it honourable and expedient, though lawful, to disappoint the Chinese Government of those concessions to them on which they might reasonably have counted in the compromise which finds its expression in the Chefoo Convention? Sir Thomas Wade drove them into that convention by threats of war—of "the extremest measure of coercion;"† and shall we refuse to abide by the recommendations which even then our Minister promised to make?

No doubt the co-operation, or at least the consent, of the other Treaty Powers is contemplated as preceding the operation of the clauses as to *li-kin* and opium. But as regards the latter, the British Government is practically the only foreign Power that has any serious interest; and if that Government should show a real willingness to give effect to this provision as to opium, there can, I believe, be little difficulty in obtaining the assent of the other Powers.

EDWARD FRY.

* Blue Book, China, No. 3, 1877, p. 119. † Ibid. p. 133.

# GOVERNMENT EDUCATION:

## THIRTY YEARS PAST, AND THIRTY YEARS TO COME.

THE present system of primary education for this country, so far as it is of Government creation, is a makeshift. It cannot last. Nevertheless, it does not follow that the foundations of our national education are artificial, or will have to be relaid; still less that our present system, whatever be its imperfections, is to be superseded by one that is wholly artificial, founded and built up from basement to pinnacle by State architects and at the public expense. There is national life and natural law at the bottom of the existing system; but the system has been extended and developed by means at variance alike with the natural laws of growth and progress, and with the standing principles of political economy.

And yet the Government system thus far may be well defended. It is abnormal, but it was contrived to meet an abnormal condition of things. It is an empirical combination of strong stimulants intended to effect a salutary revolution in what had been a condition of national torpidity and incompetence. But then it is of the highest necessity that statesmen and political thinkers should recognize that the system, so far as it is the creation of the State, is such as I have described; that it is a congeries of makeshifts, having within it—except so far as the School Board element is concerned, and that element is only partial, is working at present inequitably, and ought never to be the paramount factor in national education—no roots of life, no spring or power of spontaneity, no laws of development, no constituent forces; that its only value consists in its efficiency as a transitional arrangement, as a combination of means and stimulants, so contrived and arranged as to elicit, to revive, to fashion and train into proper forms and functions, to develop into self-sustaining and progressive vigour and growth, that national vitality for educational purposes which aulty government and defective legislation, had maintained d so feeble an existence and had assumed forms so low and The protective machinery of the United States in the t of trade and manufactures is nature and simplicity, is and legitimate, in comparison with the Governmental education in England. There would be as little unreason plating the present prohibitory system of the United States rmanent mandate of science and law of international relatrade and commerce in America, as in regarding the Privy de,—or any conceivable Government code—as a permanent ate *régime* for the education of the English people.

ment was obliged to interfere with our national education. rence came not too early but rather too late. It has been for more than thirty years—a series of experiments in the proving and extending education in the country. These its have not always proceeded on the same principles. Able smanlike a man as was Sir James Kay-Shuttleworth, it is cult, if it be not impossible, to discover from his writings hat result in the way of educational system, or permanent rovision, or natural growth and laws, he desired to work, as ional reformer. I, at least, have not been able to discover theory was, although so able a man may well have had a d an ultimate end underlying his plans and proposals, noting that these assumed a merely practical and empirical pedients intended to meet the present and pressing necessication in England, making the best, at the time, of existing As to some points, indeed, Sir James held very distinctly ple. The Normal College, the pupil teacher system, the ion, as the main basis of any educational provision for the of existing voluntary energies and agencies, these were involved in all his work, and to which he adhered to the st of these principles were already embodied in the leading al systems of education; in more than one all were embodied. s, moreover, took up a position contrary to free education, being in accord with the general feeling and practice in Europe; democratic Switzerland, primitive Norway, where m of village-communism still prevails, and France in part, in the muncipalities in which communistic principles have old, while the populations are large and include a great a of the very poor, being, so far as I know, the chief, if not xceptions to this rule. But it does not appear that Sir James ed in his own mind an ideal of the permanent future of opular education. It cannot be supposed that he expected his own system to endure; indeed in its own nature it was ly open to yearly revision, and was sure to undergo, in virtue y success, so far as it should prove successful, continual modification. There is sufficient evidence that, from an early period, if not from the first, he foresaw the probability of a supplementary municipal system, resembling in principle that of the present School Board organization, being brought into co-operation with State-aided voluntary agencies. He himself took part in the endeavour to bring into operation the Manchester and Salford scheme for uniting voluntary agency and municipal resources in the establishment and maintenance of schools; and he hailed Mr. Forster's Act as carrying out in the main his own ideas. But yet I find no trace of his having drawn out a plan of future national education for England, such as might work and be developed by properly national forces, such as should be not a mere artificial and fluctuating arrangement, but a living growth, unfolding by virtue of its own internal energies, forming a constituent and closely interwoven part of the whole educational life and organization of the country; not a system subject to regulation by the uncertain, the sometimes capricious, the rigid and uniformly enforced prescriptions of a central Board ruling the whole country from Whitehall, but actuated, extending, shaping and adapting itself, in vital harmony at once with national conditions and needs, and with local conditions, according to the laws of a real spontaneous life, and in agreement with the principles of political economy and science. It may well have been that Sir James had his private speculations as to the form which English popular education might be destined to assume after more than one generation should have passed away. But he may reasonably have thought that to encumber his practical proposals with any exposition of such views in relation to a comparatively distant future, would have only served to involve him in controversies, and would have hindered the immediate ends which, in his capacity especially of Secretary for Education, it was his proper duty to promote.

It was, however, this want of a definite and permanent principle in the original work of Sir James Kay-Shuttleworth, of some underlying law of political economy which might limit and guide the working of his plans and indicate the issue towards which they were to work, that laid the Minutes of 1846-47 open to such vigorous and reactionary handling as that of Mr. Lowe in 1861. Mr. Lowe, in his revolutionary Revised Code, as originally brought into Parliament, proceeded on very clear and definite principles of political economy, principles too which, though his application of them was violent and untimely, must still be recognized as in themselves theoretically right, as principles which must contribute to define the end towards which our existing educational administration must be led to work, if we are to attain to any stable and satisfactory settlement on this question of education.

Mr. Lowe is a follower of Adam Smith; in respect of education, no less than other things, he holds by the principles of his master. He found a system, not professedly transitional, not so arranged as visibly

...and towards the bringing about ... educational settlement—of an order of ... from itself than from that which had preceded ... his eye, seemed likely to become permanent, ... only to something more developed in the ... system offending at every point against ... principles of economical science. It was ... monopolist system applied to education of a ... Government at that time paid, out of the taxation ... and direct bounties to certificated teachers of ... schools, and to no other class of teachers; the ... paid large grants out of the public taxation to the ... schools, and to no other class of school managers. ... contrary to Adam Smith, and, as he conceived, to ... of political economy. He held, as I understand his ... ments, that whatever steps might properly be taken to ... persons from undertaking to teach, or to provide ... school inspection, it was unwarrantable for the State ... description of patented teachers into its pay, or to ... classes of schools intended for the promiscuous popu- ... He held, besides, that it was a gross and perilous ... sound principles for the State to provide, out of the ... for the education of those children whose parents ... to pay for such education themselves. To pay a ... of such education was, to his view, as really a viola- ... and a concession to communism, as to pay the whole. ... that the State was paying a large and a growing per- ... the cost of such education, and that the education provided ... more and more ambitious and costly. To him this ... of things seemed fraught with peril, and violently opposed ... tatesmanship. He was terrified at the vision of a host, a ... reasing host, of vested interests growing up under such a ... at the thought of precedents being established and multi- ... ally, which tended towards Continental communism and ... retrogression in national economy and administration. ... the system of inspection and grants in aid which Mr. ... in operation was, beyond question, one of concurrent ... the endowment directly and expressly of religious school ... ons; their endowment not by the bounty of voluntary bene- ... ing or dead, but out of the general taxation of the country. ... endowment exists no longer. It has now been ... the existing system of Government supervision and ... 1861 it was an undisguised factor in the Government ... it exists no longer, that result is, beyond question, owing ... the initiative which Mr. Lowe took in opposition to it.

... Mr. Lowe's views, it was wrong for a nation to provide

education for children except on the principle on which it provides food for the destitute. As a provision for those who otherwise must, through poverty, be left untaught, education may, and indeed must, be furnished by a wise State and a true statesmanship; even as food must be provided for those who else would starve. But it should only be provided for such; and, as the food provided for the pauper ought to be no more and no other than that which is strictly necessary and very plain, so the education provided by the State for those unable otherwise to get education ought to be limited to the plainest and the strictly necessary rudiments, such as might prepare the boy or girl for a life of honest hard work. Such being Mr. Lowe's principles, he conceived the plan of cutting down Sir James Kay-Shuttleworth's ambitiously benevolent system into one approaching as near as possible to a workhouse provision of pauper education.

At the same time, in order to do away with the principle of concurrent endowment, Mr. Lowe adopted an idea, first, I believe, suggested by Mr. Miall, in his capacity of Education Sub-Commissioner—the idea of payment according to secular results in teaching.

The results to be paid for were to be the merest rudiments of knowledge—reading, writing, and arithmetic; strictly "secular" results these; and, according to Mr. Lowe's original Bill, all other payments except for such results were to be done away.*

Payment as poor relief; payment according to the rigidly-ascertained results of secular instruction; these were the principles of the "Revised Code" as originally introduced into the House of Commons in 1861. Educationally regarded, the principle of paying according to certain results shown in a day's examination, and appraised on mechanical and yet variable principles by the personal judgment of one or more among a large corps of visiting inspectors, of all manner of tempers and attainments—many of whom, too, as a matter of fact, have had little or no real training for their work—is as indefensible a specimen of empirical legislation as can well be imagined. It is certain that no school can ever be thoroughly well taught if it is organized and conducted with a paramount regard to the production of such results as are expected to pay in an examination such as I have described. Nevertheless the convenience of the principle, in extricating the system of Government aid from any implication with the religious character of the schools inspected and aided, has led to its permanent incorporation in our educational legislation.

The other principle was very cleverly and very ruthlessly worked into Mr. Lowe's Revised Code, the principle of providing and paying for education only as poor relief. In quantity the instruction given was to be a minimum, and in quality it was to be of the plainest and most elementary description—rigidly restricted to what was deemed

* Compare, as to the whole of Mr. Lowe's scheme, Adam Smith's Wealth of Nations, book v. part 3, article 2.

[illegible] people. [illegible], was any grant for [illegible] of any child who had either reached the [illegible] of young as "infant" to undergo a [illegible] inspector in reading, writing, and arith- [illegible] for poor [illegible] children was regarded [illegible] of this proposed Code as a superfluity, while [illegible] held that children receiving a pauper dole [illegible] be away from school and to be at labour. In [illegible] none but labouring men were to be allowed [illegible] to the aided and inspected schools.

[illegible] describe Mr. Lowe's original Revised Code. It [illegible] that all the details were consistent with the general [illegible] which I have indicated. There can be no doubt [illegible] to make the Government schools such that [illegible] intelligent artisans, much more all classes of shop- [illegible] to send their children to them. As the work- [illegible] to repel all self-respecting able-bodied labourers, so [illegible] intended to repel the self-respecting and competent [illegible] well-to-do artisans, from using them. Hence every was hard, rigid, mechanical, repulsive. It is not, how- enied, as I have said, that the scheme was one which, ortunately framed and applied, proceeded on a principle portance, and one which cannot be ignored in the stitutions of our country. It is time now, I venture to e should consider how the just principle which Mr. Lowe to enforce prematurely may be gradually reinstated in nal economy of England, in such a manner as not to con- [illegible] principles of education, not to inflict any injury ls, but on the contrary to promote the highest and best [illegible] for all classes of the people.

[illegible] England was in an abnormal condition requiring [illegible]. The Government system of subsidies and direct interference was a remedial regimen intended to bring to a condition of competent educational sensibility and Mr. Lowe's Revised Code would have broken down that would have destroyed the reviving educational conscious- of the nation. Happily its worst features were removed odified, although much power for mischief was left in it, [illegible] done by it, even in the modified form in which it [illegible] imposed upon the country. It has been one chief aim [illegible] administration during the last dozen years, and [illegible] been a chief object contemplated both in Mr. Forster's [illegible] in Lord Sandon's recent measure, to undo the [illegible] Revised Code; to develop education in the most [illegible] so far as the principle, still retained, of direct pay- [illegible] secular results will allow, to promote the highest objects and motives in education. It may be hoped that the effect on the heretofore defective and backward education of the country of this generous remedial regimen—this regimen of fine stimulants and liberal diet—may have been to bring at least within the limit of contemplation the time when the nation may be trusted mainly to provide for its own education; educational energies and organs having been developed, which are adequate to that work without the need of perpetual stimulation and regulation by a Government Department.

It was the ignorance and neglect of former ages, joined to the unnatural condition—civilly, socially, and therefore also morally—of vast masses of our countrymen, which compelled the State to interfere on behalf of the public education of the lower orders of the people. The accumulated evils of the whole past history of this country,—and if there had been a growth and consolidation of good, there had also been a woeful accumulation of evil,—the inheritance of moral and intellectual degradation among certain classes, created and stored up through the centuries by the ravages of conquest, by civil strife and foreign wars, by class domination and social injustice,—all these things had contributed to compact together an appalling mass of helplessness and disorganization, presenting every variety of ignorance, demoralization, and misery, and distributed over the country, here in slower and more stubborn, there in more virulent and menacing forms. This was the legacy of the past to the England of forty years ago; this was the spectacle which offered itself to the view of the awakening Christian consciousness of the country, and to the political reflection of its alarmed rulers, at that troubled and agitated time. It might well arouse and alarm. It was a case of national destitution, which as clearly called for Government interference as the Indian famine of the past year. The Churches of the land, indeed, had long recognized—however inadequately—the gravity of the case; they had been beforehand with the Legislature, by a whole generation; they had rendered much charitable help, and had used the best remedial skill and means within their power. But the need was one which demanded direct and formal national interposition; and accordingly, at length, the Legislature shook off its apathy and began earnestly to study the case. The result has been as I have described it, an extensive and unsparing application of stimulants, a somewhat generous use of restoratives, and, of late, the upraising of a whole army of remedial Boards and agencies. But the appliances called into existence by a state of extreme constitutional derangement and feebleness are not to constitute the ordinary requirements and prescriptions of life and growth; nor ought medicine to be enforced by law as ordinary food.

All protection in matters of trade, handicraft, or profession must, as we are all agreed in this country, savour more or less of injustice. Nevertheless in the early stages of almost all industries known in the history of our country, and of every country, protection in one form [illegible] necessary. Probably it was in not a few cases [illegible] to protect the young tree in the park by a [illegible] exotic plant, at least in its earlier growth, under [illegible] of protection passed away—or ought to have [illegible] the craft or industry had taken fully and widely [illegible] well established. A continuance of protection [illegible] invention and have stunted the growth of the [illegible] venture to think it must be with our national growth [illegible] in his "Political Economy," Mr. Mill has shown under [illegible] to what extent a State might, in case of necessity, [illegible] the task of organizing a system of education for its [illegible]. But in his treatise on "Liberty," he gives his [illegible] definitive views as to the proper relations between [illegible] the nation in the matter of education in the follow- [illegible] are the more remarkable because already, at the [illegible] this book, he was beginning to verge at certain [illegible] a more communistic view of social and political science [illegible] in earlier life.

[illegible] would make up its mind," he says, "to require for every [illegible], it might save itself the trouble of providing one. It [illegible] to obtain the education where and how they pleased, [illegible] helping to pay the school fees of the poorer classes of [illegible] the entire school expenses of those who have no one [illegible] them. The objections which are urged with reason against [illegible] do not apply to the enforcement of education by the State, but [illegible] upon itself to direct that education, which is a totally [illegible]

[illegible] established and controlled by the State should only exist, if [illegible] one among many competing experiments, carried on for the [illegible] and stimulus to keep the others up to a certain standard of [illegible], indeed, when society in general is in so backward a state [illegible], or would not, provide for itself any proper institutions of edu- [illegible] Government undertook the task; then, indeed, the Government [illegible] of two great evils, take upon itself the business of schools and [illegible] may that of joint-stock companies, when private enterprise in [illegible] undertaking great works of industry does not exist in the [illegible] general, if the country contains a sufficient number of persons [illegible] provide education under Government auspices, the same persons [illegible] and willing to give an equally good education on the voluntary [illegible] the assurance of remuneration afforded by a law rendering educa- [illegible], combined with State aid to those unable to defray the expense."

[illegible] present system of Government connection with education is [illegible] main respects. It violates the principle that those who [illegible] the education of their children ought to pay for it; and it [illegible] principles of free trade. The institution of School Boards [illegible] assignable conditions, need not at all interfere with [illegible] teaching; nor is it necessary that the maintenance of [illegible] should interfere with the principle of educational self- [illegible] dependence; but the whole State-aided system, as it [illegible] in both respects as I have stated. I venture to think that the national education of the future, whilst growing out of all that now is, is capable of being gradually transformed into a system which is in harmony with the principles of liberty and political economy, as to both the points I have mentioned. When once the necessity of education has come to be acknowledged and felt by all classes of the nation, when the recognized standard of common education has come to include whatever is necessary for a citizen, in the class to which he belongs, and in the exercise of the rights and duties which belong to him, both in the family and as a member of the general community, when the possession of a competent education has become a matter of necessity enforced by the conditions of employment and even by the law of the land, education may be left to be supplied according to the operation of natural laws. This I take to be implied in the extract I have given from Mr. Mill. In a nation under such conditions there will be a true and intelligent demand for effective and adequate education, class by class, throughout the nation. The laws of free trade, in a certain sense, would hold good for education as for other things, among a people under such conditions. Demand would govern supply; supply would answer to demand. There would no longer be any need of perpetual codes, old and revised, and new and modified, eternally shifting and changing, to guide and shape the development of national education, in methods and standards, in supply and demand, in cost and price. This artificial system would then be out of time and place.

Forty years ago the condition of things was in all respects in contrast to that ideal which I have now slightly sketched, and towards which the condition of our own country is now—I venture to think—visibly approaching. At that time the demand for anything truly to be called education had to be created. The people had almost to be bribed, in the first instance, to send their children to school. Popular education rested on an eleemosynary basis; at that time it could not be otherwise. Generations of children had need to be educated by special influence and effort, before the people at large could come to understand and value education truly. Not only so, but the educational provision at that time—the supply of schools and teachers—was, for the most part, of very inferior quality; and notwithstanding the labours of Bell and Lancaster, and, above all, of that truly original and powerful master of educational principles, David Stow of Glasgow, was apparently incapable, if left to itself, or to any ordinary law of supply and demand, of developing, within any assignable period, into any growth commensurate with the needs of the country. It was under such circumstances that the Government was compelled to interpose. The eleemosynary supply, indeed, which the necessity of the case had already called forth, though inadequate, was large, the parents generally paying very low fees, but sometimes receiving a free education, such as it was, for their children. Nor, bad as things might be, could it be doubted that this supply had prevented the case from being infinitely worse, had prevented the lower strata of society from sinking more and more deeply into ignorance and destitution. Upon this basis, accordingly, Government was obliged to build; correcting, extending, completing, as best it could. It is therefore no fault of the Government if the present system of education is still largely eleemosynary. It is, on the other hand, matter for thankfulness that, not only are the entire material and means of education in the country unspeakably improved, but the people generally have learnt to pay a much higher price for the education of their children, and to pay it far more intelligently and cheerfully, than they did forty years ago. But the question which presses is, whether the Government and the Legislature should not now and henceforth definitely hold in view the object of redeeming the education of the country from its eleemosynary character, and bringing it into a condition of independence, self-support, and true nationality.

Two things are necessary in order to secure this result. One is that the people should be willing and able to pay the cost of a sound education for their children; the other, that national education should be so organized on a natural basis, and by means of properly graded and connected associations and agencies, that all the processes and operations necessary to the training of teachers and the testing of attainments should be provided for apart from the authority and prescriptions of a Government bureau.

There can be no doubt, speaking generally, that our artisan population could easily afford to pay the full cost of their children's education at a good public elementary school. It would be twice what they pay now; it need not be more, as I shall try to show; but it would still be very cheap, hardly more for a week's schooling for each child than the price of two quarts of beer, or of two ounces of tobacco; and much less than small tradespeople, with narrower means than the skilled artisan, have been accustomed to pay for education of a far inferior quality. The case would be harder for our village population; but the education at the good village school, under a trained mistress —and mistresses are, as a rule, the fittest and best teachers for village schools—would be much cheaper than at the school to which the skilled artisan sends his children. Taking into account the steady rise in labourers' wages which has set in, it would not be more in proportion than many day labourers paid for an inferior education not a great many years ago. To this point, however, I will recur by-and-by. I will only here add, on the subject, that, of course, the result I am speaking of could only be attained by degrees. The amount of public aid to schools, from whatever sources, being diminished gradually, the fees would be proportionately increased, until in the end the grant would be done away, and the entire cost paid by the parent, except in cases of proved and pressing poverty.

Leaving, however, for the present, the question of cost, let me ask attention to the other point, viz., the possibility of escaping from the present system of bureaucratic centralization, by means of a natural growth and organization of means and agencies for the training of teachers, and for testing and certifying attainments and results, both as regards the teachers and the taught.

It is encouraging to observe, then, that from natural sources of instruction and authority, from the vital activities of the old educational institutions of the country, influences have emanated and organizations have been established during the last twenty years, which begin to offer a basis on which Government might safely and constitutionally rest in its educational functions; and Government will be fulfilling one of its highest purposes by bringing these influences and organizations into relations of co-operation and unity with each other. The two ancient Universities of England, having first, for a number of years, acted separately in the way of testing and stimulating middle-class education, have now united their counsels and good offices in order to promote and to organize our first-grade education, bringing the highest schools in the country into correlation with themselves as universities, and into some sort of co-ordination with each other. It is evident that this affords only an indication of much larger and more highly organized schemes and relations which must before long grow into form and efficiency. The Universities should act conjointly not only as respects first-grade schools, but also as respects intermediate schools of secondary instruction, and middle-class schools. They should also enter into distinct co-operation with that deserving body, the College of Preceptors, which, as to many matters connected with educational organization and progress, has been very far in advance of public opinion, and, notwithstanding general apathy and heavy discouragements, has been steadily working for many years in the right direction. The Universities would thus take their natural place at the head of the educational organization of the country. On this subject the Social Science Congress has during several years past been moving; and by degrees a feeling is growing up among many earnest and leading thinkers on the subject of education, that in this direction lies our escape from some of our present difficulties, and one of the main lines of future progress.

But to complete the representation of the national education of this country, there remains to be mentioned one body besides, the National Union of Elementary Teachers. This union represents undoubtedly by far the most thoroughly trained, as well as the most numerous, body of teachers to be found in this country, nor can it be pretended that it is, in any degree, less important than either of the other branches of the profession. There is, I believe, no disposition on the part of the Universities or any other branch of the profession to ignore this important organization. In all general educational

...ferences, the elementary branch ought to be fully ... as yet the mere fact that elementary teachers act ... direction, and are a certificated and privileged ... broad separation between them and the rest of the ... The entire profession, in all its branches, will never be ... true and full harmony, until this separation is in some ... The gradual growth of public elementary schools ...dependence will be one of the conditions tending to bring ... The supply of opportunities by which middle-class teachers ...as fully trained for their profession as elementary teachers ...; and there is an important movement now going ...towards that end. The general opening of middle-class ...nd of endowed schools, working under revised and enlightened ..., to trained public elementary teachers, will be another step in ... direction. The formation of a general chartered educational ...—which should take cognizance of the whole field of national ...n in every grade, and on which, besides the Universities, as ...est link in the chain of organization, and besides the inter-...grades of schools, of which I have already spoken, the public ...ry schools of the country should be adequately represented ...be a most important step towards the establishment of a ...harmony and system of educational machinery in this country, ...might in the noblest and most comprehensive sense be regarded ...ial.

...a general chartered council of education as I have now spoken ...l constitute a natural national growth and organ, a central ...d instrument of living unity and co-operation, which, so far ...atters connected with the theory and practice of education ...erned, in every grade, and whether in schools or in colleges, ...ell at some future period supersede the present Educational ...ee of Privy Council. Such a body would have an indefeasible ...uthority; it would combine learning, experience, and science ... kind and branch of educational work; its operations would ...occult, but constitutional and intelligible; its arrangements ...e open to inspection and revision; it would, in virtue of its ...tative character, be kept continually in sympathy with the ...lucational estate of the realm.

...ey to such a reconstruction as I am endeavouring to describe ...s I have intimated, to be found in our Universities. Let me ...ed to recur to this point in order to emphasize and develop ...ght. The Universities are the natural fountain-head of educa-...fluence for the nation. There are at present two chief sources ...influence in this country—one the Universities, the other ...ent organization and stimulus in connection with the public ...ry school system. The former is a natural source of influence ...nization, the latter is factitious. What is to be desired for this country is that the former should increase, the latter decrease, or at least be greatly modified. The greatest achievement of Government legislation and administration in this matter would be for the Government to legislate and administer itself out of the field, in such wise that its place should be better supplied by the up-growth of natural life and organization. Some would have the Government organization and direction extended to secondary schools. I venture to think that that would be a serious evil. Government has done immense good by its action during the last thirty years; nevertheless it would have been vastly better if no such action had been needed. Its necessity is its only justification. We want, in this matter of national education, more of life and life's free growth, and less of State prescription; more of natural development, and less of centralized departmental rule and routine. We want a spontaneous, a self-sustaining, a self-adjusting system. We want a natural system, including alike all grades of education, from the primary schools to the Universities, and freely acting and interacting throughout.

Such a system would not be exclusive of School Boards or of Board Schools. Such Boards, on the contrary, would be necessary in order to work out into fact the idea of pervasive and intelligent educational life, of natural development, and of effective decentralization. Not only municipal boards, but in some form or other parochial or quasi-parochial boards, and, quite as emphatically, county boards, or something equivalent, would be needed. Such boards are, or ought to be, part of the natural civic life, part of the national life, of England. The county board, or something equivalent to it, is indeed the "missing link" of our national organization for all sorts of purposes, including that of education. Such boards ought, as to certain points, to exercise a responsible supervision over schools of all classes. Such boards would form a chief part of the network throughout which, from the Universities and the National Council of Education as a centre, would spread and ramify the educational life of the country. And such boards would have all possible right to establish schools, on the one condition that they entered into a fair competition with other schools, and were organized on the principle of self-support. They should be established and maintained on the principle so happily stated by Mr. Mill, "as one among many competing experiments, carried on for the purpose of example and stimulus to keep the others up to a certain standard of excellence."

The attempt to force Board Schools upon the population of the country, even where they are not required, has doubtless been pushed very far in certain localities. Such attempts are every way oppressive and evil. They are equally tyrannical and wasteful; equally opposed to liberty and to every principle of statesmanlike economy. As yet, however, the movement in this direction, however far it may have hed here and there, has on the whole signally failed. Much as may have been done in some spots, the natural instincts e people of England have thus far defeated, on the broad despotic will and counsel of our obdurate modern theorists. oard Schools constitute but a small fraction of the educa- paratus of the country, nor do they seem likely hereafter to to more than a moderate proportion. Their value and in- indeed, where they have been well and wisely placed and d, are, and will increasingly be, much greater in proportion r mere number or bulk; as the value and influence of School gain, will be out of all proportion greater and wider than inferred from the mere number of Board Schools. But still ry notable point, and one altogether pertinent to the present n, that the educational work actually done in Board Schools comparatively so small. When we are informed that more the population of England is under School Boards, and that roportion are included nearly all the towns in the country onsiderable size, and the chief manufacturing populations, resident in towns or in villages, we are apt to infer that the of Board Schools must be in a ratio somewhat corresponding rritorial extent and influence of School Boards, and that a ge share of the children of the country must be in those The facts, however, are otherwise. In schools inspected he year 1876 the number of children in average attendance at elementary schools was 1,984,573, while the number in average ce at Board Schools was only 333,234, being one-sixth of the And yet the Boards have been busily at work for six years, y of them have nearly finished their task of supplying ies.*

er with or without schools, however, with few or with many School Boards are a necessity for the educational organization ountry: county boards, municipal boards, parochial boards: ards would stand in relation, on the one hand, with the educational council of which I have spoken, the chartered Council of Education, and on the other with all classes of and of schools in the country, whether public or private, h as Eton or Harrow down to the small school of the solitary

boards would afford the means of decentralization, to the extent, for the education of the country. It is, of course, take up a general and undiscriminating objection against ation. Centralization is the necessary condition of high and organization. But, besides the great central brain, there be ganglia distributed throughout the system. There must

crease in the average attendance in voluntary schools during the same period 6) has been 500,000.

be local centres of sympathy and influence; sub-centres of intelligence, sensibility, and activity. In order to excite and sustain local interest, to develop and bring adequately under contribution local resources, to apply local knowledge and influence to the satisfaction of local demands and necessities, and, withal, to bring the intelligence, the authority, the wide inductions and experience, of the great national centre into effective communication with the intelligence, the sympathy and activity, the motive energies, of the different localities throughout the country, it is necessary that there should be provincial (or county) and district organization with local centres or sub-centres. No sole imperial centre can be brought, apart from district organization and local centres, into effective relation with all parts of the country for all local purposes. There will be, without the subordinate local organization, a want of intimate local knowledge, of living local interest, of local confidence and content, of adequate moral authority and influence within the locality. In regard to this point, it appears as if England might learn a lesson from France. The French educational economy, in the manner of combining, harmonizing, and mutually limiting the action or responsibility of the town or the commune, the province, and the national centre, appears to be planned and adjusted with great skill. Of course all the parts of the French mechanism are too much under the control and manipulation of officials nominated by the Government. The free reciprocation of influence on the part of the provincial, the municipal, the rural centres, in their relation with the national centre, is to a great extent lost sight of; and the national centre itself, though it be called by the style and title of the University of Paris, is really equivalent to a Government bureau. But this fact does not affect the symmetry and excellence of the plan, so far as respects the points to which I have referred. It is satisfactory to know that the attention of our leading statesmen is fixed upon the cardinal defect in our national organization of which I have been speaking.

By means of such a natural and comprehensive organization, such a truly national organization, as I have been endeavouring to describe, all the needs of the country for educational purposes might well be met, and a Government educational bureau would no longer be necessary, at least for any such purposes as fixing the various school standards, certifying teachers, or examining schools. Such a bureau for such purposes would no more be necessary than a Government bureau of medicine and surgery for the purpose of educating and regulating the medical profession in its various departments. At least as good a case might be made out for the creation of a Medical Department of State administration, as of a permanent Educational Department such as at present exists. If there were no medical science, capable of self-development and self-direction, in the country, it might be necessary, for a time, that Government should undertake

sairable, would be able sufficiently to enforce them without uniform requirement of law. The training of teachers would ated by the same authority acting in harmony and corre- with the various local centres or sub-centres. Degrees and s conferred or countersigned by such a council would carry n their own authority, and would enforce their own accept- nstead of Government inspection, there would be carried out school thorough examinations by gentlemen bearing a proper s examiner. The sharp distinction between primary schools rior schools, working men's schools and gentlemen's schools, done away. There would be no Government schools, and of teachers at once unduly favoured and indelibly branded r by having a monopoly of the Government certificate and overnment grant. Board Schools and other schools would the same level. Local Boards would employ their own nspectors, would accredit their own examiners. No respect- en would send his child to any school which did not admit of the inspector to regulate at the least its sanitary con- nd of some duly accredited examiner to report upon the ion of the school and the progress and attainments of the Meantime there would be as much freedom in the scholastic a as in any other, and the way would be open for all play of ingenius and enterprise.

who read these pages, such a consummation as I have ribed may seem utopian, because it implies that the system nment grants to schools will be done away. I do not imagine that any such result can be attained *per saltum.* If our Legislature and Government should have determined to work towards such a result, it would require a good many years to bring it fully about. I am not forgetting that at this moment Government grants are larger than they ever were before, and therefore the change to be effected in order to bring about what I have described might seem to be greater now than ever. This, however, is not really the case. The payments of the parents have risen higher in proportion than the Government grants. Nor can it be doubted that one effect of Government interference has been to make the expense of maintaining schools more burdensome than it need be. Government has used, at great cost, the grant system as a mighty lever for elevating and extending the elementary education of the country. They have succeeded in raising the standards of examination, age for age, and class for class, higher, both for teachers and scholars, than has yet been attained in any other country; they have made provision, now that indirect has been added to direct compulsion, for enforcing, with or without grants, regularity of attendance. The links of connection between elementary and higher education, in the way of exhibitions and otherwise, are being rapidly and extensively established; already they are more numerous and effective than in any other country; and the process of extension and multiplication is still going on rapidly, and is likely so to continue. Under such circumstances, elementary education in England should be expected henceforth to be learning to pay its own way. Before long, grants should be gradually reduced, alike to all schools. Board Schools ought not to be allowed to charge fees lower than the best large elementary schools in the same immediate neighbourhood. The rate-charge on behalf of Board Schools ought to be minimized, remission of fees being, besides the cost of enforcing compulsion, the chief ordinary charge on the rates.

Except in villages, nearly all schools in the future will be large schools, at once effectively and economically organized. Parents will have learnt to value education. It has been no uncommon thing for working men to pay, years ago, threepence, fourpence, and even sixpence a week to miserably inefficient teachers, whether dames or not, for their children's schooling. The better sort of working people will think it no hardship in the time coming to pay a somewhat higher sum for the thoroughly effective education of their children. There will —it should be remembered—be a large and valuable class of teachers, who have never been trained at college indeed, but who have been apprenticed to the profession, have acted as assistants, and have passed a good examination; and these teachers will be available and sufficient for smaller and somewhat humbler schools—schools with lower school fees—than the highly organized and superior town schools. These teachers will often supply villages, especially female

this class, and will also serve well as teachers of the most schools for the lower working-class population in towns. hools generally, indeed, will be taught at a low cost by chers, whether college-trained or not. Such a natural of schools, with corresponding grades of teachers, would ants of the people at prices varying, for the weekly payment, to ninepence. The cost would be low, the benefit roportion to the cost. Such educational provision would thin the means of the great majority of the working classes, n and country, as labour is likely to be paid after twenty passed away. If only they have in the meantime learnt here can be no doubt of the perfect ease with which, in e working classes will be able to pay the cost of such an If any really cannot pay for the good, cheaper education have spoken, they must be so poor as to stand in need of h might be afforded either by the bounty of voluntary or out of the rates. Nothing ought to be paid out of public es directly towards the cost of education for any child, the principle of poor relief. This is the only ultimate our educational problem to which we can come.

cational history of the last sixty years seems to me to war- ticipations in which I am indulging. Half a century since, village population was less removed from the condition of an it is now, when the old Poor Law was still in force, with s which that law involved, it was natural that free schools looked upon by all classes as proper to be provided for the e provided, however, as a boon rather than as a right, and ynary principles. It was found, however, that free schools rk so well, and were not regarded with so much favour, e poor, as penny schools. These accordingly came to be l rule in poor localities. Christian beneficence and private rked on this basis. But since that time the fees have been rising all the country over. In population after population in manufacturing districts, and even in villages—this pro- een repeated over and over again during the last fifty years, it is no uncommon thing, in schools largely attended by f the operative class, for sixpence a week to be charged. ge fee even of Board Schools to-day is higher than of chools forty years ago, notwithstanding the intervention in ime of Government bounty and aid, the immediate effect of t be to lower fees. Parents would gladly pay considerably s, if they could send their children to schools which were ard Schools nor schools in any way aided by Government t, still were schools certified and distinguished as under chers and as approved by high-class examiners appointed of authority. Once remove the taint of dependence, of anything like eleemosynary help or rate-aid, whilst all guarantees for high educational efficiency are retained, and it will be found that Englishmen will pay for their children's schooling a much higher fee than has yet been paid. They would cheerfully bear a fee double on the average of what has lately been paid. Such a fee ought to be sufficient.

Of course the withdrawal of grants from schools would bring with it or after it the withdrawal of grants from training colleges. Such colleges during the gradual process of such withdrawal would be obliged to make charges more and more heavy on the students who came up for training. But the course of change, by removing the taint of State aid more and more from schools, would be continually elevating the grade of the profession of trained teachers for such schools. The line of separation, also, between State-aided primary and independent middle-class schools would be gradually dying out. Consequently the candidates for entrance into the colleges would become of an increasingly well-bred class. At present young people of a superior class as a rule avoid Government schools and training colleges; they do so, notwithstanding the high salaries which are paid to certificated teachers. The reasons are two—one the taint of State aid, of dependence on public taxes or rates; the other the worry of code regulations and of martinet inspectors. As the character of the schools changed from dependent to independent, as the power of the State over them gradually relaxed, and the payment of the State faded away, a higher and higher class of candidates for training and school-keeping would press forward and seek admission into the training colleges. These would require not more than one year's training, and would be able and willing to pay the charge of that year's training, in order to secure thorough competency for their professions.

In some such way as I have now indicated, I venture to hope that the whole question of national education may be solved. The National Council of Education, universally representative as it would be, would, without any direct or compulsory power of law, give suggestion, initiation, impulse, and, to a large extent, regulation to education of every grade, by means of schools of every class. So far as elementary education is concerned, there would, under the influence of natural law, come to be a sort of ascending scale of elementary schools, in harmony with the social diversities and educational wants of the population in its various classes. There would be teachers who had never been at college, but nevertheless had been well trained as pupil teachers and assistants, and had passed a proper examination; these, as a less expensive but still competent class of purely elementary teachers, would fill the lowest class of sound but rudimentary schools in villages and in certain parts of towns for certain classes of the population. These would be cheap, but yet sound and effective

. There would be a multitude of female teachers of this ion in village schools, doing excellent service at a low cost. achers would furnish an education within the reach of the oor, if they were frugal and industrious. Above these there e all gradations of college-trained teachers, able not only to e elements after the best style, and to train pupil teachers in way, but to carry education beyond the margin which has pposed to divide primary from secondary instruction. There hus be a complete graduation of schools, each kind melting one next to it, with no gap, no arbitrary line, no prejudiced The supply and the demand would be self-adjusting. There nd would be Board Schools of higher and of lower aims and ents; there would be private schools and public schools under y management, including all diversities and gradations of d attainment.

ing at the progress made during the past thirty years, and in mind the cumulative nature of the elevating forces which tive education brings to bear on a population, and especially er in developing a worthy independence and self-reliance, I eason why in such a country as England we should despair of result being attained within the next thirty years. It would be a great and noble distinction for England if Privy Council grants to schools could be brought to an end, and if Board —which in due proportion ought, I think, always to be main- -were made to meet their own expenses, with the exception of mission of fees, in whole or in part, as might be necessary to e case of the really poor day-labouring classes, or of out-door . This would be fair between school and school, between and teacher, and would bring us out of a labyrinth of diffi- and complications from which there would appear to be no scape. Teachers indeed would need then to be trained no n now, and to be certified by a proper authority, just as at pre- s medical practitioner or apothecary must have his diploma. also would need to be examined, for a school-certificate in etter times to come will be a passport to employment and to ment. But all teachers, of all classes, would then stand in a diploma, and have the means of obtaining one; and all would have to be inspected and examined by professional ies of recognized worth and status. This is the view of the hich I always set before myself as the ideal towards which I we are already sensibly tending, and to obscure or to delay much more to obstruct or prevent it—seems to me to be to et the true principles of political economy, and to commit against the sacred cause of national progress, whether moral ctual, and therefore, I need scarcely add, of material progress

Such, and not any imitation of Continental bureaucratic centralization or of American free education,* appears to me to be the educational goal and consummation to which, in this freest and foremost of all nations, all our present educational movements should tend. It should be our aim to improve and develop, not to transmute or efface, our proper English style and school of education. In so doing, moreover, let us remember that, out of our own country, our modern English training and science of elementary education is admitted to be of the very highest excellence. English trained teachers are very highly valued in America. English lecturers on education occupy in that continent foremost places. To this country, and in particular to our training colleges, American educationists repair, that they may study our principles and methods; and they are by no means slow or stinted in acknowledging their obligations to us. Throughout the Continent also, our principles and methods are recognized as of the highest value. What are often imagined by Englishmen, who have never studied the subject at home, to be German improvements and discoveries, have, for the most part, long been familiarly known to English educationists, at least within the zone of our training colleges and trained teachers; and students of educational science alike from Russia and from Italy find in this country, rather than anywhere else, their best models of school discipline and instruction. Infant training, indeed, is a speciality of this country; here it originated and here alone has it been matured and perfected. From this country it has spread to the United States. Infant schools in Germany are the recent luxury of the better classes, not an organic element of the national system of education; and the principles so ingeniously and effectually worked up by Fröbel into the Kinder-garten system have found in this country their congenial home and their most extensive sphere of development.

If such has been our English—or let me say, for fear Scotland should

* Even in quarters where accuracy might be expected, singular errors are sometimes found as to the facts of American education. An instance of this occurs in an article on the "Social Relations of England and America," contained in the *Quarterly Review* for July, 1876. The writer says that in the United States "the knowledge of Latin, from the common school system, is more widely spread than in England, with all its time-honoured establishments." The writer is evidently unaware that, except in Boston and some other places in New England, in which section of the States more of old England survives than anywhere else, the American common school system is altogether exclusive of Latin; and that by Grammar Schools are meant, throughout the States, schools in which English grammar is taught, as distinguished from schools still more elementary in which the scholars have not yet begun to learn grammar. Except in the Latin schools of New England, Latin is only taught in the High Schools, attended by scholars from sixteen years and upwards, and these High Schools are few and far between. Even in the great city of Philadelphia, which has a distinguished reputation for its schools of "secondary education," such "secondary education" does not include Latin. There is only one public school—in that city of [illegible] inhabitants—in which Latin is taught, the Central High School, which in 1875 [illegible] 601 scholars. The course at that school is for three years, Latin being begun [illegible] second year. For a summary of the chief educational facts and statistics, r[illegible] United States, I may be allowed to refer to an article, prepared from offic[illegible] I contributed to the *Quarterly Review* in April, 1875.

seem to be lost sight of, our British—growth of educational science in the past, such the life and enterprise, the principles and methods, the art and organization, which have sprung from unfettered activity and from voluntary energy, what I plead for is that voluntary life and energy, that spontaneous activity and resources, that individual inventiveness and goodwill, should continue to lead the educational science and progress of the country, and that Government bureaux and local boards should but follow and sustain where these natural life-forces point the way; that they should do no more than furnish the basis for correlation and co-operation, and the means of extension and development.

JAMES H. RIGG.

# THE DISCOVERIES AT MYCENÆ AND CYPRUS.

*Mycenæ: Discoveries and Researches on the Sites of Ancient Mycenæ and Tiryns.* By Dr. SCHLIEMANN. London: John Murray. 1877.
*Cyprus: Its Ancient Cities, Tombs, and Temples.* By LOUIS P. DI CESNOLA. London: John Murray. 187[illegible].

ARCHÆOLOGY deserves the patient attention given to natural science. Otherwise it is impossible to convey in writing any clear ideas to a reader even with the aid of engravings. A paper on a leading theory in zoology, although up to the level of a scientific student, is carefully studied by every reader, and not only books, but galleries of natural history and zoological gardens are consulted for illustration. The writer on natural science is not afraid to be scientific, for he knows that his readers will take the pains necessary to understand what he says. Archæology has now become scientific, and cannot be written upon unscientifically. The reader, if he is convinced that the development of art, including the present question, the development of the most splendid art of antiquity, is really worthy of study, must be content to turn to the pages of Dr. Schliemann's and General di Cesnola's works to see the engravings of the text of this article, he must be ready to give a morning to the treasure from the Troad at South Kensington, and another to the bowls from Assyria and the Cyprian pottery in the British Museum, and he must look up some of my authorities in the Reading Room. If he then gets a few of the handbooks Germany, France, and England are producing, he will cease to look at antiquities as the lumber of curiosity-shops, or at best the illustrations of school-books. Of course the student must have a little interest in the history of man, in the ideas which he has endeavoured in all ages to express by his art, and in the story of their development and their decay. If he has that interest, a fragment of a rude vase from Mycenæ will attract him as much as a bone of a new saurian will captivate a naturalist. Like the naturalist, the archæologist may build up from successive documents a new theory which will supply a lost link in the history of man.

our will not be carried on amid the sights and sounds of ever-ul nature, but it will be cheered by the music of the literature h he has to seek his parallel records, and the magical associa-alled up by almost every work of ancient art. And as the list at home is fired by the heroism of his comrade abroad who quered nature for the sake of knowledge, so the archæologist study is encouraged by his admiration of an explorer who has hrough the utmost difficulties straight to the hidden treasure, ving found it has converted it into the current money of science. il lately it might have been asked in vain where in Greece and inor, and where in the museums of Europe we could point to brought from these countries which could be assigned to s age, or to the age before Homer. We may date Homer in th century before our era, and we may be sure that he knew ing of the civilization of a century before his time. We may that he described objects of metal-work such as he had seen, t he spoke of larger monuments of the earlier century with the same knowledge. Yet until the late discoveries in Cyprus, d by those in the Troad and at Mycenæ, there was scarcely eek or Græco-Asiatic work of art known of which we could say was older than about B.C. 800, for that is about the period to works of art found in the Hellenic sites can be carried up in an en series. Now we have a mass of works of an undoubtedly period, which, if they be of the age of Homer and that pre-him, may be placed side by side with his poems, as more than nentary; for monuments and books are always a mutual text mmentary. To find if we can do this it is necessary to know es of the new discoveries. In this difficult problem we have the ndent body of information afforded by the Egyptian records, l or written, of a time reaching up from the traditional date of of Troy for two or three centuries earlier, from which we gain vidence of the state of the arts at that time in Syro-Phœnicia, a certain extent in the Eastern Mediterranean. The object of t paper is to show the critical value of this independent body lence, without losing sight of the similar value of the monu-of Assyria and the works of the Phœnician craftsmen.

now nearly twenty years since Dr. Birch endeavoured to prove e Egyptians, in the time of Thothmes III., whose date may be placed in the fifteenth century B.C.,* had received tribute ertain islands of the Mediterranean. In particular he cites a in a tomb at Thebes, in which four nations are represented.†

* most probable date of his reign is, I think, B.C. cir. 1460 to 1400, but there is an ty of at least half a century, and 1600 for the accession of Thothmes III. is a rate date.

† oire sur une Patère Egyptienne (Soc. des. Ant. de France, vol. xxiv.), 1858. engraving of the subject is in Hoskins, Travels in Ethiopia, Pls. xlvi.—xlix. ncient Egyptians, vol. i. Pl. iv.

Two of these nations concern the present question. These are the Ruten (or Luden) and the Kefa. In the time of Thothmes the Ruten were the principal nation of Syria. If they did not actually hold the Phœnician coast, it must have been tributary to or allied with them. The Kefa are described as "the Kefa, islands in the midst of the great sea," and Dr. Birch conjectures, from their name and the geographical position of Cyprus, always the first island to fall into the hands of the master of Syro-Phœnicia as Thothmes was, that this people correspond to the Caphtorim or aborigines of Cyprus.* Later investigations confirm the hypothesis that people of Cyprus are here represented. In accepting it, the minimum limit of Egyptian influence towards Greece is proposed.

Let us now see how the Ruten and Kefa are represented, with the tributes that they bring.

The Ruten are of the Shemite type, bearded and wearing the hair either very short or bushy; they are clad in long dresses. Their tribute consists of gold vases of the form of kraters, adorned with blue rosettes, and with similar ornaments above their rims; ring-money of gold and silver; unguents in vases, bronze vases, no doubt containing spices, wine, or oil; a chariot, arms, horses, a bear, an elephant, and a tusk of ivory.

The Kefa resemble the Egyptians, but have long locks of hair, and are clad in short kirtles and boots. Their offerings are ring-money of silver, gold vases of the same form as those of the Ruten and adorned in the same manner, other gold vases with greater variety of adornment, special use being made of animal forms; silver vases, animals' heads of gold and silver, particularly an ox-head in silver, strings of precious stones, and a tusk of ivory. No animals are brought in tribute. It will be noticed that, while the art of the Ruten and the Kefa is similar, that of the Kefa is marked by greater fancy and elegance—is, in fact, a higher development.† It might be supposed that the ancient art of the Mediterranean island and Syria represented in the picture referred to was purely Egyptian. If, however, any one will compare the plates in which it is given with those of Egyptian pictures of the art of Egypt—and both may be seen in Rosellini's admirable "Monumenti Civili"—he will observe that the difference is very marked. Probably the origin was common, but the development in Cyprus and Syro-Phœnicia so peculiar as to be always recognizable. It need not be inquired here whether this very ancient

* Mém. p. 25 (*tirage à part*). There is, however, a doubt whether the Kefa were Cyprians or Phœnicians. Perhaps the most reasonable view is that they were Phœnicians already established in Cyprus.

† In a painting of tribute to Tutankhamen, in the fifth generation after Thothmes III., the art of the Ruten is like that of the Kefa (Lepsius, Denkmäler, iii. 115, 116), and may be compared with Egyptian art in the same picture (118). A relief of Setee I., perhaps fifty years still later, represents the same art as that of the Ruten (127). It is therefore unsafe to dwell on the difference between the art of the Ruten and the Kefa in the tribute to Thothmes III.

[illegible] the product of islanders or of Phœnicians [illegible] It is enough for the present subject [illegible] in the islands between B.C. 1400 and [illegible]

[illegible] the tribute to Thothmes is a *locus classicus* to be [illegible] the inquiry proceeds, it may be well here to point [illegible] representations of inanimate objects are marked [illegible] although there is a certain degree of conventional [illegible] ideas of symmetry. Yet this modification is [illegible] the identity of each object portrayed. If, for [illegible] of Greek vases of the best period were seen in an [illegible] they would be perfectly traceable as non-Egyptian, [illegible] identity would be no more affected than it is in the [illegible] of artists not trained to classical work. It is thus [illegible] that the tributes I have cited represent a phase of art [illegible] not Egyptian, although it may have had its origin in [illegible]

[illegible] elapsed after the publication of Dr. Birch's discovery [illegible] step was made in the direction he had thus happily [illegible] M. de Rougé then discovered the real historical relations [illegible] with the maritime Greeks and the nations of Asia [illegible] period of two centuries, ranging from B.C. 1400 or 1300 [illegible] 1100. In an Egyptian poem, that of Pentaur, which we [illegible] Rameseeis, we have the story of Ramses II. at war with [illegible] confederacy, headed by the Hittites of Upper Syria, in [illegible] Dardans and Lycians are included, perhaps even Ilium [illegible] contingent to the allied army.* The whole structure of [illegible] is like a foreshadowing of the Iliad. The king has the all- [illegible] characteristics of Achilles. Under the walls of the great [illegible] of the enemy, Kadesh on the Orontes, as before Troy, the [illegible] war is determined. It is determined by a great feat of [illegible] the king, protected by the gods, and aided by his faithful [illegible] and his horses, mentioned by name like those of [illegible]

[illegible] years earlier the same king had repelled the first recorded of [illegible] on Egypt made by the maritime Greeks. The Sar- [illegible] the Etruscans, allied with the Libyans, invaded the Delta [illegible] defeated by Ramses. Here, as in the other war, we have [illegible] of confederation which marks the Trojan period. Some [illegible] years later a more formidable invasion was nearly successful, [illegible] end of a century two great attacks, one from the east and [illegible] from the west, were repelled by Ramses III. It is on the

[illegible] of the Hittite king, the leader of the confederacy, was killed in action, [illegible] remarked, the poem of the other side has been lost.

[illegible] translation of this poem is that of M. de Rougé, Recueil de Travaux relatifs [illegible] l'Archéologie Egyptiennes et Assyriennes, p. 1, seqq.

walls of the great sepulchral temple of this Pharaoh at Medeenet-Haboo, in western Thebes, that the achievements of his life are told and pictured. There we see the long ships of the maritime Greeks in conflict on the Mediterranean with the Egyptian navy, and in many other scenes the varieties of race and the different arms of the enemies give us valuable hints for comparison with the earliest native representations of the same races. To glance aside for a moment at Homer, these descents on Egypt find their Hellenic record in the tale of a piratical expedition to Egypt with which Ulysses deceived the suitors, a tale true in every detail, such as the car of the king, his clemency, and the employment of captives taken in war in public works. Homer's knowledge of the wealth and greatness in war of Egyptian Thebes and of the medical skill of the nation is an additional evidence of the poet's truthfulness no less than is his acquaintance in the account Menelaus gives of his voyage from Troy with the only safe anchorage on the north of Egypt, where the instinct of a king who knew his Homer afterwards built the great city of Alexandria.

It may be well here to dismiss once for all an idle objection to M. de Rougé's explanations, which, had it not been urged seriously, would not deserve serious notice. It must be admitted on all hands that most of the French scholar's identifications cannot be contested. Such are those of the Dardans, Achæans, Sikels, and Sardones. But it has been objected, why do we find the Sikels and the Sardones in the Eastern Mediterranean rather than in Sicily or Sardinia? This is exactly like objecting to Genseric as a Vandal King of Carthage because we do not find that he reigned in Mecklenburg Schwerin or Mecklenburg Strelitz, or to a Gothic king in Spain or Italy, because he did not rule in Gothland. Yet this objection is calmly urged in the case of distances a tenth of those involved in the later instances. It is urged in the face of persistent traditions of movements in the general westward direction of the advance of nations. It is urged in the face of as strong traditions of great disturbances in the period immediately after that in which the Egyptian records show the nations identified with the Greeks actuated by a restless desire to make new settlements on the largest scale.

From Egypt we thus obtain a good foothold in the Greece and Asia Minor of the days before Homer. For Homer's own time there is another source, a glance at which is needed to complete this sketch. During the Egyptian supremacy in Syro-Phœnicia, we hear so little of the Phœnicians as a power, that it is still doubtful by what name the Egyptians then called them, nor have we any hint that the coast-towns of Phœnicia were then politically powerful. Much that has been written on the early history of the Phœnicians is pure speculation. The fall of the Egyptian Empire, about B.C. 1200—1100, is, at least for us, the beginning of the historical life of the Phœnicians, and two centuries later we know their place in the East. By the time of [illegible] were the great carriers of the Mediterranean [illegible] to protect their factories. They had suc- [illegible] thalassocracy. The scanty Phœnician stone [illegible] before the Greek rule are at first wholly copies [illegible] alphabet which they gave to Greece and the world [illegible] of genius, from the more comprehensive [illegible] in its usual written form, now called the hieratic. [illegible] suggest not a native style but the subtle adapta- [illegible] of foreign styles.* It is certain that there [illegible] anything, which can be called Phœnician art as [illegible] of a national instinct. A purely commercial nation, [illegible] best market, they faithfully represented the fashion- [illegible] wealthiest buyers. The types of Phœnician coinage prove this. It thus happens that Phœnician art is best [illegible] be a measure of the influence of Egypt on the one [illegible] great Eastern monarchies on the other. The use of [illegible] works for the chronology of art depends, therefore, on our [illegible] the times at which those influences prevailed.

[illegible] the art the Phœnicians produced? First of all it [illegible] to metal-work. As architects they achieved very [illegible] their works in bronze, silver, and gold, that mark their [illegible]aracter. It is now generally agreed that the likeness of the [illegible]al-work of Assyria, Cyprus, Greece, and Etruria can only be [illegible] by supposing that it was made either by Phœnicians, or at [illegible] who followed Phœnician designs. These objects, [illegible] earliest, have three styles—Egyptian, Assyrio-Egyptian, [illegible] To what date do these styles belong?

[illegible] bowls from Nemrood are our first and safest guides. [illegible] they were found was rebuilt early in the ninth [illegible] was destroyed, or, at least, lost all importance, with [illegible] Nineveh, probably B.C. 625. In a palace in this city were [illegible] of bronze bowls, which must belong to this interval, [illegible] to its earliest period, but upon this it is not [illegible] They are of the three Phœnician styles, Egyptian [illegible]ing. If we compare them with well-known Assyrian [illegible] that the so-called Assyrian style sometimes corre- [illegible] carving, such as that of the flooring of the palace at [illegible] Museum. The patterns are wholly floral, with [illegible] arrangement. The stone-work is evidently copied [illegible] was probably intended to be covered with a thin [illegible] of gold, as in the interior of Solomon's temple. [illegible] is marked by the representation of winged [illegible] with the well-known sacred tree, and also [illegible] The bowls in Egyptian style are either very

* [illegible] by Mr. Newton and Mr. Franks, as well as by M. de

simple, with plants and a few animals, or with winged figures and sphinxes of a type derived from Egypt. The mixed style combines the Assyrian and Egyptian figures. The bowls must be compared with those discovered by General di Cesnola in Cyprus, in which the purely Assyrian style is wanting.

It may be well here to point out some leading characteristics of Egyptian and Assyrian art. To understand them, the reader who cannot afford the time to turn over the splendid "Denkmäler aus Aegypten and Aethiopien" of Professor Lepsius, and the great works of Layard and Botta, will gain a good general idea of Egyptian art from Rosellini's "Monumenti Civili," and Wilkinson's "Ancient Egyptians," and of Assyrian from Layard's two smaller works. He will observe that Egyptian art is essentially architectural, Assyrian decorative.

In looking at an Egyptian sculpture or painting we are always reminded of the architectural whole of which it formed a part, whereas each Assyrian scene is a picture of itself, with no architectural relation to the structure of which it formed a part. Egyptian art is conventional and stationary, Assyrian, somewhat naturalistic and progressive. In comparing an Egyptian battle-scene with an Assyrian, which can be done in the British Museum, where casts from Beyt-el-Welee of the reliefs of Ramses II. are sufficiently near to the Assyrian sculptures of the same kind to admit of ready comparison, one sees at once that the Egyptian composition is far more skilful, though it sins against our rules of proportion, and that no perspective is attempted; in the Assyrian on the other hand the excellence of detail is marred by the weak endeavour to represent a battle-scene in something like true proportion and with a regard to aerial perspective. In feeling Egyptian art is reserved and dignified, Assyrian often violent and more frequently grotesque. The subjects in Assyrian art are battle-scenes, hunting-scenes, and a few groups in which the king worships a god, or the gods protect the king. The Egyptians in their temples, besides representing battle-scenes, had a wider range in mythology, and scarcely portrayed hunting; in other buildings gave abundant incidents of common life. The Assyrian king or deity is frequently represented slaying a single lion. The Assyrians were fond of winged figures, whereas such are very rare in Egyptian art, and the forms are different, the Assyrian wings being often curled, the Egyptian never. The ornaments are very important for the study of Phœnician art, especially as there is good reason for supposing that the decorative part of Assyrian work was executed by Phœnicians, or in their style. The Egyptian decorations are simpler and less floral than the Assyrian, which are almost all of floral forms.

The description of Solomon's temple in the First Book of Kings carries us up at least a century earlier, referring to about B.C. 1000, and illustrates Phœni[illegible] art, for when the Hebrew king prepared to

...engaged Tyrian workmen for both stone and metal-... this description, it would seem that the ... is not Egyptian, although it may have been ... Egyptian prototype. The ground-plan is more sym-... of the temples in Cyprus. In the elevation, the ... contrary to Egyptian principles, and points rather to ... however, any likeness ceases. The small dimensions, ... of metal, especially gold, are not Egyptian, nor can ... indicate Assyrian influence. They rather characterize ... of metal-workers. No architectural nation would ... the temple, walls, floor, and no doubt ceiling, with gold. ... characteristics of the art are to be looked for in the ... The pillars of brass were adorned with intertwinings of ... twists of chain-work, and lily-work, and pomegranates. ... sea was ornamented round the brim with flowers of lilies, ... upon twelve oxen. The stone-work and wood-work of the ... was plated with gold, after they had been carved with cherubim ...lm-trees, and open flowers, and the cedar ceiling, no doubt ...ted, was carved with gourds, supposed to be used for ornament ...ursting and showing the seeds, and open flowers. It is ...able that the only one of these forms of ornament found in ...cription of the tabernacle and the priests' dresses, &c., in the ...uch, is the pomegranate, which is certainly Egyptian, though ...und in Phœnician art. The others may all be recognized ...obability in Phœnician work, though we look for any but the ...vain in Egyptian. Net-work and twists characterize all pri-...art, but do not characterize Egyptian, being unusual in it, ...y naturally, for net-work is the mark of undeveloped art, which ...y repeat itself, or of declining art which has lost the power of ...ment; and twisted work is a favourite form with goldsmiths, the Egyptians never were in such a national sense as the ...ians, although they were great as jewellers. All the other ...nts named in the description of Solomon's temple are charac-... either of Phœnician or of archaic metal-work found on Hellenic ... The net-work is not usual, but twisted patterns and forms, the ...y, the pomegranate, the bursting gourd (Cesnola, pl. xxii.), and ...owers, are characteristic forms. The subjects of the temple ...nd doors, cherubim and palm-trees, recall nothing Egyptian. ...mbination of winged figures and trees is distinctly Asiatic, and ... the Assyrio-Phœnician bowls. Making due allowance for ... religious grounds, of introducing Egyptian subjects, ... here remains to show that Phœnician art was rather ... Egyptian, in objects of metal-work, as early as the date ... temple, about B.C. 1000.

... trace the influence of Assyria on Phœnician art to the ... tenth century B.C. Does history account for this?

Egypt was the mistress of Syro-Phœnicia from B.C. 1500, or 1450, to about B.C. 1200. Her power there then waned, but probably was not destroyed, until the country was conquered by an Assyrian king, about B.C. 1130. After his reign, Assyria declined, and about 1060 ceased to have any political weight in Syria—a condition which lasted for some two centuries. It is therefore natural to suppose that Phœnician art first felt Egyptian influence and then Assyrian. Its subsequent history may be illustrated by the sequence of styles in Cyprus.

Between the cities of Phœnicia and Rhodes, the outpost of Greek civilization, an easy sail from both, lies the island of Cyprus, famed for its fertility and wealth, from the beginning of Greek history until it fell under the baneful rule of Turkey. Here, with the evidence of the tribute to Thothmes before us, we might look for the oldest traces of the westward spread of the arts. Late discoveries have brought to light a great mass of archæological evidence which has yet to be classed and applied to the problem of linking together known archaic art with the remotely ancient treasures of Mycenæ and the Troad.

In the course of 1869, Mr. Lang, then manager of the Ottoman Bank at Larnaka, in Cyprus, discovered and excavated a temple at Dali, the ancient Idalium, a renowned seat of the worship of the Cyprian Aphrodite. The discoverer, in the most public-spirited manner, gave the nation the first offer of the results of his labours. Sent by the Trustees of the British Museum to report upon this collection, I had the advantage of seeing all that had been done up to the time by Mr. Lang and General di Cesnola, and of discussing with a little knot of scholars, who made their exile happy with the peaceful pursuit of archæology, the curious problems that their researches suggested. I came away convinced that the monuments of Cyprus, and the vases discovered in the tombs, reach up in a continuous series far nearer the traditional date of the taking of Troy than any antiquities found elsewhere up to the time of which I am speaking, and that very probably some are as early as the age of which Homer writes.

Here it may be well to say a word of the characteristics of Cyprian art. It is never, until the Macedonian rule, in any true sense Greek. I am not unmindful of the influence of the Greek kings, particularly Euagoras I. of Salamis, but I fail to find Hellenic art established in Cyprus, and Oriental art suppressed by it; on the contrary, Oriental art ruled until the Macedonian age. The origin and characteristics of Cyprian art must be traced to Phœnicia, and the history of Phœnician art applied to the determination of its dates. The story of the island explains this. From the time when it fell into the hands of Ptolemy the son of Lagus, until we first read of its submission to Assyria, for four centuries, from B.C. 707 downwards, the island was divided into several kingdoms, each taking its name from a chief city. Some of these kingdoms, in the early part of the seventh century, were ruled by Phœnicians, others, by Greeks. This form of government was no doubt originally Phœnician. Nowhere so constantly as in Phœnicia, do we find each city a separate state, at first, of course, a kingdom. The names of the Cyprian capitals are, probably, mostly Phœnician, some are certainly so; yet among these Phœnician towns two, at least, were ruled in the seventh century by Greek kings. The Greek kingdoms then represent Hellenic colonization following Phœnician. This Hellenic colonization, unlike that of Sicily and Magna Græcia, is referred to the heroic ages. Consequently it must have been very ancient, and we can scarcely be in error if we place the Phœnician settlement that preceded it as early as the eleventh or twelfth century B.C.

The art of Cyprus was affected by the mineral wealth of the island and the other materials there produced. The copper certainly promoted working in bronze, but the great resource of builders and sculptors was the soft limestone of the island, the qualities of which gave them a facility fatal to excellence in their work.

The temple of Dali, mainly adorned by Phœnician rulers of the united kingdoms of Citium and Idalium, in the fifth century B.C., is a curious illustration of Phœnician architecture. It had no regular plan. A very ancient shrine, where archaic statues of Egyptian style were found, was gradually increased, and the principal chamber contained a great series of statues arranged in a line with altars before them, where Mr. Lang found probable evidence of the horrible Phœnician custom of the sacrifice of children. From this temple a precious series of sculptures, inscriptions, and terra-cotta objects, as well as two finds of coins, were taken, all now placed in the British Museum. The terra-cottas were small figures of horsemen, very rudely formed by pinching the clay with the fingers: they were found in the oldest portion of the temple, and they also mark a class of tombs in the same part of the island in which nothing of importance is discovered. They have been called children's toys, but it is quite obvious that they were considered to be precious, and if so, they must be assigned to the infancy of art in the island. Very similar objects were found by Dr. Schliemann in the Troad and at Mycenæ, and by Mr. Newton in a chamber below the Mausoleum. There were two great classes of archaic statues, one in Egypto-Cyprian, the other in Assyrio-Cyprian style. The problem suggested by the temple was, whether the works of Egyptian character should be assigned to the age before the Assyrian rule of the island in the seventh century, or to the time of Egyptian influence which followed it, in the seventh and sixth centuries, and, consequently, whether the Egyptian or Assyrian style were the older. At Dali I came to the opinion that the older date for the Egyptian was the true one, and that here we had the artistic tradition of the rule of the Egyptian Empire.

The theory thus formed was strengthened by the fine collection of vases General di Cesnola had already formed from tombs in this part of the island, many examples of which may now be studied in the British Museum. Making allowance for the absence of true Greek art before Ptolemy I., I could not explain the variety of styles without the hypothesis of a great period of time. There were a series of painted vases with the upper part in the form of a human head, and the lower adorned with net-work, concentric circles, and very rude human and animal figures distributed without any sense of design. Another class was marked by incised patterns of the simplest kind, concentric circles, and parallel lines in lozenges and other forms, with a better sense of design in their ornament. A very important class of painted vases was marked by characteristics of Egyptian pottery, simple lines running round or down the vase, and sometimes a pattern round the neck, or even a subject, usually an animal, on the neck or on the body, the lotus being often used. Some one of these styles must have been prolonged to the Macedonian age, when it appears that glass vases became common, just as hieratic art was reproduced, at least to the same date, but the rudest style of vases must be of extreme antiquity. It never happens that pottery is in general far inferior to the sculpture of the same age.

The first period of General di Cesnola's excavations yielded two most important bowls, one of bronze, from Dali (p. 77), the other of silver, from the neighbouring site of Golgoi (plate xi.). These are both of Egyptian style, but singularly different. The Dali bowl is a very primitive work. The subject is a series of female dancers and musicians, with tables of offerings before a seated goddess. All are Egyptian, even the very forms of the musical instruments and the columns around, with two very important exceptions. The hair, curly on the head in all the figures but the goddess, and falling in long locks, in all cases, is that of the Kefa in the picture of the tribute to Thothmes, and but for this the subject might almost have been copied from an Egyptian scene in a tomb of that age, and scarcely of any much later, not be it remarked from an Egyptian bowl. The other exception, which General di Cesnola acutely points out, is that the vases represented are copies of the archaic pottery of Dali (pp. 78, 79), and it may be added the incised vases, a style which is not common to Egypt. This priceless bowl may be one of the very earliest efforts of Phœnician art in Cyprus. The silver patera from Golgoi is of comparatively fine style. The subjects are still Egyptian, but the artist is no longer a copyist. He has grouped together various figures without following an Egyptian design. In the centre a male and female figure, a horse, an ox, and fishes swim around. In the principal band a river is portrayed, bordered by the flowering papyrus; four boats, one in the form of a flying duck, pass in a procession. The chief boat contains a shrine in which a sacred seated statue is adored by a priestess: the others carry musicians and offerings. Between the boats, horses, cattle, [illegible] great man and his charioteer, are seen, attend- [illegible] on the bank. The only striking analogy in [illegible] is in the form of the sacred boat, for the war-ships [illegible] in the sea-fight with Rameses III. have [illegible] the shape of a wading bird's head and neck. In both [illegible] we have nothing of the ornaments of Solomon's temple, [illegible] those of the bronze bowls from Assyria. The first [illegible] product of Phœnician art, copying Egyptian paintings; [illegible] of that art wholly emancipated from servile imitation of [illegible] and as wholly untouched by Assyrian influence: the [illegible] of its antiquity is only to be settled by a laborious investigation.

[illegible] my good fortune to witness a great discovery which occurred almost immediately after I had left the kind hospitality of Cyprus. [illegible] 1870 General di Cesnola struck upon a temple at Golgoi from which he extracted a richer series of statues than Mr. Lang's find [illegible] The same styles were here represented, but the earlier were [illegible] works of greater variety and far better preservation. The reader will better understand these statues from General di Cesnola's engravings than from any description. I will only draw attention to [illegible] varieties of Egyptian style (pp. 129, 131, 154, and 145), which could scarcely have been produced within the narrow interval of Egyptian influence in the seventh and sixth centuries before our era, and to the marvellous colossal head (p. 123), probably a very early [illegible] of Assyrio-Cyprian art. The decorative details (p. 159) and [illegible] (p. 136) are also most interesting.

General di Cesnola's excavations on the site of the famous city of [illegible] did not yield very important results. On the site of Amathus he was more fortunate in a cemetery of tombs of simple but very pure [illegible] of squared stones. In one he discovered a splendid sarcophagus of marble, the sculptures of which present a remarkable [illegible] of Assyrian and archaic Greek style (Pls. xiv. and xv. p. 267). [illegible] probably of the sixth century B.C. In another tomb were found Egyptian porcelain statuettes of divinities, an extraordinary silver [illegible], and a bronze shield. The patera has two bands of Egyptian [illegible] one of Assyrian. The styles are singularly pure and the subjects only mixed, and that but little, in one of the Egyptian [illegible]. So carefully are the Egyptian divinities represented that we [illegible] most of them. The artist has admirably preserved the charac[illegible] of the two original types, which are in strange contrast, and [illegible] the Assyrians in his palm-trees, which may be recom[illegible] to the modern designer of racing plates. The Assyrian [illegible] is also curious in the occurrence of soldiers armed in Greek [illegible] (Pl. xix.).

[illegible] wonders were the result of the excavations on the site [illegible] royal city, Curium. Here the explorer opened what no doubt was the treasury of a temple, and brought to light one of the most splendid and interesting collections of gold objects ever found together. Of course, in a series of precious deposits, we cannot gain any definite idea of date except in a few instances. We can only notice dated objects and the earliest and latest styles of others. The one date is obtained from the Cyprian inscription of the golden armlets of Eteander, King of Paphos, who is reasonably identified with the prince of that name tributary to Esarhaddon, King of Assyria (B.C. 672). Unfortunately they are perfectly plain. The latest style is apparently that of fine Greek work, perhaps as late as B.C. 400, very scantily represented. The earliest style is seen in certain pateræ of purely Egyptian character, one of which is in gold (p. 316), and another of silver gilt (p. 337): both might have been executed in Egypt and dedicated by Pharaohs. A third patera of silver gilt is a splendid specimen of mixed Egyptian and Assyrian styles (p. 329). Among the works in silver a small two-handled vase is decorated with an arabesque of natural flowers, which looks like Græco-Roman work, or its prototype. (Pl. xxi.). This is one of the strangest and most suggestive objects found by General di Cesnola.

Much must be left unsaid on the many topics raised by these researches. I cannot, however, take leave of them without congratulating General di Cesnola on the excellent manner in which he has made his record. Much as Englishmen must regret that his collection has gone to America, they can at least study it in the beautiful engravings of the work, though it were well worth a voyage to New York to examine the treasures in detail. The history of the excavations is simply and clearly told, and those who are interested in the state of the Turkish Empire may not unprofitably read what General di Cesnola has to say of the administration of justice in Cyprus. The story of the sad fate of poor Hadji Jorghi, "the pioneer digger of Dali" (p. 83), is but one of a thousand pitiful tragedies which those who do not speak the local dialects, and have prepossessions in favour of the agreeable manners of the Turks, never hear, or having heard forget.

From Cyprus to Mycenæ is not an unnatural transition. We have seen in the story of discovery in Cyprus archaic works in metal which might illustrate the arms which Homer tells us Agamemnon received from Cinyras, King of Cyprus. We have gone thus far westward with the streams of Oriental art—thus far in antiquity with the gradual growth of styles. Why not cross to Hellas and see whether in the earliest works there discovered we find any traces which might link them with the earliest works discovered in this great storehouse of the very-dædalian Sidonians?

The discoveries at Mycenæ have taken the world by surprise. Nothing was more certain than that here were the tombs described by Pausanias as the traditional sepulchres of Agamemnon and his comrades: nothing more unlikely than that they should have remained unplundered. Yet these tombs have been discovered as they were left, and have yielded their treasures to Dr. Schliemann's genius.

Discarding altogether *à priori* reasoning, I shall endeavour to show what evidence of date the discoveries at Mycenæ present. I confine myself to the contents of the five tombs in the Agora, and the structure outside that enclosure, alluding to some archaic remains which are probably later. For the criticism of those objects there are three chief standards, the earliest antiquities of Cyprus, the antiquities from the Troad, and the Egyptian and other foreign evidence. And here I must turn aside for a moment to glance at the Trojan treasures.

Comparing the objects from the Troad with the earliest found in Cyprus, we are struck by the occurrence in both of two great classes of vases, those which have the upper part in the form of a human head in Cyprus, possibly an owl's head in the Trojan series, and those of the skin-like shapes, particularly the characteristic double-spouted vases. This is enough of itself to prove the high antiquity of the Trojan find. Another remarkable characteristic is the unknown type of the gold ornaments. There are two parallels elsewhere. The head-dress has characteristics that we also see in ancient German or Keltic metal-work, particularly in the use of chains; but such extremely simple forms might be common to any primitive art, and the analogies of primitive art are among the false lights of archæology, if they are used for the determination of date. For instance, all very rude representations of quadrupeds have a certain family likeness, but afford no clue to date with distinct races in widely distant countries. The head-dress when worn would give the wearer a strikingly Egyptian aspect: this, however, is not due to the technical quality of the work. On the other hand, the gold necklaces from the Troad are apparently imitations of Egyptian necklaces of beads and precious stones, and are thus consistent with extreme antiquity; while it seems that they have no analogies in later works of the kind found in Greece and the islands from about B.C. 800 downwards. There is thus reason to place the Trojan find before about B.C. 800, and not later than the earliest point to which the antiquities of Cyprus reach, perhaps the twelfth century B.C.; and it is precisely in the earlier part of this period that we should expect Egyptian jewellery to have had the widest influence.

Returning to Mycenæ, I do not propose to examine the architecture, the mode of sepulture, or the arguments in favour of the entombment of Agamemnon and his comrades in the tombs opened by Dr. Schliemann. These inquiries would be beyond the scope of this paper. I shall confine myself to the endeavour to ascertain the date of the find from Egyptian, Cyprian, and kindred evidence.

It is, however, necessary first of all to notice the positive and negative evidence of date afforded by the general character of the find. The great richness in gold points either to the time before the origin of coinage in Hellas—that is, before the eighth century B.C.—or to the time after Alexander. The discovery of very archaic pottery, in vases and little figures, in the Mycenæ soil, would favour the earlier limit. The presence of implements of stone, however scanty, carries the find into the limits of the stone age of Greece, while the occurrence of bronze weapons points to the time of the transition from the stone age to the bronze age in the same country. No doubt these ages everywhere overlapped each other, yet it is certain that the stone age in Greece ended at a very remote time, long before the beginnings of true Hellenic art. The distinctness of the art from any of Hellenic character takes it almost as high, unless it be barbarian. The idea raised by the last conjecture, that these remains are the work of some barbarous tribe which occupied the place, was at first favourably entertained by some eminent scholars. Dr. Milchover, Mr. Newton, and Mr. Gardner, were the first to repudiate it, and with true critical instinct, for it rests upon apparent similarities which a closer examination shows to be merely apparent. These similarities depend upon the common forms of primitive art, not upon the distinctive forms of primitive art at Mycenæ; and they leave these distinctive forms unexplained. So much for positive evidence of date. The negative evidence, so far as it has not been already implied, is the presence of little archaic goldsmith's work of characters hitherto known, the absence of vases of types of the later Greek ceramic art, of glass, except in beads, of coins, and inscriptions. It may be added that Mycenæ declined at a very remote time, and it is extremely unlikely that these remains are of a date at which it was not the seat of a powerful dynasty. Had such a dynasty lasted to the tenth century B.C., tradition would have remembered that it did so. It is therefore not unreasonable to place the Mycenæ treasure within the period from Homer to the usual date of the Trojan War, roughly in the tenth, eleventh, or twelfth century before our era.

The Mycenæ treasure may be divided into the following great groups of objects, in the order of their importance:—

1. Works in gold, silver, and bronze.
2. Pottery.
3. Reliefs in stone.

The extraordinary quantity of objects in gold enables one to reason inductively as to the characteristics of the art which produced them—in its general principles of ornament, and in the special forms of objects, both those made on the spot and those possibly imported. The leading forms, the concentric circle, its first developments, the S form and spiral, and the rosette, are common to Egyptian and German or Keltic ornament. Among the ancient Egyptians they were never developed; with the Northerns they reached a stage of progress which is equally seen in the Mycenæ ornaments, where the S or spiral

[illegible] essential difference between the Myce-
[illegible] statement is that the artists who
[illegible] progress enough to be able to compose
[illegible] failed in any other form, whereas the
[illegible] succeeded in making a composition to fill
[illegible] irregular. Any one who likes to try the ex-
[illegible] plate and arrange a chain in it in the form
[illegible] then develop this first form by increasing the
[illegible] using similar materials, he can fill in the inter-
[illegible] corresponding patterns; but having put two plates
[illegible] ted, on a small rectangular table, let him try
[illegible] with patterns in harmony with those of the
[illegible] the difficulty of the next step. While thus
[illegible] position, the Myceneans varied their ornaments by the
utterfly, the cuttle-fish, and a leaf, possibly that of the vine.
[illegible] objects which we may assume to have been made on the
[illegible], and it is highly probable that the same was the
[illegible] and breastplates, with similar smaller objects,
the larger vessels; for if the goldsmith's art at Mycenæ
[illegible] these diadems, the heavier vessels of gold, as well as of
[illegible] not have been imported. The masks are best compared
Egyptian custom of gilding the faces of mummies. The
ave their parallel, as Dr. Schliemann points out, in the
archaic figures of the Cyprian Aphrodite, where, however,
are in a better and later style (cf. Cesnola, Cyprus, p. 350).
d instance of this development of the technical method is
e bracelet from Curium (Cesnola, p. 311). The patterns are
art of the field, but separately affixed to it. The objects
ated with gold belong to the same style as those in gold
are chiefly valuable as a link with early Phœnician work,
obviously intended, from its extreme thinness, to be so
d further correspond to the Phœnician method in Solomon's
out B.C. 1000. The vases are of primitive forms, very like
ottery and silver vases of Cyprus, and with a more distant
e to the Trojan, though the Trojan vases in precious
much simpler and heavier in shape. With the vases
entioned the two animals' heads, the lion's mask in gold and
[illegible] silver with golden horns. Dr. Schliemann draws atten-
e parallels in the Egyptian tributes to these objects. In
in the picture of that of the Kefa there is a lion's head of
[illegible] head of silver. Mr. Gardner has convinced me that
were vase-covers, like the supposed owl-heads of the Trojan
ey had their origin, no doubt, in the Egyptian vases with the
e four genii of Amenti (Hades). The lion's mask, which can
ve been a vase-cover, is of rude design (p. 211); the ox-head
t example of metal-work from Mycenæ (pp. 216, 217). It

seems too good to be anything but a product of Phœnician art made in Egypt. Indeed, no one would have thought it out of place in an Egyptian find. It is the one work that cannot have been made by the goldsmiths who produced the metal-work of Mycenæ. Many of the smaller objects must, as already stated, have been made at the same place as the diadems and breastplates, therefore probably at Mycenæ; but there are other small portable ornaments which show much variety and more distinct relations to foreign styles. Very characteristic are little groups of quadrupeds and birds, usually two face to face, sometimes looking back, which have a general likeness to the sculpture of the Lions' Gate and an Assyrian character. The figures of Aphrodite, with one or more doves, have a Cyprian relation, and so has the golden shrine (p. 267). The cuttle-fishes, the sphinx, and the griffin, would seem to be Greek; but the griffin is also found in Egyptian jewellery. A most remarkable golden brooch (p. 193) has a very Oriental air. The lion ornament (p. 178) reminds one of archaic Greek work, unlike the solid golden lion cast and tooled (p. 36), which belongs to a separate find, that of the structure outside the Agora.

The pottery resembles the earliest Cyprian, both in forms and patterns. The net-work pattern (p. 65) is specially characteristic (Cesnola 402). There is, however, a clearly local character which separates the two. This is markedly seen in the small terra-cotta figures, as well as in the fragments of painted vases. The pottery, however, mostly comes from the soil of Mycenæ, not from the tombs. The specimens from the tombs are on the whole the most archaic. The evidence of the rest of the pottery tends to throw the date of the tombs very high.

The reliefs of the tombstones are, perhaps, the most difficult class of works in the whole series of Dr. Schliemann's discoveries. The reason is obvious. They must have been carved on the spot, and without the aid afforded to goldsmiths or potters by other works of the same kind in form if not in material. For this reason we must not expect to find in them a consistent style. The subjects are (1) a chariot at full speed, containing one man, above a lion pursuing a stag; (2) a warrior in a similar car, before whom is another on foot; (3) a warrior advancing in his car against a foot soldier. The second and third subjects are associated with patterns out of all proportion, and another tombstone has no subject but two patterns. These devices are similar to those of the work in gold found in the tombs. The subjects have no analogy with Assyrian art, in which such representations are most unusual. In Egyptian art, however, the chief personage in each scene is represented of a gigantic size compared with the rest, and in the sculptures of battles, the king in his chariot is the principal subject, and is portrayed charging at full speed. Thus, seen from a distance, an Egyptian battle-scene has the same general effect as these subjects, speaking of course very roughly.

I have purposely taken no notice of the structure outside the Agora, as its contents have a peculiar character of their own. Besides the gold lion already referred to, which is of Egyptian style, and may be compared with those presented by Algernon Duke of Northumberland to the British Museum, there were found here two very remarkable gold signet-rings, unlike anything else discovered at Mycenæ or elsewhere, a two-handled goblet of gold, the handles in the form of dogs' heads, which in this respect resembles the tributes to the Egyptian kings, and some peculiarly primitive gold beads. The more important ring is instantly seen to be a work of no known style of art. The subject is two women approaching a third seated beneath a tree, from which a fourth plucks a fruit. The women are dressed in long skirts, or tunics, with many flounces, which in two cases have broad bands decorated with a scale-pattern. If the reader will turn to the plates of the tributes to Thothmes, he will see that the women of the Kefa wear long tunics, with three skirts one above the other, and that the men wear short kirtles, with various patterns in colour on a white ground, having a general resemblance to the earliest patterns of vases at Cyprus and Mycenæ. One of these kirtles is ornamented with the scale-pattern. Thus the Egyptian picture gives us, in two of the Kefa, the form and pattern of two dresses in the ring. The other two figures wear precisely the same kind of dress as the Kefa women, except that it is doubtful whether it is a skirt or a tunic. Still more remarkably, they have the curls rising above the forehead, and the long locks which mark the Kefa men in the Egyptian picture. Above the subject are the sun and moon, as well as a Palladium or warrior; on the right are six uncertain objects. It is curious to compare this work with the very ancient Dali bowl, in which the same peculiarities of wearing the hair are seen. This is intensely naturalistic, the other thoroughly conventional. Yet the subjects are very similar. The ring seems the more archaic, for it is free from all known influences, and thus belongs to a style probably preceding the artistic supremacy of Egypt in the eastern Mediterranean. The other ring is of a kindred style. It bears an ox-head between two agalmata, somewhat resembling the so-called owl-headed Trojan vases, and below, a lion's head between two stags' heads, besides an uncertain object on the left. Are these the symbols of the primitive Pantheon? Bearing in mind the peculiarities of this tomb in the Egyptian lion, the extraordinary signet-rings, and the primitive golden beads, as well as the absence of any link with the other remains, it may be conjectured that the find there is the most ancient, and anterior to the Assyrian influence in Syria in the twelfth century.

To sum up the evidence of the discoveries at Mycenæ, the Agora tombs appear to belong to a time at which Egyptian influence had been withdrawn and Assyrian had begun to assert itself thus far west.

Side by side with larger objects which probably owe their origin to

Egyptian art, received through a Phœnician medium, are small objects on which some traces of Assyrian style may be detected. Such indications would point to the twelfth century before our era, as the highest date for these Mycenæan antiquities. How long the influence of Assyria took to extend to this distance we do not know, and so far fail to obtain the lowest date. The lowest date depends on the next considerations. The works of art of Cyprus reach up towards the time of the Trojan antiquities, which, from their marked relation in portable objects to the work of Egyptian jewellers, and the absence of all hint of Assyrian influence, are probably within the age of Egyptian supremacy, and therefore not later than the earlier part of the twelfth century B.C. The treasures of Mycenæ show a distinct advance in the forms of vases of both precious metal and pottery on those from the Trojan excavations. At the same time a wholly new art appears in the gold ornaments. This art lies midway between that of gold vases in the tributes to the Egyptian kings (B.C. 1500 or 1400 to about 1300) and that of ornaments in the oldest types of Cyprian statues and terra-cottas much before B.C. 800. Technically it is related to the most ancient gold ornaments found at Ialyssus in Rhodes, which can scarcely be later than the ninth century.

Again, both in the Trojan and Mycenæan antiquities, we find ourselves at the meeting-point of the stone and bronze ages. This points to remote dates, as stone implements are wanting in the finds of Cyprus; where, however, we may carry up some of the antiquities very near, if not actually to, the twelfth century. Making allowance for the distance and the slowness of the movement of art in the commonest objects, still I cannot hesitate to infer from this evidence a date not later than the interval from the tenth to the twelfth centuries B.C.

The one monument that carries us up to a yet earlier age than the tombs in the Agora, is the structure outside, which produced the most curious of the golden rings. In its contents we have, with a striking Egyptian work, traces of an early art, uninfluenced in form by Egyptian, and with some likeness to that of Troy. This peculiar art has the characteristics of barbarous art, striving to copy faithfully without any canon to follow.

The type of Hellenic religion as well as of Trojan, in the two great sources, is of an age before the Dorians. It is marked by the distinctly Egyptian characteristic of the worship of animal-headed divinities, a characteristic far weaker in Assyria. This strange characteristic is found in the earliest agalmata of Cyprus, but there it is far less usual. With the Trojans and the people of Mycenæ, it seems dominant. When it disappeared from Greek cultus is hard to say. Homer, in the two famous epithets of Hera and Athene, certainly preserves it, but he does so with the same instinct that made the priests preserve the old animal-headed agalmata side by side with later representations in [illegible] merely [illegible] the old ideas in epithets, and [illegible] with no further reference to the primitive [illegible] the ages of the two treasures and the date of [illegible] forms of divinities had ceased to be the rule [illegible] passed out of literature, leaving but a shade [illegible] presence. For such a change, surely two or [illegible] too great.

[illegible] that I have not taken account enough of two [illegible], the local character of many styles, and [illegible] archaism. Both must always have their weight, but [illegible] to be considered greatest when we have to deal with [illegible] and great movements, and when archaic [illegible] the obvious qualities of degradation which mark [illegible] for ages as in Cyprus by hieratic instincts.

[illegible] here to glance again at the historical evidence which [illegible] which seem not to harmonize with the results which had [illegible] before the late discoveries by archæologists in their en[illegible] to trace up the earliest remains of art found in Greece. [illegible] be no doubt on Egyptian evidence that the Cyprians or [illegible] were great metal-workers in the time of Thothmes III., at [illegible] centuries before the traditional date of the Trojan War; that [illegible] date of that war or a century earlier the maritime Greeks were [illegible] contact with the power of Egypt, in a succession of wars [illegible] least a century, when they attempted more than once to settle [illegible] and further that the Dardans joined in a Syro-Phœnician [illegible] against an Egyptian king in this later age. Thus the [illegible] of Egyptian influence and a development of art under that [illegible] would be accounted for, both in the Troad and at Mycenæ. [illegible] be objected that we find a great gap between the supposed [illegible] assigned on these grounds to the discoveries at Mycenæ and [illegible] Troad, and the oldest elsewhere found in the Greek world, [illegible] admit the antiquity of detached archaic objects from [illegible] which are moreover non-Hellenic. To this I would reply that [illegible] not allow ourselves to be absolutely guided by the analogy [illegible] progress of Greek art at the age of its independent existence. [illegible] reasonable to apply this canon of growth to Phœnician art, [illegible] not apply to the art of Egypt and Assyria. We must also [illegible] mind that great political disturbances such as the Dorian [illegible] are sufficient to account for chasms in the monumental [illegible] having probably arrested the progress that Phœnician art [illegible] shows. Lastly we must beware of a method which would [illegible] an unreasonably short space of time various styles which, [illegible], are at least marked by distinct peculiarities, and of a [illegible] would leave the absence of coins and inscriptions in the [illegible] wholly unexplained.

[illegible] question of date that a Homeric conflict will rage once more over the bodies of heroes found at Mycenæ. It is to be hoped that in the heat of battle the combatants will not forget the dignity of the subject, and most of all the generosity of the explorer, and his earnest and successful labour in the kindred field of Greek letters. Where he may be criticized is in the poetical enthusiasm with which he describes what is rude or grotesque as if produced by the highest art. This itself is Homeric, and, put into the poet's words, reads quite naturally, however perplexing to the archæologist pure and simple. To the explorer's patience, care, and truthfulness too great praise cannot be given, nor to his dignified reticence of all notice of the attacks of those who scarcely disguise their jealousy of his success. The learned world in general will be more and more grateful for the treasures he has discovered, and for the admirable manner in which he has given every means for their fullest discussion.

REGINALD STUART POOLE.

# THE COUNTY FRANCHISE.

THERE are one or two points in the discussion about the county franchise which has been carried on between Mr. Lowe in the *Fortnightly Review* and Mr. Gladstone in the *Nineteenth Century* which seem to need putting forth a little more clearly than they are put by either disputant. Or rather, there are certain considerations which Mr. Lowe, in his last article at all events, leaves out of sight altogether, and which Mr. Gladstone hardly states in such a way as to bring home their importance to readers who may happen not to have thought of them before.

Mr. Lowe (*Fortnightly Review*, December, 1877, p. 743) speaks thus:—

> "What we are asked to do is to make a new change in the power of the State, taking it away from the constituencies in whom it is now vested, and giving it altogether into the hands of persons who have hitherto been too poor and too ignorant to have any share in public affairs."

He adds on the same page:—

> "The condition of a country which, with all its institutions standing and vigorous, voluntarily strips its rulers of their power, and confers that power on classes that have hitherto had no part, directly or indirectly, in its government, has no precedent in history, and will stand out to future times as a solitary and signal instance of human levity and presumption."

Now Mr. Lowe makes these two propositions in answer to what he calls "Mr. Gladstone's proposal for equal electoral districts and manhood suffrage." He does not make them in direct answer to the lesser proposal for making the borough and county franchise uniform. It is quite possible therefore that Mr. Lowe may not mean to say that this last change would by itself amount to "conferring power on s that have hitherto had no part, directly or indirectly, in the government." He may very likely mean to apply these words only to the further proposal of manhood suffrage. But if this be his meaning, he is almost sure to be misunderstood; he is almost sure to be quoted as speaking of the mere change of the county franchise as one that would give power to classes that have hitherto not possessed it. Language of that kind has been held over and over again, and those who hold it will be delighted to quote Mr. Lowe's name on their side, whether such be his real meaning or not. And in truth both in his article and in Mr. Gladstone's the question of uniform borough and county franchise and the quite distinct question of manhood suffrage and equal electoral districts have got hopelessly mixed up together. Mr. Lowe in fact looks on the two questions as practically one. He holds "that the extension of the franchise to country householders would make necessary a complete redistribution of seats on a new principle, and that this in its turn would make it impossible to resist the accomplishment of universal suffrage." A writer in the *Times* of December 7th discusses the two articles as if they had mainly to do with the lesser question of the county franchise. But, if this last is the point at issue, such passages as I have quoted from Mr. Lowe are very likely to mislead those who read them. It may be true that the introduction of manhood suffrage would place some degree of power, or even, as Mr. Lowe seems to think, the whole power of the State, in the hands of classes which have hitherto not exercised power at all. I will not argue that point; because I do not wish now to argue the question of manhood suffrage in any detail, but rather to bring the controversy back to the point from which it has strayed—the extension of household suffrage to the counties. To this last change, taken by itself, Mr. Lowe's assertions do not apply. Such a change would not be a transfer of power from any old class to any new class, or a grant of power to any new class. It would simply be the extension of the franchise to certain additional members of two classes, both of which are largely in possession of the franchise already. It would undoubtedly make a great change in the proportion in which power is now distributed among the enfranchised classes; but it would not bestow the franchise on any new class.

This will be easily seen by looking to certain facts of which Mr. Lowe, in his last article, seems to take no notice. Yet those facts are set forth by Mr. Gladstone, not perhaps with that fulness and clearness which would be needed to bring them home to the mind of one who had never before thought about the matter, but with quite clearness and fulness enough [illegible] them home to the mind of a statesman and practised disp[illegible] Mr. Lowe. Mr. Gladstone says (*Nineteenth Century*, Novembe[illegible]:—

"Let me begin with dismis[illegible]
of essentia[illegible]

...considerable, and too large a town population in the ... little bits of counties figuring under the name of towns, ... this distinction as a barrier to a great enfranchise-

...

...on (p. 547), he again says—

"...that the peasant of Wilton and the peasant of Wilts, ...Wallingford and the peasant of Berks, the peasant of Bassetlaw ...of Notts, should be treated alike in respect of the franchise. ...with respect to the artisan, the miner, the mill-and-forge-...compared with his compeer in Dudley; and so elsewhere. ...distinctions should be intelligible and not fantastic."

...the whole gist of the matter. People constantly ...the franchise to householders in counties and giv-...to agricultural labourers were simply the same thing. ...as if both were something new. They talk as if it were ...of the present arrangement that among the town popu-...franchise should be obtained simply by the possession of a ...in the rural districts the franchise should be confined to ...own or occupy houses or other property of a certain value. ...distinction, whether reasonable or not, would be intelligible. ...object of the existing law be to establish such a distinction, ...fails of its purpose. It makes indeed a distinction ...those who live within and those who live without the ...of parliamentary boroughs. But this distinction does not ...the distinction between town and country, or to any other ...of any kind. The distinction, as Mr. Gladstone says, is ...gible, but fantastic. People talk of extending household ...the counties as if it simply meant giving the franchise to ...l labourers. It means that certainly; but it also means ...franchise to a large class which is as strictly urban as those ...the borough franchise at present. They also talk as if ...franchise to agricultural labourers was simply altogether ...evolutionary, something which would bring down the sky ...eads. If so, the revolution ought to have come, the sky ...have fallen, long ago; for large bodies of agricultural ...at this moment in possession of the franchise.

...state of the case is that, as things are at present, certain ...of the urban and the rural class, parts quite capriciously ...the elective franchise, while other parts of the same ...capriciously chosen, are shut out from it. Here is a ...a member of its own, chosen by all the householders ...Here is another town of the same size and class, which ...of its own, and whose householders have votes for ...if their holdings are of a certain value. Here is a ...which no man can vote unless his holding reaches a ...there is another rural district close by and of exactly the same character, in which every householder has his [illegible] where of course a large part of the constituency consists [illegible] tural labourers. The object of extending household [illegible] counties is, not to transfer power into the hands of any new [illegible] whether agricultural labourers or any other, but to redress the monstrous inequality which is produced by the arbitrary line which is now drawn between members of this or that class living in one [illegible] members of exactly the same class living in another place of [illegible] the same character.

Mr. Gladstone puts this forth very clearly to those who, either from general study of the subject or from particular local knowledge, happen to be familiar with the instances which he quotes. But I suspect that there are many who will hardly understand what he means by his opposition between "the peasant of Wilton and the peasant of Wilts, the peasant of Wallingford and the peasant of Berks." The reference to "Bassetlaw" will, I suspect, to many be darker still. Bassetlaw is a famous name in our parliamentary history, and "Bassetlaw reform" was at one time a proverb. Yet many will read Mr. Gladstone's article to whom the name of Bassetlaw will not suggest the singular history of the borough of East Retford. I am unavoidably writing without books, and I cannot give exact dates. But the story was something like this. Some years before the great Reform Bill the borough of East Retford was found to be notoriously corrupt. It was proposed to disfranchise it, and to transfer its members to some large unrepresented town. Instead of so doing, the borough of Retford was enlarged by throwing into it the whole adjoining hundred of Bassetlaw. Hence the phrase "Bassetlaw reform." So, at an earlier time, the corrupt electors of Shoreham were disfranchised by name, and as the remnant who had kept themselves clean were but a small body, they were strengthened by extending the franchise of the borough to the whole rape of [illegible] It thus follows that in two large agricultural districts, the [illegible] Bassetlaw and the rape of Bramber, men get votes on easier [illegible] than they do in the other parts of the counties of Notting[illegible] Sussex. In the hundred of Bassetlaw every householder [illegible] the next hundred only those householders vote whose [illegible] reach the mark fixed by the Act of 1867. That is to say, [illegible] dred of Bassetlaw the dreadful thing has happened [illegible] the agricultural labourer has the franchise. The [illegible] with Cricklade, Wilton, Aylesbury, Woodstock, [illegible] other boroughs of the same kind. Only a [illegible] stituencies is urban. The greater part [illegible] boroughs consists of the agricultural [illegible] of the surrounding rural districts, [illegible] tainly fantastic and not at all [illegible] than the inhabitants of the [illegible] the agricultural labourer already in possession of a these at all the only cases in which he enjoys that There are parts of England in which the agricultural not uncommonly a freeholder, where he gives his vote as of a certain portion of the soil of England just as much as . There are many such in my own neighbourhood in . There is then nothing novel, nothing revolutionary, votes to agricultural labourers. In England we go by pre- and for the vote of the agricultural labourer there is plenty . To extend to the whole class a right which is at t possessed by a part of the class chosen at haphazard, what- may be, will not be to give power to a class none of whose ers have ever possessed it before. And, to judge at least from perience of the rural boroughs, it does not seem that the pro- extension of the franchise from a part of the class to the whole be followed by any very revolutionary consequences. It does pear that the members for New Shoreham, for instance, have as a rule, men of specially dangerous principles. Stroud, famous for its frequent elections, is not exactly a case in point. It is ugh which covers a large surface on the map, and which must r many agricultural labourers among its electors. But it is not piece of Gloucestershire cut off from the rest by an arbitrary It is a district which has a distinct character of its own. The gh of Stroud represents the cloth district of Gloucestershire, ict which is not indeed continuously covered with houses, but contains several towns and villages which derive a certain unity he prevalence of the same kind of occupation throughout. For parate existence of the borough of Shoreham no reason can be For the separate existence of the borough of Stroud a reason given. But it does not seem to follow from that reason that abitants of the towns and villages which form the borough of should get their votes on easier terms than the inhabitants of represented towns and villages of Gloucestershire.

mention of unrepresented towns brings me to the other side of oposed change. As the extension of household suffrage to es means the raising of certain rural populations to the level of of their own kind, it no less means the raising of certain urban tions to the level of others of their own kind. At present the of household suffrage is scattered about among the smaller of England in a manner as purely capricious as the way in it is scattered about among the purely rural districts. Let me instance from my own county. Frome and Yeovil are two ing towns in Somerset, such as perhaps a Yorkshire or man might not think much of, but which seem considerable eyes. They are towns of the same class, of much the inhabited by much the same kind of people. In municipal dignity, Yeovil has the advantage, having a Mayor and Town Council, while Frome has none. But, while Frome has a member of its own, Yeovil is represented only by the members for Mid-Somerset. That is to say, every householder in Frome has a vote, but only certain householders in Yeovil have votes. Yet it is impossible to give any reason which shall be intelligible and not fantastic why a £5 or £10 householder in Frome should be thought fit to have a vote, while a householder of the same class in Yeovil should be thought unfit. We are of course not for levelling down, but for levelling up; we do not wish to lower Frome, but to raise Yeovil. To meet this case, which is a type of hundreds of cases scattered over every county in England, we wish to give household suffrage to the counties. That is, we wish to place the inhabitants of Yeovil and of other towns in the same case as Yeovil on the level with other people of their own class on whom, by a distinction purely fantastic, higher rights than their own have been bestowed.

Such is the case of these unrepresented towns, small as compared with our great cities, but locally considerable and inhabited by a really urban population. But besides them there are in the more populous parts of the country large districts, not at all inhabited by agricultural labourers, but by persons of exactly the same class as those who possess the borough franchise, to whom the proposed change would at once give the vote which they are surely as fit to have as their neighbours. Round about London, Manchester, and our other great towns, indeed in all our great centres of industry, there are "provinces covered with houses" which are not within the boundaries of any parliamentary borough. Their inhabitants therefore do not get votes on the same terms on which they are given to persons of exactly the same class within the bounds of a parliamentary borough. To these persons too, as well as to the agricultural labourers and the inhabitants of the unrepresented towns, the proposal for household suffrage in counties proposes to give votes on the same terms as their fellows within the parliamentary boroughs. Here too there is surely nothing novel or revolutionary, no transfer of power to a new class which never possessed it before. The £10 householder in the suburb is exactly the same kind of person as the £10 householder within the borough. It is a fantastic distinction indeed which gives political powers to the one and refuses them to the other.

The conclusion then to be drawn is that in the proposal to equalize the county and borough franchise, there is nothing new, nothing unprecedented, no bestowal of power on any new class. It simply proposes to bestow power on certain fresh members of two classes, of both of which classes some members hold it already. Agricultural labourers, inhabitants of small towns, inhabitants of the suburbs of large towns, at present possess the franchise in some cases and do not possess it in others. No intelligible distinction can be drawn between the cases in [illegible] in which they do not. It is proposed [illegible] to give the franchise [illegible] which it is already possessed by many. [illegible] is proposed. The further question of [illegible] which the controversy has changed in the hands [illegible] of Mr. Lowe ought to be kept distinct. It [illegible] own grounds. That change undoubtedly would [illegible] power on a new class, and arguments may fairly [illegible] prove or disprove the fitness of that class. But argu- [illegible] or unfitness of the agricultural labourer come [illegible] should have been brought in 1867 when the franchise [illegible] a large body of agricultural labourers, all those [illegible] householders within the rural boroughs. Those who [illegible] the franchise to the householders of the rest of Sussex [illegible] disfranchise the householders of the rape of Bramber. [illegible] to follow Mr. Gladstone in his curious argument about [illegible] inequality. But as to the question of fitness I would [illegible] by fitness is meant a real power—that is, in most cases [illegible] of really thinking and judging of political questions, [illegible] reason to suppose that the agricultural labourer has less [illegible] many farmers, many squires, many knights of the shire? [illegible] at some of those persons, especially of what call them- [illegible] educated classes, who have votes now, it is impossible to [illegible] hat the agricultural labourer can be lower down in the [illegible] can hardly be more ignorant; he is certainly much less [illegible] He is at the worst untaught; he is not elaborately taught [illegible] acts and reason are far more likely to weigh with him [illegible] those who still need a Sôkratês to convince them of [illegible] of knowledge without the reality. My experience of [illegible] is that men are largely made fools and kept fools by [illegible] as fools. Treat them as rational beings, and you have [illegible] step towards making them so.

[illegible]

[illegible] there is nothing novel or revolutionary in the change [illegible] be fully admitted that it is a change which must lead [illegible] changes. Mr. Lowe says, "that the extension of the suf- [illegible] householders would make necessary a complete redistri- [illegible] a new principle." It would certainly imply a large [illegible] seats; but I do not see that redistribution of seats [illegible] any new principle. I see no reason why we should [illegible] old distinctions of counties, boroughs, and univer- [illegible] is quite certain that the claims of particular [illegible] and new, would have to be examined in a far [illegible] than they have ever been examined in any [illegible] Reform Bill since the great one of 1832. And [illegible] conviction that, on one point of this argument,

Mr. Lowe has distinctly the advantage over Mr. Gladstone. It is surely better in itself and more in accordance with all English notions that parliamentary elections should be made, as far as possible, by bodies of men who have something in common with one another, who have some corporate or *quasi*-corporate feelings and interests, like the electors for counties, boroughs, or universities. At the same time, these *quasi*-corporate feelings are quicker in springing up than is sometimes thought, and it might well be that an electoral district might, sooner than one fancies, draw to itself something of the sentiment which attaches to a man's county, borough, or parish. But, however this may be, I am at a loss to see how the introduction of household suffrage in the counties would necessarily lead to equal electoral districts. We might surely have counties and boroughs, just as we have now; only it would be needful to reconsider their boundaries more thoroughly than has been yet done. If the county and borough franchises were equalized, that would not of itself do anything to take away the utterly capricious way in which seats are now distributed among the smaller towns. It would indeed bring the present inequality out in a stronger light. Take the case which I took before, of Frome and Yeovil, or that of any other two towns which stand in the same position. As it is, the distinction made between Frome and Yeovil to the advantage of Frome would seem to go on the assumption that Frome has an urban population, and that Yeovil has a rural population, and that an urban population is fit, while a rural population is unfit, to exercise the franchise. The premisses are false; but the conclusion follows reasonably enough from the premisses. But if household suffrage were extended to the counties, if a man in Yeovil got his vote on the same terms as a man in Frome, that would be a practical declaration that the people of Yeovil were as fit to exercise the franchise as the people of Frome. The question then would come even more strongly than it comes now, If a Yeovil man is as fit to vote as a Frome man, why should the vote of the Frome man go for as much as the vote of several Yeovil men? Why should a few thousand people in Frome have a member to themselves, while much the same number of people in Yeovil simply go for a few among the many thousands who are represented by the two members for Mid-Somerset? If I had figures at hand, I could easily do a sum to show how many Yeovil men would still answer to one Frome man. But the inequality is so plain that it hardly needs figures to make it understood. It comes to this, that there still would be, as there now are, favoured districts. Though a district would not, as now, get votes on easier terms than others, there would be districts where each vote counts for a great deal more than it does in others. The change in the franchise would only make this inequality stand forth even more glaringly than it does now.

But it surely does not follow that the remedy for this is to be found electoral districts, in the exact apportionment of one many electors. Indeed I believe that such an exact would be in itself unfair. Some kinds of constituencies in themselves; they have means of making their wants known, irrespective of their parliamentary representative. this some years back in a note to one of my Historical Essays ed that London, above all, should not be represented in portion to its population as compared with other parts of ry. I argued that every member of Parliament was in some mber for London. And the same argument applies in a e to all places wherever great populations are packed closely The 300,000, or whatever may be the exact number, of ts of Manchester or Birmingham have a weight in themselves, fore do not need so many members to represent them in t as the same number of men scattered over a thinly in- ounty. It would scarcely be possible to redress gross es, without bringing in absolute arithmetical precision. We ely still have counties and boroughs returning one, two, more members, in something like proportion to their size, inding ourselves to give one member to a certain number tants exactly according to the multiplication table. We e, as at present, a larger town more members, and a smaller , and we might assign those members with close regard to ve size of the towns, without destroying the corporate or orate character of the electoral bodies. Men who are used ether as citizens of the same town might act together in toral character, just as they do now.

uld still then, even though the county and borough franchise lized, go on giving members to our counties and our great h some regard to the relative amount of their populations, ut affecting the exact numerical equality. The real difficulty smaller parliamentary boroughs. At present, as I have already listribution of seats among the smaller towns is utterly capri- ollows no rule of any kind. One town has a member of its own; the same size and class has none. Here redistribution must be

members each, because the rural districts attached to them* gave them an imposing figure of twenty or thirty thousand inhabitants. While they were spared, much larger towns, like Lichfield, Dorchester, Chichester, suffered amputation. There was nothing unjust in the amputation taken by itself: those towns had clearly no claim to two members. The injustice lay in amputating them and leaving Cricklade and Shoreham whole. So again, in the last stage, when seven English boroughs were to perish to provide seven new members for Scotland, a most instructive debate took place on the question whether Wells or Evesham should be disfranchised. I have told the story elsewhere, but it is worth telling again. Several irrelevant arguments were pressed on both sides, in the course of which it came out that Sir John Pakington, now Lord Hampton, believed that Evesham abbey was still standing. In the end, Wells perished and Evesham was left alive. This decision was come to on the ground that Evesham had a population greater than that of Wells by some thirty or forty. And so the parliamentary borough of Evesham certainly had. But the town of Wells contained a larger population than the town of Evesham. The population of Wells, though small, was strictly urban; the still smaller population of Evesham was swelled by the addition of a rural district which turned the balance of apparent population in its favour. To have disfranchised both Wells and Evesham might have been perfectly just; to have grouped both Wells and Evesham with some other towns in their several counties might have been perfectly just. But to destroy Wells and keep Evesham, because an agricultural population was tacked on to Evesham, while none was tacked on to Wells, was surely a distinction altogether fantastic and not at all intelligible.

This brings me to the question as to the way in which the present haphazard distribution of members among the smaller towns is to be reformed. There are two obvious ways of doing it. One would be to make the right of distinct Parliamentary representation a privilege of towns of really considerable size, and to throw all the smaller towns, whether at present represented or not, into the counties. The seats now held by these smaller towns would of course be divided among the counties and the greater towns. This is the kind of reform which would probably suggest itself to a reformer from Yorkshire or Lancashire. And it has at least two strong arguments in its favour. It is a great deal simpler than its rival; and for party purposes it would most likely be practically better. The other is one in whose favour I have often argued in various shapes, and it is one on behalf of which a reformer from the South of England naturally has something to say. It is, [illegible]

* In the case of Cricklade, the attached district is not wholly rural, it includes one or two market towns larger than itself, among them Swindon, to which the railway has given a considerable growth. A borough of Swindon might be quite intelligible; but it is hard to understand why either the very small town of Cricklade, or the rural parishes which lie between Cricklade and Swindon, should have any privilege above the rest of Wiltshire.

intelligible point of view that, while some members counties and some to the large towns, some may also the small towns. Their inhabitants form a class apart, feelings which are not exactly the same as those of of the large towns or of the purely rural districts. have an unfair share of the representation, and their distributed among themselves. But it might to give them a smaller share, and to distribute This could only be done by grouping together towns, and giving the groups a member or members population. The system actually exists in Scotland I know nothing of the arrangements in Scotland; in groups are very badly laid out; but that does not with proper care, groups might not, both in Wales and better laid out. It is certainly absurd to yoke a huge town with two other places hardly more than villages to return member. It is no less absurd in some other parts to give a group hardly any of whose members rises above a village. hand it must be remembered that a Welsh town, the own district, has a greater relative, and therefore a positive importance than an English town of the same size. most English counties of any size, most certainly in those of ter and Somerset, it would be easy to put together a group of representing a class of electors distinct alike from the purely habitants and from the inhabitants of a great city like Bristol. se it would be a thing not to be done in a hurry. It would most careful examination of local claims and circumstances of If such an examination should be thought beyond the a mortal House of Commons to get through, there is the to fall back upon.

of these ways then the redistribution of seats which must the extension of household suffrage to counties might surely without bringing in any new principle, without bringing electoral districts, without disturbing the old English traditions and boroughs as separate elements in the national repre- There is surely nothing strange, nothing terrible, nothing in any part of the scheme. Nothing in truth is asked the householders of Yeovil may be put on a level with the of Frome, that the householders of the rest of Sussex may level with the householders of the rape of Bramber.

only to mention one or two incidental points in Mr. Whatever may be the force of Mr. Gladstone's argu- every man contributing to the public revenue and the certainly not met by Mr. Lowe's flippant excuse about and cats. It is needless to show that a dog does not contribute to the revenue in the same sense as a m namely, by his own voluntary act. A dog contributes o lucifer match might have contributed, if all Mr. Lowe's schemes had been carried out. And when Mr. Lowe goes o forth the undoubted truth that "property is not identical w dom and virtue," so far as that proves anything, it surely favour of lowering or abolishing property qualifications rathe favour of keeping them up. Then, again, it depends on the which Mr. Lowe may attach to the word "slight," whether w that "in the great Civil War it is but a slight exaggeration to the king, the nobility, and gentry were on one side, and t classes on the other." That the saying is an exaggeration M own words imply; and, when we remember how many men and gentle rank fought on the side of the Parliament, we m clined to think that the exaggeration is not a slight one. I important to note the confusions which Mr. Lowe makes wit to the constitution of the United States. Any one could ans of his references to American matters. It proves nothing "What has manhood suffrage done for America? Did it save one of the most desolating civil wars that history records?" be just as much to the purpose to say that the absolute mon France, that the balanced constitution of England, did no save either country from civil wars. If Mr. Lowe could s manhood suffrage caused the American Civil War, or that restricted suffrage would have hindered it, then, and then onl his question have the slightest point. All these are mere but it is a complete misconception of facts when Mr. Lowe s

"Other countries, such as France and America, who have adopted suffrage, have treated it more like an inevitable torment than a bene stitution. . . . . The American constitution is a monument of th which the founders of the Republic felt for the institution which obliged them to adopt. Because Congress, elected by universal suffra safely be trusted with the functions which we leave to the House of they are obliged to endure for four years a head of the executive, whom heartily wish to get rid of, and to endure a Congress which has reflect the opinion of the country. By fixed periods of time, and by of the Senate, they contrive to find a *modus vivendi* with universal su

It is passing strange if Mr. Lowe has never looked at the "Fe at any of the earlier constitutions of the several States, or eve Federal Constitution itself. Yet this passage really sounds were so. Mr. Lowe has altogether mistaken the [illegible] the principles of the authors of the Federal Constitution. not a word in the Federal Constitution about universal [illegible] indeed could there be. It is of course inaccurate to [illegible] Lowe that Congress even now is elected by universal [illegible] Lowe most likely uses the word "Congress" in [illegible] House of Representatives only. But the Federal [illegible]

... House of Representatives shall be chosen by ... nor was it so chosen in the earlier days of the ... of Representatives according to the Federal Con... by those persons who have votes for the most ... of Legislature in their several States. This rule is ... universal suffrage; it is also consistent with a franchise ... as Mr. Lowe could wish. In fact the Federal Constitu... consistent with any system of qualification, except that which ... the franchise strictly hereditary. The qualification for ... of the House of Representatives depends wholly on the ... several States. Universal suffrage is now the rule in most, ...e in all of the States. But when the Federal Constitution was ... most of the States had some qualification or other for the ... franchise, and the House of Representatives was therefore not ... universal suffrage. Universal suffrage was not an institu..., as Mr. Lowe says, the founders of the Republic were ... to adopt: as a matter of fact they did not adopt it. The ... which led the founders of the Republic to settle the powers of ... they did will be found set forth in the "Federalist," and ... will find that they had nothing whatever to do with his ... necessity of universal suffrage. And Mr. Lowe seems not ..., in a Federal Constitution, the Senate or *Ständerath*, the ...ntative of the separate being of the States, is equally neces... whether the House of Representatives or *Nationalrath* is chosen ... suffrage or not.

... this away from books, and with no power of reference ... matter, even to Mr. Lowe's former article in the *Fortnightly* ... His second article, and that of Mr. Gladstone to which it is ...ver, it will be seen that I have had by me. I trust that I have ...represented Mr. Lowe on any matter, and I feel sure that I ... my memory for my reading of the American Constitution. ...'s picture of the founders of the American Constitution is ... removed from fact than his favourite conventional picture ... and Cambridge studies. This last, untrue for many years ... have been true in some earlier time. Mr. Lowe's picture of ... of the minds of Hamilton and Madison certainly never ... being at all. As for the points on which I have myself in... is of course nothing new in them. The case of the rural ... and that of the unrepresented towns stand open to all men ... to look at them. But there certainly must be many who ... looked at them, when there are so many who talk as if ... of household suffrage to counties simply meant the ... of the agricultural labourer, and who further talk as ...chisement of the agricultural labourer was something ... never been heard of before.

EDWARD A. FREEMAN.

# DOG-POISON IN MAN.

PERIODICAL literature has developed one great change in modern life, that there is no subject too technical, none too professional, to be brought before the general reader. As regards medical questions, the great surgeon, Brodie, and the Nestor of English medicine, Sir Thomas Watson, led the way.

The subject of the present paper, that of the mode of working in man of poison from a mad dog, has one advantage, that it well illustrates the importance of viewing Biological studies as a whole; and shows that human and comparative Pathology are inseparable.

Let us consider what hydrophobia is, and how it comes to exist:—
1. How it acts. 2. How it is spread. 3. How it is to be prevented.

We must look at these from a general rather than from a medical point of view.

Hydrophobia, as all know, is the result of an animal poison operating on man. What does this mean? What are animal poisons? Whence do they come? How do they operate?

The subject of animal poisons is one of strange—nay, of fascinating interest. It is so extensive, that, if pursued in detail, it would wholly exhaust the patience of any that had not a special purpose in following it through its manifold particulars. Some idea of it, however, may be easily gained.

We are each of us constructed on a definite plan, the outcome of we know not how many myriads of ages operating under definite conditions by regular laws. We have a certain Form which varies according to the Race from which we spring. We are composed of Matter much the same in every human being, and little varying in all animal life endued with the higher kinds of consciousness. The fish, the reptile, the bird, the gentle quadruped that culls the living herb

"Information was received at 6 p.m. of November 21st, that a native boy, name and residence unknown, had died from the effects of snake-bite. It appears that the deceased had been on the Diamond Harbour Road, and, near the house of the informant, had gone into the jungle, having previously laid down on the roadside *a basket containing a snake* and some other things used by snake-charmers. He returned in a few minutes, and was observed to be rubbing his right with his left hand; on being questioned as to what was the matter, as he looked as though he was suffering, he said he had a burning sensation all over his body, and shortly after he fell down and died. *He had*, while in the jungle, *met with a snake*, the kind he did not mention, and, *on trying to catch it*, it bit him on the back of his right hand. . . . The precise time between the bite and the death is not known, but it could not have been more than from fifteen to twenty minutes, from the account I received of the circumstances of the case."*

The effect of virulent snake-poison, as, for instance, that of the cobra, is produced, *first*, by its introduction into the blood; *second*, by affecting the nerves either at their periphery, or along their course, or at their centre. Depression and faintness are the first result; then loss of co-ordinating power; then paralysis, convulsions, and asphyxia.†

It would seem by various experiments and observations on cobra-poisoned animals and men, that the motor-nerves alone, or the spinal cord, or the brain, may be each separately affected, or any combination of them.

Fayrer quotes Genesis, chapter xlix. 17, where Jacob says, "Dan is an adder in the path, that biteth the horse heels, so that his rider falleth backward"—*i.e.*, produces instant paralysis of the hinder limbs. This snake-poison is the simplest, deadliest, naturalest, healthy poison.

The poison created by the dog, our companion and friend, is in another category. It is not natural to him. He is himself a victim. The poison he transmits he has received. It works almost certainly his own destruction. He spreads it without intention. Man perhaps helps to cause it by his treatment of him. It is a consequence of his faithfulness and of his domestic relations, and of his familiarity, that he inflicts the injury on his master. The rabies which is his torment and curse, brings about the hydrophobia in his protector and guardian. It lies with man to save the dog from the sickness, which, once engendered, rebounds with terrible force on the human family.

Since the secreted poison which the dog emits when himself affected by rabies does not produce on man the same results that it produces on the dog, it might be suspected that there is something wild and uncertain in the *modus operandi* of a poison. It is not so. It has been well said by a classical writer, that there are three prime laws of poisons:—

1. That all have certain definite and specific actions.
2. That they lie latent a certain but varying period of time before these actions are set up.

* Fayrer: Thanatophidia of India, p. 30.

† This is admirably described, and [illegible] fullest manner, by Fayrer in the Proceedings of the Royal Society, 1874, p. 8.

[illegible] phenomena which result from the poison, when roused [illegible], vary according to the dose, and the condition or [illegible] character of the victim.

[illegible] of these laws, we may cite, firstly, so familiar an [illegible] that scarlet-fever poison will not produce small-pox; sec-[illegible] effect may be latent only a moment (as in the poison [illegible] and the poison of the cobra) before the symptoms [illegible] it may be latent for definite days, as in measles; or for [illegible], months, or even *years*, as in hydrophobia; and, [illegible] temperament, state of health, mode of life, race, inherit-[illegible], as well as the nature of the poison itself, produce [illegible] variations in the action of some poisons.

[illegible] is canine rabies? and how does rabies arise? Probably [illegible]taneously, or, if it ever does so, it is certainly with extreme [illegible] It is communicated from one rabid animal to another animal becomes rabid. Whether it ever does originate except by [illegible]unication is a question belonging to the interminable controversy [illegible]taneous generation.

[illegible] from Youatt a graphic description of rabies in the dog:—

[illegible] early symptoms of rabies in the dog are occasionally very obscure. In [illegible] number of cases, these are sullenness, fidgetiness, and continual [illegible] posture. Where I have had opportunity, I have generally found [illegible]stances in regular succession. For several consecutive hours, perhaps, [illegible] to his basket or his bed. He shows no disposition to bite, and he [illegible] the call upon him laggardly. He is curled up, and his face is buried [illegible] his paws and his breast. At length he begins to be fidgety. He [illegible] new resting-places; but he very soon changes them for others. [illegible] again to his own bed; but he is continually shifting his posture. [illegible] to gaze strangely about him as he lies on his bed. His countenance [illegible] suspicious. He comes to one and another of the family, and he [illegible] a steadfast gaze as if he would read their very thoughts. 'I [illegible] ill,' he seems to say; 'have you anything to do with it? or [illegible]?' Has not a dog mind enough for this? If we have observed [illegible] at the commencement of the disease, we have seen this to [illegible].

[illegible] species of dog—the small French poodle—the essence of whose [illegible] constitution is fidgetiness or perpetual motion. If this dog has [illegible] rabies is about to establish itself, he is the most irritative, rest-[illegible] can be conceived; starting convulsively at the slightest sound; [illegible] bed in every direction; seeking out one retreat after another [illegible] his wearied frame, but quiet only for a moment in any one, and [illegible] his limbs frequently simulating chorea and even epilepsy. A [illegible] is an early symptom, and one that will never deceive. A [illegible] been bitten by one of his dogs; I was requested to meet [illegible] on the subject: I was a little behind my time. As I en-[illegible] found the dog eagerly devouring a pan of sopped bread. [illegible] here,' said the gentleman. He had scarcely spoken, when [illegible] quitted the sop, and, with a furious bark, sprang against [illegible] seize some imaginary object that he fancied was there. [illegible] my reply; 'what do you think of it?' 'I see [illegible] retort; 'the dog heard some noise on the other side of [illegible] urging, however, he consented to excise the part. I procured a poor worthless cur, and got him bitten by this dog, ... disease from this dog to the third victim; they all became rabid ... other, and there my experiment ended."*

And again:—

"A terrier, ten years old, had been ill, and refused all food for th... the fourth day he bit a cat of which he had been unusually fond ... wise bit three dogs. I was requested to see him. I found him ... kitchen, and at first refused to go in, but, after observing him for ... two, I thought that I might venture. He had a peculiarly wi... look, and turned sharply round at the least noise. He often watc... of some imaginary object, and pursued with the utmost fury eve... saw. He searchingly sniffed about the room, and examined my ... eagerness that made me absolutely tremble. His quarrel with ... been made up, and when he was not otherwise employed he was ... ing her and her kittens. In the excess or derangement of his ... fairly rolled them from one end of the kitchen to another. Wh... induced his master to permit me to destroy him."

No person of ordinary observation need be told that do... children, have all their personal characters, which they ... them into their hours of sickness and suffering.

"It is not every dog that in the most aggravated state of the ... a disposition to bite. The finest Newfoundland dog that I ever ... rabid. He had been bitten by a cur, and was supposed to have be... examined in the country. No wound, however, was found: the ... was almost forgotten, and he came up to the metropolis with his ... became dull, disinclined to play, and refused all food. He wa... watching imaginary objects, but he did not snap at them. There ... nor any disposition to bite. He offered himself to be caressed, a... *satisfied except he was shaken by the paw.* On the second day I s... watched every passing object with peculiar anxiety, and follow... attention the motions of a horse, his old acquaintance; but he n... to escape, nor evinced any disposition to do mischief. I went ... patted and coaxed him, and he told me as plainly as looks and ... somewhat deepened whine could express it, how much he was gra... him on the third day. He was evidently dying. He could not ... the door of his temporary kennel; *but he pushed forward his pa... and, as I shook it, I felt the tetanic muscular action which ac... departure of life.*

"On the other hand, there are rabid dogs whose ferocity ... If they are threatened with a stick, they fly at and seize it ... shake it. They are incessantly employed in darting to the end ... and attempting to crush it with their teeth, and tearing to pieces ... or the wood-work that is within their reach. They are regard... The canine teeth, the incisor teeth are torn away; yet, unweari... sible to suffering, they continue their efforts to escape. A dog ... near a kitchen fire. He was incessant in his endeavours to esc... he found that he could not effect it, he seized, in his impotent ... coals as they fell, and crushed them with his teeth.

"If by chance a dog in this state effects his escape, he ... country bent on destruction. He attacks both the quadrupeds ... He seeks the village street or the more crowded one of the ... no dog to escape him. The horse is his frequent prey, ... not always safe from his attack. A rabid dog ...

* Youatt: The Dog, p. 181.

it no fewer than five horses, and fully as many dogs. He was seen to reacherously upon some of his victims, and inflict the fatal wound. nes he seeks the more distant pasturage. He gets among the sheep, re than forty have been fatally inoculated in one night. A rabid dog d a herd of cows, and five-and-twenty of them fell victims. In July, mad dog broke into the menagerie of the Duchess of York at Oatlands, hough the palisades that divided the different compartments of the rie were full six feet in height, and difficult, or apparently almost imposclimb, he was found asleep in one of them; and it was clearly ascerhat he had bitten at least ten of the dogs."*

subtly and by what small change of circumstance results may red, the following will show:—

re is a beautiful species of dog, often the inhabitant of the gentleman's -the Dalmatian or coach-dog. He has, perhaps, less affection for the species than any other dog, except the greyhound and the bull-dog; he sagacity than most others, and certainly less courage. He is attached table; he is the friend of the horse; they live under the same roof; are the same bed; and, when the horse is summoned to his work, the companies every step. They are certainly beautiful dogs, and it is to see the thousand expressions of friendship between them and the but, in their continual excursions through the streets, they are exposed danger, and particularly to that of being bitten by rabid dogs. It is l business when this takes place. The coachman probably did not see ay; no suspicion has been excited. The horse rubs his muzzle on the d the dog licks the face of the horse; and in a great number of cases ase is communicated from the one to the other. The dog in process of s, the horse does not long survive, and, frequently too, *the coachman their fate.* I have known at least twenty horses destroyed in this

y cases of detailed history might be quoted from the vast literathis subject—a literature, the extent of which, from Aristotle Thomas Watson, would surprise many. I would refer the to Youatt's charming book on the dog, and to the admirable haustive writings of Fleming, the industrious advocate of the of Comparative Pathology, whence I will give two passages ill show the havoc which may be caused, and how it is caused. rst, by *one* dog:—

he mad dog is not confined in a cage, but kept in a room where there liberty, it wanders about in every direction, and with all the greater n—if not accustomed to be separated from its human companions. It ually on the move, and rambles, seeks, smells, howls at the walls, flies phantoms that seem to pursue it, gnaws at the bottoms of doors, and e, and may at last make an escape through glass doors or windows. If are only separated from it by glass it does not hesitate to smash the barrier: being all the more determined to get through it when excited g them, and moved by the fatal desire to bite, which now entirely tes it. The larger the obstacles the wilder its fury, and no sacrifice is at to obtain liberty. House-dogs are trying every moment to escape eir dwelling; and those which are kept tied up or shut in a room are tly endeavouring to break their attachment, or to destroy the doors or ns that confine them, in order to satisfy their longing to be at large. hen a rabid dog makes its escape it goes freely forward, as if impelled

* Youatt: The Dog, pp. 140, 141. † Ibid. p. 134.

by some irresistible force—travelling considerable distances in a [illegible] attacking every living being it meets on its way; [illegible] to other animals, and the latter rather than mankind. Cats [illegible] next to dogs, most liable to be injured. A mad dog that had [illegible] able amount of mischief in Lancashire, in 1869, was seen, in [illegible] career, trotting along the road with a cat in its mouth, which [illegible] from a cottage, and which, some time afterwards, it dropped [illegible] Fowls, likewise, are particularly exposed to the assaults of [illegible] When it attacks, and endeavours to tear its victims, it does so in [illegible] uttering a snarl or a cry of anger; and should it chance to be injured [illegible] it emits no cry or yell of pain. Though it will not so readily [illegible] as it will other creatures, yet it is most prudent, when in the [illegible] mad dog, to allow it to pass, instead of attacking it, unless there [illegible] of killing it without the risk of being wounded by its teeth. The [illegible] ferocity would appear to be influenced very much by the natural [illegible] the dog, and the training it has received. Some, for instance, only [illegible] a slight bite in passing; while others, on the contrary, bite furiously [illegible] the objects presented to them or which they meet in their way, and [illegible] with such an extreme degree of violence as to injure their mouths [illegible] their teeth, or even their jaws. If chained up, they will gnaw the [illegible] their teeth are worn away and the jaw-bones laid bare.

"The rabid dog does not continue its progress very long. Exh[illegible] fatigue, by the fits of madness excited in it by the objects it meets [illegible] by hunger, thirst, and also, no doubt, as a consequence of the disease [illegible] limbs soon become feeble. Then it slackens its rate of travelling, [illegible] unsteadily; its drooping tail, its head inclined towards the ground, [illegible] open, and the protruded tongue of a lead-blue colour, and covered wi[illegible] all this gives the distressed creature a very striking and characteristic [illegible] nomy. In this condition, however, it is much less to be dreaded [illegible] early fits of fury. If it is still bent on attacking, it is only when it [illegible] anything directly in its track that it seeks to satisfy its rage; [illegible] longer sufficiently excitable to change its direction, or go out of its [illegible] attack an animal or a man not immediately in its path. It is extr[illegible] bable, also, that its fast-failing vision and deadened scent prevent its [illegible] easily impressed by surrounding objects as it previously was."*

The incident which is selected by Fleming concerning the [illegible] pack, though well-known, is too instructive to be unnoticed:-

"For the last seven or eight years the Durham county hounds, [illegible] management of a committee, have had Thomas Dowdswell, from [illegible] clesfield's, as their huntsman; and it is not too much to say that [illegible] breeding, with the advantage of some of the best blood, the pack [illegible] brought to a state of perfection never surpassed since the time of [illegible] Lambton, who for so many years hunted the country at present [illegible] these unfortunate hounds. The pack of forty-one couples [illegible] season under the most promising auspices, with a country well [illegible] foxes, and every prospect of success; but, alas for men's calculations [illegible] has come, and every hope apparently so well founded has been [illegible] visitation as sudden as it was unexpected.

"About five weeks ago, after a very good and severe run, in [illegible] their fox, Dowdswell observed a fine young hound, called Carver, [illegible] clesfield's Foiler, going from hound to hound in a very unusual [illegible] alarm, he had the hound led home, and by direction kept con[illegible] himself for a few days, in order to prove the nature of the [illegible] creased in intensity, and on the third day the dog was [illegible]

* Fleming: Rabies and Hydrophobia, pp. 227–[illegible]

... everything he could reach. Four hounds he had bitten previously ... . . . .

... and other hounds were seized in precisely the same ... about three or four days. As a rule the hounds so ... harmless, following the huntsman, and apparently grateful ... for them. The attacks continued, and some few began to ... of rabies. The general features of the disease were, however, what ... called dumb madness, which beyond doubt is contagious in its ... seeing that no hound, once attacked, ever recovered, the decision ... was to put them down immediately on the first appearance of the ..., in order to avoid infection.

... last week about nine couples had been attacked and died, the disease ... out. Of course hunting was dropped, and the committee, feeling ... responsibility, called a meeting of the subscribers in Durham, on ... to take into consideration the proper course to be adopted under ... painful circumstances.

... question to be decided was, whether, looking at the danger to life, and ... uncertainty as to any known mode of cure, the pack should be destroyed, ... be made to stamp out the disease by isolating every hound. Up ... it was thought the latter plan might be adopted and tried with ..., but the Monday morning's report showed the attack on several more ... had assumed unmistakable symptoms of rabies. This fact induced ... to come to an unanimous resolution:—'That it was a duty they ... the country to sacrifice the whole of their gallant pack, and to appeal ... of hounds for a few hounds to enable them to finish the season so ... cut short.' . . . .

... remarkable feature in the history of the outbreak, however, consisted ... that *some drafts of the pack were sent to India* towards the end of ..., and it was reported in Durham, at the commencement of December, that ... of these had been attacked by a 'disease of the throat' as the reporters ... it, and 'hanging of the lower jaw,' and that 'all died.'"*

Thus it is that fowls, cattle, horses, wild animals, and men are inoculated, and thus the virus is carried across Europe to the plains of India! We must apply to death brought about by rabies the same general principles as to death from snake-bite; but in the one case the poison works its fatal end at once, in the other it may lie dormant for years. It lies dormant probably by being entangled at the head of the wound, and there held in its place till some new action liberates ... lets it loose into the circulation: the view advanced by Sir Thomas Watson some years since, and now also held by others.

We have briefly considered the effect of the poison of rabies inflicted ... dog upon another, as well as the effect of virulent snake-poison ... on a man. It remains to compare the effects of the dog-poison on a man with that of the cobra upon him.

There are points of similarity and points of divergence.

The points of similarity are, first, that the poison if allowed to ... the circulation in sufficient quantity is uniformly fatal; and secondly, that the fatal termination seems certainly to be by way of the ... system.

We are not yet in a condition to say with absolute precision what

* Fleming: Rabies and Hydrophobia, pp. 65—67.

are the anatomical changes in the nervous system either in man, or in animals not man. But observations are rapidly accumulating.* It is certain that in each case the injury arises from the introduction of the animal poison into the blood. In each case, therefore, the end can be averted only by keeping the poison out of the circulation; or if in it (in a moderate quantity), *by maintaining life till it can be eliminated:* the way by which alone the Wourali can effect a cure; and this only if the poison has not wrought or set up changes destructive to the vitality or regenerative power of the nerve-elements.

The nervous symptoms in man, when once the poison has fairly entered the system, gradually increase until thirst and inability to drink remove all doubt as to the only result. The inability to drink is only a sign of deep-seated changes in the nerve-structure.

Professor Rolleston has pointed out to me that these changes, though hardly discernible, may be so great (having regard to the actual character of the force-producing nerve-cell) as to explain entirely, first, the excitement, and second, the destruction of the ordinary functions of the nerve-centres, which regulate life. In a paper to which the Professor has referred me, by Dr. Mayor, I find it noticed that "there may be differences between these delicate structures in man and other animals so slight as to be nearly inappreciable," but still differences of the widest significance and importance; and so it may quite be that fundamental changes shall take place by sudden shock or otherwise in the fine structures by which the nerve-force is developed in man, and yet the physical changes may be wholly outside the reach of our observation. It is right to add that already these changes have been observed by Dr. Gowers, though their exact import cannot yet be declared.

Hydrophobia occurring in man, after communication of the poison of rabies, is thus shown to be a "toxoneurosis." It would not be desirable, nor would it be of any use in a paper of this kind, to enter into a detailed description of the symptoms of this mode of death.† I have thought it best rather to illustrate the character of the malady in other ways. We must admit that there is, as yet, no cure known for the disease when once established in man. The most extravagant remedies have been suggested. Every form of pharmacy and charlatanism has expended itself throughout all generations—advocated

* Many persons are engaged in prosecuting researches into the actual alteration of structure which can be detected after death from hydrophobia; among whom may be named Dr. Gowers, of University College Hospital, Dr. Greenfield, of St. Thomas's, and Dr. Savage, to whom I am indebted for valuable microscopic preparations. All available knowledge will shortly be collected, under the best auspices, by a committee of the British Medical Association, including Dr. Burdon Sanderson, Dr. Lauder Brunton, Dr. Gowers, Mr. Ernest Hart, and Mr. Callender. Whether the knowledge they will certainly gain as to the *modus operandi* of the poison, and the changes it effects in vessels and nerves, will help the cure when the changes have been set up, is in the womb of the future.

† Those who desire a graphic account of a case of Hydrophobia, should consult Sir Thomas Watson's Lectures on the Practice of Medicine, vol. i. p. 590, sixth edition, 1871.

nes by otherwise great names. The pages of Coelius Aurelianus, ni, and a host of others would create considerable interest, [illegible] even amazement, on this subject. The danger is [illegible] by prompt measures taken at the time when the s inflicted. The weight of evidence seems to show that the [illegible] is the most efficacious means, excision the next, and , though sometimes sufficient, are the least to be relied upon. [illegible] I must advert to statements in various journals to ct that a case had been cured by means of Wourali poison by nburg. This is not the only case adduced. Another is reported nerica, with an excellent but cautious commentary by a great in physician, Dr. Austin Flint.

respect to Offenburg's case, I must own that from information received from Germany, through the kindness of Dr. Victor he distinguished Professor of Leipzig, I am by no means satis- t it was a true case of developed hydrophobia. Of this, as American case, I can only say that there is enough to justify and the trial of the remedy. Of all the efforts of scientific e, it would be one of the most remarkable should it turn be successful. The remedy itself is a terrible instrument, and the greatest skill in its use. That skill will not be wanting, lt of trained powers in experiment.

one evening a few weeks ago, a boy was brought to the Rad- firmary, Oxford, with the dread, if not with the signs, of hydro- He had been bitten by a dog, five years before, in the hand, in, two years before, in the leg. A pustular eruption, the size illing, had just appeared at the seat of the bite on the hand, here always had been a small scar. All connected with the e in great alarm. Now on this doubtful and slight symptom difficult questions arose :—

uld the period of incubation, if the dog had been mad, be five two years ?—On the historical evidence, Yes.

ould an eruption so occurring be likely to be the precursor of hydrophobia ?—Yes.

the genuine symptoms appeared, would the boy recover ?— he alleged cases of cure by giving the Wourali poison were en, after the symptoms arose, his death within four or perhaps s was certain.

a person die of fright, with spurious symptoms of hydro- —Yes.

strange these simple questions and answers ! Yet this is e raised in every case that occurs of dog-bite, where the n of the dog, as in this instance, could not be ascertained. t the symptoms, should they arise, Mr. Yule, Fellow of Mag- ollege, prepared for me a solution of Wourali, *whose mode of* *was able accurately to determine.* But the sore healed, and nothing remained but the old scar; and the experiment of Wourali was not called for.

This brief outline of the general character of the much-discussed malady, in our four-footed friend, and of the relation in which we stand towards it, naturally suggests the inquiry, what should be done by every State which is sufficiently organized to have an intelligent system of Sanitary Police.

If the State is in earnest to put an end to hydrophobia, it would not be worth while to do less than this, that follows:—

1st. To have a rigid dog tax, *i.e.* one which permits no unowned, unregistered dogs. Every dog should have a collar, with the name of the owner and the number of the license.

2nd. Dogs which cannot be identified by these means should be destroyed by the Sanitary Authority of the district where they are found.

3rd. No dogs should, for a certain period, be imported from abroad, except under conditions.

4th. Mr. Fleming's suggestion, that, on every dog's license, should be printed precise instructions as to the signs of rabies, and as to what should be done in case of dog-bite, should be carried out.

Practical statesmen and debates in the Houses of Parliament will doubtless suggest difficulties in these propositions. But it is hard to think that there is no agency among the Excise, the Police, the Board of Trade, the Sanitary Authorities, for carrying out with but little trouble or expense, these or any other regulations of Police for this end. Cattle, sheep, pigs, horses, do not stray unowned in the streets. I am by no means sure, that there might not be cases of exemption on payment of a much higher tax. Indeed for the sake of the poor, the cost of mere registration should be low enough to be hardly a productive tax. Packs of hounds, and some other dogs under responsible keeping, might earn immunity from the hated collar on payment of a sum quite profitable to the State, though little felt by the owners. The owner of such dogs might be safely trusted to destroy them on due cause. It has to be borne in mind that the disease may exist in all domestic animals, and notably in the wild one reserved for sport—the fox. He may perchance communicate it to the dog.

Space will not allow the distribution of rabies throughout the globe to be fully considered. Fleming has ransacked many writers in every country for records of its existence. If one should take a map of the world and mark on it with a blue wafer the countries where it is prevalent; with a red one where it exists, but is rare; and with a yellow one where it is absent, he would see, in a graphic way, that the temperate and central zones of latitude are generally occupied, rather than the extremes towards either pole. This seems to depend not upon the temperature, but upon comparative isolation of the northern and southern countries, such as Greenland, where there are many dogs and no rabies, and such as New Zealand, Australia, notwithstanding [illegible] with England, and the islands generally of [illegible]. But this matter requires more precise elucidation. Experiments at Alfort seem to show that neither thirst nor heat will [illegible] and go far to prove that it is a simple case of communi[illegible]. Great pains have been taken in France to collect a record of all known cases of persons bitten by mad dogs. M. Bouley, the learned veterinarian of France, has given in the *Comptes Rendus* for 1870 a careful and instructive abstract of reports on the subject. It will well repay perusal. In 49 departments where rabies existed, 320 persons had been bitten by mad dogs in six years. Only 129 had hydrophobia, and 123 were known to have died. No one of these 129 had the disease latent for more than six months. Most of them died on the second or third day after the symptoms appeared. Of 134 persons 92 recovered whose wounds were cauterized, and of 66 not cauterized 56 died, only 10 recovering. These statements prove the almost complete immunity through the use of actual cautery.

In the case of 785 dogs that were bitten, 527 were killed; and of 25 not killed but observed, 13 became mad. But let this be noted: of 785 thus bitten, 552 were accounted for. The authorities let 233 escape. And if these went mad in the proportion of those who were observed, there would remain 116 dogs *left at large mad*.

Statistics of this kind have been unattainable for England. But we have enough through the splendid tables of mortality, monuments alike of English civilization and of official zeal, prepared by Major Graham and Dr. Farr at Somerset House, to show that the present panic in this country depends on the horror of the complaint, not on its frequency, and upon the just conviction that it is high time to prevent its increase.

There are 22,000 cases of snake-bite annually in India, or 1 to every 10,000 of the population. In England there were in the years 1850 to 1876, 538 deaths from hydrophobia out of 12,457,265 total deaths. These occurred in 27 years, at the rate of 20 annually in a mean population of 20,781,799 persons. The annual deaths to a million persons living were 22,201, one being from hydrophobia. The cholera in Oxford, in 1854, destroyed in a few weeks 115 persons out of 26,000, which, if expressed in the proportions of the people in India, would amount to 978,077 deaths. The maximum of deaths from hydrophobia in one year, in England, from 1850 till 1876, was in 1874, viz., 61 in a population of 23,648,609; and the minimum in 1862, 1 out of 436,566 deaths among 20,371,013 persons. In the year 1876 the deaths from hydrophobia were 53, out of 510,303 deaths; or 1 in 9,628 deaths occurring among 24,244,010 persons: in other words, *one* death in a year* from hydrophobia among 457,432 living. These figures, together

* Meanwhile there was, during the eight years 1869-76, an annual average of 212 deaths among the [illegible],345 persons estimated to constitute the average population of London in the [illegible], by being run over or knocked down in the streets.

with the fact of the immunity after cautery, and the thorough attention now paid to the subject, should reduce the alarm to its natural proportions and place.

Thus I have endeavoured to present a rough sketch of a disorder which has caused too much anxiety to many. Nothing can divest the subject of its wide and weird interest. Yet nothing can be more reassuring than the knowledge of how nearly it is under our own control. The marvel is that we are and have been so careless. Often we may *prevent*, where we cannot *cure*. This has been the message of Medicine, in the present age, to Man, in more things than the poison of Rabies.

HENRY W. ACLAND.

## IN FRANCE.

PARIS, *12th December*, 1877.

ıonth of December is usually a happy month in Paris. In rate life people try to forget small grievances and quarrels, to think only of the ties of affection and goodwill existing them, that they may receive the congratulations and good the season with an easy conscience; servants, in anticipation ming *étrennes*, are unusually zealous and tractable; even the , the natural enemies of every Parisian, astonish their lodgers politeness and amiability. Society plunges into a new round and festivities, thereby affording its votaries an opportunity ing their cares and vexations in the hum of lively talk, the lights, flowers, music, and dress. The theatres reserve all their active novelties for this cheerful season. Publishers issue their handsomest works. The activity of industry and commerce to meet the increased demands upon them, and work brings some, a certain livelihood to most, and gladness to all. Nor political world escape this general tendency to tranquil activity being. Party quarrels and strifes are silenced, that more time evoted to domestic and social enjoyments, and by a sort of ement irritating questions are laid aside so as not to interfere business of the New Year. All in fact, great and small, rich masters and workmen, rulers and ruled, unconsciously review that is drawing to a close with that mixture of sadness and that bygones generally inspire; and from a disposition, o the human heart, to regret the past and regard the present favourable eyes, we forget the griefs and the trials we have ugh, and remember only the joys and the pleasures.

th very different feelings from these the French contemplate ng year, and look forward to the beginning of the new. less the year 1877 began under favourable auspices. The then in office satisfied the Republicans, and yet did not alarm ervatives; the Chamber and the Senate had shown mutual in the vote of the Budget, and seemed disposed, in order te the regular march of the Constitution, not to make an undue use of their prerogatives; the President of the Republic was regarded with universal respect, the respect due to power no doubt, beneath which more than one smile was seen to lurk, but which gave the country a feeling of security, and might in 1880 lead to the re-election of the Marshal. Finally, a hope was entertained that the war in the East might still be averted. The Universal Exhibition of 1878 promised a time of peace and fraternity to all parties, which would help France to reach the moment, always an anxious one, when a third of the Senate would have to be re-elected, a new Chamber appointed, and a new President of the Republic chosen. How have things changed since then! France has divided into two parties, separated by violent hatred and misunderstandings such as it is perhaps impossible to dissipate; all the public powers are discredited and dishonoured by abuse of their authority; all the springs of the Constitution have been strained, in some cases to breaking; and whatever the end may be that fate has in store for us, it is difficult to imagine that an orderly, happy, and peaceful state of things can result from the present conflict. Should the Republic triumph, it must give the most violent and unreasonable elements a share in the government, and dispense with the co-operation of the majority of the Conservatives, the large body, that is, who hold the wealth and the interests of the country in their hands, and who have the traditions and the habit of government. Is it possible to do without them, seeing that most of the higher posts in the magistracy, the army, and the administration are unquestionably filled by them? And on the other hand, how are they to be got rid of without disturbing social life and shaking the country to its very foundations? If the Monarchists gain the day, they must crush the Republican party; in other words, all that now represents intelligence and progress in France. The iniquity of their success, the violence and the cunning that paved the way to it, will force them to commit other iniquities and acts of violence more criminal still. They will be obliged to add military tyranny to clerical oppression; and can we suppose that in a country where more than four million of voices voted for the Republic, such a government could last long or succeed in establishing affairs on a reasonable footing?

The crisis France has gone through since the 16th of October is without parallel in contemporary history, and the most extraordinary thing is the personality of the man who has been the chief actor, if not the chief culprit. He would have been no doubt unable to do anything had he not been backed by social forces—by the clergy, by an aristocracy of wealth or birth, a bourgeoisie formerly at the head of affairs, Bonapartists longing once more to be in the possession of money and power, an army in the habit of taking the wall on every occasion—which drive him on and compel him to act. It matters little who the men who represent these different forces are,—M. de Broglie or M. de Saint Paul, Mgr. Dupanloup or Mme. de MacMahon's confessor! The forces exist, and their name is Legion. But what a singular tool they hold in their hands! What irony of fate to have placed the destinies of France in the hands of a feeble, obstinate man, who has come to believe in his own loyalty by dint of hearing it extolled, and makes it consist in keeping promises he could not make without committing a crime; who looks upon it as quite natural to violate the duties of honour his office imposes upon him, which, moreover, he [illegible] her understands nor even suspects! Never did an Emper[illegible] re more aloof [illegible] of a Republic. It is unjust to accuse him of [illegible] and treacherous combinations, because it is diffi[illegible] a depth of ignorance with regard to political matters. [illegible] believe that he really thought France would rally round [illegible] May—really thought that the Minister of Affairs, [illegible] allay the political quarrels—really wished to have [illegible]. But he always had treacherous counsellors at his [illegible] how to take advantage of his vanity and his ignorance, [illegible] his good intentions fail, and cause him to commit [illegible] which in a well-regulated State would be called [illegible] following perfectly authentic anecdote will enable one [illegible] Marshal MacMahon's capabilities as a statesman. When [illegible] with M. d'Audiffret Pasquier to ask him to form a [illegible] Ministry, the Marshal quickly rejoined, "Mais, M. Matthieu [illegible] demandes un ministère parlementaire, mais j'ai eu M. [illegible]-ce que M. Bocher n'était pas un ministre parlementaire?" [illegible] moi, M. le President," replied M. Bocher, "mais je suis M. [illegible] je n'ai jamais eu l'honneur d'être votre ministre." "Ah! [illegible] qui est-ce donc? Ah! oui, je veux dire M. Buffet!" He is [illegible]ho confuses all names, who cannot distinguish M. Bocher [illegible] Buffet, nor the National Assembly of 1875 from the Cham[illegible] of 1876, who speaks of "ma politique" and "mon [illegible]," who, in a Republic, arrogates power all but absolute to [illegible] turns M. d'Audiffret Pasquier and the representatives of [illegible] the Elysée with less ceremony than Louis XIV., who was [illegible] would have shown to the members of the Paris Parliament [illegible] came to remonstrate with him. This is the man who, [illegible] the criminal complicity of a few ambitious intriguers, and [illegible] of the timid Conservatives, has succeeded in the course [illegible] months in shaking the sentiments and the principles, [illegible] they still were, upon which a political edifice might be [illegible] France—the respect for legality, attachment to parlia[illegible], obedience to national sovereignty! His disinterested[illegible] his excuse. Had he been faithful to his duties as President [illegible] public, his name would have been honoured by the interested [illegible] of the French. He would still be talked of as the "soldat [illegible] the "Bayard des temps modernes." No one now, of his [illegible], dares to make use of these expressions, imprinted [illegible] seem to be with irony. More than this, the military [illegible] which his military reputation rested have been destroyed. [illegible] of the famous words he was said to have uttered [illegible] "J'y suis, j'y reste," has been denied; and two very [illegible] in the *Revue Politique et Littéraire* go to prove that [illegible] from having, by a bold initiative, saved the army, he had [illegible] the orders he had received, and that both tardily [illegible]. If he succeeds in destroying the Republic, he will [illegible] the one to profit by it. He will be put aside as thence[illegible] tool. One quality however, at least, cannot be denied [illegible] disinterestedness. To his friendships and his [illegible] sacrificed all that would have constituted his glory and [illegible] future.

[illegible] has likewise sacrificed the tranquillity and the future [illegible] should the French continue to look upon legality as the safeguard of their rights, and the only legitimate weapon wherewith to make their wishes triumph, if the law is made use of, by means of jesuitical interpretations and a wrong application, to deprive them of their rights and reduce them to incapacity? Why should they continue to respect the Constitution and the Parliamentary forms, if the Constitution be made use of to re-establish personal power, if the multiplicity of powers intended to secure order, moderation, and wisdom to the government be employed to create insoluble conflicts? Why should they accept the fiction of the irresponsibility of the chief of the State, when that chief usurps the responsibilities that do not belong to him? Lastly, on what basis is a Government to be established in France? How can it be expected that the citizens should unlearn revolutionary customs and revert to the peaceful course of the ballot, if the appeal made to the judgment of the country be not listened to when the caprices of one man and the wishes of a coterie are opposed to universal suffrage? How are the magistracy, the administration, and the army to be respected if the magistracy use the law as a weapon against the representatives of the majority of the country, if the administration only seek to prevent the manifestation of the national will, and if the army be employed in defending a succession of *coups d'état?*

All notions of public right and order are at present shaken, or, to speak more correctly, upset in France. The heaviest part of the responsibility falls on those whose lot it might have been to play the best part in this crisis,—on those who ought to have upheld the right interpretation of the principles of government, on those who have taken to themselves the name of "Constitutionalists." After the 14th of October they ought to have faced the situation, to have seen that the Marshal could not, either consistently with his own honour or to the advantage of the country, continue to occupy a position which had become false, through his having put himself into the hands of a party; they should, when it would have been easy, have imposed guarantees on the Republican party for the moderate Conservatives, and formed a resolute alliance with them. They could have secured the Presidency of the Republic for one of their number, and founded, both in the Chambers and country, a large Republican Conservative party. They had the wish perhaps, but, with the exception of two or three, they lacked the energy. They allowed themselves to be drawn into a series of acts of weakness. They would not condemn the De Broglie Ministry, and thus prevented the formation of a parliamentary one; they have named six new senators with the Right, who, if necessary, will vote the dissolution they themselves reject; they have encouraged the guilty hopes they themselves reprobate. A Conservative accused them the other day of betraying the party of order, saying, "I do not understand you! You betrayed M. Thiers in favour of the Monarchists; then you betrayed the Monarchists to listen to the Comte de Chambord and found the Republic; finally, you have betrayed the Republic to ally yourselves with the Right of the Senate to and vote for a dissolution. And now, you will neither give up the Marshal nor fight the Republicans! What is it you want?" A Republican might have said the same. These everlasting waverers are more fatal to the country in a time of crisis than the most violent partisans; they might say, like Racine,

> "Je ne fais pas le bien que j'aime,
> Je fais le mal que je hais."

[illegible] intentions and fine words, but, from weakness and [illegible] political crimes which they afterwards deplore [illegible] unfortunately represent but too well a considerable [illegible] party in France, which has never succeeded in [illegible] and moderation.

[illegible], at the present moment, to attempt to estimate the [illegible] degree of wisdom displayed by the different parties [illegible], to ask whether the Left of the Chamber would not [illegible] have shown more forbearance, not to have taken [illegible] the hostilities against the Government, so as not to [illegible] the Constitutionalists in the Senate an opportunity of [illegible] to the Right by their votes, to have left the Con[illegible] struggle in their impotence, and commit faults that would [illegible] the Constitutionalists over to the Left. It is quite evident [illegible] whatever the Republicans might have done would have been [illegible] them, that it was the firm intention of the Marshal's [illegible] prevent a peaceful solution of the question, and that hence[illegible] public powers or recognized Constitution exist in [illegible] but a nameless chaos, out of which by the time these [illegible] print, by dint of violence or weariness, some provisional [illegible] have sprung—a solution which, whatever it may be, can [illegible] good and lasting, in the present state of affairs.

[illegible] meantime not only the moral and political condition of France [illegible] but also her economical order. Commerce is at a standstill; [illegible] every day, and every day addresses from merchants [illegible] manufacturers beseech the Marshal to give up a policy which is [illegible] the country. Will they be listened to? It is not likely, but [illegible] minds cannot but see with dread politics becoming fatally [illegible] with economical questions. Does not this nourish the Socialist [illegible] ideas which, since 1871, seemed to be losing ground every [illegible] not the popular masses, sensible of their strength, be tempted [illegible] chimerical idea of founding a political State in which, they them[illegible] masters, they might fancy their interests would be better [illegible]? Unfortunately they are not capable of understanding that a [illegible] change cannot take place without the whole economical [illegible] of the country being disturbed. They cannot even, at the [illegible] moment, realize that the 16th of May is not the sole cause of [illegible] commercial crisis, and that the war in the East as well as [illegible] of American industry has a great deal to do with it.

[illegible] world suffers almost as much as the business world [illegible] state of France. Even the theatre, which is less [illegible] disturbances than other departments of literature [illegible] effects of the crisis.

[illegible] be a great dearth of really interesting works for M. J. [illegible] "Petites Marmites," at the Gymnase, and M. Gondinet's [illegible], to have met, the one with a partial, the other with [illegible]. Both these pieces are of a kind very much in favour [illegible] making use of some plot, no matter how unin[illegible], for the purpose of painting a malicious picture of [illegible] ridiculous sides of Parisian life. The associations [illegible] and worldly are the subject of the "Petites

Marmites," and club life that of "Le Club." The plot is not in the least interesting, the characters are not even outlined; no matter, what the author wishes to describe are the manners and customs, as if manners could show themselves in any other way than by the characters. By neglecting this essential element the author confines himself to the surface of things, to their outward aspect, and it requires a great deal of wit and fancy to hide the falseness and the emptiness of this conception of the drama. The "Cigale," by MM. Meilhac and Halévy, which is being played at the Variétés, is a piece of this kind, its chief attraction being the satire on the painters of the so-called *impressionists* school. But if the plot be based on an antiquated notion, it is revived by new and unexpected situations; amusing and stinging *mots* are profusely scattered through the dialogue; and the principal part, that of the little rope-dancer who becomes a rich heiress and a desirable *parti*, is a humorous and fanciful creation, to which the original and piquant talent of Mdlle. Chaumont lends wonderful life. It is the success of MM. Meilhac and Halévy that encourages so many young play-writers to adopt the same line. Their pieces are often nothing more than an article of the *Vie Parisienne* or the *Figaro*, diluted into two or three acts. This style is in its proper place in the Palais-Royal, where buffoonery has plenty of elbow room, or where, now and then, as in the "Panache," the "Convictions de Papa," the "Boule," some rather shrewd moral observations are hidden beneath the caricature; but when it is applied to more serious scenes, and an attempt is made to adapt it to real comedy, pictures, such as the "Club," in some sense photographic, are produced, which in spite of a certain cleverness leave the audience cold because they are wanting both in gaiety and depth.

By a strange contrast, while our *genre* theatres were all devoting themselves to this ultra-Parisian style, the drama, in its most elevated and lyrical form, was finding enthusiastic spectators elsewhere. I do not speak of Salvini and the six Shakespearian representations he gave at the Théâtre Italien. No doubt he deserved great success; he is unquestionably the greatest tragic actor living, possessing all the gifts of nature, together with all the refinements of art; a noble and expressive face, lofty stature, harmonious and powerful gestures, sonorous voice, profound and original comprehension of the works he interprets. To all who have seen him in "Othello," Othello has become identified with Salvini. Rossi was the tiger, proud, catlike, and ferocious; but Salvini is the magnanimous lion, terrible in his anger, noble and loyal throughout. Too few, unfortunately, in Paris are capable of enjoying an Italian representation, and the time is not favourable for going to the play because it is the fashion, as people did in 1875, to see Rossi. On the other hand, at the Théâtre Français, "Hernani" has excited an enthusiasm which even Victor Hugo's admirers did not anticipate. Whence this enthusiasm? It cannot be due to the subject of the drama, truly Spanish in its improbablity and exaggeration, nor to the characters which are wanting in truth and variety, for all the personages talk in the same style and are pitched in the same heroic key; it cannot be due either to the dramatic qualities of the piece, for it wants life and reality; it is conceived like an opera, and so constructed as to bring in a series of monologues resembling great arias, and dialogues that resemble duets. The success of "Hernani" is due to its poetry and eloquence, which overflow with glittering imagery and pathetic effusions. Never

... finer verses, and when spoken by the silvery voice ... Bernhardt no music could be more enchanting. Victor ... removed from this style and this harmony that we ... the classical work of an artist who is no more; and ... of the hard realities that surround us it is difficult to ... the charm of such heroic and ideal creations. We are ... for temporary consolation and some hours of noble ... and Victor Hugo had a perfect right to invite all the ... of the Parisian press without distinction of party to a ..., and, at the very height of the political crisis, say with ... authority of age and genius, "Nous nous rencontrons sur le ... des purs esprits. Il y a des orages autour de nous, il n'y en ...," and add in the words of Corneille, slightly modified,

"Au moment d'expirer, je tâche d'apaiser."

... decadence of this century, in this time of anguish and ... when all the great men who have instructed, charmed, and ... light upon France are disappearing one by one—when the ... itself seems on the point of perishing—we are glad once again ... to one of the greatest of our great writers of this century, ... his old age, to feel that time is consecrating his work, and ... the toast proposed by the manager of the Comédie Françaisc, ...ortelle jeunesse du génie!"

... not the time to try and discover what the deficiencies of this ...; but it is impossible to help noticing, in that part of his ... where he enumerated the great writers who constitute the eternal ... art, the absence of Goethe's name. Theocritus, Horace, and ... are mentioned; Goethe, the representative, *par excellence*, of the ...nth century, is left out. The truth is that Victor Hugo does ... him, has never read him, not even in a translation. And if he ... him, would he understand him?

... side with the success of "Hernani," we must place that of the ...phonic works of Berlioz. Not a Sunday but one of his com... figures in the programmes of the Pasdeloup and Châtelet .... Thus this season we have already heard the "Symphonie ...," "Romeo et Juliet," and the "Damnation de Faust." The ... these compositions has been a strange one: during their author's ... they met with nothing but coldness and hostility, whereas now ... as much admiration as the masterpieces of Beethoven. ... in this admiration. People persistently shut their ears ... passages, to others that are insignificant, to an abuse of ... music, to glaring inequalities; they forget that Berlioz has ... the wants in his musical nature, and has told us that ... capable of forming any idea of an orchestral piece until he ... played, that he often invented a subject without being ... it, or a form of instrumentation without knowing to what ... it. His *Mémoires* show that he was a *littérateur* and a ... much as a musician. A musical creation did not spring ... his brain like a complete organism, it formed itself ... Sometimes bits were missing that he could not by .... Thence the wants and the failings of this ... profound musician. But at present these defi... It is considered a duty to repair the long and grievous injustice that has been done him; our people are glad to be able to say to themselves that France too, has produced a great composer, worthy of being held up as a *pendant* or rather a rival to Wagner, whose glory is a source of secret envy and irritation to many Frenchmen. Berlioz no doubt owes his reputation in great part to the musical development that has taken place of late years, to the revolution which Schumann and Wagner have created amongst composers, but much of it he also owes to the revival occasioned by the war.

This growing enthusiasm for Berlioz is the only noteworthy fact in the musical world; for the success of the "Etoile" at the Bouffes Parisiens, will not extend beyond the horizon of the Passage Choiseul. The Opera, the Opéra Comique, the Opéra Italien, continue to revolve in a dull round either of old operas that are too well known, or new ones that do not deserve to be known; the only musical theatre that has struck out a new line for itself, and has been bringing out some interesting new works in the course of the last two years,—I allude to the Gaieté under the management of M. Vizentini,—has fallen a prey to money difficulties which will oblige it to return to operette.

Literature is far more affected by external events than the theatre. Who now has either inclination or leisure to enjoy a poem, or a novel, or a volume of criticism, when the anxious question, Where shall we be and what will have happened to us to-morrow? obtrudes itself at every turn? None of our publishers have courage to publish any works of importance. The utmost they will risk is the sale of a few volumes of posthumous works, which are the only novelties now in the market—such as the "Correspondance de Xavier de Maistre" (Lemerre), which reveals the excessive literary vanity of this pleasing writer; the "Correspondance de Jules Janin" (Jouaust)—no new revelation of the vanity of this famous critic, for it was too well known already, by his own *naïf* admission, for any one to be astonished at it. Janin's fame was one of the *bizarreries* of the time of Louis Philippe, when there were plenty of writers to admire. This big, ignorant, harmless child, who was dubbed "le prince des critiques," and whose opinions on the stage have for the last twenty years passed for oracular, was absolutely wanting in the critical faculty. He had a kind of sparkling foam of wit and imagination, a certain prettiness, the result of carelessness and caprice. His learning consisted in a mania for Latin quotations, crammed with solecisms, and his judgments in a series of apostrophes and exclamations without head or tail. But after all, this *sans façon*, this jovial vivacity, this easy way of talking about everything while knowing nothing, though most offensive in a book or even a newspaper, are not without their charm in correspondence; and it must be owned that Janin's letters are pleasant reading.

A higher kind of pleasure is afforded us in the "Nouvelles Lettres d'un Voyageur," by G. Sand (Lévy). In them we recognize the full limpid style of the great novelist, her love of nature and wondrous descriptive talent, and that philosophical optimism which had its source in profound goodness. It is strange, in the midst of the concert of lamentations, wherein the pessimism of the present day finds vent, to hear a voice saying that in the universe "tout est heureux depuis la grande âme du monde qui révèle sa joie de vivre par son éternelle activité jusqu'à l'être qui se plaint toujours, l'homme." The voice, it is true, is not a voice of the present; it proceeds from lips sealed three years ago in death. And hearing it, one is surprised that so short a time should have elapsed, so far removed is her mode of thinking and feeling from ours. Her vague pantheism and enthusiasm indistinctly spread over everything, her psychology and her equally vague and universal science, under which reality is veiled at every turn by lyricism, all appear to us to be tinged with obscurity and even with declamation; we are tempted, though wrongly, to question their perfect sincerity, and, in the long run, are wearied by them.

How far our novelists are from their great precursor! Look at M. Daudet's "Nabab," the only literary success of the moment. Is it a novel, is it art, or is it not rather a photography of life itself? Do not look for either the passionate idealism or the limpid fulness and depth of G. Sand in it; the reality is painted with a crudeness that emphasizes its ugliness, and with an impassiveness that repels sympathy as a weakness. The fever of the Parisian life it depicts is apparent in the style; it is tumultuous, disorderly, iridescent, scattering spangles of glittering gold upon the mud and rubbish of a decaying civilization. None the less for that, it is art, for in spite of the disorders, the *tohu bohu* of the composition, the breathless, inequality of the style, it gives the reader a vivid picture of the Paris of the Second Empire; the personages are living and true, and the feeling that bursts out in some of the scenes reminds one now and then, in its vivacity and freshness, of Dickens. To appreciate the merit of "Nabab," it is sufficient to read "Eugène Rougon" by M. Zola. He also tries to paint society under the Empire: his heavy hand, not guided, moreover, by personal recollection, has but produced a coarse coloured engraving. We did M. Daudet injustice when we spoke of photography in connection with "Nabab." His picture has all the clear biting relief of an etching with the brilliancy of a painting.

At this moment, when the taste for pure letters seems to be on the wane, M. P. Dalloz has embarked on a courageous undertaking. He has bought a review called the *Revue de France*, which had been vegetating for some years, and intends to turn it into an essentially literary review. We very much doubt whether he will succeed. It has been a more than once cherished dream to wrest from the *Revue des Deux Mondes* the monopoly and the kind of kingship which twenty years of obstinate struggle and twenty-five years of success have ensured to it. An influential publisher, and the Imperial Government itself, have respectively failed in the attempt with the *Revue Nationale* and the *Revue Contemporaine*. The *Revue des Deux Mondes* is the only institution of modern France that revolutions have not shaken, and which has been able to impose its authority on all parties. It would require more than a million of francs and years of patience to supplant it, and it is not the crowd of estimable and agreeable writers M. Dalloz has collected who will succeed. The only way would be to lure away its contributors from the *Revue des Deux Mondes*; and the day that is attempted, that review has only to double the pay of its writers, which it can do without materially lessening its gains, to retain them all. Any one who has anything new to say about science, travels, or literature, will always prefer to say it through the medium of a publication which already numbers more than 20,000 subscribers, and is read throughout the

If the literature of imagination be poor and meagre, the noises from without have had less effect on the more severe works of philology and history. The Ecole des Hautes Etudes has just issued two new volumes One of them, "Une Etude sur le Règne de Trajan" (Vieweg), by M. C. de la Berge, attached to the Bibliothèque Nationale, is a work of the first order. Deeply versed in epigraphy and archæology, as well as in ancient literature, a shrewd critic, and at the same time an elegant and vigorous writer, he has produced in some sense a comprehensive work on the subject. The concluding chapters on the government, customs, thought, and religion of the Roman Empire, form one of the most solid and exhaustive studies on the subject ever made. M. Giry's book on "St. Omer et ses Institutions Municipales" (Vieweg) is a very learned local monograph, the prelude to a comprehensive work by the same author on the development of the municipal institutions of France in the middle ages. For more recent epochs we have M. Forneron's book on the "Ducs de Guise" (Plon, 2 vols.), a work based unfortunately on insufficient research, with hardly any reference to original documents, but written with a spirit and warmth which give a vivid picture of the most brilliant and the most troubled period of our history. Unpublished documents have, on the contrary, been M. Valfrey's almost only source, in his conscientious study, "Ambassades de Hugues de Lionne en Italie" (Didier), as also of M. Chantelauze's, in his brilliant work on Retz's dispute with Mazarin respecting the cardinal's hat Retz solicited at Rome (Didier). MM. Valfrey and Chantelauze worked in the Archives du Ministère des Affaires Etrangères, which, with comparative liberality, have now for some years been open to scholars, and where many enjoyments and many surprises are reserved to us. M. Faugère makes us wait a long time for the unpublished letters and papers of St. Simon; and we are promised the correspondence of Cardinal de Bernis, by M. Masson. These will be invaluable documents for the history of the eighteenth century. Nor are the provinces behindhand. In the field of historical research M. Debidour, professor at Angers, has produced an excellent study on "La Fronde Angevine" (Thorin); M. Babeau of Troyes has drawn a picture, with the most minute accuracy, of the "Village sous l'Ancien Régime" (Didier), from documents collected with infinite care; M. Mége relates a curious episode of our revolutionary history in his book on the "Puy de Dôme en 1793 et le Proconsulat de Couthon" (Aubry), written with remarkable impartiality and full of new documents.

The number of workers is far more limited in the field of philology than in that of history. The principal work that has appeared in the last few weeks is the volume of "Mélanges de Mythologie et de Linguistique," by M. Bréal (Hachette). It is not a new book, seeing that it consists of a thesis on Hercules and Cacus, written in 1863 for his doctor's degree; of a memoir on the myth of Œdipus, published in the Mémoires de la Société de Linguistique; of lectures given at the Collége de France, and articles which appeared in the *Journal des Savants.* But the republication of these various studies in one volume gives them a new value, and enables one to appreciate M. Bréal's scientific ideas. He is not a creator in the field of philology; but expounds and criticizes the ideas of others with masterly soundness and elegance. He owes his reputation chiefly to a translation, that of Bopp, to which he has added some admirable prefaces. The principal merit of the work on Hercules and Cacus was its making the French public acquainted, under an ex-

[illegible] views on the solar myths, which he discovers [illegible] the old legends. His memoir on Œdipus is simply a [illegible] of the same ideas to a new legend. His [illegible] "Tables Eugubines" is a criticism and a sequel to [illegible] on the same subject. The mind of M. Bréal is a [illegible] and boldness; he is fond of new paths, not that he [illegible] himself, but he likes to follow in the steps of others: [illegible] on, then retraces his steps to be quite sure he has [illegible] one; he warns off and at times discourages those [illegible] his example but treading less surely, wish to follow in [illegible] His last volume is a striking proof of this disposition of [illegible] boldness in some cases is extreme, as in the study on the [illegible], and its timidity in others equally so, as in the articles [illegible] European roots, where, in disputing some lost children of [illegible] philology, he limits the comparative method to perhaps [illegible] bounds; and where, on account of doubtful or absurd [illegible], he seems to deny that a verbal root is invariably concealed [illegible] the substantive. It is nevertheless very evident that man was [illegible] of action and phenomenon before he conceived the wholly [illegible] idea of the object or substance whereof they are the mani[illegible] and that, psychologically if not grammatically, the verb must [illegible] before the substantive. But M. Bréal is always afraid lest [illegible] salutary novelties should be abused and in consequence dis[illegible]. He is bent on exactly defining the point where positive [illegible] stops and hypothesis begins, and does so with unquestionable [illegible]

[illegible]ould like also to draw attention to a collection that will be of [illegible] use to all engaged in the study of antiquity, namely, the last [illegible] the *Revue de Philologie d'Histoire et de Littérature Anci*[illegible] which, under the title of *Revue des Revues* (Klincksieck), forms a [illegible] publication. All the articles published in France and else[illegible] relating to antiquity, are analyzed, those that are simple reports [illegible] as others, so that no fresh discovery is overlooked. Two com[illegible] dexes make this bibliography a most useful dictionary of refer[illegible] with its help all that has been published in the course of the [illegible] about such and such a personage or author can at once be [illegible]ned.

[illegible]scholastic world does not allow itself to be disturbed in its work [illegible]re than the learned world. All the public lectures have begun [illegible] the academies are in full activity. At the Sorbonne, M. [illegible] de Coulanges, who brings his ingenious and original mind to [illegible] every question he handles, is lecturing on the Agrarian Laws in [illegible] times; at the Collége de France, M. Laboulaye, who, for some [illegible] had given up teaching for politics, has resumed his lectures on [illegible]ative Legislation. At the Académie des Sciences Morales et [illegible]ues, M. Berthold Zeller has given a very interesting course of [illegible], in which, basing his arguments chiefly on the despatches of [illegible]rentine and Venetian ambassadors, he showed that the Constable [illegible], generally regarded as a frivolous and worthless favourite [illegible] XIII., displayed the virtues of a real statesman during his [illegible] of power.

[illegible] Académie des Sciences, the subject that has excited most interest is Mr. Graham Bell's telephone, better known already in England than in France, which opens such fantastic horizons to the imagination. If the telegraph was wonderful, how much more so the telephone, which, by means of a wire and a magnet, transmits sounds to enormous distances! The idea is already entertained of being able to preserve the graphic representation of the sounds, so that they can afterwards be reproduced at will in a mechanical manner. This extraordinary invention has, for the time being, thrown M. Jablochkow's ingenious apparatus for the industrial and domestic use of the electric light into the shade, an apparatus which its inventor is continuing to improve, and which threatens to become a formidable rival to gaslight. The telephone has also for the time eclipsed MM. Frémy and Feil's remarkable discovery of the mode of making, at a very small cost, with a mixture of aluminate of lead, silicate, and bichromate of potassium, rubies as fine as real ones, and harder, which can be used for clock-work and jewelry; with the admixture of a little oxide of cobalt, they produce sapphires.

Amongst the scientific courses now going on, M. Claude Bernard's at the Museum d'Histoire Naturelle deserve special notice. The subject of his present one is the conditions and the phenomena of life. His first lectures show the ground taken by the illustrious physiologist in philosophical discussion, and the scientific precision with which he defines the limits of science. He began by examining the various definitions which philosophers and scholars have attempted to give of life, and showing that these definitions, when they are not empty phrases, are imperfect or false, and that life is a complex fact incapable of definition. Science can only seize the phenomena in the living being, the phenomena of vital creation and of organic destruction. As M. Claude Bernard very acutely observes, the former are the only phenomena that, properly speaking, constitute life—birth, nourishment, &c.; but these phenomena are interior ones; it is not by them that we become most conscious of, and most clearly manifest, our existence. On the contrary, all the acts that constitute life to us—motion, will, thought, secretion—are in reality phenomena of organic destruction, or *death*. Life only manifests itself by death. We might almost say, life is death. The professor proceeds to examine the chimerical attempts to grasp the essence of the force that governs the vital phenomena; he demonstrates the error of those vitalists who believe in a vital force acting in obedience to laws of its own, independent of the physico-chemical forces, and making it impossible accurately to determine the conditions of the development of the living being; he proves that this independent action of the vital principle is nowhere discernible, and that, on the contrary, the vital phenomena are in close and continual relation with the physical and chemical phenomena. The materialists again are equally mistaken in wishing to reduce everything to the mechanical action of the physico-chemical conditions. Such action is in fact subordinate to a plan determined beforehand, to a *vital design*. Vital force is, therefore, not an active, but a "dormant legislative force." What physiology can grasp is the manner in which the phenomena of life are determined by physico-chemical conditions. This determination is constant and absolute, but is not to be confounded with fatalism, for the very action of human liberty is determined by these physico-chemical conditions. We see how careful M. Bernard is not to allow science to encroach on the philosophical domain, and how rigidly he adheres to positive data, showing how they in nowise [illegible] with the metaphysical ideas we may entertain respecting the [illegible] of life, the final causes that govern it, and the free-will of man. On the latter point, notwithstanding, the question does not appear [illegible] entirely conclusive. M. Bernard seems to confound freedom with the possibility of acting in different ways, and of realizing one's volitions in acts. If these volitions be themselves subject to physico-chemical conditions,—and according to M. Bernard they must be so,—what becomes of freedom?

---

Those who, even less than scholars and students, have been disturbed and affected by political agitations are our little children. They have [illegible] notion of what is going on around them, nor would any one have the courage to punish them for the faults of grown-up men by depriving them of the pleasures Christmas and the New Year hold out. And such pleasures are very great in these days. Never have children been more spoiled and petted than they are now. Everybody works for them, from the pedagogue who taxes his ingenuity to discover the best ways of developing, without fatiguing, their understanding to the manufacturers of toys, who provide them with amusement and instruction combined. It would be endless to attempt to describe all the new toys and books designed for this happy age, and the improvements made in France in this respect. Children are better understood now than they used to be. The influence of England and Germany has fortunately exerted upon us. A proof of which is the change that is being introduced, little by little, in the way of celebrating the end and the beginning of the year, and the increasing importance of the Christmas festival. New Year's Day, as it used to be kept in France, and more particularly in Paris, was a somewhat dreary time for children. The day was spent in visits, some of ceremony, others of inclination, in the course of which children were smothered with presents, kisses, and bon-bons, and it ended with a great family feast. Very little time, if any, was left for the home fireside. The child was not the centre-point of the festival, as in Northern countries at Christmas, the anniversary of the day when the whole earth, symbolized by the magi and the shepherds, bowed at the feet of a Divine Child. But Christmas is beginning now to be kept in France, and even in Paris. Some Protestant and Alsatian families have set the example, and by degrees the custom of Christmas-trees is spreading. They are made for the school-children, who so often, in their poor homes, know nothing of the delights of this bright, happy, and poetical festival. One, in particular, is being prepared for the children of Alsace and Lorraine, resident in Paris since the war, and is made the occasion of a patriotic feast, held every year in the Châtelet theatre, accompanied by music, speeches, and recitations commemorative of the absent country. The Alsace-Lorraine Christmas-tree is setting a salutary example, in contributing to the spread of this patriarchal custom, which is productive of such lasting impressions on the childish imagination.

There has long been a want in France of good children's books and sensible toys. We have both now. The toys are becoming perhaps even too sensible. Everything now must be instructive; loto, the goose game, the steeple-chase, patience, the magic lantern, are transformed into geography, arithmetic, and natural history lessons, not to mention electric, pneumatic, and steam apparatus, little telegraphs, locomotive engines, and steamers, which initiate children, too early perhaps, into the secrets of modern science, and risk their becoming *blasé*. With regard to books, the progress is no less remarkable. People have learnt to write for children, to be childlike without being childish. Two publishing firms, MM. Hachette's and M. Hetzel's, have made a speciality of children's books. The former, besides the simple stories known as "La Bibliothèque Rose," have a series for a more advanced age on science and industry, called "Bibliothèque des Merveilles;" an illustrated magazine, the *Journal de la Jeunesse*, containing tales of romance and articles on science adapted to the understanding of children; and lastly, illustrated books of a handsomer form, which contain more important works of fiction. Two of the writers for this collection have earned a well-deserved reputation—M. J. Girardin and Mme. Colomb. M. Girardin began with a book in which scenes of the war of 1870-71 played an important part, called "Les Braves Gens," a story full of feeling and patriotic fervour, and the best thing he has written. The success of "Les Braves Gens" made him turn more than once to the Franco-German war for his subject, and he is wonderfully successful in painting the hard and brutal but at bottom good and upright character of the German officer. He has neither caricatured nor flattered him, which is a rare merit. M. Girardin is a shrewd observer, a painter of manners and customs rather than of character. His personages are types rather than individualities. His "Oncle Placide" is the slightly satirical portrait of a Government employé; into his "Neveu de l'Oncle Placide," he has introduced some American types drawn with a great deal of fun. He might be accused of not looking at things quite enough from a child's point of view; the humorous irony that constitutes the chief charm of his books is rather beyond even boys of twelve or thirteen, unacquainted with the world and with life. Mme. Colomb writes with more simplicity, and has a clever and pleasing imagination; but, like M. Girardin, does not know how to draw living characters. The attraction of her stories is the unlooked-for events that take place. The one she has just published, "Chloris and Jeanneton," describes the country life of the nobles and peasants of the last century, but it reminds one a little too much of the fanciful pictures of Berquin or Mme. de Genlis. Another, "La Fille de Carilès," shows very superior talent and real feeling. It is an adaptation, or rather a very clever imitation, of the "Lamplighter," a masterpiece of juvenile literature. The art of character-painting, which is one of M. Girardin's and Mme. Colomb's weak points, is Mme. de Pressensé's strong point. She has already written a number of books for children,—"Rosa," "La Maison Blanche," "Deux ans au Lycée," "Un Petit Monde d'Enfants,"—and has just published another, "Bois-Gentil" (Fischbacher), equal to her others in every respect. Mme. de Pressensé, who is well known for her unwearied labours for the relief and education of the poorer classes, is in constant contact with children. She loves and understands them. And there is nothing in her books they cannot understand; the incidents are simple, and the characters lifelike. "Bois-Gentil" is the history of a family living in the country who lose their fortune, and, nevertheless, take a little orphan niece, spoiled by a Parisian life, to live with them. Louise, the big girl who gives herself airs and is romantic and writes verses in secret; Roger, a noisy, giddy, but affectionate boy; Jeanne, the loving little sister who always forgets herself and thinks of others; Nina, the grand selfish Parisian; Suzette, the scolding but devoted cook, [illegible] people. The authoress does not describe their character; they show it by their words and actions. The whole is animated by a high [illegible], and furnishes mind and heart with wholesome food. The firm of Hetzel has shown a most fertile invention in the field of juvenile literature. Their monthly publication, *Le Magasin d'Education et de Récréation*, is remarkable both as regards drawings and letter-press, which are the work of first-class artists and writers. Froelich, the admirable Swedish draughtsman, who is so successful in catching the mingled awkwardness and grace of children, produces the most charming picture-books every year, to which Hetzel himself, under the pseudonym of Stahl, furnishes texts full of fun and simplicity. A. Daudet tells us the touching story of "Petite Chose." Lucien Biart, in his "Aventures d'un Jeune Naturaliste," unfolds a charming talent for story-telling, and an intimate acquaintance with nature. M. Macé, under the titles of "Le Serviteur de l'Estomac" and "Une Bouchée de Pain," has given us the best books of juvenile science we have. But the prince of this semi-scientific, semi-romantic literature, and a genius in his way, is Jules Verne. It is a much debated question whether his books are wholesome reading, whether the mixture of the most accurate scientific data with the wildest fancy is not calculated to give children false notions and ultimately to disgust them with real science. But no one can deny his prodigious talent and the fascination his stories exercise on readers of all ages. He has with less poetry, an imagination worthy of Edgar Poe. In "Les Indes Noires," in which he describes the life of the Scotch miners, he perhaps pushes the fantastic beyond the limits of the probable; but just now his "Hector Servadac" is making all the little heads dream of the hero's travels.

What is very much wanting in France is poetry for children. Our language and poetical form require a certain refinement; the simplicity the juvenile understanding demands easily sinks into commonplaceness in French, and exists neither in the French mind nor language. In MM. Ratisbonne's and de Grammont's collections, "La Comédie Enfantine" and "Les Bébés," in some respects so charming, there are very few pieces children are capable of enjoying. M. Marelle's "Petit Monde," in which he has tried to imitate the delightful juvenile poetry of Germany, is not poetical. An Alsatian of bold and inventive mind, M. Kuhff, who is known by some excellent German lesson books, "Form und Zahl, Rhythmus und Reim, Spruch und Sprache," has tried to collect everything in our literature that seemed to him most suitable for developing and adorning a child's mind. These collections are open to many criticisms, but they are the best we have. "Les Rimes et Dictions" (Fischbacher) contains all the proverbs in verse, verses that have become proverbs, and famous epigrams, in which French literature abounds; his "Enfantines du Bon Pays de France" is a selection of popular songs, puzzles, and childish rounds, to which the popular verse of our provinces has contributed some gems. Lastly, his "Leçons et Lectures en Vers" is a selection of short and easy verses suitable for children, and arranged under the heads of "La Nature," "Les Bêtes," "La Famille," "Dieu," and "La Patrie." Not only does it contain the most well-known pieces of our great poets, but M. Kuhff has brought to light some things, such as "Les Quatrains de Pibrac," which had been too long forgotten.

Will these young generations on whom our artists and writers are expending their best powers, grow up into men worthy to replace those who are departing? Better taught and more softly nurtured, will their ideal be as noble? In the year now drawing to a close, France has lost some of the men who were her greatest glory. Shortly after losing M. Thiers, the Liberal party was called upon to mourn the death of M. Lanfrey, one of its most noble-minded and distinguished representatives. In spite of the passion that animates it, his "Histoire de Napoléon," which he left unfinished, is a solid work, and, until now, the most complete study existing on the Imperial epoch. Timid and delicate to a degree that rendered him unfit for public life, ardent in the cause of liberty, and having lived his best years under the second Empire, he infused a tinge of bitterness and melancholy into all his works, and allowed it to colour his whole mind, which made him a "Werther of liberty." In the domain of art we have lost two colourists, Fromentin and Diaz, whose warm and dazzling palettes gladdened our eyes in the midst of the fog and gloom of our climates; and two artists who introduced the Parisian world to the simple poetical life of Alsace—Marchal and Brion. The former lost in Paris the pure and original inspiration to which he owed his best works, "Le Choral de Luther" and "Le Marché aux Servantes à Bouxwiller," and died in despair; the latter was true to the last to the mountains and patriarchal customs of Alsace. The *genre* they so well represented dies with them. Our painters do not form schools now, for the system of yearly exhibitions makes them, at any cost, go in search of what is new, to attract the attention of the ignorant and frivolous crowd. We become sadly conscious of the confusion that reigns in contemporary art in reading the beautiful work M. Charles Clément has just published on "Gleyre" (Didier), one of the greatest and truest artists of our day, but who lived aloof, despising the crowd and forgotten of them, more worthy than any other to be the head of a school, and yet exercising only a limited influence on a few select pupils. The son of a peasant of the Swiss Jura, Gleyre acquired his artistic training at the cost of unheard-of difficulties and hardships, and struggled almost all his life long with poverty. He visited the East, but in the pay of an American, who robbed him of all his drawings; in Paris, his pride and his roughness prevented him from ever gaining the popularity he was entitled to. He has nevertheless left us works of the highest order: "Le Soir," "Hercule et Omphale," "Ruth," "Les Romains passant sous le Joug," "La Cène." The fragments of his journal, which M. Clément quotes, show his profound understanding of the Eastern world; how well he had succeeded in combining antique sentiment with modern thought, the needful realism in colour and drawing to escape falling into conventionalism with the style in form and composition necessary to avoid vulgarity. Gleyre was, in painting, a brother of Andre Chenier, who

"sur des pensers nouveaux faisait des vers antiques."

He belongs, alas! to a generation that has passed away, and which has not bequeathed to its sons its soul and its spirit. If MM. Zola and Manet represent the future, whither are we tending?

GABRIEL MONOD.

[P.S.—The above pages were already written when the *coup de théâtre* of 14th December and the formation of a Ministry of the Left, under the presidency of

M. Dufaure, took place. At the very moment when violent and illegal courses—dissolution, *plébiscite*, *coup d'état*—were about to be resorted to, the change came. It is due to the Republican party, to the authority and character of M. Dufaure, to the perhaps somewhat tardy but yet courageous patriotism of two or three Constitutionalists in the Senate, MM. d'Audiffret Pasquier, Bocher, and Lambert St. Croix, and lastly to the Marshal himself, whose natural uprightness shrank from the terrible responsibilities his criminal advisers wanted to impose upon him. It was not in irony that I spoke above of his disinterestedness. The submission he has resigned himself to, perhaps, is one of the most cruel humiliations ever a political man suffered. He has accepted it, we believe, from a sense of duty and from fear of the frightful evils a longer resistance might cause. His remaining in office is better perhaps for the Republic than his removal. His presence prevents France from being drawn into too rapid a revolution, which would be dangerous, and proves that our institutions possess a certain elasticity, without which no Constitution is practicable. The Senate must not shut itself up now in a fruitless opposition that would lead to new conflicts, and the Chamber must patiently await the expiration of 1879 and 1880, which will place the Government definitively in Republican hands. If so, if the wind-up of the crisis is a real and lasting solution, we may hope that France is about to enter on a really new era. It is the first time that the Liberal party has imposed its will on the executive power and the Conservative party without using other weapons than the law and votes. This victory marks an immense progress in the political education of the country. If it be not compromised by faults, if it be the starting point of a normal development, liberty and the parliamentary *régime* will be established in France. At the moment when such prospects are opening before the Liberal patriots, it would be unjust not to pay a tribute of gratitude to the man who has contributed most to the result, by teaching the Radical party the theories of opportunism—to M. Gambetta.]

---

## IN ITALY.

FLORENCE, 14*th December*, 1877.

If one turns first to politics, what strikes us is the shortness with which that part of our task may be dismissed. Time was when what was called "the Italian Question" had a particular interest for foreign politicians, since each European Cabinet desired to have its own share of protection over our servitude, in order to impede the absolute preponderance of any other Government. That period has already long since passed. Italy has entirely changed her national physiognomy. Mere substitutions of Ministry, like that which has just happened, need not delay us. At the present time there is only one of our questions which directly preoccupies foreign Governments,—that is the relations which the new national State maintains with a Church that aims at universal empire. The seat of this Church has been fixed by Providence in our capital, and according to the increasing or diminishing of the political liberty of the Papacy, the conditions of Catholicism and its relations with Governments are modified in the various States of Europe. Hence foreign publicists are under an obligation to take a particular interest in that one question.

But in Italy, let us hasten to say, the topic has only political

tion. The fifth chapter endeavours to show the probable consequences the separation of Church from State would have upon civil society, and upon the religious future of the European nations. What are we to say of it all? In reading the book, written as it is with great impartiality, its views backed up by approved historical doctrine, we enter into the rosy-hued dream of the possibility of conciliation. But Cavour's formula—"A Free Church in a Free State"—which Signor Minghetti has not only accepted and commented upon, but, in part, as Deputy and as Minister, has put into practice, while in its terms affirming liberty twice over, has really ended in the denial of it to one of the two parties. Of course, if there had been no history in the way, the State could have ceased to occupy itself with the Church, or have treated it *tanquam non est*; or at least it could have modified the Cavourian phrase, with a very little change, into "Free Church *and* Free State." But, as the concordats prove, the two powers always clash, the one entering into he other's domain. They seem to be condemned, so long as one of the wo parties does not perish from weakness, always to embarrass one anther in the act of existing together, like the Siamese twins. Still, all iberals in Italy remain agreed that the Cavourian formula continues ie most reasonable one, being that which secures supreme liberty in ie State, while at the same time conceding to the Church the freedom ' its internal movements, allowing it to live tranquilly as long as it is the necessary strength and vital force to sustain itself. But the il was, and is, that the Church will persist in seeking to derive her rength, not from herself—that is, from her own spiritual energy and oral efficacy—but from the same material force as the State. The vil government now wishes to protect the internal liberty of the iurch with that force, but the Church desires to make it her own inrument for governing. So long as the Church does not return to her st principles—that is, rest in being a true assembly of believers—ery attempted conciliation will be in vain. The schemes are put forward minally as arrangements between Church and State, but in reality they e conflicts between two Governments, between two States equally alous of empire. In a word, for this reconciliation—more desired than excted—ever to come to pass, it will be necessary for the Church to reform rself. But the Syllabus of Pio Nono, the proclamation of the two new gmas of the Virgin's Immaculate Conception and the Spiritual Infalility of Popes, and the threatening attitude of the pretended Vatican isoner, are not indications of an approaching Liberal evolution in the iurch, such as would allow her to prosper in the bosom of modern society.

Having named the Pope, who, at the time I write, still lingers in e, we naturally think of the elective Conclaves. Though there would ot, unless one had access to the secret papers at the Vatican, seem to much to be added on this subject, or about the present Pope, after hat has been written by Cartwright and Trollope, yet a book has cently appeared which has attracted much attention. It is "Pio IX.," Ruggiero Bonghi. It treats of the present and future Pope, of the ay in which the conclaves have worked in the past, and of the possible anner in which the approaching one will be carried on. The work has ready stirred up the indifference of the Italian public, generally so rfectly heedless of all religious questions that do not necessarily in into political ones. But Bonghi has the quality of forcing even those who differ from him to read him, even those that he sometimes irritates by his cutting phrases. By translating Plato, he has acquired the potent and incisive dialectic of the Greeks. Besides this, not only has he, for thirty years past, been associated with the moderate party, which held for so many years the government of Italian affairs, but, as Minister of Public Instruction, he himself governed for a period of two years. In this office, he necessarily saw many things that the profane need not know. He gives a very lively sketch of the qualities a cardinal ought to have, or rather ought not to have, in order to be elected Pope.

But it will, perhaps, more interest foreign readers to have the judgment of an Italian, one so well fitted for forming an opinion, on Pope Pius IX. Though some of his concessions appear to me to be excessive, on the whole his account of Pius as Prince and Pope is life-like. This is what he says:—

"Pio IX. not only has not steered Church and State free from shoals, but he has led both one and the other straight into them. He has done this so completely that the one has foundered and utterly perished, while the other is in greater peril than it has ever been before. Not that he has done it from a deliberately intended policy, to which circumstances have given another effect than he might reasonably have foreseen; but it has come about because his mind—impotent, and without proper balance—has let him allow himself to be led into enterprises by others. He has shown scarcely any qualities which were really his own, unless it be great goodness of heart, great lightness of mind, and a natural and almost unconscious presumption,—three things that are exactly the worst for his position. The College of Cardinals thought they had discovered in him one of those men without extremes in good or evil, for whom they are in the habit of giving their suffrages, one of their loved mediocrities; but probably it is the first time a nature so constituted, instead of sinning by too great prudence, and inclining to conservatism, has gone so recklessly to work that it has upset everything. The ship has had a pilot; but of such a quality that another pilot was necessary to guide him, and, unfortunately, there was in Pius an absolute inability to allow himself to be knowingly directed. Enthusiasms, and dispositions of mind totally alien to the habits of the Roman Curia, have one after another, prevailed with him. But, fed from without, most of them have perished as soon as born, with the exception of his ecclesiastical enthusiasm. The advance of years, misfortunes, contrasts, and the mere not knowing what to do with himself, have increased this feeling, but because he has been, and is, wanting in spiritual and moral sympathy, it has remained without deep influence upon civil society."*

Here is another extract, prognosticating the future:—

"The Roman Pontificate," writes Bonghi, "may either be about to enter on a new and different path, or else be at the end of the centralized movement of all power and spiritual direction, which commenced ages ago, and now, under Pius IX., has arrived at its extreme limit. For it is a fact that all are mute in the Catholic camp before him. There is no private religious ardour that would rebel against him, or, without revolting, break and throw off the general submission. The forms of the National Churches have almost vanished, disappearing even to their minutest details. The obsequiousness, whether or not it arises from the depth of the heart, is general, full, and clamorous."

All this is most true, and would appear to justify only one prevision —that after this Pope there will be no others, or at least that in

* It is curious enough to observe how intellects, relatively mediocre, such as Pius IX. in Italy, Napoleon III. in France, and Bismarck in Prussia, have been able in our times to sustain political posts for so long a time, and with such numerous followers. Bismarck, it is true, has a strong personal iron will, which neither Napoleon III. nor Pius IX. possessed.

[illegible] present one, they will appear so dwarfed as to be [illegible] a series of Infallibles would be as impossible a [illegible] series of meteors is a physical one. The greatness [illegible] partly to occasions that cannot again occur, and [illegible] personal qualities, which will not be found in any of the [illegible] can never think of "the Infallibility" without think-[illegible], and it is difficult to conceive another Infallible that is [illegible] IX. himself, who caused himself to be believed in as such. [illegible] will be changed. The Duke of Sermoneta, who [illegible] blind, sees with profound mental clearness into things [illegible] the Papacy, predicts that the day will arrive when inquisitive [illegible] will ask, where was the residence of the Popes in Rome, in [illegible] manner as one now asks, Where is the house of the Grand [illegible] the Knights of Malta,—once so mighty a personage and [illegible] insignificant? So long as a man can be found to rule the [illegible] who by his personal qualities can preserve discipline in the [illegible] hierarchy, the Popes will have a widely spread and [illegible] influence in the Christian world. But it is evident that [illegible] the day arrives in which the national Churches elect their own [illegible] even do without them, they will break away from the [illegible] power of Rome. Then the Cardinals with their Pope will [illegible] themselves isolated, without authority, without efficacy,—deprived [illegible] and power, jealous of a principality without subjects, of a [illegible] without substance, of a pomp void of reality; they will be the [illegible] phantom of a splendid world which has disappeared. To [illegible] present Infallible, may indeed succeed two or three half infallibles; [illegible], third, fourth, tenth, hundredth, thousandth, millionth parts of [illegible]. The future series of Popes will, in all probability, be frag-[illegible] of the present Infallibility, dwindling progressively until we [illegible] the indivisible fraction and imperceptible atom answering to [illegible] of Sermoneta's Grand Master of Malta.

[illegible] word more as to the Papal election, and the part Italy may be [illegible] to take in it. Bonghi shows by ample evidence the succes-[illegible] efforts of the Roman Church to withdraw from all foreign [illegible] the elections of the Pontiffs. The Emperor Charlemagne [illegible] to have been the first to have exercised any supreme right in [illegible] election of the Roman Pontiffs. From the Franks this right, at [illegible] shattering of the Carlovingian Empire, passed to the German [illegible]; with Charles V. King of Spain and Emperor of Germany, [illegible] right of supreme approbation in the election of the Pontiffs was [illegible] shared between Catholic Spain and Apostolical Austria, a [illegible] of right, however, remaining to the Most Christian (*Cristian-*[illegible]) King of France. The right of these three Powers was simply [illegible] to that of the *veto*, expressed through their ambassadors. In [illegible] some Cardinals who had a chance of being elected Popes [illegible] excluded simply because they were not acceptable to one [illegible] three governments. What shall we see now that the new [illegible] Empire shows certain signs of interfering in the future con-[illegible] German publicists have seized on the question with eager-[illegible] seek to persuade the Italian Government to exercise its [illegible] in preventing the election of a Pope hostile to the Prussian [illegible]. This being the first time that a Pope will be nominated [illegible] kingdom of Italy, it may appear to some full of temptation to the King of Italy to mix himself up in the election of the Pope. So far, however, as can be foreseen, it is certain that the King of Italy and his Ministers will leave the Conclave entire They will not propose any name, nor will they oppose their nomination, but are disposed to recognize the spiritual right future Pope, whoever he may be, and his independence in the The Pope may even be the intolerant Cardinal Panebianco, t Italian Government will not change its policy.

This is how I believe the case now stands, and the only cha I see of the Papacy prolonging its existence in relative pot greatness, lies in the new Pope or Popes coming to an agreeme the Italian Government, recognizing accomplished facts, and ac the large life pension which the Italian Government offers to th Father. In this way, they would yet exercise their spiritual d over the Christian world, fortified by their position as chie national Italian Church. If the Italian Government is merely p not really more Catholic than Protestant, the fact that it trea the Papacy as with a Power, and charges itself with the duty of it respected, adds to the Papacy extraordinary prestige, which all the greater and more durable, the more the Popes know how into the true spirit of Italian life. There is, it is true, the prospec Liberal Pope would soon find arrayed against himself the ult servatives of France, Spain, Austria, Belgium, and Ireland, wh and there form small centres of reaction; but then again, there other possibility that the new Pope may infuse into Catholici life, a new spirit, more active and profound, one which will awak gious feeling and give it a more vigorous direction. At any ra not think I deceive myself when I say that the Papacy will l longer the more it remembers the history of that Rome in whic born, where it marvellously increased, and in which it threat end by petrifaction, in the form of a relic, an adorable idol, un able, perfect, infallible, but where at that moment there arose out for it a new life, and to offer it the means of prolonging it ence, an Italian Government, filial in that sense, though the seeks to pass it off for its impious executor. If the Papacy is o in remaining outside the new Italian life, and persists in con itself a stranger in Italy, it is not probable or even possib Catholicism will preserve for future Popes that reverence, that p homage and rich tribute, which Pius IX. receives. The Papa then slowly and by degrees perish.

It shows how in Italy religion, if it has ceased powerfully us socially, is mixed up with our literature, that in the importan lately published we come upon another book treating of the historically. The author, the Marquis Gino Capponi, was well kn his Guelphic sympathies,—in fact, he was the head of the Guelp torical school in Italy. In his "Introduction to the Civil Histo Popes," previously unedited, and published for the first time last few months by Senator Marco Tabarrini, is sketched morphism of the primitive Christian religions. The followi summarizes his historical conclusions:—

"With the Greeks, and all Eastern people, the imagination with great force into early Christianity. It had [illegible]

...who had no philosophers of their own, and despised ... those of other countries. But balancing in doubt ... faith, in uncertainty of mind and disorder of life, they ... hold of every superstition. The association with the ... their rites in Rome caused Christianity to be first ... the Jewish form. There was, however, one point of common ... and Hebrews finished by recognizing the vanity of ... the unity of God. In a Church constituted upon this ... head must naturally partake somewhat of the absolute ... supreme Divine Monarch. Christianity, from the first ages, ... danger of being lost from the discussions that arose among its ... the three persons of the Christian Trinity. The Popes ... supreme authority to put an end to the incautious litigation, ... in a manner which allowed of no further dispute, the divine ... they held themselves to be the direct and only representatives. ... themselves spoilt their own work, by re-constituting the pagan ... Christian saints, and by creating a special worship of the Virgin."

...he four chapters of the Marquis Gino Capponi do not carry ...ailed history far forward. The praises that he concedes to the ...idence of the Gallican Church, which always indignantly re... pay servile homage to the Church of Rome, proves that he ... intend to write an apology for the Papacy; and perhaps for ...son he left off, thinking that, as the recognized head of the new Guelphs, it would have appeared imprudent in him to exercise ...he criticism of his sharp genius upon the fundamental institu... the Guelphic doctrine.

...hould very much like to have the private "Records" of Gino ...i. It was said that in the last days of his life he dictated them ...secretary, Alessandro Carraresi. They would form one of the ...portant and interesting of modern books. But our expecta...ve been up to the present disappointed. The "Records" are ...d to only sixty pages, in which the venerable man summarily ...s, like one who is in a hurry, some of the most notable ...s of his long life. Even in their present modest form, the ...ds" offer without doubt much of interest. But readable as ... readers might find the particulars he gives of the Countess of ... and the last days of Alfieri, one cannot linger on them.

... few historical students in Great Britain may be glad to hear of ... by Professor Pasquale Villari. The events of 1849 compelled ...eek refuge in Tuscany, where he has resided for nearly thirty ...uring seventeen of which he has publicly taught modern history. ... gives us an important monograph upon Niccolo Macchiavelli,* a ... companion of his already celebrated work upon Savonarola. ...ari we have all the qualities that a great historian ought to ... I do not know if I deceive myself, but it appears to me that ...e has had a model, his principal one has been Macaulay.

... with this work I may couple another, which we owe to one of ... distinguished pupils of Villari's school at the Institute of High ... in Florence, Doctor Pier Leopoldo Cecchi. He has published a ...aph, the principal subject of which is Torquato Tasso.† Dr.

...lo Macchiavelli e suo tempo.

...rquato Tasso, e la vita Italiana nel Secolo XVI. 2. Torquato Tasso, Il Pen... Belle Lettere Italiane nel Secolo XVI.

Cecchi is of a turn of mind entirely opposed to that of his master; all dash and full of spirit, his ideas jerky, but always brilliant. In the first volume he studies Tasso as a man in connection with the habits of the sixteenth century; in the second volume he examines Tasso as a literate and philosopher, comparing the poetry and philosophy of Tasso with the poetry and philosophy of his time. This is a grave and vast argument, ranging over too great a field perhaps. The wanderings cause us to slightly forget Tasso, but in compensation the author, by rapid strokes, places before our eyes other portraits. Thus, for example, he compares the life of Pietro Bembo with that of Niccolo Macchiavelli, in a vivacious parallel.

A general reflection here arises. This book of Dr. Cecchi (of which we hear a translation into German is in preparation at Leipsic) is interesting, not only because the author examines Tasso under new aspects, but as marking the increasing attention which biographies are acquiring here amongst historical and literary studies. It is clear that in the future they will be the true and only historical romances.

I have under my eyes another recent Italian biography, highly important for our literary history. It is the life of a Piedmontese philosopher and literate, little known in Italy, still less so abroad, who has not left behind him, to tell the truth, great works, but who thought and lived as a great man. This man was Luigi Ornato, the friend of Cesare Balbo, of Santorre Santarosa, and of Luigi Provana; Victor Cousin, Vincenzo Gioberti, and Alessandro Manzoni may also be numbered amongst his admirers. Born at Caramagna, near Saluzzo, in 1787, he died in Turin, in 1842. He had upon those who surrounded him an admirably beneficent influence, by virtue of high example, by the goodness of his counsels, by the vastness of his doctrine, and by the great and generous love of country which inspired him. What he said he felt, what he felt he did. Convinced that the knowledge of truth is the means for arriving at the highest destinies of man, he was among the first to spread the Platonic doctrine, and contributed to raise the Subalpine youth from the degradation of the *sensistica* school. When, in 1832, Ornato returned to Piedmont from Paris, the philosopher Vincenzo Gioberti wrote to a friend of his, with a dash of that generous *chauvinism* which caused him to write the book "Del Primato morale e civile degli Italiani," the following:—

> "I think I can say without deceiving myself by my love of country and the affections of my heart, that Paris, in losing Luigi Ornato, is deprived of the greatest philosopher of the present time. I am the first to recognize the merits of M. Cousin, and to confess that the world has become unjust towards him. But between him and Ornato there is as great a difference as between Italian solidity and profoundness, and French lightness."

Signor Leone Ottolenghi has placed in his book—so full of interesting* notices for the civil and literary history of Piedmont—beautiful evidences of Ornato's virtues and of those of his excellent friends, adding also to his well wrought-out biography an important series of unpublished letters directed by Luigi Ornato to his intimate friends, which

* Let us, however, observe how he seems to be in the wrong, when he accepts seriously, as is shown by his references to Cousin, the assertions, often calumnious, of the famous Eugène de Mirecourt; the book of Ottolenghi also contains some superfluous citations, especially in the notes.

[illegible] and deep value, much more than do his transla-[illegible], although so much praised.

[illegible] statesmen are famous for their culture of classical [illegible] of our own public men, Signor Filippo Mariotti, a [illegible], and deputy to the Italian Parliament, employs in [illegible] the leisure left him by public affairs. He has come [illegible] new, elegant, most careful translator from the Greek. [illegible] Mariotti, a little unlike your statesmen, does not turn to [illegible] merely as a splendid æsthetical phenomenon, but he [illegible] study as a training in civil knowledge even for our own [illegible] two preceding volumes he has given us an excellent trans-[illegible] the political orations of Demosthenes, so commented upon [illegible] to associate them with our parliamentary modes. These [illegible] or contrasts seemed to us learned, ingenious, and full [illegible] instruction. Now, the Signor offers us the civil dis-[illegible] the great Athenian orator,* translated and explained in [illegible] more practical and effective manner. English orators and [illegible] since the time of Pitt know well the advantage of drawing [illegible]esh eloquence from these admirable ancient models; and [illegible]'s essay upon the Athenian orators is in the hands of all [illegible] readers. But it is a new thing in Italy for Demosthenes to be [illegible] not simply for historical and literary purposes, but with a [illegible] and civil aim. Signor Mariotti has taken from the Orations [illegible]tions of the Athenian code of laws, and all the procedure of [illegible] in civil causes, doing it with rare ability, aided by a com-[illegible]owledge of ancient and modern legislation. It is impossible [illegible] to feel a lively satisfaction in announcing the completion of [illegible]riotti's work.

[illegible] postponed mentioning until now a name which must stir every [illegible]heart—Shakspeare. An illustrious Lombard poet and man of [illegible] of the dearest disciples of Alessandro Manzoni and Giulio [illegible], the author of the "Angiola Maria," (a kind of Italian "Vicar of [illegible]"), has well deserved grateful thanks from the lovers of [illegible] and Italian literature for his excellent translation of the works [illegible]peare. Carcano's translation is anything but a hurried work. [illegible]menced it as long ago as 1840, and it is only approaching its com-[illegible] Up to the present, six volumes have been published in an elegant [illegible] in which each drama is illustrated by a special vignette.† [illegible] work will comprise ten volumes; the four which remain will [illegible] to the public within the next two years. This will form the [illegible] monument that Italy has erected to the glory of the great [illegible] poet. It may interest readers if I add a little on this subject. [illegible] Leoni attempted a translation in verse of some of the Shaks-[illegible] dramas, but it was rather a paraphrase than a translation, and [illegible] were anything but fine, containing in themselves rather [illegible]kspeare is not than what he is. This attempt passed almost [illegible]. Then followed Carlo Rusconi with a prose translation. [illegible]slator sometimes does not keep to the text, not well under-[illegible] it. In the most poetical and dramatical passages the rendering

* [illegible]tions of Demosthenes, translated and illustrated by the Advocate Filippo [illegible] to Parliament. Vol. iii.

† [illegible] Shakspeare tradotte da Giulio Carcano. Vols. i.—vi.

never approaches to the height of the original. Carlo Rusconi has, however, done good service to Italian literature in revealing to them the genius of Shakspeare. To his translations our actors generally turn when they wish to represent Shakspearean productions,—especially so does the most intelligent and powerful amongst our scenic interpreters of your poet, Signor Ernesto Rossi. But if Rusconi's translations sufficed for the general public, to whom they give a broad and popular idea of the great English poet, persons of refined taste, our writers, and such as have the good fortune to be able to appreciate Shakspeare's beauties in the original, asked for something better. They wished for a poet to translate the poet. Giulio Carcano, a refined poetical writer, put himself with every scrupulous care to the task. As his original poems in Italian were delicate, sweet, and light, we might, perhaps, have feared that Carcano would have given us an Italian Shakspeare, too languid and effeminate. But if he has gentleness of soul, there is in his mind, fortified by the study of Dante, also strength. He is himself the author of a tragedy entitled "Spartaco," which could not have been conceived and written under the Government of Austria except by a genius capable of virile ideas. It is, however, highly probable that Shakspeare, with whom Carcano has for nearly forty years lived in intimate familiarity, has contributed not a little to render robust the genius of his translator. As it is, in him we have the advantage of an exquisite writer softening in our tongue certain harshnesses of the Shakspearean style, which would offend the hearing of Italians. So great is the poetical capacity of our language that, in his first translations, Carcano had undertaken to render into verse even those passages which in the original were written in prose. But in this definite edition of his beautiful versions, he has followed better counsel. Wishing to observe more faithfully the dramatic genius of the author, he has turned into prose the previously versified portions; and this, we may add, has given him the opportunity of proving how the elegance of Italian prose is equal to a new and splendid poetry. The edition is preceded by a life of Shakspeare carefully compiled from the best sources. Each volume contains three dramas; each play is preceded by an affectionate dedication of the work to the translator's best friends, and offers a historical and critical note upon the drama, instructive, judicious, and written with much nobility of style. Both Carcano and his editor have wished to bestow on this translation of Shakspeare all possible honour. It now remains for the Italian public to honour it as it becomes them to do. But there is no doubt as to this. The version has already taken its place in contemporary literature, ranking alongside the classical versions of the "Iliad," by Vincenzo Monti, the "Odyssey," by Ippolito Pendemonte, the Greek tragedies, by Felice Bellatti, and the renderings of Schiller, Gessner, Milton, Moore, by Andrea Maffei.

Indeed, recently we in Italy have undertaken with special fervour the translation of foreign poets. For example, within the last few years, Byron's "Childe Harold's Pilgrimage," and his "Don Juan," the poems of Heine, and the "Ahasver" of Hammerling, have had not one only but several Italian translators.

But while this is going forward, a new kind of poetry, all our own, quite national, rich, sparkling, is bein ''ed with great ardour.

[illegible] songs of the various Italian provinces. These, [illegible] correspond to the local poetry of foreign peoples, [illegible] national and especially provincial character, [illegible] Florentine man of letters and ex-politician, Signor [illegible] placed in good relief in his recent work published [illegible] book would have been impossible half a century [illegible] for its construction were not collected. Popular [illegible] perhaps, even more than now. For town life is [illegible] by step into the country where these songs of the [illegible], sung by men in contact with nature; the criticism [illegible], and both chills and vitiates the rustic minstrelsy [illegible]

[illegible]

[illegible] Lombardy, Emilia, and Romagna, and probably shall never know [illegible], because the songs of the people love better the mountains [illegible] plains, and Lombardy, Emilia, and Romagna, from which we [illegible] and the least interesting songs, form notoriously a flat [illegible] So, again, with the Tuscan ones; the most beautiful and import- [illegible] from the Pistorese and Sienna mountains. The great task is [illegible] of the popular poetry in the principal provinces of Italy. [illegible] seeks the traces of this poetry as it must have existed [illegible] Etruscans and Romans, and in the middle ages; he has so [illegible] the vitality of the songs of the people that he ingeniously [illegible] ancient pious ejaculation of Cato and Varro (which has [illegible] intelligible, and upon which archæologists and philologists [illegible] present uselessly laboured) by the aid of a still-used [illegible] that also commences with a verse but slightly intel- [illegible] author will write, so we are told, another volume, to be [illegible], "History of the Italian Language." In this he will [illegible] tenacity of Italian dialects, their ancient origin, and

[illegible] della Poesia popolare in Italia. By Ermolao Rubieri.

probably their formation, before the Latin tongue had spread and corrupted itself. (We are, perhaps, already near to some national theory on this subject, judging by the quantity of notices collected by the illustrious Lombard historian, Cesare Cantu, in a dissertation inserted in the new edition of his "Storia degli Italiani," concluded this year, and entitled "Virende dei parlari d'Italia." It is there sought, under the ancient guidance of Muratori, to trace the existence of the Italian under the ancient Latin, vulgar and classical.) After having briefly pointed out in some introductory chapters how popular poetry has always accompanied the historical phases of Italian life, Signor Rubieri enters upon the main argument, and demonstrates how for several centuries the popular songs have given the impress of the peculiar life and special character of the different provinces of Italy. This thesis the author demonstrates with an acumen which renders vain all attempts at contradiction.

But since Italian love poetry has ever had an interest for all the world, foreign readers may like to hear something of the examination the author makes of the love songs, and the various modes in which the different Italian provinces demonstrate love by song. Of the amorous poetry, the most delicate, the most modest, is undoubtedly the Tuscan, and we ought therefore to conclude that Tuscany is the one Italian region where women are more chaste and men more decent than in any other. But the author, although himself a Florentine, does not pretend to lead us to this conclusion. He explains it in this way:—

"When I say that the popular poetry of Tuscany is the most moral, I do not intend to praise the character of the country, but rather the style of life that prevails there—that is, the rural life. In this in reality lies the whole secret. In no country does a more gentle, modest, and affectionate poetry abound, because in no other region does a more diffuse, full, but strict rural life predominate. This life of the Tuscan peasants is the true creator of their poetry. Or if the individual character has something to do with it, it is not because in Tuscany they are privileged in heart and intellect, but because a greater culture and activity of the heart and mind are here favoured by circumstances, by local institutions worthy of all praise. We allude to the *colon* system. Country life cannot be pure where there is no middle class, and the middle class has here no natural place except in Tuscany. The small isolated colon's house, surrounded by its farm and its peaceful wall,—which preserves it from external invasion,—is like a sanctuary of domestic affection, closed alike to the benefit and the corruption of civic concourse. Here the children grow up under the constant guard of their parents, who, void of ambition, do not seek sons and daughters-in-law distinguished for riches or gentility, and therefore are not compelled either to deceive or adulate. To them the honesty and industry of the man who takes their daughter to his home suffice, as the same qualities do in the girl whom their son brings home to them, to share the cares of the hearth and field; and they not only desire, but know how to keep far from their home any vagabond or vicious person. With both sexes, the first or indeed only scope of their love is matrimony—that to them in their isolation is a necessity, as it is also a privilege of their condition. The small Tuscan farmer, without places where he can gamble and follow other dissipations of the town, has no other joy than the fertility of his farm and the affection of his family; and he seeks for a young girl to love, that she may become his wife, and procure him the delights of domestic content, augmenting the number of hands in the colony. A poetry which is on[illegible] [illegible]oreter of a love so honest, respectful, and sincere must on its part b[illegible] [illegible]tionate and delicate. The topographical conditi[illegible] [illegible]he colon s[illegible] to nourish pure life and pure poetry. [illegible] the g[illegible]

[illegible] smiling and animated by the assiduity of a numerous [illegible] sunny spot where a house is not built, and [illegible] many others, all within a stone's throw of one another, [illegible] the eye can reach. All these houses form the knots of an [illegible] of the threads of which there is communicated from [illegible] the mysterious fluid, sympathy, which runs into rustic [illegible] between the houses and their inhabitants is not so great [illegible] interruption of this fluid, but it is sufficient to impede its

[illegible] opportune to repeat these things in Italy, since if the [illegible] of *mezzadria** were introduced into Sicily and the [illegible] it would save the people from misery and care [illegible] than brigandage. If it were brought into use on the [illegible] of the Roman Campagna, it would render ten times [illegible] produce got from those desolate plains, and would restore [illegible] and moral happiness to the heart of Italy, which now has [illegible] air to breathe, but then would be placed in more lively [illegible] with the rest of our Peninsula. It is perhaps even not [illegible] meditate upon this in England, where, if I am not in error, [illegible] of agricultural property has not yet arrived at the [illegible]fection.

[illegible] book I must not fail to mention. In the same manner as [illegible] depicts the felicity of Tuscan country life, so the Advocate Pietro [illegible] under the *nom de plume* of Hamlet's sympathetic buffoon, [illegible] describes the delights of citizen life in the fairest of the Tuscan [illegible] which is the same thing as saying, the fairest among all Italy's [illegible] all the world's cities—Florence.† Only, fortunately, he does [illegible] to speak about the popular songs heard in the streets of [illegible] They are as ugly and foul as those of the surrounding [illegible] especially in the mountains, are chaste and delicate. Those [illegible] these songs are easily convinced that Rubieri was a [illegible] times in the right when he stated that to the country [illegible] the merit of the chastity of Tuscan popular poetry. [illegible] wisely passes over this morbid excrescence of Florentine [illegible] and life, and with exquisite ability and invariable good [illegible] proposes to conduct us through the streets, and, if necessary, [illegible] houses of Florence, pointing out to us what there is in them [illegible] interest. The English reader may be surprised at seeing [illegible] things about which Yorick talks mentioned in his excellent [illegible] but the reason for it is that the foreign guides conduct the [illegible] dead Florence. Yorick, on the contrary, accompanies [illegible] living city. Foreigners who arrive at Florence by the [illegible] are taken by omnibus to the hotel recommended by [illegible] and with that volume under their arm or in their [illegible] out, as on a pilgrimage, to verify that the Italians, in [illegible] have not allowed anything famous to be de- [illegible] visiting the museums, churches, and cemeteries, and [illegible] in good order, having exhausted their guide-book

* [illegible] Tuscany the colonial system with which the master gives the [illegible] piece of land to the peasant, having for recompense the half [illegible]

† By Yorick.

inventory, they ask their hotel-keeper for his bill. Nine times out of ten this is an extortionate one, and gives them the right of arguing that the Italian people are always a little inclined to be brigands. With this falsely-formed idea of us, they visit in the same manner our other illustrious cities, receive there the same impressions, misapprehend us and our affairs in the same manner, and return to England full of enthusiasm for our past glories and of compassion for our present misery. The foreign visitor would do us a real charity if he deigned to enter a little into our houses and life, gaining from us his information concerning our affairs, and not from the cicerones and hotel-keepers, who are the same in all countries. Our houses are not so closed as travellers imagine them to be; the Italian is more benign than they think; and although without doubt there is still much to be done in Italy in the way of raising the people by instruction, I believe that the foreigner rates us very much lower than we are entitled to be estimated. I remember the admiring "oh!" with which an ex-Latin professor in an English university received the intelligence that not only Latin but Greek, not only Greek but Sanscrit, were taught by special professors, not in one only, but in several Italian universities. He did not know by name one of his Italian Latinist or Hellenist colleagues, but at the same time he appeared both happy and confused when he found that his name had reached several of our ears, although he was a man *unius libri*, and had not given proof of great literary productiveness.

I hope, however, that these periodical reviews may be the commencement of a better literary understanding between Englishmen and Italians, one that may be useful to both.

Returning to Yorick, I repeat for a moment that, with much vivacity, he introduces his readers to living Florence; in fact, he succeeds by the magic of his humorous style, in communicating to his theme a part of his own liveliness, giving the illusion that Florence is gayer, more prosperous, and happier than is really the case. One who bears the name of Yorick cannot sadden any one with sombre and desperate images; and if sometimes a tear-drop trembles in his eyes, and threatens to fall, it is only a proof of his good heart. The most curious usages of Florentine life, in the half of the year from Christmas to St. John's Day, are all described admirably. I cannot do better than advise those English who come to Florence in order to drive away their "spleen" to take Yorick for their guide; I think I can guarantee that they will find the remedy an infallible one.

By way of fittingly concluding this account of what is doing intellectually in Italy, I will in a few words sketch three "inaugurations," which I have attended on three following days. On the first day, the inauguration of the studies in the "Istituto di Studii Superiori" of Florence took place. The Abbé Antonio Stoppani, an eminent Lombard naturalist, author of a fine work describing physical Italy, entitled "Il Bel Paese," and who has now come to occupy in our institution the chair of geology, made a magnificent speech. His topic was the connection of geology with other physical sciences, and with ethics. He made a warm appeal for concord amongst all those who devote themselves to the noble search for truth, expressing his wish that the public might more interest itself in their researches. On the following day, the courses of study were solemnly inaugurated at the "Social Science

School," founded in Florence by the Marquis and Senator Carlo Alfieri. The intention of this institution is to furnish a kind of finishing class, to prepare for the political and diplomatic services those youths of well-to-do families who will not, or cannot, follow a university career. Professor Massimiliano Giarri read a discourse upon "Macchiavellism," condemning as pernicious and fatal the doctrine, but at the same time rendering a splendid tribute to the intellect and glory of Macchiavelli. Finally, at the annual meeting of the "Accademia della Crusca," the new corresponding member, Professor Fausto Lasinio, a learned Arabian scholar, read a discourse in which he demonstrated, by irrefutable evidence, the utility of associating Orientalists with the compilation of the dictionary of the Italian language.

From all this I hope it will be gathered that Italy, not contented with her merely political resurrection, is showing activity of yet higher kinds. It is only too true that most of her citizens are preoccupied with material interests, but among us are those holding high the supreme dignity of science—a dignity which ought all the more to be felt in Florence, since she aspires, once more, to merit the glorious appellation of the Athens of Italy.

ANGELO DE GUBERNATIS.

# CONTEMPORARY ESSAYS AND COMMENTS.

[*In this Section the Contributors to the* CONTEMPORARY REVIEW *are understood to express themselves with less restraint* (*as to their individual views*) *than might be thought desirable in signed and formal articles.*]

**The Cultur-Kampf.**

IN the very amusing and stimulating lecture published by Mr. Mark Pattison in the *Fortnightly Review*, he cuts a two-edged joke about a certain quotation of Ouida's ("Facilis descensus Avernus"), but one could not help wondering how many, even among ordinary journalists and men of the press, would feel both edges of the pleasantry. Yet, if critics are to be all that Mr. Pattison wants them to be, it is quite certain that the boys in our printing-offices will soon have to be capable of distinguishing between "Avernus" and "Averni." It is meanwhile undoubtedly true that a literary critic in these days, if he undertakes serious work, ought to be well-read in the older literature; to refresh by direct occasional *effort* to that end his customary knowledge even of that; and to keep up, by laborious and lively reading, a current acquaintance with what is going on in French and German literature as well as in English. In Spanish and Italian, the field of study is not very wide; but in the Scandinavian tongues and in Russia it is threatening to become so; while no man who has the true literary instinct in him can feel comfortable in reading much of what he *must* read unless he has a tincture of certain Oriental tongues, as well as of Oriental literature—which last is a matter of course. Science he must not neglect, though it will of course be hopeless to attempt to make his mind much more than an index and memorandum-book—a sort of *catalogue raisonné*—in many of these particulars. He must have general ideas—and not inaccurate ones—about a thousand topics, and he must know where to find things.

Of course all these qualifications are not required for a mere reviewer of novels, sermons, or ordinary poetry. Yet the highest work in these departments can neither be properly enjoyed nor properly criticized without large general knowledge. For example, Mr. Tennyson's poetry must contain a numerous tale of blank pages for the man who has not, at lowest, the classic commonplaces at his fingers' ends; and a man must have read somewhat widely to follow Mr. Browning. His two poems, "Christmas Eve" and "Easter Day," are on topics that are familiar, and any intelligent person can follow the argument; but what does [illegible] make of "The kingcraft of the Lucumon [illegible] The halt ar[illegible] Iketides" (the last word rhyming with "[illegible]e")?

[illegible] the stamp of Mr. Slide (in Mr. Trollope's "Phineas [illegible]")?—Nothing; they are choke-pears to him. Perhaps [illegible] to mind the very amusing note which Mr. Browning [illegible] number of his "Bells and Pomegranates" at the [illegible], and his childlike surprise that everybody had not read [illegible] it would be only too easy to multiply examples. One of [illegible] Mr. Tennyson's poetry that I ever read betrayed [illegible] ignorance of the allusion in "This is truth the [illegible]." The review was none the worse for the writer's not [illegible] Dante—though of course it might have been.

[illegible] called "The Great Cham of Literature," and his [illegible] himself is well known. At one time he was proposing to [illegible] edit a periodical general review of European literature. [illegible] objected that he would have to deal with various topics, [illegible] other, that he knew nothing about. How was he going to [illegible] Johnson made answer that he should manage as well as he [illegible] in other words that he should trust to Providence and mother-[illegible] mother-wit will carry a man far—if his mother was "witty;" [illegible] of nature will not tell a man about what 2 H — H + O = [illegible] O means, or who wrote the "Laoköon." It is not long since [illegible] a scholastic journal a review in which "Laoköon" and "Nathan [illegible]" were continuously treated as the work of "that splendid [illegible]." The explanation of such a case as that is easy. The [illegible]" the reviews, generally, for the periodical. Something [illegible] him that he does not at all understand, and he forthwith [illegible] it, rather than lose half-a-sovereign. But, after all, this was an [illegible] case. I have, indeed, read that Dr. Chalmers did not know the [illegible] between Goethe and Fichte, and publicly confounded one with [illegible]; but even that was not a hanging matter, and where is the [illegible] who could bear to have all his "secret faults" raked up and [illegible] before the sun, while men and angels hear?" I should say [illegible] greatest amount of reviewing wrong is done not by want of [illegible] but by want of aptitude and conscientiousness. For example, [illegible] er of those, cultivated or not, who know poetry at a glance, is [illegible] ly few. And of those who have a real taste in such matters, [illegible] are catholic in their appreciations? One man is for gnomic [illegible] and another for passion poetry, and each is blind to something [illegible] bound, as a critic, to see with all his eyesight. In his later [illegible] Emerson has, by certain *obiter dicta* on poets, let himself [illegible] stages as an authority. When a man of his quality calls [illegible] of Shelley "stuff" we receive once more, and with a renewal [illegible] pain, the ancient lesson that makes us sigh out, "Poor [illegible]!" And so it is all round. There are many very capable [illegible] press" who are by force of circumstances kept at inferior [illegible] may be questioned whether the less-than-half cultivated [illegible] do much harm to literature, except by helping to corrupt [illegible] by keeping up bad types of writing. This, to be [illegible]. No cultivated man can see much of the average [illegible] noting that his reading goes little farther back [illegible] his models of English are vile; and, worst of all, [illegible] slightest notion of his own ignorance, and is utterly [illegible] so clever, so full of well-meaning intelligence, [illegible] sphere, that it seems a downright sin and shame to disturb his self-complacency. But though Mr. Matthew Arnold has a most annoying way of saying true things, his estimate of the usual working literary man *is* true. Let one example serve—perhaps the anecdote, slight as it is, may be worth telling. I met a well-known and in some respects brilliant literary man (now dead) twice over in one week in full dress—bound for dinner. I rallied him upon his dissipation, and, after a very frank and humorous account from him of his daily life and work, asked, in all simplicity, "Then when do you find time to read?" The question was met by a hearty laugh—"Read? *read?* I never read anything. How can I?" I went on to remark that I had once or twice seen him in the British Museum Library, but he very plainly told me that that was only to make extracts from cyclopædias. Here are suggestions which I believe are perfectly fair, of the usual "literary" life of the usual "literary" man. Immediately above him ranks a class of public writers who do read, but who read, after all, very little, and whose estimates are in the main second-hand. For instance, if Mr. Swinburne is in vogue, they will go about from clubroom to clubroom, or from one editor's room to another, in ecstasies of quotation over such lines as—

> "The lilies and languors of virtue
> For the raptures and roses of vice"—

or over the last plum in Mr. Matthew Arnold or George Eliot. But as to serious study even of "light" literature—be it far from them as it is.

It is these half-instructed writers, those whose knowledge and judgments are essentially second-hand (though there is a decent disguise in the case), that do most harm in literature. Not so much in the way of condemning or overlooking good books, as in that of over-praising bad or indifferent ones, and following purely conventional lines of praise and blame. They know better than to use the word "period" in the vulgar sense, or "allude to" for "mention," or "transpire" for "happen;" but they are utterly incapable of making any head against new and erroneous currents of critical opinion, just at the moment when such service is most needed. Otherwise, they do not degrade literature, except by occasional flippancy and cynicism,—for they all are too "clever" by half,—and by keeping before the world a not very creditable type of literary matter. They are men who have a real liking for their work (or, as poor Mr. Slide would say, their "avocations"), and if it were not for their vanity, their readiness to take up a cry, and their extreme superficiality, there would be nothing to say against them, except what is involved in their working for money. Mr. Slide and his company cannot be so lightly let off. They elicit, and transpire, and allude, and evince, and inaugurate, and imitate the very worst of Dickens, and deliberately grind out bad copy by the foot-rule, when they might just as well be doing honest and useful work as clever engine-drivers or telegraph clerks, and they help to keep the average reader of newspapers and magazines just where he is, by their reckless pandering to his stupidity and other bad qualities. If literature, as a commodity for sale, must be produced in order to meet a given demand,—if it is right for a man with money to speculate in the literary "wants" of the populace, and proceed upon the principle of giving them just what they like,—then Mr. Slide not only has a reason of being, he is a useful and admirable citizen. But he is a [illegible]lovely object, and when we [illegible] literature together, the words Beauty and the Beast [illegible] and in truth not very appropriately. The [illegible] Barry tells an anecdote of an editor of a news[illegible] dinner, would call out—"Waiter! bread wanted [illegible] Waiter! salt wanted—for the press!" This was in [illegible] records that Lord Houghton, then Mr. Monckton [illegible] he might usually know the "press-man" at a public [illegible] quantity he ate and drank. This was partly a jest; but [illegible] well be made to yield a hundred such—cut and come [illegible] would be none the worse for it, so thick is his hide. His [illegible] own consequence, and the dignity of literature as repre[illegible] him, is something portentous. The literary man, as Mr. [illegible] Mr. Emerson draws him,—a heaven-born student, and a [illegible] of the truth he sees, ready for poverty if it must come, [illegible] anxious to avoid even Mr. Pattison's Duke's invitation to [illegible] anything else which may entangle him,—he, indeed, is a [illegible] more than respectable character. So is the simple "bread-[illegible] literature, if honest,—the man who drudges at correcting [illegible] copying extracts. But Mr. Slide, and the much more clever [illegible] who make a mere trade of their cleverness or their "bounce," or [illegible] not to be classed as noble figures, drape them as you may.

[illegible] I should like to inquire whether after all it is either Mr. Trollope's [illegible] Slide, or Mr. Carlyle's "Absconded Reporter," Dr. Phelim [illegible] (Maginn?), who does the most harm in literature—or even who [illegible] the most errors. The mere question of errors is not a serious [illegible] cultivated make as many errors as the uncultivated. Of course [illegible] is a difference between a blunder which stamps a man for stupid, [illegible] slip which, perhaps, only a man of brains and reading could [illegible]. Too much stress is laid by cultivated men of classical [illegible] upon mistakes in quotation and similar small deer of error. [illegible] George Eliot says, every schoolboy can laugh at his sister for a false [illegible], and yet the girl may be worth a dozen of the boy. Dr. Parr [illegible] Sir James Mackintosh ridiculous—in Dr. Parr's parlour—by saying, "[illegible] call it Anabásis, Jemmy, but *we* say Anábasis"—yet who was [illegible], and what was he good for? Was he not a Brummagem Dr. [illegible] made up of birch and "Gradus?" Again, no worse mistakes in [illegible] from the ancients have been made in our own time than one that [illegible] from a very distinguished pen, and had to be corrected by a [illegible] slip. It proved nothing—nor did Ouida's "Avernus," except that [illegible] had a bad headache when she put it down and read her [illegible] half an eye. I do not really know whether Hallam made [illegible] attributed to him in a note to "English Bards and Scotch [illegible]"—but if he did, it was a grave matter for an expert; and yet [illegible] prove against Hallam? Nothing in the world except that he [illegible]

[illegible] all astray in my recollection, something like this once [illegible] great novelist, who was no scholar, once advised himself [illegible] certain mythical hero with a certain real historian, and [illegible] Quintus Curtius. Some one told him he had made a [illegible]

[illegible] reviewed Payne Knight's 'Taste,' and was exceedingly severe on some [illegible] it was not discovered that the lines were Pindar's till the press [illegible] to cancel the critique, which still stands an everlasting monument [illegible] —Byron's Note.

2 F

blunder, whereupon he issued this *erratum*:—"For Quintus Curtius read Quintius Curtius." I did not verify this story, but supposing that it was quite true, it simply proves that the great writer was both ignorant and careless in a certain sphere, but even a gross mistake like this is not as bad as Slide's performances in Lord Kenyon's manner. And let me take one or two other cases. A late writer, who was a very good classic, has told the world that a leading Review once treated his Latin to some cutting sarcasm, just because the printer had turned a *u* into an *n* (or *vice versâ*). Another publicist, being in the middle of a proof, thought he would adorn an interpolated sentence with a certain bit of Latin, and, moreover, that he would add to the fire of the passage by turning plural into singular. Rash man! He began well, but when he got to the second clause, his pen betrayed him,—it ran into the long familiar plural—and the result was something like Dryden's Tonson "with two left legs." Slide could not have made such a mistake, for he did not know a singular from a plural. But Phelim McQuirk was the man to gloat over it, to tear the author with red-hot tongs, and remind him of it on high days and holydays as long as he lived. On the whole, too much stress is laid upon such matters as these. If Mr. Tennyson had been entirely serious, there would have been a tincture of insolence in his challenge to "irresponsible insolent Reviewers" to accept his "test in a metre of Catullus." A Reviewer who might be too shy, or too busy, or too little practised in Latin metre to be ready to criticize English hendecasyllabics, "so fantastical is the dainty metre," might be well read in Catullus, might know his Lucretius and Horace almost by rote, and be quite entitled to pass judgment, say upon the comparative merits of Mr. Tennyson's and Mr. Arnold's methods of rendering Homer. Paley's quantities were said to be shaky, but his opinion upon most of the more important parts of classical learning was worth infinitely more than that of the Cambridge scholar who made what he was pleased to call an epigram about Paley's pronunciation of the word *profugus*. The late Dean Alford, one of the kindest and most considerate of men, showed, in some of his otherwise very just criticisms, great ignorance of the conditions under which much of the literary work of newspapers and magazines *must* be done. A man may easily forget what he very well knows about "maddening galliambics," if he is reading or writing under the maddening roar of a printing machine, with half-a-dozen things in his head besides longs and shorts. "Then he should not handle glass when his hands are shaky." That is true, and so are all counsels of perfection; and oh, how beautifully easy!

Now "these," in Bacon's phrase, are "toys." But still confining myself to minor errors, it may be contended that the greatest of them have been made by the most distinguished writers. Did not Sir Walter Scott make the sun set in the east? Have not living men of science made errors as gross as even Molière's *Médecin malgré lui* committed? There is a living expert who, in his own sphere of criticism, committed publicly as outrageous and absurd a blunder as the malice of Swift could have invented for an enemy. It is mutual forbearance, the sense that we all live in glass houses, the honourable feeling that our common fallibility imposes upon us the duty of suppressing each other's shortcomings, that draws the covering over hundreds of mistakes. Experts spy them out, but each man is silent, because he knows, unless he is of Thersites' mood, that he too is mortal, and may,—nay, almost certainly ome day, be glad enough of a little mercy from his fellows. No ever made a mistake more nearly approaching incredibility than Mill when he showed that he mistook, as he did, a first principle Herbert Spencer's Psychology. He at once admitted his error, en was Slide, or McQuirk himself, guilty of a more astounding eption? To come nearer to the present moment, in Mr. Sidg- preface to the second edition of his "Methods of Ethics"—a book s as clear as spring water—will be found recorded by the author eptions of his meaning on the part of experts which are wild to y verge of impossibility.

impartial, absolutely indifferent reader of the best literature, in and periodicals, will, if he really *does* read, and if he has a , find it well sprinkled with both the natural and simple s, and the gross and unaccountable blunders of experts. But not all. A very strong case could be made out to support the tion not only that an age of expert authority is an age of decadence, but that it is the expert voice, the voice of "cul- he academic voice, which has most frequently led the intelli- f given ages into the dangerous by-path, or the stupid *cul-de-* his is no argument against culture or against experts, but it is ion against expert conceit, and its apparently inevitable con- it, cliquecism. I say nothing here of the difficulty of determining *reputed* experts which is *primus inter pares*. The man who s to come to the front on other grounds than that of a speciality nerally get heard first and last. Is there not high expert ty for saying that Brougham, playing "expert" once in a certain , and criticizing a certain superior of his, put back the dial of for many years? This story cuts two ways, no doubt, but how public to know?

number of the *Fortnightly Review* which contains Mr. Mark 's delightful paper, happens to supply something which may help llustrate by a case what every working man of letters finds even ads as diligently as Mr. Pattison's model critic. I may note in that Mr. Pattison's estimate of the amount of really effectual that may be got through in a year seems too low. You cannot irty pages an hour in German, especially if the print be Gothic— I seldom read twenty—but you can read so very much more in ses of French and English books that the average of thirty looks le. The great secret of reading largely, next to the formation in mechanical or quasi-mechanical habits, is to read variously. are baffled for the time by a page of Kant, go to Mill or Sainte- When you return to Kant, "unconscious cerebration" or simple ll have removed the block. But to my illustration. Every- the rhetorical everybody—knows the story of Mary Baker, and led at her oration before the Massachusetts justices, upon her viction for the offence of entering upon the duties of maternity legal sanction. Mr. John Morley tells us that the story is not d relates this very unpleasant anecdote:—

it happens, there is a piece of external evidence on the matter illustrates Raynal's curious lightheartedness as to historic . Franklin and Silas Deane were one day talking together he many blunders in Raynal's book, when the author himself d to step in. They told him of what they had been speaking.

'Nay,' says Raynal, 'I took the greatest care not to insert a single fact for which I had not the most unquestionable authority.' Deane then fell on the story of Polly Baker, and declared of his own certain knowledge that there never had been a law against bastardy in Massachusetts. Raynal persisted that he must have had the whole case from some source of indisputable trustworthiness, until Franklin broke in upon him with a loud laugh, and explained that when he was printer of a newspaper they were sometimes short of news, and, to amuse his customers, he invented fictions that were as welcome to them as facts. One of these fictions was the legend of Raynal's heroine. The abbé was not in the least disconcerted. 'Very well, doctor,' he replied, 'I would rather relate your stories than other men's truths.'"

Now how many well-read, industrious, conscientious literary men will not be surprised at all this? How many of them, even those who have well-stored book-shelves, including Franklin's autobiography, will have the means of testing the truth of Mr. Morley's correction? He gives his authority, but is it worth everybody's while to hunt it up? Every one has, of course, guessed that Miss Baker's speech was composed for her, but they have probably continued to believe the main story. In the evidence upon which we are now told to disbelieve it, I find at a glance certain difficulties:—

1. It is conceivable that Franklin should tell fibs—though this was a very disgraceful one. But,

2. It is difficult to suppose that he would have run the risk of telling *that* fib in a place where there must almost certainly have been some one who knew the law of Massachusetts in this matter. And,

3. It seems all but incredible that there should not have been a law there against bastardy.

When the new laird's wife came flaunting into her pew on her first Sunday, with a too "braw" new bonnet on, the scandalized minister, when he read the words, "Lift not up your horn on high," turned pointedly to her pew. This Mary Baker problem is typical, and may be used to point a similar moral, taken as addressed to those who flatter themselves that they can read and know everything. You can't do it. It happens to the diligent reading man every day to come upon some such problem. He strews his room with books; and after an hour's worry is, in ninety-nine cases out of a hundred, no wiser. True, the statement that in Massachusetts there never was a penal law against bastardy is so curious that the intelligent reader will be sure to bear it in mind, and check it when he has the opportunity. But, even though you should read up to twice Mr. Pattison's stint, think not that you will know everything when all is done, or even be able to tell at a glance whether a particular new course of inquiry is likely to prove fruitful or not. Remember Mary Baker, and lift not up your horn on high.

---

**The Immortality of the Soul.**

IN the recent controversy on the Immortality of the Soul, one noteworthy argument seems to have passed without comment. It was cited in an anonymous letter in the *Spectator*, and, as the [illegible] reason to believe that it influences, more or less [illegible] the minds of many thoughtful persons [illegible] face the spectre fairly. So far as I c[illegible] argument amounts to this: Granted that there is a God, and that He is absolutely benevolently disposed towards mankind,—it does not follow (as commonly assumed) that He will bestow Immortality on man, *because it is quite possible that there may be an inherent absurdity and contradiction in the idea of an Immortal Finite creature*,—it may, in short, be no more within the scope of Divine power to create an Immortal Man, than to make a triangle with the properties of a circle. If we could be first assured that the thing were *possible*, then arguments derived from the justice and goodness of the Deity might be valuable, as affording us ground for believing that He will do that possible thing. But while it remains an open question whether we are not talking actual nonsense when we speak of an ever-living created being, such reflections on the moral attributes of God are beside the mark. No justice or goodness can be involved in doing what, in the nature of things, is impossible.

Now, of course, there is a little confusion here between a *future* life—a mere *post-mortem* addition of so many years, or centuries, to this mortal existence—and an *immortal* life, which it is assumed will continue either in a series of births and deaths, or in one unbroken life, for ever and ever. In the former idea no one can find any self-contradiction. It is only the latter notion of immortality, strictly so described, which is suspected of involving a contradiction. Practically, however, the two ideas must stand or fall together, for almost every argument for the survival of the soul after death bears with double force against its extinction at any subsequent epoch of its existence.

Taking then, the Future Life of man as to all intents and purposes the Immortal Life, we are bound to confront the difficulty—"What right have we to assume that immortality and creaturehood are compatible the one with the other?"

*A priori* argument on such a matter is altogether futile. We know and can reason literally nothing about it. For anything we could urge *antecedent to the observation of man's actual state*, it was, apparently, just as probable that he could not be made immortal, as that he could be made so by any conceivable Power in the universe. But we are not quite in the position of lacking all such *à posteriori* assistance to our judgment. We can see how God has actually constituted the human race, and the problem is consequently modified to this: "Are there any signs or tokens that *Man* is meant for something more than a mere mundane existence?" It is obvious that if Immortality were an attribute, which in the nature of things he could never share, nothing in his mental or moral constitution would have been made with any reference to such an unattainable destiny. If, on the other hand, there be in his nature evidences of a purpose extending beyond the scope of this life, and stretching out into the limitless perspective of eternity, then we are authorized to draw the inference that the Author of his being planned for him a future existence, and (of course) knew that he might enjoy that divine heritage.

Here, then, the argument lies in manageable shape before us. It is true we only see a small portion of humanity, as it has yet been drawn out; but just as mathematicians can determine, from any three given points, the nature of the curve to which they belong, so we have enough indications [illegible] guide us to a conclusion respecting the character of our race. In every [illegible]ent of our nature, save our perishable bodies, we find something, [illegible] to point beyond our threescore years and ten—something inconsistent with the hypothesis that those years complete our intended existence. Our busy Intellects, persistently wrestling with the mysteries of eternity,—our human affections craving for undying love,—our sense of Justice born of no past experience of a reign of Astrea, but resolutely prophesying, in spite of experience, a perfect judgment hereafter,—the measureless meaning which moral distinctions carry to our consciences, —the unutterable longing of our spirits for union (not wholly unattained even here) with the living God, the Father of spirits;—all these things seem to show that we are built, so to speak, on a larger scale than that of our earthly life. The foundations are too deep and wide, the corner-stones are by far too massive, if nothing but the Tabernacle of a day be the design of the Architect. In brief, then, we may admit freely that, for aught we know, "God could not give to a triangle the properties of a circle;" and yet, nevertheless, hold our faith undisturbed, since we find that the line which His hand has actually drawn *is a* CURVE *already* —a few degrees of the circumference of a stupendous circle.

---

**The Uses of Imagination.**

MR. GOSCHEN is not precisely the man from whom one would have looked for a lecture on the uses of imagination to statesmen, men of business, and others. Still, he occupies a pulpit, which might well make the words of even a far less eminent man, speaking upon such a topic, pretty sure to do some good. It is true, nobody can get up imagination—you can't cram for it; so that all advice upon the subject might be said to take us back to Quintus Fixlein and the printer's errata—"There are important consequences to be drawn from all this, *and I advise you to draw them.*" And we may note, in daily life, how foolish and unreal, not to say nauseating, is all false enthusiasm. Society is more than half full of men and women who go about angling for information as to the way in which they ought to feel on such and such topics; and then we come to the state of things,—or a dozen states of things, such as are suggested by Mr. Du Maurier's delicious picture of the girls who practise Greek attitudes at lawn tennis, and "like it very much, papa; only we never hit the ball."

Some years ago Mr. Lewes was laying it down with as much fervour as if it were new, that imagination was of as much consequence to the man of science as to the poet. It is true, but what then? There are as many imaginations as there are men. In the sense of the power of making real *some* things not present, who is not imaginative? But that is not the essence of the case. The imagination which the scientific discoverer wants is the enthusiasm of forecast. This the inventor has, and the prophet, and the reformer. As for telling how other people feel, it may be a very high gift, or a very low one. A cat has it, and a Fouché, or a Talleyrand, or any successful man of business you like to name; but then its range in that case is only over a certain field. Napoleon's "imagination" would tell him what was going on in an enemy's camp; but when some one was pleading to him earnestly in a cause of heroism or affection, he asked, "How much are you to have for this?" Indeed, and of course, every "imagination" has its limits. There is not in all Shakespeare the faintest trace of conscience conce[illegible] as Wordsworth conceived it. Yet who had the most "imaginati[illegible]

The most important thing to remember for our guidance in dealing with this matter is, that the eye can only see what it brings with it. We shall find, upon close scrutiny of much poetry which for a time affects us by a certain ethical glow, that the poet has not the true ethical eye; and—for the subject is endless—it does upon the whole appear all but idle to speak of cultivating the imagination or stimulating its exercise, except, indeed, as a question of education. Here, indeed, Mr. Goschen, or any other prophet who takes up a similar strain, is on strong ground. Something—not much, but something worth the doing—may be done with the young in the way of (so to speak) cultivating the imagination, and for the present we are in danger of making even that little less than it need be. But general advice to be imaginative can only meet with some such response as Joseph Andrews gave to the clergyman who insisted on knowing whether he forgave the robbers who had torn him from his Fanny? He said, after some hesitation, that he forgave them as much as he could; and the clergyman was obliged to adjourn the question, observing vaguely that that would do.

---

Lady Nurses.

IT is much to be wished that some competent person would discuss how far it is desirable that women of education and refinement should devote themselves to the work of nursing, and, supposing it to be desirable, what are the conditions under which such work should be carried on. Does experience show that hospitals where ladies are employed are superior to other hospitals? Is it found that lady nurses, or sisters, as they called, are able to work in harmony with the medical staff? Should they be members of a regular sisterhood? Should they be paid? What should be their relation to the inferior nurses? Should they devote themselves entirely and solely to the hospital? It may perhaps make it easier for an expert to answer these questions with advantage, if an outsider lays down first what seems to him the common-sense view upon each point.

It seems to me, then, that there cannot be much difference of opinion as to some of the points mentioned. It may be taken for granted that there are ladies who, whether from natural aptitude or from the experience which may have come to them in the course of their lives, have a faculty and a liking for nursing, which do not find a sphere in their own homes. It may be taken for granted, also, that tact, refinement, intelligence, administrative power, are more likely to be found in the higher than in the lower class of society. If these are qualities needed in a hospital, then it follows that ladies are needed there. But in what capacity should they go? Dr. West, in his little book on Hospital Organization, says that they ought to go simply as ordinary nurses, sharing the same meals and the same rooms, and having only the same prospect of rising to the headship of a ward as the others have. It may be admitted that any lady who wishes to become an effective superintendent of nurses should learn to do all that an under nurse has to do; but I am unable to see why a lady, if she chooses this line of life, should be required to give up the pleasure of social intercourse with her own equals, and to undergo the ordeal of associating continually with those who must, unless by some special miracle, be less refined and less intellectual than herself, unable to share in many of her interests, and who will therefore in all probability be as much "bo by her presence as she is by theirs. When there is one mess for officers and privates of a regiment, when medical men sit dow table with their own coachmen, or, say, with their own dispense will be time for Dr. West to call upon ladies to follow their exa It is probable, too, that an ordinary nurse who was raised t head of a ward would, except in very rare cases, be as little po with her subordinates as an officer who has been raised from the r commonly is with soldiers.

It may be objected that lady nurses are apt to give themselves as we should say, while nurses of a lower class are more submissiv the medical staff. A double answer may be made to this. If w member what young medical students are, we shall not perhaps th altogether undesirable that they should be conscious of the check lady's presence in the wards; but secondly, is it not possible that, in where there has been a collision between the senior hospital autho and the ladies, this may have arisen in part from a faulty syste injudicious rules? Dr. West shows by quotations from French German writers, that the danger of collision is greatest where ladies are connected with some religious sisterhood, and he refers approval to the practice in France, and in other Roman Catholic coun where the sisters are only admitted on condition of being absol subordinate to lay authority. The Sisterhood, however, is, the extreme form of that ascetic principle which unfortunately pre among all our lady nurses, and to which I should be inclined to by far the larger part of the difficulties which have arisen be them and the medical staff, wherever the former were to Supposing men were not allowed to practise medicine exc condition of living in hospitals all the year round, seldom getting for air or exercise, with no amusements, no domestic life, nothing the constant sight of sickness and death before them, what amou common sense would they retain at the end of the year? Yet go on with this till their health breaks down altogether, and wonder that they are irritable, prejudiced, and morbid! Once it a rule that every sister gets out for a good walk whenever weather allows it, that she mixes freely in ordinary society, an possible, has one day in the week to herself, as well as an change for three months in the year, and we should hear no mo petty hospital squabbles. This would of course require a larger su of ladies to be connected with each hospital, and it would probabl found expedient to have a register of duly qualified ladies who ready to relieve those permanently connected with the hospitals.

It remains to say a word as to the payment of the sisters. Of co *à priori*, one is disposed to say, whoever does good work ought paid for it; and on several grounds it would be well if nursing be made into a profession for ladies; it would do away with the gerated idea of the work as one of pre-eminent merit; it would with the caste exclusiveness which is now too apt to be associated But here political economy enters in. If the supply exceeds the wages must fall. If there are a large number of qualified peting to be allowed to work as nurses for board and lodg cannot expect hospital authorities to offer a larger pure liberality, or any high-flown notion of the right

... has been delivering, upon a certain point in the ... of Dissenting propagandism, an address which has ... and seems bound to puzzle clear-headed people. The ... is that of association, more or less direct, with irreligious persons—I presume, the right word would be un-Christian—for the purpose of liberating Religion from ... Of course it is easy to understand, and obvious to justify, ... who will not work upon the same platform with a ... quote the phrase of a speaker who came after Dr. Parker, ... when Christianity is mentioned. The devout Christian ... the "iconoclast" (Dr. Parker, in using this word, pointed ... Mr. Bradlaugh, who for a long time lectured and wrote under ... voting on the same side, whatever be his reasons; but ... say, *non tali auxilio*—so far as personal associations ... Liberation Society might, no doubt, have refused a bequest ... if the late Mr. Mill or the late Mr. Austin had made it to ... would they? Or ought they? Was Allen, the Quaker— ... of course—wrong in employing in his journal the pen of ... against slavery? These are not easy questions. Of course ... always been two classes of Nonconformists: first, those who ... said, "We would join the National Church, if its creed, ... ritual suited us;" and secondly, those who have said, "We ... neither part nor lot in your National Church, because religion ... of government, and cannot be made one without cor... and persecution." These are, in my opinion, the only logical ... But let Dr. Parker take which side he will,—he appears to ...—his six points and his speech are illogically tied together. ... point is as follows:—"6. That the disestablishment of the ... England would be a national calamity unless it can be clearly ... the religious work which it is doing can be better done ... establishment than with it."

...uite clear that the man who holds this proposition is not a ..." Dissenter, but I think it equally clear that he cannot hold ...d consistently with an absolute reasoned faith in religion as ... a sense not to be distinguished from miraculous. The Dissen... ...n it has been my lot to know most of—men of the stamp, for ... of the late John Howard Hinton—would say, as I say myself, ... shadow of reserve:—"We have not the slightest business with ...uld happen if the Established Church were disestablished, and ... earthly means of discovering it. We have, indeed, no doubt ...gion would be a great deal better for that event, but our assu... founded, in the first instance, not upon any consideration of ... be shown as matter of fact, but upon the nature of the case." ...art from this,—and fully aware that the old-fashioned Dissenter ... is rapidly passing away into the order of troglodytes,—I ... ashamed to be a troglodyte, must still ask how Dr. Parker's ... is to be made logical and workable, if its exclusions are ... beyond the point of personal fellowship. Professor F. W. ... a pure theist. So is Miss Cobbe. Assuming them to be ... Church establishment in every form, would Dr. Parker ... with them? If not, where is the line to be drawn? ... supposition—that Mr. Matthew Arnold were to present himself in a white sheet as an opponent of all Church establishments, should he be excluded from the platform of the Liberation Society? In fine, what ground would there be for excluding any man who should maintain that the interference of the State with religion is injurious to it, whatever be the religion—that the spiritual interests of man must be let alone by the policeman?

It appears quite plain to me that, if Dr. Parker is right, the Liberationists ought at once to split into at least two bands. One of these bands would be composed of those who hold, as I do, that the interference of the State with religion in church, in school, in chamber, is in the first instance a violation of civil freedom. If such an organization had to choose between interfering on behalf of a Christian sent to prison for non-payment of Church-rates, and an Atheist sent to prison for "making mouths" at Christianity, I can conceive that the Christian would come in for help first, but the claim of the Atheist would be equally clear. That is the way I have always read the logic of Dissent. I have always refrained from actively attacking the Church of England, and would never disestablish it by a bare majority; but, after incessant study of the question, I have never been able to find a flaw in the Nonconformist position as I have now put it.

# [illegible]TEMPORARY LITERATURE.



*[illegible] to the extraordinary development of Educational Literature during the last few years, and the [illegible] of school training, we think it may not be unacceptable to many of our readers if [illegible] a portion of the space set apart for the review of Contemporary Literature to a [illegible] of the more important series dealing with what may be called the modern subjects of [illegible] History, and literature.]*

W[illegible] confess to having had some prejudice against the ruling fashion of con[illegible] knowledge in small compact doses, neatly labelled, as exemplified [illegible] the numerous series of Manuals of every kind still pouring from the [illegible] directions. Education seems in danger of becoming a thing of results [illegible] of method, of facts rather than of evidence, and less adapted to develop [illegible] than to set a premium on a mechanical memory. These hosts of [illegible] volumes seem to have a suspicious relationship to our plethoric exami[illegible] and its concomitant cramming, to the blessings of which we are [illegible] awaking. But a careful perusal of the volumes specified below* has gone [illegible] removing the prejudice, at least so far as this series is concerned. After [illegible] four volumes taken together form a connected history of Greece, if not [illegible] beginning of its life, at least from the period at which the fortunes of [illegible] became identified with those of humanity, until the epoch when the fate of [illegible] proper made little difference to the world, now that the spirit of Hellenism [illegible] abroad for ever. What higher advantage is gained by the story being written [illegible] pens it is hard to say; but we have it here in some eight or [illegible] hundred pages in a continuous form; and if for practical purposes we desire [illegible] less than the whole, we can find our epoch given separately: and it so [illegible] that ancient history, and not least that of Greece, admits conveniently [illegible] subdivisions, partly owing to the nature of affairs, and partly owing to [illegible] of our authorities.

[illegible] first epoch, "The Greeks and the Persians," corresponds to the main nar[illegible] Herodotus, and admirably has Mr. Cox reproduced the charm of the native [illegible], and at the same time supplied a running commentary on his deficiencies, [illegible] omissions. It would be difficult to find another commentary equally [illegible] and yet sufficient. Thus, Mr. Cox notices the impossibilities connected [illegible] account of the battle of Marathon; with the numbers of the army and [illegible] given by Herodotus; with the defence of Thermopylæ, the rout [illegible] at Delphi, the final struggle at Platæa, and so on. As the narra[illegible] takes the form of a reproduction and criticism of Herodotus, it is [illegible] constant references to book and chapter are not given. One of Hero[illegible] connected with the battle of Platæa, is slightly distorted in the [illegible] Sophanes, the Athenian, is not reported by Herodotus to have used [illegible] the purpose of catching his enemies—nor is it easy to see how an

* [illegible]. Edited by Rev. G. W. Cox, M.A., and Charles Sankey, M.A. London: Long-
[illegible]. By Rev. G. W. Cox, M.A.
[illegible] By Rev. G. W. Cox, M.A.
[illegible]. By C. Sankey, M.A.
[illegible]. By A. M. Curteis, M.A.

anchor would be suitable for the feat—but for the purpose of steadying himself in the press of battle; nor was the anchor "brazen," but "made of iron" (σιδηρέην). If the story was worth giving at all, it was worth giving correctly; Herodotus, too, mentions an alternative version. There is also a slip, or at least a great ambiguity in Mr. Cox's statement (p. 30), that Herodotus tells us that one of the Macedonian kings, "seeking to compete in the Olympic games, had his claim disallowed on the score of his non-Hellenic descent." What Herodotus tells us is, that the rival competitors tried to keep (ἐξεῖργον) Alexander out of the lists, but that the Hellenodicæ decided the question in his favour, and thus accredited his Hellenic descent. There are several passages in which Mr. Cox makes what we may venture to call questionable statements, as, for example, that the reason why Peisistratus observed the Solonian constitution was that he instinctively perceived that it was "sufficiently oligarchic in spirit to suit his purpose." We should rather say that, on the one hand, the deadliest enemy to the Greek tyrant was oligarchy in any and every form; and on the other, that it was the preservation of the Solonian forms by the Peisistratidæ which trained the Athenian people for the full-blown Democracy, and that the "sound instinct" of later days looked back to Solon as the first father of the Democracy. The statement, too, that the distinction between the king and the tyrant "was never very strongly marked" in the Greek cities, admits, we should say, of being completely inverted, with greater truth; as thus, that one of the most marked contrasts in Greek constitutions (as afterwards in Greek philosophy) is that between the king of right divine, and the tyrant with whom might was right: the heroic drama in democratic Athens confirms the remark. Again, Mr. Cox's analysis of causes strikes us as at times inadequate; the way in which "the old Aryan civilization" is made to explain facts of Greek political life might surprise us more, if we did not remember that he is well known for his somewhat doctrinaire explanation of Aryan myths in all their varieties as manifestations of one small set of elemental notions.

2. In the second epoch, "The Athenian Empire," Mr. Cox does for Thucydides what in the first he has done for Herodotus; but the task is simpler, as the authority is better. The volume is delightful reading, and, as in the former case, the implicit commentary on the original source of the narrative very skilful. We are, however, somewha at a loss to determine on what principle Mr. Cox decides the authenticity of the particular speeches in Thucydides. He gives his reasons for calling in question the Melian Dialogue (pp. 111, 112), and he throws a doubt on the report of the speech of the Lesbian envoys at Olympia (p. 65); but he gives without hesitation the substance of the speech of Brasidas at Akanthos, and that of Nikias at Athens in opposition to the Sicilian expedition. Nothing could be better than the compressed account of that expedition, though Mr. Cox's repeated scorn of the respectability (pp. 128, 144, 154) of Nikias must grate harshly on the average British reader. Among the causes of the deterioration of the Athenian people, and of the contrast between the generation which began and that which concluded the Peloponnesian war, Mr. Cox does not specify the actual physical incapacity and taint of a population begotten and nurtured amid the horrors of the plague, and an almost constant state of siege during the summer at least. We must notice it as an omission—though one perhaps necessitated by the exigencies of the case—that a fuller picture of the development of Athenian life and of "the Age of Pericles," which Mr. Cox eulogizes as "the most brilliant phase in the history of mankind," is not given to us. Would not the description of such a phase form a volume by itself, and deserve a place in the series?

3. Passing from the second to the third volume of the series, "The Spartan and Theban Supremacies," we seem at first to have exchanged for the terse style of Mr. Cox a flowery rhetoric, determined to atone for the dulness of Xenophon. Fortunately, however, Mr. Sankey's stylistic effervescence passes off as soon as he settles down to his proper narrative, and he ably redeems the promise of his preface, "to bring out clearly the characters of the leading men, and the causes of the chief events," in the period from the demolition of the Long Walls of Athens (B.C. 404) to the collapse of Theban supremacy on the fall of Epameinondas, "the greatest Greek of that or perhaps of any age." In general sentiment Mr. Sankey is evidently harmonious with his joint-editor; but upon occasion he knows how to substitute for "the intolerance of old Aryan civilization" a nearer though hardly less obscure set of causes for "the fatal tendency to autonomy" in "the inherent defects of the Greek character." Had more space been at his disposal, Mr. Sankey would probably have dealt more at length with the philo-Lakonism of "the pious Xenophon;" as it is, he naturally carries us with him in his censure of

[illegible] partisanship in his accounts of the battles of Leuctra and [illegible] be a question whether Mr. Sankey does not overrate the [illegible] Xenophon; are the speeches in the "Anabasis" remarkable, [illegible] other specimens of Athenian oratory? Was it the sophistic [illegible] the logic of facts, simply stated, which controlled the Ten [illegible] again? A brief chapter is devoted to Socrates, and to the [illegible] him no exception can be taken; and the characterization of [illegible] is very happy. Like Mr. Cox, Mr. Sankey seems to hold [illegible]. About the conduct of the Greek States in the Persian wars, [illegible] to us, there can hardly be two opinions; but our Atticism [illegible] shock when we admit that the policy even of Pericles was no [illegible], but definitely anti-Spartan. When, long after, the tables are [illegible] the best efforts of the times are with Epameinondas and Thebes, what [illegible] of "Attikismos" to see any special generosity in the [illegible] Athens, when she forgot past enmities, and, after the foundation of [illegible] joined hands with Sparta, out of jealousy to Thebes? In the kaleido-[illegible] politics, the slightest revolution communicated to the fabric from [illegible] without was apt to change the relations of the vari-coloured con-[illegible] a manner at first sight perhaps arbitrary-looking, but on closer [illegible] to the motives of self-preservation or aggrandisement. If the [illegible] Athenians had wished to be generous they might have exercised the [illegible] the developing liberties of Arcadia; it was indeed an abyss of [illegible] the destroyer of their own!

[illegible] Rise of the Macedonian Empire," Mr. Curteis receives the torch— [illegible] bears it to the goal. The first principles are the same, though the [illegible]; Mr. Cox's "intolerance of the old Aryan civilization," and Mr. [illegible] "inherent defect of the Greek character," is Mr. Curteis' "fatal defect [illegible] political ideas." Such stinging abstractions seem to convey a sort of [illegible], and to ignore the relativity of all political institutions, it may be [illegible]. In any case the formulæ do not disturb the narrative, and that [illegible] is compact and graphic as in the case of his predecessors. In some [illegible] an easier task, for the facts of the epoch naturally group themselves [illegible] persons of Philip and Alexander, and the latter portion of his book [illegible] itself into a biography of the latter, insomuch, indeed, that he does [illegible] the insurrection in Greece, B.C. 330, which was quelled by Antipater, [illegible] Viceroy in Macedonia. On the other hand, Mr. Curteis has the more [illegible] task of composing his narrative from less perfect sources. His geogra-[illegible] are clear and of service in following the campaigns of Alexander in [illegible] between Mesopotamia and the Indus. He does not omit to notice [illegible] mosthenes was not a full-blooded Athenian, and considering the exhausted [illegible] the population, none the worse on that account. Mr. Curteis makes no [illegible] of the condemnation and exile of Demosthenes in 325 B.C., though he [illegible] the flight of Harpalus to Athens with the treasure of Babylon, which indi-[illegible] brought about the charge of receiving bribes, on which the orator was tried. [illegible] know on what ground Mr. Curteis' renders Δημητρὸς καρπὸν in Hdt. i. 193, [illegible] (p. 94) when describing the productivity of the Babylonian soil. But [illegible] not matters of great importance. On the whole, Mr. Curteis has [illegible] his assault" with vigour; the personalities of the great father and the [illegible] are brought out into *alto relievo*; and the motives and stages of that [illegible] deplorable deterioration of the latter which made the extravagant [illegible] assumption of divine origin, the intemperance in anger and in [illegible] the murder of his foster-brother possible to the pupil of Aristotle, [illegible] marked. The fourth little volume may fairly stand beside the other [illegible]

[illegible], furnished with convenient maps and plans, written in a bright [illegible] based on the best authorities, these volumes deserve popularity. But [illegible] students, even of the humbler order, they would be still more useful if [illegible] to the original authorities were added in the margin. The [illegible] epochs needs two or three further volumes to make it complete. To [illegible] without an introductory volume, dealing with the beginnings of Greek [illegible] it is, to compare it with greater things, like a temple without a [illegible] without a fuller treatment of the age of Pericles, the epochs of the [illegible] Peloponnesian wars gape apart like the dissevered ends of the

A SIMPLE history of England, by writers who have studied the subject deeply and thoughtfully, has long been desired by the teachers of elementary schools. Up to this time they have been obliged to content themselves with works compiled by the most ordinary bookmakers, or by writers who have been devoid either of the ability or the knowledge which the task requires. It is to satisfy this demand that the present series of Historical Epochs* is now being produced, and the names of those writers who support Mr. Creighton in his work will at once prove that at least the requisite ability and knowledge are not wanting. The volumes themselves are neat and handy, well prepared for study by the arrangement of paragraphs and indexes. It remains then to consider how far the experiment has succeeded, by which writers, accustomed to compose for educated readers, are now required to make a difficult matter comprehensible to the minds of children.

1. The series opens with a volume on Early England, by Mr. York Powell, of Christ Church, and in this, at all events, we find no signs of a failure in the attempt. The volume is written in the simple English of the Bible, of which Mr. Powell shows himself a perfect master, and the thoughts are expressed in a clear yet concise manner, which will be at once intelligible and pleasant to children. The story of the foundation and development of the earlier kingdoms, of the supremacy of Wessex, and of the influence which the English empire received from and exercised over the States of the Continent, is set forth in a style which would have shown how brilliant was the literary and dramatic power of the writer in a book of more ambitious pretensions,—much more here where he is circumscribed by the space and by the purpose of his work. We notice a decided yet by no means selfish patriotism, and a strong but not prominently displayed morality, which will be certain to have the noblest influence on his young readers, yet without being too apparent to themselves. Early English history, though Mr. Freeman has done so much for us, has not yet been written in a form attractive to children; we fully believe that Mr. Powell will now have unlocked to them the charm of that most important period; even the long dull time of the Dane does not lack interest. If we must criticize, we would suggest to Mr. Powell that there is some lack of picturesqueness in the stories of Caractacus and Augustine as he tells them; that it would have been better to have related the history of Wilfrith and of Egbert all at once, without the digressions, placing these elsewhere, since the histories of these heroes are well worth bringing into strong relief; and that he has left out the causes which prevented the Britons from really attempting the conversion of our ancestors, indeed has implied that the attempt had been made and failed. But these are small blemishes in a book which so beautifully and simply develops the drama of our history, which brings the story into unity without breaking the thread of pleasant narrative.

2. In "England a Continental Power" by Mrs. Creighton, the volume which comes next in the series, we miss those constant references to geography made by Mr. Powell which have always been found so useful by teachers in varying the work and interesting children; and Mrs. Creighton has kept, with a resolution which we cannot help regretting, to the mandate in the editor's introductory notice which nearly excludes military history. Boys, at all events, and not so uncommonly girls, are devoted to descriptions of battles; and it is unwise to hesitate to humour them, even at the expense of a little space which the writer may think to employ more usefully. It seems to us, too, that Mrs. Creighton might have made the account of the Norman administrative system somewhat more agreeable by, perhaps, a little addition of personal matter, though the sketch is certainly most easy of comprehension. And when it is stated that William I. "let no man hold much land together," we cannot help thinking of the earldoms of Norfolk, Hereford, and Cornwall, and the great lordships in the Midlands, which were found so troublesome by the Conqueror's descendants, but which Mrs. Creighton does not mention in what seems meant as an exhaustive list. But it would be unwise to quarrel with a book really so excellent and so useful. The character of William I. is brilliant and vigorous, yet simple; Mrs. Creighton seems thoroughly to have understood his aims and to be able to make them easy of grasp

* English Historical Epochs. Edited by the Rev. Mandell Creighton. London: Longmans, Green, & Co.
1. Early England up to the Norman Conquest. By F. York Powell, M.A., Law Lecturer at Christ Church, Oxford.
2. England a Continental Power, from the Conquest to Magna Charta. By Louise Creighton.
3. The Rise of the People and Growth of Parliament, from the Great Charter to the accession of VII. By James Rowley, M.A., Professor of Modern History [illegible], University College.
4. The Settlement of the Constitution. By James Rowley, M.A.

to the most untrained minds; and the sketch of the struggle for the Great Charter with which the volume closes is well drawn and thoroughly interesting.

3. The third volume of the series, "The Rise of the People," by Mr. Rowley, is very inferior to its predecessors. Instead of an easy narrative, enlivening and attractive to children, a condensed account of the great features of the period is given to us, condensed not by the elimination of the less necessary facts, but by placing these lesser facts in a close and unrelieved statement. The language, too, is by no means such as children would readily understand. Before Mr. Rowley's book can be used with advantage for elementary education it will have to be written again in a different form and with simpler thoughts, omitting the technicalities which historians are now so fond of employing. Mr. Rowley seems to have imagined that his task was to cram children for competitive examinations, and even for this purpose certain inaccuracies would impair the efficiency of his book. He forgets the influence of the knights in forcing on the publication of the provisions in Westminster in October, 1259; he even attributes this great result to a party among the barons, thus losing one of the most important points in the class history of the time, and one which is so useful to a clear understanding of the growth of Parliament. Mr. Rowley tells us that Peter de la Mare, in 1376, was the first who held the office of Speaker, though he admits that he never bore the title; it appears that this position was first filled by Sir William Trussel in 1343, that is, more than thirty years earlier. We should not have noticed errors of this sort, had not Mr. Rowley attempted a nearly exhaustive sketch of the rise of Parliament, given in a long list of great councils and dates which is utterly out of place in a small book for children, and which older persons would prefer to read in the pages of Professor Stubbs. It is to be hoped that Mr. Rowley will rewrite his book in the style of Mr. Powell's, for he shows considerable comprehension of the period, and the descriptions of the wars with Wales and Scotland are decidedly interesting.

4. We have another work by the same author in "The Settlement of the Constitution," where he proposes to lay before us in a hundred pages a sketch of the political history of our country for a hundred years; beginning with the Revolution, and ending with William Pitt's final establishment as First Lord of the Treasury after the election of 1784. In other words, he begins with the successful revolt of the Great Houses against the Stewart Monarchy, and ends with the triumph of the Tories and the Hanoverian Monarch over the Great Houses. To gather so much into so small a space is a great feat; and Mr. Rowley has succeeded more than fairly in his task; for his narrative is clear and concise, and, in part at least, interesting in spite of its brevity. On the other hand, the little book has grave faults. The very title is misleading; for the man must be an ancient Conservative indeed, who holds that the "British Constitution" was "settled" by the year 1784, and that whatever has happened to it since has been only a series of modifications of an established order of things. Again, the key-note of the book is not struck true; we are not told, as we should have been, that the Revolution of 1688 was the work of the great families in revolt against the Stewarts; a fact which has affected the history of England ever since, and gives an almost dramatic interest to the struggles of George III. against the Whig oligarchy, and a special significance to Pitt's triumph in 1784. Exception may also be taken to the statement that England was divided into Jacobites and Williamites: the latter nickname is better not revived, it never gained real currency, and indeed could not have done so, as it lacked all the conditions of success. William had no personal popularity; his adherents never supported with the enthusiasm of despair a ruined cause; he did not even create a lasting belief that good government depended solely on himself; nor indeed was he even the head of a party. Therefore it is that the name of Jacobite survives, while that of Williamite is gone. We note also inaccuracies in detail in this little book. Thus, "Brandenburg, the Prussia of our own times," is a singularly misleading statement: is it intended that the young student should believe Brandenburg to be the other name for that wide aggregate of States which, under the title of the Kingdom of Prussia, has been steadily growing to right and left down to our own days? Again, the vague statement that in 1690 William III. had thoughts of going back to Holland ought not to have been repeated: Von Ranke has shown that it rests only on some impatient words uttered by the King, words which also prove that he had no such thought, and was, in fact, fully aware of the impossibility of such a step. Where again does Professor [illegible] find his "heights of Malplaquet?" Malplaquet stands on a little plain;

and the strength of the French position lay in earthworks, in the thick and broken woods, and the little ravines which intersect the country. Minorca, he tells us, was taken in 1708 and was held by the English for seventy years, without noticing that it was conquered by the French in 1756, and retained by them all through the Seven Years' War. These are statements which ought not to be laid before learners; nor indeed ought young readers to find so much of their own speech in the manuals put into their hands. "Louis XIV. had become so humble for the many beatings he had got," and affairs took "a very different turn from what they had taken," and the like, are not good phrases; nor does it make a book at all clearer to imitate little boys' language till one touches on the confines of slang.

---

Mr. Arthur's work* might have been called, with more elegance as well as propriety, a history of the Vatican Council. Its present title, like the letters in which it is emblazoned on the back of the volume, is too "loud." The work, however, is a valuable history drawn from the most authentic sources, and showing great industry and learning as well as clear and vigorous reasoning. The motives which led to the assembling of the Council are well known, and in substance not disputed by any party. The Pope and his advisers believed that the whole world was departing from the faith; men even in Catholic countries were claiming the right to think for themselves, science was asserting its supremacy over ecclesiastical dogmas, and kings were executing their office of rulers without reference to the authority of the Church. The ancient dominion of the Popes over the kings, bishops, priests, and people, had been shaken during the last three centuries in almost every country in Europe, and to some it seemed the only remedy for the evils of the present times to have that dominion restored,—in Mr. Arthur's words, "to make the Pope governor of the world by a universal reconstruction of society."

It is only by an effort that we can think of the Pope and the Jesuits as really desiring the well-being of society by their efforts to restore the dominion of the Church. Yet it is possible that they were perfectly sincere. To them the Roman Catholic Church is the kingdom of God, and therefore nothing could seem more desirable than that the kings of the earth should be subject to its head, who in their judgment is the Vicar of Heaven. But the advantages of this ecclesiastical supremacy were not apparent to Protestants, nor, indeed, to the great body of intelligent Roman Catholics. The Pope succeeded in carrying his measures notwithstanding a powerful opposition, but whether his success is to be for the good of the Church or of society is for the future to show.

Mr. Arthur begins his history with the meeting of the Congregation of Rites, on the 6th of December 1864, when the Pope communicated secretly to the Cardinals his design of holding a General Council. Incidentally he points back to the decree of the Immaculate Conception which the Pope made by his own authority, and which Dr. Döllinger, at the Bonn Conference, declared to be the *Fons et origo malorum*. On the 8th, the day of the tenth anniversary of the passing of this decree, the Pope published the Encyclical *Quanta Cura* with the Syllabus of Errors. Modern society was described as in ruins, and the first proof of it was that the Salutary force (*vis*) of the Church, which ought always to be exercised not only over individuals, but also over nations, both "peoples" and sovereigns, was set aside. The Papal States under the immediate government of the Pope might have been expected to exhibit a pattern of what the world would be when the Pope had universal sway; but from the picture given by Mr. Arthur they appear to have been the worst governed States in Europe, the villages were wretched, and the people more squalid and poverty-stricken than even in the most wretched parts of Roman Catholic Ireland.

In 1867, when the devout had gathered in Rome from all parts of the world to celebrate the eighteenth century anniversary of St. Peter, the Pope held a secret consistory, which was attended by five hundred bishops. The Syllabus received their sanction. At the same time the first public intimation was given of a General Council. This was received with great exultation, and a "Salutation" was presented to the Pope. Some of those employed to write it proposed that in this document the Pope should be proclaimed infallible, but the French bishops protested. Commissioners were appointed for the preparatory business, the year for

* The Pope, the Kings, and the People. By William Arthur. London: William Mullan & [illegible]

holding the Council was fixed, and invitations sent to those whom it was deemed proper to invite. No princes were asked to come because none were Catholic—that is, they did not put the canon law above the laws of their kingdoms. That the Council, however, might lay claim to œcumenicity, invitations were sent to all the prelates of the Oriental Churches not in communion with the See of Rome, and also "to Protestants and non-Catholics." None of these were to take any part in the Council, but they were to have an opportunity of renouncing their heresies, and submitting to the authority of Rome.

Mr. Arthur's first volume ends with some interesting chapters on the discussions and controversies which immediately preceded the opening of the Council. In these Dr. Manning is conspicuous, especially for his having assailed the historical school of Munich, for denouncing all appeals to antiquity and trusting only to the living voice of the Church. The second volume begins with the first session of the Council, and is occupied entirely with its proceedings. We have in detail the story with which we are all familiar, of the policy by which the opposition to the new dogma was gradually diminished till at last the leaders themselves submitted, and some of them became vehement advocates of that which they had once opposed. When the new rules were issued, as many as a hundred bishops protested against them, declaring it to be "a total and an astounding novelty" that a mere majority in a Council was sufficient to carry a dogma. The old rule was moral unanimity, and this they said was more necessary in the Vatican than it had been at Trent, for many bishops *in partibus* had been admitted to vote, while their right to do so had always been doubtful. But the opposition dwindled down, and the eighty-eight who said *non placet* ultimately in some form submitted to the decree of the majority, which was swollen by insignificant bishops without dioceses or from distant lands, such as are described in England in the words, "only a colonial." The submission of some eminent German bishops astonished many persons; but more remarkable still was the renunciation of the old principles of the Gallican Church by the bishops of France. The Pope's advisers had made a bold stroke; but doubtless they had been able to read something of the probable course of events. The Roman Catholic bishops and clergy in all countries, whatever might have been their private or abstract views of the Church in its essence, had begun to feel that in any collision between the Church and civil rulers they were safest on the side of the Church. Such an issue was that raised by the Vatican decree. To oppose it might be consistent with their belief of what constitutes the Catholic faith; but it was to oppose the Church which gave them shelter. The Archbishop of Munich was with the opposition till the dogma was decreed. When the Council closed he returned meekly to his diocese. It was supposed that the private manner in which he entered Munich was intended to avoid any demonstration in the way of approbation of the attitude he had assumed at Rome. But it was soon whispered that the archbishop had submitted. The Faculty of Theology, with Döllinger at its head, came with an address of congratulation on his return. After a formal reply, the archbishop said, "Rome has spoken; you, gentlemen, know the rest. We could do nothing but give in." Friedrich, who describes the scene, says that Döllinger was "boiling," and that the others were not unmoved. The archbishop continued, "We struggled long, and gained much time, also averted a deal of evil." After stating in detail the unavailing efforts of the opposition, he turned to Döllinger and said, "Shall we start afresh to work for Holy Church?" The answer was, "Yes, for the OLD one." The archbishop, repressing his rage, said, "There is only one Church; not a new one and an old one." "They have MADE a new one," said Döllinger. "There have always been alterations in the Church and in the doctrines," continued the archbishop. The startling effect of these words was at once visible on every face. That the Church was unchangeable in its doctrines was what they had learned in childhood, and what they had taught as professors to the rising priesthood. Next morning the archbishop visited Döllinger, from whom he learned what he had not learned at Rome, that after the discussion an addition was made to the decree, that the dogma was passed "not by the consent of the Church, but on the sole authority of the Pope." To this the archbishop had to reconcile himself, and then to prepare for the excommunication of Döllinger for not accepting a dogma which was contrary to the former teaching of the Church, and made without the Church's consent. Mr. Arthur's judgment of the Vatican movement is, that as to means it has been a splendid success, but as to the ultimate end a decided failure. The Church of Rome has now a decided policy, and an increase of unity which may strengthen its existence as a community, but it has declared war with all progress.

with all science, with all Christianity outside of itself, as well as with the rulers of this world, whom an apostle describes as "the ministers of God"—as divine a title as the New Testament bestows on bishops or any other ecclesiastical officers.

---

UNMINDFUL of the proverb, that good wine needs no bush, Dr. Klunzinger has prefixed to his volume* a prefatory notice by the well-known African traveller, Dr. Schweinfurth. This notice is rather a remarkable one: it commences by classing Burckhardt, Lane, and Dr. Klunzinger together; it goes on to testify to the excellent character of Dr. Klunzinger as a philanthropist; and it more than suggests that Dr. Klunzinger has in the present volume done as much, if not more, than Lane towards increasing our knowledge of Egypt; for "Lane, however trustworthy and complete his descriptions may be, concerned himself in the main with such conditions of life as exist in a large town only." Now, we think Dr. Klunzinger's wine decidedly good, but the bush is by no means attractive. In the first place, Burckhardt and Lane worked on such totally dissimilar lines that they have little in common, except that they were both consummate Orientalists and gave us consummately accurate pictures of Arab life. Dr. Klunzinger may be an excellent philanthropist, and have given a good account of Upper Egypt, but he has not the shadow of a claim to be ranked with two such men. But when we are told that his work on Egypt is as good as Lane's, if it does not even carry our knowledge further, we must decidedly demur. The book before us is the production of a keen observer, who has spent a great deal of his time amongst the poor village population of Upper Egypt, and he tells us what he saw in a simple, graphic style. His minute and accurate description of the agricultural and industrial pursuits of the provincial Egyptians is both interesting and important; and his account of the customs and superstitions which he found existing in the various districts which he visited is rendered more valuable by the comparison which he continually suggests with the customs and rites of the ancient Egyptians, as set forth in the ancient monuments. As a picture of provincial life, it is a very welcome and readable book. Not to mention, however, the deep insight into and sympathy with Egyptian character which Lane possessed, and which Dr. Klunzinger seems hardly to have attained in so high a degree, there is an absence of that absolute accuracy which makes Lane's "Modern Egyptians" a wonder to scholars. Many have tried to catch Lane tripping, and failed, and we believe the only instance of inaccuracy in his book occurs in a song, probably translated at an early period and not subsequently revised, where the poet is made to say that bright eyes have "*overthrown* him" whereas the Arabic means "*shot* him." Dr. Klunzinger's book, on the contrary, however accurate in descriptions of Fellah life and agriculture, is not immaculate from a scholarly point of view. To quote only one instance, taken at random, we are told that the Ghawazi "boast to be descended from Barmek, the well-known favourite of the Khalif Harun el Raschid" (p. 30); the favourite in question being Jaafer ibn Yahya'bn Khalid ibn Barmek, that is, Barmek's great-grandson. The translation is close, too close for the elegance of the English, and the translator has committed the mistake of leaving the Arabic words in the original German translation, which makes them read as much like Cherokee as Arabic. "Upper Egypt" is a useful, and in parts an amusing book; but it will never be classed with Lane's or Burckhardt's works, unless, perhaps, after the fashion of the Bengalee librarian, who made the following entries in his catalogue—"Mill on Liberty," "Ditto on the Floss."

---

MRS. COMYNS CARR's book† is a delightful one of a kind which is far too rare. If any one wants to really know the North Italian folk, we can honestly advise him to omit the journey and sit down to read Mrs. Carr's pages instead. The sketches she offers of town and country life on the Riviera and in the Apennines give just the information which it is hopeless to look for either in Handbooks or in volumes of full-length fiction, and which no one in passing can hastily pick up for himself. Mrs. Carr herself lived in Italy until she was penetrated by its air and its life.

What the book aims at doing, and what in a half-hidden way it is very skilfully adapted to achieve, is the producing a true impression of the social life of these parts of Italy. In saying that it is informing, it must be understood it

* Upper Egypt: Its People and its Products. By C. B. Klunzinger, M.D. With a Preface by George Schweinfurth. London: Blackie & Son.

† North Italian Folk. By Mrs. Comyns Carr. London: Chatto and Windus.

this by the way, not of first purpose. The pages are meant to be, and truly are, literature, being none the less effectively that for showing ever and again a little ease of undress, the author coming to the front and speaking in her own person. Now she describes a city, a mountain village, a stretch of the coast; now she hits off some typical personage; now she combines the scene and character in some short story, most naturally brought in. Mrs. Carr has a very picturesque pen. She can put upon her page an Italian town, whitely blazing in the sunshine, or cover it with all the coloured bustle of a Carnival scene. Indeed, we are not sure that she has not herself found this out a little too well. Once and again, the word-painting shows the rare sin of excess of colouring: the writer has used the pen a little too like a pencil, running the syllables together, giving a streak of hue. But description with Mrs. Carr is a real gift, as is shown by her power of taking up into a linked description one minute detail after another.

With light, skilful touches, Mrs. Carr makes you know nearly all the ranks of life—flower-girl, shopkeeper, housekeeper, hair-dresser, priest—showing you them holiday-making, working, loving, quarrelling; and in every instance there is enough of local atmosphere upon the page to render itself felt. Some of the illustrative short fiction is very good, in its way—rapid and brightly amusing.

If a still closer idea beforehand of the book should be wished for, it may be got if we say that its plan is not unlike that of Miss Mitford's "Our Village," only that Mrs. Carr's volume does not so much confine its scale. She speaks of cities, and includes mountains and the sea-coast; but there is the same methodical desultoriness and mixing up, in a pleasantly effective way, of reality and imaginary examples. No method could be better for producing a feeling of really knowing the places and the people.

It is rarely that a book is so happily illustrated.

---

THERE is plenty for the literary critic and the psychologist to say about Mr. Matthew Arnold, but none of it will be said in this brief notice, except what is on all hands admitted, and yet needs to be emphasized in detail: namely, that Mr. Arnold is, to adopt a familiar contrast of Goethe's, a voice and not an echo. His manner and his thought are alike his own; and the former, with all its quietness and even occasional prosaic meanness, has a singular pungency of its own. But, not to nibble at topics which might well make a feast for the muses, we must give a word of welcome to this handsome and complete edition of the poems* which many of us know and love so well. We were very glad indeed when Mr. Arnold announced his departure from a certain sphere of strife and turmoil, and hoped, against hope, that he was going back to "the two-topt mount divine"—a hope which we fear we must give up now that we see the words "complete edition," though of course that is not conclusive. But if he would only keep away from political and social wranglings,—

> "Not here, O Apollo!
> Are haunts meet for thee:
> But where Helicon breaks down
> In cliff to the sea,"—

we should at least recover to the full our old image of him in his singing robes, and get rid of the other, in which he is, if not exactly a "budge doctor of the stoic fur," something even less congenial and of a more prickly rind:—

> "Upon the Russian frontier, where
> The watchers of two armies stand
> Near one another, many a man,
> Seeking a prey unto his hand,
> Hath snatch'd a little fair-hair'd slave:
> They snatch also, towards Mervè,
> The Shiah dogs, who pasture sheep,
> And up from thence to Orgunjè,
>
> . . . . . . .
>
> The Kaffirs also (whom God curse!)
> Vex one another night and day."

Yes, all this is going on, but we should be sorry to see him set himself to write [illegible] about it. "Not here, O Apollo." But we hope he has carried [illegible] go where he will, some sense of power. His song has not been [illegible] an accordant chime:

* Poems by Matthew Arnold. London: Macmillan & Co.

"Yet, as the wheel flies round,
With no ungrateful sound
Do adverse voices fall on the World's ear.
Deafen'd by his own stir,
The rugged Labourer
Caught not till then a sense
So glowing and so near
Of his omnipotence.

"So, when the feast grew loud
In Susa's palace proud,
A white-rob'd slave stole to the Monarch's side.
He spoke: the Monarch heard;
Felt the slow-rolling word
Swell his attentive soul;
Breathed deeply as it died,
And drained his mighty bowl."

By the bye, in making this quotation, we have adhered to the early [illegible] generally we agree with other critics in disliking Mr. Arnold's [illegible] the present edition he has suppressed the first and second parts of "[illegible] at Brou." The first required emendation, but the second might [illegible] left to stand—and, indeed, a few touches would have made the first [illegible] even to fastidious readers. Several of the earlier poems, which have [illegible] escaped from the general eye, are here reprinted. We could perhaps [illegible] the "New Sirens," but the "Strayed Reveller" we are glad to have. [illegible] culties of the classification adopted by Mr. Arnold are illustrated by his [illegible] of this poem. It was in the volume by "A." which so amused Christopher [illegible] and therefore belongs to the "Early Poems,"—yet we find it elsewhere [illegible] collection.

We have already said that we do not at this moment attempt any grave [illegible] of Mr. Arnold's poetry, and will only make one remark more. Of course [illegible] not tell the principle upon which he proceeds in printing such and such [illegible] his mere criticisms of others, he has often surprised us by a certain [illegible] and want of reserve; and one or two of his poems have never ceased to [illegible] a similar surprise. Two poems anciently called "Excuse" and "Indifference" [illegible] here named anew and cut down. If we guess the reason aright, we [illegible] what justification there can be for certain lines in the last poem of what [illegible] called the Marguerite series:—

"The house! and is my Marguerite there?

"Ah, shall I see thee, while a flush
Of startled pleasure floods thy brow,
Quick through the oleanders brush,
And clap thy hands and cry: ''Tis thou!'

"Or hast thou long since wander'd back,
Daughter of France, to France thy home;
*And flitted down the flowery track,*
*Where feet like thine too lightly come?*

"*Doth riotous laughter now replace*
*Thy smile, and rouge, with stony glare,*
*Thy cheek's soft hue, and fluttering lace*
*The kerchief that enwound thy hair?*
*Or is it over? art thou dead?*"

In all Goethe we can scarcely remember anything more repelling than these [illegible] we have never found any reader who liked them. But we have put the case [illegible] the first time), and perhaps some others may be of a different mind about [illegible]

---

In the early period of the national life of a people there is always a [illegible] record stirring events and the deeds of favourite heroes in a ballad [illegible] these popular songs serve the same purpose, and have almost the [illegible] as the historic documents of a later and more civilised age. [illegible] such songs worked into a consecutive story constitutes an epic [illegible] called, and when this really faithfully represents the national [illegible] almost invariably adopted by the Rhapsodists, and the older ballads [illegible] the very fact that an epic has superseded these old ballads in popular [illegible]

[illegible] of its authenticity, for a mere work of fiction, however cleverly [illegible] constructed, could never take hold on the hearts and imaginations of a [illegible] examples of the true and false epic exist than the Iliad and [illegible] first has ever held its own as the national poem of Greece, and [illegible] incidents are in harmony with the mythology, history, and popular [illegible] of the Hellenic peoples, while every fresh discovery of the present day [illegible] accuracy as a picture of the life and manners of the age of which it [illegible] Æneid, on the contrary, has lasted only as a monument of its author's [illegible] genius, and has no place amongst the collections of popular traditional lore.

[illegible] country is perhaps so rich in epic traditions as Persia; and indeed it would [illegible] if a civilisation extending back to such remote ages, an empire so vast, [illegible] so varied, had left no traces in the popular memory, side by side with [illegible] monuments of the ancient kings. As far back as the seventh century [illegible] an Armenian writer, Moses Chorenensis, quoting certain ancient Persian [illegible] which we recognise as identical with those embodied in the great epic [illegible] which we are about to speak. The first person to make a systematic col[illegible] of these popular traditions was Naushirwan, King of Persia, and the con[illegible] of Mohammed; and the work commenced by him was carried on by [illegible] the last monarch of the Sassanian dynasty. By order of this prince [illegible] gathered together by Naushirwan were put in order by the Dihkan [illegible], and the gaps in the history filled up with the assistance of several [illegible] Magian priests. The Dihkans, to which class the new editor of the [illegible] belonged, were the ancient territorial lords of Persia, who subsequently [illegible] under the Arab Government much such a position as the old Saxon [illegible] who still retained their estates did under the Normans in England. [illegible] such a class it was only natural that the ancient local traditions should be [illegible]; and, in fact, it is to them that most of the surviving legends are due. [illegible] wrote in Pehlavi, the form of the ancient Persian language then in use, [illegible] work, which contained a history of the country from Kaiyumers, the first [illegible] to Khosraw Parviz, was called the Khodáï-Namah, or "Book of Kings." The [illegible] of this work at the hands of the lieutenant of the iconoclastic Caliph Omar, when Persia was subdued by the Moslem armies, is not very clear; but it is certain that some of it was translated into Arabic at the time, and that the greater portion at least was preserved amongst the archives of the province by the suc[illegible] Arab governors. Several Arabic translations made from this are fre[illegible] quoted by later historians. The first prince of Persian extraction who succeeded in rendering himself independent of the Caliphate in the ninth century, [illegible] Leis, at once took up the work of Naushirwan and Yezdigird, and caused Danishwer's book to be re-edited in the Persian language.

In the early part of the tenth century the power passed into the hands of the Samanides, princes descended from the old Sassanian family; the new dynasty also occupied themselves with the ancient Persian traditions, and a new edition of Danishwer's epic was undertaken by a poet named Dakiki, at the command of his sovereign. A portion of this work is preserved in that of the last and most celebrated editor, Firdousi.* A few years later the Samanides gave place in their turn to the Ghasnavides, and Mahmúd of Ghaznin, the second king of that dynasty in the year 1030 of our era, once more asserted, and to a greater extent than his predecessors, his political independence. Though a bigoted Muslim, he was much attached to the traditions of the country over which he ruled, and conceived the [illegible] of completing and perfecting the collections made by the Sassanian and Samanide kings. The most celebrated poets of the day were summoned to court [illegible] entrusted with the work: their success, however, was but mediocre, and the [illegible] was ultimately confided to a poet until then little known, but who proved [illegible] eminently fitted for the task—Abu 'l Casim, of Tùs, surnamed Firdousi.

[illegible] father himself belonged to the Dihkan class, and had given his son a [illegible] education, for we find that he was well versed in the Arabic and Pehlavi [illegible], besides being a perfect master of his own. Evincing at an early age a [illegible] research and a genius for poetry, he continually occupied himself with [illegible] the old epic traditions, and, having heard of the death of Dakiki, he [illegible] the plan of translating the entire series. One of his friends, Mohammed [illegible] procured him a copy of the Dihkan Danishwer's Pehlavi work, and [illegible] himself earnestly to the task. He had already composed a large por[illegible] history when an accidental encounter with the four poets, who then

* [illegible], par Abou 'l Kasim Firdousi, traduit et commenté par Jules Mohl. Publié par Mme.

formed the official revision committee of the ancient archives, [illegible] the notice of the sovereign, Mahmúd Ghaznavi, by whom he [illegible] entrusted with the office he had so long coveted, that of versifying the [illegible] so as to form a complete history of Persia in the form of an epic poem. [illegible]

For more than thirty years he resided at court, incessantly engaged [illegible] stupendous work; the Sultan taking great interest in its progress, and [illegible] pay a thousand pieces of gold for each thousand couplets. This money [illegible] leaving to accumulate, and stipulated that he should receive it [illegible] completion of his task. When the time arrived, however, the [illegible] long enjoyment of royal favour had raised up for him, had contrived [illegible] him to the Sultan, and the latter, instead of the promised reward, sent [illegible] pieces of silver. In his rage and disappointment Firdousi gave 20,000 [illegible] messenger who brought him the money, 20,000 to the bath-man [illegible] attended on him, and paid a passing beer-seller the remaining 20,000 [illegible] his liquor. When Sultan Mahmúd heard of this insulting conduct, [illegible] that on the morrow he would have the poet trampled to death under [illegible] his elephants, but Firdousi managed to escape to the court of [illegible] Jorjan, from whence he proceeded to Baghdad. Before leaving [illegible] Ayás, the favourite of the Sultan, a most bitter and scathing satire [illegible] which is prefixed to the epic poem and forms a curious contrast to the [illegible] eulogies on that prince contained in the introduction to the work. [illegible] he went to Kohistan, the governor of which province gave him a most [illegible] reception, and employed such good offices with the Sultan that the [illegible] to return to his native town Tús, where Mahmúd at length sent him the [illegible] was his due. But the reparation came too late. Firdousi, broken down [illegible] labour, and disappointment, one day overheard a child singing a verse [illegible] own satire, in which he laments the injustice done him in withholding the [illegible] earned by a life's labour, and contrasts his present condition with what [illegible] have been had his patron been of royal blood, and therefore capable [illegible] sentiments and princely munificence, instead of being as he was the [illegible] slave:

> "Had Mahmud's father been of royal blood,
> In gold and silver knee-deep I had stood!
> Had Mahmud's mother been a queen instead,
> A crown of gold had decked this aged head."

The incident so affected him that he fainted away, and died immediately [illegible] wards on being carried into his own house.

Such were the circumstances under which the "Sháh-Namah" or "Book [illegible] was composed; it is a most voluminous work, containing more than 60,000 [illegible] written in the purest Persian, and most musical rhythm. The traditions [illegible] relates are, as we have seen, of the highest authority that popular legend [illegible] sess, and many of them go back to a remote antiquity. Surrounded, [illegible] traditions must necessarily be, with much that is marvellous or fabulous, [illegible] scarcely an incident which does not contain some grain of historical, [illegible] or mythological truth. That Firdousi followed faithfully the ancient [illegible] which he undoubtedly had at his disposal, without giving rein to his own [illegible] amply proved both by internal and collateral evidence.

In the first place he did not dare to commence his epic in earnest [illegible] procured and carefully studied the great work of Danishwer the Dihkán; [illegible] known that he was surrounded by others of the same class, who had [illegible] moned to court for the express purpose of contributing to the work by [illegible] and addition to the existing stock of legends. The poets, too, who [illegible] have been employed on the task, and the numerous enemies which [illegible] cially in an Eastern court, always raises up, would not have failed to [illegible] they detected any interpolations or omissions in the episodes as [illegible] when completed, before Mahmúd. The very faults of the narrative, [illegible] transitions from one story to another, and the tendency to ascribe [illegible] deeds of an epoch to one favourite hero, all show that it [illegible] tradition which he followed. The *lacunæ*, also, point to the [illegible] for they are nearly always found, as in the case of his [illegible] of Alexander the Great, in parts of the history which [illegible] Persia was labouring under some national disaster, or under [illegible] foe, and these are not the events which the people love to [illegible] The Parsees, the successors of the ancient fire-worshipping [illegible] recognise so completely the identity of Firdousi's legends with [illegible]

[illegible]

[illegible] of Firdousi's work gave rise to many imitations, and we [illegible] poems mentioned by the historians of the immediately suc[illegible] of some of which have come down to us, either separately [illegible] of the "Sháh-Namah." Nor are these books mere inven[illegible] evidently based upon ancient traditions analogous to those [illegible], and supplement the history as narrated by him. The entire [illegible] Arab conquest effected in the manners, religion, language, and [illegible] would have been, no doubt, fatal to the preservation of the [illegible] legends, had it not been for the exceptional circumstances we have [illegible] the extraordinary genius of the author of the "Book of Kings." [illegible] a work we do not expect to meet with minute historical accuracy, [illegible] by the light of modern science and discovery, these old tales cannot [illegible] difficulties and fill up many gaps in the other ancient histories [illegible] been hitherto accustomed exclusively to draw our information. [illegible] impossible in the space at our disposal to give even the barest sketch [illegible] of a work filled with the most varied episodes, and embracing the period between the creation of the world and the conquest of Alexander. [illegible] say that, notwithstanding a great deal of verbiage and tedious repeti[illegible] full of interest not only for the student of history, but for the ordinary [illegible] may well take its place beside such collections as Grimm's Popular [illegible] unfortunately, Persian is not a language understanded of the common [illegible] Europe, and it might well be supposed that no one would be found with [illegible] patience and learning to give this immense volume in an intelligible form [illegible] reader. Such a person, however, has been found in M. Jules [illegible] loss the world of Oriental scholarship has had lately to deplore.

Mohl was born at Wurtemburg in 1802, educated first at Stuttgart and [illegible] at the University of Tübingen, and was destined originally for the [illegible] He subsequently relinquished the theological course, and went to Paris [illegible] his Oriental studies, and was so attracted by the society of that city [illegible] took up his abode there permanently, and in 1826 received the commission [illegible] French Government to edit and translate Firdousi's immortal work. To [illegible] undertaking he devoted over fifty years of incessant labour, and, [illegible] for the world, lived to complete it. The original edition, commenced [illegible] Monarchy and continued under the Empire and Republic, always at [illegible] cost, is a noble monument of M. Mohl's talent and industry, and of the [illegible] of the French Government; but its enormous cost places it out of the [illegible] the ordinary purchaser, and its size makes it difficult of access even in the [illegible] libraries where it is to be found. Madame Mohl has not only paid a graceful [illegible] her illustrious husband's memory, but has done the public good service, [illegible] out the French translation of the "Sháh-Namah" in a convenient and [illegible], and "Le Livre des Rois" must henceforth occupy a conspicuous place [illegible] standard works of every library that is worthy of the name.

---

JUSTIN MCCARTHY writes for "Miss Misanthrope"* a very manly and "dedication" to the friends who overwhelmed his household with inquiries [illegible] false report of his death was spread abroad some time ago. We were [illegible] number of those who were very pleased to learn that the report was [illegible] we gladly take a share of the dedication to ourselves.

[illegible] Misanthrope" is handsomely got up and characteristically illustrated; [illegible] is a novel to keep as well as to read, it is nicely suited for a present— [illegible] if the giver of the book to the lady wishes to do an oblique stroke of [illegible] of counsel: for there is much in it upon which to build alluring and [illegible] tion. Miss Misanthrope is a handsome girl, born in a country [illegible] has not had a happy or affectionate home. Forming opinions of life [illegible] bases and cherishing peculiar ideals, she says, with the young farmer [illegible] Court"—not to be confounded with "Lady Audley's Secret," though [illegible] that blunder made—who sings over the pic-nic pie, "But let me [illegible]"—meaning that she does not want much company. Woman delights [illegible] nor man neither. But a good many of the people she meets "by their [illegible] to say" that she does; and at last she gets as much entangled both [illegible] woman as it is easy to conceive. The story in detail is for the reader

* [illegible] By Justin McCarthy. In two volumes. London: Chatto and Windus.

[illegible] But, [illegible] to add [illegible] have [illegible] McCarthy [illegible] the [illegible] conceive that he might have written stories of a more "original" [illegible] this, if his career had been different; but if it had, he would [illegible] have been a very distinguished historical or biographical essayist. [illegible] have not the unconscious fluency of far inferior writers who are born with [illegible] *raconteur* gift, and have no fine faculties to embarrass them; but [illegible] as mere stories is sufficing; and all else is of a very high order. We [illegible] that intelligence—free, kindly vision—(with high conscientiousness [illegible] goodness of heart) was Mr. McCarthy's strong point as a novelist. He [illegible] understands; and he makes his readers understand. He has, also, [illegible] kindly humour. In this story, Mr. Money and Mr. St. Paul are most [illegible] studies. So is Mr. Blanchet, the poet. The sketch of the artistic clique, [illegible] the latter belonged, is exceedingly good, and so is Mr. Hopkins' picture [illegible] "unappreciated" friends.

Among the few small things which did not quite please us we may [illegible] which Mr. McCarthy knows (we are sure) as well as we do: he is too [illegible] allusions sometimes jar. For example, Miss Grey as Pippa passing is [illegible] so is Mr. St. Paul's recollection from "The Arabian Nights." It also [illegible] that the mutual intelligence between Miss Grey, Lucy, and Victor was [illegible] too suddenly and unaccountably, and that it was, on Lucy's part certainly [illegible] complete for what led up to it. As to the general drift, if there is any [illegible] the story, we do not quite see our way. It seems to us that if Miss Grey [illegible] a little more firmness and ingenuity, she might, being well off, have [illegible] her plan of living an honourable and kindly life as "Miss Misanthrope," [illegible] say, if she had been, on other grounds, the girl to do it. These are days [illegible] few men or women can effectually "wall in the sacred fire" without a [illegible] of social reticence; and nobody can understand that better than Mr. McCarthy [illegible] abundantly shows that no problem of the kind goes unconsidered by him. [illegible] case he has given us a brilliant and thoughtful novel: which may also be [illegible] if the reader pleases, as an essay of rare intelligence and fine humour, illustrated by social studies of great fidelity, wholly free from any taint of cynicism [illegible] flying sentiment. It is at once an attractive and a wholesome book: free [illegible] generous freedom, but without flippancy; and utterly without any trace of "false bottom."

---

Mr. Fleming's new story,* like its predecessor, "A Nile Novel," is [illegible] appeal only to minds of a certain tone and quality, and perhaps [illegible] to such minds in all of their moods. We can, at any rate, fully [illegible] the possibility of a most competent critic's finding the book, though [illegible] be compelled to recognize merit in it, as a whole very little to his liking [illegible] for the reader whose robust and not highly discriminating appetite [illegible] a plain tale plainly told, whether of the sensational or domestic order, he [illegible] bably throw it aside in disgust, declaring that there is nothing in it. [illegible] truth, from his own point of view, he would have very much to say for [illegible] ment; for the story is without plot, almost without anything that can [illegible] called incident; and the characters—at least the two of them who [illegible] arrest our sympathies, Constance Varley and Lawrence, the man who [illegible] been and should have been her lover—well as we may understand [illegible] seem to us suggested rather than fully drawn. The charm which the [illegible] those who find charm in it lies, we take it, in its atmosphere; [illegible] magic," as Mr. Matthew Arnold calls it, of its Eastern scenery, its [illegible] ing, the slight subtle touches and turns of thought, sentiment, [illegible] enrich it, and the deep but quiet pathos of its issue. We are conscious [illegible] fine harmony, though one far more easily felt than expressed, between [illegible] and emotions which we are here concerned in contemplating, and [illegible] surroundings. In watching the little group of American travellers [illegible] less wealthy, and some highly cultivated and sensitive to beauty, [illegible] story, we are never suffered to forget the background and setting [illegible] the Syrian landscape, now grey, arid, and desolate, now joyous [illegible]

* Mirage. By George Fleming, author of "A Nile Novel." 3 vols. London: [illegible]

spring flowers; or Damascus with its streams and rose-gardens, or its bazaars, "cool, dim, vaulted spaces, with the lustre of silks, the gleam of metal and porcelain about them, and the odour of gums and curious spices filling the dusty air." The travellers' first vision of Damascus forms a word-picture that compels quotation:—

"Beneath them lay a city and a plain—a wilderness of deep up-springing green—a curving line of warm-tinted houses and glittering mosques, and sharply-piercing minarets. And beyond that rose the violet mountains grown silver-pale in the blinding heat; and beyond that the pale border-line of infinite desert space; and all about the city a network of shining streams, a foam of blossoming trees, circled and crowned the gardens of Damascus."

As a fitting *pendant* to this we might, had we the space for it, give the description of the Plain of Esdraelon. Constance Varley is a heroine who merits a happier fate than that her loyal and patient love should at the last fail of fruition. And then the pity of it! When she thinks she is confessing to Lawrence her love for himself, believing it impossible that he should mistake her feelings, he understands the confession as one of love for the handsome young Philistine to whom he has been told she is to be married, and so takes himself out of the way. This Denis Lawrence is very life-like, though revealed to us, as we have said, chiefly by way of hint and suggestion—a true *enfant du siècle*, as he is called, a creature of the culture whose aim, as he is made to say, "is refinement, not strength; beauty, not exhilaration;" powerless to act strongly, or even desire strongly; and coming "to look back upon his past experience as on an inevitable and fatal progress from the delight of desire to the quiet acceptance of defeat." A certain Claude Davenant who flits through the story, with his art-enthusiasms and vagaries, and his frank paganism, reminds us not a little of the Mr. Rose of *The New Republic*; and the representative of worldly-wisdom and the conventionalities, Mrs. Thayer, the American lady who "has been tired ever since she was ten years old," is very amusing, and a proof, if proof were needed, that Mr. Fleming is possessed of humour and lightness of touch in addition to his other good gifts.

---

MRS. LINTON'S main object in "The World Well Lost,"* as in her previous stories, would seem to be to bring out the contrast and opposition between what may be called the religion of natural feeling and impulse and the religion of acquired notions, whether these notions stand for mere social conventionalities or are based on the accepted moral code. The same theme, it will be remembered, was powerfully treated by her in "The Atonement of Leam Dundas," in which our sympathies were claimed for the untaught child to whom right and wrong were words without a meaning, who, in a passion of loyalty to her dead mother, poisons the stepmother who shall not, she is resolved, vex that mother by occupying her place. We might almost say that the superior sanctity and obligation of the former of these two "religions" over the latter was the gospel which Mrs. Linton felt herself especially constrained to proclaim; but in the case of an artist—and that she is to be regarded as an artist we do not think there can be any manner of doubt—it is always hazardous, and, perhaps, also somewhat impertinent, to infer full moral approval even from the most effective and sympathetic representation. Not that we should have much exception to take to her gospel, if her gospel it be, accepted in the right sense, and with certain needful limitations; for, of course, the creed of what she calls "the rights of individualism and nature" may be so held and acted on as to be consistent with the very grossest selfishness and most reckless disregard of all claims that may stand in a man's way when going the road of his own will. In "The World Well Lost," the principal actors and actresses may pretty well all be divided into two groups, according as natural feeling or the recognition of social needs and obligations has greatest hold upon them. In the latter stand Lady Machell, her elder son Wilfrid and her daughter Hilda, and young Derwent Smith; in the former Derwent's mother, Mrs. Smith of Owlett, her daughter Muriel, the heroine of the piece, Arthur, the younger of the Machell brothers, and Dinah Forbes, the mannish old maid. The "situation" is admirably chosen for bringing out the moral purpose which, as we have said, seems to have animated Mrs. Linton in the composition of her book. Briefly, we may say that the mystery which all along hangs over Mrs. Smith of Owlett, the refined and gifted woman, who has persisted in living in the closest retirement, rejecting

* The World Well Lost. By E. Lynn Linton, author of "Patricia Kemball," &c. 2 vols. London: Chatto &

society altogether for herself, and as much as is possible to her [illegible] shown in the end to be due to the fact that her husband, loved [illegible] her in dishonour as in honour, has been undergoing fifteen years of [illegible] for forgery, committed in a moment of weakness to save him[illegible] ones from ruin. Then come the questions, will Derwent and Mu[illegible] cleave to the disgraced father whose strange absence receives [illegible] explanation, or put the family shame behind them and begin the [illegible] offered them? and will Arthur be loyal to the girl who, always ob[illegible] mother on the score of her poverty, is now shown to bear a [illegible] besides? The answers to these questions would take more space th[illegible] give; we will only say that they furnish occasion for some fine [illegible] scenes: the stern and somewhat harsh "chastity of honour" in De[illegible] which even his warm love for mother and sister must give way, being [illegible] portrayed with singular power, a power all the more noticeable, as that it is very far indeed from being the result of sympathy. Arthur[illegible] whilst possibly more attractive, are certainly less original. Indeed, M[illegible] disappoints us, as we are somehow led to expect from her a certain d[illegible] of action or manifestation which she never seems to exhibit. It is, we altogether as a delineator of character that Mrs. Linton is most praise; but mere gentleness and faithfulness, however idealised, do n[illegible] type with which she feels most at home.

---

MR. WEDMORE introduces his three "Pastorals"*—in which his for "form" is always conspicuous—by a preface, in which he start[illegible] that the present time offers special difficulties to the novelist [illegible] deal with contemporary life—the life of cities, the life of Society. [illegible] able time for such a novelist is, he considers, "a period of social [illegible] nothing arises to check the stream of accepted beliefs, and he [illegible] be in some measure historian and analyst of Society knows on what [illegible] and is in sympathy with the moralities to which he appeals, becau[illegible] and wrong bruited about him are the right and wrong—the good [illegible] his own mind." Such a period the present time confessedly is not. Mr. Wedmore thinks that many novelists must find perfect sincerity [illegible] hard of attainment; for either the novelist may think one thing, and he depicts another, or, if both Society and the novelist be agreed, "it [illegible] expected of him that he shall shape his work in polite and gentle [illegible] traditions both have inherited and both have cast aside." It would [illegible] prising to him, then, if many writers of fiction should, at least for [illegible] as he does here, "to such rural or outland life as by reason of its [illegible] hardly be deemed contemporary," and leave "the problems of our [illegible] deal, in remote places, with the tenderness of the old and the fancies of [illegible] We cannot attempt here to discuss this theory, for which, no doubt, [illegible] might be said; still it strikes us that Mr. Wedmore exaggerates the [illegible] difficulty he complains of, so far, at any rate, as regards writers of [illegible] power. That the ordinary novel of Society is tending to collapse [illegible] —we suspect that it is true,—but if so, we incline to think it is [illegible] of the dignified cause assigned by Mr. Wedmore than for the simple [illegible] it has been worked out.

But, theories apart, for their truthfulness, their skilful and delicate [illegible] ship, and their subdued pathos, we can give a hearty welcome to the [illegible] of life in outlying and old-world districts of France,—Pornic, [illegible] uplands at the edge of La Beauce,—to which Mr. Wedmore has given [illegible] somewhat affected name of "Pastorals of France." They are [illegible] a tale of self-sacrifice, in which the sorrow is not felt less keenly [illegible] patiently. The second of them, "Yvonne of Croisic," is the [illegible] should, on the whole, be disposed to give the preference. Y[illegible] Croisic, "a lonely country, leading nowhere," so remote that it [illegible] itself as a part of Brittany, but regards the Breton mainland [illegible] inland France almost as another world. She loves Rohan, a [illegible] to crush down her love and send her lover from her, because [illegible] needs be with his old mother at Piriac, and Piriac is "beyond [illegible] five hours' sail," an altogether unimaginable distance, whilst [illegible] Croisic, is bound to live and die among her own people. [illegible]

* Pastorals of France. By Frederick Wedmore. London: R. B[illegible]

[illegible] is unendurable. The picture Mr. Wedmore gives us of the [illegible] the still, narrow, yet not ignoble lives of its people, is one of [illegible] and beauty. Nor, as works of art, do the other two stories in [illegible] "Love at Pornic," and "The Four Bells of Chartres," come [illegible] the one we have touched on. The only exception we could [illegible] and it seems almost ungracious to take any—is that the work- [illegible] is, is perhaps allowed to be a little too much *en évidence.*

---

[illegible] by the well-known editor of the *Expositor*, is made up of a series [illegible] to a Bible-class numbering, as we are told, 150 members, [illegible] women, who were invited freely to state their difficulties for open [illegible] while the general view is much the same as that put forward by [illegible] his "Restitution of all Things," to which the author expresses [illegible] the mode of exposition is naturally more popular, and the book [illegible] better adapted to give satisfaction to the ordinary reader.

[illegible] preface the author complains that, though the dogma of everlasting [illegible] now rarely preached, and though it has been generally abandoned by [illegible] men, yet the fear of putting a stumbling-block in the way of others [illegible] them from giving free utterance to their real views. Speaking in the [illegible] the preachers, "are we," he asks, "so much wiser and better than our [illegible] that the truth which may be good for us will be injurious to them? If [illegible] is convinced that he holds any truth, let him in God's name utter his [illegible], and leave the consequences with the God who gave it to him."

[illegible] body of the work Mr. Cox grapples with those texts which are usually [illegible] support of the dogma, and which indeed are now generally admitted to [illegible] sole obstacle to the acceptance of the freer view commended by reason [illegible] by the general tone of revelation. It is shown that many of the [illegible] felt by the unlearned reader arise merely from incorrect translations, [illegible] in all probability disappear when the new version comes into use. The [illegible] "damnation," for instance, has received a new connotation since Wycliffe [illegible] the woman taken in adultery, "Hath no man damned thee?" where the [illegible] version is "Hath no man condemned thee?" Mr. Cox points out that [illegible] the word is used it represents either the Greek κρίνω to judge, or κατα- [illegible] condemn, and that in no case does it involve the idea of endless or irre- [illegible] punishment. So far there is entire agreement among scholars. It is [illegible] true that the English terms "damn," "damnation," &c., no longer [illegible] the meaning of the Greek, as they did in Wycliffe's time. Mr. Cox, [illegible] has followed an unsafe guide when he accepts Horne Tooke's derivation of [illegible] from "deem." It of course comes directly from the Latin *damnum*, [illegible] which is itself a participial form from the root *da*, to give, meaning that [illegible] is expended, like the Greek δαπάνη.†

[illegible] is more difficulty respecting the words "hell" and "eternal." The former [illegible] to represent one Hebrew and two Greek words, Gehenna, Tartarus, [illegible] The last of these, which means nothing more than the unseen world, has [illegible] a neutral force; thus Josephus uses it of the spirit of Samuel called up from [illegible] to warn King Saul of his approaching doom. It is the word used in the [illegible] chapter of Revelation, where the authorized version has "death and hell [illegible] up the dead which were in them, and they were judged every man [illegible] to his works." It is evidently, therefore, not the place of final, far less [illegible] punishment, such as we now associate with the word "hell." The only [illegible] in which the word Tartarus occurs is in 2 Pet. ii. 4, where the rebel [illegible] are said to have been "cast down to hell, to be reserved unto judgment," [illegible] appears to imply an intermediate state, but in any case has no relation to [illegible] condition of *men*. The word Gehenna is the only one of the three [illegible] of real importance in reference to our subject; and the two questions [illegible] to be asked about it are, In what sense was it understood by the Jews [illegible] of our Lord? Will this sense suit the context of the several passages [illegible] New Testament in which it is found? As regards the first question Mr. [illegible] and Dr. Dewes are referred to as authorities for the statement that there [illegible] to be found in Jewish writers, throughout the six hundred years [illegible] from 300 B.C. to 300 A.D., which would countenance the doctrine of endless

---

[illegible] By Samuel Cox. London: Henry S. King & Co.

† [illegible] Mr. Cox did not ask the assistance of some scholar to revise his proofs. In page 119, we [illegible] "eternal, comes from the Latin *aeternus*, the older form of which is *aeviternus*," and in page 58, the true text of 1 Cor. xv. 55 reads θάνατη, not ᾅδη."

[illegible] right-minded readers will agree with him in condemning the [illegible] argument, that *alώνιος* must mean everlasting when applied to [illegible] sinners, or what guarantee have we for the perfectibility [illegible]?

[illegible] of the book, the writer is on firmer ground. He shows, as [illegible] shown of late, yet not without a certain freshness which gives [illegible] earnestness of his own conviction, that the view which claims to [illegible] more opposed to reason than it is to the general teaching of [illegible] the character, the justice, and the goodness of God. Granting [illegible] can possibly be demanded for the isolated texts dealt with in [illegible] of the book, and supposing them to be incapable of any but the [illegible]tation, still the case for endless punishment is not stronger than [illegible] of Calvinism; and as the latter has ceased to darken the minds and [illegible] men, not because the texts on which it was based have been [illegible] up, but because it was felt to be inconsistent alike with reason [illegible] general voice of revelation, so we may hope that it will be with the [illegible] future destiny of our race.

---

[illegible]ry of Dr. Giles's work* ought to occupy a prominent place in the history [illegible] for freedom of speech in the Church of England in the nineteenth [illegible] three-and-twenty years ago, when Dr. Giles was a humble stipen[illegible] in the diocese of Oxford, he published that part of it which relates to [illegible], and was immediately threatened by Bishop Wilberforce with [illegible] of his license. Dr. Giles answered that his book was written only [illegible]; that a very small number of copies had been issued; that his in[illegible] concerned historical facts; and that he did not impugn any of the doc[illegible] Church. The last point, it will be noticed, is the substance of the [illegible] by Professor Smith of Aberdeen, and which rendered him invul[illegible] the artillery of the Church courts. Bishop Wilberforce was peremp[illegible] the book was only a resurrection of Toland, whose tracts he had [illegible] read, and he demanded either that Dr. Giles should withdraw his [illegible] circulation or at once resign his curacy. The book was withdrawn. [illegible] the Bishop's brother resigned his living because of his inclinations towards [illegible], and Bishop Wilberforce was among the first to advocate greater [illegible] thought within the English Church. But liberty in one direction neces[illegible] in another, and now that we have survived the panic of "Essays and [illegible] Bishop Colenso's dissertations, and a host of smaller disturbances, Dr. [illegible] publish his "Records" in their completed form, undisturbed by Bishop [illegible]tion.

[illegible] itself we shall at once say that it is the work of an excellent scholar. [illegible] is well arranged, the arguments are well put, and the whole book [illegible] clearness and elegance. Having said this, we are at liberty to express [illegible] from the main propositions, which are: (1.) That the whole of the Old [illegible] it now appears, both style of language and order of events, is due [illegible] establishment of the Hebrews in Canaan fifteen hundred years [illegible] but to the re-establishment of the nation four hundred years before [illegible] (2.) That the historical books of the New Testament did not exist in [illegible] form before the year 150 after Christ, but were then put forth with [illegible], to form the Christian Canon which we now have.

[illegible] propositions, or more properly suppositions, have their main support [illegible] of *facts* sufficient to prove the contrary. We could make hypotheses [illegible] better, that is, having greater probability of truth, and such as [illegible] supported by better arguments than Dr. Giles has for his, but the his[illegible] are too scanty and too uncertain to afford a demonstration. Dr. [illegible] and perhaps his strongest argument for the first proposition is the [illegible] historical books of the Hebrew Canon. The first five are admitted [illegible], and it is found that Joshua takes up the thread of the narrative [illegible] book of Deuteronomy ended. The same is said to be the case with [illegible], Samuel, and Kings, and the inference is that they had but one author, [illegible] compiler, who made very free use of the materials which he inherited [illegible] older documents. Now it is certainly true and admitted by the [illegible] writers, that many passages must have been inserted in the his[illegible] of the Old Testament either, as is generally believed, by Ezra, or by

* [illegible] Records. By the Rev. Dr. Giles, Rector of Sutton, Surrey. London: Trübner &

some writer who lived after the captivity. It is certainly startling [illegible] who comes for the first time to the earnest study of the Bible [illegible] books have not been treated according to our ideas of what is [illegible] and the question then arises concerning the amount of [illegible] original documents. Did Ezra merely add such passages as, for [illegible] count of the death of Moses and those explanations which [illegible] readers in his day, or did he really write, or compile in so large a [illegible] to writing, the whole of the historical books of the Old Testament? [illegible] is Dr. Giles's hypothesis, but though put in this startling form it [illegible] of indefinite modifications by the admission that Ezra had documents [illegible] nished the substance of what he wrote, and that for instance the Pentat[illegible] tains "the substance of all that Moses ever wrote, and is a correct accou[illegible] as human things admit, of what Moses did and taught." The sum of [illegible] is that there is the same uncertainty as to the origin of Hebrew literat[illegible] belongs to the literature of other nations, and consequently at least as [illegible] for Dr. Giles to suppose that the Old Testament was written by Ezra [illegible] Jesuit Hardouin to believe that the greater number of the Greek [illegible] classics were written during the middle ages. An astounding theory! [illegible] could refute it except by arguments from inherent improbability?

We might follow Dr. Giles through his chief points, and suggest [illegible] as good in the way of supposition as his arguments. For instance, it [illegible] suppose the writers of the different books to have taken up the narrat[illegible] the others left off, as to suppose that the whole was written by one [illegible] mention of the kings of Israel in Genesis xxxvi., long before Israel [illegible] may have been a comment added by a later writer, and what is said in [illegible] Book of Esdras and of the Fathers, about Ezra and the forty men [illegible] Scriptures, may only have meant that they made copies of them, or such a [illegible] as did not amount to original authorship. The argument that there were [illegible] ites in the time of Joseph is easily answered by the supposition that [illegible] became the common name for Arabs or Midianites. The inference that [illegible] were not written by persons contemporary with the events, because of [illegible] culties in the chronology, is scarcely justified. John Bunyan wrote an [illegible] his own life. He professed to follow some order, and yet a recent biogr[illegible] that "it would baffle the skill of a mathematical expert to make out [illegible] an accurate chronology of his history from the data afforded him [illegible] In the final chapters of Dr. Giles's book it is maintained that [illegible] alphabetical writings in the time of Moses, but only hieroglyphical, and [illegible] he could not have been the author of the Pentateuch. If this could [illegible] no doubt it would outweigh all conjectures on either side.

In the second volume, Dr. Giles treats of the New Testament, in [illegible] finds such a uniformity of style as leads him to the conclusion that the [illegible] is the work of one age. The uniformity of style is by some strong[illegible] indeed the great difference of style between John and the other Evangel[illegible] of the staple arguments for the late origin of the Gospel which goes under [illegible] and the impossibility of its having been written by John. The supposed [illegible] leads to the supposition of a compiler, but surely if a compiler had taken [illegible] sight of the whole, and written with a view to uniformity, he would not [illegible] many of those apparent discrepancies which seem to be the joy of many [illegible] Dr. Giles supposes that the New Testament, as we have it, originated [illegible] Christians of Antioch. Its being in Greek is reckoned evidence that it was [illegible] by Jews, whose vernacular was Hebrew. The quotations from the Old [illegible] being always made from the Septuagint is one argument, and another [illegible] Jews of Palestine did not know Greek, and consequently that the New Testam[illegible] neither have been written for them nor by them. A learned writer [illegible] book to prove that the New Testament was originally written in Latin. [illegible] ments were learned and ingenious, and certainly learning and ingenuity [illegible] many things very plausible. Dr. Giles has avoided reading the modern Germ[illegible] Had he done so, many of their theories would have upset his, and his book [illegible] wanted one of its greatest charms—originality. It is surely better to [illegible] man speak out what he thinks, than to keep him under the terrors of a [illegible] or, if he be a movable curate, the episcopal withdrawal of his licence.

---

At the time when the Sanskrit language became known to Europe[illegible] —not yet a century ago—the most sagacious observer amongst [illegible] have foreseen the influence it was soon destined to exercise upon [illegible]

[illegible] brought about by the introduction of Greek into [illegible] fifteenth century, was hardly a greater revolution than [illegible] and kindred investigations by the study of Sanskrit [illegible] comparative philology, which previous to this period had been [illegible] pastime, became at once a subject capable of scientific [illegible] yielded, at the hands of eminent Sanskrit scholars, brilliant [illegible]. Besides leading to a true appreciation of the nature, laws, [illegible] of language in general, and to a careful mapping out of the [illegible] human speech, the new science opened up the way to a know- [illegible] forms of thought and religious belief, and rendered it, in a [illegible] these forms through successive stages of development [illegible] to modern times. The science of language became thus the [illegible] branch of investigation, that of Comparative Religion. Lan- [illegible] earliest work of the human mind, and the most permanent [illegible]. More ancient than the most ancient inscriptions, older [illegible] traditions, it forms a chain of continuity between the thought of [illegible] latest times. Embedded in any modern speech we may discover [illegible] of the first lispings of the race, well-worn relics of primeval [illegible] experience. Philologists have thus been able, by singling out words to the chief members of the Aryan group of languages, and, therefore, [illegible] inheritance of each, to put together a sort of vocabulary of the [illegible] speech, before it had become developed into any of its great sub- [illegible] This vocabulary gives us a kind of mosaic picture of the civilization of [illegible] people; it furnishes us with a view—somewhat misty and unconnected, [illegible] their chief occupations, their thoughts, their religion. Our Aryan [illegible] before us in this picture as a race fairly advanced in civilization, [illegible] religion which, for rude grandeur, far excels its later developments. [illegible] books of India we may trace the growth of this ancient Aryan [illegible] its beginnings in the simple physiolatry of the earlier Vedas, through [illegible] system of Brahmanism, with its complex rites, until we find it issue in [illegible] modern descendants—Buddhism and Hinduism—systems that have [illegible] more than half of the present inhabitants of our globe. These two reli- [illegible] with Islam, which claims some 155,000,000 adherents—form the subject-matter of a series of books, undertaken by the Society for Promoting [illegible] Knowledge, of which the three mentioned below* have already appeared. [illegible]ism," by Professor Monier Williams, we have a terse though clear [illegible] the genesis and growth of a faith which has at this moment upwards [illegible],000 adherents, and boasts of a stream of sacred literature dating [illegible] the earliest ages. Judging from the changes of structure and the archaic Sanskrit, in which the hymns of the Veda are composed, [illegible] thinks that they are the work of a succession of poets writing [illegible] and 1000 B.C. In the hymns of the Rig-veda, which form by [illegible] important and oldest portion of this collection, we see reflected [illegible] worship of the parent race, outbreathings to *Dyaush-pitar* (the Heaven- [illegible] *Varuna* (the Investing Sky), appeals to the great triad *Indra* (the [illegible]atmosphere), *Agni* (the God of Fire), and *Surya* (the Sun).

In the light of the recent Indian famine, there is something approach- tragic in the piteous cry breaking forth to the great Rain-controller whom the greatest number of Vedic hymns and prayers are addressed. The hymn translated at p. 29 :—

> ". . . . Oh! let thy pitying soul
> Turn to us in compassion when we praise thee,
> And slay us not for one sin or for many."

[illegible] hymns and prayers, which come under the head of *Mantra*, there are in [illegible] writings of a later date, but, like the rest, regarded as Sruti, or revealed; the Brahmanas and Upanishads. The former, written like the Mantras in Sanskrit, consist of ritualistic precepts and illustrations in prose (pro- [illegible] from 800 to 500 B.C.), and were employed by the Brahmans in [illegible] ceremonies. They mark an advance from the simple nature- of the Mantras to a system involving numerous expiatory sacrifices, among [illegible] of human beings seems to be included.

[illegible] By Monier Williams, M.A., D.C.L., &c. Society for Promoting Christian Knowledge.
[illegible] a Sketch of the Life and Teaching of Gautama, the Buddha. By T. W. Rhys Davids, of [illegible]. Society for Promoting Christian Knowledge.
[illegible] By J. W. H. Stobart, B.A., Principal, La Martinière College, Lucknow. Society for [illegible] Knowledge.

The *Upanishads*, though standing to the Mantras in about the [illegible] the Talmud to the Old Testament Scriptures, and belonging, [illegible] period subsequent to 600 B.C., are practically the only Veda [illegible] ledged as an authority by orthodox educated Hindus at the [illegible] constitute the philosophical portion of the Veda, and introduce [illegible] the pantheistic doctrines which afterwards became distinctive of [illegible] They are the direct source of the Six Darsanas or "Demonstrations" [illegible] which, though not reckoned as revealed, exercise a powerful influence [illegible] intelligent Hindu mind.

Professor Williams devotes a chapter to the relations of Brahmanism [illegible] ism, showing their mutual influence, and pointing out that modern [illegible] with its complicated system of polytheistic doctrines and caste [illegible] the result of the blending of Brahmanism and Buddhism with the [illegible] creeds of Dravidians and aborigines. The two great epic poems, the [illegible] and Mahabharata, which are the sources of the doctrine of incarnations, [illegible] ined at some length, as well as the Puranas, which are made up from [illegible] and the Tantras. The Puranas and Tantras Dr. Williams looks upon as [illegible] ing the most corrupt phases of popular Hinduism, on which account, [illegible] books are sometimes called a fifth Veda specially designed for the [illegible] people and for women.

Mr. Rhys Davids' "Buddhism" is a most interesting book on [illegible] interesting subject. Gautama, surnamed the Buddha, has been [illegible] the region of mythology, along with Samson, King Arthur, Cyrus, [illegible] and other worthies, by some of our solar enthusiasts; but we may [illegible] ourselves to the calm and critical guidance of Mr. Davids when he [illegible] the result of his investigations, that Gautama was a contemporary of [illegible] son of a rajah in the neighbourhood of Benares, who was led by strong [illegible] impressions, when about thirty years old, to abandon his home, and devote [illegible] first, to an ascetic life, according to the rules of the Brahmans, and [illegible] had discovered the futility of those acts of penance and mortification which [illegible] looked upon as proofs of saintship, to the active service of his fellow-men, [illegible] to the preaching of a new gospel of salvation by self-control and love, [illegible] rites or ceremonies or priestly intercession of any kind. There is much [illegible] volume which bears a curious resemblance to the New Testament: *e.g.*, [illegible] tations described in pp. 32, 36—"Mara the spirit of evil appears in [illegible] promises Gautama a universal kingdom if he will give up his enterprise" [illegible] the conflict between the Saviour of the world and the prince of evil [illegible] sand appalling meteors fell; clouds and darkness prevailed;" the [illegible] miracle (p. 46), "when Gautama spoke, though he spoke in Pali, each [illegible] assembled hosts thought himself addressed in his own language;" the [illegible] parables (pp. 59, 133); the ascent to heaven (to which later tradition [illegible] scent into hell) for the purpose of teaching the new doctrine to one [illegible] been permitted to hear it on earth (pp. 71, 205); and generally the [illegible] of exclusiveness of all kinds—"Nirvana was as open to the lowest outcast [illegible] proudest of the twice-born;" "Gautama was reproached for accepting the [illegible] of sinners;" and lastly the belief in his divinity entertained by his [illegible] mere love for man he descended from his throne in heaven into his [illegible] and lived among the sorrows inseparable from finite existence."

One curious fact mentioned by Mr. Davids was noticed some years [illegible] REVIEW by Professor Max Müller, viz., that Gautama has not only [illegible] honour of deification from Buddhists, but also that he has been [illegible] Romanists; or, to speak more exactly, that a portion of the Buddhist [illegible] been connected with the name of a certain St. Josaphat, a seemingly [illegible] saint of the Romish calendar (p. 195). There is indeed a remarkable [illegible] between the system of the Church of Rome and the later developments of [illegible] such as Lamaism. While the teaching of Gautama himself, like that [illegible] Christ, was, in one of its main aspects, a protest against the formalism [illegible] of contemporary religion, we find that among the later Buddhists [illegible] nature was no more able to sustain itself at this pure spiritual [illegible] was among Christians in the middle ages. Thus we read of [illegible] "Lamaism indeed, with its shaven priests, its bells, and rosaries, [illegible] holy water, and gorgeous dresses; its service with double choirs, [illegible] and creeds, and mystic rites, and incense, in which the laity [illegible] its abbots and monks and nuns of many grades; its worship of [illegible] and of saints and angels; its fasts, confessions, and purgatory, [illegible]

... its huge monasteries, and its gorgeous cathedrals; its ... its cardinals, its Pope, bears outwardly at least a strong resem- ... in spite of the essential difference of its teachings and of its ...

... outward resemblance to Rome, Buddhism is more intimately ... different forms of belief, the mystic and the agnostic or positivist. ... "Drop then this petty foolish longing for personal happiness. ... ; the very kosmos itself is passing away, and all that you ... and mentally, of yourself will pass away like everything else: ... remain the accumulated result of all your actions, words, and ... other and kind, not lazy in thought;" when we read, "The true ... not mar the purity of his self-denial by lusting after a positive ... he himself shall enjoy hereafter," we might fancy ourselves ... George Eliot or Mr. Frederic Harrison. When again we read that ... of perfect peace, goodness, and wisdom, is the extinction of ... condition of mind and heart which would otherwise be the ... individual existence;" when we read of Jhana, the mystic trance ... in the highest of which consciousness vanishes altogether, we ... the quietism of St. Theresa and Madame Guyon, or the self-annihi- ... the older German mystics.

... "Islam," though it cannot boast of much independent research, ... interesting analysis of the teaching of the Koran on many important ... life of the prophet, from the sources at Mr. Stobart's command, is ... He appears, however, to have no knowledge of the more ... investigations upon this subject, especially as relates to the religious ... the Arabs before the time of Mohammed. There is no reference to ... labours, nor any notice taken of the papers by Osiander and ... have appeared in the *Zeitschrift der Deutschen Morgenländischen* ... Mohammed's knowledge of much of the Old Testament Scriptures ... apocryphal Gospels of the New is, we think, satisfactorily proved. ... estimate of the man, too, is one which will commend itself to most ... thinkers. Of the general tendency of his system he says that, not- ... the excellence of some of its precepts, it "poisons domestic life, ... crushes the right of private judgment, and is essentially incom- ... constitutional freedom."

... sign of the times to find books of this sort appearing under the ... the Society for the Promotion of Christian Knowledge, in place of the ... literature with which its name has been chiefly associated in former ... first to those readers for whom we may suppose them to be in the ... intended, it is a great thing that our missionaries should study the ... India, not in polemical treatises, but in impartial histories; and in the ... it is scarcely a less advantage that Englishmen in general, and our ... servants in particular, should have here brought before them in brief ... the most competent authorities, the secret of the inner life, the hopes ... imaginations and convictions, of the millions for whose welfare the ... India are responsible.

---

... to Edinburgh may recognize Sir Henry Moncreiff as a burly cleri- ... whose ringing voice dominates in that Church Parliament which ... name of "General Assembly" manages Scotch ecclesiastical matters ... Church side. They will often hear him called "Sir Harry," ... affectionate confusion of identity with his grandfather, a stately ... leader of last century. He must be distinguished from his younger ... Moncreiff, who has recently been sent to the House of Lords after ... Scotland as Whig Lord Advocate for many years; and this judge again ... confounded with Lord Moncreiff his father, the friend and contempo- ... Chalmers and of Lord Brougham.

... such family antecedents is the natural leader of conservatism in ... we open his book* with interest chiefly in one question. The Free ... known, has recently been moving strongly for Disestablishment, and ... Church is the ecclesiastical body in Scotland with the intensest ... in Church matters. How does it manage to unite the two? The ... instructive to those who wish to understand our Northern

* ... the Free Church Claim of Right. By Sir Henry Wellwood Moncreiff, Bart., D.D. With ... to alleged Facts. Edinburgh: Maclaren and Macniven.

neighbours, and to master the peculiar conditions under which an ecclesiastical problem so widely differing from ours must be solved. The Free Church stands upon a "Claim of Right" presented to Parliament and the Crown in 1843, by which it claims to be the Church of Scotland; and it consequently feels no difficulty in advocating the disestablishment of a body which it holds to be wrongfully in its own place. This natural but not therefore very amiable feeling has of course been equally appropriate to its position ever since the "Disruption"—for Sir H. Moncreiff, like his whole school, is careful to point out that his party "broke off" from the State, but never seceded from the Church. But of late years this original view has been complicated with new plans more hopeful for the future. Disestablishment of the Church which remained when Dr. Chalmers went out in 1843 is now advocated as a step, not to the substitution of the Free Church for its rival, but to a union of the whole Presbyterianism of Scotland on equal terms—a union real and co-operative, if not also formal and incorporative. And since the Patronage Act of 1874—a measure which, as Lord Hartington pointed out, has had an effect very much contrary to that intended for it—Sir Henry Moncreiff has repeatedly carried a nearly unanimous vote of the Free Assembly that the "termination of the existing connection between Church and State" in Scotland is the necessary preliminary to any good for the future. But having carried his vote, he goes no farther. The Free Church all around him streams forward in the ardour of Disestablishment and of the higher vistas opened for Scotland. In particular, it is manifestly willing to give up all active claim to restitution of its endowments, and it offers this on a score of platforms. Sir Henry Moncreiff does not in words dissent, but he retreats to his study and his ancestral traditions, and with characteristic conservatism writes his commentary on his Church's "Claim of Right."

Into this ecclesiastico-legal document we shall not follow him, highly praised though it has been. "I admire it," the Duke of Argyll writes to Mr. Taylor Innes, "as much as you do. It is the great boast of the Free Church that it has never been answered. As an argument on constitutional law, with the exception of a few paragraphs, I believe it to be unanswerable." And yet its main strength is that it bases its Scotch constitutional law upon universal law—insomuch that if its claim to exclusive privileges and endowments, founded on Scotch history and statute, were struck off, its "claim as of right" to the "inalienable liberties" of the Christian Church would still remain. But it cannot be denied that it is a hard knot of logic, and we do not recommend even Sir Henry's commentary as light reading. Those who want to get the same views in their more interesting form will go to the "Ten Years' Conflict;" to "Dr. Chalmers' Life," to "Dr. Guthrie's Life," to "Dr. Buchanan's Life," or to the more massive and formative moulds of "Dr. Cunningham's Life." Or, better still, they will go to Lord Cockburn's "Journals," and there they will get this charming portrait of the late M.P. for Greenock, who, as a young man, drew up this "Claim of Right" in 1842 :—

> "Dunlop is the purest of enthusiasts. The generous devotion with which he has given himself to this cause, has retarded, and will probably arrest the success of his very considerable professional talent and learning. But a crust of bread and a cup of cold water would satisfy all the worldly desires of this most disinterested person. His luxury would be in obtaining justice for his favourite and oppressed Church, which he espouses from no love of power or any other ecclesiastical object, but solely from piety and love of the people. There cannot be a more benevolent or honourable gentleman. I have never been able to detect the lurking in his heart of an unkindly thought."

But a historical document may be pure in motive and "unanswerable" in logic, and yet foreign to the needs of the time. The objections summarily dealt with in the appendix to this volume seem to be misapprehensions, and, in any case, being devoted to setting up what the Duke of Argyll brands as the dead and odious decisions which split the Kirk in 1843, will in Scotland be unpopular. But assuming that the Free Kirk Claim of Right has a strong constitutional standing-ground, does that go any way to solve the Church question in Scotland? Or does bringing it forward not rather tend to divide Presbyterians who, in so many ways, are already similar and united? The answer requires care. On the one hand, the Free Church position is intermediate between that of the Establishment and the Voluntaries. But on the other hand, if that middle position is too stringently insisted on, it excludes both sides and frustrates union. To all the historical positions of the Claim of Right of 1842, neither the Scotch Voluntaries nor the Scotch Established Church can agree. But what as to the more general principles of Church freedom

... contained in it? In these the vast majority of Presbyterians ... bodies will substantially acquiesce. Church independence, a ... even in English Church Congresses, has become indispensable in ... the branches of the Kirk claim it; and the only remaining question ... be done with the privileges and endowments enjoyed by one of them? ... strong passion for nationality, what does Presbyterian principle. ... There must be some change, to meet what Lord Hartington calls ... sense of injustice." Should the change be a transference of the ... and endowment, so as to include Dissenters? Or should it be a ... establishment and giving the endowments to Education, so as to put ... of the Kirk on an equality? Which does Scotland want, and how ... doubt be decided? We do not answer the question, but we recom... readers to note that in Scotland the Disestablishment cry is actually ...—it sounds like a paradox—by a passionate feeling of nationalism. ... real importance of a document like that here commented on by Sir ... comes neither from its legal nor its constitutional, but from ... position. This is a hinge of history, upon which it may be possible for the Scottish people to move over from establishment to disestablishment, without loss of respect, but with pride. Are there no wider and higher ... upon which the two remaining Presbyterian bodies, the Established Church ... United Presbyterian Voluntaries, may unite, so as to submerge in temporary ... the too narrow and too obstructive body which stands between?

---

...body, accustomed to æsthetical topics, wishes to obtain a ready bird's-eye ... so speak, of the space we have travelled over in these matters within less ... century, let him turn to, or recall Burke on the "Sublime and Beau... then read Mr. Grant Allen's highly ingenious and—we do not use the ... respectfully—very readable book.* That the removal of the discussion ... purely metaphysical to the physiological arena has not made it any easier ... ants to come to an understanding is curiously illustrated in the recent ... between the author and one of his critics, Mr. Sully (author of "Sensa... Intuition," and more recently of "Pessimism"). In *Mind* for October, ... reader will find Mr. Allen answering Mr. Sully's question, "How are ... ing the pains of ungratified desire under Mr. Allen's principle?" and ... more unsatisfactory, on both sides of the argument, we can hardly con... This, however, is only by the way, and we have furnished the curious ... a reference which will enable him to form his own opinion. Mean... attempting here to pass Mr. Allen's instances through the sieve one by ... ll remark that his book is not too long, is full of culture and fine criticism, ... intelligible to any one with the barest tincture of scientific knowledge. ... ok us with the greatest force while reading it was, that in every case ... is almost unmistakably right the results might have been stated just ... ly in the old metaphysical terminology. We will give briefly, in Mr. ... len's own words, the basis on which he has proceeded in this book:—

"... man organism is a highly complex, but not absolutely perfect self-regulating ... It differs from machines of human construction in possessing the mysterious ... of consciousness. This consciousness is specially connected with, and definitely ... a certain portion of the organism known as the cerebro-spinal nervous system, ... with particular members of that system. Every state of consciousness is a reflex ... of their states, viewed from the aspect of the various portions differentially ... *Pleasure and pain are the reflex or outcome of their states viewed from the aspect ... that is to say, so far as regards their effects on the functions of the organism, ... as a self-regulating machine. Pain is the subjective concomitant of destructive ... insufficient nutrition in any sentient tissue. Pleasure is the subjective concomitant ... amount of function in any such tissue.* . . . . . . . In the vast majority ... consensus between the organs produced by natural selection is such, that ... prejudicial or beneficial to the organism as a whole, is generally painful or ... respectively to the separate organs which it is likely to affect."

... are ours, and are merely to exhibit to the reader who may not see ... himself, a very important part of the exposition.

... desire to set over against the opening words of Mr. Grant Allen's preface ... of Mr. Ruskin's in the "Queen of the Air," and our reasons will be ... Allen writes:—

* Physiological Æsthetics. By Grant Allen, B.A. London: Henry S. King & Co.

"'Why we receive pleasure from some forms and colours and not from [illegible] Professor Ruskin, 'is no more to be asked or answered, than why we [illegible] like wormwood.' The questions thus summarily dismissed by our [illegible] on Æsthetics, are exactly the ones which this little book asks, and [illegible]

We fear Mr. Ruskin will not consider the question answered. [illegible] speaks in the chapter entitled "Athena in the Heart:"—

"It is of great consequence that you should fix in your minds, and [illegible] baseness of mere materialism on the one hand, and against the fallacies of [illegible] speculation on the other, the certain and practical sense of this word [illegible] sense in which you all know that its reality exists, as the power which [illegible] your shape, and by which you love and hate when you have received that [illegible] . . . And so long as you have that fire of the heart within you, and [illegible] of it, you need be under no alarm as to the possibility of its chemical [illegible] analysis. The philosophers are very humorous in their ecstasy of hope [illegible] the real interest of their discoveries in this direction is very small to [illegible] quite true that the tympanum of the ear vibrates under sound, and that the [illegible] water in a ditch vibrates too: but the ditch hears nothing for all that; [illegible] is still to me as blessed a mystery as ever, and the interval between [illegible] me quite as great. If the trembling sound in my ears was once of the [illegible] which began my happiness, and is now of the passing-bell which ends it, the [illegible] between these two sounds to me cannot be counted by the number of concussions [illegible] have been some curious speculations lately as to the conveyance of mental con[illegible] by 'brain-waves.' What does it matter how it is conveyed? The consciousness [illegible] not a wave. It may be accompanied here or there by any quantity of quivers [illegible] up or down, of anything you can find in the universe that is shakeable—wha[illegible] me? My friend is dead, and my—according to modern views—vibratory so[illegible] one whit less, or less mysterious to me, than my old quiet one."

If Mr. Ruskin should, as we opine he would from this passage, say, [illegible] called answer is an *ignoratio elenchi*," we should simply have to express [illegible] ment with him, but it would not follow that Mr. Allen has not made a larg[illegible] of valuable and suggestive observations.

---

THE title of Mr. Giffen's book* has not been happily chosen. It seeks [illegible] certain order in the variations of the prices of a large group of [illegible] known as the securities of the Stock Exchange, according to the [illegible] the influences which govern the motives of individuals in supplying and [illegible] these articles." The word "security" is then explained to mean the title [illegible] any kind of property which can be given as "a security" for a loan. [illegible] well-nigh all property can be pledged for loans, as even Mr. Giffen is con[illegible] include lands, houses, shares in private partnerships, capital employed in [illegible] amongst securities, we are left at a loss to discover what Stock Exchange [illegible] are. That they bear interest does not help us out of the difficulty, for lan[illegible] mortgages, and the rest, he admits to possess this quality. Thus what [illegible] specifically treats of is not defined. It would have been better if Mr. [illegible] taken the heading under which the *Times* gives the list of the Stock [illegible] prices every day—stocks, and railway and other shares. He would [illegible] given the articles in which the market of the Stock Exchange deal[illegible] funds, that is, debts and annuities due by Governments and other bodies, [illegible] nership shares in many businesses, such as railways, telegraphs, banks, [illegible] mines. That an article can be given as a security for a loan is no test o[illegible] dealt in on the Stock Exchange Market or of its being the object of [illegible] tion or gambling therein practised. To the purpose of the book, the [illegible] of the Stock Exchange, the idea of lending and pledging is entirel[illegible] except as a mere detail of some of its transactions.

But now a far graver matter presents itself for observation:—

"In inquiring into the laws of the price of a great group of articles, [illegible] inquire into is not merely the nominal money price of the articles, but [illegible] their price to that of all others which are the subject of exchange, [illegible] which is the medium of exchange. We must not think in such [illegible] the money price. What goes on at every exchange is that people sell [illegible] articles for money only in the first instance: the whole object of the sale [illegible] to purchase something else, and if purchases as a rule did not [illegible] money, the whole machinery of business would come to a stop. . . . [illegible] the ultimate transactions in money, that is, transactions in which [illegible] sense is actually acquired, and kept in the form of coin or bullion, [illegible]

* Stock Exchange Securities. By Robert Giffen. London: [illegible]

[illegible] its application is profoundly injured by the erroneous [illegible] transactions in coin or bullion "are specially important [illegible]."

[illegible] for his fundamental principle, in the explanation of prices [illegible] dealt in on the Stock Exchange, that "the quantity of [illegible] regulates the aggregate price of all articles." By money he [illegible] he uses as an illustration. He says rightly that the [illegible] by writers on political economy;" but, in the words of the [illegible] this "thought and language of a past generation on the [illegible] currency has become obsolete." It would have been well if Mr. [illegible] these words before he constructed his basis of prices. [illegible] prices of all commodities depend on the more or less coin or [illegible] in a given country, is a doctrine which is entirely false, unless [illegible] cut off from all communication with the rest of the world. In [illegible] large stock of gold was suddenly found, all prices would rise; if [illegible] swallowed up a large portion of the circulation, gold would be [illegible] would fall. But in the world we live in, gold does not, and [illegible] values in different countries. If the quantity of money in [illegible] small, attacked prices and reduced them, foreigners would rapidly [illegible] to buy these cheapened articles, and efface the difference in the [illegible]. If, on the contrary, the stock of gold were large, and prices ruled [illegible], English sellers would, on acquiring an increased amount of gold [illegible] quickly perceive that with it they could purchase a larger quantity [illegible]; they would send the gold abroad in exchange for merchandise, [illegible] would be restored very swiftly. Variations of the quantity [illegible] circulation or in stock are events of constant occurrence in England; [illegible] touch price. There is a much larger quantity of cash or money [illegible] the country in summer than in winter; but who has ever said—as [illegible] theory is bound to be said—that prices are lower in summer in the [illegible] warehouses? What happens is very simple. Coin is a tool, and very [illegible] used compared with the transactions of trade. It is a tool wanted [illegible] money payments only; and the quantity of it required varies with the [illegible] special work. Whether ready money is needed for more or fewer [illegible] transactions, what matters it? The vast selling and buying of trade [illegible] by written words—that is, by balancing accounts. If there is too much [illegible], it speedily returns back into store—if too little, it is taken [illegible] or procured from abroad. Mr. Giffen's deduction, therefore, from this [illegible] is unfounded. It is not true that "if there is a general fall in money [illegible] group of articles, this means a rise in money price in all the other [illegible]." A change of fashion or scarcity may lead ladies to give up fur dresses; [illegible] buy other clothing in their place, and so far there might be—possibly, [illegible]—a slight rise in the other clothing; but other commodities would [illegible], and assuredly the quantity of coin in the country would have nothing [illegible] the matter.

[illegible] unable, consequently, to accept Mr. Giffen's "abstract theory of the [illegible] securities and the meaning of a rise or fall," and we cannot keep company [illegible] in the practical application of this theory. Neither can we hold that an [illegible] consumable commodities, even if accompanied by an increase of stocks [illegible] on the Stock Exchange, "will cause a money fall in all articles on the [illegible] tend to a real rise in the price of these stocks," involving a lower [illegible] the money invested in purchasing them. An abundant harvest, with [illegible], cheapness of food, may lower the cost of production of many [illegible] thus stimulate their consumption that a large increase of manufac-[illegible] may be developed, resulting in higher profits and better wages, and [illegible] to buy stocks with fixed interest, except on lower prices. Cheap [illegible] anything but inconsistent with high profits and high wages and very [illegible] securities, as the agricultural products of many a colony can testify. [illegible] principle is always apt to have a large family of errors. Mr. Giffen pushes [illegible] doctrine into the region of credit—that special sphere of the Stock [illegible] declares that "the state of credit is equivalent to an increase or [illegible] the quantity of money." Let him look at the agonies of credit in a [illegible] Bank refuses to lend at a lower rate than 10 per cent.: for many of [illegible] charges much more. More venturesome banks demand still higher terms. [illegible] borrowers—though really solvent—can find no lenders. Down drop the [illegible] securities—for those who were accustomed to buy with borrowed means have vanished. And yet, during all these convulsions of [illegible] of money, of golden coin in England before, during, and after [illegible] been identically the same: there may not have been a sovereign [illegible] country. In the face of such facts, will Mr. Giffen maintain that [illegible] credit means an increase or decrease in the quantity of money? [illegible]

We fear, that in employing this formula, Mr. Giffen has [illegible] slang use of the word money in the City. In such expressions as "[illegible] dant" or "scarce," "is cheap" or "dear," the City does not speak of [illegible] made in cash, reckoned and handed over the counter by cashiers, but [illegible] of buying and lending, of purchasing power: and of what that is [illegible] the banking world, which wields and distributes it, and, we fear, even [illegible] himself, has very little idea indeed. Bankers do not know that they [illegible] of goods and nothing more. Assuredly it is not coin nor notes: yet, [illegible] had substituted the phrase "purchasing power" for "money," his [illegible] the state of credit would have been perfectly accurate; but that would [illegible] with his general argument.

Our remarks have turned on first principles involved in Mr. Giffen's [illegible] of doctrine, because in these matters their importance transcends that [illegible] elements. We have been obliged to dissent from his views: but [illegible] the details of the life, so to speak, of the Stock Exchange, we gladly [illegible] vividness and general accuracy of his description. Want of space [illegible] dwell upon them; but the reader will find much to interest him. [illegible] Exchange is admirably painted. Its methods are keenly analysed, [illegible] machinery at work by which prices are manipulated, often with [illegible] and almost as often with equal disasters. Time bargains and their [illegible] influence; the skilful handling by which the losses of a sinking [illegible] diminished by still more selling; syndicates, rigs, and corners with [illegible] names, new worlds, and new combinations; the manœuvres of perfect [illegible] gambling; the victimizing of miserable outsiders, who dream that they [illegible] the counsels of moral purity; contangos and backwardations, and their [illegible] multiplication of purchasing force; the subtle insinuations of coming [illegible] rich production of fictitious securities—are all described and explained [illegible] insight and vigorous description. Real forces too are taken into [illegible] famine, commercial prosperities and depressions, are brought upon the [illegible] complete the general effect: one only wonders how men are found [illegible] numbers into seas tossed by such uncertain and untrustworthy winds.

---

Cobbett had, in his time, much to say, and he said it effectively, [illegible] grammar in high places; while, in our own day, royal speeches ha[illegible] been found capable of standing the test of even very simple criticism [illegible] Improvement Acts, which may be considered as the work of Parl[illegible] counsel and solicitors and Parliamentary Committees united, are [illegible] found absolutely unintelligible. Public Acts, of the kind which govern [illegible] nary criminal and civil procedure, are sometimes so obscurely express[illegible] unworkable. Letters from Government clerks are sometimes inaccurate [illegible] But, in spite of all this, and the "cold shade" of Circumlocution for [illegible] Dickens is responsible, we shall not be far wrong if we affirm that there [illegible] school of accuracy as a Government office. It is next to impossible [illegible] tolerably well-practised Government official. This is no doubt partly [illegible] his having learned the art of evasion; but even that implies much [illegible] use of language; and it is far from all. The Government official [illegible] strong sense of responsibility; his work is checked and counter-checked [illegible] over again; and he gradually acquires the *hoc age* knack; gives his [illegible] what he is doing: and looks upon a mistake as Tim Linkinwater upon [illegible] uncrossed *t*. Government clerks take their time, no doubt; but [illegible] who write this notice, have had opportunities, extending over [illegible] forming an opinion upon these matters. We have handled and [illegible] of evidence which was and is matter of record in Blue-books [illegible] hundreds, perhaps thousands of written documents issuing from [illegible] offices. And, in twenty good years, we have never found a [illegible] the clerical order, in any such document. On the contrary, [illegible] to think the Government clerk wrong, to go upon a fresh [illegible] then, after wasted labour, to have to return and discover that [illegible] gentleman was right.

It is surprising, too, how rapidly a raw beginner is [illegible]

[illegible] beardless, blushing young fellow, who is afraid to [illegible] like a schoolboy, and scarcely knows whether Yorkshire is [illegible] Tweed, becomes in a year or two an accomplished circum[illegible] a mistake while on his own beat, with the eye of a lynx [illegible] the dexterity of a seraphic doctor in evading a question [illegible] "sharpened to a needle's end." A Government official, even [illegible] under cross-examination, baffle a clever Queen's Counsel, [illegible] sticking to the point, and not knowing anything, or having [illegible] that "My Lords," or the chiefs of the department wish to [illegible] therefore justified in thinking that there must be good disci[illegible] public offices—discipline, to use the words of Mr. Monkhouse's [illegible] of statement and preciseness of expression." Mr. Monkhouse [illegible] as well as a Government official, and he shows in this title that [illegible]—for, no doubt, he wrote preciseness in lieu of precision just to [illegible] the termination *sion* twice in three words. The selections from books [illegible] show reading and apprehensiveness, and we should suppose [illegible] could not fail to shorten and make more pleasant the novitiate [illegible] to enter the public service. To those who are "born" literary, [illegible] that any human being should want such teaching as Mr. Monk[illegible], but to those who need it, we can sincerely commend this book.

---

[illegible] which comes from Dr. Dawson's pen is sure to be worthy of attentive [illegible] may be doubted, however, whether the present volume,† notwith[illegible] ingenuity and learning which it displays, will advance his reputa[illegible]ologist. Its purpose may be best expressed by a sentence from the [illegible] intention of this new publication is to throw as much light as [illegible] present condition of the much-agitated questions respecting the [illegible] world and its inhabitants. To students of the Bible it will afford the [illegible] the precise import of the Biblical references to creation, and [illegible] to what is known from other sources. To geologists and biolo[illegible] to give some intelligible explanation of the connection of the [illegible] religion with the results of their respective sciences."

[illegible] is doubtless excellent, but whether Dr. Dawson has been successful [illegible]. It is, however, only fair to say that failure in this respect is [illegible] fault of the author, but (in our opinion) is inherent in the under[illegible] some years past geology and its allied sciences have been in a con[illegible] development. Facts have accumulated, and are still accumulating [illegible] while the task of co-ordination is necessarily slow. With this a vast [illegible] unexplored, and all inductions from negative evidence must be [illegible] the greatest caution. Even theories founded on positive evidence [illegible] regarded as first approximations rather than as conclusions. The [illegible] of the Scriptures. It is very far from being settled what many [illegible] Bible mean, and what may fairly be expected from it; archæolo[illegible] also is constantly throwing fresh light on the history. Any [illegible], which at the present time attempts to discuss in detail the rela[illegible] Bible history to archæology and geology must necessarily deal with [illegible], and make assumptions which experience may soon show to be

[illegible] endeavours to prove that the various days of the Mosaic record, [illegible] shows need not be limited to periods of twenty-four hours, corre[illegible] "Periods deduced from scientific considerations." The Eozoic [illegible] is supposed to be included in the "third day." To the fourth is [illegible] Metamorphism of Eozoic rocks and disturbances preceding the Cam[illegible] the present arrangement of seasons, and the beginning of existing [illegible] fifth day includes the Palæozoic and Mesozoic epochs. The sixth, [illegible] post-Tertiary. The seventh, the Period of Human History.

[illegible]ondences are worked out with much ingenuity, but the author is [illegible] to adopt theories which we had thought generally abandoned [illegible] of repute. Thus he speaks of "periodical collapses in the equatorial [illegible] regions, which form the boundaries of some of our most important [illegible]." Now it is, indeed, true that there are certain gaps in the

[illegible] book; or, Lessons in Accuracy of Statement and Preciseness of Expression. For Civil Service [illegible], and use in Schools. By W. Cosmo Monkhouse (Board of Trade). London: Crosby

† [illegible] the World according to Revelation and Science. By J. W. Dawson, LL.D., &c. London

geological records in many parts of Europe and America [illegible] used for purposes of classification, but that these gaps are [illegible] mark cataclysms, few geologists, we imagine, will maintain [illegible] whole weight of geological evidence, while admitting of local [illegible] to general uniformity. Again, Dr. Dawson, wishing to press the [illegible] tation of the Mosaic record, endeavours to limit the duration of the [illegible] some 7,000 years. To do this he is driven to the usual shifts, with [illegible] factory result. He even assumes that palæolithic stone weapons [illegible] in an unfinished state; a hypothesis startling to those who know [illegible] divergence in type, and he strains every nerve to prove that the [illegible] in the valley of the Somme can have been produced in 7,000 years. [illegible] conclude that he has never visited this or other localities where [illegible] weapons have been found, for if he had, we venture to think so [illegible] logist would have seen the improbability of such an assertion.

We doubt, then, if the book will not do as much harm as good. [illegible] seems to us to have been too ambitious. Had he been content, instead [illegible] prolix book, to write a few short essays pointing out the defects in [illegible] the part of those who think that the scientific records are so clear [illegible] sweep may be made of the Biblical, and showing that the theories of a [illegible] universe and a chance-born order of Nature present at least as many [illegible] as the belief in a Creator, we think that he would have been more likely [illegible] and less to repel.

---

Few things are more difficult than to write books for beginners, and [illegible] more competent to overcome the difficulty than Professor Huxley. [illegible] almost needless to say that, notwithstanding the numerous manuals [illegible] geography, this* volume will be a boon alike to teachers and to [illegible] lucid order, accurate statement, and clear vigorous style so characteristic [illegible] fessor Huxley's writings, are here singularly conspicuous.

The book, as is stated in the preface, has grown out of a course of [illegible] natural phenomena in general, delivered to young people at the London [illegible] the title being chosen in order to distinguish it from physical [illegible] ordinarily treated in a text-book. The student—supposed a Londoner [illegible] by the side of the Thames. What he there sees leads to the [illegible] river and its basin, to tracing its stream to the source, and to brief [illegible] the structure of the surface of the ground and the meaning of [illegible] springs welling up to form the source of the river call forth an [illegible] underground course of water, which is then traced backward till it [illegible] as rain on the earth. The explanation of rain, snow, and ice naturally [illegible] now the rain itself must be traced—whence came it? This inquiry [illegible] explanation of evaporation and atmospheric phenomena. This [illegible] subject exhausted, and the Thames water traced from the sea [illegible] the sea whence it has come, the composition of pure and natural [illegible] gated. Then the work of water is described, as rain, rivers, ice, and [illegible] the description of earth sculpture suggests the inquiry whence [illegible] materials for the carving tools? The movements of the earth's surface [illegible] fore described: earthquakes, volcanos, rise and fall of the ground, [illegible] account of the living agents which act as rock builders. Recurring [illegible] Thames basin, the lessons which have been learnt are applied to [illegible] logical structure. This suggests some account of the present [illegible] and sea, and so the student is led on to the figure of the earth, [illegible] ments, and lastly to the sun, the centre and mainspring of the [illegible]

Brevity has not been studied, and thus the information is [illegible] books—crowded too fast upon the learners. The book is a [illegible] than of lecture notes. Its appearance, too, is attractive. The [illegible] open, the illustrations numerous and generally good; though [illegible] one—the glacier of Zermatt (*i.e.*, the Gorner Glacier), copied [illegible] been replaced by something more truly physiographic, as it [illegible] historic age of mountain drawing.

* Physiography: an Introduction to the Study of Nature. By T. H. Huxley, F.[illegible] & Co.

# ON THE ORIGIN OF REASON.

THE book to which I should wish to call the attention of English philosophers bears the title of "The Origin of Language," by L. Noiré.* More clearly, however, than by the title, the real purpose of the book is set forth by a short sentence from the late Lazar Geiger's work "On the Origin of Language and Reason," printed as a motto on the title-page—"*Language has created Reason; before there was Language, man was without Reason.*" Indeed, the more appropriate title of Professor Noiré's book would have been, "On the Origin of Reason." It is a work which stands apart from the large class of treatises lately published by comparative philologists on the beginning of human speech, most of which, though containing the fruits of original thought and the results of careful research, are disappointing for one and the same reason, their authors not having perceived that the problem of the origin of language cannot be treated by itself, but must be viewed as an integral part, nay, as the corner-stone, of a complete system of philosophy.

#### The Origin of Languages, and the Origin of Language.

It is one thing to trace one language, or a number of languages, or, it may be, all languages, back to their first beginnings; it is quite another to investigate the origin of language. How languages can be arranged into families, and how all the languages and dialects belonging to one family can be broken up into their simplest constituent elements, may be seen in any of the numerous books published during the last twenty years on the science of language. While engaged in these researches, we feel that we are on firm

* Der Ursprung der Sprache, von Ludwig Noiré: Mainz, 1877.

ground. We are simply carrying on a process of analysis, and as in a chemical experiment we arrive in the end at residua, which resist further separation, so in dealing with language we find that, after having explained all that can be explained in the growth of words, there remain at the bottom of our crucible certain elements which cannot be further dissolved. It matters little how we call these stubborn residua, whether roots, or phonetic types, or elements of language. What is important is, that, when we have removed all that can be removed, the whole crust of historical growth in words, when we have broken up every compound, and separated every suffix, prefix, and infix, there remain certain simple substances, the results, not of synthetic speculation, but of experimental analysis. These simple substances being granted, we can fully understand how out of them the whole wealth of language, as treasured up in its dictionaries and grammars, could have been brought together. We can unmake a language and make it again, and it was this process of analysis and synthesis which I tried to represent as clearly as possible in my "Lectures on the Science of Language," first published in 1861.

### Roots or Phonetic Types.

Those who have read those lectures will remember how strongly I opposed any attempt on the part of the students of language to go beyond roots, such as we actually find them as the result of the most careful phonetic analysis. It was thought at the time that my protests against all attempts to ignore or skip those roots, and to derive any word or any grammatical form straight from mere cries or from imitations of natural sounds, were too vehement. But I believe it is now generally admitted, even by some of my former opponents, that the slightest concession to what, not ironically, but simply descriptively, I called the bow-wow and pooh-pooh theories in the practical analysis of words, would have been utter ruin to the character of the science of language.

But to show that a certain road, and the only safe road, leads us to a mountain wall, which from our side can never be scaled, is very different from saying that there is or that there can be nothing behind that mountain wall. To judge from the manner in which some comparative philologists speak of roots, one would imagine that they were not only *indiscernibilia*, but Palladia fallen straight from the sky, utterly incomprehensible in their nature and origin. It was in order to guard against such a view that, at the end of my lectures, I felt induced to add a few lines, just as a painter, when he has finished a landscape, dots in a few lines in the background to show that there is a world beyond. The science of language, I felt, had done its work when it had reduced the vague problem of the origin of language to a more definite form, viz., "What is the origin of roots?" How much has been gained by that change of front those will best be able to appreciate who have studied the history of the innumerable attempts at discovering the origin of language during the last century.

Beyond that point, however, where the student of language is able to lay the primary elements of language at the feet of philosophers, the science of language alone, apart from the science of thought, will not carry us. We must start afresh, and in a different direction; and it was in order to indicate that direction, in order to show to what quarter I looked for a solution of the last problem, the origin of roots, that I appealed to the fact that everything in nature, when set in motion or struck, reacts, that it vibrates, and causes vibrations. This seemed to me the highest generalization and at the same time the lowest beginning of what is meant by language. The two problems, how mere cries, whether interjectional or imitative, could develop into phonetic types, and how mere sensations could develop into rational concepts, I left untouched, trusting that philosophers by profession would quickly perceive how some of the darkest points of psychology might be illuminated by the electric light of the science of language, and fully convinced that they would eagerly avail themselves of the materials placed before them and ready for use to build up at last a sound and solid system of mental philosophy.

### Science of Language and Science of Thought.

Professor Noiré seems to me the first philosopher who has clearly perceived that in the direction indicated by the Science of Language there was a new world to discover, and who discovered it. Already in his earlier works there are repeated indications that the teaching of Comparative Philology had not been lost on him.

I confess I have often wondered at the apathy, particularly of the students of psychology, with regard to the complete revolution that has been worked before their eyes in the realm of language. They simply looked on, as if it did not concern them. Why, if language were only the outward form of thought, is it not clear that no philosophy, wishing to gain an insight into the nature of thought, and particularly into its origin, could dispense with a careful study of language? What would Hobbes or Locke have given for Bopp's Comparative Grammar? What should we say if biologists were to attempt to discover the nature and laws of organic life without ever looking at a living body? And where are we to find the living body of thought, if not in language? What are the two problems left unsettled at the end of the Science of Language—"How do mere cries become phonetic types?" and "How can sensations be changed into concepts?"—what are these two, if taken together, but the highest problem of all philosophy, viz., What is the origin of reason?

### Professor Noiré's Works.

It is impossible to do justice to Professor Noiré's last book "On the

Origin of Language," without going back to his earlier works. His last work is the last stone that finishes the arch of his philosophical system, but it is held in its place by the works which preceded it. The most important of them are :—

(1.) *Die Welt als Entwickelung des Geistes*, 1874. "The World as an Evolution of Spirit."

(2.) *Der monistische Gedanke, eine Concordanz der Philosophie Schopenhauer's, Darwin's, R. Mayer's, und L. Geiger's*, 1875. "Monistic Thought, a Concordance of the Philosophy of Schopenhauer, Darwin, R. Mayer, and L. Geiger."

(3.) *Grundlegung einer zeitgemässen Philosophie*, 1875. "Foundations of a new System of Philosophy."

(4.) *Die Doppelnatur der Causalität*, 1875. "The Double Nature of Causality."

(5.) *Einleitung und Begründung einer monistischen Erkenntnisslehre*, 1877. "Introduction to a Monistic Doctrine of Perception."

These works, though written, or at least published, within a short space of time, show a constant advance towards a clearer perception of the nature of language. Noiré is not one of those philosophers who sacrifice their delight in truth to a stationary infallibility. He is one of the few students who can still say, "I was wrong." With regard to the origin of language, he has openly retracted what he had written but a few years before. In his first book, "The World as an Evolution of Spirit," he still looked upon language as some sort of copy of the external world.

"The first human sound," he wrote (p. 255), "which deserves the name of word, cannot have differed from the warning calls of animals except by a higher degree of luminousness in the images which excited and followed these calls. They excited the idea of approaching danger among fellow-animals. . . . I assume that men were held together by the ties of social life in herds or tribes even before the beginning of language. War was then the natural state—war against animals of another species, and against neighbours of the same species. It is not unlikely that a peculiar sound or watchword united the members of a single tribe, so that they could collect by it those who were scattered abroad and had lost their way, or encourage each other while engaged in fight with other tribes. Let us suppose that but once one member of a tribe warned the other members by imitating the watchword of an hostile tribe when he saw the enemy approaching, and we have in reality the origin of the first human word, capable of doing what words have to do, viz., to excite, as they were intended to do, an idea in the mind of cognate and homogeneous creatures."

"I found afterwards," Professor Noiré continues,* "that Darwin, in his 'Descent of Man,' had started an hypothesis almost identical with my own. After declaring that he could not doubt that language owed its origin to the imitation and modification, aided by signs and gestures, of various natural sounds, the voices of other animals, and man's own instinctive cries, he says :†

* Ursprung der Sprache, p. 170.

† Descent of Man, vol. i. p. 57.

'As monkeys certainly understand much that is said to them by man, and as in a state of nature they utter signal cries of danger to their fellows, it does not appear altogether incredible that some unusually wise ape-like animal should have thought of imitating the growl of a beast of prey, so as to indicate to his fellow monkeys the nature of the expected danger; but this would have been a first step in the formation of a language.'

"The difference between my own hypothesis and that of Darwin consists only in this, that I after all see in the contents of the first sound of language something more natural, more familiar, more human, viz., the hostile neighbours, while Darwin makes the wild animal the first object of a common cognition. With a little reflection, however, it can be seen that such an attempt is utterly impossible, for the objects of fear and trembling and dismay are even now the least appropriate to enter into the pure, clear, and tranquil sphere of speech-thought (λόγος), or to supply the first germs of it. The same objection applies of course to my own theory.

"From whatever point of view we look at them, these hypotheses can never stand against serious criticism. A call of warning is a call of terror, and terror communicates itself by sympathy. But according to mine and Darwin's theories, one more particularly gifted *Homo primigenius* would have had to ruminate and reflect thus: 'How can I make my fellows conscious of the threatening danger?' and then, by some kind of momentary inspiration, he would have uttered the dreaded sound. Let us grant, what is impossible and utterly incredible, that he calculated on his being understood; how could he have been understood by others without there being the same inspiration on their part answering to his own? And that is to be the beginning of language! The fierce howling of the wild animal, the battle-shout of the enemy, are these to have been the first germ, the centre of crystallization, of that wonderful intellectual creation which, resting on the solid ground of human consciousness, has become the mirror of the world, of earth and heaven and all their marvels? Nothing is more incredible, more unlikely. And as I recognize the insufficiency of my own hypothesis, it was impossible that the whole philosophical significance of the problem, and the crying misproportion between it and his own lightly uttered guesses, could long remain a secret to the serious and profound mind of Darwin. He too in a clear and considerate confession has admitted the inadequacy of his former views, and I can do no better than to quote his last words, which dispose of our common phantasmagoria once and for ever: 'But the whole subject of the differences of the sounds produced under different states of the mind is so obscure, that I have succeeded in throwing hardly any light on it; and the remarks which I have made have but little significance.'"*

We cannot sufficiently honour the noble spirit that dictated these words, particularly if we compare it with the manner of other philosophers who seem to consider the suggestion that they could ever grow wiser as the greatest insult.

To watch the struggles of a mind impelled by a strong love of truth, and following up his prey in the right direction, though not without occasional swervings to the right and to the left, is certainly far more interesting and far more useful than to have results set before us, without our knowing how they have been obtained. Professor Noiré has evidently been for a long time under the influence of Schopenhauer and Geiger, the former by this time well known in England also; the latter, a man of high promise and full of original thought, who

* Darwin: Expression of the Emotions, p. 93. I feel bound to add that I do not see in the words of Mr. Darwin so complete a retractation of his former philosophy of language as Professor Noiré imagines.

died in 1870, after having published two books, one "On the Origin of Human Language and Reason," 1868; the other "On the Origin of Language," 1869. After a time, however, Noiré went beyond Schopenhauer and Geiger; and though he continues to express for both of them the warmest admiration, he now differs from them on some very essential points. He differs from Schopenhauer because he, Noiré, is a thorough-going evolutionist in body and mind; he differs from Geiger, because he no longer recognizes the first beginnings of language in involuntary interjectional sounds, but in sounds naturally accompanying the earliest acts of man. Where Noiré agrees with Geiger, I am generally at one with both of them; and I say this, not in order to establish any claims of priority, which are utterly out of place in a disinterested search after truth, but simply in order to define my own position in this decisive battle of thought. Whatever others have done before him, to Noiré belongs the merit of having rallied the scattered forces and led them to victory. When a student of the Science of Language points to the supreme importance of a right understanding of language for the solution of the most intricate problems in psychology or logic,—when he tries to show, for instance, that the formation of species is a question belonging in the first instance to subjective philosophy, and inseparable from the question of the formation of concepts,—when he represents the whole history of philosophy as in truth an uninterrupted struggle between language and thought, and maintains that all philosophy must in the end become a philosophy of language,—he is apt to be taken for an enthusiast. But when a philosopher by profession subscribes to every one of these positions, the case becomes different. In Germany Professor Noiré's reputation as an original thinker is by this time firmly established; and if less has been heard of him and his system in journals and newspapers, this is said to be due to the fact that, like Schopenhauer, he is not a University professor, and therefore without colleagues to support him, and without a large train of *clientes*, which originally meant *cluentes* or hearers, to swear by their master. It has also been said that the age of abstract philosophy in Germany has passed away, and that Physical Science now occupies the throne which formerly belonged to Kant, Fichte, Schelling, and Hegel. This is not so. There is no lack of philosophical productiveness, but there is certainly a lack of philosophical receptivity in Germany, so that books which thirty or forty years ago would have excited general attention, now pass unheeded, except by the smaller circle of working philosophers. Books which in England would sell by thousands, and be reviewed in all the leading journals, sell in Germany by hundreds hardly, and are generally discussed in the correspondence only that passes between the author and his friends.

There are exceptions. Some philosophical books have made a stir in Germany even in these days of iron and blood. But there is generally a reason for these exceptional successes. The same taste which finds a satisfaction in the more or less Turkish atrocities of sensational novels, is gratified, it seems, by a class of philosophical writers who try to outbid each other in startling assertions and unblushing negations, and who if they speak but loud enough, and have some friends to speak still louder, attract, at least for a time, a crowd of idle listeners. The following specimens of this kind of popular, or rather vulgar philosophy are taken from Noiré's books and elsewhere:—

"Man possesses many internal qualities, such as imagination and the milt."
"An external quality is seeing, an internal one is digestion."
"Thought is a secretion of the brain, as other secretions come from the kidneys."
"Man is what he eats. *Homo est quod est.*"

A lady published some letters addressed by her to Professor Moleschott, in which the following sentiments occur:—

"The moral rule for each man is given by his own nature only, and is different, therefore, for each individual. What are excesses and passions by themselves? Nothing but a larger or smaller overflowing of a perfectly legitimate impulse."

A philosopher* belonging to the other sex indulges in the following dithyrambus:—

"Enjoyment is good, and frenzy and love are good, but hatred also! Hatred answers well when we cannot have love. Wealth is good, because it can be changed into enjoyment. Power is good, because it satisfies our pride. Truth is good, so long as it gives us pleasure, but good is lying also, and perjury, hypocrisy, trickery, flattery, if they secure us any advantage. Faithfulness is good, so long as it pays; but treason is good also, if it fetches a higher price. Marriage is good, so long as it makes us happy; but good is adultery also for every one who is tired of marriage, or who happens to fall in love with a married person. Fraud is good, theft, robbery, and murder, if they lead to wealth and enjoyment. Life is good, so long as it is a riddle; good is suicide also after the riddle has been guessed. But as every enjoyment culminates in our being deceived and tired, and as the last pleasure vanishes with the last illusion, he only would seem to be truly wise who draws the last conclusion of all science, *i.e.*, who takes prussic acid, and that without delay."

I need hardly say that Professor Noiré's style is as far as possible removed from such ravings, at which even a Greek cynic would have smiled, but he is nevertheless by no means a timid philosopher, and never shrinks from any conclusion that is forced on him by facts or real arguments. What distinguishes him from most philosophers is his strong feeling for the history of philosophy. There is in all he writes a warm sympathy with the past, without which there is no prophet and no philosopher. He is not always anxious to impress us with the fact that his system is a new system, that his thoughts are quite his own, quite original. He knows what has been said before him on the old questions which disturb our own philosophical atmosphere, whether by the ancient philosophers of Greece, or by the schoolmen, or by any of the great leaders of philosophic thought, from Descartes to Kant. He never announces as a new discovery what may be read in any manual of the history of philosophy. He never indulges in the excited language of the raw recruit with whom every little skirmish is to rank as one of the great battles of thought. He has a clear perception that the roots of his own system of philosophy go back through Schopenhauer, Kant, and Leibniz, to Spinoza and Descartes, and it is with a full consciousness of what he owes to every one of his intellectual ancestors, that he takes his own position on the high road of philosophic thought. On the tower built up to a certain height he rears his own story, and he invites us to see whether it does not command a wider and clearer view than the loop-holes of his predecessors. If there is an evolution anywhere, it is in philosophy, and a philosophy which ignores its antecedents is like a tree without roots. The great leaders in metaphysical speculation during the last four centuries are to Noiré not only names to be cited, but living powers with whom he has to reckon, and from whom, even when he treats of the most recent problems of the day, he demands an answer in accordance with their principles.

#### Historical Antecedents of Noiré's Philosophy—Descartes.

Thus when he has to define the point from which he himself starts, in approaching the great questions of our time, and more particularly the questions of the origin of reason and language, he, like every true philosopher, feels the influence of Descartes, the founder of modern metaphysics. His *Cogito* remains the starting point of modern philosophy, whatever we may think even of the very first of his conclusions, *ergo sum*. What separated Descartes from the philosophy of the middle ages, and gave him that strong position which he still holds in the history of philosophy, was his fixing his starting point on the subjective side, and assigning to cognition the first place among all philosophical problems. We must know How we know, before we ask What we know. Every system of philosophy which plunges into the mysteries of nature without having solved the mysteries of the mind, the systems of natural evolution not excepted, is pre-Cartesian and mediæval.

But though breaking the fetters of many of the traditional ideas of the schoolmen, Descartes remained under the sway of others. He remained a Dualist, never doubting the independent existence of two separate worlds, the world of thought and the world of matter. The world of thought was given him in his *Cogito*, but the world of matter was a world by itself, beyond the reach of the *Cogito*. Mind with Descartes was a substance possessed of the property of thinking, if we use that word in its largest sense, so as to comprehend perceiving, willing, and imagining. Matter was a substance possessed of the property of extension—extension comprehending the qualities of divisibility, form, and movement. Having put asunder these two substances, how was he to join them together again? And, even if he could have joined them, how was he to prove that the knowledge which mind seemed to possess of matter was correct?

Descartes' solution sounds strange to our ears, yet it can be translated into modern philosophic thought. He starts with the conception of God which he finds impressed on his mind; and as the conception of God involves the conception of a perfect Being, Descartes considers that every possibility of delusion in the world which He has created, is *ipso facto* removed. This step, which changed the uncompromising scepticism with which Descartes begins his philosophy into an equally uncompromising faith, was influenced no doubt by the theological atmosphere of his time. But we must guard against suspecting in it a mere concession to the prejudices of the day, or, as many have done, a compromise with his own convictions. Every man, even the greatest philosopher, is a slave of the language in which he has been brought up. He may break some of its fetters; he will never break them all. If Descartes lived now, he might have expressed all that he really wished to say on the character of our cognition in the words of Dr. Martineau:—"Faith in the veracity of our faculties, if it means anything, requires us to believe that things are as they appear—that is, appear to the mind in the last and highest resort; and to deal with the fact that they 'only appear' as if it constituted an eternal exile from their reality, is to attribute lunacy to universal reason."

"Trust in God as a perfect Being," and "an unwillingness to attribute lunacy to universal reason," sound very different; but their intention is the same.

Noiré takes his first step with Descartes. He starts from the *Cogito*, as what is certain above everything else, and as that without which nothing can be certain; but he protests against the rupture between the subject and object of knowledge, and still more against any attempt to heal it by means of the *concursus divinus*, maintained by Descartes and his followers. One of the most distinguished Cartesians, Malebranche, went so far as to maintain that when our soul wills, it does not act on the body, but that God intervenes to produce the desired effect; while, when the soul perceives, it is not influenced by outward objects, but again by God only, calling forth in the soul the sensations which we ascribe to the action of the material world. Here we have the true precursor of Bishop Berkeley.

### Spinoza.

At this point Noiré, like all modern philosophy, becomes for a time and up to a certain point, Spinozistic. The very fact that we cannot bridge the gulf between two heterogeneous substances, such as mind and matter, shows us that there can be no such gulf. Thus Spinoza was led on to admit, in place of the two, or in reality three, substances of Descartes' philosophy, one substance only, of which mind and matter, or, as he would say, thought and extension, are inherent qualities. Body and soul being the same substance under two different aspects, the problem of body acting on soul, or soul on body, vanishes. Individual souls and bodies are modes or modifications, whatever that may mean, of the one eternal substance, and every event in them is at the same time both material and spiritual.

Noiré goes hand in hand with Spinoza, but only for a part, though a very important part, of his journey. The permanent gain from Spinoza's philosophy, in which we all share, is the clear perception that spirit cannot be the product of matter (materialism), nor matter the product of spirit (idealism), but that both are two sides of one and the same substance.

### Leibniz.

Noiré parts company with Spinoza where Leibniz diverged from the great monistic thinker, viz., when it became a question whether all existing things, material or spiritual, could be satisfactorily explained as so-called modes of one eternal substance. What are these modes? Whence did they arise? What would the eternal substance be without such modes? Such questions led Leibniz to postulate, as an explanation of the given universe, not one substance, like Spinoza, nor three, like Descartes, but an infinite number of individual monads. Each monad was to him a universe in itself, each was endowed with two qualities of thought and force. The two important differences between Spinoza and Leibniz were, first, Leibniz's recognition of the individual as something independent, not derivative; and secondly, his substitution of force instead of extension.

### Descartes, Spinoza, Leibniz, and Locke, on Language.

But Noiré not only turns away from Descartes and Spinoza on these points, but he declares himself most emphatically a pupil of Leibniz on another point also, viz., the proper study of language, as before all things an empirical study. He had asked Descartes what place he assigned to language in his system of philosophy, but he received from his works no answer which would show that he had ever given serious thought to the relation between his *Cogito* and the *Logos*. We might have expected that Descartes would have treated words as material sounds, as mechanical products running parallel with the ideas of the mind, but neither provoking ideas nor provoked by them, and fulfilling their purpose simply by means of the *concursus divinus*. But instead of this, he simply repeats the views then current, "that if we learn a language, we join the letters or the pronunciation of certain words, which are material, with their meanings, which are thought; so that whenever we hear the same words again we conceive the same things, and when we conceive the same things, the same words recur to our memory."*

Neither does Spinoza return a more satisfactory answer as to the mutual relation between language and thought, and we look in vain for any passage in which he might have attempted to bring the facts of language into harmony with his general system of philosophy. He distinguishes in one place very clearly between ideas or concepts on one side, and images or percepts and words on the other. But it is again the old story. Words are there to signify things,† but how they came to be there and to perform such an office, is never even asked. In another place, words and images are said to consist in corporeal movements which have nothing to do with thought (ideas). Once Spinoza asks himself the question how, on hearing the sound of *pomum*, a Roman thought of what had no similarity whatever with that sound, viz., an apple; and the answer is, by the concatenation of ideas. "The body," he says, "has frequently been affected at one and the same time by the sound of *pomum* and by the sight of an apple, and hence, on perceiving the sound of *pomum*, it perceives its frequent or constant concomitant, the apple."‡ The question, Whence that sound of *pomum*, and whence its first concomitancy with an apple? is never asked by Spinoza. One remark only shows that his thoughts must have dwelt on the difficulties of language. In one passage he compares words with footprints, and remarks that when the soldier sees the footprints of a horse, he thinks of cavalry and war, while the peasant who sees the same marks is carried away in his thoughts to the plough and the field. This shows an advance beyond the then current view of the purely conventional character of language, and some apprehension of the fact that words imply far more than they express.

Noiré, not satisfied with Descartes and Spinoza, turns to Leibniz, not, however, because that philosopher seemed to him to have solved the problem as to the relation between language and reason, but because he was the first to point out that, as in every other part of nature, so in language, it was the inductive method only that could lead to any valuable results. Before you attempt to find out how language arose, he would say, collect all that there is of language, classify, analyse, sift, label;—only when that has been done, and done thoroughly, will there be a chance of discovering the simple elements of human speech. This was the conviction which guided Leibniz in his own linguistic labours, in his collection of living dialects, in his bringing to light the earliest documents of his own language, in his

* Epist. l. 35: "Sic quum linguam aliquam addiscimus, literas sive quarundam vocum, quæ materiales sunt, pronunciationem conjungimus cum earum significationibus, quæ sunt cogitationes, ita ut auditis iterum, iisdem vocibus easdem res concipiamus, atque iisdem rebus conceptis, easdem voces in memoriam recurrant."

† Ethica, ii. Prop. xlix., schol.: "Verba quibus res significamus." Ibid.: "Verborum namque et imaginum essentia a solis motibus corporeis constituta, qui cogitationis con-

encouraging Emperors as well as missionaries in the compilation of dictionaries of hitherto unknown and barbarous tongues.* It was in this way that he became the founder of the Science of Language, as an inductive science. It was in this way also that he was led to conceive the possibility of a more perfect, or so-called universal, philosophical language. But the vital question, as to whether thought was possible without language, or language without thought, remained outside the horizon of his speculations.

At the same time, while Leibniz was laying the foundation of Comparative Philology, Locke approached nearer than any one before him to what is now called the philosophy of language. In his great, though very unequal work, "On the Human Understanding," he pointed out that words were not the signs of things, but that in their origin they were always the signs of concepts; that language begins in fact where abstraction begins, and that the reason why animals have no language is that they do not possess the power of abstraction. This observation was little regarded at the time, till it was remarked how completely, and yet how undesignedly, it had been confirmed in our own time by the discoveries of the Comparative Philology.† When it had been shown by a very considerable amount of evidence that every word in every language that had been carefully analysed was formed from a root, and that every root expressed an abstract idea, a concept, not a percept, then the coincidence between Locke and Bopp became startling, and gave a new impulse to a new philosophy both of language and thought. Lange, in his "History of Materialism," has called Locke's work "On the Human Understanding," a "Criticism of Language." We may go further, and say that, together with Kant's "Criticism of Reason," it forms the true starting point of modern philosophy.

### Leibniz's "Manadologie."

But before we leave Leibniz and the lesson which Noiré thinks should be learnt from him even at the present day, we must endeavour to see more clearly how Leibniz freed himself from the charm of Spinoza's monistic philosophy, and how Noiré, who calls his own philosophy *Monismus*, yet breaks loose from Spinoza, by admitting not one *monon*, but many *mona*. The escape from the ἓν καὶ πᾶν is not so easy to those who have once been under its spell, as Leibniz would have us believe. His well-known remark, "Spinoza aurait raison, s'il n'y avait point de monades," is rather the saying of a philosophical cavalier, and might be met by the easy retort, "Leibniz aurait raison, s'il n'y avait point de substance." Nor did Leibniz by any means shake off the almost irrepressible longing of the human mind after the One, as the source of the Many. At first sight his monads seem to form a

* Lectures on the Science of Language, vol. i. p. 158 (10th ed.).
† See M. M.'s Lectures on the Science of Language, vol. i. p. 405.

[illegible] small divinities; but not only is there for them all a [illegible] harmony," but in the end his monads are represented [illegible] monad, which itself is not created. There is an [illegible] ou substance simple originaire dont toutes les [illegible] ou dérivatives sont des fulgurations continuelles, de [illegible] moment."* Are these *fulgurations pour ainsi dire* a very [illegible] Spinoza's modes? The real solution, if there can be [illegible] what is in reality one of the so-called antinomies of the [illegible] would seem to lie in our clearly understanding that we [illegible] conceive the Many without the One, nor the One without [illegible] but it will be best to let Professor Noiré speak for him- [illegible]

[illegible] doctrine received its necessary complement through the great [illegible] that the Infinite alone exists and can be conceived by itself only; [illegible] phenomena are throughout dependent on the Eternal and the [illegible] the two true attributes of substance, viz., extension and thought, [illegible] given to us by experience, but must be conceived immediately; that [illegible] misleads us when it attempts to count and measure, where, [illegible] to their nature, counting and measuring are impossible—all these [illegible] truths which, difficult to understand, could ripen and bear fruit at [illegible] time only.

[illegible] principle of individuality remained entirely neglected in the philosophy [illegible] Individual beings are nothing but modifications, affections of the [illegible] All, the eternal and infinite God-world. Nature, however, there can [illegible] doubt, is entirely founded on individuality, and higher knowledge as [illegible] higher reality arises only through the combination of forces which were [illegible] distinct. '*Spinoza aurait raison, s'il n'y avait point de monades.*' With [illegible] the opposition of the philosophy of Leibniz to that of Spinoza [illegible] pronounced. The thought of an evolution of the world has already [illegible] through the mind of Leibniz.

[illegible] the lowest monad consists in extreme limitation, most perfect isolation [illegible]; that with the progress of evolution higher monads are formed, [illegible] with constantly brighter perception, and having the law of their [illegible] in themselves; that an inner quality is given to all beings down to [illegible] inorganic matter, determining their form and expressed in it, until the [illegible] form of existence, man, lets shine forth the light of his intelligence as [illegible] crown of creation, illuminating himself and the world around; this is [illegible] and the true kernel of Leibniz's 'Monadologie.'

[illegible] if man himself is a true individual, therefore a being in active and [illegible] relation to the rest of the world, it follows that all his endeavours, and [illegible] acts, and all his knowledge, proceed from his limited nature only. [illegible] in the Infinite would annihilate him no less than a dissolution into [illegible] atoms. His individuality exists and maintains itself only in opposi- [illegible] all the rest. Independent active force is the true character of all [illegible] the world."

### [illegible] The Intellect according to Locke, Kant, Schopenhauer, and Noiré.

[illegible] Noiré takes away with him from Leibniz are the monads, or, [illegible] to call them, the *mona*, leaving the pre-established har- [illegible] the same philosophical lumber-room with the *concursus*

* [illegible] § 42.
[illegible] und Begründung einer monistischen [illegible]

*divinus*, and pronouncing no opinion on the necessity of admitting, beyond all individual monads, one supreme or creative monad. Having settled his accounts with Leibniz, Noiré has next to pass through the ordeal of Locke, and to defend his *mona* from becoming mere canvas, or *tabula rasa*. What are the monads with which he undertakes to build up the world; and, more particularly, what are those monads of which we have to predicate the old Cartesian *Cogito*? The so-called faculties of the soul had long ago been destroyed by Spinoza, the innate ideas had fallen under the strokes of Locke. Well did Herder say,* "All the forces and faculties of our souls, and of animal souls, are nothing but metaphysical abstraction. They are effects, subdivided by us, because our weak mind cannot grasp them as one. They are arranged in chapters, not because in nature they act in chapters, but because an apprentice apprehends them most easily in this manner. In reality, the whole soul acts everywhere undivided." In Locke's philosophy there remained nothing but the perceiving subject as *tabula rasa* on one side, and on the other the objective world, throwing its picture on the white surface of the soul. Nothing was in the intellect except what had come into it through the senses; and if Leibniz rejoined, "No, nothing, except the intellect itself," the next question clearly, which philosophy, in its historical progress, had to answer was, What then is that intellect?

The answer was given from two opposite quarters, by the philosophers of France and by the philosophers of Germany. *Penser c'est sentir*, was the answer of Condillac, La Mettrie, and Diderot. Kant's answer was the "Critik der reinen Vernunft," giving to the world what is the only possible definition of the intellect, *i.e.*, the fixing of its limits. What these limits are, according to Kant, is well known by this time to all students of philosophy. Man can possess a knowledge of phenomena only; what lies beyond the phenomenal world is beyond his perception and conception. Space and time are the inevitable forms of his sensuous perception, the categories the inevitable forms of his mental conception. These forms of perception and conception are, according to Kant, neither innate nor cognate, but inevitable, irremovable; they cannot be thought away, as he expresses it, when we speak of perception and conception. They are contained in them as light is contained in colour, as number is contained in counting, analytically, not synthetically. They are that without which thought could not be conceived as possible in man. If it made their nature more intelligible, there would be no harm in calling them laws of sense, and laws of thought.

Within the charmed circle described by Kant, the human intellect is safe; outside it, it becomes entangled in antinomies or inevitable contradictions, without finding any criterion of its own to solve them. According to Kant, we have on one side man, imprisoned within the

* Noiré: Ursprung der Sprache, p. 47.

walls of his senses, and with no more freedom of movement than the categories or the chains of his intellect will allow him; on the other side we have a world, of which we know nothing except that it is, and that by its passing shadows it disturbs the repose of our prison.

As far as the prisoner is concerned, nothing that later philosophers have added has materially changed his position. Space and time have remained, what Kant was the first to prove them to be, necessary forms of our sensuous intuition. The number of the categories has been changed, and by some philosophers, in particular by Schopenhauer, they have been reduced to one, the category of causality, as the one primary form of all human thought. Thus armed, the subject, or, as we might say with Noiré, the *monos*, expects the *mona*.

But what about these *mona?* What about the outside world? Can we really know it only as it appears? Can we predicate nothing of it? It is from this question that the most powerful impulse to philosophic thought proceeded. We might follow the stream of philosophy which, starting from this point, and following the course indicated by Fichte, Schelling, and Hegel, seems for the present, like the river Sarasvati, to be lost beneath the ground. But Noiré calls us away from that enchanted valley, and bids us follow him in another direction, from Kant to Schopenhauer, and then onwards to his own system.

The transition from Kant to Schopenhauer is easy, and may be stated in the form of a single syllogism. He accepts all that Kant teaches about the subject or the I; or, if he modifies Kant's doctrines, he does so chiefly by simplifying them. But he differs from Kant in his view of the object, or the Non-I. Our only real knowledge, he says, of anything really existing is our knowledge of the I, which involves not only being, but conscious being, resisting, or, as he prefers to call it, willing. Therefore, if we say that the Non-I exists, we say at the same time that it exists as something willing, resisting, and, if not actually, at least potentially, conscious. We know no other kind of being, and therefore we cannot predicate any other. As we, the I, are to others as the Not-I, so the Not-I must be to us as the I. This is the bridge from Kant to Schopenhauer, from death to life. As soon as we have arrived on the opposite shore, as soon as we have recognized in all nature, in all that is not ourselves, something like ourselves, Noiré bids us welcome. This is the threshold of his own philosophy.

### The two Attributes of Substance.

The first question which, after he has arrived at his monads, he asks is, What are their inherent attributes? He does not ask, What is intellect? or, What is matter? but, What is essential in order to explain the whole of the subjective and objective evolution of the world? Like Descartes, like Spinoza, and like Leibniz, he requires two attributes only, but he defines them differently from his predecessors, as *motion* and *sensation*.

Out of these materials he builds up his universe, or rather, taking the universe as he finds it, he traces it back through a long course of evolution, to those simple beginnings. As Goethe said, "No spirit without matter, no matter without spirit," Noiré says, "No sensation without motion, no motion without sensation."

According to these two attributes, philosophy has to deal with two streams of evolution, the subjective and the objective. Neither of them can be said to be prior. On the one hand it may be said that motion precedes sensation, because motion causes vibration, and vibration of the conscious self is sensation. I see, I hear, I feel, I taste, I smell—all of these, translated into the highest and most general language, mean, I vibrate, I am set in motion. But, on the other hand, motion exists only where there is sensation; it presupposes sensation; it means something which is nothing except in relation to something else, and that something else capable of perceiving. The two streams of evolution run parallel, or, more correctly, the two are one stream, looked at from the two opposite shores.

### Subjective Evolution.

Taking the subjective aspect first, Noiré shows how sensation begins in its lowest form, as a mere disturbance or irritation. But even that irritation presupposes something that reacts, some force which is *conservatrix sui*, and it is that power of reacting against foreign disturbance which constitutes the beginning of real sensation. Sensation is, in fact, conscious motion or reaction.

We may define every kind of sensation as conscious vibration, and we are able now to determine the different kinds of sensation by the number of vibrations acting within a given time upon certain specially receptive organs. Let the line A B represent the $\frac{1}{1000}$ part of a second; let each straight line (|) represent 4,000,000,000 vibrations, and each curved line (‿) one vibration. Then, disturbed and set to

vibrate in unison with these vibrations, the eye within this $\frac{1}{1000}$ part of a second would see red, the skin would perceive about 31° of heat (Centigrade), and the ear would hear the tone of c'''''.*

While one *monon* maintains itself against the inroads of another, or in reality of an infinite number of other *mona*, it vibrates. It asserts its existence by vibration, *i.e.*, by a constantly and regularly repeated attempt to maintain itself against foreign inroads. Vibration in the highest sense is the struggle between being and not being. So far as

* Noiré: Grundlegung, p. 56.

for a moment one *monon* has to yield, and as it were to surrender some of the ground which belonged to itself, it recognizes in the very act of yielding the existence of something else, able to disturb, but unable to annihilate, so that when we say of something that it exists, what we really mean is that for a moment it is where we were before.

And here we have the first glimmering of the category of causality. It is by looking upon a disturbance as caused, and by fixing that cause outside ourselves, that we translate disturbance, or irritation, or vibration into the perception of an object. The gradual change from the one to the other has been so fully elaborated by the most recent school of English philosophy, that English readers will hardly find anything new in this portion of Noiré's philosophy. We must only remark, as against all philosophers from Descartes to Kant and his school, that even the most primitive perceptions or empirical cognitions are never entirely passive. Malebranche said: "In the same manner as the faculty of receiving different figures and configurations in the body is entirely passive, and involves no action whatever, the faculty also of receiving different ideas and different modifications in the mind is entirely passive, and involves no action whatever. I call this faculty, or this capacity which the mind possesses of receiving all those things, the understanding (l'entendement)." We hold, on the contrary, that every impression becomes perceived by our resistance only, and every resistance is active and self-conscious. We suffer, no doubt, in seeing and hearing, but we suffer because we resist.

Kant says: "If I take away all thought from an empirical cognition, there remains no cognition whatever of an object, for nothing is thought by mere intuition, and the fact of my sense being affected gives me nothing that relates to any object." But whatever we may do in abstract reasoning, we cannot *in rerum naturâ* take away all thought from an empirical cognition, without destroying it. This is what Schopenhauer urges with great success against Kant. He shows that even the simplest intuition involves activity, sensation, and thought. In giving to our sensuous disturbances an object, in saying of these objects that *they are*, we are not only passive; we are active, we think, we are using Kant's own category of *causality*, in addition to the intuitions of space and time. In placing the cause of our sensuous disturbance outside ourselves, we apply what Kant calls one form of our sensuous intuition, viz., *space*. In placing one disturbance by the side of another, we begin to count, and apply Kant's second form of sensuous intuition, viz., *time*. There is, in fact, according to Schopenhauer, no real sensation without the first germs of intellect in it. Kant takes the intellect as something given, as ready at hand, whenever we want to apply it to the brute material supplied by the senses. Noiré looks upon the intellect as gradually developing from the lowest indications of conscious sensation to the highest achievements of discursive reasoning. On this point he was, for a time, as it would seem, chiefly under the influence of Geiger. Geiger, speaking historically rather than psychologically, says:—

"One thing is certain, that as far as our observation reaches, man is rational. And yet he has not always been rational. Reason does not date from all eternity. Reason, like everything else on earth, had an origin and beginning in time. And like the species of living beings, reason did not spring into existence suddenly, finished, and in all its perfection, as it were by a kind of catastrophe; but it has had its own development. We have in language an inestimable and indispensable instrument for seeing this. Nay, I believe that whatever plausible theories on the descent of man may have been started elsewhere, certainty and assurance can be obtained from language only."

Geiger seems to me to mix up two ideas in the word rational. When he says that man was not always rational, he means *rationalis*, not *rationabilis*; and between these two words the difference is immense. We agree with Noiré when he says:—

"How is it possible that from unconscious and non-sentient matter consciousness and sensation should suddenly shine forth, unless the inner quality, though in a dark and to us hardly perceptible manner, belonged before to those substances from which the first animal life, in its most elementary form, was developed?" (p. 193).

It may probably be objected that the inner quality here spoken of is only a different name for the *qualitates occultæ*, which form the terror of modern philosophy. But honest philosophers must not allow themselves to be swayed by the clamour of the day. No doubt the abuse that was made of occult qualities, innate ideas, and of faculties and instincts, was very great; but because modern philosophy had shown that these terms were musty with the crust of long-accumulated misconceptions, there was no ground for throwing away these old terms, like broken toys. Every one of them, if only carefully defined, has its legitimate meaning; and with all the prejudice attaching to their name, the theory of occult qualities and their gradual manifestation rules really supreme at the present day, though thinly veiled under the new name of evolution and potential energy.

Noiré's philosophy rests on a most comprehensive theory of evolution; it is the first attempt at tracing the growth of the whole world, not only of matter, but of thought also, from the beginning of time to the present day. As the philosophy of nature strives to account for all that exists by a slow progress of evolution, beginning from the simplest elements and ascending through endless combinations to the highest effort of nature realized in man, the philosophy of thought starts from the lowest indications of conscious feeling, and follows the growth of thought through every variety of perception, imagination, and conception, to the latest work of philosophy.

### Objective Evolution.

Noiré is a true evolutionist, subjectively and objectively. But is a follower of Cuvier, not of Lamarck. He avails him-the new light which modern science, particularly through Robert Mayer and Charles Darwin, has shed on that oldest of all problems, but he is not a Darwinian, in the ordinary sense of the word. With Robert Mayer, he holds* "that there is but one universal force of nature in different forms, in itself eternal and unchangeable. Whatever we perceive, whether in the form of light, heat, sound, or anything else, is due to motion, and must be solved as a purely mechanical problem. Nor can any motion be lost; it can only be changed into a new kind of motion."

Even organic life is looked upon as a mechanical process, though it is fully admitted that science has not yet mastered it. In this respect we have, in fact, advanced but little beyond Descartes, who likewise looked upon animals, and even on the human body, as mere machines, though in the case of man the machine was connected with a new substance, the soul. Physical science is no doubt fully justified in always keeping the solution of the problem of life before its eyes; nay, in representing such a solution as the highest triumph which mechanical or chemical science could achieve. But it should never allow the anticipation of that triumph to influence philosophical speculation. We know exactly what a cell is composed of, but no synthesis has yet produced anything like a living cell, absorbing, growing, and generating, if only by self-division. We may laugh at the occult quality of vital force, but we cannot confess too openly that as yet vital force is to us an occult quality.

Leaving the origin of organic life as an open question, and remembering that even Charles Darwin requires a Creator to breathe life into matter, we may afterwards follow the progress from the lowest to the highest forms of life, with all the new light that patient research has thrown upon it. Noiré here goes entirely with the evolutionists, he believes even in the *Bathybios Haeckelii*. To me he does not seem to lay sufficient stress on the many gaps which the most laborious members of the evolutionist school are the most ready to acknowledge, nor to dwell sufficiently on the indications, supplied by Nature herself, that she may have had more than one arrow in her quiver. He differs, however, most decidedly from the evolutionists in the explanation of the process of evolution. He looks upon the struggle for life, the old πόλεμος πατὴρ πάντων, the *bellum omnium contra omnes*, on the survival of the fittest, on natural selection, influence of environment, and all the rest, as merely concomitant agencies, and places the original impulse in what Schopenhauer called Will—a word, as it seems to me, as badly chosen as could be to express what Schopenhauer wished to express. What he means by Will is simply the subjective form of what appears objectively as Force. Where other philosophers would say that everything is what it is by its own nature, what the Hindus call *svabhâvât*, Schopenhauer says it is so by its will, wishing to indicate thereby that the nature of everything, from a stone to an animal, is not determined by any other higher will, but by itself alone. He is thus driven to speak of an unconscious will in stones and plants, and he dates the beginning of a conscious will from its first manifestation in the animal kingdom.

It is not quite easy to see how far Noiré adopts Schopenhauer's theory of will. Will, as used by Schopenhauer, does not differ much from fact, however, or—from another point of view—from accident. The broader question is really this, whether we are to admit that each thing is a law to itself, or that there is a higher, universal law for all. Schopenhauer ends with a republic of separate wills, without a supreme ruler—nay, without a superintending law. Hence the aversion he felt and expressed to the theory of evolution. "What has philosophy to do with becoming?" he writes; "it ought to try to understand being."* No doubt, what exists, and is what it is by its own will, cannot easily be conceived as changing, and yet what greater change can be imagined than that from an unconscious will in stones and plants to a conscious will in animals and men? Here it is where Noiré separates himself decidedly from Schopenhauer. To him all being is becoming, and all becoming is determined from the first. There could be no consciousness in the animal world unless its undeveloped germs existed in the lower stages from which animal life proceeds. Here is the fundamental difference between Lamarck's chaotic, pangenetic evolution, and that development which is from beginning to end the fulfilment of a will, a purpose, a law, or a thought.

### Kinetics and Æsthetics.

Noiré divides the whole of philosophy, according to the views just explained, into two branches, which he calls *Kinetics* and *Æsthetics*.

By Kinetics every problem from the first motion of the atom to the revolutions of the solar system, from the formation of the first cell to the life of man, has to be solved as a purely mechanical problem.

By Æsthetics, using that word in the Kantian sense, he tries to unravel the growth of the subjective world, from the first tremor of the embryo to the brightest thoughts of man, from the first reaction of the moneres to the highest flights of human genius.

The field for the study of Kinetics is open; it is the whole realm of nature which anybody may explore who has eyes to see. It is Physical Science in the largest sense of the word. Experience and experiment are the two tools, nature the never-failing material, for those who want to work out the history of evolution in the objective world.

For the study of Æsthetics the same tools are at hand, but where is the material? where are the documents in which to study the growth or history of the sentient subject? Must we be satisfied wit

* Einleitung, p. 193.

introspection, the most uncertain of all vivisectory experiments, in which he who dissects is at the same time he who is being dissected? or with the study of that short period of growth which we call the history of the world, comprising no more than a few thousand years, filled with names of kings and battles rather than with an account of the silent growth of the mind? No wonder that men accustomed to deal with facts, and to base their theories upon them, should turn away with dismay from mental science in which every fact can be disputed by men who profess that they do not see it, and where there is hardly one technical term that admits of one definition only. An exact philosophy of the human mind seemed to become more and more hopeless the greater the achievements in the conquest of nature.

#### Language, as Subjective Nature.

And yet while philosophers complained about the scarcity or the total absence of trustworthy materials, there were old archives brimful of them, if people would only see them, open them, and read them. What should we say if we were told that in studying the growth of the earth, we must be satisfied with looking at its surface only—that everything else was hidden and lost? Were there not chronicles of the past written on that very surface, if people would only recognize them as such? Was there not a history to be read in every bit of coal, in every flake of flint? We can hardly understand how men could have been so blind as not to see what stared them in the face; and yet all mental philosophy has hitherto been struck with such blindness. Noiré is, in fact, the first philosopher by profession who has perceived what students of the science of language, more particularly Geiger, have pointed out again and again, that language is the embodiment of mind, the nature, so to say, of mind, the subjective universe in which the whole objective universe is reflected, perceived, imaged, and conceived. Here is the realm of mental science, here are materials, as real as any that physical science has to deal with. Nor have we only the surface, the living language of the day, in which to study the remnants of that unbroken series of growth which begins with the first conscious sensation. We possess in the so-called dead languages petrifactions of former stages of growth, and in the many families of human speech a wealth of form comparable only to the numberless forms of vegetable and animal life which overwhelm the student of objective nature. The evolution of sensation therefore can be studied as well as the evolution of motion, viz., in the enormous wealth of language. The history of the human mind is the history of language; the true philosophy of the human mind—true, because resting on facts—is the philosophy of language.

I quote from Noiré (Einleitung, p. 213):—

"How could such a new creation as we have in reason spring from antecedent and less perfect forms? How could what is rational and thinking proceed from what is without reason and without speech?

"If we want to know the means by which human reason worked its way from small beginnings to always-increasing clearness with reference to the qualities of things, and always higher self-consciousness, this can be done historically only, by investigating the regular development of the conceptual contents of words, which, without such contents, are empty sound. Concepts, as Geiger shows, determine each other in their genesis, so that not every one could spring accidentally from every other, but certain concepts only from certain concepts, according to rule. While there can be no science to determine the connection between concept and sound, a scientific method must be found, following the development of concepts, without reference to their phonetic forms; and in the same manner the development of phonetic forms, without reference to their meanings. We must try to find the empirical laws according to which concepts can be concatenated, laws which alone enable us to judge of real relationship of ideas, as phonetic laws of real relationship of sounds. Thus only shall we gain an insight into the nature of reason, and be enabled to ascribe to it that certainty which consists in a knowledge of a necessity determined by law."

Let us see now how Noiré works out this new discovery. What he takes as granted on the subjective side of his philosophy is sensation, corresponding to motion. That sensation, however, is something different from what we have made it, by separating from it in language what in reality can never be separated from it, viz., some kind of self-conscious thought. Even the faintest shiver is pervaded by something which we must accustom ourselves to call thought. The fact is, we suffer from the abundance of terms which have been created to signify the various manifestations of sensation as well as the faculties corresponding to them, and which, from being used loosely, have encroached on each other to that extent that it is almost impossible now to disentangle them. It would be the greatest benefit to mental science if all such words as perception, intuition, remembering, ideas, conception, thought, cognition, senses, mind, intellect, reason, soul, spirit, &c., could for a time be struck out of our philosophical dictionaries, and not be admitted again till they had undergone a thorough purification. Sensation, then, in the sense in which Noiré uses it, so far from being the lowest degree only of mental activity—so far from being what is most easy to understand and what would seem to require no explanation at all—is really the most mysterious act, the act which we can explain by no other, of which there is no simile or metaphor anywhere. Like motion, sensation will always remain an ultimate fact—a *ne plus ultra* of human philosophy. French philosophers imagined that by their tenet of *Penser c'est sentir* they were degrading thought, and such had been the influence of fashion that few only at the time could see that sensation, being at all events the indispensable antecedent of thought, was in no way a viler function, but had a perfect right to claim precedence of thought. The French tenet became faulty because Condillac and his school took *sentir* in its unnaturally sense. They had previously taken out of *sentir* all that is

then thought they could startle the world, like a juggler, by showing that the bird was still to be found in the empty egg-shell. Give us sensation, such as it really is, not such as it has been imagined to be for logical purposes, as something distinct from thought, but impregnated with thought, and everything in the human mind becomes intelligible, and *penser* may as truly be said to be *sentir* as the oak-tree is the acorn.

But then it has been asked, Is there no such thing as mind, soul, reason, intellect, &c.? Is not the soul a simple substance? Is not reason a special gift? Such is the influence of words on thought, that as soon as we throw away a word, or attempt to define its meaning, everybody thinks he is being robbed. But the sun rises just the same, though we say now that it does not rise; the moon has not been minished, though for thousands of years she has been told that she is waning; and all our mental life will remain just the same, though we deny that reason has any independent substantive existence. All the various shades of sensation from the first to the last were doubtlessly distinguished and named for some very useful purpose. The mischief was that there were too many distinctions to remain distinct, and that, as usual, what was meant as an adjective was soon changed into a substantive. Perception, intuition, remembering, ideas, conception, thought, cognition, all these exist as modes or developments of sensation, but sensation itself exists only as a quality of the *monon*, and therefore neither mind, nor intellect, nor reason, nor soul, nor spirit, being all modes or products of sensation, can claim any substantive existence beyond what they derive through sensation from the *monon*. To speak of reason as a thing by itself, as even Kant does, is simply philosophical mythology; to speak of mind, intellect, reason, soul, or spirit as so many independent beings, with limits not very sharply defined, yet each differing from the other, is neither more nor less than philosophical polytheism. A man is not, however, an atheist because he does not believe in Aphrodite as a goddess; nor is a philosopher to be called hard names because he does not believe in mind, intellect, reason, soul, or spirit as so many independent substances, or powers, or faculties, or goddesses.

Noiré sees all this quite clearly in some parts of his works; but at other times he seems still under the sway of the old philosophical theogony. Thus he sometimes identifies himself with Geiger, whose words he quotes on the title-page of his text-book:—"Language has created Reason; before there was Language, man was without Reason." I do not object to this statement so long as it is only meant as a protest against the received opinion that language is the handiwork of reason; that man, because he was possessed of reason, was able to frame for himself and others an instrument of communication in language. Geiger's words convey much truth, as calling attention to the fact that it is reason rather which was built up by language than language by reason. But what is reason without language? What shall we think of language without reason? When we say that language has been built up by reason, it is the same as when we say that a living body is built up by a vital force. Reason, like vital force, is

new word there is more reason, and every progress of reason is marked by a new word. The growth of reason and language is coral-like. Each shell is the product of life, but becomes in turn the support of new life. In the same manner each word is the product of reason, but becomes in turn a new step in the growth of reason. Reason and language, if we must separate them for our own purposes, are always held together in mutual dependence; and if we wish to arrive at a true understanding of their nature, all we can do is to break up the two words and knead them into one, viz., Logos. Then and then only shall we see that reason by itself and language by itself are nonentities, and that they are in reality two sides of one act which cannot be torn asunder.

Then what is *Logos?* it will be said. Is that term clearer than language and reason? Are we not simply placing one idol in the place of two? I believe not. Logos is the act of the *monon*, freeing itself, by means of signs, from the oppressive weight of sensations. *Logos* is what its name signifies, the act of collecting, arranging, classifying; and this act is performed by signs, and chiefly by words.

### Percepts and Concepts.

In order to understand this process of gathering and naming, we must go back to where we left the stream of the philosophy of language, and chiefly to Locke's observation that words are the signs of concepts, confirmed as it was by the later discoveries of Comparative Philology, that all words are derived from roots, and that roots express general concepts. If that is so—and no one doubts it—then the question recurs, how does sensation, which deals with percepts only, arrive at concepts,

the distinction between percepts and concepts, yet the line which separates them from each other, like that which separates sensation from reason, is by no means so sharp as we imagine. Instead of saying that we cannot think in sight nor see in thought, I should say on the contrary that we never really see without thought, and never really think without sight. There is no percept which, if we examine it closely, does not participate more or less in the nature of a concept, nor is a concept possible except on the ruins of percepts. We hardly ever take in a thing as a whole. When we look at a poppy, we see its red colour, and perhaps, to make quite sure, the shape of its leaves; but then we have done. We have here a percept which, on account of its very incompleteness, represents the first step towards a concept.

From these imperfect percepts still more drops away when the immediate impression ceases. I call this a kind of involuntary abstraction, I might also call it memory. Much difficulty has been raised about the so-called faculty of memory, but the truth is that the real problem to be solved does not lie in our remembering, but in our forgetting. If no force is ever lost, why should the force of our sensations ever become less vivid? The right answer is that their force is never lost, but determined only by new forces, and in the end changed into those faint and more general sensations which we call memory. These remembered sensations lead us another step nearer towards concepts. In one sense concepts may be called higher than percepts, and they certainly constitute, as all true philosophers have seen, the chief difference between man and brute. But from another point of view concepts are lower, less vivid, less clear and accurate than percepts, and they certainly constitute the chief source of our errors. Kant says that concepts without percepts are empty, percepts without concepts blind; it would perhaps be truer to say, that concepts and percepts are inseparable; and if torn asunder, they are nothing.

#### How are Concepts named?

The process by which percepts are constantly being changed into concepts is by no means uniform, but admits of endless variety. What concerns us, however, at present, is not so much the formation of concepts, as the process by which a concept can be fixed and named. We may understand how the faint recollection of the red colour of the poppy, separated from everything else, particularly after it has been strengthened by the red colour of other flowers, of birds, of blood, or of the sunset, becomes in the fullest sense of the word a concept. But while we can point to the flower, the bird, and the red sky, we never can point to the red as such, apart from the things to which it belongs. Unless therefore we have signs to assist our memory in the retention of concepts, they would vanish almost as soon as they have risen. This is not a merely theoretic difficulty, but it must have been felt as a very serious practical difficulty, from the first beginnings of civilized life. How to distinguish blood from water, except through the concept of red, and through some sign for red?

It is the object of Professor Noiré's last book to give an answer to this question, How are concepts framed and named? That language does not begin with mere sensation, that man never attempted to name a single subject in its completeness, he takes for granted, for the single reason that it is a superhuman task. Try to name a whole oak, and you will find that language cannot even get near it. All names are made from roots, all roots are signs of concepts. Bring the oak under a concept, under the concept of eating, for instance, and you can name it, as it was named φηγός, the eaten tree, the food tree, *par excellence;* but not otherwise. I believe, however, that one class of roots has here been overlooked, and must indeed be ascribed to the purely perceptive phase of the human mind, viz., the demonstrative or pronominal as opposed to the predicative roots. Those sounds which simply point to an object,—this, that, I, thou, he, &c.,—are in their most primitive form purely sensational. They are few in number, but they are made to render the greatest service in the later formation of words.

With the exception of this small class of roots, however, Professor Noiré is certainly right that all roots are signs of concepts. We may take any word we choose, it will invariably lead us back in the beginning, not to a single sensation, but to a concept. A *book* is originally what was made of beech. The English beech, the Latin *fagus*, the Greek *φηγός*, oak, were all so called from the root *φαγ*, to feed, to eat; that is to say, the tree was conceived as giving food to cattle, whether acorns or beech-nuts. But even *φαγ*, to eat, is a secondary root, and may be traced back to the Sanskrit root *bhag*, which has preserved the more general meaning of dividing.

Wool, *vellus*, *ἔρ-ιον*, Sanskrit ûrnâ, all come from a root *var*, to cover. A horse was called *equus*, Sanskrit asva, the swift, from a root *as*, to be sharp and quick, while the cow, in contradistinction to the runner or the horse, was called *βοῦς*, Sanskrit *gaus*, from a root *bâ* or *gâ*, to go, to move slowly. We may tap language wherever we like, the sap that runs from its veins is always conceptual.

We saw before how concepts arose ; we also saw why it was necessary that concepts should have signs. They would have vanished without signs, and it was desirable that they should not vanish. The question that remains to be answered is, how concepts were expressed in sounds.

### The Interjectional and Mimetic Theories.

The most common theories hitherto advocated on that point have been the *interjectional* and the *mimetic*, or, as they have also been called, when misapplied to etymological purposes, the Pooh-pooh and Bow-wow theories. According to the former, roots are derived from involuntary exclamations forced out by powerful impressions. According to the latter, they are formed from imitations of natural sounds, such as the barking of dogs, the lowing of cows, &c. In my lectures on Mr. Darwin's "Philosophy of Language," I tried to explain how, with certain modifications, both of these theories could be defended, not indeed as supplying actual roots, still less actual words, but as furnishing the materials out of which roots might be formed. Yet the arguments against this theory of mine are powerful. It is perfectly true, as Professor Noiré points out, that the simplest sensations which, we should think, might be expressed by interjections, are never so expressed, but are reached by language in the most circuitous way. To hunger and to thirst are two very primitive sensations; but have t[illegible] been expressed interjectionally? No

The word *hunger* is as yet without any etymology; it may possibly be connected with Sanskrit kars, to dwindle away; krisa, lean, lank; the German hager. The Latin esurio, derived from edo, means I wish to eat. The same meaning we find in the Sanskrit asanâyati, to desire food. The Greek πεῖνα, hunger, is connected with πόνος, labour, πένομαι, I labour, I strive, I reach after food; the original conception being most likely what we find in σπάω, to draw out, the German spannen, to stretch.

To *thirst*, Gothic thaursja, Sanskrit trish-yâmi, shows its original conception in Greek, τέρσομαι, I am dry; Latin, torreo; Gothic, thaursus, dry. The same root supplied material for terra, dry land; tes-ta, dried clay, bowl, French tête; testudo, turtle; probably for torrens, torrent, torris, torch, and even for French aussitôt.* This shows how language works.

And with regard to objects which might most easily have been named after the sounds which they utter, we find again that generally they are not so named, while in such words as cuckoo, *cuculus*, Noiré points out that these are not names, but rather proper names, or nicknames, and that they came in long after the concept of the bird had been framed. Sounds such as *bow wow*, or *baa* or *moo* would remind us, he thinks, of single objects only, and would never be fit to express conceptual thought.

I had tried to show, in my lecture on Mr. Darwin's "Philosophy of Language," how even out of such sounds the materials for roots or phonetic types might have been elaborated, and how in the same manner as various cries would leave the concept of crying, various sounds such as *baa* and *moo* might, by mutual friction, be raised to a root, containing the concept of to cry.

### The Sympathic Theory.

Professor Noiré has brought forward no arguments against this theory, but he has started a new theory, which, so far as it reaches, supplies certainly a better explanation of phonetic types and rational concepts than my own. He points out that whenever our senses are excited and the muscles hard at work, we feel a kind of relief in uttering sounds.† He remarks that particularly when people work together, when peasants dig or thresh, when sailors row, when women spin, when soldiers march, they are inclined to accompany their occupation with certain more or less vibratory or rhythmical utterances. These utterances, noises, shouts, hummings, songs, are a kind of reaction against the inward disturbance caused by muscular effort. These sounds, he thinks, possess two great advantages. They are from the beginning signs of repeated acts, acts performed by

* Bréal. Mélanges, p. 318.

† This point has been illustrated by Mr. Darwin in his Expression of the Emotions,

ourselves and perceived by ourselves, but standing before us and continuing in our memory as concepts only. Every repeated act can be to us nothing but a concept, comprehending the many as one, and having really nothing tangible corresponding to it in the outer world. Here, therefore, was certainly an easy bridge from perception to conception. Secondly, as being uttered not by one solitary man, but by men associated in the same work, these sounds have another great advantage of being at once intelligible. It cannot be denied that Noiré's arguments in support of his theory are very strong, nor can there be any doubt that, as most of our modern tools find their primitive types in cave-dwellings and lacustrian huts, a very large portion of our vocabulary can be derived and has been derived from roots expressive of such primitive acts as digging, cutting, rubbing, pulling, striking, weaving, rowing, marching, &c.

My only doubt is whether we should restrict ourselves to this one explanation, and whether a river so large, so broad, so deep as language may not have had more than one source.

Human language had, for instance, from a very early time, to express not only acts, but also states, or even sufferings. In fact, as Professor Noiré has himself shown, all the work of our senses admits of a double application, an active and passive one. We listen actively, and we hear passively; we watch actively, and we perceive passively; we scent and sniff, and we perceive disagreeable smells; we grope, and we feel; we taste tentatively, and we taste something bitter, whether we like it or not. Though in modern languages these two sides are often expressed by one and the same verb, the two concepts were originally quite distinct. To hear was probably to vibrate, to be moved, to be struck; and the root kru, or klu, which in all the Aryan languages means to hear, may have been connected with other roots, such as kru, to strike; krad, to sound. Where we say, I hear the thunder, the old expression might have been, I tremble, I shake from the thunder. Hence the old construction of such verbs with the ablative or genitive preserved in Sanskrit or Greek; whilst *audire* in Latin has lost every trace of the old concept, and governs the general objective case. To listen in the active sense of watching, giving ear (ausculto), might have been expressed by a root connected with the low breathing sounds uttered by a number of people who are waiting together for some great event. Instead of this, we find that in Sanskrit it is expressed by a secondary root, srush, to hear, a kind of derivative from sru, to hear, still present in the English to listen, Anglo-Saxon hlosnian, hlystan.

In some cases, again, Noiré's view comes very near the interjectional theory. Whether, for instance, the root *anh*, to choke, should be called interjectional or mimetic, or whether, as Noiré would have it, it was produced by the sympathy of activity, will be difficult to de-

If originally it was meant to express the sense of oppression and choking, it would be due to a sympathy of passivity, rather than activity; and a sound uttered from sympathy of passivity comes very near to an interjectional or mimetic sound.

Professor Noiré has, I believe, struck a new vein, but when he comes to work out his theory more in detail, he will probably find that the primitive centres of force from which the endless rays of thought radiated, do not all lie in the same direction. Locke* remarked, long ago, and others had done so before him, that all words expressive of immaterial ideas are derived from words expressive of material subjects. "By which," as he adds, "we may give some kind of guess what kind of notions they were, and whence derived, which filled their minds who were the first beginners of language." Nothing is more likely than that their daily occupations should have supplied the first concepts through which the framers of language gradually laid hold of everything that attracted their attention. If they had a word for plaiting or weaving, they could derive from it not only the name of the spider, but likewise of the poet who weaves words and thoughts together. I agree with Aufrecht that we should derive from a root vabh, to spin, the Sanskrit ûrnavâbhi, spider, Greek, ὕφος, web, and ὕμνος, poem, while Greek expressions such as δόλους καὶ μῆτιν, μύθους καὶ μήδεα, οἰκοδομήματα, ὄλβον, κακὸν ὑφαίνειν, show how many branches may spring from one single stem. The same root, in its simpler form, vay, gives us the Greek ἤτριον, warp. The roots vabh, however, and vap, before they came to mean weaving, meant throwing, also sowing; and in an intransitive sense, even our modern verb to wabble, clearly onomatopoetic, according to Mr. Wedgwood, has been traced back historically to that root by Professor Pott.

I fully agree, therefore, with Noiré, that the primitive occupations of man, and the sounds which accompany them, would supply ample materials for carving out of them a complete dictionary. I also agree with him that man finds the most natural metaphors for the expression of natural phenomena by referring them to himself, by looking upon them anthropopathically. When the colour red had to be expressed he called it a crying colour, a bitter taste was a biting taste, a shrill note was a sharp-cutting note. All this is true, and much more. But though I willingly say εὕρηκας to Professor Noiré, I still think we ought not to shut all other doors that may lead into the dark passages of language, and that we ought, in our searchings after the earliest ramifications of human thought and human language, to guard against nothing more than against the arch-enemy of all truth—dogmatism.

I hope in a future article to show more in detail how the gradual development both of the material and of the framework of reason, the so-called categories, may be studied by means of an historical analysis of language.

F. MAX MÜLLER.

* Lectures on the Science of Language, ii. p. 373.

# THE STABILITY OF OUR INDIAN EMPIRE.

> Οὐ σκοποῦντες ὅτι τυραννίδα ἔχετε τὴν ἀρχὴν καὶ πρὸς ἐπιβουλεύοντας αὐτοὺς καὶ ἄκοντας ἀρχομένους, οἳ οὐκ ἐξ ὧν ἂν χαρίζησθε βλαπτόμενοι αὐτοὶ ἀκροῶνται ὑμῶν, ἀλλ᾽ ἐξ ὧν ἂν ἰσχύι μᾶλλον ἢ τῇ ἐκείνων εὐνοίᾳ περιγένησθε.
> —THUCYDIDES, iii. 37.

THE British Empire in India stands alone in history. Its sudden and apparently casual rise, out of the struggle of a commercial Company to maintain a footing in the country; its rapid development, still mainly undesigned, and in the process of self-defence; its escape from a series of extraordinary perils, which from time to time made its subversion appear imminent; its commanding attitude and transforming influence at present, in spite of the comparatively small number of the dominant race, in a land where they must ever continue little more than fleeting strangers, with whom the very elements wage constant war:—these and other circumstances are well calculated to excite astonishment, and to provoke inquiry as to the stability of so unique a political fabric. Such an inquiry, if honestly conducted, can hardly be an unprofitable, though it may well seem a thankless task; especially when attempted by one, who may be insensibly biassed by the terrible reminiscences of life in India during the awful crisis, when the fountains of the great deep of disaffection were opened, and the pillars of our imperial structure rocked to their base. In such an investigation, optimism and pessimism are alike out of place. A practical and commercial nation should be prepared to take stock calmly of the actual outcome and ulterior tendency of its greatest trading venture, its most costly military investment, its most arduous political achievement.

The rule of the foreign conqueror must always be precarious. In this case, indeed, among a large part of the population, there is less aversion than in many others to the mere fact of the government being in the hands of strangers; for independently of the merits of the English administration, and the long-confirmed habit of subjection to foreign sway, there is, as far as we can judge, a strange indifference to the question, whose rule it is, so that the rule be tolerable, and compatible with the enjoyment of certain civil rights, traditional usages, and religious practices.

But, on the other hand, there are obviously many special circumstances, which, in spite of the undisputed ascendancy of the ruling race, contribute to impair its influence, and threaten the stability of its sway. The remoteness of England may seem a mere military disadvantage, much mitigated by our possession of intermediate stations. But it is more than this, and closely connected with our most serious danger. The tropical climate; the impossibility of transmitting to an Indian-born posterity the vigour of the European constitution,—of promoting general intermarriage between the conqueror and the conquered,—of propagating Christianity to any, politically speaking, considerable extent; the social estrangement between the European and the native, inevitable not only from Hindoo caste and food regulations, but from the conventional and rigid seclusion of women among almost all classes of Asiatics; the want of sympathy, not to say the mutual repulsion, between a large portion of the ephemeral immigrants and the bulk of those, who present to the casual observer so much that is unattractive, and have too often very slight temptation to overcome their own dislike of the *Feringhee* and exhibit their latent good qualities; the Englishman's constant thought of returning home, the native's habit of regarding him as a mere bird of passage; the perpetual non-residence of the Sovereign, and the rapid succession of Viceroys and their subordinates;—all combine to make the British Empire in India little more in reality than a gigantic, vigorous, and admirable bureaucracy, guarded in the discharge of its multifarious functions by a strong army, European and native.

In vain, in this respect, was the Company's trading monopoly destroyed. The Anglo-Indian merchant goes home "for good" far sooner than the civilian. The civilian himself is now, very commonly, unconnected by family antecedents with the service. And he visits England oftener than of old, and has his heart far less than formerly in India, and in native associations. Railways and steam-vessels enable him to mix more freely with his own countrymen, and to be much less of a *junglewallah* than Munro, or even than John Jacob, could have been. In vain the cry for colonization was at last granted. The planter cannot become a genuine colonist. He cannot plant a sturdy and abiding family tree. The army is even less identified with the country and the people than in old days. For good or for evil, the "Company's Europeans" have become general service corps. The improved *morale* of sepoy officers, the formation of the Staff Corps, and the cessation of frequent hostilities, have together relaxed the close bonds of sympathy which once made the European officer's regiment his home for life. The very bishops are more transitory than of old. In short, the English are *in* India, but not *of* India—

more numerous, more generally diffused, more powerful than in days gone by; but less even than then a component part of the permanent population; and as absolutely debarred as ever from completing their conquest by fusion with the conquered, and the harmonious adjustment of the rival pretensions and ideas, that must ever conflict so perilously until such a fusion can be effected.

The anomalous and perplexing structure of our Government, however compatible at present with working order, involves the potential elements of much discord and commotion, which the sensitiveness and ambition of native Princes, the self-confidence and energetic political propagandism of the educated class of our native subjects, the sinister influence of the seditious in India, the lively remembrance there of old political arrangements, and the half-informed dogmatism and rash speculations of politicians in England, may one day develop into dangerous activity.

Our government at home, and in most of the colonies, is strictly constitutional. But the government of India, however wise and benevolent, is still despotic, and irresponsible to the people in our own territories; while our influence is hardly less masterful, on critical points, over our avowed dependents and nominal allies, whatever amount of self-government they may be permitted to exercise in an ordinary way. Thus we have a combination somewhat resembling what would have been presented, had the Doge of Venice been elected Emperor at Constantinople, on the so-called Latin conquest: though British rule in India is as much in advance of the limited control which a Venetian Emperor would have been able to maintain in the Byzantine dominions, as English monarchical constitutionalism is in advance of the dark and grim aristocratic republicanism of the Bride of the Sea.

Whether it is not expedient to recognize in our imperial nomenclature the "un-English" fact of this despotic authority—τυραννίδα ἔχετε τὴν ἀρχήν—and on what account, will be considered later. And if so, it will appear why we are exposed to inconvenience and possible danger from the strong manifestations in England against any such recognition. And as talking, or even dreaming, of constitutionalism in the East, may not be a very desirable proceeding at home; so, it may be added, such experiments as the late trial of the Guikwar are not very encouraging examples of the result of playing at it on the spot.

The character of our Indian government involves other dangers. The Viceroy, if he is to command the respect and prompt obedience which are essential to our security, must wield great powers and be entrusted with a large discretion. His relations to the Secretary of State for India are the more delicate, because he does not follow the fortunes of the Ministry which appointed him. Though this is no new difficulty, and though it is apt perhaps to be exaggerated, the has undoubtedly raised it in a new and more serious form, compensating advantages may attend the introduction of that of time and space. It is not necessary to dwell on the that might arise from the clashing of such high authorities. though the immediate remedy may seem very obvious, and both eral regulations and personal tact on both sides may reduce such ord to a minimum, there must nevertheless be always a certain unt of risk, that either the Government may be weakened by ing differences of opinion, or that good measures may be sacrificed spirit of compromise and a desire for peace.

nother and more serious risk is the danger of rash parliamentary rference, and the crude and violent suggestions of popular senti- t, influenced by agitation. At present, indeed, the proverbial hy and stupendous ignorance, so prevalent both in and out of iament, on almost every subject relating to our greatest and most cal dependency, may seem to offer a solid bulwark against this ger. The Secretary of State for India is left much to himself—and Council; and the House narrowly escaped, on a late occasion, g counted out while the Indian Budget was being expounded. how long will this state of things continue? Many circumstances ribute to alter it, and to portend, on the part of the public, not a berate resolution to enter upon a serious and practical study of tern affairs, but a growing disposition to take (if we may say a fussy interest in them, to form offhand and vehement opinions it them, and to press those opinions imperiously upon our rulers. uld this inclination greatly increase and become chronic, it would hard to say how much irremediable mischief might not, with best intentions, be summarily accomplished; or how far our plex political mechanism could bear the strain of such inexpert hasty handling. Enlightened public opinion is invaluable. But n Bull's empirical "glimpses of the obvious" will no more avail to his Indian house in order, than a child's meddlesome curiosity to ulate a chronometer. In no case is it more true, that a little ning is a dangerous thing. And it is to be hoped rather than con- ntly anticipated, that the public may not seek to expiate its long ce of *insouciance* and obscurantism by a feverish and hysterical cise of half-awakened intelligence.

he superficial character of our relations to the inhabitants of India, inchoate stage of our conquest, the perils incident to its imperfect olidation, are forcibly announced in a question, which is daily ming more pressing. Under previous Governments the natives of country were not eclipsed and depressed as they are by us. On one hand, the capricious favouritism of the Sovereign, and the tant warfare in one quarter or another of the land, provided, even men of low station but of adventurous temper, ingratiating ners, or useful or popular accomplishments, a wide field of ambition and great prizes in the way of employment. On the other hand, well-established claims to ancient lineage were much reverenced; and the Rajput nobility, throughout the whole period of Mogul rule, presented a close resemblance to feudal barons in the middle ages, and to Highland chieftains in later times: while the sacrosanct character, social consideration, and (in Hindoo States especially) the political influence of the Brahminical order rivalled those of the mediæval clergy and of the Jesuits in Europe. The Dewan, or Prime Minister, in a Mussulman State, was often a Hindoo. And even the intolerant and suspicious Aurungzib gave the independent command of large army corps, destined to operate against Hindoos, to Rajput generals. The imperial palace was guarded by the same gallant race, under their hereditary tribal chiefs; and the emperors themselves intermarried with some of those chiefs, though Oudipoor was too proud to consign his daughters even to the imperial *zenana*. In the decline of the empire, the Mahratta and the Jat shared its highest honours, and became its political functionaries; and still later, Tippoo, fanatical Mussulman, persecutor of Hindoos, and supplanter of a Hindoo dynasty as he was, retained the Brahmin Poornea, to the last, as his Dewan.

But we have changed all that. Our rule tends to disparage the social distinctions of our Oriental subjects; to confound classes; to baffle the ambition of individuals; and to stamp the proudest native—as a native—with the badge of inferiority to members of the "Christian caste," as a Hindoo acquaintance of ours once expressed it. Both the fact and the sense of our superiority have blighted the face of Asiatic society. Native majesty and nobility pale their ineffectual fires—native ability is to a great extent paralyzed—in the presence of a system which implicity asserts, and explicitly enforces, an exclusiveness on the part of the dominant race equally incompatible with social fellowship and political equality.

The native States that still remain are organized in some measure on the old model, and give a certain scope to the old tendencies. But though they retain troops, the career of military ambition is closed by our pacifying "mission." And British regulative and sustaining influence has both precluded internal commotion, which formerly raised so many new men to high station, and has much abridged the advantages of civil office by restraining tyranny, and providing better safeguards against peculation. The importance both of the Prince and his people is impaired by the general impression, that the imperious Englishman holds them and their assumptions very cheap, or by the fear that he may be meditating their eventual subjection to his own immediate control.

If such is the case in States which still retain a vestige of independence, what is the present, as opposed to the past, condition of the native in our own territories? We began our career in the humble capacity of allies—or subordinates—of the Country Powers. And we [illegible] in those early days to the Prince, his ministers, [illegible]. But the progress of conquest and annexation, the [illegible] of European skilled agency from commercial to [illegible], [illegible] of assumed State necessity, and the indirect [illegible] codes and estimate of native ways and character, [illegible] part of India, degraded the higher classes in a [illegible] that may well seem appalling, if not intolerable, [illegible] the older state of things. The noble may display, [illegible] Durbar, the familiar finery, and wrangle for prece- [illegible] in rank, and brothers in blood and colour. But [illegible] well that he is a cipher in English estimation, and of [illegible] account than many a young civilian. The Brahmin may [illegible] regarded with reverence, though with very far diminished [illegible] by the diminishing class of orthodox Hindoos; he may still [illegible] petty political jobs; he may enter our subordinate service, [illegible] or military. But our ascendancy is fatal to all the old [illegible] higher ambition. The native gentleman may enrol him- [illegible] corps, and affect the external form and deportment of [illegible] lance" service in which his ancestors distinguished [illegible]. But what opportunities is he likely to enjoy for the [illegible] of his vocation, except in riding down insignificant [illegible]derers? And what rank can he hope to attain? The [illegible] man of worship among his people. But no native can [illegible] to command a regiment. The civil service has been [illegible] to natives; but are they likely to be preferred to very [illegible] in it? And the necessity for competing for entrance to [illegible]land is, in the case of Hindoos, almost prohibitive. Thus [illegible], and in every station of life, the predominance and [illegible] of the English are constantly and disagreeably forced [illegible]ention of men quite capable of appreciating and resenting

[illegible] exclusion from the higher offices of the State no reason can [illegible] which is likely to prove satisfactory to a native, or well cal- [illegible] propitiate him to us and our rule. "India for the English"

[illegible]wing prophetic passage is worth attention, the rather as coming not from a [illegible], and published at Ryde, Isle of Wight, in 1848, in a pamphlet [illegible] and Opinions of a Native on the present state of India and the feelings [illegible]

[illegible] a long period, been governed by foreigners. The Hindoos were not [illegible] Mahomedan rule as they are now of the English, because, under the [illegible] not excluded from a share of power in the management of their own [illegible] heavily taxed in several shapes; but, if they continue depressed [illegible] will not be surprising if, in self-defence, they may some day or other rise [illegible] from the starvation and thraldom to which they are now exposed. [illegible] materials have once caught fire, it will be difficult to arrest the rapid [illegible] flame. They are certainly treated as contemptuously by many of their [illegible] as the animals of the forest. The natives have become proverbial [illegible] all sorts of vices in the world, although the accusers will not be [illegible], with very few exceptions, to be free from so serious a charge. For [illegible] generally in the mouth of an officer, 'How like a native!'"

would be an impudently selfish provocative of disaffection. That we cannot trust the native in important stations, lest he should abuse his opportunities of turning against us, is both a national vote of want of confidence in him, and an implied confession that he has substantial reasons for risking great personal advantages in the attempt to throw off our obnoxious yoke. That he is not fit to fulfil the duties of such a station, *he* will be slow to admit, and *we* might, in many cases, find difficult to prove—at least prior to experience. "You Elphinstone Professors," a thoughtful Brahmin once said to the writer, "are always recommending to us a social revolution, but you never advocate a political one." And he proceeded to explain, that to educate their women, and give them more freedom, seemed to him a very inadequate measure of reform, unless accompanied or followed by the restoration to the natives of the government of their own country.

Thus the cry for "Home Rule" in India may be seriously raised before many years are over; and if raised at an inconvenient crisis, and aided by other influences, might become extremely embarrassing.

The want of sympathy, or rather the positive estrangement, amounting too often to strong antipathy, between our countrymen and the natives, is an evil of long standing, and likely, it is to be feared, to increase rather than diminish. To explain it fully would require more space than can here be spared, as well as very delicate handling, and at the same time very plain speaking, by no means altogether complimentary to either party concerned. But some hints may be given, which will at least serve to show that there is room for much improvement on our side; and that, unless that improvement take place, our position in the country must be proportionately insecure.

The average Englishman is not very fond of foreigners, nor much given to appreciate fairly either their good or their bad qualities. The Oriental complexion is itself a shock to him; and he is too ready to connect it with an idea of essential inferiority, which exhales not unfrequently in the elegant, complimentary, and correct epithet—*nigger*. Nursed at home in the bosom of a society which, whatever its other claims to intelligence and mental activity, systematically taboos the subject of India as a nuisance, and attaches no discredit to the grossest and most ludicrous ignorance of almost everything relating to that great country, except its field sports; proudly conscious that he is a member of the conquering and ruling race; perplexed by the peculiarity, and kept at arm's length by the social reserve, of the native manners; inquisitive, credulous, hasty in his inferences, confident and sweeping in his conclusions; finding too readily much to condemn; unsuited by temperament as by training to make due allowances, to see below the surface of a character anything but transparent, and to evoke latent good qualities by the electric affinity of an easy manner, and a considerate mode of dealing with strangers; confirmed betimes in his innate prejudices and [illegible] by the adverse and severe judgment of [illegible] room, the ball-room, in a word, the general [illegible] Presidency,—the ordinary Englishman is almost [illegible] landing in India, to entertain unreasonable and [illegible] sentiments; and so to demean himself as by [illegible] reciprocal good-will.

[illegible] observer the intellectual and moral aspects of the [illegible] are alike forbidding. While fretting daily at their bad [illegible] eyes for their good ones. The faults of children, [illegible] of hardened and unscrupulous men of the world; the [illegible] of unsophisticated savagery, and the effemi-[illegible] of a decaying civilization; the gloomy and unsocial [illegible] of the votary of abject superstition or wild fanaticism, [illegible] audacity of the man who has swallowed most moral [illegible] manner alternating between fawning and curt insolence; [illegible] irritating attempts at deception; whimsical and absolutely [illegible] caprices of conduct, but an unmistakeable and seem-[illegible] and irresistible love of crooked ways; vanity almost [illegible] egotism; vindictiveness almost diabolical in its intensity [illegible]; apathy where an expression of feeling would be [illegible]; womanish demonstrativeness where self-respect [illegible] reserve; a ridiculously obstinate adherence to sense-[illegible] and clumsy methods, and a not less ridiculous affectation [illegible] European fashions; a general unaccountableness and [illegible] inspiring at once contempt, abhorrence, and fear: such [illegible] estimate of the sort of damnatory impression likely to be [illegible] our *soi-disant* critic by what he is pleased to call his ex-[illegible] of natives and their ways.

[illegible] there is another and very different side to the picture which, [illegible] runs may not read, yet is discernible enough to the patient, [illegible]etic, and high-minded student, who fairly lays himself out (as many have done and continue to do) to decipher it, we need not pause now to trace it. Nor is it necessary to discuss [illegible] this hideous caricature is, after all, but an exaggerated [illegible]n of much that the native may fancy he observes in the white [illegible] in the increasing class of *mean* white—men.

[illegible] to take a single feature, a Mussulman, while the charge of [illegible]y and falsehood was being illustrated by the events of the [illegible] and insisted upon in the daily papers at Bombay, said to the [illegible] "When I was in England, I did go into Yorkshire; I did go [illegible] fair. They did not all speak truth, although they were [illegible]."

[illegible]ch an impression, once formed, is in too many instances not [illegible] greatly altered for the better. The eye sees only that [illegible] brings with it the power of seeing. And an Anglo-Indian [illegible] spent by too many of our countrymen (especially of the military class), and of our countrywomen, is not generally very favourable to the development of the latent power of mental vision and moral appreciation in such a subject matter. Exceptions, of course, are admitted in favour of individual natives, but only as pearls upon the Ethiop's arm, or rather as white hairs on the black camel's back. And when to the results of superficial observation are added those of religious antagonism, traditional scandal, and dark historical reminiscences, from the Black Hole and Tippoo's wholesale murder of prisoners to the well of Cawnpore, the general effect is sombre indeed.

It is less easy to say what the native really thinks and feels about the Englishman. He may appreciate our merits in maintaining good order, ruling, on the whole, justly and beneficently, and promoting material prosperity. But if he remembers the oppression, extortion, and anarchy from which we rescued the Peninsula, he remembers also the price at which that deliverance was obtained, and may sigh after the vanished glories of native Courts, and the field of enterprise now closed against him by our predominance. He is not unaware how much money is drained out of the country by our costly European establishments. He undoubtedly dislikes many of our regulations, as the former refusal to recognize the right of adoption, and the consequent extinction of many principalities; our Enam Commission, and its unsettlement of proprietary rights; our free dealings with waste lands; our salt-tax and opium monopoly; our abortive income-tax; our judicial oaths; our vaccination. The trigonometrical survey even, at one time, excited alarm, as a device to cast a spell over the land. And though we profess, and try to practise, religious toleration, our higher morality has compelled us to interfere with matters more or less associated with religion. *Thuggee* is not likely to be fondly remembered, save by its surviving and incarcerated practitioners. But the suppression of *suttee* and infanticide shocked strong native prejudices; as did the permission accorded to Hindoo widows to remarry, and the proposal to require the appearance of women in courts of justice. Though our educational system is popular with the younger generation, it excites, or certainly did some years ago, serious misgivings and great dislike among the older and more conservative classes. The Christian missionary would probably be more unpopular, if he were more successful. And though the lower classes gain by our rule, not only do the higher lose or seem to lose by it, but the general tendency of our influence to innovate upon and disturb native institutions, practices, ideas, to break down caste, and impair the typical form of native life, is probably a deeper-seated though a rather vague cause of dissatisfaction and distrust. What is the world coming to? What will become of us in the hands of these restless, inquisitorial, dogmatic strangers?

And what manner of men do we appear to the native, and how far justified by our general character and conduct in thus turning his world upside down? Whatever our political or even our personal merits may be, we are Nehushtan to both Hindoos and Mussulmans—impurer than the very Pariah, eaters of beef and of swine's flesh, with no veneration for the Brahmin or the cow, for Mahomet or the Koran. Much as we may contemn them, it is very doubtful whether we do not, on this account alone, provoke in the breast of the orthodox Hindoo and the genuine Mussulman a much stronger feeling of contempt and loathing. Hindoo heterodoxy and Mussulman laxity may have much assuaged, but have certainly not removed, this religious antipathy, which may long survive, as in analogous cases, the personal retention, in its integrity, of the faith which generated it.

The effects of the Mutiny and its suppression upon the native opinion of us have no doubt been complex. But perhaps they may be summarily expressed in the statement, that we are regarded with more fear, but also (although the annexation policy has been abandoned) with more disfavour than before. It is very doubtful, however, whether the irregularities and cruelties committed by our officers and soldiers, and which have been so much reprobated in England, were not trifling in their influence, compared to two other points which have been less dwelt upon.

Previously to that awful episode we were, so to speak, associates, though leaders, of the native States and peoples, in most of our warlike enterprises. Even the last Mahratta war was connected with the popular object of putting down the Pindaries. And we became involved in hostilities with the Peishwa as avengers of the murder of the Guikwar's envoy, whose safety we had guaranteed. Thus, except in our first and last wars with the French, which were really Oriental diversions in great European contests, and in some provinical affairs, such as the reduction of Sinde, we never fought directly and exclusively for the establishment of English rule. We were, so to speak, co-conquerors with our native allies, for the general good of India, or of a considerable portion of India. Native self-respect was thus so far saved, and a sort of mutual polite understanding assumed, that we were confederates in a *quasi*-national struggle. But on the last occasion the blow was aimed singly against English ascendancy, and, though aided by native allies, we emerged from the contest asserters simply of that ascendancy; chastisers, certainly, of a military revolt, but of one that took the form of a popular revolution on behalf of the resuscitated phantoms of Mogul and Mahratta sovereignty. It was a direct issue between the British and the native *raj*. Thenceforth there could be no mistake, no amiable fiction: we re-conquered a large part of India by the sword, and directly on our own account; by the sword we must thenceforth secure our sway everywhere. And a largely-increased European army is the best proof, how little we ourselves believe in the sentimental phrases about a grateful people submitting to our beneficent authority.

But how is this fact likely to impress the native mind? The people of India forget assuredly neither the nature of our triumph, nor the crisis which preceded it. That England rules explicitly in defiance of native titles to dominion, is a fact in which they are probably disposed to acquiesce in proportion to its inevitableness, and to the extent to which we succeed in identifying ourselves with the forms, associations, and—*mutatis mutandis*—the nomenclature of the system which we have superseded. Therefore it is that the title of Empress, as the English equivalent of the Mogul Padisha, appears most suitable under the circumstances. It may be sneeringly called a "Brummagem decoration;" but if the *nation boutiquière* will and must assume the functions of imperialism, an emblematic device with the English trade-mark as exactly represents the actual state of the case, as Persian equivalents for out-dated Sanskrit terms of supremacy denoted the authority of the Mogul—an authority in which the Hindoo long acquiesced as readily as the Mussulman. Thus the new contrivance, if strange and startling, seems also appropriate and politic. It counteracts the old claim by absorbing it. So far it would appear to be a step in the right direction. Still, on the other hand, we must lay our account, even now, for the possibility of that old claim having its lingering attractions in the minds of the natives; and the more so in proportion as we fail to diminish the breadth of the gulf which divides us from them, and unlike the Moguls, who entered into such intimate relations with them, trusted and employed them so freely in high office, and became so much assimilated to them, stand out sharply and jealously defined as a stereotyped tribe of aliens, superimposed, not commingled with the inhabitants of the country, distrustful, resentful, contemptuous of them.

This leads to the second consequence above referred to, as resulting from the Mutiny to our disfavour. No one who, like the writer, was at the time not only resident in India, but in daily, friendly, and confidential communication with educated natives, from various parts of the country, can ever forget the extraordinary and lamentable effect produced on their minds by the unmeasured terms of vituperation, insult, and scorn, so profusely lavished both in England and on the spot upon the native character, and so indiscriminately applied to all classes. They were cut to the heart, and exasperated beyond measure, by censures which they felt were not only undeserved, but which the events both of previous history and of the time utterly disproved, and which seemed to imply not only the grossest, most inexcusable, and simply invincible ignorance, but malice prepense, a determination to draw in the darkest colours an indictment against a whole people, a Pharisaic sense of our own righteousness, with the equally Pharisaic conclusion, that this people who knew not the Christian law were cursed, and a predisposition to sanction and applaud the most undistinguishing severity in our future coercion of such a mass of [illegible] and benighted reprobates. In vain it was pointed out, that such language was not to be taken literally, or as the expression of our general and habitual sentiments; that the English nation was raving in a paroxysm of sudden resentment, horror, and fear. In vain such analogies were urged as were offered by similar manifestations of feeling on occasion of the Morisco revolt in Spain, the Irish Rebellion on the eve of our great Civil War, and the Popish Plot. Englishmen, it was replied, if they were what they professed to be—a practical, just, and enlightened nation—should know better how to control themselves, and not do their utmost to make all friendly relations between themselves and their Indian fellow-subjects thenceforth almost impossible.

Lapse of time, the recovery of the national senses at home, and the conciliatory influences of good government, education, the Royal Proclamation, the Queen's personal expressions of sympathy with her distant subjects, the Star of India, the Prince of Wales's visit, and other circumstances, have (it may be hoped) much mitigated the dangerous impression produced by the ephemeral utterances of our frenzy. But though the wound may be scarred over, is it healed? Can it well be so until, as a nation, we take more trouble to gain exact knowledge of the natives, their ways, and their character, and thus qualify ourselves for judging them more intelligently and justly, and inclining them, in turn, to think better of us?

The impression they are likely to form of our national character from experience is obviously liable to the same sort of misconceptions which prevail in our conventional estimate of them. Our faults and vices are far too prominent; our virtues hidden from those who see and really know so little of our inner life. And the tendency to generalize hastily, to conclude confidently and sweepingly on inadequate *data*, and to epitomize in one confused caricature the various infirmities and bad qualities of many different descriptions of people, is not confined to us. It would not be difficult to give such a description of ourselves from a native point of view. But it might be thought a fancy picture of my own painting. And it would certainly tend to aggravate bad feelings which are already too active among us. It seems better, therefore, to suppress it. But those who are inclined to deem natives very Shylocks will do well to study Shylock's impassioned denunciation of his Christian neighbours, on the ground of a common humanity. Our natural coldness of manner—or *fierté*, as the French put it—is not conciliatory. Our idle, minute, and obtrusive curiosity, as distinct from real and benevolent sympathy, irritates Orientals, who are tenacious of their peculiarities, and very resentful of ridicule. Our persistent endeavours to convert them to a religion, the fundamental principles of which seem to be still in question among ourselves, probably amuses more than it annoys them. Our haste to be gone, when we have compassed our personal ends in the country, and secured an adequate share of its wealth, does not promote a sense of brotherhood, or a keen desire to improve acquaintance into intimacy. Our jaunty and patronizing airs are not pleasant to those, who regard us as intrusive upstarts, and themselves as the real children of the soil, in some cases as the offspring of the sun and moon. The flattering description of "nigger" can only be paralleled by certain emphatic but unquotable references to our immediate ancestry, which such a description, if fully understood, would be very apt to elicit. On the whole, we fear it must be said, that in drawing comprehensive pictures of national character, they are quite capable of rivalling our worst style, and of showing that there is little love lost between us.

Such being the relations of the Europeans and the natives, and the estimate which they are too commonly inclined to form of each other, so broad, impassable, and (it is to be feared) widening a gulf subsisting between them, the question naturally arises: Is our political security thereby seriously endangered, and, if so, to what extent? On the one hand, it may be said, the very fact of our acquisition of such an Empire, and our preservation of it amidst so many and such great perils; the vigour and promptitude with which we suppressed the great Mutiny of 1857; the quiescence at the time of the great bulk of the population; the active assistance of many native allies on that occasion; and our undisputed authority and progressive organization since, are the best indications that our dominion is secure, at least as long as we continue to rule well. On the other hand, it may be argued, that some of our original advantages we have lost, or are liable to lose; that we are already confronted by new dangers; that popular disaffection is more to be dreaded than of old; that a general combination against us may become more feasible, in proportion as our influence and institutions tend to break down the old barriers between races and classes, and to diffuse a literature which is instinct with the spirit of liberty, the glorification of patriotism, the reprobation of arbitrary government; that Princes and chiefs far more considerable and respectable than Nana Sahib and the Ranee of Jhansi have their serious and cherished grievances against our Government; and that the remoteness, the size, the climate, the geographical features of the country, may make it impossible to sustain the waste of European energy and life in a prolonged contest, especially if coincident with extensive warfare elsewhere; that if we could find the men, we might be unable to find the money for such a war, and might be thus, in one way or other, starved into the abandonment of our Indian Empire, as the indispensable condition of saving the Empire at home; lastly, that our present European peace establishment in the East both explains our tranquil ascendancy, and illustrates the precariousness of duration.

Assuming a pretty general and resolute disposition to dislodge us, there can be no doubt that our situation would be far from an enviable one. The elements of military resistance are rife in the country. Our own native army is still large; and though we may entrust the artillery exclusively to Europeans, that arm could be supplied by the native Princes. Their subsidiary forces, contingents, and other troops are very numerous and well disciplined. Then there is both in their territories and in our own a vast host of *sebundies*, *peons*, armed police, and others of the semi-military class, who would, to say the least, rapidly develop into very effective Pindaries. And the wild hill races, whom we have in some instances reclaimed to a thoroughly peaceful life, in others coerced with more or less difficulty, would, in a time of general disorder in the lowlands, readily relapse into turbulent and predatory habits, and make the confusion worse confounded. The ex-silidar, the retired sepoy, even the man who has never been an actual soldier, but has learned many soldierly lessons in the pursuit of wild beasts, would swell the ranks of our opponents. And no people are so expert as those of India in concealing their provisions and grain, to the great incommodity of a hostile army.

But it will be scornfully objected, Could such a native force, however numerous, withstand in the field a considerable English army, respectably commanded? Under ordinary circumstances, certainly not. But two contingencies are possible which, especially if coincident in their operation, might make a considerable difference to our disadvantage—the advent of a native hero, and the pressure of a great European war. It is quite conceivable that a man of political and military genius, like Hyder Ally, might arise among the inhabitants of the country, and might turn to good account the lessons which he had received in our service; that he might find many others, inferior to himself, but, being selected with care and forethought, very superior to the extemporized incapables who misled the operations against us during the Mutiny; that, like Hyder, he might import skilful and experienced officers from abroad, Orientals, Europeans, or Americans; and that he might thus be in a far better condition than we are wont to assume for confronting us even on the battle-field. In spite of the diplomatic exclusion of Europeans and Americans of unfriendly tendency from the native service; in spite of the vigilance of our cruisers and of our police; we might find too late that we had failed to prevent even a numerous body of such skilful foreign officers stealing by degrees into the country, and supplying one great desideratum of our antagonists; especially as the State with which we were at war would have an obvious interest in thus fostering so formidable a diversion against us.

It will again be scornfully retorted, Assuming all this, what could native troops, without a sustaining nucleus of European soldiers, effect, in a stricken field, against a large European army? It would scatter them, like chaff before the wind. Even this point does not seem quite certain. Hyder had few European *soldiers* in his service. But by his skilful dispositions, his careful preparation of the ground, his selection of the best sites for masked batteries, he annihilated, at Perambaukum, an army large for those days, and well supplied with Europeans. On the same ground, he made head, during a long, desperate, and very doubtful contest against Sir Eyre Coote himself; and retired at last in good order and unpursued. At Porto Novo also he stoutly resisted the same able general; changed his front during the action, to obviate Coote's stratagem of a flank march, under cover of the sand hills; and was worsted in the end by the casual intervention of an armed schooner, whose broadside was fatal to the leader of a great cavalry charge, destined to carry the key of the position. On other occasions he did much more than enough to prove the hastiness of the above assumption. And even though defeated frequently in battle, he was never conquered by us in war. Lake in Hindostan, and Wellington in the Dekkan, bore frank and emphatic testimony to the obstinate and telling, if in the end unsuccessful exertions of the native corps in the Mahratta service, though deserted by their French officers, and unsupported by European troops. Gough was very nearly defeated by the Sikhs, though the lion of the Punjab was no longer among them. And Windham gained no laurels against the mutineers, whose incompetent generalship might be set off against his own. It would be well to lay to heart such lessons, and not to discount too liberally our military superiority even in a pitched battle.

It is, however, a very vulgar and superficial view of warfare which takes account only of pitched battles, regular operations, and indeed of mere fighting of any kind. The history of every country, and of no country more than India, testifies, that extensive and powerful military Empires are liable to extraordinary and sudden collapse, from the direct and indirect operation of disturbing forces apparently contemptible, and quite inadequate to produce such momentous effects.

The Mogul Empire is a case in point. At the accession of Aurungzib it was a majestic fabric of dominion, rooted in the soil in a manner unattainable by us, mighty in military reputation and resources, tolerably organized, and, in spite of periodical disturbances and the recent internecine war of succession, commanding general reverence and a fair amount of obedience. At the close of the same Emperor's reign, it was enfeebled, incurably distracted, impoverished, discredited, practically almost dissolved. To what are we to ascribe a change so rapid, complete, and fatal? Making every allowance for Aurungzib's intolerance, and for his injudicious destruction of the kin[illegible]
and Golconda (with results not unworthy [illegible]
tionists in the present day); admitti[illegible]

[illegible] the Moguls had degenerated to an extent at all commen[illegible] the suddenness of the catastrophe; there can be no doubt that the ruin of the Empire was principally due, both directly and indirectly, to "the Mountain Rat" and his followers. Sivaji's Mahrattas were originally as unable to cope with the Moguls in the field, as a native army would now be to encounter an English one. And this continued to be the case for many years after his death, and until the work of Imperial disintegration was far advanced. But in guerilla warfare they were unrivalled. Thirty years of incessant and assiduous efforts to suppress them, efforts directed by the indefatigable and capable Emperor in person, only sufficed to prove them irrepressible and progressively more formidable. Evading, until the later years of the contest, the shock of battle, they outstripped the Imperial cavalry, cut off detachments, intercepted supplies and treasure, rendered every line of communication insecure, made profitable descents on towns, systematically plundered the country and "peeled it to the bones," and levied black-mail freely as the price of their forbearance, and compelled the inhabitants to pay so much to themselves, that little was left for the Imperial treasury. The peasant found it a more profitable game to join them, than to submit at once to their exactions and to those of the Government. Thus the area of devastation and the forces of the insurgents grew together, and by the same means. Even the Government officers themselves were fain to come to an understanding with the rebels, became often their secret allies as well as their tributaries, and withheld their payments from the exchequer on the plausible ground, that the disturbed state of the country prevented the collection of the revenue. The lesson of insubordination, meanwhile, was not lost on those more remote from the immediate theatre of the war; and *amateur* looting probably prevailed even more extensively than history has recorded. Thus the moral authority of the Empire was forfeited; its military pretensions became a laughing-stock; its administrative system was hopelessly disorganized, its exchequer verged on bankruptcy; its lieges waxed more and more independent, the whole fabric tottered to its fall, and Nadir Shah only consummated its ruin after an interval of spasmodic efforts at [illegible].

[illegible] would be absurd to attempt to establish a parallel between our [illegible] and that of the Moguls. Our circumstances differ from [illegible] such an extent that even to contrast them may seem idle. [illegible] may yet serve to point a moral to us, and not the less [illegible] though our government is so much better than theirs ever [illegible] of the Mogul *régime* are not very patent to most [illegible] though they were considerable, especially when the [illegible] race, and religion of the rulers are taken into [illegible] now to enumerate them. But putting them [illegible] challenge no comparison with the favourable aspects of our elaborate, orderly, compact, searching, progressive, law-worthy administration. And the faults of native government, as of native character, are salient enough.

On the one hand we see a Sovereign generally vigorous and beneficent as a personal ruler, but trammelled by the necessities of his position, the immaturity of the art of government, the low and selfish tone of public opinion, and a prudent fear of putting his theoretical absolutism to too severe a test; a ministry among whom personal character or court favour is of more account than the well-ascertained limits of departmental functions; a hierarchy of Subahdars, Nawabs, and their deputies, too desirous and too capable of turning their local power against each other, and against the Sovereign himself: *jaghiredars* and *zemindars*, like mediæval beneficiaries, too apt to convert a precarious leasehold into property, and to constitute themselves political potentates and social oppressors; inveterate drunkenness in the royal family; judicial corruption; frequent rebellions and malversation in the regular provinces; a turbulent independence in the wilder and more mountainous districts, even in the immediate neighbourhood of the capital; the public roads far from secure to travellers; a royal progress disastrous, as in feudal times, to the country through which it was made; law, in spite of old Hindoo codes, the Koran, and later expositors, still retaining in the Imperial mandates too much resemblance to the casual θέμιστες of patriarchal times: on the whole, little progress even under an able and mild ruler.

On the other side is a government, the foundations of which were laid in feats of heroism with which the world still rings; which has been maintained by military, and moulded by civil abilities of a high order; which has struck down every enemy that ventured to oppose it; which has risen victorious over a military revolt alike sudden, insidious, widespread, and perilously timed; which has made the vast and long-distracted area of the Peninsula as peaceable as the soil of England; which, in its calm consciousness of strength, can afford to enlist under its banners the kinsmen of the men so lately in deadly hostility to itself, and to allow the descendants of the chiefs whom it subdued to retain large armies in their service; which has reclaimed, and employed in the conservation of order, the wild tribes who were ever a perplexity and often a danger to the Mogul; which has compelled its former enemies, its allies, its dependent chiefs, to spend a considerable part of their revenues in defraying the cost of the force which constrains them to keep the peace, and conform to the will of the Paramount Power; which has organized a service of permanent civilians and picked soldiers, unrivalled in history for subordination, purity, humanity, intelligence, versatility, in a word, for efficiency; which has enforced a higher practical morality by suppress- with a firm but gentle hand cruel rites, inhuman customs, harsh restrictions, however deeply rooted in the habits and sentiments of the people; which in successive land-settlements has uniformly sought justice, and increasingly attained equity; which has recently remitted to rich natives a tax still imposed on poor and struggling Englishmen at home; which has protected industry, fostered trade and manufactures, facilitated communication—not as a matter of favour, or in a grandiose spirit of ostentation, but as a matter of enlightened policy, and of right; which, while Christian itself, and allowing free scope to Christian missionary labours, is as tolerant as it can possibly be to other religions; which is constructing abiding monuments of its wisdom and justice in codes that put to shame the unsystematic and frequently haphazard legislation of the Imperial Parliament; which in the intricate and argumentative mechanism of its records shows a decided disposition to ascertain thoroughly and settle dispassionately the merits of the perplexing problems submitted to its decision; which encourages discussion, invites criticism, and has long ago unfettered the native press; which has actively diffused popular education, and instituted Universities for higher culture;—which, in short, has, in spite of infirmities, mistakes, abuses, even occasional crimes, well sustained, on the whole, the part of an enlightened and beneficent despot, and established a strong moral claim to reciprocal allegiance.

If then, our Government is so much stronger and better organized, and so much more efficient, than that of the Moguls, and if our army is so much better disciplined, and our officers are more highly trained in the art of war than theirs, why cite the fall of the house of Baber as relevant to a speculation on our own prospects? Because it appears desirable to note the following facts:—1. The catastrophe, though proximately military, was essentially financial. 2. The military blow was struck within, not from without, the Peninsula. 3. The military resistance was not a regular, but a guerilla war, predatory expeditions, irregular, but not the less effectual and decomposing pressure applied to the non-military subjects of the Empire. 4. The character and extent of the resistance seemed at first contemptible, and was despised accordingly. And had the rebel leader been an ordinary man, it would have been presently stamped out. But, 5. The individuality of Sivaji worked wonders, baffled all calculation, ran counter to experience, and belied its familiar and positive conclusions.

Are we exposed to similar risks? No! it will be confidently answered, for we should nip the evil in the bud. In ordinary times, and in dealing with ordinary antagonists, this would no doubt be the case. But (as we have already said) it behoves us to take into account the contingency of extraordinary circumstances, and the possible emergence of an extraordinary man, such as Sivaji, Hyder Ally, or even Runjit Singh. If such a man, during a period of general embarrassment, as when we were involved in a great European war, could contrive to disseminate extensive disorder, and (as Hyder did) maintain it for several years, we should find our Indian finances, already so limited, very deficient indeed, and our credit would decline in proportion; we should, in the dearth of European soldiers, be compelled to rely most on native levies, when least able to pay them regularly (and regularity of payment has always been our strongest security for their fidelity); many of our friends would grow cold in our support, our enemies would be encouraged to strike in against us; the natural facilities and temptations which the country and the character of the people present for looting and license would aggravate the evil; piracy would probably revive, and threaten our commerce, perhaps, as French privateering did in Wellesley's day, for a time (and time in war, particularly in such a war, is everything) seriously injure it; and even if undefeated in the field, we might, like Aurungzib, be brought to the verge of bankruptcy, with ulterior consequences which may readily be conceived.

At this point it may be well to glance at our fortunes in earlier days, however different may be our actual circumstances, and remembering that the difference is not uniformly in our favour at present. Not to go further back, Warren Hastings only provided the means for saving our Indian Empire, and retrieving our ruined reputation in America, by the very rigours which laid him open to impeachment, and left a memorable warning against the abuse of authority even for such a purpose, which no future Viceroy is likely to forget. Cornwallis was fain to devote the China investment to defraying the extraordinary cost of the Mysore War. The financial embarrassments caused by Wellesley's wars produced general consternation, and were the plea for the adoption of a policy in every sense of the word illiberal, and which occasioned profuse expenditure later. Lord Hastings found in the King of Oude a seasonable—we had almost said an indispensable—paymaster, when Sir George Barlow's impecunious timidity had brought forth in the fulness of time its natural fruit, by emboldening the Nipalese to force us into a critical contest, and the Mahrattas to resume their plans for our expulsion. And in our own time all went well in Afghanistan, until the *baksheesh* began to fail. Then we quickly realized the hollowness and onerousness of the notable expedient of barricading our frontier against Russia with money-bags. And though we may not repeat the occupation, we may experience afresh the inconvenience of either paying or withholding *douceurs* in a country, where the daughters of the horseleech are so many.

The actual condition and prospects of Indian finance are not very encouraging. Whatever uncertainties may beset the subject, the following points seem pretty clear. We cannot reasonably count on any great surplus, even in quiet times. The revenue gives little hope of elasticity in proportion to our wants; and if it changes in amount, the change will too probably be for the worse. The income-tax is (we may presume) a condemned precedent. The import duties on British goods provoke much dissatisfaction in Manchester and elsewhere; and the increasing difficulty of finding other markets is not likely to abate that dissatisfaction. There is a steady set of public opinion at home against the opium trade; and interference with that trade would affect unfavourably the revenue derived from the opium monopoly. The extraordinary expenditure on public works tends more surely to increase the debt than to become promptly remunerative. And though the progress of education and other causes may gradually raise the standard of living among the lower classes, and discourage much idle outlay; and native ingenuity and enterprise, under English guidance, may make more available the teeming natural resources of the country; several causes render it far more difficult than at home for the State to appropriate its fair share of the advantages thus accruing to individuals. And the progress in this direction must be slow, while public needs are apt to become suddenly and vastly importunate. The Indian debt is already large; and our very effort to rule well, and to recognize the claims suggested by our more sensitive ideas of social obligation in the present day, can hardly fail to swell it still further. To take a single, but a colossal instance. Thrice, within little more than a decade, has famine assailed the land; and each time there has been a more imperious demand to spare no expense in mitigating or preventing, as far as possible, the sufferings thereby caused to the helpless and unthrifty *ryots*. And though a humane and Christian Government could not do otherwise, is there no reason to fear, that both the preservation of so many who must otherwise have perished, and the experience of our conduct as a *Deus ex machinâ* to them in their extremity, may tend to increase the successive demands on our benevolence, and the consequent burdens on our Indian exchequer? If *their* habits and institutions disincline them to adopt the "preventive checks to population," and *our* charitable contributions, medical skill, sanitary arrangements, pacific policy, and prohibition of infanticide and other conventionally approved forms of murder, arrest the progress of the "positive" ones; is the consequent rapid increase of a population averse to emigrate, and more inclined to continue feckless and impoverished than to rise at all rapidly in the scale of intelligence and prudence, likely to help us to keep the debt within moderate or even manageable bounds?

But it may be thought that, in a case of emergency, there are two reserve funds, upon which the Indian exchequer might, for the time at least, be able to draw—the Imperial treasury, or rather credit, and the voluntary subvention of the large class of natives who have amassed great wealth under the ægis of our protection. Neither of these sources, we fear, promises substantial aid in such a case. The rich native is often very liberal of his money; and the more so, because there is not among his people the same regard to primogeniture, and the founding of a family, that operates so strongly with us in the case of a *novus homo*. And though this, like other native sentiments, is probably in course of change, hereditary English distinctions, such as a baronetcy, suggesting an approach, in the disposal of property, to the English method, yet large donations for public objects by wealthy natives will probably continue to form a distinctive feature of Indian society. *Quasi*-patriotic contributions for the succour of the endangered government, which guarantees the security of life and property, might perhaps be coaxed or squeezed out of those who could really be convinced in time, not only that the public danger, but also their own ruin, was imminent. But there is much difference between defraying the cost of a monument that shall perpetuate the liberality and public spirit of the founder, and sinking money in the indiscriminate gulf of war-expenditure. The native, moreover, knows too well that his country has been, and is being, very heavily mulcted for the purpose of maintaining public tranquillity. He considers that he has a prescriptive right to that security, which the English Government is bound to afford "for value received." And he would not probably be very ready to open his purse to meet the extraordinary demands of a polity, whose only plea for existence in his eyes is its success, and which he would be inclined to consider had already broken faith with him, and could not fairly expect him (so to speak) to throw good money after bad. Again, we have so often been in great danger, that he would be slow to believe, and probably would not believe until too late, that the peril was so extreme as it was represented to be; while the very representation would be not only a confession of weakness, a humiliating *argumentum ad misericordiam*, but a fruitful cause of further weakness and decline—ruinous alike to our military reputation and commercial credit. And while such contributions as could be thus obtained would go but a little way towards meeting the expenses of such a war as we have supposed, the class of rich natives would suffer much by the destruction of property that it would involve. Would not many of them also be strongly inclined to "hedge," and make friends betimes of our enemies, that they might not lose all if we were overthrown? Thus we should suffer doubly: we should get less, and our foes more. Other difficulties might be raised; but perhaps enough has been said to show how little confidence can be placed in such a device for averting the evil day.

The proposal to strain the Imperial credit for the salvation of our Indian Empire is not likely to find much favour in England at any time. And at such a time as I have described, it would not only be most unpopular, but most dangerous. Burdened as we already are with so enormous a national debt, taxed so heavily to pay the interest of that debt, threatened with a continuance of the decline of our commercial and manufacturing prosperity, alive to the lavish cost of *la grande guerre* at the present day, spending as we feel obliged to do immense sums on experimental armaments and provisional munitions of war, which are promptly superseded by others equally costly, accustomed to a style of living which has a constant tendency to become more expensive;—we should find the stress of a great European war sufficiently perplexing in itself; and an attempt to add to all these sources of embarrassment a large subvention for India, and to pledge us to an indefinite outlay for such a contest there as the one in question, would be the surest way of producing formidable discontent and disturbance at home, and thus multiplying our political and military difficulties, and endangering our national credit, not to say the very existence of the Empire. Thus this resource seems quite unavailable.

What then is the conclusion of the whole matter? We have, it would appear, too good cause for grave anxiety, but none for panic fear. Though many of the unfavourable circumstances which have been noticed are undeniable, some of them are remediable; others have always existed, and our triumph over them hitherto may inspire us with confidence that they are in practice less formidable than they appear on paper; and it will be obvious that the state of things in which their combined action would be likely to prove so dangerous may never take place; though it is not the less allowable, even desirable, calmly to forecast such a possible combination. To do so may better enable us to see our way to conclusions of practical importance.

If we intend to keep India—and such is our present and firm determination—we should be very careful not to act, speak, think, or feel in such a manner as to increase the difficulty of administering its affairs, or prepare the way for a dangerous crisis. On the one hand, to ignore it systematically, as far as possible, which most people do; to acquiesce, if not almost to glory, in ignorance of its history, geography, political and social condition; and to excuse such ignorance on the pretext of want of leisure, while time is readily found for much less interesting and much more frivolous studies, is not only discreditable, but it is the abundant source of much of that prejudice, arrogance, and misconduct on the part of the ruling race in India, which contribute seriously to our insecurity. On the other hand, generous and well-meant, but rash and inapposite statements on the part of those who either habitually or occasionally do interest themselves in the natives and our government of them, are very mischievous, in so far as they foster hopes which we have no serious intention of fulfilling, and give currency to grievances which, in the first instance mainly of English conception and manufacture, may be readily adopted and exaggerated by ambitious and disaffected persons in the East, and become efficient instruments of disloyalty and disturbance.

Again, if what has been said is in the main correct, it will be clear that British interests, and the security of our Indian Empire, are little likely to be furthered, but very certain to be endangered, by the very process which is too often recommended for their vindication. Whatever our dangers in Asia may be, we may best hope to avoid them so long as we continue at peace in Europe. And so long as the seaboard of India is in our hands, and our nautical communications are secure, "out-posts of India," in the shape of new territories on the intervening mainland, would seem to be immaterial; while the additional demands which the necessity of defending them would make on our small available soldier class must *pro tanto* weaken our military position in India. But to plunge into an extensive and desperate European contest, in order to secure in the scramble such intervening territories, would surely be doubly unwise, as tending to precipitate the possible crisis which is most to be deprecated, and as risking so much to gain—not strength in the end, but harm and loss.

Once more. The policy of annexation has been renounced: indeed steps have been taken in the opposite direction, to the great satisfaction of the natives. The Oude Terai has been ceded to Nipal, in acknowledgment of assistance rendered to us during the Sepoy war. Many *sunnuds* have been granted on similar grounds to chiefs in and around the scene of disturbance. Mysore has been, so to speak, disgorged, when half-devoured by the Paramount Power. Though the Guikwar has been deposed, his dominions have been transferred to a kinsman. Rajputana and other countries have assumed a tolerably permanent form of Indo-Britannic incorporation as non-regulation provinces, and still exhibit much of their primitive aspect under *legati* of the Viceroy. The progress of Travancore while administered by Sir Madhava Rao, of the Nizam's territories under Sir Salar Jung, and of Sindia's State under Sir Dinkur Rao, is the best justification of our abrupt *volte-face* since the Mutiny; and together with other facts may point to a solution of some of our most serious difficulties, which, however distasteful and visionary it may appear now, may one day turn out to be expedient if not palatable.

However frequently and confidently it may be asserted, that lust of conquest and personal ambition were the creative causes of our Indian Empire; whatever crimes may have been committed in early days; how indefensible soever may have been such acts as led to the conquest of Sinde; however prevalent, may have been the passion, however inadequate the pretexts, for annexation under Dalhousie; the fact remains, that from Clive's time to the close of Lord Hastings' administration we fought, conquered, and acquired territory principally in self-defence. The French, Suraja Dowlah, Tippoo, and the Mahrattas successively committed us to strife, in which we had no option but to conquer, or to be despised for our timidity, discredited in native eyes, combined against, and driven out of the country. As traders, the Company sincerely disliked, dreaded, and condemned warfare. But as rulers, the wiser and more far-sighted Governors-General felt constrained to fight; and those who refused to admit the obligation only imposed it the more strictly on their successors. And for this there were, at the time, special reasons. Dupleix's policy was essentially aggressive and anti-English. Suraja Dowlah's cupidity, pride, cruelty, and faithlessness left us no option in Bengal; though the completion of our conquest there was due immediately to most scandalous misconduct and abuse of superior power on our part. With Tippoo our quarrel was as inevitable and irreconcilable as that of the Romans with Hannibal. And though our early wars with the Mahrattas, in Warren Hastings' time, may be justly condemned as the result of self-interested and rash intervention in the domestic disputes of that people, our great conquests from them were not made then, but in the later campaigns, which the Duke of Wellington as well as his brother Marquis Wellesley considered to be defensive and quite unavoidable. The same may be said of the Marquis of Hastings' final struggle with the same people, of his war with the Goorkhas, and in our day of the wars with the Sikhs.

But not only were we provoked to fight, and thus compelled to conquer, on particular occasions, but the general state of the country, which on the decline of the Mogul Empire became the prey of ambitious and lawless adventurers, and the universal hunting-ground of the Mahratta marauders, made it impossible for Englishmen, being what they were, to endure such a state of things, so offensive to their better nature, so provocative of their combative temper, and their characteristic unwillingness to go to the wall—or be pushed into the sea. *Venimus, vidimus, vicimus.* We dominated the elements of confusion, and appeased the angry storm. We disarmed the combatants, and enforced the *Pax Britannica.* But in so doing we were further and further entangled in the interior; and while some dreaded the consequences of our advance, others thought it a pity that we should not complete a process which seemed so beneficial in its operation on native India, and which promised such advantages to ourselves. Thus we were beguiled into indefinite annexation. And what the sword had begun, the pen continued, until we were suddenly awakened *en sursaut* to the formidable issues of our summary proceedings. Then we sang a loud palinode, which at least must prove that the English Government is open to conviction, and may yet be brought to see the desirableness of a further departure from principles once assumed as axioms in determining our relations to the people and States of India.

We cannot abandon the country if we would. But if our difficulties there should increase and become so obviously menacing as to incline us to seek some remedy short of that desperate measure, is there no middle course which the very facts of the case may suggest to us?

Consider the original object of our connection with the country, our constant character as an essentially nautical people, our immediate ownership of almost the whole of the coast regions and control of the rest, our command of the great rivers Indus, Jumna, and Ganges, and the comparative antiquity of our rule in the most fertile provinces, as Bengal, Behar, and Tanjore. Consider also that in the year 1800 General J. Stuart, in a remarkable paper (which will be found in the Wellesley Despatches), strongly recommended that we should confine ourselves as much as possible to the coast and its neighbourhood; that internal dangers prevented this at the time, and immersed us in the interior; that we did our work there vigorously, conquered our rivals, repressed anarchy, and annexed territory;—but that, on the other hand, we have preserved, in some cases aggrandized, and even reconstructed native States, which still occupy a considerable part of the interior. And we have done more than this. Under the shadow of our power, those States have become venerable, peaceable, progressive. They have produced not only highly-educated men, but able and high-minded statesmen, capable of appreciating many of our better political principles, of administering their masters' territories in an enlightened manner, and of preferring the gainful rivalry of civil improvement to the precarious advantages of aggressive warfare. That the people of India are adapted for representative government, after our model, it is hard indeed to believe. But that the Princes of India, aided by wise native Dewans, delivered by us from the bad habit of constantly fighting and preying on each other, and formed by us on a more peaceful model, may become equal to a moderate amount of rational self-government and mutual forbearance, does not seem a very wild vision of the future.

If so, might it not be possible, some day, for us to escape from many of our difficulties by a friendly arrangement with these native States; by which, as their fitness for self-government became more decided, and other circumstances more propitious, we should withdraw gradually from the great central plateau of the Peninsula; easing our finances by disposing to the native Princes of territories on that upland which they would covet, and we could well afford to abandon; retaining, by the convenient fiction of the imperial title, a general suzerainty over them, and a reasonable tribute in lieu of what we conceded (a tribute which they could better afford to pay, when relieved of the enormous cost of the double military establishment which several of them maintain, on our behalf and on their own); retaining also the coast districts, the great river areas of Hindostan Proper, and the northern regions, and thus commanding the same external frontiers as at present, and the resources of some of the most productive parts of the country as well as the harbours, and the facilities for foreign commerce and internal land and water traffic along the valleys of the Ganges, the Jumna, and the Indus?

Thus our responsibilities would be lessened: we should no longer vex the souls of the natives by our visible and invidious predominance everywhere: our influence would be felt more for good and less for evil, in proportion as it was more unobtrusive, though not less available in the last resort; and on the other hand, we might strengthen the hands of the native rulers by showing ourselves less jealous of their employing Europeans, when they chose to do so, on their own account, and in their own interest.

We need hardly fear, in such a state of things, any general combination against us; for there would be less motive for it than now; and we could avert it by diplomacy, by the fear of our arms, or if necessary by actual war; and no single State could withstand us in the first instance. And we should have ample warning if any such State threatened to become dangerously predominant; and the rest would have a common interest in combining with us to prevent betimes such a disturbance of the balance of power in the interior.

The military objection, that we should be reduced to depend for our defence on a vast extent of exterior lines, would be less serious, considering how rapid are modern communications by sea and land, and how speedily we could concentrate our forces on any threatened point, while fortresses, depôts, &c., could be established *en permanence* all along our line; also how much more vulnerable such improved native States would be, than the rude and wasted territories in which we made war above the Ghats of old.

The many other objections to such a process of retrogression it will be time to discuss, when a political dream, which is far enough from any prospect of speedy fulfilment, shall find favour with any influential class of politicians. But as a conceivable choice of evils, at least, its suggestion here may perhaps be condoned.

Meanwhile, a more pressing question demands solution. Is it possible to strengthen our hold over the country, by engaging in the service of Government, both civil and military, the higher classes of natives? To this effect some well-considered suggestions have been made by Colonel George Chesney, in his important and most instructive volume on "Indian Polity;" a volume which, in conclusion, we strongly commend to the attention of English statesmen, and especially of Mr. John Bright.

SIDNEY JAMES OWEN.

# FOREST AND FIELD MYTHS.

ONCE upon a time,—says a tale widely spread in Asia,—four travellers spent a night in a forest, and agreed that one of them should keep watch by turns while the others slept. The first watcher was a carpenter. By way of passing the time, he took his axe, and out of the stem of a tree lying prostrate hard by, fashioned the form of a woman, shapely in figure and comely in face. Then he woke one of his comrades, and lay down to rest. The second watcher was a tailor. And when he saw the wooden woman lying bare on the ground, he produced his work-basket and bundle of stuffs, and clothed her handsomely from head to foot. Then he too resumed his slumber, after having aroused the third of the party, who was a jeweller. And the jeweller was struck by the sight of the fair and well-dressed female form leaning against a neighbouring tree, and he opened his caskets, and decked her with rings, and necklaces, and bracelets. Then he called the last of the party, who was a holy man, strong in prayer and incantation, and went to sleep. And when the fourth watcher saw the wooden woman, so well dressed and decked, he set to work, and by spells and prayers turned her wood into flesh and blood, and inspired her with life. Just then his three companions awoke, and gazed with wonder and admiration at the lovely creature who stood before them. Simultaneously, each of the four travellers claimed her as his wife; the carpenter because he had framed her, the tailor because he had dressed her, the jeweller because he had adorned her, and the holy man because he had [illegible] fierce dispute arose. The authorities of the [illegible] were in vain appealed to; the problem, as to w[illegible] most claim to the hand of the disputed bride [illegible] to solve. At last it was resolved

court. The claimants, the judges, and the audience, all went out to the cemetery, and there prayed for a decision from on high. While the prayer went up, the woman leant against a tree. Suddenly the tree opened, and the woman entered it, and was seen no more. As she disappeared, a voice from on high was heard saying, "To its origin shall every created thing return."*

The mythological core of this story is the idea that human and tree life may be connected. The rest of it has been supplied by teachers who wished to inculcate the doctrine that all things return to their first elements, and narrators desirous of framing one of the numerous stories involving a problem or puzzle capable of various solutions. The leading idea has been better preserved in the following modern-Greek folk-tale.

There was once a childless wife, who used to lament saying, "If only I had a child, were it but a laurel berry!" And heaven sent her a golden laurel berry, but its value was not recognized, and it was thrown away. From it sprang a laurel-tree which gleamed with golden twigs. At it a prince, while following the chase, wondered greatly. And determining to return to it, he ordered his cook to prepare a dinner for him beneath its shade. He was obeyed. But during the temporary absence of the cook, the tree opened, and forth came a fair maiden, who strewed a handful of salt over the viands, and then returned into the tree, which immediately closed upon her. The prince returned and scolded the cook for oversalting the dinner. The cook declared his innocence, but in vain. The next day, just the same occurred. So on the third day the prince kept watch. The tree opened, and the maiden came forth. But before she could return into the tree, the prince caught hold of her and carried her off. After a time she escaped from him, ran back to the tree, and called upon it to open. But it remained shut. So she had to return to the prince. And after a while he deserted her. It was not till after long wandering that she found him again, and became his royal consort.†

Hahn thinks this story is founded on the Hellenic belief in **Dryads**; but it belongs to an earlier mythological family than the Hellenic, though the Dryad and the Laurel-maiden are undoubtedly kinswomen. Long before the Dryads and Oreads had received from the sculpturesque Greek mind their perfection of human form and face, trees were credited with woman-like inhabitants capable of doing good and ill, and with powers of their own, apart from those possessed by their supernatural tenants, of banning and blessing. Therefore was it that they were worshipped, and that recourse was had to them for

* For the Indian originals of the story, see Benfey's Pantchatantra, i. 489; for the variant, the Tuti-Nameh or Parrot-Book; and for a third, in which various incidents are given, the Turkish version of the Tuti-Nameh. The story [illegible] to have become domesticated in Western Europe.

† Cf. Basile's Pentamerone, No. 23; Schott's Walachische Märchen,

the strengthening of certain rites. Similar ideas and practices still prevail in Asia; survivals of them may yet be found in Europe. To this day, for instance, one of the features of a Russian marriage is the thrice-repeated walk of the bride and bridegroom around a part of the church. This ceremony is accounted for by reasons in accordance with Christian ideas, but in reality it seems to be connected with the Indian marriage ceremony of making the bride and bridegroom walk several times round a tree, a rite of which the following story gives a most remarkable form:—

A certain thief, having been caught, was impaled. After dark, a woman, who had gone out to fetch water, happened to pass by his place of torture, and accidentally touched his foot, thereby giving him great pain. Grieved thereat, she asked if she could make up for her awkwardness by rendering him any service. "You can," he replied. "It is impossible for me to die comfortably while I am unmarried. You have an unmarried daughter. Marry her to me, and I will pay handsomely for the temporary accommodation." So she went swiftly home, and brought her daughter, and married her to the dying thief —by making her walk four times round the stake on which he was impaled.*

I have told these three tales, chiefly because they are among the few important tree stories which I have not found quoted in the exhaustive work on "Ancient Cults of Forest and Field,"† recently published by one of the most painstaking and judicious of living comparative mythologists, Dr. Wilhelm Mannhardt of Dantzic. To it may be safely referred all serious students of the subjects on which it throws a copious and steady light. It is a work which no mythologist's library should be without. But as the two volumes comprise more than a thousand pages of stiff reading, they are not likely (although provided, according to Dr. Mannhardt's most laudable custom, with copious indexes) to become familiar to the general reader. It may be worth while, therefore, to give a summary of their contents, a rapid survey of the great field of thought over which they range. But first a few words about the author.

As a child (he tells us in a charming sketch of his intellectual life, prefixed to the second volume of the present work), long confinement to a couch gave him the leisure of reading such works as introduced him to the land of classic fable and "the fair humanities of old religion." Later on in healthier boyhood, during long hours spent in the greenwood or by the resounding shore, he became rapt in the study of Milton, Ossian, and the Northern Sagas and Eddas. Then came the eager perusal of Grimm's "German Mythology," and the fate of his

* Baitál Pachísí, No. 18.

† Wald-und Feldkulte, 2 vols. Berlin, 1875-77 (Gebrüder Bornträger). Ed. Eggers. The volumes are published separately. Vol. i. is [illegible] Der Baumkultus," &c., and vol. ii., "Antike Wald-und Feldkulte, aus Nordeuro[illegible] [illegible]

[illegible] Becoming in 1851 a student in the University of [illegible] himself to the study of mythology. The best-known [illegible] his "Germanic Myths," a most valuable work, [illegible] that many of its doctrines are erroneous. [illegible] an enthusiastic disciple of the "storm-myth" [illegible] Schwartz as he then was. Neither does he alto-[illegible] the "solar-myth" school; having been led, by long [illegible] the wise conclusion that it is useless to attempt to [illegible] "Key to all the Mythologies." After filling for some [illegible] chair at Berlin, he was compelled, by a return of [illegible] to give up lecturing, and to retire to the secluded post of [illegible] at Dantzic. Thence he has followed with unchanging [illegible] discoveries in Assyrian and Accadian mythology, which [illegible] light upon the early stages of Hellenic religious [illegible]ht. At the same time, his residence on the shores of the [illegible] him to study, under exceptionally advantageous [illegible] the remains of ancient Lettish and Lithuanian mytho-[illegible]—a fact to which some of the most interesting portions of his [illegible] bear witness, as well as the valuable but little-known [illegible] long ago published on "The Lettish Sun-myth." In [illegible] to Holland, Sweden, and the Baltic Provinces of Russia, he [illegible] information; and during the wars with Denmark, [illegible] France, he had frequent opportunities of talking with [illegible]ers successively sent from many parts of Europe to Dantzic; and [illegible] from them many a curious custom, legend, or song. Of [illegible]ears his studies have chiefly been directed to all that illustrates [illegible] faiths in spirits connected with the growth of herbs, corn, [illegible]ees. Some time ago he published, as specimens of his work, a [illegible]ook on the "Corn-Wolf," and another on "Corn-Demons."* But [illegible]were received by "a quite deathlike silence" on the part of the [illegible] press—merely a few kindly words from abroad, and the sym-[illegible] shown by the Universities of Berlin and Vienna, encouraged [illegible] proceed. Even the first volume of the present work was [illegible] the same discouraging manner in Prussia. Let us trust [illegible]he reception of the completed work may be one more in [illegible] with its great merits.

[illegible] the earliest times of which we know anything, men have been [illegible]d to find resemblances between human and tree life. In many [illegible] these are closely connected, as in the Iranian account of [illegible] human pair grew up as a single tree, the fingers or twigs [illegible] folded over the other's ears, till the time came when they [illegible], and infused by Ahuramazda with distinct human [illegible] the inhabitants of almost every land, trees were supposed

* [illegible] Korndämonen. The latter word sounds better than its English [illegible] to misapprehension.

to be sentient beings, and survivals of that belief linger e[illegible] present day. Thus in some places trees are informed wh[illegible] owner dies, in others woodcutters beg a sound tree's pardo[illegible] they fell it. Not only did and does a belief prevail that spir[illegible] between the tree-stem and its bark, and that therefore the b[illegible] well as the felling of a tree may dislodge demons capable [illegible] mischief, but there was a widely spread belief that trees had [illegible] their own: that either a demon lived within the stem, or tha[illegible] souls, after death, might take up their residence within it. [illegible] of a tree, also, might be linked with that of a man, and t[illegible] health and fortunes might be affected by an action done to [illegible] Thus the tremulousness of a shrew-ash might be connecte[illegible] man's ague; and the disease might be cured by immuring [illegible] shrew-mouse in the tree, which was then supposed to take [illegible] communicated malady; and thus, according to a widel[illegible] German belief, if an invalid is passed through a split tree, [illegible] then bound up, the man and the tree enter into sympathetic [illegible] with each other. If the tree flourishes, so will the man; if it [illegible] he will die. But if he dies while the tree lives on, his soul wi[illegible] it. If the tree, says Rugen tradition, is afterwards cut down [illegible] for ship-building, the dead man's ghost becomes the haunting [illegible] of the ship. Under these circumstances it is not wonderful t[illegible] should sometimes bleed when wounded. Thus, on one occasi[illegible] a musician cut a piece of wood from a tree, into which a girl [illegible] metamorphosed by her angry mother, blood flowed from the [illegible] And when he had shaped it into a fiddle bow, and played wit[illegible] his fiddle before her mother, such a sad wail made itself he[illegible] the mother repented of her hasty deed. As trees are often [illegible] of, and are connected with, a human being's life and fortu[illegible] were often introduced into birth and marriage feasts. In [illegible] many families took their names from their sacred and thus a[illegible] trees. The three families of Linnæus (or Linné), Linde[illegible] Tiliander were all called after the same tree, an ancient linde[illegible] which grew at Jonsboda Lindergård. When the Lindelius fa[illegible] out, one of the old lime's chief boughs withered; after t[illegible] of the daughter of the great Linnæus, the second main bo[illegible] leaves no more; and when the last of the Tiliander family [illegible] the tree's active life came to an end, though the dead [illegible] and is highly honoured.*

Sometimes travellers, when starting on a journey [illegible] ence with that of a tree, just as Satu, [illegible] Egyptian story of the Two Brothers, left [illegible] acacia. For trees were often suppo[illegible] influence on human life. As Vård[illegible]

* Dr. Mannhardt quotes, as his authorities [illegible] Vàrend, i. 144; Passarge, Schweden, p. 317. [illegible]

...spirit or genius, who led and guarded the men over ...watch. In the Sailors' Quarter of Copenhagen, ...H. Steffens, each house has its protecting elder-tree, ...ly guarded and watched; and similar trees have for ...connected with Lettish homes. In one Livonian ...certain Pastor Carlbom is said to have hewn down eighty ...dian trees in a single fortnight of the year 1836. It was a tree ...d which a poor Tyrolese peasant (a story tells) reverenced so ...t he refused to sell it. At length there came a storm which ...own; and amidst its roots its reverent proprietor found a rich ...

Similar to the Watch-tree was also the Boträ, or Abode... holy tree honoured by sacrifices, and tenanted by elves. ...s these are tiny beings, whose linen may be seen, in fine ...hanging out on the branches to dry. Sometimes they are ...dinary human dimensions. One of the latter kind, says a ...ry, was a nymph who appeared by day among men, but ...ent back to her willow by night. She married a mortal, ...children, and lived happily with him, till at length he cut ...willow-tree; that moment his wife died. Out of the willow ...a cradle which had the power of instantly lulling to sleep ...she had left behind her; and when the babe became a child, ...to hold converse with its dead mother by means of a pipe, ...he twigs growing on the stump which once had been that ...ome.

...he idea that trees had their peculiar spirits seems to have ..., Mannhardt thinks, a belief in wood-spirits in general. Each ...wood or forest was supposed to have its own denizens, some...en of hue and mossy of hide, at other times capable of ...uster as mortal men and women. These female spirits were ...pposed to lead joyous lives, but some of them were liable to ... and slain by the terrible Wild Huntsman who, on stormy ...ght be heard tearing at full gallop through the forest. A ...neralization may have led to the belief in a genius of tree-... f all vegetable life; a genius who was closely connected ...th and fertility, and to whom, therefore, reverence was to ...specially at the times when foliage and flowers and fruits are ...essive to the mind of man. With those seasons are con... surviving rites of time-honoured descent. In many of ... of vegetation is symbolized under the form of a ... the spring-time, when the plant world has awakened ... sleep, the May-tree, the head of the family to ... belongs, is sought for in the forest all over ...ed away in triumph, and, decked with ribbons ...lemnly planted on the village green or beside ...th the summer heats come other feasts in ...part, and when autumn gilds the fields, the last harvest waggon is adorned with a tree gaily decked and religiously honoured. When a house is finished, a similar tree is placed upon the roof; when a wedding takes place, another is set up before the door of the newly married couple. And when the short winter day begins to lengthen, the Christmas tree plays its cheery part,—a tree which, Dr. Mannhardt observes, has now become an especially German institution, and follows German emigrants over land and sea to the New World, but which, at the beginning of the present century, was known but to, comparatively speaking, few Germans; just as it remained till about 1830 all but unknown to Hungary, and was unfamiliar later still to England and France, till its observance received an impulse in those countries from the loving hands of Prince Albert and the Duchess Helen of Orleans. Its origin is plainly heathenish, though it has been claimed for the Christian Church, on the ground that the 24th of December is consecrated to Adam and Eve; and a well-known legend relates how Adam brought from Paradise a fruit or slip from the Tree of Knowledge, from which eventually sprang the tree from which the Cross was made; while another states that a branch from the Tree of Life was planted above Adam's grave, and became the tree from which Christ plucked the fruits of Redemption.

But it was not only under the forms of trees or plants that the human mind symbolized the Spirit of Growth or Vegetation, the genius of spring-tide and harvest-tide. A natural tendency towards imagining that supernatural beings are of like forms to our own led to such spirits being represented under human shapes. Of these many still survive, though many others have perished. Sometimes these figures were single; sometimes they went in pairs. Of the single figures, the best known to ourselves is the Jack-in-the-Green—our chief representative of the numerous beings who, in various lands, when spring-tide comes, are robed in dresses made of herbs and boughs. Of the coupled symbols of this kind, the most familiar to English minds, not long ago, were the King and Queen of the May. For in Old England the May-King played a prominent part in May Revels, though now we are generally accustomed to think only of the May-Queen. But in foreign countries there still exist all sorts of May-Kings and May-Counts, and the *Mairitt* is still kept up in Germany, though among ourselves the good old English custom of "going a Maying" has fallen into disrepute, and has been handed over to chimney-sweeps, or, still worse, to negro minstrels.* With these May-Ridings, and with the somewhat similar Midsummer Fire-festivals, are connected a number of customs. Most remarkable among them is that of carrying out to the forest a figure made of wood, straw, or some other like material, which is solemnly destroyed either by water or b [illegible] Similar puppets [illegible] drowned or burnt at various seasons [illegible] That [illegible]

* The blackening of faces at May-tide was [illegible] story of the aristocratic young sweep.

[illegible] least in Slavonic lands, to be a personi-[illegible] But in that which is burnt at midsummer, [illegible] to see an image of the summer vegetation, [illegible] blazing sun.. The flinging of a puppet into water [illegible] with rain-producing spells, especially as in ught the peasants in many Slavonic lands are in the [illegible] through their villages a youth or girl robed nd foliage, who is afterwards solemnly stripped and [illegible] water.

[illegible] most remarkable features of this rite of destroying a [illegible] puppet—a rite to which a historical air has been us by our burning of Guy Fawkes, a religious meaning outhern Catholics by their hanging of Judas Iscariot—are iich they retain in some lands of an ancient custom of ce. To this day in remote districts, especially in Russia, fruits and flowers destroyed along with the figure which n effigy of either the genius or the enemy of vegetation, [illegible]tures also are put to death. Thus, in olden days, the [illegible] diverted by the screams of a score of cats, which were th in the Midsummer St. John's fire on the Place de thus, at the present day, the inhabitants of Luchon in the [illegible]act great delight from the wrigglings of the snakes which, Eve, they throw into a fire which is lighted under the he clergy.* For the clergy have, in many lands, given to what is really an old heathenish custom, connected ent Baal or Moloch fires of Asia, the Palilia fires of the and the *Not-feuer* or plague-staying Need-fire of our Keltic ancestors. There seems to be good reason for at into these fires, in very ancient times, human beings ig. In some places the straw-man, or other figure repre-nan being of ordinary size, was replaced by a gigantic form. Such a figure as this, six yards high, made of sed to be burnt every July in the Rue des Ours at Paris, been led in procession through the whole city. This h lasted till 1743, was popularly supposed to date back [illegible] of a blasphemous soldier on the same spot in 1418. [illegible] version of history.† Just as figures of the Guy Fawkes [illegible] burnt in lands which never heard of a Gunpowder [illegible] similar figures to "The Giant of the Rue des Ours" [illegible] the flames in other places. Thus in Brie (Isle de [illegible] *d'osier* is said to be burnt every 23rd of June. [illegible] to compare this osier-twig figure with that in [illegible] are said to have burnt human beings to

[illegible] Mannhardt (whom nothing seems to escape) from the

[illegible] [illegible]ical explanation of a custom based on an anthropo-

death. According to the testimony of Cæsar, Strabo, and the Druids used to construct huge figures of twigs, which with human beings, and then consumed with fire. Tl murderers were preferred as sacrifices, but if there were r of them forthcoming, innocent persons also had to suffe gigantic figures, *contexta viminibus*, seem very like the osier of the Rue des Ours and his monstrous kin. And there ap good reason for supposing that the human sacrifices thus of the Britons were intended to accompany some such rites as which the inhabitants of a great part of Europe still hail th spring or midsummer, or attempt to ward off pestilence fields and homes. Within the last few years, at least o peasant has been known to sacrifice a poor relation in t staying an epidemic.

More pleasant than these sacrificial associations are t springing from the idea of a bridal pair as a representa genius of fertility. From it arose the custom of "May- still prevalent in many parts of Europe. There is an a widely-spread prejudice against marrying in May, but the in question are only fictitious and temporary alliances. In hc supposed union of the imaginary male and female repres the fertilizing powers of nature, it was, and in many parts c still is, the custom for village lads and lasses to be sportivel to each other at May-time for a year. The ceremony often beside a bonfire lighted for the purpose. The girls thus t bound are known as their lads' May-wives or *Maifraue* England might similar couples be linked for a year as Va Germany as Liebchen or Vielliebchen, in France as Pl Philippine.*

With all these spring and midsummer festivals in hor awakening, after his winter sleep, of the Genius of Veg closely linked those which take place in the autumn, when is gathered in. Nearly allied to the Tree-spirits, according t ideas, were the Corn-spirits which haunted and protected or yellow fields. But by the popular fancy they were often under the form of wolves or of "buck-men," goat-legge similar to the classic Satyrs. When the wind bows the lo waving grain, German peasants still say, "The Grass-wolf Corn-wolf is abroad;" in many places the last sheaf of rye i as a shelter for the *Roggenwulf* or Rye-wolf during the wi and in many a summer or autumn festive rite that being is r by a rustic, who assumes a wolf-like appearance. The however, was often symbolized under a human form. "Cor pass over German fields when the grain waves; a "Kirub

* Valentine has nothing to do, etymologically, with St. Valen[illegible] Galantin, a Norman word for a lover. Philippine is a corruption [illegible]

was supposed to dwell in the ears of English wheat; and by Russian eyes Rye-spirits are often seen, tall as the highest corn before harvest-time, short as the cut stems afterwards. Many a memory of the Corn-spirit is still preserved in the ceremonies of the harvest-home. All over Europe honour is shown to him in the reception of the last wain-load from a field, in the last sheaf left out in his behalf amid the deserted stubble.

Thus far does Dr. Mannhardt carry his readers in his first volume. His chief aim in it is to show how there seem to have arisen, in the minds of primitive men, a series of ideas respecting the fertilizing and fruit-bearing powers of nature. At first, he thinks, arose the belief that each tree or plant possesses spiritual as well as physical life, being tenanted either by semi-divine spirits or by the ghosts of the dead. Then came, he supposes, a generalization of this idea, according to which plants or trees collectively, the grassy meadow and the leafy wood, were credited with peculiar inhabitants. And from this a still higher generalization led to a belief in a genius of plant-life or forest-life, or, higher still, a genius of growth or fertility in general. This universal genius of growth was symbolized by a bush or tree, brought in triumph from the forest, gaily decked, and solemnly planted near the homestead or in the village: or by the effigy of a human being, or by a human being dressed in or adorned with foliage and flowers: or by a pair of similar human beings, male and female, who were at times supposed to be a wedded couple. And all these ideas, he clearly shows, prevailed as well in relation to the field as to the forest, especially to the life-supporting corn-field. His second volume is chiefly devoted to a comparison of old Greek and Roman ideas about the semi-divine inhabitants of the meadow and the grove with those prevalent among the inhabitants of the North of Europe, and of the ceremonies which in the North and South sprang out of them.

Very closely connected with the forest and field spirits of the ancient Teutons, Slavs, and Kelts, were the "wild folk" of classic lore. The tree-haunting Dryads of Hellenic times, as well as their successors, the Nereids of Modern Greece, were clearly cousins of the northern tree-nymphs. And near relations of the Teutonic and Slavonic Buck-men and Corn-demons must have been the Fawns and Satyrs of ancient days. The similarity between the legends relating to these spirits of the North and South is well illustrated by the following Tyrolese folk-tale. A peasant once hired a maid-servant of unusual strength and skill, under whose guidance his cattle prospered greatly. But after a time, as his family sat at dinner one day, they heard a voice from without cry, "Salome, come!" The maid sprang up, and disappeared. And with her seemed to go the prosperity of the house. Some years later, a butcher was passing through a neighbouring forest at midnight, when he heard a voice cry, "When thou comest to such and such a place, call out, 'Salomé is dead!'" Coming to the appointed place before daybreak, the butcher did as he had been bid. Then from the mountain recesses arose a cry of wailing and loud lament, and the butcher continued his journey full of vague alarm. Compare with this the well-known story which so greatly puzzled the Emperor Tiberius—who, whatever his failings may have been, at least was a genuine lover and investigator of the marvellous, though a little too much given to inquire, if Suetonius is to be trusted, what was the name of Hecuba's mother, what name Achilles bore among the maidens, and what songs the Sirens used to sing. As a ship was sailing from Greece to Italy, a voice from the shore hailed one of the passengers, and bade him call out when he came to a certain spot, "The great Pan is dead!" And when he had done so, a wailing cry, as of many voices, was heard resounding along the shore. Common to all Europe, also, was the idea that it was dangerous to work in the middle of the day, for that those who then laboured were liable to the wrath of some evil spirit; just as the Hellenic shepherd believed that Pan slept during the sultry noontide hour, and therefore refrained at that time from music which might awake and irritate that guardian of flocks.* So far as the field-spirits and wood-demons of Greece, Italy, and the barbaric North were concerned, there is a wealth of evidence to show that similar views of the forces of nature, as manifested in beneficial plant-growth and hostile storm-rage, produced all over Europe almost identical beliefs in supernatural inhabitants of meadow, cornfield, grove, and stream. Only the Centaurs offer a difficulty. Their horsy nature has never been quite satisfactorily explained; whether they be considered as kinsmen of the Vedic Gandharvas, or mere personifications of mountain cataracts, or as wild pre-Hellenic inhabitants of Pelion, or—from Dr. Mannhardt's point of view—as spirits of the hill and wood, descended either from Ixion, the whirlwind, or from trees, as Cheiron from a lime-tree, Pholos from an ash. Their equine nature, he thinks, must have been thrust upon them by some poet or painter, who too literally accepted a now-lost myth which compared them to horses or metaphorically bestowed upon them equine attributes. Russia seems to be the only land at any distance from Greece, we may observe, in which the Centaur has become naturalized in folk-lore. But his appearance there, under the name of Polkan,† is probably due to the Byzantine traditions which exercised for centuries so great an influence on early Russian thought and art.

Not only did similar ideas produce a similar mythological population in the woods and fields of Northern and Southern Europe, but they

* The herdsman's special friend, supposing his name not to be connected with [illegible] = all, nor to be derived from a root pu = to [illegible] to spring [illegible] guard, to pasture, &c., with which are con[illegible] pascere, pa-nis, &c.—[illegible]

[illegible] festivals and religious rites. Thus a ceremony [illegible] of Germany and the greater part of France, of [illegible] the last harvest with a gaily decorated tree or [illegible] received with all respect by the master, and planted [illegible] house, to remain there till the next harvest brings its [illegible] some rite of this sort seems to have prevailed all over [illegible] Europe. So in the autumnal harvest thanksgiving feast , it was customary to carry in sacred procession an olive- rapped in wool, called Eiresiōne, to the temple of Apollo, to leave it; and, in addition to this, a similar bough was placed beside the house-door of every Athenian who was [illegible] agriculture or fruit-culture, there to remain until replaced lar successor twelve months later.* The ceremonies with [illegible] Athenian counterpart, as Dr. Mannhardt considers it, of nic *Erntemai*, was attended to its destination, were singularly which still survive in Northern Europe as part of the rustic ome rite. In Athens, many of them were supposed to refer thical expedition of Theseus to Crete; but it was a common [illegible] olden time to combine the harvest thanksgiving with rites in commemoration of some historical or traditional e. Another interesting parallel is supplied by the spring- celebrated at Rome every March, and certain spring and estivals common to the Teutons and Slavs. To this day, in and Russia, as has already been stated, it is customary, either ly spring or at midsummer, to carry out in procession, to a e water flows, some type of the winter which has passed the spring which has reappeared, or the genius of growth ation, dead or slumbering, or brisk and full of life, and there to lave in the stream, or to fling into it from a bridge, the ck-in-the-Green, or the puppet made of straw or leafy or else (at the midsummer festivals) to pass them through next day immerse them in running water. At Rome, in [illegible] there existed twenty-four chapels, called *Argei* or *Argeorum* solemnly visited by the faithful on the 16th and 17th of And under the name of *Argei* were known the twenty-four [illegible] fashioned in human shape out of straw or rushes, and clothed [illegible], which, on the 15th of May, were carried in proces- [illegible] Sublicius, and from it were flung into the Tiber by [illegible]. An old tradition declared that, originally, human [illegible] flung into the stream as an offering to Saturnus [illegible] Dispater (Hades); but that, as time passed by, and [illegible], in place of the men more than sixty years [illegible] chosen for the purpose, were substituted types in [illegible] of *Quirites*, puppets made of straw or reeds. The

* [illegible] Scott, the Eiresiōne (*eiros* = wool) was a wool-bound *wreath*,

sacrifice was supposed to be of an expiatory nature, likely to keep off misfortune and pestilence from the city. It is possible, says Dr. Mannhardt, that at an early period the twenty-four Argei or puppets may have been carried in March to the chapels which bore the same name, and left there till the time came for their being carried away to the bridge, and thence flung into the river. At all events the puppets were no doubt closely connected with the chapels, as they seem to be also with the figures formed of or robed in foliage, which were, and still are, flung into Northern streams. In the same way, interesting parallels are supplied by Teutonic and Slavonic spring and summer festivals to the ancient rites commemorating the death of Adonis or Tammuz. In those ancient Asiatic customs, Dr. Mannhardt sees an embodiment of a pre-historic myth referring to the temporary death of the spring-tide vegetation. The spring itself, or the plant-life it vivifies, was personified as a comely youth, beloved by the goddess of fertility, and united with her during the spring. In the summer heats he leaves her and disappears, but lives on in the unseen world of the dead. He is represented by a figure which is supposed to be dead, and which is mourned over, and laved with or flung into water. At length comes the spring, and with it returns the godlike youth, who is received with joyous rites, his reunion with his divine spouse being typified by temporary unions entered into by their worshippers. So in the North of Europe, the Genius of Vegetation is still personified under the shape of a living *Laubmann*, or a Jack-in-the-Green, or a *Père-Mai*, and other figures of the same kind, or under the form of a leafy puppet, or a gaily-decked tree. And this is received in spring with a joyous greeting. But at midsummer the Russian peasant, with wailing cries such as attend a corpse, lays in a coffin a puppet, or flings into a stream a straw-figure, loudly lamenting it as one dead. But when the spring comes back, the typified Genius of Vegetation is again hailed with mirth and revel, and to the German "May-bridegroom" is given a "May-bride," and lads and lasses in many a European land enter into a kind of fictitious union, lasting for a year, as Valentines and Vielliebchen, and the like.

Lastly may be considered the fires which from time immemorial have blazed at midsummer. Just as the winter solstice has from the earliest times been honoured by what are now our Christmas revels, so has the summer solstice been for countless ages celebrated by its fires. The night which precedes St. John's or Midsummer Day is still rendered brilliant in many an European land by flames, through which spring, not only young people, but also men and women carrying their little ones in their arms. For the flames are supposed to possess a purifying, evil-averting influence. In like manner blazed of old the Phœnician fires in honour of Baal, and the Moloch-fires through which children were passed in order to secure them against evil influ- and the Purim fires into which Hama[illegible]

Babylonish demon of dearth having been confused by the Jews with their enemy Haman, just as some similar demon is now represented by a Judas Iscariot or a Guy Fawkes. In like manner do the women of modern Greece spring through a fire on Midsummer Eve, crying, "I leave my sins!" So in the early days of Rome, at the springtide festival of Palilia, when it was the custom, among other things, for men to spring through fires lighted by sparks obtained from flints: all these bonfires being closely connected also with the "need-fires," employed on special occasions to drive away evil spirits or avert plagues, fires in which even at the present day birds and beasts are frequently offered in sacrifice; just as in olden times human sacrifices were offered up, whether such criminals or unfortunates as Cæsar mentions were burnt alive in England, or other human beings were given to the flames, as Manetho asserts, in Egypt, their bodies being consumed, and their ashes scattered to the winds, during the dog-days in honour of Typhon. One interesting feature of some of these fire-feasts, was the running of the initiated barefoot over glowing coals. This was a feat annually performed in honour of the corn-goddess Feronia, at Soracte, by the men who called themselves *Hirpi* or wolves, and who were known as the *Hirpi Sorani*. In them Dr. Mannhardt is inclined to see a personification of the same idea as that which in the north of Europe has given rise to the belief in corn-wolves; a species of the corn-demon genus. With their barefoot performances he compares the similar feat performed every other harvest-tide by certain Brahmans for the edification of the Badagas in the South-Highlands of Mysore. A missionary relates how one of these Brahmans once came to him to ask for some salve for his feet, which had been burnt by the glowing ashes on which he had walked rather longer than was usual or prudent.

There is one feature of Dr. Mannhardt's work to which it is well to call special attention: the rich contribution, namely, which he has made to our knowledge of Lithuanian and Lettish mythology, superstitions, and folk-lore. But very little is known by us of those strange races, now slowly dying out, who in the north-east of Europe, in Prussia and Russia, feebly represent the once fierce and warlike inhabitants of the Grand Duchy of Lithuania, the land which so long clung to its heathenism; the land which for so many centuries, before and after its incorporation with Poland, was a constant source of danger to the growing power of the Grand Princes of Moscow, afterwards the Czars of Russia. Very few scholars are acquainted with the language spoken either by the Letts or by the Lithuanians, a language to which may almost be applied the expression so amusingly misapplied by a popular novelist in reference to Basque, that of its being a kind of "bastard Sanskrit." And still fewer know anything, [illegible] through the medium of Nesselmann's German translations, of [illegible] stores of songs and stories which exist in the memories of the

Lettish and Lithuanian people. In spite of what Dr. Mannhardt has already done, especially in his excellent monograph on "The Lettish Sun-myth," and of what has been done by Dr. W. Pierson and others, but few scholars are in a position to use the copious materials which have been recently laid up at Wilna and other Lithuanian cities. But now that he has placed upon record in his present work so much that is valuable of Lithuanian and Lettish evidence, there no longer exists any excuse for Western ignorance of the subject. All through the two volumes of the "Wald-und Feldkulte" are scattered numerous references to the customs, songs, and folk-tales of the Letts and Lithuanians, people whom Dr. Mannhardt, from his watch-tower at Dantzic, has had peculiar opportunities of observing. It will be sufficient at present, to call attention to a few of the most characteristic among their number. For this purpose may be selected the account given in the second volume of a Lithuanian harvest feast, and of a means of averting pestilence. The first is taken from the original MS. of the work (edited by Dr. W. Pierson in 1871) on Lithuanian tradition and folk-lore, compiled during the latter half of the seventeenth century, by Matthias Prätorius and other Lutheran clergymen in Prussian Lithuania, and completed but not published in 1703. In it Prätorius describes, among other things, the Lithuanian Samborios or Grain-Feast. In the early part of December, he says, when the peasants begin threshing their corn, each husbandman takes nine handfuls of every kind of seed-bearing plant which he cultivates—corn, beans, &c.—and divides each handful into three parts. He then collects the twenty-seven small sheaves thus made into one large heap, and, from part of the grain and other seeds threshed out of it, bakes a small loaf for each member of his household, mixes the rest with the other materials necessary, and therewith brews beer. The first draught of this beer is reserved for himself, his wife, and his children; the second for the rest of the household and any stranger who may, though uninvited, accidentally be present. When the beer is ready, the father of the family, at eventide, kneels down before the cask, and utters a prayer commencing with the words, "O fruit-bearing Earth,* let our rye and barley and all our grain bear fruit." Then he returns, beer-laden, to the room in which his wife and children await him, together with a cock and hen which lie pinioned on the floor. The father kneels down, holding in his hand the beer-can, and prays for a blessing on his farm and homestead. Then all lift up their hands and say, "O God, and thou, O Earth, we offer to thee this cock and hen; receive them as freely offered gifts." Then he kills the fowls with a wooden ladle, and hands them over to a maid to be plucked. The housewife then sends away the serv[illegible]

* *Zeminele*: in Russian *zemlya*. "Bless us, O Zeminele, bless our [illegible] woods and pastures too," runs a song, printed for the first time b[illegible] obtained it from a witness who heard it sung by a peasant in 18[illegible]

and labourers, and cooks the fowls in an unused pan. When ready, they are placed on a large corn-measure, which is covered with a table-cloth, along with the above-mentioned little cakes, and round this species of altar kneel all the family. The father then utters the Creed and the Ten Commandments, prays for a blessing on the coming year, and three times empties a cup of beer. Then all the others drink in turn, and the cakes and fowls are eaten. All that is eatable must be consumed. The bones must be gnawed clean by the house-dog before the master's eyes, and afterwards reverently buried in the cow-house or stable. During the whole of the day the servants and labourers must be addressed only in kindly terms.

It was not till the year 1386 that the Lithuanians accepted Christianity. Until then heathenism prevailed all over the country, except in a few towns, such as Wilna, where there were many members of the Greek Church, including the reigning family. But in that year Yagello, Grand Duke of Lithuania, married Jadwiga, Queen of Poland, passed from the Greek to the Latin Church, and made Christianity the religion of his country. The heathen Lithuanians were baptized in troops, the sacred groves were felled, the holy fires were extinguished, and an end was put to the snakes and lizards which till then had been revered if not worshipped. Heathenism, however, though scotched, was not killed, and in the gloomy recesses of Lithuanian forests it long lived on, and was represented for centuries by such feasts as that of "The Thrice-nine" which has just been mentioned, and by such other rites as the following Lettish ceremony whereby to keep off pestilence. It is described in the work published at Riga, in 1636, by a Lutheran superintendent named Einhorn, under the title of "Reformatio gentis Letticæ in Ducatu Curlandiæ." When a cattle-plague is dreaded, he says, the peasants hold a solemn feast, which they call *Sobar*. Having contributed a coin apiece, they purchase an ox or other horned beast, which they slay and cook. Each man, also, brings a certain amount of grain, from which they bake cakes and brew beer. Then, all having met together, they call upon God to avert the plague from them, and afterwards consume the victuals and drink. This was done, he goes on to say, in 1602 and 1625, years of murrain and pestilence. But it had to be done secretly, being strictly prohibited by law. "Many men have told me," he adds, "that they were warned in dreams, by the spectres which at such times show themselves, to avert a coming plague by a *Sobar*." To this day the Russian peasants in out-of-the-way places attempt by equally heathenish rites to keep off the dreaded cattle-plague from their herds. On an appointed evening the men are all confined to their homes. The women, wearing nothing but smocks, go outside the village, yoke one of their number to a plough, and [illegible] her, singing the wildest of songs, while she draws the plough [illegible] homesteads which are to be secured against pestilence.

Across the magic circle thus traced, they believe that the hostile spirit, the antagonist of the genius of growth and fertility, will not be able to pass. Should any male person be rash enough to intrude upon the rites which are being solemnized by the women, he is attacked and subjected to nearly as severe treatment as Orpheus received at the hands of his countrywomen. This strange kind of plough-driving used to be known in many lands. Akin to it was the old English custom of "ledyng of the ploughe aboute the fire as for gode begynnyng of the yere, that they shulde fare the better all the yere followyng." Later on it was partially preserved in the ceremonies still peculiar to "Plough-Monday." Still nearer to it came the German custom described by Naogeorgus in his "Regnum Papisticum," published in 1553. The lads used to pull the lasses out of their houses on Ash Wednesday, and harness them to a plough, which was then driven from street to street, and from market-place to market-place. On the plough sat a man who played and sang. Behind it went another, who, with the gestures of a sower, strewed sand and ashes behind him. Finally, the plough was driven into a brook, and the girls, after being ducked, were invited to a feast and a dance. In Leipsic a similiar rite was solemnized on Shrove Tuesday, when masked and otherwise disguised youths used to compel every girl they met to help in dragging the plough, by way of a punishment for her not having become married yet. In the year 1499, as a lad was pressing a strong-minded young woman into this compulsory plough-service, she stabbed him, and excused herself before the magistrates on the plea that what she had struck was not a man but "a spectre." To this day the custom has survived, in a mitigated form, at Hollstadt, near Neustadt, where a plough-festival is held once every seven years, in February, one of the features of which is a plough drawn by six of the fairest maidens who can be found, all arrayed in the local costume.

But it is time to stop. Of course it would be absurd to see, in every myth or fable with which the heathen world has edified or amused itself, a reference to vegetation-spirits and their foes. To do this would be merely to repeat, with a slight variation, the error of those explorers who, having gazed too earnestly at the glorious sun, can see nothing but solar myths whatever way they turn; or who, blinded by the lightning's flash and deafened by the thunder's roar, recognise a storm-myth in every creation of popular fancy. Such unwise supporters of theories which are sound enough in themselves, and which will carry the investigator safely if he does not lay unfair stress upon them, merely bring into discredit what is really well worthy of credit. The solar-myth, for instance, has done right good service while judiciously worked by such a scholar as Professor Max Müller. But some of his followers have made it ridiculous by such imaginings as that of one of their number, who suggests that the idea of Poly-

not sufficiently experienced cultivator, bring forth nothing but a kind of mythological Dead Sea apples, neither savoury nor nutritious. To

indexed it, in a manner deserving of all praise. Never before have been so clearly detailed the ideas with regard to the field and forest, and their connection with the unseen universe, possibly or probably entertained by the primitive man and his prehistoric descendants—commencing with the comparison of human life with that of the plant world, and the inclination on the man's part to attribute a soul like unto his own to the sturdy oak or the clinging ivy or the daisy's opening bud; the herb or tree being sometimes looked upon as the temporary home or husk of a human soul, torn by a violent death from its fleshy mansion, or reduced to plant life by the action of a curse or spell, at others being supposed to be the chosen habitation of some kind of demon or haunting spirit, whose good-will was to be propitiated, his ill-will deprecated by prayer and sacrifice—rising from these conceptions about the individual grass, or shrub, or tree, to views with regard to spirits collectively haunting plains and hills and woods, whether in the shape of ravenous wolves, or hirsute satyrs, or tricksy elves, or divinely beauteous Oreads and other Nymphs; and finally reaching the highest stage of this spiritual development in the imagining of such general spirits of vegetation or growth as have been variously personified by popular fancy under the form of a rustic Jack-in-the-Green or May Queen, or a princely Adonis, or divine Pan. And, certainly, never have all the thousand changing aspects, under which these ideas have been represented by popular mythology, been so clearly defined and rendered intelligible as in Dr. Mannhardt's latest contribution to our knowledge of the mystic law of the corn-field, the meadow, and the forest.

W. R. S. RALSTON.

# FRANCE BEFORE THE OUTBREAK OF THE REVOLUTION.

## I.—State of the Provinces.

DURING the night of July 14—15, 1789, the Duke de Larochefoucauld-Liancourt caused Louis XVI. to be awaked, in order to announce to him the fall of the Bastille. "Why, it is a revolt!" said the King. "Sire," returned the Duke, "it is a revolution." The event was one graver far. Not only had the power slipped from the hands of the King, but it had not fallen into those of the Assembly—it lay there on the ground, ready for use by the unrestrained populace, the violent and excited crowd, the mob that caught it up like a weapon found thrown away in the street. In fact there was no more government; the artificial edifice of human society was everywhere crumbling; men were going back to a state of nature. It was not a revolution but a *dissolution*.

### I.

Two causes excite and maintain the universal disturbance. The first, the permanent dearth prolonged during ten years, which, aggravated by the very violence it provokes, is about to exaggerate all popular passions into madness, and to change into convulsive staggering the whole march of the Revolution.

When a river is flowing on a level with its banks, a slight freshet will produce a flood. So is it with the poverty of the eighteenth century. The common people, who find it hard to live when bread is cheap, feel themselves about to die when it becomes dear. Under the pressure of anguish animal instinct revolts, and the general obedience which constitutes public peace depends upon a degree more or less of dryness or damp, heat or cold. In 1788, a very dry year, the crops had been poor, and in addition, on the eve of the harvest,* a fearful

* Marmontel: Mémoires, t. ii. 221. Albert Babeau: Histoire de Troyes pendant la Révolution, i. 91, 187 (Lettre de Huez, maire de Troyes, 30 Juillet, 1788). Archives Nationales, H, 1274 (Lettre de M. de Carar[illegible] Avril, 1789); H, 942 (Cahier des demandes des Etats du Languedoc). Roux et [illegible] Histoire parlementaire, i. 2[illegible]

hailstorm burst all around Paris from Normandy to Champagne, devastated an area of sixty leagues, and occasioned a loss of a hundred millions. The winter that succeeded was the severest known since 1709; at the end of December the Seine froze the whole way from Paris to Havre, and the thermometer stood at 18¾° below the freezing point. A third of the olive-trees in Provence died, and the remainder had so suffered as to be judged incapable of bearing fruit for two years to come. The same disaster befell Languedoc; in the Vivarais and the Cevennes entire forests of chestnut trees perished, as well as all the forage and corn of the mountain districts; and in the plains, the Rhone overflowed its bed for two months. By the spring of 1789, there was famine everywhere, and from month to month it mounted like a rising tide. In vain did the Government order farmers, proprietors, merchants, to supply the markets; in vain did it double the premium on importation, tax all its ingenuity, run into debt, expend forty millions to furnish France with corn. In vain did individuals, princes, noblemen, bishops, chapters, communities, multiply their alms,—the Archbishop of Paris contracting a debt of 400,000 livres; a certain rich man distributing 40,000 francs on the morrow of the hailstorm; a certain Bernardine convent feeding a hundred poor during six weeks.* All was not enough, neither public precaution nor private charity sufficed for such excessive need. In Normandy, where the last treaty of commerce had ruined the manufacture of linen and lace, forty thousand workmen are out of work; in numbers of parishes, a quarter of the inhabitants have to beg.† Here, "almost all the inhabitants, including farmers and proprietors, eat barley bread and drink water;" there "many poor souls eat oat bread, and others soaked bran, which has caused the death of several children." "Above all," writes the Parliament of Rouen, "let help be provided for a dying people. . . Sire, the greater number of your subjects cannot afford the price of bread, and what bread it is that is given to those who buy!" Arthur Young,‡ travelling through France at the moment, hears nothing spoken of except the dearness of bread and the distress of the people. At Troyes the loaf costs four sous the pound—that is to say, eight of our present sous—and the artisans out of work throng the workshops set up by charity, where they only earn twelve sous a day. In Lorraine, according to the testimony of all observers, "the people are nearly dead with hunger." In Paris, the number of paupers has trebled itself; there are thirty thousand in the Faubourg St. Antoine alone. Around Paris grain crops have wholly failed, or are damaged.§ At the beginning of July, at

* L'Ancien Régime, p. 45. Albert Babeau, i. 91. (The Bishop of Troyes gives 12,000 francs, and the Chapter 6,000, to the Charity Workshops.)

† L'Ancien Régime, 440, 507. Floquet: Histoire du Parlement de Normandie, vii. 502, 518 (Représentations du parlement de Normandie, 3 Mai, 1788; Lettre du Parlement au Roi, 15 Juillet, 1789).

‡ Arthur Young: Journey in France, 29th June, 2nd and 18th July. Journal de Paris, 2 Janvier, 1789: Lettre du Curé de Sainte-Marguerite.

§ Roux et Buchez, iv. 79 à 82 (Lettre du bureau intermédiaire de Montereau, 9 Juillet,

Montereau, the market is empty. "The bakers could not have baked" if the police officers had not raised the price of bread to five sous the pound; the rye and barley that the intendant sends "are of the worst quality, rotten, and in a condition to bring on dangerous diseases; nevertheless, the generality of small consumers are reduced to the dire necessity of using this damaged grain." "At Villeneuve-le-Roi," writes the mayor, "the two last consignments of rye have been too black and poor to be retailed without an admixture of wheat." At Sens the barley has "so mouldy a taste that the purchasers throw the detestable bread in the face of the dealer." At Chevreuse the barley has sprouted and has a poisonous smell. "The unfortunates," writes an official, "must be indeed pressed with hunger to put up with it." At Fontainebleau, the half-destroyed rye crop produces more bran than flour, and in order to be made bread it has to be repeatedly manipulated. This bread, however, such as it is, is furiously coveted: "they have to distribute it only through wickets;" and even those who have thus obtained their ration "are often attacked on their way back, and despoiled by the famishing who are stronger than they." At Nangis the magistrates forbid the same person to buy more than two bushels at the same market. In short, food is so scarce that it becomes a problem how to feed the soldiery; the minister sends two letters, one upon the other, ordering twenty thousand measures of rye to be cut before the harvest.* Thus we find that Paris in a time of perfect peace has the appearance of a famished town rationed at the end of a long siege, and the dearth cannot have been greater nor the nourishment worse in December, 1870, than in the July of 1789.

The nearer drew the 14th of July, says an eye-witness,† the worse became the scarcity. "Every baker's shop was surrounded by a crowd, to which bread was distributed with the utmost parsimony. . . . This bread was in general blackish, earthy, bitter, and brought on inflammation of the throat and pain in the bowels. At the Military School and in other depôts I have seen flour of a detestable quality; portions were yellow, had an offensive smell, and formed blocks so hard that they required to be broken into fragments with a hatchet. For my own part, rebuffed by the difficulty of procuring this unlucky bread, and disgusted with what was offered to me at tables d'hôte, I entirely gave up this form of nourishment. In the evenings I went to the Café du Caveau, where fortunately they were considerate enough to reserve for me two French rolls, the only bread that I ate for a whole week." But this resource was only for the rich. As for

1789; du maire de Villeneuve-le-Roi, 10 Juillet; de M. Baudry, 10 Juillet; de M. Jamin, 11 Juillet; de M. Prioreau, 11 Juillet, etc.).—Montjoie: Histoire de la Révolution de France, 2e partie, ch. xxi. p. 5.

* Roux et Buchez: ibid. "It is very grievous," writes the Marquis d'Autichamp, "to be obliged to cut standing crops; but it is dangerous to let the troops die of hunger."

† Montjoie: ibid., ch. xxxix. v. 37. De Goncourt: La Société française pendant la Révolution, p. 53. Déposition de Maillard (Enquête Criminelle du Châtelet sur les événements des 5 et 6 Octobre).

[illegible] order to obtain this dogs' food they had to stand in [illegible] together. They fight, so doing; "they snatch the [illegible] each other." No more work; "the workshops are [illegible] Sometimes after a day's waiting, the artisan has to return [illegible] handed; and if he does bring back a small four-pound [illegible] cost him three francs twelve sous—that is, twelve sous for [illegible] three francs for the lost day. In the long line of idle [illegible] beings oscillating at the doors of the shops, black [illegible] are fermenting. If the bakers lack flour to-night, we shall [illegible] thing to eat to-morrow! A dreadful idea, to confront which [illegible] force of a government is none too strong; for it is force, [illegible] force alone—present, visible, menacing—that can maintain [illegible] in the midst of famine.

[illegible] Louis XIV. and Louis XV. hunger and suffering had been [illegible] severely felt; but riots, rudely and promptly repressed, [illegible] occasioned partial and transient troubles. Some rioters were [illegible], others sent to the galleys, and at once the artisan, the peasant, [illegible] convinced of his impotence, returned to his stall or his plough. Where a wall is plainly too high, no one even thinks of [illegible] over it. But here we have the wall everywhere cracking, [illegible] all its guardians—clergy, nobility, middle class, men of letters, [illegible], the very Government itself—busy making a wide breach in [illegible] For the first time the poor, the wretched, discern an outlet; they [illegible] towards it, first in detachments, next *en masse*, and revolt is now universal, as once resignation was.

II.

The reason is, that through this aperture Hope enters like light, [illegible] reaches gradually down to the lowest levels. For the last half-[illegible] it has been rising, and its beams, that in the first instance [illegible] the higher classes in their fine first-floor apartments, next [illegible] middle-classes in their *entresol* and ground-floors, have for the last [illegible] penetrated into the cellars where the people are at work—[illegible] into the deep sinks, the dark corners where vagrants, malefactors, [illegible] unclean and swarming horde hides itself from the pursuit of [illegible]

[illegible] two first provincial assemblies, instituted by Necker [illegible] 1779, Loménie de Brienne has in 1787 added nineteen [illegible] under each of these are district assemblies; under each [illegible] parochial assemblies;* and the whole administrative [illegible] transformed. It is these new assemblies that assess [illegible] their collection; that decide on and direct all [illegible] judge at the last appeal the greater number of [illegible] intendant, the sub-delegate, the elected, thus

[illegible] la Révolution, 272—290. De Lavergne: Les [illegible] des Assemblées Provinciales, *passim*.

lose three-quarters of their authority. Between the two [illegible] whose limits are ill-defined, conflicts everywhere arise; [illegible] a floating thing, and obedience waxes less. The [illegible] feels on his shoulder the superior pressure of the one [illegible] which, without possibility of resistance or intervention, [illegible] and propelled him. In every parochial, district, or even [illegible] assembly, common people, "labourers," and occasionally [illegible] take their seats by the side of nobles and prelates. They [illegible] they bear in mind the enormous amount of taxes paid or [illegible] themselves alone—land-tax and its accessories, poll-tax, [illegible] and most certainly on their return they talk it over with their [illegible] All these figures are printed; the village attorney discusses [illegible] his clients, artisans and peasants, either on Sundays coming [illegible] mass, or at night in the common room of the inn. And these [illegible] are authorized, even encouraged, in high places. In the [illegible] of 1788, the provincial assemblies demand from the syndics [illegible] inhabitants of every parish a local inquiry; the detailed [illegible] their grievances is requested, what incomes are exempt from [illegible] what the cultivator pays and suffers, how many privileged persons are in the parish, what their fortune, whether they reside there, [illegible] sum their exemptions amount; and when the replies are given [illegible] attorney who holds the pen names and points out each privi[illegible] individual, criticizes his way of life, values his fortune, calculates [illegible] injury done to the village by his immunities, inveighs against [illegible] and officials.

On leaving these assemblies the villager ruminates long over wh[illegible] has just heard. He contemplates his misfortunes—no longer o[illegible] one, but in the aggregate and added to the immensity of misfo[illegible] that weighs down his fellows. Moreover he begins to distinguish [illegible] causes of his wretchedness. The King is said to be good: why [illegible] do his officials take so much of our money? So-and-so—Church [illegible] nitaries or noblemen—are not bad people: why do they make us [illegible] their place? Imagine a beast of burden to whom a flash of r[illegible] should suddenly reveal the equine in contrast to the human [illegible] realize, if you can, the novel thoughts that would occur to it,—f[illegible] all as to postillions and drivers by whom it is bridled and flogged, before long as to the benevolent travellers and sensitive ladies [illegible] feel for it indeed, but none the less add to the carriage load all [illegible] paraphernalia as well as their personal weight. [illegible]

In the same way now in the mind of the peasants, [illegible] reveries, slowly and gradually a new idea takes shape [illegible] oppressed multitude of which he forms part, of a great [illegible] far beyond the visible horizon, and everywhere ill-used, [illegible] fleeced. Towards the end of 1788, through the co[illegible] intendants and military commandants, one begins to [illegible] dull universal rumbling of a gathering wrath. [illegible] changing their character; they become suspicious and restive. And this is the very time when the Government, letting go the reins, summons them to direct themselves.* In the month of November, 1787, the King has declared that he convokes the States-General. The 5th of July, 1788, he requires from all public bodies and competent persons memoranda on the subject. On the 8th of August he fixes the date of the session. The 5th of October he convokes the Notables, to deliberate about it with them. The 27th of December he accords a double representation to the third estate, seeing that "his cause is bound up with all generous sentiments, and will always have public opinion on its side." The same day he introduces into the electoral assemblies of the clergy a majority of curés, "because these worthy and useful pastors occupy themselves closely and habitually with the indigence and assistance of the people," whence it follows "that they know more intimately its trials and wants." On the 27th of January, 1789, he regulates the order and form of convocation. From the date of the 7th of February, letters of convocation are sent off one by one. A week later every parochial assembly begins to draw up a report of its grievances, and excites itself by the detail and enumeration of all the distresses that it writes down. All these appeals and all these acts are so many blows struck, which re-echo in the popular imagination. "It is the desire of his Majesty," says the standing order, "that from the extremities of his kingdom and the least-known of its dwellings, every individual should feel assured of his desires and claims reaching the ear of the King." So then the thing is quite true, quite certain. They are invited to speak; they are sent for, they are consulted, they are to be relieved; henceforward their distress will be less; better times are about to begin. This is all they know. Several months later, in July,† this is the only reply that a peasant woman can make to Arthur Young: "She has been told that there are rich people who wish to do something for the poor of her class;" but as to the who and how and what she knows nothing; the matter is too complicated, out of the reach of a benumbed and mechanical intelligence. One thought only emerges thence—the hope of sudden relief, the persuasion that they are entitled to it, the resolution to help it on in every way; consequently an anxious attitude of expectation ripe for starting, a rigid tension of the will that only waits its opportunity to contract and drive action like a resistless arrow towards some unknown goal, to be all at once revealed. This goal all at once is revealed by hunger. There must needs be corn in the market-place—the farmers and proprietors must needs bring it there; the large purchasers, whether the Government or private individuals, must not transport it elsewhere; it must be cheap, the price must be fixed, the baker must sell it at twopence the pound; grain, flour, wine, salt,

* Duvergier: Collection des Lois et Décrets. Ibid. 1 à 23 et notamment, p. 15.
† Arthur Young, July 12th, 1789 (in Champagne).

and such commodities must no longer pay duty; there must no longer be any duties, neither seigniorial rights nor ecclesiastical tithes, nor royal or municipal taxes. And on the strength of this idea, in all parts of the realm, in March, April, and May, disturbances break out. Contemporary writers do not know what to think of such a scourge,* cannot in any way comprehend this innumerable quantity of malefactors who, without any apparent heads, seem by some common understanding to give themselves everywhere up to the same excesses, and just at the very time, too, when the States-General are about to meet. The fact was, that under the old *régime* the conflagration only smouldered with all apertures closed; suddenly the great door is thrown wide, air enters, and at once the flames burst forth.

III.

At first, however, there are only intermittent isolated fires, that can be extinguished or that die out of themselves; but the next moment, in the same place or hard by, cracklings begin again, and their multiplicity and repeated occurrence show the enormous mass, the depth, the raised temperature of the combustible matter about to explode. During the four months preceding the fall of the Bastille, there were more than three hundred riots in France. They occurred from month to month and week to week in Poitou, Bretagne, Touraine, Orléanais, Normandy, Ile de France, Picardy, Champagne, Alsace, Burgundy, Nivernais, Auvergne, Languedoc, Provence. On the 28th of May, the Parliament of Rouen announces pillages of grain, "violent and bloody fights, in which several men on both sides have been killed," throughout the province, at Caen, St. Lo, Mortain, Granville, Evreux, Bernay, Pont-Audemer, Elbeuf, Louviers, and other places besides. On the 20th of April, the Baron de Bezenval, military commandant of the central provinces, writes:—"I again send to M. Necker a picture of the frightful condition of Touraine and the Orléanais; each letter that I receive from those provinces contains a detailed account of three or four riots, suppressed with much difficulty by the troops."† And throughout the whole extent of the realm the same spectacle is to be seen.

Generally, as is natural, the women are the ringleaders. At Montlhéry they have ripped open the sacks of corn with their scissors. Each week, on market day, as they learn that the loaf of bread has risen three, four, seven sous, they cry out with indignation. At that price, with the poor wages earned by their husbands, and the want of work besides,‡ how are they to feed their families? Crowds gather round the sacks and the doors of the bakers; in the midst of vociferations and abuse, a rush is made; the proprietor or shopkeeper is pushed aside, thrown down; the commodity is in the hands of the

* Montjoie, 1re partie, 102. † Floquet: Histoire du Parlement de Normandie, vii. [illegible] Archives Nationales, H, 1453. ‡ Arthur Young, 29th June (at Nangis).

purchasers and the hungry; each snatches what he wants, pays, or does not pay, and runs off with his booty.

Sometimes the attack is a joint and premeditated one.* At Bray-sur-Seine, on the 1st of May, the villagers gather from a circuit of four miles, armed with stones, knives, and sticks, and numbering four thousand, force the labourers and farmers who have brought in the grain to sell it at three livres instead of four livres ten sous the bushel, and threaten to begin again next market day; then, consequently, the farmer will not return, then the market-place will be empty, and soldiers will be required to prevent the pillaging of the inhabitants of Bray. At Bagnols, in Languedoc, on the 1st and 2nd of April, the peasants, armed with cudgels and assembled by beat of drum, "traverse the town threatening bloodshed and conflagration, unless corn and money be given them." They search for grain in private houses, share it among themselves at a reduced price, "promising to pay for it next harvest;" compel the consuls to put bread at two sous the pound, and to augment the daily wage by four sous.

Indeed, this is now the customary proceeding; the people no longer obey the authorities, but the authorities the people. Consuls, sheriffs, mayors, syndics, municipal officers, grow confused and feeble in presence of this immense clamour; they feel that they are about to be trodden underfoot or thrown out of window. Others, of firmer texture, who know that a mob in revolt is demented, have a scruple about shedding blood; at all events they yield for once, hoping that on the next market day soldiers will be numerous and precautions better taken. At Amiens, after a "very sharp riot,"† they resolve to take the corn belonging to the Jacobins, and to sell it to the people at a third below its value, in a space girdled by soldiers. At Nantes, where the Hôtel de Ville has been taken possession of, they are obliged to lower the price of the loaf a penny per pound. At Angoulême, in order to avoid having recourse to arms, the Count d'Artois is requested to surrender for two months his duty on flour, the price of the bread is fixed, the bakers obtaining compensation. At Cette the authorities are so maltreated that they give up everything; the populace has sacked their houses and got the upper hand; they proclaim at the sound of the trumpet that all its demands are granted.

At other times the crowd dispenses with the administration, and acts independently. If grain fails at the market, they go to seek it wherever it may be found—at the houses of the proprietors or farmers, who dare not bring it to market for fear of pillage; in the religious houses, who are bound by a royal edict to have always a year's harvest in store; in the granaries where the Government keeps its provisions;

* Archives Nationales, H, 1453. Lettre du Duc de Mortemart, Seigneur de Bray, 4 Mai; de M. de Ballainvilliers, Intendant du Languedoc, 15 Avril.

† Archives Nationales, H, 1453. Lettre de l'Intendant M. d'Agay, 30 Avril; des Officiers Municipaux de Nantes, 9 Janvier; de l'Intendant M. Meulan d'Ablois, 22 Juin; de M. de Ballainvilliers, 15 Avril.

in the convoys despatched by the inspectors to starv
Each one for himself; so much the worse for his neighb
people of Fougères fight with and drive out those of Ernée
to buy at their market, and the same violence is shown at
inhabitants of Maine.* At Saint Léonard the people kee
grain that was setting off for Limoges, at Bost that d
Aurillac, at Saint-Didier what was to be sent to Moulin,
what was ready for despatch to Mâcon. In vain were escor
convoys: troops of men and women, armed with hatchets
lurk in the woods along the road, and jump to the bridle of
They have to be sabred in order that the procession may a
vain are reasons, explanations, kind words abundantly lavi
corn is even offered to them for money; they refuse it, cryi
convoy shall not set out. They have made up their minds
lution is that of a bull who stops up the road, with low
The corn is theirs, since it is in their country; whoever car
keeps it to himself is a thief. Nothing can root out that fi
theirs. At Chantenay, near Mans,† they prevent a miller
to his mill what he has just been buying. At Montdragon,
doc, they stone a merchant who was sending his last load
at Thiers strong bodies of workmen go and gather the
fields; a proprietor in whose possession some is found is m
they drink in the cellars, then leave the wine to run out.
the bakers having failed to stock their presses for four days
lace takes forcible possession of the granaries of private
merchants, religious communities. "The terrified merchan
grain go at whatever price is named, indeed the greater
is stolen in the presence of the guards;" and in the tumult
these domiciliary visits, a number of houses are sacked.

At this time woe to all those who are connected with the
acquisition, the traffic, the management of grain! The pop
nation needs living beings to whom it may impute its woes an
it may wreak its revenge; in its eyes that whole partic
composed of monopolizers, forestallers, and, at all events, of
the public. Near Angers the house of the Benedictines
their enclosure and woods are devastated.‡ At Amiens
were on the point of pillaging and, perhaps, burning down
of two commercial men who had constructed mills, grin
economical principle." Held in check by the soldiers, t
themselves with breaking the windows; but "other gr
destroy or pillage the houses of some private persons

* Archives Nationales, H, 1453. Lettre du Comte de Langeron, 4 Ju
Meulan d'Ablois, 5 Juin; procès-verbal de la Maréchaussée de Bost, 29 Avr
M. de Chazerat, 29 Mai; de M. de Bezenval, 2 Juin; de l'Intendant M. A

† Archives Nationales, H, 1453. Lettre de M. de Bezenval, 27 Mai; de
villiers, 25 Avril; de M de Chazerat, 12 Juin; de M. de Foullonde, 19 Avr

‡ Archives Nationales, H, 1453. Lettre de l'Intendant M. d'Aine, 1
d'Agay, 30 Avril; de M. Amelot, 25 Avril; des Officiers Municipaux de Nante

...." At Nantes, a Sieur Geslin being deputed by ... visit a certain house, and finding no corn therein, the cry ... is an embezzler, an accomplice!" The crowd falls upon ... wounded and nearly cut to pieces. It is manifest that there ... any security in France; possessions, life even, are ... The primary property of all—subsistence—is violated in ... places, and is everywhere precarious and threatened. ... the intendant and sub-delegates call for assistance, ... the mounted police impotent, and demand regular troops. ...ow it happens that public force, already insufficient, dis... tottering, finds itself set upon, not only by the blind rage ...ger, but by the mischievous instincts that profit by all disorder, ... permanent selfishness that every political convulsion frees from ...nt.

IV.

...gglers, forgers, poachers, vagabonds, beggars, convicts,* we ...een how numerous these are, and what a single year of scarcity ...o add to their number. All these are so many recruits for ... assemblies, and during the riot and under cover of it each of ... fills his sack.

... the Pays de Caux,† and even up to the environs of Rouen, at Ron...s, Quévreilly, Préaux, Saint-Jacques, and in all the surrounding district, ...f armed brigands break into the houses, especially into those of the ... and lay violent hands on whatever suits them." "To the south of ...s, three or four woodmen, out of the forests of Bellème, use their ...s against all who resist them, and get grain at the price they choose ..."

... neighbourhood of Etampes fifteen bandits enter the farms ..., and make the farmer pay a ransom by the threat of ...ism. In Cambrésis, they pillage the abbeys of Vauchelles, ..., and Guillemans, the château of the Marquis de Besselard, the ...ty of M. Doisy, two farms, the waggons of corn that pass along ...d to Saint-Quentin, and, in addition, some farms in Picardy. ... focus of this revolt is in a few villages, on the confines of ...y and Cambrésis, villages addicted to smuggling and the ... it induces." The peasants have allowed themselves to be ... by bandits; a man slips rapidly along the incline of theft, ...ch or such a one, semi-honest till then, having once taken part ...ly or reluctantly in a riot, will begin again, tempted either by ...ty or gain. In fact, "it is not extreme need that excites them." ...is "a speculative cupidity, a new kind of smuggling." An old

* ...ien Régime, 498 à 509.

† ... vii. 508 (Rapport du 27 Février). Hippeau: Le Gouvernement de Normandie, ... Lettre de M. Perrot, 23 Juin). Archives Nationales, H, 1453. Lettre de M. du ..., 29 Avril. Ibid. F. 7, 3250. Lettre de M. de Rochambeau, 16 Mai. Ibid. ... Lettre de l'Abbé Duplaquet, Député du Tiers-état de Saint Quentin, 17 Mai. ... laboureurs des environs de Saint Quentin, 14 Mai.

carabineer, sabre in hand, a forester, and "about eight persons in pretty easy circumstances, place themselves at the head of four hundred to five hundred men, repair daily to three or four villages, compel all who have corn to give it at twenty-four" and even at eighteen "livres the sack." Those of the band who declare themselves penniless carry off their portion without paying for it. The others, having paid what price they please, now proceed to sell again at a profit, and even ask forty-five livres the sack—an excellent stroke of business, in which greed goes halves with poverty. When the next harvest comes the temptation will be similar. "They have threatened to come and gather in our crops for us, and also to carry off our cattle and sell the meat at two sous the pound." In all great insurrections there are such malefactors, vagrants, outlaws, savage and desperate vagabonds, who gather like wolves wherever they scent a prey. These it is who serve as guides and executioners to private and public grudges. Near Uzès, twenty-five men, wearing masks and carrying guns and sticks, enter the dwelling of a notary, fire a pistol at him, load him with blows, destroy his furniture, burn his registers and all the title-deeds and papers deposited with him by the Count of Rouvres; of this band seven are arrested, but the people are on their side, attack the mounted police, and set them free.* They are identified by their actions, their impulse to destroy for destroying's sake, their foreign accent, their gaunt faces, and their rags. More of them come from Paris to Rouen, and for four days the town is at their mercy.† Magazines are broken into, carts of corn unloaded, convents and seminaries forced to pay ransom; they attack the house of the Procureur-Général, who has denounced them, and want to cut him to pieces; they break his mirrors, his furniture, leave laden with booty; go into the town and the outskirts to pillage manufactories, and break or burn machinery. These are henceforth the new leaders, for in every riot it is he who is most audacious, most entirely unembarrassed by scruples, who walks at the head and sets the example of havoc. The example is contagious; the crowd had begun by wanting bread, it ends by murder and conflagration, and the savagery let loose adds its unlimited horrors to the limited revolt of want.

V.

Such as it is, however, spite of scarcity and brigands, this revolt might perhaps be got under, but for that which renders it irresistible: its own belief that it is authorized, actually authorized, by those on whom the task of suppressing it is laid. Here and there break out words and acts of terrible *naïveté* which reveal beyond the

* Archives Nationales, H, 1453. Lettre du Comte de Périgord, Commandant Militaire du Languedoc, 22 Avril.

† Floquet, vii. 511 (du 11 au 14 Juillet).

so gloomy present a future more threatening still. Already on the 9th of January, 1789, there rises amidst the populace that takes possession of the Hôtel de Ville at Nantes, and lays siege to the bakers' shops,* "the cry of 'Vive la Liberté,' mingling with that of 'Vive le Roi.'" A few months later, around Ploërmel, the peasants refuse to pay tithes, alleging that the *cahier* of their assembly demands their abolition. In Alsace, dating from the month of March, the same refusal: "in many places" a number of communities even pretend that they are at liberty to pay no more taxes until their deputies to the States-General shall have definitely fixed the sum of public contributions. In Dauphiné, it is resolved in printed and published deliberations, that no more "personal duties" shall be paid, and the seigneurs who are the losers dare not go to law. At Lyons the people are persuaded that "all collection of duties should cease," and on the 29th of June the news of the reunion of the three Orders "having been received," "astonished at the illuminations and signs of public rejoicing," they believe the happy times to have really begun, and form a plan for obtaining meat at four sous and wine at the same price. The publicans think that the town dues are erelong to be abolished, and that in the meantime the King, in honour of the reunion of the three Orders, has granted a three days' exemption from all duties to Paris, and that this ought equally to apply to Lyons. Upon which the crowd rushes frantically to the barriers, to the Porte Saint-Clair, the Porte Perrache, the Bridge of La Guillotière, burns or demolishes the bureaus, destroys the registers, sacks the houses of the officials, and takes possession of the wine that is there deposited. Meanwhile the rumour has spread through the country that the entrance into the town is now free; the peasants flock in with such prodigious files of waggons laden with wine and drawn by several oxen, that in spite of the guard that has been re-established there, they are obliged to be admitted throughout the day without payment; it is only on the 7th of July that it again becomes possible to collect the duties. The same goes on in the southern provinces, where the principal taxes are levied upon articles of consumption; there, too, it is in the name of the Government that the collections are suspended. At Agde† "the people is madly persuaded that it is everything, and can do everything, by reason of the so-called will of the King as to equality of ranks"—for it is thus that it interprets, after its liking and in its own language, the double representation granted to the third estate. In consequence of this, the people threaten the town with general pillage unless the price of all provisions be lowered; and suppress the

* Archives Nationales, H, 1453. Lettre des Officiers Municipaux de Nantes, 9 Janvier; du Subdélégué de Ploërmel, 4 Juillet. Ibid. $F^7$, 2353. Lettre de la Commission Intermédiaire d'Alsace, 8 Septembre. Ibid. $F^7$, 3227. Lettre de l'Intendant Caze de la Bove, 16 Juin. Ibid. H, 1453. Lettre de Terray, Intendant de Lyon, 4 Juillet; du Prévôt des Echevins, 5 et 7 Juillet.

† Archives Nationales, H, 1453. Lettre du Maire et des Consuls d'Agde, 21 Avril; de M. de Périgord, 19 Avril et 5 Mai.

provincial duty laid on wine, fish, and meat; in addition to which, "they are determined to name consuls taken from their own class," and the bishop, the seigneur of the town, the mayor, and the notables, against whom the peasants in the country round have been gathered by force, find themselves obliged to proclaim to the sound of the trumpet that the popular demands are all complied with. Three days later they insist that the duty on grinding be diminished by half, and go to seek out the bishop to whom the mills belong. The prelate, who is ill, becomes faint in the street and seats himself on a boundary-stone; there the session is at once held, and he is obliged to sign an act of renunciation; in consequence of which "his mill, set down at 15,000 livres, is now reduced to 7,500." At Limoux, under pretext of seeking for grain, the populace break into the dwellings of the comptrollers and farmers of the taxes, carry off their registers, and throw them, together with the furniture of the officials, into the water. In Provence, things are still worse; for through an enormous injustice and an inconceivable imprudence, all the taxation of the towns rests on flour; hence it is to this taxation that the scarcity of bread is directly attributed; and this is why the fiscal agent becomes the visible enemy, and the revolts of hunger develop into insurrections against the State.

## VI.

Here, too, political novelties are the spark that sets fire to the mass of powder; everywhere it is on the very day of the electoral assembly that the people rise; in less than a fortnight there are from forty to fifty insurrections in the province. The popular imagination—like a child—goes straight to its goal; reforms having been announced, it believes them already come, and, to make still more sure, executes them on the spot; since we are to be relieved, let us relieve ourselves.

> "This is not an isolated revolt like the ordinary ones," writes the commandant of troops;* "here we have the party united and guided by uniform principles; the same errors are spread abroad in all minds. . . . The principles instilled into the people are that the King would have perfect equality, would do away with nobles and bishops, with rank, titles, and seigniorial rights. Thus these misled beings believe themselves to be in their duty and following the desire of the King."

Grand-sounding words have had their effect; they have been told that the States-General were going to bring about the "regeneration of the kingdom," they have drawn the conclusion that "the epoch of the convocation" should be that of "an entire and absolute change in

* Archives Nationales, H, 1453. Lettres de M. de Caraman, 23, 26, 27, 28 Mars; du Sénéchal Missiessy, 24 Mars; du Maire d'Hyères, 25 Mars, etc. Ibid. H, 1274; de M. de Montmayran, 2 Avril; de M de Caraman, 18 Mars, 12 Avril; de l'Intendant M. de la Tour, 2 Avril; du Procureur-Général, M. d'Antheman, 17 Avril, et rapport du 15 Juin; des Officiers Municipaux de Toulon, 11 Avril; du Subdélégué de Manosque, 14 Mars; de M. de Saint-Tropez, 21 Mars—Procès-verbal signé par 119 témoins sur l'émeute du 5 Mars à Aix, etc.

the conditions and fortunes of the community." Hence "the insurrection against the nobility and the clergy is as fierce as it is general." "In several places it has been pretty widely spread that *it was a species of war declared against proprietors and property;* and in the towns, as in the country, the people persist in declaring *that they will pay nothing whatever, neither taxes, nor duties, nor debts.*"

Naturally it is on the *piquet* or meal tax that the first assault is made. At Aix, Marseilles, Toulon, and in more than forty towns and villages, it is at once abolished; at Aupt and Luc, nothing remains of the weighing-house but the four walls; at Marseilles, the dwelling of the farmer of the slaughter-houses, at Brignolles, that of the director of the administration of leather, are sacked; the people have resolved to purge the country of all the administrative employés. This is but a beginning—bread and other commodities must be cheap, and be so at once. At Arles the corporation of sailors, presided over by M. de Barras, the consul, has just elected its representatives; by way of a finish to the meeting they insist that M. de Barras should reduce by decree the price of all victuals; and at his refusal "they throw open the window, calling out, 'We have got him; we have only to throw him into the street, others will pick him up.'" No alternative but to yield; the decree is proclaimed by the city trumpeter, and, at every taxed article named, the crowd cries, "Long live the King and M. de Barras." In presence of brute force concession was unavoidable. At the same time the perplexity is great, for by the suppression of this meal tax the towns lose all their revenue, and in addition they have to indemnify the bakers and butchers. Toulon, for example, contracted a daily debt of 2,500 livres.

In such disorder as this, woe to those suspected of having contributed directly or indirectly to the people's grievances! At Toulon, there is a demand for the heads of the mayor who signed the taxes and of the keeper of records, who had the care of the lists. At Manosque, the Bishop of Sisteron, who was visiting the seminary, was accused of favouring a monopolizer. As he was walking to his carriage he was hooted, threatened, mud was thrown at him, and then stones. The consuls in charge and the sub-delegate, who ran to protect him, were struck and thrown aside; while some madmen, under his very eyes, begin "to dig a grave in which to bury him." Defended by five or six brave men, he reaches his carriage amidst a hail of pebbles, wounded in the head and many parts of his body; and he is only saved because his horses, being also stoned, run away with him. Strangers, Italians, bandits, have joined the peasants and artisans, and words are spoken and acts committed which announce a Jacquerie. "The most frantic cry to the bishop, 'We are poor, you are rich; we mean to get all your wealth.'"* Elsewhere, "the

* Archives Nationales, H. 1274. Lettre de M. de la Tour, 2 Avril (avec mémoire détaillé et dépositions).

seditious bands place all well-to-do people under contribution." At Brignolles, thirteen houses are pillaged from top to bottom, and thirty others partially so. At Aupt, M. de Montferrat, who resists, is killed and "cut into little pieces." At La Seyne, the populace, led by a peasant, assemble to the beat of drum before the dwelling of one of the principal citizens, bidding him prepare for death, and "they will do him the honour of interring him." He flies; his house is sacked, as well as the guard-house, and on the morrow the head of the band "compels the leading inhabitants to give him money, in order, he says, to indemnify the peasants who had left their work" and employed their day in the service of the public. At Peinier, the Président de Peinier, an octogenarian, is "besieged in his château by a band of a hundred and fifty workmen and peasants," who have brought a consul and a notary with them, and with the assistance of these two functionaries force the president to sign an act renouncing all his seigniorial rights of every kind. At Sollier, they destroy the mills of M. de Forbin-Janson, sack the house of his man of business, pillage the château, demolish the roof, the chapel, the altar, the railings and armorial bearings, enter the cellars, stave in the wine-barrels, carry off all that is portable; "the carrying went on two days," the loss to the marquis amounting to 100,000 crowns. At Riez, they surround the episcopal palace with fagots, and threaten to burn it down, "but admit the bishop to terms upon a promise of 50,000 livres," and require him to burn his archives. They destroy the château of the Provost of Pignan, and seek for the Bishop of Toulon that they may kill him. In a word, the sedition is *social*, for it strikes at all who profit by or rule in the established order.

Indeed, in watching the popular actions, one would say that the theory of the *Contrat Social* had been infused into men's minds. They treat magistrates as servants, decree laws, behave as sovereigns, exercise public control, and summarily, arbitrarily, brutally establish what they hold conformable to natural rights. At Peinier they demand a second electoral Assembly, with right of suffrage for themselves. At Saint-Maximin they take on themselves the election of new consuls and officers of justice. At Sollier, they compel the magistrate's representative to give in his resignation, and break his baton of office. At Barjols, "they turn magistrates and consuls into mere valets, announce that they are the masters, and will deal out justice themselves." And in fact they do deal it out, as they are able to discern it through many exactions and thefts. So-and-so has corn, he ought to divide it with such or such another who lacks it. So-and-so has money, he ought to give some of it to those who have none wherewith to buy bread. Acting upon this principle at Barjols, they tax the Ursulines to the amount of 18,000 livres, carry off fifty loads of wheat from the chapter, eighteen from one poor artisan, forty from another, and force canons and beneficed clergy to give receipts to their farmers. Then, from house to house, cudgel in hand, they compel some to contribute money, others to renounce their claims against their debtors, "one to desist from a criminal prosecution, another to give up a decision in his favour, another, again, to reimburse the cost of a law-suit won years ago, a father to give his consent to the marriage of his son." All their grievances return to mind, and it is well known how tenacious the peasant's memory is. Now that he is master he redresses wrongs—especially those he believes to have been inflicted on himself. General restitution is the order of the day, and first of all feudal duties hitherto received. The man of business of M. de Montmeyan is deprived of all the money he has, to make up for all that during fifteen years he must have gained as notary. The former Consul of Brignolles had in 1775 inflicted fines to the value of about 1,700 or 1,800 francs and applied them to the relief of the poor: that sum is now withdrawn from his cash-box. In the eyes of the peasants not only are the consuls and lawyers a mischievous set, but all those papers that they work amongst are even worse. To the flames then with all old documents, not only clerks' registers, but also, at Hyères, all papers belonging to the town-hall and the principal notary. In the matter of papers the only good ones are the new, those bearing discharges, receipts, or obligations in favour of the people. At Brignolles, millowners are constrained to grant an act of sale by which they yield up their mills to the commune for a yearly rent of 5,000 francs, payable in ten years and not bearing interest,—a measure that ruins them; and at the sight of this signed contract the peasants shout for joy, having such confidence in stamped paper that they at once proceed to order a thanksgiving mass to be said at the Cordeliers.

Alarming symptoms these, indicating the secret disposition, the fixed resolve, the future task of the rising power. If it prove victorious, it will begin by destroying all old papers, lists, title-deeds, contracts, trusts, that it now has perforce to endure; perforce too it will have others drawn up to its own advantage, and the scribes will be the deputies, the administrators, that it holds in its rude grasp.

This causes, however, no alarm in high places; it is even thought that the revolt has something good about it, since it obliges the towns to suppress unjust taxes.* The young men of the new Marseillaise guard are permitted to go to Aubagne "to demand from M. le Lieutenant Criminel and M. l'Avocat du Roi the liberation of prisoners." There is toleration for the disobedience of Marseilles in refusing to receive the magistrates sent by letters patent to com-

* Archives Nationales, H, 1274. Lettre de M. de Caraman, 22 Avril: "Il est résulté de ce malheur un bien réel. . . . . On a reporté sur la classe aisée ce qui excédait les forces des malheureux journaliers. . . . On s'aperçoit encore d'un peu plus d'attention de la noblesse et des gens aisés pour les pauvres paysans; on s'est accoutumé à leur parler avec plus de douceur." M. de Caraman a été blessé, ainsi que son fils, à Aix, et, si les soldats lapidés ont fini par tirer, c'est sans son ordre. Ibid., Lettre de M. d'Antheman, 17 Avril; de M. de Barentin, 11 Juin.

mence informations. Better still, in spite of the remonstrances of the Parliament of Aix, a general amnesty is proclaimed; "a few ring-leaders only excepted, who are yet at liberty to leave the kingdom." The leniency of the King and of the military chiefs is admirable; it is an admitted thing that the people is a child, that it never offends except through error, that its repentance must be believed in, and that so soon as it returns to order, it must be welcomed back with paternal love; the truth being that the child is a blind giant exasperated by suffering; hence it breaks whatever it touches, not only destroying in the provinces those local wheels which after a temporary disarrangement may still be repaired, but also the central main-spring which gives movement to all the rest, and the destruction of which will throw the whole machine out of gear.

H. TAINE.

# WHAT IS IN STORE FOR EUROPE,

### AND ESPECIALLY FOR AUSTRIA-HUNGARY.

AN armistice, and with it preliminaries of peace, are under negotiation between Russia and Turkey. The apparent subject of the war, "The Eastern Question," was held to be a European one, in which both European interests, and international law founded on European treaties, are involved. Still Europe has not been admitted to a voice in the negotiations. The Czar is mighty. He bade Europe be "mum," and Europe is "mum;" even England is. The German Emperor—what from personal predilections, what from a sense of obligation for past services, and what from fear of the future is thoroughly Russian; improvidently, blindly Russian; heart and soul Russian. The Cabinet of Vienna, even more blindly improvident, is a *third party in the Russian league*. The rest of Europe is "invisible."

The Cabinet of Vienna, in this its monstrous capacity of partnership in the Russian league (firm: Gortschakoff, Bismarck, and Andrassy), has nullified Austria and Hungary for the whole course of this war, in the scales of which their very destinies are trembling; it threw cold water on the better inspirations and paralyzed the resolutions of England, whose interests are in so evident harmony with our own; and it condemned to abandonment and fall our friend, our bulwark, the Turk, who, heroically fighting for his own existence, was fighting also for the independence of Europe in general, for the safety of the position of England in the East in particular, and, in the very first line, for the future security of Austria and Hungary.

What could he do, poor wretch! bleeding from a thousand wounds; [illegible] at, bit, and hacked, right and left, front and back, by mastiff [illegible], and forsaken by all, even by those for whom he fought—[illegible] could he do?

[illegible] alternative was before him—either unfurl the banner of his Prophet, which he kept folded from a sense of humanity, su the setting half moon with an ocean of blood, and, if burial must be, bury himself under the ruins of half a shattered w ruins drearier than mankind has seen for thousands of years; bow his head in resignation before the *ineluctabile fatum*.

Poor wing-shot eagle! whom the very sparrows impudently to peck at;—he bowed his devoted head.

The pang of anguish and anxiety thrills through the heart Hungarian nation. But Count Andrassy bids her be of good "The interests of Austria and Hungary are safe; his calculati independent of the issue of the war." So he tells us. "Calcul indeed!

In the beginning he was appointed keeper of a door with wl might have pent up the winds of the hurricane. Afterwards he have chased them home with the words of Virgil's Neptune, *rate fugam*." He, instead, both unlocked the door and left fi field to the hurricane, the fury of which generations on gene shall mourn, and the long winding path of which will be by the ruins of shattered nations.

*He* unlocked the door; and then remained a spectator duri whole of the bloody drama. It is only in the last scene of act that he "calculates" to have a part to perform. Then perform, and he *will* show that our interests are safe.

Whether or not he shall be permitted to "perform" at all I tell. The signs are not encouraging. But two things I kn know that there are already facts, fatal accomplished facts, wl imaginable "performance" can undo. And I know that unless Andrassy departs from the line of policy until now pursued, not be able to save even what might yet be saved.

It is necessary to look closely into that policy in order tl Austro-Hungarian nation may see clearly her way, and deci will, and act accordingly. Where there is a will, there is a wa

Be it permitted to the love I bear to my native land, to say of Europe, to cast the light of my modest lamp on the dark the situation; perchance a ray of that modest lamp may hel bring into view the path which patriotism looks out for with solicitude.

* * *

While at Vienna Count Andrassy was being invested w Golden Fleece, at Fiume (territory of the Hungarian [illegible] to be "neutral") Russian marine officers went publicly [illegible] exercises in the art of handling the torpedoes, manufactured [illegible] Fiume, to blow up that very Turk, who (Poland being [illegible] a "living statue") is the very *last* dyke of Austria [illegible] against the flood of Panslavo-Czarism.

That Golden Fleece and that torpedo drill are each the complement of the other.

The Golden Fleece means, that the Emperor of Austria, King of Hungary, is well satisfied with the policy of his Minister for Foreign Affairs. The torpedo drill shows the colour of that policy.

I wonder whether that contented monarch has taken the pains to consider, if not the eventual consequences, at least the already-consummated actual results of that policy. For everything is not pending: there are already some accomplished facts.

There are several; I shall point out one.

A fatal connection exists between the war raging in our immediate neighbourhood and between the future of Hungary and Austria; a connection fatal as the wrath of the avenging deities, the Eumenides.

This connection originates in the fact, that in the present war not merely "The Eastern Question"—that is to say, the question of the relations between the Ottoman Porte and its Christian vassals and subjects—is put to the bloody arbitration of the sword, but that this question is complicated with another, *the question of Russian power*, which, as late as in 1854, the English Government, in open Parliament, declared to "*have grown to proportions dangerous to the liberties of Europe.*"

Whatever opinion be entertained concerning the best solution of the Eastern question if it were not complicated with the question of Russian power, this much no man having any notion of geography and ethnography will doubt: that the future of Hungary and Austria, and of the dynasty ruling these countries, will become endangered in the highest degree if one of the results of the present war be that the Roumans and the Eastern Slavs become the dependents of Russia, and get tied to the leading-strings of Russian policy. The geographical position and the ethnographical relations both of Austria and Hungary absolutely exclude even the possibility of any doubt on this point.

Therefore, whatever considerations may have influenced the determinations of the Cabinet of Vienna, so much is clear to demonstration, that *this one thing* ought not to have been permitted at any price; the instinct of self-preservation ought to have induced the Cabinet of Vienna to bring the full weight of its position, of its authority, and of its power, to bear on the point that this one thing should not be brought about. And precisely this one thing is already an accomplished fact.

Circumstances pointed out clearly to Count Andrassy what line of policy he ought to pursue.

If his opinion was, that alterations had to be made in the condition of the Turkish Empire to the profit of the Christian population, all his energies ought to have been directed to secure that the alterations deemed advisable should be the emanation, not of the pressure of victorious Russian arms, but of the spontaneous liberality of the Turkish Government, encouraged and supported by Austria and Hungary.

To have pointed out to the Porte the alterations which would have thwarted the influence of Russia without undermining the vitality of the Turkish Empire; to have presented an agreement on this basis as a condition of Austria-Hungary materially assisting Turkey in repelling Russia; to have thus brought home by facts to the understanding of the Eastern Christians that the vaunted protectorship of Russia was as feeble a reed to lean upon as it was ambitious in its aim; to have prevented the Eastern question from being complicated with the question of Russian power, thus bringing about a community of interest between the welfare and peaceful development of the Eastern Christians on the one hand, and the success of the regenerative efforts of the Turkish Empire on the other;—this was the line of policy imperatively indicated to Austria-Hungary by the exigencies of the case.

Such a policy recommended itself by advantages both obvious and essential. The Roumans and Eastern Slavs would not now be tied to the leading-strings of Russia; the totally unfounded but undeniably existing prejudice, that (I quote the very words of Count Andrassy) "Austria-Hungary had no feeling for the welfare and peaceful development of the Eastern Christians," would have been effectively removed; more yet, a community of interest would have been brought about between us, by the consideration of the requirements of future security; and last, not least, the alterations would not have exceeded the limits within which the benefits secured to the Eastern Christians would have been hailed with satisfaction by them, without undermining the vitality of the Turkish Empire, the maintenance of which is an essential postulate of the future security of Austria and Hungary. In the further course of my elucidations, I trust to be able to show that to give a reasonable satisfaction to the Eastern Christian people, and not injure materially the strength of Turkey, are two issues perfectly compatible.

Count Andrassy had it in his power to realize the manifold advantages of the above-indicated policy previous to the war, at the beginning of the war, and during the progress of the war. He did not do it. There were occasions so highly favourable to him, that they looked as if the gratuitous bounty of Providence was putting into his grasp the forelock of fleeting fortune, with these very words: "Now! take hold of it, secure the future of thy country and of thy Sovereign. Mind, that no eternity can bring the lost moment back again!"

He did not take hold of it. He rather turned his back on the good fortune offered to him; and went and became a partner in the Russian league. And in this position—truly honourable for an Austro-Hungarian Minister!—he went on, pushing the car of Russia to—Plevna, and further on.

The fall of yonder Titan there—for ever glorious even in his fall—

[illegible] fatally disastrous, not to Turkey alone, but to [illegible] Hungary, and to the Hapsburgs likewise.

[illegible] sacrifice the defeated Russian on the altar of his faith and [illegible] as his patron saint, to whom he prayeth; but many are [illegible] with the victorious Russian. Nobody would think of becoming [illegible] of the beaten Russian; of the victorious, many.

[illegible] Vienna catastrophe, Russia conquered the position of the [illegible] protector of the Roumans and of the Eastern Slavs. Her [illegible] might yet be torn from her hands by the force of arms, but to [illegible] that success by *negotiations* is absolutely impossible.

[illegible] impossible, because, whatever may be the final results of the [illegible], two things are perfectly certain.

The first is this, that if the Roumans and Eastern Slavs do not get everything their over-heated imagination is longing for, the odium of their disappointment will not fall on Russia but on others, and most [illegible] on Austria and Hungary; while Russia will certainly know how to feed the fire of their hatred with the oil of her ambitious intrigues. No doubt about that. "I felt compassion for you. I did not shrink from the immense sacrifices of a terrible war in your behalf; but to insure success it was necessary to fetter the hands of Austria-Hungary lest she might cross my road. For this end I had to make certain concessions. Therefore, if by this time all your wishes are not yet realized, you have to thank the malevolence of Austria-Hungary. But things deferred are not things lost. Just be true to me, [illegible] blade of the dagger to its handle, and what with our combined forces, what with the influence of our affinities of race, we will [illegible] Austria and Hungary. Be sure of that." So Russia will speak first and act afterwards. And it is not necessary to say that the seed so scattered will fall on a congenial soil. The odium of things not yet attained will fall on us. This is one certainty.

The second is, that everything the Roumans and the Slavs get they will set down solely and exclusively to the credit of their victorious patron, Russia; and this will, this must, fasten them unavoidably to the leading-strings of Russian policy, not as if they were in love with her, but because they found her powerful, while Europe they found "invisible;" and in invisible Europe they found Austria and Hungary miserably impotent.

Thus the very source of all the dangers menacing our future in the far-reaching consequences of the present war—the thing that had to be guarded against at every price—this very thing is by this time already a consummated event.

To realize fully in our thoughts the eventual danger implied in this [illegible], we must bear in mind that the further aspirations of the [illegible] and Servians are in a great degree directed against us (at [illegible] they are already openly, even with the authority of the [illegible], reminding the Czar of our "Transylvania"); we must bear in mind how many partisans Panslavism already numbers in the dominions of the House of Austria, and how that number is likely to increase under the influence of the nimbus surrounding the rising star of Russia in her capacity of the victorious champion of "the Slav cause;" we must bear in mind with what frenetic cheers the blood-coloured star of the rising power of Russia has been saluted from Sziszek to Prague; and when we consider what amount of auxiliary means all these fanatical aspirations and longings will impart to the evident tendencies of Russia, and with what assurance these can rely on the co-operation of the former,—on taking all this into consideration there can be no man on earth blind enough not to see that the *boa constrictor*, the *gigantic polypus* I spoke of in my former paper,* is already a material reality. The first is already hissing in our very face; the second is stretching out his tentacles. *Our frontiers are thickly beset with Russian clients.* Behind them, shattered and broken, —thanks to the suicidal improvidence of the Viennese Cabinet,—is the only friend whom we could trust, on whom we could depend. The halting-places *(étape)* are prepared for Russia on the march-route, the goal of which is Austria-Hungary!!

This success Count Andrassy has already achieved; this result he has obtained by his marvellous "calculations," so demonstratively approved of by his Sovereign.

*Plaudite!* To-day is yours: what need you care for to-morrow? what need you care for that "Fatherland" which ought still to exist when you shall be no more? The last in the file shall shut the door. *Plaudite!*

But the holy love of the native land,—the tomb of the generations that went before us, the cradle of those coming after us,—the holy love of the native country, that, with religious piety, clasps to its heart not only the Fatherland that is, but that also which ought to be, when we and the children of our children shall long have ceased to be,—this holy love feels a pang of pain that no words can express, while it looks into the "to-morrow" you did not care for.

"Like cause, like effect," is the eternal law of the eternal Lawgiver of the universe. It is not difficult to see into "to-morrow" when its shadows so evidently are cast on "to-day."

What is in store for that to-morrow?

Exactly the same thing as happened in Turkey. Word for word, the very same thing.

The patron of the Eastern Slavs and Roumans, free to dispose of them, will foment conspiracies and stir up seditions amongst the Slavs and Roumans of Austria and Hungary. There will be found plenty of such who will willingly yield to the "clinking" arguments of the victorious patron, who flatters the Slavs with the prospect of the dominion of the world, and on whose protection the Roumans rely for the reconstruction of the Dacia of the Emperor Trajan, who—as all of

*See CONTEMPORARY REVIEW for Dec., 1877.

[illegible] yesterday, some time before the migration of [illegible] thousand eight hundred years ago. The Russo-[illegible] ambitions will be repressed; the Russian will diplomati-[illegible] claiming justice and redress of "grievances" (so they [illegible] his "oppressed" (that is the term in use) kindred, and [illegible] of whom the Czar is the "natural" protector. The then [illegible] of Vienna will protest against this interference in [illegible] affairs, and either will tell the Russian that there was justice, [illegible] in Austria and Hungary; or else, with traditional [illegible] he will yield to the "benevolent advice," and to satisfy [illegible] and ally" will resort to concessions, which will not be [illegible]satisfactory—of course. In either case new conspiracies, [illegible] insurrections, will be stirred up; by-and-by Russian [illegible] "sympathisers," will openly share in the game (just [illegible]), blood will flow in streams, provinces will be devas-[illegible] cities will be burned down and sacked, inhuman [illegible] will engender inhuman retorts; Russian agents, masked [illegible] masked, in dress-coats and petticoats, will raise a hue and cry st the "sensitive" philanthropists of Europe. With the recital e new "Bulgarian atrocities," the diplomatic notes of Russia crease in number, and rise bolder and bolder in diapason, till at ter having provided for sharing partners, Russia at the proper t will declare that she cannot stand this any longer; will resort s "in the name of humanity, of freedom, of affinity of race, of and of the tranquillity of Europe;" and will step in to "restore in Hungary and Austria, and will charge some Cserkoszky to m in the holy name of liberty and of order the principle of the session of the actual proprietors and of the distribution of the soil, she did in Poland, and is doing with such splendid success now garia,—to the further glory of the wise policy of the Cabinet of [illegible].

is what will happen, word for word. Such is the habitual *modus* [illegible] of Russia. So she did with Poland, so she did with Turkey, and [illegible] do with Austria and Hungary; unless now, at the eleventh [illegible] of the nine Sibylline books are already burnt, the Cabinet [illegible] her determinations to the level of the impending peril. [illegible] slight these previsions, call them spectre-seeing or con-[illegible]. The sages of Troy, too, slighted the previsions of [illegible] and Troy fell.

[illegible] are but logical corollaries of the fact, that Russia, [illegible] allowed to vanquish in this war, has got the Roumans [illegible] Slavs (and, with these, many others likewise) tied to [illegible] her power and of her designs.

[illegible] Foreign Affairs of the Hungarian Delegation [illegible] sacrificed interests." Count Andrassy answered, [illegible] what those interests were.

I could name many; and perhaps will. One I have pointed out. It is of the highest order, because it compromises the future safety both of Hungary and of Austria.

* * *

Now what is the nature of that policy which, in spite of this fatal result, still permits Count Andrassy to rock himself in the illusion that "the interests of Hungary and Austria are safe?"

No man on earth can question the truth of the proposition that to us danger can come only from Russia, not from Turkey; that to us the maintenance of the vitality of the Turkish empire, instead of being a danger, is rather a bulwark of our safety from eventual danger.

Then by what strange reasoning could Count Andrassy arrive at the conclusion that it was not by coming to agreement with Turkey for preventing the extension of the power of Russia, he could guard that security of the Austro-Hungarian monarchy; but rather by coming to agreement with that Russia which is bent on breaking that Turkey which is the bulwark of our security?

There is such a monstrous abnormity in this proposition of the Austro-Hungarian Minister, that the official abettors of his fatal policy could find nothing better to adduce in its support than to hint at imperious pressure, at irresistible constraint, at menaces of war coming from Berlin.

All this is nothing better than a gratuitous insinuation, having no foundation whatever. The slightest acquaintance with the sentiments and interests of the German nation, and a mere cursory glance at the actual condition of Europe, are sufficient to refute it.

The Eastern broil is certainly so essentially interwoven, in different directions, with the international interests of the European Powers, that, should it become further complicated with some other European question so as to lead to a general European war, it is very likely that Austria and Hungary would not be found on the same side with Prussia.

However, to say that the Russian inclinations of the Emperor William could go so far as to resort, for the sake of Russia, to arms against Austria-Hungary, for no other reason but because the Cabinet of Vienna intended to pursue, in the Oriental question, a policy imperiously recommended by the requirements of its future safety,—to say this is to say a thing impossible.

Neither has Count Andrassy, to my knowledge, ever screened himself by any plea of constraint. He has rather always most emphatically repudiated the idea of his acting under constraint. He has always asserted, and charged the Hungarian Ministry to assert, that his hands were perfectly free.

In fact, if the case were not such, it would have been long ago the duty of Count Andrassy to bring the subject before the representative [illegible] both of Austria and of Hungary; and I am sure that [illegible] the Austro-Hungarian monarchy—with its [illegible] of 800,000 men, and with the more than 200,000 Hun[illegible] ready to march in eight days—either so sunk in [illegible] helpless in international relations as to swallow any [illegible] derogatory to the honour, dignity, and independence [illegible] monarchy, and in the highest degree injurious to its most vital [illegible] In order to repel such insult, the constitutional authorities of Hungary and Austria would certainly have granted long ago [illegible] all the required support for the realization of the [illegible]er combinations, for which the actual situation of Europe offers [illegible]d both vast and sure to the activity of a provident policy.

[illegible] the case that the Emperor William—let him be ever so [illegible]ian in his propensities—could command Francis Joseph of Austria-[illegible]gary to adopt, in favour of his natural enemy, Russia, such a line [illegible]licy as would undermine the very foundation of his existence; we would have no choice but to declare that the House of [illegible]ria is already mediatized. It depends on the whims of a patron. [illegible]ave a patron is to have a master.

[illegible]t such is not the case. It is not, because it is impossible that could be the case. Therefore, when I hear Count Andrassy [illegible] the phrase that "he did not make the Russo-Prussian alliance, [illegible]und it ready made," I feel inclined to set this to the account of [illegible]amorous propensities, by which he is wont (though not always in [illegible]roper place) to cheer the gloom of his official cares. At all events [illegible] answer is: If one finds a trap-ditch ready dug, the worst thing one [illegible] is to jump into it.

* * *

[illegible], it was not constraint, not pressure, that led Count Andrassy to [illegible]me the third partner in the Russian league: that which enticed [illegible] into that fatal abnormity was nothing else than a false starting-[illegible] in his reasonings.

[illegible] politics, as, in general, in all sorts of reasoning, everything depends [illegible]he point we start from. The foot once set upon the wheel of a [illegible]mill, one goes on treading; the wheel carries one.

[illegible] has pleased Count Andrassy to lift a little before the eyes of the [illegible]gation the veil which covered the incomprehensible mysteries of [illegible] policy. The petty details of the diplomatic circumlocutions may be a secret; the substance of his policy is no longer a secret. [illegible] little that transpired of his revelations is perfectly sufficient to [illegible]rt a clear insight into the starting-point, the direction, and the [illegible] of his policy. The rest is mere colourature, mere paraphrasis. It [illegible]ot materially alter either the drift or the issue of the case. For [illegible] in the net it is a very indifferent consolation to know with [illegible] kind of sauce he shall be served.

The situation is extremely serious.

Some years ago, when my country was standing at a fatal turning-point of its destinies, my voice—the voice of one who crieth in the wilderness—admonished the leaders of the country in these very words: "Beware how you push the nation towards surrendering her independence, by telling her that she wanted Austria to be safe from Russia. In this regard, Austria will prove to be not a protector from, but an attractor of, the lightning. Instead of strength, Austria will prove to be a weakness to Hungary as regards Russia."

The voice of the crier in the wilderness was a Cassandra voice. To-day it is already a fact that such it was.

What nameless anguish must thrill through the patriot's heart, when he considers how bright, how serene our horizon would have looked by this time, if, half-a-year ago, only half-a-year ago, the hands of Hungary had not been fettered by Vienna!

Well, they were fettered: Austria is a weakness, not a strength, to Hungary.

And at this moment I recall to memory those other words of mine: "The traditional policy of the Cabinet of Vienna will make of Hungary a funeral-pile, on which the Austrian eagle will be burnt by Russia."

Let Hungary beware lest these words, too, become the words of a Cassandra!

The time will come when appeals will be made to the hereditary heroism and the chivalric loyalty of the "magnanimous" Magyars: this I know. And the Magyar will stand his ground: this too I know. But like as that Norman of old, who to the query of St. Olav, "*In whom dost thou trust and believe?*" answered, "*In myself,*"—so we, too, can very nearly only trust and believe in ourselves. Let us keep that trust, that belief. But verily, I say, heavy times are in store for us first—and for Europe after.

KOSSUTH.

# THE NEW STAR WHICH FADED INTO STAR-MIST.

THE appearance (probably sudden) of a new star in the constellation of the Swan last autumn promises to throw even more light than was expected on some of the most interesting problems with which modern astronomy had to deal. It was justly regarded as a circumstance of extreme interest that so soon after the outburst of the star which formed a new gem in the Northern Crown in May, 1866, another should have shone forth under seemingly similar conditions. And when, as time went on, it appeared that in several respects the new star in the Swan differed from the new star in the Crown, astronomers found fresh interest in studying, as closely as possible, the changes presented by the former as it gradually faded from view. But they were not prepared to expect what has actually taken place, or to recognize so great a difference of character between these two new stars, that whereas one seemed throughout its visibility to ordinary eyesight, and even until the present time, to be justly called a star, the other should so change as to render it extremely doubtful whether at any time it deserved to be regarded as a star or sun.

Few astronomical phenomena, even of those observed during this century (so fruitful in great astronomical discoveries), seem better worthy of thorough investigation and study than those presented by the two stars which appeared in the Crown and in the Swan, in 1866 and 1876 respectively. A new era seems indeed to be beginning for those departments of astronomy which deal with stars and star-cloudlets on the one hand, and with the evolution of solar systems and stellar systems on the other.

Let us briefly consider the history of the star of 1866 in the first place, and then turn our thoughts to the more surprising and probably more instructive history of the star which shone out last November.

In the first place, however, I would desire to make a few remarks on the objections which have been expressed by an observer to whom astronomy is indebted for very useful work, against the endeavour to interpret the facts ascertained respecting these so-called new stars. M. Cornu, who made some among the earliest spectroscopic observations of the star in Cygnus, after describing his results, proceeded as follows:—

"Grand and seductive though the task may be of endeavouring to draw from observed facts inductions respecting the physical state of this new star, respecting its temperature, and the chemical reactions of which it may be the scene, I shall abstain from all commentary and all hypothesis on this subject. I think that we do not yet possess the data necessary for arriving at useful conclusions, or at least at conclusions capable of being tested: however attractive hypotheses may be, we must not forget that they are outside the bounds of science, and that, far from serving science, they seriously endanger its progress."

This, as I ventured to point out at the time, is utterly inconsistent with all experience. M. Cornu's objection to theorizing when he did not see his way to theorizing justly is sound enough; but his general objection to theorizing is, with all deference be it said, sheerly absurd. It will be noticed that I say theorizing, not hypothesis-framing, for though he speaks of hypotheses, he in reality is describing theories. The word hypothesis is too frequently used in this incorrect sense—perhaps so frequently that we may almost prefer sanctioning the use to substituting the correct word. But the fact really is, that many even among scientific writers, when they hear the word hypothesis, think immediately of Newton's famous "hypotheses non fingo," a dictum relating to real hypotheses, not to theories. It would, in fact, be absurd to suppose that Newton, who had advanced, advocated, and eventually established, the noblest scientific theory the world has known, would ever have expressed an objection to theorizing, as he is commonly understood to have done, by those who interpret his "hypotheses non fingo" in the sense which finds favour with M. Cornu. But apart from this, Newton definitely indicates what he means by hypotheses. "I frame no hypotheses," he says, "*for whatever is not deduced from phenomena is to be called an hypothesis.*" M. Cornu, it will be seen, rejects the idea of deducing from phenomena what he calls an hypothesis, but what would not be an hypothesis according to Newton's definition: "Malgré tout ce qu'il y aurait de séduisant et de grandiose à tirer de ce fait des inductions, etc., je m'abstiendrai de tout commentaire et de toute hypothèse à ce sujet." It is not thus that observed scientific facts are to be made fruitful, nor thus that the points to which closer attention must be given are to be ascertained.

Since the preceding paragraph was written my attention has been attracted to the words of another observer more experienced than M. Cornu, who has not only expressed the same opinion which I entertain respecting M. Cornu's ill-advised remark, but has illustrated in a very practical way, and in this very case, how science gains from commentary and theory upon observed facts. M. Vogel considers

"that the fear that a hypothesis" (he, also, means a theory here) "might do harm to science is only justifiable in very rare cases; in most cases it will further science. In the first place it draws the attention of the observer upon things which but for the hypothesis might have been neglected. Of course if the observer is so strongly influenced that in favour of an hypothesis he sees things which do not exist,—and this may happen sometimes,—science may for a while be arrested in its progress, but in that case the observer is far more to blame than the author of the hypothesis. On the other hand it is very possible that an observer may, involuntarily, arrest the progress of science, even without originating an hypothesis, by pronouncing and publishing sentences which have a tendency to diminish the general interest in a question, and which do not place its high significance in the proper light."

(This is very neatly put.) He is

"almost inclined to think that such an effect might follow from the reading of M. Cornu's remark, and that nowhere better than in the present case, where in short periods colossal changes showed themselves occurring upon a heavenly body, might the necessary data be obtained for drawing useful conclusions, and tests be applied to those hypotheses which have been ventured with regard to the condition of heavenly bodies."

It was, as we shall presently see, in thus collecting data and applying tests, that Vogel practically illustrated the justice of his views.

The star which shone out in the Northern Crown in May, 1866, would seem to have grown to its full brightness very quickly. Space will not permit me here to consider the history of the star's discovery; but I think all who have examined that history agree in considering that whereas on the evening of May 12, 1866, a new star was shining in the Northern Crown with second-magnitude brightness, none had been visible in the same spot with brightness above that of a fifth-magnitude star twenty-four hours earlier. On ascertaining, however, the place of the new star, astronomers found that there had been recorded in Argelander's chart and catalogue a star of between the ninth and tenth magnitude in this spot. The star declined very rapidly in brightness. On May 13th it appeared of the third magnitude; on May 16th it had sunk to the fourth magnitude; on the 17th to the fifth; on the 19th to the seventh; and by the end of the month it shone only as a telescopic star of the ninth magnitude. It is now certainly not above the tenth magnitude.

Examined with the spectroscope, this star was found to be in an abnormal condition. It gave the rainbow-tinted streak crossed by dark lines, which is usually given by stars (with minor variations which enable astronomers to classify the stars into several distinct orders). But superposed upon this spectrum, or perhaps we should rather say shining through this spectrum, were seen four brilliant lines, two of which certainly belonged to glowing hydrogen. These lines were so bright as to show that the greater part of the light of the star at the time came from the glowing gas or gases gi lines. It appeared, however, that the rainbow-tinted sp which these lines appeared was considerably brighter tha otherwise have been, in consequence of the accession of hee by and probably derived from the glowing hydrogen.

Unfortunately, we have not accordant accounts of tl which the spectrum of this star underwent as the star fa view. Wolf and Rayet, of the Paris Observatory, assert there remained scarcely any trace of the continuous sp four bright lines were still quite brilliant. But Huggins this was not the case in his observations; he was "able continuous spectrum when the bright lines could be scar guished." As the bright lines certainly faded out of view we may reasonably assume that the French observers were by the brightness of the lines from recognizing the contin trum at that particular stage of the diminution of the when the continuous spectrum had faded considerably, but gen lines little. Later, the continuous spectrum ceased in brightness, while the hydrogen lines rapidly faded. Th continuous spectrum could be discerned, and with greater distinctness as the hydrogen lines faded out.

Now, in considering the meaning of the observed chan so-called "new star," we have two general theories to con

One of these theories is that to which Dr. Huggins v to have inclined, though he did not definitely adopt it— namely, that in consequence of some internal convulsio quantities of hydrogen and other gases were evolved, whi bining with some other elements ignited on the surface and thus enveloped the whole body suddenly in a sheet of

"The ignited hydrogen gas in burning produced the light corr the two bright bands in the red and green; the remaining bright li however, coincident with those of oxygen, as might have be According to this theory, the burning hydrogen must have grea the heat of the solid matter of the photosphere, and brought it in more intense incandescence and luminosity, which may explain merly faint star could so suddenly assume such remarkable brilli liberated hydrogen became exhausted, the flame gradually abated, consequent cooling the photosphere became less vivid, and the sta its original condition."

According to the other theory, advanced by Meyer and blazing forth of this new star may have been occasio violent precipitation of some great mass, perhaps a pla fixed star, "by which the momentum of the falling mas changed into molecular motion," and result in the emiss and heat.

"It might even be supposed that the new star, [illegible] may have come in contact with one of the nebulæ, [illegible]

numbers the realms of space in every direction, and which from their gaseous condition must possess a high temperature; such a collision would necessarily set the star in a blaze, and occasion the most vehement ignition of its hydrogen."

If we regard these two theories in their more general aspect, considering one as the theory that the origin of disturbance was within the star, and the other as the theory that the origin of disturbance was outside the star, they seem to include all possible interpretations of the observed phenomena. But, as actually advanced, neither seems satisfactory. The sudden pouring forth of hydrogen from the interior, in quantities sufficient to explain the outburst, seems altogether improbable. On the other hand, as I have pointed out elsewhere, there are reasons for rejecting the theory that the cause of the heat which suddenly affected this star was either the downfall of a planet on the star or the collision of the star with a star-cloudlet or nebula, traversing space in one direction, while the star rushed onwards in another.

"A planet could not very well come into final conflict with its sun at one fell swoop. It would gradually draw nearer and nearer, not by the narrowing of its path, but by the change of the path's shape. The path would, in fact, become more and more eccentric; until at length, at its point of nearest approach, the planet would graze its primary, exciting an intense heat where it struck, but escaping actual destruction that time. The planet would make another circuit, and again graze the sun, at or near the same part of the planet's path. For several circuits this would continue, the grazes not becoming more and more effective each time, but rather less. The interval between them, however, would grow continually less and less; at last the time would come when the planet's path would be reduced to the circular form, its globe touching the sun's all the way round, and then the planet would very quickly be reduced to vapour and partly burned up, its substance being absorbed by its sun. But all successive grazes would be indicated to us by accessions of lustre, the period between each seeming outburst being only a few months at first, and gradually becoming less and less (during a long course of years, perhaps even of centuries) until the planet was finally destroyed. Nothing of this sort has happened in the case of any so-called new star." "As for the rush of a star through a nebulous mass,"

I went on,

"that is a theory which would scarcely be entertained by any one acquainted with the enormous distances separating the gaseous star-clouds properly called nebulæ. There may be small clouds of the same sort scattered much more freely through space; but we have not a particle of evidence that this is actually the case. All we certainly *know* about star-cloudlets suggests that the distances separating them from each other are comparable with those which separate star from star, in which case the idea of a star coming into collision with a star-cloudlet, and still more the idea of this occurring several times in a century, is wild in the extreme."

But while thus advancing objections, which seem to me irrefragable, against the theory that either a planet or a nebula (still less another small star) had come into collision with the orb in Corona which shone out so splendidly for a while, I advanced another view which seemed to me then and seems now to correspond well with phenomena, and to render the theory of action from without on the whole preferable to the theory of outburst from within. I suggested that, far more probably, an enormous flight of large meteoric masses travelling around the star had come into partial collision with it in the same way that the flight of November meteors comes into collision with our earth thrice in each century, and that other meteoric flights may occasionally come into collision with our sun, producing the disturbances which occasion the sun-spots. As I pointed out, in conceiving this, we are imagining nothing new. A meteoric flight capable of producing the suggested effects would differ only in kind from meteoric flights which are known to circle around our own sun. The meteors which produce the November displays of falling stars follow in the track of a comet barely visible to the naked eye.

"May we not reasonably assume that those glorious comets which have not only been visible but conspicuous, shining even in the day-time, and brandishing around tails, which like that of the 'wonder in heaven, the great dragon,' seemed to 'draw the third part of the stars of heaven,' are followed by much denser flights of much more massive meteors? Some of these giant comets have paths which carry them very close to our sun. Newton's comet, with its tail a hundred millions of miles in length, all but grazed the sun's globe. The comet of 1843, whose tail, says Sir John Herschel, 'stretched half-way across the sky,' must actually have grazed the sun, though but lightly, for its nucleus was within 80,000 miles of his surface, and its head was more than 160,000 miles in diameter. And these are only two among the few comets whose paths are known. At any time we might be visited by a comet mightier than either, travelling in an orbit intersecting the sun's surface, followed by flights of meteoric masses enormous in size and many in number, which, falling on the sun's globe with enormous velocity corresponding to their vast orbital range and their near approach to the sun—a velocity of some 360 miles per second—would, beyond all doubt, excite his whole frame, and especially his surface regions, to a degree of heat far exceeding what he now emits."

This theory corresponds far better also with observed facts than the theory of Meyer and Klein, in other respects than simply in antecedent probability. It can easily be shown that if a planet fell upon a sun in such sort as to become part of his mass, or if a nebula in a state of intense heat excited the whole frame of a star to a similar degree of heat, the effects would be of longer duration than the observed accession of heat and light in the case of all the so-called "new stars." It has been calculated by Mr. Croll (the well-known mathematician to whom we owe the most complete investigations yet made into the effect of the varying eccentricity of the earth's orbit on the climate of the earth) that if two suns, each equal in mass to one-half of our sun, came into collision with a velocity of 476 miles per second, light and heat would be produced which would cover the present rate of the sun's radiation for fifty million years. Now although it does not certainly follow from this that such a collision would result in the steady emission of so much light and heat as our sun gives out, for a period of fifty million years, but is, on the contrary, certain that there would be a far greater emission at first and a far smaller emission afterwards, yet it manifestly must be admitted that such a collision could not possibly produce so short-lived an effect as we see in the case of every one of the so-called new stars. The diminution in the emission of light and heat from the maximum to one-half the maximum would not occupy fifty millions of years, or perhaps even five million or five hundred thousand years; but it would certainly require thousands of years; whereas we have seen that the new stars in the Crown and in the Swan have lost not one-half but ninety-nine hundredths of their maximum lustre in a few months.

This has been urged as an objection even to the term star as applied to these suddenly appearing orbs. But the objection is not valid; because there is no reason whatever for supposing that even our own sun might not be excited by the downfall of meteoric or cometic matter upon it to a sudden and a short-lasting intensity of splendour and of heat. Mr. Lockyer remarks that, if any star, properly so called, were to become "a world on fire," or "burst into flames," or, in less poetical language, were to be driven either into a condition of incandescence absolutely, or to have its incandescence increased, there can be little doubt that thousands or millions of years would be necessary for the reduction of its light to its original intensity. This must, however, have been written in forgetfulness of some facts which have been ascertained respecting our sun, and which indicate pretty clearly that the sun's surface might be roused to a temporary intensity of splendour and heat without any corresponding increase in the internal heat, or in the activity of the causes, whatever they may be, to which the sun's *steady* emissions of light and heat are due.

For instance, most of my readers are doubtless familiar with the account (an oft-told tale, at any rate) of the sudden increase in the splendour of a small portion of the sun's surface on September 1, 1859, observed by two astronomers independently. The appearances described corresponded exactly with what we should expect if two large meteoric masses travelling side by side had rushed, with a velocity originally amounting to two or three hundred miles per second, through the portions of the solar atmosphere lying just above, at, and just below the visible photosphere. The actual rate of motion was measured at 120 miles per second as the minimum, but may, if the actual direction of motion was considerably inclined to the line of sight, have amounted to more than 200 miles per second. The effect was such, that the parts of the sun thus suddenly excited to an increased emission of light and heat appeared like bright stars upon the background of the glowing photosphere itself. One of the observers, Carrington, supposed for a moment that the dark glass screen used to protect the eye had broken. The increase of splendour was exceedingly limited in area, and lasted only for a few minutes,—fortunately for the inhabitants of earth. As it was the whole frame of the earth sympathized with the sun. Vivid auroras were seen, not only in both hemispheres, but in latitudes where auroras are seldom seen. were accompanied by unusually great electro-magnetic disturb

"In many places," says Sir J. Herschel, "the telegraph wires stru At Washington and Philadelphia, the electric signalmen received se tric shocks. At a station in Norway, the telegraphic apparatus wa to, and at Boston, in North America, a flame of fire followed the pen electric telegraph, which writes down the message upon chemically paper."

We see, then, that most certainly the sun can be locally ex increased emission of light and heat which, nevertheless, may for a very short time; and we have good reason for believing actual cause of the sudden change in his condition was the of meteoric matter upon a portion of his surface. We m believe that, whatever the cause may have been, it was ca might in the case of other suns, or even in our sun's own cas a much larger portion of the photosphere, in which case ther be just such an accession of splendour as we recognize in the the new stars. And as the small local accession of brillianc only a few minutes, we can well believe that an increase of brilliancy affecting a much larger portion of the photosphere, the entire photosphere, might last but for a few days or week

All that can be said in the way of negative evidence, so fa own sun is concerned, is that we have no reason for believing sun has, at any time within many thousands of years, been to emit even for a few hours a much greater amount of light a than usual; so that it has afforded no direct evidence in favou belief that other suns may be roused to many times their splendour, and yet very quickly resume that usual lustre. know that our sun, whether because of his situation in space, position in time (that is, the stage of solar development to he has at present attained), belongs to the class of stars whic with steady lustre. He does not vary like Betelgeux, for e which is not only a sun like him as to general character, but n larger and more massive orb. Still less is he like Mira, the W ful Star; or like that more wonderful variable star, Eta Argûs at one time shines with a lustre nearly equalling that of the Sirius, and anon fades away almost into utter invisibility. a variable sun, for we cannot suppose that the waxing and wa the sun-spot period leaves his lustre, as a whole, altogether un But his variation is so slight that, with all ordinary methods of metric measurement by observers stationed on worlds whic around other suns, it must be absolutely undiscernible. We do ever, reject Betelgeux, or Mira, or even Eta Argûs, from cause they vary in lustre. We recognize the fact that condition and in changes of condition, one star diff

Thus while there are excellent reasons for rejecting

[illegible] planet, or a nebulous mass like those which are [illegible] depths (the least of which would exceed many [illegible] sphere filling the entire space of the orbit of Nep[illegible] remote sun, there are no sufficient reasons for reject[illegible]ting the theory that a comet, bearing in its train a flight [illegible] of meteoric masses, falling directly upon such a sun, [illegible] to time with many times its ordinary lustre, but only [illegible] time, a few months or weeks, or a few days, or even hours. [illegible] entitled "Suns in Flames," in my "Myths and Marvels [illegible]omy," before the startling evidence recently obtained from [illegible] in Cygnus had been thought of, I thus indicated the pro[illegible] of such an event:—

[illegible] the earth has passed through the richer portions (not the actual nuclei [illegible]) of meteor systems, the meteors visible from even a single station [illegible] counted by tens of thousands, and it has been computed that millions [illegible] fallen upon the whole earth. These were meteors following in the [illegible] very small comets. If a very large comet followed by no denser a [illegible] meteors, but each meteoric mass much larger, fell directly upon the [illegible] would not be the outskirts but the nucleus of the meteoric train which [illegible] impinge upon him. They would number thousands of millions. The [illegible] of downfall of each mass would be more than 360 miles per second. [illegible] would continue to pour in upon him for several days in succession, [illegible] falling every hour. It seems not improbable that under this tremendous [illegible] continued meteoric hail, his whole surface would be caused to glow as [illegible] as that small part whose brilliancy was so surprising in the observa[illegible] by Carrington and Hodgson. In that case our sun, seen from some [illegible] whence ordinarily he is invisible, would shine out as a new sun for [illegible], while all things living, on our earth and whatever other members [illegible] solar system are the abode of life, would inevitably be destroyed."

[illegible] are, indeed, reasons for believing, not only, as I have already [illegible], that the outburst in the sun was caused by the downfall of [illegible]teoric masses, but that those masses were following in the train of [illegible] comet, precisely as the November meteors follow in the [illegible] Tempel's comet (II., 1866). For we know that November [illegible] displays have been witnessed for five or six years after the [illegible] of Tempel's comet, in its thirty-three year orbit, while the [illegible] meteoric displays have been witnessed fully one hundred and [illegible] years after the passage of their comet (II., 1862).* Now only [illegible] years before the solar outburst witnessed by Carrington and [illegible], a magnificent comet had passed even closer to the sun than [illegible] Tempel's comet or the second comet of 1862 approached the [illegible] orbit. That was the famous comet of the year 1843. Many [illegible] remember that wonderful object. I was but a child myself when [illegible]peared, but I can well remember its amazing tail, which in [illegible], 1843, stretched half-way across the sky.

* [illegible] may seem strange to say that one hundred and forty years after the passage of [illegible] which last passed in 1862, and was then first discovered, August meteors have [illegible]. But in reality, as we know the period of that comet to be about one hundred [illegible] years, we know that the displays of the years 1840, 1841, &c., to 1850, must [illegible] the preceding passage by about that interval of time.

"Of all the comets on record," says Sir J. Herschel, "that approached nearest the sun; indeed it was at first supposed that it had actually grazed the sun's surface, but it proved to have just missed by an interval of not more than 80,000 miles—about a third of the distance of the moon from the earth, which (in such a matter) is a very close shave indeed to get clear off."

We can well believe that the two meteors which produced the remarkable outburst of 1859 may have been stragglers from the main body following after that glorious comet. I do not insist upon the connection. In fact I rather incline to the belief that the disturbance in 1859, occurring as it did about the time of maximum sun-spot frequency, was caused by meteors following in the train of some as yet undiscovered comet, circuiting the sun in about eleven years, the spots themselves being I believe, due in the main to meteoric downfalls. There is greater reason for believing that the great sun-spot which appeared in June, 1843, was caused by the comet which three months before had grazed the sun's surface. As Professor Kirkwood of Bloomington, Indiana, justly remarks, had this comet approached a little nearer, the resistance of the solar atmosphere would probably have brought the comet's entire mass to the solar surface. Even at its actual distance it must have produced considerable atmospheric disturbance. But the recent discovery, that a number of comets are associated with meteoric matter travelling in nearly the same orbits, suggests the inquiry whether an enormous meteorite following in the comet's train, and having a somewhat less perihelion distance, may not have been precipitated upon the sun, thus producing the great disturbance observed so shortly after the comet's perihelion passage.

Let us consider now the evidence obtained from the star in Cygnus, noting especially in what points it resembles, and in what points it differs from, the evidence afforded by the star in the Crown.

The new star was first seen by Professor Schmidt at a quarter to six on the evening of November 24. It was then shining as a star of the third magnitude, in the constellation of the Swan, not very far from the famous but faint star 61 Cygni, which, first of all the stars in the northern heavens, had its distance determined by astronomers. The three previous nights had unfortunately been dark; but Schmidt is certain that on November 20 the star was not visible. At midnight, November 24, its light was very yellow, and it was somewhat brighter than the well-known star Eta Pegasi, which marks the fore-arm of the Flying Horse. Schmidt sent news of the discovery to Leverrier at Paris; but neither he nor Leverrier telegraphed the news, as they should have done, to Greenwich, Berlin, or the United States. Many precious opportunities for observing the spectrum of the new-comer at the time of its greatest brilliancy were thus lost.

The observers at Paris did their best to observe the spectrum of the star, and the all-important changes in the spectrum. But they had unfavourable weather. It was not till December 2 that the star was the eighth magnitude.

[His] earlier observations agreed well with Cornu's. He remarks, [howev]er, that Cornu's opinion as to the exact resemblance of the [chemic]al constitution of the star's atmosphere with that of the sierra [is not] just, for both Cornu and himself noticed one line which did [not cor]respond with any line belonging to the solar sierra; and this [line ev]entually became the brightest line of the whole spectrum. [Compa]ring his own observations with those of Cornu, Vogel points out [that th]ey agree perfectly with regard to the presence of the three [hydrog]en lines, and that of the brightest line of the air spectrum [(belong]ing to nitrogen), or the principal line of the spectrum of [nebulæ]. This is the line which has no analogue in the spectrum of the

[We] have also observations by F. Secchi, at Rome, Mr. Copeland at [Dunecht], and Mr. Backhouse of Sunderland, all agreeing in the main [with th]e observations made by Vogel and Cornu. In particular, Mr. [Backhou]se observed, as Vogel had done, that whereas in December [the gre]enish-blue line of hydrogen, F, was brighter than the nitrogen [line (als]o in the green-blue, but nearer the red end than F), on [Januar]y 6 the nitrogen line was the brightest of all the lines in the [spectru]m of the new star.

[Vogel], commenting on the results of his observations up to [March] 10, makes the following interesting remarks (I quote, with

slight verbal alterations, from a paraphrase in a weekly
journal):—

"A stellar spectrum with *bright* lines is always a highly-interestin
menon for any one acquainted with stellar spectrum analysis, and we
of deep consideration. Although in the chromosphere (sierra) of our
the limb, we see numerous bright lines, yet only dark lines appe
spectrum whenever we produce a small star-like image of the sun, and
it through the spectroscope. It is generally believed that the brigh
some few star-spectra result from gases which break forth from the
the luminous body, the temperature of which is higher than that of th
of the body—that is, the phenomenon is the same sometimes obser
spectra of solar spots, where incandescent hydrogen rushing out o
interior becomes visible above the cooler spots through the hydro
turning bright. But this is not the only possible explanation. We
suppose that the atmosphere of a star, consisting of incandescent g
the case with our own sun, is on the whole cooler than the nucleus,
regard to the latter is extremely large. I cannot well imagine how t
menon can last for any long period of time if the former hypothesis
The gas breaking forth from the hot interior of the body will impart
of its heat to the surface of the body, and thus raise the temperatu
latter; consequently the difference of temperature between the in
gas and the surface of the body will soon be insufficient to produ
lines; and these will disappear from the spectrum. This view applies
to stars which suddenly appear and soon disappear again, or at leas
considerably in intensity—that is, it applies perfectly to so-called ne
the spectra of which bright lines are apparent, *if* the hypothesis p
be mentioned is admitted for their explanation. For a more stabl
things the second hypothesis seems to be far better adapted.
Beta Lyræ, Gamma Cassiopeiæ, and others, which show the hydr
and the sierra D line bright on a continuous spectrum, with only sligh
of intensity, possess, according to this theory, atmospheres very l
tively to their own volume, the atmospheres consisting of hydrogen
unknown element which produces the D line.* With regard to the
Zöllner, long before the progress lately made in stellar physics by
spectrum analysis, deduced from Tycho's observations of the star c
him, that on the surface of a star, through the constant emission of
products of cooling, which in the case of our sun we call sun-spots, a
so that finally the whole surface of the body is covered with a colde
which gives much less light or none at all. Through a sudden a
tearing up of this stratum the interior incandescent materials which
must naturally break forth, and must in consequence, according to
of their eruption, cause larger or smaller patches of the dark envel
body to become luminous again. To a distant observer such an eru
the hot and still incandescent interior of a heavenly body must app
sudden flashing up of a new star. That this evolution of light
certain conditions be an extremely powerful one, could be explained
cumstance that all the chemical compounds which, under the influ
lower temperature, had already formed upon the surface, are again d
through the sudden eruption of these hot materials, and that this d
tion, as in the case of terrestrial substances, takes place under ev
light and heat. Thus the bright flashing-up is not only ascribed to
of the surface which through the eruption of the incandescent m

* The D line, properly speaking, as originally named by Fraunhofer,
sodium. The line spoken of above as the sierra D line is one close by the
and mistaken for it when first seen in the spectrum of the coloured promi
bright line. It does not appear as a dark line in the solar spectrum.

again become luminous, but also to a simultaneous process of combustion, which is initiated through the colder compounds coming into contact with the incandescent matter."

Vogel considers that Zöllner's hypothesis has been confirmed in its essential points by the application of spectrum analysis to the stars. We can recognize from the spectrum different stages in the process of cooling, and in some of the fainter stars we perceive indeed that chemical compounds have already formed, and still exist. As to new stars, again, says Vogel, Zöllner's theory seems in nowise contradicted

"by the spectral observations made on the two new stars of 1866 and 1876. The bright continuous spectrum, and the bright lines only slightly exceeding it at first" (a description, however, applying correctly only to the star of 1876), "could not be well explained if we only suppose a violent eruption from the interior, which again rendered the surface wholly or partially luminous; but are easily explained if we suppose that the quantity of light is considerably augmented through a simultaneous process of combustion. If this process is of short duration, then the continuous spectrum, as was the case with the new star of 1876, will very quickly decrease in intensity down to a certain limit, while the bright lines in the spectrum, which result from the incandescent gases that have emanated in enormous quantities from the interior, will continue for some time."

It thus appears that Herr Vogel regarded the observations which had been made on this remarkable star up to March 10 as indicating that first there had been an outburst of glowing gaseous matter from the interior, producing the part of the light which gave the bright lines indicative of gaseity, and that then there had followed, as a consequence, the combustion of a portion of the solid and relatively cool crust, causing the continuous part of the spectrum. We may compare what had taken place, on this hypothesis, to the outburst of intensely hot gases from the interior of a volcanic crater, and the incandescence of the lips of the crater in consequence of the intense heat of the out-rushing gases. Any one viewing such a crater from a distance, with a spectroscope, would see the bright lines belonging to the out-rushing gases superposed upon the continuous spectrum due to the crater's burning lips. Vogel further supposes that the burning parts of the star soon cooled, the majority of the remaining light (or at any rate the part of the remaining light spectroscopically most effective) being that which came from the glowing gases which had emanated in vast quantities from the star's interior.

"The observations of the spectrum show beyond doubt," he says, "that the decrease in the light of the star is in connection with the cooling of its surface. The violet and blue parts decreased more rapidly in intensity than the other parts; and the absorption bands which crossed the spectrum have gradually become darker and darker."

The reasoning, however, if not altogether unsatisfactory, is by no means so conclusive as Herr Vogel appears to think. It is not clear how the incandescent portion of the surface could possibly cool in any great degree while enormous quantities of gas more intensely heated (by the hypothesis) remained around the star. The more rapid decrease in the violet and blue parts of the spectrum than in the red and orange is explicable as an effect of absorption, at least as readily as by the hypothesis that burning solid or liquid matter had cooled. Vogel himself could only regard the other bands which crossed the spectrum as absorption bands. And the absorption of light from the continuous spectrum in these parts (that is, not where the bright lines belonging to the gaseous matter lay) could not possibly result from absorption produced by those gases. If other gases were in question, gases which, by cooling with the cooling surface, had become capable of thus absorbing light from special parts of the spectrum, how is it that before, when these gases were presumably intensely heated, they did not indicate their presence by bright bands? Bright bands, indeed, were seen, which eventually faded out of view, but these bright bands did not occupy the position where, later on, absorption bands appeared.

The natural explanation of what had thus far been observed is different from that advanced by Vogel, though we must not assume that because it is the natural, it is necessarily the true explanation. It is this—that the source of that part of the star's light which gave the bright-line spectrum, or the spectrum indicative of gaseity, belongs to the normal condition of the star, and not to gases poured forth in consequence of some abnormal state of things from the sun's interior. We should infer naturally, though again I say not *therefore* correctly, that if a star spectroscope had been directed upon the place occupied by the new star before it began to shine with unusual splendour, the bright-line spectrum would have been obtained. Some exceptional cause would then seem to have aroused the entire surface of the star to shine with a more intense brightness, the matter thus (presumably) more intensely heated being such as would give out the combined continuous and bright-line spectrum, including the bright lines which, instead of fading out, shone with at least relatively superior brightness as the star faded out of view. The theory that, on the contrary, the matter giving these more persistent lines was that whose emission caused the star's increase of lustre, seems at least not proven, and I would go so far as to say that it accords ill with the evidence.

The question, be it noted, is simply whether we should regard the kind of light which lasts longest in this star as it fades out of view as more probably belonging to the star's abnormal brightness or to its normal luminosity. It seems to me there can be little doubt that the persistence of this part of the star's light points to the latter rather than to the former view.

Let it also be noticed that the changes which had been observed thus far were altogether unlike those which had been observed in the case of the star in the Northern Crown, and therefore cannot justly be

...to the same explanation. As the star in the ...the bright lines indicative of glowing hydro- ...only the ordinary stellar spectrum remained. In ...the Swan, the part of the spectrum correspond- ...faded gradually from view, and bright lines only ...as conspicuous parts of the star's spectrum. So that ...seemed to have faded into a faint star, the other ...out into a nebula,—not merely passing into such a ...ion as to shine with light indicative of gaseity, but actually so ...ing as to shine with light of the very tints (or more strictly of ...ry wave-lengths) observed in all the gaseous nebulæ.

...strange eventful history of the new star in Cygnus did not end ...however. We may even say, indeed, that it has not ended yet. ...chapter can already be written.

...sel ceased from observing the star in March, precisely when ob- ...ion seemed to promise the most interesting results. At most observatories, also, no observations were made for about half a ... At the Dunecht Observatory* pressure of work relating to ...interfered with the prosecution of those observations which had commenced early in the year. But on September 3, Lord ...y's 15-inch refractor was directed upon the star. A star was ...where the new star's yellow lustre had been displayed last ...; but now the star shone with a faint blue colour. Under ...scopic examination, however, the light from this seeming blue ...was found not to be star-light, properly speaking, at all. It ...d no rainbow-tinted spectrum, but gave light of only a single ... The single line now seen was that which at the time of ...'s latest observation had become the strongest of the bright ...of the originally complex spectrum of the so-called new star. It ... brightest of the lines given by the gaseous nebulæ. In fact, if ...g had been known about this body before the spectroscopic ...vation of September 3 was made, the inference from the spec- ...given by the blue star would undoubtedly have been that the ... is in reality a small nebula of the planetary sort, very similar ... one close by the pole of the ecliptic, which gave Huggins the ...evidence of the gaseity of nebulæ, but very much smaller. I ...l specially direct the reader's attention, in fact, to Huggins's ...nt of his observation of that planetary nebula in the Dragon. ...August 19, 1864," he says, "I directed the telescope armed with ...pectrum apparatus to this nebula. At first I suspected some ...gement of the instrument had taken place, for no spectrum was ...but only" a single line of light. "I then found that the light of ...nebula, unlike any other extra-terrestrial light which had yet been ...ed by me to prismatic analysis, was not composed of light of ...

* ...this was written, I have learned that Mr. Backhouse of Sunderland announced ...to those obtained at Dunecht, as seen a fortnight or so earlier.

different refrangibilities, and therefore could not form a spec[illegible] great part of the light from this nebula is monochromatic, [illegible] passing through the prisms remains concentrated in a bright [illegible] more careful examination showed that not far from the brigh[illegible] a much fainter line; and beyond this, again, a third exceedin[illegible] line was seen. The brightest of the three lines was a line of [illegible] corresponding in position with the brightest of the lines in t[illegible] trum of our own air. The faintest corresponded in positio[illegible] line of hydrogen. The other has not yet been associated with line of any element. Besides the faint lines, Dr. Huggins p[illegible] an exceedingly faint continuous spectrum on both sides of th[illegible] of bright lines; but he suspected that this faint spectrum continuous, but crossed by dark spaces. Later observations [illegible] nebulæ induced him to regard this faint continuous spectrum to the solid or liquid matter of the nucleus, and as quite disti[illegible] the bright lines into which nearly the whole of the light [illegible] nebula is concentrated. The fainter parts of the spectrum gaseous nebulæ, in fact, correspond to those parts of the spe[illegible] the "new star" in Cygnus which last remained visible, be[illegible] light assumed its present monochromatic colour.

Now let us consider the significance of the evidence affo[illegible] this discovery—not perhaps hoping at once to perceive the fu[illegible] ing of the discovery, but endeavouring to advance as far as [illegible] can in the direction in which it seems to point.

We have, then, these broad facts: where no star had been an object has for a while shone with stellar lustre, in this se[illegible] its light gave a rainbow-tinted spectrum not unlike that [illegible] given by a certain order of stars; this object has graduall[illegible] with its new lustre, and in so doing the character of its spec[illegible] slowly altered, the continuous portion becoming fainter, and [illegible] lustre of the bright-line portion shifting from the hydrogen l[illegible] line which, there is every reason to believe, is absolutely [illegible] with the nebula nitrogen line; and lastly, the object has [illegible] give any perceptible light, other than that belonging to this [illegible] line.

Now it cannot, I think, be doubted that, accompanying th[illegible] lustre in this orb, there has been a corresponding loss of hea[illegible] theory that all the solid and liquid materials of the orb ha[illegible] vaporized by intense heat, and that this vaporization has ca[illegible] loss of the star's light (as a lime-light might die out with [illegible] sumption of the lime, though the flame remained as hot as[illegible] opposed by many considerations. It seems sufficient to menti[illegible] that if a mass of solid matter, like a dead sun or planet, were to an intense heat, first raising it to incandescence, and ev[illegible] altogether vaporizing its materials, although quite possibly the its intensest lustre might precede the completion of the vapo[illegible]

...as soon as the vaporization was complete, the spectrum ...vaporized mass would show multitudinous bright lines ... to the variety of material existing in the body. No ... of spectroscopic analysis lends countenance to the belief ...solid or liquid mass, vaporized by intense heat, would shine ... with monochromatic light.

... I think we are definitely compelled to abandon Vogel's ...tion of the phenomena by Zöllner's theory. The reasons ... I have urged above are not only strengthened severally by the ... which has taken place in the spectrum of the new star since ... observed it, but an additional argument of overwhelming force ... introduced. If any one of the suns died out, a crust forming ... surface and this crust being either absolutely dark or only ... with very feeble lustre, the sun would still in one respect ... all the suns which are spread over the heavens,—it ...ow no visible disc, however great the telescopic power used ...wing it. If the nearest of all the stars were as large, or even ... times as large, as Sirius, and were observed with a tele...e of ten times greater magnifying power than any yet directed to ...heavens, it would appear only as a point of light. If it lost the ...art of its lustre, it would appear only as a dull point of light. ... the planetary nebulæ show discs, sometimes of considerable ...dth. Sir J. Herschel, to whom and to Sir W. Herschel we owe ...discovery and observation of nearly all these objects, remarks that ... planetary nebulæ have, as their name imports, a near, in some ...es a perfect, resemblance to planets, presenting discs round, or ... oval, in some quite sharply terminated, in others a little hazy ...ened at the borders . . ." Among the most remarkable may ...pecified one near the Cross, whose light is about equal to that ... star just visible to the naked eye, "its diameter about twelve ...nds, its disc circular or very slightly elliptic, and with a clear ...p, well-defined outline, having exactly the appearance of a planet, ... the exception of its colour, which is a fine and full blue, verging ...what upon green." But the largest of these planetary nebulæ, ...ar from the southernmost of the two stars called the Pointers, has ...ameter of 2⅔ minutes of arc, "which, supposing it placed at a ...nce from us not greater than that of the nearest known star of ... northern heavens, would imply a linear diameter seven times ...ter than that of the orbit of Neptune." The actual volume of ... object, on this assumption, would exceed our sun's ten million ...on times. No one supposes that this planetary nebula, shining ... a light indicative of gaseity, has a mass exceeding our sun's in ...normous degree. It probably has so small a mean density as ...ikely to exceed, or perhaps barely to equal, our sun in mass. Now ... the "new star" in Cygnus presented no measurable disc, and ... as a mere blue point in the largest telescope, yet inasmuch as its spectrum associated it with the planetary and gase which we know to be much larger bodies than the stars, regarded, in its present condition, as a planetary nebul small one; and since we cannot for a moment imagine the strous planetary nebulæ just described are bodies which suns, but whose crust has now become non-luminous, whil masses of gas shine with a faint luminosity, so are we prec believing that this smaller member of the same family condition.

It *is* conceivable (and the possibility must be taken into any attempt to interpret the phenomena of the new star) shining as a star, the new orb, so far as this unusual lustr cerned, was of sunlike dimensions. For we cannot tell surface which gave the strong light was less or greater th to, that which is now shining with monochromatic light. if we had been placed where we could have seen the full of the planetary nebula as it at present exists, we should only its nuclear part glowing suddenly with increased lu after very rapidly attaining its maximum, gradually died leaving the nebula as it had been before. But that the shining with monochromatic light is, I will not say enorm but of exceedingly small mean density, so that it is enorm compared with the dimensions it would have if its entir were compressed till it had the same mean density as o must be regarded as, to all intents and purposes, certain.

We certainly have not here, then, the case of a sun which old and dead and dark save at the surface, but within wh fire has still remained, only waiting some disturbing caus it for a while to rush forth. If we could suppose that in there *could* be such changes as the spectroscope has indic the bright lines of the gaseous outbursting matter would, earlier period of the outburst, show on a bright contin ground, due to the glowing lips of the opening through matter had rushed, but later would shine alone, becoming in number, till at last only one was left,—we should still fi confronted with the stupendous difficulty that that singl line is the bright line of the planetary and other gaseous ne hypothesis accounting for its existence in the spectrum blue starlike object into which the star in Cygnus has fad be competent to explain its existence in the spectrum of th But *this* hypothesis certainly does not so explain its exist nebular spectrum. The nebulæ cannot be suns [illegible] save for the light of gaseous matter surrounding [illegible] millions, or rather millions of millions, of times [illegible] instance, a nebula, like the one above describ[illegible] southernmost Pointer, were a mass of this kind [illegible]

[illegible] lying only at the distance of the nearest of [illegible] then not only would it have the utterly monstrous [illegible] by Sir W. Herschel, but it would in the most effec- [illegible] the whole solar system. With a diameter exceeding [illegible] of the orbit of Neptune, it would have a volume, [illegible], exceeding our sun's volume and mass more [illegible] millions of millions of times. But its distance on this [illegible] would be only about two hundred thousand times the sun's, [illegible] reduced, as compared with his, on this account only [illegible] millions of times. So that its attraction on the sun [illegible] earth would be greater than his attraction on the earth, [illegible] degree that eleven millions are greater than forty thousand, [illegible] hundred and seventy-five times. The sun, despite his enor- [illegible] from such a mass, would be compelled to fall very [illegible]ly into it, unless he circuited (with all his family) around it in [illegible] one-sixteenth of a year, which most certainly he does not do. [illegible] increasing the distance at which we assume the star to lie [illegible] effect to save the sun from being thus perturbed, but the [illegible] If we double for instance our estimate of the nebula's dis- [illegible] increase eightfold our estimate of its mass, while we only [illegible] attraction on our sun fourfold on account of increased [illegible] so that now its attraction on our sun would be one-fourth [illegible] attraction multiplied by eight, or twice our former estimate. [illegible] suppose the nebula to be much nearer than the nearest [illegible], we cannot suppose that the light of these gaseous nebulæ [illegible] only from some bright orb within them of only starlike apparent [illegible]; for in that case we should constantly recognize such star- [illegible], which is not the case. Moreover, the bright-line spectrum [illegible] one of these nebulæ comes from the whole nebula, as is proved [illegible]e fact that if the slit be opened it becomes possible to see three [illegible]roscopic images of the nebula itself, not merely the three bright [illegible]

[illegible] that, if we assume the so-called star in Cygnus to be now like [illegible] objects giving the same monochromatic spectrum,—and this seems [illegible]nly legitimate assumption,—we are compelled to believe that the [illegible] now reaching us comes from a nebulous mass, not from the [illegible]y luminous envelope of a dead sun. Yet, remembering that [illegible] at its brightest this orb gave a spectrum resembling in general [illegible]teristics that of our other stars or suns, and closely resembling [illegible] in details that of stars like Gamma Cassiopeiæ, we are compelled [illegible]rity of reasoning to infer that when the so-called new star was [illegible]ming, the greater part of its light came from a sunlike mass. [illegible], then, we are led to the conclusion that in the case of this body [illegible]ave a nucleus or central mass of matter, and that around this [illegible]al mass there is a quantity of gaseous matter, resembling in con- [illegible]ion that which forms the bulk of the other gaseous nebulæ. The denser nucleus ordinarily shines with so faint a lustre that the continuous spectrum from its light is too faint to be discerned with the same spectroscopic means by which the bright lines of the gaseous portion are shown; and the gaseous portion ordinarily shines with so faint a lustre that its bright lines would not be discernible on the continuous background of a stellar spectrum. Through some cause unknown,—possibly (as suggested in my article on the earlier history of this same star in my "Myths and Marvels of Astronomy") the rush of a rich and dense flight of meteors upon the central mass,—the nucleus was roused to a degree of heat far surpassing its ordinary temperature. Thus for a time it glowed as a sun. At the same time the denser central portions of the nebulous matter were also aroused to intenser heat, and the bright lines which ordinarily (and certainly at present) would not stand out bright against the rainbow-tinted background of a stellar spectrum, showed brightly upon the continuous spectrum of the new star. Then as the rush of meteors upon the nucleus and the surrounding nebulous matter ceased,—if that be the true explanation of the orb's accession of lustre,—or as the cause of the increase of brightness, whatever that cause may have been, ceased to act,—the central orb slowly returned to its usual temperature, the nebulous matter also cooling, the continuous spectrum slowly fading out, the denser parts of the nebulous matter exercising also a selective absorption (explaining the bands seen in the spectrum at this stage) which gradually became a continuous absorption—that is, affected the entire spectrum. Those component gases, also, of the nebulous portion which had for a while been excited to sufficient heat to show their bright lines, cooled until their lines disappeared, and none remained visible except for a while the three usual nebular lines, and latterly (owing to still further cooling) only the single line corresponding to the monochromatic light of the fainter gaseous nebulæ.

RICHARD A. PROCTOR.

# THE THREE CONFLICTING THEORIES OF CHURCH AND STATE:

I. THE ERASTIAN.
II. THE LIBERATIONIST.
III. THE ANGLICAN.

A TRIANGULAR duel of the oddest kind is going on at the present time in England about the question of Church and State. Each combatant's attention is fixed on the hostile party immediately opposite him. But in point of fact, that party is harmless to hurt. He is delivering fire in quite another direction, and the attack to be really dreaded comes, in each case, from a combatant on the flank and not in the front. Such an entanglement as this is of rare occurrence in politics, and the interest of the situation is great, in proportion to its rarity and its complexity. The three combatants are the Erastian, the Liberationist, and the Anglican parties.

I. We begin with ERASTIANISM. Its singular nomenclature need not detain us long. The respectable Swiss physician, who lent his convenient name to a party he never originated, died in 1583 and was buried in peace at Basle. He was a man of sound common sense; and, being court physician in the highly Protestant atmosphere of Heidelberg, he dabbled a little in the theological squabbles of his day; and happened to propound a very clear opinion that Excommunication was a weapon largely abused, for that "heresy" alone was the proper object for Church censure, while "crime" should be dealt with exclusively by the State. It is obvious at a glance how far this notion falls short of what is understood by modern Erastianism. For that doctrine goes the length of annihilating Church censures altogether; it makes the Church neither more nor less than a department of the State, and then, if censure or discipline be needed, it devolves all such unpleasant work upon the Government of the country for the time being. The doctrine were, of course, a simple truism, if it merely meant that all coercive authority belongs, in the last resort, to the State, for this is acknowledged on all hands. It means far more than that: it is the proposal to invest the State, the country, the nation, with full power to seize and manipulate —as it might manipulate the army, the post-office, or the police—the delicate organization and the impalpable forces of religion. But how such a project could result in anything but untold disaster it is impossible either for a Liberationist or an Anglican to conceive. It appears to them like the celebrated attempt to shape a grindstone with a razor, or (in Luther's phrase) to "smite a spirit with a sword."

To what source, then, is this strange and impracticable theory to be traced? It is—like so many other notions whose essential incongruity refuses all permanent combination with English ideas—an article of foreign importation. The stamp it bears is that of Germany: the agent who introduced it into this country was Baron Bunsen: and its receiver here was Dr. Arnold of Rugby, through whose pupils it has been disseminated far and wide (especially among the laity) up and down the country. In saying this, however, not one breath of disparagement is intended against either of these two admirable men, or any of their more distinguished followers. To Dr. Arnold, in particular, as the greatest educationist of our time, this country owes an incalculable debt of gratitude. But still it does not follow, because A. B. is a good man and a first-rate schoolmaster, that therefore his theology is infallible or his theories about Church and State are to be received with implicit and uninquiring submission. Faraday was a good man and a first-rate chemist; but in theology he belonged to one of the obscurest sects in Christendom.

Now in Germany, it is well known, the exigencies of the Reformation, repudiated by the hierarchy to a man, drove Luther into the arms of the State. Amid the gloom of a bitter clerical persecution, a new light seemed to dawn on him from Holy Scripture; and a text gleamed out, in letters of fire, amid the surrounding darkness, "Ye are a chosen generation, a royal priesthood, an holy nation."* The Christian laity therefore, he argued, are all *virtually* priests; and the clergy are only *actually* so, by delegation from their brethren. Thus a Christian State, as the organized, regulative, and corrective force of the whole nation, has the right of absolute control over every part of the body politic; and the temporal Power may justly claim to define the duties of the clergy, and to punish all those whose proceedings it may disapprove.† The doctrine is plausible. It is nothing more or less, however, than the Hildebrandine theocracy presented on its reverse side. The essential idea in both cases is the same—the absolute unity and entire unchecked self-government of a Christian people. But the stress lies on the word *Christian* people: and who shall guarantee the continued Christianity either of a Church-State, whose pope may become Antichrist, or of a

* 1 Pet. ii. 9. † Address to the German Nation, 1520.

[illegible] chief magistrate may nowadays be an Atheist [illegible] nevertheless, no such *reductio ad absurdum* seems to have [illegible] mind of Luther or of any of his followers. Our own [illegible] (laying infinite stress and emphasis on the word [illegible]") says—

"[illegible] we oppose the Church and the Commonwealth, in a *Christian* society, [illegible] by the 'Commonwealth' that society in relation to all the public [illegible] —only the matter of true religion excepted; by the 'Church,' the [illegible] —with only reference unto the matter of true religion."*

[illegible]

"*Seeing that* there is not any man a member of the Commonwealth, which [illegible] of the Church of England, therefore one and the self-same multitude [illegible] in such sort be both (and *is so with us*) that no person appertaining to the one can be denied to be also of the other."†

So that he too, like Luther, makes no provision whatever for the highly probable contingency of a nation being, or becoming, only partially Christian. And since this is precisely the contingency which has befallen England now, in company with most European States, the Erastian theories of both Luther and Hooker seem to fall hopelessly to the ground; and any attempt to carry them into the field of practical politics is stricken with inevitable futility.

And yet—as if on purpose to serve as a warning to England—Prussia tried, twenty years ago, the very experiment which Erastians appear desirous of seeing repeated in this country. The Constitution of 1850 had given almost entire independence to the Romanists. But what was to be done with the Protestants? They, too, had become independent before the law; but the unhappy fact of their division into two great sections, the Lutheran (or High Church) and the Calvinist (or Low Church) parties, rendered all united action impossible. It was therefore determined to bridge over the divergence, and to yoke the two Confessions into one, by bringing into active use the dormant, but acknowledged, supremacy of the Crown. The King, by a series of edicts, organized the (so-called) Lutheran and Reformed communities into one "United Evangelical Church of Prussia." And then—having set his State-made Church upon its feet, endowed it with all that was needful for its efficiency, placed it under the friendly tutelage of a Minister of Public Worship, and discouraged all its foes by a free employment of political coercion—the good King expected it to go forth "conquering and to conquer." But in fact it would not stir one step. And, on examination, it was discovered to be dead. "An official Christendom had been set up, the willing acceptance of which *en bloc* was the test of a loyal disposition, and the condition of promotion. It was altogether overlooked that none but untrustworthy adherents could be obtained in this manner."‡ And [illegible]

* Eccles. Pol. viii. 1, 5. † Ibid. viii. 1, 2.
‡ Geffcken: Church and State, ii. 389.

the subsequent attempt to galvanize it into life, by a royal edict est ing synods, was equally unsuccessful. Certain "complaints led summary abolition, by a ministerial order, of a number of bei reforms which had obtained full legal recognition by the synod definite forms of belief gradually melted away; and at last dates for holy orders presented themselves by twos and threes, i of by tens and hundreds. Hence, to keep things together, tl of the Minister of Public Worship was intensified into a lay-p and the result is that the Church of Prussia is both "surrende the influence of the masses, and at the same time placed at the of the State."*

Such is the testimony of a German—a man (by the ackno ment of our own leading Erastians) "singularly fitted for the having "seen close at hand the ecclesiastical struggles both of E and Germany"—as to the working of Erastianism in the Fath And it is hard to imagine what more can be needed to co sensible men of the utter impracticability of the whole system. theory indeed, as an idea far away up in the clouds, nothing more beautiful. It bases itself on the hypothesis that a Ch State—unlike any other—is a sort of incarnation of the Divin earth, an organized body of the Lord, a temple of the Holy By the spread of Erastianism, prophesies Baron Bunsen, "Chri *become* the State; as, eighteen centuries ago, He became Nay, this conception is destined to swallow up, like Moses' the older theologies; for, he adds, "Is it less divine to rev essential nature of God in the purest, most intelligible form of reality [the State], than in a supposed supernatural mode of a ance [the Incarnation]?"‡ In other words, Baron Bunsen tr boldly to the Christian State all the attributes of the Ch Church; and conceives the possibility of ending, literally by *d'état*, all the religious difficulties of the one and all the theo dissensions of the other. A fiat of the royal or the parliam will is to combine into one vast system of Erastian comprehens the discordant sects; nonconformity will become henceforth disobedience to the law; the pulpit and the sacraments will be lated frankly by the Prime Minister of the day; Church discipli be directed by the police; ritual and ceremony by an Under-Sec and the hydra of schism will, once for all, be killed—not by th process of repeated decapitation, but by a scientific expos vitiated air.

But there can be no reasonable doubt that the Erastian r (whatever it might be called) would not long remain a "relig all. In an atmosphere exhausted of theological ideas, schism religion itself would perish. And no man of any hi thusiasm, no man of any saintly devotion, no man even wi

* Geffchen: Church and State, ii. 405. † Life, ii. 31. ‡ Ibid.

sense of the ridiculous, would ever consent to take orders in such a Church of the world as that. Its clergy would have to be recruited, not from the university or the diocesan college, but (like Jeroboam's priesthood) "from the lowest of the people." And as grooms and hired showmen figure in a civic pageant, clad in plumes and heraldry belonging to a bygone order of ideas, so the clergy of this so-called "Church" might indeed, for pay and provender, put on the surplice and the stole; they might, at a hint from the Prime Minister, recast the Prayer-Book and the Creeds of their Church; or even, on a vote of the House of Commons, turn Mahometans or Buddhists, Secularists or Pagans; but the people would regard them as a raree-show, and would shortly dissolve so portentous an hypocrisy amid inextinguishable laughter.

Perhaps our readers think all this a gross exaggeration. We invite them, then, to read for themselves the public statements of two well-known Erastian leaders :—

"I regard," says Mr. Thomas Hughes, "the Church of England as the nation in its relations with the invisible. The denial will not alter the fact. Supposing that all of us chose to deny that we were Englishmen, can that alter the fact of our nationality? Whatever we choose to say, we cannot take ourselves outside the Church. In *theory*, at all events, it should embrace the nation. The nation, in past times, has settled the form of Christianity which it thinks best for the people of England. The nation has formulated that Christianity in its Articles and its Prayer-book. . . . Take the burials question: we think you ought to welcome Englishmen who come forward and claim their portion in the national burying-ground. There is a national army in England. That army has charge of the parade-grounds, ranges, and other military machinery of the country. A great army of Volunteers has come forward, and is desiring to share these ranges. . . . Will these Nonconformist bodies come back to the Church? I am sorry to say, scarcely anybody in this room has the slightest hope of such a result as that. I firmly believe that we must alter our Articles; that we shall have to alter, not only our Articles, but other portions of our Prayer-book. I believe we shall be able also to provide, to a certain extent, a new framework for the Church." *

We turn to the pages of another writer, eulogized by the leaders of his own school as "a Churchman of reasonable frame of mind and true liberality of sentiment . . . whose book must be read by every one with instruction." We quote from Mr. Harwood's work, entitled "Disestablishment :"—

"The Church of England and the State of England are not now, and never have been, two separate institutions. . . A State-controlled organization may arise in one of two ways. [For instance] the Telegraph department was taken over by the State. The War department must always have existed in one form or another, as an essential part of the State. A War department independent of the State is only another name for rebellion" (p. 145). "Even if all the clergy simultaneously refused to submit to the State's conditions, the State would have to put fresh ones in their places,—and the Church of England would continue" (p. 147). "A 'National Church' means a Church teaching the religion which the nation actually holds, not that which the nation ought to hold"

* Speech at Croydon, in *Guardian*, October 17, 1877.

(p. 175). "Whatever be the religion accepted by any nation, whether it be Christianity or Mahometanism, or any other religion, it is here maintained that that religion ought to be united to the State" (p. 201). "There is no reason why the national creed cannot be modified, when necessary, as easily as any other; it is merely the creed of the nation, and can be altered by the nation whenever it likes" (p. 245). "The clergy are bound to conform to the decisions resulting from the opinions of the people" (p. 247). "Parliament, which controls other national affairs, is complete master of the Church also, and can, if the nation so wishes, make any change it likes in its doctrines and arrangements" (p. 381).

Such then is Erastianism. And we commend this clear description of its own theories and projects to the serious consideration of every Englishman, for whom the word "Church" still retains a different meaning from the word "World."

II. The second theory about Church and State, which is nowadays much in vogue, is (what may be called) the "LIBERATIONIST" theory. Its proper home and chosen field for the freest possible development is, naturally, the great Republic on the other side of the Atlantic. Indeed, there is no doubt its sympathies are, and always have been, with Republicanism. It cradle was Switzerland, its playground was the Dutch Republic, its main essay in real business was made under the English Commonwealth, its expiring failure is likely to be seen in the United States. The theory is this: that a State, as such, has no concern whatever with religion; that religion is purely a matter of individual interest; and the more entirely the individual is liberated from all interference and control in the matter, the better for him and the better for the community. Religion will then organize itself quite freely. Each person will think as he likes, and do as he likes. But as in point of fact, many persons in each neighbourhood will be found to concur in their likings, small nuclei will be formed here and there of like-minded people, who will appoint their own minister, arrange their own ritual, and (so far as any such bond may be necessary) draw up their own creed,—no man forbidding them. Thus, a Liberationist writer in this REVIEW, (January, 1871) says:—

"The only adequate conception of a Christian State is that of a nation whose whole life is saturated with Christian ideas and influences; and which gives free play to its religious beliefs and impulses, that (like the higher intellectual life of the people) they may express themselves as they see fit."

Another writer says:—

"We turn to gaze upon a vision fairer, nobler, more fruitful by far, which would realize our aspirations for the religious future of our land: the country full of a zealous and independent ministry, and each community working out, in entire freedom, its conception of what a Church ought to be."*

And again, to put it negatively, the chairman of a disestablishment meeting in London the other day (December 3) said, "he did not wish

* The *British Quarterly Review*, July, 1871, p. 154.

to make any man worship in the manner which was not consonant to his own view. He only said, let them all start free." *

Thus the Liberationist theory is fairly before us. We understand what is the Church of the future hoped for, and earnestly recommended to this country, by the eager advocates of "disestablishment." It is, in one word, *a Paradise of Sectarianism.* No man in his senses desires, nowadays, to "*make* any man worship" in this manner or that, or to make him worship at all. The question is, whether—as England is now loudly summoned to do one thing or the other—efforts shall be made to retain what religious unity we can, or whether (on the other hand) a direct encouragement shall be given, by Act of Parliament, to a system of religious dispersion. In one word, shall the nation pulverize with its own hand that grandest and most potent of all organizations which agglomerate mankind, the Brotherhood of the Church, in favour of an idea which would dissipate that system into nebulosity, and create on its ruins a world of jarring sects, either earnest and therefore mutually intolerant, or else mutually indifferent and therefore without permanent zeal or power?

For no one can seriously doubt that the present unanimity of the many Dissenting bodies in England is wholly due to transient causes. First of all, even the *interior* unity of any society must repose on a very precarious basis, if its first object is to impress all its members with the beauty, and almost the duty, of endless secession. Such teaching may fall, for a time, on unprepared ears, and evoke small practical response, so long as fervour is successfully maintained and worshippers are mainly recruited from the less intellectual classes. And so at present, no doubt, "notwithstanding this [rejection of all Church authority], Congregationalists are as much agreed in doctrine and practice as any Church which enjoins subscription. There are comparatively few Churches which would not avow their belief in the Declaration of Faith adopted by the Congregational Union." † But wait a while, till intelligence and study have caused theological divergence; wait, till the opening of the universities to Dissenters has borne its inevitable fruit; and we shall then see, for the first time in England, what intellectual divergence means when it is fostered by all the powerful influences of religion, and what chaos means when ultra-individualism is propagated amid a teeming atmosphere of conscientious nonconformity. But besides this, it is equally clear to all unbiassed observers that the present *exterior* combination of the various Dissenting bodies is almost entirely due to a transient and superficial cause. At this hour, no doubt, Mr. Dale's remark is fully justified by facts:—

"The larger Nonconformist sects have, for the most part, no controversies with each other now; the ministers are constantly exchanging pulpits, the

* *Daily News*, December 4, 1877. † Dr. Russell, in Cyclop. of Rel. Denom., p. 193.

congregations of one sect show a friendly and fraternal interest in their neighbours by going to their tea-meetings on week-days, and to their services on Sundays."*

But it is the highest compliment we can pay to these bodies, to profess our belief that this entire oblivion of all the matters which caused them originally to break with ea is but a temporary phenomenon: that it is but a lull, a tr that which foreign war often brings to intestine strife: an the very morrow of the common enemy's destruction, amid festivals which shall celebrate the downfall of the English Ch note of earnest discord would be heard afresh, and the religi would at once be recognized and acted on, of "worshipp man in the way most consonant to his own views." Individu short, all restraints being now removed, would at once rampant—and that, probably, in the State as well as in the For we have seen it all before. England is not called "Liberationism" to try a *new* experiment; but one which *already* tried, and has signally failed. On the page of histo records the great Rebellion, we may see with our own eyes "a full of a zealous and independent ministry, and each communi ing out in entire freedom its conceptions of what a Church be." And what were the results? This question shall be an not merely by a contemporary Presbyterian, who says, "This become in many places a Babel, a chaos," but—by Inde themselves. Cromwell himself complains that "our peace and are shaken and put under confusion, and ourselves rendered a scorn and contempt of strangers;"† an Independent peti sented to him laments that "our churches are like so ma launched singly, and sailing apart and alone in the vast tumultuous times, exposed to every wind of doctrine;"‡ and an Independent, rebukes Cromwell's thirty-eight "Triers" (c of Independents, Presbyterians, and Baptists) because "th their own narrow Calvinism the door of admission to Chu ferment."§

In all earnestness—as Englishmen, not as theologians; admirers of the past, and believers in the future history of o —we ask our countrymen, Do you wish those miserable stored? Do you intend, by an Act of the Legislature, to " lish" (that is, to withdraw legal sanction from) one sober, an working theory of Church and State, so long found suitabl country, in order to replace it by another—a Liberationist an "invisible Church" made visible by crowds of self-m sects—which has already been tried in this country, and bee of by our forefathers so soon as they reasonably could?

* *Fortnightly Review*, March 1, 1876, p. 319.
† Carlyle: Cromwell, ii. 302.
‡ Neal: [illegible]
§ [illegible]

tionism should fairly answer to the needs of a vast Transatlantic Republic (if it does indeed answer) forms no guarantee whatever that the system would be compatible with the adult life of a small and crowded European kingdom. The probabilities are all the other way. And the experiment of injecting into the veins of an old and healthy patient the foreign blood either of Lutheran Erastianism, or of Calvinistic-Puritan Liberationism, would bid fair to illustrate, on an enormous scale, the sad truth embodied on a celebrated tombstone: "I was well; I would be better; and here I am!"

III. We have now looked fairly in the face two of the three "theories of Church and State," which are in mutual conflict in this country. And we have found that neither *German* Lutheranism, nor *French* Calvinism, have really been able to import any ready-made system, with which we can suitably replace the long-tried *English* system which has, during twelve centuries, moulded—not wholly without success—the intellectual and moral character of this nation. It remains, therefore, to inquire what precisely is that old English system; what, in short, is the ANGLICAN theory of Church and State, which has worked well for so very long a time in this country, and is now claiming—by the voice of the most educated and thoughtful of her sons—not destruction, but adaptation to the new circumstances which have arisen in our singularly changeful epoch?

This theory is (imperfectly indeed, but perhaps most succinctly) described by the metaphor of an alliance, or a wedlock, between the Church and the State. It does not, with the Erastians, desire to blend the two powers together. It does not, with the Liberationists, long for an entire severance of mutual control. But it does desire that the great religious organization which has for twelve hundred years stood beside the English State should (in some way or other) stand beside it still. It does wish the Church of England still to speak from Lambeth to the Sovereign, from the Episcopal bench to the nobility, from the cathedral to men of science and of learning, from the parsonage to the gentry and the shopkeepers and mechanics, from the clergy-house to the swarming factory and mining population, from the "mission" to the outcasts and pariahs of our modern civilization, encouraging "all, in their several stations, to labour for the glory of God and the welfare of mankind, remembering the account that they must give." And in order to do this great national work effectively, she requires nothing in the world but that she continue to be recognized as a *public* body. She does not draw, nor wish to draw, one farthing from the State; for she lives entirely by her own endowments, supplemented and more than doubled by the voluntary gifts of her sons. But even these "gifts" the Anglican theory does not consider as private funds. The whole of this Church-property it regards as held in trust,—not for private enjoyment, but for a certain specified

public use. And it maintains that Church-buildings, Church-
Church possessions in general, are thus (like the offered first-
harvest) a perpetual recognition and standing public remi
the opposite notion of "private property" may easily l
hideous national Idol; that in fact all "property" (though
degree, as the interests involved become narrower) partal
nature of a trust; and that no nation is better warned agai
sive mammon-worship, than by the spectacle of a public mar
building, and a public endowment, planted down in every
an organized Society, older far than Parliament, and older
Realm of England itself, and working purely for the mental,
spiritual advantage of all Englishmen who may choose to a
selves of its services.

We venture to affirm,—not indeed without fear of cont
but without the slightest fear of refutation,—that no grande
generous idea of the relations between Church and State
presented itself, in tangible and working form, than this
presented now by the "Anglican" theory to the Englis
And we also allege that, while difficulties of course surround,
action, fewer and less serious difficulties by far beset the ma
of the existing alliance with the State, than are presente
other policy. Erastianism, if it succeeded, might easily co
such vast and subtle powers in the sole hands of the executiv
baleful form of tyranny might lurk not very far below the
the future. Liberationism, if it had its way, would assured
ize the nation into a concourse of mutually repulsive atoms
day of chaos, republicanism, and revolution, might be not
remote. Whereas, if practicable and honourable terms of a
are now arranged, if the too galling curb of State control
loosened, so as to allow free and effective movement with
lently throwing up the reins altogether, there is no reason
why the Church of England should not, for many a long
carry forward her beneficent mission in this land. The c
required is to give the Church, within certain limits, the
making by-laws for herself,—those limits being entirely pla
discretion of the State by the reservation to Parliament of
all important measures. The practical steps to be taken, in
instance, would be both simple and few. A power already
summon the two convocations of Canterbury and York into jo
Thus a National Church assembly becomes at once possible.
to avoid over-legislation, such a united assembly (with
representation) were summoned only once in three years, a
convention would have been constituted,—such [illegible]
excellent results, in the sister and daughter [illegible]
munion. But no Triennial Convention would be [illegible]
in which the laity of the Church were not fairly [illegible]

[illegible] therefore, that a body of lay-deputies should at [illegible] the various Diocesan Conferences throughout the [illegible] be heard before any by-law were submitted to [illegible] the State. But it is surely too obvious to need [illegible] such an arrangement could not possibly be more [illegible] expedient, interposed to give space for many neces- [illegible] and to avoid a premature application for new [illegible]. Let such a body of laymen be once assembled, [illegible] display (as they certainly would) an intelligent interest [illegible] affairs, and it is hardly too much to say that in five [illegible] would have secured their position and would be ready [illegible] Parliament actual incorporation in the Convention of [illegible]

Without the slightest wrong to any man, without peril to the [illegible] without disparagement to any other religious com- [illegible] without encroachment on any person's rights or property [illegible] just susceptibilities, the Church of England would abide [illegible] central hearth and home of this great world-wide em- [illegible] would maintain its Christian character; and would supply [illegible]tioned form of chastened, yet dignified, ceremonial into [illegible] molten feelings might run, whenever some great joy or or anxiety had, by one touch of nature, made all English- [illegible] a time akin. And of this great trust it cannot surely [illegible], even by her enemies, that she has proved herself [illegible]y. It is no longer pretended that the Church of England [illegible] asleep at her important post, for (as Mr. Dale most honour- [illegible]) "Nonconformists who are very vigorous Liberationists [illegible] to the integrity, the sanctity, and the zeal which are [illegible] the clergy of the Establishment."* It is no longer [illegible]dicted that (of all incredible assertions!) the clergy are the [illegible] of the working classes; for (as Dr. Parker nobly stated the [illegible]) "nothing is more directly contrary to the fact; in dili- [illegible], and continual service to the working classes, many of [illegible] of the Church of England certainly put him wholly and [illegible] to the blush."† It can no longer be turned even by [illegible] to her reproach that she glories—far beyond all other com- [illegible] her splendid liberty of thought and speech; for (as the [illegible] of the Baptist Union, last year, has most wisely said)—

[illegible] there were least differences, there were least life and work. If our [illegible] and moral natures were crushed, as they were by the despotism of [illegible], all would doubtless see alike, because they would all be in the [illegible] think alike, because they would be afraid to think at all."‡

[illegible] it any longer contended, as by fiery zealots of old, that our [illegible] Popish, our cathedrals "Nehushtan," our ceremonies "the

* *Fortnightly Review*, March, 1876, p. 329.

† [illegible], December 7, 1877. ‡ Ibid. October 17, 1877.

2 R 2

dregs of the beast," our methods put to shame by rival Methodisms, or our Liturgy a collection of "prayers that the mice can eat." On the contrary, our Prayer-book is used (with adaptations) in an increasing number of Dissenting chapels, and its merits are candidly acknowledged by Mr. Martineau and by many other intelligent Nonconformists. No: there is but one single attack of a formidable kind to which our attention need now be directed, and it is this: a demand that the *property of the Church shall be confiscated, and—as the first fruits of spoliation—that her Churchyards shall be seized, as a cheap makeshift for public Cemeteries, in the name of Religious Equality.* But when it comes to that, we seem to hear the surging echoes not far off, "La propriété c'est le vol," and to see unfurled that banner of "Liberté, fraternité, égalité," to which the firm reply of England has ever been (and may it ever be !), "Not equality, but willing subordination: not the jealous dead-levels of socialism, but the mutual helpfulness of constitutionalism: (in a word), not 'Liberty, Fraternity, and Equality,' but LIBERTY, FRATERNITY, and STABILITY."

G. H. CURTEIS.

# MADONNA DŪNYA.*

HREE long days o'er the barren steppe where the earth lay dead in her winding-sheet
measured the hours from dawn to down, and trod out the seconds with ceaseless feet.

ath the floor of God that is pierced by the stars, and swept by the tongues of the northern lights
wanderer lay with a load on her heart which kept out the cold of the northern nights.

ite, all white as she walked by day, from the print of her foot to the shining mist
ere the earth rose up and the heaven came down, and, glad in each other, they met and kist;

ite at night as the face of a corpse, with the dead-locked secret beneath its smile,
mask of the earth lay calm and mute, and the candles of heaven burned bright the while.

* * * * * * * * *

This poem is founded on a Russian legend which if somewhat unique in its tender ce, may yet be taken as typical of that love of children, and reverence for the maternal tion, which would seem, in these rudely conditioned lives, to be the solitary hold of timent. While few if any of the Russian sagas turn upon the love between man and nan, many are instinct with this passionate love of offspring. It is noteworthy that one of the two primary aspects of love viewed as a great natural force,—the aspect er which it is the moving cause and vital principle of all morality,—should be strongly esented in the nation now at war with that other in which the corresponding aspect he passion has long reached the ultimate limit of possible degradation. Not to inter- t the progress of the narrative with unnecessary foot-notes, it may be as well to state his place, that the allusion in the fifth couplet to the rainbow-drawn fountain, roofs, spire, is based upon a natural fact: that the eye, revolted by the insufferable unity ght upon the snowy wastes, makes for itself a sort of mirage of colour, surrounding rare objects of the scene with iridescent lines. Further, that the Russ peasant esses the poetical notion that the storms of thunder and lightning, very frequent ut St. Elijah's Day, are the result of the flash and rumbling of the prophet's fiery and steeds. It is perhaps superfluous to mention that Icon (Ikona), is a holy picture.

Broad day-light in the frozen noon,—an hour before her the village spire,
Its roofs and fountain, all rainbow-drawn,—traced on the white as with festal fire.

Slower her steps with the dwindling hour, and her failing hope is a growing fear,
When she bears her load through the empty street where the seven green cupolas stand out clear.

Still at length are the weary feet as she stands with her head o'er her burthen bowed,
Watching a door like a vagrant dog,—she whom the neighbours had called "the proud."

And the door falls back on the skirling hinge, in answer, as if to her silent prayer,
And Grunya, the stern Bolshūka,* looks out, barring her way with a stony stare.

Like a withered leaf in the stress of the storm, the wanderer sped through the guarded door,
Kneeled to the Icon, the Mother of God, then stood on her feet on the old house floor.

Fair to her greeting the Icon smiled, holding her babe to her mother's breast,
Smiled in the flickering light of her lamp, telling of comfort, and eke of rest.

Straight she turned to that ancient one who ruled the house as to her seemed good:
"We crave your grace by the yielding breast, and the pitiful heart of motherhood!"

"What brings you, Dūnya, the homeward way? Our bread and our work are as hard as of yore."
Then the wanderer looked in her face and drew the sheepskin back from the burthen she bore:

A three-months' child in its rosy sleep, a child as the Christ of the Icon fair,
Was the load which had lain on the wanderer's heart, and stood revealed to the woman there.

"What mean you, Dūnya, to lay the child on my hands that are weary, as hard, and old?"
"If you feel but a moment his breathing warmth, you will hold him safe from the peril of cold."

At a break in the infant's sleep his hand round the woman's knotted finger twined,
As a flower whose tendrils grasp a stake to keep it firm in the rock of the wind.

"Fair and soft I will keep the babe from the peril of winter's cold," quoth she;
"But go your way till St. George's day, there is nothing to bind betwixt thee and me."

"God save you for pity, my father's wife! but tie not your hands with a babe to wean;
Though your heart o'er his tender head should bleed, your breasts would be dry as they ever have been.

* Head of the House: literally, Female Big One; Big One being the title common in the days of serfage to the men or women who ruled over the large combined households.

"The Don in its banks is a wedge of ice, and the heel rings hard on the snow new snowed,
With my frozen drink and my frozen tears, his fountain failed not, but flowed, still flowed.

"I will beat your hemp, I will hew your wood, I will do your bidding both high and low,
And then in the spring if you need me not, on St. George's day I will rise and go;

"An you bid me stay, I will drive your plough, drive or draw, if your beasts are spare;
My heart is stout as my hands are strong, and my face—it is nothing now too fair."

Then the vanquished woman gave back the babe, and the door with the skirling hinge made fast:
The Icon brightened behind her flame,—the mother and child were housed at last.

When the other two women came home i' the dusk, they saw, 'neath the Virgin in gold and sheen,
A tattered pilgrim who bore a child as fair as the living Christ had been.

* * * * * * * * *

Sleep is good to the working brain, and sleep for the weary body is meet,
But the broken sleep of the nursling babe, and the nursing mother, is sweet, how sweet!

The day for the many, for trouble and care, for thankless labour and empty noise;
The night alone with the one beloved, spent in golden dreams and in silent joys;

By day, the dull, cold service within, and without the featureless mask of death;
By night, the coverlet warm and sweet with the milk and honey of infant's breath.

Not loud alarum or matin bell from her happy dreams made Dūnya start,
But the gentle suasion of longing lips, feeling their way to her mother's heart.

You may say that she dreamed by her one beloved, when the morning light broke sad and wan,
Of another belovëd who once had been—of a man who had come, a man who had gone;

I tell you no,—that not Mary's self, the Virgin Mother, the vestal soul
That of mortal passion had known no throb, had a heart for her first-born son more whole;

That the smile which went and the tear which came, having nothing to do with a foregone past,
Were the tremulous shapes of a boding love on the ground of her own dark fate forecast.

But they melted away with the urgent day, and his image, e'en as the village spire,
Rose from the colourless field of life, traced on the blank as with festal fire.

So passed the days so passed the nights; the sun rose early, and late went down;
A change came over the earth's dead face; the smell of death rose rank from the town.

Then the new-born year broke sudden and sweet, from the same dark womb that
had swallowed up death,
And out of the silence, the jubilant birds, and out of the foulness, the violets'
breath.

As the beasts came forth from their winter stalls, said Dūnya: "Now is St. George's
day,
All the winter through you have housed us two,—is it now your will we should go
or stay?"

And the women spake: "We are frail and spent, and our men from the homestead are wandering free;
We bid you to stay for your own young strength, and the sake of the child who is
frailer than we."

So she stayed and wrought; she ploughed their ground, and sowed the seed in
their plot of the Mîr,
Till, sweet in the shade of the flowering rye, she laid the flower of all the year.

Laid and left it at play with itself, as she worked her way in the fiery June,
To wear it fain on her breast again at morn, at eve, at night, and noon.

And her little lover grew jealous and coy, and learned in all love's tender wiles;
He wreathed her neck with his silken arms, and gave her back her kisses and
smiles.

One eve when behind them the sun went down, and his beams got tangled in
Dūnya's hair,
Three mowers looked on through the golden haze, and they crossed themselves
all unaware.

* * * * * * * * *

St. Peter's day had come and gone; oh the heavy heads of the ripening rye!
Oh the brazen heaven, and the breathless earth, and the sun that glowered as an
angry eye.

They sat again as the sun went down, but the air was choked with the new-mown
hay,
And she felt his weight on her weary arm, and he fell asleep in the midst of his
play.

And the beasts were lowing as if in pain, and sad over all came the feeble bleat
Of a motherless lamb; as she rose to go, a bird from the sky dropt dead at her
feet.

She stumbled and fell by the dead bird's side;—oh the bleating lamb in the distant
fold!
With the fierce red sun in the coppery sky, what meant that shudder of deadly cold?

What meant that deadly grip at the heart, the livid flesh, and the fiery breath?
She was 'ware of the fiend that was haunting the Don; she had felt the touch of
the fierce black death.

No parting kiss, no cry, no word,—she held the babe at her full arms' length,
Then laid him asleep by the way-side cross, and fled from the sight with a desperate
strength.

Three men,—the mowers who late had been,—that evening were setting their
reaping hooks,
When a woman who seemed to rise out of the ground chilled the blood in their
veins with her frozen looks.

She spoke: "For love of the Mother of God, take the child who lies by the
cross asleep,
And bear him to Grunya; so God the Son shall bless you whether you mow or
reap."

Then one of the three from the foot of the cross took the babe, and he handled
him tenderly;
She saw him carried by meadow and mere; then she cried her cry: "He is safe
from me!

"He is safe from the kiss of the foul black death I will fight with alone 'neath the
drooping rye,
I will fight for our lives in my own young strength, with an open way to God's
pitying eye."

That night with the lowing of stricken herds was mingled the voice of a woman's
moan;
And, drowning the bleat of the motherless lamb, came an infant's cry from a
cradle alone;

That dawn the voice of a woman who prayed, of a woman who sobbed in the
drooping rye:
"Oh Mother of God! feed a motherless lamb if his poisoned fountain should soon
be dry!"

In the night of that dawn the weanling child, who had wearied the day with his
cry forlorn,
Was breathing deep in his balmy sleep, and he sighed and slept till the morrow's
morn.

So night after night in his cradle alone, he gurgled, and sighed, and sweetly slept,
And day after day, passed from hand to hand, upon alien bosoms he lay and wept.

And the wondering women peered into the dark, and listened with senses keenly
bent,
For a sign, for a word, but no sound they heard, save the sighs of the infant's deep
content.

Then wondering, whispering, Grunya arose from her bed as the night and the
morning met,
And she found the babe, with his wide, bright eyes, awake with the milk on his
lip still wet.

Then she signed the sign of the cross and said,—said half in wonder and half in
fear:
"His mother, the wandering Dūnya, is dead, and the Mother of God has been with
him here.

"She has come and gone in the dead o' the night, and the babe has sucked from her
sacred breast,
If by day or night we beheld that sight, our eyes would for ever and ever be blest;

[illegible] sound for Elijah's chariot ru

[illegible] the dog in the yard

[illegible] gurgled and cro

[illegible] light leapt forth and
[illegible] breast where the laughin

[illegible] prayer, and slowly, fearfully, from her pl
[illegible] on the kneeling wives turned her so

[illegible] peace, but the face of the wandering

[illegible] reproach in the eyes which the sudde

[illegible] away, for sorrow and pity they

[illegible] as the gold-stoled woman swept

[illegible] the baby waited with wide bright ey
[illegible] of their drink, he had tasted th

[illegible] night, as they watched again the

[illegible] dark, ere a silence fell as the

[illegible] small hours,—in the light of the da

. . . . . . . .

# ILAND'S ABANDONMENT OF THE PRO-
# TECTORATE OF TURKEY.

: first week of January, 1878, brought a signal proof of the fact, which is daily becoming more apparent, that great questions w decided not by Parliament but by the nation. The last two nments resigned to the nation without waiting for a vote of f confidence in the House of Commons. By the early summon- Parliament, which the ministerial organs unanimously interpreted prelude to war measures, the Prime Minister practically put to intry the question whether it would support him in a war policy The answer was decisive; and Parliament meets only to tell me Minister in a constitutional form that he must conform to the the nation or retire. He will conform; but not without having plished great results by the policy which his speeches have dis- Beyond doubt he has hanged his Turk. Had Lord Salisbury ffectively supported at Constantinople, the Turk would have ted to measures of reform, and purchased a new lease of life. Turk, encouraged by the attitude of the English Premier, and language of the ministerial press, refused to submit to the es of reform which were necessary to render the British Protec- of Turkey compatible with British morality and with British . Thereupon the English people renounced the Protectorate, t the emancipation of Eastern Europe to take its course. That broad and to us most welcome fact, let diplomatists present it will.

istice to the war party and its organs, we must admit that the orate had been if not formally yet practically assumed, and urging the country to fight for it, they have been, in a certain defending the established policy of England. They have lefending it, one of them says, against "fools, fanatics, and professors." But the fools, fanatics, and professors have decisively triumphed, being in fact the common sense and the common morality of the country aided by a little knowledge of Turkish history, and a little ignorance of abstruse Asiatic topography and of that route of Russian aggrandisement which leads through Armenia to India, and ultimately to the Cape of Good Hope.

The Protectorate of Turkey had been assumed by English diplomacy, and England had paid a heavy price for it—the Crimean war, the Turkish loan, the enmity of Russia, who would otherwise have been a fast friend, being closely connected with this country by commerce, and having nowhere any really conflicting interest. But there was a danger, and an imminent danger, of paying a heavier price still. The world stands amazed at Machiavelli. His manual for despots is a marvellous monument reared to itself in unblushing simplicity by the wickedness of a portentous age. But for despot put imperial nation, and you will hardly find anything in Machiavelli more out of the line of ordinary morality or more likely to afford a theme to posterity than these words of the representative of a nation which has hitherto been the type of high principle, and which boasts a long line of moral teachers, reformers, and benefactors of mankind:—

"We may, indeed, and we must, feel indignant at the needless and monstrous severity with which the Bulgarian insurrection was put down, but the necessity which exists for England to prevent changes from occurring here which would be most detrimental to ourselves is not affected by the question whether it was 10,000 or 20,000 persons who perished in the suppression. We have been upholding what we knew to be a semi-civilized nation, liable under certain circumstances to be carried into fearful excesses, but the fact of this having must now been strikingly brought home to us cannot be sufficient reason for abandoning a policy which is the only one that can be followed with due regard to our own interests."

A caveat must be entered against the "we," if it means anybody beyond a select circle of diplomatists and politicians. The masses of the English people have not been consciously upholding abominations. As soon as the Bulgarian massacres revealed the truth to them, old English feeling was overwhelmingly displayed. But in eminent Turkophile journals we find the ambassador's principles even more frankly expressed:

"Was our policy in the East sound and necessary policy, as we believe, and as the Ministry believed it was? If so, it could no more be affected by the massacres at Balak and Panjurischte than by the slaughter of Christians by Mussulmans a thousand years ago. For on what was our Eastern policy founded, as it ought to remain based? Not, certainly, upon any affection for the Turks, or any admiration of the Turkish character. It was always known that the Turks were abominably cruel in war and corrupt in ways most revolting to Western civilization. But our policy in the East was not rooted in love of Turkey any more than in hatred of Russia, and it would be absurd to contend that it should be changed on a sudden because the Turks have shown, in a most horrible way, that they are now, as always, little, if at all, better than savages. Our Eastern policy, as we have conceived it, and as the Government, we trust,

> ... is founded on neither likings nor dislikings of creeds and races. ... and established by the conditions of our national existence, ... irrepressible struggle for empire in which we cannot escape taking ... embraces the whole of the Eastern and Western worlds. Are ... ground in a moment from a position which we have deliberately ... because the Turks have been guilty of loathsome cruelties in Bulgaria? ... would—unless we utterly mistake the temper of the country— ... to the contempt with which a Ministry would be visited that ... sails to the gusty sentiment of the passing hour."

ngland, then, is to maintain, over the countries of Eastern Europe, dominion of people "little if at all better than savages," a dominion loathsome cruelty" and "revolting vice," because it may be in-ctly conducive to the material greatness of the British Empire. listen to the voice of morality which protests against such a course pay a contemptible deference to the gusty sentiment of the hour. here is anything in Machiavelli more rank than this, let it be luced. To say nothing of Romilly or Wilberforce, what would nwell, Chatham, Pitt, or Canning have said to such advice? e more various causes—the plethora of wealth, the temptations mpire, the miasma of Continental militarism, the restlessness of enturers, the greediness of stock-jobbers, and the decay of old al sanctions, for which substitutes have not yet appeared, aided aps by the venial weakness which leads literary men to play warrior and diplomatist behind type—have given birth to a ous phase of opinion, and one which, if the world remains moral, be noted with interest by historians of opinion in after-times.

hat the ethics of the passage which we have cited are peculiar, able and highly-informed writer is no doubt aware. We are not ure that he and his party are distinctly conscious of the fact that ple cannot frame peculiar codes of ethics for their own exclusive ; that whatever England does to other nations, she licenses other ons to do to her; and that by steady persistence in a disregard "gusty sentiment" whenever respect for morality is inconvenient, may assume the somewhat perilous and expensive position of an my of mankind. Still less do we feel sure that the remoter con-ences of hoisting the black flag are clearly seen. In the same mns with this ultra-Chauvinism we constantly find complacent ocacy of free trade. But free trade and Chauvinism cannot live ther. Economists may lecture, but the world will not be inclined pen its ports and markets to a filibustering nation whose wealth be used as the means of unscrupulous aggrandisement; nor will e inclined to listen to such a nation when it descants in philan-pic strains on the good effects of commercial intercourse in propa-ng friendly feelings, and promoting the union of mankind. More-r, the war spirit is the spirit of taxation; taxation involves tariffs; tariffs, say what you like, will not be regulated in the interest of British manufacturer, to whom his rivals are apt to impute the same wolfish thirst of aggrandisement which some of his compatriots show in their plans for the extension of the empire. You can get rid of hostile tariffs only by reduction of expenditure; and you can bring about the reduction of expenditure only by diffusing the spirit of peace. England, like Japan, is divided between two communities with different interests, that of the "two-sword" men and that of industry. The two-sword men, with their wars, and *Alabamas* and protectorates of Turkey, are always thwarting the policy of industry and squandering its earnings; while industry has just strength enough to prevent the two-sword men from being successful in their own line. The hostile character of the present American tariff is due in no small measure to the hatred of England, excited by the conduct of our Tories in the civil war; and no doubt we shall have an equally hostile Russian tariff as a proof of gratitude for similar conduct now. It would perhaps be too sordid to suggest that Russia owes a heavy sum to English creditors, and if, rage conspiring with financial difficulty, she is driven to repudiation, the British bondholders cannot distrain.

"The irrepressible struggle for empire" is to be adopted as the basis and guiding principle of its foreign policy by a great manufacturing and commercial nation! Prove to us first the existence of this struggle. It raged no doubt with great fury among the savage or semi-savage races of the early world. It continues still to rage among the representatives of those races, in Dahomey and wherever else savagery is left now. Among the more civilized races it dies out in proportion to their civilization. It is gradually quelled by enlightened self-interest, as well as by the civilized conscience. Men learn by degrees that industry brings them more wealth than plunder. Nobody but a barbarian who was also a madman would now think of reproducing the Roman Empire; yet the Roman Empire itself, compared with its Assyrian and Persian predecessors, showed the incipient influence of the spirit of civilization; it in some degree spared nationalities, it respected national religions; it conquered, but it did not exterminate; it not only made a show of ruling, but did, to a considerable extent, actually rule, in the interest of the vanquished. Modern attempts to found empires over the civilized world, such as were made by Charles V., by Philip II., and in a less decided manner by Louis XIV., have served only to show by their failure that the time for such enterprises had irrevocably passed away. The only great exception is the Empire of Napoleon; and this is an exception which proves the rule, not only because the Empire of Napoleon was at once encountered and overthrown by the spirit of the age, but because the conqueror himself was one of an uncivilized race, though he had learned to use the ideas of civilization, like cannon, for the purposes of conquest. His nephew, attempting to repeat his barbarism, pointed anew the moral of his fate. The partition of Poland could not take place now; one at least of the partitioning [illegible] be glad to cancel the act. Two or three centuries ago, [illegible] of Alsace-Lorraine would have stood in need of no [illegible] in our day it requires the apology not only of military [illegible] but of ethnological reunion. Even empire over barbarous [illegible] has evidently had its day. We are all agreed in thinking [illegible] got the Indian Empire, we must keep it and make the [illegible] it for the natives and ourselves; but it may pretty safely be [illegible] if the political dominion of Hindostan were now offered for [illegible] time to the statesmen and the people of England they would [illegible] the offer. As to the so-called empire of Russia in Central Asia, [illegible] little more than the extension of a great and growing nation [illegible] political vacuum which surrounds it, and it really bodes [illegible], for the purpose of conquest, on any civilized power. [illegible] great wars of the last half-century, both in Europe and in [illegible] have been wars, not of empire, but of nationality and independence. They have been wars to emancipate Belgium, to emancipate Greece, to emancipate Italy, to consolidate the nationality of Germany and relieve her of the Austrian incubus, to liberate the Spanish Colonies in South America from the dominion of Spain. [illegible] true that the military spirit excited by the Napoleonic conquests, combined with jealous rivalry of British dominion in India, has led France to found an empire in Algeria; a precious empire, and a [illegible] encouragement to the advocates of Imperial aggrandisement, [illegible]. The struggle of the Americans for the preservation of their [illegible] and for the extinction of slavery was denounced by friends of the slave-owner as a struggle for empire under hypocritical pretences. [illegible] fair mind could it appear to be so. Not only was it not a struggle for empire, but it gave, at its close, a signal indication of the decline of aggrandisement. For with the war spirit excited to the utmost, with great armaments on foot, with injuries and still more stinging insults to avenge, with the defenceless frontier of Canada tempting ambition and resentment, the Republic at once sheathed her [illegible] sword, and her half-million of soldiers mingled in a few weeks with the peaceful population. Changes for the better in the general condition of the world do not take place at once or without relapses. [illegible] the age of plunder is past, and the age of industry has come.

[illegible] spirit of conquest survives, in fact, only as the vision of a filibustering class and its literary confederates. It is strong enough in this [illegible] thanks to certain abnormal influences, to stimulate to annexation, even though it be only the annexation of the Transvaal or some [illegible] of territory in Northern India. But mark the sequel. The special [illegible] aggrandisement in England is strong enough to stimulate to [illegible], but the spirit of the age prevents us from really treating [illegible] territory as empire. We shrink morally from behaving [illegible]; we draw from it no troops or tribute. It becomes not [illegible] possession, but, as has been justly said of India, a liability.

Instead of India being the slave and tributary of England, England is in a fair way to become the slave and the tributary of India. In short, under the present conditions of humanity, empire is an anachronism, and Imperialists are half-conscious that it is so.

Appealed to in the present case, in the name of the irrepressible struggle for empire, an industrial and commercial nation has decided that the irrepressible struggle for empire is not in its line, but that a quiet and neighbourly policy is, provided of course that nobody does us actual wrong. It has decided that actual wrong does not include remote and fantastic possibilities. It has decided that it is wiser to make the nations and powers of the future, on a sea which your trade must traverse, your friends, than to make them your deadly enemies. It has, we may hope, also so far deferred to "fanaticism" and "gusty sentiment" as to refuse, now that the case is fairly put before it, to make itself responsible, at the bidding of an obsolete diplomacy, for a reign of loathsome cruelty and revolting lust, for a finance of rapine, for the desolation of fair regions, for wholesale massacre and rape, for putting fire under the stomachs of Rayahs and nailing their babies to gates. The last-mentioned incident may be commended to the consideration of those aristocratic mothers of England who subscribe for the support of the gentlemanly Turk.

The special protectorate of Turkey, then, is renounced, after having, as we have said, cost this country dear. It does not follow that England is blotted out of the map of Europe, or even that she has lost her vote in the Council of Nations on such questions as the freedom of the Black Sea and the Straits, widely different matters from the balloon route of Russian invasion over the Himalayas. But England is rid of complicity with the Pachas, and she is now at liberty to watch the revolution which is going on in Eastern Europe, no longer as a fancied sufferer by the progress of humanity, but as a member of the community of nations. Fortunately the decision came before the catastrophe of the Shipka Pass, when the cause of the Pachas, supposing that England had decided to fight for it, was not yet utterly hopeless. That the immediate instrument of the change of opinion has been the Liberal party does not stamp the decision itself as an act of national self-effacement. The Liberal party is the party of Cromwell, of William III., of Marlborough, of Canning in his later and better day. It is the party that fought reactionary Spain, that fought Louis XIV., that fought, not the French Republic, but Napoleon, that, not without demonstrations of force, wrested Europe from the Holy Alliance. It is the party that, the other day, by the hand of Lord Cardwell, gave England an army capable of coping with the military science of the Continent. Of course it is and always has been the party of England, not merely as a great power, but as the head of a great European cause, and that cause it can never for any false lure of sordid self-interest betray.

... in Eastern Europe is a natural and inevitable revo- ... as natural and as inevitable as the expulsion of the ... been clearly foreseen and exactly foretold by all who, ...posing that facts could conform themselves to the pro- ...diplomacy, looked at the real forces in action and the ...logies of history. Every revolution must, of course, when ... it has come, be brought about by definite agencies; and ... of the present, secret societies may have played their part; ... secret societies being the cause of the revolution, you might ...k of their being the cause of an eclipse. European civiliza- ... sure in the end to throw off the incubus of intrusive ...ism, with its fatalism, its cruelty, its filthiness, its polygamy, ...ments, its slavishness, its tyrant anarchy of satraps under ... of a despotism. The Ottoman Empire in Europe was visibly ...ing to its grave by the same path which had conducted other ...ed, and anti-industrial empires of conquest, in numberless ...s, to the same bourne; and its downward steps were hastened ... loans, which, though commended by great statesmen as the ... means of regeneration, only aggravated the fatal malady of ...tion. Under the pressure of this alien tyranny, which, while it ... all reform, was growing weaker every day, lay young commu- ... belonging by religion and character to a higher civilization, ...ling for deliverance and encouraged by neighbours and kinsmen ...ad already thrown off the yoke. What result could be expected ...at which has at length come? That it should have come by war ...be deplored; still more that it should have come by a war of ...ing intervention, which—nobody wishes to deny it—must call ...tion whatever of military ambition there may be in the councils ...midable power. But for this England is herself responsible. ...pitalists, deluded by her statesmen, have furnished Turkey with ...ans of maintaining an army and fleet which rendered internal ...ction hopeless, and compelled the Christians to apply for aid to ..., as, when the Stuarts had a standing army, Englishmen were ...lled to apply to the Prince of Orange.

...t the revolution, though not brought about by the best means, ... good for humanity, and for England as a part of it, there can ...solutely no shadow of doubt. The fruitful lands of Eastern ... will be restored to industry, to commerce, and to civilization. ...d has an equal share with other nations in the general benefit: ... commercial benefit she has a larger share. This surely is the ...l view of the question: only a very paragon of diplomatic ...y would overlook it, and fix his eyes exclusively upon the ... danger to Herat.

...man being, we believe, imagines that the commonwealth of ...ill lose anything by the deliverance of Europe from the Otto- ... They are barbarians pure and simple. They have neither part nor lot in civilization. Their religion and its [illegible] origin, the area of their empire, their conservatism, bar [illegible] membership in the European family circle." So writes [illegible] dently does not hate them, who does hate their enemies, chief ground for finding fault with them is that, being sav affect the cant of civilization, and that they did not freely dictates of their savage nature by laying waste Bulgaria. can cant, it seems, these Turkish "gentlemen" as well a rob, and ravish; and in spite of the credit given them f every bulletin from their capital shows how their highest m Four hundred years has the Turk been quartered on Eur all that time he has done absolutely nothing for Europe, a has done nothing to reclaim him. He has consumed ever produced nothing. It seems a mockery to ask whether h tributed anything to science, to literature, to art, to manu the development of commerce, to any department of c Even his military science he has to seek from foreign services he repays with stupid suspicion and hatred. Not he made towards the foundation of a polity. His gover remained an oligarchy of Pachas, in which the most respec to eminence have been bribery and intrigue. The Circas in Bulgaria is a political handwriting on the wall. Ch nounced the employment of Red Indians in an American would he have said if George III., to obviate the danger c tion, had planted a few tribes near London, and upon the given them the signal for a promiscuous massacre? Then, agony, the Sultan calls a Parliament—a Parliament of Circa Bulgarians. He invites the Christians to take arms for pleased to call their country, and the response is once mo as to the patriotism of the slave. In finance the Turk is ficated bankrupt. War is not civilizing, but it is a test of c because it tries to the uttermost self-control and humanity. of the trial in the case of the Turk is not doubtful. He quarter; he tortures and kills the wounded; he foully mu dead. His callous neglect of his own wounded, because fight no more, signally proves how little he has raised him these ages, above the feelings and practices of the huma to the government of Constantinople, not the extremity of availed to rouse it to the exhibition of any qualities th called noble even in a savage way: it has all the time intrigue, favouritism, and revolutions of the palace. Th man was banished at once for his capacity. We find [illegible] that the most impassive of diplomatists or the most [illegible] could deliberately say that he regarded the main[illegible] rule as a thing in itself to be desired.

No doubt Plevna showed qualities which [illegible]

well as friends, and which, under better auspices, might furnish fine raw materials for civilization. But these qualities will remain. The Turkish peasantry will not die. What will die are the unspeakables of Constantinople, with their works and ways. The Turkish peasantry will live; nor will the rural Turk be a worse or a less happy man when he has to subsist by honest labour, instead of sending a bullet in a handkerchief as a draft on the cash-box of the rayah, when he is no longer able to indulge in outrage or abduction, and when he sees something like justice on the judgment-seat. Probably, under equality, he will learn to live at peace, and it is not unlikely that in course of time he will pass, or, if he is a Bosnian, return, from Islam into Christendom.

Of the Bulgarians hard things have been said. Proof or disproof is difficult amidst the turmoil of a war. The officers of a liberating army are generally disappointed with those whom they come to liberate, as those whom they come to liberate are generally disappointed with them. Englishmen and Spaniards were disappointed with each other, and probably, had the Dutch officers of William left their diaries, we should not find them flattering to our pride. That the Bulgarians, when their chain was broken, have sometimes wreaked a bloody vengeance on Turkish and Circassian fiends, is too certain; in how many cases is uncertain. What we know is, that the provocation would have fired natures of ice, and that it was very far greater than the provocation of Cawnpore. Before we call on people to bear such things tamely for the objects of our policy, we ought to consult the records of our own hearts. We suppose our own good qualities to be due in part to our free institutions; and the Bulgarians have not only not been free, they have been the downtrodden slaves of a horde of alien conquerors. It is matter of solemn European record that they have been denied the rights of men. We know that, in spite of fiscal rapine, their industry has produced a certain amount of wealth. We know that they have not been contented with their wealth, but have been willing to risk it for the rights of men, to which thousands of them have died martyrs. Slaves forbidden the use of arms, and taught to tremble, are seldom warlike, yet we know that in the desperate conflict for the Shipka Pass some of the Bulgarians fought well. But we must in reason consider, not what these people so long excluded from progress are, but what they may be. They may and probably will be like the Servians, of whom the most trustworthy observers give a pleasant and hopeful picture, and whose military character, unjustly vilified because with a raw militia they failed to vanquish the regular army of the Turk, has by their recent exploits been placed above the reach of contempt.

It would not be surprising to find that in the minds of some of those who shouted for the Turk at Guildhall, Slav and Greek were one, and alike leagued with Russia and the Panslavic societies to carry into execution the will of Peter the Great. Jealousy of the Slav has probably combined with fear of the Turkish fleet to prevent the Greek from taking part in the work of general liberation, and entitling himself to a share of the fruits of victory. British policy has driven everybody into the arms of Russia; but the emancipated Greek, when left to himself, has shown as little inclination as possible to be the tool of the Slavonic Czar. Still, one of the consequences of the overthrow of the Pachas must be an enlargement of the borders of the Greek, let diplomacy deal with the present situation as it will. And an enlargement of the borders of the Greek will be the extension and emancipation of a gifted race; a race which has already proved its capacity not only for trade and navigation, but for intellectual pursuits; a race which, whether you believe in its Hellenic pedigree or not, has partly inherited a language which was a civilization in itself. That Greece since her liberation has made no progress is an assertion sometimes heard, but confuted by the most trustworthy evidence. In government, and things which depend on government, she has made comparatively little progress because she has been saddled with a constitutional monarchy after the English pattern, the very expense of which is ridiculously disproportioned to her little territory, and with a travestie of the English party system. In things depending not on government but on the qualities of the people, such as the increase of wealth and the restoration of towns and villages, she has made a progress which astonishes those who knew her as she was when first set free. She is the Piedmont of the Greek race; small, as Piedmont was, in dimensions at present, but large in hope; and as Italian freedom marched from Turin to Rome, so will Greek freedom one day march from Athens to Constantinople.

Of Russia people are in the habit of speaking as though, unlike all other nations, she were a perfect unit, entirely unchangeable, and always bent, with undivided mind, on executing the will of Peter the Great. In reality she contains different elements, and obeys varying impulses. Her form of government lends an appearance of unity and inflexibility to her councils which the councils of a Parliament cannot wear, though French Anglophobes make a personal fiend of perfidious Albion, almost as we do of Russia. Her youth and freshness make her highly susceptible not only of the love of innovation, but of Utopi[illegible] and it is quite among the possibilities of the future that [illegible] appear upon the scene, not as a reactionary, but rather as a [illegible]tionary power. The temper and policy of her Czars vary both [illegible]ing to their personal character, and according to the in[illegible] which they fall, and which have sometimes been milit[illegible] times Encyclopedist. Alexander I. was, on one side of [illegible] an ultra-progressist and a visionary; full of philanth[illegible] humanity; ready, when he had conquered France, [illegible] Republic. Nicholas, alarmed and hardened by [illegible] revolutionary spirit on the day of his accession to the throne, was a military reactionist, a crusader against the liberties of Europe. Alexander II. is a domestic reformer, an emancipator, said to long for rest, and evidently unwilling personally to go to war.

To war he goes, as he declares, for the purpose of liberating the Bulgarians. It is said he must be insincere. If he does not liberate the Bulgarians, we shall have a right to say so; if he does, we shall have none. England was not insincere, it is to be hoped, when she liberated Spain from Napoleon, and the South American Republic from Spain. She was not insincere, it is to be hoped, when she liberated Greece. In the case of Greece, she was impelled by classic sympathy—not a stronger motive one would suppose than pity for the wrongs and sufferings of co-religionists and kinsmen. To use once more an illustration that comes home to us, why should not the Bulgarian massacre excite in the breast of a Slav of the Greek Church an emotion as genuine as that excited in English breasts by the massacre of Cawnpore? It is said that the Czar must be hypocritical in professing to emancipate the Bulgarians, because at the same time he is holding down the Poles. Ireland is the answer; and if another answer is wanted, English dealings with India and China will supply it. We have our generous impulses in spite of the flaws in our philanthropy. Nations and Governments, as well as men, do some good things and some bad. Nobody doubts the sincerity of the Czar in emancipating his serfs, though he suppressed a rebellion in Poland at the same time. Why did the worthless Polish aristocracy go hawking about their elective crown, setting all Europe by the ears, and bringing on partition with all this train of disturbances and crimes? Let us wait and see whether the Czar will liberate the Bulgarians; if he does, we repeat, his desire to liberate them must be taken to have been sincere.

On any hypothesis, the world is deeply interested in Russian character. In this war it seems on the whole to have risen. The soldiers have shown the greatest courage and the greatest endurance. Of the latter quality no army probably ever gave a higher proof than was given in the winter passage of the Balkans. The Russians have also shown civilized self-control; they have given quarter to savages who gave none, and who mutilated the slain. If their hospital arrangements have not been the best, they have treated the Turkish wounded like their own. They have shown themselves capable of respecting merit in an enemy. Excesses have been committed, no doubt; but not with the concurrence of the autherities—not at the instigation of a Russian Chevket Pacha; and before we condemn a whole army for the acts of individuals, whether in Bulgaria or Inkermann, we must think on Napier's account of Badajoz and St. Sebastian. The Russian soldiery have their vices; drunkenness above all; but their aspect in this war has been that of a strong and kindly though at present somewhat servile race. The nation has shown, no fair observer can doubt it, a great deal of generous and patriotic feeling; while, in spite of the autocracy, there is evidently a public opinion strong enough at a national crisis to set aside incapacity and bring capacity to the front. From the same lips usually come contemptuous descriptions of the utter corruption of Russia, and cries of alarm about her overwhelming power. We begin to see the real limits of both. Had her power been overwhelming, she would have conquered at once; had she been utterly corrupt, she would not have conquered at all. Her navy, which is the great bugbear, has hardly made a sign; and, therefore, the time must still be distant when she will be able to sweep England from the sea.

Liberating powers draw their pay. France drew hers when she liberated Lombardy. Russia will no doubt draw hers, and if her doing so is an evil, it is, once more, the penalty of leaving her to execute the judgment of Europe alone. But, besides this, we must expect that a great and growing nation will try to make its way to an open sea. It can be prevented from making its way to an open sea only at the cost of perpetual war: when it has gained its object there is a fair presumption that it will rest content. Manifest destiny is a dangerous doctrine: but there is such a thing as natural tendency, and it is less formidable than ambition, because it has bounds, while ambition has none. There may even in time be a natural tendency, which we shall find it difficult to resist, of the races which in the primitive shock of tribes and empires were thrust away to the North, now that the South is open to them, to draw nearer to the sun.

The personal conduct of the Czar has afforded hitherto no ground for regarding him with suspicion or for ceasing to deplore the refusal of the British Government to act heartily with him for the purpose of redressing the wrongs of Bulgaria without this hideous war. As we have said before, though an autocrat he is no usurping and reactionary Bonaparte; he is a legitimate Sovereign who, in the main, has used his power in the interest of liberty and progress. While his present assailants were cheering on *Alabamas* in support of American slavery, he, with immense effort and great risk, was emancipating the serfs. There is nothing inconsistent or suspicious in his appearance as a liberator. The sympathies of the American people, which have followed him, are not unnatural or misplaced.

Many Liberals feared a religious crusade. It cannot be said that there was no reason for the fear. The Russians are superstitious, and in a certain sense fanatical. But their religion is national and not proselytizing; they punish apostasy as a sort of treason, but they are apparently not given to forcible conversion; they seem rather [illegible] Roman Catholicism is revolt. Mahometans live [illegible] the side of Christians within the pale of the empire. [illegible] nothing as yet in this campaign of forcible baptisms [illegible] of mosques. Everything on the contrary bespeaks a [illegible].

[illegible] would blink the fact that his religion, unphilosophical [illegible] helped to sustain the Russian on the terrible fields of [illegible] amidst the storms of the wintry Balkan. His religion [illegible] to sustain him as enthusiasm in the cause of humanity [illegible] sustain the soldiers of the French Revolution. Some day [illegible] powers will be resolved into one and cleared of error and [illegible]. In the meantime the simple faith of the Russian peasant, [illegible] human nature above itself, and enabled it to do great [illegible] the race, as history will for ever pronounce over the graves [illegible].

[illegible] deprecate as robbery under the mask of hypocrisy crusades [illegible] present day; but religions are systems, and one system may be [illegible] than another. Entirely apart from dogma, Christianity is a [illegible] of Humanity; its God is the Father of all; it regards all [illegible] as "of one blood," all men as alike potential members of the [illegible] and objects of love and charity to its members. Its social idea [illegible] not predatory or military. "If any will not work neither [illegible] eat." Even the monk, in his better days, consecrated labour [illegible] with his hands; and if aristocratic idleness has intruded [illegible] Christendom, it is anti-Christian as well as anti-industrial. [illegible] who knows the Gospel can possibly believe that it warrants [illegible] living uselessly by the sweat of another man's brow. That [illegible] is monogamic, and the source of a higher ideal of mar[illegible] one will dispute. It is also a religion of moral conviction, [illegible] posed to military propagandism, of which there is not the [illegible] hint in its New Testament. "Put up again thy sword [illegible] place, for they that take the sword shall perish with the [illegible]." It was not Christianity that persecuted under Torquemada, [illegible] established Church trembling for its wealth. Put these charac[illegible] together, and you have something like the essential principles [illegible] civilization.

[illegible] on the other hand, is not a religion of humanity. It is [illegible] anti-human. Its vaunted monotheism is unreal. Its Allah [illegible] Father of all, but the single divinity of a conquering horde [illegible] sect. It is not industrial, but military and predatory, as [illegible] genuine representative, the Turk, through the four centuries [illegible] has amply proved. "To fight in the way of the Lord" [illegible] for doing God service. Its surest road to Paradise is [illegible]. Its Koran breathes a war spirit, and contains war [illegible] the law. Allah in his mercy and goodness gives up [illegible] world as lawful plunder to the true believer. Mr.

Lane in his "Modern Egyptians"* gives us the closing prayer of the boys in the schools at Cairo.

"I seek refuge with Allah from Satan the accursed. In the name of Allah the Compassionate, the Merciful. . . . O Lord of all creatures! O Allah! destroy the infidels and polytheists, thine enemies, the enemies of the religion! O Allah! make their children orphans, and defile their abodes, and cause their feet to slip; and give them, and their families, and their households, and their women, and their children, and their relations by marriage, and their brothers, and their friends, and their possessions, and their race, and their wealth, and their lands as booty to the Moslems, O Lord of all creatures!"

Being anti-industrial, Islam has always been non-political; it has never got beyond the mere despotism of the herd, never even in the political soil of Europe, founded a polity of any kind. Its political torpor, as well as its incapacity for industry, is intensified by the fatalism which is an essential part of its creed, and of the character which the creed forms, whereas predestination can only be fastened on Christianity by a pseudological process, and is conspicuously ignored in practice by the Scotch, who fancy that they specially believe the tenet. Mahometan Caliphates and Empires, touched by external influences, have sometimes shone with a precarious splendour, especially where they had sceptics or loose Mussulmans at their head; but Islam has never founded really great institutions or an enduring civilization. Its highest development was in Spain; but Spain it lost—lost by vice and corruption, and by its inability to extricate itself politically from a circle of intrigues, usurpations, and sanguinary revolutions. Its social character is of a piece with the rest. The enjoyment of polygamy may be confined to a few: so it is at Utah. But the practice degrades the sex, and kills civilization in its core. Slavery, of which Christianity has been the chief extirpator, is inherent in Islam: it is scarcely separable from the harem. With Islam it will finally depart from the abodes of civilized man. The sympathies of the party in England which upheld American slavery are now with Islam striving to perpetuate its rule over a part of Christendom. They stamp its character and seal its doom.

There is not much light in the Koran either before the battle of Bedr or after it. But there is a glow before Bedr of Arab aspiration; after it of Arab lust and rapine. Mahomet may have been a prophet and a reformer at Mecca, and while his only wife was Kadijah. At Medina he became an Arabian Brigham Young; his Koran thenceforth is a revelation of plunder and of the polygamic license of which he became in his age himself a revolting example. Devilish hatred, murderous cruelty, treachery, murder, mingle in his later history and utterances with cognate lust. And it is the Mahomet of Medina, offering mankind the choice between immoral conversion, the sword, and tribute, that is the typical man of Islam. It was the prophet's

* Quoted by Mr. Tylor in "Primitive Culture."

fortune to set rolling an avalanche which probably would in any case have fallen. Into the breaches opened by the decay of the Roman Empire, the Teuton rushed from the North, the Bedouin from the South. Teutonism, converted to Christianity, received the baptism of civilization; Bedouinism, coming into contact with a feebler and more corrupt Christianity, as well as having perhaps more power of resistance in itself, was not. A vast Bedouin raid, stimulated by fanaticism as well as by love of plunder, and now in the last stage of inevitable decay, is Islam.

Another element originally Eastern has, in the course of these elements, made us sensible of its presence in the West. For the first time perhaps Europe has had occasion to note the political position and tendencies of Judaism. In fact, had England been drawn into this conflict it would have been in some measure a Jewish war, a war waged with British blood to uphold the objects of Jewish sympathy, or to avenge Jewish wrongs. The nations of Europe, taking Judaism to be like any other form of religious belief, have acted on the supposition that by extending to it the principle of religious liberty they could make a Jew a citizen, as by the same policy citizens have been made of ordinary Nonconformists. This was a misconception, and one which may lead to unforeseen results. Judaism, like the whole circle of primitive religions, of which it is a survival, is a religion of race, the exclusiveness of the race being closely identified with the religion; much as, in the case of the Hindoo caste, social status and religion are one. The monotheism of the Jew, like that of Islam, is unreal. The Jewish God, though single, is not the Father of all, but the deity of His chosen race. The morality embodied in the Mosaic law, though distinctly tribal, and sanctioning a difference of principle between the rule of dealing with a Hebrew and that of dealing with a stranger, which the civilized conscience now condemns, was in its day a nearer approach to Humanity than any other known tribal law. At length Humanity itself appeared. The nobler part of the Jewish nation, the real heirs of David and the Prophets, heard the Gospel, and became the founders of a human religion: the less noble part, led by national pride and ceremonialism embodied in the Pharisee, rejected Humanity, and themselves fell back into a narrower and a harder tribalism than before. Exciting the hatred of other nations and the fears of the Empire, they lost their country, and wandered forth over the world with their tribal feeling intensified, and their religion more than ever identified with it, while they were bereft of the softening, elevating, and hallowing influences which, in such a patriot as Mazzini, link patriotism with the service of mankind. Cosmopolitans they could not be, as they were still in the gall of tribalism: plutopolitans they of necessity became, and learned to surpass all races in the art of handling money with profit, and in whatever is akin to that art, arts to which they were at first driven by circumstances, but which they have now carried on for eighteen centuries, have of course foundly modified the character of the race which once dwelt in As a rule they do not till the soil; they do not manufacture; the not produce; but by their financial skill they draw to themselve produce of the labour of others. Remorseful Christendom has wholly upon itself the blame of the persecutions which they end in the middle ages; but they were oppressors as well as oppre they were cruel usurers, eating the people as it were bread, an once agents and partners of royal and feudal extortion. They now been everywhere made voters; to make them patriots, they remain genuine Jews, is beyond the legislator's power. B volent and munificent they often are in the highest degree, pat they cannot be; their only country is their race, which is one their religion. The Mosaic law, with its distinctions between Hebrew and the stranger, is still theirs; an Oriental and primæval still separates them from humanity. It is putting the same thing other words to say that they cannot really share the political life European nation. Their politics are those of wealth; and the abilities, their desire to get rid of which brought them into tempo alliance with progress, being removed, they will now, as liege of wealth, pass to the side of reaction, and probably become a se addition to the forces on that side. Their religion as well as thei terest is essentially conservative: with social progress they can no sympathy. The growth of national debts has greatly incre their power. They are also becoming masters of the newspaper p The Turkophile press of Vienna is said to be greatly under the fluence of Jews. Fiery appeals may be made in the name of patrio to the war spirit, and the advocates of peace may be denounce traitors to their country, yet all the time the inspiration may be that of an Austrian, but that of a Jew.

When an empire like that of the Pachas, which is not a nationa polity but a mere military occupation, receives a crushing blow i military centre, a general break-up is likely to follow. Judea revert to the Jews, and that portion of the race which refuses to Europeanized may withdraw from Europe, where it is an alien ment, while the rest, giving up the Mosaic law and embracing a monotheism, accepts nationality and melts into the general popul of the West. It would be a danger averted from Western civiliza

As we finished writing this paper, the anticipations expresse the beginning of it seemed to be completely fulfilled. The Gov ment appeared to have submitted to the decision of the country Queen's Speech was pacific; it was announced that a war would be asked for only in case of unexpected occurrences—in words, that there was no probability of its being asked for at reasons of another kind, evidently extemporized, were given for early summoning of Parliament; and the utterances of the unfortu

# CONTEMPORARY LIFE AND THOUGHT.

## I.

## IN RUSSIA.

ST. PETERSBURG, *14th January*, 1878.

THE present period in Russia is of great interest, not only from a political, but also from a social and administrative point of view. We live in an age when the effects of war cannot be localized, even though its theatre may be, nations being far too nearly connected morally, intellectually, and economically. It is no less true that the effects of war on the internal state of a country engaged in it are incalculable, and cannot be measured by the laurels and spoils gained on the field, or summed up by the number of battles lost or won. War is now the test, not only of a country's military power, but of the worth of her institutions and government. The extraordinary efforts and sacrifices it demands, more painful as civilization advances, rouse a nation from the daily routine and political apathy consequent upon a lengthened peace. People scrutinize all, they calculate the chances of success or failure, and, though apt to grow enthusiastic, are better critics for praise or blame. In such periods there seems to be nothing stable, everything is questioned, and everybody has a new remedy to propose, a change to demand. These symptoms, that are generally found in all countries at critical times, are for various reasons more accentuated in Russia than elsewhere.

Firstly, the Russians are a young nation when compared to those of the West, and as such have the faults of youth—its vivacity, impatience, and lack of perseverance. Secondly, they possess a peculiar trait which is a wonder to foreigners, so little is it in harmony with the climate,—we mean that love of change which makes them worship the new in any form, despise the things of yesterday, rush with a vehemence worthy of a Southern from one idea, one fashion to another, and firmly believe that movement and progress are synonymous.

The peculiarities of our national character were greatly developed during the period of transition into which we entered some twenty years ago, on the accession of the Emperor Alexander II. and the termination of the Crimean war. The rapid reforms which so radically upset institutions, ideas, and habits, naturally accustomed the people to change, and led to the conviction that there is nothing really stable, but that all may be modified by law or authority.

If, on the whole, the reforms accomplished are welcomed as a boon by the great majority of the enlightened classes, they nevertheless count many formidable foes, who only await a favourable opportunity to upset [illegible] war appeared to be such an opportunity, and therefore the [illegible] has been seized on as the occasion for an attack, not only upon the civil and military authorities, but also upon the liberal [illegible] of the present reign. As long as our arms could boast of success on the two theatres of war, public opinion was unanimous in its enthusiasm, admiring not only the heroism of our gallant soldiers, but also the [illegible] and institutions that contributed to raise them to a higher [illegible] than that obtained during the autocratic reign of Nicholas.

However, the first news of our defeats, of our retreat from Kars, and the unsuccessful attacks on Plevna, proved sufficient to provoke a total change in the state of public opinion; it instantly veered in the opposite direction, and was not contented with simply condemning the military chiefs and their strategy. It went farther still, and maintained that the [illegible] of the late Emperor was preferable to the present system, that we had retrograded instead of advancing, and that the Liberal of to-day was but a disguised Nihilist and Red Radical.

This violent reaction has held part of the ground it gained during the [illegible] outburst of last autumn, in spite of the great victories since obtained, and therefore deserves the serious attention of thinking men when they reflect on the future of Russia, and the immediate consequences of the present war.

To realise the influence which this reaction may have on the situation of affairs in Russia, it is necessary to examine into the state of parties in this country and the part which each is destined to play. Though it is the fashion here to deny the existence of political parties, and to assert that they exist only in the imagination of certain over-zealous newspaper editors, it is nevertheless true that they do exist—in the government, in society, and in the press; and their character has a very evident colouring. If, in the absence of a constitution and parliament, they have not the organization and discipline possessed by those of Western Europe, there is no reason to affirm that they can exert no notable influence on affairs either through men in office or the press.

The first to be noticed, and which dates the longest, is that which calls itself the *Conservative* party, but which might be more fitly styled the *Reactionary*. Conservatives during the arbitrary and autocratic administration of the Emperor Nicholas, they are discontented with the liberal measures of the present reign. The emancipation of the serfs, the establishment of the modern courts of justice and of the jury, the municipal and provincial assemblies of the *zemstvo*, the elementary lay schools, the facilities accorded to the higher education of woman, the abolition of corporal punishment, the relaxation of the censorship, and other innovations of the sort which have so suddenly changed the face of things in Russia, have driven them into opposition. United in one common cause by these measures, which wounded their pride, attacked their purse, and robbed them of privilege and power, they formed a reactionary body that soon showed its teeth. Though mostly composed of members of the high nobility, who vainly endeavour to pass themselves off for an aristocracy such as the feudal system and chivalry created in the West, they form but a mixed class, in which the *tchin* and the favour of the Czar vie with purity of blood. As this party also looks for support on the Orthodox Church, which it would fain raise to the political status of the Roman Catholic clergy, it may be fitly called [illegible]. Unable to originate anything, even a definite programme,

they confine themselves to criticizing all that the Liberals h
dear, while their strength lies principally in their social positi
permits them to pour their griefs into the Imperial ear. Alwa
*qui vive* for symptoms of modern perversion, the result of forge
wholesome traditions of our ancestors, they seize every opport
impress on the Czar the dangers of the steps he has taken, and
salutary advice. If we examine more closely into the elements
this class is composed, we shall perceive among them aristocra
solable for their loss of authority over a herd of slaves; func
deprived of office, and hoping to regain it by a revival of
morose and melancholy old men, detesting the present and revelli
reminiscences of their youth and early prosperity. Side by side
are men in the prime of life, high in office, and playing an i
part in the country, who, less pessimistical in their doctrin
certain concessions to the spirit of the age, but must neverti
placed in the same category, their feelings at bottom being the

In the press the Extreme Right of this party is represented by
paper, the *Grajdanin* (Citizen), of which Prince Mestchersl
soul, without being its responsible editor; and its Centre by the
*Gazette*, so brilliantly edited by Mr. Katkof.

The opinions of the *Grajdanin* are most unequivocal, and
one vividly of the device of the French Legitimists, "Dieu, mon
noblesse de mes aïeux." The resemblance is at times so stril
the question involuntarily arises as to whether the author
articles is really a Russian. The veneration it professes for the
clergy, combined with aristocratic principles worthy of a
"Junker," is unique of its kind, and harmonizes but little
Russian spirit. This foreign tone of thought, however, does no
their declaring themselves Slavophiles and ultra-patriots, and
in this respect the *Moscow Gazette*, the *Rousski Mir* (Russian
the *Novoé Vrémia* (Modern Times), and their numerous satellit
which is indisputably their own is their hatred of the spirit of
and of all liberal institutions and ideas; and on this point th
and consistency are proof against all attacks.

Their Slavophilism, however, differs materially from that of
brated circle whose centre is at Moscow, and which counts a
founders such men as Aksakoff, Homiakoff, and Kireefsky. Its
are, as observed before, based on feudal and aristocratic princ
rowed from another civilization, and their national costume is
cut on a foreign pattern. In this array they are as much Ri
bad actors playing in popular pieces are peasants. If, like t
philes, they turn to the past, it is not to deplore the baneful g
Western civilization on our own by Peter the Great, but to r
loss of privileges and prestige that raised the nobles so high
rest of society. The profits they derived from their serfs are less
than the respect that was shown them and the arbitrary sway
over entire populations. They were the chosen few. In ad
their exemption from military service, the payment of taxes, an
punishment,—privileges which they shared with the clergy
"honorary citizens,"—they alone had the right of holding slaves
gave them an exceptional position.

The other classes, as belonging to an inferior race, existed
their superiors, who might tax, work, and beat them to the

content. Nowadays all that is changed: the serfs are freed, corporal punishment is abolished, everybody made liable to military service, universal suffrage introduced into the provincial and local self-governments, equality before the law established; and the last privilege enjoyed by the nobles—exemption from taxes—is universally considered to be unjust and on the point of being suppressed in its turn. One must confess this is hard to bear, especially for the older men brought up with other ideas; and one need not wonder if they try to save what they can from this universal wreck, and fill the air with their lamentations.

As we have already mentioned the *Slavophiles* when speaking of our *soi-disant* Conservatives, we will now turn to them, especially as they may be classed among the Right on account of their piety and devotion to the national Church, which both parties proclaim to be far superior to any other Christian confession, and which they esteem as a special boon from Providence to this country.

Their sympathy for the Slavs, and their faith in the special mission of Russia to deliver them from the Mussulman yoke, is another point on which they are agreed.

The profound divergence of views which separates them lies in the aristocratic principles of the one and the democratic convictions of the other. Not only do the Slavophiles deny that there is any superiority in blood, but they profess a particular reverence for the people, in whom alone they see the incarnation of a real Slav civilization and hope for its future. In their opinion the people alone can understand the God of the Orthodox, and the full grandeur of the idea of brotherhood, which forms a basis for this future civilization, and which the rural commune already realizes to a certain extent. It is not the upper classes, denationalized and spoilt by Western ideas, who have anything to teach the people; on the contrary, it is to their wisdom they must bow, and their principles they must accept. The national customs, and even dress, assume for them a particular importance, and excessive humility distinguishes them at once from their pretended allies, the reactionary Conservatives, whose immoderate pride is a characteristic feature. At the same time the humility that the Slavophiles show towards the people changes to haughtiness as soon as they have to do with their superiors and with the Government. Ever hating the products of the *rotten* civilization of the West, as it is practised in Europe, they dream of a *Sobor*, or Council of men elected from the people or *zemstvo*, whose functions and duty should not consist in limiting the prerogatives of the Sovereign, but in giving him good advice as representatives of the country, and in opposing the power of the bureaucracy. This kind of Utopia, the model of which they imagine to have found in Russia before the time of Peter the Great, is not to the taste of our bureaucrats; and notwithstanding the loyalty and patriotism of these dreamers, they do not obtain a hearing in high places. The unfavourable opinion formed of them is even so strong, that they have much more trouble in propagating their ideas than the more advanced parties. While the latter have periodical organs at their service, those of the Slavophiles could never exist, and all their attempts in this direction were checked by persecutions of the censorship. The weekly paper started several times by their present chief, Mr. Aksakoff, was subjected each time to such warnings and suppressions as to cause its ruin; and the monthly reviews founded by the same party met with a similar fate. For the very least offence their copies were publicly burnt, and they finally gave up the attempt. It is a curious fact that they remain without such an organ now when they play so brilliant a part, and have been able to organize such a vast propaganda in favour of the war, and to place themselves, without possessing an organ, at the head of this movement. They have never yet enjoyed such a brilliant triumph as when they succeeded in lifting the Slavonic question out of the region of dreams into that of diplomacy, subsequently to be decided by arms, and when their eloquence, so long an object of raillery, fascinated the nation and the Emperor himself. It is true that the triumph did not last long, and that at the first dispelling of illusions, caused by our defeats and the sad loss of the war, opinion was against the instigators of the strife, reproaching them for having driven the nation into it. But the Slavophiles do not belong to the race of the timorous, who let themselves be beaten at the least cry. Firmness of character, so rare with us, is their best quality; besides they are too well accustomed to bear injury and raillery to be much moved by them. They have, therefore, maintained all their calmness, and continue to gain strength with the conviction that the providential mission of Russia requires the deliverance of their Slavonic brethren, and that to attain this end no sacrifice is too great. If they have no journals of their own, there is no want of such as serve them for organs, now that their doctrines have obtained such a great hold and have created so many disciples.

There is even one that they might strictly claim to be the true mirror of their opinions, if it did not properly belong to its editor and only contributor, Mr. Dostoievsky. *An Author's Diary*, a monthly paper, written solely by him, clearly bears a Slavophile colouring; but as it is a literary production entirely original, it must not be ranged in the ordinary category of periodical publications. Mr. Dostoievsky, who is justly considered one of our best novelists, and whose moral character has gained him general esteem, hoped one day to be able to give to the public, once a month, a record of the ideas which pass through his mind with regard to the social and political events taking place at the present time. This kind of gossipping, without a subject or fixed programme, has received the title of *An Author's Diary*. Thanks to the talent of the author, it obtained from the very first great popularity. He touches therein, without distinction, all subjects which pass through his mind, speaking one time of the war and politics, another time about the criminal trial of the day, of the people's mania for going abroad, &c., but always and everywhere speaking of and praising the ideal qualities of the Russian people, and the incomparable beauty of the Slavonic civilization, as compared with that of Western Europe. His strong opinions expressed at the time when Russia was preparing for war, and when the Slavonic question occupied the first place, gained many converts, and contributed to the triumph of the Slavophiles.

Although the principles of this school give it a separate place, its warlike ardour brings it into connection with the party named by its opponents *Ultra-patriots*, and whose well-known chief is the celebrated Katkof. On this point, the three fractions of which I have hitherto spoken—the Reactionists, Slavophiles, and the Ultra-patriots—are perfectly in accord. Whatever may be their divergence on other questions, as soon as they touch the question of drawing the sword, it is difficult to decide which of the three displays most zeal. On all other points [illegible], which I shall mention hereafter), it is not an easy [illegible] an account of the convictions of Mr. Katkof and his [illegible] they elude all form by their flexibility and mobility. [illegible] the *Moscow Gazette*, and especially the *Rousski Vestnik* [illegible], which served him for a long time as his sole organ, [illegible] the most prodigious leaps in politics, as well as in [illegible]. Sometimes he is friendly in the extreme to the English, [illegible] their bitterest enemy; one day he is inclined towards [illegible] on her the grossest flattery, and another day abusing [illegible] against her the cause of France, to turn afterwards [illegible] latter. After that, one might suppose that the *Moscow* [illegible] in the degeneration of the West and the superiority of [illegible] world, if it did not on every occasion profess the contrary, [illegible] not put before us the West constantly as a model to [illegible]. In interior questions, the principles by which Mr. Katkof [illegible] more difficult to ascertain. We find in him liberal [illegible] tendencies side by side with the support of aristocracy, [illegible] arbitrary administration, and antiquated privileges. For [illegible] who does not know that the connecting thread of these [illegible] lies in the personal relations of the editor with the [illegible] and the members of the Government, they are a labyrinth [illegible] oneself in,—a kaleidoscope which at once shows the most fan-[illegible] and designs. In the chaos of contradictory ideas, there [illegible] two subjects that remain intact and will not be influenced by the [illegible] movement around them. These are: (1) the unity of Russia, [illegible] to him to be constantly menaced by separatism, cosmo-[illegible], and treason; and (2) instruction in the classics considered [illegible] of the country. This double preoccupation, the necessity [illegible] that the Russian nationality be not overrun by others, and [illegible] sciences and modern languages should not usurp the place [illegible] languages, has taken such hold of Mr. Katkof's mind, that [illegible] quite indifferent to all that does not come into this pro-[illegible], and he is exclusively devoted to it. Nevertheless, these two [illegible] equally dear to him, have not played an identical part in his [illegible] he has often sacrificed through one what he gained by the other. [illegible] well known that it is his excessive patriotism, and the jealous [illegible] took to defend Russian policy during the Polish insurrection [illegible], that gained for him his great popularity. Nothing is so ad-[illegible] as to touch the passions and excite national hatred during [illegible] of crisis; and at that time the feeling of hatred towards the [illegible] so violent that any one who stirred it was proclaimed [illegible] of his country. Later, when the disturbance was put down [illegible] passions were subsiding, the *Moscow Gazette*, fearing to [illegible] its high position, hastened to give them another turn, [illegible] new dangers. In its opinion, it was not only the Poles [illegible] ought to fear: the Little Russians, Finlanders, Germans of [illegible] Provinces, were not less inclined to separatist ideas, per-[illegible] threatening the unity of Russia. Society, being accustomed to [illegible] Mr. Katkof's organ as a new oracle of Delphi, lent itself but [illegible] to his instigations, and the collision which then ensued [illegible] subjects and the German subjects of the Emperor, [illegible] proportions that the Government was obliged to interfere, [illegible] to these polemics by means of the censorship. Katkof

was obliged to obey this superior order, and act with less [illegible]
his *prestige* with the people did not suffer thereby, and [illegible]
remains the Russian and the "patriot" *par excellence.*

Unfortunately for himself, he was not content with [illegible]
fanatic for the greatness of Russia; he soon found anoth[illegible]
predilection, which cost him a considerable portion of his [illegible]
Classics became his whim, and after helping to overthrow [illegible]
of Public Instruction, Mr. Golovnine, who was opposed to [illegible]
he closely allied himself to his successor, Count Tolstoy, an[illegible]
possible means to ensure the success of this reform. Up [illegible]
Latin alone was obligatory, Greek was only learnt by [illegible]
natural sciences occupied a great part in secondary edu[illegible]
college programme was entirely altered by the new Minist[illegible]
to the directions and with the concurrence of the editors of [illegible]
*Gazette.* This change caused great dissatisfaction in society, [illegible]
antipathy to the dead languages, and was irritated that igno[illegible]
Greek language was henceforth to be an obstacle to entering [illegible]
sities. This displeasure was also caused by the rude manne[illegible]
the reform was accomplished. There was a want of teac[illegible]
number of young students who commenced their studie[illegible]
former regulations saw themselves suddenly deprived of th[illegible]
career (which alone conferred rank and lucrative situations[illegible]
professors who could initiate them in the mysteries of the [illegible]
mar. They therefore murmured loudly and without restrai[illegible]
partisans of the classics, with Mr. Katkof at their head, h[illegible]
hearing of the Emperor, persuading him that the study [illegible]
and Greek authors was the only antidote against the red[illegible]
tionary propaganda which was menacing his throne, and [illegible]
sciences were but a disguised form of Nihilism, Atheism, [illegible]
versive doctrines. The Emperor, in whom revolutionists in[illegible]
dread, allowed himself to be convinced, in total oblivion of [illegible]
case, whom they made to believe the exact contrary but a [illegible]
century ago. The counsellors of Nicholas I. then absolute[illegible]
him that the study of the Greek language led directly to [illegible]
as the classical authors constantly speak in high terms [illegible]
and of liberty, and the distrustful monarch hastened to [illegible]
study of Greek in secondary education. At present, on th[illegible]
is ranged among the most conservative principles, and th[illegible]
regulates the critiques of the press on the subject. The Stat[illegible]
of the classics, and it is not without danger to declare [illegible]
opponent. During the secret and fruitless struggle of [illegible]
this new scholastic reform, the star of Mr. Katkof was pa[illegible]
When he made an attempt to regain the favour of the publ[illegible]
ing the trumpet of war, he found that others had [illegible]
lesson, and that he was not the only one to speak to the [illegible]
*Rousski Mir* (Russian World), established by the [illegible]
Tcherniaëff; the *Novoé Vrémia* (Modern Times), the [illegible]
Souvorine, passed over just then from the Liberal and [illegible]
with arms and baggage, into that of Mars; the [illegible]
*Petersburg,* and the *Grajdanin,* without reckoning [illegible]
secondary rank, all joined together in one loud [illegible]
amidst all this tumult, was unable to make [illegible]
pathies of the *Moscow Gazette* for the Slavonia[illegible]

date, and the honours of the day were incontestably shared by the Slavophiles.

Thus our Right is represented by three sections pretty clearly defined; and if we place among them the Slavophiles, notwithstanding the bad reputation they have in the upper circles, it is because at the present moment they are closely united with the war party, and because their hatred of the West makes them look unfavourably on the exigencies of modern civilization and on the principles of Liberalism. It is, however, high time to cast a glance at the other parties: those of the Centre and the Left. The first, which contains the moderate politicians, forms, whatever may be said of it, the true basis of the enlightened society and the most active national party. If it is unable always to obtain a hearing in moments of a crisis and during popular exaltation, in the end it exercises its influence as soon as minds are appeased and passions calmed down. Being strongly represented by the officials, with whom it disputes the power of the Conservatives, this party of moderate Liberals possesses two organs of the press which have a large circulation and are much esteemed in the country, namely, the *Golos*, a daily paper, and the *Messenger of Europe*, a monthly review. Accused sometimes of Radicalism and sometimes of treason, this party entertains pacific and liberal ideas as they are understood in Europe; in applauding accomplished reforms, it desires the Government to go on in the same way and complete its work. What it cherishes most is the individual and economical liberty of thought and association. Although a sworn enemy of the censorship and of arbitrary administration, it wishes that authority should be strong and remain legal. It is opposed to all useless intervention in private life, and detests "Chauvinism" and that national vanity which loves to exalt itself at the expense of other nations. The administration too, or, at least, the censor, has no sympathy for these organs, and seeks a quarrel with them on all occasions. The *Golos* and the *Messenger of Europe*, although belonging to the same political party, do not always pursue the same course; the first, as a daily paper, is much more sensible to the influences of the moment, and therefore less logical and less firm in its convictions than the latter, which, appearing but once a month, has time to reflect and express its thoughts in a consistent manner, which a paper written in haste cannot do. The pacific tendency in the *Messenger of Europe* was more strongly expressed than in the *Golos*, which, after struggling much against war, allowed itself to be carried away by the current at the last moment, and declared war to be necessary. The *Messenger of Europe*, on the contrary, was not influenced by the war enthusiasm, and notwithstanding many unfavourable circumstances continued to maintain that before delivering the Slavs we ought to think of our own affairs, and to take advantage of this propitious moment to reconcile ourselves to the Poles by giving them more liberty and by effacing the traces of the late insurrection. This party is to be found principally among the learned, the literary, professors, advocates, and judges, and also among the lower nobility; workmen of all kinds ally themselves to it more or less, and it may be boldly asserted that this is the party of action, opposed to the Extreme Right and the Extreme Left, who are given to reverie and foolish dreams.

We have perhaps succeeded in analyzing with a certain degree of precision the above-mentioned doctrines, but it will not be quite so easy to describe those of the sections of the Left, of which we [illegible] speak. The principles which the latter profess being [illegible] the parties cannot declare them openly, they are obliged to [illegible] in disguise, which embarrasses their discussions very [illegible] as republican, socialistic, and atheistic opinions are [illegible] police, and are considered as State offences, it is not only [illegible] discuss and openly to combat them, but we cannot even [illegible] by naming their organs, without placing ourselves in [illegible] secret police, and becoming informers against those whose [illegible] only in not thinking according to prescribed rules. Neverth[illegible] there are properly no opinions that are strictly forbidden [illegible] monarchical, and as there is much more indulgence for social [illegible] we may say here, putting aside all political theories, that So[illegible] held in great honour in Russia, and that it has two monthly [illegible] for its organs, viz., the *Annals of the Country* and the *Dielo* [illegible] these journals that we are able to find the opinions of our advance[illegible] explained as far as the conditions of the censorship will allow the[illegible] tone which predominates in them is raillery and satire, and the mo[illegible] questions are treated in them from this point of view, or else [illegible] with such abstruse generalities that the reader no longer knows [illegible] he still inhabits our planet or is transported to the moon. The [illegible] accustomed from an early date to the stratagems employed in [illegible] circumvent the censorship, know how to read between the lin[illegible] what would appear incomprehensible to a foreigner, not accust[illegible] the precautions necessary to cheat the censor, is perfectly cle[illegible] Russian desirous of tasting the forbidden fruit. Nevertheless th[illegible] obscurity and these shifts, so useful in their way, hardly allo[illegible] explain the ideas which are expounded in these journals. All [illegible] can say is that this party is thoroughly disgusted with the actu[illegible] of things, that the accomplished and proposed reforms do not s[illegible] and that its ill-will towards the workmen and the moderate pa[illegible] not much differ from that of the reactionists. The pessimism [illegible] fesses drew it even so near to the latter that this coincide[illegible] perceived and mentioned several times in literature as an illust[illegible] the proverb, "extremes meet." Thus only the negative side [illegible] opinions is known; as to their positive side,—*i.e.*, as to the [illegible] which the adherents of this party would propose were they [illegible] explain themselves openly,—nothing is known. There are [illegible] persons who pretend that this circumstance, far from injuring th[illegible] is somewhat favourable to it, and that it would be considerably [illegible] rassed if one asked it to speak more clearly,—and would be [illegible] pleased to be no longer surrounded by this mystery, which [illegible] greatest charm. If these sceptics are even to a certain degre[illegible] they have no proofs of what they declare, and these are [illegible] which in no way alter the situation. As regards the two [illegible] mentioned, the *Annals of the Country* has the greater [illegible] in consequence of the talents of its staff, among wh[illegible] distinguished novelists and satirists. The *Dielo*, [illegible] less interesting, has a reputation of being the [illegible] periodical organs. It owes its reputation [illegible] scholars. The group by wh[illegible] in it for truth, are [illegible] Medical Academy, Tech[illegible]

[illegible] still more anxious for novelties than here, it [illegible] partisans, consisting of young scholars ever zealous [illegible]

[illegible] parties which live in the broad light of day and [illegible] the press, there is a last party which hides in under- [illegible] whose writings are printed and spread under the [illegible] party which emerges from its darkness only to [illegible] bar to hear its doctrines condemned by a special [illegible] Senate, and to expiate them by a long and irksome [illegible] the mines of Siberia. Perhaps, however, these swarms of [illegible] out of their teens, but already fanaticised to the [illegible] their future to the propagation of a few stupid [illegible] deserve to be considered as a political party, although [illegible] with which they go on with their work in spite of its [illegible] and the rapidity with which they are succeeded by fresh [illegible] draw attention to the movement.

[illegible] done does not consist in the revolutionary propaganda [illegible] emissaries, who draw their knowledge from the pamphlets [illegible] from the cosmopolitan centres of London and Geneva; [illegible] of their activity have hitherto been naught, and the people [illegible] whatever in their teachings. Indignant at their atheism [illegible] respect for the Czar, the peasant does not even read the [illegible] productions they bring to him at the risk of their own liberty, [illegible] to hand them over to the justice of the peace or the police, [illegible] himself the denouncer of his pretended liberators. The [illegible] people are eminently religious, and a propaganda based on [illegible] has no chance of succeeding with them. On the other hand, [illegible] easily carried away by that of the dissenters who promise to [illegible] them infallible means of saving their souls; and the various [illegible] with which Russia is full lose no ground and gain daily fresh [illegible] whereas all the endeavours of the revolutionists only bring [illegible] to themselves. The evil then is not in what they do, but in [illegible] they do not, and it is pitiful to see these youths ruining themselves [illegible] without a future, depriving their country of intellectual and [illegible] powers, which it stands so much in need of. The exaggerated [illegible] with which these delinquencies, more ridiculous than culpable, [illegible] the Government, forces it to class them all under the formidable [illegible] *political crimes*, to submit them to special tribunals, and subject [illegible] exceptional penalties. This gratuitous importance given to [illegible] them in their own sight, increases the number of [illegible] adherents, and, holding out to them the crown of martyrdom, [illegible] head of many an ambitious youth seeking glory at all hazards. [illegible] State could bring itself to regard them with more calmness, [illegible] exaggerating the danger of these associations which meet with [illegible] among the people; if it refrained from molesting them so [illegible] confined themselves to the reading and spreading of their [illegible] pamphlets; or if it subjected them to police correction, instead [illegible] courts of senators in their honour, the prestige which [illegible] would quickly vanish, and their soap-bubbles [illegible] chief obstacle to the Government adopting a more sane [illegible] lies in the existence of such institutions as the [illegible] an interest in the discovery of enemies of the [illegible] which they would have no *raison d'être*. These agents, with a view of showing off their services and obtaini ment, carry on a furious pursuit of revolutionists, and fill with the innocent and inconsiderate. The case now proce Senate, and of which we shall speak more in detail on anot may serve as a sad proof; and it leaves no room for dou revolutionary group, imported from abroad, has been artifi by the unskilfulness of public functionaries; at bottom, it inoffensive, and, if it appears to assume formidable proportio when viewed from a distance and with eyes of fear.

Now that our readers know something of the colouring tions of our principal political parties, it is time to return subject, and examine the influence which the war must exert mutual relations and the internal administration of Russia. issue of the struggle will, in this respect, be of prime imp by how much a fortunate war strengthens power and the head, in so much does a military and political defeat weake arm their adversaries. It was said long ago that *nothing s success;* and if there is a domain in which this axiom suffe tion, it is certainly that of politics. Who in our days bel talents of generals or diplomatists whose campaign ends And who, on the other hand, would hesitate to bend with re the conqueror, whether in cabinets or on the field of battl do not reason otherwise with regard to their chiefs: their c obtained by success, just as their failures breed criticism for change. Accordingly, nothing guarantees so effectively *quo* at home as victory abroad, and nothing is so opposed to Without looking for instances in other countries, the Crime nishes us with a striking proof of this thesis: had the Empe come out of it victorious, his despotic power would have bee by it, and who knows how long a time Russia would have for her reforms? The humiliation felt at having been vanqui the eyes of all; the causes were searched, and were found of administration and in those of our superannuated instit pulling down of the old edifice, and the hasty erection of were commenced. The remembrance of what took place t numbers to entertain the belief that the phenomenon migh duced to-day; that a fresh defeat would be the signal for reforms, that it would inaugurate a Constitution, and raise level of other European nations. This *à priori* view of the matt is radically wrong in its very grounds, and the slightest st sufficient to convince one of it.

Of all the parties we have passed under review, these which participate in the government of the country, though totally outside the administration, and exercising no influence upon its destinies: these are the Conservatives and Reaction side, and the moderate Liberals on the other. The sition to all the progress effected in the course of the the latter are its agents and promoters. Now, the to-day between them is not the one which was the Emperor Nicholas, but rather no longer that of condemning

whether it is necessary to persevere in the same direction, or whether it was wrong to quit the beaten paths of our ancestors, and be carried away by the fallacious promises of Liberalism. Accordingly, to condemn the existing order, instead of opening the doors to progress, would be equivalent to a return to the past and a triumph to reaction. To be otherwise, it would be necessary to overthrow power by a revolution, for which there exist no elements in the country, notwithstanding the activity of our sorry revolutionary agents. The dynasty is firmly settled, and runs no risk; the lower classes and the army would allow themselves to be cut to pieces for their Czar, whom they venerate along with their orthodox God; and the nobility itself, so partial to murmuring and complaining, is too loyal at heart to undertake anything against its Sovereign. So long as he preserves this prestige in the eyes of his subjects, action is possible from above only, and the power will always be disputed by those who possess his confidence. Hitherto he has known how to balance the two contrary parties which share the power of government, and the scales have never yet perceptibly turned either one way or the other, every triumph achieved by the one having always been immediately succeeded by that of the other. To convey a more complete notion of the struggle constantly going on within the Cabinet, we may cite a few instances.

The portfolios of the Ministers being pretty equally shared between the inimical sections, it is the Minister of War, General Milutin, considered as the surest prop of the Liberals, who is the man especially detested by the Conservatives, at the head of whom stand Mr. Timasheff, Minister of the Interior; Count Pahlen, of Justice; Mr. Valouyeff, of the Public Domains; and Count Tolstoy, of Public Instruction, having under their direction the censorship on the one hand, and the secret police on the other. The reforms introduced by General Milutin in the army, the abolition of corporal punishment, and the compulsory instruction of the soldier, have raised as many enemies against him as the reorganization of the old cadet corps into military gymnasia, with a system of secondary education having nothing military in it but the name. Count Tolstoy, troubled by the competition which these schools exercise with his classical gymnasia, firmly built on the basis of the dead languages, and seeing unity of education threatened from that quarter, has declared implacable war against General Milutin, and has endeavoured in every way to ruin the military gymnasia, and get them under his own jurisdiction. Up to the present time, the efforts of the formidable coalition formed against the Minister of War have been vain, and the Emperor has not yielded to its pressure, just as he would not allow himself to be convinced by the adversaries of classicism when the question arose of sanctioning Count Tolstoy's school reform. This question, however, insignificant as it may appear to foreigners, is nevertheless of more importance to Russia than might seem at first sight. In Russia, where the State mixes itself up with private life a great deal more than elsewhere, and where public education is looked upon as quite its special matter, the sole preservative against narrow enactments is to be found in the competition of Ministers. If the schools, instead of being distributed amongst various Ministries, thus offering a free choice of systems, were all concentrated in the hands of Count Tolstoy,—that being the object of his endeavours,—the whole of Russia would be under a uniform rule,—an evil in any circumstances; and who knows if classical gymnasia, freed of all competition, would not suffer in consequence, and deteriorate under the favour of a monopoly?

The humanitarian measures and the instruction of the soldiers, inaugurated by Milutin, also raise grievous complaints against him, and the retrograde party has for a long time been proclaiming that, discipline being lost, the army would not be able to hold out against an enemy.

Another object of hatred to the Conservatives is the elementary lay instruction and the new pedagogic methods imported from Germany. It is true that much may be said against these methods, their pedantic application being frequently contrary to our manners and national character; but it is not from this point of view they are criticized by the reactionists, who are bent on finding them irreligious, and dislike and fear the intellectual development of the people. The reform of the judiciary and the institution of the jury are no more to their liking, and you frequently hear strategic faults, committed on the field of battle, attributed not only to the bad education received in military gymnasia, but likewise to the general demoralization resulting from lay schools and the partiality of juries towards malefactors.

All these facts lead us to the general conclusion that when Russia is vanquished,—be it by the Turks or by a fresh European coalition, —the reactionists alone will profit by the circumstance.

The nervous system of the Emperor would probably be unable to stand the shock, and, renouncing his present system of equilibrium, he would throw himself into the arms of the so-called Conservatives, whose first object would be to persuade him to abjure all that constitutes the glory of his reign. Schools, military and national, the superior instruction of women, the humanitarian system practised in the army, the scraps of liberty of thought allowed by the present rules of censorship, the jury itself, would run the risk of being overwhelmed in the general wreck; whilst the realization of the most urgent reforms, such as a more equitable distribution of imposts and a reduction of the taxes now burdening the peasant, would stand no chance whatever.

Thus then the speedy and glorious termination of the war is not only earnestly prayed for by patriots and warlike spirits, but no less ardently desired by reflecting minds, as leading to the real good of the country. For them it is not a question of military laurels, the nothingness of which is but too well recognized by them; nor is it even the deliverance of Bulgaria, the first article in the creed of the Slavophiles; but it is a question of the existence of liberal institutions, the development of which can alone secure the future of Russia, and they tremble to see them compromised by a failure. Herein lies the explanation of the unanimity which at this moment reigns in our country; all desire the speedy conclusion of a peace in conformity with the exigencies of Russia, and the Liberals trust that it will be the best means of making her advance in the path of progress.

At present politics absorb to such an extent all the intellectual forces of our country, that all other interests pale by the side of them, and literature and art are adjourned to a more propitious epoch. It must be hoped that peace will cause them to reflourish, and that we shall be enabled to treat of them in our next article.

T. S.

## II.

# IN FRANCE.

PARIS, 21*st January*, 1878.

[illegible] the beginning [illegible] finds all hearts singularly [illegible] joy and hope. For the first time since 1870 the [illegible] of the Republic is really in Republican hands. [illegible] MacMahon be not entirely freed from those occult [illegible] so fatally hampered preceding cabinets, and although [illegible] from an anonymous Camarilla do still from [illegible] in the nomination of functionaries, it may be [illegible] he loyally preserves the constitutional attitude to which [illegible] himself on clearly perceiving that the policy of resistance of [illegible] favourite advisers was leading him to crime. He has [illegible] the crisis greater—not, indeed, than he was before the 16th [illegible] greater than he had been from that date up to the 14th of [illegible] The authentic narrative given in *L'Estafette*, by one of the [illegible] the events of the 8th to the 13th of December, shows that [illegible] may be the reward of their discretion, and who indeed desire [illegible] progress of affairs, seem desirous of drawing nearer to the [illegible] the first time prefectoral administration rests entirely in [illegible] hands, and the Ministry is secured against finding in its [illegible] the obstacles that secret hostility, inertia, and ill-will were [illegible]. In the magistracy (although, owing to M. Dufaure, with [illegible] to the impatient), a similar change in the *procureurs* [illegible] will deprive of right to speak in the name of the [illegible] who for the last seven months have forgotten their magisterial duties in order to constitute themselves instrun ridiculous and hateful tyranny. In the army, public force will be entrusted to men capable of using it against the institutions General Ducrot has already been deprived of his comman among them General de Rochebouet, will lose theirs in [illegible] time. Finally, the municipal elections of the 6th of Jan throughout France given an immense majority to the Republi several senators of the Right, mayors of the principal tow departments, have not been re-elected members of the Municip And henceforth the majority may be looked upon as secured publicans in the Senatorial elections of December, 1878. M. [illegible] journey to Italy has been the most characteristic symbol of th change in French policy. The very man who four month condemned to prison for an offence against the Marshal is no in Rome by the French Ambassador and the King of Italy as sentative of French democracy. Wherever he went he use patriotic and moderate language, and on his return to France a speech at Marseilles, in which, nearly in the same words us chiefs of the Left Centre, MM. Calmon and Léon Renault, l out to the Republican party the rule of conduct that they oug adopted for two years past, but have been slow to recognize: th of ceasing to be an Opposition party in order to become a Gov and even a Ministerial one.

Such successes and such sagacity are well calculated to in fidence, and the spite, anger, calumnious or satirical insinuati actionary journals can but increase the satisfaction of R Nothing pleases them better than, for example, to see *Le* that journal of warped and narrow *beaux esprits*, who have themselves the *virtuosi* of calumny, and practise deceit with elegant dilettantism,—to see it wax indignant in its first arti the invasions of Radicalism, and two columns further on ri Republicans who give places to Orleanists. Such malice is parent, and it is plain that its only object is to excite a triumphant Left the jealous suspicions of the more advan Nevertheless, it would be imprudent to abandon ourselves t confidence and to close our eyes to the difficulties, the black the horizon.

These primary difficulties come from the very nature and [illegible] of the Republican party. At present, if it is desirous to [illegible] Gambetta's programme, and show itself a governing party, [illegible] patient, prudent, tolerant, and moderate. If these virtues [illegible] practice to the reasonable Republicans forming the Left Cent a portion of those forming the Left, they are singularly [illegible] the advanced Republicans of the Extreme Left. Accustomed [illegible] to lay down principles in the way dogmas are promulgat [illegible] troubling themselves to find out whether they can be [illegible] slaves of unintelligent electors who have returned [illegible] their brilliant promises,—will these ultramontanes [illegible] skilful than, but equally fanatical as those of [illegible] moderate their impatience? One is tempted to [illegible] certain journals and listening to certain [illegible] some time ago in company with [illegible] heard one of them—a very [illegible] you picture to yourself this? C—— (an influential has just been here. I asked him whether they the Jesuits, and he replied that this was not the it is hardly worth while to have a Republican ministry nothing." "There it is," said a municipal councillor, shoulders; "these men of the Left, now that they have little for the rest." Now these few words disclose all characterize the advanced democratic party: want of distrust, and envy,—sentiments unfortunately but too among popular classes. Some journals have been started and develop these sentiments; for instance, the *Reveil* and which have succeeded to the *Droits de l'Homme*, the the *Marseillaise*. Up to the present time, fortunately, their been but small, and their principal purpose seems to be that of the reactionary press with alarming quotations, and themes just as M. Paul de Cassagnac seems to have set him- the Bonapartist party by his absurd violence in the and his cynical articles in the *Pays*. Other journals, such as ublic and *Rappel*, hold themselves bound to follow suit with so as not to lose their demagogical supporters, and we find ning again to demand amnesty for the Communists,—a useless since the Senate will never entertain it, but at the same ngerous one because establishing a solidarity between the s and the enemies of social order itself. I can quite under- hard it may seem to leave unpunished such conspirators as lie, M. de Fourtou, and M. Batbie, who without the shadow e were ready to subject France to civil war, while men, many ad no other desire than to defend the endangered Republic, ned to life-long exile; but however great the moral culpa- e authors of the 16th of May, what remained in the state of tention cannot be dealt with as actual crime, and the impunity roglie and his accomplices is less dangerous to the Republic l be the justification of those who threw France into confu- e the Republic from imaginary peril.

thing is that this impatience, this impetuosity of Radical jour- mainly a matter of shop, of profit, of subscribers, the one ng to retain or gain readers. We may therefore anticipate ght embarrassment will be caused by the journalist who has nced public opinion since the 16th of May, and who has ded for it by a seat as deputy. M. Emile de Girardin, pro- he *France*, which previous to the 16th of May attained a cir- 2,500 copies, but has risen in a few weeks to one of 60,000, rardin has shown a prodigious polemical talent, an activity, a really marvellous in a man of seventy-four, and has brought the resources afforded him by the longest and the most reer as journalist that our century has witnessed. He had candidate during the crisis, in order to offer an affront to tic Government, but he was elected when the crisis was Republicans discover that they have contracted a rather compromising alliance. M. de Girardin, who has all his d up with the most daring financial enterprises, who buying journals without subscribers, and suddenly unheard-of circulation—a man above all things practical, vividly impressed for the moment, by turns Socialist, [illegible] Republican, but always a man of progress; devoid of [illegible] ever carried away by his dislikes, caprices, instincts; by [illegible] originator, but a great agitator of ideas; fond above all of [illegible] sensation, fame, and believing all to be well so long as he [illegible] and his journal sells,—M. de Girardin will probably exercise [illegible] nuity in inciting public opinion to create difficulties in order [illegible] attention to himself. He has already begun one campaign agai[illegible] *tionarism*, and another to support the retention of the Council of [illegible] a committee directing the Left, very useful during the [illegible] likely now to become the tyrant of the majority and the Minis[illegible] question, which might have become a cause of irritation owi[illegible] persistence with which the reactionary press attacked the Com[illegible] Eighteen, has been solved by the good sense of the Left, who [illegible] the present dissolved the Committee, to re-form it only in case [illegible]

Another obstacle in the way of the Government may arise [illegible] institution of Under-Secretaries of State, so useful in certain [illegible] most of them, representing more decided opinions than tho[illegible] Ministry. Yet there is danger either of the latter being [illegible] their subalterns, or of divergences capable of breaking up the [illegible] Much *savoir faire* and mutual toleration will be needed to a[illegible] rocks ahead.

In short, generally speaking, the Left has to dread the te[illegible] pointed out in my last letter—that, namely, which inclines [illegible] suffrage more and more to the choice of Radicals. Were this [illegible] to become predominant, the Republic would soon lose its m[illegible] able adherents. The municipal elections in great towns, on t[illegible] January, were not a little unfortunate in this particular. It [illegible] cially to be deplored that, in Paris, municipal councillors so [illegible] liberal as MM. Beudant, Léveillé, Degouve-Denunques, should h[illegible] set aside.

Together with the dangers springing from the very natu[illegible] Republican party, which are the most serious, there are also d[illegible] be apprehended from the action of the parties of the Right. [illegible] moment these are quiescent and powerless, but they already [illegible] certain teasing ways in the Senate, their desire to hamper, so [illegible] possible, the proceedings of Government; and on the other han[illegible] tions have been made as to the projected *coup d'état* in the [illegible] December, which prove that they would not have shrunk from [illegible] order to destroy the Republic. On the 12th of December, it [illegible] merely on the will of the Marshal whether civil war should bre[illegible] not, and as the Left was ready to meet force by force, and [illegible] side a portion of the army, it was with a military civil [illegible] appalling war of all, that we were in fact menaced. I [illegible] the anguish, the despair of all patriotic spirits obliged [illegible] this last resource, and the fall of France to the level of [illegible] horror when colonels and generals came to proffer [illegible] against the heads of the army. The remedy [illegible] worse than the disease. Yet what could have [illegible] evident that the aim of M. Bathie [illegible] throw of the Republic? And [illegible] what had to be resisted was not [illegible] a *coup d'état* concealed under the [illegible]

[illegible] it [illegible] the army should [illegible] the dis- [illegible] make [illegible] dis- [illegible] public opinion [illegible] decision [illegible] General [illegible] of having given sanguinary orders in case of disturb- [illegible] Labordère, guilty of having declared beforehand that [illegible] to obey his superior officers. The situation was so grave [illegible] large number of Republican officers who, in the event of [illegible] would have obeyed the orders of Government rather [illegible] themselves out as the interpreters of legality. They [illegible] have determined to disobey in the case of an actual *coup* [illegible] which they would have been definitively ordered to violate [illegible]

[illegible] internal dangers which threaten the new Government, whether [illegible] or left, I might add those from abroad. But here all dis- [illegible] Here we touch upon the absolutely unknown. How [illegible] Eastern Question affect us? How will the successor to Victor [illegible] devoted Prussian [illegible] his [illegible] France [illegible] to [illegible] think- [illegible] the [illegible] France [illegible] Doubtless [illegible] contrary, [illegible] Europe; [illegible] the [illegible] that [illegible] to [illegible] way [illegible] sym- [illegible] resolved [illegible] feel [illegible] re-or- [illegible] The [illegible] the [illegible] December next.

[illegible] at the recommencement of its Parliamentary labours, the [illegible] has lost its senior member, M. F. V. Raspail. He was one of [illegible] original figures of the Republican party in its heroic period. [illegible] by giving himself up to the pursuit of chemistry, and all com- [illegible] acknowledge that he showed himself possessed of true [illegible], in his researches on Vegetable Physiology and on [illegible] anticipating the discoveries of Organic Chemistry, and [illegible] on Fermentation. Unfortunately he was no sooner [illegible] political life than he replaced patient investigation by [illegible] system hastily fabricated, full of the peculiarities [illegible] diseases whatever, according to him, proceeded [illegible] and parasites, whose action he took plea- [illegible] of the Jesuits in society; and one only remedy in his opinion was needed for every form of suffering—namely, His "Manuel de la Santé," which has still a considerable c rendered superfluous both doctors and drugs, with the exception M. Raspail. There was a degree of truth in his system. It is that many maladies are purely infectious owing to organic ger brought into strong light the calming and disinfecting po camphor; but his exaggerations compromised his whole syst minds of the thoughtful. Not so with the people, who saw in friend, and found, moreover, in his "Manuel" many excellent and moral precepts. Neither did his philanthropy prevent making a large fortune by his pharmacy. His political ca more especially from the July days of 1830, when he fought o ricades. He took rank among the most ardent revolutionis was no doubt owing to his arrest, after the 15th of May, 184 was not implicated in the June insurrection. To the end of had quarrels with the law, and so late as 1875 spent a year in having in his "Manuel" defended the Commune. Nevertheless were never savagely violent, like those of many of his rev contemporaries. He never lost a kind of apostolic gentleness favourite scheme was one for changing prisons into schools, he had taken part in many guilty enterprises, and utter number of chimerical or dangerous notions, the memory he lea of a man of original and inventive mind, of a writer and spea spirit and humour, and, above all, of a pure, generous, and character.

While losing in Raspail one of its political chiefs and o scientific ornaments, the Radical party was at the same time by the death of Courbet of its greatest artist. A strange an figure that of this peasant of Franche-Comté, who died in political ideas that he did not hold and for crimes the import he did not understand. He was only a great child, uniting city of the artist to that of the rustic. Unbounded in his yet won forgiveness for it by force of *bonhommie*, or at least of *bonhommie*; for, with such natures as his, it is difficult draw the line where sincere conviction passes over into for effect. When people said to him about one of his pictures, of Velasquez," and he replied, "Velasquez was not capable of he exclaimed, "Shut me up in an island, and I will compose equal to those of Beethoven," was he speaking seriously or himself and his interlocutor? He proved on one occasion perfectly understood the art of puffing, and that his quite compatible with a certain knavishness, as is often peasants. In 1870 the Minister of Fine Arts, M. wishing to gain popularity, had Courbet sounded, in he would accept a decoration. Courbet caused the thanked with fervour, showed delight, and expressed way as to imply acceptance, without categorically went and hid himself in the country, so that the put to him more definitely. He was decorated a letter, and had it printed in all the papers name of his democratic decorated while [illegible]

ise made by Radical journals about this incident, the flattery sciples, above all the much-exaggerated praise that had been n him by Proudhon in his book on art, where he calls he Messiah of a new Æsthetic, the Democratic and Revolu- Esthetic, made the latter believe himself a politician,—he to litics were never more than matter for conversation, or rather othy talk of the brew-house and the studio. In spite of his g reputation, Courbet was never able to acquire the manners ms of a gentleman; he was a boor to the end. His *rôle* of f the Commune was only a colossal practical joke, and the own the Column of La Place Vendôme,—"that pipe that had fended him,"—was in his eyes but a gigantic trick of the studio. unals before whom he had to appear viewed it in that light. was not punished as a real insurgent; he was only condemned to ost of setting up again the monument he had destroyed. This leasantry was, however, a more serious matter than it seemed; urbet, exiled and ill, died in Switzerland in very poor circum- We may now forget his defects and his actual errors, and see ly the painter. In this respect he occupies in our contempo- school a place apart. He was wont to designate himself a *intre*, and this is the most correct definition of his talent. not indeed understand it as meaning what the word implies speak of "the masters," that is to say, the eternal models of beauty, the heads of the great schools—Titian, Raphael, , Rembrandt, Rubens. We apply the term in French to who have risen to be masters in their special calling—master- aster-enamellers, master-blacksmiths. Courbet was really a inter. No one has in our day better known his business than Do not require from him wealth of imagination, or scientific on, or a lofty ideal, or profound sensibility. But if all that is e to see well, and to render with force and truth what has he has no rival. He has the gift of immediately seeing the character of the person or the landscape before his eyes, and s it with unequalled simplicity and power. No one has been aint so well what in the language of the studio is called u. His execution is at once free and precise, the air plays is figures; his skies and his clouds give us immense distances, tints are living and warm; his inanimate objects are solid, and as living figures. When he attempts philosophic painting he triviality and pretension, except in his admirable "Casseur ," which is a study from nature; but when he paints a beautiful shows us the sea in storm, long stretches of sands, the wood- rts, where roebucks shelter timorously and stags encounter in tle—his power of vision joined to the sure and simple *maestria* ion make him a great painter. The realistic contemporary nsiders him its master. Those are entitled to do so who, like Latour, aim at adding nothing to nature, at not arranging her to a conventional ideal, but at rendering her such as she is, inging to light her most characteristic features; but those who erroneously usurp the name of realist, M. Manet and the *nalists* who have followed and caricatured him; those who hat all subjects whatever are good for painting, and that a npression and four or five correct tones thrown on canvas

suffice to make a picture,—those have no right to class [illegible]
with Courbet, that persevering and conscientious worker, wh[illegible]
difficult to satisfy himself, felt deeply the grandeur of natu[illegible]
harmony of the living being, knew how hard it is to be *mast*[illegible]
calling, and must inwardly have laughed at the formless d[illegible]
times exhibited under the pretext of realism.

This question of realism constantly recurs in [illegible]
contemporary literature and art; and I shall doubtless [illegible]
quent occasion to dwell upon it. We need not wonder th[illegible]
France that realism manifests itself with the greatest vi[illegible]
exaggeration. Romanticism, which was a reaction against t[illegible]
conventional classicism of the first Empire, was itself mix[illegible]
several factitious and conventional elements. From Cha[illegible]
down to Georges Sand, including Lamartine and Hugo, [illegible]
poets and romancists—unless, indeed, Musset—have [illegible]
certain proportion of declamation, turgidity, straining [illegible]
certain insincerities, in short. Our great historical painters [illegible]
Delacroix, do not escape the same imputation. It was [illegible]
there should be a reaction; but without speaking of the [illegible]
inferiority as regards talent, in comparison with their pred[illegible]
those who head it, this reaction is immoderate and [illegible]
order to conciliate art and nature, the best device they [illegible]
is the suppression of art. Because the beautiful has been [illegible]
sought at the expense of nature, they pursue nature at th[illegible]
of the beautiful—nay, mutilate nature out of fear and [illegible]
beautiful. The true limits of realism, the true mission [illegible]
nevertheless proclaimed at the beginning of our century, [illegible]
of genius who will remain its most complete expressio[illegible]
master,—by the one who, above all others, knew how to [illegible]
nature and love of the beautiful,—by Goethe himself. "[illegible]
der Natur—der schönen"—such was his motto, and he has [illegible]
in a celebrated sonnet, what are the bonds that unite nature [illegible]

"Natur und Kunst sie scheinen sich zu fliehen,
Und haben sich, eh Man es denkt, gefunden;
Der Widerwille ist auch mir verschwunden
Und beide scheinen gleich mich an zuziehen."

But Goethe has never exercised much influence over [illegible]
although he has been read and admired beyond any [illegible]
Daniel Stern herself, who had a real cultus for him, [illegible]
went on was able to assume, in attitude at least, [illegible]
Olympian serenity, is yet more akin to Rousseau and [illegible]
than to him. There has even been since the war of [illegible]
puerile reaction against Goethe. M. Dumas fils, in [illegible]
translation of "Faust,"—a very masterpiece of ignorance[?] [illegible]
after confessing that he does not know German, [illegible]
stones at a statue, turns the immortal work into [illegible]
siders it coarse and immoral—he, the author of [illegible]
Even M. Scherer, though with more gravity [illegible]
given way to a political rancour little worthy of [illegible]
and sought to lessen the importance of [illegible]
have sympathetic [illegible] been wanting [illegible]

l the best of M. Caro's books, the best written and most thorough of M. Mézières, as well as an excellent volume of M. Bossert, and recently furnished M. Ernest Lichtenberger with the material of the best specimens of literary criticism which has appeared in in recent years, and one of the best calculated to bring to e force and variety of Goethe's works. It only treats of Goethe's s Lyriques" (Hachette), but it is in this direction that Goethe test, and has become in Germany the favourite poet alike of s and of the people. His power and superiority as lyrical poet is sincerity. He has only written verses on real subjects to feelings that he has really experienced. He has not written etry without being in love, or sung of sorrow without having or sadness, or described what he has never seen. When he proached for not having composed patriotic songs in 1813, ied indignantly, "What! write war songs and remain in m,—that was in my line indeed! To write while bivouack-ld have been another matter." But those so true impressions, sincere sentiments, were given out according to the different of his life in most different forms, sometimes in imitation opular *Lied*, sometimes drawing inspiration from the Pindaric ow seeking to return to the rugged simplicity of Hans now rediscovering the form and elegiac accent of Tibullus, use alternately of ballad, sonnet, and distich, finally ending by ring into German—when personal inspiration began to decline, riental hyperboles and dainty graces of the *Ghazels* of Hafiz. ll worth while to follow out in this book of M. Lichtenberger the —so subtle in a psychological point of view, so delicate in a literary hich he shows us the intimate connection between Goethe's orks and personal life, and how each of the forms that he suc-y adopts corresponds to the nature and the degree of intensity elings. We subscribe to this judgment of Goethe as a genius lly lyrical, who in order to take interest in his work, needed that timent inspiring it should remain at white heat, and who ently left almost all his dramas unfinished.

deeply studied, correctly thought out, and well-written book is for a doctor's degree in letters, delivered only a few days since Sorbonne. These examinations, which they are pleased to call rsity Solemnities," afford a curious spectacle. A very small ow-roofed, dark, and most meanly furnished, a few wooden for the audience, whose number cannot be much above sixty, r closely they sit, an oval table for the candidate, and the judges ed on straw chairs, with the exception of the president,— ou have the *mise en scène* of the "solemnity." But the of the actors sets off the poverty of the theatre. The judges the most part men of rank in literature and science, members of nch Academy, like M. Mézières and M. Caro; of the Academy of ions, like M. Wallon and M. Egger; of the Academy of Moral like M. Fustel de Coulanges and M. Janet. The candidates, too, uited from among the most distinguished younger members of versity, and as their thesis is generally an elaborate one, these tions for doctors' degrees play an important part in the intel-life of the country. This does not, however, imply that the tion in itself is always a very serious affair. Often the examiners, instead of criticizing the candidate's production, as in [illegible] for dissertations, lectures, more or less brilliant, [illegible] colleagues and to the public. It is with the [illegible] much as with the debates of the Chamber—it is [illegible] guarantee publicity, but the matter is all settled [illegible] work is gone through in the Parliamentary Bureaux, [illegible] rooms of the candidate and of the judges.

Examinations for the doctor's degree have in fact a [illegible] upon study in France. The candidate begins by [illegible] Dean of Faculty the subjects that he intends to take up, [illegible] approves or criticizes, sometimes modifies, sometimes [illegible] better. The thesis written out, one of the judges is [illegible] it over; if it be defective, he requires corrections [illegible] even requires the whole to be recast. When he is [illegible] gives permission to put it in print, its delivery takes [illegible] doctor's diploma is confirmed. We see at once how [illegible] may be exercised by a learned and intelligent Dean. It is [illegible] the theses have been transformed by M. V. Leclerc. [illegible] they were short dissertations of about fifty pages on [illegible] subjects, such as "The Elegy," "Epic Poetry," &c., easily [illegible] night, and then shut up in the portfolios of the Faculty. [illegible] are books of from 300 to 500 pages, carefully planned [illegible] M. Leclerc, who was philologist and mediævalist both, [illegible] candidates towards erudite subjects, and of late no year [illegible] without our owing to this doctor's degree some important [illegible] ing an advance in the study of history, archæology, or [illegible] while the literary value of these writings has in no way been [illegible] ished, as the thesis of M. Lichtenberger proves.

It is, moreover, in the very nature of the French mind [illegible] separate substance from form, ideas from facts, life from [illegible] tice from theory. It is very rare that a Frenchman cultivates [illegible] for itself, or becomes so far a specialist as to overlook [illegible] unconnected with his own pursuits. He has ever before him [illegible] practical applications or the moral influence of the task he [illegible] and almost invariably blends some question of feeling with [illegible] he feels in scientific facts or ideas. For example, the Associ[illegible] the Encouragement of Greek Studies, of the first ten years [illegible] existence M. G. d'Eichthal has just given us a very interesting [illegible] was the work of Philhellenes, who were passionately devoted to [illegible] pendence of modern Greece, convinced that Greek literature ought to form the basis of our education—nay, some of [illegible] that Greek will ultimately become the universal language. In [illegible] way, it is not the simple interest of scientific curiosity which [illegible] erudite men now occupied with the middle ages. They [illegible] at re-awaking the love of ancient France, of restoring [illegible] national traditions, interrupted by the absolute [illegible] teenth century and by the Revolution; of opening [illegible] literature, poetry, and art. The same applies even to [illegible] Ancient French Texts, founded by MM. Paris, Meyer, [illegible] and carried out in a severely scientific spirit, but [illegible] have met with such rapid success had it not [illegible] already disposed to help on whatever might [illegible] tion of our old literature; especially among the [illegible] middle ages the era of the great power of the Church, and the type of an heroic and Christian society.

Accordingly we notice that for some time back L'Ecole des Chartes is the only government school in favour with the Catholic party, and erudite works on the middle ages are the branch of study in which the members of that party most distinguish themselves. M. Marius Sepet has just published, in the "Drame Chrétien du Moyen Age" (Didier), an excellent book in which the liturgical origin of the theatre is brought out with real erudition. But the most active and vehement representative of this school of erudite Catholicity is M. Léon Gautier, who has constituted himself the apostle of the "Chanson de Roland," of which he has already given us seven editions, and who has just published the first volume of the second edition of his great work on "Les Epopées Françaises" (Palmé). Thanks to the numerous contributions of late years to this subject, thanks too to his own researches, this second edition is an entirely new work. It is far from being a faultless one. It is a noteworthy fact that in writers of the Catholic school one hardly ever meets with exact criticism, or chastened taste, or precise and rigorous art in composition—they almost all fall into confusion, redundancy, exaggeration, florid rhetoric; their mode of argument has always a something about it that is weak, hyper-refined, childish. It may be because the Church holds them ever in a state of minority; at all events they are never thoroughly manly. This strikes us even in their greatest historians, Ozanam and Montalembert. Their best books seem less to be written by grown men than by youths full of promise, and this juvenility is very apparent in M. Gautier, but it is redeemed by many merits, by energy, contagious warmth of feeling and style, and by the audacity—I might even say the faith—necessary for such an undertaking. The critical school may smile, find fault, suggest, correct; it would never have ventured upon such a task. For that was needed an enthusiast and a believer! Just think of it, having to read and analyze more than a hundred epic poems, the greater number offering a great variety of readings, and the shortest numbering from ten to twelve thousand verses. It was a Herculean task. M. Gautier has got through it well, he has accomplished a useful work, clearing for the first time a much-encumbered ground and giving to literary workers an idea of the studies of detail open to their enterprise. Added to which the book is really pleasant reading, and makes us feel kindly to the middle age, to France, and to the author. This prodigious poetical productiveness, which began in the tenth and continued to the fourteenth century, spreading over the whole of Europe, affording inexhaustible aliment to German and Italian imaginations, gives us a grand idea of the fertility of ancient France. In the thirteenth century she was the heart and brain of Europe, and wielded an influence greater than she ever did since, even in the eighteenth century. M. Gautier has realized this greatness, and at the same time he perfectly recognizes all that there is of Germanic in the inspiration of these poems, in the ideas, feelings, and manners that they represent. Germanic and Christian in spirit, Romanic in form—such, according to him, are our ancient epics; and this definition we hold to be incontrovertible.

I have said above that nowadays it is only in these erudite researches that the Catholic school is worthily represented; in fact, in the purely

literary sphere it numbers few writers of talent,—the
century flows so far away from it that it has to accept the
promising alliances. For some time back it has adopted
After formerly gaining a reputation as romance-writer
by his stories of sword and steel, and having seen the
middle-class public gradually forsake him, this inventive
novelist, who begins his tales so well and continues them so
is now making himself a new circle of readers in the devout
satisfied with writing an apology for the Jesuits and
Etapes d'une Conversion," in which he not only confesses hi
but also those of other people, he re-edits his old romances,
them according to the counsels of ecclesiastical authori
"La Duchesse de Nemours" becomes transformed into
Tranquille."

Unfortunately M. Paul Féval no longer has any talen
Barbey d'Aurévilly, whose Catholicism is of older date, but
than that of M. Féval, has on the contrary a good deal.
d'Aurévilly is the last of the Romanticists; he still wears in 187
that was beginning to be ridiculous in 1830—a hat with broa
brim, greatcoat with collar, lapels, and velvet cuffs, and
plaited tightly about the waist. He is at once a devotee and
or rather he affects both characters. He has written books
been brought before the tribunals as outraging public
"Les Diaboliques" amongst others,—and now it is by religio
that his spicy, affected, restless, and sensual prose is so muc
it is by Catholic firms that his books are published. Wh
Because M. Barbey d'Aurévilly is an impenitent Roman
remains faithful to the dishevelled style and mystical gallan
years ago; because he would compromise any journal that
articles except Catholic journals, where the sign of the two
and sanctifies the wares. The latest book of M. d'Aurévilly's
"Les Bas Bleus" (Palmé). He has vowed mortal hatred to
presume to write—from professional jealousy, no doubt;
there is something effeminate about this old beau, who is
essences and scents, so there is also effeminacy in his talent,—
witty, imaginative, but unequal, inexact, and without creative
constantly believe ourselves to be coming to a forcible
passage, a perfect page, and suddenly the author stops
platitude or extravagance. For all that, there is much that
subtle, striking, in what he says of Mme. de Stael and Mme.
Mme. Sand, Mme. d'Agoult, Mme. Quinet, but there is
prompting his judgment, whether as regards his
towards Mme. Sand or his excessive admiration for Mme.
is a mere affair of nerves, of mood, of feminine caprice.
one most in reading this book is to see how,
numbers of women who have in the nineteenth century
in France as writers, the female author still continues
a being apart as it were, abnormal and unsexed.
who invented the expression "Bas Bleus;" it is
that the rather contemptuous estimate implied in
regard to women who write. We are still true
Romans, in whose eyes the vocation of women
stay at home, and spin, while to the Germans the

and prophetess, sharing, as Tacitus tells us, the cares and toils of her husband.

We must allow, in justice to French women, that they show a good deal of order and perseverance in asserting their rights, thereby greatly scandalizing M. d'Aurévilly, who only concedes them the one right of being beautiful. The number of female authors increases, and will increase. One of our best dramatic actresses, Mdlle. Rousseil, has just published a romance, "La Fille d'un Proscrit" (Lacroix), which has all the appearance of an autobiography, for it is the history of the daughter of a Republican workman who, in spite of poverty and insult, impelled by an invincible vocation, enters the *Conservatoire* and becomes a great artist. What makes me think that we have here a mingling of fact with fiction is, first, the passionate and occasionally eloquent tone of the book; and, next, its inequalities and incongruities. It contains some true and touching things; for instance, the story of the little beggar boy, Henri, the friend of the heroine, who becomes a painter, and dies during the siege of Paris; and yet in close connection with this we have conventional pictures of life and exaggerations that border on the ridiculous. On the whole, it is a strange book, showing plainly the mixture of idealism and vulgarity, originality and conventionalism, hyper-delicacy and want of delicacy, that is to be found in those who have lived a theatrical life.

This question of the proper sphere of women, and the rights of women, which M. Barbey d'Aurévilly treats as a clerical phantasiast, and Mdlle. Rousseil as a democrat slightly tinged with Socialism, has for several years been one of principal importance to moralists. The subject of woman's political emancipation, one of the principal themes of reformers, which still occupied attention at the close of the second Empire, is now relegated to the background; but the part played by woman in the family and in marriage is ever a burning and much-agitated question. Fifty, or even forty years ago, people still occupied the standpoint of the eighteenth century; marriage was not considered a subject for the drama or for tragedy. When a marriage was happy, it was not talked about; when unhappy, it was laughed at. At all events, conjugal infidelity was hardly more than a source of comedy; and if a separated pair were exhibited on the stage, it was only to be re-united as the curtain fell. It is so no longer. Such evils have become more serious; the indissolubility of marriage is now one of the most frequent themes of domestic dramas and of the sources of tragic and pathetic situations. The breach of the seventh commandment no longer affords the theatres (those devoted to pure farce of course excepted) plots for comedy, but for terrible tragedies, where the divided pair end—not in reconciliation, but death, suicide, or murder. Mme. Sand was the first to agitate this painful question of the indissolubility of the marriage vow with persuasive eloquence, but unfortunately her own life did not entitle her to deal with such a subject. Divorce should not be demanded or the French law attacked in the interests of our passions, but in the name of morality outraged whether by the indissoluble union of two beings who hate each other and have forfeited each other's esteem, or by such a separation as French law admits, one that leaves the separated wife at the mercy of her husband, and places both parties in a false and anomalous position, fatally conducive to disorder or despair. In all Protestant countries, where marriage is more and respected than in Catholic, divorce is admitted. It is Cat that opposes it in France. During the last fifty years has become more serious, and hence pleas in favour of become more fervent and numerous, and separations the same time the progress of the clerical party has number of those who decidedly oppose divorce through judice. Add to this the revolutionary condition of France, it natural to dread shaking society by modifying a law of standing, and renders all reforms more difficult under a Repu a Monarchy, and we shall understand how it is that divorce ously demanded by the state of our morals, finds still so many ad We even see with some surprise freethinkers range themselves side, and such a man as M. Janet declare himself, in his interesti on "Saint-Simon et Saint-Simonisme" (G. Baillière), an opp divorce. The Chamber of Deputies under Louis Philippe had lished it; the Chamber of Deputies nowadays refuses to occu with the matter, and M. Thiers commended it for so doin scandals, however, daily occur to demonstrate the iniquity of the law. A few months ago we had the unfortunate Princesse de Bau married to a man unworthy of her, and judicially separated f becoming naturalized in Saxony, and marrying the Prince G. but unable to obtain the ratification of her marriage in France, according to French law, a separated wife can accomplish no without the authorization of her husband, whence it follows whole fortune is sequestrated. A few days ago we had the la Mme. de Chevandier de Valdrôme, showing in their full h consequences of the indissolubility of marriage; both husband living immorally, and yet tyrannizing one over the other, till fin became enemies, all the more implacable because riveted to t chain. This lawsuit came to an end on the 31st December, by Valdrôme escaping to a foreign country, carrying off the of whom had been refused her by the law courts.

Such dramas of conjugal life as these, in which assassinati plays a part, are to be counted by hundreds every year in F being the only method of cutting a knot that the law refuses and thus we arrive at a monstrous but logical result: that refuses divorce to a husband outraged by his wife, but that acquits him if he kills her. Out of respect for marriage we h to authorize murder. So faulty a social condition naturally abundant material to drama-mongers; but it is but recently appeals in favour of divorce have been made from the stage. ago M. Emile Augier, in "Mme. Caverlet," put before us to escape from a wretch who deceived and ill-used her, to give up her country, live in foreign lands, and and untruth to keep her children ignorant of the false they were placed. M. Augier's piece was very amusing too, but it had one fault—Mme. Caverlet still she was happy, she loved and was beloved by a her, was able in the law's despite to lead a tranquil land, and ended by persuading her husband to Switzerland, where they obtained a divorce. All

interesting no doubt; but we do not realize their full distress since they find a happy solution. M. Legouvé has also treated this subject, but in a different manner. He saw that to make the full horror of the situation felt it was necessary to show us an irreproachable woman, replacing by no other the love she had given her husband, and enduring all the tortures and outrages which result from the *régime* of separation. Reduced to poverty, exposed to calumny as to her affections and her private life, persecuted by her husband who seeks to deprive her of her son, she would have been driven to despair, had not the cause of her separation (which she had never consented to reveal lest her son should blush for his father) come out, and her husband, known at last to have been a spy, executed justice on himself by suicide. This piece of M. Legouvé's is very cleverly constructed, has several situations that are admirably pathetic, and each catastrophe affords a commentary on some article of the Code. We see the husband empowered by law to have his separated wife watched by the police, to emancipate his son without the authorization of the mother, although it is she who has the care of this son; we see the marriage bond violated in its sweetness and sacredness, but the chain with all its weight preserved intact, and creating an unbounded hatred between the two. We see too how this rivalry and hatred between the parents produces in the children either intolerable suffering if they be noble-souled, or profound demoralization if they be frivolous and capable of profiting by this separation to extort favour from each parent and put up their own affection to auction. Unfortunately, from a theatrical point of view, M. Legouvé's "La Séparation" can hardly become popular,—it is too sad, too harrowing, too real, too, as it were, legal. Besides, looking at the demonstration aimed at, it has one great defect: the interest is divided between the mother whom the father seeks to deprive of her son, and the son whose heart is divided between his father and mother; nay, the latter interest ends by becoming predominant. From that moment we forget that we are listening to a plea in favour of divorce, since the law of divorce would not prevent children suffering cruelly when their parents parted. "La Séparation" was only played once in an afternoon at the Vaudeville, and M. Legouvé himself explained in a charming lecture what his purpose was. The piece succeeded—thanks to the admirable way in which Mme. Delaporte played the principal part, and thanks, too, to the earnest attention given by the audience to this pathetic commentary on an existing law, but we do not know if it would succeed with the more frivolous audiences that gather in an evening.

This is the only interesting theatrical novelty that we have had. "La Centième d'Hamlet," by Th. Barrière, is a posthumous drama that had better have been left unrepresented, for the credit of this vigorous and witty but incomplete writer, who has been a good deal over-praised. "La Belle Mme. Donis," by H. Malot, is without any charm, as was the romance from which it is taken. Malot is a conscientious observer, but dull, cold, and colourless, absolutely lacking in all the theatre requires. Finally, the "Bonhomme Misère," of M. d'Hervilly, is not a play at all; it is a mere putting of a popular legend into verse, an occasion for pretty costumes designed by Grévin, and for agreeable rhymes.

But this somewhat childish love of the marvellous that our authors pretend to, does not affect to us just now, when scientific discoveries give our imagination full scope for dreams that are limitless, yet have a real basis. I am not speaking of the telephone, the present delight of all family and social gatherings, but of the experiments of M. Cailletet on the liquefaction of gas. It had been long affirmed theoretically that all bodies were capable of assuming three conditions—solid, liquid, and gaseous; but it was none the less desirable experimentally to prove this theory. All gases had been liquefied except oxygen, hydrogen, and azote, when it became known, in December, that M. Cailletet, an ironmaster who devotes his fortune to the promotion of important physical enterprises, had arrived at a partial liquefaction of oxygen into the form of vapour. At once M. R. Pictet of Geneva set to work and repeated this experiment. The friends of M. Cailletet were shocked, were almost ready to accuse M. Pictet of disloyalty, for having ventured to liquefy a gas for himself; M. Cailletet, full of emulation, subjected oxygen to a new and more complete experiment, and, on the 31st December, the two last refractory gases, hydrogen and azote. M. Pictet did not consider himself beaten in this scientific steeple-chase, and he declares he has just solidified hydrogen. The partisans of M. Cailletet hint that what M. Pictet has taken for solidified hydrogen is in fact but water frozen, the combination of hydrogen at 200 degrees of cold with the oxygen of the air having produced an instantaneous congelation of water. What, however, appears more certain is that M. Pictet has obtained liquefied oxygen in quantity sufficient to be able to measure its density, which is the same as that of water. Setting aside, however, the little scientific rivalries of the friends of MM. Pictet and Cailletet, and whatever the respective merits of these bold and intelligent experimentalists may be, we can congratulate ourselves on this new triumph of science. The very process of liquefaction is interesting. The gaseous condition arising, according to theory, from the great distance between the molecules of a body, liquefaction must proceed from their increased nearness, which is brought about by pressure combined with the lowering of temperature. This pressure is easily exerted by means of a mercurial pump; but the excessive cold cannot be directly produced—it results from the sudden diminution of pressure. The gas, requiring heat to return to its original expansion, can only borrow it from itself, hence such a fall of temperature is suddenly produced that the gas liquefies. It is thus that hydrogen has been submitted to a pressure of 280 atmospheres and to 200 degrees Centigrade of cold. We may form some idea of what such a pressure is, by reflecting that a pressure of only seven atmospheres suffices to impel an ordinary locomotive, and we may imagine the power of resistance required in the tubes of iron and glass that support such pressure. Up to the present time it is not supposed that these experiments can have any other result than to establish by fact the generality of a natural law, and yet many are seeking to find in them the starting point of arguments destined to uphold such and such a theory on the composition of bodies. M. Dumas, who has constituted himself the regular champion of M. Pictet, is of opinion that the liquefaction of gas will afford a proof of the truth of the Atomic theory and of his own private theory, according to which hydrogen will prove to be a metal, carburetted hydrogen. To us these conclusions seem a little premature, but how if I should tell you the dreams that are hatching in the brains of the profane? One already sees the air reduced to tablets; gas utilized in a thousand ways, &c. Nothing is more curious than the readiness of the French intellect when once started on any given track, to follow it by logical consequences to any extremity. The telephone and liquefied gas—why here we have enough to transform the earth, if we are to believe the conversations we now hear in every *salon*. It has been sometimes said that the French want imagination and excel in common sense. I am by no means of this opinion. They owe this reputation to not having a poetic imagination and to being great arguers. But they possess in the very highest degree a logical imagination, which consists in pushing an idea from consequence to consequence up to absurdity, without taking into account the reality and complexity of things. The English are both more poetical and far more practical, because theirs is a concrete imagination, which represents to them things as they are in all their widely ramifying variety; whereas the imagination of Frenchmen is abstract and logical. This is why they are very good mathematicians, theorists of the first order, why we owe to them great theoretical discoveries in science, and very few practical inventions, why their laws are so good, and their politics so faulty.

G. Monod.

# CONTEMPORARY ESSAYS AND COMMENTS.

[*In this Section the Contributors to the* CONTEMPORARY REVIEW *are understood to express themselves with less restraint (as to their individual views) than might be thought desirable in formal articles.*]

**On Patriotism.**

DURING the last two years most of us have been forced to ask ourselves, What is the actual value and nature of Patriotism? No single feeling has taken so different an aspect according to the illustrations present to the mind of hearer or speaker; and the same person may at different times have felt inclined to protest against the halo of reverence cast around what he could only recognize as selfishness on a gigantic scale, or against a failure of loyalty towards the most permanent object of loyalty. The question what that is which assumes such different aspects has been partly answered* in a former number of this REVIEW; but the emphatic and much-needed protest there given against a distorted ideal of Patriotism prepares the way for considering the question what Patriotism actually is—a question to which the answer is not so obvious as people are apt to suppose.

In dealing with this question, we would disclaim any intention of entering on political ground. It is conceivable, though not very likely, that men agreed as to their principles might take views diametrically opposite of the desirable means of carrying them out, or that men agreed as to their actions might abhor each other's political creed. A vast and varying crowd of motives impels a nation toward peace or war; and the most passionate advocates of either might be equally passionate opponents if they dealt not with actions, but with reasons for action. We are dealing now with reasons for action solely. We are inquiring, not what Englishmen had better do, but how far a regard to the glory and interest of England is a legitimate ground for what they do. The question what particular action is for the glory and interest of England is one we carefully avoid opening.

We would guard ourselves against another misunderstanding, very likely to arise in any question of right or wrong—we mean the confusion of mind by which people suppose all merit is denied whenever one kind of merit is. To say that a particular line of conduct is not an exhibition of Patriotism, is not to deny that it may be on other grounds justifiable or even meritorious. We believe, for example, that the imperial relations of any country do not supply the field for Patriotism, any more than a man's dealings with his tenants exhibit his attitude as a father; but we are not obliged therefore to consider that England ought to cease to be an empire. An English statesman can have few subjects of deeper or wider-reaching consideration than the claims of India; while the endeavour to understand and appreciate the needs of a subject race, differing from the dominant race in almost every particular which can separate one nation from another, appears to us one in which a

* By the Duke of Argyll. See CONTEMPORARY REVIEW for July, 1877: Art. "Morality in Politics."

[illegible] helpful only so far as any particular kind of excellence is [illegible] but English dominion in India does not therefore [illegible] unrighteous. This may seem a truism, but we continually read [illegible] of the contrary. Those who do regard the British Em[illegible] mistake, who consider that our hold on India is founded [illegible] and cannot be continued without participation in the sins of [illegible] originated it, are continually blamed for their want of Patriotism. [illegible] that they are answered by the facts that England's imperial [illegible] high and dry above all questions as to their origin; that [illegible] in assuming authority over the fathers, she would sin also in [illegible] authority over the children; and that this great power, however it [illegible] is now a sacred trust which we must make the most of, and be [illegible] to defend. But the question between these two parties is not one of [illegible]tism. The object of an Englishman's Patriotism is England, not England's [illegible] over India. Patriotism can have no object but a nation.

[illegible] truth is, that the very existence of an empire is justifiable only in so far [illegible] imagine other objects more important than the development of [illegible]. If this were the only good thing in national life, it is difficult to [illegible] one nation could ever be justified in holding another in unwilling sub[illegible] The imperial State does not cease to be a nation because she is also [illegible]. But in a very important sense her subject provinces cease to be [illegible]. The empire which is in so many respects a model—in many also a [illegible] for British rule, the Empire of Rome, was a universal extinguisher [illegible]. One by one the nations taken into its vast and tenacious grasp [illegible] cease of their nationality—they gained something instead, no doubt, [illegible] was not homogeneous with the thing they lost. Carthage, Spain, [illegible] all the group of Mediterranean States, had to give up their very life [illegible] might supply Rome with subjects, and these subjects could not take [illegible] the imperial city the attitude they had lost towards their own. [illegible] looking back on the world's history, recognizing the part that Roman [illegible] Roman civilization were to play in the formation of Europe, may [illegible] that the sacrifice was not too great. But we can only do this in so [illegible] we believe that, noble and elevating as is the impulse of the Patriot, [illegible] the only influence by which the race is raised, through the progress of [illegible] to a higher level.

[illegible] indeed is less hard for an Englishman to make this concession than it [illegible] have been for a Roman. The association of antiquity which clings [illegible] the name of Patriot is no mere literary accident. Whatever else [illegible]tism may be, it is in an important sense a virtue of the old world, or of [illegible], if we were accurate, we should call the young world. To no Englishman [illegible]r day can England be altogether what any of the republics of Greece [illegible] to their citizens, or even what the Roman State was to Romans. There [illegible]rtues of youth and virtues of age in individual life, and there is the same [illegible]f contrast in the life of a nation. Patriotism, we believe, can never again [illegible]y the same proportion of a man's energies, as in the great ages of the [illegible]cal world. To an Athenian or Roman, devotion to Athens or Rome took [illegible]ace of religion. It was the devotion to an immortal being (so it seemed [illegible] men of that day), overshadowing with its grandeur the ephemeral lives [illegible] took their whole meaning and colour from their relation to it. Any [illegible]pt to return to this devotion would land us in unreality. A new spirit [illegible]assed over the world, and even when man rejects it, he cannot return to [illegible]sition of those who knew nothing of it. We have looked along the vista [illegible]other immortality; and the prospect of an endless future for every human [illegible] whether accepted or rejected, has changed the importance and meaning [illegible] national future. The destiny of England is not less important than the [illegible] of Athens; it may be far more important. But it can never fill the [illegible] of an Englishman as the destiny of Athens filled the horizon of an [illegible]. The larger thing (so we venture to believe it) occupies a smaller space of the whole field of view, because it has not [illegible] portion as the whole field of view. The individual [illegible] held in the old world. As he entered on the inheritance [illegible] took up a different position from any that had [illegible] It is not that the moderns believe in immortality, and [illegible] in it. It would be truer to say that the ancients did [illegible] do both. There is no more striking illustration of this [illegible] the great poem, which will at first sight occur to the [illegible] what we have said about it. Lucretius puts forth a very [illegible] the existence of the soul after death, no doubt. But it [illegible] student with surprise, that the philosophic poet should have [illegible] so little hope in the expectations he was combating,—that the that world

> "Where all pursuits their goal obtain,
> And life is all retouched again,"

should not have occurred to him as a possibility. He [illegible] suggested to an English poet descriptions of the domestic [illegible] death that are familiar to all,* and yet hardly match the [illegible] original, could not have been incapable of entering into the [illegible] so trite to us by frequent repetition, but they were [illegible] The continuity of love and hope and energy on both sides of [illegible] of an infinite existence carrying out to their development [illegible] and this as the lot of commonplace average men and women, [illegible] of the last century before Christ quite inaccessible. The [illegible] satisfied the instinct which in the modern world feeds on the [illegible] from another quarter. They were satisfied with the sense of [illegible] is given by union with a nation; they knew that the root [illegible] least need not—perish, and it was to them a small thing that [illegible] wither. It would take us too far to decide which was [illegible] effect in this combination, whether it was that men, having [illegible] sonal immortality, turned all their aspiration towards the [illegible] or whether the very ardour of this devotion drained off their [illegible] individual anticipation, and left the world beyond the grave [illegible] scenery that makes a background for some beloved face. It is [illegible] to note the association of the vivid national feeling with the [illegible] anticipation, and to recognize that, for limited human beings, [illegible] increase enormously one element in a complex whole [illegible] least for a time, the relative importance of the rest. The [illegible] cannot be to us quite what it was to those for whom it formed [illegible] of boundless hope, and the only stable element in a fleeting [illegible] restore the preponderance which belonged to the national [illegible] nation alone stood forth a centre of hopes and energies that were over death.

But it may be objected that many, and an increasing [illegible] day returned to the position of antiquity with regard to [illegible] "the Soul and a Future Life" suggests to us quite as much [illegible] True, but when men in our day deny Immortality, they [illegible] position of those who never thought about Immortality. [illegible] our ancestors have been profoundly moved by the [illegible] which belonged to their view have become a part of [illegible] When in our day men quit the thought of this individual [illegible] effort to return to the attitude of antiquity, they do not [illegible]

* "For them no more the blazing hearth shall [illegible]

> "Jam jam non domus accipiet te læta, [illegible]
> Optima, nec dulces occurrent oscula [illegible]
> Præripere et tacita pectus dulcedine [illegible]

[illegible] ...ition, but rather cultivate that devotion towards the [illegible] which is a disintegrating force with respect to the nation. [illegible] that, no set of men have so much drawn upon themselves [illegible] want of Patriotism as that knot of high-minded men who [illegible] the hope for a personal future, not only as an anticipation for [illegible] no basis, but as a demand for which morality offers [illegible] This part of the Comtist creed has many points of interest, [illegible] to us the unconscious tribute it bears to that very senti- [illegible] which it aims at being a protest. We measure the strength of [illegible] of Individuality by watching its reappearance in the [illegible] abstract Humanity. We are not now trying to measure the [illegible] the modern reverence for the Individual; we only speak of it as [illegible] accept it as we accept the change from youth to age. The [illegible] of Englishmen has a set of indefeasible claims that would have [illegible]gible to a Greek.

[illegible] may be said, "this is no doubt the result of our weakness and our [illegible] are we to surrender ourselves to the tendencies of our weakness [illegible]? Is not the whole of healthful national action a struggle [illegible]? If to the ancient world a man was a part of a nation, and to the [illegible] a nation is nothing but a congeries of men, so much the worse [illegible] world! There is nothing in a heightened reverence for individual [illegible], and a belief in individual immortality, to shackle the loyalty [illegible] we turn to the only stable and permanent groups of human spirits [illegible] history takes account. The expansion and elevation of the parts [illegible] to contract or degrade the whole. History is a chequered scene, [illegible] that is bright is a mere effulgence of the spirit which reverences [illegible]; it is clouded not alone by mere individual selfishness, but by the [illegible], by sectarian animosity, and all those prejudices of an order or [illegible] are poor and vulgar even when they form the link to a wider [illegible] the nation, because they are founded on a part of the nature, and [illegible] bond is founded on the whole. In our day the ignoble crowd have [illegible] ally. The love of self and the love of caste find their poverty dis- [illegible] by the allied splendour of the love of Humanity, and the banner of a wide [illegible] rallies a motley crowd, containing more elements of weakness than [illegible]gth. We do ill thus to cast from us that which throughout the whole [illegible] been the binding influence of our race, in the vain attempt to make [illegible] universal. The end of such an attempt, if it could be successful, [illegible] not the expansion of sympathy, but its extreme contraction. The [illegible] of Humanity form an ideal much too vague, too little connected with [illegible] to give any counterpoise to the steady pull of self-interest; and to set [illegible] ideal before imagination is to surrender all the motive force of life to [illegible] reality, at least in that more subtle vicarious form in which it is most [illegible]. He who is too ambitious to accept the limitations of a patriot [illegible] found at last in the numerous ranks, surely no source of strength to [illegible] of a nation, of 'ces pères de famille qui sont capables de tout.'"

[illegible] are not the considerations on which in this particular crisis of public [illegible] it seems to us specially important to dwell; but that is all we can see [illegible] against them. The part of duty to which they direct the mind is [illegible]portant. But it is not one which affords the clue to any tangled [illegible] of foreign policy. Patriotism is only one aspect of that influence [illegible] teaching us to accept corporate interests and duties, elevates as [illegible] it widens our moral nature; and the gradual development of the [illegible] through these successive groupings of sympathies—the family— [illegible] the nation—as it has been unquestionably the appointed discipline [illegible] seems to us in a less degree the school of right sympathy for the [illegible] But surely the seed of good in this discipline is the power that [illegible] the power that divides. No doubt they are inextricably combined. [illegible] tracing the origin of the conscience to the gregarious instincts of animal life, has suggested, in his picture of the swallow's [illegible] autumn as the migratory instinct called the parent birds [illegible] the first sketch, as it were, of this struggle between the two [illegible] binding power—the first hint, in all its pathetic simplicity, of [illegible] whatever binds must also sever. We have endeavoured to [illegible] illustration of the same law in contrasting the moral ideal of [illegible] that of Christendom, and there is indeed no great movement [illegible] which it is not illustrated. "Think not that I am come to [illegible] earth" has been, or might have been, the warning of every great [illegible] so far as he left among his disciples a new principle of union, [illegible] them a new principle of division also. But woe to them if this [illegible] preach! It is the warning needed by fearless enthusiasm—it is [illegible] forced from reluctant candour on any impartial view of history [illegible] becomes the foundation of a creed, the Gospel is lost.

No doubt, in all human experience, the things that bind are [illegible] the things that divide; but the binding influence is a source of [illegible] the dividing influence is a source of weakness. The very same bond [illegible] of strength or of weakness, according as it shuts in much or [illegible] Look at the lounger of the clubs side by side with the husband and [illegible] still better, watch successively the same man in both characters [illegible] luxurious trifler rouse himself to self-denial and industry; and you [illegible] that the commonest of all bonds—the one that we share with the [illegible] we look down upon—may in very truth bring a human soul salvation [illegible] look at this bond as it is a limitation. Take another kind of youth [illegible] high aims, the lofty ideals of the unshackled devotee of any [illegible] then compare this stage of early devotion with the sober mid-[illegible] sacrifices have to be shared by wife and children; and are you not [illegible] something like a descent? "This is the truth I should desire to [illegible] stood alone, and if I stood alone I could starve to set it forth; but [illegible] sacrifice my children's bread?" Many a brilliant soul, which could [illegible] remained solitary, might have been as a star to the mariner, passed [illegible] world hid in a cloud of sordid and ignoble cares, because to it [illegible] become vicarious. We accept the limitations of those to [illegible] ourselves; sympathy with an oppressed nation or a down-trodden [illegible] be wiped out of the very recollection of a noble spirit by even [illegible] frivolous need in one dear to him; and many a man, who would h[illegible] discomfort his whole life long to shed some ray of hope on t[illegible] masses beneath him, will give up the chance of such a destiny [illegible] should be obliged to go without luxuries.

The advantages and disadvantages of belonging to a group w[illegible] chooses, and indeed creates, may not seem relevant to a discussi[illegible] tie that connects him with the nation. Not only is it impossibl[illegible] separate from the larger group, but it is hardly possible tha[illegible] prove in the same manner or to the same degree a source of limita[illegible] is nothing less naturally allied with small or poor considerations th[illegible] which connects each one of us with a nation. But there is no bond [illegible] not become a limit. Even the grand perspectives of history [illegible] vistas into the past and the future which belong to a nation [illegible] from pettiness the spirit of exclusion. Though the enclosure [illegible] though it include specimens of the richest and most various [illegible] the principal thing in the minds of those who insist upon [illegible] others, the effect will be narrowing. Nay, we understate the [illegible] thus—the effect will be narrowing if those who have [illegible] any particular nation are not alive to the danger of forget[illegible] other nations. For it is always easier to see difference [illegible] mere momentum of self will be a principle of divergence [illegible] a common centre. [illegible]

What is the inference from this? [illegible]

[illegible] considerations into large considerations, not a limit put upon [illegible] to prevent their growing larger. It is one of the many [illegible] scattered through the writings of Mr. Ruskin, that Patriotism [illegible] individual;—we speak, he says, of a patriotic man or a [illegible] patriotic nation. A weighty and pregnant truth, which [illegible] by unduly extending its scope. In one sense of course all [illegible] to an individual, yet it would be easy to illustrate from history [illegible] that a nation may act justly or unjustly, generously or un- [illegible] in proportion as any action assumes a national character, it [illegible] region where Patriotism, in any sense of the word which com- [illegible] sympathy, is possible.' So far as the thing done is for the advan- [illegible] who do it, the animating principle of action is not only unlike, but [illegible] of all that wins our admiration in the attitude of the Patriot.

> "With Palinure's undaunted mood,
> Firm at his *dangerous* post he stood"

[illegible] description of the dying Pitt—just touches on the circumstance which [illegible] all its value. If you exclude not only the fact but the possi- [illegible] sacrifice, you may describe an action most justifiable, most desir- [illegible] just—we do not subtract all virtues when we subtract one—but [illegible] patriotic is merely confusing. The result may be one desired by the [illegible] but the measure of his Patriotism is his willingness to merge all [illegible] interest in national interest; and when the nation acts, this spirit [illegible] expression only in an act of national self-sacrifice. Whether such [illegible] ever be part of a nation's duty is a question on which we do

[illegible] it may be said, "but what is the practical bearing of such considera- [illegible]? Statesmen *are* individuals, the action of Government is always [illegible] the prevalence of some predominant will. Is there no meaning in [illegible] devotion to the welfare of one's country, unless a man may pay for it [illegible] life? Is it not a virtue even to discern the interests of a great nation? [illegible] such a discernment are needed the aspiring wing, the eagle eye, [illegible] a man above all things poor and petty, and obliterate the sight of [illegible] interest quite as effectually as the rush of resolve which leads an [illegible] Winkelried to gather an armful of Austrian spears into his heart, or [illegible] to crush himself to death beneath a wounded elephant. The same [illegible] shows itself in acts like these, begets the resolute prudence which [illegible] same aims by the devotion instead of sacrifice of a life, and to with- [illegible] name of Patriotism from the spirit which would produce self-sacrifice [illegible] were occasion for it, only because there is no occasion for it, is like [illegible] to change the name of a plant when it goes out of flower."

[illegible] we should deem it mere pedantry to confine the name of Patriot [illegible] who could seal it with his blood, or with any obvious and tangible [illegible] No doubt the most unselfish thing a man can do in a good many [illegible] is to take care of his own life. Hannibal showed a truer [illegible] in preserving himself for the service of his ungrateful country after [illegible] even his brother in the heroic death which wins the tribute of the [illegible] historian. We urge only that to keep unblurred the very meaning of [illegible] sacred in the long associations that gather round the name, you [illegible] that kind of devotion which one being can feel for another. [illegible] not identify the agent and the object of action. You must not [illegible] of enlightened self-interest, however justifiable, by that word [illegible] to the imagination acts of supreme self-sacrifice. There is [illegible] ashamed of in a watchful care for our own interests, or a [illegible] of our own undoubted rights. These things have their place [illegible] of all. But neither, surely, is there any need of urging [illegible] the conscience of any one. Our own interests, and the [illegible] with ourselves, will always seem to us at least a little more important than they are. No doubt, when [illegible] thing as a nation, this kind of danger is at its minimum [illegible] cease to exist in a world of varied bonds and clashing [illegible] portion as a man represents a nation he is called on to [illegible] nation. No Patriot, we believe, ever felt himself to [illegible] Hannibal struggling for sixteen terrible years to hold [illegible] empire that was throttling his country, Epaminondas lifting [illegible] dust, Mazzini watching for a chance of a united Italy—all [illegible] emotions which no man can feel for himself, or for anything [illegible] himself. So far as a man stands forth the arbiter between [illegible] and others in the comity of nations the situation is changed. [illegible] for the individual is Patriotism is for the nation Justice. [illegible] and lofty platform of national interest, a State may weigh [illegible] against those of others, but it will never be just, if it aims at [illegible]

When, in the Peloponnesian war, the noble Spartan refused [illegible] slavery any of Hellenic blood, he must have seemed to many [illegible] citizens to be playing an unpatriotic part. In the fierce stru[illegible] Athens and Sparta, the recognition of a common Greece would se[illegible] to either, as to some among our contemporaries does the [illegible] common humanity. Those who contemplate the bond on [illegible] will always consider that it is ignored by those who recognise [illegible] And yet the recognition of the wider bond is the natural devel[illegible] recognition of the narrower one. Those who feel most [illegible] are Englishmen will desire most ardently that England sh[illegible] less as the vigilant guardian of her own interests, though she [illegible] also, no doubt, than as the fearless defender of justice. Let [illegible] individuals perish when they come into collision with the interests [illegible] But when the interests of nations clash, is there no need for [illegible] of a common ground, that is to the nations of Europe what [illegible] Athens and Sparta? If Callicratidas felt that he was a Gre[illegible] Spartan afterwards, and if in this we recognize an advance on [illegible] policy, we must allow that those act most loyally to their coun[illegible] who are ready to regard it as the member of a larger whole. [illegible] of view there will be no department of political activity, [illegible] statesman will feel Patriotism less an object of conscious [illegible] in her foreign policy. Patriotism will lift him above the [illegible] be influenced by any family or personal considerations, it will [illegible] path the hindrance of a possible place or peerage, it will [illegible] "euphrasy and rue" which will purge his eyesight to discern [illegible] tage of his country. But it will not be the keynote of that pa[illegible] man's conduct which deals with the fate of other countries. [illegible] tions, while remembering that no corporate being as far transc[illegible] as the nation transcends the individual,—while realizing the [illegible] with which a man discerns, the superior efficiency with which [illegible] the welfare of those near him, and while conceding a certain [illegible] claims which he can best understand,—still at last he will not [illegible] the representative of one set of interests among many, and [illegible] impartial dealing with many interests.

If at the great crises of our history English statesmen had [illegible] bered this, would England stand lower than she does now? [illegible] who represented her had been to infuse into all her external [illegible] towards that community in which she is but a unit, would [illegible] which she is regarded by her own children be lessened in [illegible] Would not the nation which cared most for humanity be [illegible] in patriots?

It is against all analogy if it be not so. The effort [illegible] nature is towards expansion in every direction. If any [illegible] as a mere limit, it will not attract the loyalty of [illegible]

[illegible] the trades-union, not of the nation. In the national bond, [illegible] which man has not chosen, we may recognize a discipline for [illegible] which it is educated to pass the bounds it has travelled [illegible] instance. It is no true love of the familiar and the near [illegible] the spirit into a widening circle from which at last [illegible] of humanity is shut out.

---

[illegible] author of the paper in the last number of this REVIEW [illegible] Little Health of Ladies" has, some of us fancy, raised more [illegible] than can well be settled offhand upon truth in dress. She admits false teeth, and condemns false hair. She also thinks that Mrs. Haweis lays too much weight upon "the art of dress among the pursuits of women." This is, of course, a matter of feeling. As Milton says, one man's "much" or "too-much" is not necessarily commensurable with another's. I remember some lady critic was very [illegible] the *Spectator* a few years ago for suggesting that a woman's [illegible] should be "alluring." I am depraved enough to agree with the [illegible] but then my "alluring" may not be the "alluring" of that lady. She might have been thinking of some such ornament as the *suivez-moi jeune homme*; I am thinking of, say for a symbol, the attraction which "Our [illegible]" had for Heine.

[illegible] Cobbe's principles, Health, Decency, and Beauty, include "concealment [illegible] portions of the human frame"—this, under the head of decency; and [illegible]—the dress to be all genuine, with no false pads, false hair, or [illegible]." It might be largely discussed whether these three heads do cover the whole theory of human attire. No doubt Convenience, which [illegible] something to say to it, *might* be included under the head of Health, without violence. Again, a great deal of what Miss Cobbe would hold [illegible] might be smuggled in under her eleventh requirement—that of [illegible] degree of compliance with prevailing modes. Here, again, we come [illegible] upon Milton's question—how much is *your* moderate as compared with [illegible]? Still, there are laws and reasons—and we will not quibble over [illegible] head of Individuality is much more difficult: "No one body can be [illegible] in several equally suitable suits of clothes, any more than one soul [illegible] fittingly housed in twenty different bodies." To this I should reply [illegible] not-proven. Why should not one soul be capable of fit housing in different bodies, each representing its individuality *as well as it could be* [illegible], *absolute proportion being impossible?* With my utmost ingenuity, I [illegible] of no reason. A similar remark seems to me to apply still more [illegible] and decisively to the dress. A person of adequate genius, who [illegible] gave his mind to it, could probably invent an indefinite number of justly [illegible] dresses, all different, for any woman in the world. Some years ago [illegible] William Maccall, in a scheme for a Universal Church, laid down positive [illegible] ute details of dress for his chief functionaries, in this style:—

[illegible] dress of the Spiritualists must be blue as that sky which is the mantle of [illegible] when he looks serenely through the starlight on mortals. The dress of the [illegible] to be partly white, as the emblem of the love that ever forgives; partly [illegible] the emblem of the cloud that menaces; and partly red, as the emblem [illegible] lightning which destroys. The Harmonists to wear garments of four [illegible] colours: purple to represent the warm life of pictorial gorgeousness; [illegible] represent statuesque loveliness, grace, and sanctity—something like [illegible] to represent architectural grandeur and massive majesty: some-[illegible] which sunshine and cloud sinuate into each other, intervolve without [illegible] to represent the symbolical."

[illegible] Cobbe can scarcely contemplate anything like this: for example, that [illegible] great solidity of character should wear, as Mr. Maccall puts it, "something like granite;" or that a peppery dowager shall [illegible] and-lightning to indicate that she is not to be trifled with. W[illegible] of this, one can see no *necessary* limit to truthful "individuality"

It may well be a question whether the whole topic of Truth [illegible] related question of Use as suggestive of Beauty, to quote [illegible] Bothie of Tober-na-vuolich—

> "Nothing concealed that is done, but that all things be done to ad[illegible]

has yet been well cleared up. I certainly think not. But, to co[illegible] false hair; sometimes false hair is bad, but why must it alw[illegible] more than a false tooth? Take simply the one point of "conc[illegible] disgusting personal defect." What *is* disgusting?

> "My lady's cheek can boast no more . . .
> The cranberry white and pink it wore;
> And where her shining locks divide,
> The parting line is all too wide."

Now, to some male persons—nay, to some female persons—the [illegible] of "the parting line" is really and perhaps violently "disgu[illegible] would probably be worse, because it seldom if ever deceives. [illegible] is a wig necessarily wrong, on grounds of truthfulness, even [illegible] necessary on any other ground? The razor of Occam could [illegible] hairs. Then, suppose a lady loses one or two front teeth, which [illegible] and health go, she can do very well without. She will find th[illegible] disagreeable, some will say a disgusting, effect to her countena[illegible] she be wrong if she has one or two false ones inserted, merely [illegible] appearance? So keen is the feeling of most women in such ma[illegible] a fact that there are dentists who make half their income by [illegible] ladies who come to them for false teeth. The ladies wish that [illegible] be kept—from their husbands among others—and the dentis[illegible] pockets shamefully and cruelly as the price of complicity.

Now, of course this is immoral, and leads from bad to wors[illegible] indirect robbing of the husband; but that does not clear up the [illegible] What is admitted under the head of decency expressly admits [illegible] concealment. This, it will be said, goes to matters as to wh[illegible] common, not to say universal understanding. Possibly; but [illegible] contended, after all, that the understanding is actually univ[illegible] extent or character. Questions of more or less drapery, and of [illegible] assume widely differing colours among men and women of di[illegible] climate. If, however, we admit that the essence of what is [illegible] the modern sense of the word, as distinguished from that of [illegible] years ago) is the concealment, or the assumption of the conce[illegible] expression by some device of the desire to conceal, whatever m[illegible] remind one of human infirmities lying within certain [illegible] compelled to admit that the boundary lines are very fluctuating [illegible] if any number of men and women choose to say that it is [illegible] attempt to conceal the accidental want of teeth, we shall not [illegible] them. For my own part, I should say the want of hair on th[illegible] was in a woman more painful to see than the want of teeth [illegible] I was not definitely and *irrevocably* deceived, in such a [illegible] injury, by any device which concealed the defect, I should [illegible]

It is upon the saving clause that the difficulty arises. [illegible] hard upon Lady Mary Wortley Montague because she [illegible] Turkish jacket. He thought it a mannish affectation [illegible] because it gave her ease under the pangs of cancer." [illegible] supposing she had been young, and had worn such a [illegible] not for comfort only, but to conceal a deformity, [illegible] criterion shall it be determined whether the conc[illegible]

Cobbe's seventh head—"concealment, when possible, of any *disgusting* personal defect?"

Without going as far as Sir Thomas More, or Plato, or any other founder of republics in the air, all will agree that there is at least one special contract between two human beings which demands that there shall be no concealment of personal defects. Yet I have no sooner written this sentence than I see that its terms are too wide. It is anything but true that "all will agree." True, I agree, for one, and hold that the agreement ought to be general. But one finds, after a little observation of life, that among most people,—average persons, who have no particular sense of beauty, fitness, or truth,—there is a tacit understanding in favour of a certain degree of winking in this matter. A certain degree,—which is, necessarily, in practice most uncertain. It is very easy to get up caricature cases in any direction. Not to venture in the direction which would be repulsive, what can we make of a father taking a gentleman aside and saying, "My dear sir, I think I perceive you are on the point of forming a strong attachment to my daughter there,—and I feel bound in honour to let you know that she has a false submolar on each side of her lower jaw, and a false incisor in the upper"? Of course, a humourist might carry this casuistry through the whole range of both jaws. But I fail to see how Miss Cobbe's rule can be made of certain or even probably certain application:—"Where no deception is meant, and where the object is to supply a want, not to forge a claim to beauty,—*e.g.*, in the case of artificial teeth,—there is no harm involved." No doubt the incisors are required for cutting purposes, but, after all, it is the grinders that have most to do with health. And if we are to look at the case in this way, a strong case might be made out in favour of the use of false hair in certain cases, for the thinning of the hair is a common cause of taking cold and of neuralgic pains. And, as to teeth, we must bear in mind that use and beauty *cannot* be separated. Every advertisement of "Odonto," or what-not, tells women, in well-known French verse, that with good teeth no face is plain, and with bad teeth no face beautiful.

On the whole, speaking as a man, I should wind up thus:—Miss Cobbe's summary of the case, on page 283, in the last number of this REVIEW, is wonderfully good and comprehensive; and I should myself consent to any degree of stringency in the rule which would forbid the deliberate assumption by women of artificial "charms" of any kind whatever for the purpose of attracting suitors; and which would equally forbid the concealment of personal defects for the same purpose. But concealment, pure and simple, is not necessarily criminal deception. If in my wife "the parting-line" were "all too wide," I should very decidedly desire her to conceal it from strangers as far as she possibly could, by any device not seriously harmful to her health. If she could *really* improve her complexion for the eyes of strangers by paint, I should desire her to paint. If she could conceal grey hairs by the use of any harmless dye or pomade, I should wish that done too—for the eyes of strangers. And, indeed, if in an intimacy so near as married life she could successfully conceal any portion of the "disgrace and ignominy of our nature" (to quote Sir Thomas Browne) even from me, I should be only too glad. And here I am contemplating *bonâ fide* concealment, be it observed. I presume, if anybody could really *change* the complexion or the colour of the hair for the better, nobody would object. But if not, there seems no way of determining the rightness or wrongness of "concealment," except by asking two questions—Concealment from whom? Concealment for what purpose? And as I have very often and very carefully considered these questions, I have not a moment's hesitation in giving my vote, as a man, for the view which Mrs. Haweis takes of them. Perhaps I ought to add, that I have not seen her book, but that I have a minute recollection of what she wrote in *St. Paul's Magazine*, and Miss Cobbe's note gives me ample clues to the incriminated passages.

---

FOR some time past there have been murmurs of complaint, occasionally swelling into an outcry of anger, about the presence of Government clerks as competitors in the literary market. The late Mr. Mortimer Collins put into the mouth of one of his characters a condemnation of men like Sir Arthur Helps, Mr. Trollope, and others. It amounts to this:—"These gentlemen are paid by the public for their whole time and strength. They then devote a large portion of that time and strength to literary work. That is, to go no farther, a fraud, for we, their employers, are entitled to the whole of their time and energies. But in addition to this, there is the ungraciousness of their competing with us poor outsiders, who have no Government salaries to fall back upon." The "outsider" in question did not happen to say anything about the Government papers or pens,—but that is a tender point with other critics. Certain members of Parliament and Government officials were once discussing with much severity the shortcomings of another Government official. Great stress was laid upon the fact that he wrote a good deal for the reviews and newspapers. How could he possibly attend to his official duties if he did that? One of the interlocutors—a stern economist—made the suggestion, "And I daresay he writes his articles on the Government paper." This was received with some laughter, but it made a gloomy impression for all that. Some recent critics lay considerable stress upon the fact that the incriminated journalists *do* use the Government paper—it proves either that they do those articles in office hours, or that they carry the Government paper home with them.

Government Officials and Literature.

The question of unfair competition may be dismissed offhand, except as to the paper. If a Government clerk adds to his income by writing books or articles, and uses in doing so five shillings' worth of paper that he has "conveyed," he has an unfair advantage over his outside competitor, to the extent of five shillings. Let him stand "reprimanded accordingly." The rest is nonsense, so long as he does his office work properly. There are, or ought to be, some checks upon his performance of his assigned duties, as there are in the case of a banker's clerk, a Premier, a Viceroy, or a Lord Chancellor. Farther it would be impossible and undesirable to go. As a competitor in the literary market a Government clerk has just the same rights as any other man. This is a very unequal world, and we must all alike take our chance. It is a fact, and a very serious one, that without leisure, inherited or acquired, the best literary work can scarcely be done at all nowadays. Of course there are exceptions; but the excepted men are not those who complain, except to themselves or in the bosom of their family, of being handicapped in the race. Perhaps there have been few recent writers to whom literary men have been, indirectly, under so much obligation as the late Sir Arthur Helps. Almost the only men who can, with *immediate* and rapidly-diffused effect in society, "make the bounds of [intellectual] freedom wider yet," are men who have means or "something to fall back upon." On many grounds one may go in boldly for sinecures—for hard winking in a good many of these matters. There is such a fund of humorous teaching in the results. It was worth a year's interest of the National Debt to see the author of "Political Justice" placidly pocketing a salary from the nation as keeper of the Exchequer tallies.

A Government clerk is seldom in the position of a great railway manager or the head of a large commercial concern. When he is so placed that his duties are similar, he should be more jealously watched, of course. But suppose Sir Edward Watkin or some other such man (we only mention names for the sake of distinctness) were on six boards of direction at once, and were also to make a few thousands by translating the Iliad or conducting a newspaper, who would be entitled to blame him on the ground that his literary pursuits trenched upon time and energy already vowed? The only questions would be, was he a good director? was he a good translator?

The cases are very few in which a jealous supervision of a public servant's time can by any possibility be advisable. If some such official as Captain Tyler of the Board of Trade, or Captain Calver of the Thames Conservancy Board, busily engaged at a critical moment upon urgent public works, were to be found sitting up half the night seeking the perpetual motion or the philosopher's stone, it would be a matter for interference: but almost any reasonable proof of versatile energy and intelligence should be welcome in a public servant. Mr. Mill laid it down that it would be an alarming state of things if a Government were found to attract too much of the talent of the State to its service; but we are a long way from that yet.

A minor topic which has been raised is that some of the Government clerks who have been engaged in editing or contributing to "society" journals have been tempted to break confidence, and print "early and special information," dug out of the desk which should be kept locked. We should fancy, however, that a certain Foreign Office episode would even yet be remembered as a warning to Government clerks. If not, every honest man would rejoice to see the coxcomb who "broke lock and seal" well punished. Let us have his name; and then, though his breach of trust should be about no bigger a thing than "the Straits of Malacca" question, we will raise such a clatter about the ears of his department and of the Government, that a severer lot than that of dismissal on a reduced pension (I am thinking of an actual case) shall be his.

# CONTEMPORARY LITERATURE



LIFE OF THE PRINCE CONSORT.*—This third volume of Mr. [illegible]
contains a great deal that is most interesting. It covers [illegible]
of the Crimean War, with the negotiations for peace, and [illegible]
the inner workings of diplomacy, both English and Continental [illegible]
than even the innermost workings of diplomacy in relation to even[illegible]
in the past, are the accounts of the intercourse of the Prince Co[illegible]
Queen with the Emperor of the French, the visits which they [illegible]
their conversation, the impression made on the Prince by the Emp[illegible]
petuated in a vivid sketch by the Prince. The volume sustains [illegible]
opinion of the Prince's talents, good sense, accomplishments, [illegible]
character, devotion to his adopted country, and industry in wo[illegible]
service. It also sustains and even heightens the pleasant idea [illegible]
nation of the domestic life of the Royal household, and enhances ou[illegible]
untimely stroke by which an end was put to happiness so pure. T[illegible]
will be thought, we believe, in a literary point of view, to have done [illegible]
skill. He is aware, no doubt, that he writes under conditions which [illegible]
cease to exist; that posterity will apply a rude, impartial mea[illegible]
claimant of a place in history; that the political opinions of the P[illegible]
and still more the military opinions which he gave with almost equ[illegible]
though now received even with greater deference than they receiv[illegible]
lifetime, will one day be estimated without regard for his rank or [illegible]
But where critical treatment is out of the question, we are grat[illegible]
narrative free from offensive exaggeration.

We must own, however, that our sense of the biographical int[illegible]
literary merit of this volume is almost swallowed up in our sense of [illegible]
opportuneness,—or shall we say fatal opportuneness?—of its appearan[illegible]
we are convinced, could have been more at variance with the sound [illegible]
right feeling of the Prince Consort than the part which he is here [illegible]
mously to play in the diplomatic and political crisis through wh[illegible]
is at present passing. The relations between this country and R[illegible]
more in a dangerous state; there is again a question between peace [illegible]
war; and the situation, it may be presumed, is one of peculiar p[illegible]
anxiety to the Royal Family on account of the recent inter[illegible]
family of the Czar. And this is the moment chosen by Mr. Theod[illegible]
bringing the late Prince Consort from his grave into the fray, a[illegible]
apparently speak in inflammatory language against Russia and [illegible]

Lord Carnarvon says that nobody would now be so insane as [illegible]
of the policy which led to the Crimean war; and though the [illegible]
dore Martin's own writing, as well as that of some of our jo[illegible]
his lordship's assertion requires qualification to make it [illegible]
great mass of the English people now look back [illegible]
sorrow, on a policy which gave [illegible]
in the permanency of which [illegible]
alliance, and a foreign hillside [illegible]

* The Life of His Royal Highness [illegible]
[illegible]

[illegible] of the forty years' peace, and once more let loose on [illegible] fiend of war. But the situation in 1854 was widely [illegible] the present, and it is most unfair, as well as most pernicious, to [illegible] the language of the Prince Consort from one situation [illegible], and make him responsible for kindling war now, because he [illegible] in 1854. In 1854, not Alexander, the philanthropist and [illegible] but Nicholas, the iron despot and fanatical reactionist, was on the [illegible]. Nicholas had unquestionably assailed in the case of Hungary, [illegible] be deemed still to threaten, the liberties of Europe; the Turkish [illegible] had not displayed so clearly as it has now its hopeless decrepitude and [illegible]; no Bulgarian massacres had then occurred; there seemed [illegible] possibility of settling the Eastern question by means of Turkish re-[illegible], we had an ally, with an army capable of meeting that of Russia; [illegible] we have none.

[illegible] Prince Consort's defence of the war policy of 1854 is embodied in a letter [illegible]:—

"[illegible] Russia," he writes, "in her demands at Constantinople, until it [illegible] she was bent on annihilating the independence of the Porte. It was [illegible], and with a view to making a cat's-paw of other Powers, but [illegible] the possibility of war, that England pressed for the *concert Européen*. [illegible]'s faintheartedness, and regard for Russia, made our efforts in this [illegible]; therefore England and France alone took upon themselves the burden [illegible] the Porte. It is quite time that our stupid club-house politicians and [illegible] understood Russia's strength. But every statesman knew how heavy was [illegible] had undertaken. A *military* European concert might even now bring the [illegible], restore peace, and put the Porte under proper conditions. But if [illegible] France have to carry on the war single-handed against Russia, it must [illegible] of extermination; just as, if twenty men have to arrest a criminal, it is [illegible] to seize and bind him and carry him off to prison; whereas if one man [illegible] it, he does so at the risk of a struggle for life or death. All Europe, Belgium [illegible] included, have the greatest interest in the integrity and independence of [illegible] being secured for the future, but a still greater in Russia's being defeated and [illegible]. For it is to weak States, above all others, of importance as a precedent, that [illegible] neighbour seeks to oppress them, all Europe shall come to their aid and repel [illegible]. This is the true state of the case, and the politicians of the Continent [illegible] be misled by their soreness of feeling at the rough and unmeasured terms in [illegible] been expressed by the English journals. To be plain-spoken, perhaps not [illegible], is their vocation. Another mistake which people abroad make is to [illegible] England a policy based upon national interests and cold calculation. Her [illegible] pure feeling, and therefore often illogical. The Government is a popular [illegible], and the masses upon whom it rests only feel and do not think. In the [illegible] their feeling is something of this sort:—'The Emperor of Russia is a [illegible], the enemy of all liberty on the Continent, the oppressor of Poland. He wanted [illegible] the poor Turk. The Turk is a fine fellow; he has braved the rascal, let us [illegible] assistance. The Emperor is no gentleman, he has spoken a lie to our Queen. [illegible] with the Emperor of Russia! Napoleon for ever! He is the nephew of his uncle [illegible] defeated at Waterloo. We were afraid of his invading us? Quite the contrary! [illegible] all that is past and is ready to fight with us for the glorious cause [illegible] oppressor of liberty. He may have played the French some tricks, but they [illegible] and don't deserve any better. D—— all the German Princes who won't [illegible] against the Russian, because they think they want him to keep down their [illegible]. The worst of them is the King of Prussia, who ought to know better.'"

[illegible] of some of these arguments might have been questioned, even [illegible] on the case before the writer; and the medley of unthinking [illegible] which he describes the action of the British people as being founded [illegible] that the saying of Oxenstierna, which he is fond of citing, may [illegible] applicable to self-government as well as to the government of kings. [illegible], as we read the passage, that the Prince, in common with the [illegible] who had public or honest ends in view, was the dupe of the [illegible] who had manœuvred to bring on a war for the objects of his [illegible] who was aided in effecting his purpose by Lord Palmerston's [illegible] Czar, and personal desire to set aside Lord Aberdeen. But [illegible] the passage to show that the writer's words ought in justice to [illegible] before him. There was nothing in 1854 corresponding to [illegible] Constantinople in 1877, to the judgment there pronounced by [illegible] Turkish misrule, or to the refusal of Turkey to submit to necessary measures of reform which followed. Russia under Nicholas had not showed that willingness to act in concert with the other Powers which has been shown by Russia under Alexander, and we have no reason to doubt with honourable intent. Whatever Nicholas may have been, Alexander is a true "gentleman," and he has told no lies to our Queen; if there has been any lack of veracity on the present occasion, it has been in another quarter. Alexander II. is not a tyrant, nor the "enemy of all liberty" on the Continent. He has set free his own serfs, and meddled with the freedom of no other nation. The "weak and oppressed" in the present case are the Bulgarians, as the voice of united Europe has declared. A policy based on the "independence and integrity of Turkey" has been proved to be based on incurable rottenness. There is no longer any occasion for venting British expletives on German Princes as suitors to Russia for help in keeping down their own subjects. The "nephew of the uncle" has gone to his uncle after running a course of cognate crime, and our war policy now would not have the support of a single European power. It is astonishing that this last consideration at all events should not have forced itself on the mind of the writer of this biography when he was making its subject advocate a repetition of the Crimean War.

It seems needless to comment on the discretion displayed in flinging such a passage as that which we have quoted into the face of the son and heir of the Emperor Nicholas at the present juncture; to say nothing of the feelings of certain other persons who are not unconcerned in anything affecting the character of the Royal Family of Russia, and whom we should have thought entitled to some consideration in a work like the present.

When war had been declared, or had become inevitable, the Prince Consort, devoted as he was to England, would be sure to throw himself heart and soul into her cause. In his anxiety to gain allies for her, he would state her case as strongly as possible to his correspondents on the Continent, and his patriotic anger would be kindled against those who hung back or refused support. Reasonable abatement ought to be made from the warmth of his language on this ground. Perhaps if he were himself now living he would feel that a measure of justice was due from him to some of whom he spoke most harshly in 1854. The late King of Prussia may not have reasoned very strongly, and his mind may not have been of the firmest texture; but those who cherish his memory may triumphantly ask what would have been the consequences to his country if he had done what the Prince Consort would have had him do—flung himself into the arms of the French Emperor and made a deadly enemy of Russia. Surely German policy at all events has vindicated itself from contempt.

We feel sure that the Prince Consort would have objected to the employment of his confidential expressions of opinion under totally changed conditions, for the purpose of leading this country into a war with Russia. We feel not less sure that he would have objected to allowing a life of himself for which his papers had furnished the materials to be used by the biographer as a vehicle for a war agitation, or for any agitation whatever. The present volume abounds in appeals to popular passion against Russia, and in insinuations against the wisdom and patriotism of Mr. Gladstone and others who are trying to keep the peace. It is unnecessary to reproduce these passages, which in no way differ from the utterances of the journals which support the reputed policy of Lord Beaconsfield. The impropriety is not in the least diminished by supposing the opinions to be true, a supposition which in a literary review of the work we have no desire to exclude. Nor will the truth of the opinions justify want of candour in the advocate. It will not justify Mr. Martin in creating the impression that atrocities committed on a particular battle-field by a few Russian soldiers under the influence of drink and of outraged superstition, perhaps also of resentment at still greater atrocities committed by our allies the Turks, were characteristic of the Russian army as a whole, when the present war has abundantly proved that they were not. Nor will it justify him in leading his readers to infer from a manifesto issued on coming to the throne in the middle of a desperate war, that the present Emperor must be personally addicted to military aggression, when the whole of his subsequent reign has shown him to be devoted to internal improvement and averse to war. A great number of letters, it seems, written from the English camp after Inkermann, and abounding with stirring pictures, were forwarded to the Queen and Prince, and have been preserved among the Prince's papers as records of the day. One out of the whole number is selected for publication by Mr. Martin, evidently because it contains a grossly insulting description of the Russian soldiers.

Our objection extends, though in a less decided form, to criticism of the [illegible] conduct of the servants of the Crown, especially of those who are [illegible] by the accredited biographer of the Prince Consort. There are [illegible] this work, for example, which will be very unpleasant reading for [illegible] and his friends. If Mr. Martin criticizes Lord Russell, or any one [illegible] clearly emanating from himself alone, people know who is the critic, [illegible] criticised is free to reply. But a special restraint ought to be felt [illegible] of a work in which, say what you will, people will think that they [illegible] partialities and antipathies of the Court.

[illegible] Prince Consort's papers, confided to his biographer's hands, were a trust; [illegible] the living and a trust from the dead. Did not the frowning counte[illegible] dead sometimes present itself to the biographer's mental eye while [illegible] one of the most prudent, considerate, and right-minded of men [illegible] of hatred, and send forth a war-pamphlet from his tomb?

[illegible] spoken of the special interest attaching to those parts of the volume [illegible] an account of the visits interchanged by the Prince Consort and the [illegible] the Emperor and Empress of the French. To us, we confess, it is a [illegible] painful interest. Not that we for a moment fail to appreciate the [illegible] of the motives which led the Prince and Her Majesty to treat the ally [illegible] as their friend, and do everything in their power personally to [illegible] the alliance; but we cannot think without sorrow of such an episode [illegible] history of English opinion. Louis Napoleon had attained his crown by [illegible] subversive of all moral principle, of all legality, of all confidence in [illegible], of all faith in man. Twice, before fortune tossed him into Empire, [illegible] tried to levy civil war in a state enjoying peace and prosperity under a [illegible] Government. He had done this purely in his own interest, and [illegible] thereby the highest proof of criminal selfishness that man can give. [illegible] of the Republic he had not only broken his oath, but absolutely [illegible] in perjury. He had debauched the army, with which he was entrusted for [illegible] of the State. He had given orders for a hideous massacre of innocent [illegible] citizens merely to strike terror, and had deported many thousands [illegible] artisans without trial. Englishmen knew his history well, and the [illegible] reception they gave him, the eagerness with which they crowded round [illegible] wheels, when all due allowance has been made for curiosity and for the [illegible] can hardly be thought creditable to the seriousness and consistency of [illegible] national character. The man was unchanged. The schemes which he pro[illegible] to his Royal guests for the revision of the map of Europe were schemes [illegible] on a grand scale. He coolly debated whether it would be more pro[illegible] to make an alliance with Austria or to attack her and dismember her, in [illegible] of a gambler deliberating whether he had better lay his money on *rouge* [illegible]. The men about him were sharpers, and the chief of them, Morny, was [illegible] by the Prince Consort himself, and with good reason, of plotting [illegible] England in the interest of Russia at this very time. The crown of old [illegible] never came nearer to being tarnished than when it touched the crown of [illegible] III.

GOLDWIN SMITH.

---

[illegible] DEMOCRACY.*—Sir Erskine May's reputation is deservedly high. His "[illegible] History" is in every political library. When the literary world [illegible] that he was engaged on the history of Democracy in Europe, and had [illegible] extraordinary pains upon the work, great expectations were excited. [illegible] that to us the result is disappointment.

[illegible] own, however, that our disappointment arises partly from our having [illegible] a wrong notion as to the subject of the book. Europe, in the course of the [illegible] century, has been the scene of a number of momentous experiments in self-[illegible], carried on under a great variety of circumstances by nations differing [illegible] other very much in character, and by means of constitutions presenting, [illegible] a certain general resemblance, great and most important diversities of [illegible]. We were in hopes that the harvest of all these experiments was going to [illegible] in for us by the diligence, the good sense, and the calm judgment of [illegible] May. We were in hopes that he would have accurately described and [illegible] in an equal balance the effects of the different qualifications for the suf[illegible] the Unicameral and Bicameral system, of the various modes of forming a [illegible] Cabinet Government on the one hand, and the Swiss mode of electing

* [illegible] in Europe: a History. By Sir Thomas Erskine May, K.C.B., D.C.L., Author of "The Consti[illegible] History of England since the Accession of George III." London: Longmans, Green, & Co.

the executive on the other; and that he would have [illegible] of party both in its legislative and in its administrative [illegible] political architecture might be mentioned, on which [illegible] ripening, if not ripe. The relations between the social [illegible] country and the working of its political institutions [illegible] matter for investigation. The undertaking would be [illegible] a good deal of knowledge which must be gathered from [illegible] countries, not from books. But Sir Erskine May has [illegible] nities; and a grander, or more instructive, or a more [illegible] writer could desire.

Instead of this we have two volumes filled with outlines [illegible] of ancient Greece and Rome (which occupy the bulk of [illegible] Republics of Italy in the Middle Ages, Switzerland, the [illegible] England. And of these outlines we must say that, though [illegible] executed in a manner that repels any very adverse criticism, [illegible] many readers be pleasing and instructive, there is nothing [illegible] original, or which entitles them to be regarded as an addition [illegible] political science. The book, though painstaking, does not even [illegible] erudition. The authorities quoted are only the ordinary [illegible] observed not a single statement or remark bespeaking any deeper [illegible] times, indeed, the citations are such as almost to give us [illegible] Who would have expected in a note to a serious and scientific [illegible] as the sum of wisdom about English politics a flourish from [illegible] speech of Sir William Harcourt, at Oxford:—"Reverence for the [illegible] in the present, faith in the future—that is the sum of English [illegible] Sir William Harcourt, as a man of sense, no doubt knew [illegible] talking claptrap, and that the sum of English statesmanship [illegible] been said to be comprehended in the grace which, no doubt, [illegible] clergyman had just said after the dinner. Political beatitudes, [illegible] the truth, Sir Erskine May is himself a little apt to indulge, [illegible] the historical explanation of anything in the past nor the practical [illegible] problem in the present or the future.

As the work is entitled "Democracy in Europe," we have no [illegible] of it for not taking in the history of popular government in the [illegible] in the United States, and in the other free communities of the New [illegible] we must say that for the purpose of political inquiry, it is not [illegible] ment to exclude these really democratic continuations and develop[illegible] European movement, while you include the republics of ancient Gree[illegible] which were not really democratic but slaveowning, and which [illegible] essentially to a military era. Germany, Austria, Italy, Spain, Portu[illegible] Norway, Sweden, and Greece however are in Europe, and we may [illegible] why no notice should be taken of their political experiments, some [illegible] now been carried on for some considerable time, though [illegible] fortunes, and which in point of fact are better illustrations of [illegible] ordinarily called Democracy than the slaveowning communities [illegible] military oligarchy of Rome, or the aristocratic Parliament of Englan[illegible]

We fail, indeed, to apprehend clearly what the special [illegible] What force is it to which Sir Erskine May gives the name of [illegible] action of which in political history he proposes by the examples he [illegible] to illustrate? In his preface he says:—

"Montesquieu has pointed out the various senses in which the term '[illegible] understood; and 'democracy' has acquired at least as many. As [illegible] it signifies the sovereignty of the whole body of the people. [illegible] degrees and conditions of democracy as of liberty; and the term [illegible] *political power or influence of the people* under all forms of [illegible] principle or force, *and not simply an institution*; and it is in this [illegible] is to be generally understood in this history. But *it is also* [illegible] which, if not so accurate, have been sanctioned by [illegible] default of a more extended vocabulary, it is often spoken of [illegible] [illegible] *to existing institutions, if not to law and order*; and [illegible] [illegible] abroad, such a term can scarcely be misapplied. [illegible] [illegible] *citizens of a State*, as opposed to the aristocracy; [illegible] [illegible] *type of democracy*, such as the Athenian [illegible] [illegible] In short, the sense in which the word is used, [illegible] [illegible]

[illegible] Locke had set out by saying that "idea" had many [illegible] in most of them, and that its meaning in any par[illegible] was to be gathered from the context. It is a warning [illegible] which cannot fail to be accompanied in the [illegible] confusion of thought. For our own part we shall be [illegible] what the principal sense of "Democracy" [illegible] particular force the action of which this survey of [illegible] intended to illustrate. In a number of passages "Democracy" [illegible] popular agitation, mob rule, or revolutionary violence, of [illegible] history is included in the volume can hardly be deemed [illegible] signal examples. Of the two invasions of Hyde Park [illegible] it is said that "on both occasions democracy prevailed [illegible] and we are told of "constitutional measures being carried [illegible] democracy." On one page we find this:—

[illegible] changes having been made with a view to increase popular in[illegible] the State (England), have been advances towards democracy; [illegible] the legislature has borne the marks of strong popular inspiration."

[illegible] we find an apparent contradiction of the statement—

[illegible] that *democratic opinions* have gained ground among considerable [illegible] people; *but as yet they have found no representation in the legislature.*"

[illegible] perplexity, on the intervening page the British Colonies are [illegible] as democratic republics under the gentle sovereignty of [illegible] "We are waiting, sir, for your mud to settle," was the gracious [illegible] to a perplexed and hesitating disputant. We must confess [illegible] to the meaning of "democracy," and consequently with regard [illegible] of this work, our mud had not settled when we had finished

[illegible] part of the book, on the whole, as it seems to us, is the sketch of [illegible] history of Rome, though the overruling influence exercised on the [illegible] the Republic by the predominance of war and conquest, which made [illegible] to an empire inevitable, is hardly kept enough in view. That [illegible] to us least successful, perhaps because we expected most of it, is [illegible] the political history of England. The account of the great move[illegible] thirteenth century, which laid the foundation of all constitutional [illegible] producing the Great Charter and the representation of the people, [illegible] miserably curt and defective; while room is found at the end [illegible] effusive eloquence about royalty and the illness of the Prince [illegible] appropriate to the loyal pulpit or press than to a work of [illegible]. Strange to say, the all-important subject of Party and its [illegible] not the slightest consideration. No one who did not know it [illegible] gather from these pages that the Government of England was a [illegible], or that organized party was the instrument by which the [illegible] changes had been accomplished. In truth, that there have [illegible] constitutional changes of moment would not be easily inferred, for the [illegible] of constitutional drapery, which hides the real facts and forces, is [illegible] by this discreet and loyal writer.

[illegible] government," he says, "while it has in a great measure withdrawn [illegible] from that personal exercise of power which appeals to the imagination of [illegible] him from party conflicts, from responsibility for unpopular measures, [illegible] of the executive government. If he is not associated with devotion [illegible] party, neither is he pursued with the hatred of religious sects or political [illegible] rancour of his subjects is exhausted upon one another; he is himself [illegible] it; none can reach him upon his throne. *He holds an even balance [illegible] and parties:* he espouses no cause or policy. Ministers are re[illegible] exercise of his prerogatives, and take upon themselves the unpopularity [illegible] the executive. At the same time, all honours and acts of grace proceed [illegible] the Crown itself."

[illegible] sensible and so versed in politics as Sir Erskine May must know [illegible] flummery. Flummery is a very good thing in its place, but its [illegible] in a work of political science.

[illegible] May's point of view throughout is that of an English Liberal of [illegible] and highly orthodox description. We have nothing to say against [illegible]; but in order to deal successfully with a vast and varied range of [illegible] must be able to enter into phases of opinion widely different from his own, and at all events to examine them critically at [illegible] care proportioned to their importance. Even such a phenomenon [illegible] hideous as some of its manifestations have been, calls not for [illegible] but for investigation. It has already filled a considerable space [illegible] tory, and most assuredly we have not yet heard the last of [illegible] May's training, though good in its way, has been too [illegible] him, the wig and mace are always before us. With this [illegible] marks are, as might be expected, generally judicious; but [illegible] new or striking. Sometimes, we are compelled to say, he [illegible] upon platitude. Of the various movements for special objects, [illegible] establishment, marriage with a deceased wife's sister, &c., he [illegible] of their respective causes may be judged by the ultimate [illegible] tions. Where they are good, and commend themselves to the [illegible] ment of the country, they may be expected to prevail; where they [illegible] upon error or prejudice, and are coldly received or condemned [illegible] will encounter discouragement and failure." That causes coldly [illegible] demned by society will encounter discouragement, is a discovery [illegible] inclined to reward its author with a handsomely-bound copy of [illegible]

The style is clear and good, though it sometimes partakes of the [illegible] sentiment, being rather too monotonously balanced.

We do not call the book a failure; it may, as we have said, be [illegible] interesting to a considerable class of readers. There are many [illegible] its tone will please. But we repeat that it is a disappointment [illegible] looked for an important contribution to political science. The [illegible] European experience during the last century still remains almost [illegible] us hope that a reaper will soon appear.

GOLDWI[illegible]

---

FREEMAN'S OTTOMAN POWER IN EUROPE.*—Every one who [illegible] in the Eastern Question is by this time tolerably well [illegible] Mr. Freeman's opinions thereupon. From some they gain [illegible] rence, and in others they provoke passionate opposition. But [illegible] be the intrinsic merits of Mr. Freeman's views, they always have [illegible] tage of being definite, precise, and unmistakable. There is [illegible] about the bush with Mr. Freeman, no allusion to spades as [illegible] ments, no neutral tints or half-lights in his representations of [illegible] "unspeakable Turk" is not an unjust and incompetent ruler, but [illegible] Lord Derby's conduct has been not merely weak and inconsistent, [illegible] Sir Henry Elliot has become himself barbarous from long association [illegible] barians. Another advantage which Mr. Freeman can claim for his [illegible] Eastern policy is that they are not improvised for the occasion. A[illegible] panaceas, or plans for what Mr. Blackmore calls "pontooning the [illegible] have been so common of late that Mr. Freeman's book must [illegible] influence by the proofs which he gives that South-eastern Europe [illegible] him a subject of study for years. At the end of the preface to [illegible] is a list of essays contributed by Mr. Freeman to various Reviews, [illegible] chronologically from February, 1855, to March, 1877. It is not [illegible] many Englishmen besides Mr. Gladstone can boast a longer [illegible] ance with the subject that is now absorbing the interest of [illegible] Besides the merits which we have already allowed to him, Mr. [illegible] virtue without which all others are nothing worth to an author, [illegible] ably readable. Nothing can be easier than to attack his style [illegible] tonous, or clamorous, except to defend it as manly, vigorous, [illegible] as it is, it carries one over the ground, and succeeds in [illegible] continuously throughout. Its confidence may cause [illegible] create disgust. But unless a man has strong opinions of his [illegible] to influence his readers; and the intrusion of a striking [illegible] given in days when avoidance of emphasis has become a [illegible] "gossamer wings of light irony," of which George Eliot [illegible] some to most healthy minds than the expression of decided [illegible] language. But still it is possible to be "cock-sure" [illegible]

* The Ottoman Power in Europe: Its Nature, its Growth and its Decline. By [illegible] Macmillan & Co.

[illegible] opponents, and even without expressing contempt [illegible] of their moral characters. As the Bishop of [illegible] it is a mistake to regard every man who differs from [illegible]. Or at least it is a mistake to publish your [illegible] abuse of Lord Beaconsfield, Lord Derby, and Sir [illegible] made Mr. Freeman's book none the worse, and would [illegible] fewer persons attracted by the author's learning, integrity, [illegible] wish to be understood as expressing no opinion on the [illegible], or the character of the persons attacked. It is pro[illegible] admirers who will most regret the language which [illegible] these pages. A cause is not well served by attacks on the [illegible] faith of its most eminent opponent. Any one who has [illegible] published Life of Lord Beaconsfield will see reason to wonder [illegible] politician's enemies should be reduced to taunting him with [illegible]

[illegible] concerned in this volume only with the history of the Ottoman [illegible] it to be read in connection with his previously published [illegible] of the Saracens," which treats of the other Mahometan [illegible] scale of the present work is enough to show that it is one of Mr. [illegible] sketches, and not one of his detailed works. It has been flippantly [illegible] must have taken less time to accomplish the Norman Conquest than it [illegible] about it, while, on the other hand, Mr. Freeman's General [illegible] European History will almost go into the pocket of one's waistcoat. The [illegible], which summarizes the history of more than four hundred years, [illegible] pages; but from these a deduction of 62 pages, treating of what [illegible] "The Practical Question," must be made. This leaves 250 [illegible] small octavo volume for the history of Turkish dominion in Europe, [illegible] seem an extravagant allowance. In fact, if we may say so without [illegible] Mr. Freeman has given us rather a political pamphlet than a formal [illegible], as he says in his preface, "Between history and politics I can draw [illegible]. History is the politics of the past; politics are the history of the [illegible] same rules of criticism apply to judging alike of distant and of [illegible]. The same eternal laws of right and wrong are to be applied in [illegible] estimate of the actors in either case. The championship of right and [illegible] of wrong have exactly the same character in any age. A Mont[illegible], a Flambard and a Beaconsfield, must stand or fall together." [illegible] might perhaps take exception to the last sentence. Even Mr. [illegible] most enthusiastic admirers would hardly contend that it is as practi[illegible] an impartial estimate of his character and career as it is to appraise [illegible] and achievements of the father of the House of Commons. And [illegible] Lord Beaconsfield's bitterest opponents might like some more definite [illegible] object of comparison than the justiciary of William Rufus, whose [illegible] exactly a household word to the vulgar. We must refer to Mr. Free[illegible] instructive pages those who are interested in knowing why Hobart Pasha is [illegible] of St. Alban's, contenting ourselves with the assurance that it is not [illegible]. Mr. Freeman has set himself the task of showing that the rule of [illegible] over their European subjects is more irremediably bad than that of any [illegible] in the whole range of history. He maintains that this is the only [illegible] which the conquerors and the conquered have never fused and coalesced. [illegible] differ as much now from the Eastern Christians who are their subjects [illegible] five hundred years ago. The Ottoman Turks are not Aryan but [illegible], and with two exceptions, the Magyars and the Bulgarians, all the [illegible] Europe are Aryan. But the Magyars and the Bulgarians have become [illegible] of time European in habits and institutions, whereas the Ottomans [illegible] as they have always been, Asiatic, and not European. One reason for [illegible] more powerful reason than blood or language, is the difference of [illegible]. It is not simply that Christians and Mahometans cannot live together [illegible], for we govern millions of Mahometans in India. But where the govern[illegible] is Mahometan, and the subject class is Christian, there can be no toler[illegible]. For "a Mahometan Government is bound to treat its subjects [illegible] religions as a conquered race, and not to put them on a level with [illegible]." This is "a state of things which the religion of the Turks enforces [illegible] duty." "As long therefore as that Mahometan Government lasts, [illegible] be no real reform," unless indeed the Turkish rulers, like many other [illegible] better than their religious creed, which Mr. Freeman of course denies.

The rise of the Ottoman power is described in some fifty pages with clearness and power; and when he reaches its culmination under Suleiman the Lawgiver, Mr. Freeman sums up with drastic vigour its results upon the South-east of Europe. "The direct results of Turkish conquest have been that while the nations of Western Europe have enjoyed five hundred years of progress, the nations of South-eastern Europe have suffered five hundred years of bondage, and of all that follows on bondage." The decline of the Ottoman power, "so far as that decline was the work either of its own vices or of warfare with enemies beyond its borders," brings us down to the beginning of the present century, since which time there have been constant revolts against the Turks on the part of Turkey, to use Mr. Freeman's favourite distinction. Mr. Freeman is of course a warm admirer of the policy of Canning, whose last work was the Treaty of London in 1827, which secured the freedom of Greece. Since that year we have, in Mr. Freeman's opinion, abandoned ourselves to the false and wicked scheme of upholding the Turk; and it has been reserved for Russia to accomplish what the united powers of Europe should long ago have done. Mr. Freeman has stated his case with undeniable courage, conviction, and lucidity. Whether a little moderation of speech would not have increased his influence with the public is another question.

---

MANUALS OF ENGLISH HISTORY.*—Professor Stubbs' "Early Plantagenets" is a book admirably adapted to the needs of any person who is making solid advance in the study of history; but we should hesitate to recommend it unreservedly to schoolmasters, as it contains passages which boys would find it hard to understand, and is, moreover, wanting in that picturesqueness and brilliant description of personal incident and war which are so necessary to interest youthful readers. The writer commences with a short account of the reign of Stephen, thus showing convincingly how necessary was the stern despotism established by his favourite, Henry II., to put an end to the terrible anarchy which reigned in England, from 1135 to 1154. He describes with a wonderful simplicity, sympathy, and grasp of thought, that mighty struggle with the Church, which to the generality of readers will always be the most interesting part of Henry II.'s reign. We are shown in a few vivid sentences the gathering of the storm, the grand position of the Church in the days before the Conquest, the separation of Church and State which William and Lanfranc decided on and carried out, little dreaming of the terrible consequences which were shortly to follow, the antagonism roused by William Rufus and Henry I., the short-lived compromise which seemed so admirably to decide the quarrel, the growing strength of the Church in the anarchical time of Stephen, and finally, the opposing aims of the great king and the great archbishop, which made agreement impossible without the sacrifice of his dearest hopes on the part of one or the other of the contending leaders, whose rivalry was still further heightened by the position of affairs on the Continent.

It is impossible to speak too highly of Professor Stubbs' account of the foreign relations of England during the whole of this period; and not less excellent is his description of the constitutional progress of the country at home. We have a clear exposition of the causes which made parliamentary government possible in England, the hard probation which had to be passed through before the different classes which were represented were fit for the important duty committed to them, finally the course of events which, under the guidance of the master mind of Edward I., at last resulted in the great Parliament of 1295. We do not hesitate to assert that all who are interested in English history or in English politics, will do well to study the picture here given of the growth of that constitution which (to quote the author's words) "far more than any other which the world has ever seen, has kept alive the forms and spirit of free government; which has been the discipline that formed the great republic of the present day; which was for ages the beacon of true social freedom that terrified the despots abroad and served as a model for the aspirations of hopeful patriots."

Mr. Warburton's life of Edward III., which takes up the thread of English history where Professor Stubbs breaks it off, is a book of very unequal merit.

---

* The Early Plantagenets. By W. Stubbs. Second Edition. Longmans & Co.
Edward III. By the Rev. W. Warburton. Second Edition. Longmans & Co.
1. The Era of the Protestant Revolution. By F. Seebohm. 2. The Age of Elizabeth. By Rev. Mandell Creighton. 3. Life of Sir Walter Raleigh. By Louise Creighton. Longmans & Co.

[illegible] the account of the battle of Crecy, or of Edward's [illegible] with vivid descriptions and careful exami[illegible] to feel satisfied with the history of foreign [illegible] of commercial and social policy, as it is here [illegible] illustrations: Mr. Warburton has [illegible] exaggerated [illegible] Philip de Valois and his son John, kings for whom French [illegible] the strongest contempt and disgust. Under the influence of the [illegible] of Philip Augustus, Louis IX. and Philip the Fair, they did in [illegible] the absorption of the great fiefs; but both of them, and [illegible] whom our author seems to feel that unreasoning [illegible] so many English writers, were guilty of treachery [illegible] that by no means squeamish age; and John's grant [illegible] son, Philip, was the origin of great disasters and [illegible] conscious of the need of showing the history of [illegible] with the general movements of Europe, Mr. Warburton [illegible] constitutional struggle in France after the battle of [illegible] a defective knowledge of the times, and especially a [illegible] of the aims of the great party of Marcel and Lecoq, which [illegible] distinguished from those of the Jacquerie rising. Again, [illegible] very much in the dark as to the relations between the French and [illegible] also as to the position and importance of the De la Cerde family, [illegible] of England was seriously affected by both. The fortunate [illegible] in 1230, brought about the union of Castille and Leon, is [illegible] as "the annexation of Leon," though it was the heir of Leon [illegible]. Nor has Mr. Warburton been more successful in describing [illegible] aims of parties in England, which become especially involved [illegible] the end of the reign; in particular, he has failed to see the im[illegible] rivalry for office which grew up between the lawyers and the [illegible]

[illegible] obliged to point out several blemishes in this little work, but it [illegible] of supplying a simple and interesting narrative of the period [illegible] and will no doubt commend itself on this ground both to [illegible] a large class of readers.

[illegible] compressing the story of a great period into volumes of such slender [illegible] Creighton's series, of combining picturesqueness with brevity, and of [illegible] moment accuracy of detail and the attention of the reader—all [illegible] qualifications in an elementary book—is one of some difficulty; and [illegible] congratulate Mr. Seebohm and Mr. Creighton on their success. Roughly [illegible] Mr. Seebohm deals with the first, and Mr. Creighton with the second half [illegible] century: or, to put it otherwise, the one treats of the causes [illegible] the religious movement, the other of the political effects consequent [illegible]

[illegible] best feature of Mr. Seebohm's carefully prepared book is the clear[illegible] he points out the close connection which existed, especially in [illegible] between the social condition of the lowest classes and the movement for [illegible]. There is also much of interest in his remarks about the European [illegible] and the Oxford reformers. Nor must we forget the maps with which [illegible] provided, especially those which illustrate the routes of Euro[illegible] and the localities of the "Bundschuh" risings, and of the Peasant [illegible]

[illegible] of Elizabeth" is written skilfully and attractively. Following in the [illegible] Von Ranke, Mr. Creighton gives a clear and intelligent account of the [illegible] relations of Elizabeth with France, Spain, and the Papacy. [illegible] story of the Huguenot wars at a length quite sufficient to put the [illegible] to thoroughly grasp the aims of that most interesting struggle, [illegible] without depriving of their interest, the leading incidents of [illegible] work, "The Rise of the Dutch Republic." If there is per[illegible] in Mr. Creighton's description of the most spirit-stirring epoch [illegible] history, he has at any rate made some amends by his careful dis[illegible] of character, and his excellent sketch of the Elizabethan literature.

[illegible] of Raleigh, Mrs. Creighton has given to the juvenile world a simple [illegible] account of one of the most remarkable of Englishmen. It is [illegible] conceive a life more attractive than that of the Devonshire boy—half[illegible] the adventurous and ill-fated Humphrey Gilbert—himself by turns a brilliant courtier, a daring sea-rover, and a great historian ... of Essex in royal favour, at another the originator of ... last of all the victim of miserable jealousy. Perhaps the ... a little impaired from the necessity of interweaving with the ... life a good deal of the political history of the time. We should ... grateful for more frequent extracts from Raleigh's own letters ...

---

LIVES OF SIMON DE MONTFORT.*—The era of Henry III., Louis ... Frederick II., full of the problems which are still being fought ... politicians, must needs possess great attractions for historians of ... us Englishmen the central figure of this era is the "Righteous ... are not surprised to find his life an object of careful and sympathetic ... Mr. Creighton's work is intended for class use, it is brightly and ... and gives a very good idea of Earl Simon's career. The translations ... and Latin songs are very happy, good use is made of modern research ... of course, it is founded on the works of other writers, it is by no means ... There are one or two misprints on p. 162, which should be corrected.

With Professor Pauli's work in its original form most students ... subject was interesting are no doubt well acquainted, but there is ... minority in every class of readers to whom German is an unknown ... will be glad to read this careful translation. It was the first book ... anything like a clear account of the eventful years which settled ... freedom should depend on the law and not on the King's will, ... the great man whose determination, honesty, and singleness of ... so much to bring this about. The careful work, based on original ... ties (to which full references are given), and the ingenious and ... together of scattered facts, which distinguish the best German ... present here. And though on the origin of the House of Commons ... which presents almost insuperable difficulties to Continental historians ... a school of ideas which necessarily colour their theories on such ... fessor Pauli holds views which have been corrected by later English ... is a drawback which English readers, who ought by this time to know ... that such institutions are the work of generations, not of individuals ... feel. A characteristic preface by Miss Martineau adds to the interest ... in its present state.

Mr. Prothero has founded his work on original investigation, ... obligations to Professors Pauli and Stubbs, without whose help ... have been tangled and trackless indeed, are most fittingly acknowledged ... glad to have this independent confirmation, as on the whole it is, ... clusions. Mr. Prothero has given us the best picture of Simon ... constitutional position yet drawn; his accounts of the two Constitutions ... and 1264 are admirable; and if the book is perhaps in too "popular ... are still grateful for the hitherto unpublished "Office of Simon ... which he gives us in the appendix, and for the excellent maps of the ... and the careful appreciation of the value of authorities. We hope ... will some day give us the final "Life of Montfort," including, what ... his project in this work, that mass of personal detail and picturesque ... which Mr. Blaauw began to work. We would also plead for a ... Lewes Poem, which is almost needed, as the right treatment of it ... be improved on nowadays, and a perfect list, at all events, of the ... appendices of a work like this should contain just those "unedited ... the publication of which elsewhere must be deferred till more ... done; moreover such additions immensely increase the value ... student, while they do not repel the general reader. We ... notice without referring to M. Ch. Bémont's brilliant study ...

---

* Life of Simon de Montfort. By Rev. M. Creighton (Historical Biographies) ... Simon de Montfort. By R. Pauli. Translated by Iona M. Goodwin, with ... London: Trübner. 1876.
Life of Simon de Montfort, with special reference to the Parliamentary ... Prothero. London: Longmans, Green, & Co.

[illegible] Historique (Juillet), which for the first time gives [illegible] view of the episode in the south which has been [illegible] this period from Matthew of Paris downwards. It is [illegible] and in especial includes a sketch of the administra[illegible] of the provinces. M. Bémont's judgment of Simon's [illegible] Cistern and certainly gave cause for complaint, though [illegible] elsewhere, from the purest motives. It is to be hoped [illegible] historical students may be led to work the rich field which [illegible], now so easily accessible, present.

---

[illegible] of Christian Biography, etc.*—We heartily congratulate [illegible] editors, and the public, on the appearance of an instalment [illegible] "Dictionary of Christian Biography." A brief inspec[illegible] how much the standard of work of this class has risen since [illegible] the Dictionaries of Classical Antiquities, of Classical Bio[illegible] Classical Geography. Nor need the new dictionary shrink [illegible] comparison with its continental rivals. After careful comparison [illegible] "Kirchen-Lexikon" by Wetzer and Welte, the "Real-[illegible] für protestantische Theologie und Kirche" edited by Herzog [illegible] edition, of which vol. ii. to "Bandeslade," is just issued), [illegible] encyclopédie des sciences religieuses," edited by Lichtenberger (Paris, [illegible] Fischbacher; the thirteenth and last part carries the work to vol. iii. [illegible] "Croisades"), we are in a position to testify that in complete[illegible] vocabulary the English work stands entirely alone; in very many [illegible] the individual articles are more thorough and instructive than the [illegible] articles in the German and French lexicons. Nor is it merely [illegible] that this dictionary renders a service: the whole nation—indeed, [illegible] gains by the example of co-operation here set by members of [illegible] the Scotch, the French, and German Protestant Churches; scholars [illegible] communions, who work together in the revision of the English Bible [illegible] preparation of text-books for the common use of all Christian bodies, [illegible] to join together those whom sectarian newspapers would put asunder. [illegible] counted right, fifty-nine writers have contributed to this volume; in [illegible] Professors Westcott and Lightfoot undertook the editorship. [illegible] "the pressure of other engagements compelled them before long [illegible] this task. . . . On their retirement, Dr. William Smith assumed [illegible] as far as the end of the articles in B; but from the commencement [illegible] in C, Professor Wace has acted as editor." Readers will echo the [illegible] to Dr. Salmon and Mr. Hole, for the revision to which they have [illegible] proofs.

[illegible] the early contributors soon withdrew from the work. Mr. Bradshaw [illegible] short articles; Mr. Aldis Wright seven, of which only one, Abgar, [illegible] considerable length; Professor R. A. Lipsius three, each worthy of his [illegible], Abdias, Acts of the Apostles (Apocryphal), Apocalypses [illegible]; Mr. A. W. Haddan, one of the chief contributors also to the [illegible] of Christian Antiquities," too early taken from a life of hard study [illegible] suffering, has no article after B; in all he wrote thirty-five articles, of [illegible] may mention Albanus (1), as a specimen of honest criticism; Professor [illegible] contributed Agathias and Barnabas;† Dean Reeves has three articles [illegible], an author with whom his name will always be associated); [illegible] Talbot, one; Professor W. P. Dickson, three, Ambrosiaster, Aquila, [illegible] Mr. R. C. Hawkins, one, St. Anne; Mr. J. Barmby, five; the late [illegible] four, Apologists, Aristides, Aristo, Athenagoras; Mr. G. Williams, [illegible]; Mr. H. C. G. Moule, one, Arnobius; Mr. J. G. Cazenove, four, [illegible], Autpertus,‡ Caesarius; M. de Pressensé, one, Augustinus, per[illegible] disappointing article in the volume, slight of texture and far too

---

* [illegible] of Christian Biography, Literature, Sects, and Doctrines; being a Continuation of "The [illegible]." Edited by William Smith, D.C.L., LL.D., and Henry Wace, M.A., Professor of Ecclesias[illegible] College, London; Chaplain of Lincoln's Inn. Vol. i. A—D. London: John Murray.

† [illegible] "Ullmann," and two lines below "Müller," (for "Ullman" and "Möhler") also several [illegible] "Weizsäcker."

‡ [illegible] an unusual word: "This second list is ab-judged away from our Autpert, and we [illegible].

indiscriminate in eulogy; Mr. C. D. Ginsburg, one, [illegible] he wrote a special treatise in 1865; Mr. T. C. D. [illegible] editor, one; Mr. Christopher Wordsworth, nine, [illegible] Christian name which he bears as the third in succession of [illegible] ling, one, Decalogue; Mr. M. B. Cowell, two; Dr. Swainson, [illegible] on which much new light has lately been thrown, chiefly by [illegible] those of Caspari. Mr. Lupton, one, Dionysius Pseudo-Areopagita [illegible] whom his Colet publications had made him probably more [illegible] other living scholar; lastly, Mr. D. Butler, one, Capreolus. [illegible]

Dr. Hort has written some sixty-four articles, several of which [illegible] bring out his characteristic merits, exact and exhaustive research, [illegible] subtle sympathy with thought, though clothed in unfamiliar forms, [illegible] a never-failing store of ingenious conjectures, where certainty [illegible] Abrasax, Adam (books of), Adamantius, Apelles, Arsinous, [illegible] Bardaisan, Basilides, Colarbasus, Cucojo.

Dr. Lightfoot has twenty-nine articles, the chief of which [illegible] Apion, Apostolic Fathers; Dr. Westcott, thirteen; that on Clement [illegible] dria can only have been written after a complete perusal of Clement [illegible] the express purpose of noting down his characteristics one by one; [illegible] of patient labour and orderly arrangement; other important articles are Demetrius, Dionysius of Alexandria.

Mr. Venables has contributed some 216 articles, including [illegible] Atticus, Basilius of Caesareia, Chrysostom, Cosmas Indicopleustes, [illegible] salem, Diodorus. We take this occasion to do right to one of the most [illegible] and extensive labours in the field of Greek scholarship that England [illegible] which has indeed been strangely neglected abroad, but should [illegible] only the more honoured by the editor's countrymen. Mr. Venables [illegible]

"The most practically useful edition [of Chrysostom] is that contained in [illegible] of the Abbé Migne, in 13 vols. 8vo., Paris, 1863. It is in the main [illegible] Benedictine edition, but it has been enriched by a judicious use of the [illegible] modern commentators, especially those of the Rev. F. Field, in his excellent [illegible] the Homilies on St. Matthew, 8vo., Cantabr. 1839, and of those on [illegible] and Ephesians, 8vo., Oxon., 1838, sq."

Only six vols. and part of a seventh, three on St. Matthew, four on St. [illegible] Cor., Gal., Eph.) are thus accounted for. There remain of the [illegible] Paul, vol. v. 1855 (Phil., Col., Thess.), vi. 1861 (Tim., Tit., Philem.), [illegible] and ind.).

Mr. I. G. Smith gives thirty-seven articles, including Antonius, [illegible] Aniane, Benedictus of Nursia, Bonifacius Moguntinensis,* [illegible]

Mr. C. Deedes furnished thirty-one articles, including [illegible] Aidan, Alaric, Attila, Audoenus, but soon withdrew. Professor [illegible] articles, including Alcuin,† Aldhelm, Beda, Benedict Biscop. [illegible] Mr. Freeman will allow us to pair with Mr. Stubbs as a master of [illegible] has twenty-three articles, including Caedmon and (an heirloom, [illegible] Cuthbert. Dr. Schaff has thirteen articles, including Adoptianism, [illegible] Arianism, Arius, Christology. Professor Cowell has twenty-[illegible] Akiba and Buddha (this last of fifteen pages), and has given [illegible] contributors. Dr. Maclear has seven articles, all belonging to the [illegible] Augustine of Canterbury. Mr. G. H. Moberly has thirteen, [illegible] Anastasius, Callistus, Cornelius, Damasus.

Dr. Salmon's contributions, ninety in number, are among the [illegible] the volume. His mathematical skill serves him in good stead [illegible] Africanus, Chronica; and his strong common sense [illegible] mazes of Gnosticism, Clementine literature, and other [illegible] hypothesis has long run riot. See Apolinaris, Cataif[illegible] crates, Clemens Romanus, Demiurgus, Diabolus, Dionys[illegible] and Docetism, Dositheus.

Bishop Benson has twenty-eight articles, all revolving [illegible]

* [illegible]

† [illegible]

[illegible] piece of work, were it not for the omission of biblio- [illegible] e.g., Bähringer's exhaustive life (in the second edition of his [illegible] Biographieen), Marshall's translation, and Bishop Sage's [illegible] ought not to be overlooked by the careful student; [illegible] perhaps deserved to be buried in silent contempt. Mr. J. [illegible] manner grouped ten articles round Ambrose; here too the [illegible] to furnish literary references in the promised supplement, not [illegible] edition of Ballerini, of which vol. i. appeared at Milan in 1874.

[illegible] Bright contributes seven articles, all on important names, Alexander, [illegible], Coelestinus (? Caelestinus), Cyrillus of Alexandria, Didy- [illegible]. It is curious to compare the gentle, measured censure of Cyril [illegible] showed a somewhat impulsive readiness to believe the story of a [illegible] a somewhat dictatorial temper in regard to the affairs of another [illegible]") with the frank and hearty ban with which Dioscorus is dismissed: [illegible] conspicuous on a tragical but admonitory list, the list of the 'violent [illegible] Church history."

[illegible] Moxley has three interesting articles, Ammonius Saccas, Apollonius [illegible]. It is to be regretted that his references are almost exclusively [illegible] authors.

[illegible] E. M. Young has thirteen articles, including Arator, Ausonius, Avitus, [illegible], Cassiodorus, Commodianus, Corippus, Dracontius. In all these articles [illegible] of bibliography is apparent: add to Arator, C. Leimbach in Theol. Stud. [illegible] 1873, pp. 225—270; to Ausonius, *e.g.*, Hist. Lit. de la France, i. (2) Par. [illegible] 281—318, O. Clason in Heidelb. Jahrb. 1872, 461—6, A. Meurer de Aus. [illegible] Münster, 1873. On Boethius it would be easy to add a page of [illegible]; the article is certainly one of the worst in the whole book, omitting [illegible] the two volumes added in 1867 and 1871 to the Bibliotheca Teubneriana; [illegible] translations of Chaucer and Queen Elizabeth; (3) Fr. Nitzsch das System [illegible], Berl. 1860, and C. Prantl Gesch. der Logik i. (Leipz. 1855) 679—722. [illegible] Plumptre's thirteen articles (Angelolatry, Angels, Antichrist, An- [illegible] Aurelius, Caius [*sic* for Gaius nicknamed Caligula], Claudius, Com- [illegible], Decius, Diocletian, Domitian) are pleasant to read, but more suited [illegible] to beginners than as a help to scholars; the recent researches on the [illegible] of the empire are neglected, not even Lehmann's Claudius being cited. In [illegible] Cyclopaedia the history of the empire is exhaustively treated.

[illegible] Wordsworth's Constantine and his Sons has solid matter enough [illegible] volume; nor is the candour of his judgments less conspicuous than his [illegible]. His only other articles are Ammianus and Apollinaris.

[illegible] lamented Bishop Forbes began and ended with the letter B his ninety-six [illegible] of Scottish saints; but his mantle fell on Mr. James Gammack, who has [illegible] three hundred and thirty-seven.

[illegible] G. W. Boase we owe twenty-eight articles, to Mr. H. W. Yule sixteen, to [illegible] six, to Mr. W. H. Fremantle eleven, to Mr. T. R. Buchanan thirty [illegible] Popes Benedict I. and II., Boniface I.—V., Carolini libri, Charles the [illegible] to Mr. W. M. Sinclair* one hundred and sixty-six, to Mr. D. R. Jones one [illegible] and seventy-one.

[illegible] of the contributors adhere to the editor's rule: "To treat these subjects [illegible] historical point of view, and simply to give an impartial account of [illegible] believed, thought, and done in the early ages of Christianity, without [illegible] the disputable conclusions drawn from these facts by various [illegible] parties." The chief offenders against this salutary restriction appear [illegible] J. M. Fuller and Mr. E. S. Ffoulkes. Mr. Fuller's eight articles (Balaam- [illegible], Cerinthus, Caelicolae [? Coelicolae], Coptic Church, Dimoeritae, [illegible]) are wordy in the extreme; see, for instance, p. 831 b: "The [illegible] of the Eastern Church had originated these opinions, and [illegible] killed them or suffered them to give place to other and newer [illegible] time, but by God's providence for a time only, Apollinarian- [illegible] harm. It was, as Epiphanius sorrowfully puts it, the [illegible] 'who ever troubles the human race, mingling with excel- [illegible] poison, and infusing bitterness even into honey.'" Mr. [illegible] by stringing together titles of the common German [illegible] monographs or to articles in journals are valuable and

[illegible] have been dosing, when he wrote and they passed the article on [illegible] edition only at second hand (through Hoefer's Biogr. Générale), and [illegible] the Grammatici Latini, vol. 4, Teubner, 1864) is simply ignored.

cost the writer some research; but no reader need be told [illegible]
or Niedner he will find some mention, *e.g.*, of Cerinthus. [illegible]
deny that much is to be learnt from Mr. Fuller's articles. Mr. [illegible]
danger of burdening us with references to modern Germans; [illegible]
(Baptism, Charity [which should have been omitted, or a whole [illegible]
virtues added], Chiliasts, Church, Cletus, Concupiscence, Confession, [illegible]
Death and the Dead, Demonology, Dionysius Exiguus, &c.) are [illegible]
tive and cite authorities often antiquated, mostly confined to one or two [illegible]
opinion. So far as they contain a catena of texts, they no doubt [illegible]
but few English Churchmen, not to speak of Protestants of other [illegible]
would endorse such a dictum as this: "No. 67 of the 'Tracts for the [illegible]
Wilberforce on 'Baptism,' exhaust the general subject." When [illegible]
we find several lines taken up with Cave's view, we sigh: "O for [illegible]
of Lipsius." The article Demonology (which refers to Dr. [illegible]
Diabolus, a singular and instructive contrast) propounds opinion [illegible]
educated Europe since the Amsterdam pastor B. Bekker published [illegible]
Enchanted." The facts collected are no doubt valuable contributions to [illegible]
geschichte," but Roskoff's "Geschichte des Teufels," which Mr. [illegible]
cite, contains a far more complete and orderly account of this melanchol[illegible]
in the history of delusion.

We now come to the two contributors, to whom we owe the long lists [illegible]
names which make this dictionary exceptionally valuable as an [illegible]
Both began their labours, as did several other writers, with the letter [illegible]
Hole has written three hundred and ninety-two articles, and Mr. [illegible]
hundred and twenty-five. Mr. Hole has often made important additio[illegible]
collections even of Professor Stubbs, Mr. Raine, and Mr. Gammack; [illegible]
not a few cases, Scaliger's words hold good of original and supplement[illegible]
*vaut mieux que le poisson*. See Ceadda, Cedda, Centwine, Ceolfrid, Ceo[illegible]
wulf, Coenred, Coinwalch, Columba, Columbanus, two Cuthreds, Cyne[illegible]
wulf, Deusdedit. If Mr. Murray's projected "Biographia Britannica [illegible]
carried out, Mr. Hole's labours have laid a solid foundation for the [illegible]
Mr. Birks has also here and there made useful supplements, *e.g.* to Mr. [illegible]
Caesarius and to Mr. Butler's Capreolus. Sometimes he becomes wordy. [illegible]
"The whole subject of the lives of the Roman emperors in their bearing [illegible]
tunes of the Church calls for careful investigation. Late and meagre [illegible]
Pharaoh's lean kine, swallowed up the original authorities. In such [illegible]
is chiefly the gossip of the time that is preserved. And at best, the heathen [illegible]
rather delight in startling paradox, than attempt to trace the sad [illegible]
ruin of a human soul. Besides, as far and as long as they can, they [illegible]
ignore the existence of Christianity" (cf. Constantinus 1, Chrys[illegible]
same page, 402 b, the redoubtable Immanuel is spelt with a *e*, "[illegible]
perhaps have been better if so difficult an article as "Chosroes" had [illegible]
to some continental scholar, who had given his life to the study of [illegible]
sources. In p. 622 a, the father of two well-known writers is [illegible]
Stephens. The story on p. 691 b, a mere platitude of hagiography, [illegible]
been left to the nursery:

"A woman named Palladia once gave Damian three eggs, and [illegible]
that he forbade them to bury his brother in the same tomb with [illegible]
people were debating what to do with the corpse, a camel, which the [illegible]
spoke and told them it was all right, they might lay Damian with his [illegible]
been compelled by an oath to take the eggs."

On p. 308 a, Professor Stubbs says: "John the archchanter and [illegible]
at Rome:" on p. 439 b, Mr. Raine says: "John, abbot of St. [illegible]
Who shall decide when doctors disagree? Our friends will [illegible]
decision of Beda, who clearly states (H. E. iv. 18 pr.) that John [illegible]
this word we agree with Mr. Raine) of St. Martin's monastery [illegible]
with Benedict Biscop. At the end of the same chapter [illegible]
was entertained as a stranger at Tours, and that [illegible]
"propter amorem sancti Martini, cuius monasterio [illegible]

With a view to the supplement and to the remaining [illegible]
recommend the editors to engage some German, [illegible]
examine this first volume, and to furnish lists of [illegible]
(such as the Zeitschrift für Kirchengeschichte [illegible]
Niedner, and Kahnis, which is [illegible]

[illegible] the Dutch Archief of Kist and Moll; Hilgenfeld's Zeitschrift, [illegible] bibliographical works (Potthast's Bibliotheca Historica Medii [illegible] to most of the contributors: the last edition of Teuffel's [illegible] literature would have saved many a writer from grievous sins of [illegible] to compare the articles sent in with the corresponding [illegible], Wetzer and Welte, Herzog, &c., and with those in the [illegible], among which the Dutch one of Van der Aa takes a very high [illegible] all hortatory and declamatory eloquence; and to invite from [illegible] of annotated copies of such books as Cave's Historia Litteraria. [illegible] with a few titles of books taken at random. K. Werner, Beda d. [illegible] Wien, Braumüller, 1875, (reviewed with his Alcuin, ib. 1876, by [illegible] f. kath. Theol. Innsbr. 1876, pp. 131—143; by Zoepffel in Theolog. [illegible], 1877, cols. 174—176). Werner's Alcuin is reviewed by Möller, ibid. [illegible] points out that the Commentary on the Apocalypse, printed in Mai [illegible] nova coll. ix., is extracted from that of Ambrosius Autbertus), and by [illegible] Litteraturzeitung, 1877, n. 3. See further F. Hamelin, Essai sur la [illegible] Ouvrages d'Alcuin, Rennes 1873; T. Sickel, Alcuin-Studien I., Wien, 1875, 8vo, pp. 92 (from the Sitzungsber. d. Akad. lxxix.). Mr. Mullinger's [illegible] on the schools of Charles the Great also deserves to be quoted. *Sed [illegible] tabula.*

JOHN E. B. MAYOR.

---

[illegible]'s DE ECCLESIA ET CATHEDRA.*—An "Epistle" of more than a [illegible] pages, in an era of post-cards and telegrams, is in itself a portent [illegible] that the writer must needs be out of harmony with the spirit of [illegible] and therefore not the man who is likely to guide it. And this im[illegible] is strengthened by the appalling note prefixed to vol. ii., assuring [illegible] no more than an instalment is in our hands; for another volume, pre[illegible] of five hundred additional pages, is to be issued this year. The [illegible] of St. Paul's Epistles, in similar type, would occupy about thirty like [illegible] Mr. Lindsay has thus at the outset defeated his own controversial ends, [illegible] has piled up a mountain barring the way of all except professional critics, [illegible] haps a very few intimate or long-suffering friends. Hereditary Roman [illegible] will not trouble themselves to study the opinions of a recent convert, [illegible] proselytes will naturally prefer some terser and less superlunar reasons [illegible] their own way; while anti-Roman polemists will keep their artillery [illegible] formidable opponents. For the literary peculiarity of the book is a per[illegible] crotchetiness, together with a continual flow of question-begging [illegible] argument in favour of propositions which are enough to make an Ultramontane's hair stand erect, without dwelling on the fact that Mr. [illegible] by representing true Christianity as being simply Cæsarism in the [illegible] order, has quite gratuitously raised up a new objection to it in the minds [illegible] sane thinker of the present time who admits his definition. There is a [illegible] parallel between the fundamental idea of his volume and that of [illegible] most famous of Deistical writings, Tindal's "Christianity as Old as the [illegible]," which it resembles in its really destructive character, masquerading [illegible] forms of conservative exposition. Never was there a case where Talley[illegible], "Surtout, mon ami, point de zèle," might have been more appo[illegible] by Mr. Lindsay's spiritual guides, for it is not too much to say that [illegible] professedly apologetic work he has departed much further from Roman standards than he did while he was a member of the Church of England. [illegible], were he not a man of rank, ancient and distinguished family, [illegible], he would be suppressed pretty speedily by the ecclesiastical authorities [illegible] communion: but they will content themselves, as matters stand, with [illegible] their shoulders, and trusting to the extreme unlikelihood of his securing [illegible] whose opinion matters. He opens fire with a long controversial [illegible] former work from his pen, "Evidence for the Papacy," and having [illegible] against his critics in the past, goes on to provide those of the future [illegible] enough and to spare, not for mere hole-picking, but for elaborate [illegible] very small practical utility of the Infallibility dogma as a mar[illegible] sharp the theological hobbies of elderly gentlemen when they [illegible]. There is learning of a sort in the book, there is enormous

* [illegible]; or, the Empire Church of Jesus Christ. An Epistle. By the Hon. Colin [illegible] London: Longmans & Co. 1877.

labour, and there is undoubted cleverness and ingenuity [illegible] Lindsay has chosen to go a breakneck pace along the [illegible] has not had time to stop for facts or logic. Like all [illegible] on the Ultramontane side, he begins by assuming that [illegible] as to the manner in which a revelation, if made at all, [illegible] discharge its functions, are indisputable, and then has little [illegible] that only an infallible Pope can fulfil these conditions. But [illegible] circumstances, is not of the nature of proof at all. It [illegible] tion of one of Mr. Wilkie Collins's intricate plots, and [illegible] with which a number of the pre-arranged elements of the [illegible] to earlier causes, seemingly minute, but all invented for the [illegible] cisely as no one is struck with the preternatural sagacity of [illegible] racter in finding out the secret which we knew all along [illegible] author to discover, so Mr. Lindsay's so-called "proofs" have [illegible] mind of the historian or theologian, who knows that the [illegible] been invented subsequently to the chronological appearance of [illegible] they are designed to explain and justify. Mr. Lindsay has a [illegible] about the pre-Adamite world, savouring more of Talmudic [illegible] than of Christian speculation, but his step is as certain and his [illegible] in this cloud-cuckoo-town as it is when he comes to discuss the [illegible] history. Indeed, as the proposition he sets himself to establish [illegible] against the Holy See, as the embodiment of the Empire-Church [illegible] political ruin of such nations as are guilty of it, with such [illegible] England, Germany, and Italy; while, conversely, we may assume [illegible] Naples illustrate the blessings which await filial submission, it is [illegible] Lindsay is likely to be a more trustworthy guide in the [illegible] gically treated, than in the Europe of to-day. But the [illegible] voluminous epistle is that in which he sets himself to show that [illegible] not begin where the Vatican decree puts it, with the commission [illegible] Cæsarea Philippi, but that, starting from an "Original," there [illegible] of infallible Vicars of God and Supreme Rulers in temporals [illegible] from Adam to Pius IX., sixty-seven under the earlier dispensation [illegible] dred and fifty-seven Popes. The pre-Christian list contains [illegible] as Ephraim, Eli, Abiathar, the infamous Jason and Menelaus, of [illegible] of the Second Book of Maccabees speaks in such scathing language [illegible] former as "that ungodly wretch, and no high priest," and the latter [illegible] fury of a cruel tyrant, and the rage of a savage beast"), [illegible] drunkard, butcher, and fratricide, and actually Caiaphas to [illegible] "infallible in faith and morals"! No wonder that Mr. Lindsay [illegible] about John XII. and Alexander VI., not to cite any others in the [illegible]

R. F. [illegible]

---

MANNING'S INDEPENDENCE OF THE HOLY SEE.*—Cardinal [illegible] shrewder in his generation than Mr. Lindsay. The book in [illegible] for the Temporal Power, contains, inclusive of introduction and [illegible] a hundred and eighty pages, and is thus within the compass of [illegible] by a busy man. The argument is not that which his Eminence [illegible] his co-religionists, that the Temporal Power is a fundamental dogma [illegible] religion, to be believed and defended as an essential to salvation [illegible] which, by-the-bye, even in the most temperate fashion, F. C[illegible] expelled from the Jesuit body,—but a more popular and [illegible] political grounds, that it is practically inconvenient in a very [illegible] spiritual chief of Latin Christendom, looked up to by many [illegible] and often mutually hostile nationalities, should be himself the [illegible] monarch of any one such nation, and thereby be conceivably [illegible] not permissible to imagine him biassed, by the resulting relations [illegible] the case in that part of the middle ages when the Avignon [illegible] tically the registrars of the French King's will. And the Cardinal [illegible] him, might have added, still more truthfully, that the former [illegible] as sovereigns of a very small territory which they could not [illegible] their powerful neighbours, constrained them to speak and act [illegible] tion in spiritual matters, lest the penalty of forfeiture [illegible]

* The Independence of the Holy See. By Cardinal Manning. [illegible]

Pius IX. has thought it necessary to do since he has been stripped of his dominions. But where the Cardinal breaks down, as in truth having nothing to say, is in offering any reason why the Romans should immolate themselves for the political convenience of Portuguese, or French, or Bavarian, or Mexican Catholics, and return under the yoke of a government which was feeble, corrupt, meddlesome, and inefficient in the highest degree. When we take the single fact that before 1870 Rome was the most insecure of European cities for a passenger to venture into the streets after nightfall, and that a striking change for the better has ensued since they were placed under the protection of the King of Italy's police, it is not unreasonable to ask why the restoration of a *régime* which would involve the renewed impunity of brigandage should be required of those who suffered from it. If any State likes to make over a scrap of territory to the Pope, and to neutralize it, and if the population to be so transferred do not object, there are excellent reasons for trying the experiment, but nothing is more certain than that Italy, and above all Rome, does not want the Temporal Power back again, and that no crusade for its forcible replacement is politically likely or morally defensible.

R. F. LITTLEDALE.

---

RECENT CHEMICAL TEXT-BOOKS.*—So many works of this kind have been thrown upon the public during the last few years, that it might have been thought there was hardly any opening for another. On consideration, however, it will be observed that, with the exception of Dr. Odling's unfinished "Manual," the late Professor Miller's "Elements of Chemistry," and Watt's "Dictionary of Chemistry," which latter must be looked upon more as a book of reference than as a treatise, we have really no large systematic work containing the results of recent thought and investigation, brought up to the level of the present day; the latest works on chemistry having taken the form generally of elementary manuals for the use of students. The treatise on chemistry by Professors Roscoe and Schorlemmer, of which the first volume has just appeared, is a work of a very different calibre, and so far as a judgment can be pronounced from the perusal of the part now before the public, it is destined to take a high position in chemical literature.

Unlike most other text-books the volume commences with an historical sketch of the progress of the science from very early times, in which the authors pass in review the most important workers in chemistry from the time of the alchemists to that of Sir Humphrey Davy, comprehending more especially the investigations of Boyle, Black, Priestley, Scheele, Lavoisier, and Dalton; the historical details being given in a very pleasant and interesting manner. We are glad to see that in this sketch the authors pay a deserved tribute to the late Dr. Thomas Thomson as having been the first to bring forward in his teaching Dalton's atomic theory in its application to the laws of chemical combination.

The general principles of the science are next discussed, comprehending, besides the laws of chemical combination and nomenclature, the consideration of various points lying on the border-land between chemistry and physics, such as the kinetic theory of gases, the continuity of the gaseous and liquid states of matter and the diffusion of gases. While the question of chemical nomenclature is very clearly stated, the authors do not seem to advocate any one system to the exclusion of others, but content themselves with a description and explanation of the different prefixes and terminations employed generally at the present day; throughout the work also they retain, as a rule, the older and ordinary names of chemical substances. With regard to the special nomenclature of acids and salts we should have been glad of a decided opinion from them; these points are, however, left in their former somewhat unsatisfactory position. The laws of chemical combinations are stated with great clearness, and explained in a very interesting and somewhat novel manner.

The classification of the elements and compounds treated of in this volume is strictly scientific, based upon a comparison of certain chemical properties, not upon any natural relations possessed by the substances. This arrangement is one that has been rarely employed in English text-books, and we think the authors

---

* A Treatise on Chemistry. By H. E. Roscoe, F.R.S., and C. Schorlemmer, F.R.S. Vol. I. The Non-Metallic Elements. London: Macmillan & Co. 1877.

Lessons in Elementary Chemistry: Inorganic and Organic. By Henry E. Roscoe, B.A., F.R.S. London: Macmillan & Co. 1877.

Junior Course of Practical Chemistry. By Francis Jones F.R.S.E., &c., with a preface by Professor Roscoe, F.R.S. Fourth Edition, 1877. London: Macmillan & Co.

have shown sound judgment in adopting it. [illegible] in full and accurate detail, and the illustrations are, [illegible] executed; this is especially marked in the chapters [illegible] of sulphuric acid and coal gas. The authors have [illegible] collect the results of the most recent investigations, [illegible] rendered more complete by the addition of references [illegible] which it is derived.

Among the points of difference which distinguish this [illegible] English text-books, we may mention the employment of the [illegible] calculated by Stas in preference to the older and better [illegible] secondly, the consideration of such bodies as the cyanogen [illegible] volume devoted to inorganic chemistry.

While the style of writing is, on the whole, clear, and the [illegible] difficult points often admirably lucid, we notice occasional [illegible] as it would seem, from the too literal reproduction of [illegible] the present state of the science, chemical text-books must be, [illegible] compiled from the journals of other countries, but great care should [illegible] the rendering of such material into our own language. One other [illegible] must make in reference to the considerable number of typographical [illegible] found in the text. These will no doubt be corrected in a future edi[illegible] not so unimportant a matter as might at first sight appear, since [illegible] occur in equations expressing the chemical reactions, and might [illegible] the mind of a beginner, although seen at once by those possessing [illegible] of the subject. In other respects we have nothing but praise to [illegible] style and general arrangement of the volume.

Professor Roscoe's, Lessons in Chemistry have now [illegible] selves such a good hold as an elementary text-book, and have [illegible] so many editions, that any criticism of the work would be [illegible] those points can be noticed in which the latest edition seems to [illegible] former ones. Professor Roscoe has introduced considerable change[illegible] ment of the book more especially in the organic portion, [illegible] sideration of the cyanogen, carbonyl, and sulpho-carbonyl [illegible] commencement of the organic course, immediately after the [illegible] analysis, instead of, as was formerly the case, after the diatomic [illegible] derivatives. There are also some slight changes in the inorganic[illegible] most important new matters added to this division have been [illegible] namely, the absolute weights of the elementary gases, as calculated [illegible] the recent researches of this investigator on the combining weights [illegible] he has determined that of oxygen as 15·96 instead of the origi[illegible] hydrogen being taken as the unit. This number confirms the resul[illegible] in a remarkable manner, his experimental number for the actual wei[illegible] of hydrogen being 0·089578 or 1-15·96th, instead of, as formerly, 0·0[illegible] A table of the densities of several elements and compounds as [illegible] is given in the appendix, and compared with the numbers experi[illegible] mined by Regnault, Bunsen, Mitscherlich, Dumas, and others.

The book is peculiarly well adapted for the higher classes in [illegible] students in their first year.

Mr. Jones's little volume on Practical Chemistry has been [illegible] those commencing the study of this branch of the subject, [illegible] in the preface, is intended "not to supplant, but rather to [illegible] tion given by the teacher." We have had opportunities of [illegible] of the book in practical teaching, and from the results [illegible] recommend it.

The regular analytical part is prefixed by a chapter on [illegible] apparatus, gases, &c., in which ready methods are described, [illegible] changes illustrated by equations: descriptions of the more [illegible] met with in connection with analytical work are also [illegible] does not pretend to any great theoretical scope, but will [illegible] to a student who may have been unable to gain any previ[illegible] ledge, as it serves to familiarize him with certain simple [illegible] before he becomes immersed in the practical details of [illegible]

The next chapter deals with blow-pipe reactions, [illegible] examinations of substances; while the latter portion [illegible] the grouping of metallic and non-metallic substances, and the proper methods for their detection and separation from each other. In this portion there are, we think, some slight omissions which may appear minute to one advanced in the science, but are apt to lead beginners into difficulties: thus, at the commencement of the systematic analysis of metals in the wet way, no instructions are given to dissolve the substance, should it be a solid, before adding the reagents. Some of the methods employed for the detection of the metals are exceedingly good. This is especially the case in the table comprehending the separation of the iron group, where the method is very clearly stated, and as simple as circumstances permit. We would refer readers to Professor Roscoe's remarks in the preface, especially the last concerning cleanliness in manipulation.

---

FORSTER'S PHYSIOLOGY.*—This little book is peculiarly well adapted for the use of the lower classes in schools, and for youthful learners generally. The pupil is required to exert only a minimum of mental effort, since the new ideas inculcated in each definition or physiological principle are clearly enunciated, one after the other, by description and example, until finally the definition or principle itself steps in as it were of necessity; and, in case it should not have been anticipated, is duly impressed upon the attention of the learner by appearing in blacker type. Thus we escape the risk of premises being forgotten, whilst conclusions are being mastered, as might be the case did the definition precede the statement of the facts and reasoning upon which it was founded. The chapter on blood offers a good example of the method of teaching adopted throughout. Great skill is shown in the order in which the new ideas are introduced. Thus appearances, obvious to the naked eye, are first pointed out, then the microscopic corpuscles are described, hæmoglobin and amœboid motions being freely discussed under simpler names. The phenomena of coagulation naturally introduce fibrin and serum (the distinction between serum and liquor sanguinis is probably omitted to avoid mystification of the beginner). The presence of albumin in serum is demonstrated by the simple application of heat, and here the chief proteids are enumerated; lastly the ash and its more important constituents complete the list. Then follows a short paragraph summing up the whole of what has been seen. It should be added that the book is written in a pleasant and easy style. How could the student have been more easily carried down the stream, in learning the structure of the circulatory apparatus, than by being placed in the position of a blood corpuscle setting out upon its travels from artery to vein and from vein to heart? Perhaps in the chapter on respiration, the explanation of the descent of the diaphragm during expiration would have been rendered clearer if the action of the abdominal muscles had been mentioned. There are numerous diagrams and illustrations, which will be found very serviceable where practical demonstrations are not possible or convenient.

---

MIVART ON THE COMMON FROG.†—This interesting little treatise, as its title implies, appeared first in a series of papers in the journal *Nature*, and these have been reprinted in an elegant and convenient form in the volume before us.

The author's object is, according to the introductory statement, to give a special account of the structure and mode of life of the *Rana temporaria* or common Frog, and at the same time to show its relation to other animals—both those which are closely allied to it and those which, like mammals and man, are farther removed by their structure and functions from its class—and lastly, from a review of the facts stated under these heads, to bring out certain views or deductions with respect to the origin of species and the theory of descent among animals.

The author, as might be expected from him, is most successful in the first or descriptive part, presenting in clear and graphic language, with sufficiently good pictorial illustrations, a most interesting history of the life and organization of his subject. It is perhaps to be regretted that in copying some of his best figures, as he appears to have done, from Professor Ecker's careful, we may say classical work, "Die Anatomie des Frosches," Brunswick, 1864, our author has not indicated, as he has with respect to others, the source from which these figures were derived. We would also remark that he seems to us unfortunate in the substitution of the word Batrachia for that of Amphibia, as the designation of

---

* Physiology. By M. Forster, M.A., M.D., F.R.S. Fourth Edition. London: Macmillan & Co.

† The Common Frog. *Nature Series.* By St. George Mivart, F.R.S., &c. London: Macmillan & Co.

the class within which the frog and its congeners [illegible] former word, both by its origin and by general use, [illegible] as exhibited in the Anura, or frogs and toads, while [illegible] appropriate designation for most of the other [illegible] Cæcilise, Menopoma, Amphiuma, Proteus, Axolotl, and [illegible] manders or Newts, not to mention fossil genera.

In the second part of his design, Mr. Mivart is hardly so [illegible] for while he shows that there are some parts of the [illegible] amphibia, which appear to be lost, or not to be [illegible] ascending series of reptiles and birds, and which [illegible] mammals, he assumes far too much that our knowledge [illegible] he neglects some important facts connected with development, [illegible] transitions, and gives too little place to the theory of atavism, [illegible] there is the tendency to the return among the higher animals [illegible] zation belonging to those lower in the series, by means of [illegible] adaptations to external conditions, occurring at long intervals, [illegible] of beings as yet unknown.

Mr. Mivart's treatise is, however, most interesting in its [illegible] gestive in its wider views, and we can recommend it [illegible] reader, as giving him a clear insight into the structure [illegible] animal, the study of which has contributed more than that [illegible] advancement of scientific knowledge of anatomy and physiology.

---

MIVART'S ELEMENTARY ANATOMY.*—This small work has [illegible] the public for upwards of four years, and has met with [illegible] It supplied a want which was felt for a simple and [illegible] would furnish the non-medical reader with an accurate [illegible] account of the anatomy of the human body, divested of the [illegible] details which are required for the physician and surgeon, and [illegible] general principles by a comparison with the anatomy of other [illegible] It has generally been acknowledged that the author, as might [illegible] so distinguished an anatomist, has accomplished his task in [illegible] and interesting manner. In the event of a new edition being [illegible] would suggest that the introductory chapter, which treats of [illegible] logical and morphological principles, as well as of zoological [illegible] of some extension and improvement. In the zoological part [illegible] ductory lesson some revision may be desirable, and especially [illegible] figures of animals, which are on too small a scale, might be greatly [illegible]

Any attempt to criticize the matter of a work like this, going [illegible] field and embracing a multitude of details, would be unsuitable [illegible] purpose; but a remark on nomenclature connected with anatom[illegible] tion may not be out of place. In the general view of the [illegible] Mivart has, with commendable care and judgment, successfully [illegible] difficulty encountered in any attempt to bring the description of the [illegible] exceptionally erect man into accordance with that of horizontally [illegible] an attempt, we may remark in passing, too long neglected by [illegible] anatomists. By the use of such terms as "dorsal" and "ventral," [illegible] "lateral," "proximal" and "distal," the discrepancy may be [illegible] avoided. To express position of parts in the body as they lie [illegible] other extremity of the trunk, upwards and downwards in man, [illegible] wards in animals, Mr. Mivart has employed the terms [illegible] axial;" but it is unfortunate that these terms have been [illegible] Flower, as applied only to the situation of parts in each limb [illegible] axis of the limb itself. It is desirable that some terms should [illegible] by human and comparative anatomists which would express [illegible] tion without the necessity of explanation and circumlocution, [illegible] "cephalic," or "capital," and "caudal;" if not in the [illegible] clayan fashion of "cephalad" and "caudad."

---

* Lessons in Elementary Anatomy. By St. George Mivart, [illegible]

VEITCH'S HISTORY AND POETRY OF THE SCOTTISH BORDER.*—This is a genuine book. The author loves his subject and knows it, and writes, not from the desire to make a book, but from the fulness of his heart. The love of the Border-land is evidently a passion with him. In this cosmopolitan age, when all preference for the local and the national is branded as provincialism, it is refreshing to find one who loves his native dales and uplands with the simple affection of childhood confirmed by the reflection of manhood. He has wandered over those green, quiet hills, with their soft-flowing outlines, till their "pastoral melancholy" has melted into him, and coloured all his thoughts. His eye, familiar with all features of border scenery, has noted them under every season and every change of aspect. He knows by heart every peel-tower, castle, and battle-field, every house and holm, every swire and shaw in all that romantic land, and he has crooned to himself every snatch of ballad or song that still lingers around them; till imagination and reflection brooding over them have impelled him to ask, Whence comes this wonderful charm that rests on these border hills? what is it that has given to Border poetry its peculiar witchery? To find answers to this question he has ventured far back into a dim foretime, so distant that no records of it survive save the few Cymric names still borne by burns and glens. It is the poetry that drives him back on the history, in which he finds for it a substantial background. The influences which formed the poetry he traces to the successive waves of population which have swept over the country, each of which during its ascendency has been moulded by its own historic circumstances, as well as impressed by the peculiar local scenery. The earliest of these influences was the existence, from the fifth to the tenth century, of the Cymric kingdom of Strathclyde, stretching from the Frith of Clyde in the north to the River Derwent in the south, and having for its capital that rock on the Clyde, formerly called Alcluith, now known as Dumbarton, the Fort of the Britons. This is the extent attributed to that British kingdom by Mr. Skene, whom we accept *on this subject* as a better authority than Mr. Freeman, who makes it extend "from Dumbarton to Chester." While this kingdom lasted, all the high watershed whence Tweed, Clyde, Annan, Ettrick, and Yarrow run, was covered by the primeval wood of Caledon, a name that now survives only in tradition or romance. Following Mr. Skene, Professor Veitch connects King Arthur, all that is historic of him, with this British kingdom of Strathclyde. It was, according to these two authorities, in this region or in the parts adjacent, that the great Guledig or Ruler of the Britons, in their war with Saxons or Angles, fought his twelve famous battles, recorded by Nennius. Mr. Skene attempts to identify the names of these battles, as given by Nennius, with places still well known in or near the Border mountains. The seventh of these was the battle of the wood of Caledon. Professor Veitch adopting this theory of Mr. Skene's has added to it, from his minute local knowledge, one or two more confirmatory facts. Connected with this Cymric period we have a most interesting picture of Merlin, the Seer and Bard of Arthur, who, after the disastrous overthrow of his kinsmen at the battle of Ardderyd, fled to the high watershed of the Tweed, and hid his despair in the mountain wilderness of Tweedsmuir, then covered by the wood of Caledon.

"There is no wilder or more solitary moorland in the south of Scotland," writes Professor Veitch, "than those high-spreading moors; there is no scene which could be more fitly assigned to a heart-broken and despairing representative of the old Druidic nature-worship, at once past and present, of the fading faith, yet torn and distracted by secret doubts as to its truth, and not knowing well where his beloved had gone, or what was their fate in that mysterious spirit-world he felt was above and around him.

"I know no more picturesque or suggestive episode in history or in fiction, than that of the reported meeting between Merlin and Kentigern amid the birk and hazel shaws on the upland wilds of Tweeddale, when the young apostle of Christianity pressed on the nature-worshipper the claims of the new faith. One day the saint was kneeling in solitary prayer in the wilds of Drummelzier, when a mysterious figure suddenly stood before him, weird-like, unearthly in look, 'with hair growing so grime, fearful to see,' terrible as an embodied fury. The saint boldly asked who and what he was? The reply was:—'Once was I the prophet of Gwendoleu, Merlin by name, now in this solitude enduring privation. . . . . For I was the cause of the slaughter of all those who fell in the well-known battle of Arderydd, which took place between the Lidel and Carvanolow.'

"After a time the bard passed from the sight of Kentigern, more wildered, weary, and perplexed than before, to chase, if that might help him, the gleam and the shade on the

* The History and Poetry of the Scottish Border. By Professor Veitch, LL.D. Glasgow; James Maclehos

[illegible] in the pulsing of the burn and in communion with the [illegible]

[illegible] time still remain among those hills. One is [illegible] points as the grave of Merlin, where the Pow- [illegible] Glen, meets the Tweed. The other is the [illegible]—probably thrown up by the Britons of Strath- [illegible] encroaching Angles of Bernicia—which runs from [illegible] the south side of Liddlesdale. Time has [illegible] ancient landmark. Few have ever heard of it, save local [illegible] Professor Veitch has evidently traced over hill and dale every [illegible] with reverential fidelity. And his book bears marks of this [illegible] while making it not light reading for the general reader, [illegible] at all share in his tastes and associations. [illegible] Strathclyde, gradually weakened by the encroach- [illegible] east, and of Norwegian pirates on the west, at last [illegible] arms of Edmund, King of Wessex; and having been by [illegible] Malcolm, King of the Scots, became an appanage of the Scottish [illegible] Cymric population, thus merged in the northern [illegible] element that moulded Border history and poetry. [illegible] confounding the Angles of Northumbria [illegible] This charge comes from that small pedantry which, [illegible] recent writers have more pointedly distinguished [illegible] recognize the well-known fact that Saxon [illegible] besides its specific meaning, been long used as a [illegible] population of England, previous to the [illegible] Veitch need not be ashamed of a usage which has [illegible] Mr. Skene. If his use of the term is at all an error, [illegible]

[illegible] have carefully traced the change which came [illegible] begun by Malcolm Canmore and Queen [illegible] their youngest son, King David. When the earliest [illegible] twelfth century, all the lands along the Tweed and its [illegible] Angles, Normans, or Flemings. The names of all wit- [illegible] them to have been of the same races. King David's [illegible] the foundation of the great religious houses in the [illegible]—Kelso, Jedburgh, Melrose, Dryburgh. The presence [illegible] have greatly affected all Border culture and poetry. But [illegible] the influence of these immigrations, no extermination of [illegible] inhabitants seems to have taken place. However overflowed [illegible] Anglo-Norman superiors, the Cymric must still have formed [illegible] the people of the hills. We are not sure that Pro- [illegible] account of this.

[illegible] Merlin stands out in the Cymric time. In the [illegible] personages appear, who not less powerfully impressed [illegible] These were Michael Scot and Thomas of Ercildoune, [illegible] as Thomas the Rhymer. The former, as Professor Veitch shows, [illegible] beginning of the thirteenth century, who translated [illegible] treatises from Arabic into Latin, and for his learning went with the [illegible] warlock. The latter, prophet and bard, after pouring forth [illegible] which are now scattered all Scotland over, and visiting the land [illegible] disappeared to sleep in those mysterious halls beneath the Eildons [illegible] popular belief has also fixed on as the resting-place of King Arthur. [illegible] three names, Merlin, Michael Scot, and Thomas of Ercildoune, Professor Veitch assigns a large space in that background of mystery which, ever present to the imagination of the Borderers, throws such a strange glamour over all their country and the poetry that illumines it.

We have not space to follow the account of the part played by the Borderers in the wars of Independence, during which the chief man of Tweeddale, the [illegible] Simon Fraser, rode forth from his Tower of Neidpath to win the battle [illegible] and soon after to perish by a cruel doom, in London, at the hands of [illegible]. The two centuries that lay between the wars of Bruce [illegible] are well and lovingly depicted; with their peel-towers [illegible] water, their raids across the English border, their [illegible] of Hangingshaw and Cokburne of Henderland, and [illegible] across the southern hills, to put them down. All [illegible] to which not even the minutest [illegible] which form more than half of [illegible] as they are, are perhaps a little [illegible] the sequence of influence in the [illegible] has come from the author being so full of his [illegible] observations of the present and researches into the [illegible] there is in the region "Nullum sine nomine saxum."

[illegible] chapters, which describe the poetry of the Border, have a [illegible] earliest poem of known authorship connected with the dis[illegible] "Peblis to the Play," in which the accomplished King James I. [illegible] Veitch attributes this poem—pictures with graphic force [illegible] what he had seen and enjoyed at the Beltane Festival, or [illegible].

[illegible] classification of the Border ballads, somewhat different from [illegible] "The Border Minstrelsy." First, there is the historical ballad, [illegible] actual events of history. Second, come those which venture into [illegible] world or the realm of Faery. Thirdly, we have those founded [illegible] pathetic incident which befell in the district, some lament for [illegible] youth and lovelorn maid." Lastly, the ballads, or rather songs, [illegible] some localised emotion—some successful or unsuccessful love. In [illegible] we have well described wherein lies the essence of Romance. It is [illegible], in the first place, against the tyranny of materialism and of the [illegible] second, against the tyranny of commonplace.

[illegible] Veitch regards the romantic ballads as mainly an inspiration, though [illegible] from the Arthurian time, while the Fairy ballads are an echo of [illegible] mythology. So we find it written in p. 333; but a little further on, [illegible] is stated that supernatural feeling in the romantic ballad was "brought [illegible] Scandinavian north," and nursed into strength by the scenery of the [illegible] adopted land. Which of these statements are we to accept? But if [illegible] Veitch hesitates as to the source of the "eerie" feeling, there is in him [illegible] about the thing itself. He writes of the weird sights seen in the [illegible] and by the wan water, not like a modern literary man, but like a [illegible] of the Border who has known in childhood experiences of this kind of [illegible] manhood has not cared to divest itself.

[illegible] would linger over his descriptions of Tweedside and Yarrow, how "the [illegible] has been enriched, glorified, and transfigured by the return into its [illegible] wealth of imaginative creation," which its pensive beauty and pathetic [illegible] have elicited; how the traditional spirit of older nameless singers sounded [illegible] last century in the well-known strains of Hamilton of Bangour, Lady [illegible] Baillie, Jean Elliot, Mrs. Cockburn, the two last the singers of the [illegible] of the Forest," till, at the beginning of this century, it bloomed forth [illegible] Hogg, and above all in Walter Scott, the consummate flower of Border [illegible]. A few strains of later warblers are given, faint compared with the [illegible] yet still full of feeling for the old romance of Yarrow. We wish we [illegible] give one of the latest, "A Song of Yarrow," by a still-living minstrel [illegible] Selkirk." On the whole we can heartily commend Professor Veitch's [illegible] classes of readers: to all who have felt the power of Scott's "Border [illegible]" (and who with a heart has not?),—to all who care to visit and really to [illegible] delightsome land, for no other book except "The Border Minstrelsy" [illegible] open their eyes to see it,—to all dwellers in the Border-land who [illegible] as they ought to know, what constitutes the grace and the glory of [illegible] birth-land.

J. C. SHAIRP.

---

[illegible] GREEN PASTURES AND PICCADILLY.*—A learned Scottish judge—[illegible] we forget—was one day trying a case in which Jeffrey was engaged. [illegible] was called to speak to the mental capacity of a certain person. [illegible] in vain to make the witness understand what he was wanted to [illegible] "Should you say that Donald M'Alister was capable of manag[illegible]?" and other questions equally elegant, had made no impres[illegible] witness, who might as well have been spoken to in Cingalese. At

* [illegible] and Piccadilly. By William Black. 3 vols. London: Macmillan & Co.

last, the judge whispered to Jeffrey, "Let me tackle him;" [illegible] the witness, "Hae ye your mull wi' ye?" The fellow [illegible] of reason at this. "Ou ay," said he, offering the box [illegible] judge, who took a pinch. "Hoo lang, noo, hae ye kent [illegible]" said the judge. "I kent him when he was only that high," [illegible] pointing to a low stool. "Noo, atween you and me," [illegible] another pinch, and glowerin' friendlike, or geckin, or [illegible] in a way which was equal to an English wink, "is there [illegible] cratur?" The witness burst out indignantly, "I wadna [illegible] wi' a bull calf." The judge smiled, the spectators laughed, [illegible] was satisfied.

This little story, which our own ignorance of the dialect [illegible] has often occurred to us in reading some of the very best novels [illegible] far as the south is concerned, a literary Scotchman has an [illegible] Englishman which we sometimes grudge him. To the majority of [illegible] Scotland is far less known than England is to the majority of [illegible] that the Scottish novelist comes to them like a traveller full of [illegible] and readily finds his capital in local colouring and strange [illegible] fertile of all topics for his purpose is that of courtship, and Scottish [illegible] this respect—among the peasantry at least—are so different from [illegible] to the southerner as to supply the story-teller with no end of [illegible] and piquancy. If there is crime in the plot, "the fiscal" can pop in [illegible] he does. There is not much in *him*, but there he is—nearly as good [illegible] a moujik, or a kadi, or a bashi-bazouk, or whatever you like. [illegible] great thing is the dialect. It is scarcely possible to describe Gaelic [illegible] Englishman without making him laugh. Neil, the Pensioner, in "[illegible] Heth," is one of Mr. Black's happiest hits; but ordinary "Doric" [illegible] furnish a new sort of interest. Between brave and braw, away [illegible] and ken, attend and tak' tent, there is not any very great difference [illegible] to see why "my luv is like the red, red rose," should be more [illegible] "my love is like the red, red rose." No: we will not stick at [illegible] think of the mighty literary devices which still remain ready to the [illegible] Scottish novelist, when he fairly cuts his cable and launches out into [illegible] of Scotticisms. "Hallo, Jem, step inside, and let's have a chat," [illegible] novelist might say. But how poor it is by the side of "Hoot, John [illegible] ben and we'll hae a crack." The poor southerner hides his diminished [illegible] And when, from these quite elementary bypaths, the northerner [illegible] quering and to conquer, into such wild tracks of "native heath" as [illegible] find in Dr. George MacDonald, the poor Englishman succumbs. [illegible] what pathos, there must be behind all this!

Mr. Black has always been very sparing of the power he might [illegible] the poor southron in this matter, and he has not been sufficiently [illegible] it. But when we have said this, we hardly know what else to [illegible] beating so far about the bush in approaching this new novel of his, [illegible] rather wanted to put off coming closer. There is no law which [illegible] man's books must be of uniform quality—on the contrary, there [illegible] declares that fertility is accompanied by unevenness. But [illegible] neyed phrase, the novelist often proves a dangerous rival to himself. "Green Pastures and Piccadilly,"—a title which seems to [illegible] one or two quarters—stands for Town and Country: only [illegible] tended to carry with it a suggestion of "still waters" too, and [illegible] simplicity; while Piccadilly is to be read with connotations of [illegible] able intrigue of the more innocent kind. Lady Sylvia, [illegible] mistress of Willowby," with no mother and with few lady-friends [illegible] a life as innocent as that of the Willowby rabbits in "the quiet [illegible] of her father Lord Willowby's park. To her enter Hugh Balfour, [illegible] not in quite accurate drawing, we fear—but sufficiently [illegible] as a serious, reticent, rich young Scot; anxious to do good [illegible] to the poor; earnest in the study of political ways and [illegible] cable," or unworldly. He falls in love with Lady Sylvia [illegible] she takes him for a hero made of gold from head to foot [illegible] reads into her sympathy a great deal more intelligence [illegible] there is in it, or indeed can be, considering the [illegible] finds her hero has or seems to have feet of clay [illegible] both scamps; and one thing and another [illegible] a breach between these two. This situation is good and fertile; but though most of the separate passages that ensue are very lifelike, we are not made to feel that the estrangement which takes place between husband and wife is natural. With Lady Sylvia we rapidly lose all sympathy. And, after the reconciliation, we see too little of her to *feel* that she has learnt much wisdom, though we are told she has.

The episodes of American travel are most amusing, and every now and then we come to a descriptive passage which is in the author's best manner; but we are not reconciled to the device of sending Lady Sylvia to Colorado to cool down her foolish temper. The "incantation scene" of the second chapter (pp. 28, 29, vol. i.) is one of the most beautiful things Mr. Black has yet done, and it stays with the reader, who, turning back from time to time to this sweet idyllic opening, feels himself a little put upon by even the best of what follows. It was undoubtedly a good idea to set Hugh and Sylvia, both of them chastised by misfortune, to work out their happiness at last under much simpler conditions than were possible in England; but still, when we leave them in Colorado, we feel somehow as if they had gone through a trap-door, rather than as if the story had come to a full close. In fact, this novel is crowded, inconveniently crowded, with good things, and yet one would ten times rather read "Madcap Violet" or "A Daughter of Heth."

MATTHEW BROWNE.

---

SAUNDERS' JASPER DEANE.*—If this pretty tale had only been about Temple Bar, instead of St. Paul's! But Mr. Saunders has not been so lucky as to have that inspiration; though he comes as close as Shire Lane and Sir Christopher Wren, which really ought to do. The story is placed in the seventeenth century; introduces the reader to the architect of St. Paul's and Grinling Gibbons; and has touches, here and there, of historic reality which are pleasing enough. But the introduction of such touches is always hazardous, and so are even minor attempts to imitate the speech, writings, or manners of a given era. Of course, the risk is increased if the work of the narrator keeps him near at home; for to one person who thinks he can criticize Becker's "Charicles," there are a thousand who feel sure they can detect the least flaw in a story like this. In truth, however, the criticism of such a work is about as hazardous as the work itself. It is safe to affirm that tea, or coffee, or tobacco, or the potato, was not in vogue at such a date, and of course there is a wide area within which similar criticisms may be made; but none are so uncertain as those which refer to modes of speech and writing.

The safest way for the story-teller is to do as Mr. Saunders has done in "Jasper Deane"—keep for the most part to the open highway, and tell the story in the dialect of to-day. One may object to "shake his hede orful," and a few such matters; but, on the whole, the author stays on the safe side of the hedge. Even if it were otherwise, it would not be a serious matter in a book like "Jasper Deane," in which the thread of general interest is so strong, and the feeling so sweet and natural, that small antiquarian questions may well pass unnoticed. It is, we presume, a study for young people. Jasper Deane, a young apprentice with a genius for wood-carving, gets entangled in a very false situation with a bad master, but in the end escapes from it. Of course, there is a love story, and though May Engleheart is only a good, pretty girl, she lights up the narrative from end to end.

Mr. John Saunders has now been before the world as a publicist and writer of novels for a great many years, and as a dramatist he is not wholly without laurels. In all he has written, the tone has been singularly high and pure, and utterly free from the cynical taint which scarcely any of our recent novels have escaped. In one sense, he may be called a survival—so rapidly have we moved during the last five-and-twenty years. He does what is helpful and admirable in taking us back to days of simpler ethics and firmer trust, and we yet look to him for new and effective work, bright with colours of faith and hope with which we have been too little familiar of late years. Meanwhile, we can cheerfully recommend "Jasper Deane" as a story for lads and lasses. It would find a welcome in any country lending library, we should say.

MATTHEW BROWNE.

---

* Jasper Deane: Wood Carver of St. Paul's. A Tale. By John Saunders. London: Sampson Low & Co.

BLACKIE'S WISE MEN OF GREECE.*—In this curious volume Professor Blackie has attempted to throw into a dramatic form, attractive to ordinary readers, the præ-Socratic Philosophy of Greece. The mathematical speculations of Pythagoras, the simple materialism of Thales, the theological purity of Xenophanes, the mysticism of Heraclitus, the sacerdotal conservatism of Empedocles are accurately portrayed, and lucidly, if not elegantly, expounded. Anaxagoras, νήφων παρ' εἰκῇ λέγοντας, as he is described in the first book of Aristotle's Metaphysics, takes advantage of having Pericles and Aspasia for an audience to prove that mind is the origin of all things, and betrays no consciousness of being *de trop*. "The little atheist, Aristodemus," is once more confuted by Socrates, while Aristippus, one of the votaries of pleasure, whose noble lives, as Aristotle says, recommended their more questionable doctrines, is eloquent on the "limb-dissolving ecstasy of sense." Democritus alone is conspicuous by his absence. Exalted as he was by Bacon above Plato and Aristotle, and as he has been again by the latest historian of materialism, he is perhaps regarded by Professor Blackie as a charlatan, to whom kindred impostors, in the shape of modern men of science, are naturally much drawn: or it may be that he has simply recognized the fact that here he has been forestalled by Lucretius.

We find that Professor Blackie is bold enough to conclude with Socrates and Plato. Socrates at the point of death addresses his friends as follows:—

"O strange disciples, who your master love
More than the lore he taught you! Sent I not
The women from the place, for that we ought
To die by harsh protesting undisturbed,
That cuffs at Jove's high will? I pray you keep
A manly cheer, and as I lived in peace,
So let me die!"

Surely this is not the man who said, ἀλλὰ γὰρ ἤδη ὥρα ἀπιέναι, ἐμοὶ μὲν ἀποθανουμένῳ ὑμῖν δὲ βιωσομένοις· ὁπότεροι δ' ἡμῶν ἔρχονται ἐπὶ τὸ βέλτιον ἄδηλον παντὶ πλὴν ἢ τῷ θεῷ. Or perhaps Professor Blackie thinks that Plato corrupted the simplicity of his master's style, and has kindly laboured to restore it. Further we find Plato discoursing at large on love; and passages from the Symposium are translated for our benefit, not to speak of the myth from the Phædrus, concerning the charioteer and the horses. But, with all respect for Professor Blackie, we doubt whether his work will find readers beyond the class of professed scholars, who will perhaps prefer the original to any interpretation, however brilliant. "Short and easy roads" to good handwriting or anything else are very valuable, but we question the advantage of taking a John Gilpin's ride through Greek Metaphysics.

W. H. PAUL.

* The Wise Men of Greece. In a Series of Dramatic Dialogues. By John Stuart Blackie. London: Macmillan & Co.

ERRATUM.—In the January No. of the REVIEW, p. 452, line 28 from bottom, *for* "omnipotent in time as in space," *read* "omnipresent in time as in space."

# [illegible]ENGLISH LANGUAGE AS SPOKEN AND WRITTEN.

[I]T is surely needless here to set forth the importance of facilitating to foreigners, especially in Asia, a knowledge of the English [lan]guage, and of extirpating plebeian errors among ourselves. As [litt]le can it be needful to insist on the grave difficulty interposed by [th]e discord between our writing and our speaking. The topic no [lon]ger belongs to mere closet-students, for it has been taken up by [ou]r School Boards; and the enthusiastic party which would, in the [int]erest of education, revolutionize our orthography, now joins hands [wi]th kindred spirits in the United States; where especially the [Ger]mans, annoyed to find how hard to their children is the mastery [of] English orthography as compared to German, are naturally and [rig]htfully impatient of its artificial difficulties. In calling those [ent]husiastic who desire to effect uniformity and simplicity at the cost [of a s]imple *neography* (that is, as though their problem were—to [crea]te literature for a language as yet unwritten), no disparagement [of] enthusiasm is intended; indeed to achieve a conquest far less [com]plete, much enthusiasm is needed. Still, it is here contended, [that] those who fix their aim so high have no due understanding of [the task] before them, nor any discernment that to win a stronghold [is not to se]cure keeping it when won. Their argument (even that [of the w]idely learned Professor Max Müller) does not touch the [...] subject.

[...] the English language has been peculiarly unfavour[able ...] writing its sounds. No principles were laid [down by the Anglo-]Saxon writers; and Norman clerks, importing [...] a confusion, which was increased by Latin [...] In modern days Dr. Samuel Johnson's [...] other has for the present fixed our spelling, followed no intelligent principles. In different shires the pronunciation differed and differs. Between North and South England there is sensible variety, and much greater between England and Ireland. The vastness of our literature and its diffusion in foreign countries complicates the problem of converting our two languages —that which is spoken and that which is written—into a harmonious pair. A sudden jump which should break continuity of development would present to the foreigner and to the child *two* written languages instead of one, and would presently aggravate difficulty for any but very superficial knowledge. No fact is more obvious than that our spoken language (as perhaps that of all nations) varies with *time* as well as place. One function of literature is to arrest this change, as far as may be; to regulate the admission of new words, and to forbid novelties of pronunciation, especially all that promote confusion. Small indeed is the shifting in orthography, compared to the innovations in utterance, especially in a country which has many provincial dialects and no public schools in which uniformity of pronunciation is cultivated. Such exactly is our case. We barely yesterday attained any general system of national teaching, and in it we have not even begun to make elocution a substantive object of culture. Precisely because the pronunciation has changed while the orthography is nearly fixed, a far greater chasm has arisen between the written and the spoken language than existed two centuries ago. Yet, as if blind to this fact, people are vehemently urging us to take that which is ever shifting as our standard, and remodel into conformity with it that which is comparatively stable. Nor is this the only extravagance of the proposal: its advocates seem blind also to the fact, that the written medium of thought is at once more distinctive and far more copious than the spoken tongue; and they are proposing to degrade the nobler instrument into the weakness of the less noble. It is surprising to hear a learned man gravely reason that we seldom make any serious mistake in listening to a speech, as to whether a *soul* or a *sole* is intended, or in what sense *sole* is used; therefore, there will be no harm in adopting a single mode of writing the four words *right, rite, write, wright.* Undeniably it is a defect that any such ambiguity exists as the pronouncing *sole* and *soul* alike: but because we have this defect in one instance, are we therefore to introduce it, knowingly and voluntarily, in other instances. and to confound four more words because we have already confounded two? Nay, we are coolly told that we might drop the word *rite* out of the language and use *ceremonial* for it; and drop the use of *sole* in the sense of *alone, only*. No doubt the wear and tear of time does thus cast out words which are uncomfortably ambiguous; and modern Greek instructively shows how the immense degradation of the national utterance has forcibly ejected or remodelled numbers of classical words; but it is rather despotic to suggest extinction of words in the literature whose [illegible] because a corrupt pronunciation has introduced [illegible], if we must change, the more rightful way is to [illegible] pronunciation of *soul (sowl)*, which is very probably [illegible], and certainly is the more convenient. And this points [illegible] which will presently be enlarged on, that the Irish in [illegible] respects have evidently retained a purer and better [illegible] than that of London and Southern England; nay, [illegible] better than that of all England. Hence, instead of [illegible] all their peculiarities as brogue, some of them (if we are [illegible] rather be imitated and cultivated, thereby bringing our [illegible] nearer to the written standard, with advantage also to [illegible].

[illegible] it may, it is at least absolutely necessary to *define* what is *ight* pronunciation (whether or not we can persuade this gene-n to adopt it) before we can wisely begin so vast a change as a remodelling of our orthography; especially when it is possible before those die out who are "bigoted" against the new spelling, pronunciation might make new and grave deviation from the -lauded phonotype. This is every way to be expected, unless in iational schools the tendencies to slang and laziness of utterance eld in with a strong bridle. Such, according to Virgil, is the [illegible] of all things to degenerate,

> "Sic omnia fatis
> In pejus ruere . . .
> Non aliter quam qui adverso vix flumine lembum,
> Remigiis subigit,—si brachia forte remisit," &c.

e memory of the present writer, change (he would rather say ption, depravation) has been observable enough; and the remark be extended to France. Paris had an Academy, to which all ce looked up. In accordance with its *decisions* a grammar for the ish was compiled by M. de Lévizac. The seventh edition, dated , was revised by M. Stephen Pasquier of the University of Paris. ve before me my school-boy copy.) It lays down (p. 22), "H, aspirated, is sounded with *a strong guttural impulse*, as in 'harpe, , 'hideux, 'honte, and about a hundred more words." The Greek ite is prefixed to the *h*, as if to make assurance doubly sure; and inly until of late I quite believed, from old remembrance, that in t une honte," the *h* was sounded more emphatically than in [illegible] speech. But now I am informed by most decisive authority [illegible] initial *h* at all is to be heard in Parisian utterance. A decree [illegible] Academy, without schoolmasters to enforce it, apparently [illegible] unfruitful of result, although all educated France intended [illegible] submission. Other changes of pronunciation are also

[illegible] early in this century was called namby-pamby, or the [illegible] "a dandy" (itself a word quite new then), appears to be in London current and fashionable—the use of short *a* instead of broad *a* in grant, command, grass, task, and numerous other words; and besides, an entire suppression of *r* at the end of a syllable or before a consonant. Thus *lord, hard, door, lorn, pore, pork* are sounded *laud, haad, daw, lawn, paw, pawk*, without reproof, if I am rightly informed. *Arms* and *Alms* are alike corrupted into *Aams*. Are we now invited to change our writing into conformity with this corruption for the convenience of school-children, who are required to learn English quickly? Probably Northerners will say, No: but in any case we have to define what is right. My mother was a Londoner: she may have been a little old-fashioned in her tongue, but she did not confound Which with Witch, Wheel with Weal, &c., but gave to the *h* in Wh its rightful sound. In the combination Wh the English writing has deviated unwisely from the Anglo-Saxon, which had Hw for it, as in Hwilc, *which*; Hwīl, *while*; Hwistl, *whistle*; Hwīt, *white*. This corrupt sounding of Wh as mere *w* damages at least seventeen root-words, and surely ought to be rebuked as sharply as the perversion of Horse, Hand, Hedge, Hill, into 'Orse, 'And, 'Edge, 'Ill, &c. W for Hw is an especial disgrace of Southern England. At least Ireland and Scotland are staunch for the *h*; how far northward in England the mischief has now spread, may be hard to decide. My schoolmaster always sounded in Whole the *w* as well as the *h*; which was not pedantry, if (as I am told) in some counties this is the pronunciation of the peasants. To distinguish Whole from Hole, is an advantage; and in spite of Anglo-Saxon hael (hale), Whole *may* be related to Wheel. As a general remark—if any one is too old to change his utterance, he can at least confess and counsel the right way to the new generation. The word Whole suggests two small corrections which are needed in orthography: first, we ought to write Wholely (just as Solely, Vilely) so as to secure the sounding of double *l*; next, in the unseemly word Whore, we ought to omit the *w*, which is a stupid, causeless addition. Wickliffe writes *Hore*. *Wholly* ought not to rhyme to *Holy*.

Further, it may be remarked, that in many names of places the *w* of *wick* and *wich* is omitted by Londoners and others; as in Berwick, Dulwich, Greenwich, Keswick, Norwich. But in Keswick itself I observed that residents sounded the *w*, as indeed in the town of Derby its name is sounded as it is spelt; while the aristocracy call it Darby.* Names, both of places and of men, are a problem apart: and (it may seem) need first attention and summary treatment. As in manuscript it is pre-eminently important that names be clearly written, because it is impossible or hazardous to guess at them by the context; so in speech the sound of a name ought to be in close harmony with the writing. If we insist on writing Keswick, Greenwich,

* "They have learned *from their grooms*," said an old lady to me in my boyhood, "to say Darby and Barkshire."

[illegible] sound the *w*; conversely, if it be thought [illegible] in utterance, we ought not to write it. Con[illegible] attached to archives and legal documents, few will [illegible] in writing the names; and as there is no intelli[illegible] in speech, it seems evident that our pronun[illegible] go back to the earlier standard. If any one's time is [illegible] he cannot say "a gentleman," but feels constrained [illegible] of course we cannot put him into Newgate for the [illegible] can condemn it as vulgar, and such condemnation [illegible]. To speak more generally—we are forced to admit in [illegible] two pronunciations: one, which alone is correct, which [illegible] to be used on solemn occasions, or in any public ad[illegible] and serious reading; another, permissible in rapid [illegible] speech, where small deviations from accuracy may pass. [illegible] *tuppence* for *two-pence*; but not in the parable of the [illegible] Samaritan. In poetry, as we prefer the old "medicinal" to [illegible] which has mischievously supplanted it, so we may hold [illegible]" in three syllables as alone correct, though in homely [illegible] we admit "méd'cin." Are we therefore to write it *medsn*? [illegible] it seems needful to be pedantically accurate. It is [illegible] to say Ciciter when we mean Cirencéster; and many persons [illegible] sensible enough to utter the latter word in full. When [illegible]n endure the length of Chichester and Colchester, is it a great [illegible] time and strength to say Glońcester, Wórcester, and not [illegible] Wooster? If, to humour Shakespeare, we *must* say Gloster, [illegible] write Gloster, as in the old books, and admit a double [illegible]. To accept Gloucester and Gloster side by side, and pro[illegible] with three syllables, the other with two, is just what the [illegible] in poetry and prose, or in various dialects. So in Pope, [illegible] and Diomedes, Merion and Meriones. Grave remonstrance [illegible] be made to families who write themselves Beauchamp, Chol[illegible], Colquhoun, and pronounce the names Beecham, Chumley, [illegible]. If they are proud of the old spelling, ought they not to be [illegible] proud of the old pronunciation?

[illegible], I suppose, will desire to present to the foreigner two or [illegible] dialects of England, instead of a single normal language. To [illegible] we are, has its serious inconvenience; yet it does not display [illegible] arrogance of one part of the United Kingdom to another. [illegible] does not now say to the great northern towns, "We are the [illegible]; our pronunciation must be your standard;" nor to the [illegible] say, "Let us have none of your brogue." So to speak [illegible] certainly would not win their efforts to strive for a common [illegible] utterance: but this is what one county will have to say to [illegible] we attempt to fix the pronunciation without a previous [illegible] survey based on principle and right. Before proceeding [illegible] principles ought to guide us where there is local diversity, it may be permitted to make some minor suggestions as to the choice of spelling where choice is allowed, where also there is no variety of pronunciation. For this is a small field, as to which there is least occasion for controversy; in which therefore one may hope for earliest agreement. Next, I will suggest a few cautious innovations.

First, then, I place words in which a double spelling is current; and I maintain (what I hope will be generally conceded) that we ought to select that mode of writing which agrees the better with the soun[d]. According to which principle we ought to write:

Jail, *not* Gaol.
Jailer, *not* Gaoler.
Show, *not* Shew.
Hiccup, *not* Hiccough.
Hocks, *not* Houghs.
Chesnut, *not* Chestnut.
Guage, *not* Gauge.
Lackey, *not* Lacquey.
Licorice, *not* Liquorice.
Alchymy, as of old.
Chymist, *not* Chemist.
Chymistry, *not* Chemistry.
Accounts, *not* Accompts.
Accountant, *not* Accomptant.
Harken, *not* Hearken.
Cartridge, *not* Cartouch.
Vial, *not* Phial.
Skeptic, *not* Sceptic; and
perhaps a few others.

Assailants who aim at a total upturn swell their forces by producing some of these words. Their argument, without these, is abundantly strong in favour of partial change and other aids. By not conceding this, we strengthen them.

Gaol, Gaoler, stand alone in English with *g* soft before *a*. Of course the French *Geôle* is the origin; but in this, *e* follows the *g*. Few now write *Shew;* but the word is produced by Phonotypists to reproach us. Strew and Strow are (I believe) both good, as verbs; identical in sense, differing slightly in pronunciation. To Straw is a third variety, but nearly obsolete. Hiccough is confessed to be a mere fancy. Hough, Houghs, are quite isolated in giving to *gh* the sound of *k*. To retain the *t* before *n* in Chesnut *because* it comes from Latin Castanus, is as weak as it would be to write Lacrme, Poulsser in modern French. Skeptic is the American way of writing.

Secondly, where irregularity is *unique*, or nearly so, the public will never be sorry to get rid of it. A few illustrations shall be ventured.

1. *Schedule* is the only word in use in which *Sch* has the German sound. (How the obsolete Seneschal was pronounced, I do not know.) I think we ought to write Shedule, in conformity with Sheet from *scida;* also Scism (as Scissors), not Schism. Then every remaining *Sch* means *Sk*. 2. Clerk, Serjeant, and Heart, Hearth, have *er* or *ear* for *ar*. Clerk has a new sense, diverse from Cleric. Might we not extinguish these exceptions? 3. *Yacht*, alone in the language, has *ch* mute. Who will regret the loss of the *ch?* We shall only need then some fit mark on the *a* to denote the right sound. 4. By collating Conceive, Conceit; Deceive, Deceit, we see that Receive ought to form Receit. The *p* in Receipt is surely a mere vexation. 5. The word Guild until

[illegible] at least) used to rhyme to Mild, Child, Wild. I [illegible] in my early days Guild, Guildhall, sounded with short *i*. [illegible] Guild is gratuitously confounded with Gild. On Aris[illegible] principle, that perspicuity is the first excellence of language, we [illegible] to go back to the long *i* in this word, though we cannot help [illegible] Guilt with Gilt in our utterance. 6. That *ia* has no [illegible] in *Parliament*, has been pointed out by Mr. E. Jones of [illegible] and, no doubt, by others. *Parlement* is the old and only [illegible] spelling, and the sooner it is resumed the better. 7. *Busy*, *Busi*[illegible] with *u* sounded as *i*, is a peculiar anomaly, and without historical [illegible]: *Busy* is in Dutch Besig, in Anglo-Saxon Bisig. Surely [illegible] without hesitation, to write *Bisy*, Bisiness, if not rather Biziness. 8. Perhaps ten words end in *mb*, with *b* mute. [illegible] got its *b* from the French, which probably had it from the Mas[illegible] Greek; *Womb*, *Lamb*, have *b* from the Anglo-Saxon; but Dutch Wam, Swedish Vame, Danish Vom; also German has Lamm, [illegible]h and Danish Lam. In Latin, Tum-ulus has Tum for root. [illegible] if we wrote *Toom*, *Woom*, *Lam*, no one would miss the *b*. But [illegible]mb, Numb (Benumb), Thumb, the *b* has no support in etymology, [illegible]n kindred languages. In Dumb it has perhaps a small excuse Icelandic. *Lam* would presently look to us as natural as Ram, Jam, Sham, Slam; *Lim* (the true Anglo-Saxon) as Slim, Dim, Brim, Prim; *Num*, *Benum*, *Thum*, as Gum, Hum, Rum, Sum. But [illegible] word *Climb*, the *b* has both etymological reason (compare French [illegible]per) and potential life, as Clamber shows. In Cumberland I have [illegible] Climb sounded with short *i* and vocal *b*, which I doubt not is [illegible]ld and only true pronunciation; nor is it more difficult than to [illegible] *p* in Limp, Imp, Jump. Here, to write Clime for Climb would [illegible]ere depravation. 9. In two words, beginning with Bu, the *u* is [illegible]gely superfluous. I do not mean in *Buoy*; for careful speakers [illegible]ly sound the *u*, and do not confound the word with Boy; but [illegible]n, *Build* and *Buy*. The German *Bild* at once ought to warn us [illegible]hat is right, and embolden us to drop the *u*. In Wedgwood's [illegible]ed and valuable dictionary I find that to Build was in old English [illegible]essed by to *Bylle*, even the *d* being unessential, as in Sound, Soun: [illegible] or *u* there seems no pretence. The verb Buy was in old English [illegible]e, again without *u*. Wycliffe writes Bigger for Buyer. Unless [illegible]re going to extirpate *gh* in Nigh, High, and many other words, it [illegible]vious to correct Buy, Buyer, into Bigh, Bigher. The past tense, [illegible]ght, still displays the *gh*. 10. The eccentric word *Women* ought [illegible]inly to be written Wimen. 11. Nephew should be Nevew, [illegible]evew. Dabitur licentia sumta pudenter.

[illegible] resume the general question, "How is the best pronuncia[illegible] settled?" Here we may rest on two principles: first, that [illegible] gives (mentally) most distinction of sense; secondly, [illegible] are equal, that is best which (orally) is best heard.

The second condition is almost identical with preference of long Italian vowels, which are melodious, or fitted to music. Each topic admits much illustration; but I will advert to the latter first. Consonants are not so well heard as vowels, or at least as long vowels. In the hum of an assembly the hearers of vowels are often able to guess at consonants which they cannot hear. Men with large lungs, as practised singers, can peal forth long vowels with a strength hard to limit, because these vowels can be dwelt upon; but liquids and sibilants are the only consonants on which the voice can dwell; and of vowel sounds, the Italian are the clearest, especially broad *a*, long *o*, and long *u*. Of all vowels, the short *i* is the hardest to utter audibly, as will easily be found in shouting out such a name as Dickson or Hickson (Dixon, Hixon). On the ground of melody and ease of hearing, I claim for our old-fashioned southern broad *a* (Italian *a*) and for the still fuller-voiced *aw, au* (modern Greek ω), a preference over the narrower sounds by which the more northern counties have been invading the south for fifty years past. Let me denote Italian broad *a* by à. To me the standard pronunciation in the following words (and many others) is:

> àss, gràss, pàss ; àsk, tàsk, gràsp, bàsket ; grànt, commànd, plànt ; Frànce, trànce, glànce ; fàst, làst, pàst ; fàsten, vàst, càst ; càstle, fàther, ràther, &c. ;

in which the utterance of short *a* is by many thought elegant. Again, let me denote Greek ω (English *au, awe*) by ò. In my mother tongue I learnt: òff, dòff, tòss, cròss, sòft, òft, lòft, còffee, còffer, òffer, &c.; but I am told that a short *o* is the now prevalent fashion, and is much prettier. Further, the clipping of words, to which a slipshod pronunciation ever tends, by omitting vowels, lessens the number of syllables and crams consonants together. This surely ought to be resisted with all our might. The greatest defect of our language as to melody (which is nearly measured by penetration of the air) is its excess in consonants; a mischief which the contraction of words by elision of the vowels ever tends to aggravate. The vulgar are not satisfied with *'peach* for impeach, *'prentice* for apprentice, *spose* for suppose; but they would confound pelisse and police in *plice*. Nothing more distinguishes careful and cultured pronunciation than the accurate utterance of the *un*accented vowels, generally short—a task which often is not easy. In Hystérical and Histórical the contrast of the accented vowels is clear enough; but it is not so easy to distinguish *e* from *o* in Mystery and History, Literal and Littoral, or to discriminate Accessary from Accessory, if indeed they ought to be two words. When unaccented vowels are long, as in Cóntrīte, Fínīte, Fémāle, no embarrassment arises: but when they are short, they are obscured and confused, and *a* is undistinguishable from *u*, or even from *e, i*. If we learned by the ear alone the words Mútăble, E'mphăsis

Púrpŏse, Fávŏurăble, Plĭănt, Líŏn, we might suppose the ă and the ŏ to be ŭ. Similarly Dámage, Rávage, Sávage, O'range, might seem to be Damej or Damij, Ravij, Savij, Orenj or Orinj. Again, *e* and *i* ending an unaccented syllable, cannot be discriminated; as in Pérmĕate, Végĕtate, Gérmĭnate, Persĕvére, Pársimony, Púrity. Such being the *natural* result of the stress accent placed strongly on one syllable, it would be a great error to invent a set of short vowels to define these varied utterances. It suffices to know on which syllable the stress falls; and this for the foreigner is sometimes the chief matter, in words of more than two syllables—a circumstance out of which will presently arise some discussion.

But, with such facts before us, it is evident that no recasting of our orthography can make the ear alone a guide to correct writing, unless we make disgraceful havoc of words.

But, continuing the argument of melody, we must admit, that if it is to dictate that the broad vowels â, ô, of the South shall dominate the narrow ones of the more northern counties, it equally decides against the Southerners in favour of the long Italian û as the true sound of *oo*. In Hull, for instance, they say *Book* with the long *oo* of southern *Fool*, and (as far as known to me) never give to *oo* the short southern sound. In the Midland counties also Room, Groom, have *oo* = û, but in my native London I learned to pronounce near twenty words with *oo* short; equivalent to the vowel of Puss, Full. They are Book, Brook, Cook (Cookery), Crook, Hook, Look, Nook, Rook (Rookery), Shook, Took; Broom, Room (Roomy), Groom (Bridegroom); Good, Hood (Hoodwink), Wood (Woody, Wooden), Stood, Foot, Wool (Woolly, Woollen). Not a single inconvenience appears from sounding every *oo* long; and if any high authority will enunciate that Yorkshire and the North are here right (hard as I might find it to adapt my tongue to the change), I should rejoice in it as removing arbitrary anomalies, and in some measure promoting audible speech. The new generation would grow up into the better way. Blood, Flood, Soot, remain anomalous in the South, as Foot in Lancashire,—sounded so as to rhyme with Nut!

I go back to illustrate the principle, that, of two rival pronunciations, that is better which better discriminates words, and aids to fix the sense. In the culture which ennobles a language there is a constant striving towards sharper distinction, which (by a perverted use of the word) Herbert Spencer would call "differentiation." In the Iliad ἕλκος and ὠτειλὴ indifferently mean a wound; but in prose Greek τραῦμα is a wound, ἕλκος an ulcer or sore, ὠτειλὴ a scar, ἐσχάρα the scab over a burn. This is a single illustration of a general fact. Accurate thought leads to distinctive phrase. Poets, for metre or rhyme, or to avoid prosaic accuracy, take liberties; so too do silly persons, thinking themselves witty when they are only coarse—as in saying the *hide* of a man for his skin; his *shell* (testa, tête) for his head; his *beak* or *snout* for his nose; *amalgam* (μάλαγμα) for gold; *tin* for silver; *gizzard* and *pluck* (odious word!) for heart; and so on. Moreover by lazy pronunciation words slightly differing in sound are confounded, which above was illustrated by *police* and *pelisse*. We are bound to struggle against every such degradation of our tongue. The enemy is ever at work, attacking in detail; and we must resist in detail, or he beats us. Moreover our written tongue is sedulously cultivated for accuracy, while our spoken tongue has been left to the untender whims of slang and laziness. Necessarily our written medium of thought is both more copious and more accurately distinctive: we must vehemently refuse in a single word to degrade it, where it is more exact, in compliment to the spoken tongue. As said above, better to pronounce Soul *sowl*, as the Irish do, than deliberately confound it with Sole. I have compiled a list of 207 groups of words, pairs or triplets, in which the written language makes distinctions unknown to us in speech. Granting that in very few cases of this list can a distinctive utterance be suggested, that is no reason for renouncing the written distinction. We are traitors if we surrender any point of superiority which our higher organ possesses. But sometimes it is not impossible to elevate the lower organ, the spoken tongue, by recovering for it lost discriminations. I have already named the Wh (Hw), but I proceed to treat of the *r*.

How far the Scots retain the full vibration of *r*, I less perfectly know: but every Irish gentleman seems to me accurately to pronounce it, and I cannot doubt that he has the true primitive sound, which we from carelessness have lost. For instance, we have three words, Or, Ore, Oar; for which the Irish have three sounds, but the English only two. The same is the case with For, Fore, Four. Notoriously in many languages the *r* is liable to transposition, but that does not necessarily lead to a weakening of its vibratory force. R is indeed among the consonants easiest to hear. At least, I think that in a room full of people Mirror would be better heard than even Miller; Merry certainly than Mewy (the "dandy" substitute), Roar than Lone, Lawn, though the last is a mouth-filling word. We emasculate the language by getting rid of as many *r*s as possible. See the process in the word Iron. Its proper sound is exactly as in Irony, and what can be better? This is still the Irish pronunciation; is also that which we English instinctively give to it in poetry or other solemn reading. But in the uneducated mouth the *r* was first transposed, as if we wrote I-orn, next it became I-ern, very similar to the Welsh Haiarn. Anglo-Saxon has Iren and Isen, German Eisen. It is open to possibility that the Welsh modified our pronunciation. Be that as it may, I-arn has almost been softened into I-an in careless lips, the *r* quite vanishing. But this is only one word out of a hundred.

So few persons seem to have pondered on the topic here brought forward that yet further illustration may be expedient. We have no difficulty in distinguishing Own from Owen; nor if we sounded Bowl so as to rhyme with Fowl, should we be prone to mistake Bowl for Bowel, or Growl for Growel (if Gruel were so sounded, rhyming with Bowel); yet we cannot in speech discriminate Flour from Flower. Why is this? It is because we do not fully vibrate final *r*, but insert a furtive short vowel between it and the *ou*, converting Flour into Flou-ăr, Flou-ĕr. Growl is a monosyllable, but an Englishman seems forced to make Flour into two syllables.

We have almost made two letters out of *r*, which may be distinguished as the perfect *r* and the imperfect or broken *r*. Of these, the latter must be carefully noted for its influence on the vowel preceding. Our *r* is broken, when it ends a syllable or precedes a consonant; then a part of its vibration is lost, and the previous vowel is elongated and modified. Hereby *e*, *i*, *u*, lose all distinction, as in Her, Fir, Fur; Hers, Furze; Pert, Flirt, Spirt, Spurt. Indeed, when the syllable is unaccented, even ă and ŏ seem to be merged in ŭ; as in Friăr, Briăr, Liăr, Buyĕr, Mirrŏr, Honŏr or Honour. Nor only so, but a peculiar sound (elsewhere unheard in English) is assigned to *a*, *e* long, before broken *r*, which seems to be the French grave è, as in Stare, Wary, There, Hair, Bear, Heir, Wear, Were, Ere, which all rhyme perfectly. Thus Tear is really two words, Tear (to rend) sounded as Tare, and Tear (larme, lacruma) sounded as Tier. The Irish, on the contrary, ignore this French è sound, and consistently sound Mare, Fare, Pair, &c., with the vowel of Mane, Fane, Pain, retaining for *r* its full vibration: likewise, as I think, they give the same vowel sound to There as to Here, Mere, Near. It is not at all likely that we shall ever follow them throughout. If just enough difference remain to mark nationality, who can grudge it? a compatriot of Bellerophon might surely talk Doric! But if we cannot go the Irish length, and pronounce Ore, Fore, with a fully vibrated *r*, with long Italian ô, and without any interpolated vowel, any "Patahh furtive" of the Hebrews, before *r*;—yet we may strongly insist that in every *r* *something* of vibration shall be heard; that Born shall not rhyme to Gòne and Lawn, nor Car to Ah! nor Or to Paw; that Arms shall not sound as Alms; nor Order, Lord, be as Awder, Laud; in short, that in Corn, Cart, Court, Mortal, Murky, War, Worn, Short, and all other words with *r*, this letter shall have a most unmistakable roughness. Even so, we do not solve the whole question how *r* is to be sounded where our counties differ,—as, how to discriminate Ore from Oar or Or, which is a type of many other words; whether Door, Floor, Four, Pour, are to rhyme with Oar, or with Or, Nor, For. Until such questions are settled, we cannot adopt a complete consistent Phonotype.

It may here be added, that Irish ladies, without the smallest affectation or effort, pronounce Calm, Palm, Alms, just as they are written, retaining the *l* and making the *a* sharp and short as in Măn. About

Half and Calf I am not so sure, but it seems impossible to doubt that such was the English pronunciation at no distant time, and such it *ought* to be now. The lip has been unschooled and wilful: we must not let it be master of the situation. There is no more *difficulty* in sounding the *l*, than in Elm, Helm, Elf, Pelf, Shelf, in all which we sound the *l*, and make the vowel short. A specious compromise would be, to allow breadth to the à in Calm, Palm, Psalm, Alms, &c., to lay down, that *in strictness* the *l* ought to be at least slightly heard, and that its omission in homely talk is a regrettable liberty. Whoever approves this as a theory, will perhaps extend it to Walk, Stalk, Talk, Chalk, Balk or Baulk, in all of which *a* has the sound of *au*. So in Falcon we utter *a* as *au*, yet do not with the French omit to sound the *l*. Indeed, no good case is made out to Phonotypists for eliding the *l*.

Another topic opens upon us with initial Kn, Gn, Ps—combinations which people seem to imagine are unpronounceable to English lips. Yet no English schoolboy finds difficulty as to these in Greek, nor even to the yet harder initial sounds Kt, Khth, Pt, Bd, Phth, Mn, Pn. No one thinks of dropping the first consonant in ψάλλω, ψαλμὸς, μνήμη, κνήμη, γνήσιος, γνωτὸς, γνόφος, δνόφος, βδελυρος, κνίζω, κνάω, &c. Not inability, but mere laziness or inobservance, make the English say Salm for Psalm, Nife for Knife, Nat for Gnat, Night for Knight, Nave for Knave. German accuracy here rebukes us. They do not boggle over the K of Knabe and Knecht, which at bottom are the same words as our Knave and Knight. To one (German or English) who comes to us with the request that we will drop the K in order to accommodate the popular speech which confuses Knave with Nave, Knight with Night, we may respectfully but firmly reply: "Sir! you mistake the culprit (the spoken language): he has debased himself; and now to please him, you try to wheedle his comrade (the orthography) into like debasement. The only cure is, that he repent and retrace his steps. We may wink at his laziness, but we will not sanction it. If we are implicated in his offence, we will not justify ourselves, nor plunge into new mischief by tampering with sound literature." For Knife the French have Canif; and it surely were better to pronounce a furtive vowel between K and *n* than to lop the K off; and similarly of the other words. Difficulties in detail remain. The *g* in Cognizance will probably ere long be sounded, since Recognize gives the hint. Just so, Ignore, which forty years ago was sounded with Italian *gn* as in Signor, now is assimilated to Ignorant and Ignoble with *g* hard. The *g* in Sign, Benign, Malign, cannot be spared. It has potential life. *Sign* must not be confounded with mathematical *Sine*, nor divorced from Signal. Some mark must be devised to show that *g* is mute. When *mn* ends a word, it is hardly needful to tell that *n* is mute; for the tongue naturally fails. But since with derivatives the *n* reappears in vigour, as in Solemn, Solemnity; Condemn, Condemnable; most of [illegible] Salem, Condemn, as the opposite of improvement. One [illegible] reveres his native English may well feel indignation, [illegible] who shrink from enunciating initial K, G, P in the com- [illegible] /Gn, Ps, as harsh,—at the same time, by clipping or [illegible] our vowels, crowd our consonants into unpronounceable [illegible] Who first made *diddest*, *hoddest* into didst, hadst, we [illegible] In Shakespeare the ending *ation* makes three syllables [illegible]. Poets, whose task is to develop and conserve melody, [illegible] seem rather to have studied to cram words and thought [illegible] smallest possible compass, and thus (perhaps!) to make poetry [illegible]phy. Whenever two vowels come together, they must (forsooth) [illegible] their belonging to different syllables. Thus *-tion* became *-shun* [illegible]ance; Chariot, Warrior, became two syllables instead of three, [illegible] Heaven, Tower, Power, &c., were clipped into monosyllables. In [illegible]hood I used to hear from modest, unlearned, but not unrefined [illegible] in Hampshire such plurals as Birdis, Nestis, Houndis, according [illegible] the old melodious principle which forbids great agglomeration of [illegible]. If we can manage to utter Nests, Breasts, Sixths, it is [illegible] to complain of initial Kn, Ps, as hard. The Germans say [illegible] Sonne, the sun; Mein Sohn, my son: we, by shortening the vowel [illegible] Sohn corrupt Sun and Son into one sound. Our poets bear a strong responsibility for much of this depravation. Nay, some of them, not unadmired, write as if aiming to get into one syllable as much as possible, as, viewst for viĕwĕst, rigidst for rigidest, and a hundred of other examples; whereby they produce a lumbering jumble of consonants comparable to those of some old Latin tragedian. If we are to fix the language now, let us first define its noblest and least unmelodious state, and not assume that every depravation is to be acquiesced in as a κτῆμα ἐς ἀεί.

If in this generation we protest in favour of a right pronunciation, and schools do their duty, the next generation will grow up with *a new ideal.* The defective utterance will gradually be thought vulgar, and it will become possible, without diverting attention injuriously from the matter to the manner, to pronounce rightly upon all high occasions. That is the proper way of healing the discord between our literature and our speech, *whenever the former is wholly right and the [illegible] wholly wrong.* The argument applies even to initial Wr. The [illegible] was certainly once sounded. It is more difficult to be heard than [illegible] K, the G, or the P just discussed; therefore, no doubt, it insensibly [illegible] out *of use.* In Dutch and Scandinavian the Wr becomes Vr, [illegible] is as well heard as Fr. If we seriously tried to utter the [illegible] Wry, Writhe, Write, &c., *probably* either Vr or Hr would be the [illegible] result. Just so, in ancient Greek, when the old digamma [illegible] before an ρ, in few dialects could it stand. It either vanished [illegible] (V?) or was converted into the aspirate (H): thus [illegible]. The root Ϝριχ (Sanscrit, Vrih), according to

Benfei, "to roar," generated *βρύχω*. It is also possible that the effort to sound W before *r* would introduce a furtive vowel, as in Worite, Worý, Worénch, Worést.

The words just written down show the immense importance of the stress accent. In the Greek language, each dialect having strictly conformed its orthography to its local pronunciation, nothing more was needed after the Macedonian conquest of Western Asia to facilitate the use of Greek to Asiatics, than the adding of accents,—*three* indeed, the distinction of which is lost to the modern Greeks. To Indians and others who try to learn English from a book, the information concerning our accent can hardly be given in grammars, since it is matter of detail, and to consult the dictionary for every word separately is most laborious. Practically no one can so learn; every one must have an oral teacher, until grammars are written in Indian languages for learners in English, and accent the English words. But it would be a great assistance to have the right accent printed in all the English pieces set before them, at least on polysyllables. How unintelligible do words become with the accent misplaced; as Capáble, Tabérnacle, Penultíma, Modérate, Bravéry! But even dissyllables sometimes change their sense with the accent, and contrast a verb with a noun. I have no complete list of such, nor is usage quite uniform with some words. The following are a specimen:—

| *Verb.* | *Noun.* | *Verb.* | *Noun.* | *Verb.* | *Noun.* |
|---|---|---|---|---|---|
| insúlt | ínsult | objéct | óbject | detaíl | détail |
| accént | áccent | colléct | cóllect | convért | cónvert |
| desért | désert | ejéct | éject | commúne | cómmune |
| transpórt | tránsport | digést | dígest | defíle | défile |
| condúct | cónduct | incréase | íncrease | prodúce | próduce |
| refúse | réfuse | ally′ | álly (′) | prefíx | préfix |
| subjéct | súbject | perfúme | pérfume | suffíx | súffix |

*Not unlike are* preténd, prétext; compóse, cómpost.

More peculiar is it that to Móderate (*verb*) has a secondary accent on the last syllable, and its *a* is long (German ä), while Móderate (*adjective*) has no secondary accent on the last, and the *a* is, in consequence, almost an *e* (móderet), nearly as the *a* in O′range (Orenj).

In numerous cases the accent has been thrown back in this century from the penultima to the antepenultima, or even to the fourth syllable from the end, against all law of Greek and Latin euphony, and generally with damage to the sound. In my early childhood I learned to say Indústry (as Indústrious) and Contráry (as Contrárious), and was surprised to be afterwards told that In′dustry, Cóntrary were [illegible] correct. (The Nursery Rhyme has—"Mary, Mary! quite contráry," [illegible] Alexánder was the first pronunciation, which ere long changed (
for the worse) into A′lexander, reversing the [illegible]
accent. Accéptable, Accéssary, have been [illegible]

... Parliamentary into Párliamentary, monstrously throw-
... on to the fifth syllable from the end. Contémplate,
... have been changed to Cóntemplate, I'llustrate, perhaps to
... some versifier; Medicinal to Medicinal, much for the
... It is remarkable that the tendency appeared in Athens, about
... Pericles. The melodious τροπαῖον, ὁμοῖος were changed to
... ὅμοιος. But plenty of old-fashioned people among us
... against throwing the accent farther back than the antepen-
... of these words; indeed insist on retaining Contémplate,
... Desirous and Sonōrous stand firm against their rivals Décor-
... Sónorous, which I believe are going out. Decádence has of
... supplanted by Décădence, imported from France; rhymesters
... prefer Décadence; but perhaps the verb Decáy will keep
..., aided also by the noun Cadence. The time may shortly
... when a middle class well educated from books, and not reared
... trail of aristocratic pronunciation, will restore to the language
... better accentuation and add to our long vowels. Already they
... on saying Opposite, Maritime, Dȳnasty. Before long they
... give us Medicīne, Infinīte, and Literāry instead of the obscure
... We cannot fix the language: but it would be something
if we could guide the movement aright. The foreigner needs to be
informed that in words of Greek and Latin origin the accent shifts
by a law of its own; as in Démocrat, Demócracy; Hármony, Harmó-
nious; Mélody, Melódious; expressly that it may *not* be thrown further
back than the antepenultima. There is also a frequent tendency to
shorten in a trisyllable the vowel which was long in a monosyllable; as
Grāve, Grăvity; Cāve, Căvity; Suāve, Suăvity; but this rule will mislead us, if applied to Saxon words, as appears in Brāve, Brăvery. For
this and very many reasons the pupil, especially the foreign learner,
requires a text in which the length and quality of vowels is marked.
How deceptive are Fīnīte and I'nfinite! Divīne an iamb with accent
on the last; Fīnīte, a pure spondee, accented on the first. If Direct is
known to be an oxytone, the doubt remains whether it be an iamb or
a spondee. In fact this is not at the speaker's will; though preva-
lently perhaps the adjective Dīrect is a spondee, and the verb Direct
... has *i* short. It is easy so to mark our vowels as to set all these
... at rest in that part of our language which is derived from Latin
... Greek. It is the Saxo-Norman portion which contains the words
... so capriciously written as to puzzle us, even when we
... throw the fault on pronunciation changing with lapse of time.
... are the greatest vexation. Final *e* mute is held not
... because it lengthens the vowel next preceding it,
... between Pan and Panė; the latter being = Pän.
... apt to be obtruded out of place, where it only
... dozen words in which (seemingly) *e* ought
... to Live, Love, Glove, Shove, Dove;

Shone, Bade, Sate, Ate. In the three first I advise its omission, also in all verbal adjectives from Latin -ivus, as Activ, Plaintiv, Fugitiv. A properly dotted *o* sets right the four next words; the four last are antiquated forms,—what may be called first aorist, co-existing with the more popular second aorist, Shon, Bad, Sat, Et.

With a simple mark to denote that a letter is mute* (say a compact little mathematical zero), our worst difficulties of notation vanish. The cedilla and the Greek aspirate, to modify consonants, remove a large number of uncertainties concerning consonantal sounds. How to mark S when it has the sound of Z is difficult, only because there are so many solutions. Here let the remark be dropt, that the dot on *i* and *j* ought to be removed from print. Neither is found with the capital letters I and J. With *j* the dot is useless even in MS. In hand-writing the loop of *e* is apt to blot, which leads to writing *e* almost like *i*; therefore alone a dot is of use even in MS. All useless dots dull the eye to the perception of useful ones, and ought to be cleared off. Reserving (′) to denote the stress accent, we at once have at our disposal for modified vowels, ä ë ï ö ü; à è ì ò ù; â ê î ô û, of which some are superfluous, *viz.*, ì ù; indeed ê is wanted for three English words only, *viz.*, brêak, grêat, stêak, sounded as brake, grate, stake, from which they differ in sense. Nevertheless this triple row of vowels is not sufficient, unless we largely alter our received spelling. I want double dots under a e o u (a̤ e̤ o̤ ṳ).

Thus armed, we can make our received orthography suggest to a learner precisely the right sounds, with very few and insignificant exceptions which perhaps ought to be summarily dealt with.

Here may be noticed a very few words in which the spoken tongue may vaunt itself as more discriminating than our manuscript. But a few marks added will give equal precision to the latter.

Böw, of an archer or of a shoe-tie; Bow, bend the head.

To Söw (seed); Sow, female pig.

To Röw (a boat); Row (ignoble word), tumult.

Döes, female deer; Does, doeth.

To Möw (grass); a Barley Mow, rick, stack.

Any other such ambiguities can by easy devices be removed.

The problem of teaching the foreigner or the child to read correctly a book set before him is but *half* the problem of Phonotype. It is complex enough in our received mode of writing, yet with a sufficiency of well-devised marks, it can be solved; and may be made simpler by very moderate correction, also without disfiguring the text, especially if by slight change we revert to better pronunciation. To solve this half of the problem would be of immense importance, and in my judgment ought not to be delayed. To solve the other half would be so to write and print that he who hears the sounds of our

* But *g* is certainly wrong in Foreign, Sovereign, and may perhaps be well dropt also in Feign and Deign. The *t* can well be spared in -tch.

tongue shall at once be able to write them down from his ear in the very way which we hold to be orthographic. This would require a total reconstruction of the written language. To attempt it I account to be irrational, and believe all effort for it to be a misdirection of energies which might otherwise be of avail: moreover, such effort damages the hope of attainable reform, inasmuch as it stirs up disgust against all change. But there is a remark, not yet made, which may bear usefully on a large class of words.

The Phonotypists make very light of diligently confounding Rain, Rein, Reign, under a single spelling (and this is but one example out of 200), arguing that we could well endure *Rane* as expressing all three, because in every language words have many ambiguities. For instance, Box means: 1. A certain shrub or tree; 2. A coffer made of boxwood, and hence, any wooden coffer; 3. A blow on the cheek; 4. A *bakhshiesh*, or small gift at Christmas. What hardship, then, would it be if *Rane* had three very different senses? The reply is, that if we could write the sound Box in four different ways answering to the four different senses, it would facilitate the learning of English. Suppose that we wrote—1. Bocs; 2. Boks; 3. Box; 4. Bokhs, sounding all alike, the pupil would at once be warned of four different senses, and would *the better remember them* by reason of the different writing, which acts as a *memoria technica*. Also, inasmuch as bad reasoning chiefly rises out of ambiguous words, nothing so aids accurate thought as accurate marks of distinction. If it were possible, we ought to remove ambiguities both to the ear and to the eye; or at least to the eye, if we cannot to the ear. But we are unable thus to create distinctions at will. Surely, then, when tradition itself freely gives us in certain words distinctions for which we vainly wish in others, it were great folly to throw away the advantage. This would be a *levelling down*, and not a *levelling up*.

Finally, to fix ideas, I briefly explain one vowel system which would be efficient and sufficient. I say *one* system; for there are, of course, many possible, and in twenty-five years' effort I have changed my mind often enough.

1. System of circumflexed vowels:

   â, âll fâll fâlcon âltar âlter wâter wâr wârd.
   ê, *only in* brêak grêat stêak.
   î (French *i* long), marine machîne suite.
   ô, môve tômb shôe.
   û (Italian long *u*), rûe rûle blûe roûte.

2. System of grave accents:

   à (Italian broad *a*), tàsk fàther fàst.
   ò, òrder òft lòft lòst. (è ì ù are in general superfluous.)

3. System of double dots *above* the vowel:

ä, mäne ängel chämber dänger cäpable sävour, *to* moderäte.
ë, lëver ëvil këy concëit wëir hëar tëar ëqual.
ï, sïgh tïe lïe whïlom ïron sïnecure divïne.
ö, böne böld öld öar möw töw gö.
ü, ünite mule türeen valüe nätüre.

These might, with excellent result, be printed in *all* our literature.

4. System of double dots beneath the vowels:

a̤ (after W or Qu), wa̤sp wa̤s wa̤tch qua̤rrel ëqua̤l.
e̤ he̤ad ple̤asure. (Better to drop *a* in seventy words.)
o̤, so̤n to̤n co̤ver co̤vet wo̤rry o̤nion fro̤nt.
ṳ, pṳt pṳsh pṳll bṳshel bṳtcher bulwark.

5. Long ā and ē (only before *r*), as in Māre, Thēre.

Besides the omission of *a* in about seventy words, such as Deaf, Dead, Dreamt, Early, &c., the *u* should be dropt in Honour, Favour, &c. No one approves *u* in Rector, Editor, Tutor, &c. To printers, writers, and learners, all really superfluous letters are an annoyance. Happily we have got rid of *k* in Publick, Musick, &c. For One, Once, I propose to write 'o̤ne, 'o̤nce.

Many have suggested marks for our consonants. Webster's Dictionary has a complete system, and many others would succeed. The practical question is, Which least offends the eye, and will meet least opposition? It is not requisite here to lay before the reader what most pleases the present writer. Suffice it to insist that the problem has more than one good solution.

F. W. Newman.

# THE FUTURE OF FAITH.

*"Son of man, can these bones live?"*

"MEN die of many diseases; creeds of only one: that of being found out." Such is a recent utterance of Mr. Leslie Stephen's; and it has naturally a special reference to the Christian creed in particular. The sentence is a remarkable one, though not for its intrinsic merits. Judged by these, it is manifestly but a terse untruth. Creeds of course may in some cases die of detection; but detection is not the only, nor is it the chief, thing that is fatal to them. Often they are left to die, just as many women are, not for any falsehood that has been found out in them, but for some greater attraction that has been found out in a rival. They have been superseded, forgotten, and abandoned; they have not been detected. But Mr. Stephen's sentence, if not remarkable for the truth of what it tells us about creeds, is remarkable for the truth with which it represents to us a certain tone of mind with regard to them. And looked on in this light, it is well worth attention. For this tone of mind is essentially the modern tone; it is the special tone of to-day. It may not yet be dominant; perhaps it never will be; but at the present moment it is at any rate tending to become so. It is the tone that is the supposed result of a clear view of things, moral and scientific; and it professes to be luminous with the high and dry light of the intellect. Mr. Stephen's sentence shows us its main characteristics. The first is the assumption that all creeds (that is, all definite assertions as to things beyond the reach of experience) are impostures. There is something knavish in them; there is something hostile. The human race has to *find them out*. The second is the assumption that this process of finding out is on the eve of completion. The winking virgin is cut open, and all who have eyes sharp enough can peep in and see the machinery. The third characteristic is the feeling that our antagonist being thus utterly prostrate, thus utterly past making the least resistance, it may be insulted safely by any shallow falsehood that can give point to an epigram.

Such, or something such, is the modern tone in its pure state; a tone of confident and supercilious animosity, that is gradually dying into triumph. It is true that this leaven in its full bitterness is to be found only in a narrow circle; but flavours of it, more or less diluted, meet us far and wide. Indeed, it is difficult to find any place where they are not traceable. There is doubtless much definite religion left around us, and many firm believers. But the modern tone has its influence even on these. Religion must be changed in some ways by the neighbourhood of irreligion. If it is persecuted, it may burn up with a greater fervour; but if it is not persecuted, it must in a certain way be chilled. Believers and unbelievers, separated as they are by their tenets, are yet in these days mixed together in all the acts and relations of life. They are united by habits, by blood, and by friendship; and they are each accustomed to ignore or to excuse what they hold to be the errors of the other. In a state of things like this, it is plain that the conviction of believers can neither have the fierce intensity found in a minority under persecution, nor the placid confidence that belongs to an overwhelming majority. They can neither hate the unbelievers, for they daily live in amity with them; nor despise altogether their judgment, for the most eminent thinkers of the day belong to them. The believers are forced into a sort of compromise, which is a new feature in their history. They see that the age is against them; and yet they are obliged to make excuses for their enemy. This enemy denies daily all that they hold most sacred, and most surely true. Yet the utmost they can do is to talk patiently with it. They can neither call it absurd nor wicked. By such conditions as these, even the strongest faith cannot fail to be affected. It may not lose its firmness, but it must lose something of its fervour; and it is a significant fact that even men who most devoutly believe in God would smile at the simplicity of any one who should presume, in a mixed company, that His existence would be taken as an axiom.

If the modern tone has thus affected even those who are most opposed to it, what must not be its effect upon those who have, in part of their own free will, adopted it? And these form to-day a great mass of our educated public. A large number of these still call themselves Protestants; and were the matter to be treated lightly, they might afford countless studies for the humorist. The state to which they have reduced their religion is indeed a curious one. With a facile eclecticism that is based on no principle, and that changes from year to year, or more probably from mood to mood, they pick and choose their doctrines, saying. "I keep this and I reject this," in some such manner as the following: "Of course, the Apostles' Creed is true: and of course the Athanasian Creed is false. And then, after all, suppose neither is true, the meaning of the thing is the real heart of

Such is the Protestant language of to-day; nor is it ...foolish or of ignorant people; it is the language of ...men who have much to do, and of countless clever ...have nothing to do. The actual value of such faith as this ...is very often and very easily tested. A great sorrow ...great temptation comes. At once the tone of to-day grows ...ed, and a new set of arguments suggest themselves ...singular readiness. "God is not good, or He would never have ...of so good a husband;" or, "God is not good, or He would ...have let me marry such a bad one." And then follows, as a ...lary to these propositions, "God is nothing if not good, and there- ...here is no God at all." Or the syllogism, especially in the feminine ..., takes not uncommonly some such form as this: "If there was a ...He would put me into hell for being in love with so and so; but ...certain in my own mind that I do not deserve hell: therefore I ...ertain in my own mind that there can be no God to put me ..." In former times, when such thoughts occurred to men, the ...weight of the world's opinion was always ready to condemn ...as vain and wicked. But now the case is just reversed. How- ...foolish may be the actual conduct of such reasoning, the opinion ...e enlightened world is ready to corroborate the conclusion.

...ain, beyond this circle there is a probably far larger one. It is ...up of men who are in suspense altogether. They see much to ...e and to regret in Christianity, but they make no pretence of be- ...g in its details. They do not even think them worth arguing ...st. Much of the Christian spirit they may perhaps still cherish, ...ope that in time it will again rule the world. But it must take, ...hink, a quite new shape,—it must free itself of its old associations; ...h what its new shape will be they can probably not even ...ecture.

...d lastly, there are the extreme destroyers, who would break alto- ...r with the past; and who, though probably wishing to retain some ...emotions that were once directed to God and to heaven, would ...them an entirely different object in the shape of humanity, and ...l never suffer them to wander from the earth's surface.

...ch are the various parties that the world of thought now shows to ...There is a small body who cling heart and soul to the past; ...is a small body that would utterly break with the past; and ...een them is a vast and varied crowd, tinged in various proportions ...the colours of each extreme. And amongst them all there is a con- ...arguing, and anxiety, and perplexity. But meanwhile it cannot be ...ed that the modern tone is spreading. To all except a small mino- ...ith, in the old sense of the word, is growing a cold and shadowy ... The dogmas, the services, the ministers of the Church, are ...all of them to have a belated look for us. They seem out of ...in the busy world around us. Ever and again we hear of a new

Catholic miracle; and the fame of some new pilgrimage. And the strange effect that these things have on us shows us how far our minds have travelled. Do such things still exist? we ask in surprise and irritation: and we set them down as "the grimacings of a dead superstition," galvanized into a ghastly imitation of life. And then from the modern miracles the mind goes back to the older ones, once held so sacred and so certain. And they, too, have undergone a change for us. Not only are Lourdes and Paray-le-Monial contemptible, but Calvary is disenchanted. There may have been a death there, but there was never a sacrifice. Scales have fallen from our eyes. We see it all clearly. The creed we were brought up in is an earthly myth; not a heavenly revelation. We know exactly whence it came; and we see pretty certainly whither it is going. The signs of it still survive; but they signify nothing. They will soon be swept away, and will make place, we hope earnestly, for something better.

Some feel all this with regret and doubt; others with triumph and expectation. At any rate in their various ways, the great body of men feel it. The old conception of things is supposed to be dead and done with.

The question which I wish to discuss calmly is, how far this supposition is well founded; how far it results from actual proof and reasoning: and how far it represents a mere mood of the world's feeling. Christianity is at present prostrate. But it may possibly be only stunned with the noise of the powder, and not pierced by the ball. We should try to clear away the smoke a little, and see more clearly what is the real state of the case. We should examine carefully the fallen body, to see if any wounds are to be found upon it: and if so, whether these wounds are mortal. The actual truth of Christianity I have no wish to discuss; but the prospects merely of its again recovering power, and, whether true or not, being accepted as true by humanity. This is an inquiry that, in the interest of all parties, should be made more calmly than it has been hitherto. Supposing, on examining it more closely, we are led to think that Christianity has more life left in it than it seems to have, those who long for a God (and there are about us many such) may be glad to hope that their children may again find Him, though they themselves most likely never will. To those on the other hand who hate a God, and who look on the idea of Him as a sort of paper hawk, flown above the world to keep down humanity, it will be of some interest to see whether, to change the metaphor, they have scotched the snake or killed it; so that, if the former be the case, they may repeat their blow. For it is quite possible that we may assure ourselves too soon of the result of the great struggle; and a fate fo [illegible] present opinions may be [illegible] gested by that of the Eastern con [illegible] was surveyi [illegible] evening, the field of [illegible] 's vict [illegible] lenly a [illegible] sprang up and stab [illegible]

To begin then, let us first briefly take stock of the various ways in which thought and knowledge, as they now stand, are supposed to have discredited Christianity. These will be seen to divide themselves into two main sets of objections. The one set is *à priori*, and is opposed to all religion, natural as well as revealed; the other set is *à posteriori*, and is opposed to revealed religion only. Of both sets, some are old and some are new; but modern knowledge has much to do with all of them. It is supposed to have strengthened the old objections, as well as to have raised the new. I shall try to estimate both at their present, and their extremest strength.

Analyzed, and summed up briefly, they may be thus stated:—

In the first place it is said that modern physical science can explain the universe without the hypothesis of a God. It thus reduces Him to a superfluity. We can find nothing in nature that so much as suggests Him to us. And the same too may be said of a future life. Nor is this all. There is a deeper objection yet. God is nothing if not good; He is nothing if not omnipotent. No one would care to be the prophet of a bad or a feeble deity. How then can evil, how can misery exist, if a Being has anything to do with the world whose only wish is for its good, and who has but to wish a thing to accomplish it? Thus, then, the *à priori* objections to all religion amount to this. The existence of God is a superfluous premiss; and it leads to impossible and self-contradictory conclusions.

These primary objections are of necessity somewhat vague. But when we pass from religion in general to the Christian religion in particular, from a spontaneous faith to a definite revelation, many more points of attack present themselves; and these in general are far more easy to realize. For a Revelation must have a history; it cannot have passed through the world without leaving footprints behind it; and these are open to examination. Modern historical science professes to have examined them, and to have found about them nothing that is superhuman. And not only is Christianity thus assailed by history, but physical science and the moral sense are busy against it too: the one disproving its miracles, the other discrediting some of its main doctrines.

Such are the forces and the objections that now assail religion, and that, in the opinions of many, have been already fatal to it. I will now proceed to examine them, something in the above order, and will try to estimate fairly what lasting force there is in them.

To begin, then, with the *à priori* objections above mentioned, what has physical science really done to destroy our belief in a God, or an intelligent first cause of things? Let us not under-estimate the new facts it has revealed to us, or the force of its magical touch, at which [illegible] whole view of nature has expanded. It has shown law and [illegible] surrounding us on every side; it has traced their common [illegible] the darkest and least accessible places. For the most mysterious phenomena it has discovered the most homely parentage. What once seemed to be special acts of God, resolve themselves into inevitable combinations of unchanging laws. The animate and inanimate world seems all to point to one common origin, and to have grown from it without break and without disorder. The more we study nature, the more hopeless does it seem to discern in it any trace of the supernatural; and the traditional proofs of God's existence, and of His daily providence, keep falling momentarily about us, like so many dead flies. But what is the real result of all this? The old difficulty is still unsolved. It is only pushed further back. When we get to the primal material from which all we see has evolved itself, what do we know of that? what can we say of that? It is true that many of our modern men of science endow matter with eternity and automatism, and deny the necessity of any external and forming cause. But this is assumption only: it is not proof. In this matter there can be no experience, and no verification, of the kind that science demands. The question is one of logic and of metaphysics; and it is daily becoming plainer that metaphysics is the sea to which all physics in the end must bring us. As we travel far and farther backwards in the history of matter, the character of the inquiry insensibly changes around us; and, often unperceived by themselves, the confidence of our physicists begins to fail them in those blank and silent regions. Such words as first and final cause, they stammer in uttering. Their voice may be loud enough, but its sound seems to bewilder them; and they seem doubtful what they themselves have said. They talk much of space and of time; but as a rule they can give no account of their notions of either. They talk much of doubt and of certainty; but what they really mean by knowledge they are quite unable to tell us. They are like men who have followed a line of light, through countless difficult and seemingly impassable places, in the hope of tracking it to some self-luminous source; but who, after a certain point, find it growing dimmer and dimmer, till at last they discover that it vanishes into a dark cavern. Of what is concealed in the darkness they know nothing. No method of theirs can fathom it, or can say whether it is full or empty. All that physical science can say of a God is that it can find no trace of Him; though possibly, when the logical opinions of the world become more settled, it may discover that His existence is a necessary postulate. But at the worst, so far as proof or reasoning goes, it can but leave the matter doubtful. And the same, too, is the case with a future life. Science cannot disprove that; it can only say that it can show us no ground for expecting it.

The moral difficulty that arises from the presence of evil is more positive. As we look at the condition of the world around us, the argument seems to be completely unassailable, that, if there be a God, He cannot be good, or else He cannot be omnipotent. Nor does any one really hold it possible to escape from this dilemma, by any doctrine of seeming or partial evil, conducing in reality to the general good. Such theories for the most part have had no thinkable meaning: and even at their best they could but justify pain; they could not justify vice. If virtue be the supreme good that any moral system assumes it to be, then it is an unmixed evil that any human being should not be virtuous. We have in vice an eternal blemish, an eternal discord that is not to be hid or silenced; and reason can never reconcile it with God's power, or, what is morally the same thing, with God's existence. But if, for this reason, we get rid of the notion of God, do we at all escape our difficulty? Do we arrive at a more satisfactory view of the world? Not in the least. The same difficulty confronts us, only in a slightly altered shape. The very moment we discern between good and evil, it is there. It is found dogging our moral sense, like a shadow. We cannot conceive the existence of good without being utterly bewildered by the existence of evil. For good, as we conceive it, is not the best thing only, but the strongest and most enduring also. And thus when we find it perpetually being marred by evil, the sight the mind is called to contemplate is something that in its very nature seems to be impossible; it is the sight of supreme strength being thwarted by what is not supreme strength—the eternal in the toils of the transitory. In striking the balance, then, between any views of life that give man any moral dignity, and his existence any serious meaning, we must remember that this difficulty is common to all of them, not to theism only; and that therefore it is practically a factor that is to be cancelled out. It is a knot we must all agree to cut; for it is certain that it can be untied by none of us.

The *à priori* objection to religion, then, amounts logically to no more than this. The moral objections must be set deliberately aside by all except the most despairing pessimists. The scientific objections consist of a destruction of a number of what were once thought proofs; but they supply us with nothing that even approaches to a disproof. But though, logically, modern thought can only leave us in doubt, yet practically it can affect us in another and more powerful way. Though it cannot convince the intellect, it can paralyze the imagination. I shall speak of this again by-and-by. But I pause for a moment to note one most fruitful source of error—that is, the confusion of the logical certainty that a thing does not exist, with an inability of the imagination to picture it as existing. And it may on the whole be safely said, that if, from the friction of some unlooked-for catastrophe, or the unlooked-for production of some new theistic evidence, the religious imagination of men should once again take fire, they would find nothing in all that modern science can prove to them to hinder their instant adoption of the most fervent natural theism. Their faith, they would find, had not been dead but sleeping. It had taken a narcotic only, and not a poison.

But though this may be the case with a merely natural theism, with religion (that is) unencumbered with any doubtful history, it by no means follows that the same will hold good of Christianity. Against this the boasts of knowledge are more formidable. It could merely make good, in the former case, that it was powerless to prove. Here it loudly claims that it is powerful to disprove. It simply succeeded in not finding the natural God; it professes, as Mr. Stephen puts it, to have "found out" the revealed one. And the boast has every appearance of being well founded. Christianity is not a thing to be judged *à priori* only. It is closely bound up with a long earthly history, which it has itself written in one way, binding itself to stand or fall by the truth of it; and this all the secular wisdom of the world is re-writing in quite another. The new view is sustained by two different lines of study. One is a critical examination of Christianity, taken by itself—its sacred books, and the growth of its doctrines. The other is a critical examination of Christianity as compared with other religions. And the result of both these lines of study is, to those brought up in the old faith, in the last degree startling, and, in appearance at least, altogether disastrous.

Let us but glance, to begin with, at what criticism has accomplished on the Bible. The Biblical account of the creation it has shown to be an impossible fable. To many of the sacred books it has assigned new dates and origins. To passages thought prophetic it has given the most homely meanings. Everywhere at its touch all that seemed supernatural has become humanized. The divinity that hedged the records has rapidly abandoned them. And now, looked at in the common daylight, and judged by a common standard, stories that we once accepted with a solemn reverence, seem childish, ridiculous, and grotesque, and not unfrequently barbarous. To put the case in the mildest form, this at least has been sufficiently established, that the Bible, if it does not give the lie itself to the astonishing claims that have been made for it, contains nothing, at any rate, that can really avail to support them. This applies to the New Testament just as much as to the Old. And the consequences are here even more momentous. Weighed as mere human testimony, the value of the Gospels becomes doubtful or insignificant. For the miracles of Christ, and for his superhuman nature, they can bring no evidence, that even tends to be satisfactory; and even his daily words and actions it seems probable may have been inaccurately reported, in some cases perhaps invented; and in others supplied by a deceiving memory. When we pass from the Gospels to the Epistles, a kindred sight presents itself. We discern in them the writings of men not inspired from above; but, with many disagreements amongst themselves, struggling upwards from below, influenced by a variety of existing views, and doubtful which of them to assimilate. We discern in them, as we do in other writers, the products of their age and of [illegible]. The materials of which they formed their doctrine, [illegible] the world around them. And as we follow the Church's [illegible] and examine her great dogmas, as they grow more [illegible] articulate, we shall be able to trace all of them to a [illegible] religion. We shall see how, in part at least, men conceived [illegible] the Trinity from the teachings of Greek Mysticism; and [illegible] idea of the Atonement was shaped by ideas of Roman Juris- [illegible]. Everywhere, in fact, in the holy building supposed to [illegible] come down from God, we discern fragments of older structures, [illegible] of earthly workmanship.

[illegible] the matter does not end here. Historical science not only [illegible] our own religion in this new light, but it sets other religions [illegible] side of it, and shows us that their course through the world [illegible] precisely similar. They, too, have their sacred books, and [illegible] superhuman prophets; their priesthoods, and their traditions, [illegible] their growing bodies of doctrine; there is nothing in Christianity [illegible] cannot find its counterpart. All have sprung, it seems, from a [illegible] and an earthly root, though some of the branches may have [illegible] large and fruitful, and their leaves for the healing of the nations, [illegible] others weak or barren. And thus another blow has been dealt to a faith that has been already weakened. Not only can our religion not prove itself in any supernatural sense to be sacred, but even in a natural sense it has been proved not to be singular. It has not come down from heaven: it is not alone even in its attempt to rise to it.

Such are the broad conclusions which in these days seem to be [illegible] upon us, and which knowledge, as it widens on every side, would seem to be daily strengthening. But are they altogether of necessity so destructive as they seem? Many of us have, doubtless, been confounded as our eyes have first been opened to these *diræ facies*. We have felt much as Æneas felt:

> "Tum vero omne mihi visum considere in ignes
> Ilium."

[illegible]

[illegible] if we are determined to find it, is there no loophole left through [illegible] we may escape, even though it be so as by fire, and carry the [illegible] treasure with us?

[illegible] look on Christianity in what is commonly considered as its [illegible] rational form, to this question I think we must certainly answer [illegible] Christianity relies for support on the external evidence of its [illegible] never again hope to convince men. These supports are [illegible] inadequate to the weight that is put upon them. [illegible] possibly serve as props, but they crash and crumble [illegible] used as pillars. And it is as pillars that the [illegible] Christianity uses them. It will be enough in this [illegible] attention to the Bible, and consider the weight that Protestantism lays on that. There, it says, is the Word of God; there is my infallible guide: I listen to none but that. It is my first axiom that the Bible is infallible; and granting that, history teaches me that all other Churches are fallible. On the Bible, and the Bible only, I rest myself. Out of its mouth shall you judge me. And for a long time this language had much force in it, for the Protestant axiom was received by all parties. It is true that it might be hard to decide what God's Word meant; but still every one admitted that God's Word was there, and it at any rate meant something. But now all this is changed. The great axiom is received no longer. Many indeed consider it not an axiom, but an absurdity; at best it appears but as a very doubtful fact; and if external proof is to be what guides us, we shall need more proofs to convince us that the Bible is the Word of God, than that Protestantism is the religion of the Bible.

We need not pursue the matter farther, nor inquire how Protestantism will fare at the hands of Comparative Mythology. The blow dealt by Biblical criticism is to all appearance mortal; there is no need to look for another. Now in this country, at least, nearly all the ablest attacks upon supernatural religion have been directed against it as embodied in the Protestant form; and they have widely, and not unnaturally, been regarded as quite victorious. But it seems to escape the assailants that though they may have burnt the outworks, there is still a citadel inside, which, though it seems to them almost too contemptible to take account of, may yet not prove combustible, and when the conflagration outside has subsided, may still remain to annoy them. They forget altogether, I mean, the Church of Rome; nor do they seem to consider that, though for other causes she may perhaps be dying, yet many of their logical darts can do nothing to hasten her end.

This to many may be doubtless a distasteful consideration. But it is at this moment one of great importance; and whether we like it or no, we must look it fairly in the face.

We have glanced briefly at the chief points at which modern thought and science have assailed revealed religion. We have seen how vulnerable at these points Protestantism has proved. But we must observe that the Catholics have one characteristic which fundamentally separates them from the Protestants with respect to these. To its past history, and to external evidence, Protestantism bears one relation, Catholicism quite another.

Protestantism offers itself to the world as a strange servant might, bringing with it a number of written testimonials. It asks us to examine them, and by them to judge of its merits. It expressly begs us not to trust to its own word. "I cannot," it says, "rely upon my memory. It has failed me often; it may fail me again. But look at these testimonials in my favour, and judge me only by them." And the world looks at them, examines them carefully; it at last sees that they look suspicious, that they may very possibly be forgeries; it asks the Protestant Church to prove them genuine, and the Protestant Church cannot.

But Catholicism comes to us in an exactly opposite way. It too brings with it the very same testimonials; but it knows their apparent weakness, and it does not at first lay much stress on them. First, it asks us to make some acquaintance with it; to look into its living eyes, to hear the words of its mouth, to watch its ways and works, and to feel its inner spirit; and then it says to the world, "Can you trust me? If so you must trust me all in all, for the first thing I declare to you is that I have never lied. Can you trust me thus far? Then listen, and I will tell you my story. You have heard it told one way, I know; and that way often goes against me. I admit, myself, that it has many suspicious circumstances. But none of them positively condemn me. All are capable of a guiltless interpretation; and now you know me as I am, you will give me the benefit of every doubt." It is in this spirit that Catholicism offers us the Bible. "Believe the Bible for my sake," it says, "not me for the Bible's." And the book, as thus offered us, changes its whole character. We have not the formal testimonials of a stranger, but the intermittent memoranda of a friend. We have now that presumption in their favour, which in the other case was altogether lacking; and all that we ask of the records is, not that they contain any inherent evidence of their truth, but that they contain no inherent and conclusive evidence of their falsehood. There is this farther point to remember. Catholic and Protestant alike declare the Bible to be inspired; but the Catholics can afford to attach to *inspiration* a far wider and less assailable meaning; for their Church claims for herself a perpetual living power, which can always detect and concentrate the essence of the divine truth, be it never so diffused. And to a definite statement as to what inspiration is, the Roman Church, as a fact, has never yet committed herself. As Catholicism, then, stands at the present moment, it seems hard to say that, were we for any other reasons inclined to trust it, it makes any claim for the Bible that would absolutely prevent our doing so.

Let us now go farther, and consider its various doctrines, which, though it is claimed that they are all implied in the Bible, are confessedly not expressed in it, and were confessedly not consciously assented to by the Church till long after the sacred canon was closed. And here let us grant the extreme position of the Church's most hostile critics. Let us grant that all the doctrines in question can be traced to external and often to non-Christian sources. And what is the result on Romanism? Does this go any way whatever towards logically discrediting its claims? If we do but consider the matter fairly, we shall see that it does not even tend to do so. Here, as in the case of the Bible, the Roman doctrine of infallibility meets all objections. For the real question here is not in what storehouse of opinions the Church found its doctrines; but why it selected those it did, and why it rejected and condemned the rest? History cannot answer this. History can show us only who made the separate bricks; it cannot show us who made and designed the building. No one believes that the devil made the plans of Cologne Cathedral; but were we inclined to think he did, the story would not be in the least disproved by our discovering from what quarries every stone had been taken. And the doctrines of the Church are but as the stones in a building, the lettors of an alphabet, or the words of a language. Many are offered and few chosen. The supernatural action is to be detected in the choice. The whole history of the Church in fact, as she herself tells it, is a history of supernatural selection. It is quite possible that she may claim it to be more than that; but could she vindicate for herself but this one faculty of an infallible choice, she would vindicate to the full her claim to be under a superhuman guidance. The Church may be conceived of as a living organism, for ever and on all sides putting forth feelers and tentacles, that seize. try, and seem to dally with all kinds of nutriment. A part of this she at length takes into herself. A large part she at length puts down again. Much that is thus rejected she seems for a long time on the point of choosing. But however slow may be the final decision in coming, however reluctant or hesitating it may seem to be, when it is once made, it is claimed for it that it is infallible. And this claim when we once understand its nature, will be seen, I think, to be one that neither our knowledge of ecclesiastical history, or of comparative mythology, can invalidate now or even promise ever to do so. Nor is this last expectation in any way a rash one. The Church knows the difficulties that her past records present to us; especially that of the divine character of the Bible. But she knows too that this divinity is at present protected by its vagueness; nor is she likely to expose it more openly to its enemies, till some sure plan of defence has been devised for it. And here in passing is a singular fact to notice. Rigid as were the opinions entertained as to Biblical inspiration, throughout the greater part of the Church's history, the Church has never formally assumed them as articles of faith. Had she done so. she might indeed have been convicted of error, for many of these opinions are demonstrably at variance with fact. But though she lived and breathed for so many centuries amongst them, though for ages none of her members perhaps ever doubted their truth, she has not laid them on succeeding ages. She has left them opinions still. A Catholic might well adduce this as an instance, not indeed of supernatural selection, but of its counterpart, supernatural rejection. And now to turn from the past to the future, the possible future conduct of the Church in this matter will afford us a very luminous illustration of her past procedure. It may be that before the Church defines inspiration exactly (if she ever does so), she will wait till hostile criticism has done all it can do. The Church may then consider what views of [illegible] historically tenable, and what not; and may faithfully [illegible] by the learning of this world, though it may have [illegible] together for the express purpose of overthrowing her. [illegible] may be quoted in her councils; and supercilious and [illegible] philologists, could they live another hundred years, might [illegible] their discoveries, even their words and phrases, em[illegible] ecclesiastical definition. To the outer world such a [illegible] might seem to be a mere natural production. But in the [illegible] Catholic it would be as truly supernatural, as truly the work [illegible] Spirit, as if it had come down ready-made out of heaven, [illegible] the accompaniments of a rushing mighty wind, and of visible [illegible] of flame.

[illegible]us far we have seen only that the Catholic Church can still claim, [illegible]e face of all the new lights thrown on her history, to be sprung [illegible] a supernatural root. But it still may be, that when we come to [illegible]ct them in detail, she will be found to be betrayed by her fruits. [illegible] primary dogmas, and her general sacred character, we may be [illegible]ng at first to concede to her; but there may be numberless deduc[illegible] from them, and indirect consequences, that revolt our common [illegible] and our moral sense, though we have no exact means of dis[illegible]ing them. And such difficulties undoubtedly do exist. But if [illegible]xamine them carefully, many, at least, will be found to rest upon [illegible]ceptions.

[illegible] consider those first which are of this nature. There are some [illegible] are not explained away so easily; and I will keep these till last.

[illegible] begin, then, it is commonly urged against Catholicism, that it [illegible]s salvation depend on our assenting to a number of obscure pro[illegible]ions, to which it is hard for any man to attach a meaning, and for [illegible] men quite impossible. But in the first place, the number of points [illegible] are actual dogmas are far fewer than is commonly supposed; [illegible] in the next place, it is by no means required that even these be [illegible] comprehended by all. No Catholic teacher, for instance, ever [illegible]osed that a peasant, or even a busy politician, should be able to [illegible] such matters as *ousia* and *hypostasis*, or that they should know [illegible] enough philosophy to discriminate accurately between accident and [illegible]ance. The truth seems to be that few outside the Roman Church [illegible] fully the way in which that Church regards her dogmas. They [illegible]ardly understand that she regards them as statements of objective [illegible] which have an infinite number of sides and bearings, and which [illegible] an order of things as yet only partly known to us; and that [illegible] part of these facts, with great profit to ourselves, with[illegible] others on which these of necessity depend, and without [illegible] these save under their simplest aspect. Theology is to [illegible] what anatomy and medicine are to the human body. It [illegible] utmost importance to the world in general that doctors [illegible] should arrive at right conclusions with regard to the subtlest and most complex questions, incomprehensible to any except specialists; but the world in general may learn from them the practical rules of health, and yet know little or nothing of the hidden facts which these rules imply or are founded on. To say, then, as has often been said, that Catholicism makes salvation depend on the "balancing the mind on an intellectual tight-rope," is about as true as to say that anatomy and medicine make health depend on the accuracy with which a man can draw the human skeleton, or explain the action of a pill.

Again, the intricacies of Catholic ritual seem to many to be integral parts of the Church's mystical body, and salvation not to hang only on an assent to occult propositions of philosophy, but upon altar-candles, and the coloured clothes of priests. This is the external view, and it has been adopted by our English ritualists. But the Catholic Church views these things in a very different light. To her they are things by the way. They are, as it were, the natural flush on a cheek, that comes of natural exercise. But no simile must be ridden to death. We cannot follow out this analogy, and allow each congregation to express its feelings as it pleases. A rule more or less definite has had to be introduced, enjoined by the Church, and enforced by her authority. And thus in these days it might well be a deadly sin for a priest to celebrate Mass without lighted candles on the altar. But would this prove that the presence of God depended on the lighting of a candle? Not so. The candles are not essential, but obedience is. If such writers as Professor Huxley would consider the matter in this light, they would see reason, I think, to moderate their usual tone. Professor Huxley speaks of the God of dogmatic theology as "a sort of pedantic drill-sergeant of mankind, to whom no valour, no long-tried loyalty, could atone for the misplacement of a button of the uniform." The answer to which is, that the misplacement of the button might itself be no great harm, but that the soldier had no business to be meddling with the buttons at all. Such an act, though it might prove nothing against the soldier's valour, would betray germs of insubordination, which might develop themselves much farther. And a body of common men that would march together and do just what their generals told them, would form a far better army than a body of heroes, of whom each at any moment might choose to go his own way.

There is a yet subtler characteristic of the Church, which makes her a rock of offence to many; and that is the temper and the intellectual tone which she seems to develop in her members. But such a tone and temper, we must remember, is not necessarily Catholicism. The temper of the Church may change, and as a matter of fact does change. It is not the same in any two countries or in any two eras. And it may have a higher future in store for it. It may become bolder, and broader, and more rational. But if it ever does so, it will, in the opinion of Catholics, be not growing false to the spirit of the Church. It will be finding out that spirit more fully. Thus some people associate Catholic conceptions of extreme sanctity with a neglect of personal cleanliness; and must imagine that a clean Catholic can, if his faith be true, never come very near to his Master. But it was never the teaching of the Church that dirt was sacred; she has added no ninth beatitude in favour of an unchanged shirt. Dirty saints were dirty not because of the Church they belonged to, but because of the age they lived in. Such an expression of sanctity for themselves it is probable will be loathed by the saints of the future: and yet for all that, they may none the less reverence the saints who so expressed it in the past. And this may serve as a type of the great variety of changes that the Church as a living organism, still full of vigour and power of self-adaptation, will be able to develop and sustain, and yet lose nothing of her supernatural identity.

And thus the doctrine of the Church's infallibility has a side that is just the opposite of that which is commonly thought to be its only one. It is supposed to have simply gendered bondage; not to have gendered liberty. But as a matter of fact it has done both; and if we view the matter fairly, we shall see that it has done the latter at least as completely as the former. The doctrine of infallibility is undoubtedly a rope that tethers those that hold it to certain real or supposed facts of the past; but it is a rope that is capable of indefinite lengthening. It is not a fetter only; it is a support also; and those who cling to it can venture fearlessly, as explorers, into currents of speculation that would sweep away altogether men who did but trust to their own powers of swimming. Nor does, as is often supposed, the centralizing of this infallibility in the person of one man present any difficulty from the Catholic point of view. It is said that the Pope might any day make a dogma of any absurdity that might happen to occur to him; and that the Catholic would be bound to accept these, however strongly his reason might repudiate them. And it is quite true that the Pope *might* do this any day, in the sense that there is no external power to prevent him. But he who has assented to the central doctrine of Catholicism knows that he never *will*. And it is precisely the obvious absence of any restraint from without that brings home to the Catholic his faith in the guiding power from within.

There are again another set of misconceptions to be removed, that tend to fix an imaginary gulf between Catholicism and the world in general. These refer to a number of miraculous legends and quaint beliefs, which are or have been prevalent amongst Catholics, but which very certainly are in no way vouched for by the Church; and [illegible]h the Church might repudiate to-morrow, were she in any way [illegible] to give an opinion on the matter. She is no more pledged to [illegible] she is to an untenable view of the solar system. It is true [illegible]s for a long time lived and moved amongst such opinions;

and to the external eye they have naturally seemed a part of her. But time moves on, and we see that she can cast them off. She has cast off some; she will probably cast off many others; not in any petulant anger, but with a composed and gentle quiet, as some new light gravely dawns upon her. This is a point that, in estimating the future chances of Catholicism, the world in general is too apt to forget. If it does so, it may find itself in the position of a man who engages to fight another, believing that his strength and movements will be hampered by a number of cloaks and wrappages, which he wears as he enters the ring, but which suddenly, if the occasion calls for it, he flings aside in a moment, and steps forth as free of limb as his challenger.*

The real fact is this. If we would estimate dispassionately the chance Catholicism has of again becoming a power in the world, we must not judge it by the way in which it appeals to our taste in the present. We may, perhaps, not think such an estimate worth making; but if we do, we must remember that it will take us some care and some discrimination to make. We must separate the teachings of Catholicism from the opinions of Catholics; the miracles it vouches for from the miracles they believe in; its temper from their temper.

These difficulties, that I have just been dwelling on, will thus be seen to be not really formidable. If we merely desire reflections that will deepen our distaste for the Church, these difficulties will no doubt serve to deepen it. But they will hardly avail to repel us, if our inclinations are the other way. But difficulties worse than these are yet left for us. Granting that the discoveries of historical and physical science, and the growth of a liberal temper and intellectual independence, do not thus far preclude our believing in the truth and the infallibility of the Catholic Church, we have yet to encounter certain moral objections to her scheme altogether, and objections of science and common sense to other necessary parts of it.

The moral objections consist principally of these: the exclusiveness of the Church, which leaves the rest of mankind uncared for; the Church's doctrine of rewards and punishments, which are barbarous or ridiculous in their details, and which, besides that, make all virtue venal; and the doctrine of a vicarious satisfaction for sin, which to many minds carries its own condemnation on the face of it. Lastly, besides these, there is the entire question of miracles. Is the natural order ever interfered with? Or are there two orders of things at all? The

* It is a common fault with anti-religious critics to judge Christianity in general, and Romanism in particular, by the most ill-considered utterances of entirely unauthorised exponents. Some time since, Sir James Stephen discovered a passage in Bellarmine, in which hell is spoken of as situated in the middle of the earth; and the immortality of the soul is vouched for by the accounts of travellers, who have seen certain truant souls of the wicked, lamenting their eternal torments at the edge of the crater of Hecla, and trying for a few moments to snatch a furtive breath of fresh air. He immediately published this valuable discovery to the world; and argued from thence that Catholicism is untenable.

[illegible] teaches that there are. If we reject this teaching [illegible] Church. No matter how good otherwise her case might [illegible] be overthrown utterly if we decide against her here.

[illegible] exclusiveness of the Catholic Church, it must be of course [illegible] that much perplexity is caused by any view of the world [illegible] us to think of the most saving truths, and the most [illegible] helps to a right life, being confined to a minority of the human [illegible] But supposing we attach to a knowledge of the truth any real [illegible] let us hold the supreme truths of life to be what we may, [illegible] whole human race are unanimous about them, we shall have [illegible] part, probably through no fault of their own, as condemned [illegible] error. But of all creeds, Catholicism is the one that does [illegible] alleviate this perplexity. Of all religious bodies, the Roman [illegible] has the largest hope and charity for those outside her own [illegible] She condemns men not for not accepting her teaching, but only [illegible] it; and they cannot reject it until they know it, what it [illegible] its inner spirit, as well as its outward forms and formulas. [illegible] knowledge, in the opinion of many Catholics, it may be a very [illegible] to convey to some men. Prejudices for which they them[illegible] not responsible, may have blinded their eyes; and if they [illegible] blind, they will not have had sin. They will be able [illegible] invincible ignorance: and the judgments the Church pro[illegible] are not against those who have not known, but against those who have known and hated. Nor is it too much to say, that a [illegible] Catholic can afford to harbour more hope for an infidel, than a [illegible] Protestant can afford to harbour for a Catholic.

[illegible] now consider the moral and common-sense objections so [illegible] raised to-day against the Christian doctrine of rewards and [illegible]ments. These are condemned for two reasons; first, because [illegible] necessarily tend to make all virtue venal; and secondly, [illegible] the punishments threatened us are vindictive and barbarous; [illegible] rewards either ridiculous or degraded, or else unthinkable. [illegible] number of modern writers, from whom one might have ex[illegible] more continence of judgment, seem seriously to think the [illegible] committed to the statement that hell is literally something [illegible] fire-place, full of hot coals, and of non-Catholics. Nor do [illegible] to conceive of the heaven of Theology as really a change [illegible]ter. Mr. Frederic Harrison, for instance, speaks of the [illegible] there as one of "ceaseless psalmody," and an "eternity of [illegible] it must be confessed that there has been much in [illegible] certain Christians to justify such misconceptions. [illegible] described as if it were the inside of a Scotch [illegible] were the back-scene in a Christmas [illegible] God, the eternal communion with [illegible] of all the longings of the [illegible] us as a body of people in white night-gowns, set in a circle round an enormous petroleum lamp, and wondering at it with a foolish face of praise. But such are not the teachings of religion, though many religious people have taught them. Least of all is the Catholic Church in any way responsible for them. The galled jade may wince; her withers are unwrung. How true this is will at once become plain when we examine the notion that the hope or the fear of a future will make all virtue venal. This notion again is based on a radical misconception. The opponents of religion always speak of heaven and hell, as though they were an arbitrary payment for certain classes of acts; and as if they were not rather their inevitable consequences; consequences which can be only augured here, not realized. To such men, God promising heaven, seems like a gardener who should promise, if a pear-tree grew well this year, not that next year it should bring forth pears, but that he could graft a peach upon it. But the only view of the matter for which theology is responsible is something very different from this. It is the very essence of the supernatural conception of virtue, that it contains potentially more than it can actualize here. It brings peace, it is true, to those that possess it; but the peace comes to them like a bud, not like a blossom or a fruit. The fruit, as the Church teaches, is the full sight of God; the sight of God is the very essence of heaven; nor need writers like Mr. Harrison be offended because Catholics are unable to describe or even imagine it on this imperfect earth; for their earthly existence is imperfect, mainly because of this inability. It simply proves, on their grounds, that they are not in heaven yet, not that they never will be. Virtue, therefore, is no more rendered venal by being practised with a view to heaven than a painter need be because he makes his rough sketch with a view to completing his picture.

With future punishment the case is just the same. The essence of the punishment is not something alien to the acts that have merited it. There is something in sin itself that at the moment of its commission is creating hell for the sinner. Hell in its essence is nothing but a state of intense self-consciousness; the sight of what we have ourselves done to ourselves; a sight which we can now have only through a glass darkly, but then face to face. The entire doctrine on this subject cannot be expressed more clearly than it has been in a very remarkable sonnet called "Lost Days," by Mr. D. G. Rossetti, beginning thus:—

> "The lost days of my life, until to-day,
> What were they, could I see them in the street,
> Lie as they fell?"

And it ends with these memorable lines:—

> "I do not know them now, but after death
> God knows I know the faces I shall see;
> Each one a murdered self, with last low breath,
> 'I am thyself, what hast thou done to me?
> And I, and I, thyself,' to each one saith,
> 'And thou thyself to all eternity.'"

Could any hell be a truer hell than this, or any more deserved? How shall we be able to arraign its justice, when we ourselves shall be our own tormentors, and it is our own inexorable anger, under which we shall be for ever cowering?

I do not mean to deny, in what I have just said, that the Church may menace sinners with some positive *pœna sensûs*, in addition to the *pœna damni*, the internal tortures I have just been dwelling on. But even if she does, there is nothing in it that need shock the moral sense, when we remember these two points. In the first place the prospect of such a grosser form of punishment may be necessary, in many cases, as a beginning. It may lash the soul forcibly away from lower things; and though not giving it, by that, a taste for things that are higher, it may at any rate drive it within the sphere of their attraction. And besides this, the scourge, be it never so coarse, must in a great measure be self-applied. The vengeance threatened is remote; and unless we make some effort ourselves, it may easily fade out of our imagination. When imagined it may be unspiritual; but there is something spiritualizing in the laborious effort that is required effectually to imagine it. Nor can such fear as is thus engendered properly be called servile or degrading, when we ourselves, of our own free-will, become a part of that which terrifies us, and are ourselves assessors of the judge before whom we tremble.

And now, what is to be said of the doctrine still more distinctively Christian—the doctrine of vicarious satisfaction, which has so often, and by such high authorities, been called immoral, or morally impossible?

Here again, it cannot be denied, we have a great difficulty. But the fact must be, I think, a sufficient answer to objectors, that we can only get rid of it by giving place to a greater one. For let us once acknowledge the supreme importance of virtue, let us once realize how hard it is to attain to it, and we shall immediately become conscious of the inexpressible enormity of sin, and of the extent to which we ourselves are sullied by it. Further, as no act dies barren and without its consequences, we shall feel that our sins, whether only against ourselves, or against others, are still surviving in their effects. They have passed beyond our own control.

> "All things are taken from us, and become
> Portion and parcel of the dreadful Past."

Or, to use the words of another poet, we shall realize this:—

> "The moving finger writes, and having writ
> Moves on, nor all your piety nor wit
> Shall move it back to cancel half a line,
> Nor all your tears wash out a word of it."

The sense is thus, inevitably, born in us, that we have chained ourselves to the evil of the world. We cannot rise towards God. In this situation, what is to be done? Our burthen is greater than we can bear. If it is to be borne at all, it must be borne by another. But how? The thing is impossible. It can only be done by a moral miracle; and by a miracle that in its very nature is absurd and unthinkable. Precisely: and such a miracle is the central doctrine of the Church—a doctrine as unthinkable, but not more so, than is God's power and goodness, when we confront these attributes with the existence of pain and evil.

And now, lastly, as to the whole question of miracles altogether—is it possible that the world, with its eyes opened by science as they now have been, can ever again yield assent to these? Our impulse at the present day is at once to reply, Never. "Believe in the Pope!" said the late Dr. Arnold; "I would as soon believe in Jupiter." And we now think of miracles much as Dr. Arnold did of the Pope. But this saying I have just quoted is a very instructive one. To Dr. Arnold it seemed like the profoundest sense. And yet Dr. Arnold believed in the Divine nature of Christ, and in the story of His miraculous birth. What then will the present generation think of his logic, who have been brought up to regard Christianity with the same unsympathizing criticism that he applied to Popery? It is surely a greater tax on our credulity to believe that Christ was the Son of God, than, having believed that, to believe that the Pope is the representative of Christ. And now let us see whether we ourselves may not in a few years be seen to have been condemning religion in general as illogically as Dr. Arnold now seems to us to have condemned a particular form of it. Though those who call themselves our advanced thinkers repudiate all faith in Christianity, they yet talk of morality and moral responsibility. These are to them matters of the highest importance, and all the reverence they have is consecrated to these. But it seems quite possible, indeed it seems not improbable, that as the years go on, we shall grow to feel certain teachings of science more strongly than we do now. As it is, we know them,—our reason grasps them; but they are not yet brought home to our daily imagination. In a short time more they may be. And then perhaps we shall grow to see that, in the face of that unvaried necessity, that inevitable sequence of things that science alone reveals to us, every notion of choice and of moral responsibility will be seen to be as antagonistic to reason as is the story of the birth and the resurrection of Christ. To the eye of reason, could the world only bring itself to regard the matter steadily with that, the existence of free-will, and therefore of morality itself, may seem as much a miracle as any grotesque cure or transformation related in the *Acta Sanctorum*.

Looking, then, at the Church of Rome from a strictly logical standpoint, it is hard to see how, if we believe in free-will and morality in the face of these modern discoveries, which, as far as they go, show us all life as nothing but a vast machine—it is hard to see how we can consider the Church of Rome as logically in any way wounded, or crippled, or in a condition, should occasion offer, to be less active than she was in the days of her most undisputed ascendency. I conceive of her as a ship, that seems now unable to go upon any voyage, or to carry men anywhere, but that this is not because, as was said not long since, that her "hull was riddled by logic," or that she is dismasted or has lost her sails, but merely because she has no wind to fill them. In other words, with regard to supernatural religion, and Catholicism as its one form that still survives unshattered, I conceive that the imagination of the world has been to a great measure paralyzed; but that it may be seen eventually that it never has been in any way convinced; and that nothing is wanting to revive the Roman Church into stronger life than ever, but a craving amongst men for the certainty, the guidance, and the consolation that she alone offers them.

The only question is, whether such an outburst of feeling is in any way probable. It is possible that the world may be outgrowing such a craving as that I speak of; or that it may find some new way of appeasing it. This is a question that is well worth considering; and I propose to refer to it in some future paper.

W. H. MALLOCK.

(Griechenland, vi. 274), which are omitted by Finlay. If these had been supplied, and references added to Gervinus' history, where it differs from the present narrative of recent affairs, the work before us would have been more unquestionably the best on the later history of Greece. But perhaps this is an unreasonable demand from an editor, and went beyond the limits which he justly imposed upon himself. Indeed it is captious to qualify in any respect the praise which the excellent though unassuming contributions of Mr. Tozer richly deserve. Finlay's love of large principles and his dislike of long and minute details, while it saved him from the melancholy ponderousness of most German historians, made him sometimes careless of smaller points, on which the reader regrets his silence. In his account of the battle of Navarino (vii. 17), he is extremely curt as to the circumstances before the battle, and his narrative leads us to believe that the allied commanders sailed in with the deliberate purpose of fighting, and only allowed the Turks to fire the first shot because they were not themselves in position. Other accounts, which he must have known perfectly, state that the battle was forced on by the Turks firing on English boats which carried peaceful messages, and that the English admiral even then stayed his fire in the hope of avoiding bloodshed. This is the account, for example, of Gervinus, in the sixth volume of his history of this century. We should like to know whether Finlay deliberately rejected it, but he contents himself with merely referring to a manuscript account of the battle as his authority.

On the other hand, his work is full of broad philosophic generalizations, drawn from long study of the facts, combined with the native shrewdness of the Scot; and these give a distinct character to his writing, and raise him above the ordinary pedant or the servile chronicler. Yet it would not be difficult to find in different volumes conflicting propositions, which give an air of hesitation to his thinking. In the portraits of individual Greek leaders, whom he knew during the War of Liberation, these generalities often obscure the likeness by suggesting inconsistent features; and yet these portraits he evidently thought his strong point, and the portions of his history on which he had bestowed much care. He differs indeed very widely from the Greek popular notions of the military adventurers, or bandit chiefs, who became national heroes in the memories of the people. His honourable and chivalrous, but tame, character had no sympathy for Kolokotrones or for Odysseus, the latter of whom he paints as an atrocious compound of every vice (vi. 249), while his sketch of the former is not much more favourable. Probably the most interesting to the general reader is that of Lord Byron, with whom he spent much of his time at Mesolonghi, just before the poet's death, and which I will quote, as not being known so well as it deserves, and as a good specimen of the author's style:—

"The genius of Lord Byron would in all probability never have unfolded either political or military talent. He was not disposed to assume an active part in public affairs. He regarded politics as the art of cheating people, by concealing one half of the truth and misrepresenting the other; and whatever abstract enthusiasm he might feel for military glory was joined to an innate detestation of the trade of war. Both his character and his conduct presented unceasing contradictions. It seemed as if two different souls occupied his body alternately. One was feminine, and full of sympathy; the other was masculine, and characterized by clear judgment, and by a rare power of presenting for consideration those facts only which were required for forming a decision. When one arrived, the other departed. In company, his sympathetic soul was his tyrant. Alone, or with a single person, his masculine prudence displayed itself as his friend. No man could then arrange facts, investigate their causes, or examine their consequences, with more logical accuracy, or in a more practical spirit. Yet, in his most sagacious moment, the entrance of a third person would disarrange the order of his ideas; judgment fled, and sympathy, generally laughing, took its place. Hence he appeared in his conduct extremely capricious, while in his opinions he had really great firmness. He often, however, displayed a feminine turn for deception in trifles, while at the same time he possessed a feminine candour of soul, and a natural love of truth, which made him often despise himself quite as much as he despised English society for what he called its brazen hypocrisy. He felt his want of self-command; and there can be no doubt that his strongest reason for withdrawing from society and shunning public affairs was the conviction of his inability to repress the sympathies which were in opposition to his judgment."

Perhaps most of us would not recognize the great poet in this portrait, which avoids his salient and public features for the sake of bringing out minor points of no less interest. But if this principle be carried out in the description of more obscure, but more important men to modern Greek history, we can understand how the present generation of Greeks have complained of Finlay's History, and asserted that it did not do either the nation or its leaders full justice. Indeed, it appears that while in the *form* of his character-painting he was very fond of introducing antitheses and contrasts, perhaps in imitation of the style of Gibbon, he really made too little allowance for that strong mixture of motives which, especially in half-civilized people, produces such inconsistencies as no logic can reconcile. Thus we may well imagine that among the bandit chiefs, who led armed troops of robber patriots against the Turks, there may have been real patriotism, as well as selfishness, personal ambition, and a great deal of dishonesty. It requires not only ancestral traditions, but a clear social atmosphere, for the development of high principles, and still more for the staunch adherence to them. It is therefore enough, it is even a great deal, to expect from a degraded and disorganized people that the general tendency of their leaders should be towards better and higher things, and we should condone the frequent relapses into selfishness and cruelty which result from the violence of hereditary passions, and the weakness of hereditary principles.

These considerations seem supported by his constant reiteration of the remark that the Greek nation were so much more earnest, and so much more unselfish, than their leaders. Indeed, the whole history of the War of Liberation is only to be explained by the unflinching patriotism and devotion of the mass of the people, and to this feature Finlay does ample justice. It is needless to point out that a nation of pure patriots can never be led by a parcel of pure knaves, and that even the most savage and unprincipled of the Greek leaders must have shown some higher warrant to obtain the confidence of devoted and determined followers. It is easy to show this by examples.

According to Finlay's own account (vi. 221), Kolokotrones, who was a man of considerable military ability, by an exhibition of avarice and dishonesty in the matter of booty at Tripolitza lost both his fair chance of leading the Revolution and the moral influence he had accidentally gained, and relapsed into a mere klepht or party chief. On the other hand, the incompetent Mavrocordatus, who had no military reputation, was called five times from an inferior or private station to occupy the highest rank in the government of Greece. In every case he made shipwreck of his own reputation, and left public affairs as bad, or worse than he found them. Yet even when he forfeited the nation's confidence, he retained a place in their esteem. This arose from a conviction that he was less influenced by love of money than the other politicians. Thus his unsullied reputation conferred on him a greater popularity than he could have obtained, had ministerial corruption and financial peculation not been considered the direct causes of most political evils by the Greeks (vi. 246, abridged). How strongly we are reminded of Grote's account of Nikias and the Athenians in these remarks, and how strikingly they contradict the dark picture which many parts of Finlay's book give us of the dishonesty of the nation!

There are, indeed, few nationalities more distinct than that of the Greeks, either ancient or modern; and it is, perhaps, the best possible introduction to a study of their present claims and prospects, to read, through Finlay's volumes, the history of their later antecedents, and the causes which have made them what they now are. Of course, the present people have made great capital out of their ancestry—a feature which often rouses Finlay's sarcasm and his ire. It is argued, with a good deal of force, that this illustrious descent, or the belief in it, has done the Greeks great practical harm, that it has made them vain and self-assuming, and impaired their reliance upon present virtues by dazzling them with bygone glories. But, on the other hand, those who maintain that Greece should start as a perfectly new nation, if she desires to succeed, seem to underrate the force of Greek traditions, however remote, in kindling enthusiasm and sustaining trial.

Be this as it may, when Finlay first wrote on the subject, the practical side of the question had been obscured by historical speculations, which denied the alleged descent of the modern from the old Greeks altogether, and brought evidence to show that, while the Greek language had survived, the people who now speak it were not Greeks in [illegible], but a mixed race, made up of Sclavonians, Albanians, and [illegible] late immigrants. It was a question on which evidence was [illegible] scanty and difficult to be found. In the earlier volumes of [illegible]'s book, the history of Greece is made to embrace the history of [illegible]tinople and its empire, otherwise all the extant materials must [illegible] down from two volumes (ii. and iii.) to a few pages, which relate [illegible] and there the invasions of Northern tribes, and the miseries of [illegible] inhabitants. The foundation of such all-important places as [illegible]vasia is even shrouded in mist, and we can only infer their [illegible] from the necessity felt in the sixth century of removing from [illegible] inland highroads of Sclavonian invasion to the seaboard, where an escape by ships remained open to the beleaguered Greeks.*

According to Hopf, it was the high authority of Finlay which, for a season at least, placed a seal upon the bold theory advanced by Fallmerayer, that not a single old Hellene could now be traced in Greece, but that the whole country having been ravaged and desolated—Athens even for four hundred years—the present people were northern immigrants, southern and eastern pirates, in fact, a collection of mixed nationalities, in which Slavs and Albanians predominated. It was thought by most Germans that so shrewd and able a critic as Finlay, who lived on the spot, would not have accepted Fallmerayer's quotations from archives at Athens without proper evidence; and so for a good many years the Hellenic parentage of the present Greeks was consistently denied and even ridiculed.

The reaction, which began with exclamations of sentimental disgust and illogical patriotism, gradually gained a firmer position by the special researches of Ellissen, Zinkeisen, and Ross, who rather, however, brought out facts inconsistent with the Slav theory than direct disproof of the evidence on which it was based. But the day of reckoning has come at last. The chronicle of Monemvasia has been proved by Hopf a late and perfectly worthless compilation of the Turkish period, and its authority not only small, but inconsistent with itself. The case is still worse with the alleged records of the Anargyri convent, and the public letters preserved by the house of Ajacciuoli, said to be in a monastery at Athens. Fallmerayer, it seems, objected very much to the publication of this piece of evidence, but asserted that the copy in his possession was authentic and conclusive, though he was refused access to the original, as soon as his theory excited the hostility of the offended Greeks. The Greek authors, Surmelis and Paparrhigopoulos, first openly declared the Anargyri fragments to be mere forgeries. At last Pittakis published the original in the

* The chronicle of Monemvasia, which is shown by Hopf to be a very untrustworthy document, does, however, describe the founding of this city in 567 A.D., and this account [illegible] probable. The terrible ravages of the pirates in the seventeenth and eighteenth [illegible] through all the coasts and islands led afterwards to an opposite result, and the [illegible] and culture of Greece removed again from the seaboard, as was the case in the [illegible] days of Phœnician and Carian adventure.

Athenian Archæological Journal, when the four hundred years of the desolation of Athens were suddenly reduced to three! Hopf roundly asserts that Pittakis forged the whole thing, that he prepared the first copy to suit Fallmerayer, for ready money, and afterwards another to suit Greek taste; but that the paper on which the so-called archives are written is undoubtedly Venetian paper of the eighteenth century, and that the whole of the so-called evidence is a deliberate imposture.

This is the sum of the remarks (pp. 100—119) in Hopf's History of Mediæval Greece, to which Mr. Tozer briefly refers. It is perhaps the most readable passage in the German Professor's profound but dull essay. He seeks to establish afterwards, but not, I think, on very satisfactory evidence, that the only districts in the Morea which were really Sclavized were the very districts commonly supposed to contain the purest and noblest Hellenic stock—I mean the Tsakonian and Mainot districts. If this conclusion holds its ground, the result is most curious; for the former condition of the question will be exactly reversed. The other parts of Greece are reinstated into their long-suspected legitimacy. The Mainots and Tsakonians are ousted from their proud title of Spartans, and degraded into cousins of the Bulgarians and Servians.

Nevertheless, it seems to me that on both sides of the controversy the really important issue has been overlooked. The question whether foreign blood has been introduced into a nation's ancestry is of little import, provided the habits, the traditions, and the sentiments of the people have not changed. And this is quite possible, even in cases where the admixture of blood is so large as to warrant at first sight the assertion of a total change of race. For there are races which easily disappear and lose themselves by admixture, whereas there are others so tenacious that, even when they are numerically inferior, they keep out-breeding their rivals, like the little leaven which gradually leavens the whole lump. I will take a remarkable case under my own eye. The people of the city and county of Dublin have been for many centuries so largely invaded by the Danes, and then reinforced by English settlers and adventurers, nay, even so often exiled from its pale, and excluded by these strangers, that the Irish language has long disappeared (except in the local names), and it may be questioned whether a single person now in the district can claim pure Irish descent. Yet if another Fallmerayer were to bring up all this evidence, and infer from hence that the people of Dublin were really English adventurers and Norse pirates, he would be justly disbelieved and ridiculed by all such as had studied not merely the history, but even the present manners and traditions of the place. It would not require a minute analysis of the derivations of the names of places, or a painful examination of old pedigrees, to show that Irish blood was really dominant in the county of Dublin up to the present day. Any traveller [illegible] Kingstown knows in five minutes that he is not among Englishmen or Norsemen, but in Ireland, and finds that the town of Dublin is now as distinctly Irish in character as any town in the west of the country. The climate of course has had some influence. But other cases—those of Glasgow and Liverpool, and of American towns—seem to show that the Irish Celts have the power of out-breeding even stronger and higher races, and forcing their obtrusive nationality upon the strangers who have conquered and who despise them. Thus the Sclavonians may have invaded and occupied many parts of Greece, which remained Greek, or reverted into Greek districts by the natural action of physical and social laws which the foreign conquerors could not control. And if the Irish have maintained their nationality in spite of the almost total loss of their language, how much stronger is the case of the Greeks, who have not only preserved their tongue, but even imposed it upon most of the Albanians, who came into the country in its lowest state of misery and depopulation, and occupied deserted tracts without necessary fusion with older inhabitants!

The real question therefore which is worth discussing about Greek nationality is this: Has the Hellenic race, which had become effete, and which would probably have become extinct without the infusion of foreign blood, maintained its characteristics during this process, or has it changed in type, and become a new people, with no claims to the great heritage of its predecessors in the same country? It is on this question that Finlay's History affords us the evidence of those darker and less-known centuries through which Greece has passed since the paralyzing grasp of Rome destroyed her political vitality. There is indeed little material up to the Frankish conquest, yet even that little serves as a connecting thread with the days when a series of occupations by Western conquerors again brought Greece within the ken of accessible chroniclers.* But, although not a word can be said against the strict impartiality and love of justice of our historian, it is to be regretted that the disappointment of his hopes, and the sense of failure in his life, has made him a severe judge and a very uncompromising exponent of the faults and weaknesses of mediæval, as well as of modern Greeks.

This harsh estimate from so great an authority is the more likely to mislead us in the inquiry which I have proposed, as the usual pictures of the classical Greeks are very much exaggerated in the opposite direction, and it is more than probable that these extravagant notions had much to do in producing the bitter feelings of disappointment in such phil-Hellenes as Finlay, who never thought of sifting the evidence for the current pictures of ancient Greek society. The splendour of the extant literature and the art of Attic culture was

* Hopf has detected a good many important facts from the records of the bishoprics and the lives of saints through this dark epoch, all of which tend to support the theory of a persistent Hellenic culture through Greece, even in the days of barbarian conquest and occupation.

accepted as evidence of the highest qualities in the bulk and average of the nation, and so an ideal Spartan or Athenian type was created, which was nearly as imaginary then as it would be now. Of course any actual people must appear miserably degraded in comparison with such a picture.

In estimating the relations of the old to the new Hellenes, a correction of these classical prejudices seems to me vital, and the conclusion which we form will chiefly depend on our not starting from a false basis.* But if we lay aside rhodomontade and twaddle, and draw common-sense inferences from our evidence as men of the world, and not as pedant professors who are eaten up with the importance of the objects of their study, we shall find that both the virtues and the vices of the mediæval and modern Greeks have their direct prototypes in classical times. I will not repeat what I have elsewhere shown at length, and what is confirmed by the delicate social tact of such men as Ernest Renan, Georges Perrot, and Émile Burnouf, who combine the quick and subtle intuitions of Frenchmen with a thorough knowledge both of classical Greek books and modern Greek people. Let any one take up Finlay's seventh volume on Greece since 1829, and he will find reproduced with curious exactness the indelible features which appear through all the twelve volumes of Grote. There is the same constant love of liberty in the body of the people, and faith in leaders who have once served them well. There is the same duplicity and craft in most of the leaders, the same openness to bribes, and, what is more striking, the same passion to wield despotic power in individuals, combined with the same hatred of despotism in the masses. There is a curious persistence in the jealousy of greatness, along with the confidence in it just named; there is, moreover, the same combination to be found of patriotism and knavery, of warlike tastes and personal cowardice. There is the same preponderance of intellectual acuteness over moral uprightness; the same love of learning and enlightenment rather than of honour and purity.

These are of course mere predominating tendencies, nor is it for one moment possible to affirm that the moral qualities which are put in the second place are not also respected. It is in fact rather in contrast to the Northern and Western nations of Europe, that a certain difference of balance is felt, which makes many of us greatly overrate the vices and underrate the virtues of a semi-Eastern people. For even this feature, the Oriental complexion of modern Greece, which most people ascribe to Turkish domination, is a far older, nay, even an original feature, which separated the earliest Hellenic culture in tone and temper from that of Italy and the further West.

The parallel I have here indicated is between the old free Greeks

* I must apologize for referring to my own "Social Life in Greece," as an attempt to form a more reasonable estimate on this matter.

and the Greeks of to-day, and is instituted between the present people, and their ancestors when in their highest and noblest condition. But it is needless to insist that this comparison is hardly fair, for that long before the Greeks could be suspected of having suffered contamination in blood, their higher features were impaired and their meannesses stimulated by the despotism of Rome. Their political talents found no scope, save in the direction of intrigue, and their quick intellects were devoted to the gaining of wealth by trade, or of influence by acting upon the weakness of their masters. These unfortunate conditions, together with the rapid depopulation of the country, are ably sketched in the general essays which form Finlay's first volume, and which show us the pure Greeks in a state of melancholy degradation without any admixture of baser blood. Indeed, as he notices, the "Hero" of Musæus, the epigrams of Agathias, and many historical works written late in this period, prove that even Greek literature in a higher sense—the surest token of Hellenic culture—was not dead. He might well have added the "Daphnis and Chloe," a work of genius which would have gained a reputation in any age.

In the division of the empire the Greeks again rose to a prominent position, but it is now the Greeks, and not Greece, which become the subject of Hellenic history. Indeed so large a portion of Finlay's History treats of their fortunes in the Byzantine empire, that the very title of his book is a misnomer, for there were centuries when the History of the Greeks hardly alludes to the condition of Greece.* The Asiatic provinces and the Euxine colonies furnished a larger contingent of successful men to the Byzantine empire than the deserted Attica or Lacedæmon. Yet still it was the Greek race which, by its superior intelligence and higher education, monopolized all the administration of law and religion in the empire. These two engines of government, the one obtained from Roman genius, the other from the victory of Christianity over Paganism, gave an unity to the Greek nation which it had never before possessed; "but, unfortunately for the law, Latin continued to be the language of legal business in the East until after the time of Justinian. This fact explains the comparatively trifling influence of the legal class in establishing the supremacy of the Greek nation in the Eastern empire, and accounts also for the undue influence which the clergy were enabled to acquire in civil affairs. Had the language of the law been that of the people, the Eastern lawyers could hardly have failed, by combining with the Church, to form a systematic and constitutional barrier against the arbitrary exercise of imperial authority" (i. 152).

The influence of the Church was far more prominent, and is certainly not underrated by Finlay. If there is in fact any fundamental

* The limits of this paper compel me to pass by in silence all such parts of the work as do not affect Greece directly, though there are many points of interest and of valuable research in every part of it

difference between old and new Greeks, it is probably derived from the spread of orthodox Christianity, with its centralizing and systematizing tendencies. But it seems to have merely replaced the distinction of Hellene and barbarian by that of orthodox and heretic, and even to have saved the love of autonomy and municipal independence by setting up the local bishop, and the spiritual head, as a sort of counterpoise to the central tyranny of the government at Constantinople. Finlay, though not consistent with himself on this point, asserts that Hellenic nationality, during the middle ages, became nothing but orthodoxy, and that the Greeks were no longer held together by race and language, but by the bond of a Church which happened to adopt their language. This theory, which he was obliged to abandon in the face of his own experience in modern Greece, is only intelligible if we recognize the fact that the Eastern Church took up within it and satisfied those elements of old Hellenism which survived within the hearts of the people. We know that innumerable Pagan legends, among the lower classes, were accommodated to saints, and that the more educated found scope for their love of subtlety and disputation in the metaphysical controversies of their faith. And while orthodoxy thus preserved and protected old Hellenic features in the people, it was a powerful engine for helping the amalgamation of foreign settlers in Greece, and bringing them within the influence of the older and tougher nationality. Indeed, what strikes us most forcibly in the account of the Norman incursions into Greece, is the small effect which the bold and turbulent Sclavonians had made, after centuries, upon a population which, owing to prolonged Byzantine despotism, had developed what we may call its Jewish qualities, its love of peace and of gain. Thebes, Corinth, and Eubœa, are then described (iii. 161) as full of wealth and manufacture, of rich citizens and fair women, but unable to offer the slightest resistance to the invaders, and even surrendering the Acrocorinthus without a struggle. It is, however, certain that the city populations, which then suffered, were least affected by barbarian inroads, and that these peaceful and submissive inhabitants must have been almost purely Hellenic.

When the Frankish knights' conquest of Greece supervened, we arrive at a period of more light and fuller information, but the chroniclers are too busy recording the splendour of the courts of Thebes and Athens, of Klarentza and Karytena, to tell us how Greek nationality presented itself to their eyes. The military resistance of the people was small, for the knights were very brave and well-disciplined, and able to overcome in their panoply any European infantry, previous to its organization by the Spaniards. They moreover offered good terms to the people, and their rule may have been accepted as a chance of some escape from the fiscal oppression of the Byzantine government. But many untoward circumstances prevented this interesting historical experiment of bringing Greece into Western politics

...culture from obtaining a fair trial. The chivalry of ...Greeks was ruined by the disaster near Orchomenus, which ...Thebes at the mercy of the rapacious and bloodthirsty ...mercenaries. The princes of the Morea only partially con...d that country; the momentary successes of William of Ville...uin being sacrificed to release him from captivity. There was ...a Byzantine province in the peninsula, not to speak of Vene...ports, to interfere with the peaceable development of feudalism. ...causes, combined with the perpetual quarrels and wars of ...arious princes, and above all the pretensions and exactions of ...atin clergy who accompanied them, made it but too natural that ...reeks should desire and revert to the known evils of Byzan...dominion, now mitigated by the growing apprehension of the ... Still later, when the central power became weak and helpless, ...rong hand of Mohammed II. seemed the only salvation from the ...s of piracy and anarchy with which the country was tormented. ...ms to me, therefore, that Hopf is misled by his familiarity with ...alogies of the Frankish courts in the chronicles, when he criti... Finlay's estimate of this period, and thinks that the condition of ...eople was happy under their Western rulers. The shrewd instinct ... Scotch historian was not misled by the onesidedness of the ...nce.

...therefore impossible to maintain that the Greeks had a fair offer ...bracing Western culture, which was indeed, at that time, in many ...ts far behind the East, and of which the noblest features de...d, as Finlay well explains, on hereditary associations, and upon ...ents which written laws could not convey. But if we study the ...ty of the Hellenic race through the rest of its history, we shall ...posed to decide that under no circumstances would the Frankish ...ts have made Greece one of the members of Western Europe.*

...this period, during the conquest by Mohammed II., the Alba... begin to act a prominent part in the Morea, and even attempt ...arate policy. This idea was crushed by the Sultan, but we may ...hat the Albanian element, originally brought in to colonize waste ... and fill material gaps, did far more important service in refresh...e political deficiencies of the Greeks, and in reintroducing that ...and warlike love of independence which marks both the ancient ...e modern Hellenes. Even up to the War of Liberation those ...ns of the country which are known to be Albanian have taken ...d in warlike affairs, but they became so thoroughly amalgamated ...y with the Hellenes during Turkish despotism, that we may ...them to have restored to the population one of its oldest and ... features, which had been well-nigh crushed out with misery

* ...of forming States in the East by conquest and colonization from the West ... have lasted a long time after the Crusades. As late as 1628 the Huguenots ... after the siege of Rochelle, to buy Rhodes from the Sultan, and set up a ...nt kingdom there under the Duc de Rohan.

and misgovernment. There are still portions of Greece, even in Attica, where Albanian is commonly spoken. Certain districts and islands, such as Megara, Hydra, Poros, Spetza, and most of Ægina, are said to be purely Albanian. Yet even here I think a strong Greek element must have remained, or reappeared, together with the language and the old traditions. So much I know from personal observation, that there are in Ægina old Greek types not a whit inferior to those upon the Parthenon frieze.

But however the infusion of a military spirit may have been caused by the Albanians, we have Finlay's testimony that the bulk of the nation was not changed in character. In discussing (in his fifth volume) the second attempt to render the Morea a dependency of the West,—that of the Venetians, 1684-1718,—he quotes (p. 208) the Venetian pictures of Greek character as being the same as those of Cantacuzenos in the fourteenth century. The causes of the failure of this attempt* are more curious and interesting than those of the failure of the Frankish knights, for the Venetians governed carefully and generously after their notions, and even held a balance between their own and the Greek Church—an instance of remarkable enlightenment for that age. As the Crusaders' conquest is compared to the Norman invasion of England, so this crisis in the history of Greece is even more aptly compared to the management of the Ionian islands by England, or the new kingdom of Greece by Bavaria.†

The conduct of the Venetians, and the permanent benefits, especially in education, which they conferred upon the Greeks, make the easy reconquest of the country by the Turks in 1718 a very strange fact, especially as the decay of the Porte had commenced, and the vices of Ottoman rule had been already known and felt by the Greeks. Finlay attributes to the Venetians the first kindling of the sparks of independence in the nation, and suggests that the good example of the Catholic clergy had a permanent effect upon their degraded and lethargic Orthodox rivals in the affections of the people. He thinks that the generation educated under the Venetians was of a newer and better type, though his picture of the Greek character at this very period of his work (v. 203, 204) is anything but flattering. It is indeed hard to

* By far the longest experiment of Western feudalism on the Greeks was that which subsisted (under Venice) at Corfu and the other Ionian islands. But it seems to have left the population no less Greek than the rest; the Corfiotes, even after the later rule of the English, seem to possess all the weaknesses of the other Greeks, and do not seem to have acquired any special Western virtues. Hopf thinks (vii. 188, 6) that a traveller passing from the Ionian islands into Greece can even now see the good results of Venetian occupation. This curious statement ignores the English influence completely, though it has long since overlaid most Venetian traces of culture.

† Finlay adds that the Venetian rule "would not suffer by the comparison" (v. p. 197), a statement which Hopf translates into an assertion of a decided superiority in the Venetians (vii. 187). This seems to show that he does not know the English language more accurately than the English treatment of these islands. I am certain Finlay wrote the sentence loosely, and meant to apply the comparison chiefly, if not wholly, to the Bavarians. Among other analogies the government of Chios by a Genoese Company under the sanction of the State affords a comparison with our own East India Company.

see in the conduct of the people at this period any signs of the higher qualities which presently manifested themselves. They seem rather to have grown up first from a more complete fusion of the Albanian families with the rest of the nation,* thus giving a certain element of sturdiness to the national character, which had been depraved by long servility and corruption. Secondly, we must not forget the ingrained love of learning in the nation, which Finlay constantly calls love of pedantry, and most unjustly stigmatizes as a weakness, whereas it is really a clear sign of intellectual superiority in the Greek over the other nations of the east of Europe. This love of learning, this intellectual curiosity, became stimulated, not only by the great strides of liberty among the nations of Europe in the eighteenth century, but by the constant intrigues of Russia, which kept promoting insurrections in the Christian provinces of the Sultan. There should be added the gradual relaxation of Turkish despotism, and the constant advancement to high honours of the Phanariot members of the Greek race. These causes are more proximate and more obvious in explaining the gradual rise of Greek spirit, than the transitory occupation by the Venetians, which, in spite of its ability and mildness, perhaps, as Hopf thinks, on account of the mildness, failed to heal the distempers and secure the affections of the people. But as Finlay remarks over and over again, no foreign domination, however well meant, has ever satisfied the Greeks; it remains to be seen, whether they will be contented by a Government of their own.

The interest of Finlay's volumes increases as he brings us nearer to the present time and within the range of the first beginnings of the Eastern question. The character and policy of the Ottoman rulers, their great virtues and brilliant abilities, are painted with a very sympathetic hand, and in the War of Liberation there is no figure which stands out more prominently than that of Sultan Mahmud II.,† whose whole life was a patient and almost heroic attempt to hold together an empire which even sixty years ago was thought in the crisis of its dissolution, and had its vultures wheeling around in anticipation of their prey. Yet it would indeed be surprising if the wonderful military, political, and mercantile organization which the historian describes in the splendid opening chapter of his fifth volume had decayed without flashing out again into brilliant moments of greatness.

The neighbouring nations seem ever to have been underrating the Ottoman power. From the ridiculous campaign of Peter the Great

* Finlay observes (vi. p. 28) that within the greater part of the limits of Greece occupied by the Albanians, the Greeks have been as completely expelled as the Celtic race by the Saxons in England. Is it at all clear that many Celtic elements do not underlie the Saxon population of England, though lapse of time has fused the nation into one homogeneous whole? In any case, the districts which are really Albanian, and where Albanian is now spoken, were rather deserted tracts colonized than districts conquered from expelled Greeks.

† Cf. vi. 209 and 309, which are very interesting passages.

on the Pruth, in 1711, to the campaign of last year, when the Russian officers were boasting that they would hunt the Turk without a struggle into Constantinople, the enemies of Turkey have been deceiving themselves about her power of resistance. She has seldom failed to produce able generals when they were required. In the War of Liberation, it appears from Finlay's narrative that Reshid Pasha was far the ablest officer on either side. Her diplomacy has on the whole been marked by more honesty and straightforwardness than those of most of her Christian neighbours. In fact the conduct of the Western powers about the time of the battle of Navarino was a mere tissue of duplicity. Nevertheless the fact that the Sultan has been a professed despot, and that he has regarded his Christian subjects as his slaves—this combined with an utterly corrupt officialism—has permitted Christian sovereigns who were practically as despotic, and whose officials were not less corrupt, to assume that the existence of the Porte in Europe is intolerable, and that even breaches of faith in dealing with it are excusable, as with heretics in the middle ages. These remarks apply specially to Russia, whose policy is sketched by Finlay with clearness, and apparently with fairness, but not without a strong conviction that her meanness, her duplicity, and her selfishness, have been more consistent than those of her neighbours.

With regard to Finlay's estimate of the Greeks, I have intimated already that his judgments seem harsh and unintentionally unfair. It was impossible that such a war as that of the liberation of Greece could have been fought out without bringing to the surface every adventurer and miscreant in the nation. Long degradation had, as a matter of course, intensified those feelings of revenge, and that love of cruelty, which were dark features in the old Athenians, the most humane people of the most civilized times in Greece. The consistent treachery in the massacre of prisoners, and the breaking of capitulation treaties, which disgraced the Greek armies, are the common feature of all slave insurrections, and, dreadful as these things are, it must be urged, in common justice, that humanity in war is a very late and partial outcome of civilization, and that greater nations than the Greeks seem not to have learned it even at the present day.

The really melancholy spectacle, and that which must have painfully affected all such enlightened phil-Hellenes as Finlay, was the utter ignorance among the Greeks of the very meaning of freedom, when they had attained it. To the mass of the country population, it meant relief from the Ottoman yoke, and yet "during the whole war with the Sultan, the administrative organization of civil and financial business remained the same in free Greece as in Turkey. No improvement was made in taxation, no measures were adopted for rendering property more secure, no attempt made to obtain an equitable administration of justice; no courts of law were established, or financial accounts published" (vi. 230). A people of slaves were suddenly enfranchised, and it was imagined that they would at once know what to do with their liberty.

The fact is that even their leaders were equally ignorant of its meaning. With most of them liberty meant personal aggrandisement, and license to pay dependents and followers out of the public revenue. Accordingly "governments were formed, constitutions were drawn up, national assemblies met; orators debated, and laws were passed according to the fashion of the Liberals of the day. But no effort was made to prevent the Government being virtually absolute, unless it was by rendering it absolutely powerless. The national assemblies were nothing but conferences of parties, and the laws passed were intended to fascinate Western Europe, not to operate with effect in Greece" (ibid.). When the unhappy nation sought to place itself under the control of some political head who would frame a new order of things, and save the land from anarchy, they only found men of two classes, the very few who attempted honest government, but who had no notion of that municipal freedom which alone trains a country to independence; or the many who at once turned to their own aggrandisement, and made their power a mere source of wealth to themselves and their adherents. It is quite possible that the theory of Capodistrias was the true one, and that Greece would have been best governed during her years of political infancy by a strong and somewhat despotic hand. But the despot should have been some Solon, or Timoleon, some real patriot who, while he crushed out anarchy and disorder, and secured personal safety and the rights of property, set himself at once to establish the law above government officials, and to teach the people the management of their local affairs by selecting the best men among themselves. It was the dire misfortune of Greece that in this crisis she developed no Washington, and that she fell instead under the hands of a Capodistrias.*

Still more luckless was the refusal of Leopold to become King, and the selection of a prince from Bavaria, a country which, even in the Germany of that day, was noted for parochial despotism. Otho cannot possibly have had the least inkling of the practical meaning of constitutional liberty, though of course all the petty German princes of that period had read enough about it to fear it thoroughly, and to apprehend that the day of reckoning must soon come for themselves. Consequently after the frightful anarchy which followed the death of Capodistrias, Greece fell into the clutches of a Bavarian clique, who did

* "To live or die free was the firm resolve of the peasantry of Greece when they took up arms; and no sufferings ever shook that resolution. They never had the fortune to find a leader worthy of their cause. No eminent man stands forward as the type of the nation's virtues; too many are famous as representatives of the nation's vices. From this circumstance the records of the Greek Revolution are destitute of one of history's most attractive characteristics: it loses the charm of a hero's biography. But it possesses its own distinction. Never in the records of States did a nation's success depend more entirely on the conduct of the mass of the population" (vii. 181).

what they could to centralize everything, to subdue the people again into political nullity, and to neutralize either by tyranny or by base intrigue all the efforts of Greek patriots to complete the liberation of their sorely tried people.

The Revolution of 1843, a most honourable and reasonable movement, only partially cured these evils, for the country was still ruled by a dishonest king, and his ministers were still the men who had been trained in old and evil times. At last the Revolution of 1862, though accompanied by some painful excesses, got rid of the real source of the evil, and by the banishment of Otho made way for a constitutional sovereign. It is from this year, and not from 1829, the date of the battle of Navarino, that the freedom of Greece really dates. At last Greece has been relieved from the pressure of a centralizing government, and to a great extent from the frightful evil of brigandage which was almost fostered by the Bavarian king for political purposes. Accordingly Greece has since steadily improved. The Piræus is now full of factories, and the Morea, so long devastated and isolated, is now a well-cultivated and secure country. The provinces along the Turkish frontier have not yet revived, for they have only lately escaped from the oppression, and hardly from the fear, of brigands. But when the frontiers of Greece are rectified, as must surely soon come to pass, when Thessaly and Epirus are joined to the kingdom, and the Turk is no longer within a day's journey of Athens, we may fairly expect that more rapid progress will be made.

I dare not prophesy greater things of the future of the Hellenic people, though in the momentous changes which seem to be impending, they may be called to fulfil a greater destiny, and occupy in the world's history a place more worthy of their ancient fame.

J. P. Mahaffy.

# HERBERT SPENCER AND MR. G. H. LEWES:

## APPLICATION OF THE DOCTRINE OF EVOLUTION TO THOUGHT.

### Part II.—Mr. Spencer on the Independence of Matter.

In the December number of this Review we entered on an inquiry into the "Independence" of matter or the object, as expounded by Mr. Spencer in the seventh Part of his Psychology. He there identifies the object with a certain aggregate of vivid states of consciousness, which he makes out to be independent of another aggregate, consisting of faint states, and identified with the subject. We ventured to express a doubt whether, notwithstanding his express statements to that effect, his view of the independence of the object was thus fairly expressed, on the twofold ground that the "vivid aggregate," as he describes it in detail, is not really independent of what he describes as the "faint," and that the constituents of the objective world cannot properly be reduced to vivid states of consciousness or to "clusters" of such states. Enough was said to show that if we are to accept Mr. Spencer's account of the objects of the sensible world as clusters of states of consciousness, and his division of these states into the vivid and the faint, we must at least maintain that vivid states enter into the objects only in combination with, and as qualified by, faint ones, and in dependence upon an intellectual action which, whatever it may be, is certainly not a vivid state. It remains to be seen next whether "vivid states" enter at all into the objective world, as such—into the "things" or "phenomena" which we are said to perceive; and finally whether any states of consciousness so enter in a sense in which the distinction between the vivid and the faint applies to them. We shall then be nearer a conclusion as to the nature of the independence and persistency which Mr. Spencer ascribes to matter.

Let us revert to one of Mr. Spencer's illustrations, which we were considering in the previous article. "When for any consequent in the vivid series we can perceive the antecedent, that antecedent exists in the vivid series. . . . Thus, in the vivid series, after the changing forms and colours which, as united, I call a curling breaker, there comes a sound made by its fall on the beach." We have already endeavoured to show that the perceived antecedent in this instance, the "curling breaker," is not wholly or merely a collection of vivid states. But is any element of it a vivid state? And can the perceived consequent, "the sound made by its fall on the beach," be rightly considered a vivid state either? These are in fact questions as to the relation between Sensation and Perception. That there is some necessary relation between them—that no object can be perceived without sensation, that a man must have felt in order to perceive—we shall not dispute, but this relation may be understood in very different ways. Those who would admit that sensible objects—breakers, headlands, umbrellas, &c.—are wrongly regarded as "clusters of vivid states," independent of faint ones, and that a confusion between sensation and perception is at the bottom of the mistake, would still be apt to maintain that sensation was an element in perception and that vivid states, though not constituting the objects we perceive, were yet necessarily included in them. Otherwise it is supposed there would be no difference between an object perceived and one merely conceived, nor would there be any meaning in the verification of conceptions by reduction to possible perceptions. But is this a true account of the matter? We shall find reason, on the contrary, for holding that, whereas perception in its simplest form is already a consciousness of relation, a sensation neither is so, nor, remaining a mere sensation, can become one of the related elements of which in every perception there is a consciousness.

The first part of the thesis here advanced—that all perception is consciousness of relation—will probably find general acceptance. Perception, it will be admitted, is of facts—a perceived object is resoluble into certain facts—and facts consist in relations. But upon what ground, it will be asked, can we doubt that a sensation may—not to say must—enter into such a relation as one of its constituents? When, feeling a pain or pleasure of heat, I perceive it to be connected with the action of approaching the fire, am I not perceiving a relation of which one constituent, at any rate, is a simple sensation? The true answer is, No. That which is perceived to be related to the action mentioned is not a sensation, but the fact that a sensation is felt—a fact to which the designation "vivid," appropriate to the sensation, is inappropriate. If, in order to make sure of the existence of the relation, I try walking backwards and forwards, out of the range of the fire's heat and into it again, the related facts are equally before my mind all the time. It is not the case that one of them vanishes from consciousness and returns again, as would be the case if one of them were the sensation which ceases when I have withdrawn to a certain distance from the fire. On the contrary, the consciousness of it as a related fact becomes most clear just when, with a last step backward from the fire, the feeling of warmth passes away—clearness of perception increasing as vividness of sensation grows less. We conclude, then, that "facts of feeling," as perceived, are not feelings as felt; that, though perception presupposes feeling, yet the feeling only survives in perception as transformed by a consciousness, other than feeling, into a fact which remains for that consciousness when the feeling has passed. If it is suggested that consistency will require us to ascribe a like consciousness to many of the animals, it will be sufficient to reply that this, if true, would be no valid objection to a conclusion founded on an accurate analysis (if it be so) of our own experience. We must remember, however, that there is no reason to suppose, because the burnt dog shuns the fire, that he perceives any relation between it and the pain of being burnt. A sequence of one feeling upon another is not a consciousness of relation between them, much less of relation between facts which they represent. The dog's conduct may be accounted for by the simple sequence of an imagination of pain upon a visual sensation, resembling one which actual pain has previously followed. There may be cases of canine behaviour which could with difficulty be explained in this way, but, till dogs can talk, what data have we on which to found another explanation?

The case of perception just considered, however, is by no means, it may be said, the simplest possible. It is a perception of relation between two distinct phenomena. May not each of these be separately perceived, and, as so perceived, would it not be merely a sensation—a state of consciousness fitly called vivid? In answering this question we must first ask another: What would these perceptions severally be? Apparently, the perception that I am warm, and the visual perception of the fire. As to the former of these, its distinction from the sensation of warmth would be recognized, on occasion, by Mr. Spencer himself. In exposing the fallacy of the "postulate" with which he strangely supposes that "all metaphysical reasoning sets out"—viz., that "we are primarily conscious only of our sensations"—he rightly insists on the difference between "having a sensation and being conscious of having a sensation."* To feel warm, then, is not the same as to perceive that I am warm, or that my body is so. The perception is of something qualified by the feeling, or of the feeling as a change from a previous state. Whether that which is qualified, or which is the subject of the change, is or is not distinctly conceived as inward or as outward, as self or not self, makes no difference to the fact that in the perception the feeling is no longer what it is as a feeling, but takes its character from a relation to something else—it may be to what has been previously felt—established by a consciousness which, because it is a consciousness of change, cannot itself be one of the feelings that form the changes.

* Principles of Psychology, §§ 404 and 405.

[illegible] that there may be anything
[illegible] must precede infere
[illegible] sensation, and does not suc
[illegible] also inference
[illegible] my eyes on that fire
[illegible] element along w
[illegible] phenomenon I perceiv
[illegible] view of what may
[illegible] necessarily involves s
[illegible] be perceived
[illegible] sensation ex
[illegible] something else
[illegible] then the questi
[illegible] persuasion is
[illegible] proper, exc
[illegible] objects. O
[illegible] in feeling, a
[illegible] we have tall
[illegible] on
[illegible] our seeing a
[illegible] words
[illegible]
[illegible]
[illegible]
[illegible]
[illegible]
[illegible] seeing
[illegible] anythin
[illegible]

[illegible] supposed, the affection of the retina is not an image at all, [illegible] which we are apt to attach to the word, as a conveyance [illegible] of some likeness of an object. It is so only when interpreted as representing something, and for the person in the fit of [illegible] it is not so interpreted. For him it is an image only in that sense in which the reflection of an object in a mirror would be an image in the absence of any consciousness of relation between it and the object. The affection of the retina by rays of light proceeding from certain points is not in itself a recognition of the points from which the rays proceed, or of relation between them. Yet, from speaking of the affection as an image, we are apt to think of it as if it were such a recognition. Hence our habit of overlooking the essential difference between the "phenomenon" as it issues from the process of attention—the proper object of perception—and the sensation which precedes that process, or any of the sensations which accompany it, including the last. The sensation has no parts, or related elements, as the phenomenon has. Any notion to the contrary can only arise from a confusion either between a sensation and its organ—between the retina, for instance, of which manifold parts are excited when we see anything, and the vision itself—or between sensation and the sensible thing. A plurality of objects, or of parts of an object, which I am said to see at once, is a plurality for consciousness only in virtue of a twofold intellectual act. In the first place, upon the simple visual sensation there must have supervened successive acts of attention, in which what by anticipation are called the parts of the luminous area are traversed (we say "by anticipation" because it is only through the process of attention that for consciousness they become such parts); and, secondly, upon these successive acts there must have supervened a synthesis by which the elements, successively detached in the acts of attention, are held together in negation of the succession as co-existing parts of a whole. These elements are not elements of the original sensation, which must have been constantly replaced by others as the eye moves during the process of attention, nor of any of those which have succeeded it. They are elements of something by which these sensations of light and colour are accounted for. Nor, on the other hand, do any of these sensations form such elements. The several sensations which are received as the eye traverses any area of vision are not parts of that area. As this area itself is, for consciousness, the object by which a visual sensation is accounted for, conceived simply as extended, so its parts are the objects by which the sensations, arising upon motion of the eye during the process of attention, are accounted for, conceived in a similar way.

It appears then that perception in its simplest form—in a form which may be supposed prior to any reference of an object to a class or any inference to possibilities of sensation—perception as the first sight or touch of an object in which nothing but what is seen or touched is

recognized—neither is nor contains sensation. [illegible]
of its stages. It is true of that original interpretation [illegible]
a change, which excites the attention necessary to [illegible]
change or thing changed is, and which must be other than th
so interpreted. It is true again of that process of attention its
momentarily changing sensations become facts [illegible]
parison with other experience. It is true, finally, of the [illegible]
or "total impression"—the whole of related parts, or [illegible]
fied elements—which results. If, then, Mr. Spencer's vivid
means the world of sensible objects, as the instances whic
of its components require us to suppose, we must deny the
vivid states of consciousness, according to the only
meaning of that phrase, enter into its composition as [illegible]
other mental action, but that they enter into it at all.
however, for that reason to be supposed that it consists of
The distinction between faintness and vividness does not
to such objects, or to their elements or relations. If it did,
indefinite degrees of vividness and faintness, so each objec
related element of the object, would be susceptible of b
nitely more or less what it is, while at some unascertainal
the scale of diminished intensity, it would pass from an "
into a merely "subjective" existence. If Mr. Spencer's u
instance, were what he calls it, "a cluster of vivid states o
ness," and no less if it were a cluster of faint ones, it would
be more or less of an umbrella, as the vividness or faintnes
degree; and, if his theory is to hold, there must be some p
gradual abatement of liveliness at which, from being a
ceived umbrella, it would become an imaginary or merely
one. No doubt it does affect, and is perceived as affecting
more or less vividly, but the vivacity or faintness of this
not a vivacity or faintness of the object or of its qualities.

As to the primary, or, in Mr. Spencer's language, "statical
this will scarcely be disputed. No one will seriously s
figure or motion of a sensible object, either in reality or a
are states of consciousness to which the designation of viv
is applicable. In regard to the secondary, or "dynamical
more hesitation may be felt. Is not green colour, it ma
a quality of the umbrella, and is it not at the same tim
consciousness which admits of being more or less vivid
that, in the sense in which the green colour is a [illegible]
sciousness, it is not a quality of an object, not [illegible]
not perceived. The sensible qualities of a [illegible]
either in possibilities of producing sensation, or [illegible]
and such sensations are being produced; and [illegible]
nor the fact of a sensation being produced, wh[illegible]
vivid or faint, is itself vivid or faint. It [illegible]

[illegible], in an unenlightened person, does not thus interpret the [illegible] which it ascribes to objects. It knows nothing of the [illegible] between sensations and their formal causes. It supposes [illegible] colour to belong to the umbrella irrespectively of its relation [illegible] or to the eye. But it is a fallacy to say on that account [illegible]'s consciousness the sensation is the quality perceived. [illegible] of the quality's relation to sense does not mean its iden-[illegible] with a feeling. For the consciousness of the perceiver in all [illegible] the colour perceived is a quality which does not cease, as it [illegible] if it were a sensation, when he turns to look at something else, [illegible] for him—if he be uninstructed, as a colour; if he be [illegible], as a possibility of colour—though actually unseen. "But [illegible]," it may be rejoined, "the umbrella may be more or less [illegible]: its perceived colour has the variable vividness which you say [illegible] only to sensation." Not quite so. Doubtless colour as a [illegible] is vivid, and may be vivid in various degrees, but the quality [illegible] is the fact that the umbrella is green of a certain shade. [illegible] the fact or it is not the fact; it is not more or less the fact, nor [illegible] more or less vivid. In a different light the shade of colour might deepen or otherwise; the sensation produced might become more lively or less so; but the vividness or variability in degree of the [illegible] produced is not a vividness or variability in degree either of [illegible] possibility of its being produced, or of the fact that the colour is [illegible] presented with a particular degree of vivacity. And either such [illegible] or such fact is what I perceive in perceiving the colour.

It may be suggested, indeed, that although neither the perceived object nor any of its qualities is a vivid state of consciousness, yet the act of perception is so. Since, however, it is not acts of perception, but things perceived, that Mr. Spencer has in view when he speaks of the objective world as a vivid aggregate of states of consciousness, this suggestion, if accepted, would not help to rehabilitate his doctrine. But it could only be accepted through a confusion between clearness and vividness. Vividness is not an attribute of perception, but of the sensation which perception interprets, and which, as in the case of a blinding sight or deafening sound, may be so vivid as to render perception for the time impossible. A perception is clear when the relations between the elements, in the consciousness of which as related it consists, are distinctly, coherently, and completely conceived. [illegible] becomes less clear in proportion as any of the elements drop out of [illegible], or as the relations between them become confused; [illegible] clear as more elements are distinguished, or relations discovered [illegible] those not previously known to be connected. Each element [illegible] distinguished or not distinguished, each relation known or not [illegible]; there is no more or less of vividness in the knowledge or [illegible]; nor do the knowledge or distinction become more possible [illegible] becomes more lively, less possible as it becomes less so.

To revert to Mr. Spencer's illustration of the headland; approach it, my perception of it becomes more clear, proportion as my sensations become more vivid, but see more of the marks by which I recognise it. When recognized the green patch as down, the grey patch as of liveliness to the colours makes any difference to the does make a difference to it is the increasing number of which I am able to identify the particular down or these features are in no case sensations of which vividness They are not sensations but sensible facts,—relative to actu sensation and relations of such facts,—and every one sees a fact or relation that can be either vivid or faint. In when once a clear perception of the headland has been gradual abatement in the liveliness of the accompanyin does not mean a gradual loss of the perception. gathering of the sea-fog, according to Mr. Spencer's green and grey colours become less lively, the perception land need not become less clear. Unless attention is something else, it may very well be as clear the moment plete obscuration as it was when the sensations of colou lively. Why, then, it may be asked, so soon as the ol complete do we regard the perception as over? Not, because it is the cluster of sensations, which may become lively without its being affected, but because our conscio object is not reckoned a perception unless a relation to pres is included in that of which we are conscious; and in which, in the case supposed, we are conscious, when reached a certain density, no such relation is included.

So much for Mr. Spencer's "vivid clusters," as independ ones. Taking these as he describes them, we find that tuents are not such as can fitly be called vivid states of co and that they are only independent of faint states in the distinction of faint and vivid has no application to them, them is independent of qualification by conditions of which, according to Mr. Spencer's principle of division, vivid aggregate and the faint, could not belong to the "clusters of faint states, partially independent of the detain us long. According to his instances, just as the states are objects perceived, so those of faint states bered, imagined, or conceived. If, after perceiving my eyes but continue to think of it, a cluster of the headland, is supposed to take the place of the so called. Now it is true, as we have just state, relation to which as present was one of the object as perceived, ceases with the object then of which I contin that which I perceived as the headland in so far as the fact consisting in this relation is no longer predicable of it. I have to say of it that it was related instead of that it is. In every other respect, so long as the memory of it remains clear and full, the object as represented in imagination or conception remains what it was as perceived. All that can be said of the one can be said of the other. All the facts, consisting in *possibilities* of sensation, thought of in the perception of the headland, are equally thought of in the remembrance of it, till the conception of it becomes inadequate or indistinct, as it does, not through any abatement of liveliness, but through the disappearance from consciousness, owing chiefly to distraction by competing experiences, of the constituent facts. Thus the distinction between objects of consciousness perceived and such objects remembered is not one between a "cluster" relatively vivid and a "cluster" relatively faint. Of each alike the truth is that it is neither faint nor vivid. The difference is that one fact or relation belonging to the perceived cluster, and which differentiates it as perceived, is absent from the conceived, while in every other respect they may be the same and, when they differ, do so only through causes which affect the correspondence between the conception I may have of an object to-morrow and that which I have of it to-day just as much as the correspondence between the conception of to-day and the perception of yesterday. That the conceived "cluster" should be even "partially independent" of the perceived, when the constituents of the one are thus carried on into the other, is clearly impossible. Only if the perceived object were the "vivid state of consciousness," or sensation as felt, which we have seen is not even one of its constituents, could the conceived object be said to be independent of it.

An objection may here be anticipated to some such effect as the following:—"You are finding fault with Mr. Spencer on the strength of a misinterpretation of his meaning due to a misunderstanding on your own part. If by 'clusters of vivid states of consciousness' he meant the objects of perception in the sense which you attach to such objects, their independence of faint states could not be maintained. But he does not. You first misconceive the true nature of the object of perception, confusing it with the mere logical 'thing'—the subject of sensible qualities—corresponding to a connotative name, and then, on the supposition that Mr. Spencer's vivid clusters, because they are objects of perception, are so in this fictitious sense, you conclude that they have not the independence which he ascribes to them since such logical 'things' have not. We are said indeed to perceive things, but the real objects of perception are not logical things but the associated facts of which the logical thing is the mere symbol used in thinking. These, in the language of an older school, are real essences, [illegible] the things which we are said to conceive are merely nominal [illegible] the groups of attributes signified by general names. So soon as we explain to ourselves what these attributes mean for us—

to interpret our logical symbol—we find that we are remembering, or anticipating the recurrence of, events or facts previously perceived or felt. But there is a clear and essential difference between the original events in the way of sensation on the one hand, which are perceptions or perceived, and are properly called 'vivid states of consciousness,' and on the other hand the events in my mental history, consisting in memory or anticipation as explained, which are properly faint states. The former are objective, the latter subjective. Nor can there be any doubt as to the independence of the former on the latter. If Mr. Spencer errs at all, it is only in respect of the partial independence which he allows to the faint states."

It would not be difficult to show that the distinctions, whatever they may be worth, which we here suppose to be made on Mr. Spencer's behalf are not made by him. Fact and logical thing, real essence and nominal essence, events in the way of sensation and events in our mental history, are all blended or confused in his "constituents of the vivid aggregate." This is not said to his disadvantage. If, as we hold, none of these distinctions, however important in the history of thought, are finally valid, there is something to be said for an author who writes as if he were not aware of them, though it causes an opponent the difficulty of not knowing how far back he ought to go in explaining his opposition. In examining Mr. Spencer's notion of the two "aggregates" we have not felt bound explicitly to take account of distinctions which he ignores, but have supposed ourselves warranted on the strength of his examples in applying to the constituents of the vivid aggregate the doctrine which he shares with the modern "empirical school" as to the nature of the objects of perception. If we have, with a qualification, identified the objects of perception with those of conception, this is not due to our understanding the former as mere logical "entities," but to our being unable so to understand the latter. The sensible object, alike as perceived and as conceived, we have taken to consist in facts or groups of facts, consisting in relations to actual or possible feeling—relations which, when the object is merely conceived, are all relations to possible feeling, whereas, when it is perceived, though most of the relations are so, some are relations to actual or present feeling. This being so, we have found that between an aggregate of perceivable facts and an aggregate of objects represented in memory or imagination, no such separation, or relation of mutual independence, is possible as Mr. Spencer supposes to exist between the aggregates, called vivid and faint, which he identifies severally with object and subject. So long as we regard perceivable facts, the constituents of the vivid aggregate, as objects for consciousness, or as being really what they are for the subject that perceives and knows aright, this conclusion is unavoidable. Are we then to understand that our error has lain in treating them as objects of consciousness, and that since they are events in nature as opposed to events in our mental history, real facts in opposition to facts conceived, they are "beyond consciousness," in the sense of having some other existence than that which they have for consciousness, yet one compatible with their being perceived? Is that what Mr. Spencer means? Is it an intelligible or significant proposition?

This question leads us to another aspect of Mr. Spencer's doctrine as to the "independence of matter" than that which we have been so far considering. Hitherto we have dealt with it as meaning, according to his own explanation of what he understands by "matter" or "the object," that the "vivid aggregate of conscious states" is independent of the faint. We have sought to show that, if the representation of the objective and subjective worlds respectively as such aggregates were admissible, their separation could not be maintained; but that, in fact, it is inadmissible. We have now to notice Mr. Spencer's transition to another way of understanding the independence of matter, according to which the independence does not exist on the part of the "vivid aggregate," but on the part of something, antithetical to the subject of consciousness, on which that aggregate depends.

If we were to hold Mr. Spencer bound by the ordinary rules of consistency, it might seem that his repeated account of the "vivid aggregate" as an aggregate of states of consciousness was incompatible with his regarding the object which he identifies with it as in any sense "beyond consciousness." How can he hold, it may be asked, that the facts or objects which he calls states of consciousness are anything else than what they are for consciousness? It is quite a tenable position to deny that an object is a *state of* consciousness, and yet to hold that only for a thinking consciousness has it any reality; but the converse position, which affirms it at once to be a state of consciousness and to be a fact beyond consciousness, does not seem to admit of coherent statement. A reader of Mr. Spencer, however, soon discovers that he must not be held too tightly to his declarations about "states of consciousness." That is a phrase which, like "phenomena" with other writers, seems to slip from him without determinate meaning. Perhaps it serves to give a philosophical character to descriptions of experiences, on the sea-shore and elsewhere, which might otherwise be thought to be written too much after the manner of a newspaper correspondent. A plain man, whom it strikes as bad sense to have his umbrella called a "cluster of vivid states of consciousness," may be the more ready on that account to believe it good psychology. At any rate, having already seen* that the objective world, with which Mr. Spencer identifies the "vivid aggregate," has been previously determined simply as the negation of all or any states of consciousness, we shall not be surprised to find it constantly implied that the members of this aggregate, though it is an aggregate of states of consciousness, are not such states after all.

* CONTEMPORARY REVIEW for December, 1877, p. 38.

When he speaks, for instance, of antecedent and consequent in the "vivid series," he is not really thinking of states of consciousness, of which one happens to come before the other, but of a relation in the way of cause and effect, which no number or order of sequent feelings can constitute. Thus in illustrating the separateness of the two aggregates by the example of the "curling breaker," and the "sound made by its fall on the beach," he remarks, "No combination of faint feelings serves to initiate this vivid feeling of sound; nor when I receive the vivid visual feelings from the curling breaker, can I prevent the vivid feeling of sound from following."* Very true, we reply, if by to "initiate" is meant to cause; but in that sense a combination of vivid states serves to initiate it as little. Mr. Spencer, it is to be presumed, does not consider the sensations which the vivid feeling of sound immediately follows to be the cause of the "sound made by the breaker's fall on the beach." If he does, not the "vivid visual feelings," merely, which I am said to receive from the curling breaker, but the odours, pressures, and sounds present along with them, will have a right to be so considered. On the other hand, if to "initiate" means merely to precede, faint states of consciousness may initiate the sound just as well as vivid ones; nor, "while I am physically passive," can I prevent its sequence upon states of the one sort any more than upon states of the other. In respect of "initiation," then, vivid and faint states stand on the same footing. We do not require a philosopher to teach us that no one

> ". . . . can hold a fire in his hand
> By thinking on the frosty Caucasus,
> Or cloy the hungry edge of appetite
> By mere imagination of a feast;"

but no antecedent "cluster of vivid states" will save the hand from burning, or fill the belly any better. Vivid states of feeling do not cause vivid states, nor do faint states cause faint states. A certain faint state may precede a certain vivid one as immediately and unfailingly as a certain vivid state precedes it. In the instance before us the precedence of the sight, as a vivid state of consciousness, to the sound is not more direct or uniform than is the precedence to it of those "faint states" which must be associated with the sight in order to render it a sight of a "curling breaker," or of anything whatever. If we do not reckon such precedence causation, neither may we reckon the representation in memory of a curling breaker the cause of the sequent representation of a sound. The relation of cause and effect does not in either case consist in the sequence of states of consciousness, but in the relation between this sequence and something else which determines it.

The essential difference, therefore, does not lie between an initiation of the sound by vivid states and impossibility of its initiation by faint ones, but between its initiation by states of consciousness, whether vivid or faint, and the real causation of it. The cause of the sound

* Principles of Psychology, § 455.

lies in the event called the fall of the breaker on the beach, but in this only as determined by complex laws of matter and motion, and as related through specific vibrations of a medium to a particular nervous organism. Neither the event, nor its conditions or relations, are reducible to a succession or coincidence of feelings. The sound itself, again, as an effect or as determined by relation to such a cause, is much more than a feeling of this or that man, or of any number of men, as he or they happen to be conscious of it. It is a feeling of which the nature lies in conditions and relations not present to the consciousness of the subjects of it. To call it a state of consciousness is to ignore this nature, and thus to convey either no meaning at all or one that is false. How little meaning Mr. Spencer himself attaches to the phrase becomes apparent when we find him saying* that "in the vivid aggregate"—an aggregate of states of consciousness—"the antecedent to any consequent may or may not be within the limits of consciousness;" a statement which, taken as it stands, amounts simply to this, that a state of consciousness may be beyond the limits of consciousness. In the immediate sequel, the directness of this contradiction is avoided by an altered formula, which, however, scarcely conveys a more intelligible meaning. Whereas "in the series of faint states the antecedent to each consequent" can always be found, in the vivid aggregate it is not so. "Into that part immediately present there are ever entering new components, which make their appearance out of some region lying beyond consciousness,"—a region afterwards said to be one "of potential antecedents and potential vivid states." Fine word—potential! But a potential state of consciousness—a state not present, a feeling not felt—is not a state of consciousness at all. We can only suppose it to exist as a potential state in relation to a subject contemplating the possibility of its being felt, and Mr. Spencer, by placing it in a "region beyond consciousness," excludes this supposition. Except as related to such a subject, an "aggregate of states of consciousness," of which the greater part are thus absent or potential, is not less essentially nonsense than is a "state of consciousness beyond the limits of consciousness." Nor, if we seek to translate words into thoughts, shall we find it possible to make much of a "series of vivid states," to any consequent in which the antecedent state may not be the antecedent, nor of states of consciousness which make their appearance "out of a region" where they are not.

Mr. Spencer's illustrations of the characteristics of the vivid aggregate thus described, though they make his meaning clearer, also make it clear that what he means is not what he says, and that his doctrine of the "aggregates" collapses as soon as stated.

"The white cumulus which has just come over the blue sky on the left constitutes a change in the vivid series that was not preceded by anything I

* Principles of Psychology, § 456.

could perceive. Sudden as it was, the sensation of cold I lately had on the back of my hand took me by surprise; since, not having seen the cloud behind, I did not anticipate the rain-drop which caused the sensation. . . . If I consider simply the pebble which just shot across my area of vision and fell into the sea, I can only say that it was a change in the vivid aggregate, the antecedent of which was somewhere outside the vivid aggregate. But such motions of pebbles have in past cases had for their visible antecedents certain motions of boys, and with the vivid states now produced by the falling pebble, there cohere in consciousness the faint states representing some similar antecedent outside the aggregate of vivid states."*

Now it will scarcely be denied that every vivid state has another state before it, just as much as every faint state. If the coming of the cumulus, then, over the blue sky, and the shooting of the pebble across the area of vision, are vivid states, they have vivid states before them. These, however, according to Mr. Spencer, are not their antecedents. Yet clearly, if we say with him that the state preceding a faint state is its antecedent, and that the "vivid visual feeling" which we experience immediately before we hear the sound of the breaking wave is the antecedent of that sound, we cannot with him deny that the states preceding those of which he speaks in the passage just quoted are their antecedents, without using either "antecedent" or "state of consciousness," or both, in an equivocal sense.

A little attention will show that the equivocation is twofold, or rather that it affects "antecedent" and "states of consciousness" correlatively. If we look to Mr. Spencer's account of the phenomena of which "the antecedents are outside the vivid aggregate," we find that, although according to him they are "components" of this aggregate,—*i.e.*, states of consciousness,—they are also more particularly described as changes in it. In truth the one description is incompatible with the other. A change is not any single state of consciousness, nor any number of states; it is a relation between them arising out of or determined by their relation to something else, which is not one of the states, but is persistent throughout them. A change in the vivid aggregate, then, cannot be a component of the aggregate—cannot be one, or more than one, of the states of which the aggregate is supposed to consist. Not being one among the series of vivid states at all, it is as impossible that it should have an antecedent in this series as, were it one of the series (as Mr. Spencer takes it to be), it would be impossible for it not to have such an antecedent. In what sense, then, can it be said to have an antecedent at all? "In the sense of cause," will be the ready answer. We have already shown, however, that the cause of the phenomena, natural or mental—such as the sound of the breaker or any representation in memory—from which Mr. Spencer distinguishes those now under consideration, is just as little a preceding state of [illegible] those cases in which, according to him, the anteo limits of consciousness," just as much as in th

* Principles of Psychology, §§ [illegible]

neither is the "consequent," if it means effect, consequent upon a state of consciousness, nor is the "antecedent," if it means cause, antecedent to a state of consciousness. The consequent, to which a cause is correlative, is not a state of consciousness, but a change; the antecedent, to which a change is correlative, is not a state of consciousness, but a cause. If, then, we are to allow ourselves to follow Mr. Spencer in speaking (*a*) of the antecedent of the sound from the breaker, (*b*) of the antecedent of So-and-so's imagination of the breaker, (*c*) of the antecedents of the changes called the coming of a cumulus over the blue sky, or the shooting of a pebble across the area of vision, and if we want to keep the term "antecedent" to the same sense throughout, we must take it in each case to mean a cause which is not a state of consciousness. And not less, if we are to keep "consequent" to the meaning correlative to that thus given to "antecedent," must we take it in each case to mean a determined sequence of states—a change either of nature or the mind—which cannot therefore be a sequent state.

Is there then no real distinction between the cases distinguished above as *a* and *c*? Undoubtedly there is, but it is not a distinction between a case where a phenomenon has a state of consciousness before it, and one where it has not. The statement that the coming of the cumulus over the blue sky "was not preceded by anything I could perceive," obviously untrue as it stands, really means that the motion of the cumulus is not perceived as a continuation of a previous motion. The perception of it is preceded by another, but the object perceived in the previous perception is not one of which it can be conceived to be the effect, consistently with other experience. Every perceived object is also conceived, but not every conceived object is also perceived; and in the supposed case the cause of the phenomenon, which, as in every case, is an object of conception, has not also been perceived, *i.e.*, has not been related to a present sensation, or vivid state of consciousness. It is otherwise with the sound of the breaker. Its cause is as much an object of conception, as little a vivid state, as that of the cloud's transit, but it is related to a sensation that has been actually felt. Thus, though there is no more sense in talking of a "potential antecedent" than of a "potential vivid state" or unfelt feeling—for whether "antecedent" means cause or previous sensation, it is alike actual—we may truly say that in one case the antecedent, as meaning cause, is actually related to sensation, while in the other it is but potentially so.

By degrees the mysterious region in which, according to Mr. Spencer, states of consciousness are not, but out of which they make their appearance, has taken an intelligible character. It is simply the [illegible] of nature, the realm of cause and effect, to which the pheno-[illegible] called by him "members of the vivid series," always belong [illegible] they never quit. They so belong, however, only because they are not what he says they are. What do not belong never in it, are mere states of consciousness,—feelings as determination by relations which are not feelings,—but these ever "make their appearance out of it." When it is state of consciousness makes its appearance out of a region is not, "state of consciousness" changes its meaning between clauses of the proposition. The state of consciousness, wh its appearance," &c., is a feeling as determined by th nature, not consisting in feelings, of which it is a changed The state of consciousness, on the other hand, which is "region" or order of nature is a fiction of certain "idealis whom Mr. Spencer ineffectually exclaims without havin himself from their mode of thinking. It is a *mere* feeling simply as one of a series of "vivid states;" a feeling, minus the reality derived from conditions which are not fe such abstraction it is a nonentity, a word to which no re sponds; for no real feeling has ever not been in that orde that "region," out of which it is said to appear.

This change of meaning, however, is not recognized by himself. He leaves us to suppose that the objects of world are all alike vivid states of consciousness, more or less that these divide themselves into two orders according as t have not other states of consciousness for their antecedent the distinction, in respect of which they so divide them one affecting the intrinsic nature which entitles them in the designation "states of consciousness." It is to the gives of his meaning, not to his own statement of it, that our justification for interpreting it in a different way. learn that, whereas all states of consciousness are characte by sequence in time upon other states of consciousness, dependence upon conditions which are not such states at every case the dependence, not the sequence, which nature ascribed to "constituents of the vivid aggregate so, such a description is essentially a misnomer. It is a de the objects of the real world as being just that which they are not, and which Mr. Spencer himself does not being. In all the instances of vivid states of conscious describes we have found a nature implied which such states—which is not a succession or coincid this lies the explanation of the paralogism alread to the "independence" of the object. throughout the reasoning is claimed for the ness, is in the conclusion ascribed to and absolutely independent of it, under the name "states of consc tacitly understood a determinat

what is predicable of states of consciousness has to be denied. The abstraction of this something else, which, because the negation of all *states of* consciousness, is supposed to be "absolutely independent" of consciousness, yields Mr. Spencer's conception of matter. It is on the possibility of claiming for this abstract object an existence independent of, and separate from, thought, that the possibility of claiming such existence for the vivid aggregate—the world of sensible objects—ultimately depends. We have seen that of these objects, as objects of consciousness, no such independence can be rightly asserted. Facts perceived or presented form one organic whole of experience with facts conceived or represented. But Mr. Spencer at bottom supposes them to have an existence in relation to a "matter," which is independent and separate, other than that in relation to consciousness, and thus to be independent of thought in the sense of being dependent on that which is independent of it. It is the validity of this view which we have now to examine.

At the risk of iteration let us first make sure that the point at issue is understood. It is not the question whether the objective world, can or cannot be reduced to a succession of states of consciousness. To attempt so to reduce it, as we have sufficiently seen, is a self-contradictory abstraction. Feelings sequent on each other, apart from a world, a nature, an order of things, which is not one or any number of them, would properly be nothing at all: nor by supposing them indefinitely vivid could we give any real meaning to a supposition which in effect leaves nothing to be vivid. Though Mr. Spencer himself sometimes writes as if lively feelings constituted "the object," which he denounces idealists for seeking to suppress, we have given him credit for meaning to be more consistent than he seems. He regards all states of consciousness as related to "something else beyond them," and as deriving their nature from this relation. So far the idealist is quite at one with him. The difference arises upon the question, what this something else is. Mr. Spencer's views about it seem to form a series, in which (to use an Aristotelian distinction) what is φύσει πρότερον may perhaps have been γενέσει ὕστερον. His first or last thought about it, is that it cannot be conceived at all. It is the unknowable. His second thought is that it is either matter as including force, or force as that of which "matter and motion are differently conditioned manifestations," and that this is the *alterum quid* by relation to which all phenomena or states of consciousness indifferently are determined. But then it is "objective," and this in Mr. Spencer's view implies antithesis to a co-ordinate subject—a separation of *ego* and *non-ego*. Hence a third conception of it, under which it breaks into two—a subjective something else, and an objective something else, a mind and a matter.

ally, no doubt, these conceptions exclude each other, but not pencer's philosophy. If we might hazard a conjecture as to his mental history, we should surmise that the one last stated had come first in it, and that the other two had gradually supervened without any recognition of their incompatibility with it and with each other. In his writings they are alternately dominant and in abeyance, and may sometimes be found struggling for existence against each other in the same chapter, the sign of conflict being the strangely ambiguous use of the terms objective and subjective. Attempts to reconcile them, it is true, from time to time appear. An instinctive desire to adjust the third and the first finds expression in the occasional statement that subject and object are alike "manifestations of the unknowable." What then is the subject and what the object? If the subject is consciousness, the object that which is beyond consciousness, the latter is no "manifestation;" it does not differ from the unknowable; and all phenomena—the "vivid aggregate" no less than the "faint"—are alike subjective. It may be suggested indeed, according to another mode of Mr. Spencer's philosophy, that the object, though beyond consciousness, is still other than the unknowable, being a manifestation of it as matter or force; but we shall then have the additional difficulty of finding anything not derived from consciousness by which to distinguish such matter from the unknowable, without being any nearer to a distinction between objective and subjective phenomena. If the distinction lies between consciousness as the subject, and what is beyond it as the object, all phenomena, as constituents of consciousness, must be subjective, whether the "object" beyond be simply "the unknowable," or the unknowable plus a double of itself called force or matter. Such a division, in short, of the world of consciousness, as Mr. Spencer adopts, into "antithetical and independent halves," presupposes a dualism of "things beyond consciousness" as its ground. Though it is itself appealed to as the ground of the separation between subject and object, it has become clear from our previous inquiry that Mr. Spencer's thoughts have really followed another course—that the presupposed and misunderstood antithesis of subject and object is the basis of the untenable separation between "faint and vivid aggregates." If by the subject is meant consciousness as a succession of states, the constituents of both "aggregates" are alike subjective. If by the object, again, is meant a sole "thing in itself" beyond consciousness, the same conclusion follows. Only if the subject is regarded as one thing "beyond consciousness," but producing certain modes of it—as "mind" in itself—and the object as another thing also beyond consciousness, but producing certain other modes of it—as "matter" in itself—can Mr. Spencer's distinction be maintained.

It is here that the idealist joins issue. Are there two "somethings else" than states of consciousness, or only one something else? Are *ego* and *non-ego* separate things, severally "lying beyond" separate aggregates of conscious states, or are they correlative factors of one reality ? And is this reality—which is doubtless other than any or all states of consciousness, vivid no less than faint, so long as these are regarded in fictitious abstraction as that which passes apart from that which passes not,—is it for that reason other than thought ? Or does it only seem to be so because we understand by thought something different from thought in its truth ; either the thought of each of us, which is related to thought in its truth as the undeveloped to the full actuality, or thought in a sense in which it is the creature of a false philosophical abstraction, and is related to true thought as the imaginary to the real—thought conceived as separate from the object, which is nothing without it and without which it is nothing?

We have already seen how Mr. Spencer appeals to the experience of resistance as "giving concreteness to the conceptions of self and not-self." We have seen also that, according to his own showing, in giving concreteness to them it presupposes them—that, in fact, the experience appealed to is not in a feeling or any succession of feelings, but a complex theory of such succession, which proves much indeed as to what is "beyond" the feelings, but nothing as to what is beyond the theorizing mind.* Its testimony, in short, is not the testimony of sense, nor is it a testimony to the existence of an independent object. Still it is and will remain the stronghold of the popular conviction that I am not matter and that matter is not me—a conviction which welcomes as independent evidence of its truth what is really its expression, and which, suspicious of metaphysics so long as Mr. Spencer is asseverating the objectivity of the object as an aggregate of conscious states, feels at home with him when it finds that the object is an outward force, a force not mine, pulling the other way from a force which I put forth from within. It is thus when the doctrine of subject and object as independent aggregates of conscious states—the doctrine which we have so far been examining—is for the time in abeyance, and when the independence of matter, either as a source or as a manifestation of force, is being asserted, that Mr. Spencer commands the most ready assent. It is with this latter form of his doctrine that we have now to deal. For the statement of it we must apply chiefly to the work entitled "First Principles." This indeed often appeals for the detailed justification of its doctrine to the "Principles of Psychology ;" but we have already found that its realism does not gain from the "transfiguration" which, in being psychologically justified, it has to undergo.

[illegible] essential to Mr. Spencer's doctrine, as he constantly shows [illegible] that the announcement of an independent *non-ego* [illegible] immediate and primitive deliverance of con- [illegible] either itself a simple sensation, or such [illegible] sensations as is effected by the action [illegible] announcement were found to be itself [illegible] of intellectual synthesis, the

* [illegible], 1877, p. 43.

independence of the object announced could, to say [illegible] be accepted as a matter of course. Hence in [illegible] taken as a sample of many, we find Mr. Spencer [illegible]

"A single impression of force is manifestly receivable by [illegible] devoid of mental forms: grant but sensibility, with no [illegible] thought, and a force producing some nervous change will still [illegible] the supposed seat of sensation."*

Now what is meant by the "single impression of force" whic[illegible] told is thus "manifestly receivable by a sentient being d[illegible] mental forms?" According to the meaning assigned to it, position becomes either a truism or a fallacy. "Grant se[illegible] and a sensation is possible; grant a nervous system, and a irritation, constituting a change from the previous state of the is possible"—so far we have only a truism. It becomes [illegible] when sensation is rendered into "impression of force," and irritation into a "presentation of some force at the seat of sen[illegible] for this rendering, understood as it must be understood if it is the purpose of Mr. Spencer's theory, implies that for sensatio[illegible] stituted a judgment that force is being exercised. The "im[illegible] of force" in fact covers three meanings. It may mean eithe[illegible] occurrence of a certain event in the way of feeling, or (b) th[illegible] tions of such an event, or (c) the judgment that it has occu[illegible] been conditioned in a certain way. It is only by an equi[illegible] between these essentially different meanings that Mr. Spe[illegible] find acceptance for the dictum that "matter, as opposing our [illegible] energies, is immediately present to consciousness in terms [illegible] A force, "presented at the seat of sensation," is felt simply as [illegible] tion. The sensation may be of a kind which we come to e[illegible] one of pressure, or effort, or resistance; but in itself, i.e., ap[illegible] relations which are not feelings or felt, it is not a force any m[illegible] a vision of colour is a vibration of æther. We may say, if that though "on the subjective side" it is a feeling, yet [illegible] objective" it is a particular exercise of force. But it is quite [illegible] thing to say that, as "received by a being devoid of mental f[illegible] distinguishes these opposite aspects of itself. We may not so fuse the two sides as to suppose that the feeling is [illegible] sentient subject that which perhaps it really and [illegible] which it is only for the intelligent subject: and we [illegible] confusion when, on the ground that the feeling [illegible] being and really is an effect of force, we take it [illegible] force. A feeling of force can only mean some [illegible] and a consciousness of force implies at least [illegible] —i.e., of a succession of states in something [illegible] states—which the force produces. Now the [illegible] ing, as an event which force produces, [illegible]

* First Princ[illegible]

[illegible] of successive states no one, and no number, can [illegible] of the succession. No feeling, then, as an effect [illegible] by "mental forms" other than itself, can be a [illegible] a relation of succession between it and other such [illegible]ly, a consciousness of itself as a change. Thus, [illegible] on its objective side," a change produced by force, a [illegible] "on its subjective side," unless the subject thinks in [illegible] consciousness of itself either as such a change or as a [illegible]ing a change. In other words, it cannot be a conscious-[illegible] of external force or of muscular energy. It cannot with [illegible] propriety be called an impression of force at all.

[illegible] objector may perhaps ask by what right we restrict the use of [illegible]" to express a state succeeding another state, and why it [illegible] not also express that consciousness permanent throughout the [illegible] and distinguishing itself from them, which is necessary to the [illegible]tation of them as a process of change, and thus as a manifes-[illegible] of force. The answer is that there is of course no intrinsic [illegible] to the use of feeling, or any other word, in any sense what-[illegible] that we may not take feeling at once to be such a conscious-[illegible] and to be that of which the "objective side," or formal cause, is [illegible]ous irritation or transmission of force. If it is the change pro-[illegible] by a transmission of force—a feeling to which a previous feel-[illegible] given place—it cannot also, for the reason given, be the consciousness of the change. Yet Mr. Spencer's theory requires it to be [illegible]. Feeling must be these incompatible things; it must at once be [illegible] state, caused through nervous irritation by the exercise of a [illegible] and the consciousness of relation between such states as so [illegible], if it is to yield immediate evidence—evidence independent of "[illegible] constructions"—either of *ego* or *non-ego* as exercising force.

[illegible]ssions are occasionally made by Mr. Spencer himself, which in a more coherent writer would imply some approach to a recognition of this equivocation. Thus in the immediate sequel of the passage on which we have been commenting, he proceeds—"Though no single [illegible] of force so received" (*i.e.* received by a sentient being [illegible] of mental forms) "could itself produce consciousness, which [illegible] relations between different states, yet a multiplication of such [illegible], differing in kind and degree, would give the materials for [illegible]ment of relations, *i.e.* of thought. And if such relations [illegible] their forms as well as in their contents, the impressions of [illegible] would be organized simultaneously with the impressions [illegible]. Thus all other modes of consciousness are derivable [illegible] of force."

[illegible] so derivable, if the "experience of force," is to [illegible]ing all that in the two previous sentences has [illegible] no one would care to dispute. The real [illegible] experience of force is itself an effect of force, and whether the consciousness in which it consists is derivable from such impressions of force as Mr. Spencer previously told us were "manifestly receivable by a sentient being devoid of mental forms." "No single impression so received," it now appears, "could itself produce consciousness." At first sight this statement might seem to imply that the "impression of force" is not to be understood as a feeling at all. What meaning, it may be asked, can there be in a statement that a single feeling, a state of consciousness, cannot produce consciousness? Must not "impression of force" be here taken to mean, not a feeling as felt, but the nervous irritation transmitting force, which is its cause? Such questions, however, turn upon a distinction which, as we have seen, Mr. Spencer ignores. If by an "impression of force" he understood anything distinct from feeling, he would not in the same sentence have spoken of it as "a presentation at the seat of sensation." He understands by it, in fact, neither the "molecular change" in the nervous system producing a state of consciousness, as distinct from the state of consciousness so produced, nor the state of consciousness as distinct from the molecular change, but something which is indifferently both or either of them. If we took his statements strictly, we should be left in doubt whether, in saying that no single impression of force can produce consciousness, he meant more than that, since (as he afterwards puts it) "consciousness consists of changes," the *non-ego*, as force, must have produced more feelings than one before it could make a consciousness.

To say, however, that consciousness "consists of changes," or "implies relations between different states," does not accurately express either the truth, or, as we venture to think, what Mr. Spencer means to say about it. A statement to the effect that, since consciousness is a noun of multitude standing for a multiplicity of feelings, one feeling cannot constitute what is so called, would scarcely be worth making. In that sense of consciousness in which alone it can be said with any significance that a single feeling, "received by a subject void of mental forms," does not produce or constitute it, consciousness not merely implies relations between different states: that might be said of the line which my pen is writing: it is a recognition of these different states as related. It not merely consists of changes, but is a consciousness of itself as a subject of change. And the essential question is whether this cognition of change, which is implied no less in the most elementary experience of force than in the most abstracted self-consciousness, can be any more constituted by a multiplication of feelings, which we will provisionally allow to be effects of force, than by one of these singly.

This question is not touched by Mr. Spencer. "The multiplication of impressions differing in kind and degree," he tells us, "would give the materials for the establishment of relations, *i.e.*, of thought." Upon this we have to ask whether it is meant (*a*) that the multiplied impressions are recognized by the subject of them as differing in kind and degree, and (*b*) that the relations, which come to be established, are understood or (at least) perceived relations—relations of which there is a consciousness on the part of the subject of the related impressions. If the passage quoted is to be other than tautological, the former part of the question must be answered in the negative, the latter in the affirmative. Differences in kind and degree between impressions already are relations; impressions recognized as differing in kind and degree imply already a consciousness of relation, *i.e.*, thought. If, then, the passage is to mean anything more than that relations give the materials for the establishment of relations, or that the consciousness of relations gives the materials for the establishment of such consciousness, it must mean that the multiplication of impressions, differing in kind and degree but not recognized as so differing by the subject of them—differing merely as the successive atmospheric influences to which a plant is subject—would give the materials for the establishment of the consciousness of relations, *i.e.*, of thought. And upon this the remark is obvious that, though in such multiplied impressions we may indeed have "materials for the establishment of relations, *i.e.*, of thought," yet in the absence of thought which, *ex hypothesi*, has yet to be established, there is nothing to effect the establishment. We cannot suppose the mere multiplication of the impressions to effect it without tacitly supposing that they are, to begin with, recognized as differing in kind and degree—that they are, in fact, not changing impressions, but a consciousness of change; and this is to anticipate the establishment in question, and to invest them with the form, to which at the same time they are opposed as being merely materials.

There can be little doubt, however, that Mr. Spencer does make this supposition, and that the correct interpretation of the passage before us is that which reduces it to a tautology. Just as he thinks of the single feeling, "received by a subject devoid of mental forms," as an impression of force, at the very time when he is admitting that it does not amount to the process of change which the impression of force presupposes, so he thinks of the multiplication of impressions as already involving a recognition of their relations, even when he is treating of it as the efficient cause which is gradually to result in such recognition. The one consciousness, equally present to, yet distinguishing itself from, successive feelings, without which there could be no such synthesis of them as is necessary to a recognition of their difference in kind and degree, and to their constituting a consciousness of change, is first taken for granted and then represented as resulting from the synthesis which presupposes it. It must be presupposed, in order to the possibility of feelings being held together as related by the subject which experiences them, and except as so held together they give no "materials for its establishment." In

truth, if they are to be called its materials at all, it can only
Aristotelian δύναμις, to which the corresponding ἐνέργεια is "pri
mere materials of it, they have as little reality as any other "
in abstraction from "form." Here as elsewhere Mr. Spencer
chogenesis" is an affair of nomenclature. He assumes as
certain elementary feelings, which are in fact nothing at
from determination in a system of self-consciousness, or in a co
consciousness of nature, and to which both he and his reade
ascribe the character derived from such determination....
traces a genesis out of them of the system which they pre
So long as he can find one set of terms for the "materials"
fictitious abstraction, another for the supposed concrete re
here the materials are called "multiplied impressions differing
and degree," the result a "consciousness implying relations
different states"—he takes and is allowed the credit of havin
a discovery in the natural history of mind.

So far, then, we have found no help from Mr. Spencer in re
the question whether the consciousness, called experience of
itself an effect of force. This is the question which must be a
affirmatively if, under any transfiguration, we are to accept
trine that (in vulgar language) mind tells us of matter as acti
it, as the source of its being what it is. In favour of an af
answer at first sight is the apparent possibility of treating ou
successive feelings as events of which the invariable anteced
nervous irritations produced by force. Against it is the diffic
say the least—of so treating the synthetic principle withou
the successive feelings could not, for the subject of them, b
mined by mutual relation and thus could not form the cons
of change which that of force presupposes. Mr. Spencer ign
synthetic principle. Confusing succession of feelings with c
of succession, changes of consciousness with consciousness of
he virtually supposes the feelings, as apart from it, to be tha
they doubtless really are, but which they only are in relatio
He then extracts from them, as the result of their multiplica
through them the result of force, that unified consciousne
they must be in order to become. It remains to be seen whe
paralogistic procedure is essential or accidental to his doctri
the experience of force be treated as an effect of force withou

This question will be found to involve the following:—(a)
"synthetic principle" spoken of be dispensed with altoge
formative condition of experience? (b) If not, can it be
be, though primary in consciousness, as much an effect of
at any rate, of physical antecedents) as the successive fee
supposed to be; or (c) to be not primary at all, but to result fr
—to result from them in the proper sense and without co
supposition of itself? In the current psychologies, which a

physical theory of the origin of mind, these questions, as occasion requires, are all implicitly answered in the affirmative. To render the answers explicit is the best criticism of the theory which involves them. We shall not expect, of course, to find any philosophical writer who, having distinctly asked himself whether or no experience (in the shape of an experience of force, or any other) is a mere succession of feelings, void of a unifying principle, has distinctly answered, yes. By help of sundry familiar figures—those of the thread, the stream, &c.—our psychologists avoid the ultimate analysis by which the question is necessarily raised, and are able by turns to avail themselves of a virtually affirmative and a virtually negative answer to it. The phrase "states of consciousness," as equivalent to feelings, has come conveniently into fashion as a further shelter for the ambiguity. We cannot employ this phrase of feelings without implying the persistence of a subject throughout them, their relation to which forms their nexus with each other. Thus by the use of it the physical psychologist can disguise that disintegration of experience which is logically involved in its reduction to a succession of feelings, corresponding to a series of occurrences in the nervous organism. The embarrassment, which might be caused by a demand for a physiological account of this persistent subject, he can avoid by saying that to him experience is merely the succession of feelings. The question which might then arise as to the possibility of the successive feelings being also an experience of succession he can take out of his critic's mouth by the assumption that feelings are states of consciousness—states of a subject which recognizes them as its successive modes.

The critic of any theory, however, should make it his first care to find its best representative, and when we speak of physical psychology, we may properly be asked what particular statement of it we have in view. We are examining the question whether our experience testifies to the action of an "independent matter" or "*non-ego*" as its source, and we have found Mr. Spencer's answers fail us owing to his defective analysis of experience. Before we assume, however, a negative answer to the question in consequence, we should make sure whether a more thorough account of experience might not be given, which would avoid the confusions previously noticed, deal fairly by the questions stated at the beginning of the preceding paragraph, and yet be compatible with a physical theory of its origin. As the best hope of obtaining such an account we propose in another article to turn to Mr. Lewes, in whom every candid critic must recognize a philosophical [illegible] who thoroughly understands his business, and in whose hands [illegible] will suffer for want of the best possible mode of statement. [illegible] too, we find the same confusions latent, we shall have strong [illegible] charging them upon the essential nature of the doctrine, [illegible] exponent.

T. H. GREEN.

# THE ABUSE OF CHARITY IN LONDON:

## THE CASE OF THE FIVE ROYAL HOSPITALS.

IN order that the reader may form a clear idea of the great abuses which at present exist, and which year by year are becoming greater, in the administration of some of the chief London charities, it will be necessary to give a very brief description of the origin of our five great Royal Hospitals.

I.

Most people are aware that, by the dissolution of the religious houses at the time of the Reformation, the poor were deprived of the charitable relief which had been bequeathed to them by the piety of former ages. This was especially the case in London, where the indigent had to be supported by the private charity of the citizens, who were not only called upon to relieve their own poor, but multitudes of others still more wretched, who, tempted by its great reputation for wealth, flocked into the City. By the dissolution of the religious houses not only was much misery caused, but disorder, demoralization, and robbery were increased to such an extent that the administration of justice, sanguinary as it was in those days, could not entirely subdue them. It is to the credit of the clergy of the Reformed Church that they exerted themselves manfully in the cause of the poor, and insisted in vigorous language on a more liberal distribution of alms for their support, not only from the City authorities, but the nobility and clergy as well. Bishop Latimer, when preaching a sermon at Paul's Cross on the subject of the distress among the poor of the City of London, and the wealth of the citizens, nobility, and clergy, said that

"byshopes, abbotes, pryores, parsons, canons resident, pristes, and all, were strange theves, yea dukes, lordes, and all; the king, quod he, made a mar-

[illegible] of parliamente that certayne men shoulde sowe every of them [illegible] hempe, but it was all to littel were it so muche more to hang the [illegible] in England. Byshopes, abbotes, and such others, should not [illegible] many servauntes, nor so many dysches, but to goo to their first foundation, and kepe hospitalite, to fede the nedye people, not jolye felows with [illegible] chaines and velvet gownes; ne let them not ones come into the houses of religious men; let them call them knave byshope, knave abbote, knave pryor, yet fede none of them all, nor ther horses nor ther dogges."*

Again, Bishop Ridley, in a letter he wrote to Cecyl for permission to use Bridewell as an asylum for the poor, says:—

"Good Mr. Cecyl, I must be a suitor to you in our master Christ's cause. I beseech you to be good unto him. The matter is, sir, alas! he has been too, too long abroad as you do know without lodging in the streets of London, both hungry, naked, and cold. Now thanks be unto Almighty God the citizens are willing to refresh him, and to give him both meat, drink, clothing, and firing, but, alas! sir, they want lodging for him, for in some one house I dare to say they are fain to lodge three families under one roof."

Again, Stowe, quoting from a pamphlet published at Nurenberg, says:—

"O ye citizens, if ye would turn but even the profits of your chauntries and your obits to finding of the poor with a politic and godly religion! Whereas now London being one of the flowers of the world, and touching worldly riches, hath so many, yea an innumerable number of poor people forced to go from door to door and to sit openly in the streets a begging, and many not able to do for others, but lie in their houses in most grievous pain, and die for lack of aid of the rich, to great shame of thee, O London! I say if ye would redress these things as ye are bound, and sorrow for the poor, so should ye be without dishonour of them which also have cried unto God against you. . . ."

And again:

"I think, in my judgment, under heaven is not so little provision made for the poor, as in London of so rich a city."

The poverty and misery in the City of London at length reached such a height that in the thirtieth year of the reign of King Henry VIII. (1538), the mayor and commonalty of the City of London prayed that they might from henceforth have the order, rule, government, and disposition of the Hospitals or Spitals, commonly called St. Mary's Spital, St. Bartholomew's Spital, St. Thomas' Spital, and the new abbey at [illegible]-hill, with the rents and revenues appertaining to the same, [illegible] only relief of the poor, sick, and needy persons." Nor did the [illegible] body in any of their supplications attempt to conceal from [illegible] the real state of the poor in the City of London, for they [illegible] that the three great Spitals named were

[illegible] by auncyent fathers, and endowed with great [illegible], comforte, and ayde of the poore and [illegible] theymselffe, and not to the mayn[illegible] lyvyng as they of late have

[illegible], then curate of St. Margaret's,

doon, nothyng regardyng the myserable people lying in the streete, offendyng every clene person passyng by the way wt theyre fylthye and nastye savors . . . so that all impotent persones not hable to labor shalbe releved by reason of the sayd hospitalles and abbey, and all sturdy beggers not wyllyng to labor shalbe punisshed so that wt Godd's grace we or no persones shalbe seene abrode to begge or aske almesse; for the whyche doyng yo^r^ grace shall not alonely meryt more toward God, and yo^r^ people, than any of yo^r^ most noble progenitors whiche have fownded so many abbeys."

Although his Majesty granted the prayer of the corporation to have the above-named Spitals placed under their management, a lapse of six years seems to have taken place before any direct system was organized for their management. The first Spital which was handed over to the civic authorities was that of St. Bartholomew, which was for ever after to be styled "the House of the Poor in West Smithfield, in the suburbs of the City of London, of King Henry VIII.'s foundation," in order, as Stowe tells us, "that there might be comfort to the prisoners, visitation to the sick, food to the hungry, and drink to the thirsty, clothes to the naked, and a sepulchre to the dead." In consideration of his Majesty's bounty the citizens agreed that within three months after their charter was sealed they would sustain a priest, to be called Visitor of Newgate, and provide other priests for Christ Church; and that they would also make and provide at the Spital sufficient lodging for one hundred "poor" men and women, and for one matron, and twelve women under her, to make the beds, and watch and attend on the sick men and women, finding for all of them perpetually sufficient meat, drink, bedding, clothing, wood, coals, and all other things necessary; and also eight persons to be beadles, to bring to the said hospital such poor, sick, and impotent people as should be found going abroad in the City and suburbs, not having wherewith to be sustained. Also that they would find one physician and one surgeon, and provide "all manner of 'pothecary ware, and other things meet, necessary, and convenient for the help or healing of the poor, sick, or impotent people." They further undertook that after supporting the vicars, priests, ministers, and other officers, the whole of the endowments of the hospital should go *to the relief and sustentation of the poor.*

In the thirty-eighth year of the reign of Henry VIII. (27th of December, 1546) the King further granted that the said mayor, commonalty, and citizens, and their successors, should be masters, rulers, and governors of the hospital or house called St. Mary of Bethlem, without and nigh the gate called Bishopsgate; and should have the order, rule, and government of the said hospital and people there; and should have full power and authority to see and cause the rents, revenues, and profits of the lands and possessions of the same hospital to be employed and bestowed to the relief of the poor distracted people there, according to the true meaning of the foundation of the same, or otherwise as it shall please the King.

Although St. THOMAS'S HOSPITAL did not then receive its charter, the King granted all the endowments which had formerly belonged to the hospital by way of purchase to the City for the sum of £2,461 2*s*. 6*d*. It seems to have been intended for the relief of the poor,—or, in other words, was an institution somewhat similar to our parish workhouses,—and not solely for the cure of the sick. In his letters-patent the King says:—

"Know ye that we, weighing and considering the exhausted and miserable state and condition of the poor, sick, and infirm persons going about and begging in the public streets and places of our City of London, *and suburbs thereof*, and also for the cure and support of the poor as aforesaid, . . . and further, of our more ample grace, we will for us, our heirs and successors, and do grant, that the said hospital in Southwark from henceforth may and shall be a place and house for poor persons there to be relieved and supported; and shall be called the House of the Poor in Southwark, in the county of Surrey, of our foundation."

The Hospital of BRIDEWELL did not receive its charter from Edward VI. till the year 1552. Although the sick poor, and infirm and impotent persons, had been greatly relieved by the establishment of the three royal hospitals already named, two other sources of anxiety were perpetually pressing themselves on the notice of the mayor and aldermen. The City, it appears, was at that time infested by a vast number of sturdy rogues and lazy vagabonds, who, too indolent to work, lived upon alms they extorted from the citizens by their audacity, and occasionally caused great disturbances. There were also numbers of destitute and helpless children whose parents were dead or had deserted them. At length the citizens petitioned the King to assist in establishing hospitals or refuges for both classes—one, where the vagabonds should be obliged to work; the other for the reception of poor and destitute children. The supplication made in the name of the poor to the King's Majesty for obtaining the house of Bridewell, in 1552, says:—

"For Jesu Christ's sake, right dear and most dread sovereign lord, we the humble, miserable, sore, sick, and friendless people, beseech your Majesty to cast upon us your eyes of mercy and compassion. . . . But, most gracious lord, unless we find favour in the eyes of your Majesty, our hope of deliverance from our wretched and vile state cannot be obtained, for lack of harbour and lodging; and therefore, most gracious Sovereign, hear us speaking in Christ's name, and for Christ's sake have compassion on us, that we may lie no longer in the streets for lack of harbour. And that our old sore of idleness may no longer vex us nor grieve the commonweal, our suit, most dear Sovereign, is for one of your Grace's houses called *Bridewell*, a thing no doubt most unmeet for us to ask of your Majesty, and also to enjoy, if we ask the same for our sinful living and unworthiness' sake. But we are the poor members of our Saviour Jesu Christ, sent by Him most humbly to sue your Majesty, in our said Master's name Jesu Christ, that we for His sake, and for the service He hath done your Grace and all the faithful commons in your realm, in spending His most dear and precious blood, may all be in reward at your Majesty's hand."

The original charter of CHRIST'S HOSPITAL resembles so closely in its wording those of the other hospitals, and the full control of its funds and management is given to the Lord Mayor, commonalty, and citizens of London in such equally explicit terms, that it would be a useless waste of the reader's time to go into the details. Stowe, in his summary, 1556, when speaking of Christ's Hospital says: "It was established to take the chylde out of the streete, which was the seede and increase of beggary, by reason of ydle bringing up. And to nourysh the said chylde in some goode learninge and exercise profitable to the commonweale." He goes on to say, that in one month from the opening of the school, November 21st, 1552, "chyldren had been taken from the streetes to the number of fower hundred." Machyn also, in his "Diary" about the same time, makes frequent mention of the children in this school, all tending to prove that they were taken from precisely the same class of children as those which now come under the authority of the Poor-law Board.

## II.

From this short description of the foundation of the five Royal Hospitals the reader will easily perceive in them the original model of the present Poor-law administration in the metropolis. If further proofs were wanting they might be produced in abundance from different records still existing in the City archives, all tending to show that for more than a century after they received their charters the hospitals strictly fulfilled the uses for which they were instituted. Nor were they solely dependent upon their endowments, for, in case of any insufficiency of funds for their maintenance, the Corporation had the power to levy taxes for their support. For example, the Corporation, by an Act (5 Philip and Mary), which on several occasions was put in force, had granted to them the profits of sundry offices, &c., for the use of the hospitals, especially duties on "the balance commonly called the King's Beame, the gawginge of wyne and fyshe, and the measurynge or measurs of silk and woollen clothes, &c." The revenue of St. Bartholomew's Hospital, in consequence of its expenditure being more than its income, was supplemented by a tax levied on the citizens, and one curious circumstance connected with the power of raising money for the support of this charity was that the Livery Companies were called upon to supply a large portion of the amount required. In the year 1548, an Act was passed by the City Council for assessing the City Companies in the sum of 500 marks, to be paid annually to St. Bartholomew's Hospital. The Livery Companies afterwards attempted to relieve themselves from the responsibility, but the governors of the hospital, in the year 1712, commenced a suit in Chancery against the Companies, and obtained a decree in their favour which exists now. Again, in the first year of the reign of Edward VI. (1547), the Common Council made a grant of half of a fifteenth to be assessed on the citizens and inhabitants of the metropolis, "towards sustaining, maintaining, and finding the poor personages in the house or hospital lately erected and founded by King Henry VIII." Again, on the 26th of July, 1552, a rate was levied on the citizens for the repairing of the Gray Friars' house for poor fatherless children. These and other passages, far too numerous to cite, all tend to show how closely the original institution of the five great Royal Hospitals resembled our present Poor-law administration.

Nor was the legal authority possessed by the Corporation less than that at present placed in the hands of our Poor-law authorities. We find the following order issued by the Lord Mayor, on the 13th day of October, in the eleventh year of Elizabeth's reign:—

"On the Quenes Majesties behalf, we straightlie charge and command you that ye forthwith, callinge before you your deputie constables, bedell and bedelles of your said warde, doe give unto them straightlie in charge that they doe make searche from time to time betweene this and the Feaste of All Saintes next cominge, for all such poore people sicke and disseased, and having no place to dwell in of their owne, or shall be founde lyinge under stalles, or at mens dores within your said warde. And such as they finde as aforesaide, forthwith to cause to be hadd and conveyed to one of the hospitalles of *St. Bartholomew* in *West Smithfielde*, or of *St. Thomas* Hospitall in *Southwarke*, where we have given order they shalbe received in avoidinge of further daunger of infection that might happen and growe by their lyinge in the fields. Faile you not hereof, as ye will answer to the contrarie at your perrill. Given at the Guildhall of the Citye of *London*, the xiiith daie of *October* above written."—*Letter-Book* V., fol. 259 b.

The duties of the governors of the hospitals were not then by any means the sinecures or honorary appointments they appear to be in the present day. In the rules of St. Thomas's Hospital, as they stood in the reign of Elizabeth, we find, where they treat of the duties of the hospital beadles:—

"And also on all such days as the governors of this house shall sit in this hospital for the affairs of the same, ye shall separate and divide yourselves into sundry parts of the city and liberties thereof, every man taking his several walks. And if in any of your walks ye shall happen to espy any person infected with any loathly grief or disease which shall fortune to be in any notable place in this city to the noyance and infection of the passers by, and slander of this house, ye shall give knowledge thereof unto the almoners of this hospital, that they may take such order therein, as to them shall seem meet."

From the foregoing it will be seen that the medical charities were not solely used for acute diseases as they are in the present day, but for all infectious and incurable cases, and also for sheltering the aged and impotent. Beyond that, they were asylums for lying-in women; and a clause in the charter of St. Bartholomew's ordains that in case of the death of the mother, the child shall be maintained by the hospital authorities till it is seven years of age, and then be transferred into

Of the latter hospital, as also of Bridewell, we must say a few words, if only that the reader may be the better able to judge how widely they both now differ from their original uses.

Christ Church for more than a century continued to perform strictly the work for which it was originally instituted, that of being the pauper school of the metropolis. The education received by the children was such as would enable them to obtain the means of existence by honest industry; in fact, it was such an education as that at present given in our better-class pauper schools. In a rule published about the time of Charles I., we find it ordered that,—

"The treasurer with one other of the governors at the least shall put forth any of the children of this house to service, having a careful regard to whom they be put, chiefly that they be honest persons, and such as will be well able to keep them, and to bring them up to such faculty, service, or occupation as they may hereafter be good members of the commonwealth, whereas without such regard taken they may happen to become more poor than their poor parents . . . and before they are put forth, being men children, they may write and read and cast accounts, *being found apt thereto.* And that such of the children as may be very pregnant and very apt at learning, be reserved and kept in the grammar school, in hope of preferment to the Universities, where they may be virtuously educated, and in time become learned and good members of the commonweale."

Of Bridewell itself, beyond the fact that it was intended for the reception of sturdy vagabonds,—in other words, was the City workhouse, —little need be further said, excepting that the school which was established in it might almost be considered as an industrial school attached to Christ's Hospital. One item connected with Bridewell may be quoted as tending to show that the training of the children in Christ's Hospital and Bridewell was identical:—

"Yt was orderyd and agreyd by this courte that th' aldermen and governors of th' ospitalles of *Brydewell* and *Christes* Hospitalle shall consyder of the request made unto the same courte by *Nycholas van Benscenn*, a pynne maker, for the havinge and injoyinge of a convenyent place within th' ospitalle of St. *Thomas* or *Brydewell* to make pynnes, and there to teache and instructe certeyn of the poore chyldren of *Christies* Hospitall in the sayd arte of makynge of pynnes, and to make reporte unto this courte of their doynges therein."—*Ref.* 18, fol. 396 b.

Altogether the organization of the five Royal Hospitals, as originally instituted, did immense credit to the citizens of London, not only in the way of humane, charitable feeling, but also by the admirable, shrewd common sense they showed in their administration. A certain Bishop of Durham, quoted by Strype, says of these Hospitals, particularly Bridewell:—

"Look ye into London what hospitals be there founded in the Gospel time; the poor indeed relieved, youth godly brought up, and the idle set to work. Popery would sometimes feed the hungry, but seldom correct the unprofitable drones that suck the honey from the labouring bees, nor bring up children in the fear of God. But to feed the belly and not teach virtue is to increase vice. Well forth Bridewell, for it is a good school."

But though the foundation endowments of the five Royal City Hospitals were supplemented by the voluntary contributions of the citizens, it will certainly strike the reader, that these institutions, admirable in their conception and administration, would be totally inadequate to the requirements of the present day. The population of the City in the latter end of the reign of Edward VI. and the beginning of that of Elizabeth numbered, perhaps, 100,000, and we learn, from a note in [illegible]ingham's Diary, that there were of these no fewer than 30,000 dependent, more or less, upon charitable relief. It would, of course, be impossible now, when the population of the metropolis exceeds four millions, for the hospitals, much as their buildings have been increased in size, to supply our present wants. At the same time, it may be shown that the disparity in their means for that purpose is not as great as might at first be imagined; even when taking into consideration the difference in the value of money in the time of Edward VI. and in the present day. When St. Bartholomew's Hospital received its charter in the time of Henry VIII. its endowment amounted to only £666 per annum,—half of this sum being bestowed by the King from confiscated ecclesiastical property, the other half derived from endowments of landed property given by the Corporation of the City of London. The balance necessary for its maintenance was derived from voluntary contributions from the citizens. At the latter end of the reign of Edward VI. the revenue of St. Thomas's Hospital does not seem to have exceeded £3,291 per annum. And of this sum £2,914 was contributed from the private purses of the citizens. In the time of James I. the population of the City greatly increased, and with it the poor increased in equal ratio. But it can be shown that the value of the hospital endowments,—the greater portion of which was in lands or houses, either in the City or suburbs,—had increased in greater ratio. With every further growth of population in the City of London the advance in value of the hospital endowments not only kept pace, but was further augmented by legacies and charitable donations, till, in the year 1750, we find the expenditure of the Royal Hospitals * amounted to the sum of £10,000 per annum. From that time to the present, the revenues of these hospitals, mainly in consequence of the rise in the value of land in the metropolis, have continuously increased in far greater proportion than the population. The endowments in the time of Edward VI. may be set down as at most worth £50,000, but now, if we take into the reckoning the amount of the actual revenues, the value of the hospitals themselves and the ground they stand on, together with the reversionary value of the leases about to fall in, the total value cannot be less, in round numbers, than from ten to eleven millions sterling. This, whether adequate or not, is at least an astounding sum.

Let us now turn to the amount of benefit derived from this

* Strype, on Stowe.

enormous capital, and inquire to what extent the present application of the income is made according to the stipulations of the hospital charters.

In the case of Bridewell, there appears to be but one of the many duties formerly insisted on that is in any way now fulfilled. This hospital is no longer used as a house of detention. Originally vagrants were first taken there to have their cases inquired into: the blind and impotent, the paralyzed, and pregnant women, were sent to St. Bartholomew's Hospital; the curable sick carried to St. Thomas's Hospital; the idle were set to work at the hand-mills and other labour; the disorderly were punished; and unruly apprentices and servants were incarcerated for longer or shorter periods. Of all these duties none is now performed; the only injunction mentioned in the charter which is at present carried out is that for the maintenance of charity children, some three hundred of whom appear to receive an education of no higher description than that given to the children in the Metropolitan District Schools.

As regards funds, it appears from the Governors' Report for 1869 that the income then of Bridewell Hospital was admitted to be £18,175 16*s.* 6*d.* To this, however, should be added the value of the ground and building opposite the London, Chatham, and Dover Railway in New Bridge Street, Blackfriars, now used solely as a residence for the clerk and for the meetings of the governors of the school, which itself has lately been removed into Surrey. This building is estimated to be worth at least £2,000 a year. Besides this, since the report alluded to was published, a very large plot of ground at the back of the building, belonging to the hospital, which had remained idle and unproductive for more than twenty years, has been covered with magnificent houses, the rents of which will raise the gross income to at least £25,000 a year. It follows that, reckoning the reversionary interests in the increase of rents from leases falling in, the hospital's gross assets cannot amount to much less than a million sterling.

We will now see what, in 1869, was the expenditure of this hospital for the maintenance of 217 charity children, for at that time there were no more. The salaries paid in Blackfriars, which are wholly additional to those of the school officials, amount to no less than £565 16*s.* a-year. The stipends of the officials at the school, for the education and superintendence of the 217 *charity* children, are given at £1,840 a-year; the majority of the officers being also boarded and lodged. Although the pupils of these schools are certainly treated with great kindness, their education, as before stated, is no better than that given in our National schools, nor are their food and raiment superior to those of the children in any respectable orphanage. To look after the spiritual welfare of these 217 charity children there were two chaplains, the senior having a residence, partly furnished, and a salary of £450 a-year; the assistant receiving £124. Besides these, there were twenty-four schoolmasters, trade instructors, and other officials, employed in the establishment,—being at the rate of one official or servant for every nine of these charity children. Without dwelling longer on Bridewell Hospital, we ask the reader, whether the above was a sufficient result for a gross capital not much less in value than a million sterling.

Injudicious and extravagant as the administration of the funds belonging to Bridewell Hospital may be, it sinks into utter insignificance in those respects when compared with that of Christ's Hospital. With respect to the funds of the latter it would appear, from a report drawn up by Mr. Thomas Hare for the Charity Commissioners in the year 1864, and which appears to be as just and impartial a document as was ever published, that the expenditure in that year for the working staff of this charity, including masters, teachers, officers, clerks, and servants, amounted to no less than £21,444. Mr. Hare further calculated that the gross cost per head of the children, including house-rent, was £58 2*s.* 6*d.* per annum. In 1864 he valued the premises and grounds in Newgate Street at £200,000. But property has vastly increased in value in that locality since the date of his report, as may be gathered from the fact that, three years since, the trustees were offered for the Newgate Street property alone—about five acres in extent—no less a sum than £600,000, and declined it as being insufficient. The property is now considered, on competent authority, to be fairly worth £700,000. In 1864 the gross annual revenue of the hospital, including house-rent, was reckoned at about £70,000 a-year, to which should be added some £20,000 a-year more for the increased value of its ground and house property since that date, and the reversions on the falling-in of leases of the hospital's property in the neighbourhood of Great Queen Street, Westminster. The gross total of the hospital revenue may be fairly computed at £100,000 a-year, representing a capital of something more than three millions sterling.

It is very pertinent now, we think, to ask what amount of benefit the population of London derives from the enormous income belonging to Christ's Hospital; for it should be understood that, although governed by nominees of the City Corporation, it was to be open for the reception of children from the whole of the metropolis. The gross number at present in the schools, including those at Hertford, is about 1,200; of these about 650 are residing in Newgate Street. It is estimated that not above 16 of the whole of the 1,200 pupils are really eligible for admission under the original charter; the remainder are the children of middle-class parents whose incomes may average about £300 a-year. It may be urged, however, and rightly, that assuming the gross present and reversionary income of the school to be £100,000 a-year, there should be deducted £7,000 for the blind charity, and some few thousands a year more for the mathematical school, which would lessen by that amount its annual revenue for general educational

Hospital
the disor
were inc
none is n
which is
children.
of no hig
politan l
As re
1869 th
be £18.
the gro
Railway
dence f
which
estimat
report
back o
idle an
with n
to at l
interes
gross
We
for th
no m
tional
a-yea
tion

proportion with the growth of the population, a new building was erected for their reception in Moorfields. This, again, notwithstanding the providing, by private charity, of St. Luke's Hospital for the Insane, became so crowded that it was at length determined, about the year 1809, to remove to the present site in St. George's Fields. A large space of ground was there purchased by the Corporation for that purpose, and the present building erected upon it. The reader should bear in mind that Bethlem Hospital, unlike St. Luke's, is really, by its charter, the property of the inhabitants of the metropolis, and is managed by their trustees, a body selected by the Corporation of the City of London, so that every ratepayer has a pecuniary interest in the institution. What the gross income of the hospital now is, it would be difficult to say, but three years ago it was admitted, in the Governors' Report, to be no less than £23,854 per annum. This, as is the case with the reports issued by the other hospitals, does not include the value of the building, nor of the enormous space of ground surrounding it, which for ground rents alone is estimated to be worth £6,000 a-year. Looking to the general increase in the value of property in the metropolis during the last seven or eight years, this would raise the real gross revenue of Bethlem Hospital to a sum certainly in excess of £30,000 a-year, representing a capital of fully a million sterling. For this sum, seven years since, it managed to maintain about 260 patients, and it appears from the report of the last Parliamentary Committee that the number does not now exceed 270, notwithstanding the increase in its revenue.

According to the above report, the cost of the staff of Bethlem Hospital, for the care of less than 270 insane patients, including the superior officials, nurses, and servants, was no less than £5,108 8*s.* a-year, and this, it should be understood, does not include house-rent. What the present salaries amount to it would be impossible to say; but, assuming that they do not exceed the sum named, the reader will admit that the salaries of the staff are most liberal, if not extravagant. This may be judged from the fact that in the Idiot Asylum at Caterham, where the patients are in every respect as well treated as in Bethlem Hospital, the building being far more commodious, and the staff in every respect equal in point of excellence to that of Bethlem, the cost of the management of 1,800 patients does not exceed £6,361 per annum. It may possibly be said that the patients in Bethlem Hospital are of a description more difficult to manage than those at Caterham. Admitting that patients suffering from acute mania require a greater amount of supervision than imbeciles, let us contrast the expenditure of Bethlem with that of the late Criminal Lunatic Asylum at Fisherton—the criminal class of insane patients being the most difficult of all to thoroughly control and superintend. At Fisherton we find that the total cost of the patients, including the salaries of officials of every description, as well as house-rent, did not exceed 11*s*. a-week per head. But even taking into consideration the great increase in the price of provisions, the cost of the 270 patients at present in Bethlem, including house-rent and establishment charges, should be defrayed for the sum of £12,000 a-year, leaving a surplus of nearly £20,000 per annum, which might be applied to the use of "the distracted poor" of the metropolis, for whom the hospital was instituted, or for easing the pockets of the ratepayers to that amount.

But before quitting the subject of Bethlem Hospital, a curious fact connected with it may be placed before the reader, as showing the total disregard paid by the Court of Chancery to the original purposes of many of our charitable institutions. By its deed the charity of Bethlem Hospital was intended solely for those too poor to contribute to their support. All others were obliged to pay a moderate weekly sum, in proportion to their means, to indemnify the hospital for the care bestowed on them. By a decision of Lord Chancellor Eldon, all patients too poor to contribute anything to the charity are now rigorously excluded from receiving any benefit from the institution, and are thrown upon the ratepayers for relief; while those who to a greater or lesser extent are able to pay for the benefits they receive are admitted gratuitously.

One reason given for the maintenance of Bethlem Hospital in its present position and management is, that it serves as a model school for the study of mental diseases, and that on this account alone it ought not to be interfered with by interlopers or reformers. But, excellent as the management of Bethlem undoubtedly is, the treatment of the patients is not superior to that witnessed in any of the large lunatic asylums in the kingdom; nor would it appear that any great improvement has been made in its management since the middle of the last century, about which time great and beneficial changes were introduced into the treatment of the insane. Strype tells us (1754), "By God's blessing, for twenty years ending 1753, there have been in Bethlem two patients in three cured." It may be further added that in 1754 there were 200 patients under treatment in Bethlem Hospital. At the present time, although its income is at least ten times the amount it was at that date, there are, as we have said, only 270 patients under treatment.

The two Royal Hospitals which now remain to be mentioned, St. Bartholomew's and St. Thomas's, being each used solely for medical purposes, may be taken together. The joint income of these two institutions, without taking into account the value of the ground on which they stand, is certainly in excess of £100,000 per annum. The revenue of St. Thomas's alone is admitted by the Governors, in their Report to the Charity Commissioners, to be £42,000 per annum. A few years since it was quoted at £48,000, the reduction being caused by the enormous expenditure on the present building. The income of St. Bartholomew's is certainly not less than £60,000 a year; but that does not represent the whole, inasmuch as recently the Governors were threatening to enforce the payment of a rate of 2*s.* 9*d.* in the pound on the rack-rental of the parish of Christ Church, Newgate Street, as well as calling for arrears amounting to £30,000, to which they are indisputably entitled by their charter. At present we believe the suit is in abeyance, inasmuch as their title to this immense revenue is based on the charter given by Henry VIII., which provided for the relief of the sick, aged, blind, and impotent poor, and pregnant women. A trial might raise the curious question, by what right they have relieved themselves of these responsibilities. We must, also, in estimating the income of this hospital, take into consideration the reversionary value of the leases about to fall in, which will certainly add a considerable sum to the revenue account. The value of the hospital buildings and grounds also is enormous. Judging by the sum offered by the Railway Company for Christ's Hospital, the value of St. Bartholomew's would certainly be £400,000; while on the buildings and ground of St. Thomas's alone no less than £600,000 have been expended. These figures, together with the capital from which income is derived, will raise the gross assets of these two Hospitals to a sum fully equal to £5,000,000 sterling.

Possibly the best example which could be given of the mode in which the revenues of St. Bartholomew's might be made most useful to the inhabitants of London, is furnished by the hospitals erected under the supervision of the Local Government Board. Of these there are several, but the one which will best suit our purpose as an illustration is that known as the Poplar and Stepney Sick Asylum. In excellence of construction and sanitary appliances, no hospital in Europe can excel it; no cost has been spared in thoroughly adapting it for hospital uses; and yet the whole cost of the building of this magnificent hospital for 600 patients did not exceed £100 per bed, while that of St. Thomas's was certainly not less than £800. Indeed, it has been estimated that had the present inmates of St. Thomas's Hospital, 300 in number, been located in mansions in Belgrave Square, they would have been accommodated at less than half the house-rent they incur in the present hospital.

But another fault may be found with the management of these two wealthy hospitals,—the locality in which each is placed deprives the poor of much of the advantages which might be derived from them. In the commencement of the present century, St. Bartholomew's was situated in the centre of a densely-populated poor neighbourhood, to which it was indisputably a great advantage. Since that time more than 120,000 of the working classes have been driven from the City of London, their dwellings being destroyed. So few, in fact, now live near it that the average distance patients have to walk to the hospital for advice is estimated to be a mile and a-half, the great majority of them living in Hackney, Shoreditch, Kingsland, and other thickly-peopled districts. The present position of St. Thomas's Hospital is equally objectionable. It was originally situated in the Borough of Southwark, and remained there till the site was purchased by a railway company. Much discussion then arose as to where the new hospital should be built. The City authorities in this case, greatly to their credit, insisted on its being erected in some populous poor district. The medical staff, however, most of whom resided in the West End of the town, insisted on its being built in its present position, apparently indifferent to the fact that there were as few—perhaps fewer—of the working classes resident in that vicinity as there were near St. Bartholomew's Hospital. How far this was justifiable on their part, may be judged when we remember that in the north-eastern and south-eastern districts of the metropolis, there is to be found an aggregate population of not less than a million souls without a general hospital for their relief—a state of things which can be found in no other metropolis in the world. The reader may probably remember the case of a poor girl who, a few years since, died from wounds inflicted on her at Eltham in Kent. When she was discovered she was in an almost moribund condition, but notwithstanding this, she was placed upright beside a policeman in a street cab, which had to be driven over Blackheath. through Greenwich, Deptford, Rotherhithe, and Bermondsey, a distance of eight miles, to Guy's Hospital, that being the nearest.

Besides the inconvenience of their positions, none can deny that the expenditure of these two hospitals—which by their charters are nothing more than metropolitan sick asylums—is far in excess of the benefits the poor derive from them. But although it is impossible to get rid of this fact, a plausible, and, alas! an effectual defence is set up in their favour—that, owing to their admirable and scientific management, they should be accepted as models for other similar institutions to imitate; and that the professors attached to them are men unequalled in Europe for skill and medical science, as is proved by the multitude of pupils who flock to them for instruction, and afterwards disseminate over England and her vast colonies the knowledge they have acquired under such able instructors. These statements have been repeated so frequently that the public at last appear to have accepted them as an article of faith. A calm, unprejudiced inquiry into the facts of the case, however, would go far to dispel the mischievous errors. Not unnaturally, non-medical persons feel that it would be an act of presumption on their part to sit in judgment on the scientific reputation of the eminent men who are the professors in these schools, and who devote the whole of their lives to alleviating the sufferings of the sick, and instructing others to follow their example. They may remember that Sir James Paget, of St. Bartholomew's, has no superior in the world as a surgeon, and that the other chairs there, as well as in St. Thomas's Hospital, are filled [illegible] men, scarcely less eminent. That Sir James Paget has no superior in Europe we are perfectly ready to admit, but we are equally certain that men might be named in England, attached to different hospitals, who are unknown beyond the immediate localities in which they live, but who are, if the tree is to be judged by its fruits, at least the equals of Sir James Paget. If the practical test be applied, it will be found that in other medical schools in London, and in that in some of the provincial hospitals, the professors are equal in scientific attainments to those of St. Thomas's and St. Bartholomew's.

Skilful, as a rule, as the surgeons of St. Thomas's and St. Bartholomew's Hospitals indisputably are, and strong as is their position in public favour, it is a singular fact that the mortality attending their operations, in common with those in other great hospitals, has by no means improved during the last fifty years or more. In order to show that this statement is not put forward without good data to support it, we will quote verbatim the words of one of the most eminent surgeons of the day, Mr. Erichsen, of University College Hospital. In his work on "Hospitalism" he says, "It would be worse than useless, and it would be reprehensible, to deny the fact that the mortality resulting from or consequent upon the greater operations has not only not diminished of late years, but has, there is every reason to believe, in some cases actually increased. The present death-rate after lithotomy—even when making allowance for the application of lithotrity to the more dangerous cases—is quite as great as it was in the days of Cheselden (1760), or the great Norwich surgeons. Herniotomy is at least as fatal as it was in the hands of Hey and of Cooper. And the mortality consequent on amputations—the operations as to which we possess the most extended statistics—has certainly not decreased, but, if anything, is rather on the increase, since Phillips and Lawrie published their tables." The only hospital operations which Mr. Erichsen admits to have improved are those known under the name of ovariotomy, and that improvement has been made at such a cost as to throw serious doubts on the value of the operation, certainly as performed in large hospitals; and of the justice of this opinion the reader may judge for himself, from the startling fact given in Skölberg's report of one year's practice in five of the large London hospitals—in which, by the way, St. Thomas's is not mentioned. In this report he states, that out of ninety-three operations fifty-one of the patients died. Of this number St. Bartholomew's had twelve cases, of which only four recovered. In a valuable work published by Mr. Lawson Tait last year (1877), he says, "I have collected 271 cases of ovariotomy performed in hospitals having more than one hundred beds; of these 58 per cent. have died,—a mortality worse than that displayed in Dr. Skölberg's statistics. Mr. Spencer Wells and Dr. Keith have already proved, as fully as any fact in statistics can be displayed, that in a small hospital the mortality from this operation should not much exceed 28 per cent., and that in private practice it probably would be less than 20 per cent. These figures have convinced me that this operation should not be performed in a hospital, in the ordinary sense of the term, of any kind whatever; and I think that the most enthusiastic conservative will hardly dare venture to support its performance in large hospitals." With respect to the medical practice in these two large hospitals we will not detain the reader further, beyond saying that, judging from the mortality returns (and it should be understood that no incurable cases are admitted into these hospitals), not the slightest improvement has taken place during the last quarter of a century, notwithstanding the constant laudation we hear of the skill of the professors.

But we may be told that in the schools attached to, or rather which have absorbed, these two large hospitals, there is another branch of science taught which deserves especial respect at the hands of the community at large, and of which the professors are admitted to be the most learned in England, if not in the world,—and that is sanitary science, the great object of which is the prevention of disease. So highly indeed is the authority of the professors esteemed on this subject that their opinions on any matter connected with sanitary science are accepted as law, not only by the public, but by our magistrates and judges as well. And yet if the matter were thoroughly investigated it might appear that great doubts could be thrown on the infallibility of their opinions. Let us take, in support of our view, the very hospitals which are immediately under their control, and what is the result? This: that while St. Bartholomew's Hospital during the last ten years has certainly improved in its sanitary condition, it is still not one jot superior to any of the large Metropolitan Sick Asylums under the control of the Local Government Board. From an article in *The British Medical Journal*, October, 1876, we find that during the previous year in the surgical wards alone of these two hospitals there were no fewer than 114 cases of pyæmia and erysipelas, and out of these 34 proved fatal, two-thirds of them being in St. Thomas's Hospital, which had more sanitary science displayed in its erection than St. Bartholomew's! Of the reasons given for this excess of mortality, the principal one is, that its situation is a most unhealthy one, in consequence of the atmosphere around it being impregnated with gas from the sewage in the river. But is this excuse, or any of the others which have been urged, really valid? If so, let us contrast it with another hospital under still more unfavourable circumstances—the Seamen's Hospital at Greenwich. Here, unlike St. Thomas's Hospital, which receives only such patients as are deemed curable, [illegible] s are admitted without any selection whatever, whether infec[illegible] d, or consumptive. And what are the results? We find [illegible] f 1 [illegible] t the gross death-rate was o[illegible] about 8 per cent., the surgical below 3 per cent. In this hospital, containing 250 beds, only 50 less than there are at present in St. Thomas's Hospital, the mortality, reckoning cases of pyæmia and erysipelas, is lower than in any general hospital in London. And let it not be forgotten that while the cost of St. Thomas's Hospital, owing to its scientific sanitary arrangements, averaged more than £800 per bed, a better hospital than the Seamen's could be erected for £80 a bed. But a still stronger contrast might be drawn between St. Thomas's Hospital and the Poplar Hospital for surgical cases, in which during one year more serious cases were received than in St. Thomas's in three years, while there was not one death from either pyæmia or erysipelas.

A singular silence is maintained by the hospital authorities on the causes of this enormous number of cases of pyæmia and erysipelas, as well as of enteric fever. It has been attributed to the large number of medical students attached to the schools; and it is urged as most objectionable that the dissecting rooms should be allowed to remain on the ground plan of the hospitals, or even near them. During the winter session at least eighty dead bodies are required for the dissecting rooms of St. Bartholomew's Hospital alone, and the students using these are allowed to walk the wards during the visits of the surgeons and physicians, as well as assist them with the out-door patients. Nay, more, it is a common practice, in a large London medical school, for pupils fresh from the dissecting rooms to be allowed to attend married women in their confinements, the average age of these young gentlemen possibly not exceeding eighteen years. Of the mortality in this class of patients little is known, but of those attended by the pupils of St. Bartholomew's Hospital, if the authorities did their duty, a tolerably correct idea might be obtained, as by its charter the children of all women dying in child-bed under its care should be maintained at its expense until seven years of age, instead of their being, as now, thrown upon the ratepayers. It may be said it is necessary that these young gentlemen should be under the supervision and instruction of the hospital physicians, so that they may learn that branch of their profession. But there are the wards of the workhouse infirmaries, in which, thanks to the skill of the parish surgeons, the mortality is not one-sixth (according to Dr. Edward Smith's statistics) of that occurring under hospital superintendence, and in these they might learn that branch of their profession.*

One word more with respect to these Royal Medical Hospitals. It

* During the six years that the lying-in wards in King's College Hospital were open, the mortality was not less than one in every twenty-three cases. In eleven London workhouses, comprising Bermondsey, Kensington, Chelsea, Clerkenwell, Fulham, St. James's, and five others, out of 2,413 deliveries, there was not one death. Notwithstanding this enormous hospital mortality, though it included cases of pyæmia, erysipelas, and enteric fever in St. Thomas's Hospital, no coroner's inquest was held, nor official inquiry instituted. Had a similar calamity occurred in the foreign cattle market at Deptford, there would have been no lack of prosecutions under the Contagious Diseases (Animals) Act. It should, however, be added, that, for some unexplained reason, the Local Government Board is not allowed to interfere in the administration of the metropolitan hospitals.

is generally supposed that the physicians and surgeons are actuated solely by philanthropic motives in their attendance on the patients. This, however, is a great fallacy, for the appointments are valuable from a pecuniary point of view. In these two hospitals alone, there are no fewer than 700 pupils, paying on an average £30 a year each, making an income of no less than £21,000 a year. Nor is this all, for by way of increasing the attractions of these schools, the Charity Commissioners have not only allowed the professors of St. Bartholomew's to appropriate land for their use to the value of £40,000, besides donations of £5,000 or upwards, but within the last month they have permitted them to apply the sum of £50,000 of the Hospital Charity Funds towards the extension of the building and the advancement of the school of medicine; the latter sum being sufficient for the erection of a branch hospital for 500 beds, equal in every respect to the excellent Sick Asylum at Stratford already mentioned, in one of the crowded districts of the metropolis. We will leave it for the reader to determine whether the charitable funds bequeathed to the poor of London should be applied to the furtherance of a private speculation. It may be added that in the West End hospitals no contributions whatever are made from the funds towards the maintenance of the schools. Nay, more, at University College Hospital, a portion of the funds received from the pupils has been applied to the use of the patients, and yet the professors are not a whit behind those of St. Thomas's and St. Bartholomew's.

IV.

Surely the metropolitan public are interested in this perversion of the funds of the five Royal Hospitals from their original uses; the educational charities being only to a very small extent applied for the benefit of the poor, and the medical ones being used almost entirely for the advantage of the professors—no cases being admitted into the hospitals but such as tend (indirectly) to their personal benefit. In their defence it may be urged that the poor are no losers by the present system; that all who require gratuitous medical relief, or need education for their children, are supplied in abundance by taxes levied on the ratepayer; and that nothing can be fairer than this system, since all pay in just proportion, without regard to social status,—the rich and the poor alike. But is this really true? Let us take the case of a man with an independent income of £10,000 a-year, who lives in a mansion costing £1,000 a-year, of which the rates and taxes amount to £200 per annum. Now there are at least a hundred persons whose independent income does not exceed £1,000 a year for every one with [illegible] a-year, and each will pay in rates an average of £50 per [illegible] e aggregate £5,000 a-year, in [illegible] cash; and so on downward, the tradesman and professional man paying in a greater proportion the smaller their profits may be, till we reach a man of the dockyard and bricklayer's labourer class, whose average earnings do not exceed £1 per week. Out of this sum he pays 4*s.* a week for his lodgings, in which is included at least £3 10*s.* a-year for rates and taxes. Admitting that there are only five thousand of this class to one man of £10,000 a-year, the total sum they contribute to municipal taxation is no less than £17,500 a-year against the [illegible] a-year of the latter. Again, the labourer has another tax to submit to, namely, to pay school-fees for his children, while at the same time it can be shown that if all educational charities and endowments were applied to their original uses, there would be sufficient funds in the metropolis for the elementary education of the whole of the population. Nay more, if to the revenues of the *whole* of the medical charities, supplemented as they now are by private contributions, there were added one-half the amount spent by the City guilds on their feasts and on their halls, there would be (this was the opinion of the late Lord Brougham) sufficient to do away with the whole amount at present levied for Poor-law relief within the area of the London Local Boards.

It is frequently urged by those who uphold the present system of rating, that if it were abolished the amount at present levied on the poor for rates and taxes would be still paid by them in the increased rents which would be levied by their landlords. But the experience of the last ten or twelve years in the metropolis tends to show a totally different result. Formerly, the rates in the parish of St. George's, Hanover Square, were 3*d.* in the pound, and in Paddington 2*d.*; now they are as proportionately high as in other parts of the metropolis; and the rents have increased in some cases nearly 50 per cent. In Blackfriars and St. George's, Southwark, the rates ten years ago were 6*s.* in the pound, but the rents of the working classes have not increased 5 per cent., and their dwellings are better. But admitting that the educated classes, having the power of remonstrance against it, are justified in allowing the poor to be deprived of their life interest in the valuable charities and endowments from which they have been so ruthlessly shut out, is it not most unfair that we also should allow the poor of the next two generations to be heavily taxed for the *laches* of the present one? Take for example the rate levied by the School Board, to pay off the five and a-half millions they [illegible] raised. Of this vast sum they have spent two millions and [illegible]; the other three millions represent the accruing interest during [illegible] fifty years, which will, the greater part at least, have to be paid [illegible] children. Our whole system of education and charitable ad[illegible] is full of anomalies and corruption, which nothing short [illegible] Royal Commission will be able to rectify.

WILLIAM GILBERT.

# CARDINAL MANNING'S TRUE STORY OF THE VATICAN COUNCIL.

IT was quite natural that Dr. Manning, one of the chief actors in the preparations for the Vatican Council and in carrying through the question of Infallibility, as well as one of the best writers among the Romish prelates, should have considered himself called upon to write a history of the Vatican Council. This idea seems also to have been entertained in the Vatican, as we now learn from France that the Pope caused the official documents of the Council to be handed over to Dr. Manning that he might write the history. And indeed, it is well known that, during the Council, he was one of those prelates who were charged with guiding contemporary literature into the right sense of its proceedings—that is, the sense of the Curia. That he did this is, however, rather surprising, as just before the Council he gave vent, in a Pastoral Letter, to his hatred of all writers of history. He could not sufficiently denounce the "pretensions of the historical science" and certain "learned writers of history," as well as "their historical criticism;" and during the Council he said to all, "We have to fear but one school, the school of history." How then does it come to pass that he also is among the historians? The answer is simple. Interest demands it. From Dr. Manning also proceeded another winged word, "Dogma must conquer history;" and this ground principle he now applies to the history of the Vatican Council, which must not be set forth as it is read in official documents known to the whole world, but must be written so as to agree with the doctrine of Papal Infallibility proclaimed on the 18th of July, 1870. Whatever interferes with this definition by a Council will be ignored or treated as calumny according to the canon set forth at the Council in relation to historical inquiry by the so-called Commission of Faith; historical facts which contradict a truth of faith a [illegible] certainly to be regarded as fa[illegible]

[illegible] they contradict such a truth.* Dr. Manning even confirms this in his writing, where he says he has weighed together all the things which "will incline future historians to sum up the contest for the definition of the infallibility in some such way as this."† So then we have to expect, from the Cardinal's character as well as his own confession, NO TRUE history, but one written for a doctrinal purpose. This will sufficiently appear from what follows.

Regarded from the scientific point of view, Dr. Manning's book is really of no importance. Its significance it owes entirely to the author's position in the Romish hierarchy, and to the efforts of the Ultramontane party to bring it into a wide circulation among the masses of the people in other countries, as well as in England. But the more it tries to obscure the truth concerning the Council, so much the more urgent is the duty to set forth its utter poverty and its perversion of history. The book in fact is written without regard to the elementary principles of historical science.

By the history of an event is understood not merely the chronological enumeration of external circumstances, but also the representation of its inward connections with the past and also other contemporary historical factors, and more especially the exhibition of the internal motives and the collisions of parties, until at length the event itself took place. Of all this Dr. Manning appears not to have the least idea. He begins his history with the first proposal to hold an Œcumenical Council made by Pius IX. (December 6th, 1864), and the questions addressed to the Cardinals resident in Rome concerning its convocation. What he gives on this subject is merely an extract from Ceçconi's first volume of the history of the Council, which was written by order of the Pope. He indeed keeps so close to this book that he even repeats Cecconi's incidental reflections, which, however, does not prevent him from here and there pressing somewhat further than Cecconi had done the "prudent economy" with the full truth, or, in his precipitate zeal, uttering words which must at least be offensive to good Roman ears; for instance, that one Cardinal stated his opinion "that the necessity of the temporal power of the Pope in the present time" should be maintained. We refrain from any remark on this, and only recall what the Jesuit Curci, on the other hand, rightly asks the irreconcilable Ultramontanes—if the loss of the States of the Church, which has already continued seven years, was not also by permission of [illegible] providence as well as their first coming into the possession of the [illegible]? and if it was really a Christian spirit stiffneckedly to oppose this [illegible] of Providence? Singularly enough, Dr. Manning believes [illegible] only a few of the Cardinals, in their Opinions, which were [illegible] by the Syllabus which had meanwhile appeared, men[illegible] of the definition of Infallibility and of the Syllabus,

* [illegible] historiæ facta opponantur, ea certissime, quatenus opposita videantur, [illegible] Cf. Relatio super Observationibus . . . in Schema de Rom. [illegible] Friedrich's Documenta, ii. 309.

† Page 157.

"that if the course of history does not prove that a [illegible] spiracy controlled the programme of the Council, the [illegible] *usque ad nauseam*, that 'Rome, by hidden schemes of [illegible] conceived the design of concentrating all power, ecclesiastical [illegible] hands of the Supreme Pontiff, and setting up in the Church [illegible] tant authority by the *servility* of the bishops,' will be irreparably [illegible]

No one indeed can see what this remark means in this pl[illegible] Cardinals when first asked their opinion, as Dr. Manning hi[illegible] pressly says, had not the task of making the programme for th[illegible] It follows further that the Cardinals did not speak of Infal[illegible] that Infallibility must have come into the programme fro[illegible] quarter, and since neither Manning nor Cecconi says what p[illegible] Pius IX. made for the Council, and by whom the particu[illegible] were suggested to him, the argument goes for nothing. An[illegible] Manning seriously believe that the "prudent economy" of [illegible] Commission for the preparation of dogmas spoke in ref[illegible] Infallibility, and which they confess to have put in practic[illegible] already influence the Curia and the Pope in 1865?

And in the following section, concerning the appointing o[illegible] mission of Cardinals to consult on the question of the convo[illegible] General Council, the Cardinal should not have begun with t[illegible]

"Many might expect that Pius IX. would have proceeded to [illegible] the convocation of the Council of the Vatican. Indeed, many hav[illegible] he was so strongly bent upon it for the special purpose of his own '[illegible] that he waited for no consultation and endured no advice. History t[illegible] tale" (p. 12).

From Cecconi the fact is certain that Pius IX. could not w[illegible] the Cardinals had given their opinions. Six were still silent. [illegible] an extract to be made from those opinions that had bee[illegible] and consultations again to be held. In other things Dr. Man[illegible] closely to Cecconi's book, certainly with "prudent econo[illegible] only the remark concerning the question whether Cathol[illegible] should be invited to the Council is his own unhistorical [illegible] stands in direct contradiction with what went before, whe[illegible] says the Commission of Cardinals thought fit "that [illegible] Sovereigns should be invited to appear by their legates [illegible] of the Vatican." The opinion of Giannelli, the secretary [illegible] mission, he perfectly ignores, and puts down his own [illegible]

"At this day Governments are not Catholic. . . . [illegible] therefore, no longer represent Catholic kingdoms; they [illegible] states as such to have no religion (*sic*), and have withdrawn [illegible] from the unity of the Church and faith, and from [illegible] To invite them to sit in an Œcumenical Council would [illegible] authorities of the United States to sit in the British [illegible]

(*Omne simile claudicat!*) But the [illegible] reflections, otherwise it would [illegible] sion to invite the princes. Pe[illegible] party which afterwards prevente[illegible]

Further, Dr. Manning, following Cecconi, records the constitution of a [illegible] of Direction, and taking the opinion of thirty-six Occidental [illegible] Oriental bishops. He adds only a few remarks, but these, like all the others, give evidence of remarkable confusion. Thus he says: "Every bishop is, in virtue of his office, a doctor or teacher of the faith. It matters not how large or how small his diocese may be, whether it be in the Catholic unity or *in partibus infidelium*, whether he have a flock under his jurisdiction or not. The bishop of the least see in this is equal to the bishop of the greatest. He has been constituted a guardian of the faith by a divine commission, and his testimony as a witness is not greater or less in weight because the city over which he rules is greater or less in magnitude. It is the same in all" (p. 24). Dr. Manning, as he here reckons it necessary to vindicate the bishops *in partibus infidelium*, seems as if he wished to say that among the thirty-six bishops whose names neither he nor Cecconi dares to mention, there were bishops *in partibus*. These bishops, we must say, would certainly find themselves in a strange condition should they have to answer for the circumstances of their dioceses *in partibus infidelium*—that is, in heathen lands, which they themselves only know by name—and for what necessities of the heathen they held a universal Council to be necessary. Whether their dioceses are great or small is in itself unimportant, but not if the diocese is an old one, or a new one, perhaps, just founded by a missionary sent out by the Propaganda. The old Church at least made this difference very important, though neither the Roman Curia nor Dr. Manning cares to remember it. But for whom bishops *in partibus infidelium* are constituted guardians of the faith, Dr. Manning himself can scarcely know. In any case, he can point to no Divine command. They are a late Romish invention, of which the old Church knew nothing, and which on that account could not come into consideration in the old Councils. Their existence cannot be justified, nor can anything be said in defence of their right to sit in a Council of the Church. Dr. Manning must have felt this, as he says nothing further about them. Only the Roman Curia which created them required such "guardians of the faith." After the Cardinal has given an extract from the opinions of the thirty-six bishops, which treat of all things possible and impossible, he once more makes the clever remark, since only a few bishops recommended the definition of Infallibility, and many pointed to the Syllabus now in their hands as giving the best outlines of matters to be treated by the Council, that the object for which [illegible] Council was said to be called—namely, the Infallibility definition [illegible] only mentioned by a few bishops, and was not at all in the [illegible] But this argument is as easily understood as the other. We [illegible] yet neither the majority of the Cardinals nor of the [illegible] the definition of Infallibility. The con[illegible] not think it was necessary to define Infal[illegible] came into the programme, it must have [illegible] source. Was it from some party, or from the Pope counselled and influenced by some party? We shall see before long. But first it is necessary to notice that Cardinal Manning's arguments have nothing to do with the subject, as the bishops had not to make a programme, and still less could they say for what particular object the Pope wished to convoke the Council. This was always hidden in the profoundest silence. If Dr. Manning will discuss this point, he must for the future keep more closely before his eyes the fact that the Pope, and afterwards the Commission of Direction, alone knew the special object of the Council, and had prepared the programme for it. The other Cardinals, those who did not sit in this commission, as well as the whole actual episcopate of Christendom, not that of the heathen, were apparently excluded from this office. Dr. Manning must prove that the Pope and the Commission of Direction had not from the beginning contemplated the definition of Infallibility as a subject for the Council; and if this is done, then it stands so much the more certain that it was brought into the programme by some party who must have been active in relation to the Council from the first.

What has been said will serve for the criticism of the introduction to the following chapter, "Recapitulation—The situation in Europe—The war between Austria and Prussia (1866)—The invitation to the Centenary of St. Peter (1867)." Although Dr. Manning has spent some pages over the question just discussed, he once more assures us that the initiative to the Council was altogether the act of Pius IX., and the motive was the wish to find an extraordinary remedy for the extraordinary evils of the Christian world; so it was not the definition of Infallibility. Dr. Manning cannot surely be aware of the insufficiency of his argument. Along with the question of initiative and that of motive, the remedy whereby this world's evils are to be healed had to be discussed. After the Council, at least universally by the Ultramontanes, Infallibility was reckoned the remedy for the evils; and for this we can appeal to the Cardinal himself, when he says:—

"When the generation of to-day is past, and they who may have opposed or reluctantly acquiesced in what was not familiar to their youth are passed away, when the definitions of the Vatican shall have pervaded the living world-wide faith of the Church [and so it appears these things have not hitherto pervaded the faith of the Church!] like the definitions of Nicæa and Trent, then it will be seen what *was needed in the nineteenth century*, and what the Vatican Council has accomplished" (p. 204).

But was not this remedy clear to the Pope and the Commission of Direction from the beginning, or did it first occur to them after the [illegible] and the commencement of the Council? This we do not [illegible], and further on we shall give proof of the contrary. The [illegible], which follows of the evils of the time, which forms a (*Om*[illegible] of the hi[illegible] the Church, we do not notice further, reflect[illegible] [illegible] reader already familiar with Ultra-sion to i[illegible] refuse to look somewhat nearer at party whic[illegible] [illegible]lanning says:—

"The separations of the sixteenth century were not of this sort. They were the formal going out of nations from the world-wide family of Christendom, based and defended upon the principle that participation in the unity of the Catholic Church was not necessary, and that every nation contained within itself the fountain of faith and of jurisdiction, and, being independent of all authority external to itself, was therefore self-sufficing" (p. 33).

If any one but considers these words, he will naturally ask, Does Dr. Manning here intentionally utter an untruth, or does he really not know history better? We prefer taking the latter alternative, since the Cardinal shows himself in these passages to be very ignorant of theology. What people which in the sixteenth century received the Reformation formally declared that it came out or even intended to come out from the family of Christendom scattered throughout the world? Did they wish no more to be Christians, or did they only wish to reform the concrete Christianity which they saw around them, and which they believed to be corrupt? They certainly did not mean that they were to come out from Christianity, but only from obedience to the Pope and the bishops until they were reformed "in head and members," &c. But if by Christianity Dr. Manning understands the Romish Church, he makes a strange mistake. Everybody knows that there existed in the world the Greek Oriental Church, which is not in union with Rome, and whose pretensions it rejects. But this Church not only declares itself Christian, but is reckoned so by others, yea, even by the Roman Curia.

A Romish Cardinal really ought not to require to have such elementary things brought home to him. Of the same kind is the assertion that the Reformation rested on the principle that "participation in the unity of the Catholic Church was not necessary;" which is quite false, unless by "Catholic" Dr. Manning understands Romish, which, indeed, at that time the Catholic Church had become. That the Reformation ultimately set forth the principle "that every nation contained within itself the fountain of faith," is not merely a novel statement, unsupported by history, but is evidence of incredible theological ignorance. Dr. Manning does not know, or at least affects not to know, what is understood by "source of faith." With Catholics it is the Bible and tradition, with Protestants the Bible. Only one who does not know this, or is willingly ignorant of it, could ever arrive at Dr. Manning's assertions. But perhaps we shall better understand what is meant, if we remember that for Dr. Manning and the Roman Curia, "the Pope is actually the source of faith;" according to the saying of Cardinal Perrone and different bishops and Ultramontane doctors, he no longer requires either Bible or tradition (the last taken in the specially Catholic sense). By this the dogma of the Immaculate Conception was justified both before and after 1854. This is also the line of thought from which proceeded the famous application by the Pope [illegible]self of the words "I am the Way, the Truth, and the Life" [illegible] Dr. Manning has surely no right to transfer his corrupt idea of the source of faith to the Reformed Churches. [illegible] is the Cardinal's idea that "the Revolution . . . [illegible] throne and in almost every government and legislature [illegible] world," and that "the public laws even of the [illegible] people are Catholic are Catholic no longer" (pp. 35, 36). S[illegible] to be Catholic that is, not to be Romish, is to be revolutiona[illegible] life, and this revolution will only end when the public l[illegible] become Catholic, that is, Romish. And then the Cardinal [illegible] usual Ultramontane threat, which ought to make all dynast[illegible] perpetual terror—

"If, as political foresight has predicted, all nations are on th[illegible] democracy, the Church will know how to meet this new and strang[illegible] the world. The high policy of wisdom by which the Pontiffs held t[illegible] dynasties of the Middle Age, [and did not crush and exterminate t[illegible] know how to hold together the peoples who still believe" (p. 36).

The only piece of information in this section concerning t[illegible] of the Council is the fact, not related even by Cecconi, that "[illegible] had at one time thought of fixing" for the opening of the Co[illegible] 29th of June, 1867, on which the eighteenth centenary of [illegible] martyrdom would fall" (p. 40). That on this day also the Pro[illegible] of Infallibility was fixed, as was believed in France, Dr. M[illegible] course does not say, as it was not to be allowed that in R[illegible] was any thought of Papal Infallibility in the calling of a Co[illegible]

Of the second chapter, which treats of the time from the p[illegible] of the Bull of Convocation to the opening of the Council, the [illegible] is entirely Dr. Manning's own. Cecconi says nothing of the d[illegible] concerning the definition of the Immaculate Conception, of t[illegible] zation of the Japanese Martyrs, and especially of the centena[illegible] relation to the Vatican Council. We quite agree with the [illegible] when he says:—

"There can be little discernment in any man who cannot see how [illegible] events brought out the Infallibility of the Roman Pontiff,—that of [illegible] defining of a dogma of faith, and that of 1862," &c. (p. 44).

We also agree almost entirely with what follows on the nex[illegible]

"It is not too much to say that of the proximate causes of the d[illegible] the Infallibility, the centenary of St. Peter's martyrdom was the most [illegible]

Indeed, it was always our conviction that these celebrations [illegible] the way for the definition of Infallibility. We perhaps only [illegible] the Cardinal in this, that we maintain, while he is silent [illegible] that the two last were especially used for this end, an[illegible] absolutely necessary. The truth of the last [illegible] will probably admit, as he has shown a remarkable [illegible] appreciation of the meaning of the definition of 18[illegible] seriously declared that in no case so directly [illegible] and the Episcopate worked together [illegible] while Bishop Malou, writing [illegible] Pope, on this question, [illegible]

[illegible] Immaculate Conception.* In the book before us, Dr. [illegible] writes in entire agreement with Malou. He will perhaps [illegible] progress under the guidance of the Jesuit Schrader. [illegible] himself says, "If Pius IX. did not bear an infallible [illegible] was the act of 1854? . . His act was therefore infallible, [illegible] (p. 42). It is explained thus: "It is certain that the [illegible] 1854 powerfully awakened in the minds of both clergy [illegible] the thought of Infallibility" (p. 48). But this is not the [illegible]. The Act of 1854, as Schrader describes it, was a [illegible]. He says, "It is an act quite peculiar to the pontifi[illegible] Pius IX., as no previous pontificate had pointed to it."† [illegible] usurpation some authority must be produced. This the Pope [illegible] provides, so far as he can do it, for himself. It is found [illegible] twenty-third thesis of the Syllabus, where he teaches that [illegible] Roman Popes . . . have never overstepped the bounds of their [illegible] . . . and have never erred in determining faith and morals." [illegible] was only a judgment in a particular matter. The usurpation [illegible] could only be done away by the definition of the Infallibility [illegible] Pope. The assemblies of bishops in Rome in 1862 and 1867, [illegible] their two addresses (though important means of agitation, full of [illegible] and often meaningless phrases), were unable to effect this. In [illegible] interpretation of these addresses we cannot at all agree with [illegible]. What he says of the address of 1867 is directly opposed [illegible]. Some members of the Commission which prepared it caused [illegible] word "infallible," which frequently occurred, to be struck out, because they did not wish to speak of Infallibility. The same is the case with the words "Peter has spoken by Leo." They were described as [illegible] acclamations (*Beifallsrufe*), and it is expressly remarked that ac[illegible] "define nothing, and can neither be the object of faith nor end any controversy." These things being so, of course Infallibility could not be contained in the address, nor the Syllabus described as in[illegible]. Moreover on the opposition of the Papal Commissary, repre[illegible] the Roman prelates, the proposal to mention the Syllabus in the [illegible] was set aside, for, as he remarks, "the Syllabus is no act of the [illegible]."‡ The facts do not admit of Dr. Manning's interpretation: that [illegible] prepared by a commission and taken from house to house to [illegible] signatures, are worthless in matters for the determination of [illegible]. But so far we recognize the addresses to be of great value, [illegible] they were actually understood by the Curia and the majority of [illegible] in Dr. Manning's sense. Much more important, however, [illegible] the Conference of 1867, another proceeding which [illegible] of in Dr. Manning's pages. Here he does not act [illegible] economy." If he had, it would have been better to

* [illegible] of Christendom, p. 58, seq.

† [illegible] und als König, 1865, s. 12.

‡ [illegible], nach Angabe eines Commissions-Mitgliedes.

have passed over the document in silence. Not indeed in this place, but in several other places, does he tell us:—

"The majority [of the five hundred bishops assembled in Rome in 1867] desired that at the coming Council all questions on this doctrine [the Infallibility of the Pope] should be closed, and all future controversies ended" (p. 158);

and that they, "since the centenary of St. Peter, had fixed their minds upon it" (p. 193). So that, already in 1867, the Infallibilist majority of the Council was constituted, and on their side the subject of Infallibility was brought into the programme, perhaps directly in consequence of the address debates, concerning which the reader may consult Lord Acton's History of the Vatican Council, and take note of the circumstance that one bishop did not subscribe the address and had to leave Rome. Everything that proceeded from this majority, as Dr. Manning's book on the centenary, with all that was done under their influence and with their sanction, had for its object to agitate for the definition of Infallibility. The establishment by the Jesuits of the Infallibility League, with the celebrated vow of the *sacrificio dell'intelletto,* should not be left unmentioned, though for Cardinal Manning it seems to have no existence.

On the sketches of the historical development of the doctrine of Infallibility appended to this section (p. 56, ff.) we shall not enlarge. Dr. Manning speaks of history as a blind man speaks of colours. The first period, he says, in which men knew nothing of Infallibility, was that in which they simply believed the truth; others call it the time of latent traditions. But in this period (which, according to the Jesuit Schrader, begins from 1854) the truth was acted upon. Results like these can of course only be reached by depraving and perverting the clearest and best assured facts in history. Among other proofs of Infallibility, Dr. Manning says, that on the authority of Innocent I. and Gelasius "alone the doctrine of original sin and the Canon of Holy Scripture rested down to the Council of Trent!" (p. 58). We may safely say that no student of Romish theology in Germany would dare to make such a statement. According to Dr. Manning, the Infallibility of the Pope was believed down to the Council of Constance. Through it was this faith first shaken when the distinction arose between *sedes et in ea sedentem.* It was then said that the Apostolic See, and not the Pope, was infallible. This doctrine, it is added, was held especially by the Sorbonne and the Gallican Church, and the controversy concerning it has continued to our time. The German Church, which corresponds to the old and mediæval one, holds, the Curialists of course being excepted, that neither the *sedes* nor the *in ea sedens* is infallible, but only the Church in General Council in union with the Pope. Strange it is that of this view Dr. Manning knows nothing whatever! It fares still worse with his parallel between the development of the Infallibility doctrine and the Immaculate Conception. It is a pity that he does not

all points. Even Denzinger, the disciple of the Jesuits, in his book on the Immaculate Conception, says that the definition of it had been a contest between the Jesuits and the Dominicans, and that it could only be proceeded with when the latter had lost their power. But in what way the power of the Dominicans was completely broken we learn from the Jesuit Perrone, in his book concerning the Acts of the Immaculate Conception. He says that Pope Pius IX., in 1847, simply commanded the Dominicans to insert in their Missal and Breviary the Immaculate Conception,—that is, they had to believe it at the command of the Pope. This is the way by which, in the Romish Church, a "latent tradition" becomes a univetsal one. From that time the Immaculate Conception becomes definable. Perrone now writes his book concerning its definability, dedicates it to the Pope (1847), and so the business floats on the stream. There are yet other like parallels in relation to Infallibility which we shall see anon; but concerning these of course the Cardinal is silent.

After Dr. Manning has spoken, in the second section of this chapter, of the fixing of the day for the opening of the Council, and of the Bull of Convocation, he comes to the reception of the summons by opponents, with their open and secret machinations, and the consequences of them. We ought really to quote the whole of this chapter as a remarkable specimen of the perversion of history. Let us try to set forth the substance of the matter. The Count de Maistre and Lamennais had represented as the only remedy for the evils in Church and State the full and absolute declaration of Papal Infallibility. It is well known what influence both these men had, and how their views were soon embodied in the Ultramontane party. The first especially—for Lamennais afterwards departed from the faith of the Romish Church—became the classical author for the Ultramontanes of all countries, and, according to Montalembert, his principles in the fourth decade of the century had become commonplaces for the Catholic youth of France. In the time of Gregory XVI., under the leadership of Gousset, a theological, and under that of Gueranger, a liturgical "revolution," as the Ultramontanes themselves call it, took place. Non-infallibilist writings and catechisms were removed from schools, and replaced by infallibilist. In 1848 the French Ultramontane party had set forth as its programme the definition of the Immaculate Conception and of Papal Infallibility. Soon after prophecies, dreams, miracles, were contrived to favour it. Pius IX. entered so far into this programme as to take the lead in furthering the "revolution;" the pastorals of the bishops that leaned to Gallicanism he denounced in allocutions, and caused to be condemned by the Congregation of the Index. This congregation had marvellous work to do, for the oldest and most highly-esteemed text-books were put on the Index. Whilst the non-infallibilist writings were thus rendered suspicious, the old infallibilist literature was more widely circulated, and a new infallibilist literature created. [illegible] the desired episcopal approbation to all [illegible] Infallibility. The bishops had to hold [illegible] Infallibility was to be brought forward. In [illegible] the Jesuit Perrone said after the Vatican, "All arrang[illegible] the definition of Infallibility) were made beforehand, n[illegible] wanting." The Curia also, in the preparations for the Vati[illegible] confessed that these provincial synods had mainly prepar[illegible] for the Vatican Council. Then came, in 1867, the centenary with the events already mentioned. Concerning the kind in favour of the Infallibility League, Bishop Dupanloup h[illegible] some particulars in his declaration immediately before t[illegible] The majority of the bishops assembled in Rome in 1867, w[illegible] the definition of Infallibility by a Council, continued by Dr[illegible] own confession, to agitate. The Commissioners for P[illegible] partly constituted before the centenary but completed were composed — as Cardinal Schwarzenberg complai[illegible] letters to Antonelli, who in his answer admitted th[illegible] one-sided and genuine Ultramontane theologians. Conc[illegible] correspondence, by the way, both Manning and Cecconi Doubtless Archbishop Cardoni was even then at work, auspices of the Commission of Direction, on his opinion bility, which was afterwards published. Dr. Manning publish[illegible] on the Centenary in vindication of Infallibility, in which th[illegible] of it is plainly announced, so that the *Civilta Cattolic[illegible]* it as the first and most important of the writings conn[illegible] the Council. In 1868 lists of the members of the Infallibil[illegible] were sent to the Pope. In all countries 1868 begins a [illegible] ture, both in books and periodicals, in favour of Infallib[illegible] Ultramontane press of France demanded openly, and with a long before the Council, their two dogmas—Infallibility [illegible] bodily ascension into heaven. In the first days of the appeared a treatise on the Council, by Bishop Fessler, afte[illegible] first Secretary of the Council, with a discourse on Infa[illegible] which the Ultramontane party read the wish for the de[illegible] Infallibility. Renouf's treatise on Honorius was not [illegible] against, but also put in the Index. Maret's book, which h[illegible] appeared, was nevertheless the cause of a vigorous and bit[illegible] versy in the *Univers*. In Germany alone everything was still the end of 1868 Dr. Manning went to Rome, there to spend [illegible] Scarcely had he arrived when the English Ultramo[illegible] nounced that he would not return without a Cardinal's [illegible] was also intended for Archbishop Darboy of Paris, if [illegible] his opposition to the Curia. Dr. Manning was sent [illegible] mission to Darboy, to persuade him to do this; [illegible] days of 1869 are the most important. In Manning's [illegible]

[illegible] determined on, and that it was to be by acclama- [illegible] undertook to promote the acclamation, as Haneberg, [illegible] consulter of one of the Preparation Commissions, [illegible] from Rome, and as was known in France.

[illegible] of the Civilta Cattolica were preparing their famous [illegible] of February, 1869, the Commission of Faith were [illegible] same subject. In that article the "true Catholics" in [illegible] the proclamation of Infallibility by acclamation, also [illegible] the bodily ascension of Mary into heaven, and the pro- [illegible] Council of the Syllabus. Of the contemporaneous [illegible] the Commission of Faith, Cecconi says:—

> [illegible] sitting of the 14th and 21st of January, 1869, the Commission dis- [illegible] subject of the primacy, and determined the chief things which the [illegible] were to put into the Schema of the decree; after which, [illegible] the standing order, it was to be examined by the Commission [illegible] the 11th, 18th, and 25th of February, they treated of Papal Infalli- [illegible] the questions which came under consideration were the follow- [illegible] If Papal Infallibility could be defined as an article of the faith? (2.) [illegible] defined as an article of the faith? The first question was affirmed [illegible] in the Commission. As to the second, all the consulters, with the [illegible] of one only, agreed that the subject should not be brought before [illegible] unless proposed by the bishops. . . . In consequence of this con- [illegible] standing deputation, when they prepared the Schema of the [illegible] bishops on the 22nd of April, avoided the subject of Infallibility, as is [illegible] Protocol, from that prudent economy of which we have spoken [illegible] Not the less did the question continue to be agitated not only in [illegible] sittings, but also in that of the 18th of June following, where [illegible] of a decree was discussed, which was to be kept in readiness for [illegible] mentioned above. The Commission discussed a multitude of modifi- [illegible] this project, but the overwhelming number of other urgent questions [illegible] the return to the subject of Papal Infallibility. So the work [illegible] unfinished."

[illegible]e same time the Pope, who was not idle, through the *Civilta* [illegible]*lica*, on the 6th of February, announced to the world his sublime [illegible]ve. We learn from various later writings that through briefs [illegible] his blessings he animated the members of the Agitation [illegible] and the Infallibilist authors. One letter is dated on that same [illegible] February on which the Commission adopted the significant [illegible]e. On the 13th and 14th of February appeared the *Civilta* article [illegible] papers of the Ultramontane party. Three times the *Univers* [illegible] expressly to its "importance" and "its altogether exceptional [illegible]ance," while Bishop Plantier, on the same day, had his book [illegible]ed in the *Univers*, which was to serve as a commentary on the [illegible]e in the *Civilta*, and to vindicate acclamation. In France many [illegible]ers appeared, but the most important polemical articles were those [illegible] *Augsburger Allgemeine Zeitung*, from March 9th to 15th, as they [illegible] in "Janus," which was published in the end of August, 1869. [illegible] does Dr. Manning set forth these events? He proceeds [illegible] nothing at all about them. The Centenary, he says, and [illegible] of the Pope and the bishops on that occasion, kindled the zeal of the party hostile to the authority of Rome. The origin of this party in France is traced to the condemnation of Lamennais by Gregory XVI., and in Germany of certain professors by Pius IX. because they wished to liberate politics and science from the guidance of revelation (or the Curia?). What appeared in France is too insignificant to be noticed. Much more important is Germany.

"There in the year 1868 (*sic*), appeared the work entitled 'Janus,' an elaborate attempt of many hands (*sic*) to destroy, by profuse misquotations from history, the authority of the Pope, and to create animosity against the future Council. The fable that the Infallibility was to be defined by acclamation was first formally announced in 'Janus.' The work was promptly translated into English, French, and Italian" (p. 67).

It is also said, in order to take away all doubt about the chronological order and the connection of events, that "the Council was scarcely announced when 'Janus' appeared." In connection with "Janus," Dr. Manning brings on the stage Prince Hohenlohe, at that time Bavarian Foreign Minister. He mentions not merely the well-known Circular Despatch of the 9th April, which he wrongly says was sent to all European Governments, but also the so-called Hohenlohe theses submitted to the judgment of the theological faculty of Munich, by whom "answers were returned in the sense desired." A diplomatic anti-Council League was formed. In June, 1869, Prince Hohenlohe addressed a second despatch to the Governments of Europe, and finally, in alliance with the Italian Government, a third despatch to the Cabinet of Paris, "urging the withdrawal of the French troops during the Council, *to insure the freedom of its deliberations*, or, in other words, to anticipate the 20th of September, 1870, and the seizure of Rome" (p. 69). The newspapers which "Janus" had supplied with "a large vocabulary of vituperation" began "to assail the future Council." The effect of this deliberate widespread and elaborate attempt to hinder the definition of the Infallibility of the Head of the Church by controlling the Council and obstructing its freedom was as might be expected. It "insured the proposing and passing of the definition" (p. 70). So that "Janus," according to Dr. Manning, did the whole business. Certainly this is an extraordinary method of expounding history!

But will any one believe that in the whole of this there is scarcely one word of truth? This is evident, even from what Dr. Manning himself has recorded, but much more from the chronological analysis of the events which we have made. In Rome Infallibility had long been in the programme and discussed. The article in the *Civilta*, with the demand for acclamation, had been sent forth into the world and widely disseminated by the Ultramontane press, and the Pope had issued his briefs in favour of Infallibility just as the opposition began in France and Germany. Of "Janus," until August, 1869, not a word had been said, as it had not yet appeared. If or how far Prince Hohenl[illegible] hised with the German sition need not be here determined. But in any case Dr. Manning need not wonder at the statements in the despatch of the 9th of April, as what happened in Rome in January and February, 1869, had been in part blabbed out by the *Civilta Cattolica* and was otherwise known to the whole world, though the Cardinal professes not to know it. Either from ignorance of the collected original documents, which if it were the case would be little flattering to so pretentious an author, or through a bias which is quite natural, Manning represents the Hohenlohe theses to have been directed only to the Munich faculty of theology, whilst they went at the same time to the theological faculty in Würzburg and the legal faculty in Munich. And by all was returned an answer; in fact from the Munich theologians two, with the opinions of both a minority and majority. Of Hohenlohe's second circular despatch in June, 1869, nobody before this knew anything, and as Dr. Manning does not say one word either concerning its contents or its object, it seems as if he knew nothing either, unless the notification of it was discovered by himself, as in the case of the assumed despatch of the Bavarian and Italian Governments to the Cabinet of Paris. After special investigation into the subject, we are in a position formally to declare that the whole discovery is "a mare's nest."* That Infallibility was proposed and passed in consequence of this opposition is a subject on which we need not say one word more. It stands in glaring contradiction to the ascertained facts, and is manifestly false. We might also remind Dr. Manning that in the well-known "Reflessioni d'un Teologo," translated from the French, of which several editions appeared during the Council, and were distributed in Rome without receiving any contradiction, it stands written :—

> "Although in Orleans it was not supposed that the question of Infallibility would be raised in the Council, Orleans is not the whole world. In a hundred other regions the contrary was believed, and a great number of bishops, priests, and believers have always thought and hoped that this question would be brought before the Council and definitely settled, and this indeed long before the *Univers* and the *Civilta Cattolica* had given an impulse to any such movement. We will say further, Must not Bishop Dupanloup by some chance have been the only person who did not know that Pius IX. has always had in his mind the definition of this dogma and the condemnation of Gallicanism? Do not the acts of his Pontificate point to this as its goal and its special crown? Yes, we will proclaim it openly. Pius IX. believed that he had received a special mission to define Immaculate Conception and Papal Infallibility."

J. FRIEDRICH.

(*To be continued.*)

* "Ein lächerliche Erfindung," which is Hohenlohe's expression in ... inquiries concerning the second despatch.—TR.

# " PHILOCHRISTUS."

*Memoirs of a Disciple of the Lord.* London: Macmillan & Co. 1878.

THE winning beauty of this book, and the fascinating power with which the subject of it appeals to all English minds, will secure for it many readers, and many of those who read it will be puzzled what to think of it. It is a work which ranks rather with "Ecce Homo" than with Canon Farrar's "Life of Christ." It is associated, indeed, with the former book by the dedication :—"To the author of 'Ecce Homo,' not more in admiration of his writings than in gratitude for the suggestive influence of a long and intimate friendship." I do not recognize however in "Philochristus" any signs of such influence as would warrant its being called an imitation of "Ecce Homo." It is like it in being an original study of the life and work of Jesus Christ, not an illustrated or a critical reproduction of the New Testament narratives. But, being distinctly original, it is wholly independent of "Ecce Homo," from which it differs in style and method and point of view. "Ecce Homo" was a series of chapters on the designs and working of Christ as the founder of a society. Who can have forgotten the lucent clearness of exposition, the force and stateliness and precision of language, the freshness of idea, the insight into social motives, the delicate appreciation of certain aspects of Christ's character and aim, which made that work one of the chief objects of interest in its day? "Philochristus" will not seize on the general mind as "Ecce Homo" did; nor does it indeed, by occupying the same ground, enter into any rivalry with it. But it has attractions of no ordinary class. It combines poetic tend[illegible] with scholarly [illegible] learning, an almost painful boldness with the re[illegible] a devout Christian. Every one will have som[illegible] but no one will read it without [illegible] joyment.

The book purports to be written by "a disciple of the Lord," one Joseph the son of Simeon, who was born at Sepphoris in Galilee in the twentieth year of the reign of Augustus. Sepphoris was an important place, about three miles north of Nazareth, well known to readers of Josephus, though it does not happen to be mentioned in the New Testament. Joseph, afterwards named Philochristus, lives to a very advanced age, and addresses these autobiographical "memoirs" to the members of the Church in Londinium, of which he has been one of the founders. He intimates in a Postscript that he designs to complete the history of his life; but this volume gives the first part of it only, bringing down the narrative to the Day of Pentecost. He tells us of his youth and education in Galilee, and how he shared the feelings and counsels of the Galilean patriots; of a visit to Alexandria, which brought him into contact with Philo; then of the preaching of John the Baptist and the ministry of our Lord. Philochristus was one of the small company of those who followed Jesus wherever he went, who accompanied him on his last visit to Jerusalem and saw him after he had risen from the dead, and who kept together till the descent of the Holy Ghost quickened and organized them into a living body. Of the scenes in which he thus bore a part Philochristus gives his personal recollections, telling the story of his discipleship in pure and simple English of the time of our Received Version. The portrait he is made to draw of himself is that of a docile, receptive, affectionate nature, thoroughly loyal, but of a somewhat feminine gentleness. The author seeks to give us, through the descriptions of this disciple, a living picture of the country and the age of Jesus. Most of his readers will feel, I think, that they did not know Galilee so well before. Its imported civilization, its traditional religion, its mongrel government, the fierce discontent and eager hopes of its Jewish population, the soft beauty of its scenery, have received touches which make the whole environment in the midst of which Jesus lived and taught more real to us. But the author's aim is not merely to describe this environment. He wishes to make Jesus himself, his nature and character and mode of working, more real to [illegible] modern Christian. A high and difficult attempt! Philochristus, [illegible] of the tenderest and most unreserved devotion to his Master, [illegible] what we call a rationalizing treatment to the life and work of [illegible] He adds something to what the Evangelists relate, and by [illegible] excisions from their respective narratives he makes the [illegible] some sense more natural than they are in the Gospels. [illegible] on the whole bring us nearer to the real original [illegible] Jesus, is a question on which I shall offer some

[illegible] Lord's time were hoping for a Messiah who [illegible] off the Roman yoke, is a fact of which [illegible] takes note. Every commentator on the life of Christ has some view of the relation in which Jesus stood to that expectation. He was an almost mythical product of the Messianic idea,—that is one view. He was one of many enthusiasts, though immeasurably the noblest of them, who were inspired and inflated by it, —that is another view. He had the happy thought of assuming to be the Messiah in order that he might transform the popular Messianic ideal into one of self-suppression and sweet reasonableness,—is a third. The author of "Philochristus" holds most earnestly the Christian belief in Jesus as the Divine Redeemer of Israel and of mankind; but he brings the popular expectation into the innermost circle of the followers of Jesus, and uses it as a key to solve the mystery of the discipleship and the treason of Judas Iscariot. An attempt to explain, even by a plausible conjecture, so perplexing a mystery will be welcome to many. From his early youth Philochristus is involved in the restless agitation which Jewish patriotism and the hatred provoked by the conqueror kept stirring in Galilee. The preaching of John the Baptist, we are told, gave a vigorous impulse to it.

"Many other rumours were noised abroad, and this rumour prevailed most, that 'One from the East would come forth to rule the world,' which saying had spread even to Italy and Spain. But we in Galilee thought that this conqueror from the East would be our Messiah. Thus, the hearts of all men everywhere being in expectation, it came to pass that many of my friends (who were the leaders of the sect called the Patriots or Galileans), having proposed these many weeks to hold a council determined at this time to confer together in a little valley between Sepphoris and Nazareth, there to resolve what should be done. Most of those present were from the inland parts of Galilee: of these Barabbas the son of Josiah was from Jotapata. Only Hezekiah the son of Zachariah (a Scribe who was thought to be well-affected towards the Galileans) came from Jerusalem. But from Capernaum came my cousin Baruch, the son of Manasseh, with three others. There were present also from the region of Gaulonitis James and John and Manahem, sons of the famous Judas of Galilee. James the son of Judas spake first, giving his judgment for war, and saying that Israel had slept too long: 'for while we sleep,' said he, 'the leaven spreadeth; Greek cities cover our land; our own cities are being defiled with Gentile abominations. They are stealing from us even our language. No man may earn a living in Galilee now, unless he speak Greek. With Greek theatres and amphitheatres, and baths, and market-places; with Greek pictures and images, feasts and games; with Greek songs and poems and histories, they purpose, by easy degrees, to beguile the hearts of our young men from the religion of their forefathers. Our princes are Edomites in the pay of Rome. Our rich men long for the flesh-pots of Rome, and call themselves by the name of Herod. Our Scribes, our wise men, cry peace when there is no peace, and wink at the payment of tribute. Publicans and harlots bring down the wrath of God upon the nation, and go unpunished. All these things are as the meshes of the net wherein Rome is encompassing our land. And lo, the fowler layeth the net and the silly bird stayeth still'" (pp. 18, 19).

This conference of the patriots ends in a resolve that they will wait to see how the new prophet declares himself. And they agree that they will go and hear him where he was reported to be teaching and baptizing. Some new touches are given to the teaching of the Baptist, but in this part of his work the author has a comparatively easy task. He shows how the ferment about an insurrection was allayed for the time in the astonishment and awe produced by the warnings of John, but he describes the minds of the people as being more profoundly unsettled, and the hopes of a coming Deliverer as growing more defined and more eager.

The reader also, if I mistake not, will have been prepared to look forward with sympathetic interest to the appearing of the Deliverer upon the author's stage. It seems to me beyond the reach of human and Christian art, that the introduction of our Lord in a work of fiction should be so managed as not to create disappointment and a sense of inadequacy in the minds of readers of the Gospels. The more the narrative succeeds in resembling real life, the less likely is the reader to feel satisfied. Our author has deliberately chosen to confront this difficulty, and to do as well as he could what he must have known he could not do satisfactorily. He tells us in a Note that he has not put words into the mouth of Jesus that are not found either in the Gospels or amongst the twenty traditional sayings which, according to Professor Westcott, "seem to contain, in a more or less altered form, traces of words of our Lord." He has only allowed play to his invention in the field of looks and gestures, and in the observations and interpretations put into the mouths of disciples. No one can doubt the loving and cautious reverence with which the person and bearing of Jesus are presented. My own impression—and this is hardly such faint and negative praise as it might at first appear to be—is not one of any resentment against the author as having detracted on the whole from the marvellous dignity of the New Testament portraiture of the Son of God. The most essential principle of the nature of Jesus, according to all the Gospels, was his dependence on the Father; and this, which in "Ecce Homo" remains a blank, is illustrated with much tenderness and beauty in "Philochristus." The author's aim, it is clear, is to develop those ideas as to the spiritual consciousness of Christ which form the heart of the Evangelical narratives.

Of course Philochristus endeavours to explain to the inhabitants of Britain the phenomena of demoniac possession,—a mysterious subject, on which some light, perhaps, yet remains to be thrown.* The possessed with devils were to be found, our author says, almost exclusively in the lowlands about the Lake and in the Valley of Jordan. Besides the symptoms of epilepsy and lunacy, the demoniacs suffered apparently from some local malady which had its consciousness shaped by traditional beliefs and fancies. In any case, demoniac possession was a name for a miserable class of afflictions. In an early chapter of this book, Philochristus relates the proceedings of an exorcist who attempted to cast out a devil from a boy named Raphael at Capernaum. The attempt had a temporary success; but, a few days after,

* I remember to have seen in some account of Abyssinia, descriptions of cases closely resembling the Galilean possessions.

Philochristus, going to the house of Raphael's father to inquire about the boy, hears the well-known demoniac cries. He finds a stranger also at the door; and the two enter together.

"So I went in, following the stranger till we both came to the door of the upper room: and there I stood, and durst not enter into the chamber; for my heart was empty of comfort, neither knew I how to console the old man in his affliction. But the stranger that was with me, going forward, spake first of all to Joazar the father, and said some words of kindness to him. Now so it was, that when the stranger first entered into the chamber, the evil spirits ceased not, but raged yet more fiercely than before, crying aloud and saying, 'Depart from us; let us alone; let us alone;' and the youth also rent his cheeks so that the blood gushed out; and he would fain have leaped up from his bed. But the stranger (whose face I had not yet seen), hearing the voices of the spirits, turned himself round from the old man to the son: and going up to the bed-side he stood there, steadfastly looking at the youth. Now when he thus turned himself, then for the first time I beheld his countenance; and, as I remember, I marvelled thereat, and also at the manner of his dealing with the youth. For, first of all, when he looked upon the youth, his face seemed swallowed up with pity; and then of a sudden it changed again, and he stretched out his arm as one having authority, and as if on the point to bid the evil spirits depart, and this he did twice; but twice again he drew back his arm, as if changing his purpose. Then, at the last, the pity came back upon his face all in an instant, so that his features seemed even melted therewith; and he stooped down and embraced the boy, and kissed him: and, as I thought, he whispered words in his ear. But this I know not for certain; howbeit the boy, in any case, ceased from his raging and no longer struggled, but lay still and quiet, only muttering and moaning a little. Hereat the stranger turned himself to Joazar to take his leave; but I (perchance because my mind misgave me that I had played the eavesdropper, albeit unwittingly, or for whatever other reason) feared to wait and meet the stranger; so I turned my back, and went forth in haste from the house."

On the same day he sees at some distance the same stranger, and is told that it is Jesus of Nazareth. A certain space of time intervenes, containing the visit to John the Baptist and a sojourn at Alexandria, and then Philochristus meets with Jesus again. He had become much bewildered and depressed, and was tormented by various doubts and questionings. He had gone from teacher to teacher, and found no sure guidance. He was resting one day on the road between Sepphoris and Nazareth, and had fallen on his face to pray that the Redeemer might come, and that he might see him.

"As I arose, there came one behind me unperceived and touched my shoulder; and he said unto me, 'Wherefore weepest thou?' I started at his voice, for there was a power in it; but I looked not up for weeping, but made answer and said, 'Because of the yoke of the Law; for it is written "Whoso receiveth upon him the yoke of the Law, THEY remove from him the yoke of oppression and the yoke of the path of the world." But it is not so with me. For from a child I have settled my heart to study the Law and to take upon me the yoke thereof, yet have I not attained to the knowledge thereof. But the yoke of the world and the yoke of the oppression of Israel weigheth heavily upon me.' Then he that spake said unto me, 'Cast away the heavy yoke and take upon thee the light yoke.' So I looked up, marvelling at such words, and behold, it was not the face of a stranger, for I knew it; and yet again I knew it not, neither could I bring to mind the name of him that spake to me. But I saw strength in his countenance, and his face was as the morning-star in brightness; and I rejoiced with a great joy, for I knew that the Lord had sent unto me a teacher to guide my feet into the path of life. So I replied, 'What yoke, O master?' And he answered and said, 'Take my yoke upon thee, and learn of me; for I am meek and lowly of heart.' When I heard that, I was speechless and as one astonied; to hear such a saying, which seemed in part the words of a king, and in part the words of a child. But when speech came back to me, I said, 'My heart is afflicted because of the wonder of the ways of the Lord, and because His paths are past finding out.' But he answered, 'They that wonder shall reign, and they that reign shall rest.' Now I perceived not all the meaning of his words at the time; but thus much I did most clearly perceive, that here was one that could guide me through all wonderment and perplexity, even unto the haven of rest. But a sudden fear fell upon me that peace would depart from my soul, if my Master should depart; therefore with many entreaties I besought him to tarry that night at my mother's house. So when he had consented we straightway went to the city. But, as we went, my mind still beat upon the thought that I had seen my Master's countenance before; yet could I not call to mind the when and where.

"But even as we entered into the house, behold, my mother was crying aloud, being tormented beyond measure by her disease: and when my Master heard it, he asked who cried thus, and I answered and told him concerning my mother's condition. Then straightway he desired to go into the upper chamber where she lay; and having gone in, he looked steadfastly at her, and took her by the hand, and said, as one having authority, 'Arise:' and immediately my mother arose and went about as one whole. Now it came to pass, that when he looked steadfastly at my mother, even in that instant I knew his face, that it was the face of the stranger that had looked after the like manner upon Raphael the son of Joazar, even the face of Jesus of Nazareth; and then also in that same instant it was borne to my mind that this was he of whom Jonathan had spoken, namely he concerning whom John the Prophet had prophesied saying that he was the Messiah of Israel: and I marvelled that I had not known him before; but I perceived that, albeit the same, yet was he not the same; so great a glory and a brightness of the Holy Spirit now reigned in his countenance. All this, I say, I perceived even when he was gazing on my mother; but I durst not for my life speak to him then. But when my mother was made whole and arose from her bed, then straightway I fell down on my knees and bowed before him; and I spake also to my mother all the words of Jonathan the son of Ezra, how that John had affirmed my Master to be the Redeemer of Israel: and I believed, and my mother also, and all our household."

After this, he hears Jesus in the synagogue, and sees him healing diseases. "Incurable" diseases, Philochristus reports, Jesus passed by; but he healed those who were possessed by evil spirits, or who were lunatic or sick of the palsy or of fever, or who had impediment in their speech. For he "had a marvellous power to discern, not only them that had faith from them that had not, but also such diseases as were to be cured from such as were not to be cured because it was not prepared for him that he should cure them" (p. 97). In several places Philochristus endeavours to describe the actual process by which the healing was accomplished, always referring the curative power to the effect wrought on the mind of the sufferer. Thus in the account of the cure of the palsied man whose bed was let down through the roof, and to whom Jesus said first, "Thy sins be forgiven thee,"—

"His countenance shone as the sun: pity and sorrow were there, but pity and sorrow swallowed up in the brightness and glory of joy and triumph; and the sick man's face gave back the brightness. But when Jesus perceived that the time had come, and that the word of God had gone forth, and that the chains in heaven had been broken, then Jesus spoke and broke the chains on earth. . . . 'But that ye may know that the Son of man hath authority even upon the earth to forgive sins'—here he paused and stood up, and behold, the whole of the congregation was constrained to stand up with one consent; insomuch that I saw even Eliezer the son of Arak standing up with the rest, and his face was kindling as the faces of the rest, and the silence was even such as could be felt, and the palsied man himself seemed half to raise himself in his bed in expectation: and, like a shock, there fell on us the word 'Arise.' And lo, the man arose at once, and stood straight up, and Jesus said to him, 'Take up thy bed, and go thy way into thy house.'"

Perhaps the most striking chapter of the book, for novelty of interpretation, dramatic interest, and power of description, is that in which the author develops and illustrates the conversation begun by the question, "Whom do men say that I, the Son of man, am?" "Philochristus" aims at tracing a historical continuity in the events which the Gospels record. The Disciple makes the death of John the Baptist the culminating moment of the popular feeling and expectation concerning Jesus. For a while, the eager Galilean patriots, amongst whom our author places Barabbas as well as Judas Iscariot (or, of Kerioth), set their hopes upon the prophet of Nazareth, and follow him, as one who will deliver the land from Herod and from the Romans. When John is imprisoned, they suppose that the time has come for prompt aggressive action, and they expect that Jesus will put himself at the head of a popular army and march to the rescue of the Baptist. They trust, for victory, to the supernatural aid which Jesus can invoke from heaven. When the Baptist is put to death, they cannot but believe that Jesus will avenge his murder. A chilling disappointment falls on the Galilean multitudes, and affects even the most devoted followers of Jesus, when they find that he makes no sign of calling out an insurrection, but by silence and occasional flight seems to be refusing all aggressive enterprise. The bearing of Jesus at this season, as described by Philochristus, is chiefly what we should call wistful. Sorrow, pity, anxiety, love, are blended in his behaviour. He speaks more with looks than in words. The multitudes fall away; the twelve and a few more remain with him, but are depressed and perplexed. The Master retains his personal hold upon them, but they are conscious that they do not understand him, and they begin to be haunted by misgivings. This change in the relations between Jesus and his disciples is pictured with much delicacy by Philochristus. He relates how Jesus, not long after the death of the Baptist, led his small band of followers on an apparently aimless journey northwards. They travelled on towards the snow-covered cone of Hermon, one of the landmarks of Israel, until they had [illegible] boundary-line of Galilee and arrived at the place [illegible] was a heathen city, previously named after the god Pan, [illegible] there, and whose name still survives in the modern [illegible]. The most copious fountain of the Jordan rises in [illegible] at the base of Hermon, and above this cavern Herod [illegible] a beautiful temple of white marble dedicated to the emperor [illegible]. To this spot Jesus leads his silent and dejected band. [illegible] down together facing the source and the temple. The dis[illegible] sure, from the manner of their Master, that some new [illegible] or some crisis was at hand. "A deep silence and a [illegible] fell on us; and we saw the lips of Jesus moving as if in prayer." They had heard him repeating to himself sentences from the Psalms in which the word "congregation" occurred. When at last the question came, "Whom do men say that I the Son of man am?" their "hearts were lightened," and they readily gave their various answers. But "the lips of Jesus still moved as if in prayer, and his eyes were fixed upon the temple on the rock before him; and his mind was not with us nor with our words, but with something that was still to come from the depths of the future." Presently, "he turned himself round and set his eyes full upon us who were sitting before him," and asked the question upon which the whole future of the kingdom of heaven was to turn, "But whom say ye that I am?" Let Philochristus continue the story in his own words:

"A few Sabbaths before, we should have been very ready with an answer; for then all men said that Jesus was the Redeemer, the Christ, and we had often said the same thing. But now many stumblingblocks lay in our path. The Scribes and the pious and the learned, all save a very few, had rejected Jesus. The patriots had joined themselves to him for a long time, but they too had cast him off; yea, and even the rest of the men of Galilee had been led away with them. The poor, as well as the rich, were now against us. In fine, none were now on our side except a few of the lowest of the people, sinners and tax-gatherers and the like. Besides all this, John himself, a prophet, and one whom Jesus had called the greatest of the prophets, even he seemed to have wavered in his faith in Jesus; and when he had besought help in prison, Jesus had helped him not. Yea, and Jesus himself of late seemed to have cast off faith in himself. For when he had been challenged to work a sign in heaven, which seemed an easy thing for a prophet to do, he had refused to do it. Also, he had fled from the face of Herod and from the Pharisees, and seemed to have become a wanderer rather than a deliverer. Else, why were we, children of Abraham and inheritors of the Land of Promise, sitting there like exiles, looking on the temples of false gods in a foreign land? Even in the words wherein he had questioned us, Jesus had spoken of himself as the Son of man. Might it not be indeed that he was, and knew that he was, naught [illegible] than one of the common sons of man? When had he called himself the [illegible]? Never. . . .

[illegible] for this cause did the Lord lead us into the wilderness together with [illegible] in sorrow and in exile, to the intent that there, being apart from [illegible] might weigh, as it were in a balance, on the one side all the [illegible] other side the Son of man; a man of sufferings and sorrows, [illegible] and exiles, acquainted with rejections and contempts; [illegible] weighed the two, we might prefer the Son of man, [illegible] in our hearts which cried within us, 'Whom have [illegible] and there is none on earth that we desire in comparison of thee.' And this, as I judge, was the faith that Jesus desired of us: and to this faith was the Lord leading our hearts, while Jesus was patiently waiting for our answer. But though it needeth many words to show even a very little of the searchings of our hearts in that sore extremity, yet the time thereof was short, not more (as I said before) than while a man could count nine or ten very slowly.

"Then Peter rose up. If it were possible to judge from their countenances, some of the other disciples also were very nigh unto speaking; for their features were as it were in a flux, dissolving in passion, and speech seemed welling upward through them, and the lips of John the son of Zebedee were trembling as if upon the brink of utterance. Notwithstanding it was reserved for Simon Peter to set forth in words and to shape by the force of his soul the thoughts of John and all the rest. He therefore rose up and spake as I never heard man speak before, neither think I ever to hear man speak again saying, 'Thou art the Christ, the Son of the living God. . . . .'

"Again and again, pondering that saying of Simon Peter in my mind, I have thought of the words of Nathanael, how he said that Jesus gave a voice to all visible things even though they be voiceless by nature; and, in the same way, it might have been said also that Jesus had power to give a kind of light to sounds: such brightness did he seem to cast upon the words of Simon Peter, insomuch that the words, though old, seemed new, yea quite new, and never heard before. For the tongue and the voice seemed the tongue and the voice of Peter, but the spirit and the light thereof seemed to proceed from Jesus; so that one scarce knew whether it were truer to say that it was Jesus speaking through Peter, or that it was Peter speaking in the spirit of Jesus.

"But when Jesus heard the words of Peter, he turned and looked upon all the disciples and upon Peter, and he rejoiced with an exceeding joy, as if in that utterance of faith the first seed had been sown which was to grow up into the Tree of Life; or as if he had seen before his very eyes the laying of the foundations of a great temple, not like unto the marble temple of Augustus built upon the visible rock, but a temple of human souls compacted together by no hands of man, but by the Spirit of God, and destructible by no power in earth or hell. Howbeit he called it not Temple but rather (using the word which our fathers had used in old days concerning Israel) Congregation" (pp. 258—262).

Judas of Kerioth, however, did not like this word Congregation so well as Kingdom. He was accustomed to say that he did not see how the Forgiveness of Sins could drive Herod from Tiberias or the Romans from Jerusalem. But when Jesus, on the next day after the blessing of Simon Peter, announced that they were to go up to Jerusalem for the next Passover, Judas at first "smote his hands together for very gladness," counting on an inevitable collision with the Romans, in which Jesus must put forth his supernatural power and destroy them. This is the key which the writer uses to unlock the mystery of the action of Judas. Many doubts will occur to the reader as he considers this explanation, but he will not fail to be interested by it. That Judas was prompted to his act of betrayal by the desire to precipitate a collision, mixed with some real hope that Jesus might thus be forced to assert his power, is not a new theory. I learn from Dr. [illegible] article on Judas in the Dictionary of the Bible that it [illegible] by Archbishop Whately, who was himself following Paulus, the ingenious rationalizer of the Gospel [illegible] method of our author enables him to give it [illegible] it could not previously claim. What needs to be [illegible] much the treachery of Judas,—avarice, disappoint-[illegible], wounded self-love, or many another evil motive, will [illegible]—but his discipleship. How came he to be attracted [illegible] to be chosen by him as one of the twelve, to live with [illegible] brother with brethren, to follow the Master into the very [illegible] destruction? In "Philochristus" we see all the disciples [illegible] originally in the popular belief in Jesus as a leader of insur-[illegible], and never able, to the very last, completely to shake it off. [illegible] uses Nathanael for the expression of the most spiritual [illegible] concerning our Lord's mission which any disciple in his lifetime [illegible] to entertain. But Simon Peter and the sons of Zebedee, the leading Apostles, though they are possessed and governed by devotion [illegible] person of their master, expect that in some way or other he will triumph over the enemies of Israel by a display of heavenly power. Judas, according to Philochristus, was a zealous and sincere follower of Jesus, but of coarser grain and with a larger mixture of external motives than the rest of the twelve. He is not without sensibility for the gracious aspects of Christ's character, but they do not conquer him; his *rôle* in the Apostolic company is to insist upon practical action and to complain of what seems to him the unduly gentle hesitancy of Jesus. He thinks, as many followers have thought, before and after him, that his leader needs to be pushed on. It becomes to him a duty to apply this pressure; but he succeeds so little that at last he is driven to despair. As the disciples move towards Jerusalem, they are all full of anxiety about a conflict with the Romans, and the excitement of Judas is intense. When they learn that Jesus proposes to make a public entry into Jerusalem, Simon Peter, according to Philochristus, observes:—

"When that cometh to pass, then doubtless he will be moved to perform some mighty work. I say not that he will smite with the sword; for he ever shrinketh from the sword. But perchance he will pray unto the Lord, and the earth will open for our enemies, even as it opened for the children of Korah, or fire will go forth from the presence of our Master himself, and he will consume his enemies with the fervency of his breath."

Judas is shown to us struggling against his despair, but more and more angered by the calmness of Jesus; and the last moments of the [illegible] betrayal are thus described:—

"[illegible] who was the guide of the armed men, ran swiftly before the rest [illegible] and said, 'Hail, Master,' and saluted him. And, as I was told by [illegible], Judas seemed as if he knew not, even at the last, [illegible] scarce what he himself was doing. For he [illegible] the soldiers that followed behind him, as if [illegible] fire upon them. But Jesus looked [illegible] him such answers as to shew [illegible] back, they said, as one [illegible]

[illegible]—of which Philochristus himself did not see much, though he approached the Cross in time to hear the last words,—Judas is introduced once more, mad with remorse as the New Testament represents him. Having come across Philochristus, he utters words of horror, and leaves him.

I do not here take space to discuss the question whether the Judas of this book makes the Judas of the Gospels on the whole more intelligible. I am not unaware of objections that may be raised to the character of the Betrayer as drawn by Philochristus, when I say that I am myself disposed to retain the thought of Judas as a tragical example of what the choice of a lower ideal and the obstinate rejection of a higher may come to, rather than as an utterly base and odious nature. But an expression used by Judas in this his last meeting with Philochristus serves as a starting-point for a brief notice of what the author has to say about the Resurrection. No real Philochristus—no disciple of the Lord and elder of the Church in Londinium—would have given this account of it. It is a modern lover of Christ who speaks. Judas hisses out "He is not dead; these three times I have seen him." The words begin to haunt Philochristus. As he goes up the mountain to Bethany, "all things thereon seemed to cry aloud with one consent, 'He is not dead.'" He throws himself on the ground in his sorrow and exhaustion, and falls asleep; and sees a vision of Jesus carried up in triumph to heaven. Waking on the morrow after day-break, he goes to the house of Mary and Martha and finds all the Apostles there. For a while they all sit silent; then they begin to touch on the miserable events of the day before, but also on the serenity and majesty of Jesus; but the last words, "Why hast thou forsaken me?" bring them to silence again. Presently one of the women remarks that Jesus had prophesied his own rejection and death. This reminds them that he had also spoken of a victory over death. He had often quoted the words of Hosea, "Come and let us return unto the Lord, for he hath torn and he will heal us; he hath smitten. and he will bind us up. After two days will he revive us; in the third day he will raise us up, and we shall live in his sight." These words "after two days he will revive us" take hold of them, and they all sit brooding upon them. There is a stirring of hope in their hearts. It is beautifully suggested that the words "Why hast thou forsaken me?" are the opening words of a psalm which was familiar to Jesus, and which advances from despairing utterances to trust and triumphant praise. Mary of Magdala passionately refused to believe that Jesus could be dead for ever; "God were no God unless Jesus were restored to life." Thus expectation was nourished until the women went with their spices to embalm the body, and found the stone rolled away from the tomb, and saw an angel or angels, and heard the words "He is not here, he is risen." But what had happened to the body laid there?—Philochristus tells us that, when he was leaving the Cross after the death of Jesus, he met Hezekiah the Rabbi, who taunted him and said, "Ye Galileans (as is reported to us) hope to steal his body from the grave and so to feign that he has risen; but that shall not be. For though your patron Joseph of Arimathæa may have his will to-day, yet will we take good order that we have our will to-morrow. For the body of a false prophet deserveth not honourable burial." Another remarkable incident is recorded by Philochristus. When the sun had set on the day after the Crucifixion, he determined to go down to see whether the tomb were beset by guards or not, and whether the women with their spices would have easy access to it. Whilst he was looking at the tomb, which then had the stone at its mouth, he saw a party of men arrive with torches, and Hezekiah the Rabbi among them. These men proceeded to surround the tomb, whilst they sent out watchers to spy if any one were near; and Philochristus had to fly, and was nearly taken. What was then done, he leaves it to his readers to imagine. The return of the women to Bethany was soon followed by that of Peter and John, who had gone into the tomb, and found it empty. Thereupon Philochristus and others determined to go at once into Galilee, and in a few days Peter and James and others of the disciples joined them at Capernaum. Philochristus proceeds to describe how the highly wrought expectation of the disciples, acting upon the nervous system of men who had been long fasting and praying, resulted in repeated appearances of Jesus as they were breaking bread in remembrance of him and at other times. The author is here on common ground with all the non-Christian critics; and I do not find that his detailed account, as by an eye-witness, of the apparitions, makes the theory at all the more acceptable. He invents such stories as this: "James had taken an oath that he would neither eat nor drink until he had seen Jesus risen from the dead. Therefore on the night after the vision of angels which had been seen by the women, James was in the house at Bethany with Simon Peter and John, and the table was spread for supper; but James would not eat. Then suddenly Jesus was seen sitting in the midst of them, breaking bread and blessing it, and bidding James to partake thereof." It is a comfort to reflect that no such oath is recorded in the Gospels or alluded to by St. Paul. And we are compelled to ask, was the bread which was broken and of which James was bidden to partake, as unreal as the vision of the Lord?

It is needless to say, that the Ascension and the Descent of the Holy Spirit on the Day of Pentecost are similarly rationalized. These events, however, are delayed in "Philochristus" for a year beyond the time named in the Gospels. That year the disciples spend in Galilee, seeing continual apparitions of the Lord Jesus. When they return for the next Passover to Jerusalem, they have a vision of him on the day of the Feast; but for the following forty days "Jesus revealed himself not to any one of us, neither by sight nor by voice," until the eve of the Pentecost, when he was seen ascending in the flames of a glorious sunset, and "we knew that we were now bidding farewell to the Lord Jesus for ever." On the next day followed the Pentecostal effusion. And at this point the history pauses. But there is a concluding chapter in which Philochristus professes his earnest and confirmed faith in the Divinity and the government of Jesus Christ,—a faith beautifully and eloquently expressed in these final words:

"Verily to thee, O Lord, and to thy Kingdom, all things in heaven and earth do bear witness.

"The faces of all children, whom thou didst call thy little ones, give back the brightness of thy countenance; the goodness of all good men testifieth unto thee, the supreme pattern of all good; yea even the bad and the weak proclaim their need of thee, O Lord our Redeemer, in whom alone is power to create goodness in the worst, and to make the weakest strong. To thy word the seed-time and harvests bear witness; the flowers also do sing of thy trustfulness and hope. If I look unto the earth, thou hast trodden and sanctified it; if to the heaven, thou hast gone up into it and dost possess it: if I think of the terrors of the depths beneath the earth, behold, thou knowest them, and hast passed through them, and overcome them, and hast broken the bars thereof; that they shall no more keep captive them that shall follow in thy footsteps, passing through the darkness of the grave. Thus hast thou, O Eternal Word (by whom in ages past the worlds were created), now in these last times created the universe anew for them that love thee: so that all things do serve thee and proclaim thy Good Tidings, and the world is become unto thee as a vesture, and the elements are become thy servants: yea, death itself thou hast subdued to be thy minister, and sin thou shalt subdue to be thy bond-slave."

It is evident from this hasty sketch that "Philochristus" cannot be read without the intrusion of those anxious and disturbing thoughts which modern criticism and philosophy awaken. It is a pity that a study like this cannot be quietly contemplated, as if it were a picture by Holman Hunt. But the author himself manifestly intends it to be one of the attempts with which this age is familiar, to bring the advanced thought of the time to bear upon Christianity. Though he has no preface or introduction, he tells us in the "Scholia" at the end of the volume upon what method he has proceeded. He assumes that "Philochristus had in his mind a certain Original Gospel (whether it were a book or tradition)," from which the Evangelists derived that part of their narratives which is common to the first three Gospels. As to the fourth Gospel,

"Anchinous saith that Philochristus, although he make no mention of any of the acts, nor of the long discourses, nor set dialogues of that Gospel, nevertheless useth the doctrine of that Gospel as the foundation of the whole of his history. Notwithstanding, saith Anchinous, Philochristus seemeth not to attribute this doctrine to John the son of Zebedee (who ever speaketh after a different manner, and rather as one of the Sons of Thunder, or as the writer of the book of Revelation, than as the writer of the Fourth Gospel), but to Nathanael and Quartus."

By these critical assumptions, a certain number of so-called miracles, including several of the most miraculous, are put aside. Of the remainder, some—such as most of the acts of healing—are described

said, "Ye Galileans (as is reported to us) hope to steal his body from the grave and so to feign that he has risen; but that shall not be. For though your patron Joseph of Arimathæa may have his will to-day, yet will we take good order that we have our will to-morrow. For the [illegible] of a false prophet deserveth not honourable burial." Another remarkable incident is recorded by Philochristus. When the sun had set on the day after the Crucifixion, he determined to go down to see whether the tomb were beset by guards or not, and whether the women with their spices would have easy access to it. Whilst he was looking at the tomb, which then had the stone at its mouth, he saw a party of men arrive with torches, and Hezekiah the Rabbi among them. These men proceeded to surround the tomb, whilst they sent out watchers to spy if any one were near; and Philochristus had to fly, and was nearly taken. What was then done, he leaves it to his readers to imagine. The return of the women to Bethany was soon followed by that of Peter and John, who had gone into the tomb, and found it empty. Thereupon Philochristus and others determined to go at once into Galilee, and in a few days Peter and James and others of the disciples joined them at Capernaum. Philochristus proceeds to describe how the highly wrought expectation of the disciples, acting upon the nervous system of men who had been long fasting and praying, resulted in repeated appearances of Jesus as they were breaking bread in remembrance of him and at other times. The author is here on common ground with all the non-Christian critics; and I do not find that his detailed account, as by an eye-witness, of the apparitions, makes the theory at all the more acceptable. He invents such stories as this: "James had taken an oath that he would neither eat nor drink until he had seen Jesus risen from the dead. Therefore on the night after the vision of angels which had been seen by the women, James was in the house at Bethany with Simon Peter and John, and the table was spread for supper; but James would not eat. Then suddenly Jesus was seen sitting in the midst of them, breaking bread and blessing it, and bidding James to partake thereof." It is a comfort to reflect that no such oath is recorded in the Gospels or alluded to by St. Paul. And we are compelled to ask, was the bread which was broken and of which James was bidden to [illegible], as unreal as the vision of the Lord?

[illegible] needless to say, that the Ascension and the Descent of the [illegible] on the Day of Pentecost are similarly rationalized. These [illegible] are delayed in "Philochristus" for a year beyond the [illegible] Gospels. That year the disciples spend in Galilee, [illegible] of the Lord Jesus. When they return for [illegible] Jerusalem, they have a vision of him on the day [illegible] following forty days "Jesus revealed him[illegible] by sight nor by voice," until the eve of [illegible] ascending in the flames of a glorious

our faith in Christ and God on miracles. He invites them to believe in a forgiving Father, revealed and known through his Son, who is now ruling and breathing his Spirit into men from heaven, but who once lived and was put to death as Jesus of Nazareth. He calls upon them thus to acknowledge Christ, not because he interfered with the course of nature, but because he manifested heavenly qualities and powers, to be accounted for in no other way than by supposing him to be what he declared himself to be, the Son of God. I entirely believe this to be the right and evangelical method. But can we persuade ourselves for a moment that this Gospel will have nothing "miraculous" in it to one who believes in an immutable course of nature? I hope I may be mistaken; but from all that I have learned as to the views of those who decline to believe in miracles, I should infer that such a Divine Man as Philochristus worships would be to them the most transcendent and impossible of miracles.

Certainly, one who believes in Jesus Christ after the manner of Philochristus cannot think of this Son of God as a casual product of natural evolution. The appearance of such a Being upon the world's stage cannot be classed with that of extraordinary men such as Socrates or Shakespeare. It must be regarded as an altogether exceptional fact, an intervention descending from heaven upon the natural succession of human beings. This Son of God, miraculous in himself, is admitted to have performed cures transcending the known powers of other men, to have arrested the course of fevers with a word or a look, to have given sudden restoration from chronic paralysis, permanent deliverance from epilepsy and lunacy. He is represented as rising after death to a higher condition of life and consciousness, of a kind which we fail to detect in any observed order of natural phenomena. And from that time to this he is alleged to be exercising an effective government of human affairs, so that men's lives are moulded, not only by the impulse of evolution, but by free relations of their spirits with an invisible Lord.

The histories called the Gospels, from which we learn nearly all that we know of this Divine Man, tell us these things which Philochristus accepts as true, and add to these some other wonderful statements concerning him. They report, for example, in their uniformly simple and matter-of-fact style, that he restored the sight of certain blind persons. Philochristus stumbles at such a miracle, and gives a spiritual interpretation to the statement. Again they tell us that, when his body had been laid in the grave, it was not left to natural decay, but underwent some exceptional change and left the tomb empty in which it lay. Philochristus substitutes for this account a story that the Jewish priests sent men by night who carried off the body of Jesus and dishonoured and destroyed it. We are led therefore to this question. Is it reasonable to suppose that those who have been brought to accept the great wonder of the Divine personality of Jesus [illegible] hopeless stumbling-blocks in these lesser wonders? We may sympathise, indeed, with the feeling that turns away from prodigies. The Gospels themselves teach us not to imagine that we can ascend from prodigies to the recognition of a Divine Saviour. There is no ground for the system which lays down as a first article of faith that every statement in the New Testament is absolutely and literally true. But as we read the Gospels with the reverence which we acknowledge to be due to them, we shall at least ask whether there is sufficient reason for rejecting this and the other statement which they contain. When the grace and truth of Christ have persuaded us to believe in him as the Son of God, and we come down with him from heaven to follow the steps of his so exceptional appearance on earth, are we likely to pronounce that an alleged event in his history cannot possibly be true, because it is out of the common course of nature? I will not affirm that the Christian faith in a risen Saviour is bound up with the received view as to the mode of his resurrection; the substantial fact for our faith is that Jesus lives, not that his body was transmuted. But it is a serious thing for those who inherit the faith of the Apostles to amend what all the Apostles believed on such a point. An unbeliever who thinks that the faith of the Apostles was a complete delusion, and that the Gospels are a mass of untrustworthy legends, is in a different position from that of the author of "Philochristus." This author, going so far as he does in reverent acceptance of the Gospel narrative, feels himself bound to explain what he would substitute for it when he diverges from it. Accordingly, he gives what seems to me a very lame account indeed of the occurrences which followed the Crucifixion. He makes Hezekiah, one of the enemies of Jesus, tell Philochristus that it is reported that "ye Galileans hope to steal his body and so to feign that he is risen;" but that he and his friends will take good care that the disciples shall not do so. Such a report implies that the idea of a resurrection was not unfamiliar to the disciples; but we are presently told how the hope of it began to germinate in their minds after the Crucifixion. The threat of Hezekiah, so shocking to a reverent disciple, makes no impression [illegible] mind of Philochristus, who neither communicates what he has [illegible] any other disciple nor keeps it in his own memory. But, [illegible] to the tomb to see whether the women would have [illegible] access to it, he happens to see Hezekiah evidently doing, [illegible] of agents of the chief priests, what he had [illegible] Philochristus, barely escaping out of their hands, [illegible] what he had seen, and they were "sore [illegible] strange to say, makes no difference to [illegible] hopes. It scarcely appears there[illegible] them. No anger against the enemies [illegible] to steal and dishonour his body [illegible] Hezekiah and his accomplices are [illegible] so foolish as not to see that, if *they* steal the body and all the many persons who must have been privy to the act keep their secret ever after, they are serving the very design which they intended to defeat. For it was the same thing for the fiction of the disciples, whether the body of the Lord disappeared by their act or by the act of his enemies. In truth, the rationalizing process, as applied to the Gospel narratives, has never given much satisfaction except to those who have exercised their ingenuity upon it.

The value of this book, then, does not appear to me to consist in its likeliness to find favour as a new version of the Gospel, but in the testimony it bears to *the spiritual authority of the Lord Jesus Christ*. It is a task of this age of ours, by many forms of its activity, to give their due supremacy to the righteousness and love which were manifested as the very Divine nature in Jesus of Nazareth. It is only in revealing these to the heart and conscience that the Gospel does its appointed work. When once orthodoxy has entangled and fettered the minds of Christians in evidential miracles or intellectual systems of doctrine or methods of discipline, it has ceased to be a blessing to mankind. Then it is good that men's minds should be agitated and shaken; yes, let us confess it, whatever the cost of such disturbance may be. When the constriction of opinion is loosened, and men are set free to speculate on Divine nature and revelation, it is certain that there will be many attempts to propound new theories of religion; the soil will be fertile in varieties of Gnosis. There will be much suffering, much apparent waste of moral strength. If it were ours to guard the Church from such dangers, we should no doubt do our best to avert them. But we must accept the conditions of our time. And do we not see, in the midst of the doubts and inquiries of the age, all things bearing their witness in one voice or another to the spiritual authority of Jesus Christ? On the one hand, we are made to feel the utter inadequacy of all merely naturalistic theories of existence, the absolute need of an authority for the conduct of life and of a stay and comfort in the contemplation of death, which no system of evolution can supply. On the other hand, we find those who are completely emancipated from the restraints of orthodoxy turning their reverent thoughts with a yearning which they will not disguise to the heavenly dignity of the Son of man. It is not for the most of us to discard our orthodoxy; we may remember the words of the Lord, "These things ought ye to have done, and not to leave the other undone." But we have reason to be grateful for any voice, whose tones are evidently not tuned by orthodoxy, which calls men to worship the righteousness and love supremely shown in a self-humbling Divine Man. And such a voice, of real freshness and sweetness and power, we seem to hear in the words of Philochristus.

J. LLEWELYN DAVIES.

# MR. FROUDE'S LIFE AND TIMES OF THOMAS BECKET.

MR. FROUDE'S appearance on the field of mediæval history will hardly be matter of rejoicing to those who have made mediæval history one of the chief studies of their lives. They cannot welcome him as a partner in their labours, as a fellow-worker in the cause of historic truth. On the other hand they cannot afford to pass by his appearance without notice. He cannot be treated as one of the crowd of blunderers who may be left to perish of their own insignificance. Mr. Froude has a name and a following. What he writes will be read by many and will be believed by some. Even if he were now beginning as an unknown writer, he would be sure of a more attentive and favourable hearing than falls to the lot of most unknown writers. His style is admired by many, and it undoubtedly has its merits. When Mr. Froude can keep himself both from metaphors and from vulgarisms, he knows how to tell a story clearly and attractively. It would be a pleasure to read a narrative by Mr. Froude about times, places, and persons of which one had never heard before, among which there would therefore be no means of judging whether his statements were accurate or inaccurate. In such a case the critical faculty would slumber, and we might simply enjoy what we might be sure would supply much for us to enjoy. And there can be little doubt that there are many with whom the influence of Mr. Froude's style goes very much further than this. His way of writing is eminently fitted to impose on those who have not the means of judging for themselves. When Mr. Froude is most inaccurate, when he is most thoroughly ignorant of the subject on which he writes, he still writes with an air of quiet confidence which is likely to take in all whose own studies have not qualified them to answer him. It is because the air of confidence is so quiet that it is so dangerous. As a rule, those who write on subjects which they have not mastered betray their lack of mastery in their manner. But there is nothing in Mr. Froude's manner to suggest either lack of knowledge or unfair treatment of materials. Never surely did a false prophet succeed so thoroughly in putting on the outward garb of the true. There can be no doubt that many who read in perfect good faith and with a sincere desire of knowledge are led away by this singular appearance of knowledge and fairness where both are in truth absent. Still it is lucky that, even when Mr. Froude is most plausible, he is almost sure to let something out to startle the reader who reads in good faith, however small may be his amount of critical knowledge. Many were doubtless tempted to accept Mr. Froude's new theory of Henry the Eighth,—a theory which Hallam so vigorously demolished beforehand,—who drew back when they were asked to believe that Henry beheaded Anne one day and married Jane the next from no motive but the severest sense of public duty. So Mr. Froude, in his present attempt to paint the picture of the great men of the twelfth century, puts on the outward garb of one who has read and tested his materials, and has come to a critical judgement on what he has read and tested. But he happily leaves a little cranny open which enables us to look within. The very first words of Mr. Froude's Life and Times of Thomas Becket* are enough to show us that the seeming historical inquiry is really designed as a manifesto against a theological party which once numbered its author among its members. To those who know the whole literature of the subject, it has a look more unpleasant still. Those whose study of twelfth-century history goes back to times when those who are now in their second half-century were young, will not fail to remember a time when the name of Froude reminded them of another, an earlier, and I have no hesitation in saying a worthier, treatment of the same subject. And some of those who go back so far may be tempted to think that natural kindliness, if no other feeling, might have kept back the fiercest of partisans from ignoring the honest work of a long-deceased brother, and from dealing stabs in the dark at a brother's almost forgotten fame.

Of the historical work of the elder Froude with regard to the great controversy of the reign of Henry the Second I shall have a few words to say presently. I am as yet concerned rather with the relation of the younger bearer of that name to the reign of Henry the Second and to mediæval history generally. Mr. J. A. Froude has mainly confined himself to later periods of English history; in one of his works he has dealt with times which a few living men can still remember. He has appeared as the apologist of Henry the Eighth and as the apologist of Flogging Fitzgerald. The way in which he has treated his subjects has been commonly such as now and then to suggest the thought that the whole thing is an elaborate joke. The thought will force itself

* *Nineteenth Century*, June, 1877, p. 548.

[illegible] the mind that Mr. Froude is simply laughing at his readers, and trying to see what amount of paradox they may be made to swallow. That any man could venture, in a civilized, not to say in a Christian, community, to put forth some of the moral theories which Mr. Froude puts forth, to defend some of the acts which Mr. Froude defends, might indeed seem beyond human belief. Yet some very astounding utterances in this line are no more than might be looked for from one who turned from legendary hagiography to write "Shadows of the Clouds" and the "Nemesis of Faith." On purely moral points there is no need for me now to enlarge; every man who knows right from wrong ought to be able to see through the web of ingenious sophistry which tries to justify the slaughter of More and Fisher. Still the apologist of King Harry has hardly done the best that might be done for his own hero. Mr. Froude's flattering picture comes hardly nearer to the real man than the vulgar Bluebeard portrait of which he very rightly complains. Both pictures alike slur over the distinguishing lines in a character which is in truth a most singular moral study. In Mr. Froude's lofty contempt for ecclesiastical details he perhaps hardly thought it a fact worthy of his attention that Henry the Eighth himself drew up the statutes of some of the cathedral churches which he refounded, that he drew them up with his own hand, and that the statutes so drawn up breathe a spirit worthy of the most pious founders on record. That this same man had robbed those very churches of their most sacred treasures, that he had squandered and gambled away all that men before his time had agreed to respect, that his hand had been stretched out to lay waste and to spoil the very resting-places of the dead, seems at first one of the strangest of moral contradictions. Yet both are parts of a strangely mixed character, the character of a tyrant the form of whose tyranny has no exact parallel elsewhere. Mr. Froude's belief that Henry married Jane Seymour as "an indifferent official act," which he went through for the good of the nation, quite wipes out the peculiar character of Henry's tyranny with regard to his marriages as with regard to anything else. A tyrant who was determined to have his own will in all things, but who always strove to find something like legal sanction for the gratification of his own will, was specially ingenious in finding out pretexts which gave some kind of legal sanction to his divorces, beheadings, and remarriages. We can well believe that, when Henry had beheaded Anne and married Jane, he returned thanks that he had reformed his "old and detestable life," that he was no longer an adulterer as other kings were, not even as his friend and brother, Francis of France. A character like this deserved drawing in its minutest lights and shadows; but all its characteristic features have been daubed out by the indiscriminate apology of Mr. Froude. From the purely artistic point of view, it is to be regretted that so remarkable a specimen of human nature has not had better justice done to it. From the point of view of historic and of moral truth, it is to be regretted that a portrait so wide of the reality should be accepted as genuine. It is still more to be regretted, if any have been found at once to accept Mr. Froude's statement of Henry's acts and to accept his judgement upon them.

Mr. Froude, it may be remembered, made his first appearance as a writer on historical subjects—for his contribution to the Lives of the Saints can hardly be looked on as history—in a paper in one of the volumes of Oxford Essays, which deservedly drew to itself much attention, and in which truth and error were mingled in a remarkable way. Mr. Froude's main proposition was that English history ought to be studied in the Statute-Book. Taken with some qualifications, the proposition is a thoroughly true one. It is perfectly true that many readers and writers of history have devoted themselves to personal matters, or at the most to battles and negotiations, and have left legislation and all that legislation touches too much in the background. Mr. Froude did really good service by calling attention to the necessity of giving to the internal legislation of any country at least as prominent a part in its history as any of those aspects of the story by which internal legislation has often been overshadowed. But, in putting forth this really important truth, Mr. Froude was led into two errors. One of these lurks in the word "Statute-Book." If we are allowed to extend the meaning of the word "Statute-Book" so as to take in our earliest written *Dooms*, and our scattered notices of laws and institutions yet older than our earliest written *Dooms*, then we may fully admit that the Statute-Book is the true text-book of English history. Still the use of the phrase "Statute-Book" might seem to imply a somewhat modern way of looking at things; it might seem to imply that the study of the laws and history of England could safely begin at some arbitrary point later than their beginning. And while Mr. Froude did right in claiming for acts of parliament and for other public documents their due value among the sources of history, he went further, and seemed to claim for them a kind of infallibility which the lawyers themselves do not venture to assert. It is, I believe, an acknowledged legal rule that the preamble of an act of parliament need not be received as of any binding force. Mr. Froude seems to think otherwise. He seems to look on the statements of motives and causes set forth in any public document as being of necessity the real motives and causes. On this point, Gibbon and Sismondi held quite another view from Mr. Froude.* Acts of parliament, proclamations, public documents of every kind, have indeed their use; but it is not the particular use which was claimed for them by Mr. Froude. The motives

* I am unavoidably writing without the means of reference to books, except such as I have brought with me for the express purpose in hand. But I have discussed Mr. Froude's way of treating documents, and quoted the passages from Sismondi and Gibbon, in an article in the *Fortnightly Review* (No. 57, September, 1871,) on "The Use of Historical Documents."

which are set forth in a public proclamation are by no means necessarily the real motives of the potentate who puts forth the proclamation. But they have their historical value none the less. For it is often important to know, not only by what motives a man really acted, but by what motives he wished that others should believe that he acted. Now these two forms of error, which disfigured an argument which was highly ingenious and to a great extent true, are both of them worth studying, because they point to one great cause of error in Mr. Froude's writings. They are exactly the errors of a novice; they are the errors of a man who had taken up historical writing and historical study in the middle instead of at the beginning. Mr. Froude had clear-sightedness enough to see at a glance the importance of documentary evidence. But the conviction had to him something of the charm of a discovery; an official proclamation, judgement, assertion of any kind, became in his eyes clothed with a kind of sacred character, before which the ordinary rules of morals and the ordinary rules of historical evidence had to give way. All this could hardly have happened to one who had made history the study of his life. But Mr. Froude, by his own statement, had not made history the study of his life. Nor was he, like Mr. Finlay, led to the study of the past because he saw that no otherwise could he find the key to what he saw around him in the present. Mr. Froude, in that singular confession which he once published,* explained that he took to the writing of English history chiefly because he had nothing else to do. The consequence naturally was that he rushed at a particular period without any preparation from the study of earlier periods. No one who really knows English history can fail to see in almost every page of Mr. Froude's account of Henry the Eighth signs of imperfect knowledge of the days before Henry the Eighth. This fault mends itself to some extent as he goes on; but its effects can never be fully got rid of. Constant inaccuracy of reference and quotation betray the man who has begun to write without having gone through any thorough discipline of reading. Endless displays of ignorance on points of detail bear the same witness. The man who insisted on the Statute-Book being the text-book of English history showed that he had never heard of *peine forte et dure* and had no clear notion of the nature of a bill of attainder. A crowd of mistakes on ecclesiastical and foreign points have been pointed out by Mr. Froude's reviewers. And there is one point in which Mr. Froude shows a striking contrast to Lord Macaulay. One of the best points in Lord Macaulay's History is the vivid way in which he brings before his readers the past history and present state of every place which witnessed any event of importance in his story. Lord Macaulay clearly made it his business to see with his own eyes the places of which he had to speak. Mr. Froude seems never to have done anything of the kind. He can vividly describe a place which he has seen; but it is plain that a

* It appeared in a fly-leaf of "The English in Ireland."

large part of the places which figure in his story he has never seen. Take the story of the martyrdom of Hooper. As far as personal incident goes, Mr. Froude tells his story well; but Lord Macaulay would have added a vivid picture of Gloucester city in its transition state, when the abbey had so lately become the cathedral church. In Mr. Froude's hands the story, full of personal life, is utterly without that local life which it would certainly have received at the hands of Lord Macaulay.

But, besides all this, Mr. Froude's treatment of later times displays one characteristic which goes yet further than all these to disqualify him for treating any subject of mediæval history. This is his fanatical hatred towards the English Church at all times and under all characters. Reformed or unreformed, it is all the same; be it the Church of Dunstan, of Anselm, or of Arundel, of Parker, of Laud, or of Tillotson, it is all one to Mr. Froude. It is a hatred compared to which I should think that the enmity of any Nonconformist, religious or political, must be a lukewarm feeling. It certainly surpasses anything into which an ordinary layman can throw himself even dramatically. It is, I should guess, a degree of hatred which must be peculiar to those who have entered her ministry and forsaken it, perhaps peculiar to the one man who first wrote Lives of the Saints and then "Shadows of the Clouds." How deep-set and bitter Mr. Froude's anti-ecclesiastical feelings are is shown by the fact that they are consistent with the fullest artistic perception of whatever is touching and poetic in the ecclesiastical system. Mr. Froude, as a writer, never reaches so high a point as in several passages where he describes various scenes and features of monastic life. To do justice to a bishop or a monk is what Mr. Froude can never bring himself to; but to paint this and that poetic aspect of a bishop or a monk is what few men can do better. Hatred must be fierce indeed which is in no way softened by so remarkable a power of merely artistic appreciation. In a student of mediæval history Mr. Froude's artistic appreciation is undoubtedly no contemptible help; but it will hardly stand in the place of unswerving justice. What the mediæval Church asks from the student of mediæval history is simply justice. And justice will never be done to her either by fanatical votaries or by fanatical enemies. Mr. Froude has tried both characters; and both characters are alike incompatible with justice, incompatible with truth.

Thus prepared or unprepared, Mr. Froude has made more than one raid, as it may be called, on the history of times earlier than those with which he deals in his chief work. It is curious to mark the exactly opposite way in which his mediæval sketches have been received by those who have, and those who have not, studied the times in which Mr. Froude has ventured himself. The sketches, simply as sketches, are brilliant and effective; the only unlucky thing is that the things sketched have, for the most part, no existence except in Mr. Froude's imagination. By those who are not themselves historical students, who have not the means of testing the truth of the pictures which Mr. Froude has given them, these pictures have naturally been admired. They have been admired as a well-executed picture, good in drawing and colour, may be admired by those who have not the means of knowing that it bears no likeness whatever to the scene or the buildings which it professes to represent. But historical scholars, those who have lived and made their homes in the ages in which Mr. Froude shows himself only as an occasional marauder, have passed a different judgement. These lesser writings have indeed seriously affected their estimate of Mr. Froude's greater work. They are no longer inclined to look on the defence of Henry the Eighth as a mere ingenious paradox. They are now fully convinced that, even in dealing with the relations between Henry and his wives, Mr. Froude really meant what he said. They are now disposed to set down Mr. Froude's vagaries of narrative and judgement to an inborn and incurable twist, which makes it impossible for him to make an accurate statement about any matter. They see in these lesser writings that when Mr. Froude undertakes one of the simplest of tasks, that of fairly reporting the statements made by a single writer, he cannot do it. By some destiny which it would seem that he cannot escape, instead of the narrative which he finds—at least which all other readers find—in his book, he invariably substitutes another narrative out of his own head. That Mr. Froude can hardly be called a free agent in this matter appears from the nature of the points of difference between his narratives and those of the writers whom he professes to copy. That Mr. Froude should colour his story in accordance with his own ideas is not very wonderful: everybody does so more or less; Mr. Froude could hardly fail to do so a great deal. That Mr. Froude, in writing the history of a monastic house, turns everything as far as may be to the discredit of monasticism and of the ecclesiastical system generally might have been taken for granted beforehand. But it is the smallest instances which best prove a law; and the law which compels Mr. Froude to tell his story in a different way from his authority is best illustrated by those instances which are of no controversial and of little historical importance. Be the matter in hand what it may, be the interest of the story great or small, Mr. Froude finds the same necessity laid upon him. Come what may, Mr. Froude's story must not be the story in the book. If the book calls a man by one name or title, Mr. Froude must give him another name or title. If the book says that a thing happened in one place, Mr. Froude must say that it happened in another place. If the book says that it happened on one day of the week, Mr. Froude must say that it happened on another day. It is only on this theory of overwhelming necessity that some of Mr. Froude's astounding departures from his text can be explained. It cannot be supposed that a man who has undertaken to write any part of the

history of England can be ignorant of the name of Robert
Marshal of the army of God and of the Holy Church.
could not have been a free agent when, meeting
filius *Walteri*," fully and clearly described, he
"Sir Robert Fitz*william*," without any description at all.
be supposed that a man who has been Fellow of
really believe that "prædictæ rationes" means "shortene
or that "sæcularis potestas" means "rude policemen from
But the necessity was upon him; as his book said
Mr. Froude was bound to say something else.

Now all this opens a serious question with regard to M
earlier writings. In those writings Mr. Froude's narrative
depends on authorities which very few of us can examin
whether they bear out the statements which Mr. Fro
from them. Very few of us can test references to
Simancas; it is not every one who can, at a moment's
references to manuscripts much nearer home. But every
has learned Latin can test statements which profess to b
on the volumes published by authority of the Master of
When we find that, whenever Mr. Froude professes to
story which is found in those volumes, he nine times out o
us a quite different story, we are tempted to argue from the
the unknown, and to suspect that the Simancas manuscript
Mr. Froude's narrative of later times in the same relation in
Saint Albans History stands to Mr. Froude's narrative
times. The feeling is the same as when a profound inq
early Eastern history expects us to take his word for his
of Hamite, Scythic, and Babylonish, while he shows in the
his argument that he does not understand Greek, Latin,
English. It may be that the suspicion is unjust in both cas
be that some special guidance is afforded to walkers in ro
which is not to be looked for by those who keep in smoot
Still, rightly or wrongly, the thought will force itself upon
that the man who cannot be trusted for a single detail in
where every educated man can test him is not likely to
trustworthy in a narrative where he has the vast major
readers at his mercy.

Mr. Froude's present attempt at mediæval history is the
efforts in the same field. Their scale has grown with eac
He first dealt with the life of Saint Hugh of Lincoln, pr
found his story on the "Magna Vita Sancti Hugonis" pu
Mr. Dimock in the Master of the Rolls' series. This
appeared in one of the earlier volumes of Mr. Froude's
on Great Subjects." The last volume of that collection
Annals of an English Abbey," which profess to
series of Saint Albans Histories—beginning with the

of Matthew Paris—which are also published in the Chronicles and Memorials. In both of these cases the relation between Mr. Froude's narrative and the original which he professes to copy is of the kind which has been already described. If there is any difference between the two, it is that the departures from the original narrative are far more numerous and glaring in Mr. Froude's second mediæval study than they were in the first. Mr. Froude's Annals of Saint Albans are in no sense the same story as the Annals of Saint Albans of the only writers to whom Mr. Froude has to go for his facts. Mr. Froude's narrative differs from the original on countless points great and small, some of which may serve for controversial purposes, while in others the departure from the original seems to be wholly arbitrary. Mr. Froude's annals are in short annals of his own devising, of which the utmost that can be said is that most of the names and many of the incidents seem to have been suggested by the original annals. The narrative was not long ago so minutely examined in one of the weekly journals that it is needless to go again through the whole of the evidence which shows the real character of Mr. Froude's imaginary history of the greatest of English abbeys. I will only once more remind the reader that this is not a case for any deep research, nor a case where there is any field for difference of opinion. It is not a case where the truth has to be got by comparing various and sometimes conflicting statements. In such cases men of equal learning, equal judgement, and equal honesty may often come to different conclusions. In the Saint Albans History there is no such balancing of statements to be gone through. There is only one detailed narrative; there is nothing to confirm or to contradict its statements, except when our one source for the local history of Saint Albans comes into contact with some of our many sources for the general history of England. In all other cases we must take our story for what it is worth, and judge it by internal evidence only. It is open to Mr. Froude or to anybody else to make any objections which he may think good to its authority. But Mr. Froude makes no objections to its authority. He professes to follow it as an authentic narrative, and then gives us a quite different narrative of his own instead. And, as an instance of Mr. Froude's singular indifference to accuracy in local matters, it is plain that he wrote nearly the whole of his Saint Albans narrative in the belief that the abbey church, lately raised to cathedral rank, was a ruin like Rievaux or Tintern.

In his third undertaking Mr. Froude has ventured upon a subject of far greater importance and far greater difficulty than the life of Saint Hugh or the Annals of Saint Albans Abbey. The Life and Times of Thomas Becket form a subject which has been surrounded with controversy from the days of Thomas to our own day. It is a subject which involves the treatment of some of the greatest questions which ever divided Western Christendom. It is a subject which involves the portraiture of some of the foremost men of our own history, and which is not dealt with in its fulness without some notice of men in other lands who were famous on a yet wider field. It is a subject which involves the examination of a state of things when causes which had been long working were bringing forth their final results; it calls for the treatment of the time when we see the issue of the Norman Conquest and of the causes which led to the Norman Conquest, and when we see that that issue was, not to turn Englishmen into Normans, but to turn Normans into Englishmen. It calls too for the treatment of that time in its œcumenical, as well as in its insular aspect. The days of the first Angevin King were days when the immediate rule, not of England but of her ruler, stretched from the Pyrenees to the Cheviots, and when his policy took in all lands from Ireland to Jerusalem. Emperors and Popes, Sicilian Kings and Lombard commonwealths, should be as familiar to him who would write the "Life and Times of Thomas Becket" as the text of the Constitutions of Clarendon or the relations between the sees of Canterbury and York. And the mastery of so vast a subject calls, not for the study of a single narrative, the biography of a single man, or the annals of a single monastery, but for familiarity with a whole contemporary literature. The "Life of Thomas Becket" has to be read in a crowd of independent biographies, and yet more in the endless correspondence of himself, his friends, and his enemies. All these writings have to be carefully studied, carefully weighed, alike in their actual statements and in the colouring with which their statements are overlaid. And to master the "Times of Thomas Becket" needs a further study of the general sources of English, and indeed of European, history. Nor is contemporary history enough either in England or elsewhere. No man can understand the twelfth century, who has not thoroughly mastered the eleventh. And no man can master the eleventh century who has not gone pretty deep into the centuries before it. A man who should begin his studies of the eleventh century in the eleventh century itself, will certainly find it a hard matter to grasp the true position either of William King of the English or of Henry Emperor of the Romans.

But, beyond all this, the Life and Times of Thomas Becket is, of all subjects, that which should least be approached in the spirit of the fanatic or of the partisan. It is a time of controversy, of controversy from which we should, as far as may be, shut out the passions and even the memories of our own times. There are times, distant times, whose controversies are absolutely the same in principle as the controversies of our own day. Both in the earlier and the later shape of those controversies, we must do all that we can to be fair to the supporters of both sides; but we cannot help taking a side ourselves. We feel that, being what we are, we must, if we had lived in those [illegible] thrown in our lot with one side against the other. In the controversies of the twelfth century there is no absolute need thus to take a side. The controversies are quite unlike anything which we can conceive going on in our own times. Looking at the dispute between Henry and Thomas by the light of earlier and of later ages, we see that the cause of Henry was the right one; that is, we see that it was well that the cause of Henry triumphed in the long run. But we cannot feel at all certain whether, being what we are, we should, if we had lived in the days of Henry and Thomas, have taken the side of Henry or the side of Thomas. We feel that, with the same sense of right and wrong which we have now, we must, whether we had been clerk or layman, earl or churl, have gone along with Stephen Langton and Simon of Montfort. In those controversies right is distinctly on one side and wrong is distinctly on the other. In the dispute between Henry and Thomas, we now see that right was on one side, but it would be too much to say that wrong was on the other side. Given the same sense of right and wrong which we have now, our application of it to the points at issue would most likely have varied, according as we might have been clerks or laymen, earls or churls. In estimating such a time and its actors, we ought to be specially able to throw ourselves into the position of the men of both sides, to understand how both sides felt, and fully to take in that there were wise and good men on both sides. There are those who hold that, in any dispute between a king and a bishop, the king must necessarily be right and the bishop wrong. There are others who hold that, in any such dispute, the bishop must necessarily be right and the king wrong. Some on each side go so far as instinctively to set down the king or the bishop not only as being necessarily in the wrong in the controversy, but as being necessarily an evil man in himself. Fanatics of either of these kinds can never deal fairly with the great controversy which Mr. Froude has taken in hand. If we look calmly at the matter, we shall see that both Henry and Thomas acted as, being the men that they were and placed in the position in which they were placed, they could hardly fail to have acted. We may give our sympathy to both as far as the general case of each side goes. We must refuse our sympathy to very many of the particular acts and sayings of both. Both disputants have sadly degenerated from an earlier pair of disputants in a quarrel which has many points of connexion with their own. Henry the First and Anselm knew how to carry on a controversy without loss of dignity on either side, and even without breach of personal friendship. Henry the Second and Thomas had doubtless their predecessors before them as their models; but the copy was in either case very far from reproducing the better points of the original.

Such is, according to my notions, the way in which the Life and Times of Thomas Becket ought to be approached. And I do not fear that any one who knows what the twelfth century was, whether his view either of King or Archbishop be more or less favourable than mine, will think any other way of approaching it likely to be of service to the cause of historic truth. Let us contrast Mr. Froude's way of approaching it. He is controversial, something more than controversial, from the beginning. He undertakes the study, not to throw fresh light on the history of the twelfth century, but to deal a blow at a party in the nineteenth. His first words are—

"Among the earliest efforts of the modern sacerdotal party in the Church of England was an attempt to re-establish the memory of the martyr of Canterbury."

It is not everybody who reads this who will fully take in what is here meant. The first attempt made, within the memory of our own generation, to examine and compare the materials for the great controversy between King and Primate, was made by Richard Hurrell Froude, of Oriel College—the Froude of the once famous "Remains," the elder brother of the man who makes this somewhat unbrotherly reference. The elder Froude doubtless belonged to what the younger calls "the modern sacerdotal party." His wish undoubtedly was "to re-establish the memory of the martyr of Canterbury." To those with whom historic truth comes foremost, and who have no special fanaticism, sacerdotal or anti-sacerdotal, the effort of a "sacerdotal party" to re-establish the memory of Thomas of Canterbury may seem at least as worthy an object as to re-establish the memory of Flogging Fitzgerald or of King Harry himself. To re-establish the memory of Thomas is at the worst a question of words and names, and of a certain law; it does not, like the two other "re-establishments," imply the defence of any matter of wrong or wicked lewdness. And the elder Froude's history of the controversy, if undertaken with a purpose of theological partisanship, was still a piece of creditable historical work. Done forty years or so ago, it was of course not up to the level of modern criticism on the subject. But it was the beginning of modern criticism on the subject. The elder Froude is entitled, at the hands of every one who writes or reads the story of Thomas, to that measure of respectful thanks which belongs to a pioneer on any subject. As for his spirit of partisanship, those who stand outside the arena of all such partisanship might say that, when the elder Froude wrote, it was time that the other side should be heard in its turn. The name of "Thomas à Becket" had been so long the object of vulgar and ignorant scorn; his character and objects had been treated with such marked unfairness, even by historians of real merit, that fair play might welcome a vindication, even if it went too far the other way. Such a vindication was the object of the elder Froude: in the course of it he got rid of several prevalent errors, and made ready the way for more impartial and critical examination at the hands of others. The elder Froude did something to put one who, whatever were his objects, whatever were his errors, was still a great and heroic Englishman, in a historic place more worthy of him.' At all events, he deserves better than to have his work thus sneeringly spoken of by his own younger brother :—

"And while Churchmen are raising up Becket as a brazen serpent, on which the world is to look to be healed of its incredulities, the incredulous world may look with advantage at him from its own point of view, and if unconvinced that he was a saint, may still find instruction in a study of his actions and his fate."

This way of speaking may seem startling to those who know the relation between the long-deceased champion of the one side and the living champion of the other. It may cease to be startling to those who have read Mr. Froude's slenderly veiled works of fiction, and who know the key to them. But to come to more general questions, the point of view of those whose sole object is historic truth may well be different either from the point of view of "Churchmen" or from that of "the incredulous world." At all events, historic truth has nothing to do with the point of view of either. From that point of view which regards historic truth alone, Thomas appears in more than one character of which Mr. Froude takes no notice. In the wider view of history, the primate and martyr may perhaps hardly claim a larger space than the Englishman of Norman descent whose career shows before all things how soon England turned her foreign conquerors and settlers into her own children. The canonized saint may, perhaps, hardly claim a larger space than the great Chancellor who did more than any holder of that office to raise it to its later greatness, and who, in that office, was the right-hand man of one of our greatest kings, in bringing back peace and order after the days of anarchy. Had Thomas never become primate, martyr, and saint, he would still have been entitled to no small place in English history. Indeed, with him as with not a few characters in history, a world-wide fame of one kind has gone far to defraud him of a fame less brilliant, but perhaps more solid, of another kind. Leaving "Churchmen" and "the incredulous world" to dispute about his saintship, both may perhaps "find instruction in the study of his actions" in that part of his life when he appears as the great minister of a great king.

And here I would ask leave for a word or two of a more personal kind. In approaching the Life and Times of Thomas Becket, I may perhaps be allowed to speak as one who cannot call himself a novice in the study of the subject. It is a subject which has been before my eyes, I might say, from my childhood. I long ago said what I had to say on the matter, in an essay which was reprinted in the first series of my collected Historical Essays. I have since had occasion to give a summary of the tale in the last volume of the History of the Norman Conquest. And I feel that, at both stages, I have laboured, with whatever success, to extract the simple truth out of conflicting statements, and to deal fairly with the disputants on either side. I have drawn my picture of Thomas according to my light; and I suspect that I have not drawn him exactly according to the pattern either of those whom Mr. Froude calls "Churchmen," or of those whom he calls "the incredulous world." That Mr. Froude has ever done me the honour to read those writings of mine I cannot venture to think. I am vain enough to believe that, if he had, he would have altered, not perhaps any expressions of opinion, but possibly some statements about plain facts. But I discern in Mr. Froude's treatment of his subject signs of a far greater lack than failure to read anything of mine. I see no sign of his having made use of the advantages which are offered in a special degree to him who studies the English history of the latter half of the twelfth century. To the popular mind, Mr. Froude probably seems to be, before all other men, the historian of Henry the Eighth; he seems to be, in those days at least, master of a domain which is thoroughly his own. It is perhaps only a scholar here and there who knows that the domain which seems to be Mr. Froude's is in truth the rightful possession of Mr. Brewer. But there is at least no doubt to whose domain the reign of Henry the Second belongs. The Angevin reigns are the immediate possession of the great master of English history. He must be a bold man who shall venture to paint King Henry and King Richard, Bishop Hugh of Puiset and Bishop William of Longchamp, in rivalry or in ignorance of the living portraits which have been given to us by Professor Stubbs. In his great prefaces, the Professor has set before us the reign of Henry the Second in every aspect but one. Unhappily the Master of the Rolls has given the special memorials of Thomas to another hand, and has thus hindered us from having the whole reign of Henry, in all its relations, dealt with by the one man who could do justice to it.* Had Professor Stubbs directly told the story of Thomas, the appearance of Mr. Froude in the same field would have been grotesque indeed. As it is, one would have thought that no man would have ventured to deal with any matter in the Angevin period without mastering the writings which make the men of the

* Let me do all justice to the editor, Mr. J. C. Robertson, who has been actually chosen for this work. On the score of minute accuracy, nothing is to be said against him. Some time back he wrote a Life of Thomas, which forms a very useful summary, and in which he has cleared up several points of detail. Its fault is a sneering and carping spirit, the result, it would seem, of sheer inability to understand men of the scale of Henry and Thomas. Even local association—for Mr. Robertson is described on his title page as a Canon of Canterbury—cannot raise him to the level of his subject. But in all minute points, Mr. Robertson's hard-working accuracy is most praiseworthy. In the volumes of the Memorials which have already appeared, we have to thank him for a good text, well edited, to take the place of the helpless attempts of Dr. Giles. And in his Prefaces he gives us many sound and useful editorial remarks. But the master-hand would have given us all this, and much more. The whole materials for the Angevin reigns from the hands of the editor of Benedict and Roger of Howden would have been a possession indeed.

Angevin period, the state of England and Europe during the Angevin period, stand out in full life before us. But Mr. Froude's sketch of the state of things when Henry and Thomas come on the stage shows no sign of any such studies. Even where Mr. Froude does not directly misconceive everything, nothing can be more meagre than his general picture. There is not a word to show how the controversy came about, not a word to connect it with earlier controversies. Yet the reign of Henry the Second cannot be understood without going back to the reigns of William the Conqueror, of William Rufus, and of Henry the First. Mr. Froude, in his introductory sketch, has something to say about Gregory the Seventh; he has not a word to say about Anselm. Yet the position of Thomas cannot be understood without understanding the career of Anselm. Of the great work of the century, the fusion of Normans and English, that fusion of which Thomas himself is the most illustrious example, Mr. Froude clearly knows nothing. Nothing is more certain than the origin of Thomas. The idea that he was of Old-English descent, the conscious champion of English nationality against the Norman, is a dream of Thierry's, which is now as thoroughly exploded as the wild legend of his Saracen mother, which Mr. Froude rejects indeed, but still seems to think worthy of discussion. Some of Thierry's kindred dreams I trust that I have myself dispelled; but this one was dispelled long ago by Dr. Giles and Mr. Robertson, following out hints given by the elder Froude. The mistake was most likely owing to the fact that Thomas was the first Englishman—in the sense of a native of England of whichever race—who rose to the metropolitan throne after the Norman Conquest. This fact might easily be so misunderstood as to represent him as having been an Englishman in the sense of being of Old-English descent. The fact that, from the Conquest to the elevation of Thomas, no Archbishop of Canterbury, and not very many bishops of any see, were natives of England is in itself one of importance; but it has not the meaning which Thierry puts upon it. To Mr. Froude the fact seems to suggest nothing one way or another. But a point of far more importance in the history of Thomas and his age is the fact that Thomas himself, born in London of Norman parents, in the second decade of the twelfth century, was in all but actual descent a thorough Englishman. He has the warmest national patriotism for England, the warmest local patriotism for London. Of the feeling conventionally attributed to men of Norman descent in his age, there is not a trace in his story. There is not a word in the history of the writings of himself, his friends, or his enemies, which could suggest that Thomas was looked on by any man in the land as a stranger, or that he looked on any man in the land as other than his countryman. The importance of all these facts in forming our conception of the "Life," and still more of "the Times of Thomas Becket," can hardly be over-rated. But Mr. Froude is so far from being able to make any inferences from the facts that he has not yet mastered the most elementary facts themselves. We seem to have gone back a generation or so when we read—

> "Thomas Becket was born in London in the year 1118. His father, Gilbert Becket, was a citizen in moderate circumstances. His name denotes Saxon extraction. Few Normans as yet were to be found in the English towns condescending to trade. Of his mother nothing authentic is known, except that she was a religious woman who brought up her children in the fear of God."

Mr. Froude adds in a note—

> "The story that she was a Saracen is a late legend. Becket was afterwards taunted with the lowness of his birth. The absence of any allusion to a fact so curious if it was true, either in the taunt or in Becket's reply to it, may be taken as conclusive."

The argument doubtless is conclusive; but at this time of day the historical scholar as little needs conclusive arguments to prove that Thomas' mother was not a Saracen as the astronomer needs conclusive arguments to prove that the moon is not made of green cheese. As for the other point, Mr. Froude does not vouchsafe to explain how either the name Gilbert or the surname or nickname Becket "denotes Saxon extraction." As however Thomas' father was a Norman of Rouen, while his mother came from Caen,* Mr. Froude's etymological speculations do not greatly matter. And, as Gilbert Becket was not engaged in trade,† Mr. Froude's somewhat hasty assumption against the likelihood of a Norman "condescending to trade" does not much matter either. These assumptions are important only as showing with how little knowledge of his subject a man may undertake to describe the Life and Times of one of the most representative characters in English history, when his avowed object is, not to discover or to set forth historic truth, but to run a tilt against a theological party which he has forsaken.

In short Mr. Froude, in his opening picture, gives us no picture at all of the state of Europe or of England. We get, to be sure, a few grotesque misstatements.

> "Over Scotland the English monarchs asserted a semi-feudal sovereignty, to which Stephen, at the battle of the Standard, had given a semblance of reality."

What form of the threefold relation in which the English overlord stood to Scotland proper, to Lothian, and to the old Scottish fief of

* The whole matter of Thomas' parentage is discussed by Mr. Robertson: see "Becket, Archbishop of Canterbury: A Biography," p. 14.

† I think that the witness of William Fitz-Stephen must be accepted on this head. He says (p. 183, Giles) that Thomas was born "ex legitimo matrimonio et honestis parentibus; patre Gilberto, qui et vicecomes aliquando Londoniæ fuit, matre Matilde, civibus Londoniæ mediastinis neque fœnerantibus neque officiose negotiantibus, sed de reditibus suis honorifice viventibus." The Lambeth writer, on the other hand, makes Gilbert a merchant.

Cumberland, may be darkly hinted at in Mr. Froude's queer phrase of "semi-feudal sovereignty," it might be vain to ask. But Mr. Froude seemingly thinks that Stephen was present at the battle of the Standard; he clearly thinks that the English supremacy over Scotland was more firmly established after the battle of the Standard than it was before. He plainly never took in that David, worsted in the battle, was successful in the war; he would seem never to have heard how the Northumberland of Waltheof and the Cumberland of Rufus were granted to a Scottish prince as its result. So we presently read—

> "In 1159 Pope Adrian died. Alexander the Third was chosen to succeed him with the usual formalities, but the election was challenged by Frederic Barbarossa, who set up an antipope."

This is an odd way of expressing the fact that, in a disputed election, the Emperor took the side of the candidate who, as his party was in the end unsuccessful, appears in ecclesiastical history as an antipope. In short, Mr. Froude took no trouble at all to master the real state of things in England or in Europe; he had work on hand much more to his liking; he had lighted on a contemporary writer whose witness he thought would tell with killing effect against the contemporary Church.

Mr. Froude's excuse for thus giving an opening picture of "the Times of Thomas Becket" in which every characteristic feature of the man and his times is slurred over is that "characteristic incidents, particular things which men representative of their age indisputably did, convey a clearer idea than any general description." In a certain sense this is true: a particular story is likely to fix itself more strongly on the mind than any general description. But, if only the general description be a true one, the idea given by the particular incident, though it may be clearer, is not likely to be more accurate, unless the particular incidents are chosen with great care both as to the actors and as to the particular acts chosen. It may always be a question what are "characteristic incidents," what men are "representative of their age." If any man in a prominent position, a king, a bishop, or the like, may be taken as a representative man, and if anything that he indisputably did may be taken as a characteristic incident, it would be possible to give several ideas of the age, all of which might be very clear, but which would be singularly inconsistent with one another. One chooser of anecdotes might represent all twelfth-century bishops as being like Saint Hugh; another might represent them as being all like William of Longchamp. Nay it would be easy to convey most opposite ideas by picking out different anecdotes of the same man. By taking this or that act which Henry the Second or his son Richard, to go no further, indisputably did, one might make a series of remarkably incongruous pictures of the ideal king of the twelfth century. Mr. Froude picks out the story of the death of the young king Henry, son of Henry the Second,* as showing "one aspect of the twelfth century, the darkest crimes and the most real superstition existing in the same character." To me the story is a very touching one. I am not clear that, under the circumstances, Mr. Froude's language is not a little too strong. That Henry rebelled against his father, that, having rebelled against his father, he carried on the war according to the brutal fashion of the time, are indisputable facts. The "burning towns and churches," and so forth, of which Mr. Froude complains, was bad enough, but it was at least not worse than the kind of warfare waged in Scotland by Edward Earl of Hertford at the express bidding of Henry the Eighth. And blameworthy as was young Henry's rebellion, it should be remembered that his mother and his overlord had a share in it as well as himself. If the elder Henry had been a better husband, he might have had more dutiful sons. And if, as Mr. Froude says, young Henry "drew on himself general hatred," he also drew to himself the deep affection of some. There is a contemporary narrative which even strives to make him out to be a saint and martyr.† And I can at least see nothing to sneer at in the deep and solemn repentance of his death-bed. I do not know whether Mr. Froude would have thought better of him, if his life had been equally criminal and his latest hours had not been equally penitent.

Mr. Froude next wishes to prove that "men who had so little pity on themselves were as pitiless to others." He tells—from Stowe‡—the story of the heretics who were condemned at Oxford in 1166. It is a very remarkable story in many ways. I suspect that their tale concerns Mr. Tylor at one end and Mr. Arthur Evans at the other. At all events, Mr. Froude would have done well to mention that they are the only recorded heretics in English history for several centuries, and that they made only one English proselyte. They seem to have belonged to some of the sects which passed from Asia into Bulgaria and Bosnia, and thence into various parts of Western Europe,

* The hand of a novice is curiously displayed in Mr. Froude's description of the young king, Henry the Third, as some called him in his own day. He becomes "Henry Plantagenet, eldest son of Henry the Second, Prince of Wales as we should now call him, called then the 'young king,' for he was crowned in his father's lifetime." This is not the way in which those who are familiar with the young king and with his coronation would speak of him. The phrase "Henry Plantagenet" shows that Mr. Froude is one of those who fancy that the nickname of Count Geoffrey was borne as a hereditary surname by his grandchildren. And why "Prince of Wales as we should now call him"? We call the present heir-apparent Prince of Wales, because his mother and sovereign has so created him. If the creation had not taken place—and in the case of several heirs-apparent it did not take place till long after their birth—we should not call him Prince of Wales. But why anybody should have dreamed of the eldest son of the king of England being Prince of Wales in the twelfth century, no man can guess. It is like the Dauphin who, in so many histories, is made to invade England in the time of John, a good deal more than a hundred years before the Viennese Dauphiny became the possession of the eldest son of the French king. Elsewhere Mr. Froude talks about "Prince William," "Princess Margaret," exactly as if they had belonged to the illustrious House of Hanover.

† This is a piece by Thomas Agnellus, a Canon of Wells, printed, I think, in one of Mr. Robertson's volumes.

‡ Not that Stowe is to be despised. He was the only writer who made use of the contemporary life of Edward the Confessor while it was still in manuscript. Still it is odd to quote from him rather than from a contemporary writer.

Southern Gaul above all. They were not burned or put to death in any way; they were whipped and branded, and turned loose, all men being forbidden to help them. Mr. Froude truly calls this "a fate more piteous than the stake." I think that we may see in this sentence a feeling of superstition—I can this time freely use the word—deeper than Mr. Froude seems to suspect. It is of a piece with various ways in which men have sought to cause death without incurring the responsibility of taking life, especially in the form of shedding blood. It is of a piece with the imprisonment of Antigonê in the tomb; it is of a piece with Bishop Odo's club on the day of Senlac. I will not say that it is of a piece with the substitution of mutilation for death in the legislation of the Conqueror, because I believe that that was honestly meant to be a legislation of mercy, however different it may now seem in our eyes. But in any case the partisans of Thomas may comfort themselves with the thought that with this act he and his friends had nothing to do; it was wholly the doing of the King and of the Bishops of his party.

Mr. Froude then goes on to ask, "What were the bishops and clergy like themselves?" The answer which any fair inquirer into the time would give is that there were among them, as among other men, both good and bad. The fault lay not at all in the absence of the good, but in the toleration of the bad. The Bishops of Henry the Second's reign—setting aside the saint of Lincoln who had not yet shown himself, and numbering among them some men who were strongly opposed to Thomas—were by no means a contemptible set of men, either in attainments or in character. Age had tamed the fire of Henry of Winchester; Gilbert of London, Bartholomew of Exeter, Hilary of Chichester, were by no means men to be thrust aside in a few general words. Some of them had distinctly risen by personal merit. But all that Mr. Froude has to say in answer to his own question is to tell, and—what Mr. Froude surely need not have done—to spoil in the telling, the grotesque story of the scuffle between the two archbishops in the Council of 1176. As Mr. Froude has given an extract from Stowe, I will send my readers to enjoy the story in its fulness in Godwin's Catalogue of Bishops. Here the chief performer was Roger Archbishop of York, Thomas' great enemy. Of him it is perfectly true that John of Salisbury repeats, as Mr. Froude says, a tale of crime than which nothing could be worse. But I suspect that Mr. Froude has hardly stopped to think on what light evidence such stories were told and believed in days when the restraints which in our day put a check on both speaking and writing were quite unknown. A man must have a large faith in the depravity of mankind, if he believes that all the enemies of Giraldus were quite so black as Giraldus paints them. John of Salisbury was a man of higher stamp than Giraldus; but it is easy to believe that even he would not bring the severest rules of evidence to bear on a story which told so strongly against the chief of the other party. And against the report which described Archbishop Roger as the most infamous of mankind, we may fairly set the fact, that his early promotions were due to the favour of such a man as Archbishop Theobald.

Mr. Froude then goes on to say:—

"As to the inferior clergy, it might be enough to quote the language used about them at the conference at Montmiraux in 1169, where their general character was said to be atrocious, a great number of them being church-robbers, adulterers, highwaymen, thieves, ravishers of virgins, incendiaries, and murderers."

Mr. Froude gives the original in a note, and adds the reference, "John of Salisbury to the Bishop of Exeter. Letters, 1169." A reader who did not verify the reference might be tempted to think that it was John of Salisbury who gave this description of his brethren. But happily the letters of John of Salisbury are not at Simancas, and the passage may be found with an effort, even in the edition of Dr. Giles. He who makes the effort will find that the words come from the mouth of King Henry. The reader may judge how much or how little qualification is to be made on this account; but at all events when Mr. Froude says, "it is said," he should have added who it was that said it.

One specimen more does Mr. Froude give before he comes to his strong point of all. This is the character of Abbot Clarembald of Saint Augustines. Nothing, except the story about Roger, can be worse, and there is no reason to doubt the truth of an official report. Some might whisper that one cause of evil in this case was the exemption of the monastery from ordinary jurisdiction. But this is just the kind of point which Mr. Froude is not likely to stop and think about. The case of Clarembald—a strong partisan of the King's, as Mr. Froude does not conceal—undoubtedly proves a fearful lack of discipline when such a man could have been endured for a day. But it does not prove, as Mr. Froude evidently wishes to imply, that the clergy in general, or that abbots in general, were men of the same type. It would be just as fair to describe the virtues of Saint Hugh or of Saint William of York, and to infer that all other bishops were like them.

But Mr. Froude has a stronger point than all. He loves to take some one book or some one author, and to make use of him as a kind of text. It is not always a fair way of handling a subject; but it is often an effective way. Mr. Froude, we know, has tried it with the "Magna Vita Sancti Hugonis" and with the "Gesta Abbatum." He now tries it with the satires, prose and verse, of Nigel of Canterbury, printed among the "Satirical Poems" in the Chronicles and Memorials. Here beyond sea I have not the book at hand; but I remember its general purport, and Mr. Froude gives large extracts. Mr. Froude says with truth:—

"In reading him we feel that we are looking at the old England through an extremely keen pair of eyes. We discern, too, perhaps that he was a clever fellow, constitutionally a satirist, and disappointed of promotion, and we make "the necessary allowances."

A man must have a much deeper acquaintance with the writings of those times than we can fairly give Mr. Froude credit for before he fully understands how much allowance is necessary in such a case. Mr. Froude, in drawing his black picture of the twelfth century, has left out one of its chief vices, utter unscrupulousness of statement in the whole class of writings of which these of Nigel are specimens. I have mentioned some examples already. It is a case in which goodness of purpose is no guaranty of literal truth. No man was so likely to draw an utterly one-sided, a grossly exaggerated, picture, as a man who was really stirred up by righteous zeal against the vices of his age. As a rule, no sinner uses fiercer, or even fouler, language than a saint in a rage. One chief motive which imposes some measure of restraint on a modern reformer was absent. In our times, with our endless variety of sects and parties, each is a check on every other. Each is on its good behaviour in the presence of all the rest. Gross scandals are less likely to happen, and, when they do happen, if there are those whose interest it is to expose them, there are those whose interest it is to hush them up. Every man observes some moderation in denouncing the vices of his own party, lest, in denouncing its vices, he should chance to endanger either its principles or its success. Every disputant now remembers the saying about washing one's dirty linen at home. But when all Western Europe, setting aside Jews and Saracens, was of one theological mind, none of these motives had any play. Wherever the dirty linen was washed, it was equally at home. Wherever and to whomever the fierce reformer made his declamation, there were no Nonconformists, no outsiders of any kind, to hear it. He might rebuke the vices of priests, bishops, and popes, without being supposed to shake the foundations of the priesthood, the episcopate, or the popedom. The greater was his faith in the thing itself, the more unsparing, the more reckless, would be his denunciations of all its abuses. In such a case we must take off at least as much from the denunciations of an internal reformer as we should now take off from the denunciations of an external enemy. In both cases the charges are sure to have some foundation in fact: in both cases they are sure to be exaggerated; in both cases there is sure to be that particular form of exaggeration which consists in taking the worst case that can be found and making it typical of the whole class. In this way it would be easy to draw a very black picture of almost any class of men in almost any age. It would certainly be easy to draw a very black picture of classes of men whose average is far higher than that of the English clergy in the twelfth century. When we turn to the particular charges made by Nigel, we shall see that some of them, allowing for exaggeration, are true enough, while others seem quite wide of the mark. When he complains that the officers of the king's court and household were forced as bishops upon unwilling chapters and convents, he describes one of the chief abuses of the time, and it is quite possible that in this or that particular case all the scandalous details which he describes may have taken place. But when he speaks of the sons of nobles being put into bishoprics while they were still children, he is describing an abuse which was rather continental than English. The English bishops of that age did not, as a rule, belong to great families, and they were not, as a rule, appointed in extreme youth. Henry of Winchester, grandson, nephew, and brother of kings, stands alone among the bishops with whom Thomas had to deal as an example of a bishop belonging to the highest rank.* Most of the prelates of his time had made their way to high places by personal qualifications of some kind, though those qualifications were not always of a kind for which we should now think ecclesiastical office the fitting reward. On one point there is little doubt that Mr. Froude has failed, through lack of familiarity with the language of the time, to understand the formulas of reviling employed by his author. Hugh Nonant, Bishop of Chester, Coventry, or Lichfield, whichever we choose to call him, drove out the monks of Coventry and put secular canons in their stead. Richard of Devizes bewails the act as well as Nigel. In an age when change more commonly was the other way, the act of Bishop Hugh was indeed startling. Any one who knows the age will understand how any monastic writer would speak of it. The monk Nigel speaks of the monastery being turned into a brothel and of harlots being openly brought into cloister and chapter-house. Most likely all this means nothing more than that some of the canons were married.

I do not undertake the defence of an age when the deepest abuses were undoubtedly rife. But I ask for justice. I ask that a whole class of men shall not be described from the portraits of the very worst among them. And, leaving this matter aside, I ask that a picture of the faults of one class of men in that or in any other age shall not be taken as a sufficient picture of that age. To understand the Life and Times of Thomas Becket, it is indeed necessary to take in the great and crying evils which prevailed in the Church of that day. But it is also necessary to take in a great many other things, to the understanding of which Mr. Froude gives no help whatever. Having thus cleared the way by giving the reader some help towards forming an estimate of Mr. Froude's capacity for dealing with twelfth-century history, I may go on in another paper to see how he deals in detail with the "Life and Times" of the man whose age he has so thoroughly failed to understand, and whose own origin and position he has so utterly mistaken.

EDWARD A. FREEMAN.

* Saint William of York is also said to have been a nephew of King Stephen; but the pedigree is hard to make out. The custom of using bishoprics as provisions for cadets or bastards of the royal family, so common in some other countries, never prevailed in England. Bishops of noble families were not wholly unknown at any time, but they became much more common some centuries later.

# CONTEMPORARY LIFE AND THOUGHT.

## I.

## IN ITALY.

FLORENCE, 18*th February*, 1878.

TWO months only have elapsed since my last article was written, and Italy seems in that time to have grown older by many years. That which has happened to us is known to all Europe, and in our national mourning her interest has been as keen as unanimous. The foreign press has been occupied with relating our loss, and shown us a sympathy that demands our deepest gratitude.

The death of our first King has proved to us that we are not isolated, living only to ourselves; but that we form one of the recognized family of European nations, and *that* not only by being recognized diplomatically and officially,—a distinction we should have, whatever might be our form of government, whether suitable or not. For example, Spain has seen, since the expulsion of Queen Isabella, during the short space of ten years, five or six different changes of government, and all have been recognized by foreign Powers as legitimate, or at least tolerated as such. But in Italy the same government has continued uninterruptedly for the space of eighteen years. It sprang from the ruins of several kingdoms protected by the Holy Alliance. Its origin may appear, at first sight, illegal and antagonistic to the law of Divine right; while that which Italy subsequently had the daring to accomplish in 1870, in Rome, appeared a bold revolutionary act, which might have put her beyond the pale of international law. But Italy pursued her course with so much certainty of success, with such intrepidity, and with such a unanimous desire to attain the goal of her aspirations, that all which but a few years since appeared illegal and impracticable, seems now but a necessary and consequential act. She has used her successes with so much moderation, shown herself so prudent in the exercise of her liberty, that all thought has ceased of contesting her possession of that which for ages had been denied her, worthy though she proved herself to hold it. And when the European peoples heard that Italy's heart was bleeding for the loss of her first King, they pressed forward as one man to offer sympathy and weep with her the premature death of the Prince who had made of divided Italy one family, and by so doing acknowledged in the most eloquent manner the legitimacy of our strongly constituted nationality. What, indeed, are we mourning in Victor Emmanuel? The maker of Italian unity. And the more poignant and universal the grief for the death of the King, the more consolidated does it prove the unity of the people of Italy.

I had the sad comfort of being one of the 80,000 persons who, forming the funeral *cortège* of the 17th January, preceded or followed the bier of King Victor Emmanuel, and accompanied him to his last glorious resting-place in the Pantheon, in the temple consecrated to all the gods and to the divine Raphael, and where the affection of the Romans willed that the defunct King of Italy should be rather amongst the deified than among the buried. I saw the religious gathering of the people of Rome, crowding the ways where passed the funeral *cortège*. Rome seemed transformed into a magnificent temple, where were being celebrated more than the obsequies of a single prince—those of an entire nation. Joined to the family of Italy but seven years since, the Romans yet felt so certainly that Victor Emmanuel had become also *their* King, that they with one accord put forth their pious desire that the royal remains should rest in Rome, where they would be guarded and protected from all outrage—where Italy would be always found to be gathering fresh inspirations to renewed great deeds, whatever national peril might arise. It was feared that taking the body of Victor Emmanuel from Rome might give rise to the idea at the Vatican that the House of Savoy did not consider itself sufficiently secure of its permanent tenure of Rome. The good sense of the Italian people comprehended the evil that might accrue had the clerical party a pretext of affirming that the House of Savoy carried away their dead from the field of battle like an acknowledgment of their defeat. No! Italy was to avow nothing of the kind, and in spite of the profound disappointment of the Turinese at being deprived of the remains of their Piedmontese King, and the personal feeling of the new King Humbert against separating the body of his father from that of his grandfather, the voice of the Italian people spoke so eloquently that the decision was made that King Victor Emmanuel should inaugurate in Rome the tombs of the Kings of Italy. And in listening from the first day of his reign to the voice of the people, King Humbert has shown himself a worthy successor of Victor Emmanuel, who gained from his people the name of the *Galantuomo* ("The Honest Man") because tempted often to withdraw the "Statute," he was always the jealous guardian of it. From his soldiers he gained the name of "hero" for the intrepidity with which, on the field of battle, he defied more than once the balls of the enemy; and from Europe the name of "Great," not only for the great deeds achieved in his name during his reign, and for the crowning act, the independence, the unity, the liberty of Italy, but because these great deeds were performed in the most meritorious manner, not following his own instincts, or his own aspirations, but putting them aside and carrying out, guided by an admirable good sense, the will of his people. I know not if there be a genius of good sense and a genius of honesty; if there be such, these two geniuses existed personified in King Victor Emmanuel. No king had ever been more strictly educated in the etiquette of a Court, or was more scrupulous in the observance of ancient ceremonials, or had such high aristocratic principles instilled in him from his birth. Yet he became the most democratic sovereign of our time.

The feelings of respect that he owed to the House of Austria, whence came his mother, would have led him naturally into cultivating the most cordial relations with it; but the well-being of his people, and that Star of Italy in which the Savoyard Princes have an almost superstitious faith, moved him to make war against Austria and to make himself the champion of Italian independence. Naturally devout and religious, he would never of his own free-will have put his name to the decree that abolished in Piedmont the ecclesiastical court; and still less to the decree that incorporated the property of the convents with that of the State; and still less would he have deprived the Head of the Church of the city in which was his temporal abode. But though a prince he had learned the virtue of sacrifice; as a constitutional king, he knew that the more he could temper and assimilate himself to the wishes and dispositions of his people the more perfect would be his rule. And of this power of adaptability in an extraordinary degree one reads in those foreign journals which show the greater sympathy for and appreciation of our country, a panegyric so flattering to us; for Italy, while possessing a soil and a sky unmatched, and producing under its sky and on its lands the most æsthetic of the European peoples, has also been able, while rising in civilization, to show in Victor Emmanuel that she can also produce ideal kings. In other countries the death of a king is wont to give rise to strange agitations, to unexpected demonstrations. In young Italy [illegible] that the death of Victor Emmanuel consolidates more firmly [illegible], and the succession from father to son has passed as facilely as [illegible] hereditary monarchy had existed for ages in the kingdom. It is true [illegible] Savoy is now the most ancient dynasty wearing a crown, but that [illegible] which took place peaceably when the Lords of Savoy were Counts [illegible] and Dukes of Savoy or Kings of Sardinia, might have become [illegible] in a new reign, which extended over the ruins of several other [illegible], over people composed of elements so diverse, and which had been [illegible] so few years ago. All passed, however, in the most perfect and orderly manner possible. King Humbert has reigned but a few days, and the Italians have already given him proofs of affection such as few reigning princes can boast of. A reign that commences with such happy auspices reassures both prince and people. Italy then, even in the days of her deepest sorrow, can find reason for her brightest hopes.

Italy is saved from much peril by the natural love of moderation, the sign of true wisdom, in her people. They may also be considered a fortunate people. It may be remarked, that until the 18th March, 1876, the Government had been always in the hands of one party only, that of the moderate party, called the Right. So that one might almost think that Italy had been made free only to benefit that party; that monarchy was a species of exclusive privilege of the Right. If Victor Emmanuel had been taken from us before two years ago, it might have been feared that the Left, excluded until that time from power, with its Republican tendencies, would have attempted to create some agitations, which might have ended in throwing the whole of Italy into a state of anarchy. Fortunately the 18th of March, 1876, saw the Left in power, and still holding it, when called upon to render the last homage to the first King of Italy, and the first honours to his worthy successor. So that before the tomb of King Victor Emmanuel, while all Italy was raising one earnest cry of mingled regret and sorrow, she could feel assured that no attempt would be made to change her form of government, and at the same time acknowledge the truth of the words uttered by Signor Crispi, now Minister of the Interior, on the day he publicly separated himself from Mazzini and all the Republican party—"Monarchy unites us, Republicanism divides us."

They say that the late Pope, in his voluntary seclusion in the Vatican, not only showed a sincere grief for the death of the King, but astonishment that he was so beloved by the Italian people and so mourned by them. He complained to his intimate friends around him, that he had been deceived concerning the true sentiments of the Italians. However true or false may be this story that spread from street to street in Rome, one thing remained patent—the impotency of the enmity and anger of the Vatican against Italy, and the uselessness of its opposition.

I said in my last letter, that the future Pope would have but only one means of raising the Catholic Church again in Italy, and this would be by associating himself sincerely with the Italian Liberal movement, aiding the civil progress of the young kingdom of Italy, and breathing on it, as if from on high, a spirit of Christian charity.

No one could have imagined, when I thus wrote, so near and unforeseen an event as that of Italy's first King preceding the aged Pope to his tomb, whose pontificate was begun with blessings on Italy. As the King's end approached, and it became bruited abroad that the Pope was sensibly affected by the announcement, hopes were raised that the Pontiff would seize the occasion to reconcile himself with Italy, and repair in person to the Quirinal to give his benediction to the dying liberator of Italy. It was hoped that Pius IX., showing himself great in mind and heart, would have gone forth from his Vatican prison to save his Church, taking to his bosom the kingdom of Italy, knowing that, while blessing, his own superiority and no weakness would be shown. The

Italian people would have been mad with delight [illegible] 1847, and, returning amid the acclamations of [illegible] forgiveness and blessing would have aggrandised [illegible] dent. Religion also would have been a gainer by [illegible] is the place where real religious sentiment and C[illegible] found. In the Vatican they love not, but hate and [illegible] Pius IX., which perhaps was already prepared to [illegible] arrested by the artful designs of adverse counsellors, [illegible] Papacy to its ruin—men who until now were thought [illegible] Church's cause.

And now Pius IX. has unexpectedly gone to his grave [illegible] after the death of the first King of Italy; and, instead of [illegible] by blessing Italy a second time at the end of his P[illegible] enough to permit Cardinal Simeoni to make a sterile protest [illegible] of Victor Emmanuel, because he had inaugurated his reign with [illegible] of the Pope, contenting himself with that of all the Italian [illegible] death of Pius IX. change the situation of the Papacy [illegible] Fear and hope put in evidence the names of some cardinals [illegible] Papacy: fear, those of Cardinals Panebianco and [illegible] Cardinals Pecci and Di Pietro. But nothing is more difficult [illegible] result of a Papal election. If the cardinals assembled [illegible] maintain the popularity attached to Pius IX. by calling [illegible] they are deceiving themselves. The glory of Pius IX. [illegible] which none of his successors can inherit.

To King Victor Emmanuel, prince, warrior, liberator of [illegible] King Humbert, who, though a valiant soldier in the field, [illegible] reign, and begins to show a lively interest in the progre[illegible] throughout the kingdom. Let us hope that to the Pope [illegible] agitating, may succeed one bent on reconciling and [illegible] between the Church and State, which have tended only to [illegible] the Italian people too superstitious, the other too irreligious.

The book of Father C. M. Curci,* which has made so much [illegible] and elsewhere during the last two months, has confirmed [illegible] ing ground in the consciences of the Italians—that the [illegible] isolated herself from Italian life, that she has now no [illegible] over it. It is well known that for his new opinions, [illegible] the counsellors of the Vatican too liberal and heretic, [illegible] expelled from that same Society of the Jesuits of which [illegible] been a most zealous champion. The fault of Father Curci [illegible] covering too late that the Church was on the road to [illegible] before now have opened his eyes to the truth, before now [illegible] maledictions launched by the Pope against Italy, the new [illegible] complicate and overload Catholicism, the Syllabus, the [illegible] were all means that isolated from the Papacy its natural [illegible] faith, the affections, and the sympathy of the Italian people. [illegible]

The Pontifical reign of Pius IX. has been a sequel [illegible] authors of which have been those very Jesuits to which [illegible] But it is much that a Jesuit should become cognisant of [illegible] them, and lose, by so doing, all the advantages which [illegible] learning, highly cultivated mind, honesty of life, had [illegible] remain alone, poor and persecuted, for having told [illegible] The clerical journals treat Father Curci as a [illegible] by reproving and mortifying the author, to [illegible] But the truth is that all the Italian liberal clergy [illegible] central Italy than the Vatican likes to [illegible]

* Il Moderno Dissidio [illegible]

[illegible] between Church and State which Father Curci has pointed out,—[illegible] which, according to him, would cease when the Church should [illegible] deplore the loss of her temporal power, cease to meddle with the civil [illegible] affairs of the State, and become alone the wise ruler of spiritual [illegible]. The ills the Church laments, she has brought on herself. Father Curci [illegible] not praise the spoliators, but finds it just that the Church should be [illegible] of a power that was not formed for her, and he repeats the words of [illegible], "Injusta patimur, sed non injuste."

[illegible] accuse the Church of being in the wrong, when that same Church is [illegible] by a Pontiff who created the dogma of the Infallibility, appears [illegible] an unheard-of temerity at the Vatican; but it is to be doubted if the Vatican be still the faithful interpreter of the interests and needs of the Church. If the present temper of the Vatican continue, the approximate ruin of the Papacy may be easily foreseen. In Italy at least it will lose all prestige and [illegible], will reduce itself to a sect, in an age when sects in Italy have no longer any power; and all this will be its own dark work. Deprived of the [illegible] enlightenment of the age, it will become an enemy to all civilization. The Church alone can become great when her representatives become pious charitable evangelists, beloved of men, ceasing to care for things temporal and political, or for the material affairs of the state. This is the wholesome conclusion to which the bold and eloquent pamphlet of Father Curci leads us. Whatever may be the prejudices against the author, on account of his previous position, it is certain that all the friends of religion rejoice over the publication of this book, which, while denouncing the gravest evils, leads us to hope that some one of the eminent cardinals predestined to the glory, or punishment, of the Pontificate may set himself to work to remedy them.

Father Curci deplores the want of sympathy in Italy for important religious questions, but if these themes have not become popular they have nevertheless been discussed for years in many of our political papers,—such as *Opinione* and *Diritto* of Rome, *Nazione* of Florence, *Perseveranza* of Milan, *Corriere Mercantile* of Genoa,—by the most cultivated, learned, and moderate writers, with perfect impunity. Further, our best reviews publish from time to time articles full of serious matter on the relations of Church and State, which denote a signal progress in criticism, even though the writers be attached to one or other party; as in the case of the *Civiltà Cattolica*, the organ of the Jesuits, which comes out twice a month in two small sheets; in that of the *Rivista Universale*, representative of that Catholic party which wishes at the same time to show respect for the Pope and the King, and conciliate religious faith with love of country; also in that of the *Nuova Antologia*, the most eminent and trustworthy of our literary reviews, now published every fortnight in an elegant form under the direction of Professor Protonotari, and to which during the last twelve years the most distinguished writers have contributed. In the *Nuova Antologia* appeared, in detached articles, the interesting work of Signor Bonghi on Pius IX. mentioned in my last letter; and [illegible], Villari, Mamiani, Minghetti, and other eminent men, have written [illegible] learned articles on political, social, and religious questions. In the *Nuova Antologia* there is not perhaps unity of purpose, but there is always most ample liberty of discussion, so that one there finds nearly all the most antagonistic opinions on the most diverse subjects. The choice among these [illegible] opinions belongs to the reader, who generally cares little for these [illegible], and therefore selects none of them. To gain a really lasting [illegible] on his mind it is necessary that the journal that comes to his hand be [illegible] constant in the defence of one class of ideas, and revealing an ardent [illegible] towards propagandism. This spirit of liberal propagandism has [illegible] forth in Florence, in the beginning of this year, a new review, which [illegible] brought before the English reader. It bears the simple title of the [illegible] *Settimanale*, and is modelled on the plan of the *Saturday Review*. It proposes, in a series of short articles, generally anonymous, but written by eminent men, to write, regardless of criticism, the truth, such as it appears to politicians, legislators, teachers, men of science, letters, and art, with the hope of weaning the Italians from that style of vain complimentary rhetorical and academical pomp, that *esprit de routine* which so often, by doing and undoing for the sake of ameliorating, leaves a worse production. The intention is excellent, and the two talented young men who have placed themselves at the head of the direction have both mind, hearty will, energy, and pecuniary means to carry it on. And warmly we sympathize with the idea that incited Leopoldo Franchetti and Sidney Sonnino to commence the *Rassegna Settimanale;* and in the first numbers now before us, we see a promise of the realization of it. We fear at the same time that some of their contributors may take too literally the obligation to be veracious, and that, with some, to write the bare truth may mean to be uncivil, to fail to recognize anything of good, to find all bad, or to be silent about the meritorious and speak only of the undeserving, demolishing wholesale; a system which, if continued, is to be deplored, seeing that Italy has to be always working onward and progressing. Flattery is not required, and caricaturing should be forbidden, but to render its criticisms useful, and not odious, the new journal must show a little more respect towards the few Italians who work and by their publications do good service to learning. For example, the notices of Rubieri's book and Mariotti's translation of Demosthenes are simply irritating, from the manner in which they coolly neglect the merits and enlarge on the defects of these well-known publications. Let us hope that the new journal, with time and age, may acquire that indulgence that springs from mature judgment. There is wanting neither talent nor learning in Italy: and the contributors to the new review have a large share of both; there needs but a good spirit among them. This is the great and ardent wish of myself, among many who desire to see literature take its old place among us.

Poets might also aid in the work, but for the moment modern writers seem not to occupy themselves much with this needed branch of letters. One of the latest poets risen to notice is Dr. Olindo Guerrini of Bologna (a contributor to the *Rassegna Settimanale*, in which, until now, has appeared but the most materialistic, pernicious poetry), who writes under the name of a deceased friend, that of Dr. Lorenzo Stecchetti. The volume, which is published by Zanichelli of Bologna, under the title of "Posthumous Poems," is distinguished not less for the simple elegance of the style than for the bold realistic images it contains. He possesses in an eminent degree the plastic art of Italian verse, but of this happy gift he makes too ample use. In a sonnet which serves as an introduction, he calls his verses "rime discrete" (but it would be difficult to admit their discretion), and he bids them tell his lady of his love:

"Quanto, quanto l'amai voi le direte."

(" How, oh! how I loved her, you will tell her.")

Let us see, then, what is Signor Stecchetti's idea of love. He relates his coming into the world on a wild night, when the witches had assembled to celebrate their orgies. The horoscope promises but little; the verses depict vividly the gloom of the moment:

" Come nembo di furie agitatrici,
   Dei Satanici amplessi al rito immondo
Sceser le streghie dalle lor pendici.
   Triste colui che in quel terror profondo
Trasse della sua vita i primi auspici!
   Io quella notte son venuto al mondo."

("As a cloud of agitated furies
   Of the Satanic [illegible] [illegible]pure rite
Descend the witche[illegible] [illegible]ghts.
   Sad must he be [illegible]
Draws the first [illegible]
   On that night [illegible]

In the following verses the poet laments that his lady-love had left him without giving him a parting embrace, and asks if she be dead, or become false to him, or if she be married; and tortures himself with the thought that she may [illegible] children that are not the fruit of his love. But the poet recalls [illegible] embraces, the joyful night, the secret voluptuousness and pleasures, [illegible] on his couch his solitude, and, in his despair, curses God who has separated him from her. In the following sonnet he paraphrases the verse of Béranger:—

"Maudit printemps, reviendras-tu toujours?"

and curses the spring which brings back the memory of the embraces of yore, but not the embraces themselves. Then follows a mediæval legend, in which a defunct princess arises, and says to her lover:—

"Guardami, tocca;
Son la figlia del re, baciami in bocca."

("Look at me—touch me;
I'm the daughter of a king.
Kiss me on my lips.")

The strophes that follow paraphrase the verses of Horace—

"Si fractus illabatur orbis
Impavidum ferient ruinæ"—

and the poet invites his Nerina to sit on his knee, to bind her arms about his neck, so that, with his face buried in her bosom, he may, in that heroic attitude, defy the ruin of the world. Observe how many poets retain their monotonous characteristic and betray their particular taste; one will speak for ever of light, another of smiles, or flowers, or eyes. The weak side of Signor Stecchetti displays itself in the constant introduction of "bosoms" and "knees." These are the two images that occur the most frequently in his poems. Among many to be noticed, and having much originality, we find one sonnet of Signor Stecchetti's that ends—

"Sono poeta o sono un imbecille?"

("Am I a poet, or a fool?")

A similar verse, strange to say, is found in a mediocre French poet—Benjamine Antier—who sings:

"Poëtes ou fous. . . .
C'est un peu notre histoire à tous."

But after asking himself this question, the poet seems again serious, and, in the midst of a carnival, himself begins to mock at

"Danze, fiori, chiome fluenti,
Candidi petti, voluttà cocenti."

("Dances, flowers, flowing hair,
White breasts, burning desires.")

[illegible] the poet laments that his love, after having

"Messo nel sangue un novo istinto
Che scalda il cor tediato e lo tramuta"

("Put into my blood a novel instinct
That warms the tired heart and transforms it"),

[illegible] looking at him. He sees her again in his dream:

"[illegible] vestita, e il crin disciolto
[illegible] sui ginocchio."

("Her vesture was white, and her flowing hair
Descended to the knees.")

The poet, though healthy and rubicund, thinks himself about to die, and invites his love beforehand to his tomb, and asks of her a kiss for the dead. The verses that express this more absurd than natural idea are among the most beautiful that Stecchetti has written—

"Là vieni, o donna; il tuo fedel t'invita;
Là sulla tomba mia, cogli commossa
L'erba che amavi, del mio cor nudrita,
O! non negarle un bacio e liete l'ossa
Come ai tuoi baci già soleano in vita
Tremeranno d'amor dentro alla fossa."

("Come there, O lady; thy faithful one invites thee;
There, on my tomb, gather afflicted
The herb thou lovedst, nourished by my heart.
Oh! do not deny it a kiss, and my bones, o'er-joyful,
As they were wont in life at your kisses,
Will tremble for love within their grave.")

Here at least is some trace of refinement and poetry; but evidently this very modern poet, wishing to be realistic, come what may, has some scrupulous feelings after having written the above, and breaks off into the grotesque. Wishing to be thought witty, he gives an imitation of Soulary, in which the ass and the ox, at the birth of Jesus Christ, lament the part allotted to them, for the ass will be beaten when carrying the Redeemer into Jerusalem, and the ox will be devoured as beefsteaks at the marriage at Cana.

"Ed il bue: Le mie costole sapranno
Un giorno a Cana se redente le hanno,
Quando in bisteeche me le mangeranno."

("And the ox: My ribs will know,
One day at Cana, if they have been redeemed,
When they shall be eaten as beefsteaks.")

In the Maremma the poet experiences an hour of true ennui, and represents it most graphically. He fears he will die there or become imbecile, when he remembers the pleasant spots inhabited or passed through in his youth. This thought becomes a poetic terror, given in perhaps one of the best sonnets of the collection:—

"Nella capanna, in fondo al mio cortile,
Il luppolo alle canne s'attorciglia,
Nell'aria fresca c'è un odor gentile,
Odor di gelsomino e di vaniglia,
Un' Ebe quasi nuda alta e sottile,
Sorride e spia colle marmoree ciglia,
Dei palombi gli amor sotto al sedile,
E il vento del mattin passa e bisbiglia,
Bisbiglia e narra di lontane aiaole,
Gli amor lontani ad un popol giocondo,
Di gerani fiammanti e di viole,
Quanto amor, quanta gioia in questo mondo
Di pochi passi che si desta al sole!
O! quanta vita! ed io son moribondo."

("In my cottage, at the end of my inner court,
The hop twines itself among the reeds;
In the fresh air, there comes [illegible] odour—
An odour of jessamine a[illegible]
A Hebe, almost nude, tall [illegible]
Smiles and spies with [illegible]

The loves of the doves under their eaves,
And the winds of the morning, passing and sighing,
Whisper and tell of distant gardens,
Their distant loves to joyous folk,
Of flaming geraniums and the violets.
What love! what joy in this little world,
Which rises with the sun!
Oh, how much life! and I am dying!")

What poetry in these different situations! The dying man would have had [illegible] life had he not fixed his love on a single object, and that an ignoble one,—had he, instead of devoting himself to the Paphian goddess, hiding his face in the bosom of a female, and blaspheming Christ, cultivated in his soul a higher and purer love. Even although he threw off all reserve respecting what is sacred, he need not have exclaimed, in a moment of satiety—

"Ma Taide, mima a saziar la fame
Tenta le reni dei moderni drudi
Levando il piede nella danza infame,
Ma noi giacciamo nauseati e stracchi
Senza un affetto in cor, sul reo letame
Di questa sozza età! noi siam vigliacchi."

("But Thais, to satisfy the hunger,
Excites the senses of the modern paramour,
Raising her foot in the shameless dance;
But we lie nauseated and wearied,
Without an affection in our heart, on the guilty bed
Of this vicious age. We are cowards!")

Yes, we are cowards indeed! How we admire this Thais! how we chant her! how we praise and applaud those who sing her praises! This is what we call in our days love of the truth, hatred of rhetoric, war to Arcadia; yet critics are to be found, who, I regret to say, excuse, pity, even encourage this tendency in poetry.

If thirty years ago we had had such poets in Italy, Italy would never have been united; and I fear if the style be not changed, if our youth get enamoured of that kind of poetry, Italy will be undone morally, if not materially. Excess of poetry is an evil, but that of sensual common productions is infinitely worse, and can be corrected with less facility than the former. This sympathetic defect is attributed to Signor Edmondo de Amicis, the most elegant and, in our time, the most popular among living Italian writers—ex-officer in the army; writer of sketches and novelettes full of life; traveller, and most original writer of travels, written so graphically that he seems to be taking us through a gallery of vividly coloured pictures. De Amicis is an enthusiast; his enthusiasm begins before he starts forth on his travels, his imagination increases as he proceeds, till he works up his reader to a state of delirious excitement, and maintains the interest, as he relates, with admirable refinement, his reminiscences of travel and the feelings he experienced. There is perhaps a little exaggeration in them; but it is so rare in these days to find writers who feel sympathy with the countries they visit and for the men they are judging, that to find a writer like De Amicis ready to show benevolence, and pity, and admiration while travelling even among the Turks, makes the reader still more [illegible] than he naturally is; for we must remember that malevolence in criti[illegible] always antipathy in the reader's mind, whom we may always conceive [illegible] interested in the question treated. The second part of De Amicis' [illegible] Constantinople was published only last month; but it cannot be called [illegible] Constantinople as it is, for the journey to the Turkish capital [illegible] ago. The work was written about the end of 1877, [illegible] Milan, seized on the present lucky moment to issue [illegible], the last picturesque aspect of the city before the rumours of war had reached it,—in fact, in its normal state. What fate lies in store for Constantinople one cannot predict. Will it be always a Turkish city? or a Greek city? or an international one? A year will solve the problem. In the meantime it is interesting to see what impression the grand Oriental city made on the mind of an Italian traveller, with an imagination like that of De Amicis. We must, however, in all the works of De Amicis, make allowances for poetic license, and for his desire to produce brilliant effects, and obtain the sympathy of his readers. Still there is so much variety in his word-pictures,—his scenes of life, his descriptions,—that Constantinople stands out before us in the most life-like manner. The traveller himself is always before us, for his temperament, his character, his mind, give an impress of originality to every figure that passes in review. After having visited Constantinople with De Amicis, we cannot pretend that we have nothing more to learn about the city, or to have seen it under the only aspect worth knowing, but we shall have received impressions that no other traveller will have made, and will also feel a conviction of the truth of them. De Amicis saw the poor Sultan Abdul Aziz, and he seemed to him a man weary and worried. After having sketched his biography, his physical and moral portrait, De Amicis gives his final opinion of him thus:—"He is there between Europe and Asia, in his vast palace, —bathed by the sea like a ship ready to set sail,—in the midst of an infinite confusion of ideas and objects, surrounded by fabulous pomp, immense misery. no longer *nè un nè due* (Dante would say), no longer a true Mussulman, and not a true European; reigning over a mixed people, a barbarian by birth; of double-faced aspect like Janus; served as a god, watched as a slave, adored, flattered, blinded; and, in the meanwhile, every day that passes he extinguishes a ray of his halo, and unlooses a stone from his pedestal. Were I like him,— wearied with his strange position in the world, satiated with sensual pleasures and adulations, depressed with having always to suspect all around him, indignant against the government, insecure and careless of the immeasurable disorders existing,—I would, when the immense Seraglio was steeped in sleep, throw myself into the Bosphorus like a fugitive galley-slave, and go and pass the night in a tavern at Galata, in the midst of a group of sailors, with a glass of beer in my hand and a clay pipe in my mouth, and roar out the 'Marseillaise.'" The chapter on the Turkish women is perhaps the most important and the cleverest, flavoured with a little touch of maliciousness, that both conquers and pleases the reader. See, for example, with what talent he describes the impression the Turkish women's veils made on him:—"Such is the art with which they adjust the *jasmaec*, that the pretty seem beautiful and the ugly passable. One cannot describe what they do with these two veils; with what elegance they twine them like crowns and turbans—with what luxuriance and wealth of folds they twist them around—with what lightness and carelessness they loosen them and let them fall—how they use them to discover, to hide, to promote, to propose enigmas, to reveal unexpectedly little surprises. Some seem as if they had around their heads a white transparent cloud that could be dispersed with the slightest breeze. Others seem garlanded with lilies and jessamine; they seem to have white skins that, protected by their veils, acquire an enchanting softness and freshness. 'Tis a head-gear at once severe and pleasing, and has something of the sacerdotal and virginal about it, under which there should rise nought but gentle thoughts and innocent caprices; instead there rises—a little of everything." Each traveller has a special world of his own which interests him: the Oriental world seen by De Amicis is not the same that occupied Lamartine, Chateaubriand, Lady Wortley Montague, De Nerval, Prince Puckler, Theophilus Gautier, and other illustrious travellers; for we learn many things from him of Constantinople that the others would not have known how to tell us, because it would never have entered their heads to observe them; besides, each nation, Russians, French, Germans, Italians, travel differently from the English, as we see from their books. The Italian who, seen at home, seems heedless, abroad shows himself the most diligent of observers. Amongst the ancient records of travel, the most vivid and copious notices are those of Italians. And now our Italian travellers are affording us most important details of travel.

Professor Enrico Giglioli, who himself made a voyage round the world in the *Magenta*, the description of which was published two years since in one bulky volume, has given in the *Nuova Antologia* several most interesting accounts of travel and discoveries made by two intrepid Italian naturalists, D'Albertis and Odoardo Beccari, who have rendered and still hope to render much valuable service to geographical science. It is from the scientific matter brought together by these two voyagers, that the best of our anthropological writers, Professor and Senator Paolo Mantegazza, founder of our Anthropological Museum, has for the most part composed his monograph entitled, "Anthropological and Ethnological Studies in New Guinea." The work is dedicated to Odoardo Beccari, the eminent botanist and intrepid traveller. The author founds his ethnological inductions on the study of the Papuan skulls collected from the group of Mysore Islands in the Gulf of Geelvinck.

"We are not, unfortunately," writes he, "in that period in which we can form sure and broad syntheses, but must instead content ourselves with bringing to the common field our tribute of measures and inductions. But that will not suffice, for every anthropological school, or rather every anthropologist, measures skulls according to his own method, puts aside elements considered by others as of ultra-importance, and while some load their memories with a mass of figures, others content themselves with a few. Let us hope that the International Congresses (Anthropological), instead of occupying themselves exclusively with prehistoric hardware goods, may dedicate themselves to solve some of these problems of scientific philosophy and method which serve to decide an epoch in the history of science, and, what is better, serve to range in order the dispersed energies of individuals under the banner of one sole direction."

The discussion in which Professor Mantegazza, after having defined Papuan craniums (craniology is the especial science in which no one can surpass him), employed himself, is a series of ethnological problems of the greatest interest. The spirited criticism that he undertook on the pretended proboscis of the elephant, which was believed to have been found near Papua, and which was thought a still stronger indication of the Indian origin of the Papuans, is an excellent correction to all the ethnological inductions too hastily arrived at; though it would be imprudent to give any absolute negation to the ancient Indian origin of the Papuans, knowing so little as we do as yet of the real ethnical character of many indigenous Dravidian peoples of the Deccan. Beccari and Giglioli may well, with the scarcity of proofs at hand, have come to a too hasty conclusion on the Indian origin of the Papuans; but Professor Mantegazza would perhaps risk still more if the possibility of such a migration were to be denied; since *Indian* by no means signifies *Aryan*, India comprising, as it is well known, under the dominating Aryan type, a numerous people, belonging to various tribes, who have come in contact with lower types of the human family. The illustrated pages that accompany the learned minutes of Professor Mantegazza show in every way, in the several objects they delineate, an art and an incipient and rugged industry, as well as an advanced civilization, which cannot be explained by the present state of the Papuans, who appear to travellers as perfect savages. It is necessary to suppose that there has been a time in which the Papuans have been more civilized; nothing can be more logical than to suppose it, as they were in Asia, and therefore in contact with civilized people.

Archæology, like philology, has its claims on ethnology, and this point must not be denied, for it is only by their agreement that these three sciences can possibly advance beneficially. Our archæological studies have been progressing for some years past with a singular alacrity. I will here mention the recent discoveries which were made of the ancient city of Sipontum, in Apulia, near Manfredonia, the excavations of which are being worked with some energy, since there have been unearthed a temple to Diana, a colonnade sixty feet long, and a part of a Necropolis. The Museum of Naples has already enriched itself with several interesting objects from the new excavations. However, it would be vain to expect discoveries at Sipontum equal in importance to those of Pompeii, since by reason of its position in an unhealthy and marshy part, and its having become Roman after the Second Punic war, this Greek colony could never have been flourishing or have held an important position amongst the ancient cities. When King Manfred in 1251 founded a city on a more elevated site, the old low-lying Sipontum was deserted, and by successive earthquakes was, by degrees, not totally destroyed, but entirely covered over.

We have able searchers after the antiquities in the Terra d'Otranto, where Signor Luigi de Simone utilizes the spare hours which remain to him from his duties as judge of Lecce, in illustrating successively, with great intelligence, all the memorials of his native province, which was among the first of Italian provinces to become civilized. In past times excavations were abandoned to private persons, who, on their own account, often drew forth objects of great value from their own lands. These were seldom of any benefit to science, for they were sometimes injured through the inexperience of the excavators, or left to decay, or shut up in some private houses in town or country, or fell to the lot of some foreigner, not always appreciative, who retained them rather as relics of travel or objects of curiosity than those of study. A decree of the Minister of Public Instruction in 1869 instituted special Commissioners for the provinces, in order that the excavations should be regularly carried on and watched, and the greatest possible profit for the study of archæology extracted therefrom, and to see that the objects discovered should not be dispersed or injured.

Signor de Simone is one of the Commissioners for the excavations in the province of Lecce, and the work which we have before us, entitled "Note Yapigo—Messapiche" (Turin, 1877), shows us already how precious must have been the assistance of so erudite an archæologist. The modest title of the publication sufficiently justifies the author's not having given a complete scientific colouring to the matter related, but Signor de Simone is not wanting in critical acumen; he wished rather to communicate to archæologists such notices as he considered interesting than to criticize completely and exhaustively the great problem of the true character of the antique Yapigian and Messapian people, about which there have been such useless disputations in our schools. The author has still faith that time may disclose the intimate relations, both ethnographic and linguistic, that bind together the ancient Italian peoples—and also that the Messapii, in spite of the opinion that excludes them from the Italian family, may be found in strictest relations with the Osci.

Among recent historical Italian publications, I am pleased to signal out two volumes by Giovanni de Castro of Milan, entitled "I Popoli dell'antico Oriente," (Milan, Hoepli, 1878), not as a learned work, neither as a model of popular history; for though the Italians can write learnedly they have not yet found the way of writing on serious subjects popularly. However, Signor de Castro sets us a good example in putting his great learning in such an attractive form that subjects which hitherto it has been the privilege of only the erudite to grasp, have been brought to the level of the young. Had the author been wiser in the choice of his lectures, sometimes excellent, but occasionally insufficient and fallacious, with the real talent he possesses of grasping the matter he studies, he would [illegible] us a work worth [illegible] high commendation. Whatever defects there [illegible] in his work [illegible] rather ascribe to the nature of the materials [illegible]al. The [illegible] treats of the Egyptians and Assyrians; the second of the Babylonians, Hebrews, Phœnicians, of the Aryans in general (but rather too succinctly, the volume of Duncker on the Aryans might have served the author as an excellent guide), the people of Asia Minor, the Medes and Persians.

The popular style of writing is to be found up to this time less in historic literature than in that of science. The charming book of Professor Antonio Stoppani, called "Il bel Paese," published by Agnelli of Milan (the first edition came out last year, the last bears the date of 1878), describes all Italy, physical and geological, in a series of pleasant conversations. The work was duly rewarded with a premium by the Lombard Institute of Milan, as the best of the new popular writings presented at the competition which the institute had announced. Professor Stoppani, who is among the most distinguished Italian naturalists, adds to his great scientific learning an enviable descriptive talent. Italy has never till now been described geologically. There are excellent works on the geology of *some* of the provinces, but no geologist has gone through the entire peninsula with the object of representing its geology under a popular form. I know not if in its present perfectly Italian, almost Manzonian form, the work will be acceptable to the general public; but I feel certain that all who wish to make themselves acquainted with the natural beauties of our country can find no surer guide than Professor Stoppani's book, in which people and places are placed before us under an animated and highly-coloured aspect.

To the city of Milan, its writers and publishers, signal merit is due for the efforts they make to produce popular scientific literature. Professor Mantegazza is of Lombardy. His works on hygiene, the "Almanac Hygienic," his works on the physiology of pleasure, grief, love, have had a most extraordinarily rapid sale. Mauro Macchi also is a Lombard. He publishes yearly at Milan an almanac and popular annual of history. In Milan are brought out the popular scholastic editions of Gnocchi and Agnelli, and the cheap journals of Sonzogno and Treves. This latter eminent publisher issues every year a valuable scientific annual, to which, each in his special style, several distinguished scientific Italian writers contribute. One of these is the Genoese Professor Girolamo Boccardo, who, besides having a special reputation as an economist, also shows a great versatility of power in treating, with much variety of argument, many scientific subjects in a kind of popular scientific annual (Treves & Co., Milan) entitled, "Novità della Scienza," in which are put forth, in a clear, bright, easy style, the results of the most recent scientific research. Some critics rebel against this popular scientific literature, and think the scientific man lowers himself too much, and science loses its dignity, by becoming popular. But science is valuable in the ratio of its usefulness. Science as science, and art as art, are lovely things; but, like gold unspent, they are useless if not propagated.

Our country has much to do to overtake other nations in culture and learning: why then arrest a movement which, if not yet perfectly organized, is having an immense effect on our national instruction? Professor Arthur Issel of Genoa once proposed that a forced circulation should be given to certain popular books, and that they should be used by the people as money. The idea, be it remembered, came from a Genoese, a people whom Dante flagellated for their avarice; but it seemed too visionary, and was abandoned. This does not detract from its excellence, and it might receive attention now, when Italy is struggling for the application of the law for compulsory education.

ANGELO DE GUBERNATIS.

## II.

## IN FRANCE.

PARIS, [illegible]

OUR over-confiding optimists, ready to believe [illegible] once, have had in these early days of February [illegible] to slacken in their vigilance. On the 4th of [illegible] suddenly spread of grave dissensions between the President [illegible] and his Ministers, of his threatening to resign, and [illegible] nominations presented to him; while on the other hand a conflict [illegible] between the Senate and the Chamber of Deputies, the latter [illegible] the Budget so long as the Senate deferred voting the laws of [illegible] to the State of Siege and *Colportage*, and the Upper Chamb[illegible] against a pressure that it considered unconstitutional. This [illegible] kindle imaginations on both sides, Conservatives fancying the [illegible] of a return to power, Republicans perceiving with dismay [illegible] them against another 16th of May. It was indeed but a false [illegible] soon dispelled. But it none the less revealed the actual state [illegible] the precarious character of political institutions in France w[illegible] upon so factitious a basis as the union of the four fractions of [illegible] the Executive power is in the hands of a man who, having [illegible] front, may do so a third time, and while the majority in the S[illegible] upon that whimsical group of Constitutionalists which knows [illegible] wants nor what it does. One might have supposed that after [illegible] 14th of December, helped to maintain the Republican *régime*, [illegible] Legitimist or Bonapartist *coup d'état*, it would frankly have give[illegible] to the Ministry. But it is the nature of this party so soon as they [illegible] to seek forthwith to nullify it, because of the possible consequences [illegible] Fortunately these fluctuations have dislocated the Senatorial ma[illegible] may expect the new laws proposed by Ministers to find acc[illegible] Senate. Nay, it is even probable that an alliance may now be formed [illegible] Left and the Constitutionalists for the election of life-senators [illegible] efforts of the latter to nominate the Duc Decazes in spite of [illegible] attitude since the 16th of May, and the small degree of personal [illegible] that he enjoys, must have convinced them that they have perman[illegible] the members of the Extreme Right. Indeed they have been hu[illegible] as to have to sacrifice their candidate for that of the Right, [illegible] Latour.

Another cause tending to bring them nearer the Left is the [illegible] which the contest becomes limited to Republicans and Bonapa[illegible] Chamber of Deputies, although the Royalists outnumber the [illegible] never open their mouths, except noisily to interrupt the [illegible] authorized representatives, the only speaking-trumpets, [illegible] party are Bonapartists,—MM. Rouher, Haentjens, Paul [illegible] d'Ornano,—who with habitual want of principle can indiffe[illegible] laws either from the conservative point of view, as [illegible] democratic, as illiberal. Thus they have demanded [illegible] political criminals whatever, while a few months [illegible] Senate to get M. Dufaure's limited scheme of amnesty [illegible] stood how in presence of such unscrupulous [illegible] are but weapons of attack or matter for [illegible] viction—the Republican party should [illegible]

Nevertheless it does wrong in letting itself [illegible] of a powerful majority to show itself [illegible] doubt whether the Republican Deputies [illegible] political sagacity in the late verification of elections. At all events foreigners [illegible] wonder at the number invalidated, and among them some in which the deputy was returned by a majority of from two to three thousand. The view taken by the majority in the Chamber is this: all elections of official candidates of the Government are vitiated and might be lawfully annulled for the very reason that they were recommended by white placards. But, out of indulgence, this is only done when the majority was very small, or the pressure exercised manifestly undue. There is sense in this; MM. De Broglie and De Fourtou themselves revealed the value they attached to official candidature by their belief that it would secure them a majority. The very official deputies themselves who have been unseated virtually acknowledged that they considered their success due to the pressure of Government, since out of seven cases of re-election five of the candidates did not venture to stand again. Still however right the theory of the majority, one may venture to point out mistakes in its application. The rule has not been by any means the same in all cases. The confirming or annulling has depended on much that was unconnected with the facts of the elections—on the more or less popular character of the new deputy and his rival, on the greater or smaller chances of Republicans winning in a fresh contest, on his having opposed one of the three hundred and sixty-three of the former Chamber, or a new candidate. It would have been better to adopt a uniform procedure, and to unseat official deputies who had obtained a large majority only in cases of serious misconduct. One may know but too well that universal suffrage is accessible to threats and promises, but it is not good loudly to proclaim this in a country where it forms the sole basis of political order. In short, it would be sad indeed that the Republican majority should use its right of verification to carry out party revenge, or itself put pressure on electors. Men were justified in their indignation against M. de Broglie, who used to say, "If the Chamber be Republican we will dissolve it again and again till it become what we wish;" but they should not appear to be saying to electors, "It is not worth while to name Conservative Deputies, we shall unseat them." In the election reports one is often pained to see Republicans citing, as reasons for so doing, newspaper articles, or more or less violent speeches, as though they for their part had scrupled to employ all the resources of the press and of public speaking. This is as ridiculous in them as it was in the Ministry of the 16th May to affirm that the Republican propaganda had put pressure on the conscience of electors.

It would, however, be a mistake to suppose that the leadership of the Republican party belongs to men of extreme views. Such are just now in abeyance. The noisiest among them have had to vanish successively from the political arena, where their function was to damage those alone capable of founding a durable government. M. Bonnet Duverdier, who had distinguished himself in 1877 by fraternizing with the refugees of the Commune in London, who had been chosen as deputy by the Lyons workmen merely on account of his uncompromising Radicalism, had to give in his resignation on grounds of personal character. M. Duportal, the editor of the *Reveil*, who never ceased harassing M. Gambetta by all manner of calumnies, has been expelled from the meetings of the Extreme Left because he was found to have, in 1852, written to Prince Louis Napoleon soliciting a situation as Librarian or Under-[illegible]. Lastly, M. Yves Guyot, who went and asked the suffrage of the [illegible] of Bordeaux without any other plea than the violent character of [illegible], merely obtained a contemptible minority. It is true that the [illegible] about to commit a great political fault by electing, in the [illegible] Blanqui, the most incorrigible of conspirators; but this [illegible] to nothing.

[illegible] has this advantage, that the Deputies not only [illegible] Ministry by inopportune motions, but vote the [illegible] unprecedented rapidity. They feel that they [illegible] shake the Ministry and furnish to the reactionaries in the Senate occasion for [illegible] aim is to restore to the country the peace [illegible] and to leave it to the Ministry to prepare [illegible]

While the whole of Europe is occupied with [illegible] France has the privilege (that none need envy [illegible] fortunes) of only attending to her own internal [illegible] do under peculiarly favourable circumstances, for [illegible] saves her from the temptation to run diplomatic [illegible] she has undergone have infused public spirit [illegible] society. We have a proof of this in the [illegible] Lyons, and evincing the progress made by their [illegible] economic science. No doubt, more than one of the [illegible] of the Collectivist or Communist Socialism; but [illegible] an echo, and the Congress is almost unanimous in [illegible] harmony established between different classes, and [illegible] and violent solutions.

One of the spheres in which there is most to do [illegible] in requiring reform, is that of public instruction. [illegible] already begun to act. M. Bardoux has brought forward [illegible] restoring to the rectors the nomination of primary [illegible] gave to prefects, thus securing that body against [illegible] for rendering primary instruction gratuitous by means of [illegible] communes. In theory, gratuitous primary instruction is [illegible] It is not well to burden the State with expenses that [illegible] viduals, or to free parents able to pay from an expense [illegible] as experience shows that we value most what we pay for [illegible] better to extend this gratuitous system only to the [illegible] say nothing of the democratic and levelling side of the [illegible] Republicans, there is another reason for this law. All [illegible] are in favour of compulsory primary instruction, such as [illegible] but the clerical party opposes it might and main, [illegible] parental authority, and is even supported by some men [illegible] that the State cannot force citizens to pay for instruction, [illegible] communes are not provided with schools adequate to the [illegible] Hence, the first duty of the State is to provide schools [illegible] to all. This will entitle it to insist upon the attendance [illegible] for the sacrifice it makes. Gratuitous instruction is [illegible] direction of compulsory.

We are not told whether M. Bardoux means to [illegible] projected reform of the higher instruction. Meanwhile, [illegible] preparing to second this reform by inquiry and agitation. [illegible] the purpose has just been formed, at the instigation of M. [illegible] guished director of the Free School of Political Science, [illegible] rence of our leading men of science—MM. Pasteur, [illegible] Renan, Taine, Paris, &c. The best way to stimulate [illegible] assure success to the desired reforms, will be to point out [illegible] countries, and the functions of the great universities [illegible] instruction flourishes most.

We have recently been shown at the Academy of [illegible] how far from enlightened the general mind is on [illegible] the hold of routine on men who think themselves [illegible] of the causes impeding the development of the [illegible] the existence of Special Schools, such as the [illegible] the Central, carrying off the best and [illegible] to subject them to a uniform [illegible] sarily limited, all who [illegible] cannot be made to [illegible]

[illegible] is not insisted on as in Germany; but diplomas suffice, often indeed [illegible] diploma of Bachelor, that is, of secondary studies. Thus the great [illegible] youth is deprived of all advanced intellectual and scientific culture; [illegible] not for the sake of science, but for that of the diploma to be obtained [illegible] be occupied. Hence in all branches, but especially in State depart- [illegible] positive inferiority whether as to acquirement or intellectual [illegible] only remedy would lie in the creation of large universities, and in [illegible] laid on all intended for liberal and administrative careers to [illegible] three years there, together with the transformation of special [illegible] which should be attached to the university. And yet just at the time [illegible] evils of these special schools are so complained of, we see men, who [illegible] liberals, intent on creating a fresh one—a School of Administration for [illegible] Sub-Prefects and Ministerial officials. This measure, already brought [illegible] Senate, was held up to eulogy the other day by M. Jules Simon [illegible] Academy of Moral Science. M. Hippolyte Passy and M. de Parieu [illegible] no difficulty in proving that this would be to establish a true [illegible], to lessen still further the force and influence of higher instruc- [illegible] place serious difficulties in the way of the Government by conferring [illegible] young men who might personally be quite unfitted for the parts they [illegible] play, that in short it would be to take away the spirit of liberty and [illegible] from the very branch that needs it most. The foundation of such a [illegible] would be the more absurd that the Free School of Political Science [illegible] exists and does the required work admirably, while it is open to all, [illegible] teaching harmonizes intimately with legal, historical, and literary [illegible]. Let the State, as M. Boutmy proposed in an excellent measure [illegible] to all special schools, connect the School of Political Science with [illegible] Faculty of Law, let it while leaving intact its organization and funds, [illegible] its lectures and examinations with those of that Faculty and require [illegible] diploma from all who aspire to diplomatic or administrative functions. This would be the true way of solving the problem, and it would have the further advantage of costing the State nothing, and leaving the widest field for freedom in study.

[illegible] is one branch of learning in which the progress made since 1870 has been strikingly rapid—geography, to wit. On inquiring into the cause of our [illegible]—outside those purely military—it was unanimously held that the [illegible] of the Germans rested on three facts: their widely diffused primary [illegible], the excellence of their higher education, and their geographical [illegible]. We have just dwelt on the efforts still needed to reform our Schools and Faculties in general. As regards geography, it was more easy to [illegible] work. Government increased the number of hours devoted in Lyceums to the subject, entrusted it wherever it was possible to special professors, [illegible] Geographical Chairs in several Faculties of Letters,—at Nancy, Bordeaux, Lyons,—and furnished fresh supplies of maps and globes. On all [illegible] and geographical manuals began to appear. Well-known men, such as M. Levasseur and M. Perigot, became, as it were, the apostles of geo- [illegible], and the Geographical Congress of 1875 showed the progress that had [illegible] made. We must not, indeed, exaggerate it; there has been a [illegible] that is hasty and feverish in this new pursuit. Bookselling specula- [illegible] it up, and we have been deluged by elementary books,—sometimes [illegible] well-known names, but carelessly written,—maps drawn at random, [illegible] compilations. Our cartography in particular, spite of the praise- [illegible] efforts of some engravers, amongst whom M. Erhard occupies the [illegible], remains sadly inferior to the German. But the impulse, having [illegible], will not stop short. The Geographical Society, which [illegible] before the war, has tripled the number of its members, and a [illegible] has sprung up by its side, under the presidency of [illegible] the leading classical publisher's house in Paris, that of

Hachette, has, by a series of bold and skilful enterprises, given a strong impetus to geography as interpreted by the requirements of modern science. After bringing out the excellent "Dictionnaire de la Géographie de la France," by M. Joanne, it has undertaken works on historical and modern geography both. M. Desjardins has given us the first volume of his intended four, "Géographie de la Gaule Romaine," in which archæology and epigraphy combine to throw light on the origin of our history, administration, division of territory, commercial development, system of roads, &c. It gives us, too, one of the most important aspects of the history of the Roman Empire, studied with the minuteness and precision of modern erudition. A few days ago M. Longnon published his "Géographie de la Gaule au Sixième Siècle," a capital book, in which profound science, seconded by an excellent method and a wonderful gift of geographical intuition, is combined with a clear and elegant explanatory faculty. It furnishes us with the best commentary on our Merovingian chroniclers, and is a sure guide through the history of the early Frank Kings. Finally, M. Vivien de Saint Martin sums up the results of a life of labour and research in his "Dictionnaire de Géographie Ancienne et Moderne," and in his large atlas, which many compare with the best in Germany. For modern geography the house of Hachette has had the good fortune to find a man endowed with the patience of the compiler, the special knowledge of the savant and geologist, and the most vivid imagination. M. Elisée Reclus, after having travelled much, and studied long all questions of physical geography, has undertaken a great work, "Géographie Universelle," to consist of ten large volumes, three of which have already appeared, devoted to Southern Europe, Central Europe, and France. As is indicated by the title, "La Terre et l'Homme," M. Reclus, without neglecting administrative and political geography, merely attaches a secondary importance to it. The description of the soil, climate, inhabitants, their customs and employments, the reciprocal action of man and of surrounding nature, occupy the principal place in his book. One is amazed at the mass of exact information therein contained, the picturesque talent which makes us, as it were, see all described, the new ideas that are suggested by its facts, the light thrown on the history of the world. Excellent maps interposed at almost every other page add to the clearness of the description. On certain historical or philological points it may be said that the conclusions of M. Reclus are sometimes a little premature, but that is a secondary matter; what we especially admire in him is his calmness, the moderation of his views, the mental agility which seizes both sides of subjects, understands the varied characters of nations, and the freedom from passion and prejudice with which he depicts them. This is the more striking that M. Reclus is best known for the absolute and chimerical nature of his political opinions, and for the part he took, more thoughtless and imprudent than culpable, in the events of the Commune, and which he paid for dearly by exile. One cannot read without emotion the final sentences of his description of French character: "It is seldom that strangers do not enjoy themselves in France; it is still more seldom that Frenchmen do not feel unhappy far from their country; there are few men on whom the burden of exile more heavily falls."

The primary condition for forming good geographers is travel. In this respect, too, France has advanced of late. No doubt she has always boasted energetic and courageous men who explored distant lands; the names of Bougainville, Lapeyrouse, and Dumont d'Urville have ranked side by side with those of Cook and Franklin; the missionaries of the seventeenth and eighteenth centuries undertook journeys pronounced almost impracticable nowadays; but it is none the less certain that France in the nineteenth century cannot, as regards voyages of discovery, compete with England and Germany. For some years past, however, such voyages have been more frequent, and, above all, more rich in results. Some of them, like those of M. de Beauvoir and the Marquis de Compiègne, have been chiefly undertaken in the interests of the picturesque; but others have led to important scientific results, such as those of Guillaume

Raffray in Abyssinia, M. Garnier and M. Lagrenée in Cochin China, and M. Delaporte in Cambodia. The charming periodical publication *Tour du Monde* (Hachette) will teach us to appreciate the amount of information due to French explorers. The success of M. de Lesseps' great enterprise at the isthmus of Suez has acted as a spur to the French traveller who up to that time had looked on Africa rather from the standpoint of a painter than that of a pioneer of civilization. Since then M. Roudaire has pursued studies which have led to his magnificent scheme for the formation of an inland sea in the Sahara; M. Largeau, with an energy and perseverance above praise, has sought to trace out ways across the Sahara which might lead to openings for French commerce. He has related his first journeys in a volume of the highest interest, "Le Sahara" (Fischbacher). M. de Sémellé is engaged in a similar exploration of the Coast of Senegal. The State, which unfortunately has but meagre resources for the purpose, endeavours as much as may be to multiply scientific missions, having just voted funds for a journey of exploration into the interior of Africa; and on the 23rd of January last the Ministry inaugurated in the Palace of Industry a Musée Provisoire d'Ethnographie, where for the present all the objects brought back by explorers will be kept. Imperfect as the museum is, we may by its aid follow them in more than one remarkable journey: we can with M. Ujfalvy penetrate into Central Asia up to the cradle of the Indo-European race. We can find, somewhat in confusion indeed, types of Turks, Mongols, Tartars, and Persians; architecture and ornaments illustrative of Persian and Chinese arts, while dressed-up figures help us to form an idea of the weapons and attire of soldiers who fought against the Russian conquerors. M. Wiener brings before us the whole of Peru, from the grand Cyclopean structures left by the Incas, or even by the races—no doubt of Asian origin—that peopled Peru before the rule of the Incas, down to the sordid huts in which vegetate the Indians of to-day, or the elegant *hacienda* where a fair proprietor, descended from the Spaniards, languidly leans on her balcony. M. Pinart carries us to Mexico, M. André to Columbia, making us descend with him into the appalling gulf into which, hanging to a rope, he plunged to find natural curiosities. Nay, we even meet with *ex votos* from the temple of Tanit, brought from Carthage by M. Sainte-Marie, showing some singular aspects of Carthaginian civilization. Each of these explorers is to explain at public reunions the aim and results of his particular mission.

But if it be useful to traverse the world in order to study foreign manners and customs and to gather up the remnants of vanished civilizations, we must not forget that the country in which we live is far from having been thoroughly explored. If there be a study with which engineers, who better than any others know the details connected with the soil they work in, may well amuse their leisure hours, it is that of geographical archæology. This is plainly perceived by M. Kerviler, who has made valuable pre-historic discoveries at Saint-Nazaire, and also by M. Lentheric, the author of two charming volumes on Provence and Languedoc,—"Les Villes Mortes de la Méditerranée," and "La Grèce et l'Orient en Provence" (Plon),—where descriptions of nature and the scientific observations of the geologist and engineer are happily blended with historic interest. A new association has been formed with this object of exploring France, the Club Alpin Français, founded and managed by M. Joanne. It does not resemble the English Alpine Club, in exacting from its members a sort of initiation and having for its chief aim the climbing of virgin peaks. It is a society open to all, of whatever age or sex, and it includes many who have never climbed anything higher than Montmartre. M. Joanne's purpose has not only been to encourage the ascent of difficult mountains like those of Dauphiné, but to subject the whole of France to scientific exploration, and to spread abroad the love of travel as one of the best means of education for youth. The success of this club has been brilliant; it has already in four years numbered 3,000 subscribers; the three volumes of its Annual Reports

are full of interesting papers; several [illegible]
genuine exploits, amongst others the [illegible]
last year in the Dauphiné where La Meije, [illegible]
been conquered. But in one point M. Joanne [illegible]
cible prejudices. He wished to organize [illegible]
districts. Railroads offered reduced fares, [illegible]
up to the present time nothing has been done. [illegible]
dangers their children may run, but the [illegible]
give up a part of their holidays for the [illegible]
manliness, that bane of French education, in [illegible]
place. Mothers wish to keep their boys tied [illegible]
prefer displaying themselves with their gloves, [illegible]
the sands of Etretat or Trouville, to tasting the [illegible]
overcome fatigue and danger, and thereby gained [illegible]
panorama or made some fresh scientific observation. [illegible]
mountain scenery is making great progress in France. [illegible]
sufficient to name two books on Mont Blanc recently [illegible]
by M. Eugène Viollet-le-Duc, is written from the [illegible]
other, by M. Durier ("Le Mont Blanc," Fischbacher), [illegible]
the work of a historian and a poet, nay, even of a [illegible]
delightful emotions excited in him by his dear [illegible]

M. Joanne is very right in wishing to bring about a [illegible]
dolence and effeminacy. A healthy manly education [illegible]
if she desires regeneration, and this, too, is the starting [illegible]
—that constant subject of thought with our politicians, [illegible]
slowly. The law on army administration, so carefully [illegible]
remains buried in the Chamber, which seems little [illegible]
are powerless in comparison with morals; the latter [illegible]
cient military institutions. This has been expounded [illegible]
remarkable article published in the *Revue des deux Mondes* [illegible]
Army Organization, and the first of a series on military [illegible]
ceding article he had dealt with the important subject of [illegible]
commissioned officers, whom it becomes more and more [illegible]
the service, and who yet form the indispensable [illegible]
his article of the 1st of February, he examines into the [illegible]
decadence, and analyzes them with the completeness of [illegible]
and the insight of the thinker. What we lack in France [illegible]
tions, formed in time of peace and meant to keep up [illegible]
patriotic mission by which an army should be [illegible]
in general the consciousness of their military duties, and [illegible]
preserve them from military vanity and to prevent the [illegible]
legends that ruin armies and nations. M. Trochu [illegible]
in France war has always been improvised, and how [illegible]
they are of brilliant offensive warfare, have ever [illegible]
because of a want of military intelligence and military [illegible]
campaigns have been disastrous in this respect. [illegible]
an excellent military school, but in point of fact [illegible]
insubordination into the army, taught war on a [illegible]
vented military legends in which brave heads of [illegible]
into great generals; made soldiers believe that [illegible]
led to the neglect of tactics and science, without [illegible]
is unavailing. M. Trochu stands forward as the [illegible]
army organization, and compulsory service for [illegible]
looks upon an army less as a weapon of [illegible]
national independence and a means of [illegible]
him such an education requires [illegible]

[illegible]

[illegible] victories in order to a reflorescence of our literature and art. [illegible] this, of a soldier requiring peace to form a good [illegible] demanding war to ensure the flourishing condition [illegible] The book, or rather the unfinished pages, in which [illegible] forth this idea (more ingenious than practical) were written [illegible] last weeks of his life, and are published by his widow under the title, [illegible] de l'Art Grec" (Dentu), with notes that, unfortunately, are five [illegible] as long as the text. Quinet had always passionately loved Greece. He [illegible] there shortly after the War of Independence, and although his genius [illegible] to the profundity of the German mind than to the serene radiance [illegible] Greek, he felt himself a citizen of Athens, as indeed Germans often do. [illegible] des Religions" contained beautiful pages upon Greece, and in the [illegible] now given us we also find several happy passages and noble [illegible] In his opinion, Greek genius is the offspring of Greek victories [illegible] barbarians; it is made up of happiness, heroism, and noble pride. He fol[illegible] this idea through Herodotus, Æschylus, Sophocles, and Plato. Demos[illegible] his heroes, is filled with the spirit of the Persian wars, and it is this [illegible] which constitutes his glory. As a contrast, Quinet instances [illegible]tarch, the spiritless and timid burgher of Cheronea, who is ever ready to [illegible] the conquerors of Greece. Whatever may be the objection to this [illegible] of Hellenic civilization, it is very certain that the Persian wars were [illegible] moment of the blossoming-out of Greek genius which in the fifth [illegible] before Christ attained its most complete originality, and that all the [illegible] of Athens bear on their brows a ray of the glory of Salamis. There [illegible] touching about the sight of an aged man returning from exile, to find his own country conquered, humiliated, torn by reactionary passions, and [illegible] consolation in the state of antiquity and in the pious and credulous [illegible] that similar victories might generate similar *chefs d'œuvre* at home.

Meanwhile, while awaiting these victories and masterpieces, we have to content ourselves for the most part with reading posthumous works: this fragment of Quinet; M. de Remusat's drama on "Le Saint Barthélemy" (Lévy), so true from the historical point of view, and so profound from that of the psychologist—a worthy pendant to "Abélard;" "Correspondance de Sainte-Beuve" (Lévy), of which the first volume is just out. The literary interest of this correspondence is not great. Sainte-Beuve did not write letters for posterity, or seek to show off his intellect or style. He wrote briefly and simply, merely to tell facts or express feelings. Hence his letters are all the more valuable, as serving to make us acquainted with [illegible] that unique and accomplished type of the literary critic. The [illegible] made is very favourable to Sainte-Beuve. We see that throughout [illegible] remained independent and incapable of insincere criticism. When Mme. [illegible] asked him to alter a few words in a notice of her father, he preferred to withdraw the paper which preceded the edition on which he had bestowed so much care. When he was requested to write on M. Granier de Cassagnac, he declined to praise one "who used his pen like a stick." It is known, too, that he declined to review the "Life of Cæsar" by Napoleon III., in spite of his [illegible] with imperial circles. In reading his letters, one learns to understand [illegible] himself be drawn into these relations, for which he has been so [illegible] and how he became able to approve the *régime* of 1852. We notice [illegible] never given to politics, who in his dealings with the most marked [illegible] under the monarchy of July had found many of them mean-spirited [illegible] low and malicious. M. Villemain flattered him in public, and [illegible] in private. M. Cousin published, as discoveries of his own, [illegible] Sainte-Beuve had had the *naïve* generosity to lend him—a [illegible] which he reproaches Cousin in a letter that is a master[illegible]. When the Revolution of 1848 came, Sainte-Beuve [illegible] of having been paid out of secret funds by the [illegible] Philippe, and he had the greatest difficulty in dispelling this calumny. He saw France, as he thought, [illegible] clericalism or socialistic anarchy. The imperial [illegible] tion, but he never spared it advice or warnings, [illegible] unstained by a political attitude that we feel [illegible] greatest weaknesses were—as he himself avowed [illegible] which led King Solomon to disgust of all things [illegible] acknowledges that he thus quenched his own spirit [illegible] some nameless aridity and secret *ennui* to hang about [illegible] when young, and whom the man survived." And yet he [illegible] these weaknesses never perverted his heart. Thus [illegible] and earnest—to Mme. Desbordes Valmore or to [illegible] equipped for war nor treading the Parisian boards, he [illegible] hearty, tender, and trusty, able to understand every [illegible] thought. But the distinguishing merit of Sainte-Beuve [illegible] intellectual sincerity and honesty which never forsook him [illegible] to some young *littérateur* who asks his advice, he does not [illegible] ventional and deceptive praise, as was customary with [illegible] day—Lamartine and Hugo, above all. He gives him the advice of a clear-sighted intelligence.

It is a severe ordeal for a man to go through this publi[illegible] and it is seldom that he comes out of it unscathed. [illegible] respondence has just been completed by a third volume ([illegible] anything more lamentable than these continual sarcasms [illegible] bitterness, those forced jests, those heroic-comic dispatch[illegible] Campe, and his family—incomparable poet that he wa[illegible] grace, and imagination, but neither lofty, upright, nor [illegible] strange fate that of this "Prussian Libéré," this Fran[illegible] wrote against France at the expense of Louis-Philippe, [illegible] whilst adoring her, and despised France while sheltered a[illegible] nightingale that had made its nest in M. de Voltaire's per[illegible] expressed it, is now rejected and banned by Germans, whi[illegible] the popularity of a national writer.

It would be easy to trace his influence over our [illegible] seldom happy, for there is nothing more difficult than [illegible] sentiment in the way he did, or to express philosop[illegible] fanciful or even fantastic form. M. Bouchor has just [illegible] in his "Faust Moderne" (Charpentier), and we cannot [illegible] ceeded. M. Bouchor began his literary career by [illegible] praising drunkenness and debauchery, but merely of [illegible] not from serious conviction. It was like firing a pist[illegible] make passers-by turn round. His next book, "Poëmes de l'[illegible] showed facility, but little originality, and made no impressio[illegible] of his friend Jean Richepin, whose first production, "La [illegible] succeeded by scandalizing, and whose second, "Les Cas[illegible] noticed. I fear that "Le Faust Moderne," spite of a fe[illegible] brilliant passages, will fare the same. Its great fault is [illegible] reading it twice, I seem to make out that love leads to d[illegible] to *ennui*, but this is expressed in such unconnected and [illegible] one is perpetually in danger of losing the thread. [illegible] to see our young poets trying their powers on [illegible] express in their verse something more than a [illegible] While M. Bouchor was attempting a "Faust," [illegible] purer and more ample, was launching a "[illegible] beautiful verses, and M. Aicard [illegible] published for some time. But [illegible] or less successful adaptation, [illegible] crushes the imitator; and [illegible] rest and pleasure in returning [illegible]

[illegible] “Parfums et Chansons” (Charpentier), by a gentle poet recently dead, [illegible] Mathieu, whose song, negligent but graceful in its ease, was of spring, [illegible] swallows, of forests, or the fair Cendrinette, but who sometimes too found [illegible] words in which to scourge tyranny or evoke liberty.

As is always the case nowadays, works of erudition prevail over those of imagination. The three most striking books that have appeared this month are historical. M. Aubé, who had already brought out a remarkable volume on the much exaggerated Persecutions of the Church in the two first centuries, reducing these to their true proportions, now gives us “La Polémique païenne au Deuxième Siècle” (Didier). The prominent figure in this work is that of Celsus. By keen insight into the historical medium, and much patient ingenuity, M. Aubé has almost entirely restored the real “Discourse of Celsus against the Christians,” and he enables us to enter into the [illegible] and elevation of his polemics, hitherto so difficult to judge of, since we only knew them by the refutations of his adversaries. Fronto and Lucian have also been studied, but less in detail than Celsus, for whom M. Aubé's work amounts to a resurrection. Indeed Christianity has no longer to contend against a mocker and calumniator or persecutor in Celsus, but against a moderate and almost equitable adversary, one worthy, in short, to combat Origen.

We pass on, with M. Rocquain, to the eighteenth century, to the epoch when Christianity after seventeen hundred years' dominion finds itself once more exposed to the same attacks as those it endured in the second century. Voltaire and the English Deists added less than may be supposed to the arguments employed by Celsus. M. Rocquain has made a study of “L'Esprit révolutionnaire avant la Révolution” (Plon)—that is, the manifestations of public opinion which from the early part of the century announced an overthrow of the social and political condition. The ingenious idea occurred to him of seeking the history of these manifestations in manuscripts not hitherto utilized; in the Series of Decrees of Parliament, and of Decrees of the King's Council. Parliament was almost entirely composed of Jansenists and Gallicans, so that it pursued with its censures all books attacking Gallican doctrine and supporting Ultramontane theories; while the King's Council, where Jesuit influence prevailed, condemned what the Parliament approved, and even its decrees. This conflict of decrees enables us to trace the stir of ideas that from the middle of the century declare themselves definitely and energetically opposed to the political system of the *Ancien Régime*, and above all increasingly hostile to the Jesuitic tendencies of Catholicism. M. Rocquain's book brings into full light the important part that religious disputes played in developing revolutionary ideas. After reading it we no longer wonder that a great portion of the most influential members of revolutionary assemblies sprang from Parliaments, and were imbued with Gallican ideas. One of the acts that most tended to hurry on the Revolution, and to give it a persecuting and violent character, namely, the Civil Constitution of the Clergy, was the work not of irreligious men, but of pious and conscientious Gallicans.

M. Rocquain brings us up to the threshold of the Revolution. M. Taine [illegible] us the drama itself. The second volume of his great work on “Les [illegible] de la France Contemporaine” (Hachette) is devoted to the earlier stages [illegible] Revolution up to 1791. This book will doubtless raise many storms, [illegible] the Revolution, even in its most moderate period, in blackest [illegible]. After pointing out the troubled, and already anarchic medium in [illegible] States-General met in 1789, he analyzes the work done by the [illegible], and, instead of discerning in it the creation of a new [illegible], and social dissolution erected into a system. He [illegible] applied engendered, on all sides, anarchy, poverty, [illegible] is a good deal of truth in the picture drawn by [illegible] merely words but facts. He has laid under [illegible] original and unpublished documents, studied national life in its least details, and all these facts, [illegible] forcible style peculiar to him, stand out in [illegible] added many mournfully true pages to the history of [illegible] he attained his aim? Has he given us the philosophy [illegible] explained their results, and the way in which modern [illegible] them? We may be allowed to doubt it. As he represents [illegible] was but a disease, an attack of furious mania. But [illegible] account for the enthusiasm that it has inspired [illegible] influence it has exercised even over the nations [illegible] it was accompanied by disorders; and the attempt [illegible] Assembly to create a universal order according to [illegible] fallacious and unrealizable. But on the one hand, the [illegible] social order began long before the Revolution, which [illegible] pleted it; and on the other, almost all the social and [illegible] liberty, civil equality, and equity by which we now live, [illegible] seeking to realize, were affirmed by the Constituent Assembly [illegible] and imprudently no doubt—but with a faith and courage which [illegible] not to admire. If it be objected that whatever is good [illegible] has prevailed in other European nations without their having [illegible] upheaval to which the Revolution sentenced France, we may [illegible] French Revolution did much to spread these ideas, and [illegible] tion of the country under the *Ancien Régime* such as [illegible] depicts it in his first volume, the change could not come about [illegible] vulsion and general overthrow. Absolutely to condemn the Rev[illegible] it was accompanied by violence, is to judge of it as [illegible] Reformation, or as Pagans did of Christianity. Great changes [illegible] the world's history without great shocks. When the Cond[illegible] was a prisoner in the Luxembourg, and waiting to be sent to [illegible] wrote out for his son "Observations on the History of France [illegible] says:—"To-day that the Revolution, the most pure in its [illegible] complete in its effects, has executed justice on all usurpations [illegible] a new day dawns on our history. . . . You will be able [illegible] the necessity for the Revolution, and consequently of the obli[illegible] all to do all we can for its success." When a man can [illegible] *régime* that puts him to death, there must needs be something [illegible] weakness and crime. The Revolution has been too long [illegible] book denotes the inevitable reaction against a blind admirati[illegible] shows us one side of the question, which however it is well [illegible] ought to understand why the Revolution failed in part, and what [illegible] in its conceptions. Unfortunately, there will not be many [illegible] M. Taine's work the lessons there to be found. Some will reject [illegible] as decrying the Revolution, and others will exalt it for that [illegible] the public at large this result of earnest and laborious erudition [illegible] a reactionary pamphlet.

In the scientific world we have to-day only to recount losses [illegible] of Science, that a few months ago had to mourn one of [illegible] Verrier, has been deprived in the course of a few days [illegible] men that did it most honour, of M. Becquerel, M. Regnault [illegible] Claude Bernard, the most illustrious of the three. M. [illegible] a very advanced age; he was eighty-seven, but he [illegible] scientific activity: last year even he was engaged [illegible] capillary phenomena, fifty-seven years after the [illegible] electricity. All his life has been devoted to [illegible] Electro-Chemistry, that is, the chemical reactions [illegible] prolonged action of electricity. In 18[illegible] on Electricity" in seven volumes. [illegible] tinction, in the time of the Restoration, [illegible]

[illegible] methods of unsealing letters. M. Regnault, though much younger than M. Becquerel, has for years past been lost to science. The tragic death of his son, the great painter, Henri Regnault, at the battle of Buzenval, January [illegible] 1871, and the mental derangement of another brilliantly-gifted son, broke down before his time this man—cold and ironical outwardly, but feeling and benevolent at heart. Regnault does not leave behind such a scientific reputation as his really superior talent seemed to promise. His name is linked with no great discoveries, but he has defined, corrected, and developed the achievements of his predecessors or contemporaries. His researches into the [illegible] and expansion of gases, and on the substitution of equivalents in chemistry, [illegible] connected with the discoveries of Laurent, Dumas, and Dulong. They have set science on the way that led of late to the beautiful experiments of M. Cailletet. M. Regnault had the great merit, both as savant and professor, of not believing formulated laws to be absolute, and of ever remaining the docile disciple of experiment. He was indeed an experimentalist of the first order, and his labours almost constantly led to important practical results. His investigations of steam-engines were undertaken for the Government, and he rendered important services both as Engineer of the Gas Company, and as Director of the Sèvres Manufactory.

Claude Bernard was neither broken down by years like Becquerel, nor by domestic sorrows like Regnault. He was in full possession of all his powers when struck down by disease and death. Nothing can fill the void he leaves in the learned bodies to which he belonged: the French Academy, the Museum, the Academy of Science, the College of France. There he exercised an uncontested authority, not only by his intellectual superiority, but by the uprightness of his character and the soundness of his judgment. If he gave advice, or recommended a candidate, it was always felt that there was no favour in the matter, that he was guided solely by the interests of science. Claude Bernard was not only a sagacious observer and skilful experimenter, he was an eminent thinker as well. It is not so much because of his discoveries on the action of the nervous system, on digestion, on the pancreatic functions, that he was widely famous, but because he laid down with masterly hand the rules of the experimental method, because he so perfectly understood how to avoid straying beyond the purely scientific domain, while never pretending, in the name of science, to resolve problems that defy experiment. No one has kept science more free from metaphysical hypotheses, without, on the other hand, ever denying the claims of metaphysic. France had no purer nor more universally respected scientific luminary, and his death has been a public grief. The State undertook the care of his funeral.

But if our eminent scientists and literary lights are vanishing from our midst, the taste for science and the efforts made for its propagation are daily increasing. Two scientific associations have entered into a noble rivalry, the "Society for the Advancement of Science," whose aim is to bring men of science together, and rouse scientific interest in the provinces by its annual meetings; and the "French Scientific Association," whose chief purpose is to supply funds for the promotion of scientific research. It has already laid out 200,000 francs in experiments and subsidies to savants, and has recently very brilliantly inaugurated at the Sorbonne a course of public meetings. M. Dumas opened them by a tribute to M. le Verrier, founder of the association; M. Cailletet repeated his experiments on the liquefaction of gases, and M. Jablochkoff his on electric [illegible]. The results he has obtained may really be called dazzling, for as yet [illegible] only fault consists in this, that they do dazzle, and that the light pro[illegible] not soft enough for the eyes to bear. It is a fine sight that of 2,000 [illegible] assembled in the great amphitheatre of the Sorbonne attentively [illegible] account of the most recent scientific discoveries.

[illegible] fine-art department there seems, on the contrary, little [illegible] reserving itself no doubt for the opening of the

Universal Exhibition, when it will have to do the honours of France to foreigners. Still we have two small exhibitions of painting open at present, the one at "Le Cercle Artistique et Littéraire," Rue St. Arnaud, the other at "L'Union Artistique," in the Place Vendôme; and these are the annual prelude to the "Salon de Peintures" in the Champs Elyseés. This year the former has nothing very remarkable to show; but the latter has a true masterpiece of detail, and two portraits by Harlamoff, which place him not only before all living portrait-painters, but even alongside of the great masters of the past—Rembrandt or Franz Hals. Every one is waiting for the great tournament in the Champ de Mars. It repays better to go, if one can, to the studios and see the last touches given to the works destined to compete there. Two of the most remarkable of these are tombs, the one that of General de La Moricière, the last defender of the Papacy, by M. H. Dubois, where four monumental figures, Courage, Charity, Faith, and Thought, keep guard at the foot of the hero's statue. Inspired by Florentine art, these statues have at the same time an air of morbid melancholy, quite modern, and the noble sadness befitting a vanquished cause. The other tomb, which is very different, is that of our great historian Michelet. This has been entrusted to M. Mercié, the bold and inspired sculptor of the "Gloria Victis." Michelet lies dead on a Sarcophagus, before him stands the Muse of History, who, holding in one hand the book of Fate, writes with the other on the wall the author's motto, "History is a Resurrection." Nothing can be grander or more noble than this idea.

The theatres give us nothing striking to report. At the Gymnase, "La Femme de Chambre" is an amusing farce; at the Odéon, the "Nid des Autres" might have furnished material for a powerful and interesting play, but in spite of its wit and talent we find it somewhat empty. We may, however, console ourselves by reading over the history of the theatre during the past year given us by MM. Noel and Stoullig: "Le Théâtre et la Musique en 1877" (Charpentier). It is convenient to have such repertories to aid the memory that, alas! has so many insignificant things to retain. M. Daniel has rendered us the same sort of service in another direction by his "Année Politique," a historical record written with much impartiality and liberal feeling. The principal attraction in the book of MM. Noel and Stoullig is a paper written by our excellent comedian, M. Got, on the provincial theatre. He exhibits its deplorable condition and irreparable decadence, and proposes to form companies in Paris to circulate in the provinces, and go from town to town. I confess myself alarmed by this excessive centralization. I see the time when, thanks to the telephone, we shall only have throughout France one single orchestra playing in Paris for the whole of the provinces, one single University, where the professors will transmit lessons by wire to all corners of the land! This utter absorption of France by Paris seems to me adverse to progress; and I cannot wonder that such hypertrophy of the head at the expense of the body should lead from time to time to attacks of brain fever.

G. Monod.

# CONTEMPORARY ESSAYS AND COMMENTS.

[*In this Section the Contributors to the* CONTEMPORARY REVIEW *are understood to express themselves with less restraint (as to their individual views) than might be thought desirable in formal articles.*]

**The Theory of Belief.—Dr. Newman and Mr. Leslie Stephen.**

SINCE there appeared in this REVIEW (November, 1877) a brief outline of Dr. Newman's statement of the position of the English Church contained in the re-issue of his "Lectures on the Prophetical Offices of the Church," and of the refutation of his former theories with which he has accompanied them, the second volume of the same work ("The Via Media of the Anglican Church," 2 vols.: Pickering) has been published; and we have also had in the pages of the *Fortnightly Review*, from the vigorous pen of Mr. Leslie Stephen, an elaborate examination and estimate of what he calls "Dr. Newman's Theory of Belief." Concerning this examination we propose to offer a few remarks; but let us first devote a word or two to Dr. Newman's volume.

The most interesting portion of its contents are, beyond question, the republication, with an introductory "Notice" and appended notes, of Tract for the Times, No. 90, "Remarks on Certain Passages in the Thirty-nine Articles," the famous pamphlet which, in its day, "fluttered the dovecotes" of our ecclesiastical Corioli even more thoroughly than "Essays and Reviews" themselves, and the letters regarding it addressed by the author to Dr. Jelf and to the then Bishop of Oxford, Dr. Bagot. It is just thirty-seven years since Tract 90 was published, and looking back on the matter after that lapse of time, and with sundry decisions of the Judicial Committee of the Privy Council in our memory, it is not a little difficult to understand why it should have caused the commotion it did. Indeed, Dr. Newman is able to point out, with a certain natural triumph, that, in 1868, Dr. Forbes, Bishop of Brechin "was suffered to repeat the very same statements, without protest, which were considered so disingenuous and disgraceful in Tract 90." If it was to be shown that, as Mr. Leslie Stephen puts it, "the English Church may be legitimately affiliated to that primitive Church whose unity was a visible and palpable phenomenon, not a matter of careful inference and accommodation," it was necessary to show that she taught Catholic doctrine as the primitive Church taught it. For, if she did not, she was not a branch of the Church Catholic; and in that case Dr. Newman asks, "What had we to do with her?" The interpretation of the Thirty-Nine Articles in a Catholic sense was, then, for him, and those like-minded with him, at once a logical necessity and a moral duty. He clearly foresaw that it would be said concerning the explanations he gave of the anti-[illegible] Articles—some of which he admits now are not a little forced—that [illegible] notorious that the Articles were drawn up by Protestants, and intended [illegible]blishment of Protestantism, it was an evasion of their meaning to [illegible] other than a Protestant drift. To this he replies in advance, [illegible] which we owe, both to the Catholic Church and to our own, [illegible] confessions in the most Catholic sense they will admit; [illegible]wards their framers." Farther, the injunction that the [illegible] in the "literal and grammatical sense" "relieves us from the necessity of making the known opinions of their fr[illegible] upon their text."

> "Their framers constructed them in such a way as [illegible] did not go so far in Protestantism as themselves. Anglo-Catho[illegible] the successors and representatives of those moderate reformers; [illegible] been directly anticipated in the wording of the Articles. It [illegible] not perverting, they are using them for an express [illegible] their authors framed them. The interpretation Anglo-Catho[illegible] tended to be admissible; though not that which those authors [illegible]

"The Protestant confession," says Dr. Newman in conclu[illegible] up with the purpose of including Catholics; and Catholics [illegible] included. What was an economy in the Reformers is a [illegible]

From the standpoint he occupied in the year 1841, we [illegible] was anything "disgraceful or disingenuous" in the [illegible] he applied to the Articles; though, of course, the results of [illegible] *tour de force* could not have been very satisfactory to an[illegible] failed to satisfy him. He was not seeking to [illegible] Broad-Churchmen—"Latitudinarians" he would then [illegible] his interpretation of the Articles was the necessary [illegible] was addressing those more or less at one in faith and feeling [illegible] endeavouring to soothe them by showing that though [illegible] "there are real difficulties to a Catholic Christian in the [illegible] our Church at this day, the statements of the Articles are [illegible]

And the attitude which Dr. Newman assumes in Tract 90 [illegible] he rarely departs. Seldom, if ever, do we find him doing [illegible] declared enemies, bringing forward arguments with a view [illegible] a thoroughgoing sceptic of the truth of Christianity, [illegible] Protestant of the validity of the claims of the Catholic Chur[illegible] which he appeals are those which have already much in [illegible] which stand, so to say, very much on the same plane of th[illegible] are already really on the same road as himself, though the[illegible] advanced so far, and he would urge and encourage them on[illegible] method of Dr. Newman's has attracted the attention of Mr. [illegible] whose criticisms we now turn. Any student of Dr. Newma[illegible] writings, he says, must be struck by one remark :—

> "The man, he will say, is an Anglican, or has become a Ca[illegible] he not defend himself by proving his creed to be true? Let hi[illegible] or an *à posteriori* test, as he pleases; exhibit its philosophical [illegible] any straightforward mode of confronting it with facts. [illegible] apparently most natural method, we are involved in a [illegible] Instead of examining with an earlier school of apologists the [illegible] internal of the position, our attention is invited at length to [illegible] analogies, such as the relations between Anglicans and semi-A[illegible] tion of the internal consistency of the Creed, instead of its corres[illegible]

Mr. Stephen attributes the indifference to or aversion fro[illegible] of proof in theological matters, which he discerns in Dr. New[illegible] scepticism as to their power of producing conviction. He i[illegible] man to hold "that although a reality as well as a show o[illegible] producible to duly prepared minds for the central doctrines [illegible] a matter of plain undeniable fact, no system of independ[illegible] theology, such as philosophers have dreamed, has ever [illegible] world." For direct proof then of the Catholic system, [illegible] substitutes another kind of test, and for questions as to [illegible] creeds gives us questions as to their practical vitality [illegible] creeds live in proportion to the amount of truth [illegible] plainest facts written on the very surface of history [illegible] truest." In Dr. Newman's "Essay on the [illegible] this method is applied by him in a masterly [illegible]

[illegible] the elementary doctrines of Christianity, but hesitate between [illegible] Catholicism, in favour of the latter. But those with whom the [illegible] does not lie merely between Anglicanism and Catholicism are untouched [illegible] argument; for, of course, the mere logical coherence and consistency of [illegible] of themselves sufficient evidence of its truth. This, as Mr. [illegible] admits, has been fully recognised by Dr. Newman who has "supplied [illegible] theory of belief" with other mental bases besides that of the simple [illegible] of a creed. These bases are set forth by him in the "Grammar of [illegible]," with an examination of which work a considerable portion of Mr. [illegible] Stephen's criticisms is occupied. We have in it, he says, "an elaborate [illegible] assents or beliefs, varying from the faintest to the most vivid, and from [illegible] most abstract to the most concrete." We have, too, a careful analysis of the [illegible] by which the mind draws remote inferences without a conscious syllogistic [illegible] to which the name of "the Illative Sense" is given. And here again, says [illegible] Stephen, "we are struck by the absence of the direct logical method."

[illegible] A Grammar of Assent, one would say, ought to correspond to a treatise on logic. [illegible] ought to assent to true propositions, and therefore should begin by inquiring [illegible] is the test of truth. But the very name of the treatise seems designedly [illegible] to set aside such inquiries, and contemplates at least the possibility of a divorce between the faculty of believing and the faculty of perceiving the truth."

The method employed is one that evades the purely logical question. "Indeed, Dr. Newman lays it down as a principle that 'in no class of concrete reasoning . . . . . . is there any ultimate test of truth and error in our reasonings besides the trustworthiness of the illative sense that gives them its sanction.'" The conditions of belief investigated in the treatise are, says Mr. Stephen, simply the conditions of belief in general, not the conditions of right and reasonable belief. As a theory of the methods by which men are in fact convinced he considers the Grammar of Assent masterly and unassailable. In large classes of belief the grounds of conviction are too complex and delicate to be expressible in syllogistic form, and among these are beliefs as to matters of fact and religious beliefs. Such beliefs as we form on these subjects are due—primarily, we understand Mr. Stephen to mean—to the testimony of the illative sense. "I perceive, by a process analogous to the use of the external senses, that this or that belief is on the whole congruous to my other established beliefs. Therefore it is true. I can go no farther." And accordingly Dr. Newman says that "a proof, except in abstract demonstration, has always in it, more or less, an element of the personal." That men do by these methods become convinced of certain beliefs, or, in other words, yield "assent" to them, Mr. Stephen holds to be undeniably true; but all this, he says, is "entirely irrelevant to the logical problem." "When a man's mind is constituted in a certain way, and certain evidence is brought before him, it will inevitably produce a certain opinion. That is as true as that any action whatever is a function of the organism and the medium. But it has simply no bearing upon the other question whether the man's mind is rational, or whether he deals with the evidence in accordance with logical rules." If, he says again, "the difference between men's minds were such that no two people could hold the same opinion, the pursuit of a truth independent of personal variation would be chimerical." But this is not so; and therefore "the difficulty of summing up and (so to speak) packing into a single formula the whole pith and essence of so complex an assent as that to the truth of a religion," does not "diminish in the slightest degree the importance of applying logical tests other than that of the direct testimony of the 'illative sense,'" or of ordering our minds, in [illegible] with Locke's canon, not to entertain any proposition "with greater [illegible] than the proofs it is built on will bear." In fine, Mr. Stephen accuses [illegible] of constructing a theory of belief which virtually ignores the dis-[illegible] belief of any sort and right and logical belief, and the tests [illegible] employ to satisfy himself, more or less, whether or not his [illegible] conformity with facts. Dr. Newman, he says in effect, accepts

Catholicism on the testimony of his "illative sense," and with the Protestant or sceptic who asks for proof that the system of Catholicism is in harmony with the teachings of history and science, or with what we call civilization, he will not argue, because they do not admit his first principles. So far as other people hold his first principles, the illative sense working in them may bring them to the same results that he has arrived at. "But any attempt at a common measure of truth as an 'objective test' is explicitly pronounced impossible."

> "The whole pith of the Grammar of Assent, so far as it is original, is in the assertion that belief is a personal product in such a sense that no common measure between different minds is attainable. Therefore agreement can only be produced by supernatural intervention; or, in other words, rational agreement is impossible."

We do not at all charge Mr. Leslie Stephen with unfairness or inaccuracy in his analysis of Dr. Newman's "Theory of Belief," but we think he is in error in assuming, as he seems to do, that the theory has been framed by its author under pressure of an argumentative necessity, and that "the direct logical method" of proof is set aside or made light of from a consciousness that it will not serve the purpose in hand. We do not think that Mr. Stephen has taken enough account of Dr. Newman's views as to First Principles—views which, if we consider them, seem a sufficient explanation why his "theory of belief" should be what it is. In a remarkable passage at the end of one of his University sermons,* Dr. Newman says, "Half the controversies in the world are verbal ones; and could they be brought to a plain issue, they would be brought to a prompt termination. Parties engaged in them would then perceive, either that in substance they agreed together, or that their difference was one of first principles. This is the great object to be aimed at in the present age, though confessedly a very arduous one. We need not dispute, we need not prove—we need but define. . . . When men understand what each other mean, they see, for the most part, that controversy is either superfluous or hopeless." References to these "first principles," a difference as to which between disputants thus renders controversy hopeless, are frequent in Dr. Newman's writings, but perhaps he has never spoken so fully and explicitly concerning them as in the seventh of the "Lectures on the Present Position of Catholics in England." These "first principles" are there defined as being "opinions and beliefs which do not depend on previous grounds, which are not drawn from facts, for which no reasons can be given, or no sufficient reasons, which proceed immediately from the mind, and which the holder considers to be, as it were, part of himself. If another person doubts them, the holder has nothing to show for their truth, except that he is sure that they are true; he cannot say, 'I will reconsider my reasons,' for he has no reasons to consider." They are such simple persuasions or sentiments as "come to the holder, he cannot tell how, and which, apparently, he cannot help holding." "No man alive," says Dr. Newman, "but has some first principles or other." "If you trace back your reasons for holding an opinion, you must stop somewhere; the process cannot go on for ever; you must come at last to something you cannot prove." These First Principles "are the means of proof, and are not themselves proved; they rule, and are not ruled."

> "They are our guides and standards in speculating, reasoning, judging, deliberating, deciding, and acting; they are to the mind what the circulation of the blood and the various functions of our animal organs are to the body. They are the conditions of our mental life; by them we form our view of events, of deeds, of persons, of lines of conduct, of aims, of moral qualities, of religions. They constitute the difference between man and man; they characterize him."

Such, then, are first principles in Dr. Newman's eyes—"sovereign, irresponsible, and secret"—secret, because they are so close to the mind, so completely a part of it that a man is very likely to hold them without being aware of them—and, thinking thus of them, he may well say as he does, "What an awful form of government the human mind is under from its very constitution!"

* "Faith and Reason contrasted as Habits of Mind."

It is no wonder then that we find him saying that "a proof, except in abstract demonstration, has always in it, more or less, an element of the personal," because the man's acceptance of it as a proof must depend upon those first principles which are to him, though perhaps unconsciously, his "guides and standards" in almost every field of mental activity. To attempt direct logical proof of a philosophical or theological position to an opponent whose first principles were different from his own would necessarily seem to Dr. Newman a mere waste of time. Whilst the other's first principles remained what they were he could not influence him. The utmost he could accomplish would be to induce him to go back upon himself, and examine into his first principles. If a man's first principles are sound—and their soundness depends much more on the ethical temper than the intellect—on the "heart," not the "head"—his "illative sense" working from them will arrive at true conclusions, which have no need to be subjected to any formal logical tests. Reasoning, says Dr. Newman, in the sermon on "Implicit and Explicit Reason"—the thirteenth of the "University Sermons"—or the exercise of reason, "is a living, spontaneous energy within us, not an art." Logic is but the analysis of the reasoning process, and "the exercise of analysis is not necessary to the integrity of the process analyzed. The process of reasoning is complete in itself, and independent. The analysis is but an account of it; it does not make the conclusion correct; it does not make the inference rational. . . . How a man reasons is as much a mystery as how he remembers." Faith, which is the illative sense of a religious man exercised in the religious sphere, is a legitimate exercise of reason, though it is content with weaker evidence than would satisfy what is commonly called "Reason," which demands direct and definite proof, because it proceeds not only on the grounds it may be able to put forward, but on antecedent considerations—"previous notices, prepossessions, and (in a good sense of the word) prejudices"—in fact on first principles. Thus it is a moral faculty, "because created in the mind, not so much by facts, as by probabilities; and since probabilities have no definite ascertained value, and are reducible to no scientific standard, what are such to each individual depends on his moral temperament. A good and a bad man will think very different things probable." And Dr. Newman in the sermon from which we have already quoted, states it as a heavy drawback upon the value of what are called the "Evidences" of Christianity that "defenders of Christianity naturally select as reasons for belief, not the highest, the truest, the most sacred, the most intimately persuasive, but such as best admit of being exhibited in argument; and these are commonly not the real reasons in the case of religious men. Nay," he adds, "they are led for the same reason to select such arguments as all will allow; that is such as depend on principles which are a common measure for all minds," implying that the validity of arguments does not depend on their standing the test of the application of any such "common measure."

Thus, as it seems to us, Dr. Newman's theory of belief and methods of argument, which Mr. Leslie Stephen regards as so unsound and indirect, spring necessarily from his fundamental conception of the constitution of the human mind, and are in perfect consistency with that conception. In a sense, in his view, the soul is even here alone with God—*sola cum solo.* The human mind is so constituted that belief is so far a personal product that a common measure between different minds is only approximately attainable. "It is probable," writes Dr. Newman, "that a given opinion, as held by several individuals, even when of the most congenial views, is as distinct from itself as are their faces." He would hold it no less true of us intellectually than morally that

"Each in his hidden sphere of joy or woe
Our hermit spirits dwell, and range apart."

Of course what we are to think of this fundamental conception of Dr. Newman's, and the conclusions to which it has led him, is not here the question. Our object has simply been to point out that his theories had an intellectual basis which Mr. Leslie Stephen seemed to have overlooked.

**Obiter Dicta in Public Discussion.**

OUR newspapers informed us the other morning that in a debate upon the Burials Bill, "Mr. Talbot complained of the hard language used by the Marquis of Hartington at Edinburgh—not so much in speaking of 'the miserable attempt of the Conservative party' to settle this question, but in referring to what he termed 'the odious privilege claimed by the clergy.' It was not the claiming of a privilege, but the maintenance of a right."

As Mr. Talbot could hardly have intended a simple begging of the question we may take this to mean that his complaint was that the clergy were represented as claiming what they knew to be a mere "privilege," and in such a way as to make it "odious." As the Marquis of Hartington, though not a subtle and over-refined speaker, is scrupulously fair and very clear-headed, we may safely presume that between his speech and this comment of the mild and gentlemanly Mr. Talbot there lies some mistake in reporting or otherwise. But in most speakers and writers there is a very general tendency to indulge in casual judgments of men and things which are outside the limits of the assumptions upon which they are supposed to be working, or which are otherwise unfair.

We are long past the time when angry controversialists treated even superficial difference of opinion as proofs of a depraved heart; or, to say the least, the spheres within which this is not true are small. There are, no doubt, questions of morals and even of æsthetics, which are seldom discussed without the flinging of the old-fashioned firebrands. There are also certain small arenas of ecclesiastical controversy in which very bad language is used. But on the other hand, the spirit of modern courtesy makes not a few religious writers unfaithful to the logic of their own beliefs—they refrain from imputations when in their secret hearts they feel that it would be just to make them. A clear head, a tenacious memory, and a keen sense of justice do not always go together; even when they exist together they are not all equally wide-awake at the same moment; and nothing less than this could ever sweep controversy clear of imputations.

Nobody will deny that there are cases in which the imputation of bad motives more or less consciously entertained may very justly enter into public discussion. A writer might advocate community of goods or community of wives in such a way as to stamp him for one "of the baser sort." But nobody who was at all fit to handle difficult questions of that order could very well criticize, say, Mr. Noyes of Oneida Creek and Proudhon (on the one hand) upon the same footing with, say, Jack Wilks and Jack Sheppard on the other. It is, admittedly, difficult to draw the line in such instances; but it *is* to be drawn; and, usually, by treating the difficulty as a psychological problem to begin with. A critic who is capable of seeing the real difficulty raised by a case like that of "Brother Noyes," soon comes to conclude that he is a man in whom certain fibres of head, heart, and fancy are weak, but a man who means well and may claim to be treated with respect. But let us put the case—an actual one, for it occurred in this very REVIEW—of a reviewer's calling the Oneida Creek men "hogs,"—would that necessarily imply that the reviewer thought them wholly stupid or unworthy of respect? Certainly not; the use of that particular word went to one point only—want of delicacy of feeling, and readiness to take physical plenty and make too much of it, come as it might. Discussion would have no life in it, if the disputants were always to speak through gags or fight with buttoned foils. Nor is that all, or the chief point. Arguments addressed to moral questions should have moral power in them; it is not enough that they should be free from logical flaws. The same may be said of political discussion. Now there is no example, from the Gospels and Epistles downwards, of writing or speaking full of moral power, and at the same time free from the imputation of motives and from vehement moral censure. The thing is impossible. We may sometimes have the choice of saying to an opponent, "You are a fool," or "You are a bad man;" but we may be driven to make the choice. The force of epithets is, of course, relative. If one man calls another a fool or a beast in the middle of an ordinary drawing-room conversation, everybody is struck with the incongruity, and the words strike like pistol-shots. They are quite out of the key of the intercourse. But when passions run high, and the key-note of strong language has once been fairly struck, it constantly happens that what under other circumstances would be received as an insult, passes with but little notice, or, at all events, is regarded as a mere incident of allowed give and take. "If you bite my dog's tail, I'll bite *your* dog's tail." Unless we know at the time that personal hatred lies behind, we can most of us put up with a good deal of abuse—so long as there is room for retaliation. The retaliation, however, must be as public as the attack, and must be addressed to the same audience.

It is at this point that we approach the question of the inconvenience and injustice of mere *obiter dicta* of condemnation. But, before passing on, it may be observed that the imputation of questionable motive, or, at least, of feeling, is, upon a large view, almost inseparable from three-fourths of any critical writing that is at present possible. To say, for example, that Southey softened down certain parts of the story of Nelson might involve an imputation upon Southey's impartiality. This would be a small fault, if any; but partiality in history or biography is not always an error to be treated leniently—even when the erring person is quite sincere. If politician A thinks that politician B has written in a prejudiced or reckless vein, it is the duty, or it may be the duty, of A to say what he thinks, leaving B to whatever remedy he can get. It may very well be that no remedy is open to him. As things go in this lopsided world, we must take our chance in such matters, just as we do with regard to the daily gossip of our neighbours, who assuredly utter a good many unjust things about us. Of course, in the case of public criticism, the attitude of the critic is supposed to be strictly judicial: but this cuts both ways.

One thing is clear, that, barring trifles—with which the sense of humour ought to be competent to deal—public criticism, when it condemns, should give its reasons. The indictment should set forth clearly what is incriminated, and the argument should go before judgment. This rule—with another rule, one of common fairness—excludes from the sphere of right criticism the majority of mere *obiter dicta* of condemnation; perhaps all, and especially if they carry any odium with them. An argument cannot be clearly attached to an epithet flung in by the way. That is one reason; the other is that in ninety-nine cases out of a hundred the person thus casually incriminated has no fair chance of reply. So we find, both in public oratory and in literary criticism, a casual scrap of condemnation proves the most fertile source of small personality. The world is surprised some fine morning to find Professor John Doe, in the middle of a paper on Thomas Aquinas and Nominalism, stigmatizing Professor Richard Roe's work on Pascal and the Jansenists as a flippant and ill-digested treatise. The world may well be surprised, but the fact is that about two years previously Professor Richard Roe, quite suddenly, and if not irrelevantly yet under no pressure of necessity, went out of his way in an essay on Kant's Categories, to call Professor John Doe's book on Theism thinly disguised Pantheism of the lowest order. To say nothing of the question of literary dignity, the injured, insulted Doe had no present remedy, so he drew out his bare bodkin when he could. Literature is crowded with *misères* of this kind.

In the third year of the Chancellorship of Brougham occurred this very disagreeable incident. "The House was thinly attended, and the Dukes of Wellington and Cumberland were sitting close to each other, conversing in a low tone of voice. The debate was a dull one, and the Lord Chancellor when speaking took occasion to remark that the epithet 'illustrious' was sometimes used in a conventional sense implying no real merit or eminence in the person so designated. 'For instance,' said he looking sharply in the direction of the two conversing dukes, 'the Duke of Cumberland is illustrious by "courtesy" only, but the Duke of Wellington is illustrious by his character and services.' A bombshell falling at the feet of the astonished dukes could not have more startled them—Wellington probably not so much. His Royal

Highness of Cumberland was exceedingly indignant. 'Why,' he angrily demanded, 'had he, who had taken no part in the discussion, was not even listening to it, been dragged into it in that unseemly manner?' The Lord Chancellor coolly replied, that it had suddenly occurred to him that his Royal Highness and the Duke of Wellington afforded apt illustration of the truth he was endeavouring to enforce—that there was a vast and essential difference between individuals illustrious by 'courtesy' and those who were illustrious by achievements and success."

Now this was not only indefensible on the part of Brougham, it was cowardly, because the Duke of Cumberland was about the best-hated man of his time. And we may surely say that an *obiter dictum* of the attacking order becomes ignoble in proportion to the amount of odium it is likely to create, and the *quality* of the odium in question. For instance, the *odium theologicum* is a very bad *odium* indeed, and one should be very careful in awaking it. It is not at all a question of abuse: we stand in but small danger from that nowadays. Besides, it does not hurt much. If Mr. Milton says, "I mean not to dispute Philosophy with this Pork, that never had any"—his opponent may, and surely will, retort by calling Mr. Milton "an Hyæna,"—this is all in the bargain and breaks no bones. But it is quite another thing when Samuel Clarke—just in passing—labels a doctrine of an opponent as "a shameful fallacy," or, "a wicked folly." This high style is very fit for a Busby addressing his scholars, or a Pope of Rome promulgating a Bull; but the law of controversy between presumed equals is that one view is as good as another till it is proved false. Hence, though casual expressions of opinion about the views of other people are, when qualified, allowable or inevitable, mere blunt *obiter dicta* are forbidden. And they certainly are not inevitable.

---

**Toilet Artifices.**

THERE is a story told of a blind gentleman, who married a very plain woman, under the impression that she was a great beauty. The poor fellow indulged himself in many dreams of her charms, and his friends charitably kept up the delusion, smiling unseen at his unfounded boasts. In particular, her splendid hair—which he was able actually to feel and measure—was often the subject of the fond husband's remarks; till one unhappy night he chanced to rise and move about his bedroom, while his wife lay asleep. In the course of his peregrinations his hand came upon a very surprising substance hanging on the looking-glass. He grasped it with both hands, felt it over and over, and then rushed to the bedside, thrust aside his wife's nightcap, and touched her head. Alas! alas! that head bore but the shortest and scantiest covering of hair! The object on the looking-glass was a wig, and the husband's pride, faith, and love were all mortified together.

I should like to commend this instructive little tale to the kindly critic who, in the last number of the CONTEMPORARY REVIEW, expresses his willingness that his wife should, if she could, conceal her grey hairs, or any other "disgrace" (assuming grey hairs to be a disgrace), from strangers, or even from himself. Would he not have shared the poor blind gentleman's sentiments under the same trying circumstances?

It is quite true, as my critic very justly reminds me, that there is no defining strictly or drawing a hard and fast line between the *concealment of a defect*—which may amount almost to a duty of decency—and the *assumption of an artificial beauty*, which I look upon as equally a mistake in æsthetics and a fault in the minor moralities. Nevertheless, I think, the *principle* is tolerably clear, and may generally be applied pretty safely. Let us keep to this matter of false hair as a good case in point.

The artificial hair which I condemn consists in coils, *chignons*, plaits, curls, &c., added to a woman's natural head of hair to make it appear that, instead of the small or moderate allowance which Nature has given her, she has a plentiful chevelure. This is distinctly *deception*, deliberate falsification, done not for the sake of disguising an ugliness, but of pretending to a beauty. The prevalence of the late fashion in this respect went so far and the heads became so preposterous, that the women who wore the *chignons* at last grew hardened, and ceased to care whether anybody believed their stupendous erections to be genuine or otherwise. But at the commencement of the mania we can well recollect the panic which seized the ladies in Rotten Row one day, when a mischievous young gentleman stuck a *chignon* on the top of his whip and rode round, pretending that he had picked it up and was looking for its owner; and how scores of fair equestrians betrayed their consciousness that their hair *could* come off, by hurriedly putting up their hands to their heads to feel if it were still *in situ*.

This pretence to a beauty which the wearer does not possess is, I think, beyond a doubt a demoralizing thing; but no one can say the same of an effort to hide a disagreeable defect, such as baldness would be in woman. Fortunately, I believe, Nature has taken some special precautions in making a woman's scalp, so that there should very rarely exist such a thing as the terrible spectre described so long ago as in the "Golden Ass" of Apuleius,—a woman otherwise beautiful, but perfectly bald. It is usually quite possible to cover decently, and even ornamentally, with a little lace or muslin, any deficiency from which a woman suffers even in very advanced old age. Our charity, therefore, outruns itself if we are ready to grant plenary indulgence to a false-haired woman on the time-honoured ground that

"He who has no hair must needs wear a wig."

But the principle for which I contend comes out still more clearly in the matter of dyed hair and painted skin, both of which Jezebel contrivances I find, with horror, my critic is ready to condone, *if* they effect their purpose of improvement; a ground on which every woman who uses them will *by the hypothesis* take her stand.

Now, grey hairs and a faded complexion are the outward and visible signs of the fact that the woman is no longer twenty or thirty, but is forty, fifty, or sixty years of age, as the case may be. The question then is, Does the woman who dyes her hair wish it to be supposed she is only twenty when she is fifty? Notoriously she does so; and what is the result? That her whole life is, so to speak, played in a false key. The position she assumes in society, her carriage, demeanour, opinions, the degree of experience, knowledge of the world, and authority wherewith she can and ought to speak at fifty, must be carefully hidden and forgone if she wish to appear twenty years younger. Of course, she never succeeds, and the whole thing is æsthetically a failure—a particularly frightful, ghastly kind of failure. The black or golden hair and brilliant complexion jar miserably with the faded eyes, and all the indescribable changes of lines and contours which distinguish age from youth. But these physical disharmonies are nothing to the moral discord which takes place between the inward character and the outward appearance. As years go on, the unhappy woman is caught in a trap of her own making, for she dare not wash and be clean, lest she reveal all at once what a deception she has practised, or appear in white hair to-day having worn raven locks yesterday. She is actually obliged to keep up her artifices even when she may wish to renounce them; till, at last, the assumption of youth is too obviously monstrous to be endured, and then some propitious illness or journey is made the occasion of a sudden transformation from twenty-five to seventy.

And what a price the poor soul had paid all those years for her mock juvenility! What lack of wholesome ablutions! What dependence on the fidelity of her confidential maid, or the secresy of that room at the hair-dresser's so ominously marked PRIVATE on the door! Or, still worse, what peril of exposure, from a shower of rain-water or from the too hasty kisses of a child, of the fact that she employs the witch-ointment of Madame Rachel! And all this for a wretched, paltry purpose, for which, in her inmost heart, she must despise herself! We have all laughed at the pious grocer, who told his shop-boy to "sand the sugar, and then come to prayers." It hardly seems a more appropriate preparation for a lady's repose that she should make her maid dye her hair and enamel her face before

> "Her gentle limbs doth she undress,
> And lies down in her [artificial] loveliness."

When women cease to be taught that the only honour and purpose of their lives is to obtain that kind of admiration which is given to youth and beauty, they will look on all these "Toilet Artifices" with the same contempt men feel for a braced-up, padded, be-wigged, and be-rouged old dandy of the masculine gender. They will come to the opinion that, far from being a "disgrace," the "hoary head" is—for a woman, as well as for a man—"a crown of glory," if it be found in the way of sense, dignity, and goodness.

F. P. C.

---

"Reform" Associations.

IN a volume of sermons on "week-day" subjects, which was published by Mr. Strahan several years ago, Mr. R. W. Dale had something to say, as was natural, about Dancing and the Stage. And, as was to be expected, all he said was liberal and intelligent. He had high praise for comedy as an intellectual refreshment, and of the highest art in tragedy there was really nothing new to remark. But he wound up by anticipating—with frankly expressed regret on *æsthetic* grounds—the time when, owing to the triumphs of religion and morality, human life would no longer present such striking examples of conflict of passion as were necessary for the purpose of the tragic poet, or such anomalies as supplied the basis of comedy. At least, we are sure about the tragedy, and, of course, whether Mr. Dale said it or not, the question of the continuance of comedy would have to be treated from a corresponding, though not similar point of view.

It was scarcely possible for the meditative reader to turn the page without a smile. These remarks of the preacher raised, with a touch, the most profound question of philosophy on the one side, and went straight to the innermost difficulties of the heart on the other. To take the latter first,—who could think, without a pang, of giving up humour? "Smiles from reason flow, to brute denied," sang Milton. Perhaps this is not true; it is maintained that brutes *do* smile; but is it possible to conceive of any moral life in which variety of character should be absent? And can we conceive of variety of character without scope for humour? Similar questions may be asked with regard to passion, and before we well know where we are we find ourselves landed on the dreary shores upon which the relativity of all human apprehension falls to be considered. Briefly, we find that although we can frame abstract sentences about what we call perfection, we are unable to make to ourselves pictures of any life for finite creatures from which conflicts and anomalies are excluded.

Coming down, however, from these heights, we may take a little repose upon the table-land of continuous indefinite improvement. No man who is in pain but seeks to be rid of it; and few who try to escape it, wholly fail. No good man in presence of a vicious society or a vicious institution but wishes to see it improved. And societies and institutions do occasionally get improved. But when we come to the question of organized efforts to improve particular institutions, we find ourselves beset with doubts and difficulties.

We have all heard something lately of an organized effort to improve, or reform, or elevate the stage, or the drama, or both. It is impossible to state the objects of any such society except in vague terms. A society for helping to enforce particular laws may be considered precise in its object; and a voluntary association of religious persons or other propagandists for the promotion of given objects in religion or morals is sufficiently, though not exactly, amenable to definition of purpose and plan. It would seem to be otherwise, however, where the "objects" of the association are conversant with the most confusedly mixed questions of æsthetics, morals, and commercial success. The presence or absence of the commercial element makes a highly embarrassing difference in the state of facts. One understands and sees the way of a band of "total abstainers;" they want to persuade others to leave off drinking certain liquors, and to encourage them by social support. Equally easy is it to follow the *rationale* and methods of a Particular Baptist, or Free Methodist, or Quaker society. Simple enough, too, might be the motive and plans of, say, a body of ladies and gentlemen who should associate to cultivate a high dramatic taste,—that is, what they considered a high taste,—by the joint study of great plays and the acting of them among themselves. So long as no pecuniary object was proposed, and so long as the general public were not of the council, directly or indirectly, the course of such a society might be smooth enough. If it ran to cliquesism, as it would,—if it went off in unseemly quarrels, and indeed in smoke, as it *probably* would,—nobody would be hurt, or much hurt, but the volunteers who had been engaged in the scheme. Nay, some good would perhaps have been done; though those who have seen a little of such enterprises will be rather sceptical about the good.

It is a very different case, and a dangerous one, when "the field is the world," and the seed has to be cast into the furrow amid a hurly-burly of moral, æsthetic, and commercial difficulties and disagreements. Here we may, with confidence, predict that any organization which has general ideas of amendment, "elevation," and suppression behind it will fail. Some will say that it is neither uncharitable nor unphilosophical to wish that it may. Not, surely, from any want of sympathy with certain high objects. The theatre has long been a weariness of the flesh to cultivated men and women. In this enormous capital, with all its wit and wealth, its luxury and art, it ought to be possible for a tired man to be able to find somewhere among twenty or thirty theatres a wholesome and pleasant evening's entertainment, let the want strike him when it will. On the contrary, this is just the thing which is not. In the general result, the most cursory examination shows us that art, money, and morals are inextricably jumbled together in the state of facts which is behind all this. If any organization proposes to deal with the æsthetic part of the question, it is foredoomed to final failure, even though it should appear to win some transient successes. There is no authority to appeal to; there is no *consensus* of opinion: and, if there were, the question of "drawing the line" in practice would prove fatal. In approaching moral questions, the difficulties redouble themselves. No organization that ever existed has ever been able to deal fairly with such questions, when these two elements, (1) the element of bread-winning, and (2) the inevitable invocation of general public opinion, entered into the case. Protestant Christian Churches have dealt with such matters more or less fairly, but they have not appealed to "public opinion;" and they have not meddled with the question of bread-winning. Neither have they been (necessarily) inquisitorial; for the act of uniting with a given religious body is voluntary and implies submission to a discipline which is both mutual and above-board. Scrupulously conscientious persons who have seen, with any degree of closeness, the working of associations that profess to seek the improvement of morals by availing themselves of the pressure of the law, or of public opinion, have seldom been agreeably impressed by what went on behind the scenes. We have not the slightest knowledge of the association which has the elevation of the drama or the stage for its object. We do not even know its exact title—much less its plan. What we have written is general. But we have a strong feeling that more is lost than gained by even the most favourably devised and carefully worked associations *of this order*. Perhaps the true history of organized effort in general would tell a tale not too flattering to the *Zeit-Geist* of the last fifty years.

# CONTEMPORARY LITERATURE.



EPOCHS OF MODERN HISTORY.*—Messrs. Longman were very fortunate when they persuaded the Dean of St. Paul's to write their introductory volume. It was by far the most difficult in the series, and we are inclined to think, on the whole, that it has proved to be the most valuable. To bridge over the gulf between ancient and modern history in two hundred short pages is in itself a feat; to have done it in an admirable style, clear and easy, and at times very spirited and strong, with no sense of effort, nor the slightest confusion, even where the history is in itself most incoherent, is a real triumph, and shows a masterly command of the historian's best resources. The Dean's work stands completely clear of the whole tribe of common manuals; it affords us a delightful summary of periods which few students care to work out in detail, and takes its place at once by the side of Michelet's bright and workmanlike "Précis de l'Histoire Moderne."

We may describe the Dean's work as, in its main lines, a sketch of the great struggle for domination in Europe between the influences of the Germanic and the Latin races. It is true that Eastern history also finds due place in the book; but it is confined to a single chapter, and all the rest treats of the different Teutonic incomers as they dealt with and are in turn influenced by the climates, races, religion, institutions, with which they met in their career. The Dean's colleague in this series, Professor Stubbs, would probably say, and with solid grounds, that he underrates the permanence of the general effect of these Germanic influences in central Europe. He does, perhaps, give too little prominence to Germanic modes of thought and institutions;—the word "feudal" finds no place in his index, though the book comes down to the eleventh century. It is clear that the Dean takes a pleasure in recording how the Latin influences beat back their antagonists in a large part of Europe, after the death of Charles the Great; we discern that his sympathies lie rather with the south than the north.

Like a true historian, Dean Church deals in a singularly temperate tone with the religious questions which again and again agitated Christendom. He treats the Arian kingdoms with complete fairness, recognizing the broad spread of Arian opinions, their freedom from violence, their tolerant spirit: the matters at issue between the Eastern and Western Churches in the ninth century, and the hot, disastrous quarrels which split Christendom in twain, are handled with a clearness and fairness deserving of all praise. It was perhaps inevitable, in so narrow a space, that the author should decline to work out the characters of the chief personages he meets with in the course of his history. It is much to be regretted, for the Dean could do it so well. The catena of causes and events is excellently drawn out; the more important subjects are sketched with the firm free hand of a master; and when, as in the case of Charles the Great, he does make a pause over a period, the result is a true and brilliant picture, full of life and energy.

A series which includes this book, the "Angevins" of Professor Stubbs, and Mr.

---

* Epochs of Modern History: Longmans & Co.:—
1. The Beginning of the Middle Ages. By R. W. Church, D.D., Dean of St. Paul's. 1877.
2. The Normans in Europe. By Rev. A. H. Johnson. 1877.
3. The Crusades. By G. W. Cox, M.A. 1877.
4. House of Lancaster and York, with the Conquest and Loss of France. By James Gairdner. 1875. Maps. Second Edition.
5. The Thirty Years' War. By S. R. Gardiner, M.A., formerly Student of Christ Church, Oxford. 1877.
6. The Age of Anne. By E. E. Morris, M.A. 1877.
7. War of American Independence, 1775–83. By J. M. Ludlow. 1876.

Mr. Gardiner's "Thirty Years' War," to say nothing of other members of it, has secured a permanent position far above the crowd of small books on large subjects which have become the fashion of our day.

We cannot commend "The Normans in Europe;" there is nothing in it which the young student cannot easily find elsewhere, while the general reader will probably prefer to read the subject in those works of Professor Stubbs and Mr. Freeman, of which the greater part of this little book is a mere epitome.

The title is a misnomer, as the author indeed confesses; but even within the limits he has chosen for himself, his work is neither adequate nor even altogether correct. To take a few examples from the earlier chapters: the "Elder Edda" is, at all events, not "a collection of Sagas," and these so-called "Sagas" do not "belong to a period anterior to the movement of the Scandinavian people." Again, "Nái" is not a "region," but "a corpse" (dat. sing. of Nár), nor does "Valfadir" mean "god of battle." No one now doubts that the "Northmen" discovered Vinland (wineland), on the coast of North America. Later on in the book Harold's brothers are said to have all fallen at Senlac, and the song made by the English at the exile of Belesme is given as an exclamation of Orderic Vitalis himself. Reference to such books as B. Thorpe's translation of the Edda, and Laing's "Sea-kings of Norway," would have prevented such mistakes as the former, and a fresh perusal of the standard English authorities the latter. Still these are such mistakes as by themselves do not necessarily damage a book much; but when we come to the substance of the work, we find no traces of acquaintance with the original authorities, save such as are implied in a few quotations from the A. S. Chronicle. Thus, to give one material instance, Domesday Book is neither sufficiently noticed by, nor familiar to the author, and accordingly his treatment of feudalism in England is misleading in several points. In short, the book can neither interest the public nor be a safe guide to the beginner. We hope to see the same subject better treated ere long, for it is important and interesting both in itself and in its bearings on many historical problems.

The author of the tiny "Gesta Dei per Francos," Mr. Cox, does not hold that the crusading "Franks" were much inspired or controlled by Him in whose name they wandered forth and fought. He paints their dense ignorance, their neglect of the simplest rules of prudence, their mixed motives, their grossness and sensual triumphs, with a merciless hand. In his preface he tells us he has followed in the footsteps of "the illustrious author of the 'History of Latin Christianity;'" and he is even less inclined than his master to give any credit to the Crusaders for noble aim or disinterested piety. This want of dignity in the treatment of the subject seems to drag it down, and to suck away all its interest.

The introductory portion of the volume is well worth reading, especially in its clear account of what is called the gradual localization of Christianity, though it is perhaps a little out of place in a school-book. The first Crusade receives, as it deserves, the most attention, and this part of the book is clear and interesting; the account of the Latin Empire of Constantinople is also well done, though in some places the late Dean of St. Paul's is too closely followed; thus the well-known passage describing the taking of the city is reproduced in all its dark and thrilling details, with almost literal fidelity.

On the whole, however, the volume is not one of the more successful members of the series. The Crusades belong to "the romance of history," and demand graphic narrative, minute description, plentiful "local colouring." Such characteristics are inevitably wanting in a summary of the whole epoch. On the other hand, a short book on the Crusades ought to pay especial attention to whatever may be available to connect its periods together, and to bring into prominence all points which may give some unity to the subject. The nine Crusades, like the beads of a necklace, must be strung on some thread, if they are to hold together. And this is where the book is weak: the author does not work out the varying feudalism which runs through them all, or trace the effects of the Crusades in modifying the earlier Germanic institutions of Western Europe; he fails to point out the influence of revived religious energies on the feudal life; we see it neither in war nor in government, neither at Antioch nor at Mansourah, neither in the rule of Baldwin of Flanders at Constantinople, nor in the Great Assise of Jerusalem, nor in the sad fortunes of St. Louis in Egypt. Nor is the religious movement of the age so clearly indicated as it might have been. The Crusades were the Athanasian Creed of mediæval history; they were the strongly-marked expression of vehement religious passion, called forth by the antagonism of the "miscreant;" they were the enthusiasm of Latin dogma written in act, instead of being embodied in stern and strange affirmations. A thoughtful treatment of this exposition of the fierce spirit of late Latin Christianity, as it dealt with the Greek Church, with the Paynim, with the Albigensian heretic, as it swept from Constantinople all round the eastern and southern shores of the Mediterranean, and thence crossed into France, would have given the book a tone of unity and coherence which it seems to lack. A more careful handling of the geographical questions involved, a study of the different routes towards the East, of the reasons why now one, and now another point was attacked, might have been helpful towards the same end. This part of the work, however, is but weak: and the one map which acts as frontispiece to the volume is positively bad. The boundaries of states are often wrong; the Lombards did not have the Rhone for their western limits; the Arelat, whether kingdom or republic, is altogether unnoticed; all Burgundy is put outside France, though the Duchy was a fief of the kingdom; Lorraine did not have the lower Rhine as its north-eastern frontier: the March of Ancona is made to swallow up all the Duchy of Spoleto; the limits of Croatia, Dalmatia, Bosnia, are far too definite; the map gives little or no help to any one who wishes to trace the routes followed by land; the "Empire of Trebizond" is unfairly merged in that of "Rum." There is a most scanty supply of names of places; neither Tunis nor Mansourah is marked.

Finally, the latter part of the book is too brief and hurried, as if the author were weary of his task. The crusade of St Louis, which might have been drawn in fine contrast with much that disfigures the earlier part of the history, is given in a very few pages; hardly a word is said respecting his four years' sojourn in Palestine; no question is asked as to the reason for his prolonged and useless stay, or as to the causes of the weakness shown by the Saracens; the Christians at that time held only Ptolemais and Tyre: why were they left so unmolested? These are interesting points, which Sir G. Cox could have discussed clearly and well. Nor is the volume closed, as we might have expected, with a general view of the results which certainly flowed from the whole movement. All that is said on this is placed near the beginning of the book, and lays no claim to completeness. In a word, though there is much that is really praiseworthy in the volume, it still fails to be successful; and we regret that the able author should have fallen below his proper level; for he could certainly have written a better book, in spite of the inherent difficulties of his task.

Mr. Gairdner's book helps to fill a gap in English history which has not received adequate attention since Sharon Turner wrote. It is strange that this should have been so, for much new matter has turned up, and fresh light has been thrown on the subject by the labours of foreign scholars, and by Mr. Gairdner's own excellent edition of the Paston Letters, which is of course the chief authority on the social state of the England of that day. The story is well and accurately told in the little work before us, the brief biographical notices interesting, the mention accorded to literature judicious, while the strictly political aspect of the times is certainly better given here than by any other writer; for the Constitutional history we must wait for Professor Stubbs' third volume. Still we confess that when we had read it through, we felt disappointed that Mr. Gairdner had not given us a big book, instead of cramping his subject, as he has been obliged to do here. The period is certainly one that demands plenty of room; it is rich in detail and broad in area, belonging really to continental rather than English history. Mr. Gairdner has given, indeed, full attention to the foreign aspects of the question he considers, but it is impossible to treat it fairly in the space. The book will be found especially useful to the teacher, as an excellent *précis* of the best authorities. We must also thank Mr. Gairdner for the appreciative criticism of the "chroniclers" in his preface. They have been too much neglected, latterly, by students of our language and history.

Mr. S. Gardiner's book is just what a good manual ought to be. The ordinary reader will find it well worth reading; the student will be very thankful for its help. Till it appeared, the Thirty Years' War must have seemed to the world to be a dull and chaotic period; the only available source of general information respecting it being Schiller's wearisome work. And it is an especial advantage to the English student of this age, that while important books on the period, or on parts of it, or on personages involved in it, thicken around him, he has this clear, well-written sketch to make the outline of his knowledge firm, ere he ventures into the labyrinth before him.

Mr. Gardiner's book is one of those rare works which become more and more useful the more knowledge the reader brings with him to the perusal of it; and yet, though he does not write for children, his treatment of seventeenth century problems is so sound, and his colouring so firm and true, that any intelligent boy would read the book with interest and profit. He is not overwhelmed either by the great difficulties of the subject, or by the extent and minuteness of his own reading and knowledge. The narrative is clear and characteristic; the historical judgments sound and convincing; the sketches of personal character have the stamp of truthfulness and reality. The growth of the principle of religious toleration, with its varying features, in Germany, France, and England, forms the basis of the book; and that this semi-religious struggle had side by side with it a cognate struggle for the establishment of the unity of Germany, is well brought out. This parallelism shows clearly in Mr. Gardiner's admirable sketch of Wallenstein's standpoint, in which he makes it clear that the imperial general distinctly recognized the relation of the two subjects, and assured Ferdinand, first, that the union of Germany must depend on the establishment of a new military empire, supported by an emperor's army distinct from the forces of either league or union; and next that, just as that army was composed indifferently of Catholics and Protestants, so the new empire, of which that body was the only true parliament and representative force, must also be erected on the basis of religious equality. It is Wallenstein's title to real greatness that he alone of all the commanders in this terrible war can be compared with Gustavus Adolphus, both in skill as a general and as the representative of the national yearning after unity, which certainly still survived in Germany. This it is that renders his command of the first of modern imperialist armies specially significant; he was the first man who displayed before the eyes of Europe the true meaning of that new form of imperialism which we have seen but too often since his day—the imperialism which is based on a great standing army. Gustavus Adolphus also desired to achieve the unity of Germany; but far in advance of his great rival, he sought to found first a political union as the basis of his military strength, and believed that the great result would follow the triumph of his arms, as a natural and wholesome outgrowth of the liberties of the German States and cities. To Wallenstein the army was everything; Ferdinand, like Napoleon after him, should go down to posterity as "Head of the Army," an emperor borne aloft on his warriors' shields; to Gustavus political life came first, and the army was but the temporary instrument of his grand designs. The morality of Wallenstein's army never rose much above the level of those marauding bands which had ravaged Germany early in the war, while Gustavus took care that his troops should, as far as possible, spare the districts through which they passed. In the shock of these two opposing champions of German unity, the interest of the war rises to a dramatic height; the drama becomes tragedy when Gustavus falls on the field of Lützen, and Wallenstein, two years after, perishes at Eger, victim to the rage and jealousy of those who feared his imperialist ideas. When these two chiefs, who, like so many others in the war, were foreigners in Germany, had fallen, a new phase of the conflict began. It became once more a dreary scramble of selfish princes; even the greatness of Bernard's character does not lift him above the position of a splendid and self-seeking partisan; and after the defeat of the Swedes at Nordlingen, in 1634, French influences rise supreme, and the war becomes inexpressibly dreary. Mr. Gardiner, therefore, condenses the last thirteen years of it into a few pages, although even thus he manages to give sufficient attention to the grand figures of Richelieu and Turenne, who swayed the fortunes of this last period of the war. The section which describes Richelieu's character and aims is one of the best things in this excellent book. In fine, Mr. Gardiner's work, as we have said, is just what a good manual ought to be: arrangement admirable, balance between historical fact and reflection well sustained, style perfectly clear; nothing trivial let in, nothing valuable for a sketch of the kind left out; a delightful map as introduction to the volume. If there is a fault, it arises out of the very goodness of the workmanship; we fail, as we read, to be aware of the terrible confusion of the time, though the ruin wrought by the war is brought before us in a few clear touches, which lift a little corner of the dark veil that shrouds the awful misery to which Germany was reduced.

Mr. Morris, in his preface to "The Age of Anne," is so frank and straight-

forward, that he at once secures a friendly and favoura
confess to a smile at seeing Thackeray gravely rebuked fc
de St. George over to England, in 1714, in the teeth of his
exists no more truthful picture of Queen Anne's times tl
pages of "Esmond;" and surely the historical novelist is
of fact, so long as his accuracy of general impression anc

The main difficulty of Mr. Morris' subject lies here: h
chief prominence to Queen Anne and English affairs, wl
Louis XIV. was still great in France, and the wild and l
Peter and Charles XII. was attracting all eyes toward
management of the period might have linked these thi
but this is just where Mr. Morris seems to fall short.
the whole reign of Louis XIV., though his subject de
and more melancholy portion of it: in his appendix c
account of Pascal, who died in 1662; Molière, in 1673; Co
in 1699;—all before Queen Anne began to reign.

The ground is also sometimes twice trodden, as in t
memorable interview between Charles XII. and Marlbor
Mr. Morris say it took place at Dresden; and why should
going to the "Court of Charles?" The great soldiers
camp at Alt Ranstadt; and the rough young king's Spa
to be called his Court.

The statistical chapter deals with England only, thoug
on the state of the other European nations; the colonial
time receives very scanty notice. These seem to us the
which otherwise is accurately and pleasantly written.
and clear maps.

In his "War of American Independence," Mr. Ludlo
sketch, in a singularly attractive style, of a time which is
of us, and he has contrived, without losing himself in d
deal of clearly digested, well arranged information, o
English reader generally knows very little. The introd
mirable, but the summing up of the whole case, in chap.
piece of work in the book. The references to the Indians,
of the characters of the leading *dramatis personæ*, the
American opinion at the various stages of the struggle,
as especially good and novel.

---

Historical Handbooks.*—Mr. Smith's book is ju
recommend to a foreigner who wished to get a general nc
tions. It is well arranged, accurate, contains a vast amou
means badly written. For purposes of instruction, wher
Stubbs, Hallam, and May cannot be used, we prefer it to
Taswell-Langmead; it lends itself more easily to the want
use it as a centre to work round, and it is not a mere
reader will find it useful for reference.

The "History of Modern English Law" relates to a
demanded, but not hitherto received, adequate treatmer
book, and really accomplishes the author's design of givi
view of the whole field of English Law since the work of
a book was wanted by the law-student, and will be welc
especially to the sociologist. In the present day it is only
a Sir James Stephen which could uphold the chaotic a
superstitions presented to us in the pages of Blacksto
embodiment of common sense. To those who suffered
must indeed have been intolerable, but for the fact th
sheltered many a rogue, often left a way of escape to tl
it was, on the whole, administered by men whose one
stantial justice, irrespective either of court favour or
worst of it is, that, though the labours of Romilly, H

* Historical Handbooks, London: Rivingtons:—
1. History of English Institutions. By P. V. Smith.
2. History of Modern English Law. By Sir Roland K. V

[illegible] all of Bentham, to whose splendid gifts and noble efforts a fitting tribute [illegible] paid, have swept away much that was evil, much evil still remains. The [illegible] is still in a disgraceful state; the position of women but little alle-[illegible]; we cannot bring a civil action without incurring an expense it is seldom [illegible] while to face unless very important interests are at stake. We allow [illegible] grocer to adulterate our food, our debtors to defraud us, our stockbroker [illegible] agent to swindle us, because it would cost too much to go to law with-out the certainty of recovering our just dues. We have progressed, it is true, but certainly much remains to do, and as long as our statesmen prefer to let the interests of the legal profession override those of the public, we can hardly share the somewhat sanguine hopes of our author. In concluding our notice, by wishing this little book the success it deserves, we may further mention that it contains a useful chronological appendix, the indispensable index, and a short summary of the present law on the observance of Sunday, giving the whole state of the case as it now stands in a few words, an excellent example of the concise and exhaustive style of the whole book.

---

LATHAM ON EXAMINATIONS*.—Mr. Latham has done good service in putting the results of his long experience at Cambridge before the world in this book, in which shrewd observation and careful analysis are combined with practical common sense, and set forth in a lively vigorous style, full of apt and racy illustration.

The question of Examinations has become in the last five-and-twenty years, both more important and more widely interesting in consequence of the extent to which they have been made use of for the purpose of awarding office and emolument, not only at Oxford and Cambridge, where the action of the last Commission led to a great increase in the number and value of Fellowships and Scholarships open to general competition, but also in connection with the Civil Service of India, the Military and Naval Services, and finally the Home Civil Service. The mode of estimating merit and the value to be assigned to different subjects, which were once cherished mysteries of the Universities, have now been divulged to the criticising and not wholly impartial world of tutors, parents, and politicians. At the same time, what for brevity's sake may be called modern subjects have been rising in general estimation, and their cultivators have claimed for them equality with, or even preference to, the staple subjects of English education. And this leads to a serious practical difficulty. While on the one hand a subject which obtains little or no recognition in examinations for emoluments, is, as Mr. Latham often reminds us, a subject doomed to neglect; on the other hand, until a subject has been prepared and manipulated for this special purpose, its qualities as a subject of competitive examination have not been determined, and the best methods of dealing with it have not yet been discovered. People are apt to imagine that, because a subject is well worth study, it is therefore well fitted for examination; and that because we can examine our own pupils in what we have taught them, therefore our examinations will be suitable for a mixed collection of students, taught nominally the same subject, but by a great variety of teachers and methods; and lastly, that, because an examination is good for educational purposes, therefore it will bear the strain of being made the means of awarding large emoluments, and consequently of being studied by skilled tutors with a view to evasion.

Here lies one of the great merits of Mr. Latham's book. It forces into serious and practical consideration a distinction which is often too little regarded, between examinations which are educational and examinations which are merely for the purpose of selection. It is not uncommon to take an examination of the one class and apply it to the purpose of the other, or at least to draw conclusions from examinations in use and credit already, as if they were convertible equally to any subject we chose. The Indian Civil Service Examination at its first starting was [illegible] to serve simply the purpose of selecting young men for appointments in [illegible]. It was framed mainly on the principle of teaching the existing subjects, [illegible] according to the proficiency displayed in them. But it was soon [illegible] some of the subjects were more susceptible of cramming than others, [illegible] where great prizes are to be awarded by examination, efforts

---

* [illegible] of Examinations, considered as a Means of Selection. By Henry Latham, M.A., Fellow and [illegible] Hall, Cambridge. Cambridge: Deighton, Bell & Son.

were not wanting to make rapidity of acquisition and kna place of well-grounded knowledge and of less ready but m

Nor does the evil end here. The examination react especially the weaker schools. And now it does not come ir of the subjects thought best for education, but to encoura pay best in the examination, and discourage those, ofter which are less susceptible of being readily acquired and If a school refuses to become the slave of the "Exam." tl tutor who is more submissive and less scrupulous.

We do not hesitate to assert that this is almost an unm far from saying that all quick acquisition for an immec that the power of making the best use of the knowledge either discreditable or undesirable. But both these ca sphere, or ought to be brought within the sphere, of o business of special preparation for the Indian or other main not educational at all, but simply an ingenious and resources with a view to obtain the selection of a c would not succeed. If a candidate could succeed anyhow, is unnecessary and the time might be better spent. If s short special preparation, who would not have won witl many against his turning out the best in the long run.

The question how to award emoluments is not that t book; but supposing emoluments to be awarded by com shows what are the tendencies created or developed by their mischiefs may be avoided or corrected and their guarded and distributed. He discusses fully the cautions n ation is regarded simply as a test of knowledge, and the where it is intended to infer from the knowledge displaye mental or moral, of the candidate. If the examination find therein much help in judging how far the candid attention, memory in various shapes, delicacy of perceptio ation and reasoning power, and, besides all these, ener qualities connected with action, and all that involves beings or the power of influencing them, all that have and personal manner, lie outside the range of our testin qualities do so also. We cannot even tell whether to refe the other of the two types which are foci round which a l is grouped: we cannot see whether he is likely in any give or as little in the way of duty as he possibly can." Thi reason for adding to an examination other evidences of an appointment is in question. But those who make use the authority of examinations should remember that if of the whole, that is no reason for disregarding what i or more; and that a candidate shown to possess good i is at least as likely to possess the necessary or desirable r he were ignorant and commonplace; not to mention that are more often the cause of mischievous actions than imm

It would be impossible here to discuss the various s Latham. One point may be noticed. He thinks that in m language, it might be well to allow the candidates the use way the examination might fairly be made to depend mc than upon set books. We think this well worth trying. nuisance to schools, and afford a very favourable guide less sanguine as to the result of Mr. Latham's further app where he suggests that, when candidates have to write a Greek History, they should be allowed access to the texts Dramatists, and Orators, and also to works on Chronology ample time" would be given. But unless the "ample t the candidates like a non-unanimous jury, for a week, w the candidates to find themselves in a better position rel which their essay would be judged than when, as at prese the best they can with the material which they may hav memories. It would be fortunate indeed if a painstaking surface at all; and the lighter spirits would do as well witl

[illegible] Scholae Academicae.*—A book by a Cambridge man on [illegible], especially as carried on at Cambridge, deserves high praise, [illegible] character and merits are as different from Mr. Latham's as possible. [illegible]'s book is a book of facts, very carefully compiled from a great [illegible] sources, and stated with particulars of date and biographical details [illegible] an antiquary. To all who have a desire to see what University [illegible] methods, and examinations were a hundred or a hundred and fifty [illegible] ago, the book is full of interest and information. The appendix contains [illegible] a number of letters from Wm. Reneu, a student at Jesus College, Cambridge, to John Strype, about the beginning of last century, and some [illegible] part of the diary of Wm. Gooch of Caius, towards the end of that century, all printed from MSS. in the Cambridge *Library*, and giving a lively account of Cambridge ways at the time. Specimens of the old disputations, [illegible] books recommended by various tutors, and brief annals of the Cambridge University Press, will also be found in this somewhat multifarious but amusing collection. Those who complain of the tendencies of modern examinations, may derive some comfort from a study of the disputations which preceded them. Few mathematicians would wish to revive the custom of debating mathematics orally in Latin, subject to syllogistic forms; and no admirer of Latin can regret the time when the moderator could be heard to say "*Verte canem ex*," or "*Facimus tam bene sine quam cum*," or when to the moderator's dismissal of a disputant in the words "*Descendas domine*," the student answered "*Non descendebo*."

---

Bishop Thirlwall's Remains.†—The first two volumes of Bishop Thirlwall's Remains were noticed last year in the June number of this Review. They consisted entirely of "Charges," the ordinary mode in which a Bishop expresses what he has to say on all current or contemporary questions. The present volume is made up of "Essays, Speeches, Sermons, &c.," and they are mostly of the same character as the Charges, marked by strong individuality, and setting forth clearly and definitely the bishop's judgment on many questions that occupied the public mind during the course of his long episcopate. The Essays are chiefly reprinted from the *Philological Museum*, a journal which was started by Bishop Thirlwall and his friend Julius Hare, the object of which was to forward "the knowledge and the love of ancient literature." The first is on "The Irony of Sophocles," described truly by the editor, Dr. Perowne, as "a masterpiece of philosophical criticism." The next is on Memnon, which reviews all the legends concerning him, as well as all modern theories, and tries to answer the question who he was. Two of the most interesting are those entitled "Hannibal's Passage of the Alps," and "Some Traditions of Submerged Cities." The first of the "Speeches" is on "The Disabilities of the Jews," delivered as far back as 1848. In opposition to the Primate and almost the whole of the bishops, Thirlwall defended the admission of Jews to Parliament. He did not believe in the bitterness which they were supposed to manifest towards our Lord, and ascribed much of their aversion to Christianity to the treatment they had received at the hands of Christians. Their admission to Parliament would not unchristianize the Legislature, which would still remain Christian in the same degree that the country itself was Christian. Two hundred years ago, when, under Cromwell, the Jews were allowed to settle in England, the country in this sense was unchristianized. The clergy vehemently opposed their settlement, but Cromwell remonstrated that it was surely better to allow the Jews to settle in England where they would see Christianity in its purest form, than suffer them to remain in countries where it was disfigured by numberless corruptions. There was a time when all "heretics and schismatics" were excluded from Parliament, but their admission was a sign of the flexibility and expansiveness of the English constitution, and these would still further appear by the admission of Jews. On the Irish Church question, Bishop Thirlwall advocated concurrent endowment. He was not satisfied with its position as the Established Church of Ireland; [illegible] he did not see the solution of the question which he wished, he [illegible] the measure as the best that could be obtained. One of the last

* [illegible]: Some Account of the Studies at the English Universities in the Eighteenth Century. [illegible] M.A. Cambridge: At the University Press.

† [illegible] and Theological, of Bishop Thirlwall. Vol iii. London: Daldy, Isbister & Co. 1877.

public questions in which Bishop Thirlwall took a deep interest was that which concerned the Athanasian Creed. He did not think the Church would lose anything by having it excluded from the public services. All of it which contained any clear doctrinal statements existed in other creeds, and the rest was what Jeremy Taylor calls "opinions speculative, curiosities of explication, and minute particularities." He believed that among those who were most zealous for the use of this creed there was, unconsciously, a large amount of "pernicious Apollinarian and Eutychian heresy." Of the Sermons here given, one is on "The Apostolical Commission," in which it is shown that even by the interpretation of those "whose language and practice appear to trench most upon this Divine prerogative," none but God only can forgive sins. The words, therefore, "Whose soever sins ye remit are remitted," can only mean a declaration general or particular that sins have been forgiven by God, and such a declaration is made whenever the gospel is preached. Absolution, it is said, in whatever form it may be pronounced, can effect no real change in the state of any man before God. One of the most characteristic and most memorable documents in this volume is the letter to Archbishop Longley on the "Pan-Anglican" gathering in 1867. Bishop Thirlwall could see no good end that was to be gained by it. He feared that it was only a paltry imitation of the great assemblies of bishops which the late Pope was in the habit of convoking at Rome, and he was not without some shrewd suspicions that the ultimate object was to get a declaration on some doctrinal questions, such as those raised by the "Essays and Reviews" or Bishop Colenso's publications. The Bishop of St. David's had an intense dislike to the clerical habit of mind which seeks to effect its purpose by side-winds. There are many other subjects discussed in this volume of great interest to those who are studying the ecclesiastical questions which have of late been agitated in the Church of England.

---

PUBLICATIONS OF THE THEOLOGICAL TRANSLATION FUND.*—Of the works issued by the Theological Translation Fund, those now before us are among the ablest, though, indeed, where all are so able and remarkable, comparisons can hardly be at once general and accurate. The works named below are without both the historical importance and the ability at once critical and constructive which distinguish Baur's celebrated Essay on "Paul" and Kuenen's well-known "History of the Religion of Israel;" but while they cannot claim, like these, to be books that make and mark an epoch, they yet, for more solid reasons, deserve to rank beside them. Zeller has more literary ability than Baur, and as much critical ingenuity, though less inventiveness or originality, and his qualities were never more conspicuously displayed than in the work now before us. Keim and Pfleiderer, again, are superior to both Baur and Kuenen in the insight that comes of spiritual sympathy, in the apprehension that belongs to vivid appreciation of the person, character, and system studied. It is not meant either that Baur was, or that Kuenen is, deficient in the latter quality; but in both cases historical theories and critical aims were too strong to allow the sympathy that begets insight full or even fair play. Their deficiencies were, perhaps, due to their peculiar work, and their deficiencies is but another name for their power to stimulate. When men do so much that what they leave undone is a conspicuous blank, those who see it and feel its danger are impelled to stand forward and attempt to fill it up. Baur has done more than any man in this century to promote the literary and historical criticism of the New Testament, to make our study of it a real and fruitful study, and what he did for the New Testament Kuenen is doing for the Old. His works are works that all scholars must welcome, and most of all those who least agree with him.

Of the works specified above, Zeller's is the oldest. It originated in a series of articles contributed, in 1848-51, to the *Theological Journal*, which Zeller started and edited, and which, as his father-in-law, F. C. Baur, declared, offered "a platform to such as without any reservation or ulterior end whatever, cultivated

---

* The Contents and Origin of the Acts of the Apostles Critically Investigated. By Dr Edward Zeller. To which is prefixed Dr F. Overbeck's Introduction to the Acts, from De Wette's Handbook. Translated by Joseph Dare, B.A. Williams & Norgate.

The History of Jesus of Nazara, freely Investigated in its Connexion with the National Life of Israel, and related in Detail By Dr Theodor Keim. Vols. i and iii., translated by Arthur Ransom: vol. ii. by Rev E. M. Geldart. Williams & Norgate.

Paulinism: a Contribution to the History of Primitive Christian Theology. By Dr. Otto Pfleiderer. Translated by Edward Peters. Williams & Norgate.

[illegible] its own sake alone." The articles were collected, revised, and en-[illegible] in 1854 published as the work now translated. It thus belongs to [illegible] when the Tübingen school was at its zenith, when its inquiries were most promising, its spirit most hopeful, and its literary activity greatest; and [illegible] had no more classic product than this. It is full of the spirit and [illegible] that then reigned in the school. A year or two later all was changed, and Zeller, disappointed in theology, was cultivating Greek philosophy with a [illegible] success that were to make him its most brilliant and genial expositor. [illegible] work on the Acts may be regarded as one of a cycle, completing lines [illegible] that had been opened years before, and making it necessary to open [illegible] and new accesses to the old before further progress was possible. The cycle had commenced with Schneckenburger's well-known work on "The Object or Aim of the Acts." He showed that there ran through the book a parallel between the apostles Peter and Paul, and concluded that its design was apologetic, an apology for Paul addressed to his Jewish antagonists. Baur appropriated the results of Schneckenburger, but interpreted them differently, in harmony with his own critical and historical theory. The design of the Acts was not apologetic, but conciliatory. If Peter was shown in harmony with Paul, Paul was also set in harmony with Peter; Paul was made Petrine, Peter Pauline, in order that the union of the Gentile and Judaic parties into the Christian Church might be promoted. Schwegler, in his "Nachapostolisches Zeitalter," developed these positions still further. Paul was Judaized, the original apostles Paulinised, and so an attempt at mediation and peace made in the form of a history. This theory Zeller accepted, and strove to prove it by a fine and searching criticism of the book, both on its literary and historical sides. He held that the book was "the draft of a proposal for peace presented to the Judaists by the Pauline party," who hoped "by means of concessions to Judaism, to purchase the recognition of the Gentile Christians by the Jewish Christians." Now, the criticism of the Tübingen school was throughout dominated by its historical theory. This theory was based on a given interpretation of certain passages in the great Pauline Epistles, and was rigorously applied to the determination of all the questions concerning the literary and historical criticism of the other books of the New Testament. It was made to determine their aim, their date, their authorship, the place where written, and the readers they addressed. Its influence on Zeller's treatment of the Acts is evident. It made him formulate its aim in the terms quoted above, and it made him fix the date so late as the period 110—125 A.D. It could not be placed earlier, simply because conciliation, on the Tübingen historical theory, was not possible at any earlier point. If the object of the book be not what Zeller affirms, his main evidence of its late origin fails him, and its object cannot be what he says it is, unless his theory as to the historical evolution of primitive Christianity be true. We have thus as nice a case of *petitio principii* as any one could desire. Overbeck, in the essay here prefixed to Zeller, has made it pretty evident that "all we know of the development of the ancient Catholic Church makes such a concession (as Zeller seeks to prove) on the part of the Pauline Christians appear incomprehensible;" and there can now be little doubt that he is right. Overbeck himself is not much more successful in the theory he would substitute, and uses it to prove a late origin of the book. But as Zeller was arbitrary on one side, Overbeck is arbitrary on the other, and together they help us to see that a really scientific criticism must discuss neither the internal nor the external evidences too exclusively, but rather review, co-ordinate, and combine both. It is significant that, since Zeller's work appeared, the tendency has been to assign an older date to the Acts. While Volkmar would, indeed, bring it down to as late as 100—110, critics as dissimilar as Scholten and Meyer, Renan and Lekebusch, Ewald and Trip, think its origin must be placed about the year 80, at least within the first decade after the destruction of Jerusalem. By the way, it is a wonder, in these days of translations, that no one has been moved to translate Lekebusch's "Die Composition und Entstehung der Apostelgeschichte."

Keim's is a very different book from Zeller's,—in every respect a greater book. It is everywhere distinguished by thoroughness, the strenuous struggle of the writer to realise from his own standpoint, and to exhibit to others, the person who forms the centre of his history. Keim is not like Zeller, the representative of a particular school. He is too conservative for Tübingen (as it was when its criticism lived), but much too progressive and advanced for Leipzig and Erlangen. He is a theologian, and believes not simply in the eminence, but in the pre-eminence of Jesus, though it is a pre-eminence that must be denoted by the term historical rather than by the term supernatural. Strauss once complained that Baur's courage had deserted him in the presence of the resurrection of Christ, that he wrote of it with most uncharacteristic obscurity and reserve. So Keim, however critical elsewhere, seems to become as spiritual as intellectual in the presence of Jesus, and surprises now and then by the fresh light he can shed on the character and words of the person he studies. Men who confound free with negative criticism, do not like his interpretation and representation of Jesus,—they do not understand how the history may master the man who tries to master it. Men who think a free critic simply a dangerous person, best unknown or avoided, turn away from him, and miss the advantage of seeing the Christ they love from the standpoint of a man who, while without many of their beliefs and prepossessions, has yet singular freshness and strength of eye. The work is one that satisfies neither the simply natural nor the simply supernatural idea and interpretation of Jesus, but it is also one that no man who wishes to study and understand the Evangelical History, whatever his critical position or doctrinal views, can afford to ignore.

Keim thus speaks as to his temper and standpoint:—

"As to the second point (impartiality), I cannot, it is true, pretend to have attained altogether to Strauss' freedom from pre-supposition. I, like so many kindred minds in Germany and Switzerland, have not sacrificed my heart's interest in the religious sphere of Christianity to a cold neutrality-standpoint, the very neutrality of which becomes the rallying point of a party, and which, in the case of Strauss, in spite of a perceptible, indeed, successful, striving after calm objectivity, has emerged from its chrysalis in the form of a predilection for philosophical pre-suppositions."—P. ix.

And again:—

"It is incumbent upon the history of the life of Jesus, if light is to pierce this darkness, to let the facts speak for themselves as clearly, fully, and impartially as possible; to do this even more conscientiously than in any other department of history; and cautiously and carefully, with the reservation of the right of an independent judgment upon every detail, to restrict the province of supposition and inference and general verdict, to the narrowest possible limits. This implies an equal, impartial attention to the facts which support the one or the other standpoint, and an equal, impartial renunciation of those points of view which do violence to history, whether, Strauss-like, they strike miracle out of history beforehand, or, with the opposite school, recognize miracle as belonging to the idea of history; for in controverted questions the decision belongs to history alone, and if history cannot decide, no one can. This is an impartiality which certainly is not granted to all, but only to those who have freed themselves from the narrow rules of the Church on the one hand, and from the formulas of Science on the other, because their mental characters have been nourished, not merely by one or the other, but by both mothers. Nevertheless, a fundamental conviction cannot be dispensed with—one that is ever present to give light and warmth to the whole from the beginning: and this must be such a conviction as, so far as the subject permits, is built upon a careful logical induction from the facts, and must be held without attempting to force the opinion of any who may not be able to follow. To betray in one sentence our own latest sentiments, no conviction has become more certain to us, in our contemplation of this life, than that there, where the most genuine and unadulterated humanity dwelt, was revealed at the same time, not only a religious genius, but the miracle of God and His presence upon earth; the person itself, and nothing else, is the miracle; the God-confederated man is the living temple of God."—Vol. i. pp. 9, 10.

The work is not yet fully translated, though the last volume of the German edition was published so long ago as 1872. The time has thus not yet come for an exhaustive review, and all that is here possible is to express our general idea of the work. It is a model of German thoroughness—nothing that could illustrate its great Subject or was in any way related to Him has been neglected. Geography, physiography, chronology, history, religion, literature, art, all are laid under contribution. And as the author has spared himself no labour, he spares his readers none. We have his processes as well as his results, and those are often better than these. It is not a book for an indolent man, or a hasty or ignorant reader, but essentially a book written by a student for students. It is a book that eminently requires the exercise of reason, and, indeed, the reason informed and practised. The competent reader, whatever his school of theology, will find himself often differing from the author and for reasons supplied by himself. His interpretations are often violent and arbitrary; his criticism often rash and wayward. His resolution of the six husbands of the Samaritan woman into the five heathen religions and the maimed, impure religion of Jehovah known in Samaria (though he is anything but singular in this interpretation, as it is essentially that of men so unlike as Strauss and Hengstenberg), and of the parable of the Prodigal Son into a story of late origin, which had arisen out of the post-apostolic reconciliation of the two opposed parties in the Church, are cases in point. The critical discussions in the first volume are full of judgments we cannot but question, and conclusions we dispute. We cannot allow that Mark's Gospel is an epitome of Matthew and Luke, written by "an author in a flower-bedecked garment," and that it did not originate till about the year 100. While recognizing the merit of his full and vigorous discussion of the Johannean question, we cannot allow that he is either warranted or quite consistent in his denial of the Johannean authorship of the Fourth Gospel. But these are points which cannot be discussed here. We conclude our notice with an extract that may be regarded as indicating Dr. Keim's peculiar and distinctive theological position.

"The more human, the more deeply imbedded in the historic growth of the race these facts discover themselves, the less will they let us doubt. But if there are points in this life, such for example as the moral faultlessness of Jesus, his unsullied sense of God, his sunbright conception of his Fatherhood, his wonders, his resurrection, his boundless self-assertion, which far transcend at once all the attainments and all the consciousness of the soundest and most signally commissioned links in the chain of humanity, and hence, at the same time, transcend that chain itself, as regards the law of its experience: we confess our inability, to begin with, to call in question inviolable certainties with the levelling arts of a Strauss; but as little are we able either—though it be at the risk of again laying ourselves fairly open to the charge of having strayed out of history into the old false dogmatism and mysticism at the hands of the most advanced spirit of the age—to refrain from the acknowledgment that in the person of Jesus a higher human organisation than heretofore was called into being by that creative will of God, that runs in parallel though viewless course side by side with the processes of creaturely procreation. If it must have a name, it can bear no better one than that which Paul found for it at the outset: a new creation in mankind, a consummation, a desensualization, a spiritualization, a deification, of the Godlike image."—Vol. ii. pp. 63, 64.

"But here the divine energy, say we rather the divine self-communication, is one that with unbroken might breaks through; it is a whole, full, blameless life, no piecework, no mixture of the lofty and the base; it is a divine creation in full force of largest love; for it is the completion of man as man, the issuing of the creation into the being of the Creator, the blest repose of God in the work of His own hands. It is the realized ideal of God in His creation, and it is more than a creation; to speak in figures, for of the Highest we can use no other language, a divine formation of His own being's kin and being's like in humanity, a coming of the essential Godhead to men, inasmuch as above and beyond all unlikeness between the divine and human nature rises the higher unity of holy life and inseverable communion in spirit, mind, and love, the presage of an ever-broadening breach of sundering boundaries, which the eternal God has yet in store, in regions wider than the earth, for his eternities; yes, for his mankind of the future."—Vol. ii. p. 66.

Dr. Keim is not an easy writer to translate. His style is full of the qualities that most tax a translator's skill—is graphic, forcible, often laden with suppressed thought, too vivid to be subdued, marked at times by great beauty, but also by phrases and turns of expression that startle at once by their vigour and questionable taste. The translators have been tolerably successful, though, as in the above passages, the rendering is not the happiest and best possible.

Pfleiderer's work professes to be "a contribution to the History of Primitive Christian Theology," and no scholar will deny that what it professes to be it in great measure is. Dr. Pfleiderer is one of the ablest of the younger German theologians. His work "Die Religion," with its sequel, "Die Moral," was distinguished by equal fineness of philosophical criticism and historical analysis. And the same qualities are apparent here, and find ample scope for their exercise. This work was suggested, like so many more of our latest works on Paul, by the striking and able essays of Holsten. Pfleiderer says:—

"It was Holsten's brilliant idea of starting from Paul's conversion, and the psychological pre-suppositions and inferences connected with it, in order to grasp the kernel of his Gospel in its peculiarity, that suggested to me the task of endeavouring to understand how, from this nucleus of Paul's faith in Christ, on the one hand, and the pre-supposition of his Jewish theology, on the other, the Pauline [illegible] existence; and what is the particular [illegible]

The method is the right one; the man and [illegible] the personality is revealed, becomes articulate, [illegible] derer is right, too, in regarding Paul as hardly [illegible] culture was essentially Hebrew. His theology, [illegible] throughout the traces of his Jewish training, in his [illegible] of sacrifice, of sin and righteousness. In his very revolt [illegible] homage to its power over his spirit, confessed the might of [illegible] once embodied and buried, and which he, by the light [illegible] transfigured and universalized. His revolt was due to [illegible] "the revelation of Jesus Christ," the memorable [illegible] His Son in him. The new circle of thought, in which [illegible] him had as its centre the crucifixion of Christ. "As [illegible] grace, the expiatory death was the means of creating a [illegible] *ness*, which is no longer in any respect a human achievement [illegible] entirely a gift of God, which is not obtained by works of [illegible] in the new divine scheme of salvation by the death and [illegible] We differ, at times radically, from Dr. Pfleiderer's inter[illegible] Pauline and post-Pauline theology, but none the less we [illegible] form a book that had been familiar and useful to us in its [illegible]

---

MATHESON'S GROWTH OF THE SPIRIT OF CHRISTIANITY.* — [illegible] Mr. Matheson, is equivalent to development, and in the [illegible] developments of Christianity, he shows its own natural [illegible] of its growth, while he traces the inner causes of events as the[illegible] selves in history. The book is essentially philosophical, and [illegible] seems to be a Protestant of a very orthodox school, he is [illegible] reason, but rather delights in looking upon Christianity as a [illegible] sophical religion. While hesitating to admit the principle of the [illegible] Christian religion was nothing more than the flower of [illegible] entire disagreement with those who depict Paganism as [illegible] that Christianity may shine by the contrast. That [illegible] reversal of all previous beliefs is shown to have been the [illegible] among early Christian writers; it is not until the time of [illegible] sharp separation is made between nature and grace, and that [illegible] against the earth as its antithesis and destroyer. Augustine, [illegible] have gone too far in picturing the virtues of the heathen as [illegible] own nature prevented him doing injustice to the speculations of [illegible] For Christianity to have been altogether a new thing in the [illegible] Matheson says, be much commendation. "A revelation which [illegible] original would have been altogether useless. Whatever reve[illegible] must reveal itself to my experience, and the deeper that experie[illegible] speaks the more perfect will be the revelation. The book which [illegible] be that book which awakens most, which stirs up the longest [illegible] which strikes the oldest chord in our nature."

These sentiments will explain the ground from which Mr. [illegible] survey of Christianity. It had old truth, but it had also [illegible] new it met the defects of Paganism. The old world never [illegible] Cross. It worshipped what was strong, but could not [illegible] Spirit as united to what was weak or lowly. But Christianity [illegible] it found the remedy for the world's evils in suffering. [illegible] which is on the preparation for the Cross, treats of the [illegible] having least affinity to Christianity being regarded as the [illegible] Chinese, which is at the utmost possible distance from [illegible] Divine sacrifice. Its chief idea of God is immutability [illegible] Hinduism, where God is continually undergoing changes, [illegible] a multitude of incarnations. Here we approach Christian[illegible] volves a cross, or the limiting of an infinite nature. [illegible] vague, and the human mind ceased to have a grasp of [illegible]

---

* The Growth of the Spirit of Christianity. By the Rev. George [illegible] Clark. 1877.

[illegible] Buddhism, or the religion of despair. Man looked at nothingness in [illegible] worship, and saw no blessedness but in ceasing to be. Parsism, [illegible] the same sense of unrest, finds its origin in a principle of evil [illegible]. The soul of man found that its misery is in its absence from the [illegible] light. Perhaps at this moment Abraham was called from Ur of the [illegible]. In Judaism appears with a new force the recognition of the secret of [illegible] perception of a violated moral power. The worship of Adonis in [illegible] a tendency in the direction of the worship of suffering, and in the [illegible] the Egyptians we see the human soul struggling to free itself from its [illegible] chains. In Greece man deifies himself. He rises to the gods, conquering [illegible] nature, and though the idea is not so much God becoming man as man [illegible] God, yet Greece first grasps the possibility of a permanent union between [illegible] and the Divine. Christianity gathered into itself the chief ideas of [illegible] world. "There are," says Mr. Matheson, "only three ways in which [illegible] think of God,—either as the unknown being dwelling above all his [illegible] or as the Spirit which pervades and animates these works, or as endued with a human form and found in fashion as a man. Between these views the [illegible] world was divided; and when there appeared a religion which blended and [illegible] them all in one, it inevitably gathered to itself those beliefs which had [illegible] scattered and discordant."

The work consists of thirty-two chapters, the very titles of which would occupy more than the space at our command. After the three preliminary chapters of which we have spoken, the author treats of the birthplace of the spirit of Christianity, and how it stood related to the Pharisees, the Sadducees, and the Essenes. He then comes to the transition from infancy to childhood, when Christ appears among men and his Spirit informs the Church. The rise of different parties is traced, and the departure of Christianity from its birthplace to become a great power in the Gentile world. The early centuries of Christianity pass in review, with the great events of the first Councils, the struggles with Paganism, and the contentions in the Church of North Africa. This is followed by a history of the rise of Mohammedanism and the beginning of the scholastic ages. Then comes a history of the rise of the Papacy, and its long conflict with the civil rulers. The Church in the dark ages had become the world. Justice is done to the great Churchmen, such as Hildebrand, and to the zeal of St. Francis and St. Dominic, with the orders which they founded. The influence of the Mystics is also prominently set forth, with that of all the precursors of the Reformation. Mr. Matheson's work is fresh, vigorous, learned, and eminently thoughtful.

---

ZOECKLER'S CROSS OF CHRIST.*—Dr. Zoeckler has set out with an excellent subject, and if he had somewhat narrowed his lines and then kept strictly within them, would have produced a work such as we have none too many of. He might have taken one of two courses and, following either of them, would have produced a very readable book. He might have treated the cross as a branch of Christian symbolism, and written a work such as those of Mrs. Jameson or Mr. Hemans. The cross as a symbol enters largely into questions of art and archæology, and though this branch of the subject is interesting chiefly to a small circle of art critics, it would have its specialty as such, and perhaps would throw some side-lights on the opinions and practices of the early or mediæval Church. On the other hand, Dr. Zoeckler might have discarded symbolism and taken up *symbolik*, or the comparative history of creeds. He might have handled the question exclusively as a theologian, and presented to us a history of Christian doctrine as seen in the light of the cross. Either of these lines of argument would have furnished material for a monograph, but the desire for completeness has led Dr. Zoeckler to attempt too much. As it is, we are confused between the symbolical and the doctrinal chapters. Much of the former is curious reading for those who are interested in the history of iconography. The chapters, for instance, on the cross in the pre-Christian and extra-Christian religious systems contain some good hints mixed with much that is fanciful and which will not bear criticism. What Dr. Zoeckler describes as staurosophic mysticism might be passed on one side as irrelevant if not trifling. We do not care to discuss whether

* The Cross of Christ. Studies in the History of Religion and the Inner Life of the Church. By Otto Zoeckler, D.D., Professor of Theology, in Greifswald. Translated, with the co-operation of the author, by the Rev. [illegible] J. Evans, B.A. London: Hodder and Stoughton. 1877.

Christ was crucified on a three-armed cross, or to know
of the Egyptian Ansate cross may be. It is now admit
constantly occurring in Egyptian hieroglyphics has no r
ever, or that it was in any sense an anticipation of th
Christian faith. The day is long past for these wild s
as to the prefiguration of this mystery in heathen art.
these correspondences of certain external symbols in h
the author seems to find a strange fascination in them.
vein is in the fibre of his mind, and, repressed in one
another. The following illustrates our meaning:—

"In the uplifted banner of Salvation, which is to the Jews
a folly, we see all at once intersecting each other the two lin
of man and the Divine call of grace; lines running side by sid
separation throughout all previous ages. They intersect e
opposition, and with such mighty impact that the dark line c
the heart with deadly effect by the bright line of salvation.
Life, towards which the longing of all nations had been dire
the poisonous Tree of Knowledge, fruitful in misery, bef
trembled, and under whose death-shade they had sighed; th
formed into one: and over that figure, lifeless and bare, but
hope of salvation, stands written in the fiery characters of D
swallowed up in victory.'"

The underlying thought here contained is a good one,
and the metaphors broken, through the writer's straining
"the Tree of Knowledge, before whose arrows they had t
death-shade they had sighed." This is a fine "derangen
expression, "the sin-curse was pierced to the heart by th
is obscure for the same reason. It is an old conceit
the two trees of Paradise joined together made up the t
upright one being taken from the Tree of Life, the trans
the Tree of Knowledge. But applications of this kind
They are of as little help in elucidating sound doctri
Jewish Cabbalists, such as the names of the Sephiroth o
were grouped together to represent, at one time a tree wi
and at another an erect human being. The field of sta
exhaustless one for those who care to explore it. The la
symbol lifted upon the air, and in this sense a sign of Ch
in the upper and under world, and against spiritual wick
been urged by many of the Eastern Fathers. In modern
of Nettelsheim to Jacob Bohmen and others, the same v
Much of the work is taken up with enumerating these fa
has little space left for the sober, spiritual exegesis of t
"I am crucified with Christ."

As a whole, then, the work, notwithstanding its var
spirit, disappoints us, since it is neither one thing nor th
symbolism it has been anticipated by writers like the la
the other hand, as an outline of Christian doctrine, it is t
matic to be of much use to the theological student. A l
one thing, of Christian doctrine another—it is only a Ge
thus run symbolism and *symbolik* into one mould. Th
confused image, and we are reminded of old Horace's r

> "Amphora cœpi
> Institui, currente rotâ cur urceus exi
> Denique sit quidvis simplex dumtax

---

Adler's Creed and Deed.*—These Lectures (with
motto from Æschylus, ἔργῳ κοὺ λόγῳ (which we need not
thing as the title), were published first in New York, by
Society of Ethical Culture;" of which we have many of
and then. Dr Adler appears to be a cultivated Jew.
without the name, the Positivist faith—if we must

* Creed and Deed. A Series of Discourses. By Felix Adler, Ph.D L

"creed" is to be set aside. We say *if* we must, because it is obvious that, however we may talk of placing our deeds before our creeds, our actions must on the whole and ultimately be governed by what we think. The position of him who says, "I cannot make up my mind as to this, that, or the other creed, but I can and will go and do the deed which is everywhere pronounced good by cultivated man," is intelligible enough. True, action will ultimately compel the mind to evolve consciously a creed of some kind, and unconsciously a creed there always is; but plain duties carry with them much comfort to the storm-tossed or doubting spirit, especially if they be such as make large demands upon its sympathies. A society of ethical culture, *irrespective* of creed, is also intelligible as a conception; but in practice it will be found that in such a society there is always at work a very pronounced creed of negations.

We have no desire to say anything hard, or to underrate the generosity or the usefulness of any sincere effort to promote human good,—heaven knows the field is large enough and the labourers few enough,—but we think scarcely any one new to the subject could read these discourses on such matters as Immortality, the New Ideal, the Priest of the Ideal, and the like, without a chill, and, in addition, a sense of emptiness. "There is no God; no future life; let us console ourselves with—this fine spring day; that pretty picture; the kindness of our friends; and the probability that those who come after us will be the better for our lives and labours." That is all; and it would be idle to deny that goodness may exist with no more approach to a "creed" than this. But on what scale? for how long? whether as more than a cut flower in water? or with what propagating power? are of course vital questions. It would be unjust to Mr. Adler to conceal that the one who writes this notice holds, with the very utmost intensity of conviction, that the whole of this business is foredoomed to failure, and is in itself illogical. Those who fancy that they take a purely disinterested pleasure of mere forecast in the happiness of future generations, deceive themselves. They are like old Featherstone, in "Middlemarch," who, when he made his will, imagined himself *alive* in his coffin, enjoying what took place above ground.

As an expounder, Dr. Adler has strongly-marked capacities. The papers which he has reprinted in the appendix belong to the most destructive school of Biblical criticism, and are open to plenty of comment; but they are remarkably clear, and well adapted to the author's purpose.

---

TAIT'S SERMONS.*—A volume of occasional sermons by a Continental chaplain would scarcely, as a rule, call for remark. They have served the purpose for which they were printed if they are read by the members of the British Diaspora for whom they were prepared in the first instance. But these sermons of Mr. Tait's, and especially the Appendix on the Incarnation, have this merit, that, while they are written on the old lines of Evangelical orthodoxy, they also bring out that view of the Person of Christ which is the true key to His mission and work. The question which the four first councils were supposed to have set at rest by the dogma of "two natures in one person" was not an end of all strife, as it was intended to be. The question took a new point of departure with the Monothelite controversy. If there were two natures in one person, by which nature were the miracles wrought, and in which nature did Christ suffer and die? It is no explanation of the mystery to fall back on such a metaphor as that of Hooker, viz., that "the sword which is made fiery doth not only cut by reason of the sharpness which it hath, but also burn by means of the heat which it hath from the fire." For the question will recur, When was it the cutting sword, and when the fiery sword, by which our Master wrought and suffered? The true key to the doctrine of the Incarnation is the expression, Phil. ii. 7, He emptied Himself. This was practically overlooked by the early Church, and the Lutheran school of divines only touched upon it when, for their own controversial ends, they wished to establish the theory of the *communicatio idiomatum*. The expression in Phil. ii. 7 teaches us that the Eternal Logos, who was with God and who was God, used His equality with God not as an opportunity for self-exaltation, but for self-abasement. And this brings us to the point which Mr. Tait has so well and carefully worked out. Starting with a statement of Ebrard that it is "only an Absolute Being who is able to limit

---

* Sermons, Expository and Practical, preached in England and France. With Appendices on Incarnation, Atonement, and Ritual. By William Tait, M.A., Incumbent of Trinity Church, Pau, France. London: Hamilton, Adams, & Co. 1877.

himself, and that because he is Absolute and his own Lor
that this is the abiding contrast between the creature an

"We cannot limit ourselves. They tell of the great New induced to learn the propositions of Euclid. He saw their *and could not help doing so.* And Lord Macaulay, as is wel that he was not able to forget. But the Son of the Blessed, b among men are not—absolute and His own Lord, was able divine prerogative. This is the true key to the Incarnation. 'Christ emptied Himself of all but love.'"

We may add that it is this which explains the otherwise Messianic prophecy, "Who is blind as my servant? or de sent?" (Isaiah xlii. 19). Our Lord was, all through His He had no self-will; His hour was not come when, in co of the disciples was always ready. He was the only be breath, in whom the Divine Spirit was as the breath of life separate from God, and to whom the Spirit was measure. This is a topic which we have not space to en remark that the short paper on the Incarnation is a mo explains the apparent contradictions of the union of the old dogmatic definitions fail to do. We should wish that for such studies, would expand this lecture into a trea purged of that mystical conception of a continued incarn detracts from such works as that of the late Archdeacon who see beyond the *Cur Deus Homo* of Anselm.

---

WOOD'S NATHAN THE WISE.*—The first question ask up a new book is what is its *raison d'être*, to which the an none, the book ought never to have been brought into exis must be our verdict in the present case. If Lessing had wri might have been grateful for any translation that gave original, whatever might be its shortcomings in other re from a German work which has certainly twice already one very readable and idiomatic, if not always perfectly Norwich, the other more accurate, though less spirited, by expected to show a competent knowledge of the German la command of English style and an acquaintance with the The latest translation of "Nathan" fails in all respe allow us to quote a few lines in which his English makes but, wherever we have compared the three versions, w by far the least satisfactory.

Act I., Scene 2. Recha *loq.*

"Ihr musstet über
Den Euphrat, Tigris, Jordan; über—wer
Weiss was für Wasser all?"

*Wood*:—"You must have crossed Euphrates, Tigris,
I know not all what streams you must hav

*Taylor*:— "You had to cross
The Jordan, Tigris, and Euphrates, and
Who knows what rivers else?"

Act V., Scene 6. Sittah *loq.*

"So jung! so klug
Was du nicht alles weisst! nicht alles mus
Gelesen haben!"

*Wood*:— "So young! so pr
So innocent! What all know'st thou? W
Must thou have read!"

*Taylor*:—"So young, so good, so prudent, so much kn
You must have read a great deal to be thu

* Nathan the Wise Translated into English blank verse. By Andrew burgh. W. P Nimmo.

Act I., Scene 2. Nathan *log.*

"Der Wunder höchstes ist,
Dass uns die wahren, echten Wunder so
Alltäglich werden können, werden sollen."

Wood:—"The greatest wonder is that real wonders
To us so common can, and should become."

Reich:— "The greatest of all wonders
Is that to us the real true wonders can
Become so commonplace, and must become so."

---

THOMAS COOPER'S POETICAL WORKS.*—Whether the revival of his name in the "Life of Charles Kingsley" has induced Mr. Cooper to favour the public with a collection of his poems, we are unable to say, but we think some reason was required for their reproduction besides the literary merits of the poems themselves. It may be necessary to inform some of our readers that Mr. Cooper was once a Chartist and a Freethinker, and that, unlike George Grote, he has retained his radicalism though he has parted with his theological heterodoxy. "The Purgatory of Suicides," which was a work of his unregenerate days, is now republished, though "without hesitation I have expunged lines and stanzas which I found contained misstatements of fact, or which I thought violated right feeling." But "errors which have been repeatedly confessed and openly abandoned" are retained, "as part of a mind-history." Thus we have the suet of iniquity without the plums of naughtiness. It may be doubted whether "Every man his own Bowdler" is a sound principle of literary action, and whatever the "Purgatory of Suicides" may once have been, we do not think it will now entrap the unwary or scandalize the sensitive. We do not know that we can give a better idea of the poem, which consists of ten books and extends over 272 pages, than by quoting a stanza, selected *ad aperturam libri*, and neither better nor worse, so far as we can see, than any other:—

"But lo! a sudden, silent pallor seized
The hostile crew, beholding where upreared
A shape threatening as spectre unappeased
By devilish wizard, who beholds afeard
The power his sable mischief hath unsphered,
But lacks the deeper skill to lay. Atween
Two cirque-stones vast the huge gray shape appeared
So stone-like, and so blind, yet stern of mien,
That naught proclaimed it human save its gaberdine."

"Sable mischief," is, we presume, a pleasing variation for "black art;" but we challenge Mr. Cooper to explain what "unsphering a power" may be. What precise amount of humanity remains in a being which has nothing human about it but a "gaberdine," we are unable to conjecture, but we feel sure that this sort of thing cannot do much harm; only, if the "Purgatory of Suicides" still finds readers, it would appear that "the Many," to use Mr. Cooper's phrase, who do not publish verses, have not yet "ceased their slavery to the Few" who do.

Perhaps the best of Mr. Cooper's shorter pieces, which are allowed small space, by the portentous length of the "Purgatory of Suicides" and the "Paradise of Martyrs," is "The Chartist Chaunt," from which, in justice to him, we quote the first stanza.

"Truth is growing—hearts are glowing
With the flame of liberty;
Light is breaking—thrones are quaking—
Hark! the trumpet of the free!
Long, in lowly whispers breathing,
Freedom wandereth dimly,
Still in faith her laurel wreathing
For the day when there should be
Freemen shouting 'Victory!'"

---

* The Poetical Works of Thomas Cooper. London: Hodder & Stoughton.

But if all the people who could write up to this level were to take advantage of their power, it is appalling to think what a consumption of ink and paper there would be.

Happily for Mr. Cooper, his fame does not rest solely upon his verses, which cannot interfere with the popularity of his Autobiography. It is easy to see from that work that its author has always been, notwithstanding his change of opinions, a man of sincere convictions and honest purposes, as well as of popular sympathies and unselfish character. Chartism is now regarded as an extinct chimera, but beside the mischievous nonsense of the "Young England" party, which obtained a brief immortality from the muse of Lord John Manners and still lives in the pages of "Sybil," the principles of Mr. Cooper and his friends appear triumphs of statesmanlike wisdom. Parson Lot and the Christian Socialists have had their day, and Mr. Greg's essay upon them seems now like a slaughter of the slain. But the historical interest of a struggle survives the cause of conflict, and as a veteran friend of the people, Mr. Cooper is entitled to rank with Charles Kingsley and Frederick Maurice.

---

PROMETHEUS THE FIRE-GIVER.*—This is "an attempted restoration of the lost first part of the Promethean Trilogy of Æschylus." The author addresses to Æschylus a poetical dedication, in which the following impressive, but slightly obscure lines occur :—

"I lean into the ghost-filled night,
And my will pierces on to dreams
Of shapes and shades that seem to sight—
Till one, thine own, so sought for! seems."

The drama opens with our old friends Clotho, Lachesis, and Atropos, each of whom sings a short song. Lachesis, we are sorry to see, has not kept up her Greek prosody, and so begins—

"We, Ourānos' ancient might,"

and so forth (p. 4). She is, however, kept in countenance by Prometheus himself, who speaks of (p. 59)

"Where the dread might of Oceănus reigns."

Nor is the chorus of Oceanides unassailable from a metrical point of view, such a line as (p. 18)

"On his foes Empire and Victory heaped ruin and rout"

being easier to admîre than to scan. Our poet is, as many poets are, rather fond of blood, and perhaps the following example of his taste may serve as a warning to others. Man personified offers a sacrifice to the gods, that they

"May have full gladness, and the scent of blood,
Slowly out-dripped from agonizing veins,
May fill your pleasured nostrils through red hours."

The work before us, which seems modelled on Mr. Swinburne's Erechtheus, abounds in strophes and antistrophes, though our author (pp. 23, 24), does not seem to be aware that the antistrophe is expected to correspond with the strophe in metre. However, a στιχομυθία extending over thirteen pages (33—46) makes up for many technical shortcomings, especially when it is so happily conceived in the spirit, if not the form, of Bohn. It may perhaps be necessary to say that this volume describes the gift of fire by Prometheus to man; and if the reader consults p. 56, and is not reminded of the Chinaman and the roast pig, it will be because he has not read Lamb. We take our leave of this pretentious volume, which is apparently designed to rank with the contributions of Æschylus and Shelley on the same subject by quoting the last line, which runs,

"And thinking of thy gains shall ease my pains."

Surely the music of Shelley and the force of Æschylus are united in such poetry as this. Is it by Alderman Cotton?

---

* Prometheus the Fire-Giver.

BENNOCH'S POEMS.*—It has long been proverbial how hard it is to unite poetry and business. But Mr. Bennoch has succeeded in doing it. In this volume, he, a successful man of business, offers to his readers a collection of poetry not much less in bulk than the works of his countryman Burns. It is true he has had the advantage of a longer stretch of time. The first sentence of his preface runs—"Nearly forty years ago, I published a small volume of poems." During this long period Mr. Bennoch, in all the busy activity of mercantile life, has kept the flame of poetry burning brightly.

Taking the book as a whole, it may safely be affirmed of it, that it is a volume of sound healthy verse. A number of the pieces will win laughter,—some of them will go near to earn a tear. In the earlier compositions, the influence on Mr. Bennoch of Wordsworth, with whom he was upon terms of friendship, seems to us to be visible. At any rate, the most lengthy poem, "The Storm," shows a similar choice of homely subject, with a liking for pushing incident to a point of rude tragedy; and there is, though in a lesser degree, and of a less recluse kind, the same out-door feeling for the joys of the country, and the changing seasons of the year. In the course of the volume, nearly the whole calendar is celebrated. The second chief poem of the book, "Sir Ralph de Rayne and Lilian Grey," exhibits ability for finding a theme in old legend, such as Scott would have revelled in. The "Noviomagian Brotherhood," to whom the poem is dedicated, will not often have a "laureate" of equal merit. If this sounds rather mysterious, we can only say that the reader will find it all explained by referring to Mr. Bennoch's notes.

The special charm of the book to us lies in the striking illustration it affords of how literature can be the companion of daily life, heightening its common matters by special touches of enjoyment in the mere glad recital of them. The volume is a kind of poetical autobiography. Few things have happened to Mr. Bennoch that he has not turned into verse. He has made the muse walk by his side and sing to him of his own concerns. Of late years poetry has grown very high and mighty; bards can no longer spare a sonnet to a friend. Mr. Bennoch has kept up the older more genial habits. Besides celebrating his own domestic happiness and his friendships,—in which he must have been very fortunate,—he shows a plentiful interest in public matters. Always the sympathy is broad and robust, whether he is writing a song for the Switzers, hymning the old Covenanters, or pleading—when it was not fashionable to do so—for Ireland. However, it is his native Scotland which always touches him most.

---

THE LOVE-LETTERS OF JOHN KEATS.†—This book is inscribed to Mr. Severn, and whatever reminds us of his heroic friendship for Keats is welcome. Heroic the friendship must have been, for apart from the more obvious aspects of the case (which Mr. Severn would be the last to think of) there was poor Keats's awful temper, and the peculiarly distressing character of the illness which at last made an end of him—a sore trial it must have been to the most patient nurse. The volume before us has an etching by Mr. W. B. Scott, from a drawing of the sufferer's head made by Mr. Severn (to keep him awake), at three o'clock one morning, less than a month before the end came. It is a most painful thing to look at—the hair matted with the death-dew, and the face drawn with pain. But we did not *need* Mr. Cowden Clarke's assurance to Mr. Forman that the likeness is good. It is easy enough to recognize in this mask of the grave the same features as those which are familiar in the portrait in which Keats is looking out upon us with his chin upon his hand. If any one should find the recognition difficult, there is help in another portrait, that is or was in the National Portrait Gallery, in which Keats is seated (in nankeen trousers, under a tree, as we remember) reading. This gives an intermediate view of the face, which is instructive.

If the fireside talk over these letters could be collected from half-a-dozen cultivated homes, and published, it would constitute a more edifying comment than any reviewer can write. But the fireside talk could never get printed, even if it

---

* Poems, Lyrics, Songs, and Sonnets By Francis Bennoch. London · Hardwicke and Bogue

† Letters of John Keates to Fanny Brawne, written in the years MDCCCXIX. and MDCCCXX., and now given from the Original Manuscripts: with Introduction and Notes by Harry Buxton Forman London: Reeves & Turner.

were collected. Nor will any reviewer say a tenth part of what he thinks about this love story.

One thing is exceedingly obvious, though perhaps not always remembered. Love-letters cannot tell their story truly unless we are made welcome to the part which both the lovers took in the correspondence. Nor even then can we pluck out the heart of the mystery. The happiest and most straightforward courtship under the sun is only a series of attempts and experiments on both sides. Now it is Strephon that draws back, and now it is Chloe. To-day Strephon is "plunging and curvetting in his course," goaded by impulses that he cannot command; to-morrow Chloe writes oddly, lest she should betray that she is "sick with love." The lovers have the key to the cryptograph no other soul has or can have. In Letter V. of this series (16th August, 1819) Keats draws back. In Letter VI. (14th September) he is more "coming-on," and a great deal more full of notes of interrogation. In letter VII. (11th October) we find his reserve, whatever was the secret of it, has broken down—*an affectionate movement towards him on the lady's part* appears to have clinched the engagement. "My sweet girl, I am living to-day in yesterday. . . . Tell me you will never, for ever, be less kind to me than yesterday. . . ." And the letter ends, after the signature, with a sigh—"Ah herté mine!" The next letter (13th October) is similar in tone, and Keats says to the lady, "I have ceased to reason against the reasons of my love." Now, there were reasons enough why Keats, whether as a young poet, as a penniless adventurer, or as a man who was, to use an Americanism, "shot," should reason against his love, and hold back; but nobody can tell how much reasoning intent there was in the reserve which he had just practised, or how much of the mere practical logic of love. Of course a lover is not satisfied till he sees the beloved is at his mercy, and, of course, in every impassioned courtship there comes a time when he has to break her stiff neck; and it is naturally some accident which determines this time. We all understand a man like Goethe, when he really tells us that he "tries" if he can "renounce" Lili or some other *holde wesen*; he had no reason but his own resolve not to give himself away. But it was otherwise with Keats. On the one hand he was poor, and more than half conscious that his chances of life were, at the best, worth little, and he had a lurking sense that for so young a man, with such ambitions, to marry would be, from one point of view, suicidal. On the other hand, the intimacy had now gone to some length, and he was a pledged man.

These particular letters, then (one of which Mr. Forman rightly calls "extraordinary"), stand unexplained, until we know the other side of the correspondence. A score of explanations may be suggested, but either of them might all just as easily prove wrong as right. This, indeed, is the inherent difficulty of the case. Some of Keats's letters are very angry and bitter, but with the exception of what he says about poor Brown, who was evidently a good friend, we can by no means decide how much of these outbreaks was excusable or more than excusable.

Some of the letters display, as was to be expected, great force of expression, but the light in which, on the whole, they present Keats to us is very painful, and not instructive in proportion. Of the lady we gather nothing, except what is confirmed by the silhouette portrait of her,—namely, that she had a strong will, a full share of self-reliance, and a good understanding prone to specialities of pursuit. Whether she had or had not the unworldliness or the capacity of responding to downright passion which the nature of a man like Keats would have looked for, not to say exacted, we have scant means of judging. The picture that burns itself into our mind is that of the author of "Hyperion" and the "Ode to a Nightingale," very poor, and tormented in a thousand ways. He was under sentence of death, and he knew it: and yet he is nearly always trying to flatter himself out of the knowledge. There are traces—some subtle, and some very plain—that he was not at ease in the depths of his nature even about the quality and chances of this passion, *as* a passion. He must have feared that this marriage, under any possible circumstances, could only hamper him as a poet; and so he went on fretting his life away under the falsehood of the situation. "The world is too brutal for me; I am glad there is such a thing as the grave. . . . I wish I was in your arms, full of faith, or that a Thunderbolt would strike me. God bless you. J. K." These are the last words, so far as we know, that Keats ever wrote in the way of love-letters.

The lady appears to have been much wiser than he was, and so does "Brown." Both seem to have understood that, however the company of the betrothed might please the lover, the quickening of the pulse and the breathing was not all good for

[illegible] —[illegible] how hard it is to unite poetry [illegible] But Mr. Bennoch has succeeded in doing it. In this volume, he [illegible] offers to his readers a collection of poetry not much [illegible] the words of his countryman, Burns. It is true he has had the [illegible] stretch of time. The first sentence of his preface runs— [illegible] I published a small volume of poems." During this [illegible] Mr. Bennoch, in all the busy activity of mercantile life, has kept the [illegible].

[illegible] as a whole, it may safely be affirmed of it, that it is a volume [illegible] verse. A number of the pieces will win laughter,—some of them [illegible]. In the earlier compositions, the influence on Mr. [illegible] Wordsworth, with whom he was upon terms of friendship, seems to us [illegible] at any rate, the most lengthy poem, "The Storm," shows a similar [illegible] homely subject, with a liking for pushing incident to a point of rude [illegible] there is, though in a lesser degree, and of a less recluse kind, the [illegible] feeling for the joys of the country, and the changing seasons of the year. In the course of the volume, nearly the whole calendar is celebrated. [illegible] chief poem of the book, "Sir Ralph de Rayne and Lilian Grey," [illegible] ability for finding a theme in old legend, such as Scott would have [illegible] The "Noviomagian Brotherhood," to whom the poem is dedicated, [illegible] often have a "laureate" of equal merit. If this sounds rather mysterious, [illegible] only say that the reader will find it all explained by referring to Mr. [illegible] notes.

The special charm of the book to us lies in the striking illustration it affords of how literature can be the companion of daily life, heightening its common matters by special touches of enjoyment in the mere glad recital of them. The volume is [illegible] of poetical autobiography. Few things have happened to Mr. Bennoch that he has not turned into verse. He has made the muse walk by his side and sing to him of his own concerns. Of late years poetry has grown very high and mighty; [illegible] can no longer spare a sonnet to a friend. Mr. Bennoch has kept up the [illegible] more genial habits. Besides celebrating his own domestic happiness and his friendships,—in which he must have been very fortunate,—he shows a plentiful interest in public matters. Always the sympathy is broad and robust, whether he is writing a song for the Switzers, hymning the old Covenanters, or pleading—when it was not fashionable to do so—for Ireland. However, it is his native Scotland which always touches him most.

---

The Love-Letters of John Keats.†—This book is inscribed to Mr. Severn, and whatever reminds us of his heroic friendship for Keats is welcome. Heroic the friendship must have been, for apart from the more obvious aspects of the case (which Mr. Severn would be the last to think of) there was poor Keats's awful temper, and the peculiarly distressing character of the illness which at last made an end of him—a sore trial it must have been to the most patient nurse. The volume before us has an etching by Mr. W. B. Scott, from a drawing of the sufferer's head made by Mr. Severn (to keep him awake), at three o'clock one morning, less than a month before the end came. It is a most painful thing to look at—the hair matted with the death-dew, and the face drawn with pain. But we did not need Mr. Cowden Clarke's assurance to Mr. Forman that the likeness is good. It is easy enough to recognize in this mask of the grave the same features [illegible] which are familiar in the portrait in which Keats is looking out upon us [illegible] upon his hand. If any one should find the recognition difficult, [illegible] another portrait, that is or was in the National Portrait Gallery, [illegible] Keats is seated (in nankeen trousers, under a tree, as we remember) [illegible]. This gives an intermediate view of the face, which is instructive.

[illegible] fireside talk over these letters could be collected from half-a-dozen cultivated homes, and published, it would constitute a more edifying comment than [illegible] can write. But the fireside talk could never get printed, even if it

---

[illegible] Poems, Lyrics, Songs, and Sonnets. By Francis Bennoch. London: Hardwicke and Bogue.

† [illegible] Fanny Brawne, written in the years MDCCCXIX. and MDCCCXX., and now [illegible] with Introduction and Notes by Harry Buxton Forman. London: Reeves [illegible]

We have not yet succeeded in reconciling the two ends of employment and dispersion, but we have, or had, a Discharged Prisoners' Aid Society; and we have institutions like the one in the South-Western District of London, where Mr. Gilbert (without naming it) has gone for the purpose of getting a start for his story. A ticket-of-leave woman, who is an inmate of this Refuge or Reformatory, steals a pair of boots. Neither she nor anybody else can ever put them on without getting into trouble. The sad story of "Them Boots," with the poor woman's theory as to their manufacture, we shall leave to be found out in Mr. Gilbert's own pages.

But we cannot part with the story without noticing that the work suffers greatly by the "temperance" chapter at the end. The moral needed no such pointing, and the narrative itself is made *suspect* by it. In another place we should have been glad enough to see Mr. Gilbert throwing ridicule upon the prosecution of a grocer for selling preserved peas with an infinitesimal taint of copper in them, while the adulteration of beer and spirits goes unnoticed, or nearly so. But we cannot agree that publicans are *never* prosecuted for adulteration—we have certainly seen a few cases in which they have been fined.

---

LADY VERNEY'S SKETCHES FROM NATURE.*—This volume, like all Lady Verney's books, has much good work in it. If she has contented herself in some of the sketches with rather small topics, they are skilfully treated, a turn of novelty being always given to the page, either from some instance of close personal observation brought in, or else from some gleaning of out-of-the-way reading. The book consists of twenty essays and short tales, several of them now published for the first time, though the bulk have seen the light before. All kinds of subjects are dealt with, ranging from anthropology to cookery classes at South Kensington. But the larger part of the contents will not disappoint readers who may have more rustic expectations stirred by the title. There are charming papers on "Bees in the Past and Present," "Ants," "Tendrils and Climbing Plants," "Swallows," "The Names of Plants," "Birds of Passage" For young readers, who want a touch of the horrible in their natural history, we can recommend the sketch of "The Bottle-Nosed Shark," in which are given several delightfully fearful shark stories. The book, in a great part of it, specially appeals to young readers. To our thinking, among its most successful contents are the two juvenile stories at the end, "Little Mary Cradock" and "A Pair of Friends" They are touchingly sad. On the other hand, we expect the young folks will get quite as much fun as, according to good morals, they ought to do, out of the account of "The Lighthouse Donkey," which commits a murder. The victim is a pony. If, however, youthful perusers will like the book, older readers will find in it much that asks an adult mind to enjoy it fully. There are some exquisite bits of landscape sketching, and Lady Verney always has an eye to a good joke. The page is never long without a little flash of humour. Penetrating readers will take note that a new kind of moral feeling towards the lower creatures is fitfully taught,—a recognition of the distinctness of their interests from ours. The book enforces habits of close observation of natural scenes and the inferior animals in the best of all ways,—by a very successful example. The most modern results of science are brought in whenever the subject gives an opportunity, making the volume indirectly instructive as well as entertaining. It has a number of well-executed engravings.

---

KEIGHTLEY'S MYTHOLOGY.†—We welcome a new and handy edition of Keightley's excellent and too little appreciated manual. Our recollection of Dr. Schmitz's articles on mythology in Dr. Smith's Dictionary, which may perhaps be ranked along with those on Greek literature by another distinguished and most excellent man, the late Bishop Cotton, as among the least valuable portions of that generally useful book, had not led us to expect much from the editor's revision; and, in fact, little seems to have been done beyond the changing of the Greek names. Dr. Schmitz claims to have introduced the correct spelling, by which he appears to mean the illogical hybrids so popular with the schoolmasters of the day. *Phœbus* we know, and Φοῖβος we know, but where did *Phœbos* spring from? If we are to read of *Herodotos*, why not of *Hesiodos?* If *Thraké* is the correct

---

* Sketches from Nature with Pen and Pencil. By Lady Verney London · Daldy, Isbister, & Co.

† The Mythology of Ancient Greece and Italy. By Thomas Keightley. Fourth Edition. By Leonard Schmitz, LL.D. London · Bell and Sons.

thing, why not *Athenai?* But there is no reasoning with those who have once tasted of this insane root.

---

ZELLER'S SOCRATES.[1]—Zeller's excellent History of Greek Philosophy is now so well known that it is unnecessary to do more than point out the changes which have been made in the present edition. The English edition of 1868 was from the second German edition, which appeared in 1859; the present is from the third German edition, which appeared in 1875, and is enlarged by more than fifty pages. The translation has also been most carefully revised; in fact there is hardly a sentence which has not undergone some alteration, so as to make it a more correct and idiomatic expression of the original, of which it may now be taken as a thoroughly worthy representative. We are glad to see that the translation of the two remaining volumes, on the Pre-Socratic Schools and the Older Peripatetics, is announced as in preparation.

---

ARBER'S REPRINTS.—Mr. Arber (of Southgate, London, N.) has just issued a new prospectus of his publications, which can only be obtained "by postal application" to him, and are sent post free to all parts of the world.

They include—(A.) Thirty numbers of "English Reprints," viz., Milton's *Areopagitica* (with a decree of the Star-Chamber, 1637, and an order of the Lords and Commons, 1643); Latimer's Sermon on the Ploughers and Seven Sermons before Edward VI.; Stephen Gosson's Schoole of Abuse and Apologie of the Schoole of Abuse (1579); Sir Philip Sidney's Apologie for Poetrie (1595); The [illegible] thinges which Edward Webbe hath seene (1590); Selden's Table Talk; Ascham's Toxophilus (1545) and Scholemaster (1570); Addison's Criticisms of Milton's *Paradise Lost*; Lyly's Euphues (1579), Euphues and his England (1580); The Rehearsal of George Villiers, Duke of Buckingham (1672); George Gascoigne's Steele Glas (1575-1576) with other pieces; John Earle's Micro-cosmographie (1628); More's Utopia, translated by Raphe Robynson (1556); Puttenham's Arte of English Poesie (1589); Howell's Instructions for Forreine Travell (1642 and 1656); Udall's Roister Doister (1566); The Revelation to the Monk of Evesham (cir. 1485); James I., The Essayes of a Prentise in the Divine Art of Poesie (1585) and A Counter-Blaste to Tobacco (1604); Naunton's Fragmenta Regalia (1653); Thomas Watson's Centurie of Love (1582), and other pieces; Habington's Castara (1640); Tottel's Miscellany (1557); Thomas Lever's Three Sermons (1550); William Webbe's Discourse of English Poetrie (1586); Bacon's Essays, with the variations of the nine critical texts; William Roy's Rede me and be nott Wrothe (1528); with two tracts by Jerome Barlow, (1.) Against the Ambicion of the Clergye; (2.) A [illegible] howe that we ought to have the Scripture in Englysshe; three tracts (by Sir W. Raleigh, G. Markham, and J. H. v. Linschoten) on the last Fight of the Revenge (1591); Barnabe Googe's Eglogs, Epitaphes and Sonettes (1563).

(B.) The only known fragment of the first printed English New Testament, by William Tyndale, assisted by William Roy. 4to (photolithographed; with a critical introduction).

(C.) The Paston Letters, (1422-1509) including upwards of four hundred letters, etc., hitherto unpublished. Edited, with notes and indices, by James Gairdner, 3 vols., 8vo.

(D.) A transcript of the Registers of the Company of Stationers (1554-1640). To be completed in five vols., four of which are ready. Two hundred copies are printed on small paper at five guineas a volume, and thirty on large paper at [illegible] 2s. 6d. a volume. All copies not subscribed for (and eighty subscriptions are still wanting) will be destroyed on the publication of vol. v.

(E.) The first three English books on America. (1 vol. will probably appear in 1878.)

(F.) Petruccio Ubaldini's Discourse concerning the Spanish fleete invadinge Englande in the yeare 1588. . . . [with] certain tables expressinge the generall exploites, and conflictes had with the said fleete. (These plates are being engraved in facsimile.)

---

[1] Socrates and the Socratic Schools. Translated from the Third German Edition of Dr. E. Zeller. By Oswald J. Reichel. Second Edition. London: Longmans, Green, & Co.

(G.) Two new series are announced:

I. An English Garner. "Its prose will comprise over one hundred distinct works (from manuscript or printed originals) illustrating English history, biography, trade, social life, poetry, criticism, sports, military and naval affairs, &c.; in association with integral passages, important extracts, and elegant prefaces. Its verse will include some two thousand poems; as psalmic paraphrases, anthems, hymns, elegies, sonnets, pastorals, canticles, ballads, epigrams, idylls, songs, odes, &c.: most of which are now utterly forgotten. Many of these pieces are of the utmost rarity: so that no two public libraries in the world could at present produce all their original editions." Three or four volumes, of about 650 pp. each, may be looked for annually at the price of seven shillings small, fifteen shillings large paper. The "principal contents" of vol. i. (now ready) fully bear out the promise of this prospectus, comprising many rare and interesting pieces published in the sixteenth and seventeenth centuries, *e.g.*, The Captivity of Captain Rob. Knox in Ceylon (1660-1679); the Expedition in Scotland under the conduct of the Earl of Hertford (1544); A. Munday's captivity of John Fox, of Woodbridge, by the Turks, and his wonderful escape from Alexandria (1577); The voyage of the first Englishman [T. Stevens, S. J.] known to have reached India by the Cape of Good Hope (1579). Among the contents of vols. ii. and iii. will be Dr. Caius on Dogs (1536-1576); The triumphs of Boulogne and Calais in October 1532; The Coronation Procession of Queen Anne through London (31st May, 1533); W. Patten's Expedition into Scotland (1548).

II. The English Scholar's Library. Three or four parts (of about 500 pp. each) may be looked for annually, price seven shillings each part, small paper, and fifteen shillings large paper.

It will comprise (1) early printed translations; (2) romances, "histories," satires, epigrams, "love pamphlets," poems by Braithwaite, Breton, T. Campion, Chettle, Churchyard, Daniel, B. Rich, &c.; (3) quaint sermons or other characteristic books by Puritans; twenty to twenty-five tracts of the Marprelate controversy (1588-90); (4) a selection from the drama, pageants, court revels, masks, &c., to the time of Dryden, with books attacking or defending the stage; (5) remarkable books, like Sir T. Elyot's Governor; Sir T. Wilson's Rhetoric and Logic; The Mirror for Magistrates; Col. S. Allen's Killing no Murder, &c.; (6) the Controversy with Rome in the first stage of the English Reformation, as represented by the works of Tyndale, More, C. St. German, R. Barnes, J. Rastell, G. Joye, &c.; (7) characters, essays, &c.; (8) quarrels of authors, *e.g.*, of Gabriel Harvey and Tom Nash; (9) travels, as Lithgow's Peregrination and Coryat's Crudities; (10) philosophical books, as Sir J. Elliot's Monarchie of Man; J. Hales' Golden Remains; T. Hobbes' Leviathan; Bishop Wilkins' Real Character; (11) books of emblems.

Part I. (to be ready about March 1st, 1878) will include Caxton's History of Reynard the Foxe (June 1481); John Knox's First Blast of the Trumpet against the Monstrous Regiment of Women (1558); Clem. Robinson's Handefull of Pleasant Delites (1584); a sketch of the Marprelate controversy; John Udall's State of the Church of Englande (1588); The Return from Pernassus (1606); Decker's Seven Deadly Sinnes of London (1606).

The accuracy of Mr. Arber's reprints, and the exact research displayed in his introductions, are universally acknowledged. Almost alone he has published a series which would do honour to a society of learned editors, and at a price which leaves no margin for advertising. It is to be hoped that eighty subscribers will be forthcoming for the copies still on hand of the Registers of the Stationers' Company.

Lightning Source UK Ltd.
Milton Keynes UK
UKHW021445281218
334535UK00010B/1937/P

9 781527 701663